CURRENT LAW STATUTES ANNOTATED
1992

VOLUME TWO

AUSTRALIA
The Law Book Company
Brisbane ● Sydney ● Melbourne ● Perth

CANADA
Carswell
Ottawa ● Toronto ● Calgary ● Montreal ● Vancouver

Agents:
Steimatzky's Agency Ltd., Tel Aviv;
N. M. Tripathi (Private) Ltd., Bombay;
Eastern Law House (Private) Ltd., Calcutta;
M.P.P. House, Bangalore;
Universal Book Traders, Delhi;
Aditya Books, Delhi;
MacMillan Shuppan KK, Tokyo;
Pakistan Law House, Karachi

CURRENT LAW

STATUTES

ANNOTATED

1992

VOLUME TWO

SWEET & MAXWELL EDITORIAL TEAM
SARAH ANDREWS
CAROLINE EADIE
BARBARA GRANDAGE
PHILIPPA JOHNSON
SOPHIE LOWE
BETHAN OWEN
ROSANNA ROTHERY
CLARE TURNER
HELEN WAUCHOPE

W. GREEN EDITORIAL TEAM
ELANOR BOWER
ALISON GAY
PETER NICHOLSON
IAN YOUNG

LONDON

SWEET & MAXWELL

EDINBURGH

W. GREEN

1993

Published by
SWEET & MAXWELL LIMITED
of South Quay Plaza, 183 Marsh Wall, London E14 9FT
Typeset by MFK Typesetting Ltd., Hitchin, Herts.
Printed in Great Britain
by The Bath Press,
Bath, Avon.

ISBN This Volume only : 0 421 48660 0
As a set   : 0 421 48690 2

CONTENTS

CHRONOLOGICAL TABLE

VOLUME TWO

VOLUME TWO

INDEX OF SHORT TITLES

STATUTES 1992

(References are to chapter numbers of 1992)

BINGO ACT 1992*

(1992 c. 10)

An Act to amend the Gaming Act 1968 with respect to bingo; and for connected purposes. [6th March 1992]

PARLIAMENTARY DEBATES
Hansard, H.L. Vol. 533, col. 1426; Vol. 535, col. 546; Vol. 536, col. 171.

INTRODUCTION AND GENERAL NOTE
This Act relieves licensed bingo clubs from some of the stringent restrictions that are contained in s.42 of the Gaming Act 1968. Subject to some exceptions, this prohibits any advertisement informing the public that gaming takes place on any premises or inviting the public to participate in gaming or to subscribe money for that use. Apart from the placement of formal notices in the press, advertising is limited to notices on the premises indicating that gaming takes place there.

The concessions that are introduced by this Act are intended to assist the bingo industry to reverse the decline in its fortunes over recent years. The Government has accepted that bingo clubs offer their membership the opportunity to participate in an innocent and congenial social occasion which is unlikely to encourage excessive gambling. They do not therefore require the same close control as does casino gaming. From the commencement of the Act it will be lawful for bingo clubs to advertise their existence and to indicate what prizes can be won there, but they are not permitted to do both simultaneously. "The overall objective . . . is separation of the advertising of bingo club premises, on the one hand, and inducement to play bingo or to become members of a bingo club, on the other". (Viscount Astor, *Hansard*, H.L. Vol. 535, col. 550 (February 10, 1992)).

The Act was promoted by Lord Harmar-Nicholls and the Bingo Association of Great Britain, and was supported by the Gaming Board for Great Britain and the Government.

COMMENCEMENT AND EXTENT
The Act comes into force on May 7, 1992. It does not extend to Northern Ireland.

ABBREVIATION
the 1968 Act: the Gaming Act 1968.

Bingo advertising

1.—(1) Section 42 of the Gaming Act 1968 (restrictions on advertisements relating to gaming) shall be amended as follows.

(2) In subsection (1), at the end of paragraph (c) there shall be inserted "or

(d) containing an inducement to the public to take part as players in a game of bingo, or to become members of a club to which section 20 of this Act applies, or

(e) containing any such matter relating to any relevant premises, to any activities carried on at any relevant premises or to any club operating from any relevant premises as may be specified or described in regulations made by the Secretary of State."

(3) After that subsection there shall be inserted—

"(1A) For the purposes of this section any advertisement displayed on a sign or notice which—

(a) is within 400 metres of any relevant premises;

(b) contains sufficient information about the premises to indicate their location; and

(c) contains anything which constitutes an inducement to attend the premises or to become a member of a club operating from the premises,

---

*Annotations by Dr David Miers, Reader in Law, Cardiff Law School.

shall be taken to fall within subsection (1)(a) of this section whether or not it indicates that the premises are relevant premises and notwithstanding that it does not inform the public that any premises are premises on which gaming takes place or is to take place."

(4) In subsection (2), for "The preceding subsection" there shall be substituted "Subsection (1) of this section".

(5) In subsection (3)(a), after "force" there shall be inserted "other than bingo club premises".

(6) At the end of paragraph (c) of subsection (3) there shall be inserted "or

   (d) the display on any bingo club premises (whether or not so as to be visible from outside those premises) of a sign or notice indicating the amount, value or description of anything that has been or may be won in a game of bingo—

      (i) by a player present on those premises, or

      (ii) by a player present on premises which (by virtue of section 20(2) of this Act) are regarded as the same as those premises for the purposes of section 12(1) of this Act,

   or

   (e) the display on any bingo club premises, so as not to be visible from outside those premises, of a sign or notice indicating the amount, value or description of anything that has been or may be won in a game of bingo by a player regarded, by virtue of section 2(1) of the Gaming (Bingo) Act 1985 (multiple bingo), as present on those premises for the purposes of section 12(1) of this Act, or

   (f) the inclusion in an advertisement in a newspaper circulating throughout England and Wales or Scotland of information as to the amount, value or description of anything that has been or may be won by a player in a game of multiple bingo, or

   (g) the inclusion in an advertisement to which subsection (3A) or (3B) of this section applies of—

      (i) the information that any bingo club premises are premises on which gaming in the form of the playing of bingo takes place, or is to take place; or

      (ii) an invitation to the public to take part in gaming in that form;".

(7) After that subsection there shall be inserted the following subsections—

"(3A) This subsection applies to any advertisement displayed on a sign or notice where—

   (a) the advertisement does not contain a relevant inducement, and

   (b) the sign or notice is displayed either—

      (i) on the bingo club premises in question, whether inside or outside the premises; or

      (ii) at a place which is not within 400 metres of any sign or notice on which an advertisement containing a relevant inducement is displayed.

(3B) This subsection applies to any other advertisement in documentary form where the advertisement—

   (a) does not contain a relevant inducement, and

   (b) is neither published in, nor distributed with—

      (i) a newspaper circulating throughout England and Wales or Scotland; or

      (ii) any other publication or document in which there is a relevant inducement contained in another advertisement.

(3C) References in subsections (3A) and (3B) of this section to a relevant inducement are references to anything which (with or without indicating that they are relevant premises) constitutes an inducement—

   (a) to attend any relevant premises which are at the same location as

the premises to which the information or invitation mentioned in
subsection (3)(g) of this section relates, or

(b) to become a member of a club operating from premises at that
location."

(8) For subsection (8) there shall be substituted—

"(8) In this section—

'advertisement' includes every form of advertising, whether in a
publication or by the display of notices or by means of circu-
lars or other documents or by an exhibition of photographs or
a cinematograph film, or by way of sound broadcasting or
television or by inclusion in a programme service (within the
meaning of the Broadcasting Act 1990) that is not a sound or
television broadcasting service and references to the issue of
an advertisement shall be construed accordingly;

'bingo club premises' has the meaning given by section 20 of this
Act;

'inducement' in relation to taking part as a player in a game of
bingo, to attending any premises or to becoming a member of
any club, means any of the following so far as they appear to
be connected with taking part in such a game, attending those
premises or becoming such a member, namely—

(a) any promise of a gift,

(b) any offer of, or information about, an opportunity to
receive a gift or to win a prize,

(c) any information as to the amount, value or description
of anything that has been or may be won in any game;

'multiple bingo' has the same meaning as in the Gaming (Bingo)
Act 1985;

'public' means the public in Great Britain, and includes any section
of the public in Great Britain, however selected;

'relevant premises' means any bingo club premises or premises
containing bingo club premises or any premises which are at
the same location as any bingo club premises and are occupied
with, or used in association with, those bingo club premises."

(9) Section 2(4) of the Gaming (Bingo) Act 1985 and paragraph 14 of
Schedule 20 to the Broadcasting Act 1990 (which are spent in consequence
of the preceding provisions of this section) are hereby repealed.

DEFINITIONS
  "advertisement": s.1(8).
  "bingo club premises": s.1(8).
  "England and Wales": Interpretation Act 1978, Sched. 1.
  "gaming": s.52(1) of the 1968 Act.
  "inducement": s.1(8).
  "multiple bingo": s.1(8).
  "public": s.1(8).
  "relevant premises": s.1(8).
  "Secretary of State": "one of Her Majesty's Principal Secretaries of State", Interpretation
Act 1978, Sched. 1.

GENERAL NOTE
  The sum of these amendments is that, with the exception of multiple bingo, the prizes of
which may be advertised, but only in the national newspapers, all advertising of bingo prizes
away from club premises is prohibited. Individual clubs are permitted to advertise inside (and
sometimes outside) their premises the value of any prizes that have been or may be won by
those playing at their premises. Clubs are, in addition, permitted to advertise locally on a sign or
notice, or in documentary form, their location as bingo clubs, the fact that bingo is played there
and to invite applications for membership; but these advertisements cannot be accompanied by
or be associated with any inducements, which include statements about the value of any prizes
that have been or may be won by those playing at their premises.

Subs. (2)

This extends s.42(1) of the 1968 Act so as to prohibit (subject to what follows) any advertisement which contains an inducement to participate in bingo or to become a member of a licensed bingo club or which contains such matter in respect of any "relevant premises", that is, premises that are used for or, broadly speaking, are connected with, bingo club premises.

To which section 20 of this Act applies. This means a club licensed under para. 25 of Sched. 2 to the 1968 Act whose licence is limited to the playing of bingo.

Subs. (3)

This adds subs. (1A) to s.42 of the 1968 Act. It provides that any advertisement within 400 metres of bingo club premises which contains both sufficient information to identify their location and anything in the form of an inducement shall as a matter of law be presumed to be an advertisement "informing the public that any premises in Great Britain are premises on which gaming takes place or is to take place" (s.42(1)(a)), whether or not it actually says so.

Subs. (6)

This extends the list of exceptions in s.42(3) of the 1968 Act so that it will be lawful to display (within or outside the premises) the value of any prizes that have been or may be won by a person playing bingo there (which includes linked bingo). In the case of multiple bingo, it will be lawful to display the value of such prizes within the premises only, and to advertise them in a newspaper provided that it has a national circulation.

Together with subss. (7) and (8), subs. (6) further provides that it is lawful to advertise the location of bingo club premises and to invite the public to participate in bingo at those premises, so long as that advertisement, where it appears on a sign or notice, does not also include an inducement to play, and, if it is not situated inside or outside the premises, is not within 400 metres of an advertisement containing such an inducement. It will also be lawful to publish documentary advertisements of the location of the premises (and inviting participation), provided that they neither appear in a national newspaper nor are associated with any inducements relating to those premises.

Subs. (8)

Programme service. This refers to the Broadcasting Act 1990, s.201.

Gift. This means a transfer without consideration of a beneficial interest (*Rose, Re, Rose* v. *I.R.C.* [1952] Ch. 499).

Offer. This is presumably to be taken in its contractual sense (*Fisher* v. *Bell* [1961] 1 Q.B. 394).

Short title, commencement and extent

2.—(1) This Act may be cited as the Bingo Act 1992.

(2) This Act shall come into operation at the end of the period of two months beginning with the date on which it is passed.

(3) This Act does not extend to Northern Ireland.

INDEX

References are to section numbers

AGGRAVATED VEHICLE-TAKING ACT 1992*

(1992 c. 11)

An Act to make provision with respect to persons who commit offences
under section 12(1) of the Theft Act 1968 in relation to a mechanically
propelled vehicle where additional circumstances are present relating to
the driving of or damage to the vehicle.   [6th March 1992]

PARLIAMENTARY DEBATES
    Hansard, H.C. Vol. 200, col. 620; H.L. Vol. 534, col. 480; Vol. 535, col. 690; Vol. 536, cols.
241, 812.

INTRODUCTION AND GENERAL NOTE
    On December 9, 1991 the Secretary of State for the Home Department, Mr Kenneth Baker,
moved in the House of Commons that the Aggravated Vehicle-Taking Bill be read for the
second time (*Hansard*, H.C. Vol. 200, col. 621).
    The Bill had been introduced to the House of Commons as a response to what was perceived
as a serious crimewave involving motor vehicles. The Secretary of State informed the House
that in the 12 months to June 1991 over 550,000 motor vehicles had been stolen, and that there
had been 800,000 thefts from vehicles. Crime relating to motor vehicles accounted for approximately one-third of all recorded serious crime, and was rapidly rising, accounting for more than
a third of the overall increase in recorded crime for 1991.
    Section 1 is the heart of the Act. It makes provision for a new aggravated form of the existing
offence under s.12(1) of the Theft Act 1968 of taking a conveyance without consent or
knowingly driving or being carried in one which is so taken, by adding a s.12A to that Act. The
offence is triable either way.
    Liability under the offence arises where it is established that a person has committed an
offence under s.12(1) and in addition it is established that before the recovery of the motor
vehicle, that vehicle was driven dangerously or was damaged or was driven in a way which led to
personal injury or damage to other property. Section 1 also sets out defences to the offence.
    Section 2 provides that the offence must be tried summarily if the only aggravating element of
the offence was damage and the value is below a specified amount. The section also sets out
formulae for valuing the damage. The section inserts a new paragraph into Sched. 2 to the
Magistrates' Courts Act 1980 and makes amendments and further insertions to the main body
of that Act.
    Section 3 provides for obligatory disqualification and endorsement and for the imposition of
penalty points on conviction of a person of an offence under the new s.12A, by amending the
Road Traffic Offenders Act 1988.
    Section 4 provides, *inter alia*, for the commencement and extension of the Act.

New offence of aggravated vehicle-taking

    1.—(1) After section 12 of the Theft Act 1968 (taking conveyances with-
out authority) there shall be inserted the following section—
        "**Aggravated vehicle-taking**
        12A.—(1) Subject to subsection (3) below, a person is guilty of
    aggravated taking of a vehicle if—
        (a) he commits an offence under section 12(1) above (in this section
            referred to as a "basic offence") in relation to a mechanically
            propelled vehicle; and
        (b) it is proved that, at any time after the vehicle was unlawfully
            taken (whether by him or another) and before it was recovered,
            the vehicle was driven, or injury or damage was caused, in one or
            more of the circumstances set out in paragraphs (a) to (d) of
            subsection (2) below.
        (2) The circumstances referred to in subsection (1)(b) above are—
        (a) that the vehicle was driven dangerously on a road or other public
            place;

---

* Annotations by G. P. Scanlan, LL.B., Solicitor, Lecturer in Law, University of Liverpool.

(b) that, owing to the driving of the vehicle, an accident occurred by which injury was caused to any person;

(c) that, owing to the driving of the vehicle, an accident occurred by which damage was caused to any property, other than the vehicle;

(d) that damage was caused to the vehicle.

(3) A person is not guilty of an offence under this section if he proves that, as regards any such proven driving, injury or damage as is referred to in subsection (1)(b) above, either—

(a) the driving, accident or damage referred to in subsection (2) above occurred before he committed the basic offence; or

(b) he was neither in nor on nor in the immediate vicinity of the vehicle when that driving, accident or damage occurred.

(4) A person guilty of an offence under this section shall be liable on conviction on indictment to imprisonment for a term not exceeding two years or, if it is proved that, in circumstances falling within subsection (2)(b) above, the accident caused the death of the person concerned, five years.

(5) If a person who is charged with an offence under this section is found not guilty of that offence but it is proved that he committed a basic offence, he may be convicted of the basic offence.

(6) If by virtue of subsection (5) above a person is convicted of a basic offence before the Crown Court, that court shall have the same powers and duties as a magistrates' court would have had on convicting him of such an offence.

(7) For the purposes of this section a vehicle is driven dangerously if—

(a) it is driven in a way which falls far below what would be expected of a competent and careful driver; and

(b) it would be obvious to a competent and careful driver that driving the vehicle in that way would be dangerous.

(8) For the purposes of this section a vehicle is recovered when it is restored to its owner or to other lawful possession or custody; and in this subsection "owner" has the same meaning as in section 12 above."

(2) The provisions of subsection (4) of section 12A of the Theft Act 1968 are without prejudice to the operation of—

(a) section 30 of the Powers of Criminal Courts Act 1973 (under which a Crown Court has a general power to fine an offender convicted on indictment); and

(b) section 17 of, and Schedule 1 to, the Magistrates' Courts Act 1980 (under which, with certain exceptions not material to section 12A, offences under the Theft Act 1968 are triable either way).

(3) Nothing in section 12A of the Theft Act 1968 applies to—

(a) an offence under section 12(1) of that Act which was committed before this section comes into force; or

(b) any driving, injury or damage which occurred before this section comes into force.

DEFINITIONS
"dangerously": s.12A(1)(7).
"mechanically propelled vehicle": Road Traffic Act 1988, s.185(1)
"recovered": s.12A(1)(8).

GENERAL NOTE
This section, which inserts a new s.12A into the Theft Act 1968, is the heart of the legislation. The new section initially requires proof beyond reasonable doubt of the commission by a party of an offence under s.12(1) of the Theft Act 1968. A vehicle must accordingly either (a) be taken and driven away by a party for his own or another's use, without the owner's consent or other lawful authority; or (b) a party must drive or allow himself to be driven or carried in or on the vehicle knowing that the vehicle has been taken without lawful authority.

The proof of such an offence, "the basic offence", is a condition precedent to liability under s.12A. The section, in addition to the commission of a "basic offence", requires proof beyond reasonable doubt that the vehicle was driven or injury or damage caused in one or more aggravating circumstances. These "aggravating circumstances", which are set out in s.12A(1) (b) must occur after the vehicle was first unlawfully taken, but before it is recovered (see s.12A(1)(8)). The drafting of the section is wide and it is apparent that an accused initially involved as a party to a commission of a basic offence may also be held to be a party to the complete offence under the section though at the time when an aggravating circumstance occurs he is no longer in or on the vehicle.

An accused is provided with defences to a charge under the section. As is common with such statutory defences, it is for the accused to establish any such defence on a balance of probabilities. One difficulty in the interpretation of s.12A(1)(3) lies in determining what is to be regarded as being in the immediate vicinity for the purposes of the defence set out in s.12A(3) (b). It would tend to suggest that anything less than a very close proximity to the vehicle, both in terms of space and time, would excuse an accused from liability for the subsequent occurrence of any aggravating circumstance that took place therefore in the absence of the accused.

Section 12A(1)(4) provides for a maximum custodial sentence for an offence where death has occurred of five years. Notwithstanding this provision, it cannot affect the permitted maximum sentence of a juvenile for such an offence which is currently permitted by legislation.

Section 12A(1)(5) and (6) permits a person charged with an offence under the section to be convicted purely of an offence under s.12(1) of the Theft Act 1968: and where the offence is tried on indictment (the offence is one triable either way) for the Crown Court to have the same powers and duties as a magistrates' court where a person is found guilty by virtue of s.12A(1)(5) of an offence under s.12(1) of the Theft Act 1968.

Section 12A(1)(7) provides a definition of what constitutes dangerous driving for the purposes of the section. It is a twofold test and mirrors the test of dangerous driving provided in the Road Traffic Act 1991. It constitutes in essence negligent driving and it is determined accordingly purely on an objective standard.

It should be noted that the section refers not to a conveyance (which would be capable of including all vehicles) but to the taking and driving of mechanically propelled vehicles. This is defined by s.185(1) of the Road Traffic Act 1988 as "a mechanically propelled vehicle intended or adapted for use on roads".

Section 12A(2) and (3) contain both transitional and saving provisions concerning, *inter alia*, the general powers of the Crown Court to fine offenders convicted on indictment and the powers of a magistrates' court to deal with offences under the Theft Act 1968 which are triable either way.

Offence to be tried only summarily if value of damage is small

2.—(1) In Schedule 2 to the Magistrates' Court Act 1980 (offences for which the value involved is relevant to the mode of trial) after paragraph 2 there shall be inserted the following paragraph—

"3. Offences under section 12A of the Theft Act 1968 (aggravated vehicle-taking) where no allegation is made under subsection (1) (b) other than of damage, whether to the vehicle or other property or both.	The total value of the damage alleged to have been caused.	(1) In the case of damage to any property other than the vehicle involved in the offence, as for the corresponding entry in paragraph 1 above, substituting a reference to the time of the accident concerned for any reference to the material time. (2) In the case of damage to the vehicle involved in the offence— (a) if immediately after the vehicle was recovered the damage was capable of repair— (i) what would probably then have been the market price for the repair of the damage, or

(ii) what the vehicle would probably have cost to buy in the open market immediately before it was unlawfully taken,

whichever is the less; or

(b) if immediately after the vehicle was recovered the damage was beyond repair, what the vehicle would probably have cost to buy in the open market immediately before it was unlawfully taken."

(2) In the Magistrates' Courts Act 1980, at the end of section 22 (which introduces Schedule 2) there shall be added the following subsection—

"(12) Subsection (8) of section 12A of the Theft Act 1968 (which determines when a vehicle is recovered) shall apply for the purposes of paragraph 3 of Schedule 2 to this Act as it applies for the purposes of that section."

(3) In section 33 of the Magistrates' Courts Act 1980 (maximum penalties on summary conviction in pursuance of section 22)—

(a) in subsection (1), at the beginning of paragraph (a) there shall be inserted the words "subject to subsection (3) below"; and

(b) after subsection (2) there shall be inserted the following subsection—

"(3) Paragraph (a) of subsection (1) above does not apply to an offence under section 12A of the Theft Act 1968 (aggravated vehicle-taking)."

GENERAL NOTE

This section provides that the new offence must be tried summarily if the only aggravating circumstance occurring is damage and the value thereof is below a specified sum. The section also inserts a new para. 3 into Sched. 2 to the Magistrates' Courts Act, 1980 which concerns offences for which the value involved is relevant to the mode of trial. This new paragraph sets out formulae for valuing the damage in different circumstances.

Obligatory disqualification

3.—(1) In Schedule 2 to the Road Traffic Offenders Act 1988 (punishment of offences, etc.), in Part II (disqualification, endorsement and penalty points for offences under Acts other than the Traffic Acts) after the entry relating to manslaughter and culpable homicide there shall be inserted the following entry—

| "An offence under section 12A of the Theft Act 1968 (aggravated vehicle-taking). | Obligatory. | Obligatory. | 3–11". |

(2) In section 34 of the Road Traffic Offenders Act 1988 (disqualification for certain offences), after subsection (1) (obligatory disqualification except for special reasons) there shall be inserted the following subsection—

"(1A) Where a person is convicted of an offence under section 12A of the Theft Act 1968 (aggravated vehicle-taking), the fact that he did not drive the vehicle in question at any particular time or at all shall not be regarded as a special reason for the purposes of subsection (1) above."

GENERAL NOTE

Section 3, by an insertion in Pt. II of Sched. 2 to the Road Traffic Offenders Act 1988 which concerns punishment of offences, provides for obligatory disqualification and endorsement, and for penalty points to be imposed when a person is convicted of an offence under s.12A(1).

Short title, commencement and extent

4.—(1) This Act may be cited as the Aggravated Vehicle-Taking Act 1992.

(2) This Act shall come into force on such day as the Secretary of State may by order made by statutory instrument appoint, and different days may be so appointed for different purposes.

(3) This Act extends to England and Wales only.

INDEX

References in roman type are to sections of this Act: references in italic are to the new section
12A of the Theft Act 1968

TAXATION OF CHARGEABLE GAINS ACT 1992*

(1992 c. 12)

ARRANGEMENT OF SECTIONS

PART I

CAPITAL GAINS TAX AND CORPORATION TAX ON CHARGEABLE GAINS

General

PART II

GENERAL PROVISIONS RELATING TO COMPUTATION OF GAINS AND ACQUISITIONS AND DISPOSALS OF ASSETS

CHAPTER I

INTRODUCTORY

CHAPTER II

ASSETS AND DISPOSALS OF ASSETS

General provisions

---

* Annotations by Ian Ferrier, M.A., Barrister.

PART V

TRANSFER OF BUSINESS ASSETS

CHAPTER I

GENERAL PROVISIONS

Replacement of business assets

Stock in trade

Transfer of business to a company

Retirement relief

CHAPTER II

GIFTS OF BUSINESS ASSETS

PART VI

COMPANIES, OIL, INSURANCE ETC.

CHAPTER I

COMPANIES

Groups of companies

Transactions within groups

Losses attributable to depreciatory transactions

Companies leaving groups

PART VII

OTHER PROPERTY, BUSINESSES, INVESTMENTS ETC.

Private residences

An Act to consolidate certain enactments relating to the taxation of chargeable gains.   [6th March 1992]

PARLIAMENTARY DEBATES
   Hansard, H.L. Vol. 534, cols. 117, 477; Vol. 535, col. 843; H.C. Vol. 205, col. 264.
   The Bill was discussed in Joint Committee on January 22 and 29 and February 5, 1992.

INTRODUCTION
   Although income tax was first introduced at the end of the eighteenth century and has been charged continuously since 1842, gains of a capital nature remained exempt from tax until well after the Second World War. In 1962 the Conservative government introduced a new Case VII of Sched. D charging to income tax capital gains on the disposal of land within three years of its acquisition and on the disposal of other assets within six months.
   In 1965 the incoming Labour government introduced a general capital gains tax ("C.G.T."). It also introduced a new system of taxing companies through corporation tax in place of income tax and profits tax. Strictly, the capital gains of companies were assessed to corporation tax on chargeable gains, while the capital gains of other taxpayers were assessed to C.G.T., but the same principles applied. The rate of C.G.T. was set at 30 per cent. Case VII was retained for gains realised within 12 months of the acquisition of assets, but this charge was repealed by the next Conservative government in 1971.
   The provisions relating to the chargeable gains of companies subject to corporation tax were consolidated into the Income and Corporation Taxes Act 1970 and these sections were not consolidated into the Income and Corporation Taxes Act 1988. The provisions relating to taxation of capital gains generally were consolidated into the Capital Gains Tax Act 1979.
   The 1970s were a period of severe inflation, at times reaching a level of more than 20 per cent. a year. In these circumstances C.G.T. was perceived as an unjust tax on purely notional gains and this led to a number of highly artificial avoidance schemes which evoked the development by the House of Lords of the "new approach" in *Ramsay (W.T.)* v. *I.R.C.* [1982] A.C. 300, *I.R.C.* v. *Burmah Oil Co.* (1981) 54 T.C. 200 and *Furniss* v. *Dawson* [1984] A.C. 474.
   Meanwhile, steps had been taken to mitigate the injustice of C.G.T. by introducing an indexation allowance for gains realised after April 1982 and later by rebasing the tax to 1982 market values from 1965 market values. There was a departure from the general 30 per cent. rate, with companies being charged at their appropriate corporation tax rate, individuals at the basic rate, or at the higher rate if their income reached that level, and trusts at the basic rate, or at the sum of the basic and additional rates in the case of accumulation and discretionary settlements.
   The new consolidation brings together again all the provisions relating to the taxation of chargeable gains. The relatively simple tax introduced in 1965 has now evolved into what Lord Wilberforce described in the second reading debate in the House of Lords as "legislation of unimaginable complexity ... absolutely impossible for the ordinary citizen to understand ... impossible for many accountants to understand ... as I know from personal experience ... also impossible for the officials of the Inland Revenue to understand. Sections are piled upon sections and schedules are piled upon schedules in order to deal with supposed cases of evasion ... We now have a monster tax which ... has outgrown the possibility of being handled ... the unfortunate taxpayer and his advisers are landed with a Frankenstein's monster that they must use".

Structure of the Act
   Against the background of this warning it would obviously be naïve to expect an Act which is easy to use. However, the draftsman has attempted to impose some kind of logical order on a mass of provisions.

Part I, ss.1–14 and Sched. 1, introduces the basic concept of the tax and deals with the question of residence. This is of great importance, since the tax is normally levied only on persons resident or ordinarily resident in the U.K.

Part II, ss.15–57 and Scheds. 2–4, deals with the computation of the tax and introduces several anti-avoidance provisions. There are several important general principles—first, no gains accruing before April 6, 1965 are brought into charge; secondly, the tax is generally rebased to values as at March 31, 1982; and thirdly, from that date arithmetical gains are adjusted for inflation.

Part III, ss.58–103 and Sched. 5, deals with the liabilities of individuals, partnerships, settlements and unit and investment trusts. It includes the complex régime which has grown up over the years to counter tax avoidance through moving the residence of settlements overseas.

Part IV, ss.104–151, covers the provisions relating to shares and similar instruments and the difficult problems which arise on reconstructions and amalgamations.

Part V, ss.152–169 and Scheds. 6 and 7, is concerned mainly with three important reliefs relating to businesses, "roll-over" relief on replacement of assets, retirement relief on sales by the elderly, and the relief on gifts of businesses. The latter is more significant since the abolition of the general relief for gifts which operated for much of the 1980s.

Part VI, ss.170–221, covers the provisions relating to groups of companies and continues with the special legislation for the oil, mining and insurance industries, building societies and various public authorities.

Part VII, ss.222–271 and Sched. 8, is somewhat miscellaneous in character. It opens with the private residence relief, the most important exemption from C.G.T., and goes on to cover the exemptions for employee share ownership trusts ("ESOTs") and pension funds. The special provisions relating to land, particularly the treatment accorded to leases, come next, followed by groups of sections dealing with debts, charities and various miscellaneous exemptions.

Part VIII, ss.272–291 and Scheds. 9–12, contains a number of provisions of general and supplemental character and includes the usual interpretation section and schedules dealing with consequential amendments of other statutes, transitional provisions and repeals.

ABBREVIATIONS

CGTA 1979	:	Capital Gains Tax Act 1979.
B.E.S.	:	Business Expansion Scheme.
ESOTs	:	Employee Share Ownership Trusts.
FA	:	Finance Act (of year indicated).
F(No. 2)A 1975	:	Finance (No. 2) Act 1975.
FIFO	:	First In First Out.
ICTA 1988	:	Income and Corporation Taxes Act 1988.
I.H.T.	:	Inheritance Tax.
IHTA 1984	:	Inheritance Tax Act 1984.
LIFO	:	Last In First Out.
TMA 1970	:	Taxes Management Act 1970.

PART I

CAPITAL GAINS TAX AND CORPORATION TAX ON CHARGEABLE GAINS

General

The charge to tax

1.—(1) Tax shall be charged in accordance with this Act in respect of capital gains, that is to say chargeable gains computed in accordance with this Act and accruing to a person on the disposal of assets.

(2) Companies shall be chargeable to corporation tax in respect of chargeable gains accruing to them in accordance with section 6 of the Taxes Act and the other provisions of the Corporation Tax Acts.

(3) Without prejudice to subsection (2), capital gains tax shall be charged for all years of assessment in accordance with the following provisions of this Act.

GENERAL NOTE

This is the general charging section, bringing into tax capital gains, *i.e.* chargeable gains accruing to persons other than companies, and chargeable gains accruing to companies, which are subject to corporation tax rather than capital gains tax as such.

Persons other than companies are charged with reference to years of assessment, April 6 to April 5 of the following year, while companies are charged with reference to accounting periods (see s.8).

The tax is applicable to all disposals of assets, including those by way of gift, unless an exemption applies (*Turner* v. *Follett* (1979) 48 T.C. 614).

Capital gains tax

Persons and gains chargeable to capital gains tax, and allowable losses

2.—(1) Subject to any exceptions provided by this Act, and without prejudice to sections 10 and 276, a person shall be chargeable to capital gains tax in respect of chargeable gains accruing to him in a year of assessment during any part of which he is resident in the United Kingdom, or during which he is ordinarily resident in the United Kingdom.

(2) Capital gains tax shall be charged on the total amount of chargeable gains accruing to the person chargeable in the year of assessment, after deducting—

(a) any allowable losses accruing to that person in that year of assessment, and

(b) so far as they have not been allowed as a deduction from chargeable gains accruing in any previous year of assessment, any allowable losses accruing to that person in any previous year of assessment (not earlier than the year 1965–66).

(3) Except as provided by section 62, an allowable loss accruing in a year of assessment shall not be allowable as a deduction from chargeable gains accruing in any earlier year of assessment, and relief shall not be given under this Act more than once in respect of any loss or part of a loss, and shall not be given under this Act if and so far as relief has been or may be given in respect of it under the Income Tax Acts.

GENERAL NOTE

Subs. (1)

The charge to C.G.T. applies in general to persons who are resident or ordinarily resident in the U.K. during the year of assessment. There are special exceptions for non-residents with a U.K. branch or agency (s.10) and in relation to the continental shelf (s.276).

The Inland Revenue's practice with regard to residence and ordinary residence is explained in their booklet IR 20. By extra-statutory concession, D2, they will normally treat a person leaving the U.K. and relinquishing residence and ordinary residence as outside the scope of C.G.T. from the moment of his departure, but they will refuse this relief in cases where they consider tax avoidance is involved (*R.* v. *I.R.C.*, ex p. *Fulford-Dobson* [1987] Q.B. 978).

Subs. (2)

Capital losses are allowable as an offset against capital gains, and may be carried forward to set against future gains.

Subs. (3)

This denies any carry-back of losses, except in the case of a deceased individual, where a three-year carry-back is allowed under s.62(2), and any double relief for losses, against either C.G.T. or income tax.

Annual exempt amount

3.—(1) An individual shall not be chargeable to capital gains tax in respect of so much of his taxable amount for any year of assessment as does not exceed the exempt amount for the year.

(2) Subject to subsection (3) below, the exempt amount for any year of assessment shall be £5,500.

(3) If the retail prices index for the month of December preceding a year of assessment is higher than it was for the previous December, then, unless Parliament otherwise determines, subsection (2) above shall have effect for

that year as if for the amount specified in that subsection as it applied for the previous year (whether by virtue of this subsection or otherwise) there were substituted an amount arrived at by increasing the amount for the previous year by the same percentage as the percentage increase in the retail prices index and, if the result is not a multiple of £100, rounding it up to the nearest amount which is such a multiple.

(4) The Treasury shall, before each year of assessment, make an order specifying the amount which by virtue of this section is the exempt amount for that year.

(5) For the purposes of this section an individual's taxable amount for a year of assessment is the amount on which he is chargeable under section 2(2) for that year but—

  (a) where the amount of chargeable gains less allowable losses accruing to an individual in any year of assessment does not exceed the exempt amount for the year, no deduction from that amount shall be made for that year in respect of allowable losses carried forward from a previous year or carried back from a subsequent year in which the individual dies, and

  (b) where the amount of chargeable gains less allowable losses accruing to an individual in any year of assessment exceeds the exempt amount for the year, the deduction from that amount for that year in respect of allowable losses carried forward from a previous year or carried back from a subsequent year in which the individual dies shall not be greater than the excess.

(6) Where in a year of assessment—

  (a) the amount of chargeable gains accruing to an individual does not exceed the exempt amount for the year, and

  (b) the aggregate amount or value of the consideration for all the disposals of assets made by him (other than disposals gains accruing on which are not chargeable gains) does not exceed an amount equal to twice the exempt amount for the year,

a statement to the effect of paragraphs (a) and (b) above shall, unless the inspector otherwise requires, be sufficient compliance with any notice under section 8 of the Management Act requiring the individual to make a return of the chargeable gains accruing to him in that year.

(7) For the year of assessment in which an individual dies and for the next two following years, subsections (1) to (6) above shall apply to his personal representatives as they apply to an individual.

(8) Schedule 1 shall have effect as respects the application of this section to trustees.

GENERAL NOTE

This introduces the annual exemption for individuals. The system now in operation was introduced in 1980 with an exemption of £3,000. In 1982 it was raised to £5,000, with provision for future indexation by Treasury order by reference to the retail price index. In 1987 it reached £6,600, but the following year it was reduced to £5,000 in view of the rebasing of C.G.T. to 1982. In 1991 it was increased to £5,500 by the Capital Gains Tax (Annual Exempt Amount) Order 1991 (S.I. 1991 No. 736) and this is the amount carried forward in the consolidation. The indexation is not automatic, since it can be overridden by Parliament.

Subs. (5)

The set-off of losses against gains applies only to the amount which exceeds the exemption.

Subs. (6)

Where an individual's gains do not exceed the exempt amount and his disposals do not exceed twice the gains, a note to this effect on his tax return is sufficient disclosure.

Subs. (7)

This applies the exempt amount to executors for the year of an individual's death and the two subsequent years.

Subs. (8)
Schedule 1 deals with the exemption for trustees. Generally they have half the individual's exemption.

Rates of capital gains tax

4.—(1) Subject to the provisions of this section and section 5, the rate of capital gains tax in respect of gains accruing to a person in a year of assessment shall be equivalent to the basic rate of income tax for the year.

(2) If income tax is chargeable at the higher rate in respect of any part of the income of an individual for a year of assessment, the rate of capital gains tax in respect of gains accruing to him in the year shall be equivalent to the higher rate.

(3) If no income tax is chargeable at the higher rate in respect of the income of an individual for a year of assessment, but the amount on which he is chargeable to capital gains tax exceeds the unused part of his basic rate band, the rate of capital gains tax on the excess shall be equivalent to the higher rate of income tax for the year.

(4) The reference in subsection (3) above to the unused part of an individual's basic rate band is a reference to the amount by which the basic rate limit exceeds his total income (as reduced by any deductions made in accordance with the Income Tax Acts).

GENERAL NOTE
From the introduction of C.G.T. until 1988, tax was charged at a single rate of 30 per cent. Since then the rates of C.G.T. and income tax have been unified. C.G.T. is charged at 25 per cent., but if an individual's total income and chargeable gains exceed the basic rate limit, the excess is charged at 40 per cent.

Accumulation and discretionary settlements

5.—(1) The rate of capital gains tax in respect of gains accruing to trustees of an accumulation or discretionary settlement in a year of assessment shall be equivalent to the sum of the basic and additional rates of income tax for the year.

(2) For the purposes of subsection (1) above a trust is an accumulation or discretionary settlement where—
(a) all or any part of the income arising to the trustees in the year of assessment is income to which section 686 of the Taxes Act (liability to income tax at the additional rate) applies, or
(b) all the income arising to the trustees in the year of assessment is treated as the income of the settlor, but that section would apply to it if it were not so treated, or
(c) all the income arising to the trustees in the year of assessment is applied in defraying expenses of the trustees in that year, but that section would apply to it if it were not so applied, or
(d) no income arises to the trustees in the year of assessment, but that section would apply if there were income arising to the trustees and none of it were treated as the income of the settlor or applied as mentioned in paragraph (c) above.

GENERAL NOTE
For accumulation or discretionary settlements the rate of C.G.T. corresponds to the rate of income tax, *i.e.* the basic plus the additional rate (see ICTA 1988, ss.1(2)(a) and 832(1)).
The liability generally applies to settlements caught by ICTA 1988, s.686.

Other special cases

6.—(1) References in section 4 to income tax chargeable at the higher rate include references to tax chargeable by virtue of section 353(4), 369(3A), 683(1) or 684(1) of the Taxes Act (restriction to basic rate of relief on certain interest etc. and settlements) in respect of excess liability (that is, liability to income tax over what it would be if all income tax were charged at the basic rate to the exclusion of any higher rate); and

    (a) where for any year of assessment a deduction is by virtue of section 353(4) or 369(3A) not allowed in computing the total income of a person for the purposes of excess liability then, whether or not he is chargeable to tax otherwise than at the basic rate, that deduction shall not be allowed for the purposes of section 4(4);

    (b) where for any year of assessment income is treated by virtue of section 683(1) or 684(1) as the income of a person for the purposes of excess liability then, whether or not he is chargeable to tax otherwise than at the basic rate, it shall also be treated as his income for the purposes of section 4(4).

(2) Where for any year of assessment—

    (a) by virtue of section 549(2) of the Taxes Act (gains under life policy or life annuity contract) a deduction of an amount is made from a person's total income for the purposes of excess liability, or

    (b) by virtue of section 683(1) or 684(1) of that Act an amount of a person's income is treated as not being his income for those purposes, or

    (c) by virtue of section 699(1) of that Act (income accruing before death) the residuary income of an estate is treated as reduced so as to reduce a person's income by any amount for those purposes,

section 4(4) shall have effect as if his income for the year were reduced by that amount.

(3) Where by virtue of section 547(1)(a) of the Taxes Act (gains from insurance policies etc.) a person's total income for a year of assessment is deemed to include any amount or amounts—

    (a) section 4(4) shall have effect as if his total income included not the whole of the amount or amounts concerned but only the appropriate fraction within the meaning of section 550(3) of that Act, and

    (b) if relief is given under section 550 of that Act and the calculation required by section 550(2)(b) does not involve the higher rate of income tax, section 4(2) and (3) shall have effect as if no income tax were chargeable at the higher rate in respect of his income.

(4) Nothing in subsection (1) above shall be taken to reduce, and nothing in subsections (2) and (3) above shall be taken to increase, the amount of the deduction which a person is entitled to make from his total income by virtue of any provision of Chapter I of Part VII of the Taxes Act which limits any allowance by reference to the level of his total income.

GENERAL NOTE

    This section includes special provisions consequent on the unification of the rates of income tax and capital gains tax.

Subs. (1)

    This brings into account for determining whether higher rate tax is payable the exclusion of higher rate relief on mortgage interest and the charge to higher rate tax on the income of settlements where the settlor retains an interest.

Subs. (2)

    This subsection likewise allows the deduction from income for higher rate purposes for losses on life policies, settlement income where the settlor is not chargeable and residuary income of an estate chargeable to inheritance tax.

Subs. (3)

    This extends the relief to cases where gains on life policies are mitigated for income tax purposes.

Subs. (4)

The foregoing provisions do not affect any restriction on personal reliefs by reference to total income.

Time for payment of tax

7. Capital gains tax assessed on any person in respect of gains accruing in any year shall be payable by that person on or before 1st December following the end of that year, or at the expiration of a period of 30 days beginning with the date of the issue of the notice of assessment, whichever is the later.

GENERAL NOTE

The time for payment of C.G.T. is December 1 in the year following the year of assessment in which the gain arises, or, if later, 30 days after the issue of an assessment.

If a tax return is not rendered by October 31, the Inland Revenue will consider charging interest under TMA 1970, s.88, on any assessment to C.G.T. made late (see Statement of Practice SP6/89).

Corporation tax

Company's total profits to include chargeable gains

8.—(1) Subject to the provisions of this section and section 400 of the Taxes Act, the amount to be included in respect of chargeable gains in a company's total profits for any accounting period shall be the total amount of chargeable gains accruing to the company in the accounting period after deducting—

(a) any allowable losses accruing to the company in the period, and

(b) so far as they have not been allowed as a deduction from chargeable gains accruing in any previous accounting period, any allowable losses previously accruing to the company while it has been within the charge to corporation tax.

(2) For the purposes of corporation tax in respect of chargeable gains, "allowable loss" does not include a loss accruing to a company in such circumstances that if a gain accrued the company would be exempt from corporation tax in respect of it.

(3) Except as otherwise provided by this Act or any other provision of the Corporation Tax Acts, the total amount of the chargeable gains to be included in respect of chargeable gains in a company's total profits for any accounting period shall for purposes of corporation tax be computed in accordance with the principles applying for capital gains tax, all questions—

(a) as to the amounts which are or are not to be taken into account as chargeable gains or as allowable losses, or in computing gains or losses, or charged to tax as a person's gain; or

(b) as to the time when any such amount is to be treated as accruing, being determined in accordance with the provisions relating to capital gains tax as if accounting periods were years of assessment.

(4) Subject to subsection (5) below, where the enactments relating to capital gains tax contain any reference to income tax or to the Income Tax Acts the reference shall, in relation to a company, be construed as a reference to corporation tax or to the Corporation Tax Acts; but—

(a) this subsection shall not affect the references to income tax in section 39(2); and

(b) in so far as those enactments operate by reference to matters of any specified description, account shall for corporation tax be taken of matters of that description which are confined to companies, but not of any which are confined to individuals.

(5) This Act as it has effect in accordance with this section shall not be affected in its operation by the fact that capital gains tax and corporation tax are distinct taxes but, so far as is consistent with the Corporation Tax Acts,

shall apply in relation to capital gains tax and corporation tax on chargeable gains as if they were one tax, so that, in particular, a matter which in a case involving two individuals is relevant for both of them in relation to capital gains tax shall in a like case involving an individual and a company be relevant for him in relation to that tax and for it in relation to corporation tax.

(6) Where assets of a company are vested in a liquidator under section 145 of the Insolvency Act 1986 or Article 123 of the Insolvency (Northern Ireland) Order 1989 or otherwise, this section and the enactments applied by this section shall apply as if the assets were vested in, and the acts of the liquidator in relation to the assets were the acts of, the company (acquisitions from or disposals to him by the company being disregarded accordingly).

GENERAL NOTE

This section contains further provisions about the charge to corporation tax on chargeable gains of companies imposed by s.1(2).

Subs. (1)

The general rule applies that chargeable gains are added to profits after deducting allowable losses for that period or brought forward. Under ICTA 1988, s.400, government investment written-off extinguishes a company's losses to the extent of the write-off.

Subs. (2)

Losses are not allowable in circumstances where a gain would be exempt, *e.g.* on intra-group transactions.

Subs. (3)

The general principles of C.G.T. apply for the purposes of computing corporation tax on chargeable gains.

Subs. (4)

References to income tax in the Act are to be taken, *mutatis mutandis*, to refer to corporation tax except where they are obviously inapplicable. Section 39(2) excludes from deduction expenditure on assets allowable against income.

Subs. (5)

For purposes of cases where the liability of more than one person is involved, *e.g.* provisions related to connected persons, C.G.T. and corporation tax on chargeable gains are to be treated as one tax.

Subs. (6)

Where a company is in liquidation, the liquidator steps into its shoes for the purposes of corporation tax on chargeable gains.

Residence etc.

Residence, including temporary residence

9.—(1) In this Act "resident" and "ordinarily resident" have the same meanings as in the Income Tax Acts.

(2) Section 207 of the Taxes Act (disputes as to domicile or ordinary residence) shall apply in relation to capital gains tax as it applies for the purposes mentioned in that section.

(3) Subject to section 10(1), an individual who is in the United Kingdom for some temporary purpose only and not with any view or intent to establish his residence in the United Kingdom shall be charged to capital gains tax on chargeable gains accruing in any year of assessment if and only if the period (or the sum of the periods) for which he is resident in the United Kingdom in that year of assessment exceeds six months.

GENERAL NOTE

Subs. (1)
Residence and ordinary residence have the same meaning as for income tax (see ICTA 1988, ss.334–336).

Subs. (2)
As with income tax, disputes as to domicile or ordinary residence are heard by the Special Commissioners.

Subs. (3)
An individual is not chargeable to C.G.T. if he is only in the U.K. for a temporary purpose and not for more than six months in any year (*cf.* ICTA 1988, s.336(1)).

Non-resident with United Kingdom branch or agency

10.—(1) Subject to any exceptions provided by this Act, a person shall be chargeable to capital gains tax in respect of chargeable gains accruing to him in a year of assessment in which he is not resident and not ordinarily resident in the United Kingdom but is carrying on a trade in the United Kingdom through a branch or agency, and shall be so chargeable on chargeable gains accruing on the disposal—
  (a) of assets situated in the United Kingdom and used in or for the purposes of the trade at or before the time when the capital gain accrued, or
  (b) of assets situated in the United Kingdom and used or held for the purposes of the branch or agency at or before that time, or assets acquired for use by or for the purposes of the branch or agency.
(2) Subsection (1) above does not apply unless the disposal is made at a time when the person is carrying on the trade in the United Kingdom through a branch or agency.
(3) For the purposes of corporation tax the chargeable profits of a company not resident in the United Kingdom but carrying on a trade or vocation there through a branch or agency shall be, or include, such chargeable gains accruing on the disposal of assets situated in the United Kingdom as are by this section made chargeable to capital gains tax in the case of an individual not resident or ordinarily resident in the United Kingdom.
(4) This section shall not apply to a person who, by virtue of Part XVIII of the Taxes Act (double taxation relief agreements), is exempt from income tax or corporation tax chargeable for the chargeable period in respect of the profits or gains of the branch or agency.
(5) This section shall apply as if references in subsections (1) and (2) above to a trade included references to a profession or vocation, but subsection (1) shall not apply in respect of chargeable gains accruing on the disposal of assets only used in or for the purposes of the profession or vocation before 14th March 1989 or only used or held for the purposes of the branch or agency before that date.
(6) In this Act, unless the context otherwise requires, "branch or agency" means any factorship, agency, receivership, branch or management, but does not include any person within the exemptions in section 82 of the Management Act (general agents and brokers).

GENERAL NOTE
Non-resident persons carrying on a trade in the U.K. through a branch or agency are chargeable on gains accruing on the disposal of assets in the U.K. used for the purposes of the trade or branch or agency.

Subs. (4)
This charge does not apply if double taxation relief is available under a treaty (see s.277). Treaties now normally allow U.K. taxation in the circumstances of this section.

Subs. (5)
The charge extends to non-residents carrying on a profession or vocation, as from March 14, 1989.

Subs. (6)
The extended definition of "branch or agency" in TMA 1970, s.118(1), applies, as does the important exemption for brokers under *ibid.* s.82.

Visiting forces, agents-general etc

11.—(1) A period during which a member of a visiting force to whom section 323(1) of the Taxes Act applies is in the United Kingdom by reason solely of his being a member of that force shall not be treated for the purposes of capital gains tax either as a period of residence in the United Kingdom or as creating a change in his residence or domicile.

This subsection shall be construed as one with subsection (2) of section 323 and subsections (4) to (8) of that section shall apply accordingly.

(2) An Agent-General who is resident in the United Kingdom shall be entitled to the same immunity from capital gains tax as that to which the head of a mission so resident is entitled under the Diplomatic Privileges Act 1964.

(3) Any person having or exercising any employment to which section 320(2) of the Taxes Act (staff of Agents-General etc.) applies (not being a person employed in any trade, business or other undertaking carried on for the purposes of profit) shall be entitled to the same immunity from capital gains tax as that to which a member of the staff of a mission is entitled under the Diplomatic Privileges Act 1964.

(4) Subsections (2) and (3) above shall be construed as one with section 320 of the Taxes Act.

GENERAL NOTE
Diplomatic immunity applies for C.G.T. as for other taxes, and is similarly extended to visiting forces and the agents-general of British colonies and states or provinces of Commonwealth countries and their staffs.

Foreign assets of person with foreign domicile.

12.—(1) In the case of individuals resident or ordinarily resident but not domiciled in the United Kingdom, capital gains tax shall not be charged in respect of gains accruing to them from the disposal of assets situated outside the United Kingdom (that is, chargeable gains accruing in the year 1965–66 or a later year of assessment) except that the tax shall be charged on the amounts (if any) received in the United Kingdom in respect of those chargeable gains, any such amount being treated as gains accruing when they are received in the United Kingdom.

(2) For the purposes of this section there shall be treated as received in the United Kingdom in respect of any gain all amounts paid, used or enjoyed in or in any manner or form transmitted or brought to the United Kingdom, and subsections (6) to (9) of section 65 of the Taxes Act (under which income applied outside the United Kingdom in payment of debts is, in certain cases, treated as received in the United Kingdom) shall apply as they would apply for the purposes of subsection (5) of that section if the gain were income arising from possessions out of the United Kingdom.

GENERAL NOTE
This important provision accords exemption from C.G.T. to the foreign assets of individuals resident or ordinarily resident but not domiciled in the U.K., unless the gains are remitted to the U.K.

Subs. (2)
The rules for constructive remittance in connection with Cases IV and V of Sched. D in ICTA 1988, s.65(6)–(9), are applied for the purposes of C.G.T.

Attribution of gains to members of non-resident companies

13.—(1) This section applies as respects chargeable gains accruing to a company—
  (a) which is not resident in the United Kingdom, and
  (b) which would be a close company if it were resident in the United Kingdom.

(2) Subject to this section, every person who at the time when the chargeable gain accrues to the company is resident or ordinarily resident in the United Kingdom, who, if an individual, is domiciled in the United Kingdom, and who holds shares in the company, shall be treated for the purposes of this Act as if a part of the chargeable gain had accrued to him.

(3) That part shall be equal to the proportion of the assets of the company to which the person would be entitled on a liquidation of the company at the time when the chargeable gain accrues to the company.

(4) If the part of a chargeable gain attributable to a person under subsection (2) above is less than one-twentieth, that subsection shall not apply to that person.

(5) This section shall not apply in relation to—
  (a) any amount in respect of the chargeable gain which is distributed, whether by way of dividend or distribution of capital or on the dissolution of the company, to persons holding shares in the company, or creditors of the company, within two years from the time when the chargeable gain accrued to the company, or
  (b) a chargeable gain accruing on the disposal of assets, being tangible property, whether movable or immovable, or a lease of such property, where the property was used, and used only, for the purposes of a trade carried on by the company wholly outside the United Kingdom, or
  (c) a chargeable gain accruing on the disposal of currency or of a debt within section 252(1), where the currency or debt is or represents money in use for the purposes of a trade carried on by the company wholly outside the United Kingdom, or
  (d) to a chargeable gain in respect of which the company is chargeable to tax by virtue of section 10(3).

(6) Subsection (5)(a) above shall not prevent the making of an assessment in pursuance of this section but if, by virtue of that paragraph, this section is excluded, all such adjustments, whether by way of repayment or discharge of tax or otherwise, shall be made as will give effect to the provisions of that paragraph.

(7) The amount of capital gains tax paid by a person in pursuance of subsection (2) above (so far as not reimbursed by the company) shall be allowable as a deduction in the computation under this Act of a gain accruing on the disposal by him of the shares by reference to which the tax was paid.

(8) So far as it would go to reduce or extinguish chargeable gains accruing by virtue of this section to a person in a year of assessment this section shall apply in relation to a loss accruing to the company on the disposal of an asset in that year of assessment as it would apply if a gain instead of a loss had accrued to the company on the disposal, but shall only so apply in relation to that person; and subject to the preceding provisions of this subsection this section shall not apply in relation to a loss accruing to the company.

(9) If the person owning any of the shares in the company at the time when the chargeable gain accrues to the company is itself a company which is not resident in the United Kingdom but which would be a close company if it were resident in the United Kingdom, an amount equal to the amount apportioned under subsection (3) above out of the chargeable gain to the shares so owned shall be apportioned among the issued shares of the second-mentioned company, and the holders of those shares shall be treated

in accordance with subsection (2) above, and so on through any number of companies.

(10) The persons treated by this section as if a part of a chargeable gain accruing to a company had accrued to them shall include trustees owning shares in the company if when the gain accrues to the company the trustees are neither resident nor ordinarily resident in the United Kingdom.

(11) If any tax payable by any person by virtue of subsection (2) above is paid by the company to which the chargeable gain accrues, or in a case under subsection (9) above is paid by any such other company, the amount so paid shall not for the purposes of income tax, capital gains tax or corporation tax be regarded as a payment to the person by whom the tax was originally payable.

GENERAL NOTE

The purpose of this section is to attribute to resident shareholders their part of the gains of non-resident companies which would be close companies if they were resident in the U.K. The definition of "close company" is contained in ICTA 1988, ss.414–415, and means basically a company controlled by five or fewer participators, subject to certain exceptions. The attributable part of the gains corresponds to the proportion of the assets to which the shareholder would be entitled on a liquidation.

There is a *de minimis* exemption of five per cent., and exemption also where the gain is distributed within two years (although this does not preclude a protective assessment in respect of the gain), where the gain is in respect of tangible assets or foreign currency or debt used for a non-U.K. trade, or where the gain is already chargeable under s.10.

Subs. (7)

Where a tax charge is paid by a person under this section and not reimbursed, it is allowable as a deduction against a gain accruing on the disposal of the underlying shares.

Subs. (8)

This allows proportionate relief in relation to losses accruing to the company, but only for the purposes of this section.

Subs. (9)

This allows sub-apportionment where the shareholder is another close company, and so on.

Subs. (10)

This applies the charge to non-resident trustee shareholders (with a view to resident beneficiaries).

Subs. (11)

Where the charge is paid by the company concerned, this is not treated as a payment to the shareholder.

For a relief for delayed remittances, see s.279.

Non-resident groups of companies

14.—(1) This section has effect for the purposes of section 13.

(2) Sections 171 to 174 and 175(1) shall apply in relation to non-resident companies which are members of a non-resident group of companies, as they apply in relation to companies resident in the United Kingdom which are members of a group of companies.

(3) Sections 178 to 180 shall apply for the purposes of section 13 as if for any reference therein to a group of companies there were substituted a reference to a non-resident group of companies, and as if references to companies were references to companies not resident in the United Kingdom.

(4) For the purposes of this section—

(a) a "non-resident group" of companies—

(i) in the case of a group, none of the members of which are resident in the United Kingdom, means that group, and

(ii) in the case of a group, two or more members of which are not resident in the United Kingdom, means the members which are not resident in the United Kingdom;
(b) "group" shall be construed in accordance with section 170 without subsections (2)(a), (9) and (12) to (14).

GENERAL NOTE
The effect of s.13 is mitigated for companies which are members of non-resident groups. The "no-gain/no-loss" provisions of ss.171–175 apply, subject to the charge under ss.178–180 where a company leaves a group.

PART II

GENERAL PROVISIONS RELATING TO COMPUTATION OF GAINS AND ACQUISITIONS AND DISPOSALS OF ASSETS

CHAPTER I

INTRODUCTORY

Computation of gains

15.—(1) The amount of the gains accruing on the disposal of assets shall be computed in accordance with this Part, subject to the other provisions of this Act.
(2) Every gain shall, except as otherwise expressly provided, be a chargeable gain.

GENERAL NOTE
This introduces the general computational provisions of Pt. II and provides that any gain so thrown up is chargeable unless otherwise excluded.

Computation of losses

16.—(1) Subject to section 72 of the Finance Act 1991 and except as otherwise expressly provided, the amount of a loss accruing on a disposal of an asset shall be computed in the same way as the amount of a gain accruing on a disposal is computed.
(2) Except as otherwise expressly provided, all the provisions of this Act which distinguish gains which are chargeable gains from those which are not, or which make part of a gain a chargeable gain, and part not, shall apply also to distinguish losses which are allowable losses from those which are not, and to make part of a loss an allowable loss, and part not; and references in this Act to an allowable loss shall be construed accordingly.
(3) A loss accruing to a person in a year of assessment during no part of which he is resident or ordinarily resident in the United Kingdom shall not be an allowable loss for the purposes of this Act unless, under section 10, he would be chargeable to tax in respect of a chargeable gain if there had been a gain instead of a loss on that occasion.
(4) In accordance with section 12(1), losses accruing on the disposal of assets situated outside the United Kingdom to an individual resident or ordinarily resident but not domiciled in the United Kingdom shall not be allowable losses.

GENERAL NOTE
The general rule is that losses are to be computed in the same way as gains. This is made subject to FA 1991, s.72, which allows unincorporated businesses relief for trading losses against capital gains.

Subs. (2)
Provisions distinguishing gains from chargeable gains are to be applied, *mutatis mutandis*, for distinguishing losses from allowable losses.

Subs. (3)

Losses accruing to a non-resident are not allowable in the same way as gains are not chargeable, except where he is within the charge under s.10.

Subs. (4)

Non-domiciled residents who are outside the charge to C.G.T. on unremitted gains on foreign assets are *pari passu* excluded from relief on losses.

Disposals and acquisitions treated as made at market value

17.—(1) Subject to the provisions of this Act, a person's acquisition or disposal of an asset shall for the purposes of this Act be deemed to be for a consideration equal to the market value of the asset—

(a) where he acquires or, as the case may be, disposes of the asset otherwise than by way of a bargain made at arm's length, and in particular where he acquires or disposes of it by way of gift or on a transfer into settlement by a settlor or by way of distribution from a company in respect of shares in the company, or

(b) where he acquires or, as the case may be, disposes of the asset wholly or partly for a consideration that cannot be valued, or in connection with his own or another's loss of office or employment or diminution of emoluments, or otherwise in consideration for or recognition of his or another's services or past services in any office or employment or of any other service rendered or to be rendered by him or another.

(2) Subsection (1) shall not apply to the acquisition of an asset if—

(a) there is no corresponding disposal of it, and

(b) there is no consideration in money or money's worth or the consideration is of an amount or value lower than the market value of the asset.

GENERAL NOTE

This section imposes a market value rule in cases where assets are acquired or disposed of otherwise than by a bargain at arm's length, *e.g.* gifts, transfers into settlement or distributions from companies, and also where the consideration cannot be valued or where the consideration relates to an employment.

In some of these cases there may be in any event a charge to income tax.

Subs. (2)

This excludes the market value rule in cases where there is no corresponding disposal of the asset and the consideration is either nil or less than the market value. The purpose of this provision is to prevent the market value rule from being used to increase artificially the acquisition cost of an asset, as in the "reverse Nairn Williamson" avoidance scheme, inspired by the decision in *Harrison* v. *Nairn Williamson* [1978] 1 W.L.R. 145 (see [1977] B.T.R. 110).

Transactions between connected persons

18.—(1) This section shall apply where a person acquires an asset and the person making the disposal is connected with him.

(2) Without prejudice to the generality of section 17(1) the person acquiring the asset and the person making the disposal shall be treated as parties to a transaction otherwise than by way of a bargain made at arm's length.

(3) Subject to subsection (4) below, if on the disposal a loss accrues to the person making the disposal, it shall not be deductible except from a chargeable gain accruing to him on some other disposal of an asset to the person acquiring the asset mentioned in subsection (1) above, being a disposal made at a time when they are connected persons.

(4) Subsection (3) above shall not apply to a disposal by way of gift in settlement if the gift and the income from it is wholly or primarily applicable for educational, cultural or recreational purposes, and the persons benefiting from the application for those purposes are confined to members of an association of persons for whose benefit the gift was made, not being persons all or most of whom are connected persons.

(5) Where the asset mentioned in subsection (1) above is an option to enter into a sale or other transaction given by the person making the disposal a loss accruing to the person acquiring the asset shall not be an allowable loss unless it accrues on a disposal of the option at arm's length to a person who is not connected with him.

(6) Subject to subsection (7) below, in a case where the asset mentioned in subsection (1) above is subject to any right or restriction enforceable by the person making the disposal, or by a person connected with him, then (where the amount of the consideration for the acquisition is, in accordance with subsection (2) above, deemed to be equal to the market value of the asset) that market value shall be—

(a) what its market value would be if not subject to the right or restriction, minus—

(b) the market value of the right or restriction or the amount by which its extinction would enhance the value of the asset to its owner, whichever is the less.

(7) If the right or restriction is of such a nature that its enforcement would or might effectively destroy or substantially impair the value of the asset without bringing any countervailing advantage either to the person making the disposal or a person connected with him or is an option or other right to acquire the asset or, in the case of incorporeal property, is a right to extinguish the asset in the hands of the person giving the consideration by forfeiture or merger or otherwise, the market value of the asset shall be determined, and the amount of the gain accruing on the disposal shall be computed, as if the right or restriction did not exist.

(8) Subsections (6) and (7) above shall not apply to a right of forfeiture or other right exercisable on breach of a covenant contained in a lease of land or other property, and shall not apply to any right or restriction under a mortgage or other charge.

GENERAL NOTE
    This section deems an acquisition and disposal of an asset to be other than at arm's length where the parties are "connected persons". For the interpretation of "connected persons", see s.286.

Subs. (3)
    This denies relief on any loss on the disposal, except against a gain on some other disposal to the same connected person. A scheme designed to avoid the effect of this provision was considered in *Shepherd (Inspector of Taxes)* v. *Lyntress*; *News International* v. *Shepherd (Inspector of Taxes)* [1989] S.T.C. 617. An attack on such schemes and the scheme used in *Burman* v. *Hedges & Butler* [1979] 1 W.L.R. 160 was launched by FA 1989, ss.135–138, now consolidated in ss.30–34 *infra*.

Subs. (4)
    This excludes from the ambit of subs. (3) gifts to educational, cultural or recreational purpose trusts, so long as the beneficiaries are not all or mostly connected persons.

Subs. (5)
    This extends the mischief of the section to options. For the general treatment of options, see ss.143–148 *infra*.

Subs. (6)
    Where the asset is subject to any right or restriction, the market value of the asset is reduced by the market value of the right or restriction or by the amount of the increase in value of the asset if this were removed, whichever is less.

Subs. (7)
    However, where the right or restriction could destroy or substantially impair the value of the asset without bringing any countervailing advantage, it is to be ignored.

Subs. (8)
    The foregoing two subsections do not apply to mortgages or covenants under leases.

Deemed consideration in certain cases where assets disposed of in a series of transactions

19.—(1) For the purposes of this Act, in any case where—

(a) by way of two or more material transactions which are linked (a series of linked transactions), one person disposes of assets to another person with whom he is connected or to two or more other persons with each of whom he is connected, and

(b) the original market value of the assets disposed of by any of the transactions in the series, as determined under section 20, is less than the appropriate portion of the aggregate market value of the assets disposed of by all the transactions in the series, as so determined,

then, subject to subsection (2) below, the disposal effected by any linked transaction in the series in respect of which the condition in paragraph (b) above is fulfilled shall be deemed to be for a consideration equal to the appropriate portion referred to in that paragraph.

(2) Where the disposal effected by a material transaction is one to which section 58 applies, nothing in subsection (1) above shall affect the amount which, for the purposes of this Act, is the consideration for that disposal.

(3) Subject to subsection (5) below, any reference in this section to a material transaction is a reference to a transaction by way of gift or otherwise; and, for the purposes of this section, two or more material transactions are linked if they occur within the period of six years ending on the date of the last of them.

(4) This section shall apply or, as the case may be, shall again apply—

(a) when a second material transaction causes a series of linked transactions to come into being; and

(b) whenever, on the occurrence of a further material transaction, an existing series is extended by the inclusion of that transaction (whether or not an earlier transaction ceases to form part of the series);

and all such assessments and adjustments of assessments shall be made as may be necessary to give effect to this section on each such occasion.

(5) Where a member of a group of companies disposes of an asset to another member of the group in circumstances such that, by virtue of section 171, both companies are treated, so far as relates to corporation tax on chargeable gains, as if the consideration for the disposal were of such an amount as would secure that neither a gain nor a loss would accrue, the transaction by which that disposal is effected is not a material transaction; and a disposal in these circumstances is in this section referred to as an "inter-group transfer".

(6) In any case where—

(a) a company ("company A") disposes of an asset by way of a material transaction, and

(b) company A acquired the asset after 19th March 1985 by way of an inter-group transfer, and

(c) the disposal by company A is to a person who is connected with another company ("company B") which at some time after 19th March 1985 disposed of the asset by way of an inter-group transfer, and

(d) either the disposal by way of inter-group transfer which is referred to in paragraph (c) above was the occasion of the acquisition referred to in paragraph (b) above or, between the disposal and that acquisition, there has been no disposal of the asset which was not an inter-group transfer,

then, for the purpose of determining whether subsection (1) above applies in relation to a series of linked transactions, the disposal by company A shall be treated as having been made by company B; but any increase in the consideration for that disposal resulting from the application of subsection (1) above shall have effect with respect to company A.

GENERAL NOTE

This section, together with s.20, was introduced in 1985. The purpose of the provisions is to prevent avoidance of tax by fragmentation of assets. They replaced a previous unsatisfactory formulation in CGTA 1979, s.151.

Subs. (1)

The section bites where assets are disposed of between connected persons (see s.286) in a series of transactions and the "original market value" of these assets is less than the appropriate portion of the "aggregate market value". In such a case the value is increased to the appropriate portion. For definitions of these terms see s.20(3), (4). This would apply, for example, to a case where a father distributed the shares of a company equally among his five children. Each holding, instead of being valued at the discount appropriate to a 20 per cent. holding, would be valued at a fifth of the whole.

Subs. (2)

The foregoing does not apply to disposals between spouses, which are on a no gain/no loss basis under s.58.

Subs. (3)

Transactions are linked if they occur within a six-year period.

Subs. (4)

The section's operation is reactivated if a further series of transactions commences.

Subs. (5)

The section does not apply to intra-group transfers treated under s.171 on a no gain/no loss basis.

Subs. (6)

This is aimed at the case where intra-group transfers take place, followed by a disposal to a connected person. This disposal is treated as being made at the aggregate market value, although the charge applies to the company actually making the disposal.

Original market value and aggregate market value for purposes of section 19

20.—(1) This section has effect for determining the original market value of assets and the aggregate market value of assets as mentioned in subsection (1)(b) of section 19.

(2) Expressions used in this section have the same meaning as in that section.

(3) Where there is a series of linked transactions, the original market value of the assets disposed of by each transaction in the series shall be determined as follows—

(a) if at the time in question the transaction is the most recent in the series, the original market value of the assets disposed of by that transaction is the market value which, apart from section 19, would be deemed to be the consideration for that transaction for the purposes of this Act; and

(b) in the case of any other transaction in the series, the original market value of the assets disposed of by that transaction is the value which, prior to the occurrence of the most recent transaction in the series, was or would have been deemed for the purposes of this Act to be the consideration for the transaction concerned (whether by virtue of the previous operation of section 19, or by virtue of any other provision of this Act).

(4) Subject to subsections (6) to (9) below, in relation to any transaction in a series of linked transactions—

(a) any reference in this section or section 19 to the aggregate market value of the assets disposed of by all the transactions in the series is a reference to what would have been the market value of all those assets for the purposes of this Act if, considering all the assets together, they had been disposed of by one disposal occurring at the time of the transaction concerned; and

(b) any reference in section 19 to the appropriate portion of the aggregate market value of the assets disposed of by all the transactions in the series is a reference to that portion of the market value determined in accordance with paragraph (a) above which it is reasonable to apportion to those of the assets which were actually disposed of by the transaction concerned.

(5) The reference in subsection (4)(a) above to considering all the assets together includes a reference not only to considering them as a group or holding or collection of assets retaining their separate identities but also (if it gives a higher market value) to considering them as brought together, physically or in law, so as to constitute either a single asset or a number of assets which are distinct from those which were comprised in each of the transactions concerned.

(6) If any of the assets disposed of by all the transactions in a series of linked transactions were acquired after the time of the first of those transactions, then, in the application of subsections (4) and (5) above in relation to each of the transactions in the series—

(a) no account shall be taken of any assets which were acquired after the time of that transaction unless they were acquired by way of an inter-group transfer; and

(b) subject to subsection (7) below, the number of assets of which account is to be taken shall be limited to the maximum number which were held by the person making the disposal at any time in the period beginning immediately before the first of the transactions in the series and ending immediately before the last.

(7) If, before the first of the transactions referred to in paragraph (b) of subsection (6) above, the person concerned (being a company) disposed of any assets by way of an inter-group transfer, the maximum number of assets referred to in that paragraph shall be determined as if the inter-group transfer had occurred after that first transaction.

(8) In the application of subsection (6) above in a case where the assets disposed of are securities, the assets disposed of by any of the transactions in a series of linked transactions shall be identified with assets acquired on an earlier date rather than with assets acquired on a later date.

(9) In subsection (8) above "securities" includes any assets which are of a nature to be dealt in without identifying the particular assets disposed of or acquired.

GENERAL NOTE
This is the interpretation provision for s.19.

Subs. (3)
"Original market value" is the market value apart from the operation of s.19.

Subs. (4)
"Aggregate market value" is the market value of the whole if disposed of in one transaction and the "appropriate portion" is the amount which it would be reasonable to apportion to the assets concerned.

Subs. (5)
Marriage value is to be considered in reaching aggregate market value.

Subs. (6)
Assets acquired after the commencement of the linked series of transactions otherwise than by way of intra-group transfer are ignored and the number of assets taken into account is limited to the maximum held by the person making the disposal during the series.

Subs. (7)

The latter limitation does not apply where there was an intra-group transfer prior to the beginning of the series.

Subss. (8) and (9)

In applying subs. (6), securities and other assets without earmark are identified on a FIFO rather than a LIFO basis.

CHAPTER II

ASSETS AND DISPOSALS OF ASSETS

General provisions

Assets and disposals

21.—(1) All forms of property shall be assets for the purposes of this Act, whether situated in the United Kingdom or not, including—

(a) options, debts and incorporeal property generally, and

(b) any currency other than sterling, and

(c) any form of property created by the person disposing of it, or otherwise coming to be owned without being acquired.

(2) For the purposes of this Act—

(a) references to a disposal of an asset include, except where the context otherwise requires, references to a part disposal of an asset, and

(b) there is a part disposal of an asset where an interest or right in or over the asset is created by the disposal, as well as where it subsists before the disposal, and generally, there is a part disposal of an asset where, on a person making a disposal, any description of property derived from the asset remains undisposed of.

GENERAL NOTE

Subs. (1)

This is a crucial provision, defining the subject-matter of the tax, and doing so in wide terms. However, para. (a) does not catch trade debts, except for the curiously named "debt on a security" (see further s.251(1)). Examples of assets caught by para. (c) include copyright in books and works of art. It does not include the issue of shares by a company, since the disposal coincides with the creation.

The following are issues which have been decided under the subsection:

(1) Rights of an employee under a contract of service are an "asset" within para. (a): *O'Brien* v. *Benson's Hosiery (Holdings)* [1980] A.C. 562 H.L.;

(2) so also is the right to deferred consideration on the disposal of an asset: *Marren* v. *Ingles* [1980] 1 W.L.R. 983;

(3) and also a statutory right to compensation for irretrievable loss: *Davenport (Inspector of Taxes)* v. *Chilver* [1983] Ch. 293;

(4) and the right to bring an action for negligence: *Zim Properties* v. *Procter (Inspector of Taxes)* (1984) 58 T.C. 371;

(5) and the goodwill disposed of under a covenant not to trade given by a company: *Kirby (Inspector of Taxes)* v. *Thorn EMI* [1988] 1 W.L.R. 445, C.A.

In each case the "incorporeal property" concerned was in the nature of a "chose in action".

Subs. (2)

A common example of a part disposal is the grant of a lease out of a freehold (see Sched. 8, para. 2(1)). It was held in *Berry* v. *Warnett* [1982] 2 All E.R. 630, H.L., that a transfer of assets to a settlement with retention of a life interest was not a part disposal. In *Anders Utkilens Rideri A/S* v. *O/Y Lovisa Stevedoring Company Co. A/B* [1985] 2 All E.R. 669 it was held that a compromise of an action on terms that the defendant sell the property and divide the proceeds with the plaintiff imposed an immediate trust for sale and effected a part disposal of the property.

Disposal where capital sums derived from assets

22.—(1) Subject to sections 23 and 26(1), and to any other exceptions in this Act, there is for the purposes of this Act a disposal of assets by their owner where any capital sum is derived from assets notwithstanding that no asset is acquired by the person paying the capital sum, and this subsection applies in particular to—

(a) capital sums received by way of compensation for any kind of damage or injury to assets or for the loss, destruction or dissipation of assets or for any depreciation or risk of depreciation of an asset,

(b) capital sums received under a policy of insurance of the risk of any kind of damage or injury to, or the loss or depreciation of, assets,

(c) capital sums received in return for forfeiture or surrender of rights or for refraining from exercising rights, and

(d) capital sums received as consideration for use or exploitation of assets.

(2) In the case of a disposal within paragraph (a), (b), (c) or (d) of subsection (1) above, the time of the disposal shall be the time when the capital sum is received as described in that subsection.

(3) In this section "capital sum" means any money or money's worth which is not excluded from the consideration taken into account in the computation of the gain.

GENERAL NOTE

Subject to the special provisions regarding insurance claims and mortgages, the receipt of a capital sum "derived from assets" is treated as a disposal, even if no asset is acquired by the person paying the sum. Paragraphs (a)–(d) give specific examples.

The cases discussed under s.21(1) *supra* are also relevant to this section. Important exclusions from its scope are compensation for the termination of a lease under the Agricultural Holdings Act 1986 (*Davis* v. *Powell* [1977] 1 W.L.R. 258), and the Landlord and Tenant Act 1954 (*Drummond* (*Inspector of Taxes*) v. *Brown* (*Austin*) [1986] Ch. 52, C.A.) and also compensation received for the destruction of business premises by terrorists (*Lang* (*Inspector of Taxes*) v. *Rice* [1984] S.T.C. 172, C.A.), since these related rather to the extinction of assets. However, compensation for the revocation of planning permission to conduct drag racing under a licence did fall under the section, since it was derived from the licence (*Pennine Raceway* v. *Kirklees Metropolitan Council* (*No. 2*) [1989] S.T.C. 122, C.A.).

Payments for the relinquishing of an option are also chargeable under this section (*Golding* (*Inspector of Taxes*) v. *Kaufman* (1984) 58 T.C. 296; *Welbeck Securities* v. *Powlson* (*Inspector of Taxes*) [1987] S.T.C. 468, C.A.).

Receipt of compensation and insurance money not treated as a disposal

23.—(1) If the recipient so claims, receipt of a capital sum within paragraph (a), (b), (c) or (d) of section 22(1) derived from an asset which is not lost or destroyed shall not be treated for the purposes of this Act as a disposal of the asset if—

(a) the capital sum is wholly applied in restoring the asset, or

(b) (subject to subsection (2) below), the capital sum is applied in restoring the asset except for a part of the capital sum which is not reasonably required for the purpose and which is small as compared with the whole capital sum, or

(c) (subject to subsection (2) below), the amount of the capital sum is small, as compared with the value of the asset,

but, if the receipt is not treated as a disposal, all sums which would, if the receipt had been so treated, have been brought into account as consideration for that disposal in the computation of the gain shall be deducted from any expenditure allowable under Chapter III of this Part as a deduction in computing a gain on the subsequent disposal of the asset.

(2) If the allowable expenditure is less than the consideration for the disposal constituted by the receipt of the capital sum (or is nil)—

(a) paragraphs (b) and (c) of subsection (1) above shall not apply, and

(b) if the recipient so elects (and there is any allowable expenditure)—

(i) the amount of the consideration for the disposal shall be reduced by the amount of the allowable expenditure, and

(ii) none of that expenditure shall be allowable as a deduction in computing a gain accruing on the occasion of the disposal or any subsequent occasion.

In this subsection "allowable expenditure" means expenditure which, immediately before the disposal, was attributable to the asset under paragraphs (a) and (b) of section 38(1).

(3) If, in a case not falling within subsection (1)(b) above, a part of a capital sum within paragraph (a) or paragraph (b) of section 22(1) derived from an asset which is not lost or destroyed is applied in restoring the asset, then if the recipient so claims, that part of the capital sum shall not be treated as consideration for the disposal deemed to be effected on receipt of the capital sum but shall be deducted from any expenditure allowable under Chapter III of this Part as a deduction in computing a gain on the subsequent disposal of the asset.

(4) If an asset is lost or destroyed and a capital sum received by way of compensation for the loss or destruction, or under a policy of insurance of the risk of the loss or destruction, is within one year of receipt, or such longer period as the inspector may allow, applied in acquiring an asset in replacement of the asset lost or destroyed the owner shall if he so claims be treated for the purposes of this Act—

(a) as if the consideration for the disposal of the old asset were (if otherwise of a greater amount) of such amount as would secure that on the disposal neither a gain nor a loss accrues to him, and

(b) as if the amount of the consideration for the acquisition of the new asset were reduced by the excess of the mount of the capital sum received by way of compensation or under the policy of insurance, together with any residual or scrap value, over the amount of the consideration which he is treated as receiving under paragraph (a) above.

(5) A claim shall not be made under subsection (4) above if part only of the capital sum is applied in acquiring the new asset but if all of that capital sum except for a part which is less than the amount of the gain (whether all chargeable gain or not) accruing on the disposal of the old asset is so applied, then the owner shall if he so claims be treated for the purposes of this Act—

(a) as if the amount of the gain so accruing were reduced to the amount of the said part (and, if not all chargeable gain, with a proportionate reduction in the amount of the chargeable gain), and

(b) as if the amount of the consideration for the acquisition of the new asset were reduced by the amount by which the gain is reduced under paragraph (a) of this subsection.

(6) This section shall not apply in relation to a wasting asset.

GENERAL NOTE

Subs. (1)

In the special case of capital sums under s.22 derived from an asset which is not lost or destroyed, the taxpayer may opt to be excluded from s.22, if the sum is wholly, or to the maximum extent reasonable, applied in restoring the asset, or the amount is small. The receipt will, however, be deducted from the base cost on any subsequent disposal.

Subs. (2)

If the base cost is less than the compensation, the recipient may elect to set the base cost against it.

Subs. (3)

If part of the compensation is applied in restoring the asset, the recipient may elect to have that part excluded from s.22, subject to deduction from the base cost on a subsequent disposal of the asset.

Subs. (4)

If the sum received is compensation for loss or destruction, and the recipient applies the amount within a year (or longer if the inspector allows) to replacing the asset, he may elect to have the deemed disposal of the old asset treated on a no-gain/no-loss basis. The acquisition cost of the new asset will be reduced by any excess of the compensation, together with any residual or scrap value, over the consideration for the deemed disposal.

Subs. (5)

Where part only of the sum is applied, the recipient may claim, if the part not applied is less than the gain, to have the gain reduced to the amount of that part. The consideration for the acquisition is correspondingly reduced.

Subs. (6)

The section does not apply to a wasting asset (see s.44).

Disposals where assets lost or destroyed, or become of negligible value

24.—(1) Subject to the provisions of this Act and, in particular to section 144, the occasion of the entire loss, destruction, dissipation or extinction of an asset shall, for the purposes of this Act, constitute a disposal of the asset whether or not any capital sum by way of compensation or otherwise is received in respect of the destruction, dissipation or extinction of the asset.

(2) If, on a claim by the owner of an asset, the inspector is satisfied that the value of an asset has become negligible, he may allow the claim and there-upon this Act shall have effect as if the claimant had sold, and immediately reacquired, the asset for a consideration of an amount equal to the value specified in the claim.

(3) For the purposes of subsections (1) and (2) above, a building and any permanent or semi-permanent structure in the nature of a building may be regarded as an asset separate from the land on which it is situated, but where either of those subsections applies in accordance with this subsection, the person deemed to make the disposal of the building or structure shall be treated as if he had also sold, and immediately reacquired, the site of the building or structure (including in the site any land occupied for purposes ancillary to the use of the building or structure) for a consideration equal to its market value at that time.

GENERAL NOTE

An asset may become valueless, *e.g.* shares in a company which becomes bankrupt. In such a case the taxpayer may crystallise his loss if the inspector is satisfied that the value of the asset has become negligible. A building may be treated as a separate asset from the land, but the market value of the land must be brought into account. A claim under this section cannot be antedated to a year of assessment prior to the claim (*Williams* v. *Bullivant* (1982) 56 T.C. 159; *Larner* v. *Warrington* [1985] S.T.C. 442).

Forfeited deposits are dealt with under s.144.

Non-residents: deemed disposals

25.—(1) Where an asset ceases by virtue of becoming situated outside the United Kingdom to be a chargeable asset in relation to a person, he shall be deemed for all purposes of this Act—

(a) to have disposed of the asset immediately before the time when it became situated outside the United Kingdom, and

(b) immediately to have reacquired it,

at its market value at that time.

(2) Subsection (1) above does not apply—

(a) where the asset becomes situated outside the United Kingdom contemporaneously with the person there mentioned ceasing to carry on a trade in the United Kingdom through a branch or agency, or

(b) where the asset is an exploration or exploitation asset.

(3) Where an asset ceases to be a chargeable asset in relation to a person by virtue of his ceasing to carry on a trade in the United Kingdom through a branch or agency, he shall be deemed for all purposes of this Act—
   (a) to have disposed of the asset immediately before the time when he ceased to carry on the trade in the United Kingdom through a branch or agency, and
   (b) immediately to have reacquired it,
at its market value at that time.

(4) Subsection (3) above shall not apply to an asset by reason of a transfer of the whole or part of the long term business of an insurance company to another company if section 139 has effect in relation to the asset by virtue of section 211.

(5) Subsection (3) above does not apply to an asset which is a chargeable asset in relation to the person there mentioned at any time after he ceases to carry on the trade in the United Kingdom through a branch or agency and before the end of the chargeable period in which he does so.

(6) In this section—
   "exploration or exploitation asset" means an asset used in connection with exploration or exploitation activities carried on in the United Kingdom or a designated area, and
   "designated area" and "exploration or exploitation activities" have the same meanings as in section 276.

(7) For the purposes of this section an asset is at any time a chargeable asset in relation to a person if, were it to be disposed of at that time, any chargeable gains accruing to him on the disposal—
   (a) would be gains in respect of which he would be chargeable to capital gains tax under section 10(1), or
   (b) would form part of his chargeable profits for corporation tax purposes by virtue of section 10(3).

(8) This section shall apply as if references to a trade included references to a profession or vocation.

GENERAL NOTE
   This section is designed to prevent avoidance of tax under s.10 by moving assets outside the U.K. In such a case there is a deemed disposal when the asset is so moved. This does not apply where the carrying on of a business in the U.K. through a trade or agency ceases at that time or the asset is an "exploration or exploitation asset". This latter applies basically to assets used in the North Sea (see s.276), which are dealt with under s.199. Where there is a cesser of a business, however, there is also a deemed disposal at that time, unless the asset continues to be within charge.
   The section does not apply to the transfer of the long-term business of an insurance company (see Insurance Companies Act 1982, Sched. 1) if s.139 applies by virtue of s.211.

Mortgages and charges not to be treated as disposals

26.—(1) The conveyance or transfer by way of security of an asset or of an interest or right in or over it, or transfer of a subsisting interest or right by way of security in or over an asset (including a retransfer on redemption of the security), shall not be treated for the purposes of this Act as involving any acquisition or disposal of the asset.

(2) Where a person entitled to an asset by way of security or to the benefit of a charge or incumbrance on an asset deals with the asset for the purpose of enforcing or giving effect to the security, charge or incumbrance, his dealings with it shall be treated for the purposes of this Act as if they were done through him as nominee by the person entitled to it subject to the security, charge or incumbrance; and this subsection shall apply to the dealings of any person appointed to enforce or give effect to the security, charge or incumbrance as receiver and manager or judicial factor as it applies to the dealings of the person entitled as aforesaid.

(3) An asset shall be treated as having been acquired free of any interest or right by way of security subsisting at the time of any acquisition of it, and as being disposed of free of any such interest or right subsisting at the time of the disposal; and where an asset is acquired subject to any such interest or right the full amount of the liability thereby assumed by the person acquiring the asset shall form part of the consideration for the acquisition and disposal in addition to any other consideration.

GENERAL NOTE
This section takes mortgages and charges on assets outside the scope of the tax, since they do not involve a disposal of the beneficial interest. Dealings by the mortgagee are treated as if done by the mortgagor. However, the section does not apply to transfers of property pursuant to an order made on decree nisi, even where the recipient gives undertakings in respect of proceeds of sale (*Aspden* (*Inspector of Taxes*) v. *Hildesley* [1982] 1 W.L.R. 264).

Subs. (3)
Assets are treated as being acquired and disposed of free of any charge. Where a purchaser assumes liability for a charge, this comprises part of the consideration (see the Stamp Act 1891, s.57, for an analogous provision).

Disposals in cases of hire-purchase and similar transactions

27. A hire-purchase or other transaction under which the use and enjoyment of an asset is obtained by a person for a period at the end of which the property in the asset will or may pass to that person shall be treated for the purposes of this Act, both in relation to that person and in relation to the person from whom he obtains the use and enjoyment of the asset, as if it amounted to an entire disposal of the asset to that person at the beginning of the period for which he obtains the use and enjoyment of the asset, but subject to such adjustments of tax, whether by way of repayment or discharge of tax or otherwise, as may be required where the period for which that person has the use and enjoyment of the asset terminates without the property in the asset passing to him.

GENERAL NOTE
A hire-purchase or "other transaction" under which property in goods passes after a period during which the hirer enjoys the use of the asset is treated as a disposal *ab initio*, subject to adjustment if the property does not in fact pass. An agreement for the sale by instalments of a taxi and its licence plate was held to be an "other transaction" for the purposes of the section (*Lyon* (*Inspector of Taxes*) v. *Pettigrew* (1985) 58 T.C. 452).

Time of disposal and acquisition where asset disposed of under contract

28.—(1) Subject to section 22(2), and subsection (2) below, where an asset is disposed of and acquired under a contract the time at which the disposal and acquisition is made is the time the contract is made (and not, if different, the time at which the asset is conveyed or transferred).

(2) If the contract is conditional (and in particular if it is conditional on the exercise of an option) the time at which the disposal and acquisition is made is the time when the condition is satisfied.

GENERAL NOTE

Subs. (1)
This important provision treats the disposal and acquisition of an asset for C.G.T. as taking place where a binding contract is made. However, capital sums derived from assets, as under insurance policies, are chargeable when received (s.22(2)). For a consideration of the provision in the context of a tax avoidance scheme, see *Magnavox Electronics Co.* (*In Liquidation*) v. *Hall* (*Inspector of Taxes*) (1986) 59 T.C. 610, C.A.

Subs. (2)
In the case of a conditional contract, the disposal takes place when the condition is satisfied.

The nature of a conditional contract was considered in *Eastham* v. *Leigh London & Provincial Properties* [1971] Ch. 871, C.A. It was held that a contract the fulfilment of which depended on the due performance by the parties of its terms was not conditional for this purpose.

Value shifting

General provisions

29.—(1) Without prejudice to the generality of the provisions of this Act as to the transactions which are disposals of assets, any transaction which under the following subsections is to be treated as a disposal of an asset—

    (a) shall be so treated (with a corresponding acquisition of an interest in the asset) notwithstanding that there is no consideration, and

    (b) so far as, on the assumption that the parties to the transaction were at arm's length, the party making the disposal could have obtained consideration, or additional consideration, for the disposal, shall be treated as not being at arm's length and the consideration so obtainable, or the additional consideration so obtainable added to the consideration actually passing, shall be treated as the market value of what is acquired.

(2) If a person having control of a company exercises his control so that value passes out of shares in the company owned by him or a person with whom he is connected, or out of rights over the company exercisable by him or by a person with whom he is connected, and passes into other shares in or rights over the company, that shall be a disposal of the shares or rights out of which the value passes by the person by whom they were owned or exercisable.

(3) A loss on the disposal of an asset shall not be an allowable loss to the extent to which it is attributable to value having passed out of other assets, being shares in or rights over a company which by virtue of the passing of value are treated as disposed of under subsection (2) above.

(4) If, after a transaction which results in the owner of land or of any other description of property becoming the lessee of the property there is any adjustment of the rights and liabilities under the lease, whether or not involving the grant of a new lease, which is as a whole favourable to the lessor, that shall be a disposal by the lessee of an interest in the property.

(5) If an asset is subject to any description of right or restriction the extinction or abrogation, in whole or in part, of the right or restriction by the person entitled to enforce it shall be a disposal by him of the right or restriction.

GENERAL NOTE

"Value-shifting", *e.g.* the transference of value from one class of shares in a company to another, had long been used for the avoidance of stamp duty by the device known as the "pref-trick". Its potential for the avoidance of C.G.T. was recognised and these provisions, apart from subs. (3), derive from the original legislation in FA 1965, Sched. 7, para. 15; subs. (3) was added by F(No. 2)A 1975, s.60. Experience showed that these provisions were inadequate to counter more sophisticated forms of value-shifting and ss.30–34 were added by FA 1977, s.43, and FA 1989, ss.135–137.

Subs. (1)

This opens a general attack on value-shifting by providing for the substitution of market value for actual values in the circumstances of the section.

Subs. (2)

This is the key component of the 1965 provisions, attacking the classic example of value-shifting by a person controlling a company. The leading case on value-shifting is *Floor* v. *Davis* [1980] A.C. 695, which was finally settled in favour of the Inland Revenue by a 3–2 majority of the House of Lords on the basis that "person" was to be interpreted as including "persons". It is clear from the subsequent House of Lords decision in *Ramsay (W.T.)* v. *I.R.C.* [1982] A.C. 300 that the *Floor* v. *Davis* scheme would also have been vulnerable under the "new approach" enunciated in that case (see *per* Lord Wilberforce at p. 185 and *per* Lord Fraser of Tullybelton at p. 198).

Subs. (3)
This extends the scope of subs. (2) to cover schemes designed to create allowable losses.

Subs. (4)
This attacks value-shifting through the adjustment of terms in leases.

Subs. (5)
This provides that the abrogation of a right or restriction is to be treated as a disposal of it.

Tax-free benefits

30.—(1) This section has effect as respects the disposal of an asset if a scheme has been effected or arrangements have been made (whether before or after the disposal) whereby—
    (a) the value of the asset or a relevant asset has been materially reduced, and
    (b) a tax-free benefit has been or will be conferred—
        (i) on the person making the disposal or a person with whom he is connected, or
        (ii) subject to subsection (4) below, on any other person.
    (2) For the purposes of this section, where the asset disposed of by a company ("the disposing company") consists of shares in, or securities of, another company, another asset is a relevant asset if, at the time of the disposal, it is owned by a company associated with the disposing company; but no account shall be taken of any reduction in the value of a relevant asset except in a case where—
    (a) during the period beginning with the reduction in value and ending immediately before the disposal by the disposing company, there is no disposal of the asset to any person, other than a disposal falling within section 171(1),
    (b) no disposal of the asset is treated as having occurred during that period by virtue of section 178 or 179, and
    (c) if the reduction had not taken place but any consideration given for the relevant asset and any other material circumstances (including any consideration given before the disposal for the asset disposed of) were unchanged, the value of the asset disposed of would, at the time of the disposal, have been materially greater;
and in this subsection "securities" has the same meaning as in section 132.
    (3) For the purposes of subsection (1)(b) above a benefit is conferred on a person if he becomes entitled to any money or money's worth or the value of any asset in which he has an interest is increased or he is wholly or partly relieved from any liability to which he is subject; and a benefit is tax-free unless it is required, on the occasion on which it is conferred on the person in question, to be brought into account in computing his income, profits or gains for the purposes of income tax, capital gains tax or corporation tax.
    (4) This section shall not apply by virtue of subsection (1)(b)(ii) above if it is shown that avoidance of tax was not the main purpose or one of the main purposes of the scheme or arrangements in question.
    (5) Where this section has effect in relation to any disposal, any allowable loss or chargeable gain accruing on the disposal shall be calculated as if the consideration for the disposal were increased by such amount as appears to the inspector, or on appeal the Commissioners concerned, to be just and reasonable having regard to the scheme or arrangements and the tax-free benefit in question.
    (6) Where—
    (a) by virtue of subsection (5) above the consideration for the disposal of an asset has been treated as increased, and

(b) the benefit taken into account under subsection (1)(b) above was an increase in the value of another asset,

any allowable loss or chargeable gain accruing on the first disposal of the other asset after the increase in its value shall be calculated as if the consideration for that disposal were reduced by such amount as appears to the inspector, or on appeal the Commissioners concerned, to be just and reasonable having regard to the scheme or arrangements in question and the increase made in relation to the disposal mentioned in paragraph (a) above.

(7) References in this section to a disposal do not include references to any disposal falling within section 58(1), 62(4) or 171(1).

(8) References in this section, in relation to any disposal, to a reduction in the value of an asset, where the asset consists of shares owned by a company in another company, shall be interpreted in accordance with sections 31 to 33 and, in those sections, the disposal, the asset and those companies are referred to respectively as "the section 30 disposal", the principal asset", "the first company" and "the second company".

(9) In relation to a case in which the disposal of an asset precedes its acquisition the references in subsections (1)(a) and (2) above to a reduction shall be read as including a reference to an increase.

GENERAL NOTE

This widens the scope of s.29 by attacking any scheme to reduce the value of an asset and confer a tax-free benefit on the disponor or a connected person (see s.286) or anyone else unless tax avoidance was not the purpose of the scheme. The schemes involved usually included either a shift in value from an equitable interest which was a chargeable asset to one which was not, or the reduction in value of a chargeable debt.

Subs. (2)

The section catches in certain circumstances the disposal of shares in a company by an associated company (*i.e.* a member of the same group: see ss.33(9) and 170). It is aimed particularly at cases where a member of a group pays a dividend or disposes of an asset within the group and is then transferred itself to another member of the group, which in turn is sold on.

Subs. (5)

The section operates by increasing the consideration for a disposal by such amount as appears "just and reasonable" to the inspector or the Commissioners.

Subs. (6)

As a consequence, the consideration on the next disposal of the asset will be adjusted on a "just and reasonable" basis.

Subs. (7)

The section does not apply to disposals between spouses, to legatees or within a group.

Subs. (8)

This ties the section in to the subsequent anti-avoidance provisions in ss.31–33.

Subs. (9)

This applies the section to cases where a disposal precedes an acquisition with a reference to an increase rather than a reduction in the value of an asset.

Distributions within a group followed by a disposal of shares

31.—(1) The references in section 30 to a reduction in the value of an asset, in the case mentioned in subsection (8) of that section, do not include a reduction attributable to the payment of a dividend by the second company at a time when it and the first company are associated, except to the extent (if any) that the dividend is attributable to chargeable profits of the second company and, in such a case, the tax-free benefit shall be ascertained without regard to any part of the dividend that is not attributable to such profits.

(2) Subsections (3) to (11) below apply for the interpretation of subsection (1) above.

(3) Chargeable profits shall be ascertained as follows—

(a) the distributable profits of any company are chargeable profits of that company to the extent that they are profits arising on a transaction caught by this section, and

(b) where any company makes a distribution attributable wholly or partly to chargeable profits (including any profits that are chargeable profits by virtue of this paragraph) to another company, the distributable profits of the other company, so far as they represent that distribution or so much of it as was attributable to chargeable profits, are chargeable profits of the other company,

and for this purpose any loss or other amount to be set against the profits of a company in determining the distributable profits shall be set first against profits other than the profits so arising or, as the case may be, representing so much of the distribution as was attributable to chargeable profits.

(4) The distributable profits of a company are such profits computed on a commercial basis, as, after allowing for any provision properly made for tax, the company is empowered, assuming sufficient funds, to distribute to persons entitled to participate in the profits of the company.

(5) Profits of a company ("company A") are profits arising on a transaction caught by this section where each of the following three conditions is satisfied.

(6) The first condition is that the transaction is—

(a) a disposal of an asset by company A to another company in circumstances such that company A and the other company are treated as mentioned in section 171(1), or

(b) an exchange, or a transaction treated for the purposes of section 135(2) and (3) as an exchange, of shares in or debentures of a company held by company A for shares in or debentures of another company, being a company associated with company A immediately after the transaction, and is treated by virtue of section 135(3) as a reorganisation of share capital, or

(c) a revaluation of an asset in the accounting records of company A.

In the following conditions the "asset with enhanced value" means (subject to section 33), in the paragraph (a) case, the asset acquired by the person to whom the disposal is made, in the paragraph (b) case, the shares in or debentures of the other company and, in the paragraph (c) case, the revalued asset.

(7) The second condition is that—

(a) during the period beginning with the transaction referred to in subsection (6) above and ending immediately before the section 30 disposal, there is no disposal of the asset with enhanced value to any person, other than a disposal falling within section 171(1), and

(b) no disposal of the asset with enhanced value is treated as having occurred during that period by virtue of section 178 or 179.

(8) The third condition is that, immediately after the section 30 disposal, the asset with enhanced value is owned by a person other than the company making that disposal or a company associated with it.

(9) The conditions in subsections (6) to (8) above are not satisfied if—

(a) at the time of the transaction referred to in subsection (6) above, company A carries on a trade and a profit on a disposal of the asset with enhanced value would form part of the trading profits, or

(b) by reason of the nature of the asset with enhanced value, a disposal of it could give rise neither to a chargeable gain nor to an allowable loss, or

(c) immediately before the section 30 disposal, the company owning the asset with enhanced value carries on a trade and a profit on a disposal of the asset would form part of the trading profits.

(10) The amount of chargeable profits of a company to be attributed to any distribution made by the company at any time in respect of any class of shares, securities or rights shall be ascertained by—

(a) determining the total of distributable profits, and the total of chargeable profits, that remains after allowing for earlier distributions made in respect of that or any other class of shares, securities or rights, and for distributions made at or to be made after that time in respect of other classes of shares, securities or rights, and

(b) attributing first to that distribution distributable profits other than chargeable profits.

(11) The amount of chargeable profits of a company to be attributed to any part of a distribution made at any time to which a person is entitled by virtue of any part of his holding of any class of shares, securities or rights, shall be such proportion of the chargeable profits as are attributable under subsection (10) above to the distributions made at that time in respect of that class as corresponds to that part of his holding.

GENERAL NOTE

This section, introduced together with the three following sections as FA 1989, ss.135–137, makes a more focused attack on value-shifting within groups of companies. It deals with the payment of an intra-group dividend prior to a disposal. The anti-avoidance provisions do not apply unless the dividend is attributable to chargeable profits.

Chargeable profits are profits arising on three types of transaction: (a) an intra-group disposal; (b) a reconstruction of capital between associated companies; and (c) a revaluation of assets.

These profits will be chargeable if no other actual or deemed disposal of the asset took place before the disposal was caught by s.30 and after that disposal the asset is owned outside the group.

The section does not apply to trading transactions or where no gain or loss could accrue on the disposal because of the nature of the asset.

The amount of chargeable profits to be attributed to a dividend is allocated among the shareholders in proportion to their holdings, taking other profits before chargeable profits.

Disposals within a group followed by a disposal of shares

32.—(1) The references in section 30 to a reduction in the value of an asset, in the case mentioned in subsection (8) of that section, do not include a reduction attributable to the disposal of any asset ("the underlying asset") by the second company at a time when it and the first company are associated, being a disposal falling within section 171(1), except in a case within subsection (2) below.

(2) A case is within this subsection if the amount or value of the actual consideration for the disposal of the underlying asset—

(a) is less than the market value of the underlying asset, and

(b) is less than the cost of the underlying asset,

unless the disposal is effected for bona fide commercial reasons and does not form part of a scheme or arrangements of which the main purpose, or one of the main purposes, is avoidance of liability to corporation tax.

(3) For the purposes of subsection (2) above, the cost of an asset owned by a company is the aggregate of—

(a) any capital expenditure incurred by the company in acquiring or providing the asset, and

(b) any other capital expenditure incurred by the company in respect of the asset while owned by that company.

(4) For the purposes of this section, where the disposal of the underlying asset is a part disposal, the reference in subsection (2)(a) above to the market value of the underlying asset is to the market value of the asset acquired by the person to whom the disposal is made and the amounts to be attributed to the underlying asset under paragraph (a) and (b) of subsection (3) above shall be reduced to the appropriate proportion of those amounts, that is—

   (a) the proportion of capital expenditure in respect of the underlying asset properly attributed in the accounting records of the company to the asset acquired by the person to whom the disposal is made, or

   (b) where paragraph (a) above does not apply such proportion as appears to the inspector, or on appeal the Commissioners concerned, to be just and reasonable.

(5) Where by virtue of a distribution in the course of dissolving or winding up the second company the first company is treated as disposing of an interest in the principal asset, the exception mentioned in subsection (1) above does not apply.

GENERAL NOTE

This section brings s.30 into operation if a subsidiary makes an intra-group disposal of an asset at less than market value and cost unless there is a bona fide commercial reason. In the case of a part disposal, a "just and reasonable" proportion is applied. The charge does not apply to disposals during liquidation.

Provisions supplementary to sections 30 to 32

33.—(1) For the purposes of sections 30(2) and 31(7) to (9), subsections (2) to (6) below apply for the purpose of determining in the case of any asset ("the original asset") whether it is subsequently disposed of or treated as disposed of or owned by any other condition is satisfied in respect of it.

(2) References in sections 30(2)(a) and (b) and 31(7) to a disposal are to a disposal other than a part disposal.

(3) References to an asset are to the original asset or, where at a later time one or more assets are treated by virtue of subsections (5) or (6) below as the same as the original asset—

   (a) if no disposal falling within paragraph (a) or (b) of section 30(2) or, as the case may be, of 31(7) has occurred, those references are to the asset so treated or, as the case may be, all the assets so treated, and

   (b) in any other case, those references are to an asset or, as the case may be, all the assets representing that part of the value of the original asset that remains after allowing for earlier disposals falling within the paragraphs concerned,

references in this subsection to a disposal including a disposal which would fall within the paragraphs concerned but for subsection (2) above.

(4) Where by virtue of subsection (3) above those references are to two or more assets—

   (a) those assets shall be treated as if they were a single asset,

   (b) any disposal of any one of them is to be treated as a part disposal, and

   (c) the reference in section 30(2) to the asset owned at the time of the disposal by a company associated with the disposing company and the reference in section 31(8) to the asset with enhanced value is to all or any of those assets.

(5) Where there is a part disposal of an asset, that asset and the asset acquired by the person to whom the disposal is made are to be treated as the same.

(6) Where the value of an asset is derived from any other asset in the ownership of the same or an associated company, in a case where assets have been merged or divided or have changed their nature or rights or interests in or over assets have been created or extinguished, the first asset is to be treated as the same as the second.

(7) For the purposes of section 30(2), where account is to be taken under that subsection of a reduction in the value of a relevant asset and at the time of the disposal by the disposing company referred to in that subsection—

   (a) references to the relevant asset are by virtue of this section references to two or more assets treated as a single asset, and

   (b) one or more but not all of those assets are owned by a company associated with the disposing company, the amount of the reduction in the value of the relevant asset to be taken into account by virtue of that subsection shall be reduced to such amount as appears to the inspector, or on appeal the Commissioners concerned, to be just and reasonable.

(8) For the purposes of section 31, where—

(a) a dividend paid by the second company is attributable to chargeable profits of that company, and

(b) the condition in subsection (7), (8) or (9)(c) of that section is satisfied by reference to an asset, or assets treated as a single asset, treated by virtue of subsection (3)(b) above as the same as the asset with enhanced value,

the amount of the reduction in value of the principal asset shall be reduced to such amount as appears to the inspector, or on appeal the Commissioners concerned, to be just and reasonable.

(9) For the purposes of sections 30 to 32 and this section, companies are associated if they are members of the same group.

(10) Section 170(2) to (11) applies for the purposes of sections 30 to 32 and this section as it applies for the purposes of that section.

GENERAL NOTE
This contains provisions supplementary to ss.30–32. The sections do not apply to part disposals, but if there is a part disposal, the asset acquired by this will be treated as the same as the original asset. An asset the value of which is derived from another asset within the group is treated as the same asset. References to an asset include all such deemed assets and a disposal of any one is treated as a part disposal. In all such cases, reductions in values of assets are to be adjusted on a "just and reasonable" basis.

Transactions treated as a reorganisation of share capital

34.—(1) Where—

(a) but for sections 127 and 135(3), section 30 would have effect as respects the disposal by a company ("the disposing company") of an asset consisting of shares in or debentures of another company ("the original holding") in exchange for shares in or debentures of a further company which, immediately after the disposal, is not a member of the same group as the disposing company, and

(b) if section 30 had effect as respects that disposal, any allowable loss or chargeable gain accruing on the disposal would be calculated as if the consideration for the disposal were increased by an amount,

the disposing company shall be treated for the purposes of section 128(3) as receiving, on the reorganisation of share capital that is treated as occurring by virtue of section 135(3), that amount for the disposal of the original holding.

(2) For the purposes of subsection (1) above it shall be assumed that section 136 has effect generally for the purposes of this Act, and in that subsection "group" has the same meaning as in sections 30 to 33.

GENERAL NOTE
This extends the effect of s.30 to cases which would otherwise have been outside its ambit because of the provisions relating to exchanges and reorganisation of share capital.

CHAPTER III

COMPUTATION OF GAINS: GENERAL PROVISIONS

Re-basing to 1982, and assets held on 6th April 1965

Assets held on 31st March 1982 (including assets held on 6th April 1965)

35.—(1) This section applies to a disposal of an asset which was held on 31st March 1982 by the person making the disposal.

(2) Subject to the following provisions of this section, in computing for the purpose of this Act the gain or loss accruing on the disposal it shall be assumed that the asset was on 31st March 1982 sold by the person making the disposal, and immediately reacquired by him, at its market value on that date.

(3) Subject to subsection (5) below, subsection (2) above shall not apply to a disposal—
   (a) where a gain would accrue on the disposal to the person making the disposal if that subsection did apply, and with a smaller gain or a loss would so accrue if it did not,
   (b) where a loss would so accrue if that subsection did apply, and either a smaller loss or a gain would accrue if it did not,
   (c) where, either on the facts of the case or by virtue of Schedule 2, neither a gain nor a loss would accrue if that subsection did not apply, or
   (d) where neither a gain nor a loss would accrue by virtue of any of—
         (i) sections 58, 73, 139, 171, 172, 215, 216, 218 to 221, 257(3), 258(4), 264 and 267(2) of this Act;
         (ii) section 148 of the 1979 Act;
         (iii) section 148 of the Finance Act 1982;
         (iv) paragraph 2 of Schedule 2 to the Trustee Savings Banks Act 1985;
         (v) section 130(3) of the Transport Act 1985;
         (vi) section 486(8) of the Taxes Act; and
         (vii) paragraph 2(1) of Schedule 12 to the Finance Act 1990.

(4) Where in the case of a disposal of an asset—
   (a) the effect of subsection (2) above would be to substitute a loss for a gain or a gain for a loss, but
   (b) the application of subsection (2) is excluded by subsection (3),
it shall be assumed in relation to the disposal that the asset was acquired by the person making the disposal for a consideration such that, on the disposal, neither a gain nor a loss accrues to him.

(5) If a person so elects, disposals made by him (including any made by him before the election) shall fall outside subsection (3) above (so that subsection (2) above is not excluded by that subsection).

(6) An election by a person under subsection (5) above shall be irrevocable and shall be made by notice to the inspector at any time before 6th April 1990 or at any time during the period beginning with the day of the first relevant disposal and ending—
   (a) two years after the end of the year of assessment or accounting period in which the disposal is made, or
   (b) at such later time as the Board may allow;
and "the first relevant disposal" means the first disposal to which this section applies which is made by the person making the election.

(7) An election made by a person under subsection (5) above in one capacity does not cover disposals made by him in another capacity.

(8) All such adjustments shall be made, whether by way of discharge or repayment of tax, the making of assessments, or otherwise, as are required to give effect to an election under subsection (5) above.

(9) Schedule 2 shall have effect in relation to disposals of assets owned on 6th April 1965 in cases where neither subsection (2) nor subsection (4) above applies.

(10) Schedule 3, which contains provisions supplementary to subsections (1) to (8) above, shall have effect.

GENERAL NOTE

This important provision, introduced as FA 1988, s.96, rebases C.G.T. to March 31, 1982, and so leaves gains accruing before that date out of account. The rebasing does not apply in cases where it would be disadvantageous for the taxpayer, *e.g.* where the 1982 value is lower than cost or in cases where the no gain/no loss rule applies, but the taxpayer may irrevocably elect within two years of his first relevant disposal, or such longer period as the Board may allow, to have the rebasing apply to his disposals.

The section is supported by two Schedules. Schedule 2 deals with particular cases where the April 6, 1965 valuation may still be relevant and Sched. 3 has detailed provisions relating to the rebasing to March 31, 1982. See further the General Note to these Schedules.

Deferred charges on gains before 31st March 1982

36. Schedule 4, which provides for the reduction of a deferred charge to tax where the charge is wholly or partly attributable to an increase in the value of an asset before 31st March 1982, shall have effect.

GENERAL NOTE

This introduces a relief to taxpayers who acquired assets after March 31, 1982, and where acquisition costs were reduced as a result of holdover, rollover or like reliefs. In such a case a relief of one-half of the gain is given. See further the General Note to Sched. 4.

Allowable deductions

Consideration chargeable to tax on income

37.—(1) There shall be excluded from the consideration for a disposal of assets taken into account in the computation of the gain any money or money's worth charged to income tax as income of, or taken into account as a receipt in computing income or profits or gains or losses of, the person making the disposal for the purposes of the Income Tax Acts.

(2) Subsection (1) above shall not be taken as excluding from the consideration so taken into account any money or money's worth which is—

(a) taken into account in the making of a balancing charge under the 1990 Act, including the provisions of the Taxes Act which are to be treated as contained in the 1990 Act but excluding Part III of the 1990 Act, or

(b) brought into account as the disposal value of machinery or plant under section 24 of the 1990 Act.

(3) This section shall not preclude the taking into account in a computation of the gain, as consideration for the disposal of an asset, of the capitalised value of a rentcharge (as in a case where a rentcharge is exchanged for some other asset) or of the capitalised value of a ground annual or feu duty, or of a right of any other description to income or to payments in the nature of income over a period, or to a series of payments in the nature of income.

(4) The reference in subsection (1) above to computing income or profits or gains or losses shall not be taken as applying to a computation of a company's income for the purposes of subsection (2) of section 76 of the Taxes Act (expenses of management of insurance companies).

GENERAL NOTE

To avoid double taxation, amounts brought into charge to income tax are excluded from a C.G.T. computation, subject to an exception in relation to balancing charges under the Capital Allowances Act 1990 and capitalised income payments. In *Hirsch (Inspector of Taxes)* v. *Crowthers Cloth* [1990] S.T.C. 174 an attempt to obtain a double deduction under earlier provisions was rejected.

Acquisition and disposal costs etc.

38.—(1) Except as otherwise expressly provided, the sums allowable as a deduction from the consideration in the computation of the gain accruing to a person on the disposal of an asset shall be restricted to—

(a) the amount or value of the consideration, in money or money's worth, given by him or on his behalf wholly and exclusively for the acquisition of the asset, together with the incidental costs to him of the acquisition or, if the asset was not acquired by him, any expenditure wholly and exclusively incurred by him in providing the asset,

(b) the amount of any expenditure wholly and exclusively incurred on the asset by him or on his behalf for the purpose of enhancing the value of the asset, being expenditure reflected in the state or nature of the asset at the time of the disposal, and any expenditure wholly and exclusively incurred by him in establishing, preserving or defending his title to, or to a right over, the asset,

(c) the incidental costs to him of making the disposal.

(2) For the purposes of this section and for the purposes of all other provisions of this Act, the incidental costs to the person making the disposal of the acquisition of the asset or of its disposal shall consist of expenditure wholly and exclusively incurred by him for the purposes of the acquisition or, as the case may be, the disposal, being fees, commission or remuneration paid for the professional services of any surveyor or valuer, or auctioneer, or accountant, or agent or legal adviser and costs of transfer or conveyance (including stamp duty) together—

(a) in the case of the acquisition of an asset, with costs of advertising to find a seller, and

(b) in the case of a disposal, with costs of advertising to find a buyer and costs reasonably incurred in making any valuation or apportionment required for the purposes of the computation of the gain, including in particular expenses reasonably incurred in ascertaining market value where required by this Act.

(3) Except as provided by section 40, no payment of interest shall be allowable under this section.

(4) Any provision in this Act introducing the assumption that assets are sold and immediately reacquired shall not imply that any expenditure is incurred as incidental to the sale or reacquisition.

GENERAL NOTE

The section defines in fairly narrow terms the expenditure allowable in computing chargeable gains.

To qualify as expenditure "wholly and exclusively for the acquisition of the asset", the main object of incurring it must be its acquisition: *Clevelys Investment Trust Co.* v. *I.R.C.* (*No.* 2) (1975) 51 T.C. 26. Fees paid to a solicitor for obtaining probate and a commission paid on a subsequent sale of shares have been held to be within subs. (1)(b) and (c) respectively (*I.R.C.* v. *Richards' Executors* [1971] 1 W.L.R. 571), but an insurance premium paid as a term of an agreement by which settled property ceased to be held as such did not qualify (*Allison* v. *Murray* [1975] 1 W.L.R. 1578).

Where a company acquired a portfolio of securities in exchange for its own shares it was held that market value could not be substituted for the agreed value in the contract, since that had been honestly agreed by the parties in an arm's-length bargain (*Stanton* v. *Drayton Commercial Investment Co.* [1983] A.C. 501). Arrears of rent paid to obtain a lease which was then assigned with the landlords' consent was held not to be enhancement expenditure, since it was the discharge of the obligation under the lease (*Emmerson* v. *Computer Time International* (*In Liquidation*) [1977] 1 W.L.R. 734). "Expenditure" must be in money or money's worth, so that an individual's personal labour in enhancing the value of an asset is not allowable (*Oram* v. *Johnson* [1980] 1 W.L.R. 558).

In *Chaney* v. *Watkis* (*Inspector of Taxes*) (1986) 58 T.C. 707 it was held that the requirement for the expenditure to be reflected in the state of the asset at the time of its disposal did not preclude expenditure between contract and completion.

Exclusion of expenditure by reference to tax on income

39.—(1) There shall be excluded from the sums allowable under section 38 as a deduction in the computation of the gain any expenditure allowable as a deduction in computing the profits or gains or losses of a trade, profession or vocation for the purposes of income tax or allowable as a deduction in computing any other income or profits or gains or losses for the purposes of the Income Tax Acts and any expenditure which, although not so allowable as a deduction in computing any losses, would be so allowable but for an insufficiency of income or profits or gains; and this subsection applies irrespective of whether effect is or would be given to the deduction in computing the amount of tax chargeable or by discharge or repayment of tax or in any other way.

(2) Without prejudice to the provisions of subsection (1) above, there shall be excluded from the sums allowable under section 38 as a deduction in the computation of the gain any expenditure which, if the assets, or all the assets to which the computation relates, were, and had at all times been, held or used as part of the fixed capital of a trade the profits or gains of which were (irrespective of whether the person making the disposal is a company or not) chargeable to income tax would be allowable as a deduction in computing the profits or gains or losses of the trade for the purposes of income tax.

(3) No account shall be taken of any relief under Chapter II of Part IV of the Finance Act 1981 or under Schedule 5 to the Finance Act 1983, in so far as it is not withdrawn and relates to shares issued before March 19, 1986, in determining whether any sums are excluded by virtue of subsection (1) or (2) above from the sums allowable as a deduction in the computation of gains or losses for the purposes of this Act.

GENERAL NOTE
Conversely to s.37, expenditure allowable or potentially allowable for income tax purposes cannot be deducted for C.G.T. purposes.

Subs. (3)
This contains a transitional provision relating to the Business Expansion Scheme (see ICTA 1988, s.289).

Interest charged to capital

40.—(1) Where—
(a) a company incurs expenditure on the construction of any building, structure or works, being expenditure allowable as a deduction under section 38 in computing a gain accruing to the company on the disposal of the building, structure or work, or of any asset comprising it, and
(b) that expenditure was defrayed out of borrowed money,
the sums so allowable under section 38 shall, subject to subsection (2) below, include the amount of any interest on that borrowed money which is referable to a period or part of a period ending on or before the disposal.

(2) Subsection (1) above has effect subject to section 39 and does not apply to interest which is a charge on income.

(3) In relation to interest paid in any accounting period ending before 1st April 1981 subsection (1) above shall have effect with the substitution for all following paragraph (b) of—
"and
(c) the company charged to capital all or any of the interest on that borrowed money referable to a period or part of a period ending on or before the disposal,
and the sums so allowable under section 38 shall include the amount of that interest charged to capital.";
and subsection (2) above shall not apply.

GENERAL NOTE
Interest incurred by a company on loans incurred for capital expenditure and charged to capital is deductible. This does not apply to interest allowable as a charge on income.

Restriction of losses by reference to capital allowances and renewals allowances

41.—(1) Section 39 shall not require the exclusion from the sums allowable as a deduction in the computation of the gain of any expenditure as being expenditure in respect of which a capital allowance or renewals allowance is made, but the amount of any losses accruing on the disposal of an asset shall be restricted by reference to capital allowances and renewals allowances as follows.

(2) In the computation of the amount of a loss accruing to the person making the disposal, there shall be excluded from the sums allowable as a deduction any expenditure to the extent to which any capital allowance or renewals allowance has been or may be made in respect of it.

(3) If the person making the disposal acquired the asset—

   (a) by a transfer by way of sale in relation to which an election under section 158 of the 1990 Act was made, or
   (b) by a transfer to which section 78(2) of that Act applies,

(being enactments under which a transfer is treated for the purposes of capital allowances as being made at written down value), the preceding provisions of this section shall apply as if any capital allowance made to the transferor in respect of the asset had (except so far as any loss to the transferor was restricted under those provisions) been made to the person making the disposal (that is the transferee); and where the transferor acquired the asset by such a transfer, capital allowances which by virtue of this subsection can be taken into account in relation to the transferor shall also be taken into account in relation to the transferee (that is the person making the disposal), and so on for any series of transfers before the disposal.

(4) In this section "capital allowance" means—

   (a) any allowance under the 1990 Act, including the provisions of the Taxes Act which are to be treated as contained in the 1990 Act, other than an allowance under section 33(1) of the Taxes Act (relief for cost of maintenance of agricultural land),
   (b) any relief given under section 30 of the Taxes Act (expenditure on sea walls), and
   (c) any deduction in computing profits or gains allowable under section 91 of the Taxes Act (cemeteries).

(5) In this section "renewals allowance" means a deduction allowable in computing the profits or gains of a trade, profession or vocation for the purpose of income tax by reference to the cost of acquiring an asset for the purposes of the trade, profession or vocation in replacement of another asset, and for the purposes of this Chapter a renewals allowance shall be regarded as a deduction allowable in respect of the expenditure incurred on the asset which is being replaced.

(6) The amount of capital allowances to be taken into account under this section in relation to a disposal include any allowances falling to be made by reference to the event which is the disposal, and there shall be deducted from the amount of the allowances the amount of any balancing charge to which effect has been or is to be given by reference to the event which is the disposal, or any earlier event.

(7) Where the disposal is of machinery or plant in relation to expenditure on which allowances or charges have been made under Part II of the 1990 Act, and neither section 79 (assets used only partly for trade purposes) nor section 80 (wear and tear subsidies) of that Act applies, the capital allowances to be taken into account under this section are to be regarded as equal to the difference between the capital expenditure incurred, or treated as incurred, under that Part on the provision of the machinery or plant by the person making the disposal and the disposal value required to be brought into account in respect of the machinery or plant.

GENERAL NOTE

   This contains provisions relating to cases where capital allowances or renewal allowances (as defined in subss. (4) and (5)) have been made on an asset.

Subs. (2)

Capital and renewal allowances must be excluded where this would produce a loss.

Subs. (3)

Where there has been a previous transfer of assets at written-down value, this value is carried through to a subsequent disponor of the asset.

Subs. (6)

Balancing charges are taken into account where computations have to be made under this section.

Subs. (7)

For machinery and plant, the capital allowances to be taken into account are the difference between the original capital expenditure and the disposal value to be brought into account, save where the assets have not been used wholly for trade purposes or there has been a wear and tear subsidy.

Part disposals

42.—(1) Where a person disposes of an interest or right in or over an asset, and generally wherever on the disposal of an asset any description of property derived from that asset remains undisposed of, the sums which under paragraphs (a) and (b) of section 38(1) are attributable to the asset shall, both for the purposes of the computation of the gain accruing on the disposal and for the purpose of applying this Part in relation to the property which remains undisposed of, be apportioned.

(2) The apportionment shall be made by reference—

(a) to the amount or value of the consideration for the disposal on the one hand (call that amount or value A), and

(b) to the market value of the property which remains undisposed of on the other hand (call that market value B),

and accordingly the fraction of the said sums allowable as a deduction in the computation of the gain accruing on the disposal shall be—

$$\frac{A}{A + B}$$

and the remainder shall be attributed to the property which remains undisposed of.

(3) Any apportionment to be made in pursuance of this section shall be made before operating the provisions of section 41 and if, after a part disposal, there is a subsequent disposal of an asset the capital allowances or renewals allowances to be taken into account in pursuance of that section in relation to the subsequent disposal shall, subject to subsection (4) below, be those referable to the sums which under paragraphs (a) and (b) of section 38(1) are attributable to the asset whether before or after the part disposal, but those allowances shall be reduced by the amount (if any) by which the loss on the earlier disposal was restricted under the provisions of section 41.

(4) This section shall not be taken as requiring the apportionment of any expenditure which, on the facts, is wholly attributable to what is disposed of, or wholly attributable to what remains undisposed of.

(5) It is hereby declared that this section, and all other provisions for apportioning on a part disposal expenditure which is deductible in computing a gain, are to be operated before the operation of, and without regard to, section 58(1), sections 152 to 158 (but without prejudice to section 152(10)), section 171(1) or any other enactment making an adjustment to secure that neither a gain nor a loss occurs on a disposal.

GENERAL NOTE

This contains the important rule that where part of an asset is disposed of, the base cost is apportioned by reference to the consideration for the part disposal as compared with the market value of the part undisposed of. This applies in priority to the provisions of s.41 and is subject to other provisions relating to no gain/no loss disposals.

Assets derived from other assets

43. If and so far as, in a case where assets have been merged or divided or have changed their nature or rights or interests in or over assets have been created or extinguished, the value of an asset is derived from any other asset in the same ownership, an appropriate proportion of the sums allowable as a deduction in the computation of a gain in respect of the other asset under paragraphs (a) and (b) of section 38(1) shall, both for the purpose of the computation of a gain accruing on the disposal of the first-mentioned asset and, if the other asset remains in existence, on a disposal of that other asset, be attributed to the first-mentioned asset.

GENERAL NOTE

Where an asset is derived from another asset, an appropriate apportionment may have to be made. An extinction of one asset in favour of another cannot be described as a merger (*Aberdeen Construction Group* v. *I.R.C.* [1978] A.C. 885). A new lease granted under the Landlord and Tenant Act 1954 does not merge with the original lease (*Bayley* v. *Rogers* (1980) 53 T.C. 420).

Wasting assets

Meaning of "wasting asset"

44.—(1) In this Chapter "wasting asset" means an asset with a predictable life not exceeding 50 years but so that—
  (a) freehold land shall not be a wasting asset whatever its nature, and whatever the nature of the buildings or works on it;
  (b) "life", in relation to any tangible movable property, means useful life, having regard to the purpose for which the tangible assets were acquired or provided by the person making the disposal;
  (c) plant and machinery shall in every case be regarded as having a predictable life of less than 50 years, and in estimating that life it shall be assumed that its life will end when it is finally put out of use as being unfit for further use, and that it is going to be used in the normal manner and to the normal extent and is going to be so used throughout its life as so estimated;
  (d) a life interest in settled property shall not be a wasting asset until the predictable expectation of life of the life tenant is 50 years or less, and the predictable life of life interests in settled property and of annuities shall be ascertained from actuarial tables approved by the Board.
  (2) In this Chapter "the residual or scrap value", in relation to a wasting asset, means the predictable value, if any, which the wasting asset will have at the end of its predictable life as estimated in accordance with this section.
  (3) The question what is the predictable life of an asset, and the question what is its predictable residual or scrap value at the end of that life, if any, shall, so far as those questions are not immediately answered by the nature of the asset, be taken, in relation to any disposal of the asset, as they were known or ascertainable at the time when the asset was acquired or provided by the person making the disposal.

GENERAL NOTE

A special régime is provided under the Act for "wasting assets", defined in general as an asset with a predictable life of less than 50 years. In the case of such an asset, the allowable expenditure will usually be restricted.

Exemption for certain wasting assets

45.—(1) Subject to the provisions of this section, no chargeable gain shall accrue on the disposal of, or of an interest in, an asset which is tangible movable property and which is a wasting asset.

(2) Subsection (1) above shall not apply to a disposal of, or of an interest in, an asset—

(a) if, from the beginning of the period of ownership of the person making the disposal to the time when the disposal is made, the asset has been used and used solely for the purposes of a trade, profession or vocation and if that person has claimed or could have claimed any capital allowance in respect of any expenditure attributable to the asset or interest under paragraph (a) or paragraph (b) of section 38(1); or

(b) if the person making the disposal has incurred any expenditure on the asset or interest which has otherwise qualified in full for any capital allowance.

(3) In the case of the disposal of, or of an interest in, an asset which, in the period of ownership of the person making the disposal, has been used partly for the purposes of a trade, profession or vocation and partly for other purposes, or has been used for the purposes of a trade, profession or vocation for part of that period, or which has otherwise qualified in part only for capital allowances—

(a) the consideration for the disposal, and any expenditure attributable to the asset or interest by virtue of section 38(1)(a) and (b), shall be apportioned by reference to the extent to which that expenditure qualified for capital allowances, and

(b) the computation of the gain shall be made separately in relation to the apportioned parts of the expenditure and consideration, and

(c) subsection (1) above shall not apply to any gain accruing by reference to the computation in relation to the part of the consideration apportioned to use for the purposes of the trade, profession or vocation, or to the expenditure qualifying for capital allowances.

(4) Subsection (1) above shall not apply to a disposal of commodities of any description by a person dealing on a terminal market or dealing with or through a person ordinarily engaged in dealing on a terminal market.

GENERAL NOTE

Tangible movable assets which are wasting assets are removed from the ambit of the tax, save in the case of dealings on terminal markets. Also, the exemption does not apply to cases where capital allowances have applied in whole or part to the asset. The asset must actually have been brought into use for the exemption to be disapplied (*Burman (Inspector of Taxes)* v. *Westminster Press* (1987) 60 T.C. 418).

Straightline restriction of allowable expenditure

46.—(1) In the computation of the gain accruing on the disposal of a wasting asset it shall be assumed—

(a) that any expenditure attributable to the asset under section 38(1)(a) after deducting the residual or scrap value, if any, of the asset, is written off at a uniform rate from its full amount at the time when the asset is acquired or provided to nothing at the end of its life, and

(b) that any expenditure attributable to the asset under section 38(1)(b) is written off from the full amount of that expenditure at the time when that expenditure is first reflected in the state or nature of the asset to nothing at the end of its life,

so that an equal daily amount is written off day by day.

(2) Thus, calling the predictable life of a wasting asset at the time when it was acquired or provided by the person making the disposal L, the period from that time to the time of disposal T(1), and, in relation to any expenditure attributable to the asset under section 38(1)(b), the period from the time when that expenditure is first reflected in the state or nature of the asset

to the said time of disposal T(2), there shall be excluded from the computation of the gain—
   (a) out of the expenditure attributable to the asset under section 38(1)(a) a fraction—

$$\frac{T(1)}{L}$$

   of an amount equal to the amount of that expenditure minus the residual or scrap value, if any, of the asset, and
   (b) out of the expenditure attributable to the asset under section 38(1)(b) a fraction—

$$\frac{T(2)}{L-(T(1)-T(2))}$$

   of the amount of the expenditure.
   (3) If any expenditure attributable to the asset under section 38(1)(b) creates or increases a residual or scrap value of the asset, the provisions of subsection (1)(a) above shall be applied so as to take that into account.

GENERAL NOTE
   In the case of a wasting asset, original cost and enhancement expenditure are written off on a straightline basis. For the special rules applying to leases of land, see Sched. 8, para. 1.

Wasting assets qualifying for capital allowances

   47.—(1) Section 46 shall not apply in relation to a disposal of an asset—
   (a) which, from the beginning of the period of ownership of the person making the disposal to the time when the disposal is made, is used and used solely for the purposes of a trade, profession or vocation and in respect of which that person has claimed or could have claimed any capital allowance in respect of any expenditure attributable to the asset under paragraph (a) or paragraph (b) of section 38(1), or
   (b) on which the person making the disposal has incurred any expenditure which has otherwise qualified in full for any capital allowance.
   (2) In the case of the disposal of an asset which, in the period of ownership of the person making the disposal, has been used partly for the purposes of a trade, profession or vocation and partly for other purposes, or has been used for the purposes of a trade, profession or vocation for part of that period, or which has otherwise qualified in part only for capital allowances—
   (a) the consideration for the disposal, and any expenditure attributable to the asset by paragraph (a) or paragraph (b) of section 38(1) shall be apportioned by reference to the extent to which that expenditure qualified for capital allowances, and
   (b) the computation of the gain shall be made separately in relation to the apportioned parts of the expenditure and consideration, and
   (c) section 46 shall not apply for the purposes of the computation in relation to the part of the consideration apportioned to use for the purposes of the trade, profession or vocation, or to the expenditure qualifying for capital allowances, and
   (d) if an apportionment of the consideration for the disposal has been made for the purposes of making any capital allowance to the person making the disposal or for the purpose of making any balancing charge on him, that apportionment shall be employed for the purposes of this section, and
   (e) subject to paragraph (d) above, the consideration for the disposal shall be apportioned for the purposes of this section in the same proportions as the expenditure attributable to the asset is apportioned under paragraph (a) above.

The restriction under the previous section does not apply to assets qualifying for capital allowances and used solely for business purposes. An apportionment is made in cases of partial qualification.

Miscellaneous provisions

Consideration due after time of disposal

48. In the computation of the gain consideration for the disposal shall be brought into account without any discount for postponement of the right to receive any part of it and, in the first instance, without regard to a risk of any part of the consideration being irrecoverable or to the right to receive any part of the consideration being contingent; and if any part of the consideration so brought into account is subsequently shown to the satisfaction of the inspector to be irrecoverable, such adjustment, whether by way of discharge or repayment of tax or otherwise, shall be made as is required in consequence.

GENERAL NOTE
This provides the important rule that where the consideration for a disposal is postponed, no account is taken of this initially. Contingencies not within the section were considered in *Randall* v. *Plumb* [1975] 1 W.L.R. 633 and *Marson* v. *Marriage* (1979) 54 T.C. 59.
For the treatment of payments by instalment, see s.280.

Contingent liabilities

49.—(1) In the first instance no allowance shall be made in the computation of the gain—
  (a) in the case of a disposal by way of assigning a lease of land or other property, for any liability remaining with, or assumed by, the person making the disposal by way of assigning the lease which is contingent on a default in respect of liabilities thereby or subsequently assumed by the assignee under the terms and conditions of the lease.
  (b) for any contingent liability of the person making the disposal in respect of any covenant for quiet enjoyment or other obligation assumed as vendor of land, or of any estate or interest in land, or as a lessor,
  (c) for any contingent liability in respect of a warranty or representation made on a disposal by way of sale or lease of any property other than land.
(2) If it is subsequently shown to the satisfaction of the inspector that any such contingent liability has become enforceable, and is being or has been enforced, such adjustment, whether by way of discharge or repayment of tax or otherwise, shall be made as is required in consequence.
(3) Subsection (2) above also applies where the disposal in question was before the commencement of this section.

GENERAL NOTE
Various contingent liabilities, mainly in relation to disposals of land, are initially left out of account. Others not specifically mentioned may be taken into account (*Randall* v. *Plumb* [1975] 1 W.L.R. 633).

Expenditure reimbursed out of public money

50. There shall be excluded from the computation of a gain any expenditure which has been or is to be met directly or indirectly by the Crown or by any Government, public or local authority whether in the United Kingdom or elsewhere.

GENERAL NOTE
This excludes from a computation any expenditure met by a government or public authority.

Exemption for winnings and damages etc.

51.—(1) It is hereby declared that winnings from betting, including pool betting, or lotteries or games with prizes are not chargeable gains, and no chargeable gain or allowable loss shall accrue on the disposal of rights to winnings obtained by participating in any pool betting or lottery or game with prizes.

(2) It is hereby declared that sums obtained by way of compensation or damages for any wrong or injury suffered by an individual in his person or in his profession or vocation are not chargeable gains.

GENERAL NOTE

Subs. (1)
  Winnings in gambling are excluded from charge.

Subs. (2)
  Compensation for damages for personal or professional injury are exempt from C.G.T. For the comparable exemption from income tax, see ICTA 1988, s.329.

Supplemental

52.—(1) No deduction shall be allowable in a computation of the gain more than once from any sum or from more than one sum.

(2) References in this Chapter to sums taken into account as receipts or as expenditure in computing profits or gains or losses for the purposes of income tax shall include references to sums which would be so taken into account but for the fact that any profits or gains of a trade, profession, employment or vocation are not chargeable to income tax or that losses are not allowable for those purposes.

(3) In this Chapter references to income or profits charged or chargeable to tax include references to income or profits taxed or as the case may be taxable by deduction at source.

(4) For the purposes of any computation of the gain any necessary apportionments shall be made of any consideration or of any expenditure and the method of apportionment adopted shall, subject to the express provisions of this Chapter, be such method as appears to the inspector or on appeal the Commissioners concerned to be just and reasonable.

(5) In this Chapter "capital allowance" and "renewals allowance" have the meanings given by subsections (4) and (5) of section 41.

GENERAL NOTE
  This section contains some general supplementary and explanatory provisions.

Subs. (4)
  The general power to apportion on a "just and reasonable" basis is of importance.

CHAPTER IV

COMPUTATION OF GAINS: THE INDEXATION ALLOWANCE

General

The indexation allowance and interpretative provisions

53.—(1) Subject to any provision to the contrary, an allowance ("the indexation allowance") shall, on the disposal of an asset, either be set against the unindexed gain or, as the case may be, added to the unindexed loss so as to give the gain or loss for the purposes of this Act as follows—
  (a) if there is an unindexed gain, the indexation allowance shall be deducted from the gain and, if the allowance exceeds the unindexed gain, the excess shall constitute a loss;

(b) if there is an unindexed loss, the indexation allowance shall be added
to it so as to increase the loss; and

(c) if the unindexed gain or loss is nil, there shall be a loss equal to the
indexation allowance;

and any reference in this Act to an indexation allowance or to the making of
an indexation allowance shall be construed accordingly.

(2) For the purposes of subsection (1) above, in relation to any disposal of
an asset—

(a) "the unindexed gain or loss" means the amount of the gain or loss on
the disposal computed in accordance with this Part, and, if neither a
gain nor a loss on the disposal is so given, the unindexed gain or loss
shall be nil; and

(b) "relevant allowable expenditure" means, subject to subsection (3)
below, any sum which, in the computation of the unindexed gain or
loss was taken into account by virtue of paragraph (a) or paragraph
(b) of section 38(1).

(3) In determining what sum (if any) was taken into account as mentioned
in subsection (2)(b) above, account shall be taken of any provision of any
enactment which, for the purpose of the computation of the gain, increases,
excludes or reduces the whole or any part of any item of expenditure falling
within section 38 or provides for it to be written-down.

(4) Sections 54 and 108 and this section have effect subject to sections 56,
57, 109, 110, 113, 131 and 145.

GENERAL NOTE

The indexation allowance, first introduced in 1982, remedied the perceived unfairness of
C.G.T. in taxing gains which were purely inflationary. In general, gains and losses are adjusted
by reference to changes in the retail prices index (R.P.I.) on a monthly basis starting from
March 31, 1982.

For the application of indexation to assets held on April 6, 1965, where apportionment may
also be necessary, see the Note to Sched. 2, para. 16.

Calculation of indexation allowance

54.—(1) Subject to any provision to the contrary, the indexation allowance is the aggregate of the indexed rise in each item of relevant allowable
expenditure; and, in relation to any such item of expenditure, the indexed
rise is a sum produced by multiplying the amount of that item by a figure
expressed as a decimal and determined, subject to subsections (2) and (3)
below, by the formula—

$$\frac{(RD-RI)}{RI}$$

where—

RD is the retail prices index for the month in which the disposal occurs;
and

RI is the retail prices index for March 1982 or the month in which the
expenditure was incurred, whichever is the later.

(2) If, in relation to any item of expenditure—

(a) the expenditure is attributable to the acquisition of relevant securities, within the meaning of section 108, which are disposed of within
the period of 10 days beginning on the day on which the expenditure
was incurred, or

(b) RD, as defined in subsection (1) above, is equal to or less than RI, as
so defined,

the indexed rise in that item is nil.

(3) If, in relation to any item of expenditure, the figure determined in
accordance with the formula in subsection (1) above would, apart from this

subsection, be a figure having more than 3 decimal places, it shall be rounded to the nearest third decimal place.

(4) For the purposes of this section—

(a) relevant allowable expenditure falling within paragraph (a) of subsection (1) of section 38 shall be assumed to have been incurred at the time when the asset in question was acquired or provided; and

(b) relevant allowable expenditure falling within paragraph (b) of that subsection shall be assumed to have been incurred at the time when that expenditure became due and payable.

GENERAL NOTE

This provides for the calculation of the indexation allowance. The Inland Revenue publish monthly tables giving the increase in the R.P.I. from March 1982 to the current month, rounded to three decimal places.

Acquisition expenditure is deemed to have been incurred when the asset was acquired or provided and enhancement expenditure when it became due and payable.

Assets owned on 31st March 1982 or acquired on a no gain/no loss disposal

55.—(1) For the purpose of computing the indexation allowance on a disposal of an asset where, on 31st March 1982, the asset was held by the person making the disposal, it shall be assumed that on that date the asset was sold by the person making the disposal and immediately reacquired by him at its market value on that date.

(2) Except where an election under section 35(5) has effect, neither subsection (1) above nor section 35(2) shall apply for the purpose of computing the indexation allowance in a case where that allowance would be greater if they did not apply.

(3) If under subsection (1) above it is to be assumed that any asset was on 31st March 1982 sold by the person making the disposal and immediately reacquired by him, sections 41 and 47 shall apply in relation to any capital allowance or renewals allowance made in respect of the expenditure actually incurred by him in providing the asset as if it were made in respect of expenditure which, on that assumption, was incurred by him in reacquiring the asset on 31st March 1982.

(4) Where, after 31st March 1982, an asset which was held on that date has been merged or divided or has changed its nature or rights in or over the asset have been created, then, subject to subsection (2) above, subsection (1) above shall have effect to determine for the purposes of section 43 the amount of the consideration for the acquisition of the asset which was so held.

(5) Subsection (6) below applies to a disposal of an asset which is not a no gain/no loss disposal if—

(a) the person making the disposal acquired the asset after 31st March 1982; and

(b) the disposal by which he acquired the asset and any previous disposal of the asset after 31st March 1982 was a no gain/no loss disposal;

and for the purposes of this subsection a no gain/no loss disposal is one on which, by virtue of section 257(2) or 259(2) or any of the enactments specified in section 35(3)(d), neither a gain nor a loss accrues (or accrued) to the person making the disposal.

(6) Where this subsection applies to a disposal of an asset—

(a) the person making the disposal shall be treated for the purpose of computing the indexation allowance on the disposal as having held the asset on 31st March 1982; and;

(b) for the purpose of determining any gain or loss on the disposal, the consideration which, apart from this subsection, that person would be treated as having given for the asset shall be taken to be reduced by deducting therefrom any indexation allowance brought into account by virtue of section 56(2) on any disposal falling within subsection (5)(b) above.

GENERAL NOTE
This provision, introduced in 1985, applies indexation to the market value of an asset held on March 31, 1982, rather than on its original cost. There are various modifications to this rule.

Subs. (2)
Unless the taxpayer has elected for rebasing to 1982, the section will not apply where it would be disadvantageous to him.

Subs. (3)
Capital and renewal allowances are also appropriately adjusted.

Subs. (4)
Appropriate adjustment is also made in the case of merged or divided assets.

Subss. (5) and (6)
These deal with the position where an asset has been acquired after March 31, 1982 on a no-gain/no-loss basis. In such a case the disponor will be treated as having held the asset on March 31, 1982, and the indexation allowance from that date will be deducted from the consideration for the disposal.

Part disposals and disposals on a no-gain/no-loss basis

56.—(1) For the purpose of determining the indexation allowance (if any) on the occasion of a part disposal of an asset, the apportionment under section 42 of the sums which make up the relevant allowable expenditure shall be effected before the application of section 54 and, accordingly, in relation to a part disposal—

(a) references in section 54 to an item of expenditure shall be construed as references to that part of that item which is so apportioned for the purposes of the computation of the unindexed gain or loss on the part disposal; and

(b) no indexation allowance shall be determined by reference to the part of each item of relevant allowable expenditure which is apportioned to the property which remains undisposed of.

(2) On the disposal of an asset which, by virtue of any enactment, is treated as one on which neither a gain nor a loss accrues to the person making the disposal ("the transferor")—

(a) the amount of the consideration shall be calculated for the purposes of this Act on the assumption that, on the disposal, an unindexed gain accrues to the transferor which is equal to the indexation allowance on the disposal, and

(b) the disposal shall accordingly be one on which, after taking account of the indexation allowance, neither a gain nor a loss accrues;

and for the purposes of the application of sections 53 and 54 there shall be disregarded so much of any enactment as provides that, on the subsequent disposal of the asset by the person acquiring the asset on the disposal ("the transferee"), the transferor's acquisition of the asset is to be treated as the transferee's acquisition of it.

GENERAL NOTE
This deals with two special cases, one where there is a part disposal and the other where there is a no-gain/no-loss disposal, *e.g.* between spouses or within groups of companies. In the first case, apportionment under s.42 is applied before indexation, in the second the transferee takes the transferor's indexation allowance in the form of an uplifted base cost.

Receipts etc. which are not treated as disposals but affect relevant allowable expenditure

57.—(1) This section applies where, in determining the relevant allowable expenditure in relation to a disposal of an asset, account is required to be taken, as mentioned in section 53(3), of any provision of any enactment which, by reference to a relevant event, reduces the whole or any part of an item of expenditure as mentioned in that subsection.

(2) For the purpose of determining, in a case where this section applies, the indexation allowance (if any) to which the person making the disposal is entitled, no account shall in the first instance be taken of the provision referred to in subsection (1) above in calculating the indexed rise in the item of expenditure to which that provision applies but, from that indexed rise as so calculated, there shall be deducted a sum equal to the indexed rise (determined as for the purposes of the actual disposal) in a notional item of expenditure which—

(a) is equal to the amount of the reduction effected by the provision concerned; and

(b) was incurred on the date of the relevant event referred to in sub-section (1) above.

(3) In this section "relevant event" means any event which does not fall to be treated as a disposal for the purposes of this Act.

GENERAL NOTE
Where there is a restriction on allowable costs (*e.g.* under s.125) the restriction applies also to the indexation allowance.

PART III

INDIVIDUALS, PARTNERSHIPS, TRUSTS AND COLLECTIVE INVESTMENT SCHEMES

CHAPTER I

MISCELLANEOUS PROVISIONS

Husband and wife

58.—(1) If, in any year of assessment, and in the case of a woman who in that year of assessment is a married woman living with her husband, the man disposes of an asset to the wife, or the wife disposes of an asset to the man, both shall be treated as if the asset was acquired from the one making the disposal for a consideration of such amount as would secure that on the disposal neither a gain nor a loss would accrue to the one making the disposal.

(2) This section shall not apply—

(a) if until the disposal the asset formed part of trading stock of a trade carried on by the one making the disposal, or if the asset is acquired as trading stock for the purposes of a trade carried on by the one acquiring the asset, or

(b) if the disposal is by way of donatio mortis causa,

but this section shall have effect notwithstanding the provisions of section 18 or 161, or of any other provisions of this Act fixing the amount of the consideration deemed to be given on a disposal or acquisition.

GENERAL NOTE
Disposals between spouses are treated on a no-gain/no-loss basis, except in the case of assets which have been or will become trading stock and disposals by way of *donatio mortis causa*, which are exempt from C.G.T. under s.62(5).

References to "a married woman living with her husband" are to be construed in accordance with ICTA 1988, s.282 (s.288(3)). The effect of this, prior to the amendment of ICTA 1988, s.282, following on the introduction of independent taxation for wives, was considered in *Gubay* v. *Kington* [1984] 1 W.L.R. 163.

Partnerships

59. Where 2 or more persons carry on a trade or business in partnership—

(a) tax in respect of chargeable gains accruing to them on the disposal of any partnership assets shall, in Scotland as well as elsewhere in the United Kingdom, be assessed and charged on them separately, and

(b) any partnership dealings shall be treated as dealings by the partners and not by the firm as such, and

(c) section 112(1) and (2) of the Taxes Act (residence of partnerships) shall apply in relation to tax chargeable in pursuance of this Act as it applies in relation to income tax.

GENERAL NOTE
The capital gains of partnerships are treated as being the gains of the partners and partnership dealings as being those of the partners.

Under ICTA 1988, s.112(1) and (2), partnerships controlled and managed abroad are deemed to be non-resident and are charged on U.K. profits on the same basis as any other non-resident.

This brief provision is inadequate to cover dealings within the partnership. The Inland Revenue practice in this regard is dealt with in their Statement of Practice D12.

Nominees and bare trustees

60.—(1) In relation to assets held by a person as nominee for another person, or as trustee for another person absolutely entitled as against the trustee, or for any person who would be so entitled but for being an infant or other person under disability (or for 2 or more persons who are or would be jointly so entitled), this Act shall apply as if the property were vested in, and the acts of the nominee or trustee in relation to the assets were the acts of, the person or persons for whom he is the nominee or trustee (acquisitions from or disposals to him by that person or persons being disregarded accordingly).

(2) It is hereby declared that references in this Act to any asset held by a person as trustee for another person absolutely entitled as against the trustee are references to a case where that other person has the exclusive right, subject only to satisfying any outstanding charge, lien or other right of the trustees to resort to the asset for payment of duty, taxes, costs or other outgoings, to direct how that asset shall be dealt with.

GENERAL NOTE
The acquisitions and disposals of nominees and trustees for persons absolutely entitled to the assets as against them are treated as being those of the beneficial owner.

Subs. (2)
This enlarges on the meaning of "absolutely entitled as against the trustee". The provision is of some importance in view of the charge under s.71 when a person becomes so entitled, but its construction has given rise to some difficulty.

The leading case on the topic is *Crowe* v. *Appleby* [1975] 1 W.L.R. 1539 (see (1976) 51 T.C. 457 p. 470 *et seq.*, *per* Goff J.). This followed on earlier decisions in *Tomlinson* v. *Glyns Executor & Trustee Co.* [1970] Ch. 112, C.A. and *Stephenson* v. *Barclays Bank Trust Co.* [1975] 1 W.L.R. 882. A residuary legatee in Scotland was held not to be "absolutely entitled" as against the administrators of the estate (*Cochrane's* v. *I.R.C.* [1974] S.T.C. 335). In England joint tenants and tenants in common are both absolutely entitled (*Kidson* v. *Macdonald* [1974] Ch. 339). However, the members of a club are not absolutely entitled as against the trustees of its property (*Worthing Rugby Football Club Trustees* v. *I.R.C.* [1987] 1 W.L.R. 1057) and the owner of shares in a private company may not be (*Lloyds Bank* v. *Duker* [1987] 1 W.L.R. 1324). Where assets such as shares (*Booth* v. *Ellard* [1980] 1 W.L.R. 1443) or farm land (*Jenkins* (*Inspector of Taxes*) v. *Brown* [1989] 1 W.L.R. 1163) are pooled for business purposes the owners remain jointly absolutely entitled as against the trustees, provided that their interests are concurrent.

Funds in court

61.—(1) For the purposes of section 60, funds in court held by the Accountant General shall be regarded as held by him as nominee for the persons entitled to or interested in the funds, or as the case may be for their trustees.

(2) Where funds in court standing to an account are invested or, after investment, are realised, the method by which the Accountant General effects the investment or the realisation of investments shall not affect the question whether there is for the purposes of this Act an acquisition, or as the case may be a disposal, of an asset representing funds in court standing to the account, and in particular there shall for those purposes be an acquisition or disposal of shares in a court investment fund notwithstanding that the investment in such shares of funds in court standing to an account, or the realisation of funds which have been so invested, is effected by setting off, in the Accountant General's accounts, investment in one account against realisation of investments in another.

(3) In this section "funds in court" means—

(a) money in the Supreme Court, money in county courts and statutory deposits described in section 40 of the Administration of Justice Act 1982, and

(b) money in the Supreme Court of Judicature of Northern Ireland and money in a county court in Northern Ireland,

and investments representing such money; and references in this section to the Accountant General are references to the Accountant General of the Supreme Court of Judicature in England and, in relation to money within paragraph (b) above and investments representing such money, include references to the Accountant General of the Supreme Court of Judicature of Northern Ireland or any other person by whom such funds are held.

GENERAL NOTE
    The beneficiaries of funds in court in England and Wales and Northern Ireland are to be treated as absolutely entitled to them.

Death: general provisions

62.—(1) For the purposes of this Act the assets of which a deceased person was competent to dispose—

(a) shall be deemed to be acquired on his death by the personal representatives or other person on whom they devolve for a consideration equal to their market value at the date of the death, but

(b) shall not be deemed to be disposed of by him on his death (whether or not they were the subject of a testamentary disposition).

(2) Allowable losses sustained by an individual in the year of assessment in which he dies may, so far as they cannot be deducted from chargeable gains accruing in that year, be deducted from chargeable gains accruing to the deceased in the three years of assessment preceding the year of assessment in which the death occurs, taking chargeable gains accruing in a later year before those accruing in an earlier year.

(3) In relation to property forming part of the estate of a deceased person the personal representatives shall for the purposes of this Act be treated as being a single and continuing body of persons (distinct from the persons who may from time to time be the personal representatives), and that body shall be treated as having the deceased's residence, ordinary residence, and domicile at the date of death.

(4) On a person acquiring any asset as legatee (as defined in section 64)—

(a) no chargeable gain shall accrue to the personal representatives, and

(b) the legatee shall be treated as if the personal representatives' acquisition of the asset had been his acquisition of it.

(5) Notwithstanding section 17(1) no chargeable gain shall accrue to any person on his making a disposal by way of donatio mortis causa.

(6) Subject to subsections (7) and (8) below, where within the period of two years after a person's death any of the dispositions (whether effected by

will, under the law relating to intestacy or otherwise) of the property of which he was competent to dispose are varied, or the benefit conferred by any of those dispositions is disclaimed, by an instrument in writing made by the persons or any of the persons who benefit or would benefit under the dispositions—

(a) the variation or disclaimer shall not constitute a disposal for the purposes of this Act, and

(b) this section shall apply as if the variation had been effected by the deceased or, as the case may be, the disclaimed benefit had never been conferred.

(7) Subsection (6) above does not apply to a variation unless the person or persons making the instrument so elect by notice given to the Board within six months after the date of the instrument or such longer time as the Board may allow.

(8) Subsection (6) above does not apply to a variation or disclaimer made for any consideration in money or money's worth other than consideration consisting of the making of a variation or disclaimer in respect of another of the dispositions.

(9) Subsection (6) above applies whether or not the administration of the estate is complete or the property has been distributed in accordance with the original dispositions.

(10) In this section references to assets of which a deceased person was competent to dispose are references to assets of the deceased which (otherwise than in right of a power of appointment or of the testamentary power conferred by statute to dispose of entailed interests) he could, if of full age and capacity, have disposed of by his will, assuming that all the assets were situated in England and, if he was not domiciled in the United Kingdom, that he was domiciled in England, and include references to his severable share in any assets to which, immediately before his death, he was beneficially entitled as a joint tenant.

GENERAL NOTE

Originally there was a charge to C.G.T. on death, but this was abolished in 1971. However, a revaluation to market value at death was retained.

A right is given to the beneficiaries under a will to vary any of the dispositions within two years of the death without any C.G.T. consequences, provided that they so elect within six months of the variation (for the comparable provision relating to inheritance tax, see IHTA 1984, s.142).

Legatees take assets from the personal representatives without a charge to C.G.T., but they may not add any sum paid to them to obtain possession of the assets (*Passant* v. *Jackson* (*Inspector of Taxes*) (1987) 59 T.C. 230). Foreign assets must be valued in sterling as at the date of death (*Bentley* v. *Pike* (1981) 53 T.C. 590).

Allowable losses sustained by individuals in their year of death may be carried back three years.

The definition of "competent to dispose" in subs. (10) is comparable to that for estate duty in FA 1894, s.22(2)(a), but differs in detail.

Death: application of law in Scotland

63.—(1) The provisions of this Act, so far as relating to the consequences of the death of an heir of entail in possession of any property in Scotland subject to an entail, whether sui juris or not, or of a proper liferenter of any property, shall have effect subject to the provisions of this section.

(2) For the purposes of this Act, on the death of any such heir or liferenter the heir of entail next entitled to the entailed property under the entail or, as the case may be, the person (if any) who, on the death of the liferenter, becomes entitled to possession of the property as fiar shall be deemed to have acquired all the assets forming part of the property at the date of the deceased's death for a consideration equal to their market value at that date.

GENERAL NOTE

The provisions of s.62 are applied on the death of an heir of entail or liferenter in Scotland.

Expenses in administration of estates and trusts

64.—(1) In the case of a gain accruing to a person on the disposal of, or of a right or interest in or over, an asset to which he became absolutely entitled as legatee or as against the trustees of settled property—

(a) any expenditure within section 38(2) incurred by him in relation to the transfer of the asset to him by the personal representatives or trustees, and

(b) any such expenditure incurred in relation to the transfer of the asset by the personal representatives or trustees,

shall be allowable as a deduction in the computation of the gain accruing to that person on the disposal.

(2) In this Act, unless the context otherwise requires, "legatee" includes any person taking under a testamentary disposition or on an intestacy or partial intestacy, whether he takes beneficially or as trustee, and a person taking under a donatio mortis causa shall be treated (except for the purposes of section 62) as a legatee and his acquisition as made at the time of the donor's death.

(3) For the purposes of the definition of "legatee" above, and of any reference in this Act to a person acquiring an asset "as legatee", property taken under a testamentary disposition or on an intestacy or partial intestacy includes any asset appropriated by the personal representatives in or towards satisfaction of a pecuniary legacy or any other interest or share in the property devolving under the disposition or intestacy.

GENERAL NOTE

This allows a legatee or beneficiary disposing of assets to deduct from his gain any costs incurred by him or the trustees in relation to the transfer of assets to him.

Liability for tax of trustees or personal representatives

65.—(1) Capital gains tax chargeable in respect of chargeable gains accruing to the trustees of a settlement or capital gains tax due from the personal representatives of a deceased person may be assessed and charged on and in the name of any one or more of those trustees or personal representatives, but where an assessment is made in pursuance of this subsection otherwise than on all the trustees or all the personal representatives the persons assessed shall not include a person who is not resident or ordinarily resident in the United Kingdom.

(2) Subject to section 60 and any other express provision to the contrary, chargeable gains accruing to the trustees of a settlement or to the personal representatives of a deceased person, and capital gains tax chargeable on or in the name of such trustees or personal representatives, shall not be regarded for the purposes of this Act as accruing to, or chargeable on, any other person, nor shall any trustee or personal representative be regarded for the purposes of this Act as an individual.

GENERAL NOTE

C.G.T. accruing to trustees or personal representatives may be charged on any or all of them who are resident in the U.K. They are charged in their capacity as trustees, not as individuals. For a case in which these provisions operated in a rather penal way, see *Roome* v. *Edwards* [1982] A.C. 279, H.L.

Insolvents' assets

66.—(1) In relation to assets held by a person as trustee or assignee in bankruptcy or under a deed of arrangement this Act shall apply as if the assets were vested in, and the acts of the trustee or assignee in relation to the assets were the acts of, the bankrupt or debtor (acquisitions from or disposals to him by the bankrupt or debtor being disregarded accordingly), and tax in respect of any chargeable gains which accrue to any such trustee or assignee shall be assessable on and recoverable from him.

(2) Assets held by a trustee or assignee in bankruptcy or under a deed of arrangement at the death of the bankrupt or debtor shall for the purposes of this Act be regarded as held by a personal representative of the deceased and—

(a) subsection (1) above shall not apply after the death, and

(b) section 62(1) shall apply as if any assets held by a trustee or assignee in bankruptcy or under a deed of arrangement at the death of the bankrupt or debtor were assets of which the deceased was competent to dispose and which then devolved on the trustee or assignee as if he were a personal representative.

(3) Assets vesting in a trustee in bankruptcy after the death of the bankrupt or debtor shall for the purposes of this Act be regarded as held by a personal representative of the deceased, and subsection (1) above shall not apply.

(4) The definition of "settled property" in section 68 shall not include any property as being property held by a trustee or assignee in bankruptcy or under a deed of arrangement.

(5) In this section—

"deed of arrangement" means a deed of arrangement to which the Deeds of Arrangement Act 1914 or any corresponding enactment forming part of the law of Scotland or Northern Ireland applies, and

"trustee in bankruptcy" includes a permanent trustee within the meaning of the Bankruptcy (Scotland) Act 1985.

GENERAL NOTE

No charge to C.G.T. arises on the transfer of insolvents' assets to their trustee or assignee in bankruptcy and the latter's disposals are treated as those of the former. The assignee, however, remains liable for the tax (*McMeekin, A Bankrupt, Re* (1973) 48 T.C. 725).

Provisions applicable where section 79 of the Finance Act 1980 has applied

67.—(1) In this section "a claim" means a claim under section 79 of the Finance Act 1980 ("section 79") and "relief" means relief under that section (which provided general relief for gifts).

(2) Where a disposal in respect of which a claim is or has been made is or proves to be a chargeable transfer for inheritance tax purposes, there shall be allowed as a deduction in computing (for capital gains tax purposes) the chargeable gain accruing to the transferee on the disposal of the asset in question an amount equal to whichever is the lesser of—

(a) the inheritance tax attributable to the value of the asset; and

(b) the amount of the chargeable gain as computed apart from this subsection;

and in the case of a disposal which, being a potentially exempt transfer, proves to be a chargeable transfer, all necessary adjustments shall be made, whether by the discharge or repayment of capital gains tax or otherwise.

(3) Where an amount of inheritance tax—

(a) falls to be redetermined in consequence of the transferor's death within seven years of making the chargeable transfer in question; or

(b) is otherwise varied,

after it has been taken into account under subsection (2) above (or under section 79(5)), all necessary adjustments shall be made, whether by the making of an assessment to capital gains tax or by the discharge or repayment of such tax.

(4) Where—

(a) a claim for relief has been made in respect of the disposal of an asset to a trustee, and

(b) the trustee is deemed to have disposed of the asset, or part of it, by virtue of section 71(1) or 72(1)(a),

sections 72(1)(b) and 73(1)(a) shall not apply to the disposal of the asset, or part by the trustee, but any chargeable gain accruing to the trustee on the disposal shall be restricted to the amount of the held-over gain (or a corresponding part of it) on the disposal of the asset to him.

(5) Subsection (4) above shall not have effect in a case within section 73(2) but in such a case the reduction provided for by section 73(2) shall be diminished by an amount equal to the proportion there mentioned of the held-over gain.

(6) Section 168 shall apply where relief has been given—

(a) with the substitution for subsection (1) of the following—

"(1) If—

(a) relief has been given under section 79 of the Finance Act 1980 in respect of a disposal made after 5th April 1981 to an individual ("the relevant disposal"); and

(b) at a time when he has not disposed of the asset in question, the transferee becomes neither resident nor ordinarily resident in the United Kingdom,

then, subject to the following provisions of this section, a chargeable gain shall be deemed to have accrued to the transferee immediately before that time, and its amount shall be equal to the held-over gain (within the meaning of section 67) on the relevant disposal."; and

(b) with the substitution in subsections (2), (6) and (10) for the references to section 165(4)(b) of references to section 79(1)(b).

(7) In this section "held-over gain", in relation to a disposal, means the chargeable gain which would have accrued on that disposal apart from section 79, reduced where applicable in accordance with subsection (3) of that section, and references to inheritance tax include references to capital transfer tax.

GENERAL NOTE

The general hold-over relief for gifts between individuals, introduced by FA 1980, s.79, and extended to gifts into trust by FA 1981, s.78, was abolished by FA 1989, s.124. Where such a gift took place, and the gift subsequently proves to be liable to I.H.T., the chargeable gain on a disposal can be reduced by the amount of I.H.T. payable if this is advantageous. Variations in I.H.T. payable due to the death of the transferor or otherwise are taken into account.

Where a claim for hold-over relief has been made on a gift into trust, the chargeable gain on a subsequent deemed disposal by the trustee is restricted to the amount of the held-over gain. The same applies in relation to the charge on emigration of a donee under s.168.

CHAPTER II

SETTLEMENTS

General provisions

Meaning of "settled property"

68. In this Act, unless the context otherwise requires, "settled property" means any property held in trust other than property to which section 60 applies.

GENERAL NOTE

This defines settled property as any property held in trust, except where the beneficiaries are absolutely entitled as against the trustee, as to which see the Note to s.60.

Trustees of settlements

69.—(1) In relation to settled property, the trustees of the settlement shall for the purposes of this Act be treated as being a single and continuing body of persons (distinct from the persons who may from time to time be the trustees), and that body shall be treated as being resident and ordinarily resident in the United Kingdom unless the general administration of the trusts is ordinarily carried on outside the United Kingdom and the trustees or a majority of them for the time being are not resident or not ordinarily resident in the United Kingdom.

(2) Notwithstanding subsection (1) above, a person carrying on a business which consists of or includes the management of trusts, and acting as trustee of a trust in the course of that business, shall be treated in relation to that trust as not resident in the United Kingdom if the whole of the settled property consists of or derives from property provided by a person not at the time (or, in the case of a trust arising under a testamentary disposition or on an intestacy or partial intestacy, at his death) domiciled, resident or ordinarily resident in the United Kingdom, and if in such a case the trustees or a majority of them are or are treated in relation to that trust as not resident in the United Kingdom, the general administration of the trust shall be treated as ordinarily carried on outside the United Kingdom.

(3) For the purposes of this section, and of sections 71(1) and 72(1), where part of the property comprised in a settlement is vested in one trustee or set of trustees and part in another (and in particular where settled land within the meaning of the Settled Land Act 1925 is vested in the tenant for life and investments representing capital money are vested in the trustees of the settlement), they shall be treated as together constituting and, in so far as they act separately, as acting on behalf of a single body of trustees.

(4) If tax assessed on the trustees, or any one trustee, of a settlement in respect of a chargeable gain accruing to the trustees is not paid within six months from the date when it becomes payable by the trustees or trustee, and before or after the expiration of that period of six months the asset in respect of which the chargeable gain accrued, or any part of the proceeds of sale of that asset, is transferred by the trustees to a person who as against the trustees is absolutely entitled to it, that person may at any time within two years from the time when the tax became payable be assessed and charged (in the name of the trustees) to an amount of capital gains tax not exceeding tax chargeable on an amount equal to the amount of the chargeable gain and, where part only of the asset or of the proceeds was transferred, not exceeding a proportionate part of that amount.

GENERAL NOTE

The section provides that the trustees of a settlement are to be treated as a single body of persons resident and ordinarily resident in the U.K., unless the administration is outside the U.K. and the trustees or majority of them are not so resident.

A trust administrator of property derived from a person not domiciled, resident or ordinarily resident in the U.K. is treated as carrying it on outside the U.K. if the non-residence test regarding trustees is satisfied.

Parts of a settlement vested in different trustees are treated as a single settlement. For the operation of this provision, see *Roome* v. *Edwards* [1982] A.C. 279, H.L.

Where tax charged on trustees is not paid within six months, recourse may be had on a beneficiary within two years.

Transfers into settlement

70. A transfer into settlement, whether revocable or irrevocable, is a disposal of the entire property thereby becoming settled property notwithstanding that the transferor has some interest as a beneficiary under the settlement and notwithstanding that he is a trustee, or the sole trustee, of the settlement.

GENERAL NOTE

A transfer into settlement is a disposal of the entire property, even though the transferor retains an interest (other than absolute entitlement). The section was slightly modified following its consideration in *Berry* v. *Warnett* [1982] 2 All E.R., H.L.

Person becoming absolutely entitled to settled property

71.—(1) On the occasion when a person becomes absolutely entitled to any settled property as against the trustee all the assets forming part of the settled property to which he becomes so entitled shall be deemed to have been disposed of by the trustee, and immediately reacquired by him in his capacity as a trustee within section 60(1), for a consideration equal to their market value.

(2) On the occasion when a person becomes absolutely entitled to any settled property as against the trustee, any allowable loss which has accrued to the trustee in respect of property which is, or is represented by, the property to which that person so becomes entitled (including any allowable loss carried forward to the year of assessment in which that occasion falls), being a loss which cannot be deducted from chargeable gains accruing to the trustee in that year, but before that occasion, shall be treated as if it were an allowable loss accruing at that time to the person becoming so entitled, instead of to the trustee.

(3) References in this section to the case where a person becomes absolutely entitled to settled property as against the trustee shall be taken to include references to the case where a person would become so entitled but for being an infant or other person under disability.

GENERAL NOTE

This introduces a charge to C.G.T. when a beneficiary becomes absolutely entitled as against the trustee. Mitigated for a time by the general relief for gifts, this charge is once again a serious consideration.

Additional complication is added by the fact that trustees may become absolutely entitled as against themselves in relation to assets advanced under powers contained in a trust. This problem has been considered in a number of cases, notably *Hoare Trustees* v. *Gardner*; *Hart* v. *Briscoe* [1979] Ch. 110, *Roome* v. *Edwards* [1982] A.C. 279, *Bond (Inspector of Taxes)* v. *Pickford* [1983] S.T.C. 517, C.A., *Ewart* v. *Taylor (H.M. Inspector of Taxes)* [1983] S.T.C. 721 and *Swires* v. *Renton* [1991] S.T.C. 490. The general rule which has emerged is that where trustees are exercising an administrative power no charge will arise, but if they are exercising a dispositive power then a charge may be in point. The distinction is akin to that between a general and a special power of appointment.

Termination of life interest on death of person entitled

72.—(1) On the termination, on the death of the person entitled to it, of a life interest in possession in all or any part of settled property—
   (a) the whole or a corresponding part of each of the assets forming part of the settled property and not ceasing at that time to be settled property shall be deemed for the purposes of this Act at that time to be disposed of and immediately reacquired by the trustee for a consideration equal to the whole or a corresponding part of the market value of the asset; but
   (b) no chargeable gain shall accrue on that disposal.

For the purposes of this subsection a life interest which is a right to part of the income of settled property shall be treated as a life interest in a corresponding part of the settled property.

(2) Subsection (1) above shall apply where the person entitled to a life interest in possession in all or any part of settled property dies (although the interest does not then terminate) as it applies on the termination of such a life interest.

(3) In this section "life interest" in relation to a settlement—
   (a) includes a right under the settlement to the income of, or the use or occupation of, settled property for the life of a person other than the person entitled to the right, or for lives,

(b) does not include any right which is contingent on the exercise of the discretion of the trustee or the discretion of some other person, and

(c) subject to subsection (4) below, does not include an annuity, notwithstanding that the annuity is payable out of or charged on settled property or the income of settled property.

(4) In this section the expression "life interest" shall include entitlement to an annuity created by the settlement if—

(a) some or all of the settled property is appropriated by the trustees as a fund out which the annuity is payable, and

(b) there is no right of recourse to settled property not so appropriated, or to the income of settled property not so appropriated;

and, without prejudice to subsection (5) below, the settled property so appropriated shall, while the annuity is payable, and on the occasion of the death of the annuitant, be treated for the purposes of this section as being settled property under a separate settlement.

(5) If there is a life interest in a part of the settled property and, where that is a life interest in income, there is no right of recourse to, or to the income of, the remainder of the settled property, the part of the settled property in which the life interest subsists shall while it subsists be treated for the purposes of this section as being settled property under a separate settlement.

GENERAL NOTE

Where a life interest in settled property comes to an end on death, this gives rise to a deemed disposal, but without any chargeable gain (this corresponds to the general relief on death; see s.62). There are detailed provisions defining "life interest" and explaining how far the term includes annuities created by the settlement.

Death of life tenant: exclusion of chargeable gain

73.—(1) Where, by virtue of section 71(1), the assets forming part of any settled property are deemed to be disposed of and reacquired by the trustee on the occasion when a person becomes (or would but for a disability become) absolutely entitled thereto as against the trustee, then, if that occasion is the termination of a life interest (within the meaning of section 72) by the death of the person entitled to that interest—

(a) no chargeable gain shall accrue on the disposal, and

(b) if on the death the property reverts to the disponer, the disposal and reacquisition under that subsection shall be deemed to be for such consideration as to secure that neither a gain nor a loss accrues to the trustee, and shall, if the trustee had first acquired the property at a date earlier than 6th April 1965, be deemed to be at that earlier date.

(2) Where the life interest referred to in subsection (1) above is an interest in part only of the settled property to which section 71 applies, subsection (1)(a) above shall not apply but any chargeable gain accruing on the disposal shall be reduced by a proportion corresponding to that represented by the part.

(3) The last sentence of subsection (1) of section 72 and subsection (5) of that section shall apply for the purposes of subsection (2) above as they apply for the purposes of section 72(1).

GENERAL NOTE

Where the occasion when a person becomes absolutely entitled to settled property is the death of a life tenant, there is a deemed disposal, but without any chargeable gain. Where the property reverts to the disponor, the disposal is deemed to be on a no-gain/no-loss basis, or at pre-1965 values if applicable.

Effect on sections 72 and 73 of relief under section 165 or 260

74.—(1) This section applies where—

(a) a claim for relief was made under section 165 or 260 in respect of the disposal of an asset to a trustee, and

(b) the trustee is deemed to have disposed of the asset, or part of it, by virtue of section 71(1) or 72(1)(a).

(2) Sections 72(1)(b) and 73(1)(a) shall not apply to the disposal of the asset or part by the trustee, but any chargeable gain accruing to the trustee on the disposal shall be restricted to the amount of the held-over gain (or a corresponding part of it) on the disposal of the asset to him.

(3) Subsection (2) above shall not have effect in a case within section 73(2) but in such a case the reduction provided for by section 73(2) shall be diminished by an amount equal to the proportion there mentioned of the held-over gain.

(4) In this section "held-over gain" has the same meaning as in section 165 or, as the case may be, 260.

GENERAL NOTE

Where a claim for relief is made under the provisions relating to gifts of business or gifts subject to inheritance tax, then a charge will arise under ss.72 or 73, but restricted to the amount of any held-over gain under those provisions.

Death of annuitant

75. Sections 71(1) and 72(1) shall apply, where an annuity which is not a life interest is terminated by the death of the annuitant, as they apply on the termination of a life interest by the death of the person entitled thereto.

In this section "life interest" has the same meaning as in section 72.

GENERAL NOTE

An annuitant, *i.e.* the recipient of an annual payment not necessarily for life, is treated in the same way as a life tenant for the purposes of ss.71 and 72.

Disposal of interests in settled property

76.—(1) No chargeable gain shall accrue on the disposal of an interest created by or arising under a settlement (including, in particular, an annuity or life interest, and the reversion to an annuity or life interest) by the person for whose benefit the interest was created by the terms of the settlement or by any other person except one who acquired, or derives his title from one who acquired, the interest for a consideration in money or money's worth, other than consideration consisting of another interest under the settlement.

(2) Subject to subsection (1) above, where a person who has acquired an interest in settled property (including in particular the reversion to an annuity or life interest) becomes, as the holder of that interest, absolutely entitled as against the trustee to any settled property, he shall be treated as disposing of the interest in consideration of obtaining that settled property (but without prejudice to any gain accruing to the trustee on the disposal of that property deemed to be effected by him under section 71(1)).

GENERAL NOTE

This confers an important exemption from C.G.T. where an interest under a settlement is disposed of, except where it has been acquired for consideration. Where this leads to absolute entitlement, the charge under s.71 is not excluded.

The exemption does not apply where absolute entitlement already exists (*Harthan* v. *Mason* [1980] S.T.C. 94). For an attempt to use the section in the context of a tax avoidance scheme, see *Eilbeck* v. *Rawling* [1982] A.C. 300.

Charge on settlor with interest in settlement

77.—(1) Subject to subsections (6), (7) and (8) below, subsection (2) below applies where—

(a) in a year of assessment chargeable gains accrue to the trustees of a settlement from the disposal of any or all of the settled property,

(b) after making any deductions provided for by section 2(2) in respect of disposals of the settled property there remains an amount on which the trustees would, disregarding section 3 (and apart from this section), be chargeable to tax for the year in respect of those gains, and

(c) at any time during the year the settlor has an interest in the settlement.

(2) Where this subsection applies, the trustees shall not be chargeable to tax in respect of the gains concerned but instead chargeable gains of an amount equal to that referred to in subsection (1)(b) above shall be treated as accruing to the settlor in the year.

(3) Subject to subsections (4) and (5) below, for the purposes of subsection (1)(c) above a settlor has an interest in a settlement if—

(a) any property which may at any time be comprised in the settlement or any income which may arise under the settlement is, or will or may become, applicable for the benefit of or payable to the settlor or the spouse of the settlor in any circumstances whatsoever, or

(b) the settlor, or the spouse of the settlor, enjoys a benefit deriving directly or indirectly from any property which is comprised in the settlement or any income arising under the settlement.

(4) A settlor does not have an interest in a settlement by virtue of subsection (3)(a) above if and so long as none of the property which may at any time be comprised in the settlement and none of the income which may arise under the settlement can become applicable or payable as mentioned in that subsection except in the event of—

(a) the bankruptcy of some person who is or may become beneficially entitled to that property or income;

(b) any assignment of or charge on that property or income being made or given by some such person;

(c) in the case of a marriage settlement, the death of both the parties to the marriage and of all or any of the children of the marriage; or

(d) the death under the age of 25 or some lower age of some person who would be beneficially entitled to that property or income on attaining that age.

(5) A settlor does not have an interest in a settlement by virtue of subsection (3)(a) above if and so long as some person is alive and under the age of 25 during whose life none of the property which may at any time be comprised in the settlement and none of the income which may arise under the settlement can become applicable or payable as mentioned in subsection (3)(a) above except in the event of that person becoming bankrupt or assigning or charging his interest in that property or income.

(6) Subsection (2) above does not apply where the settlor dies during the year.

(7) In a case where the settlor has an interest in the settlement only for either or both of the following reasons, namely—

(a) that property or income is, or will or may become, applicable for the benefit of or payable to the settlor's spouse, and

(b) that the settlor's spouse enjoys a benefit from property or income,

subsection (2) above does not apply where the spouse dies, or the settlor and the spouse cease to be married, during the year.

(8) Subsection (2) above does not apply unless the settlor is, and the trustees are, either resident in the United Kingdom during any part of the year or ordinarily resident in the United Kingdom during the year.

GENERAL NOTE

The unification of the rates of income tax and capital gains in 1988 under what is now ss.4 and 5 created an incentive to avoid the higher rate by settling property. This section seeks to negate such an advantage by a charge on the settlor where he has an interest in the settlement. A settlor has an interest where he or his spouse enjoys a benefit from the settlement or may have the property in the settlement applied for their benefit. This does not apply in cases of a contingency depending on bankruptcy, assignment, the deaths of the parties under a marriage settlement, the deaths under 25 of individuals beneficially entitled to the property on attaining such an age, the bankruptcy of or assignments by such an individual, or where the spouse dies or the marriage ceases during the year.

The section only applies in cases of a resident or ordinarily resident settlor and trustees.

Right of recovery

78.—(1) Where any tax becomes chargeable on and is paid by a person in respect of gains treated as accruing to him under section 77(2) he shall be entitled—

(a) to recover the amount of the tax from any trustee of the settlement, and

(b) for that purpose to require an inspector to give him a certificate specifying—

(i) the amount of the gains accruing to the trustees in respect of which he has paid tax, and

(ii) the amount of tax paid;

and any such certificate shall be conclusive evidence of the facts stated in it.

(2) In order to ascertain for the purposes of subsection (1) above the amount of tax chargeable for any year by virtue of section 77(2) in respect of gains treated as accruing to any person, those gains shall be regarded as forming the highest part of the amount on which he is chargeable to capital gains tax for the year.

(3) In a case where—

(a) gains are treated as accruing to a person in a year under section 86(4), and

(b) gains are treated as accruing to the same person under section 77(2) in the same year,

subsection (2) above shall have effect subject to section 86(4)(b).

GENERAL NOTE

A settlor charged under s.77 is entitled to recovery from the trustees against a certificate provided by the inspector. Where there is also a charge on the settlor under s.86(4), the gains are deemed to be the highest part of the gains on which he is chargeable for that year.

Provisions supplemental to sections 77 and 78

79.—(1) For the purposes of this section and sections 77 and 78 a person is a settlor in relation to a settlement if the settled property consists of or includes property originating from him.

(2) In this section and sections 77 and 78—

(a) references to settled property (and to property comprised in a settlement), in relation to any settlor, are references only to property originating from that settlor, and

(b) references to income arising under a settlement, in relation to any settlor, are references only to income originating from that settlor.

(3) References in this section to property originating from a settlor are references to—

(a) property which that settlor has provided directly or indirectly for the purposes of the settlement,

(b) property representing that property, and

(c) so much of any property which represents both property so provided and other property as, on a just apportionment, represents the property so provided.

(4) References in this section to income originating from a settlor are references to—

(a) income from property originating from that settlor, and

(b) income provided directly or indirectly by that settlor.

(5) In subsections (3) and (4) above—

(a) references to property or income which a settlor has provided directly or indirectly include references to property or income which has been provided directly or indirectly by another person in pursuance of reciprocal arrangements with that settlor, but do not include references to property or income which that settlor has provided directly or indirectly in pursuance of reciprocal arrangements with another person, and

(b) references to property which represents other property include references to property which represents accumulated income from that other property.

(6) An inspector may by notice require any person who is or has been a trustee of, a beneficiary under, or a settlor in relation to, a settlement to give him within such time as he may direct, not being less than 28 days, such particulars as he thinks necessary for the purposes of this section and sections 77 and 78.

(7) The reference in section 77(1)(a) to gains accruing to trustees from the disposal of settled property includes a reference to gains treated as accruing to them under section 13 and the reference in section 77(1)(b) to deductions in respect of disposals of the settled property includes a reference to deductions on account of losses treated under section 13 as accruing to the trustees.

(8) Where the trustees of a settlement have elected that section 691(2) of the Taxes Act (certain income of maintenance funds for historic buildings not to be income of settlor etc.) shall have effect in the case of any settlement or part of a settlement in relation to a year of assessment, sections 77 and 78 subsections (1) to (7) above shall not apply in relation to the settlement or part for the year.

GENERAL NOTE

The section contains provisions amplifying ss.77 and 78. For a parallel provision applying to income tax, see ICTA 1988, s.679.

The inspector is entitled to obtain information from interested parties.

Section 77 applies to gains accruing to resident shareholders of non-resident close companies under s.13, but not to cases where the provisions regarding maintenance funds for historic buildings under IHTA 1984, Sched. 4 have been applied by virtue of an election under ICTA 1988, s.691(2).

Migration of settlements, non-resident settlements and dual resident settlements

Trustees ceasing to be resident in U.K.

80.—(1) This section applies if the trustees of a settlement become at any time ("the relevant time") neither resident nor ordinarily resident in the United Kingdom.

(2) The trustees shall be deemed for all purposes of this Act—

(a) to have disposed of the defined assets immediately before the relevant time, and

(b) immediately to have reacquired them,

at their market value at that time.

(3) Subject to subsections (4) and (5) below, the defined assets are all assets constituting settled property of the settlement immediately before the relevant time.

(4) If immediately after the relevant time—

(a) the trustees carry on a trade in the United Kingdom through a branch or agency, and

(b) any assets are situated in the United Kingdom and either used in or for the purposes of the trade or used or held for the purposes of the branch or agency, the assets falling within paragraph (b) above shall not be defined assets.

(5) Assets shall not be defined assets if—

(a) they are of a description specified in any double taxation relief arrangements, and

(b) were the trustees to dispose of them immediately before the relevant time, the trustees would fall to be regarded for the purposes of the arrangements as not liable in the United Kingdom to tax on gains accruing to them on the disposal.

(6) Section 152 shall not apply where the trustees—

(a) have disposed of the old assets, or their interest in them, before the relevant time, and

(b) acquire the new assets, or their interest in them, after that time, unless the new assets are excepted from this subsection by subsection (7) below.

(7) If at the time when the new assets are acquired—

(a) the trustees carry on a trade in the United Kingdom through a branch or agency, and

(b) any new assets are situated in the United Kingdom and either used in or for the purposes of the trade or used or held for the purposes of the branch or agency,

the assets falling within paragraph (b) above shall be excepted from subsection (6) above.

(8) In this section "the old assets" and "the new assets" have the same meanings as in section 152.

GENERAL NOTE

This section, introduced in 1991, imposes a charge to C.G.T. when a settlement is exported from the U.K. The charge applies by way of a deemed disposal of all the assets in the settlement, save any used for the purposes of a trade carried on in the U.K. or protected by double taxation relief.

Roll-over relief under s.152 is also excluded for migrant trusts, again subject to an exception where assets are used for a trade in the U.K.

Death of trustee: special rules

81.—(1) Subsection (2) below applies where—

(a) section 80 applies as a result of the death of a trustee of the settlement, and

(b) within the period of 6 months beginning with the death, the trustees of the settlement become resident and ordinarily resident in the United Kingdom.

(2) That section shall apply as if the defined assets were restricted to such assets (if any) as—

(a) would be defined assets apart from this section, and

(b) fall within subsection (3) or (4) below.

(3) Assets fall within this subsection if they were disposed of by the trustees in the period which—

(a) begins with the death, and

(b) ends when the trustees become resident and ordinarily resident in the United Kingdom.

(4) Assets fall within this subsection if—

(a) they are of a description specified in any double taxation relief arrangements,

(b) they constitute settled property of the settlement at the time immediately after the trustees become resident and ordinarily resident in the United Kingdom, and

(c) were the trustees to dispose of them at that time, the trustees would fall to be regarded for the purposes of the arrangements as not liable in the United Kingdom to tax on gains accruing to them on the disposal.

(5) Subsection (6) below applies where—

(a) at any time the trustees of a settlement become resident and ordinarily resident in the United Kingdom as a result of the death of a trustee of the settlement, and

(b) section 80 applies as regards the trustees of the settlement in circumstances where the relevant time (within the meaning of that section) falls within the period of 6 months beginning with the death.

(6) That section shall apply as if the defined assets were restricted to such assets (if any) as—

(a) would be defined assets apart from this section, and

(b) fall within subsection (7) below.

(7) Assets fall within this subsection if—

(a) the trustees acquired them in the period beginning with the death and ending with the relevant time, and

(b) they acquired them as a result of a disposal in respect of which relief is given under section 165 or in relation to which section 260(3) applies.

GENERAL NOTE

The charge under s.80 might operate unfairly where a settlement became non-resident because of the death of a trustee. Accordingly in such a case the charge is excluded if the settlement reverts to U.K. residence within six months.

The exemption does not apply to disposals within the period of non-residence or if the settlement is protected from charge by double taxation relief.

Conversely, where a settlement becomes resident through the death of a trustee, a six-month grace period is given to emigrate. The relief does not extend to assets acquired during the period to which roll-over relief under ss.165 or 260(3) applied.

Past trustees: liability for tax

82.—(1) This section applies where—

(a) section 80 applies as regards the trustees of a settlement ("the migrating trustees"), and

(b) any capital gains tax which is payable by the migrating trustees by virtue of section 80(2) is not paid within 6 months from the time when it became payable.

(2) The Board may, at any time before the end of the period of 3 years beginning with the time when the amount of the tax is finally determined, serve on any person to whom subsection (3) below applies a notice—

(a) stating particulars of the tax payable, the amount remaining unpaid and the date when it became payable;

(b) stating particulars of any interest payable on the tax, any amount remaining unpaid and the date when it became payable;

(c) requiring that person to pay the amount of the unpaid tax, or the aggregate amount of the unpaid tax and the unpaid interest, within 30 days of the service of the notice.

(3) This subsection applies to any person who, at any time within the relevant period, was a trustee of the settlement, except that it does not apply to any such person if—

(a) he ceased to be a trustee of the settlement before the end of the relevant period, and

(b) he shows that, when he ceased to be a trustee of the settlement, there was no proposal that the trustees might become neither resident nor ordinarily resident in the United Kingdom.

(4) Any amount which a person is required to pay by a notice under this section may be recovered from him as if it were tax due and duly demanded of him; and he may recover any such amount paid by him from the migrating trustees.

(5) A payment in pursuance of a notice under this section shall not be allowed as a deduction in computing any income, profits or losses for any tax purposes.

(6) For the purposes of this section—

(a) where the relevant time (within the meaning of section 80) falls within the period of 12 months beginning with 19th March 1991, the relevant period is the period beginning with that date and ending with that time;

(b) in any other case, the relevant period is the period of 12 months ending with the relevant time.

GENERAL NOTE

In practice it may be difficult to collect tax where the trustees are non-resident. Accordingly, the Board are given power to serve a notice within three years of the time when the amount of tax is finally determined on a trustee during the period of a year before the settlement was exported, requiring him to pay within 30 days any tax due, plus interest.

There is a let-out from the section if the trustee can show that at the time he retired there was no proposal to export the settlement. He also has a right of recovery against the offshore trustees.

Trustees ceasing to be liable to U.K. tax

83.—(1) This section applies if the trustees of a settlement, while continuing to be resident and ordinarily resident in the United Kingdom, become at any time ("the time concerned") trustees who fall to be regarded for the purposes of any double taxation relief arrangements—

(a) as resident in a territory outside the United Kingdom, and

(b) as not liable in the United Kingdom to tax on gains accruing on disposals of assets ("relevant assets") which constitute settled property of the settlement and fall within descriptions specified in the arrangements.

(2) The trustees shall be deemed for all purposes of this Act—

(a) to have disposed of their relevant assets immediately before the time concerned, and

(b) immediately to have reacquired them,

at their market value at that time.

GENERAL NOTE

This section attacks settlements which become dual resident for double taxation relief purposes. In such a case there is a deemed disposal at market value of assets protected from C.G.T. by the relief.

Acquisition by dual resident trustees

84.—(1) Section 152 shall not apply where—

(a) the new assets are, or the interest in them is, acquired by the trustees of a settlement,

(b) at the time of the acquisition the trustees are resident and ordinarily resident in the United Kingdom and fall to be regarded for the purposes of any double taxation relief arrangements as resident in a territory outside the United Kingdom,

(c) the assets are of a description specified in the arrangements, and

(d) were the trustees to dispose of the assets immediately after the acquisition, the trustees would fall to be regarded for the purposes of the arrangements as not liable in the United Kingdom to tax on gains accruing to them on the disposal.

(2) In this section "the new assets" has the same meaning as in section 152.

GENERAL NOTE

Roll-over relief on disposals of business assets does not apply to dual resident trustees where a disposal of the newly acquired assets would be protected by double taxation relief.

Disposal of interests in non-resident settlements

85.—(1) Subsection (1) of section 76 shall not apply to the disposal of an interest in settled property, other than one treated under subsection (2) of that section as made in consideration of obtaining the settled property, if at the time of the disposal the trustees are neither resident nor ordinarily resident in the United Kingdom.

(2) Subject to subsections (4) and (9) below, subsection (3) below applies where—

(a) section 80 applies as regards the trustees of a settlement,

(b) after the relevant time (within the meaning of that section) a person disposes of an interest created by or arising under the settlement and the circumstances are such that subsection (1) above prevents section 76(1) applying, and

(c) the interest was created for his benefit, or he otherwise acquired it, before the relevant time.

(3) For the purpose of calculating any chargeable gain accruing on the disposal of the interest, the person disposing of it shall be treated as having—

(a) disposed of it immediately before the relevant time, and

(b) immediately reacquired it,

at its market value at that time.

(4) Subsection (3) above shall not apply if section 83 applied as regards the trustees in circumstances where the time concerned (within the meaning of that section) fell before the time when the interest was created for the benefit of the person disposing of it or when he otherwise acquired it.

(5) Subsection (7) below applies where—

(a) section 80 applies as regards the trustees of a settlement,

(b) after the relevant time (within the meaning of that section) a person disposes of an interest created by or arising under the settlement and the circumstances are such that subsection (1) above prevents section 76(1) applying,

(c) the interest was created for his benefit, or he otherwise acquired it, before the relevant time, and

(d) section 83 applied as regards the trustees in circumstances where the time concerned (within the meaning of that section) fell in the relevant period.

(6) The relevant period is the period which—

(a) begins when the interest was created for the benefit of the person disposing of it or when he otherwise acquired it, and

(b) ends with the relevant time.

(7) For the purpose of calculating any chargeable gain accruing on the disposal of the interest, the person disposing of it shall be treated as having—

(a) disposed of it immediately before the time found under subsection (8) below, and

(b) immediately reacquired it,

at its market value at that time.

(8) The time is—

(a) the time concerned (where there is only one such time), or

(b) the earliest time concerned (where there is more than one because section 83 applied more than once).

(9) Subsection (3) above shall not apply where subsection (7) above applies.

GENERAL NOTE

Subs. (1)

   This provision, introduced in 1981, excludes the relief under s.76(1) on disposals of interests in settled property where the settlement is non-resident.

The remainder of the section, which was introduced in 1991, provides a relief from the charge which would otherwise arise under subs. (1) in cases where there has already been a charge under ss.80 or 83. The relief operates by rebasing the value of the interest to its market value at the time the relevant charge occurred.

Attribution of gains to settlors with interest in non-resident or dual resident settlements

86.—(1) This section applies where the following conditions are fulfilled as regards a settlement in a particular year of assessment—
  (a) the settlement is a qualifying settlement in the year;
  (b) the trustees of the settlement fulfil the condition as to residence specified in subsection (2) below;
  (c) a person who is a settlor in relation to the settlement ("the settlor") is domiciled in the United Kingdom at some time in the year and is either resident in the United Kingdom during any part of the year or ordinarily resident in the United Kingdom during the year;
  (d) at any time during the year the settlor has an interest in the settlement;
  (e) by virtue of disposals of any of the settled property originating from the settlor, there is an amount on which the trustees would be chargeable to tax for the year under section 2(2) if the assumption as to residence specified in subsection (3) below were made;
  (f) paragraph 3, 4 or 5 of Schedule 5 does not prevent this section applying.
  (2) The condition as to residence is that—
  (a) the trustees are not resident or ordinarily resident in the United Kingdom during any part of the year, or
  (b) the trustees are resident in the United Kingdom during any part of the year or ordinarily resident in the United Kingdom during the year; but at any time of such residence or ordinary residence they fall to be regarded for the purposes of any double taxation relief arrangements as resident in a territory outside the United Kingdom.
  (3) Where subsection (2)(a) above applies, the assumption as to residence is that the trustees are resident or ordinarily resident in the United Kingdom throughout the year; and where subsection (2)(b) above applies, the assumption as to residence is that the double taxation relief arrangements do not apply.
  (4) Where this section applies—
  (a) chargeable gains of an amount equal to that referred to in subsection (1)(e) above shall be treated as accruing to the settlor in the year, and
  (b) those gains shall be treated as forming the highest part of the amount on which he is chargeable to capital gains tax for the year.
  (5) Schedule 5 (which contains provisions supplementary to this section) shall have effect.

GENERAL NOTE

  This section, also introduced in 1991, allows the gains of non-resident or dual resident settlements to be attributed to a settlor domiciled, resident or ordinarily resident in the U.K. where he has an interest in the settlement. Attributed gains are taxed at the settlor's highest rate of tax.
  See further the Note to Sched. 5.

Attribution of gains to beneficiaries

87.—(1) This section applies to a settlement for any year of assessment during which the trustees are at no time resident or ordinarily resident in the United Kingdom if the settlor or one of the settlors is at any time during that year, or was when he made his settlement, domiciled and either resident or ordinarily resident in the United Kingdom.

(2) There shall be computed in respect of every year of assessment for which this section applies the amount on which the trustees would have been chargeable to tax under section 2(2) if they had been resident or ordinarily resident in the United Kingdom in the year; and that amount, together with the corresponding amount in respect of any earlier such year so far as not already treated under subsection (4) below or section 89(2) as chargeable gains accruing to beneficiaries under the settlement, is in this section and sections 89 and 90 referred to as the trust gains for the year.

(3) Where as regards the same settlement and for the same year of assessment—

(a) chargeable gains, whether of one amount or of 2 or more amounts, are treated as accruing by virtue of section 86(4), and

(b) an amount falls to be computed under subsection (2) above,

the amount so computed shall be treated as reduced by the amount, or aggregate of the amounts, mentioned in paragraph (a) above.

(4) Subject to the following provisions of this section, the trust gains for a year of assessment shall be treated as chargeable gains accruing in that year to beneficiaries of the settlement who receive capital payments from the trustees in that year or have received such payments in any earlier year.

(5) The attribution of chargeable gains to beneficiaries under subsection (4) above shall be made in proportion to, but shall not exceed, the amounts of the capital payments received by them.

(6) A capital payment shall be left out of account for the purposes of subsections (4) and (5) above to the extent that chargeable gains have by reason of the payment been treated as accruing to the recipient in an earlier year.

(7) A beneficiary shall not be charged to tax on chargeable gains treated by virtue of subsection (4) above as accruing to him in any year unless he is domiciled in the United Kingdom at some time in that year.

(8) In computing an amount under subsection (2) above in respect of the year 1991–92 or a subsequent year of assessment, the effect of sections 77 to 79 shall be ignored.

(9) For the purposes of this section a settlement arising under a will or intestacy shall be treated as made by the testator or intestate at the time of his death.

(10) Subsection (1) above does not apply in relation to any year beginning before 6th April 1981; and the reference in subsections (4) and (5) to capital payments received by beneficiaries do not include references to any payment received before 10th March 1981 or any payment received on or after that date and before 6th April 1984 so far as it represents a chargeable gain which accrued to the trustees before 6th April 1981.

GENERAL NOTE

This section mainly derives from FA 1981, s.80, and was introduced in view of the inadequacy of the previous provisions (as to which, see *Leedale (Inspector of Taxes)* v. *Lewis* [1982] 1 W.L.R. 1319). It allows the gains of non-resident settlements to be attributed to resident beneficiaries who receive capital payments from the settlement, where the settlor is, or was when he made the settlement, domiciled and either resident or ordinarily resident in the U.K. A double charge under ss.86 and 87 is prevented. A non-domiciled beneficiary cannot be charged. The charge on a settlor with an interest in a resident settlement under s.77 is ignored for the purposes of this section.

A trust arising under a will or intestacy is treated as having been made at the time of death. For the meaning of "capital payment" see s.97(1).

Gains of dual resident settlements

88.—(1) Section 87 also applies to a settlement for any year of assessment beginning on or after 6th April 1991 if—

(a) the trustees are resident in the United Kingdom during any part of the year or ordinarily resident in the United Kingdom during the year,

(b) at any time of such residence or ordinary residence they fall to be regarded for the purposes of any double taxation relief arrangements as resident in a territory outside the United Kingdom, and

(c) the settlor or one of the settlors is at any time during that year, or was when he made his settlement, domiciled and either resident or ordinarily resident in the United Kingdom.

(2) In respect of every year of assessment for which section 87 applies by virtue of this section, section 87 shall have effect as if the amount to be computed under section 87(2) were the assumed chargeable amount; and the reference in section 87(2) to the corresponding amount in respect of an earlier year shall be construed as a reference to the amount computed under section 87(2) apart from this section or (as the case may be) the amount computed under section 87(2) by virtue of this section.

(3) For the purposes of subsection (2) above the assumed chargeable amount in respect of a year of assessment is the lesser of the following 2 amounts—

(a) the amount on which the trustees would be chargeable to tax for the year under section 2(2) on the assumption that the double taxation relief arrangements did not apply;

(b) the amount on which, by virtue of disposals of protected assets, the trustees would be chargeable to tax for the year under section 2(2) on the assumption that those arrangements did not apply.

(4) For the purposes of subsection (3)(b) above assets are protected assets if—

(a) they are of a description specified in the double taxation relief arrangements, and

(b) were the trustees to dispose of them at any relevant time, the trustees would fall to be regarded for the purposes of the arrangements as not liable in the United Kingdom to tax on gains accruing to them on the disposal.

(5) For the purposes of subsection (4) above—

(a) the assumption specified in subsection (3)(b) above shall be ignored;

(b) a relevant time is any time, in the year of assessment concerned, when the trustees fall to be regarded for the purposes of the arrangements as resident in a territory outside the United Kingdom;

(c) if different assets are identified by reference to different relevant times, all of them are protected assets.

(6) In computing the assumed chargeable amount in respect of a particular year of assessment, the effect of sections 77 to 79 shall be ignored.

(7) For the purposes of section 87 as it applies by virtue of this section, capital payments received before 6th April 1991 shall be disregarded.

GENERAL NOTE

The provisions of s.87 are extended as from April 6, 1991, to a dual resident settlement. The chargeable amount is the lesser of the total charge on the settlement and the charge on assets protected by the double taxation relief arrangement.

Migrant settlements etc.

89.—(1) Where a period of one or more years of assessment for which section 87 applies to a settlement ("a non-resident period") succeeds a period of one or more years of assessment for each of which section 87 does not apply to the settlement ("a resident period"), a capital payment received by a beneficiary in the resident period shall be disregarded for the purposes of section 87 if it was not made in anticipation of a disposal made by the trustees in the non-resident period.

(2) Where—

(a) a non-resident period is succeeded by a resident period, and

(b) the trust gains for the last year of the non-resident period are not (or

not wholly) treated as chargeable gains accruing in that year to
beneficiaries,
then, subject to subsection (3) below, those trust gains (or the outstanding
part of them) shall be treated as chargeable gains accruing in the first year of
the resident period to beneficiaries of the settlement who receive capital
payments from the trustees in that year; and so on for the second and
subsequent years until the amount treated as accruing to beneficiaries is
equal to the amount of the trust gains for the last year of the non-resident
period.
(3) Subsections (5) and (7) of section 87 shall apply in relation to subsection (2) above as they apply in relation to subsection (4) of that section.

GENERAL NOTE
This provision, deriving, like s.87, mainly from FA 1981 grants a relief from tax where a
resident period for a settlement is succeeded by a non-resident period. Capital payments made
during the resident period are ignored unless they were made in anticipation of a disposal
during the non-resident period.
Conversely, gains made during a non-resident period may be attributed to capital payments
made to beneficiaries during subsequent resident periods until they are exhausted.

Transfers between settlements

90.—(1) If in a year of assessment for which section 87 or 89(2) applies to a
settlement ("the transferor settlement") the trustees transfer all or part of
the settled property to the trustees of another settlement ("the transferee
settlement") then, subject to the following provisions—
   (a) if section 87 applies to the transferee settlement for the year, its trust
      gains for the year shall be treated as increased by an amount equal to
      the outstanding trust gains for the year of the transferor settlement or,
      where part only of the settled property is transferred, to a proportion-
      ate part of those trust gains;
   (b) if subsection (2) of section 89 applies to the transferee settlement for
      the year (otherwise than by virtue of paragraph (c) below), the trust
      gains referred to in that subsection shall be treated as increased by the
      amount mentioned in paragraph (a) above;
   (c) if (apart from this paragraph) neither section 87 nor section 89(2)
      applies to the transferee settlement for the year, subsection (2) of
      section 89 shall apply to it as if the year were the first year of a resident
      period succeeding a non-resident period and the trust gains referred
      to in that subsection were equal to the amount mentioned in para-
      graph (a) above.
(2) Subject to subsection (3) below, the reference in subsection (1)(a)
above to the outstanding trust gains for the year of the transferor settlement
is a reference to the amount of its trust gains for the year so far as they are not
treated under section 87(4) as chargeable gains accruing to beneficiaries in
that year.
(3) Where section 89(2) applies to the transferor settlement for the year,
the reference in subsection (1)(a) above to the outstanding trust gains of the
settlement is a reference to the trust gains referred to in section 89(2) so far
as not treated as chargeable gains accruing to beneficiaries in that or an
earlier year.
(4) This section shall not apply to a transfer so far as it is made for
consideration in money or money's worth.

GENERAL NOTE
The charge under ss.87 and 89 applies in the case where property has been transferred
between settlements other than for consideration in money or money's worth.

Increase in tax payable under section 87 or 89(2)

91.—(1) This section applies where—

(a) a capital payment is made by the trustees of a settlement on or after 6th April 1992,

(b) the payment is made in a year of assessment for which section 87 applies to the settlement or in circumstances where section 89(2) treats chargeable gains as accruing in respect of the payment,

(c) the whole payment is, in accordance with sections 92 to 95, matched with a qualifying amount of the settlement for a year of assessment falling at some time before that immediately preceding the one in which the payment is made, and

(d) a beneficiary is charged to tax in respect of the payment by virtue of section 87 or 89(2).

(2) The tax payable by the beneficiary in respect of the payment shall be increased by the amount found under subsection (3) below, except that it shall not be increased beyond the amount of the payment; and an assessment may charge tax accordingly.

(3) The amount is one equal to the interest that would be yielded if an amount equal to the tax which would be payable by the beneficiary in respect of the payment (apart from this section) carried interest for the chargeable period at the rate of 10 per cent. per annum.

(4) The chargeable period is the period which—

(a) begins with the later of the 2 days specified in subsection (5) below, and

(b) ends with 30th November in the year of assessment following that in which the capital payment is made.

(5) The 2 days are—

(a) 1st December in the year of assessment following that for which the qualifying amount mentioned in subsection (1)(c) above is the qualifying amount, and

(b) 1st December falling 6 years before 1st December in the year of assessment following that in which the capital payment is made.

(6) The Treasury may by order substitute for the percentage specified in subsection (3) above (whether as originally enacted or as amended at any time under this subsection) such other percentage as they think fit.

(7) An order under subsection (6) above may provide that an alteration of the percentage is to have effect for periods beginning on or after a day specified in the order in relation to interest running for chargeable periods beginning before that day (as well as interest running for chargeable periods beginning on or after that day).

(8) Sections 92 to 95 have effect for the purpose of supplementing subsections (1) to (5) above.

GENERAL NOTE

This section, introduced in 1991, is designed to counteract the advantage which would arise to beneficiaries from delays in capital payments which would be chargeable under ss.87 or 89(2) if these payments were made immediately. For capital payments made after April 6, 1992, there is a notional interest charge of 10 per cent. per annum on the tax payable, up to a maximum of 60 per cent. The charge is calculated by reference to a period running from December 1 to November 30 in the following year. The Treasury have power to substitute a different percentage by order.

Sections 92 to 95 apply for matching capital payments with gains which have accrued.

Qualifying amounts and matching

92.—(1) If section 87 applies to a settlement for the year 1992–93 or a subsequent year of assessment the settlement shall have a qualifying amount for the year, and the amount shall be the amount computed for the settlement in respect of the year concerned under section 87(2).

(2) The settlement shall continue to have the same qualifying amount (if any) for the year 1990–91 or 1991–92 as it had for that year by virtue of

paragraph 2 of Schedule 17 to the Finance Act 1991 (subject to subsection (3) below).

(3) Where—

(a) capital payments are made by the trustees of a settlement on or after 6th April 1991, and

(b) the payments are made in a year or years of assessment for which section 87 applies to the settlement or in circumstances where section 89(2) treats chargeable gains as accruing in respect of the payments,

the payments shall be matched with qualifying amounts of the settlement for the year 1990–91 and subsequent years of assessment (so far as the amounts are not already matched with payments by virtue of this subsection).

(4) In applying subsection (3) above—

(a) earlier payments shall be matched with earlier amounts;

(b) payments shall be carried forward to be matched with future amounts (so far as not matched with past amounts);

(c) a payment which is less than an unmatched amount (or part) shall be matched to the extent of the payment;

(d) a payment which is more than an unmatched amount (or part) shall be matched, as to the excess, with other unmatched amounts.

(5) Where part only of a capital payment is taxable, the part which is not taxable shall not fall to be matched until taxable parts of other capital payments (if any) made in the same year of assessment have been matched; and subsections (3) and (4) above shall have effect accordingly.

(6) For the purposes of subsection (5) above a part of a capital payment is taxable if the part results in chargeable gains accruing under section 87 or 89(2).

GENERAL NOTE

The general rule is that undistributed gains and capital payments are matched on a FIFO basis.

Matching: special cases

93.—(1) Subsection (2) or (3) below applies (if the case permits) where—

(a) a capital payment is made by the trustees of a settlement on or after 6th April 1992,

(b) the payment is made in a year of assessment for which section 87 applies to the settlement or in circumstances where section 89(2) treats chargeable gains as accruing in respect of the payment, and

(c) a beneficiary is charged to tax in respect of the payment by virtue of section 87 or 89(2).

(2) If the whole payment is matched with qualifying amounts of the settlement for different years of assessment, each falling at some time before that immediately preceding the one in which the payment is made, then—

(a) the capital payment ("the main payment") shall be treated as being as many payments ("subsidiary payments") as there are qualifying amounts,

(b) a qualifying amount shall be attributed to each subsidiary payment and each payment shall be quantified accordingly, and

(c) the tax in respect of the main payment shall be divided up and attributed to the subsidiary payments on the basis of a just and reasonable apportionment,

and section 91 shall apply in the case of each subsidiary payment, the qualifying amount attributed to it and the tax attributed to it.

(3) If part of the payment is matched with a qualifying amount of the settlement for a year of assessment falling at some time before that immediately preceding the one in which the payment is made, or with qualifying amounts of the settlement for different years of assessment each so falling, then—

(a) only tax in respect of so much of the payment as is so matched shall be taken into account, and references below to the tax shall be construed accordingly,

(b) the capital payment shall be divided into 2, the first part representing so much as is matched as mentioned above and the second so much as is not,

(c) the second part shall be ignored, and

(d) the first part shall be treated as a capital payment, the whole of which is matched with the qualifying amount or amounts mentioned above, and the whole of which is charged to the tax,

and section 91, or that section and subsections (1) and (2) above (as the case may be), shall apply in the case of the capital payment arrived at under this subsection, the qualifying amount or amounts, and the tax.

(4) Section 91 and subsections (1) to (3) above shall apply (with appropriate modifications) where a payment or part of a payment is to any extent matched with part of an amount.

GENERAL NOTE

Where a capital payment is made in respect of undistributed gains for different years, the tax is to be divided up on a "just and reasonable" basis. Only tax in respect of matched amounts is to be taken into account.

Transfers of settled property where qualifying amounts not wholly matched

94.—(1) This section applies if—

(a) in the year 1990–91 or a subsequent year of assessment the trustees of a settlement ("the transferor settlement") transfer all or part of the settled property to the trustees of another settlement ("the transferee settlement"), and

(b) looking at the state of affairs at the end of the year of assessment in which the transfer is made, there is a qualifying amount of the transferor settlement for a particular year of assessment ("the year concerned") and the amount is not (or not wholly) matched with capital payments.

(2) If the whole of the settled property is transferred—

(a) the transferor settlement's qualifying amount for the year concerned shall be treated as reduced by so much of it as is not matched, and

(b) so much of that amount as is not matched shall be treated as (or as an addition to) the transferee settlement's qualifying amount for the year concerned.

(3) If part of the settled property is transferred—

(a) so much of the transferor settlement's qualifying amount for the year concerned as is not matched shall be apportioned on such basis as is just and reasonable, part being attributed to the transferred property and part to the property not transferred,

(b) the transferor settlement's qualifying amount for the year concerned shall be treated as reduced by the part attributed to the transferred property, and

(c) that part shall be treated as (or as an addition to) the transferee settlement's qualifying amount for the year concerned.

(4) If the transferee settlement did not in fact exist in the year concerned, it shall be treated as having been made at the beginning of that year.

(5) If the transferee settlement did in fact exist in the year concerned, this section shall apply whether or not section 87 applies to the settlement for that year or for any year of assessment falling before that year.

GENERAL NOTE

Where property is transferred from one settlement to another, an appropriate adjustment is made, on a "just and reasonable" basis if necessary, where there are undistributed gains not wholly matched by capital payments.

Matching after transfer

95.—(1) This section applies as regards the transferee settlement in a case where section 94 applies.

(2) Matching shall be made under section 92 by reference to the state of affairs existing immediately before the beginning of the year of assessment in which the transfer is made, and the transfer shall not affect matching so made.

(3) Subject to subsection (2) above, payments shall be matched with amounts in accordance with section 92 and by reference to amounts arrived at under section 94.

GENERAL NOTE
The rules for matching are carried forward to the transferee settlement where s.94 applies.

Payments by and to companies

96.—(1) Where a capital payment is received from a qualifying company which is controlled by the trustees of a settlement at the time it is received, for the purposes of sections 87 to 90 it shall be treated as received from the trustees.

(2) Where a capital payment is received from the trustees of a settlement (or treated as so received by virtue of subsection (1) above) and it is received by a non-resident qualifying company, the rules in subsections (3) to (6) below shall apply for the purposes of sections 87 to 90.

(3) If the company is controlled by one person alone at the time the payment is received, and that person is then resident or ordinarily resident in the United Kingdom, it shall be treated as a capital payment received by that person.

(4) If the company is controlled by 2 or more persons (taking each one separately) at the time the payment is received, then—

(a) if one of them is then resident or ordinarily resident in the United Kingdom, it shall be treated as a capital payment received by that person;

(b) if 2 or more of them are then resident or ordinarily resident in the United Kingdom ("the residents") it shall be treated as being as many equal capital payments as there are residents and each of them shall be treated as receiving one of the payments.

(5) If the company is controlled by 2 or more persons (taking them together) at the time the payment is received and each of them is then resident or ordinarily resident in the United Kingdom—

(a) it shall be treated as being as many capital payments as there are participators in the company at the time it is received, and

(b) each such participator (whatever his residence or ordinary residence) shall be treated as receiving one of the payments, quantified on the basis of a just and reasonable apportionment,

but where (by virtue of the preceding provisions of this subsection and apart from this provision) a participator would be treated as receiving less than one-twentieth of the payment actually received by the company, he shall not be treated as receiving anything by virtue of this subsection.

(6) For the purposes of subsection (1) above a qualifying company is a close company or a company which would be a close company if it were resident in the United Kingdom.

(7) For the purposes of subsection (1) above a company is controlled by the trustees of a settlement if it is controlled by the trustees alone or by the trustees together with a person who (or persons each of whom) falls within subsection (8) below.

(8) A person falls within this subsection if—

(a) he is a settlor in relation to the settlement, or

(b) he is connected with a person falling within paragraph (a) above.

(9) For the purposes of subsection (2) above a non-resident qualifying company is a company which is not resident in the United Kingdom and would be a close company if it were so resident.

(10) For the purposes of this section—

(a) the question whether a company is controlled by a person or persons shall be construed in accordance with section 416 of the Taxes Act, but in deciding that question for those purposes no rights or powers of (or attributed to) an associate or associates of a person shall be attributed to him under section 416(6) if he is not a participator in the company;

(b) "participator" has the meaning given by section 417(1) of the Taxes Act.

(11) This section shall apply to payments received on or after 19th March 1991.

GENERAL NOTE
It was possible to avoid the charge under s.87 by channelling payments through a company. This section, introduced in 1991, imposes a charge where a capital payment is received from a company controlled by trustees or from the trustees by a non-resident company controlled by residents. The concept of control is widened to include control by the trustees together with the settlor and persons connected with him. The definitions for close companies in ICTA 1988, ss.416 and 417, apply, except that rights of a person's associates are not to be attributed to him if he is not a participator.

Where the payment is received by a non-resident company it is attributed to the residents controlling it, if necessary on a "just and reasonable" basis, subject to a five per cent. *de minimis* exclusion.

Supplementary provisions

97.—(1) In sections 87 to 96 and this section "capital payment"—

(a) means any payment which is not chargeable to income tax on the recipient or, in the case of a recipient who is neither resident nor ordinarily resident in the United Kingdom, any payment received otherwise than as income, but

(b) does not include a payment under a transaction entered into at arm's length if it is received on or after 19th March 1991.

(2) In subsection (1) above references to a payment include references to the transfer of an asset and the conferring of any other benefit, and to any occasion on which settled property becomes property to which section 60 applies.

(3) The fact that the whole or part of a benefit is by virtue of section 740(2)(b) of the Taxes Act treated as the recipient's income for a year of assessment after that in which it is received—

(a) shall not prevent the benefit or that part of it being treated for the purposes of sections 87 to 96 as a capital payment in relation to any year of assessment earlier than that in which it is treated as his income; but

(b) shall preclude its being treated for those purposes as a capital payment in relation to that or any later year of assessment.

(4) For the purposes of sections 87 to 96 the amount of a capital payment made by way of loan, and of any other capital payment which is not an outright payment of money, shall be taken to be equal to the value of the benefit conferred by it.

(5) For the purposes of sections 87 to 90 a capital payment shall be regarded as received by a beneficiary from the trustees of a settlement if—

(a) he receives it from them directly or indirectly, or

(b) it is directly or indirectly applied by them in payment of any debt of his or is otherwise paid or applied for his benefit, or

(c) it is received by a third person at the beneficiary's direction.

(6) Section 16(3) shall not prevent losses accruing to trustees in a year of assessment for which section 87 of this Act or section 17 of the 1979 Act applied to the settlement from being allowed as a deduction from chargeable gains accruing in any later year (so far as they have not previously been set against gains for the purposes of a computation under either of those sections or otherwise).

(7) In sections 87 to 96 and in the preceding provisions of this section—
"settlement" and "settlor" have the meaning given by section 681(4) of the Taxes Act and "settlor" includes, in the case of a settlement arising under a will or intestacy, the testator or intestate, and
"settled property" shall be construed accordingly.

(8) In a case where—
(a) at any time on or after 19th March 1991 a capital payment is received from the trustees of a settlement or is treated as so received by virtue of section 96(1),
(b) it is received by a person, or treated as received by a person by virtue of section 96(2) to (5),
(c) at the time it is received or treated as received, the person is not (apart from this subsection) a beneficiary of the settlement, and
(d) subsection (9) or (10) below does not prevent this subsection applying,
for the purposes of sections 87 to 90 the person shall be treated as a beneficiary of the settlement as regards events occurring at or after that time.

(9) Subsection (8) above shall not apply where a payment mentioned in paragraph (a) is made in circumstances where it is treated (otherwise than by subsection (8) above) as received by a beneficiary.

(10) Subsection (8) above shall not apply so as to treat—
(a) the trustees of the settlement referred to in that subsection, or
(b) the trustees of any other settlement,
as beneficiaries of the settlement referred to in that subsection.

GENERAL NOTE
This contains general interpretative provisions for the purposes of ss.87–96, and also deals with the interaction of these sections with ICTA 1988, s.740. See further *ibid.*, s.740(6).

Power to obtain information for purposes of sections 87 to 90

98.—(1) The Board may by notice require any person to furnish them within such time as they may direct, not being less than 28 days, with such particulars as they think necessary for the purposes of sections 87 to 90.

(2) Subsections (2) to (5) of section 745 of the Taxes Act shall have effect in relation to subsection (1) above as they have effect in relation to section 745(1), but in their application by virtue of this subsection—
(a) references to Chapter III of Part XVII of the Taxes Act shall be construed as references to sections 87 to 90; and
(b) the expressions "settlement" and "settlor" have the same meanings as in those sections.

GENERAL NOTE
Wide powers are given to the Revenue to obtain necessary information, subject to certain restrictions contained in ICTA 1988, s.745(2)–(5).
The powers are backed by the penalty provisions in TMA 1970, s.98.

CHAPTER III

COLLECTIVE INVESTMENT SCHEMES AND INVESTMENT TRUSTS

Application of Act to unit trust schemes

99.—(1) This Act shall apply in relation to any unit trust scheme as if—

(a) the scheme were a company,
(b) the rights of the unit holders were shares in the company, and
(c) in the case of an authorised unit trust, the company were resident and ordinarily resident in the United Kingdom,

except that nothing in this section shall be taken to bring a unit trust scheme within the charge to corporation tax on chargeable gains.

(2) Subject to subsection (3) below, in this Act—

(a) "unit trust scheme" has the same meaning as in the Financial Services Act 1986,

(b) "authorised unit trust" has the meaning given by section 468(6) of the Taxes Act.

(3) The Treasury may by regulations provide that any scheme of a description specified in the regulations shall be treated as not being a unit trust scheme for the purposes of this Act; and regulations under this section may contain such supplementary and transitional provisions as appear to the Treasury to be necessary or expedient.

GENERAL NOTE

A unit trust scheme, defined in the Financial Services Act 1986, s.75(8), as "a collective investment scheme under which the property in question is held in trust for the participants", is treated as if the unit-holders were shareholders. This conforms with the treatment of unit trusts authorised under *ibid.*, s.78 for the purposes of ICTA 1988, s.468.

Exemption for authorised unit trusts etc.

100.—(1) Gains accruing to an authorised unit trust, an investment trust or a court investment fund shall not be chargeable gains.

(2) If throughout a year of assessment all the issued units in a unit trust scheme (other than an authorised unit trust) are assets such that any gain accruing if they were disposed of by the unit holder would be wholly exempt from capital gains tax or corporation tax (otherwise than by reason of residence) gains accruing to the unit trust scheme in that year of assessment shall not be chargeable gains.

(3) In this Act "court investment fund" means a fund established under section 42 of the Administration of Justice Act 1982.

GENERAL NOTE

Gains accruing to the entities mentioned are exempt from C.G.T. The definition of "investment trust" in ICTA 1988, s.842, applies.

Subs. (2)

This provides an exemption for unit trusts which are not authorised under the Financial Services Act, but whose unit-holders are exempt in any case, *e.g.* charities and approved superannuation schemes.

Transfer of company's assets to investment trust

101.—(1) Where section 139 has applied on the transfer of a company's business (in whole or in part) to a company which at the time of the transfer was not an investment trust, then if—

(a) at any time after the transfer the company becomes for an accounting period an investment trust, and

(b) at the beginning of that accounting period the company still owns any of the assets of the business transferred,

the company shall be treated for all the purposes of this Act as if immediately after the transfer it had sold, and immediately reacquired, the assets referred to in paragraph (b) above at their market value at that time.

(2) Notwithstanding any limitation on the time for making assessments, an assessment to corporation tax chargeable in consequence of subsection (1) above may be made at any time within six years after the end of the accounting period referred to in subsection (1) above, and where under this

section a company is to be treated as having disposed of, and reacquired, an asset of a business, all such recomputations of liability in respect of other disposals and all such adjustments of tax, whether by way of assessment or by way of discharge or repayment of tax, as may be required in consequence of the provisions of this section shall be carried out.

GENERAL NOTE
   Where roll-over relief under s.139 has applied on the transfer of a company's business to another company which was not an investment trust at that time, then a charge on the rolled-over gain will arise on any assets still held if that company becomes an investment trust.
   Assessments under this section may be made within six years of the event triggering the charge.

Collective investment schemes with property divided into separate parts

   102.—(1) Subsection (2) below applies in the case of arrangements which constitute a collective investment scheme and under which—
   (a) the contributions of the participants, and the profits or income out of which payments are to be made to them, are pooled in relation to separate parts of the property in question, and
   (b) the participants are entitled to exchange rights in one part for rights in another.
   (2) If a participant exchanges rights in one such part for rights in another, section 127 shall not prevent the exchange constituting a disposal and acquisition for the purposes of this Act.
   (3) The reference in subsection (2) above to section 127—
   (a) includes a reference to that section as applied by section 132, but
   (b) does not include a reference to section 127 as applied by section 135; and in this section "participant" shall be construed in accordance with the Financial Services Act 1986.

GENERAL NOTE
   This section was introduced in 1989 to remove an advantage previously enjoyed by offshore umbrella funds by which participants could switch between sub-funds without a charge to tax.
   The definition of "collective investment scheme" in the Financial Services Act 1986, s.75, applies.

Restriction on availability of indexation allowance

   103.—(1) An indexation allowance shall not be made in the case of a disposal if each of the two conditions set out below is fulfilled.
   (2) The first condition is that the disposal is of rights in property to which arrangements which constitute a collective investment scheme relate.
   (3) Subject to subsection (4) below, the second condition is that, at some time in the relevant ownership period, not less than 90 per cent. of the market value (at that time) of the investment property then falling within the arrangements was represented by—
   (a) non-chargeable assets,
   (b) shares in a building society, or
   (c) such assets and such shares.
   (4) In a case where—
   (a) the arrangements are ones under which the contributions of the participants, and the profits or income out of which payments are to be made to them, are pooled in relation to separate parts of the property in question, and
   (b) the disposal is of rights in property falling within a separate part, subsection (3) above shall have effect as if the reference to the arrangements were to the separate part.
   (5) For the purposes of subsection (3) above the relevant ownership period is the period which begins with the later of—

(a) the earliest date on which any relevant consideration was given for the acquisition of the rights, and

(b) 1st April 1982,

and ends with the day on which the disposal is made.

(6) For the purposes of subsection (3) above investment property is all property other than cash awaiting investment.

(7) For the purposes of subsection (3) above an asset is a non-chargeable asset if, were it to be disposed of—

(a) at the time the rights are disposed of, and

(b) by a person resident in the United Kingdom,

any gain accruing on the disposal would not be a chargeable gain.

(8) For the purposes of subsection (5) above relevant consideration is consideration which, assuming the application of Chapter III of Part II to the disposal of the rights, would fall to be taken into account in determining the amount of the gain or loss accruing on the disposal, whether that consideration was given by or on behalf of the person making the disposal or by or on behalf of a predecessor in title of his whose acquisition cost represents (directly or indirectly) the whole or any part of the acquisition cost of the person making the disposal.

GENERAL NOTE

This section, introduced in 1990, was designed to counteract the creation of allowable losses by collective investment funds through the use of the indexation allowance (see s.53). The funds concerned are those invested at least 90 per cent. in non-chargeable assets, such as gilts, and building society shares.

PART IV

SHARES, SECURITIES, OPTIONS ETC.

CHAPTER I

GENERAL

Share pooling, identification of securities, and indexation

Share pooling: general interpretative provisions

104.—(1) Any number of securities of the same class acquired by the same person in the same capacity shall for the purposes of this Act be regarded as indistinguishable parts of a single asset growing or diminishing on the occasions on which additional securities of the same class are acquired or some of the securities of that class are disposed of.

(2) Subsection (1) above—

(a) does not apply to any securities which were acquired before 6th April 1982 or in the case of a company 1st April 1982; and

(b) has effect subject to sections 105, 106 and 107.

(3) For the purposes of this section and sections 105, 107, 110 and 114—

"a new holding" is a holding of securities which, by virtue of subsection (1) above, is to be regarded as a single asset;

"securities" does not include relevant securities as defined in section 108 but, subject to that, means—

(i) shares or securities of a company; and

(ii) any other assets where they are of a nature to be dealt in without identifying the particular assets disposed of or acquired; and

"relevant allowable expenditure" has the meaning assigned to it by section 53(2)(b) and (3);

but shares or securities of a company shall not be treated as being of the same class unless they are so treated by the practice of a recognised stock exchange or would be so treated if dealt with on a recognised stock exchange.

(4) This section and sections 110 and 114—

(a) shall apply separately in relation to any securities held by a person to whom they were issued as an employee of the company or of any other person on terms which restrict his rights to dispose of them, so long as those terms are in force, and

(b) while applying separately to any such securities, shall have effect as if the owner held them in a capacity other than that in which he holds any other securities of the same class.

(5) Nothing in this section or sections 110 and 114 shall be taken as affecting the manner in which the market value of any securities is to be ascertained.

(6) Without prejudice to the generality of subsections (1) and (2) above, a disposal of securities in a new holding, other than a disposal of the whole of it, is a disposal of part of an asset and the provisions of this Act relating to the computation of a gain accruing on a disposal of part of an asset shall apply accordingly.

GENERAL NOTE
This section opens a fasciculus of sections (ss.104–114) dealing with general provisions regarding the pooling of shares and identification of securities for the purposes of indexation.

Subs. (1)
Securities of the same class acquired by the same person are treated as a single entity.

Subs. (2)
Subsection (1) does not apply to securities acquired before the introduction of indexation in 1982 and is subject to rules contained in ss.105–107.

Subs. (3)
This contains definitions for the purposes of this fasciculus of sections.

Subs. (4)
Shares issued to an employee on restrictive terms are to be treated separately from other holdings of such shares which he may have.

Subs. (5)
The sections do not affect the calculation of the market value of securities.

Subs. (6)
Disposals of part of a holding are to be treated as a part disposal (see s.42).

Disposal on or before day of acquisition of shares and other unidentified assets

105.—(1) The following provisions shall apply where securities of the same class are acquired or disposed of by the same person on the same day and in the same capacity—

(a) all the securities so acquired shall be treated as acquired by a single transaction and all the securities so disposed of shall be treated as disposed of by a single transaction, and

(b) all the securities so acquired shall, so far as their quantity does not exceed that of the securities so disposed of, be identified with those securities.

(2) Subject to section 106, where the quantity of the securities so disposed of exceeds the quantity of the securities so acquired, then so far as the excess is not required by any provision of section 104 or 107 or Schedule 2 to be identified with securities acquired before the day of the disposal, it shall be treated as diminishing a quantity subsequently acquired, and a quantity so acquired at an earlier date, rather than one so acquired at a later date.

GENERAL NOTE

This provision, originally introduced in 1971 and superseded in 1982, was brought back into force in 1985. It treats securities acquired or disposed of on the same day as being acquired or disposed of by a single transaction. Securities acquired are to be identified with securities disposed of. Where disposals exceed acquisitions, they are identified with them on a FIFO basis.

Disposal of shares and securities by company within prescribed period of acquisition

106.—(1) For the purposes of corporation tax on chargeable gains, shares disposed of by a company shall be identified in accordance with the following provisions where—
  (a) the number of shares of that class held by the company at any time during the prescribed period before the disposal amounted to not less than 2 per cent. of the number of issued shares of that class; and
  (b) shares of that class have been or are acquired by the company within the prescribed period before or after the disposal.

(2) Where a company is a member of a group, shares held or acquired by another member of the group shall be treated for the purposes of paragraphs (a) and (b) of subsection (1) above as held or acquired by that company and for the purposes of paragraph (b) any shares acquired by that company from another company which was a member of the group throughout the prescribed period before and after the disposal shall be disregarded.

(3) References in subsection (1) above to a company's disposing, holding and acquiring shares are references to its doing so in the same capacity; and references in that subsection to the holding or acquisition of shares do not include references to the holding or acquisition of shares as trading stock.

(4) The shares disposed of shall be identified—
  (a) with shares acquired as mentioned in subsection (1)(b) above ("available shares") rather than other shares; and
  (b) with available shares acquired by the company making the disposal rather than other available shares.

(5) The shares disposed of shall be identified with available shares acquired before the disposal rather than available shares acquired after the disposal and—
  (a) in the case of available shares acquired before the disposal, with those acquired later rather than those acquired earlier;
  (b) in the case of available shares acquired after the disposal, with those acquired earlier rather than those acquired later.

(6) Where available shares could be identified—
  (a) with shares disposed of either by the company that acquired them or by another company; or
  (b) with shares disposed of either at an earlier date or at a later date,
they shall in each case be identified with the former rather than the latter; and the identification of any available shares with shares disposed of by a company on any occasion shall preclude their identification with shares comprised in a later disposal by that company or in a disposal by another company.

(7) Where a company disposes of shares which have been identified with shares disposed of by another company, the shares disposed of by the first-mentioned company shall be identified with the shares that would, apart from this section, have been comprised in the disposal by the other company or, if those shares have themselves been identified with shares disposed of by a third company, with the shares that would, apart from this section, have been comprised in the disposal by the third company and so on.

(8) Where shares disposed of by one company are identified with shares acquired by another, the sums allowable to the company making the disposal under section 38 shall be—

(a) the sums allowable under subsection (1)(c) of that section; and
(b) the sums that would have been allowable under subsection (1)(a) and (b) of that section to the company that acquired the shares if they have been disposed of by that company.

(9) This section shall have effect subject to section 105(1).

(10) In this section—

"group" has the meaning given in section 170(2) to (14);

"the prescribed period" means—

(a) in the case of a disposal through a stock exchange or Automated Real-Time Investments Exchange Limited, one month;

(b) in any other case, six months.

(11) Shares shall not be treated for the purpose of this section as being of the same class unless they are so treated by the practice of a recognised stock exchange or would be so treated if dealt with on such a stock exchange.

(12) This section applies to securities as defined in section 132 as it applies to shares.

GENERAL NOTE

This section, originally introduced by F(No. 2)A 1975, s.58, was introduced to control "bed-and-breakfasting", the practice of crystallising a loss by selling shares and buying them back again, and to preclude "double-banking", whereby prior to the sale of shares at a loss other shares of the same type were purchased. It should be noted that it only applies to companies and only where the holding amounts to more than two per cent. of the shares in question. The timescale of the section is one month for shares disposed of on the stock exchange or through ARIEL, six months in other cases.

Subs. (2)

Holdings within a group are aggregated and transactions within the group are disregarded.

Subs. (3)

Shares held as trading stock are excluded from the operation of the section.

Subs. (4)

Shares disposed of are to be identified with shares acquired during the timescale of the section rather than with other shares.

Subs. (5)

The shares disposed of are to be matched with shares acquired previously on a LIFO basis and with shares acquired later on a FIFO basis.

Subs. (6)

Within a group, shares should first of all be identified with shares held by the same company. Generally, a FIFO rule applies.

Subs. (7)

Shares disposed of by a company which have already been identified with shares disposed of by another company are to be identified with the shares that would have been comprised in that company's disposal, and so on in relation to third and other companies.

Subs. (8)

Costs of acquisition are attributed to the company making the disposal.

Subs. (9)

The section is subject to the rules governing securities acquired and disposed of on the same day in s.105.

Identification of securities etc.: general rules

107.—(1) Where a person disposes of securities, the securities disposed of shall be identified in accordance with the provisions of this section with securities of the same class acquired by him which could be comprised in that disposal.

(2) This section applies notwithstanding that securities disposed of are otherwise identified by the disposal or by a transfer or delivery giving effect to it (but so that where a person disposes of securities in one capacity, they shall not be identified with securities which he holds or can dispose of only in some other capacity).

(3) Without prejudice to section 105 if, within a period of 10 days, a number of securities are acquired and subsequently a number of securities are disposed of and, apart from this subsection—

(a) the securities acquired would increase the size of, or constitute a new holding, and

(b) the securities disposed of would decrease the size of, or extinguish, the same new holding,

then, subject to subsections (4) and (5) below, the securities disposed of shall be identified with the securities acquired and none of them shall be regarded as forming part of an existing new holding or constituting a new holding.

(4) If, in a case falling within subsection (3) above, the number of securities acquired exceeds the number disposed of—

(a) the excess shall be regarded as forming part of an existing new holding or, as the case may be, as constituting a new holding; and

(b) if the securities acquired were acquired at different times (within the 10 days referred to in subsection (3) above) the securities disposed of shall be identified with securities acquired at an earlier time rather than with securities acquired at a later time.

(5) If, in a case falling within subsection (3) above, the number of securities disposed of exceeds the number acquired, the excess shall not be identified in accordance with that subsection.

(6) Securities which, by virtue of subsection (3) above, do not form part of or constitute a new holding shall be treated for the purposes of section 54(2) as relevant securities within the meaning of section 108.

(7) The identification rules set out in subsections (8) and (9) below have effect subject to section 105 but, subject to that, have priority according to the order in which they are so set out.

(8) Securities disposed of shall be identified with securities forming part of a new holding rather than with other securities.

(9) Securities disposed of shall be identified with securities forming part of a 1982 holding, within the meaning of section 109, rather than with other securities and, subject to that, shall be identified with securities acquired at a later time rather than with securities acquired at an earlier time.

GENERAL NOTE

These provisions, introduced in 1985, apply to acquisitions and disposals of securities within a timescale of 10 days. In such a case, the disposals are to be identified with the acquisitions and no pooling takes place. However, excess acquisitions go into the pool on a FIFO basis and excess disposals come out of the pool. Securities caught by the section do not qualify for indexation. Subject to the same-day rules in s.105, disposals are to be identified firstly with acquisitions rather than with other holdings, secondly with pre-1982 share pools held in 1985 rather than with other holdings, and otherwise on a LIFO basis.

Identification of relevant securities

108.—(1) In this section "relevant securities" means—

(a) securities, within the meaning of section 710 of the Taxes Act;

(b) deep discount securities, within the meaning of Schedule 4 to that Act; and

(c) securities which are, or have at any time been, material interests in a non-qualifying offshore fund, within the meaning of Chapter V of Part XVII of that Act;

and shares or securities of a company shall not be treated for the purposes of this section as being of the same class unless they are so treated by the practice of a recognised stock exchange or would be so treated if dealt with on a recognised stock exchange.

(2) Where a person disposes of relevant securities, the securities disposed of shall be identified in accordance with the rules contained in this section with the securities of the same class acquired by him which could be comprised in that disposal, and shall be so identified notwithstanding that they are otherwise identified by the disposal or by a transfer or delivery giving effect to it (but so that where a person disposes of securities in one capacity, they shall not be identified with securities which he holds or can dispose of only in some other capacity).

(3) Relevant securities disposed of on an earlier date shall be identified before securities disposed of on a later date, and the identification of the securities first disposed of shall accordingly determine the securities which could be comprised in the later disposal.

(4) Relevant securities disposed of for transfer or delivery on a particular date or in a particular period—

(a) shall not be identified with securities acquired for transfer or delivery on a later date or in a later period; and

(b) shall be identified with securities acquired for transfer or delivery on or before that date or in or before that period, but on or after the date of the disposal, rather than with securities not so acquired.

(5) The relevant securities disposed of shall be identified—

(a) with securities acquired within the 12 months preceding the disposal rather than with securities not so acquired, and with securities so acquired on an earlier date rather than with securities so acquired on a later date, and

(b) subject to paragraph (a) above, with securities acquired on a later date rather than with securities acquired on an earlier date; and

(c) with securities acquired at different times on any one day in as nearly as may be equal proportions.

(6) The rules contained in the preceding subsections shall have priority according to the order in which they are so contained.

(7) Notwithstanding anything in subsections (3) to (5) above, where, under arrangements designed to postpone the transfer or delivery of relevant securities disposed of, a person by a single bargain acquires securities for transfer or delivery on a particular date or in a particular period and disposes of them for transfer or delivery on a later date or in a later period, then—

(a) the securities disposed of by that bargain shall be identified with the securities thereby acquired; and

(b) securities previously disposed of which, but for the operation of paragraph (a) above in relation to acquisitions for transfer or delivery on the earlier date or in the earlier period, would have been identified with the securities acquired by that bargain—

(i) shall, subject to subsection (3) above, be identified with any available securities acquired for such transfer or delivery (that is to say, any securities so acquired other than securities to which paragraph (a) above applies and other than securities with which securities disposed of for such transfer or delivery would be identified apart from this subsection); and

(ii) in so far as they cannot be so identified shall be treated as disposed of for transfer or delivery on the later date, or in the later period, mentioned above.

(8) This section shall have effect subject to section 106 but shall not apply—

(a) where the disposal is of quoted securities (within the meaning of paragraph 8 of Schedule 2), unless an election has been made with respect to the securities under paragraph 4 of that Schedule or under section 109(4), or

(b) where the disposal is of securities as respects which paragraph 17 or 18 of Schedule 2 has effect.

GENERAL NOTE

This section deals with stocks and bonds (excluding company shares), deep discount securities, *i.e.* redeemable stock issued at a heavy discount, and securities which are material interests in non-qualifying offshore funds (see ICTA 1988, ss.759, 760).

Such securities are firstly identified on a FIFO basis, secondly with securities acquired earlier rather than later in a particular period, and thirdly with securities acquired within the 12-month period preceding the disposal. However, where there is a single bargain for the acquisition and disposal of securities, these will be identified and previous disposals reallocated accordingly. The section applies subject to s.106 but not for quoted securities unless an election for pooling has been made under the provisions cited.

Pre-April 1982 share pools

109.—(1) This section has effect in relation to any 1982 holding, and in this section "1982 holding" means a holding which, immediately before the coming into force of this section, was a 1982 holding for the purposes of Part II of Schedule 19 to the Finance Act 1985.

(2) Subject to subsections (3) to (5) below—

(a) the holding shall continue to be regarded as a single asset for the purposes of this Act, but one which cannot grow by the acquisition of additional securities of the same class, and

(b) every sum, which on a disposal of the holding, would be an item of relevant allowable expenditure shall be regarded for the purposes of section 54 as having been incurred at such a time that the month which determines RI in the formula in subsection (1) of that section is March 1982.

Securities of a company shall not be treated for the purposes of this section as being of the same class unless they are so treated by the practice of a recognised stock exchange or would be so treated if dealt with on a recognised stock exchange.

(3) Nothing in subsection (2) above affects the operation of section 127 in relation to the holding, but without prejudice to section 131.

(4) If a person so elects, quoted securities, as defined in paragraph 8 of Schedule 2 which are covered by the election—

(a) shall be treated as an accretion to an existing 1982 holding or, as the case may be, as constituting a new 1982 holding; and

(b) shall be excluded from paragraph 2 of that Schedule;

and the relevant allowable expenditure which is attributable to that 1982 holding shall be adjusted or determined accordingly.

(5) Paragraphs 4(8) to (13) and 5 to 8 of Schedule 2 shall apply in relation to an election under subsection (4) above as they apply in relation to an election under paragraph 4(2) of that Schedule, but with the substitution for any reference to 19th March 1968 of a reference to 31st March 1985 in the case of holdings or disposals by companies and 5th April 1985 in any other case.

(6) For the purpose of computing the indexation allowance (if any) on a disposal of a 1982 holding, the relevant allowable expenditure attributable to the holding on the coming into force of this section shall be the amount which, if the holding had been disposed of immediately before the coming into force of this section, would have been the relevant allowable expenditure in relation to that holding on that disposal, and for the purposes of section 54(4) relevant allowable expenditure attributable to a 1982 holding shall be deemed to be expenditure falling within section 38(1)(a).

GENERAL NOTE
    This section deals with "1982 holdings", *i.e.* share pools which existed on the introduction of
indexation. Such pools are frozen but attract indexation as from March 1982. This is subject to
the provisions of ss.127 and 131 regarding reorganisations and to an election to have quoted
securities added to the pool. The rules in Sched. 2 apply with the substitution of 1985 for 1968.
Indexation applies to 1992 values, based on acquisition cost.

New holdings: indexation allowance

110.—(1) This section and section 114—
   (a) apply in place of section 54 in relation to a disposal of a new holding
        for the purpose of computing the indexation allowance;
   (b) have effect subject to sections 105 and 106.
   (2) On any disposal of a new holding, other than a disposal of the whole of
it—
   (a) the qualifying expenditure and the indexed pool of expenditure shall
        each be apportioned between the part disposed of and the remainder
        in the same proportions as, under this Act, the relevant allowable
        expenditure is apportioned; and
   (b) the indexation allowance is the amount by which the portion of the
        indexed pool which is attributed by the part disposed of exceeds the
        portion of the qualifying expenditure which is attributed to that part.
   (3) On a disposal of the whole of a new holding, the indexation allowance
is the amount by which the indexed pool of expenditure at the time of the
disposal exceeds the qualifying expenditure at that time.
   (4) In relation to a new holding, the qualifying expenditure is at any time
the amount which would be the aggregate of the relevant allowable expenditure in relation to a disposal of the whole of the holding occurring at that
time.
   (5) Subject to subsection (6) below and section 114 the indexed pool of
expenditure shall come into being at the time that the holding comes into
being or, if it is earlier, when any of the qualifying expenditure is incurred
and shall at the time it comes into being be the same as the qualifying
expenditure at that time.
   (6) In relation to a new holding which was in existence immediately before
the coming into force of this section, the indexed pool of expenditure on the
coming into force of this section shall be the same as it was for the purposes
of Part III of Schedule 19 to the Finance Act 1985 immediately before then.
   (7) Any reference below to an operative event is a reference to any event
(whether a disposal or otherwise) which has the effect of reducing or
increasing the qualifying expenditure referable to the new holding.
   (8) Whenever an operative event occurs—
   (a) there shall be added to the indexed pool of expenditure the indexed
        rise, as calculated under subsection (10) or (11) below, in the value of
        the pool since the last operative event or, if there has been no
        previous operative event, since the pool came into being; and
   (b) if the operative event results in an increase in the qualifying expendi-
        ture then, in addition to any increase under paragraph (a) above, the
        same increase shall be made to the indexed pool of expenditure; and
   (c) if the operative event is a disposal resulting in a reduction in the
        qualifying expenditure, the indexed pool of expenditure shall be
        reduced in the same proportion as the qualifying expenditure is
        reduced; and
   (d) if the operative event results in a reduction in the qualifying expendi-
        ture but is not a disposal, the same reduction shall be made to the
        indexed pool of expenditure.
   (9) Where the operative event is a disposal—
   (a) any addition under subsection (8)(a) above shall be made before the

calculation of the indexation allowance under subsection (2) above; and

(b) the reduction under subsection (8)(c) above shall be made after that calculation.

(10) At the time of any operative event, the indexed rise in the indexed pool of expenditure is a sum produced by multiplying the value of the pool immediately before the event by a figure expressed as a decimal and determined, subject to subsection (11) below, by the formula—

$$\frac{RE-RL}{RL}$$

where—

RE is the retail prices index for the month in which the operative event occurs; and

RL is the retail prices index for the month in which occurred the immediately preceding operative event or, if there has been no such event, in which the indexed pool of expenditure came into being.

(11) If RE, as defined in subsection (10) above, is equal to or less than RL, as so defined, the indexed rise is nil.

GENERAL NOTE

This contains the general rules for computing the indexation where there is a disposal out of a share pool. The indexation allowance is apportioned to the part disposed of or applied to the entire pool in the case of a total disposal. The pooling is carried forward from FA 1985, Sched. 19, Pt. III, to this Act. Appropriate adjustments are made to the pool on an acquisition or disposal, by reference to changes in the R.P.I. since the previous acquisition or disposal.

Indexation: building society etc. shares

111. An indexation allowance shall not be made in the case of—
(a) shares in a building society, or
(b) shares in a registered industrial and provident society as defined in section 486 of the Taxes Act.

GENERAL NOTE

Indexation is not available in the case of shares in building societies or registered industrial and provident societies. This is to prevent unrealistic losses being created.

Parallel pooling regulations

112.—(1) The Capital Gains Tax (Parallel Pooling) Regulations 1986 made by the Treasury under paragraph 21 of Schedule 19 to the Finance Act 1985 shall continue to have effect notwithstanding the repeal by this Act of that Schedule, and for the purposes of section 14 of the Interpretation Act 1978 that paragraph shall be deemed not to have been repealed.

(2) An election under Schedule 6 to the Finance Act 1983 which has not been revoked before 6th April 1992 shall not have effect in relation to any disposal after 5th April 1992 and may, if the Board allow, be revoked by notice to the inspector.

(3) All such adjustments shall be made, whether by way of discharge or repayment of tax, or the making of assessments or otherwise, as are required in consequence of a revocation under subsection (2) above.

GENERAL NOTE

Subs. (1)

The Capital Gains Tax (Parallel Pooling) Regulations 1986 (S.I. 1986 No. 387) continue in force and may be amended subsequently. Parallel pooling was introduced by FA 1983, s.34 and Sched. 6, and allowed companies to elect retrospectively to April 1, 1982 for pooling in respect of each holding of shares. The regulations were introduced following amendments to the indexation system in 1985.

Subs. (2)
  An election under FA 1983 may be revoked if the Revenue allow, with consequent adjustments to assessments.

Calls on shares

113.—(1) Subsection (2) below applies where—
  (a) on a disposal to which section 53 applies, the relevant allowable expenditure is or includes the amount or value of the consideration given for the issue of shares or securities in, or debentures of, a company; and
  (b) the whole or some part of that consideration was given after the expiry of the period of 12 months beginning on the date of the issue of the shares, securities or debentures.
  (2) For the purpose of computing the indexation allowance (if any) on the disposal referred to in subsection (1)(a) above—
  (a) so much of the consideration as was given after the expiry of the period referred to in subsection (1)(b) above shall be regarded as an item of expenditure separate from any consideration given during that period; and
  (b) section 54(4) shall not apply to that separate item of expenditure which, accordingly, shall be regarded as incurred at the time the consideration in question was actually given.

GENERAL NOTE
  This deals with cases where shares are issued part paid, with subsequent calls. Where such a call is made more than a year after the issue, it is indexed separately.

Consideration for options

114.—(1) If, in a case where section 110(8)(b) applies, the increase in the qualifying expenditure is, in whole or in part, attributable to the cost of acquiring an option binding the grantor to sell ("the option consideration"), then, in addition to any increase under section 110(8)(a) or (b), the indexed pool of expenditure shall be increased by an amount equal to the indexed rise in the option consideration, as determined under subsection (2) below.
  (2) The indexed rise in the option consideration is a sum produced by multiplying the consideration by a figure expressed as a decimal and determined, subject to subsection (3) below, by the formula—

$$\frac{RO\text{-}RA}{RA}$$

where—
  RO is the retail prices index for the month in which falls the date on which the option is exercised; and
  RA is the retail prices index for the month in which falls the date in which the option was acquired or, if it is later, March 1982.
  (3) If RO, as defined in subsection (2) above, is equal to or less than RA, as so defined, the indexed rise is nil.

GENERAL NOTE
  Where part of the pool relates to the cost of acquiring an option to buy shares, the cost of the option is indexed between its acquisition and its exercise.

Gilt-edged securities and qualifying corporate bonds

Exemptions for gilt-edged securities and qualifying corporate bonds etc.

115.—(1) A gain which accrues on the disposal by any person of—
  (a) gilt-edged securities or qualifying corporate bonds, or

(b) any option or contract to acquire or dispose of gilt-edged securities or qualifying corporate bonds,

shall not be a chargeable gain.

(2) In subsection (1) above the reference to the disposal of a contract to acquire or dispose or gilt-edged securities or qualifying corporate bonds is a reference to the disposal of the outstanding obligations under such a contract.

(3) Without prejudice to section 143(5), where a person who has entered into any such contract as is referred to in subsection (1)(b) above closes out that contract by entering into another contract with obligations which are reciprocal to those of the first-mentioned contract, that transaction shall for the purposes of this section constitute the disposal of an asset, namely, his outstanding obligations under the first-mentioned contract.

GENERAL NOTE

Gilt-edged securities and corporate bonds are exempt from C.G.T. For a definition of gilt-edged securities and a list of those in existence when this Act was passed, see Sched. 9. For a definition of qualifying corporate bonds, see s.117.

The exemption extends to options on such securities, whether they are disposed of or closed out by entry into another option with reciprocal obligations. For further provisions relating to options, see ss.143–148.

Reorganisations, conversions and reconstructions

116.—(1) This section shall have effect in any case where a transaction occurs of such a description that, apart from the provisions of this section—
  (a) sections 127 to 130 would apply by virtue of any provision of Chapter II of this Part; and
  (b) either the original shares would consist of or include a qualifying corporate bond and the new holding would not, or the original shares would not and the new holding would consist of or include such a bond;

and in paragraph (b) above "the original shares" and "the new holding" have the same meaning as they have for the purposes of sections 127 to 130.

(2) In this section "relevant transaction" means a reorganisation, conversion of securities or other transaction such as is mentioned in subsection (1) above, and, in addition to its application where the transaction takes place after the coming into force of this section, subsection (10) below applies where the relevant transaction took place before the coming into force of this section so far as may be necessary to enable any gain or loss deferred under paragraph 10 of Schedule 13 to the Finance Act 1984 to be taken into account on a subsequent disposal.

(3) Where the qualifying corporate bond referred to in subsection (1)(b) above would constitute the original shares for the purposes of sections 127 to 130, it is in this section referred to as "the old asset" and the shares or securities which would constitute the new holding for those purposes are referred to as "the new asset".

(4) Where the qualifying corporate bond referred to in subsection (1)(b) above would constitute the new holding for the purposes of sections 127 to 130, it is in this section referred to as "the new asset" and the shares or securities which would constitute the original shares for those purposes are referred to as "the old asset".

(5) So far as the relevant transaction relates to the old asset and the new asset, sections 127 to 130 shall not apply in relation to it.

(6) In accordance with subsection (5) above, the new asset shall not be treated as having been acquired on any date other than the date of the relevant transaction or, subject to subsections (7) and (8) below, for any consideration other than the market value of the old asset as determined immediately before that transaction.

(7) If, on the relevant transaction, the person concerned receives, or becomes entitled to receive, any sum of money which, in addition to the new asset, is by way of consideration for the old asset, that sum shall be deducted from the consideration referred to in subsection (6) above.

(8) If, on the relevant transaction, the person concerned gives any sum of money which, in addition to the old asset, is by way of consideration for the new asset, that sum shall be added to the consideration referred to in subsection (6) above.

(9) In any case where the old asset consists of a qualifying corporate bond, then, so far as it relates to the old asset and the new asset, the relevant transaction shall be treated for the purposes of this Act as a disposal of the old asset and an acquisition of the new asset.

(10) Except in a case falling within subsection (9) above, so far as it relates to the old asset and the new asset, the relevant transaction shall be treated for the purposes of this Act as not involving any disposal of the old asset but—

(a) there shall be calculated the chargeable gain or allowable loss that would have accrued if, at the time of the relevant transaction, the old asset had been disposed of for a consideration equal to its market value immediately before that transaction; and

(b) subject to subsections (12) to (14) below, the whole or a corresponding part of the chargeable gain or allowable loss mentioned in paragraph (a) above shall be deemed to accrue on a subsequent disposal of the whole or part of the new asset (in addition to any gain or loss that actually accrues on that disposal); and

(c) on that subsequent disposal, section 115 shall have effect only in relation to any gain or loss that actually accrues and not in relation to any gain or loss which is deemed to accrue by virtue of paragraph (b) above.

(11) Subsection (10)(b) and (c) above shall not apply to any disposal falling within section 58(1), 62(4), 139, 171(1) or 172, but a person who has acquired the new asset on a disposal falling within any of those sections (and without there having been a previous disposal not falling within any of those sections or a devolution on death) shall be treated for the purposes of subsection (10)(b) and (c) above as if the new asset had been acquired by him at the same time and for the same consideration as, having regard to subsections (5) to (8) above, it was acquired by the person making the disposal.

(12) In any case where—

(a) on the calculation under subsection (10)(a) above, a chargeable gain would have accrued, and

(b) the consideration for the old asset includes such a sum of money as is referred to in subsection (7) above,

then, subject to subsection (13) below, the proportion of that chargeable gain which that sum of money bears to the market value of the old asset immediately before the relevant transaction shall be deemed to accrue at the time of that transaction.

(13) If the inspector is satisfied that the sum of money referred to in subsection (12)(b) above is small, as compared with the market value of the old asset immediately before the relevant transaction, and so directs, subsection (12) above shall not apply.

(14) In a case where subsection (12) above applies, the chargeable gain which, apart from that subsection, would by virtue of subsection (10)(b) above be deemed to accrue on a subsequent disposal of the whole or part of the new asset shall be reduced or, as the case may be, extinguished by deducting therefrom the amount of the chargeable gain which, by virtue of subsection (12) above, is deemed to accrue at the time of the relevant transaction.

(15) In any case where—

(a) the new asset mentioned in subsections (10) and (11) above is a qualifying corporate bond in respect of which an allowable loss is treated as accruing under section 254(2), and

(b) the loss is treated as accruing at a time falling after the relevant transaction but before any actual disposal of the new asset subsequent to the relevant transaction,

then for the purposes of subsections (10) and (11) above a subsequent disposal of the new asset shall be treated as occurring at (and only at) the time the loss is treated as accruing.

GENERAL NOTE

This section deals with the situation where there is a company reorganisation, conversion or reconstruction within ss.127–130 and either the original shares or the new holding, but not both, contain a qualifying corporate bond. In such a case the rules in this section apply in place of ss.127–130.

These rules are as follows:

(1) The new asset, whether a qualifying corporate bond or not, is treated as being acquired for the market value of the old asset at that time, plus or minus any money paid or received.

(2) If the old asset is a qualifying bond no chargeable gain arises on the reorganisation.

(3) If the old asset is not a qualifying bond, the chargeable gain that would have arisen had it been disposed of at market value at the time of the reorganisation is calculated. This gain is held over until a subsequent disposal of the new asset. In the cases mentioned in subs. (11), the charge falls on the person acquiring the asset.

(4) Where cash is received on the reorganisation, then a charge arises in proportion to the cash as compared to the market value, but this may be waived by the inspector if the amount is small.

(5) Where relief is given for a loss on qualifying bonds under s.254 a subsequent disposal of the bond is treated as occurring at the time the loss accrued.

Meaning of "qualifying corporate bond"

117.—(1) For the purposes of this section, a "corporate bond" is a security, as defined in section 132(3)(b)—

(a) the debt on which represents and has at all times represented a normal commercial loan; and

(b) which is expressed in sterling and in respect of which no provision is made for conversion into, or redemption in, a currency other than sterling,

and in paragraph (a) above "normal commercial loan" has the meaning which would be given by sub-paragraph (5) of paragraph 1 of Schedule 18 to the Taxes Act if for paragraph (a)(i) to (iii) of that sub-paragraph there were substituted the words "corporate bonds (within the meaning of section 117 of the 1992 Act)".

(2) For the purposes of subsection (1)(b) above—

(a) a security shall not be regarded as expressed in sterling if the amount of sterling falls to be determined by reference to the value at any time of any other currency or asset; and

(b) a provision for redemption in a currency other than sterling but at the rate of exchange prevailing at redemption shall be disregarded.

(3) For the purposes of this section "corporate bond" also includes a security which is not included in the definition in subsection (1) above, and which—

(a) is a deep gain security for the purposes of Schedule 11 to the Finance Act 1989 ("the 1989 Act"), or

(b) by virtue of paragraph 21(2) of Schedule 11 to the 1989 Act falls to be treated as a deep gain security as there mentioned, or

(c) by virtue of paragraph 22(2) of that Schedule, falls to be treated as a deep gain security as there mentioned, or

(d) by virtue of paragraph 22A(2) or 22B(3) of that Schedule, falls to be treated as a deep gain security as mentioned in the paragraph concerned.

(4) For the purposes of this section "corporate bond" also includes a share in a building society—

(a) which is a qualifying share,

(b) which is expressed in sterling, and

(c) in respect of which no provision is made for conversion into, or redemption in, a currency other than sterling.

(5) For the purposes of subsection (4) above, a share in a building society is a qualifying share if—

(a) it is a permanent interest bearing share, or

(b) it is of a description specified in regulations made by the Treasury for the purposes of this paragraph.

(6) Subsection (2) above applies for the purposes of subsection (4) above as it applies for the purposes of subsection (1)(b) above, treating the reference to a security as a reference to a share.

(7) Subject to subsections (9) and (10) below, for the purposes of this Act, a corporate bond—

(a) is a "qualifying" corporate bond if it is issued after 13th March 1984; and

(b) becomes a "qualifying" corporate bond if, having been issued on or before that date, it is acquired by any person after that date and that acquisition is not as a result of a disposal which is excluded for the purposes of this subsection, or which was excluded for the purposes of section 64(4) of the Finance Act 1984.

(8) Where a person disposes of a corporate bond which was issued on or before 13th March 1984 and, before the disposal, the bond had not become a qualifying corporate bond, the disposal is excluded for the purposes of subsection (7) above if, by virtue of any enactment—

(a) the disposal is treated for the purposes of this Act as one on which neither a gain nor a loss accrues to the person making the disposal, or

(b) the consideration for the disposal is treated for the purposes of this Act as reduced by an amount equal to the held-over gain on that disposal, as defined for the purposes of section 165 or 260.

(9) Subject to subsection (10) below, for the purposes of this Act—

(a) a corporate bond which falls within subsection (3)(a) above is a qualifying corporate bond, whatever the date of its issue;

(b) a corporate bond which falls within subsection (3)(b) above is a qualifying corporate bond as regards a disposal made after the time mentioned in paragraph 21(1)(c) of Schedule 11 to the 1989 Act, whatever the date of its issue;

(c) a corporate bond which falls within subsection (3)(c) above is a qualifying corporate bond as regards a disposal made after the time the agreement mentioned in paragraph 22(1)(b) of that Schedule is made, whatever the date of its issue;

(d) a corporate bond which falls within subsection (3)(d) above is a qualifying corporate bond as regards a disposal made after the time mentioned in paragraph 22A(1)(c) or 22B(2)(b) of that Schedule (as the case may be);

and subsections (7) and (8) above shall not apply in the case of any such bond.

(10) A security which is issued by a member of a group of companies to another member of the same group is not a qualifying corporate bond for the purposes of this Act except in relation to a disposal by a person who (at the time of the disposal) is not a member of the same group as the company which issued the security; and references in this subsection to a group of companies or to a member of a group shall be construed in accordance with section 170(2) to (14).

(11) For the purposes of this section—

(a) where a security is comprised in a letter of allotment or similar instrument and the right to the security thereby conferred remains provisional until accepted, the security shall not be treated as issued until there has been acceptance; and

(b) "permanent interest bearing share" has the same meaning as in the Building Societies (Designated Capital Resources) (Permanent Interest Bearing Shares) Order 1991.

(12) The Treasury may by regulations provide that for the definition of the expression "permanent interest bearing share" in subsection (11) above (as it has effect for the time being) there shall be substituted a different definition of that expression, and regulations under this subsection or subsection (5)(b) above may contain such supplementary, incidental, consequential or transitional provision as the Treasury thinks fit.

(13) This section shall have effect for the purposes of section 254 with the omission of subsections (4) to (6), (11) and (12).

GENERAL NOTE

This section contains the definition of "qualifying corporate bond" for the exemption under s.115.

The following points should be noted:

(1) The bond must be a security, *i.e.* a loan stock or similar security, whether secured or unsecured, which represents a normal commercial loan and is exclusively denominated in sterling. The definition of "normal commercial loan" in ICTA 1988, Sched. 18, para. 1(5) applies, *mutatis mutandis*.

(2) This definition is extended to cover deep-gain securities within FA 1989, Sched. 11, and permanent interest-bearing shares in building societies and such other building society shares as may be specified in Treasury regulations.

(3) The exemption covers bonds issued after March 13, 1984, or acquired after that date, unless the disposal is a no-gain/no-loss one or relief under ss.165 or 260 is available. Special rules cover deep-gain securities.

(4) Securities issued within a group of companies do not qualify.

Deep discount securities, the accrued income scheme etc.

Amount to be treated as consideration on disposal of deep discount securities etc.

118.—(1) Subject to subsections (2) and (3) below, in the computation of the gain accruing on the disposal by any person of any deep discount securities (within the meaning of Schedule 4 to the Taxes Act)—

(a) section 37 shall not apply but the consideration for the disposal shall be treated as reduced by the amount mentioned in paragraph 4(1)(a) of that Schedule (including any amount mentioned in paragraph 3 of that Schedule); and

(b) where that amount exceeds the consideration for the disposal, the amount of the excess shall be treated as expenditure within section 38(1)(b) incurred by that person on the security immediately before the disposal.

(2) Subsection (3) below applies where—

(a) there is a conversion of securities to which section 132 applies and those securities include deep discount securities; or

(b) securities including deep discount securities are exchanged (or by virtue of section 136(1) are treated as exchanged) for other securities in circumstances in which section 135(3) applies.

(3) Where this subsection applies—

(a) subsection (1) and section 37 shall not apply but any sum payable to the beneficial owner of the deep discount securities by way of consideration for their disposal (in addition to his new holding) shall be treated for the purpose of the computation of the gain as reduced by the amount of the accrued income on which he is chargeable to tax by virtue of paragraph 7(3) of Schedule 4 to the Taxes Act or, in a case where paragraph 3 of that Schedule applies, on which he would be so chargeable if that paragraph did not apply; and

(b) where that amount exceeds any such sum, the excess shall be treated as expenditure within section 38(1)(b) incurred by him on the security immediately before the time of the conversion or exchange.

(4) Where a disposal of a deep discount security is to be treated for the purposes of this Act as one on which neither a gain nor a loss accrues to the person making the disposal, the consideration for which the person acquiring the security would, apart from this subsection, be treated for those purposes as having acquired the security shall be increased by the amount mentioned in paragraph 4(1)(a) of Schedule 4 to the Taxes Act (including any amount mentioned in paragraph 3 of that Schedule).

(5) Where by virtue of paragraph 18(3) of Schedule 4 to the Taxes Act trustees are deemed for the purposes of that Schedule to dispose of a security at a particular time—

(a) they shall be deemed to dispose of the security at that time for the purposes of this Act, and

(b) the disposal deemed by paragraph (a) above shall be deemed to be at the market value of the security.

(6) Where by virtue of paragraph 18(4) of Schedule 4 to the Taxes Act trustees are deemed for the purposes of that Schedule to acquire a security at a particular time—

(a) they shall be deemed to acquire the security at that time for the purposes of this Act, and

(b) the acquisition deemed by paragraph (a) above shall be deemed to be at the market value of the security.

GENERAL NOTE

This section contains the capital gains provisions applicable to the régime for deep-discount securities contained in ICTA 1988, Sched. 4. The following rules apply:

(1) The amount of deep discount already charged to income tax is excluded from the consideration for the disposal.

(2) Where there is a conversion or reorganisation involving deep-discount securities, any consideration paid to the holder is reduced by the amount of deep discount chargeable to income tax.

(3) On a no-gain/no-loss disposal of a deep-discount security the deemed consideration is increased by the amount of the deep discount chargeable to income tax.

(4) Deep-discount securities held in premiums trust funds at Lloyd's are deemed to be disposed of on December 31 of each year, and reacquired on the following January 1.

Transfers of securities subject to the accrued income scheme

119.—(1) Where there is a transfer of securities within the meaning of section 710 of the Taxes Act (accrued income scheme)—

(a) if section 713(2)(a) or (3)(a) of that Act applies, section 37 shall be disregarded in computing the gain accruing on the disposal concerned;

(b) if section 713(2)(b) or (3)(b) of that Act applies, section 39 shall be disregarded in computing the gain accruing to the transferee if he disposes of the securities;

but subsections (2) and (3) below shall apply.

(2) Where the securities are transferred with accrued interest (within the meaning of section 711 of the Taxes Act)—

(a) if section 713(2)(a) of that Act applies, an amount equal to the accrued amount (determined under that section) shall be excluded from the consideration mentioned in subsection (8) below;

(b) if section 713(2)(b) of that Act applies, an amount equal to that amount shall be excluded from the sums mentioned in subsection (9) below.

(3) Where the securities are transferred without accrued interest (within the meaning of section 711 of the Taxes Act)—

   (a) if section 713(3)(a) of that Act applies, an amount equal to the rebate amount (determined under that section) shall be added to the consideration mentioned in subsection (8) below;

   (b) if section 713(3)(b) of that Act applies, an amount equal to that amount shall be added to the sums mentioned in subsection (9) below.

(4) Where section 716 of the Taxes Act applies—

   (a) if subsection (2) or (3) of that section applies, section 37 shall be disregarded in computing the gain accruing on the disposal concerned, but the relevant amount shall be excluded from the consideration mentioned in subsection (8) below; and

   (b) if subsection (4) of that section applies, section 39 shall be disregarded in computing the gain accruing on the disposal concerned, but the relevant amount shall be excluded from the sums mentioned in subsection (9) below.

(5) In subsection (4) above "the relevant amount" means an amount equal to—

   (a) if paragraph (b) below does not apply, the amount of the unrealised interest in question (within the meaning of section 716 of the Taxes Act);

   (b) if section 719 of the Taxes Act applies—

      (i) in a case falling within subsection (4)(a) above, amount A (within the meaning of section 719);

      (ii) in a case falling within subsection (4)(b) above, amount C (within the meaning of section 719).

(6) In relation to any securities which by virtue of subsection (7) below are treated for the purposes of this subsection as having been transferred, subsections (2) and (3) above shall have effect as if for "applies" (in each place where it occurs) there were substituted "would apply if the disposal were a transfer".

(7) Where there is a disposal of securities for the purposes of this Act which is not a transfer for the purposes of section 710 of the Taxes Act but, if it were such a transfer, one or more of the following paragraphs would apply, namely, paragraphs (a) and (b) of section 713(2) and paragraphs (a) and (b) of section 713(3) of that Act, the securities shall be treated—

   (a) for the purposes of subsection (6) above, as transferred on the day of the disposal, and

   (b) for the purposes of subsections (2) and (3) above, as transferred with accrued interest if, had the disposal been a transfer for the purposes of section 710, it would have been a transfer with accrued interest and as transferred without accrued interest if, had the disposal been such a transfer, it would have been a transfer without accrued interest.

(8) The consideration is the consideration for the disposal of the securities transferred which is taken into account in the computation of the gain accruing on the disposal.

(9) The sums are the sums allowable to the transferee as a deduction from the consideration in the computation of the gain accruing to him if he disposes of the securities.

(10) Where on a conversion or exchange of securities a person is treated as entitled to a sum under subsection (2)(a) of section 713 of the Taxes Act an amount equal to the accrued amount (determined under that section) shall, for the purposes of this Act, be treated as follows—

   (a) to the extent that it does not exceed the amount of any consideration which the person receives (or is deemed to receive) or becomes

entitled to receive on the conversion or exchange (other than his new
holding), it shall be treated as reducing that consideration; and

(b) to the extent that it does exceed that amount, it shall be treated as
consideration which the person gives on the conversion or exchange;

and where on a conversion or exchange of securities a person is treated as
entitled to relief under subsection (3)(a) of that section an amount equal to
the rebate amount (determined under that section) shall, for the purposes of
the computation of the gain, be treated as consideration which the person
receives on the conversion or exchange.

(11) In subsection (10) above "conversion" means conversion within the
meaning of section 132 and "exchange" means an exchange which by virtue
of Chapter II of this Part does not involve a disposal.

GENERAL NOTE

The accrued income scheme in ICTA 1988, s.710 *et seq.*, was designed to counter the practice
known as bond-washing by charging interest on bonds to tax on an accrual basis by time to the
vendor or purchaser. Where amounts are charged to income tax or rebated under the scheme,
the consideration given or received on a disposal of the bond is appropriately adjusted for
capital gains tax purposes. The various situations in which this may apply are set out in *ibid.*,
ss.713, 716 and 719. The same adjustment applies in the case of deemed disposals for the
purposes of this Act which are not transfers for purposes of *ibid.*, s.710, and on a conversion or
exchange of securities.

Increase in expenditure by reference to tax charged in relation to shares etc.

120.—(1) Where an amount is chargeable to tax under Chapter II of Part
III of the Finance Act 1988 on a person who acquires shares or an interest in
shares, then on the first disposal of the shares (whether by him or by another
person) after his acquisition, section 38(1)(a) shall apply as if a sum equal to
the amount chargeable had formed part of the consideration given by the
person making the disposal for his acquisition of the shares; and this subsection shall apply with the appropriate modifications in a case to which
section 83 of that Act applies.

This subsection shall be construed as if it were contained in Chapter II of
Part III of the Finance Act 1988.

(2) Section 38(1)(a) applies as if the relevant amount as defined in the
following provisions of this section in the cases there specified had formed
part of the consideration given by the person making the disposal for his
acquisition of the assets in question.

(3) Where an amount is chargeable to tax by virtue of section 162(5) of the
Taxes Act in respect of shares or an interest in shares, then—

(a) on a disposal of the shares or interest, where that is the event giving
rise to the charge; or

(b) in any case, on the first disposal of the shares or interest after the
event,

the relevant amount is a sum equal to the amount so chargeable.

(4) If a gain chargeable to tax under section 135(1) or (6) of the Taxes Act
is realised by the exercise of a right to acquire shares, the relevant amount is
a sum equal to the amount of the gain so chargeable to tax.

(5) Where an amount is chargeable to tax under section 138 of the Taxes
Act on a person acquiring any shares or interest, then on the first disposal
(whether by him or another person) of the shares after his acquisition, the
relevant amount is an amount equal to the amount so chargeable.

(6) Where an amount was chargeable to tax under section 185(6) of the
Taxes Act in respect of shares acquired in exercise of any such right as is
mentioned in section 185(1) of that Act, the relevant sum in relation to those
shares is an amount equal to the amount so chargeable.

(7) Subsections (3), (4), (5) and (6) above shall be construed as one with
sections 162, 135, 138 and 185 of the Taxes Act respectively.

GENERAL NOTE

The provisions mentioned in FA 1988 are designed to charge to income tax initially artificial benefits given under unapproved employee share schemes. Where such a charge arises, the amount of the charge is treated as part of the base value on the occasion of the first subsequent disposal of the shares.

A similar adjustment is also made in the case of charges to income tax under ICTA 1988, s.162 (charge on employees for purchase price of shares left outstanding), s.135 (charge on employees for gain on exercise of share options), s.138 (charge on employees acquiring shares, now replaced by the provisions in FA 1988) and s.185 (charge on employees for gain under share option schemes).

Saving certificates etc.

Exemption for government non-marketable securities

121.—(1) Savings certificates and non-marketable securities issued under the National Loans Act 1968 or the National Loans Act 1939, or any corresponding enactment forming part of the law of Northern Ireland, shall not be chargeable assets, and accordingly no chargeable gain shall accrue on their disposal.

(2) In this section—

(a) "savings certificates" means savings certificates issued under section 12 of the National Loans Act 1968, or section 7 of the National Debt Act 1958, or section 59 of the Finance Act 1920, and any war savings certificates as defined in section 9(3) of the National Debt Act 1972, together with any savings certificates issued under any enactment forming part of the law of Northern Ireland and corresponding to the said enactments, and

(b) "non-marketable securities" means securities which are not transferable, or which are transferable only with the consent of some Minister of the Crown, or the consent of a department of the Government of Northern Ireland, or only with the consent of the National Debt Commissioners.

GENERAL NOTE

Savings certificates and non-marketable government securities are exempt from C.G.T.

Capital distribution in respect of shares etc.

Distribution which is not a new holding within Chapter II

122.—(1) Where a person receives or becomes entitled to receive in respect of shares in a company any capital distribution from the company (other than a new holding as defined in section 126) he shall be treated as if he had in consideration of that capital distribution disposed of an interest in the shares.

(2) If the inspector is satisfied that the amount distributed is small, as compared with the value of the shares in respect of which it is distributed, and so directs—

(a) the occasion of the capital distribution shall not be treated for the purposes of this Act as a disposal of the asset, and

(b) the amount distributed shall be deducted from any expenditure allowable under this Act as a deduction in computing a gain or loss on the disposal of the shares by the person receiving or becoming entitled to receive the distribution of capital.

(3) A person who is dissatisfied with the refusal of the inspector to give a direction under this section may appeal to the commissioners having jurisdiction on an appeal against an assessment to tax in respect of a gain accruing on the disposal.

(4) Where the allowable expenditure is less than the amount distributed (or is nil)—

(a) subsections (2) and (3) above shall not apply, and
(b) if the recipient so elects (and there is any allowable expenditure)—
    (i) the amount distributed shall be reduced by the amount of the allowable expenditure, and
    (ii) none of that expenditure shall be allowable as a deduction in computing a gain accruing on the occasion of the capital distribution, or on any subsequent occasion.
In this subsection "allowable expenditure" means the expenditure which immediately before the occasion of the capital distribution was attributable to the shares under paragraphs (a) and (b) of section 38(1).
(5) In this section—
(a) the "amount distributed" means the amount or value of the capital distribution,
(b) "capital distribution" means any distribution from a company, including a distribution in the course of dissolving or winding up the company, in money or money's worth except a distribution which in the hands of the recipient constitutes income for the purposes of income tax.

GENERAL NOTE
A capital distribution from a company is in general to be treated as consideration for disposal of an interest in the shares (distributions chargeable to income tax such as dividends are excluded). For the construction of this provision and its interaction with s.171, see *Innocent* (*Inspector of Taxes*) v. *Whaddon Estates* [1982] S.T.C. 115.
The inspector may allow the distribution to be netted off if he considers that it is small in relation to the value of the shares. In *O'Rourke* (*Inspector of Taxes*) v. *Binks* [1991] S.T.C. 455, Vinelott J. refused to accept that a distribution amounting to 15 per cent. of the value of the shares was "small", but he held that this did not affect the taxpayer's right under subs. (4) to have the base cost set off against the distribution.

Disposal of right to acquire shares or debentures

123.—(1) Where a person receives or becomes entitled to receive in respect of any shares in a company a provisional allotment of shares in or debentures of the company and he disposes of his rights, section 122 shall apply as if the amount of the consideration for the disposal were a capital distribution received by him from the company in respect of the first-mentioned shares, and as if that person had, instead of disposing of the rights, disposed of an interest in those shares.
(2) This section shall apply in relation to rights obtained in respect of debentures of a company as it applies in relation to rights obtained in respect of shares in a company.

GENERAL NOTE
Where bonus or rights issues in respect of the shares or debentures of a company are disposed of, this is treated as a distribution within s.122.

Close companies

Disposal of shares: relief in respect of income tax consequent on shortfall in distributions

124.—(1) If in pursuance of section 426 of the Taxes Act (consequences for income tax of apportionment of income etc. of close company) a person is assessed to income tax, then, in the computation of the gain accruing on a disposal by him of any shares forming part of his interest in the company to which the relevant apportionment relates, the amount of the income tax paid by him, so far as attributable to those shares, shall be allowable as a deduction.

(2) Subsection (1) above shall not apply in relation to tax charged in respect of undistributed income which has, before the disposal, been subsequently distributed and is then exempt from tax by virtue of section 427(4) of the Taxes Act or in relation to tax treated as having been paid by virtue of section 426(2)(b) of that Act.

(3) For the purposes of this section the income assessed to tax shall be the highest part of the individual's income for the year of assessment in question, but so that if the highest part of the said income is taken into account under this section in relation to an assessment to tax the next highest part shall be taken into account in relation to any other relevant assessment, and so on.

(4) For the purpose of identifying shares forming part of an interest in a company with shares subsequently disposed of which are of the same class, shares bought at an earlier time shall be deemed to have been disposed of before shares bought at a later time.

GENERAL NOTE

Where the income of a close company has been apportioned among its shareholders for income tax purposes under ICTA 1988, s.426, the tax paid is allowable as a deduction on a subsequent disposal of the shares, unless the income has been subsequently distributed.

Section 426 has now been repealed by FA 1989, Sched. 17, Pt. V with regard to accounting periods beginning after March 31, 1989.

Shares in close company transferring assets at an undervalue

125.—(1) If a company which is a close company transfers, or has after 31st March 1982 transferred, an asset to any person otherwise than by way of a bargain made at arm's length and for a consideration of an amount or value less than the market value of the asset, an amount equal to the difference shall be apportioned among the issued shares of the company, and the holders of those shares shall be treated in accordance with the following provisions of this section.

(2) For the purposes of the computation of the gain accruing on the disposal of any of those shares by the person owning them on the date of transfer, an amount equal to the amount so apportioned to that share shall be excluded from the expenditure allowable as a deduction under section 38(1)(a) from the consideration for the disposal.

(3) If the person owning any of the shares at the date of transfer is itself a close company an amount equal to the amount apportioned to the shares so owned under subsection (1) above to that close company shall be apportioned among the issued shares of that close company, and the holders of those shares shall be treated in accordance with subsection (2) above, and so on through any number of close companies.

(4) This section shall not apply where the transfer of the asset is a disposal to which section 171(1) applies.

(5) In relation to a disposal to which section 35(2) does not apply, subsection (1) above shall have effect with the substitution of "6th April 1965" for "31st March 1982".

GENERAL NOTE

This section is designed to prevent the creation of artificial losses on shares by the transfer of assets by close companies at an undervalue. In such a case the undervalue is apportioned among the shares. A sub-apportionment is carried out where the holder of the shares is itself a close company.

The section does not apply to transfers within groups of companies.

For the definition of close company, see ICTA 1988, ss.414 and 415.

CHAPTER II

REORGANISATION OF SHARE CAPITAL, CONVERSION OF SECURITIES ETC.

Reorganisation or reduction of share capital

Application of sections 127 to 131

126.—(1) For the purposes of this section and sections 127 to 131 "reorganisation" means a reorganisation or reduction of a company's share capital, and in relation to the reorganisation—

(a) "original shares" means shares held before and concerned in the reorganisation,

(b) "new holding" means, in relation to any original shares, the shares in and debentures of the company which as a result of the reorganisation represent the original shares (including such, if any, of the original shares as remain).

(2) The reference in subsection (1) above to the reorganisation of a company's share capital includes—

(a) any case where persons are, whether for payment or not, allotted shares in or debentures of the company in respect of and in proportion to (or as nearly as may be in proportion to) their holdings of shares in the company or of any class of shares in the company, and

(b) any case where there are more than one class of share and the rights attached to shares of any class are altered.

(3) The reference in subsection (1) above to a reduction of share capital does not include the paying off of redeemable share capital, and where shares in a company are redeemed by the company otherwise than by the issue of shares or debentures (with or without other consideration) and otherwise than in a liquidation, the shareholder shall be treated as disposing of the shares at the time of the redemption.

GENERAL NOTE

This fasciculus of sections, ss.126–131, deals with reorganisation or reduction of the share capital of a company. An attempt to use the sections to crystallise a loss in *I.R.C.* v. *Burmah Oil Co.* (1981) 54 T.C. 200, was defeated by the application of the House of Lords' new approach to pre-arranged tax schemes.

In *Dunstan (Inspector of Taxes)* v. *Young, Austen and Young* [1989] S.T.C. 69 the Court of Appeal held that the examples of reorganisation given in subs. (2) were not exhaustive but provided for the avoidance of doubt.

Equation of original shares and new holding

127. Subject to sections 128 to 130, a reorganisation shall not be treated as involving any disposal of the original shares or any acquisition of the new holding or any part of it, but the original shares (taken as a single asset) and the new holding (taken as a single asset) shall be treated as the same asset acquired as the original shares were acquired.

GENERAL NOTE

A reorganisation does not involve a disposal, the original shares being carried forward to the new shares.

The interaction of this section with ss.171 and 135 was considered in *Westcott (Inspector of Taxes)* v. *Woolcombers* [1987] S.T.C. 600, C.A. The effect of the decision was subsequently reversed by what is now s.171(3).

Consideration given or received by holder

128.—(1) Subject to subsection (2) below, where, on a reorganisation, a person gives or becomes liable to give any consideration for his new holding or any part of it, that consideration shall in relation to any disposal of the new holding or any part of it be treated as having been given for the original shares, and if the new holding or part of it is disposed of with a liability attaching to it in respect of that consideration, the consideration given for the disposal shall be adjusted accordingly.

(2) There shall not be treated as consideration given for the new holding or any part of it—

(a) any surrender, cancellation or other alteration of the original shares or of the rights attached thereto, or

(b) any consideration consisting of any application, in paying up the new holding or any part of it, of assets of the company or of any dividend or other distribution declared out of those assets but not made,

and, in the case of a reorganisation on or after 10th March 1981, any consideration given for the new holding or any part of it otherwise than by way of a bargain made at arm's length shall be disregarded to the extent that its amount or value exceeds the relevant increase in value; and for this purpose "the relevant increase in value" means the amount by which the market value of the new holding immediately after the reorganisation exceeds the market value of the original shares immediately before the reorganisation.

(3) Where on a reorganisation a person receives (or is deemed to receive), or becomes entitled to receive, any consideration, other than the new holding, for the disposal of an interest in the original shares, and in particular—

(a) where under section 122 he is to be treated as if he had in consideration of a capital distribution disposed of an interest in the original shares, or

(b) where he receives (or is deemed to receive) consideration from other shareholders in respect of a surrender of rights derived from the original shares,

he shall be treated as if the new holding resulted from his having for that consideration disposed of an interest in the original shares (but without prejudice to the original shares and the new holding being treated in accordance with section 127 as the same asset).

(4) Where for the purpose of subsection (3) above it is necessary in computing the gain or loss accruing on the disposal of the interest in the original shares mentioned in that subsection to apportion the cost of acquisition of the original shares between what is disposed of and what is retained, the apportionment shall be made in the like manner as under section 129.

GENERAL NOTE

Where consideration is given for new shares on a reorganisation, it is treated as having been given for the original shares. However, surrender or cancellation of rights or the application of assets of the company in paying up the new holding is not treated as consideration, and consideration otherwise than by way of a bargain at arm's length is disregarded to the extent of the excess over market value. Where other consideration is received from the company or other shareholder this is treated as a disposal, but without otherwise affecting the identity of the old and new shares. An apportionment is made in such a case in line with s.129.

Part disposal of new holding

129. Subject to section 130(2), where for the purpose of computing the gain or loss accruing to a person from the acquisition and disposal of any part of the new holding it is necessary to apportion the cost of acquisition of any of the original shares between what is disposed of and what is retained, the apportionment shall be made by reference to market value at the date of the disposal (with such adjustment of the market value of any part of the new holding as may be required to offset any liability attaching thereto but forming part of the cost to be apportioned).

Any necessary apportionment of value is made by reference to market values at the date of disposal.

Composite new holdings

130.—(1) This section shall apply to a new holding—

(a) if it consists of more than one class of shares in or debentures of the company and one or more of those classes is of shares or debentures which, at any time not later than the end of the period of three months beginning with the date on which the reorganisation took effect, or of such longer period as the Board may by notice allow, had quoted market values on a recognised stock exchange in the United Kingdom or elsewhere, or

(b) if it consists of more than one class of rights of unit holders and one or more of those classes is of rights the prices of which were published daily by the managers of the scheme at any time not later than the end of that period of three months (or longer if so allowed).

(2) Where for the purpose of computing the gain or loss accruing to a person from the acquisition and disposal of the whole or any part of any class of shares or debentures or rights of unit holders forming part of a new holding to which this section applies it is necessary to apportion costs of acquisition between what is disposed of and what is retained, the cost of acquisition of the new holding shall first be apportioned between the entire classes of shares or debentures or rights of which it consists by reference to market value on the first day (whether that day fell before the reorganisation took effect or later) on which market values or prices were quoted or published for the shares, debentures or rights as mentioned in subsection (1)(a) or (1)(b) above (with such adjustment of the market value of any class as may be required to offset any liability attaching thereto but forming part of the cost to be apportioned).

(3) For the purposes of this section the day on which a reorganisation involving the allotment of shares or debentures or unit holders' rights takes effect is the day following the day on which the right to renounce any allotment expires.

This section applies to new holdings which consist of more than one class of shares or debentures or more than one class of rights of unit holders. Where it is necessary to apportion costs of acquisition, this is done, where there is a quoted market value within three months, or longer if allowed by the Revenue, by reference to that value on the day it was first quoted.

Indexation allowance

131.—(1) This section applies where—

(a) by virtue of section 127, on a reorganisation the original shares (taken as a single asset) and the new holding (taken as a single asset) fall to be treated as the same asset acquired as the original shares were acquired; and

(b) on the reorganisation, a person gives or becomes liable to give any consideration for his new holding or any part of it.

(2) Where this section applies, so much of the consideration referred to in subsection (1)(b) above as, on a disposal to which section 53 applies of the new holding, will, by virtue of section 128(1), be treated as having been given for the original shares, shall be treated for the purposes of section 54 as an item of relevant allowable expenditure incurred not at the time the original shares were acquired but at the time the person concerned gave or became liable to give the consideration (and, accordingly, section 54(4) shall not apply in relation to that item of expenditure).

Where additional consideration is given on a reorganisation for the new holding, this is treated for purposes of the indexation allowance as given at the time it was paid and not at the time of acquisition of the original holding.

Conversion of securities

Equation of converted securities and new holding

132.—(1) Sections 127 to 131 shall apply with any necessary adaptations in relation to the conversion of securities as they apply in relation to a reorganisation (that is to say, a reorganisation or reduction of a company's share capital).

(2) This section has effect subject to sections 133 and 134.

(3) For the purposes of this section and section 133—

(a) "conversion of securities" includes—

(i) a conversion of securities of a company into shares in the company, and

(ii) a conversion at the option of the holder of the securities converted as an alternative to the redemption of those securities for cash, and

(iii) any exchange of securities effected in pursuance of any enactment (including an enactment passed after this Act) which provides for the compulsory acquisition of any shares or securities and the issue of securities or other securities instead,

(b) "security" includes any loan stock or similar security whether of the Government of the United Kingdom or of any other government, or of any public or local authority in the United Kingdom or elsewhere, or of any company, and whether secured or unsecured.

GENERAL NOTE
The provisions of ss.127–131 regarding reorganisations of a company's capital apply, *mutatis mutandis*, to the conversion of securities, *i.e.* the new holding is identified with the old holding. "Conversion of securities" and "security" are both given wide definitions.

Premiums on conversion of securities

133.—(1) This section applies where, on a conversion of securities, a person receives, or becomes entitled to receive, any sum of money ("the premium") which is by way of consideration (in addition to his new holding) for the disposal of the converted securities.

(2) If the inspector is satisfied that the premium is small, as compared with the value of the converted securities, and so directs—

(a) receipt of the premium shall not be treated for the purposes of this Act as a disposal of part of the converted securities, and

(b) the premium shall be deducted from any expenditure allowable under this Act as a deduction in computing a gain or loss on the disposal of the new holding by the person receiving or becoming entitled to receive the premium.

(3) A person who is dissatisfied with the refusal of the inspector to give a direction under subsection (2) above may appeal to the Commissioners having jurisdiction on an appeal against an assessment to tax in respect of a gain accruing to him on a disposal of the securities.

(4) Where the allowable expenditure is less than the premium (or is nil)—

(a) subsections (2) and (3) above shall not apply, and

(b) if the recipient so elects (and there is any allowable expenditure)—

(i) the amount of the premium shall be reduced by the amount of the allowable expenditure, and

(ii) none of that expenditure shall be allowable as a deduction in computing a gain accruing on the occasion of the conversion, or on any subsequent occasion.

(5) In subsection (4) above "allowable expenditure" means expenditure which immediately before the conversion was attributable to the converted securities under paragraphs (a) and (b) of section 38(1).

GENERAL NOTE

On a conversion of securities, the holder sometimes receives a premium in cash. Where the premium is small in relation to the value of the converted securities, the inspector may simply deduct the premium from the base cost carried forward. If the base cost is less than the premium, the taxpayer may elect to have it set off against the premium.

For the operation of similar provisions under s.122, see *O'Rourke* (*Inspector of Taxes*) v. *Binks* [1991] S.T.C. 455.

Compensation stock

134.—(1) This section has effect where gilt-edged securities are exchanged for shares in pursuance of any enactment (including an enactment passed after this Act) which provides for the compulsory acquisition of any shares and the issue of gilt-edged securities instead.

(2) The exchange shall not constitute a conversion of securities within section 132 and shall be treated as not involving any disposal of the shares by the person from whom they were compulsorily acquired but—
(a) there shall be calculated the gain or loss that would have accrued to him if he had then disposed of the shares for a consideration equal to the value of the shares as determined for the purpose of the exchange, and
(b) on a subsequent disposal of the whole or part of the gilt-edged securities by the person to whom they were issued—
  (i) there shall be deemed to accrue to him the whole or a corresponding part of the gain or loss mentioned in paragraph (a) above, and
  (ii) section 115(1) shall not have effect in relation to any gain or loss that is deemed to accrue as aforesaid.

(3) Where a person to whom gilt-edged securities of any kind were issued as mentioned in subsection (1) above disposes of securities of that kind, the securities of which he disposes—
(a) shall, so far as possible, be identified with securities which were issued to him as mentioned in subsection (1) above rather than with other securities of that kind, and
(b) subject to paragraph (a) above, shall be identified with securities issued at an earlier time rather than those issued at a later time.

(4) Subsection (2)(b) above shall not apply to any disposal falling within the provisions of section 58(1), 62(4) or 171(1) but a person who has acquired the securities on a disposal falling within those provisions (and without there having been a previous disposal not falling within those provisions or a devolution on death) shall be treated for the purposes of subsections (2)(b) and (3) above as if the securities had been issued to him.

(5) Where the gilt-edged securities to be exchanged for any shares are not issued until after the date on which the shares are compulsorily acquired but on that date a right to the securities is granted, this section shall have effect as if the exchange had taken place on that date, as if references to the issue of the securities and the person to whom they were issued were references to the grant of the right and the person to whom it was granted and references to the disposal of the securities included references to disposals of the rights.

(6) In this section "shares" includes securities within the meaning of section 132.

(7) This section does not apply where the compulsory acquisition took place before 7th April 1976.

GENERAL NOTE
This provision was originally introduced during the term of office of the 1974–79 Labour government on the occasion of the nationalisation of the aircraft and shipbuilding industries. It applies where company shares are compulsorily acquired in exchange for gilts. If s.132 applied, the shares would be rolled over into the gilts, and the subsequent disposal of the gilts would be exempt under s.115. To prevent this happening, the gain that would have accrued on an actual disposal of the shares is calculated, and charged to tax on a subsequent disposal of the gilts. Where other gilts of the same kind are held, disposals are to be identified as far as possible with those received for the compulsorily acquired shares on a FIFO basis. The accrued charge is passed on when a no-gain/no-loss disposal occurs. The section applies as from the date of take-over, even if the gilts are issued later.

Company reconstructions and amalgamations

Exchange of securities for those in another company

135.—(1) Subsection (3) below has effect where a company ("company A") issues shares or debentures to a person in exchange for shares in or debentures of another company ("company B") and—
   (a) company A holds, or in consequence of the exchange will hold, more than one-quarter of the ordinary share capital (as defined in section 832(1) of the Taxes Act) of company B, or
   (b) company A issues the shares or debentures in exchange for shares as the result of a general offer—
      (i) which is made to members of company B or any class of them (with or without exceptions for persons connected with company A), and
      (ii) which is made in the first instance on a condition such that if it were satisfied company A would have control of company B.
   (2) Subsection (3) below also has effect where under section 136 persons are to be treated as exchanging shares or debentures held by them in consequence of the arrangement there mentioned.
   (3) Subject to sections 137 and 138, sections 127 to 131 shall apply with any necessary adaptations as if the two companies mentioned in subsection (1) above or, as the case may be, in section 136 were the same company and the exchange were a reorganisation of its share capital.

GENERAL NOTE
This fasciculus of sections, ss.135–140, deals with more complex situations, such as company take-overs.
   The rule under this section is that where one company issues securities in exchange for securities in another and will as a consequence hold more than 25 per cent. of the ordinary share capital of the other company, then the reorganisation provisions of ss.127–131 apply, *mutatis mutandis*. The section also applies to securities issued as the result of a take-over bid. "Ordinary share capital" is given its special meaning under ICTA 1988, s.832(1), of "all the issued share capital (by whatever name called) of the company, other than capital the holders of which have a right to a dividend at a fixed rate but have no other right to share in the profits of the company".
   Before the introduction of the provisions in s.137, the section was much used in the context of tax avoidance schemes, and the development of case law in this area may be seen in *Floor* v. *Davis* [1980] A.C. 695, *Furniss* v. *Dawson* [1984] A.C. 474 and *Craven (Inspector of Taxes)* v. *White* [1988] 3 W.L.R. 423.
   The interaction of this section with ss.127 and 171 was considered in *Westcott (Inspector of Taxes)* v. *Woolcombers* [1987] S.T.C. 600, C.A., but the decision in that case was subsequently reversed by what is now s.171(3).

Reconstruction or amalgamation involving issue of securities

136.—(1) Where—

(a) an arrangement between a company and the persons holding shares in or debentures of the company, or any class of such shares or debentures, is entered into for the purposes of or in connection with a scheme of reconstruction or amalgamation, and

(b) under the arrangement another company issues shares or debentures to those persons in respect of and in proportion to (or as nearly as may be in proportion to) their holdings of shares in or debentures of the first-mentioned company, but the shares in or debentures of the first-mentioned company are either retained by those persons or cancelled,

then those persons shall be treated as exchanging the first-mentioned shares or debentures for those held by them in consequence of the arrangement (any shares or debentures retained being for this purpose regarded as if they had been cancelled and replaced by a new issue), and subsections (2) and (3) of section 135 shall apply accordingly.

(2) In this section "scheme of reconstruction or amalgamation" means a scheme for the reconstruction of any company or companies or the amalgamation of any two or more companies, and references to shares or debentures being retained include their being retained with altered rights or in an altered form whether as the result of reduction, consolidation, division or otherwise.

(3) This section, and section 135(2), shall apply in relation to a company which has no share capital as if references to shares in or debentures of a company included references to any interests in the company possessed by members of the company.

GENERAL NOTE
   This extends the operation of s.135 to cases where there is no actual exchange of securities but rather an issue of securities by another company in pursuance of a scheme of reconstruction or amalgamation as defined in subs. (2).

Restriction on application of sections 135 and 136

137.—(1) Subject to subsection (2) below, and section 138, neither section 135 nor section 136 shall apply to any issue by a company of shares in or debentures of that company in exchange for or in respect of shares in or debentures of another company unless the exchange, reconstruction or amalgamation in question is effected for bona fide commercial reasons and does not form part of a scheme or arrangements of which the main purpose, or one of the main purposes, is avoidance of liability to capital gains tax or corporation tax.

(2) Subsection (1) above shall not affect the operation of section 135 or 136 in any case where the person to whom the shares or debentures are issued does not hold more than 5 per cent. of, or of any class of, the shares in or debentures of the second company mentioned in subsection (1) above.

(3) For the purposes of subsection (2) above shares or debentures held by persons connected with the person there mentioned shall be treated as held by him.

(4) If any tax assessed on a person (the chargeable person) by virtue of subsection (1) above is not paid within six months from the date when it is payable, any other person who—

(a) holds all or any part of the shares or debentures that were issued to the chargeable person, and

(b) has acquired them without there having been, since their acquisition by the chargeable person, any disposal of them not falling within section 58(1) or 171,

may, at any time within two years from the time when the tax became payable, be assessed and charged (in the name of the chargeable person) to all or, as the case may be, a corresponding part of the unpaid tax; and a person paying any amount of tax under this subsection shall be entitled to recover a sum of that amount from the chargeable person.

(5) With respect to chargeable gains accruing in chargeable periods ending after such day as the Treasury may by order appoint, in subsection (4) above—

(a) for the words "the date when it is payable" there shall be substituted "the date determined under subsection (4A) below";

(b) for the words "the time when the tax became payable" there shall be substituted "that date"; and

(c) for the words "a sum" onwards there shall be substituted "from the chargeable person a sum equal to that amount together with any interest paid by him under section 87A of the Management Act on that amount";

and after that subsection there shall be inserted—

"(4A) The date referred to in subsection (4) above is whichever is the later of—

(a) the date when the tax becomes due and payable by the chargeable person; and

(b) the date when the assessment was made on the chargeable person."

(6) In this section references to shares or debentures include references to any interests or options to which this Chapter applies by virtue of section 136(3) or 147.

GENERAL NOTE

The widespread use of s.135 in connection with tax avoidance schemes led to the enactment of the predecessor to this section. Modelled on the income tax provisions directed against dividend-stripping in ICTA 1988, s.703, it denies relief unless the arrangement in question is effected for bona fide commercial reasons and does not form part of a tax avoidance scheme.

There is a *de minimis* exemption in the case of a holding of less than five per cent. (including connected persons under s.286).

Where tax assessed under this section remains unpaid for six months, the Revenue may assess within two years any other person who holds the securities in question without there having been any other disposal except a no-gain/no-loss disposal between spouses or within a group of companies. This provision will be appropriately modified by Treasury order when the Pay and File system for corporation tax becomes applicable.

The ambit of the section was considered in *Young and Young* v. *Phillips* (*Inspector of Taxes*) (1984) 58 T.C. 232. It was held that, although the primary purpose of the scheme in question was avoidance of capital transfer tax, the machinery involved C.G.T. avoidance as well, so that the scheme was caught by this section.

Procedure for clearance in advance

138.—(1) Section 137 shall not affect the operation of section 135 or 136 in any case where, before the issue is made, the Board have, on the application of either company mentioned in section 137(1), notified the company that the Board are satisfied that the exchange, reconstruction or amalgamation will be effected for bona fide commercial reasons and will not form part of any such scheme or arrangements as are mentioned in section 137(1).

(2) Any application under subsection (1) above shall be in writing and shall contain particulars of the operations that are to be effected and the Board may, within 30 days of the receipt of the application or of any further particulars previously required under this subsection, by notice require the applicant to furnish further particulars for the purpose of enabling the Board to make their decision; and if any such notice is not complied with within 30 days or such longer period as the Board may allow, the Board need not proceed further on the application.

(3) The Board shall notify their decision to the applicant within 30 days of receiving the application or, if they give a notice under subsection (2) above, within 30 days of the notice being complied with.

(4) If the Board notify the applicant that they are not satisfied as mentioned in subsection (1) above or do not notify their decision to the applicant within the time required by subsection (3) above, the applicant may within 30 days of the notification or of that time require the Board to transmit the application, together with any notice given and further particulars furnished under subsection (2) above, to the Special Commissioners; and in that event any notification by the Special Commissioners shall have effect for the purposes of subsection (1) above as if it were a notification by the Board.

(5) If any particulars furnished under this section do not fully and accurately disclose all facts and considerations material for the decision of the Board or the Special Commissioners, any resulting notification that the Board or Commissioners are satisfied as mentioned in subsection (1) above shall be void.

GENERAL NOTE

A procedure for clearance in advance is provided by this section. It is normal practice for such a clearance to be sought, often in tandem with one under ICTA 1988, s.707, in cases where the anti-avoidance provisions might inadvertently have effect. Clearance after full disclosure will protect the transactions from a subsequent tax charge.

A time limit of 30 days is prescribed for a reply by the Revenue to an application under the section. A similar time limit applies to requests and responses regarding further particulars and to an appeal to the Special Commissioners against a refusal of clearance.

Reconstruction or amalgamation involving transfer of business

139.—(1) Subject to the provisions of this section, where—
  (a) any scheme of reconstruction or amalgamation involves the transfer of the whole or part of a company's business to another company, and
  (b) at the time of the transfer both the companies are resident in the United Kingdom, and
  (c) the first-mentioned company receives no part of the consideration for the transfer (otherwise than by the other company taking over the whole or part of the liabilities of the business),
then, so far as relates to corporation tax on chargeable gains, the two companies shall be treated as if any assets included in the transfer were acquired by the one company from the other company for a consideration of such amount as would secure that on the disposal by way of transfer neither a gain nor a loss would accrue to the company making the disposal, and for the purposes of Schedule 2 the acquiring company shall be treated as if the respective acquisitions of the assets by the other company had been the acquiring company's acquisition of them.

(2) This section does not apply in relation to an asset which, until the transfer, formed part of trading stock of a trade carried on by the company making the disposal, or in relation to an asset which is acquired as trading stock for the purposes of a trade carried on by the company acquiring the asset.

Section 170(1) applies for the purposes of this subsection.

(3) This section does not apply in relation to an asset if the company acquiring it, though resident in the United Kingdom—
  (a) is regarded for the purposes of any double taxation relief arrangements as resident in a territory outside the United Kingdom, and
  (b) by virtue of the arrangements, would not be liable in the United Kingdom to tax on a gain arising on a disposal of the asset occurring immediately after the acquisition.

(4) This section does not apply in the case of a transfer of the whole or part of a company's business to a unit trust scheme to which section 100(2) applies or which is an authorised unit trust or to an investment trust.

(5) This section does not apply unless the reconstruction or amalgamation is effected for bona fide commercial reasons and does not form part of a

scheme or arrangements of which the main purpose, or one of the main purposes, is avoidance of liability to corporation tax, capital gains tax or income tax; but the foregoing provisions of this subsection shall not affect the operation of this section in any case where, before the transfer, the Board have, on the application of the acquiring company, notified the company that the Board are satisfied that the reconstruction or amalgamation will be effected for bona fide commercial reasons and will not form part of any such scheme or arrangements as aforesaid.

Subsections (2) to (5) of section 138 shall have effect in relation to this subsection as they have effect in relation to subsection (1) of that section.

(6) Where, if the company making the disposal had not been wound up, tax could have been assessed on it by virtue of subsection (5) above, that tax may be assessed and charged (in the name of the company making the disposal) on the company to which the disposal is made.

(7) If any tax assessed on a company ("the chargeable company") by virtue of subsection (5) or (6) above is not paid within six months from the date when it is payable, any other person who—

(a) holds all or any part of the assets in respect of which the tax is charged; and

(b) either is the company to which the disposal was made or has acquired the assets without there having been any subsequent disposal not falling within this section or section 171,

may, within two years from the time when the tax became payable, be assessed and charged (in the name of the chargeable company) to all or, as the case may be, a corresponding part of the unpaid tax; and a person paying any amount of tax under this section shall be entitled to recover a sum of that amount from the chargeable company.

(8) With respect to chargeable gains accruing in chargeable periods ending after such day as the Treasury may by order appoint, in subsection (7) above—

(a) for the words "when it is payable" there shall be substituted "when it is due and payable or, if later, the date when the assessment is made on the company";

(b) for the words "the time when the tax became payable" there shall be substituted "the later of those dates"; and

(c) for the words "a sum" onwards there shall be substituted "from the chargeable company a sum equal to that amount together with any interest paid by him under section 87A of the Management Act on that amount".

(9) In this section "scheme of reconstruction or amalgamation" means a scheme for the reconstruction of any company or companies or the amalgamation of any two or more companies.

GENERAL NOTE

This section, consolidated along with the following section from the provisions in ICTA 1970 regarding corporation tax on chargeable gains, deals with the position where a reconstruction or amalgamation involves the transfer of a business from one company to another.

There has been a similar relief for stamp duty purposes and some of the cases relevant for that may also be in point here, *e.g. Wild* v. *South African Supply and Cold Storage Co.* [1904] 2 Ch. 268, *Brooklands Selangor Holdings* v. *I.R.C.*; *Kuala Pertang Syndicate* v. *I.R.C.* [1970] 1 W.L.R. 429, *Crane-Fruehauf* v. *I.R.C.* [1975] 1 All E.R. 429 and *Swithland Investments* v. *I.R.C.* [1990] S.T.C. 448.

Where a transfer of assets comes within the section, it is treated on a no-gain/no-loss basis. The acquiring company is treated for the purpose of apportionment of gains on assets held in 1965 as if it had acquired them when the disposing company did.

The section does not apply to trading assets, to dual resident or non-resident companies, or to transfers to unit trusts and other entities exempt under s.100. It also does not apply unless the arrangement is for bona fide commercial reasons and does not form part of a tax avoidance scheme. The clearance procedure under s.138 applies for this purpose.

There are provisions, similar to those under s.137, for recovering tax in default from the acquiring company.

Postponement of charge on transfer of assets to non-resident company

140.—(1) This section applies where a company resident in the United Kingdom carries on a trade outside the United Kingdom through a branch or agency and—
- (a) that trade, or part of it, together with the whole assets of the company used for the purposes of the trade or part (or together with the whole of those assets other than cash) is transferred to a company not resident in the United Kingdom;
- (b) the trade or part is so transferred wholly or partly in exchange for securities consisting of shares, or of shares and loan stock, issued by the transferee company to the transferor company;
- (c) the shares so issued, either alone or taken together with any other shares in the transferee company already held by the transferor company, amount in all to not less than one quarter of the ordinary share capital of the transferee company; and
- (d) either no allowable losses accrue to the transferor company on the transfer or the aggregate of the chargeable gains so accruing exceeds the aggregate of the allowable losses so accruing;

and also applies in any case where section 268A of the Income and Corporation Taxes Act 1970 applied unless the deferred gain had been wholly taken into account in accordance with that section before the coming into force of this section.

Section 170(1) shall apply for the purposes of this section.

(2) In any case to which this section applies the transferor company may claim that this Act shall have effect in accordance with the following provisions.

(3) Any allowable losses accruing to the transferor company on the transfer shall be set off against the chargeable gains so accruing and the transfer shall be treated as giving rise to a single chargeable gain equal to the aggregate of those gains after deducting the aggregate of those losses and—
- (a) if the securities are the whole consideration for the transfer, the whole of that gain shall be treated as not accruing to the transferor company on the transfer but an equivalent amount ("the deferred gain") shall be brought into account in accordance with subsections (4) and (5) below;
- (b) if the securities are not the whole of that consideration—
  - (i) paragraph (a) above shall apply to the appropriate proportion of that gain; and
  - (ii) the remainder shall be treated as accruing to the transferor company on the transfer.

In paragraph (b)(i) above "the appropriate proportion" means the proportion that the market value of the securities at the time of the transfer bears to the market value of the whole of the consideration at that time.

(4) If at any time after the transfer the transferor company disposes of the whole or part of the securities held by it immediately before that time, the consideration received by it on the disposal shall be treated as increased by the whole or the appropriate proportion of the deferred gain so far as not already taken into account under this subsection or subsection (5) below.

In this subsection "the appropriate proportion" means the proportion that the market value of the part of the securities disposed of bears to the market value of the securities held immediately before the disposal.

(5) If at any time within six years after the transfer the transferee company disposes of the whole or part of the relevant assets held by it immediately before that time there shall be deemed to accrue to the transferor company

as a chargeable gain on that occasion the whole or the appropriate proportion of the deferred gain so far as not already taken into account under this subsection or subsection (4) above.

In this subsection "relevant assets" means assets the chargeable gains on which were taken into account in arriving at the deferred gain and "the appropriate proportion" means the proportion which the chargeable gain so taken into account in respect of the part of the relevant assets disposed of bears to the aggregate of the chargeable gains so taken into account in respect of the relevant assets held immediately before the time of the disposal.

(6) There shall be disregarded—

(a) for the purposes of subsection (4) above any disposal to which section 171 applies; and

(b) for the purposes of subsection (5) above any disposal to which that section would apply apart from section 170(2)(a) and (9);

and where a person acquires securities or an asset on a disposal disregarded for the purposes of subsection (4) or (5) above (and without there having been a previous disposal not so disregarded) a disposal of the securities or asset by that person shall be treated as a disposal by the transferor or, as the case may be, transferee company.

(7) If in the case of any such transfer as was mentioned in section 268(1) of the Income and Corporation Taxes Act 1970 there were immediately before the coming into force of this section chargeable gains which by virtue of section 268(2) and 268A(8) of that Act were treated as not having accrued to the transferor company, subsection (4) above shall (without any claim in that behalf) apply to the aggregate of those gains as if references to the deferred gain were references to that aggregate and as if references to the transfer and the securities were references to the transfer and the shares, or shares and loan stock, mentioned in section 268(1).

(8) If in the case of any such transfer as was mentioned in section 268A(1) of the Income and Corporation Taxes Act 1970 there were immediately before the coming into force of this section deferred gains which by virtue of section 268A(3) were treated as not having accrued to the transferor company, subsections (4) and (5) above shall (without any claim in that behalf) apply to those deferred gains as they apply to gains deferred by virtue of subsection (3) above (as if the references to the transfer and the securities were references to the transfer and securities mentioned in section 268A(1)).

GENERAL NOTE

This section applies where a U.K. resident company carries on a trade outside the U.K. through a branch or agency and transfers the assets of the trade to a non-resident company in exchange for securities, provided that it has at least 25 per cent. of the ordinary share capital (see ICTA 1988, s.832(1)) of the transferee company.

In such a case the transferor company may claim relief on terms that any gain will be deferred until it disposes of the securities. A charge may also arise if the transferee company disposes of any of the assets in question within six years. The transferor company's gain may be rolled over into another group company.

There are transitional provisions carrying forward relevant parts of the previous versions of this section in ICTA 1970, s.268, and ICTA 1970, s.268A (substituted by FA 1977, s.42(1)).

CHAPTER III

MISCELLANEOUS PROVISIONS RELATING TO COMMODITIES, FUTURES, OPTIONS AND OTHER SECURITIES

Stock dividends: consideration for new holding

141.—(1) In applying section 128(1) in relation to the issue of any share capital to which section 249 of the Taxes Act (stock dividends) applies as involving a reorganisation of the company's share capital, there shall be allowed, as consideration given for so much of the new holding as was issued as mentioned in subsection (4), (5) or (6) of section 249 (read in each case with subsection (3) of that section) an amount equal to what is, for that much of the new holding, the appropriate amount in cash within the meaning of section 251(2) of the Taxes Act.

(2) This section shall have effect notwithstanding section 128(2).

GENERAL NOTE
A stock dividend is subject to income tax in certain circumstances under ICTA 1988, s.249, when received by individuals, personal representatives or trustees. In such a case the amount subjected to income tax is allowed as consideration for the new holding under s.128.

Capital gains on certain stock dividends

142.—(1) This section applies where a company issues any share capital to which section 249 of the Taxes Act applies in respect of shares in the company held by a person as trustee, and another person is at the time of the issue absolutely entitled thereto as against the trustee or would be so entitled but for being an infant or other person under disability (or two or more other persons are or would be jointly so entitled thereto).

(2) Notwithstanding paragraph (a) of section 126(2) the case shall not constitute a reorganisation of the company's share capital for the purposes of sections 126 to 128.

(3) Notwithstanding section 17(1), the person who is or would be so entitled to the share capital (or each of the persons who are or would be jointly so entitled thereto) shall be treated for the purposes of section 38(1)(a) as having acquired that share capital, or his interest in it, for a consideration equal to the appropriate amount in cash within the meaning of section 251(2) to (4) of the Taxes Act.

GENERAL NOTE
In the case of stock dividends caught by s.249 to which a beneficiary is absolutely entitled as against the trustees, the beneficiary is treated as having acquired the stock for the amount subjected to income tax.

Commodity and financial futures and qualifying options

143.—(1) If, apart from section 128 of the Taxes Act, gains arising to any person in the course of dealing in commodity or financial futures or in qualifying options would constitute, for the purposes of the Tax Acts, profits or gains chargeable to tax under Schedule D otherwise than as the profits of a trade, then his outstanding obligations under any futures contract entered into in the course of that dealing and any qualifying option granted or acquired in the course of that dealing shall be regarded as assets to the disposal of which this Act applies.

(2) In subsection (1) above—

(a) "commodity or financial futures" means commodity futures or financial futures which are for the time being dealt in on a recognised futures exchange; and

(b) "qualifying option" means a traded option or financial option as defined in section 144(8).

(3) Notwithstanding the provisions of subsection (2)(a) above, where, otherwise than in the course of dealing on a recognised futures exchange—

(a) an authorised person or listed institution enters into a commodity or financial futures contract with another person, or

(b) the outstanding obligations under a commodity or financial futures contract to which an authorised person or listed institution is a party are brought to an end by a further contract between the parties to the futures contract, then, except in so far as any gain or loss arising to any person from that transaction arises in the course of a trade, that gain or loss shall be regarded for the purposes of subsection (1) above as arising to him in the course of dealing in commodity or financial futures.

(4) In subsection (3) above—

"authorised person" has the same meaning as in the Financial Services Act 1986, and

"listed institution" has the same meaning as in section 43 of that Act.

(5) For the purposes of this Act, where, in the course of dealing in commodity or financial futures, a person who has entered into a futures contract closes out that contract by entering into another futures contract with obligations which are reciprocal to those of the first-mentioned contract, that transaction shall constitute the disposal of an asset (namely, his outstanding obligations under the first-mentioned contract) and, accordingly—

(a) any money or money's worth received by him on that transaction shall constitute consideration for the disposal; and

(b) any money or money's worth paid or given by him on that transaction shall be treated as incidental costs to him of making the disposal.

(6) In any case where—

(a) a person who, in the course of dealing in financial futures, has entered into a futures contract does not close out that contract (as mentioned in subsection (5) above), and

(b) the nature of the futures contract is such that, at its expiry date, the person concerned is entitled to receive or liable to make a payment in full settlement of all obligations under that contract,

then, for the purposes of this Act, he shall be treated as having disposed of an asset (namely, his outstanding obligations under the futures contract) and the payment received or made by him shall be treated as consideration for that disposal or, as the case may be, as incidental costs to him of making the disposal.

GENERAL NOTE

These provisions, originally introduced in 1985, deal with commodity or financial futures, traded options and financial options. Where profits on dealings in these did not constitute profits of a trade, they were liable to income tax under Case VI of Sched. D. What is now ICTA 1988, s.128, removed this charge. This section subjects them instead to C.G.T.

The section applies to dealings on recognised stock or futures exchanges (as to which see s.289(1) and (6)) or with persons or institutions authorised under the Financial Services Act 1986.

Where a contract in commodity or financial futures is closed out by entering into another contract with reciprocal obligations, the transaction is treated as a disposal of an asset for C.G.T. purposes.

Where a financial futures contract is not closed out, any payment received or made on the expiry of the contract is brought into account for C.G.T.

Options and forfeited deposits

144.—(1) Without prejudice to section 21, the grant of an option, and in particular—

(a) the grant of an option in a case where the grantor binds himself to sell what he does not own, and because the option is abandoned, never has occasion to own, and

(b) the grant of an option in a case where the grantor binds himself to buy what, because the option is abandoned, he does not acquire,

is the disposal of an asset (namely of the option), but subject to the following provisions of this section as to treating the grant of an option as part of a larger transaction.

(2) If an option is exercised, the grant of the option and the transaction entered into by the grantor in fulfilment of his obligations under the option shall be treated as a single transaction and accordingly—

   (a) if the option binds the grantor to sell, the consideration for the option is part of the consideration for the sale, and

   (b) if the option binds the grantor to buy, the consideration for the option shall be deducted from the cost of acquisition incurred by the grantor in buying in pursuance of his obligations under the option.

(3) The exercise of an option by the person for the time being entitled to exercise it shall not constitute the disposal of an asset by that person, but, if an option is exercised then the acquisition of the option (whether directly from the grantor or not) and the transaction entered into by the person exercising the option in exercise of his rights under the option shall be treated as a single transaction and accordingly—

   (a) if the option binds the grantor to sell, the cost of acquiring the option shall be part of the cost of acquiring what is sold, and

   (b) if the option binds the grantor to buy, the cost of the option shall be treated as a cost incidental to the disposal of what is bought by the grantor of the option.

(4) The abandonment of—

   (a) a quoted option to subscribe for shares in a company, or

   (b) a traded option or financial option, or

   (c) an option to acquire assets exercisable by a person intending to use them, if acquired, for the purpose of a trade carried on by him,

shall constitute the disposal of an asset (namely of the option); but the abandonment of any other option by the person for the time being entitled to exercise it shall not constitute the disposal of an asset by that person.

(5) This section shall apply in relation to an option binding the grantor both to sell and to buy as if it were two separate options with half the consideration attributed to each.

(6) In this section references to an option include references to an option binding the grantor to grant a lease for a premium, or enter into any other transaction which is not a sale, and references to buying and selling in pursuance of an option shall be construed accordingly.

(7) This section shall apply in relation to a forfeited deposit of purchase money or other consideration money for a prospective purchase or other transaction which is abandoned as it applies in relation to the consideration for an option which binds the grantor to sell and which is not exercised.

(8) In subsection (4) above and sections 146 and 147—

   (a) "quoted option" means an option which, at the time of the abandonment or other disposal, is quoted on a recognised stock exchange;

   (b) "traded option" means an option which, at the time of the abandonment or other disposal, is quoted on a recognised stock exchange or a recognised futures exchange; and

   (c) "financial option" means an option which is not a traded option, as defined in paragraph (b) above, but which, subject to subsection (9) below—

      (i) relates to currency, shares, securities or an interest rate and is granted (otherwise than as agent) by a member of a recognised stock exchange, by an authorised person within the meaning of the Financial Services Act 1986 or by a listed institution within the meaning of section 43 of that Act; or

      (ii) relates to shares or securities which are dealt in on a recognised stock exchange and is granted by a member of such an exchange, acting as agent; or

      (iii) relates to currency, shares, securities or an interest rate and is granted to such an authorised person or institution as is referred to in sub-paragraph (i) above and concurrently and in association with an option falling within that sub-paragraph which is granted by that authorised person or institution to the grantor of the first-mentioned option; or

    (iv) relates to shares or securities which are dealt in on a recognised stock exchange and is granted to a member of such an exchange, including such a member acting as agent.

(9) If the Treasury by order so provide, an option of a description specified in the order shall be taken to be within the definition of "financial option" in subsection (8)(c) above.

GENERAL NOTE

Subs. (1)
The grant of an option is treated as a disposal of an asset, namely the option. The provisions of ss.144–148 give a code for the treatment of options, but this does not preclude a charge under general principles where an option is not exercised (*Strange* v. *Openshaw* (*Inspector of Taxes*) (1983) 57 T.C. 544) or is abandoned in return for a payment (*Golding* (*Inspector of Taxes*) v. *Kaufman* (1984) 58 T.C. 296, *Welbeck Securities* v. *Powlson* (*Inspector of Taxes*) [1987] S.T.C. 468, C.A.).

Subss. (2) and (3)
Where the option is exercised, the two transactions are merged, so that for a grantor in the case of a call option the cost of the option is part of the sale consideration and in the case of a put option the proceeds of the option are deducted from the acquisition cost and *vice versa* for the person entitled to exercise the option.

Subs. (4)
The abandonment of an option is not the disposal of an asset under this section unless it is a quoted share option, a traded or financial option or an option to acquire trading assets.

Subs. (5)
A combined put and call option is treated as two options with half the consideration attributed to each.

Subss. (6) and (7)
These cover options to grant a lease for a premium and forfeited deposits.

Subss. (8) and (9)
These provide definitions of various types of option for the purposes of this section and ss.143, 146 and 147, subject to a power of the Treasury to widen the definition of "financial option" by order.

Call options: indexation allowance

145.—(1) This section applies where, on a disposal to which section 53 applies, the relevant allowable expenditure includes both—

    (a) the cost of acquiring an option binding the grantor to sell ("the option consideration"); and

    (b) the cost of acquiring what was sold as a result of the exercise of the option ("the sale consideration"),

but does not apply in any case where section 114 applies.

(2) For the purpose of computing the indexation allowance (if any) on the disposal referred to in subsection (1) above—

    (a) the option consideration and the sale consideration shall be regarded as separate items of expenditure; and

    (b) subsection (4) of section 54 shall apply to neither of those items and, accordingly, they shall be regarded as incurred when the option was acquired and when the sale took place, respectively.

(3) This section has effect notwithstanding section 144, but expressions used in this section have the same meaning as in that section and subsection (5) of that section applies for the purpose of determining the cost of acquiring an option binding the grantor to sell.

GENERAL NOTE
In the case of a call option (except where the provisions regarding share pools in s.114 apply) the option and its exercise are treated as separate events for the purposes of the indexation allowance.

Options: application of rules as to wasting assets

146.—(1) Section 46 shall not apply—
  (a) to a quoted option to subscribe for shares in a company, or
  (b) to a traded option, or financial option, or
  (c) to an option to acquire assets exercisable by a person intending to use them, if acquired, for the purpose of a trade carried on by him.

(2) In relation to the disposal by way of transfer of an option (other than an option falling within subsection (1)(a) or (b) above) binding the grantor to sell or buy quoted shares or securities, the option shall be regarded as a wasting asset the life of which ends when the right to exercise the option ends, or when the option becomes valueless, whichever is the earlier.

Subsections (5) and (6) of section 144 shall apply in relation to this subsection as they apply in relation to that section.

(3) The preceding provisions of this section are without prejudice to the application of sections 44 to 47 to options not within those provisions.

(4) In this section—
  (a) "financial option", "quoted option" and "traded option" have the meanings given by section 144(8), and
  (b) "quoted shares or securities" means shares or securities which have a quoted market value on a recognised stock exchange in the United Kingdom or elsewhere.

GENERAL NOTE
The types of option covered by subs. (1) are not wasting assets for the purposes of s.46. However, under subs. (2), options to buy and sell stock exchange securities are dealt with under the wasting asset rules.

Quoted options treated as part of new holdings

147.—(1) If a quoted option to subscribe for shares in a company is dealt in (on the stock exchange where it is quoted) within three months after the taking effect, with respect to the company granting the option, of any reorganisation, reduction, conversion or amalgamation to which Chapter II of this Part applies, or within such longer period as the Board may by notice allow—
  (a) the option shall, for the purposes of that Chapter be regarded as the shares which could be acquired by exercising the option, and
  (b) section 272(3) shall apply for determining its market value.

(2) In this section "quoted option" has the meaning given by section 144(8).

GENERAL NOTE
Where a quoted option to subscribe for shares is dealt in within three months of any company reorganisation to which ss.126–140 apply, the option is treated for the purposes of these sections as being the shares which could be acquired by exercising it. The middle price on the Stock Exchange list is used for determining its value.

Traded options: closing purchases

148.—(1) This section applies where a person ("the grantor") who has granted a traded option ("the original option") closes it out by acquiring a traded option of the same description ("the second option").

(2) Any disposal by the grantor involved in closing out the original option shall be disregarded for the purposes of capital gains tax or, as the case may be, corporation tax on chargeable gains.

(3) The incidental costs to the grantor of making the disposal constituted by the grant of the original option shall be treated for the purposes of the computation of the gain as increased by an amount equal to the aggregate of—

(a) the amount or value of the consideration, in money or money's worth, given by him or on his behalf wholly and exclusively for the acquisition of the second option, and

(b) the incidental costs to him of that acquisition.

(4) In this section "traded option" has the meaning given by section 144(8).

GENERAL NOTE

This provision, introduced in 1991, deals with the common situation where an option contract is closed out by the grantor acquiring an option of the same description. In such a case the closing out is not treated as involving a disposal, but is the grantor's base cost for the first option as increased by the consideration for the second option, together with any incidental costs.

Rights to acquire qualifying shares

149.—(1) This section applies where on or after 25th July 1991 (the day on which the Finance Act 1991 was passed) a building society confers—

(a) on its members, or

(b) on any particular class or description of its members,

any rights to acquire, in priority to other persons, shares in the society which are qualifying shares.

(2) Any such right so conferred shall be regarded for the purposes of capital gains tax as an option granted to, and acquired by, the member concerned for no consideration and having no value at the time of that grant and acquisition.

(3) In this section—

"member" includes a former member, and

"qualifying share" has the same meaning as in section 117(4).

GENERAL NOTE

This forms part of a series of provisions introduced in 1991 to allow building societies to issue permanent interest-bearing shares which would be exempt from C.G.T. (see s.117(11)(b)), while deducting income tax at basic rate on the interest. A preferential right to acquire such shares granted to members is treated as an option acquired for no consideration.

Business expansion schemes

150.—(1) In this section "relief" means relief under Chapter III of Part VII of the Taxes Act, Schedule 5 to the Finance Act 1983 ("the 1983 Act") or Chapter II of Part IV of the Finance Act 1981 ("the 1981 Act") and "eligible shares" has the meaning given by section 289(4) of the Taxes Act.

(2) A gain or loss which accrues to an individual on the disposal of any shares issued after 18th March 1986 in respect of which relief has been given to him and not withdrawn shall not be a chargeable gain or allowable loss for the purposes of capital gains tax.

(3) The sums allowable as deductions from the consideration in the computation for the purposes of capital gains tax of the gain or loss accruing to an individual on the disposal of shares issued before 19th March 1986 in respect of which relief has been given and not withdrawn shall be determined without regard to that relief, except that where those sums exceed the consideration they shall be reduced by an amount equal to—

(a) the amount of that relief; or

(b) the excess,

whichever is the less, but the foregoing provisions of this subsection shall not apply to a disposal falling within section 58(1).

(4) Any question—

(a) as to which of any shares issued to a person at different times, being shares in respect of which relief has been given and not withdrawn, a disposal relates, or

(b) whether a disposal relates to shares in respect of which relief has been given and not withdrawn or to other shares,

shall for the purposes of capital gains tax be determined as for the purposes of section 299 of the Taxes Act, or section 57 of the Finance Act 1981 if the relief has only been given under that Act; and Chapter I of this Part shall have effect subject to the foregoing provisions of this subsection.

(5) Notwithstanding anything in section 107(1) and (2), section 107 does not apply to shares in respect of which relief has been given and not withdrawn.

(6) Where an individual holds shares which form part of the ordinary share capital of a company and the relief has been given (and not withdrawn) in respect of some but not others, then, if there is within the meaning of section 126 a reorganisation affecting those shares, section 127 shall apply separately to the shares in respect of which the relief has been given (and not withdrawn) and to the other shares (so that shares of eack kind are treated as a separate holding of original shares and identified with a separate new holding).

(7) Where section 58 has applied to any eligible shares disposed of by an individual to his or her spouse ("the transferee"), subsection (2) above shall apply in relation to the subsequent disposal of the shares by the transferee to a third party.

(8) Where section 135 or 136 would, but for this subsection, apply in relation to eligible shares issued after 18th March 1986 in respect of which an individual has been given relief, that section shall apply only if the relief is withdrawn.

(9) Sections 127 to 130 shall not apply in relation to any shares in respect of which relief (other than relief under the 1981 Act) has been given and which form part of a company's ordinary share capital if—

(a) there is, by virtue of any such allotment for payment as is mentioned in section 126(2)(a), a reorganisation occurring after 18th March 1986 affecting those shares; and

(b) immediately following the reorganisation, the relief has not been withdrawn in respect of those shares or relief has been given in respect of the allotted shares and not withdrawn.

(10) Where relief is reduced by virtue of subsection (2) of section 305 of the Taxes Act—

(a) the sums allowable as deductions from the consideration in the computation, for the purposes of capital gains tax, of the gain or loss accruing to an individual on the disposal, after 18th March 1986, of any of the allotted shares or debentures shall be taken to include the amount of the reduction apportioned between the allotted shares or (as the case may be) debentures in such a way as appears to the inspector, or an appeal to the Commissioners concerned, to be just and reasonable; and

(b) the sums so allowable on the disposal (in circumstances in which subsections (2) to (8) above do not apply) of any of the shares referred to in section 305(2)(a) shall be taken to be reduced by the amount mentioned in paragraph (a) above, similarly apportioned between those shares.

(11) There shall be made all such adjustments of capital gains tax, whether by way of assessment or by way of discharge or repayment of tax, as may be required in consequence of the relief being given or withdrawn.

GENERAL NOTE
The Business Expansion Scheme ("B.E.S."), which originated in 1981 as the business

start-up scheme, allowed individuals to invest in new businesses and set the investment off against their income. The income tax provisions are now found in ICTA 1988, ss.289–312. The B.E.S. is due to be terminated at the end of 1993.

An exemption from C.G.T. is also accorded to B.E.S. shares issued after March 18, 1986. For B.E.S. shares issued before that date the base cost on a disposal ignores the income tax relief, except that where the base cost exceeds the consideration it is reduced by the lesser of the relief or the excess (this does not apply to a no-gain/no-loss disposal between spouses).

B.E.S. relief is withdrawn under ICTA 1988, s.289(12), if the shares are disposed of within five years. Where this happens the withdrawal occurs on a FIFO basis (*ibid.*, s.299). This rule is adopted for C.G.T. Otherwise, the rules for identification of securities in s.107 do not apply.

Where an individual holds shares some of which qualify for B.E.S. relief and some do not, they are treated separately on a s.126 reorganisation.

The exemption from C.G.T. may be passed on between spouses. Where a B.E.S. company is involved in a s.135 or s.136 take-over situation, these sections only apply if B.E.S. relief is withdrawn. The reorganisation provisions of ss.127–130 also do not apply where there has been a rights issue and relief has not been withdrawn.

Under ICTA 1988, s.305, where consideration is received by a B.E.S. shareholder on a s.126 reorganisation, the income tax relief is reduced by the difference in market value of the shares immediately before and after the reorganisation. The base cost of the shares for C.G.T. purposes will on the reorganisation and on any subsequent disposal be similarly reduced by an apportionment on a just and reasonable basis.

Appropriate adjustments for C.G.T. purposes will be made, if necessary, on the giving or withdrawal of B.E.S. relief.

Personal equity plans

151.—(1) The Treasury may make regulations providing that an individual who invests under a plan shall be entitled to relief from capital gains tax in respect of the investments.

(2) Subsections (2) to (5) of section 333 of the Taxes Act (personal equity plans) shall apply in relation to regulations under subsection (1) above as they apply in relation to regulations under subsection (1) of that section but with the substitution for any reference to income tax of a reference to capital gains tax.

(3) Regulations under this section may include provision securing that losses are disregarded for the purposes of capital gains tax where they accrue on the disposal of investments on or after 18th January 1988.

GENERAL NOTE

Personal Equity Plans ("PEPs") were introduced in 1986. Investments in PEPs are exempt from income tax on reinvested dividends and from C.G.T. so long as they are held for at least a complete tax year after the year in which the investment is made. Losses on PEPs are likewise disregarded.

The relevant regulations are to be found in the Personal Equity Plan Regulations 1989 (S.I. 1989 No. 469), as amended by S.I. 1990 No. 678 and S.I. 1991 No. 733.

PART V

TRANSFER OF BUSINESS ASSETS

CHAPTER I

GENERAL PROVISIONS

Replacement of business assets

Roll-over relief

152.—(1) If the consideration which a person carrying on a trade obtains for the disposal of, or of his interest in, assets ("the old assets") used, and used only, for the purposes of the trade throughout the period of ownership is applied by him in acquiring other assets, or an interest in other assets ("the new assets") which on the acquisition are taken into use, and used only, for the purposes of the trade, and the old assets and new assets are within the classes of assets listed in section 155, then the person carrying on the trade shall, on making a claim as respects the consideration which has been so applied, be treated for the purposes of this Act—

(a) as if the consideration for the disposal of, or of the interest in, the old assets were (if otherwise of a greater amount or value) of such amount as would secure that on the disposal neither a gain nor a loss accrues to him, and

(b) as if the amount or value of the consideration for the acquisition of, or of the interest in, the new assets were reduced by the excess of the amount or value of the actual consideration for the disposal of, or of the interest in, the old assets over the amount of the consideration which he is treated as receiving under paragraph (a) above,

but neither paragraph (a) nor paragraph (b) above shall affect the treatment for the purposes of this Act of the other party to the transaction involving the old assets, or of the other party to the transaction involving the new assets.

(2) Where subsection (1)(a) above applies to exclude a gain which, in consequence of Schedule 2, is not all chargeable gain, the amount of the reduction to be made under subsection (1)(b) above shall be the amount of the chargeable gain, and not the whole amount of the gain.

(3) Subject to subsection (4) below, this section shall only apply if the acquisition of, or of the interest in, the new assets takes place, or an unconditional contract for the acquisition is entered into, in the period beginning 12 months before and ending three years after the disposal of, or of the interest in, the old assets, or at such earlier or later time as the Board may by notice allow.

(4) Where an unconditional contract for the acquisition is so entered into, this section may be applied on a provisional basis without waiting to ascertain whether the new assets, or the interest in the new assets, is acquired in pursuance of the contract, and, when that fact is ascertained, all necessary adjustments shall be made by making assessments or by repayment or discharge of tax, and shall be so made notwithstanding any limitation on the time within which assessment may be made.

(5) This section shall not apply unless the acquisition of, or of the interest in, the new assets was made for the purpose of their use in the trade, and not wholly or partly for the purpose of realising a gain from the disposal of, or of the interest in, the new assets.

(6) If, over the period of ownership or any substantial part of the period of ownership, part of a building or structure is, and part is not, used for the purposes of a trade, this section shall apply as if the part so used, with any land occupied for purposes ancillary to the occupation and of that part of the building or structure, were a separate asset, and subject to any necessary apportionments of consideration for an acquisition or disposal of, or of an interest in, the building or structure and other land.

(7) If the old assets were not used for the purposes of the trade throughout the period of ownership this section shall apply as if a part of the asset representing its use for the purposes of the trade having regard to the time and extent to which it was, and was not, used for those purposes, were a separate asset which had been wholly used for the purposes of the trade, and this subsection shall apply in relation to that part subject to any necessary apportionment of consideration for an acquisition or disposal of, or of the interest in, the asset.

(8) This section shall apply in relation to a person who, either successively or at the same time, carries on two or more trades as if both or all of them were a single trade.

(9) In this section "period of ownership" does not include any period before 31st March 1982.

(10) The provisions of this Act fixing the amount of the consideration deemed to be given for the acquisition or disposal of assets shall be applied before this section is applied.

(11) Without prejudice to section 52(4), where consideration is given for the acquisition or disposal of assets some or part of which are assets in relation to which a claim under this section applies, and some or part of which are not, the consideration shall be apportioned in such manner as is just and reasonable.

GENERAL NOTE

It was appreciated that if tax was charged on the disposal of assets, used for a trade, which had to be replaced, this would place an undue burden on business. Accordingly, a roll-over relief is granted where the proceeds of disposal are applied in acquiring new assets. The relief must be claimed and operates by treating the disposal on a no-gain/no-loss basis. The base cost of the new assets is reduced accordingly.

The new assets must be taken into use for the purposes of the trade on acquisition. Assets purchased with a view to such use, but not actually used, do not qualify (*Temperley* v. *Visibell* [1974] S.T.C. 64. Where the acquisition of a freehold was followed later by the acquisition of an underlease which gave possession of the premises, the relief does not apply to the acquisition of the freehold (*Campbell Connelly & Co.* v. *Barnett* [1992] S.T.C. 316).

In the case of assets held in 1965, the roll-over is restricted to the chargeable gain.

A condition for the relief is that the new assets should be acquired up to one year before and three years after the disposal of the old assets, unconditional contracts being accepted on a "wait-and-see" basis.

The relief is excluded where the acquisition is made with a view to realising a gain.

Apportionments are made where a building is not wholly used for the purposes of a trade or when an asset is not so used throughout the period of ownership. In *Todd* (*Inspector of Taxes*) v. *Mudd* (1986) 60 T.C. 237, it was held that where an individual making a disposal of the old assets acquired a 75 per cent. interest in new assets, only three-quarters of which were to be used for business purposes, roll-over relief was restricted to 75 per cent. of the three-quarters, despite his claim that it was the 75 per cent. which was used entirely for business purposes. Subsection (9), excluding periods of ownership before 1982 from consideration, was passed to reverse the decision in *Richart* (*Inspector of Taxes*) v. *J. Lyons & Co.* [1989] S.T.C. 665, C.A.

All trades carried on by a person are to be treated as one trade, so that it is not necessary to roll over into the same trade.

The section applies subject to the provisions relating to deemed disposals, and any necessary apportionments are to be made on a just and reasonable basis.

Assets only partly replaced

153.—(1) Section 152(1) shall not apply if part only of the amount or value of the consideration for the disposal of, or of the interest in, the old assets is applied as described in that subsection, but if all of the amount or value of the consideration except for a part which is less than the amount of the gain (whether all chargeable gain or not) accruing on the disposal of, or of the interest in, the old assets is so applied, then the person carrying on the trade, on making a claim as respects the consideration which has been so applied, shall be treated for the purposes of this Act—

(a) as if the amount of the gain so accruing were reduced to the amount of the said part (and, if not all chargeable gain, with a proportionate reduction in the amount of the chargeable gain), and

(b) as if the amount or value of the consideration for the acquisition of, or of the interest in, the new assets were reduced by the amount by which the gain is reduced (or as the case may be the amount by which the chargeable gain is proportionately reduced) under paragraph (a) of this subsection,

but neither paragraph (a) nor paragraph (b) above shall affect the treatment for the purposes of this Act of the other party to the transaction involving the old assets, or of the other party to the transaction involving the new assets.

(2) Subsections (3) to (11) of 152 shall apply as if this section formed part of that section.

GENERAL NOTE

This section applies where only part of the proceeds is reinvested. In such a case a claim can still be made if the part of the consideration not reinvested is less than the gain. The part of the gain not reinvested is immediately chargeable and the remainder goes to reduce the base cost of the new assets.

New assets which are depreciating assets

154.—(1) Sections 152, 153 and 229 shall have effect subject to the provisions of this section in which—
 (a) the "held-over gain" means the amount by which, under those sections and apart from the provisions of this section, any chargeable gain on one asset ("asset No. 1") is reduced, with a corresponding reduction of the expenditure allowable in respect of another asset ("asset No. 2"), and
 (b) any reference to a gain of any amount being carried forward to any asset is a reference to a reduction of that amount in a chargeable gain coupled with a reduction of the same amount in expenditure allowable in respect of that asset.
 (2) If asset No. 2 is a depreciating asset, the held-over gain shall not be carried forward, but the claimant shall be treated as if so much of the chargeable gain on asset No. 1 as is equal to the held-over gain did not accrue until—
 (a) the claimant disposes of asset No. 2, or
 (b) he ceases to use asset No. 2 for the purposes of a trade carried on by him, or
 (c) the expiration of a period of 10 years beginning with the acquisition of asset No. 2,
whichever event comes first.
 (3) Where section 229 has effect subject to the provisions of this section, subsection (2)(b) above shall have effect as if it read—
 "(b) section 232(3) applies as regards asset No. 2 (whether or not by virtue of section 232(5)), or".
 (4) If, in the circumstances specified in subsection (5) below, the claimant acquires an asset ("asset No. 3") which is not a depreciating asset, and claims under section 152 or 153—
 (a) the gain held-over from asset No. 1 shall be carried forward to asset No. 3, and
 (b) the claim which applies to asset No. 2 shall be treated as withdrawn (so that subsection (2) above does not apply).
 (5) The circumstances are that asset No. 3 is acquired not later than the time when the chargeable gain postponed under subsection (2) above would accrue and, assuming—
 (a) that the consideration for asset No. 1 was applied in acquiring asset No. 3, and
 (b) that the time between and disposal of asset No. 1 and the acquisition of asset No. 3 was within the time limited by section 152(3),
the whole amount of the postponed gain could be carried forward from asset No. 1 to asset No. 3; and the claim under subsection (4) above shall be accepted as if those assumptions were true.
 (6) If part only of the postponed gain could be carried forward from asset No. 1 to asset No. 3, and the claimant so requires, that and the other part of the postponed gain shall be treated as derived from 2 separate assets, so that, on that claim—
 (a) subsection (4) above applies to the first-mentioned part, and
 (b) the other part remains subject to subsection (2) above.
 (7) For the purposes of this section, an asset is a depreciating asset at any time if—
 (a) at that time it is a wasting asset, as defined in section 44, or

(b) within the period of 10 years beginning at that time it will become a wasting asset (so defined).

GENERAL NOTE

This section is designed to prevent the disappearance of gains by their roll-over into depreciating assets. A depreciating asset is a wasting asset, *i.e.* one with a predictable life not exceeding 50 years, or an asset which will become such within 10 years. In such a case, the gain is not deducted from the base cost of the new asset but is held over for whichever is shortest of 10 years after the acquisition, the disposal of the new asset and cessation of its use for the purposes of the trade. The roll-over rules may be reapplied if the gain is rolled back into a non-depreciating asset before the occurrence of the first of these events.

The section also applies for the purposes of the new relief for employee share ownership trusts (ESOTs) introduced in 1990 (see s.229).

Relevant classes of assets

155. The classes of assets for the purposes of section 152(1) are as follows.

CLASS 1

Assets within heads A and B below.

Head A

1. Any building or part of a building and any permanent or semi-permanent structure in the nature of a building, occupied (as well as used) only for the purposes of the trade
2. Any land occupied (as well as used) only for the purposes of the trade. Head A has effect subject to section 156.

Head B

Fixed plant or machinery which does not form part of a building or of a permanent or semi-permanent structure in the nature of a building.

CLASS 2

Ships, aircraft and hovercraft ("hovercraft" having the same meaning as in the Hovercraft Act 1968).

CLASS 3

Satellites, space stations and spacecraft (including launch vehicles).

CLASS 4

Goodwill.

CLASS 5

Milk quotas (that is, rights to sell dairy produce without being liable to pay milk levy or to deliver dairy produce without being liable to pay a contribution to milk levy) and potato quotas (that is, rights to produce potatoes without being liable to pay more than the ordinary contribution to the Potato Marketing Board's fund).

GENERAL NOTE

This defines the classes of assets which qualify for relief. These have been added to over the years to bring in new types of asset such as hovercraft, satellites and milk quotas.

Head A

It was held in *Anderton* v. *Lamb* (1980) 55 T.C. 1 that houses occupied by partners in a farming business were not occupied as well as used only for the purposes of the trade.

Head B

The word "fixed" qualifies "machinery" as well as "plant", so that movable equipment does not qualify (*Williams* v. *Evans* (*Inspector of Taxes*); *Jones* v. *Evans*; *Roberts* v. *Evans* [1982] 1 W.L.R. 972.

Assets of Class 1

156.—(1) This section has effect as respects head A of Class 1 in section 155.

(2) Head A shall not apply where the trade is a trade—

(a) of dealing in or developing land, or

(b) of providing services for the occupier of land in which the person carrying on the trade has an estate or interest.

(3) Where the trade is a trade of dealing in or developing land, but a profit on the sale of any land held for the purposes of the trade would not form part of the trading profits, then as regards that land, the trade shall be treated for the purposes of subsection (2)(a) above as if it were not a trade of dealing in or developing land.

(4) A person who is a lessor of tied premises shall be treated as if he occupied (as well as used) those tied premises only for the purposes of the relevant trade.

This subsection shall be construed in accordance with section 98(2) of the Taxes Act (income tax and corporation tax on tied premises).

GENERAL NOTE

Land development and associated activities, for long a trade not favoured for fiscal purposes, is excluded from roll-over relief, except in the case of land the disposal of which would not form part of the trading profits.

The owner of tied premises within ICTA 1988, s.98(2), is treated as if he occupied as well as used them for the purposes of the trade.

Trade carried on by family company: business assets dealt with by individual

157. In relation to a case where—

(a) the person disposing of, or of his interest in, the old assets and acquiring the new assets, or an interest in them, is an individual, and

(b) the trade or trades in question are carried on not by that individual but by a company which, both at the time of the disposal and at the time of the acquisition referred to in paragraph (a) above, is his family company, within the meaning of Schedule 6,

any references in sections 152 to 156 to the person carrying on the trade (or the 2 or more trades) includes a reference to the individual.

GENERAL NOTE

Assets owned by an individual but used by his family company qualify for relief. For the meaning of "family company", see the General Note to Sched. 4.

Activities other than trades, and interpretation

158.—(1) Sections 152 to 157 shall apply with the necessary modifications—

(a) in relation to the discharge of the functions of a public authority, and

(b) in relation to the occupation of woodlands where the woodlands are managed by the occupier on a commercial basis and with a view to the realisation of profits, and

(c) in relation to a profession, vocation, office or employment, and

(d) in relation to such of the activities of a body of persons whose activities are carried on otherwise than for profit and are wholly or mainly directed to the protection or promotion of the interests of its members in the carrying on of their trade or profession as are so directed, and

(e) in relation to the activities of an unincorporated association or other body chargeable to corporation tax, being a body not established for

profit whose activities are wholly or mainly carried on otherwise than for profit, but in the case of assets within head A of class 1 only if they are both occupied and used by the body, and in the case of other assets only if they are used by the body,
as they apply in relation to a trade.

(2) In sections 152 to 157 and this section the expressions "trade", "profession", "vocation", "office" and "employment" have the same meanings as in the Income Tax Acts, but not so as to apply the provisions of the Income Tax Acts as to the circumstances in which, on a change in the persons carrying on a trade, a trade is to be regarded as discontinued, or as set up and commenced.

(3) Sections 152 to 157 and this section shall be construed as one.

GENERAL NOTE

Relief is extended to a certain number of other activities which are not within the ambit of trade, but can be regarded as carrying on business activities.

The expressions "trade", "profession", "vocation", "office" and "employment" have the same meaning as for income tax, but not so as to import the provisions relating to deemed cessations of a trade (see ICTA 1988, s.113).

Non-residents: roll-over relief

159.—(1) Section 152 shall not apply in the case of a person if the old assets are chargeable assets in relation to him at the time they are disposed of, unless the new assets are chargeable assets in relation to him immediately after the time they are acquired.

(2) Subsection (1) above shall not apply where—

(a) the person acquires the new assets after he has disposed of the old assets, and

(b) immediately after the time they are acquired the person is resident or ordinarily resident in the United Kingdom.

(3) Subsection (2) above shall not apply where immediately after the time the new assets are acquired—

(a) the person is a dual resident, and

(b) the new assets are prescribed assets.

(4) For the purposes of this section an asset is at any time a chargeable asset in relation to a person if, were it to be disposed of at that time, any chargeable gains accruing to him on the disposal—

(a) would be gains in respect of which he would be chargeable to capital gains tax under section 10(1), or

(b) would form part of his chargeable profits for corporation tax purposes by virtue of section 10(3).

(5) In this section—

"dual resident" means a person who is resident or ordinarily resident in the United Kingdom and falls to be regarded for the purposes of any double taxation relief arrangements as resident in a territory outside the United Kingdom; and

"prescribed asset", in relation to a dual resident, means an asset in respect of which, by virtue of the asset being of a description specified in any double taxation relief arrangements, he falls to be regarded for the purposes of the arrangements as not liable in the United Kingdom to tax on gains accruing to him on a disposal.

(6) In this section—

(a) "the old assets" and "the new assets" have the same meanings as in section 152,

(b) references to disposal of the old assets include references to disposal of an interest in them, and

(c) references to acquisition of the new assets include references to acquisition of an interest in them or to entering into an unconditional contract for the acquisition of them.

(7) Where the acquisition of the new assets took place before 14th March 1989 and the disposal of the old assets took place, or takes place, on or after that date, this section shall not apply if the disposal of the old assets took place, or takes place, within 12 months of the acquisition of the new assets or such longer period as the Board may by notice allow.

GENERAL NOTE
   This provision, introduced in 1989, debars roll-over relief where the old assets are chargeable assets in relation to the owner, unless the new assets are also chargeable assets in relation to him. The assets referred to are those chargeable under s.10(1) and 10(3), *i.e.* assets used by non-resident persons or companies for the purposes of a trade in the U.K. through a branch or agency. The exclusion does not apply where the owner becomes resident, unless the assets are protected by a double tax treaty, under which the owner is treated as a dual resident.

Dual resident companies: roll-over relief

160.—(1) Where a company is a dual resident company at the time it disposes of the old assets and at the time it acquires the new assets, and the old assets are not prescribed assets at the time of disposal, section 152 shall not apply unless the new assets are not prescribed assets immediately after the time of acquisition.

(2) In this section—
   "dual resident company" means a company which is resident in the United Kingdom and falls to be regarded for the purposes of any double taxation relief arrangements as resident in a territory outside the United Kingdom; and
   "prescribed asset", in relation to a dual resident company, means an asset in respect of which, by virtue of the asset being of a description specified in any double taxation relief arrangements, the company falls to be regarded for the purposes of the arrangements as not liable in the United Kingdom to tax on gains accruing to it on a disposal.

(3) In this section—
   (a) "the old assets" and "the new assets" have the same meanings as in section 152,
   (b) references to disposal of the old assets include references to disposal of an interest in them, and
   (c) references to acquisition of the new assets include references to acquisition of an interest in them or to entering into an unconditional contract for the acquisition of them.

(4) Where the acquisition of the new assets took place before 14th March 1989 and the disposal of the old assets took place, or takes place, on or after that date, this section shall not apply if the disposal of the old assets took place, or take place, within 12 months of the acquisition of the new assets or such longer period as the Board may by notice allow.

GENERAL NOTE
   Similar to s.159, relief is denied in the case of a dual resident company, where assets not protected by double taxation relief are rolled over into assets which are.

Stock in trade

Appropriations to and from stock

161.—(1) Subject to subsection (3) below, where an asset acquired by a person otherwise than as trading stock of a trade carried on by him is appropriated by him for the purposes of the trade as trading stock (whether on the commencement of the trade or otherwise) and, if he had then sold the asset for its market value, a chargeable gain or allowable loss would have accrued to him, he shall be treated as having thereby disposed of the asset by selling it for its then market value.

(2) If at any time an asset forming part of the trading stock of a person's trade is appropriated by him for any other purpose, or is retained by him on his ceasing to carry on the trade, he shall be treated as having acquired it at that time for a consideration equal to the amount brought into the accounts of the trade in respect of it for tax purposes on the appropriation or on his ceasing to carry on the trade, as the case may be.

(3) Subject to subsection (4) below, subsection (1) above shall not apply in relation to a person's appropriation of an asset for the purposes of a trade if he is chargeable to income tax in respect of the profits of the trade under Case I of Schedule D, and elects that instead the market value of the asset at the time of the appropriation shall, in computing the profits of the trade for purposes of tax, be treated as reduced by the amount of the chargeable gain or increased by the amount of the allowable loss referred to in subsection (1), and where that subsection does not apply by reason of such an election, the profits of the trade shall be computed accordingly,

(4) If a person making an election under subsection (3) is at the time of the appropriation carrying on the trade in partnership with others, the election shall not have effect unless concurred in by the others.

GENERAL NOTE
The section deals with appropriations of assets to and from trading stock.

Subs. (1)
Where an asset is appropriated to trading stock a deemed disposal at market value occurs.

Subs. (2)
Where an asset is appropriated from trading stock it is deemed to be acquired for the amount brought into the accounts of the trade. This will normally be market value (*Sharkey* v. *Wernher* [1956] A.C. 58, H.L.

Subs. (3)
The trader may elect not to have subs. (1) apply, but instead to have the value of the asset on his books reduced by the amount of the gain (or increased by the amount of any loss).

Subs. (4)
Partners must all concur in a subs. (3) election.
For two attempts to use the section to crystallise losses, with partial success in one case, see *Coates* (*Inspector of Taxes*) v. *Arndale Properties*; *Reed* (*Inspector of Taxes*) v. *Nova Securities* [1984] 1 W.L.R. 1328.

Transfer of business to a company

Roll-over relief on transfer of business

162.—(1) This section shall apply for the purposes of this Act where a person who is not a company transfers to a company a business as a going concern, together with the whole assets of the business, or together with the whole of those assets other than cash, and the business is so transferred wholly or partly in exchange for shares issued by the company to the person transferring the business.

Any shares so received by the transferor in exchange for the business are referred to below as "the new assets".

(2) The amount determined under subsection (4) below shall be deducted from the aggregate of the chargeable gains less allowable losses ("the amount of the gain on the old assets").

(3) For the purpose of computing any chargeable gain accruing on the disposal of any new asset—

(a) the amount determined under subsection (4) below shall be apportioned between the new assets as a whole, and

(b) the sums allowable as a deduction under section 38(1)(a) shall be reduced by the amount apportioned to the new asset under paragraph (a) above;

and if the shares which comprise the new assets are not all of the same class, the apportionment between the shares under paragraph (a) above shall be in accordance with their market values at the time they were acquired by the transferor.

(4) The amount referred to in subsections (2) and (3)(a) above shall not exceed the cost of the new assets but, subject to that, it shall be the fraction—

$$\frac{A}{B}$$

of the amount of the gain on the old assets where—

"A" is the cost of the new assets, and

"B" is the value of the whole of the consideration received by the transferor in exchange for the business;

and for the purposes of this subsection "the cost of the new assets" means any sums which would be allowable as a deduction under section 38(1)(a) if the new assets were disposed of as a whole in circumstances giving rise to a chargeable gain.

(5) References in this section to the business, in relation to shares or consideration received in exchange for the business, include references to such assets of the business as are referred to in subsection (1) above.

GENERAL NOTE

This provides a roll-over relief for the transfer to a company of a business as a going concern together with all the assets of the business (other than cash) wholly or partly in exchange for shares.

The amount of gain rolled over is restricted proportionally in so far as there is consideration other than shares, and is deducted from the base cost of the shares on a subsequent disposal, being apportioned among different classes of shares in accordance with their market value at the time they were acquired.

In *Gordon* v. *I.R.C.* [1991] S.T.C. 174, C.S., the Revenue argued that the transfer of a farming business to a company with a view to facilitating its disposal and roll-over into another farming business did not qualify for relief because it was not a "going concern", but this was rejected.

Retirement relief

Relief for disposals by individuals on retirement from family business

163.—(1) Relief from capital gains tax shall be given, subject to and in accordance with Schedule 6, in any case where a material disposal of business assets is made by an individual who, at the time of the disposal—

(a) has attained the age of 55, or

(b) has retired on ill-health grounds below the age 55.

(2) For the purposes of this section and Schedule 6, a disposal of business assets is—

(a) a disposal of the whole or part of a business, or

(b) a disposal of one or more assets which, at the time at which a business ceased to be carried on, were in use for the purposes of that business, or

(c) a disposal of shares or securities of a company (including a disposal of an interest in shares which a person is treated as making by virtue of section 122),

and the question whether such a disposal is a material disposal shall be determined in accordance with the following provisions of this section.

(3) A disposal of the whole or part of a business is a material disposal if, throughout a period of at least one year ending with the date of the disposal, the relevant conditions are fulfilled and, in relation to such a disposal, those conditions are fulfilled at any time if at that time the business is owned by the individual making the disposal or—

(a) the business is owned by a company—
    (i) which is a trading company, and
    (ii) which is either that individual's family company or a member of a trading group of which the holding company is that individual's family company; and

(b) that individual is a full-time working director of that company or, if that company is a member of a group or commercial association of companies, of one or more companies which are members of the group or association.

(4) A disposal of assets such as is mentioned in subsection (2)(b) above is a material disposal if—

(a) throughout a period of at least one year ending with the date on which the business ceased to be carried on the relevant conditions are fulfilled and, in the relation to such a disposal, those conditions are fulfilled at any time if at that time either the business was owned by the individual making the disposal or paragraphs (a) and (b) of subsection (3) above apply; and

(b) on or before the date on which the business ceased to be carried on, the individual making the disposal had either attained the age of 55 or retired on ill-health grounds below that age; and

(c) the date on which the business ceased to be carried on falls within the permitted period before the date of the disposal.

(5) A disposal of shares or securities of a company (including such a disposal of an interest in shares as is mentioned in subsection (2)(c) above) is a material disposal if, throughout a period of at least one year ending with the operative date, the relevant conditions are fulfilled and, in relation to such a disposal, those conditions are fulfilled at any time if at that time—

(a) the individual making the disposal owns the business which, at the date of the disposal, is owned by the company or, if the company is the holding company of a trading group, by any member of the group; or

(b) the company is the individual's family company and is either a trading company or the holding company of a trading group and the individual is a full-time working director of the company or, if the company is a member of a group or commercial association of companies, of one or more companies which are members of the group or association;

and, except where subsection (6) or subsection (7) below applies, the operative date for the purposes of this subsection is the date of the disposal.

(6) In any case where—

(a) within the permitted period before the date of the disposal referred to in subsection (5) above, the company concerned either ceased to be a trading company without continuing to be or becoming a member of a trading group or ceased to be a member of a trading group without continuing to be or becoming a trading company, and

(b) on or before the date of that cessation, the individual making the disposal attained the age of 55 or retired on ill-health grounds below that age,

then, subject to subsection (7) below, the operative date for the purposes of subsection (5) above is the date of the cessation referred to in paragraph (a) above; and, where this subsection applies, the reference in subsection (5)(a) above to the date of the disposal shall also be construed as a reference to the date of that cessation.

(7) If, throughout a period which ends on the date of the disposal referred to in subsection (5) above or, if subsection (6) above applies, on the date of

the cessation referred to in paragraph (a) of that subsection and which begins when the individual concerned ceased to be a full-time working director of the company or, if that company is a member of a group or commercial association of companies, of one or more companies which are members of the group or association—

(a) the company concerned was his family company and either a trading company or the holding company of a trading group, and

(b) he was a director of the company concerned or, as the case may be, of one or more members of the group or association and, in that capacity, devoted at least 10 hours per week (averaged over the period) to the service of the company or companies in a technical or managerial capacity,

the operative date for the purposes of subsection (5) above is the date on which the individual ceased to be a full-time working director as mentioned above.

(8) For the purposes of this section—

(a) any references to the disposal of the whole or part of a business by an individual includes a reference to the disposal by him of his interest in the assets of a partnership carrying on the business; and

(b) subject to paragraph (a) above, at any time when a business is carried on by a partnership, the business shall be treated as owned by each individual who is at that time a member of the partnership.

(9) Part I of Schedule 6 shall have effect for the interpretation of this section as well as of that Schedule.

GENERAL NOTE

From the inception of C.G.T. it was recognised that some relief should be accorded to individuals who disposed of their businesses by sale or gift on retirement. Originally contained in one section, FA 1965, s.34, it has now burgeoned into three sections and two schedules, filling more than 20 pages of the statute book. Disposals by sale and disposals by gift were separated in 1978 and in 1985 the relief for disposals by sale was entirely recast to include in the legislation a number of practices and extra-statutory concessions which had developed over the years. The relief for disposals by sale is now contained in ss.163, 164 and Sched. 6 and for disposals by gift in s.165 and Sched. 7.

It should be noted initially that it is not actually essential under this section for the individual to go into retirement, unless he is doing so on grounds of ill-health under the age of 55. It should also be noted that under subs. (2) the relief covers the disposal of the whole or part of a business, assets which were in use for the purposes of a business when it ceased to be carried on or shares in certain companies. In three cases involving farmers (*McGregor* v. *Adcock* [1977] 1 W.L.R. 864; *Atkinson (Inspector of Taxes)* v. *Dancer*; *Mannion (Inspector of Taxes)* v. *Johnston* [1988] S.T.C. 758) it was held that the disposal of part of their acreage by farmers who continued working was a disposal of assets rather than the disposal of part of their business, and so relief was not available.

The Revenue may also take a somewhat restrictive view of what constitutes a business. In an activity such as running a rooming-house, some personal activity by the proprietor other than collecting rent is desirable, for example.

Subs. (3)

The business must have been owned throughout a period of one year ending with the disposal either by the individual or by a family company which is trading or the holding company of a trading group. In the latter case he must also be a full-time working director of the company or of a company which is a member of a group or commercial association of companies along with it. These terms are further defined in Sched. 6, para. 1(2).

Subs. (4)

Where the disposal is of assets, the business should have ceased within the previous year.

Subss. (5)–(7)

These provide further conditions governing the relief for the disposal of shares. Where the company ceases to trade or the individual ceases to be a full-time director (but continues to work part-time) the disposal should be within a year.

Subs. (8)

The relief applies to members of a partnership.

Other retirement relief

164.—(1) Relief from capital gains tax shall be given, subject to and in accordance with Schedule 6, in any case where an individual—

(a) who has attained the age of 55, or

(b) who has retired on ill-health grounds below the age of 55,

makes a relevant disposal of the whole or part of the assets provided or held for the purposes of an office or employment exercised by him; and, if he ceases to exercise that office or employment before the date of the relevant disposal, the date on which he ceased to exercise it is in subsection (2) below referred to as the "prior cessation date".

(2) For the purposes of subsection (1) above, a disposal of the whole or part of the assets provided or held as mentioned in that subsection is a relevant disposal if—

(a) throughout a period of at least one year ending with the date of the disposal or, where applicable, the prior cessation date, the office or employment was the full-time occupation of the individual making the disposal; and

(b) that office or employment is other than that of director of a company which is either the family company of the individual concerned or is a member of a trading group of which the holding company is his family company; and

(c) where there is a prior cessation date, the individual either had attained the age of 55 on or before that date or on that date retired on ill-health grounds below that age; and

(d) where there is a prior cessation date, the disposal takes place within the permitted period after the cessation date.

(3) Relief from capital gains tax shall be given, subject to and in accordance with Schedule 6, where—

(a) the trustees of a settlement dispose of—

(i) shares of securities of a company, or

(ii) an asset used or previously used for the purposes of a business,

being, in either case, part of the settled property; and

(b) the conditions in subsection (4) or, as the case may be, subsection (5) below are fulfilled with respect to a beneficiary who, under the settlement, has an interest in possession in the whole of the settled property or, as the case may be, in a part of it which consists of or includes the shares or securities or the asset referred to in paragraph (a) above, but excluding, for this purpose, an interest for a fixed term; and in those subsections that beneficiary is referred to as "the qualifying beneficiary".

(4) In relation to a disposal of shares or securities of a company (including such a disposal of an interest in shares as is mentioned in section 163(2)(c)), the conditions referred to in subsection (3)(b) above are—

(a) that, throughout a period of at least one year ending not earlier than the permitted period before the disposal, the company was the qualifying beneficiary's family company and either a trading company or the holding company of a trading group; and

(b) that, throughout a period of at least one year ending as mentioned in paragraph (a) above, the qualifying beneficiary was a full-time working director of the company or, if the company is a member of a group or commercial association of companies, of one or more companies which are members of the group or association; and

(c) that, on the date of the disposal or within the permitted period before that date, the qualifying beneficiary ceased to be a full-time working director as mentioned in paragraph (b) above, having attained the age of 55 or retired on ill-health grounds below that age.

(5) In relation to a disposal of an asset, the conditions referred to in subsection (3)(b) above are—

(a) that, throughout a period of at least one year ending not earlier than the permitted period before the disposal, the asset was used for the purposes of a business carried on by the qualifying beneficiary; and

(b) that, on the date of the disposal or within the permitted period before that date, the qualifying beneficiary ceased to carry on the business referred to in paragraph (a) above; and

(c) that, on or before the date of the disposal or, if it was earlier, the date on which the qualifying beneficiary ceased to carry on that business, he attained the age of 55 or retired on ill-health grounds below that age.

(6) In any case where—

(a) by virtue of section 163, relief falls to be given, in accordance with Schedule 6, in respect of a material disposal of business assets which either consists of the disposal by an individual of his interest in the assets of a partnership or is of a description falling within subsection (5) of that section, and

(b) the individual making that material disposal makes an associated disposal of assets, as defined in subsection (7) below,

relief from capital gains tax shall also be given, subject to and in accordance with that Schedule in respect of the associated disposal.

(7) In relation to a material disposal of business assets, a disposal of an asset is an associated disposal if—

(a) it takes place as part of a withdrawal of the individual concerned from participation in the business carried on by the partnership referred to in subsection (6)(a) above or, as the case may be, by the company which owns the business as mentioned in section 163(5)(a); and

(b) immediately before the material disposal or, if it was earlier, the cessation of the business mentioned in paragraph (a) above, the asset was in use for the purposes of that business; and

(c) during the whole or part of the period in which the asset has been in the ownership of the individual making the disposal the asset has been used—

    (i) for the purposes of the business mentioned in paragraph (a) above (whether or not carried on by the partnership or company there referred to); or

    (ii) for the purposes of another business carried on by the individual or by a partnership of which the individual concerned was a member; or

    (iii) for the purposes of another business in respect of which the conditions in paragraphs (a) and (b) of subsection (3) of section 163 were fulfilled.

(8) In subsections (6) and (7) above "material disposal of business assets" has the same meaning as in section 163 and Part I of Schedule 6 shall have effect for the interpretation of this section as well as of that Schedule.

GENERAL NOTE

This section extends retirement relief to certain cases not covered by the previous section. Generally, see further the General Note to s.163 and Sched. 6.

Subs. (2)

The relief is extended to cases where an individual holds assets for the purposes of an office or employment held by him.

Subss. (3)–(5)

It is also extended to cover trustees where a beneficiary with an interest in possession otherwise fulfils the conditions for relief.

It also covers cases where a retiring partner or shareholder holds assets for the use of the partnership or company.

CHAPTER II

GIFTS OF BUSINESS ASSETS

Relief for gifts of business assets

165.—(1) If—

(a) an individual ("the transferor") makes a disposal otherwise than under a bargain at arm's length of an asset within subsection (2) below, and

(b) a claim for relief under this section is made by the transferor and the person who acquires the asset ("the transferee") or, where the trustees of a settlement are the transferee, by the transferor alone,

then, subject to subsection (3) and sections 166 and 167, subsection (4) below shall apply in relation to the disposal.

(2) An asset is within this subsection if—

(a) it is, or is an interest in, an asset used for the purposes of a trade, profession or vocation carried on by—

(i) the transferor, or

(ii) his family company, or

(iii) a member of a trading group of which the holding company is his family company, or

(b) it consists of shares or securities of a trading company, or of the holding company of a trading group, where—

(i) the shares or securities are neither quoted on a recognised stock exchange nor dealt in on the Unlisted Securities Market, or

(ii) the trading company or holding company is the transferor's family company.

(3) Subsection (4) below does not apply in relation to a disposal if—

(a) in the case of a disposal of an asset, any gain accruing to the transferor on the disposal is (apart from this section) wholly relieved under Schedule 6, or

(b) in the case of a disposal of shares or securities, the appropriate proportion determined under paragraph 7(2) or 8(2) of Schedule 6 of any gain accruing to the transferor on the disposal is (apart from this section) wholly relieved under that Schedule, or

(c) in the case of a disposal of qualifying corporate bonds, a gain is deemed to accrue by virtue of section 116(10)(b), or

(d) subsection (3) of section 260 applies in relation to the disposal (or would apply if a claim for relief were duly made under that section).

(4) Where a claim for relief is made under this section in respect of a disposal—

(a) the amount of any chargeable gain which, apart from this section, would accrue to the transferor on the disposal, and

(b) the amount of the consideration for which, apart from this section, the transferee would be regarded for the purposes of capital gains tax as having acquired the asset or, as the case may be, the shares or securities;

shall each be reduced by an amount equal to the held-over gain on the disposal.

(5) Part I of Schedule 7 shall have effect for extending the relief provided for by virtue of subsections (1) to (4) above in the case of agricultural property and for applying it in relation to settled property.

(6) Subject to Part II of Schedule 7 and subsection (7) below, the reference in subsection (4) above to the held-over gain on a disposal is a reference

to the chargeable gain which would have accrued on that disposal apart from subsection (4) above and (in appropriate cases) Schedule 6, and in subsection (7) below that chargeable gain is referred to as the unrelieved gain on the disposal.

(7) In any case where—

(a) there is actual consideration (as opposed to the consideration equal to the market value which is deemed to be given by virtue of section 17(1)) for a disposal in respect of which a claim for relief is made under this section, and

(b) that actual consideration exceeds the sums allowable as a deduction under section 38,

the held-over gain on the disposal shall be the amount by which the unrelieved gain on the disposal exceeds the excess referred to in paragraph (b) above.

(8) Subject to subsection (9) below, in this section and Schedule 7—

(a) "family company", "holding company", "trading company" and trading group" have the meanings given by paragraph 1 of Schedule 6, and

(b) "trade", "profession" and "vocation" have the same meaning as in the Income Tax Acts.

(9) In this section and Schedule 7 and in determining whether a company is a trading company for the purposes of this section and that Schedule, the expression "trade" shall be taken to include the occupation of woodlands where the woodlands are managed by the occupier on a commercial basis and with a view to the realisation of profits.

(10) Where a disposal after 13th March 1989, in respect of which a claim is made under this section, is (or proves to be) a chargeable transfer for inheritance tax purposes, there shall be allowed as a deduction in computing (for capital gains tax purposes) the chargeable gain accruing to the transferee on the disposal of the asset in question an amount equal to whichever is the lesser of—

(a) the inheritance tax attributable to the value of the asset, and

(b) the amount of the chargeable gain as computed apart from this subsection,

and, in the case of a disposal which, being a potentially exempt transfer, proves to be a chargeable transfer, all necessary adjustments shall be made, whether by the discharge or repayment of capital gains tax or otherwise.

(11) Where an amount of inheritance tax—

(a) falls to be redetermined in consequence of the transferor's death within seven years of making the chargeable transfer in question, or

(b) is otherwise varied,

after it has been taken into account under subsection (10) above, all necessary adjustments shall be made, whether by the making of an assessment to capital gains tax or by the discharge or repayment of such tax.

GENERAL NOTE

This relief was first introduced along with retirement relief in FA 1965, s.34, and was recast on its own by FA 1978, s.46, and consolidated into CGTA 1979, s.126. It became less significant when the general relief for gifts was introduced by FA 1980, s.79. When the general relief for gifts was abolished by FA 1989, s.124, this relief was recast by *ibid.*, Sched. 14, paras. 1–3, together with some anti-avoidance provisions which follow.

The relief applies where a disposal is made otherwise than under a bargain at arm's length and a claim is made by the transferor and the transferee, or by the transferor alone in the case of a transfer into a settlement. The assets covered are assets used for the purposes of a trade, profession or vocation carried on by the transferor, his family company (see Sched. 6, para. 1) or a member of a trading group of which the holding company is his family company (see *ibid.*). Similarly, shares of a trading company or of the holding company of a trading group are covered where they are neither quoted on the Stock Exchange nor dealt in on the USM or the company concerned is the transferor's family company.

Subs. (3)
The relief does not apply where relief is otherwise available, *i.e.* retirement relief, relief on corporate bonds and relief for gifts on which inheritance tax is payable.

Subs. (4)
Where a claim is made, the gain is held over and the transferee takes the assets at the transferor's base value.

Subss. (5) and (6)
These refer to detailed provisions in Sched. 7. See further the General Note to that Schedule.

Subs. (7)
Where there is actual consideration for the transfer and this exceeds the base cost under s.38, the excess reduces the held-over gain.

Subs. (8)
This refers to definitions.

Subs. (9)
This extends relief to commercial woodlands.

Subss. (10) and (11)
These deal with the interaction of C.G.T. and inheritance tax (I.H.T.) on a gift which is, or proves to be, a chargeable transfer for the purposes of I.H.T. Where the asset concerned is disposed of by the transferee, the chargeable gain is reduced by whichever is the lesser of the I.H.T. attributable to the asset and the chargeable gain as otherwise computed. Any necessary adjustment is made where the transferor makes a potentially exempt transfer and dies within seven years.

Gifts to non-residents

166.—(1) Section 165(4) shall not apply where the transferee is neither resident nor ordinarily resident in the United Kingdom.

(2) Section 165(4) shall not apply where the transferee is an individual or a company if that individual or company—

(a) though resident or ordinarily resident in the United Kingdom, is regarded for the purposes of any double taxation relief arrangements as resident in a territory outside the United Kingdom, and

(b) by virtue of the arrangements would not be liable in the United Kingdom to tax on a gain arising on a disposal of the asset occurring immediately after its acquisition.

GENERAL NOTE
The relief does not apply to gifts to non-residents, or dual residents under a tax treaty where a subsequent disposal would be protected by the treaty.

Gifts to foreign-controlled companies

167.—(1) Section 165(4) shall not apply where the transferee is a company which is within subsection (2) below.

(2) A company is within this subsection if it is controlled by a person who, or by persons each of whom—

(a) is neither resident nor ordinarily resident in the United Kingdom, and

(b) is connected with the person making the disposal.

(3) For the purposes of subsection (2) above, a person who (either alone or with others) controls a company by virtue of holding assets relating to that or any other company and who is resident or ordinarily resident in the United Kingdom shall be regarded as neither resident nor ordinarily resident there if—

(a) he is regarded for the purposes of any double taxation relief arrangements as resident in a territory outside the United Kingdom, and

(b) by virtue of the arrangements he would not be liable in the United Kingdom to tax on a gain arising on a disposal of the assets.

GENERAL NOTE

The relief does not apply to gifts to companies controlled by non-residents or persons connected with them. A person controlling a company by virtue of holding assets relating to the company is regarded as non-resident if he would be protected by a double tax treaty from U.K. tax on a disposal of the assets.

Emigration of donee

168.—(1) If—

(a) relief is given under section 165 in respect of a disposal to an individual or under section 260 in respect of a disposal to an individual ("the relevant disposal"); and

(b) at a time when he has not disposed of the asset in question, the transferee becomes neither resident nor ordinarily resident in the United Kingdom,

then, subject to the following provisions of this section, a chargeable gain shall be deemed to have accrued to the transferee immediately before that time, and its amount shall be equal to the held-over gain (within the meaning of section 165 or 260) on the relevant disposal.

(2) For the purposes of subsection (1) above the transferee shall be taken to have disposed of an asset before the time there referred to only if he has made a disposal or disposals in connection with which the whole of the held-over gain on the relevant disposal was represented by reductions made in accordance with section 165(4)(b) or 260(3)(b) and where he has made a disposal in connection with which part of that gain was so represented, the amount of the chargeable gain deemed by virtue of this section to accrue to him shall be correspondingly reduced.

(3) The disposals by the transferee that are to be taken into account under subsection (2) above shall not include any disposal to which section 58 applies; but where any such disposal is made by the transferee, disposals by his spouse shall be taken into account under subsection (2) above as if they had been made by him.

(4) Subsection (1) above shall not apply by reason of a person becoming neither resident nor ordinarily resident more than six years after the end of the year of assessment in which the relevant disposal was made.

(5) Subsection (1) above shall not apply in relation to a disposal made to an individual if—

(a) the reason for his becoming neither resident nor ordinarily resident in the United Kingdom is that he works in an employment or office all the duties of which are performed outside the United Kingdom, and

(b) he again becomes resident or ordinarily resident in the United Kingdom within the period of three years from the time when he ceases to be so, without having meanwhile disposed of the asset in question;

and accordingly no assessment shall be made by virtue of subsection (1) above before the end of that period in any case where the condition in paragraph (a) above is, and the condition in paragraph (b) above may be, satisfied.

(6) For the purposes of subsection (5) above a person shall be taken to have disposed of an asset if he has made a disposal in connection with which the whole or part of the held-over gain on the relevant disposal would, had he been resident in the United Kingdom, have been represented by a reduction made in accordance with section 165(4)(b) or 260(3)(b) and subsection (3) above shall have effect for the purposes of this subsection as it has effect for the purposes of subsection (2) above.

(7) Where an amount of tax assessed on a transferee by virtue of subsection (1) above is not paid within the period of 12 months beginning with the date when the tax becomes payable then, subject to subsection (8) below, the transferor may be assessed and charged (in the name of the transferee) to all or any part of that tax.

(8) No assessment shall be made under subsection (7) above more than six years after the end of the year of assessment in which the relevant disposal was made.

(9) Where the transferor pays an amount of tax in pursuance of subsection (7) above, he shall be entitled to recover a corresponding sum from the transferee.

(10) Gains on disposals made after a chargeable gain has under this section been deemed to accrue by reference to a held-over gain shall be computed without any reduction under section 165(4)(b) or 260(3)(b) in respect of that held-over gain.

GENERAL NOTE

This section, originally introduced by FA 1981, s.79, was designed to prevent abuse of the general relief for gifts. It now applies to cases where relief has been given under ss.165 or 270, and the donee subsequently becomes non-resident. In such a case the held-over gain is deemed to accrue to the donee prior to his emigration. The mischief of the section disappears after six years and it does not apply if the donee goes to work overseas and comes back within three years without having disposed of the asset.

Where a donee does not pay the tax due under this section within a year, then it may be assessed on the donor up to six years after the donee emigrates. The donor has a right of recovery against the donee.

The held-over gain is ignored for the purposes of a charge under this section.

Gifts into dual resident trusts

169.—(1) This section applies where there is or has been a disposal of an asset to the trustees of a settlement in such circumstances that, on a claim for relief, section 165 or 260 applies, or would but for this section apply, so as to reduce the amounts of the chargeable gain and the consideration referred to in section 165(4) or 260(3).

(2) In this section "a relevant disposal" means such a disposal as is referred to in subsection (1) above.

(3) Relief under section 165 or 260 shall not be available on a relevant disposal if—

(a) at the material time the trustees to whom the disposal is made fall to be treated, under section 69, as resident and ordinarily resident in the United Kingdom, although the general administration of the trust is ordinarily carried on outside the United Kingdom; and

(b) on a notional disposal of the asset concerned occurring immediately after the material time, the trustees would be regarded for the purposes of any double taxation relief arrangements—

(i) as resident in a territory outside the United Kingdom; and

(ii) as not liable in the United Kingdom to tax on a gain arising on that disposal.

(4) In subsection (3) above—

(a) "the material time" means the time of the relevant disposal; and

(b) a "notional disposal" means a disposal by the trustees of the asset which was the subject of the relevant disposal.

GENERAL NOTE

This section, originally introduced by FA 1986, s.58, debars relief where an asset has been disposed of to trustees who are treated as resident in the U.K. for the purposes of s.69 of this Act but are treated as non-resident for the purposes of a double tax treaty and so not liable to C.G.T.

PART VI

COMPANIES, OIL, INSURANCE ETC.

CHAPTER I

COMPANIES

Groups of companies

Interpretation of sections 171 to 181

170.—(1) This section has effect for the interpretation of sections 171 to 181 except in so far as the context otherwise requires, and in those sections—
  (a) "profits" means income and chargeable gains, and
  (b) "trade" includes "vocation", and includes also an office or employment.
Until 6th April 1993 paragraph (b) shall have effect with the addition at the end of the words "or the occupation of woodlands in any context in which the expression is applied to that in the Income Tax Acts".
  (2) Except as otherwise provided—
  (a) references to a company apply only to a company, as that expression is limited by subsection (9) below, which is resident in the United Kingdom;
  (b) subsections (3) to (6) below apply to determine whether companies form a group and, where they do, which is the principal company of the group;
  (c) in applying the definition of "75 per cent. subsidiary" in section 838 of the Taxes Act any share capital of a registered industrial and provident society shall be treated as ordinary share capital; and
  (d) "group" and "subsidiary" shall be construed with any necessary modifications where applied to a company incorporated under the law of a country outside the United Kingdom.
  (3) Subject to subsections (4) to (6) below—
  (a) a company (referred to below and in sections 171 to 181 as the "principal company of the group") and all its 75 per cent. subsidiaries form a group and, if any of those subsidiaries have 75 per cent. subsidiaries, the group includes them and their 75 per cent. subsidiaries, and so on, but
  (b) a group does not include any company (other than the principal company of the group) that is not an effective 51 per cent. subsidiary of the principal company of the group.
  (4) A company cannot be the principal company of a group if it is itself a 75 per cent. subsidiary of another company.
  (5) Where a company ("the subsidiary") is a 75 per cent. subsidiary of another company but those companies are prevented from being members of the same group by subsection (3)(b) above, the subsidiary may, where the requirements of subsection (3) above are satisfied, itself be the principal company of another group notwithstanding subsection (4) above unless this subsection enables a further company to be the principal company of a group of which the subsidiary would be a member.
  (6) A company cannot be a member of more than one group; but where, apart from this subsection, a company would be a member of two or more groups (the principal company of each group being referred to below as the "head of a group"), it is a member only of that group, if any, of which it would be a member under one of the following tests (applying earlier tests in preference to later tests)—
  (a) it is a member of the group it would be a member of if, in applying subsection (3)(b) above, there were left out of account any amount to

which a head of a group is or would be beneficially entitled of any profits available for distribution to equity holders of a head of another group or of any assets of a head of another group available for distribution to its equity holders on a winding-up,

(b) it is a member of the group the head of which is beneficially entitled to a percentage of profits available for distribution to equity holders of the company that is greater than the percentage of those profits to which any other head of a group is so entitled,

(c) it is a member of the group the head of which would be beneficially entitled to a percentage of any assets of the company available for distribution to its equity holders on a winding-up that is greater than the percentage of those assets to which any other head of a group would be so entitled,

(d) it is a member of the group the head of which owns directly or indirectly a percentage of the company's ordinary share capital that is greater than the percentage of that capital owned directly or indirectly by any other head of a group (interpreting this paragraph as if it were included in section 838(1)(a) of the Taxes Act).

(7) For the purposes of this section and sections 171 to 181, a company ("the subsidiary") is an effective 51 per cent. subsidiary of another company ("the parent") at any time if and only if—

(a) the parent is beneficially entitled to more than 50 per cent. of any profits available for distribution to equity holders of the subsidiary; and

(b) the parent would be beneficially entitled to more than 50 per cent. of any assets of the subsidiary available for distribution to its equity holders on a winding-up.

(8) Schedule 18 to the Taxes Act (group relief: equity holders and profits or assets available for distribution) shall apply for the purposes of subsections (6) and (7) above as if the references to subsection (7), or subsections (7) to (9), of section 413 of that Act were references to subsections (6) and (7) above and as if, in paragraph 1(4), the words from "but" to the end and paragraphs 5(3) and 7(1)(b) were omitted.

(9) For the purposes of this section and sections 171 to 181, references to a company apply only to—

(a) a company within the meaning of the Companies Act 1985 or the corresponding enactment in Northern Ireland, and

(b) a company which is constituted under any other Act or a Royal Charter or letters patent or (although resident in the United Kingdom) is formed under the law of a country or territory outside the United Kingdom, and

(c) a registered industrial and provident society within the meaning of section 486 of the Taxes Act; and

(d) a building society.

(10) For the purposes of this section and sections 171 to 181, a group remains the same group so long as the same company remains the principal company of the group, and if at any time the principal company of a group becomes a member of another group, the first group and the other group shall be regarded as the same, and the question whether or not a company has ceased to be a member of a group shall be determined accordingly.

(11) For the purposes of this section and sections 171 to 181, the passing of a resolution or the making of an order, or any other act, for the winding-up of a member of a group of companies shall not be regarded as the occasion of that or any other company ceasing to be a member of the group.

(12) Sections 171 to 181, except in so far as they relate to recovery of tax, shall also have effect in relation to bodies from time to time established by or under any enactment for the carrying on of any industry or part of an industry, or of any undertaking, under national ownership or control as if

they were companies within the meaning of those sections, and as if any such bodies charged with related functions (and in particular the Boards and Holding Company established under the Transport Act 1962 and the new authorities within the meaning of the Transport Act 1968 established under that Act of 1968) and subsidiaries of any of them formed a group, and as if also any two or more such bodies charged at different times with the same or related functions were members of a group.

(13) Subsection (12) shall have effect subject to any enactment by virtue of which property, rights, liabilities or activities of one such body fall to be treated for corporation tax as those of another, including in particular any such enactment in Chapter VI of Part XII of the Taxes Act.

(14) Sections 171 to 181, except in so far as they relate to recovery of tax, shall also have effect in relation to the Executive for a designated area within the meaning of section 9(1) of the Transport Act 1968 as if that Executive were a company within the meaning of those sections.

GENERAL NOTE

This fasciculus of sections, ss.170–181, is consolidated from ICTA 1970. Its purpose is to ensure that disposals of assets within a group of companies are treated broadly on a fiscally neutral basis, while preventing the use of this for tax avoidance.

Section 170 provides the essential definitions for the purposes of the succeeding sections. It should be noted that they apply only to U.K. resident companies. The general rule is that a company and all its 75 per cent. subsidiaries form a group and this can extend to 75 per cent. subsidiaries of 75 per cent. subsidiaries and so on. However, this is subject to the limitation that no company which is not "an effective 51 per cent. subsidiary" of the top company can be a member of the group, and a top company cannot itself be a 75 per cent. subsidiary. The latter rule may be superseded where the 51 per cent. rule prevents a 75 per cent. subsidiary and its parent from being members of the same group, unless it would allow a further company to be a top company.

Subs. (6)

This provides a series of "tie-breaks" for determining which group a company belongs to when there is a possible choice. The tests, in order of application, are the 51 per cent. rule, entitlement to profits, entitlement to assets on a winding-up, and percentage ownership of ordinary share capital.

Subs. (7)

This defines an effective 51 per cent. subsidiary in terms of entitlement to more than 50 per cent. of the profits and 50 per cent. of the assets on a winding-up.

Subs. (8)

This applies, *mutatis mutandis*, provisions of ICTA 1988 directed against the formation of artificial groups. For the operation of these provisions, see *J. Sainsbury* v. *O'Connor* (*Inspector of Taxes*) [1991] S.T.C. 318, C.A.

Subs. (9)

The provisions apply only to legally constituted companies, registered industrial and provident societies and building societies.

Subs. (10)

Groups can be amalgamated if the top company becomes a member of another group.

Subs. (11)

A winding-up does not make a company cease to be a member of a group.

Subss. (12)–(14)

The provisions also apply to nationalised industries and similar bodies, subject to specific rules in the ICTA 1988 relating to such bodies as the Electricity Council, the Atomic Energy Authority and the British Airways Board (ss.511–513).

The provisions regarding transfers within groups were used to avoid tax through the use of "envelope" companies (see, *e.g. Burman* v. *Hedges & Butler* [1979] 1 W.L.R. 160), but anti-avoidance provisions have now been introduced, both in these sections and in those dealing with value-shifting (ss.29–34, *supra*).

Transactions within groups

Transfers within a group: general provisions

171.—(1) Notwithstanding any provision in this Act fixing the amount of the consideration deemed to be received on a disposal or given on an acquisition, where a member of a group of companies disposes of an asset to another member of the group, both members shall, except as provided by subsections (2) and (3) below, be treated, so far as relates to corporation tax on chargeable gains, as if the asset acquired by the member to whom the disposal is made were acquired for a consideration of such amount as would secure that on the other's disposal neither a gain nor a loss would accrue to that other; but where it is assumed for any purpose that a member of a group of companies has sold or acquired an asset, it shall be assumed also that it was not a sale to or acquisition from another member of the group.

(2) Subsection (1) above shall not apply where the disposal is—

(a) a disposal of a debt due from a member of a group of companies effected by satisfying the debt or part of it; or

(b) a disposal of redeemable shares in a company on the occasion of their redemption; or

(c) a disposal by or to an investment trust; or

(d) a disposal to a dual resident investing company; or

(e) a disposal to a company which, though resident in the United Kingdom—

(i) is regarded for the purposes of any double taxation relief arrangements as resident in a territory outside the United Kingdom, and

(ii) by virtue of the arrangements would not be liable in the United Kingdom to tax on a gain arising on a disposal of the asset occurring immediately after its acquisition;

and the reference in subsection (1) above to a member of a group of companies disposing of an asset shall not apply to anything which under section 122 is to be treated as a disposal of an interest in shares in a company in consideration for a capital distribution (as defined in that section) from that company, whether or not involving a reduction of capital.

(3) Subsection (1) above shall not apply to a transaction treated by virtue of sections 127 and 135 as not involving a disposal by the company first mentioned in that subsection.

(4) For the purposes of subsection (1) above, so far as the consideration for the disposal consists of money or money's worth by way of compensation for any kind of damage or injury to assets, or for the destruction or dissipation of assets or for anything which depreciates or might depreciate an asset, the disposal shall be treated as being to the person who, whether as an insurer or otherwise, ultimately bears the burden of furnishing that consideration.

GENERAL NOTE

Subs. (1)
The general rule is that disposals of assets within a group of companies are treated on a no-gain/no-loss basis.

Subs. (2)
This provides exceptions to the rule in the circumstances mentioned.

Subs. (3)
This was passed to reverse the decision in *Westcott (Inspector of Taxes)* v. *Woolcombers* [1987] S.T.C. 600 and excludes the section in cases involving company reorganisation under ss.127 and 135.

Subs. (4)
Where the consideration for the disposal consists of compensation, the disposal is treated as being to the person who ultimately provides it, *e.g.* an insurer.

Transfer of United Kingdom branch or agency

172.—(1) Subject to subsections (3) and (4) below, subsection (2) below applies for the purposes of corporation tax on chargeable gains where—
  (a) there is a scheme for the transfer by a company ("company A")—
      (i) which is not resident in the United Kingdom, but
      (ii) which carries on a trade in the United Kingdom through a branch or agency,
    of the whole or part of the trade to a company resident in the United Kingdom ("company B"),
  (b) company A disposes of an asset to company B in accordance with the scheme at a time when the two companies are members of the same group, and
  (c) a claim in relation to the asset is made by the two companies within two years after the end of the accounting period of company B during which the disposal is made.
  (2) Where this subsection applies—
  (a) company A and company B shall be treated as if the asset were acquired by company B for a consideration of such amount as would secure that neither a gain nor a loss would accrue to company A on the disposal, and
  (b) section 25(3) shall not apply to the asset by reason of the transfer.
  (3) Subsection (2) above does not apply where—
  (a) company B, though resident in the United Kingdom,—
      (i) is regarded for the purposes of any double taxation relief arrangements as resident in a territory outside the United Kingdom, and
      (ii) by virtue of the arrangements would not be liable in the United Kingdom to tax on a gain arising on a disposal of the asset occurring immediately after its acquisition, or
  (b) company B is either a dual resident investing company or an investment trust.
  (4) Subsection (2) above shall not apply unless any gain accruing to company A—
  (a) on the disposal of the asset in accordance with the scheme, or
  (b) where that disposal occurs after the transfer has taken place, on a disposal of the asset immediately before the transfer,
would be a chargeable gain and would, by virtue of section 10(3), form part of its profits for corporation tax purposes.
  (5) In this section "company" and "group" have the meanings which would be given by section 170 if subsections (2)(a) and (9) of that section were omitted.

GENERAL NOTE
This section, introduced by FA 1990, s.70, gives relief where a non-resident company transfers a trade carried on in the U.K. through a branch or agency to a U.K. resident company. Previously such a transaction would have attracted a charge under ss.10 or 25. On a claim being made within two years by both companies, the transfer is treated as being made on a no-gain/no-loss basis. The general conditions for relief under s.171 apply.

Transfers within a group: trading stock

173.—(1) Where a member of a group of companies acquires an asset as trading stock from another member of the group, and the asset did not form part of the trading stock of any trade carried on by the other member, the member acquiring it shall be treated for purposes of section 161 as having acquired the asset otherwise than as trading stock and immediately appropriated it for the purposes of the trade as trading stock.

(2) Where a member of a group of companies disposes of an asset to another member of the group, and the asset formed part of the trading stock of a trade carried on by the member disposing of it but is acquired by the other member otherwise than as trading stock of a trade carried on by it, the member disposing of the asset shall be treated for purposes of section 161 as having immediately before the disposal appropriated the asset for some purpose other than the purpose of use as trading stock.

GENERAL NOTE

Where a member of a group of companies acquires an asset from another member as trading stock and it was not trading stock of that other member, it is treated as having been acquired other than as trading stock. In such a case the asset would be deemed to be transferred to trading stock at market value (*Sharkey* v. *Wernher* [1956] A.C. 58 H.L.).

Where the converse situation applies, *i.e.* trading stock is acquired otherwise than as trading stock, then there is a deemed appropriation immediately before the disposal. In *Coates (Inspector of Taxes)* v. *Arndale Properties*; *Reed (Inspector of Taxes)* v. *Nova Securities* [1984] 1 W.L.R 1328 it was held that this provision did not operate because of the fiscal motive.

Disposal or acquisition outside a group

174.—(1) Where there is a disposal of an asset acquired in relevant circumstances, section 41 shall apply in relation to capital allowances made to the person from which it was acquired (so far as not taken into account in relation to a disposal of the asset by that person), and so on as respects previous transfers of the asset in relevant circumstances.

(2) In subsection (1) above "relevant circumstances" means circumstances in which section 171 or 172 applied or in which section 171 would have applied but for subsection (2) of that section.

(3) Subsection (1) above shall not be taken as affecting the consideration for which an asset is deemed under section 171 or 172 to be acquired.

(4) Schedule 2 shall apply in relation to a disposal of an asset by a company which is or has been a member of a group of companies, and which acquired the asset from another member of the group at a time when both were members of the group, as if all members of the group for the time being were the same person, and as if the acquisition or provision of the asset by the group, so taken as a single person, had been the acquisition or provision of it by the member disposing of it.

(5) Subsection (4) above does not apply where the asset was acquired on a disposal within section 171(2)(c).

GENERAL NOTE

Where an asset has been transferred within a group and is subsequently disposed of outside the group at a loss, the amount of the loss is diminished by the expenditure on the asset for which capital allowances have been given within the group.

For the interaction of subs. (4) with other provisions, see *Innocent (Inspector of Taxes)* v. *Whaddon Estates* [1982] S.T.C. 115.

Replacement of business assets by members of a group

175.—(1) Subject to subsection (2) below, for the purposes of sections 152 to 158 all the trades carried on by members of a group of companies shall, for the purposes of corporation tax on chargeable gains, be treated as a single trade (unless it is a case of one member of the group acquiring, or acquiring the interest in, the new assets from another or disposing of, or of the interest in, the old assets to another).

(2) Subsection (1) above does not apply where so much of the consideration for the disposal of the old assets as is applied in acquiring the new assets or the interest in them is so applied by a member of the group which is a dual

resident investing company or a company which, though resident in the United Kingdom—

(a) is regarded for the purposes of any double taxation relief arrange-ments as resident in a territory outside the United Kingdom, and

(b) by virtue of the arrangements would not be liable in the United Kingdom to tax on a gain arising on a disposal of, or of the interest in, the new assets occurring immediately after the acquisition;

and in this subsection "the old assets" and "the new assets" have the same meanings as in section 152.

(3) Section 154(2) shall apply where the company making the claim is a member of a group of companies as if all members of the group for the time being were the same person (and, in accordance with subsection (1) above, as if all trades carried on by members were the same trade) and so that the gain shall accrue to the member of the group holding the asset concerned on the occurrance of the event mentioned in section 154(2).

(4) Subsection (2) above shall apply where the acquisition took place before 20th March 1990 and the disposal takes place within the period of 12 months beginning with the date of the acquisition or such longer period as the Board may by notice allow with the omission of the words from "or a company" to "the acquisition".

GENERAL NOTE

For the purposes of roll-over relief on replacement of business assets, all the trades carried on by the members of a group are treated as a single trade, except in the case of an intra-group disposal.

This is excluded in the case of a dual resident investing company (see ICTA 1988, s.404) or a dual resident company under the terms of a double tax treaty the gains of which would be protected from U.K. tax under the terms of the treaty.

All members of a group are treated as one for the purposes of s.154(2), which restricts roll-over into depreciating assets.

Losses attributable to depreciatory transactions

Depreciatory transactions within a group

176.—(1) This section has effect as respects a disposal of shares in, or securities of, a company ("the ultimate disposal") if the value of the shares or securities has been materially reduced by a depreciatory transaction effected on or after 31st March 1982; and for this purpose "depreciatory transaction" means—

(a) any disposal of assets at other than market value by one member of a group of companies to another, or

(b) any other transaction satisfying the conditions of subsection (2) below,

except that a transaction shall not be treated as a depreciatory transaction to the extent that it consists of a payment which is required to be or has been brought into account, for the purposes of corporation tax on chargeable gains, in computing a chargeable gain or allowable loss accruing to the person making the ultimate disposal.

(2) The conditions referred to in subsection (1)(b) above are—

(a) that the company, the shares in which, or securities of which, are the subject of the ultimate disposal, or any 75 per cent. subsidiary of that company, was a party to the transaction, and

(b) that the parties to the transaction were or included two or more companies which at the time of the transaction were members of the same group of companies.

(3) Without prejudice to the generality of subsection (1) above, the cancellation of any shares in or securities of one member of a group of companies under section 135 of the Companies Act 1985 shall, to the extent that immediately before the cancellation those shares or securities were the

property of another member of the group, be taken to be a transaction fulfilling the conditions in subsection (2) above.

(4) If the person making the ultimate disposal is, or has at any time been, a member of the group of companies referred to in subsection (1) or (2) above, any allowable loss accruing on the disposal shall be reduced to such extent as appears to the inspector, or, on appeal, the Commissioners concerned, to be just and reasonable having regard to the depreciatory transaction, but if the person making the ultimate disposal is not a member of that group when he disposes of the shares or securities, no reduction of the loss shall be made by reference to a depreciatory transaction which took place when that person was not a member of that group.

(5) The inspector or the Commissioners shall make the decision under subsection (4) above on the footing that the allowable loss ought not to reflect any diminution in the value of the company's assets which was attributable to a depreciatory transaction, but allowance may be made for any other transaction on or after 31st March 1982 which has enhanced the value of company's assets and depreciated the value of the assets of any other member of the group.

(6) If, under subsection (4) above, a reduction is made in an allowable loss, any chargeable gain accruing on a disposal of the shares or securities of any other company which was a party to the depreciatory transaction by reference to which the reduction was made, being a disposal not later than six years after the depreciatory transaction, shall be reduced to such extent as appears to the inspector, or, on appeal, the Commissioners concerned, to be just and reasonable having regard to the effect of the depreciatory transaction on the value of those shares or securities at the time of their disposal, but the total amount of any one or more reductions in chargeable gains made by reference to a depreciatory transaction shall not exceed the amount of the reductions in allowable losses made by reference to that depreciatory transaction.

All such adjustment, whether by way of discharge or repayment of tax, or otherwise, as are required to give effect to the provisions of this subsection may be made at any time.

(7) For the purposes of this section—

(a) "securities" includes any loan stock or similar security whether secured or unsecured,

(b) references to the disposal of assets include references to any method by which one company which is a member of a group appropriates the goodwill of another member of the group, and

(c) a "group of companies" may consist of companies some or all of which are not resident in the United Kingdom.

(8) References in this section to the disposal of shares or securities include references to the occasion of the making of a claim under section 24(2) that the value of shares or securities has become negligible, and references to a person making a disposal shall be construed accordingly.

(9) In any case where the ultimate disposal is not one to which section 35(2) applies, the references above to 31st March 1982 shall be read as references to 6th April 1965.

GENERAL NOTE

This is an anti-avoidance provision to prevent the creation of artificial losses using intra-group transactions. The situation envisaged is where assets are transferred at an undervalue between group companies and there is then a disposal (or cancellation) of shares, throwing up an apparent loss. The book loss may be reduced on a just and reasonable basis. If there have been other similar transactions in the opposite direction, these may be taken into account. Where a gain is subsequently realised within six years by another company which was a party to the depreciating transaction, this may be reduced by not more than the loss previously disallowed.

The section was originally based on April 6, 1965, but the relevant date in most cases now will be March 31, 1982.

Dividend stripping

177.—(1) The provisions of this section apply where one company ("the first company") has a holding in another company ("the second company") and the following conditions are fulfilled—

(a) that the holding amounts to, or is an ingredient in a holding amounting to, 10 per cent. of all holdings of the same class in the second company,

(b) that the first company is not a dealing company in relation to the holding,

(c) that a distribution is or has been made to the first company in respect of the holding, and

(d) that the effect of the distribution is that the value of the holding is or has been materially reduced.

(2) Where this section applies in relation to a holding, section 176 shall apply, subject to subsection (3) below, in relation to any disposal of any shares or securities comprised in the holding, whether the disposal is by the first company or by any other company to which the holding is transferred by a transfer to which section 171 or 172 applies, as if the distribution were a depreciatory transaction and, if the companies concerned are not members of a group of companies, as if they were.

(3) The distribution shall not be treated as a depreciatory transaction to the extent that it consists of a payment which is required to be or has been brought into account, for the purposes of corporation tax on chargeable gains, in computing a chargeable gain or allowable loss accruing to the person making the ultimate disposal.

(4) This section shall be construed as one with section 176, and in any case where the ultimate disposal is not one to which section 35(2) applies, the reference in subsection (1)(c) above to a distribution does not include a distribution made before 30th April 1969.

(5) For the purposes of this section a company is "a dealing company" in relation to a holding if a profit on the sale of the holding would be taken into account in computing the company's trading profits.

(6) References in this section to a holding in a company refer to a holding of shares or securities by virtue of which the holder may receive distributions made by the company, but so that—

(a) a company's holdings of different classes in another company shall be treated as separate holdings, and

(b) holdings of securities which differ in the entitlements or obligations they confer or impose shall be regarded as holdings of different classes.

(7) For the purposes of subsection (1) above—

(a) all a company's holdings of the same class in another company are to be treated as ingredients constituting a single holding, and

(b) a company's holding of a particular class shall be treated as an ingredient in a holding amounting to 10 per cent. of all holdings of that class if the aggregate of that holding and other holdings of that class held by connected persons amounts to 10 per cent. of all holdings of that class,

and section 286 shall have effect in relation to paragraph (b) above as if, in subsection (7) of that section, after the words "or exercise control of" in each place where they occur there were inserted the words "or to acquire a holding in".

GENERAL NOTE

This section applies where one company (and persons connected with it) holds at least 10 per cent. of another company otherwise than as dealing stock, receives a dividend from it and then realises a loss on a disposal of the shares. Such a disposal may be treated in the same way as a depreciatory transaction under s.176. A distribution which is brought into account in computing a gain or loss is not caught by the section.

Companies leaving groups

Company ceasing to be member of group: pre-appointed day cases

178.—(1) If a company ("the chargeable company") ceases to be a member of a group of companies, this section shall have effect as respects any asset which the chargeable company acquired from another company which was at the time of acquisition a member of that group of companies, but only if the time of acquisition fell within the period of six years ending with the time when the company ceases to be a member of the group; and references in this section to a company ceasing to be a member of a group of companies do not apply to cases where a company ceases to be a member of a group by being wound up or dissolved or in consequence of another member of the group being wound up or dissolved.

(2) Where two or more associated companies cease to be members of the group at the same time, subsection (1) above shall not have effect as respects an acquisition by one from another of those associated companies.

(3) If, when the chargeable company ceases to be a member of the group, the chargeable company, or an associated company also leaving the group, owns, otherwise than as trading stock—

(a) the asset, or
(b) property to which a chargeable gain has been carried forward from the asset on a replacement of business assets,

the chargeable company shall be treated for all the purposes of this Act as if immediately after its acquisition of the asset it had sold, and immediately reacquired, the asset at market value at that time.

(4) Where, apart from subsection (5) below, a company ceasing to be a member of a group by reason only of the fact that the principal company of the group becomes a member of another group would be treated by virtue of subsection (3) above as selling an asset at any time, subsections (5) and (6) below shall apply.

(5) The company in question shall not be treated as selling the asset at that time; but if—

(a) within six years of that time the company in question ceases at any time ("the relevant time") to satisfy the following conditions, and
(b) at the relevant time, the company in question, or a company in the same group as that company, owns otherwise than as trading stock the asset or property to which a chargeable gain has been carried forward from the asset on a replacement of business assets,

the company in question shall be treated for all the purposes of this Act as if, immediately after its acquisition of the asset, it had sold and immediately reacquired the asset at the value that, at the time of acquisition, was its market value.

(6) Those conditions are—

(a) that the company is a 75 per cent. subsidiary of one or more members of the other group referred to in subsection (4) above, and
(b) that the company is an effective 51 per cent. subsidiary of one or more of those members.

(7) Where—

(a) by virtue of this section a company is treated as having sold an asset at any time, and
(b) if at that time the company had in fact sold the asset at market value at that time, then, by virtue of section 30, any allowable loss or charge-

able gain accruing on the disposal would have been calculated as if the consideration for the disposal were increased by an amount,
subsections (3) and (5) above shall have effect as if the market value at that time had been that amount greater.

(8) For the purposes of this section—

(a) two or more companies are associated companies if, by themselves, they would form a group of companies,

(b) a chargeable gain is carried forward from an asset to other property on a replacement of business assets if, by one or more claims under sections 152 to 158, the chargeable gain accruing on a disposal of the asset is reduced, and as a result an amount falls to be deducted from the expenditure allowable in computing a gain accruing on the disposal of the other property,

(c) an asset acquired by the chargeable company shall be treated as the same as an asset owned at a later time by that company or an associated company if the value of the second asset is derived in whole or in part from the first asset, and in particular where the second asset is a freehold, and the first asset was a leasehold and the lessee has acquired the reversion.

(9) If any of the corporation tax assessed on a company in consequence of this section is not paid within six months from the date when it becomes payable then—

(a) a company which on that date, or immediately after the chargeable company ceased to be a member of the group, was the principal company of the group, and

(b) a company which owned the asset on that date, or when the chargeable company ceased to be a member of the group,

may, at any time within two years from the time when the tax became payable, be assessed and charged (in the name of the chargeable company) to all or any part of that tax; and a company paying any amount of tax under this section shall be entitled to recover a sum of that amount from the chargeable company.

(10) Notwithstanding any limitation on the time for making assessments, an assessment to corporation tax chargeable in consequence of this section may be made at any time within six years from the time when the chargeable company ceased to be a member of the group, and where under this section the chargeable company is to be treated as having disposed of, and reacquired, an asset, all such recomputations of liability in respect of other disposals, and all such adjustments of tax, whether by way of assessment or by way of discharge or repayment of tax, as may be required in consequence of the provisions of this section shall be carried out.

GENERAL NOTE

This section, together with the following three sections, deals with the situation where a company leaves a group within six years of having acquired an asset from another member of the group. In such a case, it is treated as having disposed of the asset at market value at that time.

The structure of ss.178–180 takes account of two changes in the law, one already in force and one prospective. The first was the introduction of a new definition for groups of companies, effective from March 14, 1989, by FA 1989, s.138. The second is the introduction of new machinery for the collection of corporation tax, known as Pay and File, by F(No. 2)A 1987, ss.82–88, 90, 91, 95 and Sched. 6, from a day to be appointed by the Treasury. This is now expected to be October 1, 1993.

Section 178 has effect from the coming into force of this Act, April 5, 1992, but will be replaced by s.179 when Pay and File comes into force.

For the definitions governing "75 per cent. subsidiary" and "effective 51 per cent. subsidiary", see s.170 and the Note thereto.

The charge is carried over to new assets on the acquisition of which roll-over relief has been obtained and to an asset which derives its value from the asset transferred, *e.g.* where a lease is transferred and the reversion is subsequently obtained.

There are provisions for collecting the tax due from other companies involved, with a right to reimbursement from the chargeable company.

Company ceasing to be member of group: post-appointed day cases

179.—(1) If a company ("the chargeable company") ceases to be a member of a group of companies, this section shall have effect as respects any asset which the chargeable company acquired from another company which was at the time of acquisition a member of that group of companies, but only if the time of acquisition fell within the period of six years ending with the time when the company ceases to be a member of the group; and references in this section to a company ceasing to be a member of a group of companies do not apply to cases where a company ceases to be a member of a group by being wound up or dissolved or in consequence of another member of the group being wound up or dissolved.

(2) Where two or more associated companies cease to be members of the group at the same time, subsection (1) above shall not have effect as respects an acquisition by one from another of those associated companies.

(3) If, when the chargeable company ceases to be a member of the group, the chargeable company, or an associated company also leaving the group, owns, otherwise than as trading stock—

    (a) the asset, or

    (b) property to which a chargeable gain has been carried forward from the asset on a replacement of business assets,

then, subject to subsection (4) below, the chargeable company shall be treated for all the purposes of this Act as if immediately after its acquisition of the asset it had sold, and immediately reacquired, the asset at market value at that time.

(4) Any chargeable gain or allowable loss which, apart from this subsection, would accrue to the chargeable company on the sale referred to in subsection (3) above shall be treated as accruing to the chargeable company as follows—

    (a) for the purposes for which the assumptions in section 409(2) of the Taxes Act (group relief) apply, it shall be assumed to accrue in the notional or actual accounting period which ends when the company ceases to be a member of the group; and

    (b) subject to paragraph (a) above, it shall be treated as accruing immediately before the company ceases to be a member of the group.

(5) Where, apart from subsection (6) below, a company ceasing to be a member of a group by reason only of the fact that the principal company of the group becomes a member of another group would be treated by virtue of subsection (3) above as selling an asset at any time, subsections (6) to (8) below shall apply.

(6) The company in question shall not be treated as selling the asset at that time; but if—

    (a) within six years of that time the company in question ceases at any time ("the relevant time") to satisfy the following conditions, and

    (b) at the relevant time, the company in question, or a company in the same group as that company, owns otherwise than as trading stock the asset or property to which a chargeable gain has been carried forward from the asset on a replacement of business assets,

the company in question shall be treated for all the purposes of this Act as if, immediately after its acquisition of the asset, it had sold and immediately reacquired the asset at the value that, at the time of acquisition, was its market value.

(7) Those conditions are—

    (a) that the company is a 75 per cent. subsidiary of one or more members of the other group referred to in subsection (5) above, and

    (b) that the company is an effective 51 per cent. subsidiary of one or more of those members.

(8) Any chargeable gain or allowable loss accruing to the company on that sale shall be treated as accruing at the relevant time.

(9) Where—

(a) by virtue of this section a company is treated as having sold an asset at any time, and

(b) if at that time the company had in fact sold the asset at market value at that time, then, by virtue of section 30, any allowable loss or chargeable gain accruing on the disposal would have been calculated as if the consideration for the disposal were increased by an amount,

subsections (3) and (6) above shall have effect as if the market value at that time had been that amount greater.

(10) For the purposes of this section—

(a) two or more companies are associated companies if, by themselves, they would form a group of companies,

(b) a chargeable gain is carried forward from an asset to other property on a replacement of business assets if, by one or more claims under sections 152 to 158, the chargeable gain accruing on a disposal of the asset is reduced, and as a result an amount falls to be deducted from the expenditure allowable in computing a gain accruing on the disposal of the other property,

(c) an asset acquired by the chargeable company shall be treated as the same as an asset owned at a later time by that company or an associated company if the value of the second asset is derived in whole or in part from the first asset, and in particular where the second asset is a freehold, and the first asset was a leasehold and the lessee has acquired the reversion.

(11) If any corporation tax assessed on a company in consequence of this section is not paid within six months from the date determined under subsection (12) below, then—

(a) a company which on that date, or immediately after the chargeable company ceased to be a member of the group, was the principal company of the group, and

(b) a company which owned the asset on that date, or when the chargeable company ceased to be a member of the group,

may, at any time within two years from the date so determined, be assessed and charged (in the name of the chargeable company) to all or any part of that tax; and a company paying any amount of tax under this subsection shall be entitled to recover from the chargeable company a sum of that amount together with any interest paid by the company concerned under section 87A of the Management Act on that amount.

(12) The date referred to in subsection (11) above is whichever is the later of—

(a) the date when the tax becomes due and payable by the company; and

(b) the date when the assessment was made on the chargeable company.

(13) Where under this section the chargeable company is to be treated as having disposed of, and reacquired, an asset, all such recomputations of liability in respect of other disposals, and all such adjustments of tax, whether by way of assessment or by way of discharge or repayment of tax, as may be required in consequence of the provisions of this section shall be carried out.

GENERAL NOTE

This section closely mirrors s.178, with necessary changes to reflect the change in administration of corporation tax on the introduction of the "Pay and File" system, expected on October 1, 1993.

Transitional provisions

180.—(1) Subject to the following provisions of this section—

(a) section 178 has effect where the chargeable company referred to in section 178(4) ceases to be a member of the group in an accounting period beginning after 5th April 1992, but shall not apply where section 179 has effect, and

(b) section 179 has effect where the accounting period in which the chargeable company referred to in section 179(5) ceases to be a member of the group ends after such day as the Treasury by order appoint,

and in any case where section 178 or section 179 has effect in respect of tax for any accounting period, that section shall also have effect in respect of tax for earlier accounting periods, to the exclusion of the corresponding enactments repealed by this Act.

(2) Subject to subsection (1) above—

(a) section 178(5) to (7) apply where a company which apart from section 278(3C) of the Income and Corporation Taxes Act 1970 would by virtue of subsection (3) of that section have been treated as selling an asset (unless it has already been treated, by virtue of section 278(3C), as if it had sold the asset in question), and

(b) section 179(6) to (9) apply where a company which, apart from section 278(3C) of the Income and Corporation Taxes Act 1970 or section 178(4) of this Act, would by virtue of section 278(3) or section 178(3) have been treated as selling an asset (unless it has already been treated, by virtue of section 278(3C) or section 178(4), as if it had sold the asset in question).

(3) Where by virtue of section 138(8) of the Finance Act 1989 a company which, by virtue of the substitution of the new definition for the old definition, ceased to be a member of a group at the beginning of 14th March 1989 was not treated as selling an asset at any time unless the conditions in section 138(9) became satisfied, then that company shall continue not to be treated as selling the asset at that time unless the conditions in subsection (4) below become satisfied, assuming for that purpose that the old definition applies.

(4) Those conditions are—

(a) that for the purposes of section 178 or 179 the company in question ceases at any time ("the relevant time") to be a member of the group referred to in subsection (3) above,

(b) that, at the relevant time, the company in question, or an associated company also leaving that group at that time, owns otherwise than as trading stock the asset or property to which a chargeable gain has been carried forward from the asset on a replacement of business assets, and

(c) that the time of acquisition referred to in section 178(1) or 179(1) fell within the period of six years ending with the relevant time.

(5) Where, under any compromise or arrangement agreed to on any date before 14th March 1989 in pursuance of section 425 of the Companies Act 1985 and sanctioned by the court, one company acquires at any time, directly or indirectly, an interest in ordinary share capital of another company and immediately after that time—

(a) under the old definition the two companies are, by virtue of that acquisition, members of a group for the purposes of the group provisions, but

(b) the second company is not an effective 51 per cent. subsidiary of the first company,

subsection (6) below applies; and in that subsection those companies and any other members of the group are referred to as "relevant companies".

(6) In respect of the period beginning with the time of acquisition and ending with—

(a) the expiry of the six months beginning with the date of the agreement, or

(b) if earlier, the date when, under the old definition, the other company
ceases for the purposes of the group provisions to be a member of the
group referred to in subsection (5)(a) above,
the old definition shall apply in relation to the relevant companies for the
purposes of the group provisions and, in relation to those companies, the
reference in subsection (3) above to 14th March 1989 shall be read as a
reference to the day following the end of that period.

(7) In subsections (3) to (6) above—
"arrangement" has the same meaning as in section 425 of the Companies Act 1985,
"effective 51 per cent. subsidiary" has the meaning given by section
170(7);
"group provisions" means sections 170 to 181 (excluding subsections (3)
to (6) above);
"the new definition" means section 170; and
"the old definition" means section 272 of the Income and Corporation
Taxes Act 1970 as it had effect on 13th March 1989,
and section 178(8) or 179(10) shall apply for the purposes of those
subsections.

GENERAL NOTE
This contains transitional provisions governing the carry-forward from ICTA 1970, s.278 to
ss.178 and 179, *supra*.
The three important dates are as follows: (1) March 14, 1989 (introduction of new definition
of groups of companies); (2) April 5, 1992 (coming into force of this Act); (3) October 1, 1993,
"the appointed day" (expected introduction of Pay and File system).

Exemption from charge under 178 or 179 in the case of certain mergers

181.—(1) Subject to the following provisions of this section, neither
section 178 nor section 179 shall apply in a case where—
(a) as part of a merger, a company ("company A") ceases to be a member
of a group of companies ("the A group"); and
(b) it is shown that the merger was carried out for bona fide commercial
reasons and that the avoidance of liability to tax was not the main or
one of the main purposes of the merger.

(2) In this section "merger" means an arrangement (which in this section
includes a series of arrangements)—
(a) whereby one or more companies ("the acquiring company" or, as the
case may be, "the acquiring companies") none of which is a member
of the A group acquires or acquire, otherwise than with a view to their
disposal, one or more interests in the whole or part of the business
which, before the arrangement took effect, was carried on by company A; and
(b) whereby one or more members of the A group acquires or acquire,
otherwise than with a view to their disposal, one or more interests in
the whole or part of the business or each of the businesses which,
before the arrangement took effect, was carried on either by the
acquiring company or acquiring companies or by a company at least
90 per cent. of the ordinary share capital of which was then beneficially owned by two or more of the acquiring companies; and
(c) in respect of which the conditions in subsection (4) below are fulfilled.

(3) For the purposes of subsection (2) above, a member of a group of
companies shall be treated as carrying on as one business the activities of
that group.

(4) The conditions referred to in subsection (2)(c) above are—
(a) that not less than 25 per cent. by value of each of the interests
acquired as mentioned in paragraphs (a) and (b) of subsection (2)

above consists of a holding of ordinary share capital, and the remainder of the interest, or as the case may be of each of the interests, acquired as mentioned in subsection (2)(b), consists of a holding of share capital (of any description) or debentures or both; and

(b) that the value or, as the case may be, the aggregate value of the interest or interests acquired as mentioned in subsection (2)(a) above is substantially the same as the value or, as the case may be, the aggregate value of the interest or interests acquired as mentioned in subsection (2)(b) above; and

(c) that the consideration for the acquisition of the interest or interests acquired by the acquiring company or acquiring companies as mentioned in subsection (2)(a) above, disregarding any part of that consideration which is small by comparison with the total, either consists of, or is applied in the acquisition of, or consists partly of and as to the balance is applied in the acquisition of, the interest or interests acquired by members of the A group as mentioned in subsection (2)(b) above;

and for the purposes of this subsection the value of an interest shall be determined as at the date of its acquisition.

(5) Notwithstanding the provisions of section 170(2)(a), references in this section to a company includes references to a company resident outside the United Kingdom.

GENERAL NOTE

This provides an exemption from the effects of ss.178 or 179 in cases where a company leaves a group as the result of a merger and the transaction meets the tests of bona fide commerciality and no tax avoidance motivation.

The type of arrangement envisaged involves an exchange of shares or bonds between two groups of companies of substantially the same value.

Restriction on indexation allowance for groups and associated companies

Disposals of debts

182.—(1) Subject to subsection (3) below, where—

(a) there is a disposal by a company of a linked company debt on a security owed by another company, and

(b) the two companies are linked companies immediately before the disposal,

there shall be no indexation allowance on the disposal.

(2) Subject to subsection (3) below, where—

(a) there is a disposal by a company of a debt on a security owed by another company which is not a linked company debt on a security, and

(b) the two companies are linked companies immediately before the disposal,

then, in ascertaining any indexation allowance due on the disposal, RD as defined in section 54(1) shall be taken as the retail price index for the first month after the acquisition of the debt in which the two companies were linked companies (or, if later, March 1982).

(3) Where—

(a) there is a disposal by a company of a debt on a security owed by another company,

(b) the debt constituted or formed part of the new holding received by the company making the disposal on a reorganisation, and

(c) subsection (1) or (2) above would apply in relation to the disposal but for this subsection,

neither of those subsections shall apply in relation to the disposal, but any indexation allowance which, apart from this subsection, would be due on the disposal shall be reduced by such amount as appears to the inspector, or, on appeal, the Commissioners concerned, to be just and reasonable.

(4) For the purposes of this section a debt on a security owed by a company is a linked company debt on a security where immediately after its acquisition by the company making the disposal the two companies were linked companies.

(5) Where—

(a) there is a disposal by a company of a debt on a security owed by any person,

(b) the company and that person are not linked companies immediately before the disposal, and

(c) the debt was incurred by that person as part of arrangements involving another company being put in funds,

subsections (1) to (4) above shall have effect if and to the extent that they would if the debt were owed by that other company.

GENERAL NOTE

This section, together with s.183, is designed to prevent the exploitation of the indexation allowance by transactions between linked companies (see s.184(1)). Section 182 deals with disposals of debts on a security. The expression "debt on a security" has caused difficulty in interpretation; see *Aberdeen Construction Group* v. *I.R.C.* [1978] A.C. 885.

The indexation allowance is denied altogether on the disposal where the two companies were linked at the time of the acquisition of the security, or the date when they become linked. Where the security was issued as part of a reorganisation, relief may be given by the inspector on a "just and reasonable" basis.

The section covers arrangements involving third parties putting a linked company into funds.

Disposals of shares

183.—(1) This section applies—

(a) where there is a disposal by a company of—

    (i) a holding of redeemable preference shares of another company, or

    (ii) a holding of shares, other than redeemable preference shares, of another company which has at all times consisted entirely of, or has at any time included, linked company shares, or

(b) where—

    (i) there is a disposal by a company of a holding of shares of another company which is not a holding falling within paragraph (a) above,

    (ii) the holding constituted or formed part of the new holding received by the company making the disposal on a reorganisation, and

    (iii) but for section 127 that reorganisation (or in a case where the holding disposed of derives, in whole or in part, from assets which were original shares in relation to an earlier reorganisation, that reorganisation or any such earlier reorganisation) would have involved a disposal in relation to which section 182(1) would have applied or this section would have applied by virtue of paragraph (a) above,

if the two companies are linked companies immediately before the disposal.

(2) Where this section applies, any indexation allowance which, apart from this section, would be due on the disposal shall be reduced by such amount as appears to the inspector, or on appeal the Commissioners concerned, to be just and reasonable.

(3) For the purposes of this section, shares of a company are linked company shares where—

(a) immediately after their acquisition by the company making the disposal the two companies were linked companies,

(b) their acquisition by the company making the disposal was wholly or substantially financed by one or more linked company loans or linked company funded subscriptions (or by a combination of such loans and subscriptions), and

(c) the sole or main benefit which might have been expected to accrue from that acquisition was the obtaining of an indexation allowance on a disposal of the shares.

(4) In subsection (3) above—

"linked company loan" means a loan made to the company making the disposal by another company where immediately after the acquisition of the shares by the company making the disposal the two companies were linked companies, and

"linked company funded subscription" means a subscription for shares in the company making the disposal by another company where—

(a) immediately after the acquisition of the shares by the company making the disposal those two companies were linked companies, and

(b) the subscription was wholly or substantially financed, either directly or indirectly, by one or more linked company subscription-financing loans.

(5) In subsection (4) above "linked company subscription-financing loan" means a loan made by a company to the subscribing company or any other company where immediately after the acquisition of the shares by the company making the disposal—

(a) the company making the loan, and

(b) the subscribing company, and

(c) where the company to which the loan was made was not the subscribing company, that company,

were linked companies.

GENERAL NOTE

This applies to disposals of redeemable preference shares, linked company shares (see subs. (3)), or shares acquired on a reorganisation where the two companies concerned are linked companies before the disposal. Subsections (4) and (5), defining "linked company loan," "linked company funded subscription" and "linked company subscription-financing loan" are designed to catch sophisticated methods of avoiding the application of the section.

Where it does apply, the indexation allowance falls to be reduced on a "just and reasonable" basis.

Definitions and other provisions supplemental to sections 182 and 183

184.—(1) For the purposes of this section and sections 182 and 183 companies are linked companies if they are members of the same group or are associated with each other; and for the purposes of this section—

(a) "group" means a company which has one or more 51 per cent. subsidiaries together with that subsidiary or those subsidiaries (section 838 (meaning of 51 per cent. subsidiary) of the Taxes Act having effect for the purposes of this paragraph as for those of the Tax Acts), and

(b) two companies are associated with each other if one controls the other or both are under the control of the same person or persons (section 416(2) to (6) (meaning of control) of the Taxes Act having effect for the purposes of this paragraph as for those of Part XI of that Act).

(2) Where a disposal of a holding of shares follows one or more disposals of the same holding to which section 171(1) or 172 applied, section 183(3) to (5) shall have effect as if the references to the company making the disposal were references to the company which last acquired the asset otherwise than on a disposal to which either of those sections applied.

(3) In section 183 "redeemable preference shares" means shares in a company which are described as such in the terms of their issue or which

fulfil the condition in paragraph (a) below and either or both of the conditions in paragraphs (b) and (c) below—
  (a) that, as against other shares in the company, they carry a preferential entitlement to a dividend or to any assets in a winding up or both;
  (b) that, by virtue of the terms of their issue, the exercise of a right by any person or the existence of any arrangements, they are liable to be redeemed, cancelled or repaid, in whole or in part;
  (c) that, by virtue of any arrangements—
      (i) to which the company which issued the shares is a party, or
      (ii) where that company and another company are linked companies at the time of the issue, to which that other company is a party,
    the holder has a right to require another person to acquire the shares or is obliged in any circumstances to dispose of them or another person has a right or is in any circumstances obliged to acquire them;
and for the purposes of paragraph (a) above shares are to be treated as carrying a preferential entitlement to a dividend as against other shares if, by virtue of any arrangements, there are circumstances in which a minimum dividend will be payable on those shares but not on others.
  (4) In sections 182 and 183 the expressions "reorganisation", "original shares" and "new holding" have the meanings given by section 126 except that, in a case where sections 127 and 128 apply in circumstances other than a reorganisation (within the meaning of section 126) by virtue of any other provision of Chapter II of Part IV those expressions shall be construed as they fall to be construed in section 127 and 128 as they so apply.
  (5) In this section and sections 182 and 183—
    "holding", in relation to shares, means a number of shares which are to be regarded for the purposes of this Act as indistinguishable parts of a single asset,
  "security" has the same meaning as in section 132.

GENERAL NOTE
  This is the definition section for the purposes of ss.182 and 183.
  "Linked companies" includes members of the same group and companies under common control.
  Shares can be traced through disposals within a group.
  "Redeemable preference shares" includes shares covered by arrangements covering their disposal to other parties.

Non-resident and dual resident companies

Deemed disposal of assets on company ceasing to be resident in U.K.

  185.—(1) This section and section 187 apply to a company if, at any time ("the relevant time"), the company ceases to be resident in the United Kingdom.
  (2) The company shall be deemed for all purposes of this Act—
  (a) to have disposed of all its assets, other than assets excepted from this subsection by subsection (4) below, immediately before the relevant time; and
  (b) immediately to have reacquired them,
at their market value at that time.
  (3) Section 152 shall not apply where the company—
  (a) has disposed of the old assets, or of its interest in those assets, before the relevant time; and
  (b) acquires the new assets, or its interest in those assets, after that time,
unless the new assets are excepted from this subsection by subsection (4) below.
  (4) If at any time after the relevant time the company carries on a trade in the United Kingdom through a branch or agency—

(a) any assets which, immediately after the relevant time, are situated in the United Kingdom and are used in or for the purposes of the trade, or are used or held for the purposes of the branch or agency, shall be excepted from subsection (2) above; and

(b) any new assets which, after that time, are so situated and are so used or so held shall be excepted from subsection (3) above;

and references in this subsection to assets situated in the United Kingdom include references to exploration or exploitation assets and to exploration or exploitation rights.

(5) In this section—

(a) "designated area", "exploration or exploitation activities" and "exploration or exploitation rights" have the same meanings as in section 276;

(b) "exploration or exploitation assets" means assets used or intended for use in connection with exploration or exploitation activities carried on in the United Kingdom or a designated area;

(c) "the old assets" and "the new assets" have the same meanings as in section 152;

and a company shall not be regarded for the purposes of this section as ceasing to be resident in the United Kingdom by reason only that it ceases to exist.

GENERAL NOTE

This section was introduced in 1988 as part of an overhaul of the rules concerning company residence. Under ICTA 1988, s.765, it was a serious criminal offence to move the residence of a company outside the U.K. without Treasury permission. In *R.* v. *H.M Treasury and Customs and Excise Commissioners, ex p. Daily Mail and General Trust* [1989] Q.B. 440, the European Court held that s.765 did not infringe community law in its present state. However, it was felt to be inappropriate in its present form, and that part of s.765 was repealed and replaced by FA 1988, s.66, which provides that after a transitional period all companies incorporated in the U.K. are to be regarded as resident here wherever the place of central management and control. Non-U.K. incorporated companies will be resident here, as at present, only where their central management and control is here.

To complete these measures, this section introduces a charge on the deemed disposal of a company's assets on ceasing to be resident in the U.K., although in view of FA 1988, s.66, it will be of limited application. Roll-over relief under s.152 is withdrawn if the company migrates before acquiring the new assets unless it continues to trade here through a branch or agency. North Sea assets are included in the U.K. for this purpose.

Deemed disposal of assets on company ceasing to be liable to U.K. taxation

186.—(1) This section and section 187 apply to a company if, at any time ("the relevant time"), the company, while continuing to be resident in the United Kingdom, becomes a company which falls to be regarded for the purposes of any double taxation relief arrangements—

(a) as resident in a territory outside the United Kingdom; and

(b) as not liable in the United Kingdom to tax on gains arising on disposals of assets of descriptions specified in the arrangements ("prescribed assets").

(2) The company shall be deemed for all purposes of this Act—

(a) to have disposed of all its prescribed assets immediately before the relevant time; and

(b) immediately to have reacquired them,

at their market value at that time.

(3) Section 152 shall not apply where the new assets are prescribed assets and the company—

(a) has disposed of the old assets, or of its interest in those assets, before the relevant time; and

(b) acquires the new assets, or its interest in those assets, after that time, and in this section "the old assets" and "the new assets" have the same meanings as in section 152.

GENERAL NOTE

The charge extends to cases where a company while continuing to be resident in the U.K. acquires non-residence for the purposes of a double tax treaty. In such a case there is a deemed disposal of all assets protected by the treaty from U.K. tax and a denial of roll-over relief under s.152 where protected assets are acquired.

Postponement of charge on deemed disposal under section 185 or 186

187.—(1) If—

(a) immediately after the relevant time, a company to which this section applies by virtue of section 185 or 186 ("the company") is a 75 per cent. subsidiary of another company ("the principal company") which is resident in the United Kingdom; and

(b) the principal company and the company so elect, by notice given to the inspector within two years after that time,

this Act shall have effect in accordance with the following provisions.

(2) Any allowable losses accruing to the company on a deemed disposal of foreign assets shall be set off against the chargeable gains so accruing and—

(a) that disposal shall be treated as giving rise to a single chargeable gain equal to the aggregate of those gains after deducting the aggregate of those losses; and

(b) the whole of that gain shall be treated as not accruing to the company on that disposal but an equivalent amount ("the postponed gain") shall be brought into account in accordance with subsections (3) and (4) below.

(3) If at any time within six years after the relevant time the company disposes of any assets ("relevant assets") the chargeable gains on which were taken into account in arriving at the postponed gain, there shall be deemed to accrue to the principal company as a chargeable gain on that occasion the whole of the appropriate proportion of the postponed gain so far as not already taken into account under this subsection or subsection (4) below.

In this subsection "the appropriate proportion" means the proportion which the chargeable gain taken into account in arriving at the postponed gain in respect of the part of the relevant assets disposed of bears to the aggregate of the chargeable gains so taken into account in respect of the relevant assets held immediately before the time of the disposal.

(4) If at any time after the relevant time—

(a) the company ceases to be a 75 per cent. subsidiary of the principal company on the disposal by the principal company of ordinary shares of the company;

(b) after the company has ceased to be such a subsidiary otherwise than on such a disposal, the principal company disposes of such shares; or

(c) the principal company ceases to be resident in the United Kingdom, there shall be deemed to accrue to the principal company as a chargeable gain on that occasion the whole of the postponed gain so far as not already taken into account under this subsection or subsection (3) above.

(5) If at any time—

(a) the company has allowable losses which have not been allowed as a deduction from chargeable gains; and

(b) a chargeable gain accrues to the principal company under subsection (3) or (4) above,

then, if and to the extent that the principal company and the company so elect by notice given to the inspector within two years after that time, those losses shall be allowed as a deduction from that gain.

(6) In this section—

"deemed disposal" means a disposal which, by virtue of section 185(2) or, as the case may be, section 186(2), is deemed to have been made;

"foreign assets" means any assets of the company which, immediately after the relevant time, are situated outside the United Kingdom and are used in or for the purposes of a trade carried on outside the United Kingdom;

"ordinary share" means a share in the ordinary share capital of the company;

"the relevant time" has the meaning given by section 185(1) or, as the case may be, section 186(1).

(7) For the purposes of this section a company is a 75 per cent. subsidiary of another company if and so long as not less than 75 per cent. of its ordinary share capital is owned directly by that other company.

GENERAL NOTE

The charge under ss.185 or 186 can be postponed in the case of a 75 per cent. subsidiary of a U.K. resident company, if both companies so elect within two years. The net gain on the deemed disposal of foreign assets, *i.e.* assets outside the U.K. and used for a trade outside the U.K., is held over and only brought into charge, on the parent company, in respect of assets disposed of within a six-year period. The charge also crystallises on a disposal of the shares or migration of the parent. Allowable losses in the subsidiary may be used to mitigate these gains if both companies so elect.

Dual resident companies: deemed disposal of certain assets

188.—(1) For the purposes of this section, a company is a dual resident company if it is resident in the United Kingdom and falls to be regarded for the purposes of any double taxation relief arrangements as resident in a territory outside the United Kingdom.

(2) Where an asset of a dual resident company becomes a prescribed asset, the company shall be deemed for all purposes of this Act—

(a) to have disposed of the asset immediately before the time at which it became a prescribed asset, and

(b) immediately to have reacquired it,

at its market value at that time.

(3) Subsection (2) above does not apply where the asset becomes a prescribed asset on the company becoming a company which falls to be regarded as mentioned in subsection (1) above.

(4) In this section "prescribed asset", in relation to a dual resident company, means an asset in respect of which, by virtue of the asset being of a description specified in any double taxation relief arrangements, the company falls to be regarded for the purposes of the arrangements as not liable in the United Kingdom to tax on gains accruing to it on a disposal.

GENERAL NOTE

This supplements the charge under s.186 by providing that a company which already has dual resident status under a double tax treaty is deemed to have disposed of and reacquired at market value any asset which becomes protected from U.K. tax by the treaty.

Recovery of tax otherwise than from tax-payer company

Capital distribution of chargeable gains: recovery of tax from shareholder

189.—(1) This section applies where a person who is connected with a company resident in the United Kingdom receives or becomes entitled to receive in respect of shares in the company any capital distribution from the company, other than a capital distribution representing a reduction of capital, and—

(a) the capital so distributed derives from the disposal of assets in respect of which a chargeable gain accrued to the company; or

(b) the distribution constitutes such a disposal of assets;
and that person is referred to below as "the shareholder".

(2) If the corporation tax assessed on the company for the accounting period in which the chargeable gain accrues included any amount in respect of chargeable gains, and any of the tax assessed on the company for that period is not paid within six months from the date determined under sub-section (3) below, the shareholder may by an assessment made within two years from that date be assessed and charged (in the name of the company) to an amount of that corporation tax—

(a) not exceeding the amount or value of the capital distribution which the shareholder has received or become entitled to receive; and

(b) not exceeding a proportion equal to the shareholder's share of the capital distribution made by the company of corporation tax on the amount of that gain at the rate in force when the gain accrued.

(3) The date referred to in subsection (2) above is whichever is the later of—

(a) the date when the tax becomes due and payable by the company; and

(b) the date when the assessment was made on the company.

(4) Where the shareholder pays any amount of tax under this section, he shall be entitled to recover from the company a sum equal to that amount together with any interest paid by him under section 87A of the Management Act on that amount.

(5) The provisions of this section are without prejudice to any liability of the shareholder in respect of a chargeable gain accruing to him by reference to the capital distribution as constituting a disposal of an interest in shares in the company.

(6) With respect to chargeable gains accruing in accounting periods ending on or before such day as the Treasury may by order appoint this section shall have effect—

(a) with the substitution for the words in subsection (3) after "above" of the words "is the date when the tax becomes payable by the company"; and

(b) with the omission of the words in subsection (4) from "together" to the end of the subsection.

(7) In this section "capital distribution" has the same meaning as in section 122.

GENERAL NOTE

This section and the following section, consolidated from ICTA 1988, ss.346 and 347, allow the recovery of tax in certain circumstances from a shareholder or another group company.

A shareholder may be liable where he is a person connected with the company (see s.286) and receives from the company a capital distribution (see s.122) other than on a reduction of capital and the distribution derives from a disposal of assets or constitutes such a disposal. If the tax due on such a disposal is not paid within six months of the due date, then it may be assessed on the shareholder within two years, in proportion to his share of the distribution. The shareholder has a right of recovery from the company.

The section is without prejudice to any possible liability of the shareholder under s.122.

Tax on one member of group recoverable from another member

190.—(1) If at any time a chargeable gain accrues to a company which at that time is a member of a group of companies and any of the corporation tax assessed on the company for the accounting period in which the chargeable gain accrues is not paid within six months from the date determined under subsection (2) below by the company, then, if the tax so assessed included any amount in respect of chargeable gains—

(a) a company which was at the time when the gain accrued the principal company of the group, and

(b) any other company which in any part of the period of two years ending with that time was a member of that group of companies and owned the asset disposed of or any part of it, or where that asset is an interest or right in or over another asset, owned either asset or any part of either asset,

may at any time within two years from the date determined under subsection (2) below be assessed and charged (in the name of the company to whom the chargeable gain accrued) to an amount of that corporation tax not exceeding corporation tax on the amount of that gain at the rate in force when the gain accrued.

(2) The date referred to in subsection (1) above is whichever is the later of—
  (a) the date when the tax becomes due and payable by the company; and
  (b) the date when the assessment is made on the company.

(3) A company paying any amount of tax under subsection (1) above shall be entitled to recover a sum of that amount—
  (a) from the company to which the chargeable gain accrued, or
  (b) if that company is not the company which was the principal company of the group at the time when the chargeable gain accrued, from that principal company,

and a company paying any amount under paragraph (b) above shall be entitled to recover a sum of that amount from the company to which the chargeable gain accrued, and so far as it is not so recovered, to recover from any company which is for the time being a member of the group and which has while a member of the group owned the asset disposed of or any part of it (or where that asset is an interest or right in or over another asset, owned either asset or any part of it) such proportion of the amount unrecovered as is just having regard to the value of the asset at the time when the asset, or an interest or right in or over it, was disposed of by that company.

(4) Any reference in subsection (3) above to an amount of tax includes a reference to any interest paid under section 87A of the Management Act on that amount.

(5) Section 170 shall apply for the interpretation of this section as it applies for the interpretation of sections 171 to 181.

(6) In relation to any chargeable gains accruing in accounting periods ending on or before such day as the Treasury may by order appoint this section shall have effect—
  (a) with the substitution for the words in subsection (2) after "above" of the words "is the date when the tax becomes payable by the company"; and
  (b) with the omission of subsection (4).

GENERAL NOTE

Where a company which is a member of a group does not pay tax due on a chargeable gain within six months, the tax may be assessed within two years on the parent company or any other company within the group which had any interest in the asset disposed of during that period. The company paying the charge has a right of recovery.

Tax on non-resident company recoverable from another member of group or from controlling director

191.—(1) This section applies where—
  (a) a chargeable gain has accrued to a company not resident in the United Kingdom (the tax-payer company) on the disposal of an asset on or after 14th March 1989,
  (b) the gain forms part of its chargeable profits for corporation tax purposes by virtue of section 10(3), and
  (c) any of the corporation tax assessed on the company for the accounting period in which the gain accrued is not paid within six months from the time when it becomes payable.

(2) The Board may, at any time before the end of the period of three years beginning with the time when the amount of corporation tax for the accounting period in which the chargeable gain accrued is finally determined, serve on any person to whom subsection (4) below applies a notice—

(a) stating the amount which remains unpaid of the corporation tax assessed on the tax-payer company for the accounting period in which the gain accrued and the date when the tax became payable, and

(b) requiring that person to pay the relevant amount within 30 days of the service of the notice.

(3) For the purposes of subsection (2) above the relevant amount is the lesser of—

(a) the amount which remains unpaid of the corporation tax assessed on the tax-payer company for the accounting period in which the gain accrued, and

(b) an amount equal to corporation tax on the amount of the chargeable gain at the rate in force when the gain accrued.

(4) This subsection applies to the following persons—

(a) any company which is, or during the period of 12 months ending with the time when the gain accrued, was, a member of the same group as the tax-payer company, and

(b) any person who is, or during that period was, a controlling director of the tax-payer company or of a company which has, or within that period had, control over the tax-payer company.

This subsection shall have effect in any case where the gain accrued before 13th March 1990 with the substitution of "beginning with 14th March 1989 and" for "of 12 months".

(5) Any amount which a person is required to pay by a notice under this section may be recovered from him as if it were tax due and duly demanded of him; and he may recover any such amount paid by him from the tax-payer company.

(6) A payment in pursuance of a notice under this section shall not be allowed as a deduction in computing any income, profits or losses for any tax purposes.

(7) In this section—

"director", in relation to a company, has the meaning given by subsection (8) of section 168 of the Taxes Act (read with subsection (9) of that section) and includes any person falling within subsection (5) of section 417 of that Act (read with subsection (6) of that section);

"controlling director", in relation to a company, means a director of the company who has control of it (construing control in accordance with section 416 of the Taxes Act);

"group" has the meaning which would be given by section 170 if in that section references to residence in the United Kingdom were omitted and for references to 75 per cent. subsidiaries there were substituted references to 51 per cent. subsidiaries.

GENERAL NOTE

This section is designed to facilitate the collection of tax due from a non-resident company on the disposal of an asset after March 14, 1989. Where the tax is unpaid within six months, the Revenue may within three years serve a notice requiring payment within 30 days on any other company in the same group in the year before the gain accrued or a controlling director of the company or of a company which controlled it. The demand may be for the lesser of any unpaid corporation tax or the corporation tax on the amount of the gain. There is a right of recovery.

Subs. (7)

This defines "director", "controlling director" and "group" for this purpose.

Demergers

Tax exempt distributions

192.—(1) This section has effect for facilitating certain transactions whereby trading activities carried on by a single company or group are divided so as to be carried on by two or more companies not belonging to the same group or by two or more independent groups.

(2) Where a company makes an exempt distribution which falls within section 213(3)(a) of the Taxes Act—

 (a) the distribution shall not be a capital distribution for the purposes of section 122; and

 (b) sections 126 to 130 shall, with the necessary modifications, apply as if that company and the subsidiary whose shares are transferred were the same company and the distribution were a reorganisation of its share capital.

(3) Subject to subsection (4) below, neither section 178 nor 179 shall apply in a case where a company ceases to be a member of a group by reason only of an exempt distribution.

(4) Subsection (3) does not apply if within five years after the making of the exempt distribution there is chargeable payment; and the time for making an assessment under section 178 or 179 by virtue of this subsection shall not expire before the end of three years after the making of the chargeable payment.

(5) In this section—

 "chargeable payment" has the meaning given in section 214(2) of the Taxes Act;

 "exempt distribution" means a distribution which is exempt by virtue of section 213(2) of that Act; and

 "group" means a company which has one or more 75 per cent. subsidiaries together with that or those subsidiaries.

(6) In determining for the purposes of this section whether one company is a 75 per cent. subsidiary of another, the other company shall be treated as not being the owner of—

 (a) any share capital which it owns directly in a body corporate if a profit on a sale of the shares would be treated as a trading receipt of its trade; or

 (b) any share capital which it owns indirectly and which is owned directly by a body corporate for which a profit on the sale of the shares would be a trading receipt.

GENERAL NOTE

A relief for demergers, *i.e.* the division of trading activities carried on by a single company or group so as to be carried on by two or more companies not belonging to the same group or by two or more independent groups, was introduced by FA 1980, s.117 and Sched. 18. The provisions relating to income tax are now contained in ICTA 1988, ss.213–218. This section carries forward the provisions relating to capital gains tax.

A distribution of shares which ranks as a demerger is excluded from the operation of s.122 and is treated as a reorganisation under ss.126–30. It is also excluded from the operation of ss.178 or 179 unless a chargeable payment within ICTA 1988, s.214(2) is made within five years, in which case an assessment under ss.178 or 179 may be made within a further three years.

CHAPTER II

OIL AND MINING INDUSTRIES

Oil exploration and exploitation

Roll-over relief not available for gains on oil licences

193.—(1) A licence under the Petroleum (Production) Act 1934 or the

Petroleum (Production) Act (Northern Ireland) 1964 is not and, subject to subsection (2) below, shall be assumed never to have been an asset falling within any of the classes in section 155.

(2) Nothing in subsection (1) above affects the determination of any Commissioners or the judgment of any court made or given before 14th May 1987.

GENERAL NOTE

Oil licences are denied roll-over relief under s.155. This provision was introduced to reverse a decision of Special Commissioners to the opposite effect (*Hansard*, H.C. Vol. 116, col. 287, Written Answers).

Disposals of oil licences relating to undeveloped areas

194.—(1) In this section any reference to a disposal (including a part disposal) is a reference to a disposal made by way of a bargain at arm's length.

(2) If, at the time of the disposal, the licence relates to an undeveloped area, then, to the extent that the consideration for the disposal consists of—

(a) another licence which at that time relates to an undeveloped area or an interest in another such licence, or

(b) an obligation to undertake exploration work or appraisal work in an area which is or forms part of the licensed area in relation to the licence disposed of,

the value of that consideration shall be treated as nil for the purposes of this Act.

(3) If the disposal of a licence which, at the time of the disposal, relates to an undeveloped area is part of a larger transaction under which one party makes to another disposals of two or more licences, each of which at the time of the disposal relates to an undeveloped area, the reference in subsection (2)(b) above to the licensed area in relation to the licence disposed of shall be construed as a reference to the totality of the licensed areas in relation to those two or more licences.

(4) In relation to a disposal of a licence which, at the time of the disposal, relates to an undeveloped area, being a disposal—

(a) which is a part disposal of the licence in question, and

(b) part but not the whole of the consideration for which falls within paragraph (a) or paragraph (b) of subsection (2) above,

section 42 shall not apply unless the amount or value of the part of the consideration which does not fall within one of those paragraphs is less than the aggregate of the amounts which, if the disposal were a disposal of the whole of the licence rather than a part disposal, would be—

(i) the relevant allowable expenditure, as defined in section 53; and

(ii) the indexation allowance on the disposal.

(5) Where section 42 has effect in relation to such a disposal as is referred to in subsection (4) above, it shall have effect as if, for subsection (2) thereof, there were substituted the following subsection—

"(2) The apportionment shall be made by reference to—

(a) the amount or value of the consideration for the disposal on the one hand (call that amount or value A), and

(b) the aggregate referred to in section 194(4) on the other hand (call that aggregate C),

and the fraction of the said sums allowable as a deduction in computing the amount of the gain (if any) accruing on the disposal shall be—

$$\frac{A}{C}$$

and the remainder shall be attributed to the part of the property which remains undisposed of."

GENERAL NOTE
Together with the following two sections, this gives certain relief in relation to the North Sea oil industry.

Where a licence for an undeveloped area is disposed of in exchange for another such licence or an obligation to undertake exploration or appraisal work in the area disposed of, the consideration is treated as nil.

The provision applies, *mutatis mutandis* and with appropriate apportionments, to multiple and part disposals.

Allowance of certain drilling expenditure etc.

195.—(1) On the disposal of a licence, relevant qualifying expenditure incurred by the person making the disposal—

(a) in searching for oil anywhere in the licensed area, or

(b) in ascertaining the extent or characteristics of any oil-bearing area the whole or part of which lies in the licensed area or what the reserves of oil of any such oil-bearing area are,

shall be treated as expenditure falling within section 38(1)(b).

(2) Expenditure incurred as mentioned in subsection (1) above is relevant expenditure if, and only if—

(a) it is expenditure of a capital nature on scientific research; and

(b) either it was allowed or allowable under section 137 of the 1990 Act (capital expenditure on scientific research) for a relevant chargeable period which, or the basis year for which, began before the date of the disposal or it would have been so allowable if the trading condition had been fulfilled; and

(c) the disposal is an occasion by virtue of which section 138 of the 1990 Act (termination of user of assets representing scientific research expenditure of a capital nature) applies in relation to the expenditure or would apply if the trading condition had been fulfilled and the expenditure had been allowed accordingly.

(3) In subsection (2) above and subsection (4) below, the expression "if the trading condition had been fulfilled" means, in relation to expenditure of a capital nature on scientific research, if, after the expenditure was incurred but before the disposal concerned was made, the person incurring the expenditure had set up and commenced a trade connected with that research; and in subsection (2)(b) above—

"relevant chargeable period" has the same meaning as in section 137 of the 1990 Act; and

"basis year" has the same meaning as in subsection (6)(c) of that section.

(4) Relevant expenditure is qualifying expenditure only to the extent that it does not exceed the trading receipt which, by reason of the disposal—

(a) is treated as accruing under section 138(2) of the 1990 Act; or

(b) would be treated as so accruing if the trading condition had been fulfilled and the expenditure had been allowed accordingly.

(5) On the disposal of a licence, sections 37 and 41 shall apply in relation to any such trading receipt as is mentioned in subsection (4)(a) above as if it were a balancing charge falling to be made by reference to the disposal.

(6) Where, on the disposal of a licence, subsection (1) above has effect in relation to any relevant qualifying expenditure which had not in fact been allowed or become allowable as mentioned in subsection (2)(b) above—

(a) no allowance shall be made in respect of that expenditure under section 137 of the 1990 Act; and

(b) no deduction shall be allowed in respect of it under section 138(3) of that Act.

(7) Where, on the disposal of a licence which is a part disposal, subsection (1) above has effect in relation to any relevant qualifying expenditure, then, for the purposes of section 42, that expenditure shall be treated as wholly

attributable to what is disposed of (and, accordingly, shall not be apportioned as mentioned in that section).

GENERAL NOTE
   On the disposal of an oil licence, certain expenditure in searching for oil or ascertaining the extent of an oil-bearing area or the reserves of oil therein is allowed relief. The following conditions apply:
   (1) it must be capital expenditure on scientific research;
   (2) it must be of a type eligible for relief under the Capital Allowances Act 1990, s.137;
   (3) the disposal must be an occasion to which *ibid.*, s.138 would have applied;
   (4) the expenditure must not exceed the trading receipt treated as accruing under s.138(2).
   The trading receipt is treated as a balancing charge. Double relief under this section and C.A.A. 1990 is precluded. On a part disposal, no apportionment of the expenditure is made.

Interpretation of sections 194 and 195

196.—(1) For the purposes of section 194, a licence relates to an undeveloped area at any time if—
   (a) for no part of the licensed area has consent for development been granted to the licensee by the Secretary of State on or before that time; and
   (b) for no part of the licensed area has a programme of development been served on the licensee or approved by the Secretary of State on or before that time.

   (2) Subsections (4) and (5) of section 36 of the Finance Act 1983 (meaning of "development") shall have effect in relation to subsection (1) above as they have effect in relation to subsection (2) of that section.

   (3) In relation to a licence under the Petroleum (Production) Act (Northern Ireland) 1964 any reference in subsection (1) above to the Secretary of State shall be construed as a reference to the Department of Economic Development.

   (4) In relation to a disposal to which section 194 applies of a licence under which the buyer acquires an interest in the licence only so far as it relates to part of the licensed area, any reference in subsection (1) or subsection (3) of that section or subsection (1) above to the licensed area shall be construed as a reference only to that part of the licensed area to which the buyer's acquisition relates.

   (5) In sections 194 and 195 and the preceding provisions of this section "oil", "licence", "licensee" and, subject to subsection (4) above, "licensed area" have the meaning assigned by section 12(1) of the Oil Taxation Act 1975.

   (6) In section 194—
   (a) "exploration work", in relation to any area, means work carried out for the purpose of searching for oil anywhere in that area;
   (b) "appraisal work", in relation to any area, means work carried out for the purpose of ascertaining the extent or characteristics of any oil-bearing area the whole or part of which lies in the area concerned or what the reserves of oil of any such oil-bearing area are.

GENERAL NOTE
   This is the interpretation section for the purposes of the two previous sections. The special tax provisions relating to the North Sea are found mostly in the Oil Taxation Acts 1975 and 1983 and in ICTA 1988, ss.492–502.

Disposals of interests in oil fields etc: ring fence provisions

197.—(1) This section applies where in pursuance of a transfer by a participator in an oil field of the whole or part of his interest in the field, there is—
   (a) a disposal of an interest in oil to be won from the oil field; or
   (b) a disposal of an asset used in connection with the field;

and section 12 of the Oil Taxation Act 1975 (interpretation of Part I of that Act) applies for the interpretation of this subsection and the reference to the transfer by a participator in an oil field of the whole or part of his interest in the field shall be construed in accordance with paragraph 1 of Schedule 17 to the Finance Act 1980.

(2) In this section "material disposal" means—

(a) a disposal falling within paragraph (a) or paragraph (b) of subsection (1) above; or

(b) the sale of an asset referred to in section 178(3) or 179(3) where the asset was acquired by the chargeable company (within the meaning of that section) on a disposal falling within one of those paragraphs.

(3) For any chargeable period in which a chargeable gain or allowable loss accrues to any person ("the chargeable person") on a material disposal (whether taking place in that period or not), subject to subsection (6) below there shall be aggregated—

(a) the chargeable gains accruing to him in that period on such disposals, and

(b) the allowable losses accruing to him in that period on such disposals, and the lesser of the 2 aggregates shall be deducted from the other to give an aggregate gain or, as the case may be, an aggregate loss for that chargeable period.

(4) For the purposes of tax in respect of chargeable gains—

(a) the several chargeable gains and allowable losses falling within paragraphs (a) and (b) of subsection (3) above shall be left out of account; and

(b) the aggregate gain or aggregate loss referred to in that subsection shall be treated as a single chargeable gain or allowance loss accruing to the chargeable person in the chargeable period concerned on the notional disposal of an asset; and

(c) if in any chargeable period there is an aggregate loss, then, except as provided by subsection (5) below, it shall not be allowable as a deduction against any chargeable gain arising in that or any later period, other than an aggregate gain treated as accruing in a later period by virtue of paragraph (b) above (so that the aggregate gain of that later period shall be reduced or extinguished accordingly); and

(d) if in any chargeable period there is an aggregate gain, no loss shall be deducted from it except in accordance with paragraph (c) above; and

(e) without prejudice to any indexation allowance which was taken into account in determining an aggregate gain or aggregate loss under subsection (3) above, no further indexation allowance shall be allowed on a notional disposal referred to in paragraph (b) above.

(5) In any case where—

(a) by virtue of subsection (4)(b) above, an aggregate loss is treated as accruing to the chargeable person in any chargeable period, and

(b) before the expiry of the period of two years beginning at the end of the chargeable period concerned, the chargeable person makes a claim under the subsection,

the whole, or such portion as is specified in the claim, of the aggregate loss shall be treated for the purposes of this Act as an allowable loss arising in that chargeable period otherwise than of a material disposal.

(6) In any case where a loss accrues to the chargeable person on a material disposal made to a person who is connected with him—

(a) the loss shall be excluded from those referred to in paragraph (b) of subsection (3) above and, accordingly, shall not be aggregated under that subsection; and

(b) except as provided by subsection (7) below, section 18 shall apply in relation to the loss as if, in subsection (3) of that section, any reference to a disposal were a reference to a disposal which is a material disposal; and

(c) to the extent that the loss is set against a chargeable gain by virtue of paragraph (b) above, the gain shall be excluded from those referred to in paragraph (a) of subsection (3) above and, accordingly, shall not be aggregated under that subsection.

(7) In any case where—

(a) the losses accruing to the chargeable person in any chargeable period on material disposals to a connected person exceed the gains accruing to him in that chargeable period on material disposals made to that person at a time when they are connected persons, and

(b) before the expiry of the period of two years beginning at the end of the chargeable period concerned, the chargeable person makes a claim under this subsection,

the whole, or such part as is specified in the claim, of the excess referred to in paragraph (a) above shall be treated for the purposes of section 18 as if it were a loss accruing on a disposal in that chargeable period, being a disposal which is not a material disposal and which is made by the chargeable person to the connected person referred to in paragraph (a) above.

(8) Where a claim is made under subsection (5) or subsection (7) above, all such adjustments shall be made whether by way of discharge or repayment of tax or otherwise, as may be required in consequence of the operation of that subsection.

GENERAL NOTE

For general tax purposes, a "ring fence" is put round North Sea activities to preclude the set-off of profits and losses against other activities. This section applies that system for capital gains.

Each year gains and losses on North Sea disposals (or deemed disposals on companies leaving groups) are aggregated. This aggregate is then chargeable to tax. If there is a loss, it may be carried forward to set off against future North Sea gains, subject to an election within two years to set it off against general gains. Losses accruing on disposals made to connected persons (see s.286) are treated separately.

Replacement of business assets used in connection with oil fields

198.—(1) If the consideration which a person obtains on a material disposal is applied, in whole or in part, as mentioned in subsection (1) of section 152 or 153, that section shall not apply unless the new assets are taken into use, and used only, for the purposes of the ring fence trade.

(2) Subsection (1) above has effect notwithstanding subsection (8) of section 152.

(3) Where section 152 or 153 applies in relation to any of the consideration on a material disposal, the asset which constitutes the new assets for the purposes of that section shall be conclusively presumed to be a depreciating asset, and section 154 shall have effect accordingly, except that—

(a) the reference in subsection (2)(b) of that section to a trade carried on by the claimant shall be construed as a reference solely to his ring fence trade; and

(b) subsections (4) to (7) of that section shall be omitted.

(4) In any case where sections 152 to 154 have effect in accordance with subsections (1) to (3) above, the operation of section 175 shall be modified as follows—

(a) only those members of a group which actually carry on a ring fence trade shall be treated for the purposes of those sections as carrying on a single trade which is a ring fence trade; and

(b) only those activities which, in relation to each individual member of the group, constitute its ring fence trade shall be treated as forming part of that single trade.

(5) In this section—

(a) "material disposal" has the meaning assigned to it by section 197; and

(b) "ring fence trade" means a trade consisting of either or both of the activities mentioned in paragraphs (a) and (b) of subsection (1) of section 492 of the Taxes Act.

GENERAL NOTE

The "ring-fence" principle is also applied to roll-over relief under ss.152 or 153. "Ring-fence trade" is defined in ICTA 1988, s.492, to include any oil extraction activities or the acquisition, enjoyment or exploitation of oil rights.

The replacement asset is conclusively presumed to be a depreciating asset within s.154, so allowing a maximum 10-year hold-over.

Exploration or exploitation assets: deemed disposals

199.—(1) Where an exploration or exploitation asset which is a mobile asset ceases to be chargeable in relation to a person by virtue of ceasing to be dedicated to an oil field in which he, or a person connected with him, is or has been a participator, he shall be deemed for all purposes of this Act—
  (a) to have disposed of the asset immediately before the time when it ceased to be so dedicated, and
  (b) immediately to have reacquired it,
at its market value at that time.

(2) Where a person who is not resident and not ordinarily resident in the United Kingdom ceases to carry on a trade in the United Kingdom through a branch or agency, he shall be deemed for all purposes of this Act—
  (a) to have disposed immediately before the time when he ceased to carry on the trade in the United Kingdom through a branch or agency of every asset to which subsection (3) below applies, and
  (b) immediately to have reacquired every such asset,
at its market value at that time.

(3) This subsection applies to any exploration or exploitation asset, other than a mobile asset, used in or for the purposes of the trade at or before the time of the deemed disposal.

(4) A person shall not be deemed by subsection (2) above to have disposed of an asset if, immediately after the time when he ceases to carry on the trade in the United Kingdom through a branch or agency, the asset is used in or for the purposes of exploration or exploitation activities carried on by him in the United Kingdom or a designated area.

(5) Where in a case to which subsection (4) above applies the person ceases to use the asset in or for the purposes of exploration or exploitation activities carried on by him in the United Kingdom or a designated area, he shall be deemed for all purposes of this Act—
  (a) to have disposed of the asset immediately before the time when he ceased to use it in or for the purposes of such activities, and
  (b) immediately to have reacquired it,
at its market value at that time.

(6) For the purposes of this section an asset is at any time a chargeable asset in relation to a person if, were it to be disposed of at that time, any chargeable gains accruing to him on the disposal—
  (a) would be gains in respect of which he would be chargeable to capital gains tax under section 10(1), or
  (b) would form part of his chargeable profits for corporation tax purposes by virtue of section 10(3).

(7) In this section—
  (a) "exploration or exploitation asset" means an asset used in connection with exploration or exploitation activities carried on in the United Kingdom or a designated area;
  (b) "designated area" and "exploration or exploitation activities" have the same meanings as in section 276; and
  (c) the expressions "dedicated to an oil field" and "participator" shall be

construed as if this section were included in Part I of the Oil Taxation Act 1975.

GENERAL NOTE

This applies the charge under s.25 on a deemed disposal when an asset ceases to be situated in the U.K. to the special circumstances of the North Sea. There are deemed disposals in the following circumstances:

(1) when a mobile asset ceases to be dedicated to an oil field in which the taxpayer, or a connected person, has participated. No definition of "mobile asset" is provided;

(2) when a non-resident person ceases to carry on a trade in the U.K. through a branch or agency. This applies to any exploration or exploitation asset other than a mobile asset. It does not apply, however, if the asset continues to be used for these purposes in the U.K. or a designated area (basically the continental shelf);

(3) when an asset so used ceases to be so used.

Limitation of losses on disposal of oil industry assets held on 31st March 1982

200.—(1) This section applies to a disposal of an oil industry asset where the following conditions are fulfilled—

(a) the person making the disposal held the asset on 31st March 1982 or, by virtue of paragraph 1 of Schedule 3, is treated as having held the asset on that date for the purposes of section 35;

(b) disregarding the following provisions of this section, for the purposes of this Act, a loss would accrue on the disposal; and

(c) in the application of section 35 subsection (2) of that section does not apply because of the operation of subsection (3)(b) of that section.

(2) For the purposes of this section, the following are "oil industry assets"—

(a) a licence under the Petroleum (Production) Act 1934 or the Petroleum (Production) Act (Northern Ireland) 1964;

(b) shares falling within paragraph 7(2)(d) of Schedule 3;

(c) oil exploration or exploitation assets, which expression shall be construed, subject to subsection (3) below, in accordance with paragraph 7(5) and (6) of Schedule 3; and

(d) any interest in an asset falling within paragraph (a) to (c) above.

(3) In the application of paragraph 7(5)(b) of Schedule 3 for the purposes of subsection (2)(c) above, for the words from "the company whose shares" to "that company" there shall be substituted "the person making the disposal or a person connected with him".

(4) Where this section applies to a disposal, there shall be determined for the purposes of this section the loss or gain which would accrue on the disposal on the following assumptions—

(a) that section 35(2) continues not to apply on the disposal; and

(b) that, in calculating the indexation allowance on the disposal, section 55(1) does not apply;

and in the following provisions of this section the loss or gain (if any) on the disposal, determined on those assumptions, is referred to as the non-rebased loss or, as the case may be, the non-rebased gain.

(5) If there is a non-rebased loss on a disposal to which this section applies and that loss is less than the loss which accrues on the disposal as mentioned in subsection (1)(b) above, it shall be assumed for the purposes of this Act that the loss which accrues on the disposal is the non-rebased loss.

(6) If there is a non-rebased gain on a disposal to which this section applies, it shall be assumed for the purposes of this Act that the oil industry asset concerned was acquired by the person making the disposal for a consideration such that, on the disposal, neither a gain nor a loss accrues to him.

(7) If, on the determination referred to in subsection (4) above, there is neither a non-rebased loss nor a non-rebased gain on a disposal, subsection

(6) above shall apply in relation to the disposal as if there were a non-rebased gain on the disposal.

GENERAL NOTE
    This section was introduced, along with what is now Sched. 3, para. 7, to restrict the effects of rebasing to 1982 in the case of North Sea oil assets. This is because the value of such assets was relatively high at that time due to the price of oil. Where such an asset is disposed of, the indexation allowance is calculated on the basis of acquisition cost rather than March 1982 value. If this produces a lower loss than the loss calculated on 1982 values, the former prevails. If this produces a gain or neither a loss nor a gain, the disposal is assumed to be on a no-gain/no-loss basis.

Mineral leases

Royalties

    201.—(1) A person resident or ordinarily resident in the United Kingdom who in any chargeable period is entitled to receive any mineral royalties under a mineral lease or agreement shall be treated for the purposes of this Act as if there accrued to him in that period a chargeable gain equal to one-half of the total of the mineral royalties receivable by him under that lease or agreement in that period.
    (2) This section shall have effect notwithstanding any provision of section 119(1) of the Taxes Act making the whole of certain kinds of mineral royalties chargeable to tax under Schedule D, but without prejudice to any provision of that section providing for any such royalties to be subject to deduction of income tax under section 348 or 349 of that Act.
    (3) The amount of the chargeable gain treated as accruing to any person by virtue of subsection (1) above shall, notwithstanding any other provision of this Act, be the whole amount calculated in accordance with that subsection, and, accordingly, no reduction shall be made on account of expenditure incurred by that person or of any other matter whatsoever.
    (4) In any case where, before the commencement of section 122 of the Taxes Act, for the purposes of the 1979 Act or corporation tax on chargeable gains a person was treated as if there had accrued to him in any chargeable period ending before 6th April 1988 a chargeable gain equal to the relevant fraction, determined in accordance with section 29(3)(b) of the Finance Act 1970, of the total of the mineral royalties receivable by him under that lease or agreement in that period, subsection (1) above shall have effect in relation to any mineral royalties receivable by him under that lease or agreement in any later chargeable period with the substitution for the reference to one-half of a reference to the relevant fraction as so determined.

GENERAL NOTE
    Mineral royalties under a mineral lease or agreement (see ICTA 1988, s.122 (5)–(7)) are taxable half to income tax and half to capital gains tax. Under ICTA 1988, s.119, rents payable in connection with mines are subject wholly to income tax, and are liable to deduction at source under *ibid.*, ss.348 and 349. The distinction is governed by the Mineral Royalties (Tax) Regulations 1971 (S.I. 1971 No. 1035).
    The capital gain is charged to tax without any deduction for allowable expenditure.

Subs. (4)
    This preserves for transitional purposes a charge computed by reference to betterment levy, which existed from 1970 to 1971.

Capital losses

    202.—(1) This section has effect in relation to capital losses which accrue during the currency of a mineral lease or agreement, and applies in any case where, at the time of the occurrence of a relevant event in relation to a mineral lease or agreement, the person who immediately before that event occurred was entitled to receive mineral royalties under the lease or agreement ("the taxpayer") has an interest in the land to which the mineral lease or agreement relates ("the relevant interest").

(2) For the purposes of this section, a relevant event occurs in relation to a mineral lease or agreement—

    (a) on the expiry or termination of the mineral lease or agreement;

    (b) if the relevant interest is disposed of, or is treated as having been disposed of by virtue of any provision of this Act.

(3) On the expiry of termination of a mineral lease or agreement the taxpayer shall, if he makes a claim in that behalf, be treated for purposes of tax in respect of chargeable gains as if he had disposed of and immediately reacquired the relevant interest for a consideration equal to its market value, but a claim may not be made under this subsection—

    (a) if the expiry or termination of the mineral lease or agreement is also a relevant event falling within subsection (2)(b) above; nor

    (b) unless, on the notional disposal referred to above, an allowable loss would accrue to the taxpayer.

(4) In this section "the terminal loss", in relation to a relevant event in respect of which a claim is made under subsection (3) above, means the allowable loss which accrues to the taxpayer by virtue of the notional disposal occurring on that relevant event by virtue of that subsection.

(5) On making a claim under subsection (3) above, the taxpayer shall specify whether he requires the terminal loss to be dealt with in accordance with subsection (6) or subsections (9) to (11) below.

(6) Where the taxpayer requires the loss to be dealt with in accordance with this subsection it shall be treated as an allowable loss accruing to him in the chargeable period in which the mineral lease or agreement expires.

(7) If on the occurrence of a relevant event falling within subsection (2)(b) above, an allowable loss accrues to the taxpayer on the disposal or notional disposal which constitutes that relevant event, the taxpayer may make a claim under this subsection requiring the loss to be dealt with in accordance with subsections (9) to (11) below and not in any other way.

(8) In subsections (9) to (11) below "the terminal loss" in relation to a relevant event in respect of which a claim is made under subsection (7) above means the allowable loss which accrues to the taxpayer as mentioned in that subsection.

(9) Where, as a result of a claim under subsection (3) or (7) above, the terminal loss is to be dealt with in accordance with this subsection, then, subject to subsection (10) below, it shall be deducted from or set off against the amount on which the taxpayer was chargeable to capital gains tax, or as the case may be corporation tax, for chargeable periods preceding that in which the relevant event giving rise to the terminal loss occurred and falling wholly or partly within the period of 15 years ending with the date of that event.

(10) The amount of the terminal loss which, by virtue of subsection (9) above, is to be deducted from or set off against the amount on which the taxpayer was chargeable to capital gains tax, or as the case may be corporation tax, for any chargeable period shall not exceed the amount of the gain which in that period was treated, by virtue of section 201(1), as accruing to the taxpayer in respect of mineral royalties under the mineral lease or agreement in question; and subject to this limit any relief given to the taxpayer by virtue of subsection (9) above shall be given as far as possible for a later rather than an earlier chargeable period.

(11) If in any case where relief has been given to the taxpayer in accordance with subsections (9) and (10) above there remains an unexpended balance of the terminal loss which cannot be applied in accordance with those subsections, there shall be treated as accruing to the taxpayer in the

chargeable period in which the relevant event occurs an allowable loss equal to that unexpended balance.

GENERAL NOTE

This section gives relief for capital losses which accrue during the currency of a mineral lease or agreement. The relief can arise on two occasions:

(1) the expiry or termination of the lease. In this case the taxpayer may claim to be treated as having disposed of his interest in the land and reacquired it at market value. If this produces a loss, the taxpayer may opt either to have it treated as accruing to him in the year of expiry or to have it set off so far as possible against his gains arising from the lease over the previous 15 years.

(2) an actual or deemed disposal of the lease. This can only be dealt with by set-off against previous gains, with only the balance treated as accruing in the year of disposal.

Provisions supplementary to sections 201 and 202

203.—(1) Subsections (5) to (7) of section 122 of the Taxes Act (meaning of "minerals" etc.) shall apply for the interpretation of this section and sections 201 and 202 as they apply for the interpretation of that section.

(2) No claim under section 202(3) or (7) shall be allowed unless it is made within 6 years from the date of the relevant event by virtue of which the taxpayer is entitled to make the claim.

(3) All such repayments of tax shall be made as may be necessary to give effect to any such claim.

GENERAL NOTE

Relevant definitions for ss.200–202 are in ICTA 1988, s.122 (5)–(7).

Claims under s.202 must be made within six years.

CHAPTER III

INSURANCE

Policies of insurance

204.—(1) The rights of the insurer under any policy of insurance shall not constitute an asset on the disposal of which a gain may accrue, whether the risks insured relate to property or not; and the rights of the insured under any policy of insurance of the risk of any kind of damage to, or the loss or depreciation of, assets shall constitute an asset on the disposal of which a gain may accrue only to the extent that those rights relate to assets on the disposal of which a gain may accrue or might have accrued.

(2) Notwithstanding subsection (1) above, sums received under a policy of insurance of the risk of any kind of damage to, or the loss or depreciation of, assets are for the purposes of this Act, and in particular for the purposes of section 22, sums derived from the assets.

(3) Where any investments or other assets are or have been, in accordance with a policy issued in the course of life assurance business carried on by an insurance company, transferred to the policy holder on or after 6th April 1967, the policy holder's acquisition of the assets and the disposal of them to him shall be deemed to be, for the purposes of this Act, for a consideration equal to the market value of the assets.

(4) In subsections (1) and (2) above "policy of insurance" does not include a policy of assurance on human life and in subsection (3) "life assurance business" and "insurance company" have the same meaning as in Chapter I of Part XII of the Taxes Act.

GENERAL NOTE

Rights of insurer and insured under a policy of insurance (other than a policy on human life, as to which see s.210) are largely protected from C.G.T. by subs. (1) which was amended to reverse the decision in *I.R.C.* v. *Montgomery* [1975] Ch. 266. However, this is without prejudice to the possible charge under s.22.

Subs. (3)
This was introduced originally by FA 1967, s.35, and imposes a deemed disposal at market value when assets are in accordance with a life assurance policy transferred to the policy-holder. See ICTA 1988, s.443 for a parallel provision.

Disallowance of insurance premiums as expenses

205. Without prejudice to the provisions of section 39, there shall be excluded from the sums allowable as a deduction in the computation of the gain accruing on the disposal of an asset any premiums or other payments made under a policy of insurance of the risk of any kind of damage or injury to, or loss or depreciation of, the asset.

GENERAL NOTE
Insurance premiums are disallowed for C.G.T., whether or not they are an allowable deduction for income tax.

Underwriters

206.—(1) An underwriting member of Lloyd's shall, subject to the following provisions of this section, be treated for the purposes of this Act as absolutely entitled as against the trustees to the investments of his premiums trust fund, his special reserve fund (if any) and any other trust fund required or authorised by the rules of Lloyd's or required by the underwriting agent through whom his business or any part of it is carried on, to be kept in connection with the business.

(2) The trustees of any premiums trust fund shall, subject to subsections (3) and (4) below, be assessed and charged to capital gains tax as if subsection (1) above had not been passed.

(3) Tax assessed by virtue of subsection (2) above for a year of assessment shall be assessed at a rate equivalent to the basic rate of income tax for the year; and if an assessment to tax at a higher rate is subsequently made on an underwriting member in respect of the same gains, an appropriate credit shall be given for the tax assessed on the trustees.

(4) The assessment to be made on the trustees of a fund by virtue of subsection (2) above for any year of assessment shall not take account of losses accruing in any previous year of assessment, and if for that or any other reason the tax paid on behalf of an underwriting member for any year of assessment by virtue of assessments so made exceeds the capital gains tax for which he is liable, the excess shall, on a claim by him, be repaid.

(5) For the purposes of subsections (2) to (4) above the underwriting agent may be treated as a trustee of the premiums trust fund.

GENERAL NOTE
This section, together with the three following, deals with the special situation of underwriters at Lloyd's. The individual underwriting member is treated as being absolutely entitled to the investments of his premiums trust fund, his special reserve fund and any other trust fund required or authorised by the rules of Lloyd's or by the underwriting agent. However, C.G.T. is in practice assessed on the underwriting agent as trustee of the fund at the basic rate. Higher-rate tax and relief for previous years' losses are settled direct with the underwriting member.

Disposal of assets in premiums trust fund etc.

207.—(1) Subject to subsection (6) below, the chargeable gains or allowable losses accruing on the disposal of assets forming part of a premiums trust fund shall be taken to be those allocated to the corresponding underwriting year.

(2) The amount of the gains or losses so allocated at the end of any accounting period shall be such proportion of the difference mentioned in subsection (3) below as is allocated to the underwriting year under the rules or practice of Lloyd's.

(3) That difference is the difference between the valuations at the beginning and at the end of the accounting period of the assets forming part of the fund, the value at the beginning of the period of assets acquired during the period being taken as the cost of acquisition and the value at the end of the period of assets disposed of during the period being taken as the consideration for the disposal.

(4) Subsection (5) below applies where the following state of affairs exists at the beginning of an accounting period or the end of an accounting period—

(a) securities have been transferred after 18th August 1989 by the trustees of a premiums trust fund in pursuance of an arrangement mentioned in section 129(1) or (2) of the Taxes Act (stock lending),

(b) the transfer was made to enable another person to fulfil a contract or to make a transfer,

(c) securities have not been transferred in return, and

(d) the transfer made by the trustees constitutes a disposal which by virtue of section 271(9) is to be disregarded as there mentioned.

(5) The securities transferred by the trustees shall be treated for the purposes of subsection (3) above as if they formed part of the premiums trust fund at the beginning concerned or the end concerned (as the case may be).

(6) Subsections (1) to (3) above do not apply to gilt-edged securities and qualifying corporate bonds.

GENERAL NOTE

Subss. (1)–(3) and (6)
These derive originally from FA 1973, Sched. 16, paras. 6 and 7. They provide that the gains and losses on assets in a premium trust fund are to be allocated to an underwriting year under the practice of Lloyd's. This allocation is a proportion of the difference between the valuations of the fund at the beginning and the end of a period, taking into account acquisitions and disposals as at that time.

Subss. (4) and (5)
These subsections, introduced by FA 1989, s.91(2), allow Lloyd's underwriters to lend stock to market makers without a C.G.T. liability. The stock in question is treated as still being in the trust fund.

Premiums trust funds: indexation

208. Sections 53 to 57, 104, 108, 109, 110, 113, 114, 131 and 145 shall apply with any necessary modifications in relation to assets forming part of a premiums trust fund as they apply in relation to other assets, and for the purposes of the application of those sections in accordance with this section, it shall be assumed—

(a) that assets forming part of a fund are disposed of and immediately reacquired on the last day of each accounting period; and

(b) that the indexation allowance computed for that accounting period is allocated to the corresponding underwriting year in the same proportion as the gains or losses referred to in section 207(2).

GENERAL NOTE
The provisions relating to indexation and the rules relating to securities are applied to premiums trust funds. A fund for this purpose is deemed to be disposed of at the end of each accounting period and the indexation allowance is allocated in line with s.207(2).

Interpretation, regulations about underwriters etc.

209.—(1) Expressions used in this section or sections 206 to 208 and in sections 450 to 456 of the Taxes Act (Lloyd's underwriters) have the same meanings as they have for the purposes of sections 450 to 456.

(2) The Board may by regulations provide—

   (a) for the assessment and collection of tax charged in accordance with section 207;

   (b) for modifying the provisions of that section in relation to syndicates continuing for more than 2 years after the end of an underwriting year;

   (c) for giving credit for foreign tax.

(3) Subsection (4) below applies in the case of any provision of the Tax Acts, the Management Act, this Act or any other enactment relating to capital gains tax, which imposes a time limit for making a claim or an election or an application.

(4) The Board may by regulations provide that where the claim or election or application falls to be made by an underwriting member of Lloyd's or his spouse (or both) the provision shall have effect as if it imposed such longer time limit as is specified in the regulations.

(5) Regulations under subsection (4) above may make different provision for different provisions or different purposes.

(6) Regulations under subsection (2) or (4) above may make provision with respect to any year or years of assessment; and the year (or any of the years) may be the one in which the regulations are made or any year falling before or after that year (including years earlier than 1992–93), but regulations under subsection (2) may not make provision with respect to any year of assessment which precedes the next but one preceding the year of assessment in which the regulations are made.

GENERAL NOTE

   This is a general interpretative and administrative provision regarding Lloyd's underwriters and corresponds with ICTA 1988, s.451. It originated in FA 1973, Sched. 16, para. 17 and was amended by FA 1989, s.92 to allow regulations to be made retrospective, subject to a limit of the year of assessment which precedes the next but one preceding the year of assessment in which the regulations are made. There is also a power to extend time limits for claims, elections and applications by underwriters and their spouses. The regulations in force are contained in the Lloyd's Underwriters (Tax) (1989–90) Regulations 1992 (S.I. 1992 No. 511).

Life assurance and deferred annuities

210.—(1) This section has effect as respects any policy of assurance or contract for a deferred annuity on the life of any person.

(2) No chargeable gain shall accrue on the disposal of, or of an interest in, the rights under any such policy of assurance or contract except where the person making the disposal is not the original beneficial owner and acquired the rights of interest for a consideration in money or money's worth.

(3) Subject to subsection (2) above, the occasion of—

   (a) the payment of the sum or sums assured by a policy of assurance, or

   (b) the transfer of investments or other assets to the owner of a policy of assurance in accordance with the policy,

and the occasion of the surrender of a policy of assurance, shall be the occasion of a disposal of the rights under the policy of assurance.

(4) Subject to subsection (2) above, the occasion of the payment of the first instalment of a deferred annuity, and the occasion of the surrender of the rights under a contract for a deferred annuity, shall be the occasion of a disposal of the rights under the contract for a deferred annuity and the amount of the consideration for the disposal of a contract for a deferred annuity shall be the market value at that time of the right to that and further instalments of the annuity.

GENERAL NOTE
   Life assurance policies and deferred annuity contracts are exempt from C.G.T., except when disposed of by someone, other than the original owner, who purchased it. In the latter case, occasions of charge may arise on the maturity or surrender of the policy. Also, with a deferred annuity, on the payment of the first instalment of the surrender, there is a disposal at market value of the rights under the contract.

Transfers of business

   211.—(1) This section applies where there is a transfer of the whole or part of the long term business of an insurance company ("the transferor") to another company ("the transferee") in accordance with a scheme sanctioned by a court under section 49 of the Insurance Companies Act 1982.

   (2) Subject to subsection (3) below, where this section applies section 139 shall not be prevented from having effect in relation to any asset included in the transfer by reason that—

   (a) the transfer is not part of a scheme of reconstruction or amalgamation,
   (b) the condition in paragraph (c) of subsection (1) of that section is not satisfied, or
   (c) the asset is within subsection (2) of that section;

and where section 139 applies by virtue of paragraph (a) above the references in subsection (5) of that section to the reconstruction or amalgamation shall be construed as references to the transfer.

   (3) Section 139 shall not have effect in relation to an asset by virtue of subsection (2) above unless—

   (a) any gain accruing to the transferor—
         (i) on the disposal of the asset in accordance with the scheme, or
         (ii) where that disposal occurs after the transfer of business has taken place, on a disposal of the asset immediately before that transfer, and
   (b) any gain accruing to the transferee on a disposal of the asset immediately after its acquisition in accordance with the scheme,

would be a chargeable gain which would form part of its profits for corporation tax purposes (and would not be a gain on which, under any double taxation relief arrangements, it would not be liable to tax).

GENERAL NOTE
   This provision, introduced by FA 1990, Sched. 9, para. 1, grants relief from tax on the transfer of the whole or part of the long-term business of an insurance company to another company under a scheme sanctioned by the court, notwithstanding that some of the conditions in s.139 are not complied with. It does not apply where either company is covered by double tax treaty relief.
   "Long-term business" is defined in the Insurance Companies Act 1982, Sched. 1.

Annual deemed disposal of holdings of unit trusts etc.

   212.—(1) Where at the end of an accounting period the assets of an insurance company's long term business fund include—

   (a) rights under an authorised unit trust, or
   (b) relevant interests in an offshore fund,

then, subject to the following provisions of this section and to section 213, the company shall be deemed for the purposes of corporation tax on capital gains to have disposed of and immediately reacquired each of the assets concerned at its market value at that time.

   (2) Subsection (1) above shall not apply to assets linked solely to pension business or to assets of the overseas life assurance fund, and in relation to other assets (apart from assets linked solely to basic life assurance and general annuity business) shall apply only to the relevant chargeable fraction of each class of asset.

(3) For the purposes of subsection (2) above "the relevant chargeable fraction" in relation to linked assets is the fraction of which—

(a) the denominator is the mean of such of the opening and closing long term business liabilities as are liabilities in respect of benefits to be determined by reference to the value of linked assets, other than assets linked solely to basic life assurance and general annuity business or pension business and assets of the overseas life assurance fund; and

(b) the numerator is the mean of such of the opening and closing liabilities within paragraph (a) above as are liabilities of business the profits of which are not charged to tax under Case I or Case VI of Schedule D (disregarding section 85 of the Finance Act 1989).

(4) For the purposes of subsection (2) above "the relevant chargeable fraction" in relation to assets other than linked assets is the fraction of which—

(a) the denominator is the aggregate of—

(i) the mean of the opening and closing long term business liabilities, other than liabilities in respect of benefits to be determined by reference to the value of linked assets and liabilities of the overseas life assurance business, and

(ii) the mean of the opening and closing amounts of the investment reserve; and

(b) the numerator is the aggregate of—

(i) the mean of such of the opening and closing liabilities within paragraph (a) above as are liabilities of business the profits of which are not charged to tax under Case I or Case VI of Schedule D (disregarding section 85 of the Finance Act 1989), and

(ii) the mean of the appropriate parts of the opening and closing amounts of the investment reserve.

(5) For the purposes of this section an interest is a "relevant interest in an offshore fund" if—

(a) it is a material interest in an offshore fund for the purposes of Chapter V of Part XVII of the Taxes Act, or

(b) it would be such an interest if the shares and interests excluded by subsections (6) and (8) of section 759 of that Act were limited to shares or interests in trading companies.

(6) For the purposes of this section the amount of an investment reserve and the "appropriate part" of it shall be determined in accordance with section 432A(8) and (9) of the Taxes Act.

(7) In this section "trading company" means a company—

(a) whose business consists of the carrying on of insurance business, or the carrying on of any other trade which does not consist to any extent of dealing in commodities, currency, securities, debts or other assets of a financial nature, or

(b) whose business consists wholly or mainly of the holding of shares or securities of trading companies which are its 90 per cent. subsidiaries; and in this section and sections 213 and 214 other expressions have the same meanings as in Chapter I of Part XII of the Taxes Act.

(8) Subject to section 214, this section shall have effect in relation to accounting periods beginning on or after 1st January 1991 or, where the Treasury by order appoint a later day, in relation to accounting periods beginning on or after that day (and not in relation to any earlier accounting period, even if the order is made after 1st January 1, 1991 and the period has ended before it is made).

GENERAL NOTE

This section, together with the two following, implements an annual charge on rights under an authorised unit trust (see s.99) or relevant interests in an offshore fund (see subs. (5)), held in an insurance company's long-term business fund (see the Companies Act 1982, s.96(2)). It does not apply to assets linked solely to pension business or assets of the overseas life assurance fund and applies in relation to other assets (apart from assets linked only to basic life assurance and general annuity business) only to the relevant chargeable fraction (see subss. (3) and (4)).

Spreading of gains and losses under section 212

213.—(1) Any chargeable gains or allowable losses which would otherwise accrue on disposals deemed by virtue of section 212 to have been made at the end of a company's accounting period shall be treated as not accruing to it, but instead—

(a) there shall be ascertained the difference ("the net amount") between the aggregate of those gains and the aggregate of those losses, and

(b) one-seventh of the net amount shall be treated as a chargeable gain or, where it represents an excess of losses over gains, as an allowable loss accruing to the company at the end of the accounting period, and

(c) a further one-seventh shall be treated as a chargeable gain or, as the case may be, as an allowable loss accruing at the end of each succeeding accounting period until the whole amount has been accounted for.

(2) For any accounting period of less than one year, the fraction of one-seventh referred to in subsection (1)(c) above shall be proportionately reduced; and where this subsection has had effect in relation to any accounting period before the last for which subsection (1)(c) above applies, the fraction treated as accruing at the end of that last accounting period shall also be adjusted appropriately.

(3) Where—

(a) the net amount for an accounting period of an insurance company represents an excess of gains over losses,

(b) the net amount for one of the next six accounting periods (after taking account of any reductions made by virtue of this subsection) represents an excess of losses over gains,

(c) there is (after taking account of any such reductions) no net amount for any intervening accounting period, and

(d) within two years after the end of the later accounting period the company makes a claim for the purpose in respect of the whole or part of the net amount for that period.

the net amounts for both the earlier and the later period shall be reduced by the amount in respect of which the claim is made.

(4) Subject to subsection (5) below, where a company ceases to carry on long term business before the end of the last of the accounting periods for which subsection (1)(c) above would apply in relation to a net amount, the fraction of that amount that is treated as accruing at the end of the accounting period ending with the cessation shall be such as to secure that the whole of the net amount has been accounted for.

(5) Where there is a transfer of the whole or part of the long term business of an insurance company ("the transferor") to another company ("the transferee") in accordance with a scheme sanctioned by a court under section 49 of the Insurance Companies Act 1982, any chargeable gain or allowable loss which (assuming that the transferor had continued to carry on the business transferred) would have accrued to the transferor by virtue of subsection (1) above after the transfer shall instead be deemed to accrue to the transferee.

(6) Where subsection (5) above has effect, the amount of the gain or loss accruing at the end of the first accounting period of the transferee ending after the day when the transfer takes place shall be calculated as if that accounting period began with the day after the transfer.

(7) Where the transfer is of part only of the transferor's long term business, subsection (5) above shall apply only to such part of any amount to which it would otherwise apply as is appropriate.

(8) Any question arising as to the operation of subsection (7) above shall be determined by the Special Commissioners who shall determine the question in the same manner as they determine appeals; but both the transferor and transferee shall be entitled to appear and be heard or to make representations in writing.

(9) It is hereby declared that amounts to which section 47(1)(b) and (c) of the Finance Act 1990 applied immediately before the commencement of this section shall continue to be subject to the provisions of this section (with any necessary modifications).

GENERAL NOTE
The charge under s.212 does not accrue immediately. One-seventh is charged immediately and the remainder spread over the following six accounting periods. Where a loss arises in one of these periods, it may be carried back on a claim being made within two years.

The entire gain crystallises when a company ceases to carry on long-term business, except when this occurs under a transfer approved by the court, in which case the transferee company assumes the liability. In cases of a partial transfer, this will apply to an appropriate amount, subject to determination by the Special Commissioners.

Transitional provisions

214.—(1) In this section—
(a) "section 212 assets" means rights under authorised unit trusts and relevant interests in offshore funds which are assets of a company's long term business fund;
(b) "linked section 212 assets" means section 212 assets which are linked assets;
(c) "relevant linked liabilities", in relation to a company, means such of the liabilities of its basic life assurance and general annuity business as are liabilities in respect of benefits under pre-commencement policies or contracts, being benefits to be determined by reference to the value of linked assets;
(d) "pre-commencement policies or contracts" means—
     (i) policies issued in respect of insurances made before 1st April 1990, and
     (ii) annuity contracts made before that date,
but excluding policies or annuity contracts varied on or after that date so as to increase the benefits secured or to extend the term of the insurance or annuity (any exercise of rights conferred by a policy or annuity contract being regarded for this purpose as a variation);
(e) "basic life assurance and general annuity business" means life assurance business, other than pension business and overseas life assurance business.

(2) The assets which are to be regarded for the purposes of this section as linked solely to an insurance company's basic life assurance and general annuity business at any time before the first accounting period of the company which begins on or after 1st January 1992 are all the assets which at that time—
(a) are or were linked solely to the company's basic life assurance business or general annuity business, or
(b) although not falling within paragraph (a) above, would be, or would have been, regarded as linked solely to the company's basic life assurance business, were its general annuity business treated as forming, or having at all times formed, part of its basic life assurance business and as not being a separate category of business.

(3) Where within two years after the end of an accounting period an insurance company makes a claim for the purpose in relation to the period, section 212(1) shall not apply at the end of the period to so much of any class

of linked assets as it would otherwise apply to and as represents relevant linked liabilities.

(4) For the purposes of subsection (3) above assets of any class shall be taken to represent relevant linked liabilities only to the extent that their value does not exceed the fraction set out in subsection (5) below of such of the company's relevant linked liabilities as are liabilities in respect of benefits to be determined by reference to the value of assets of that class.

(5) The fraction referred to in subsection (4) is—

$$\frac{A \times C \times 110}{B \times D \times 100}$$

where—

A is the amount at the end of 1989 of such of the company's relevant linked liabilities as are liabilities in respect of benefits to be determined by reference to the value of linked section 212 assets;

B is the amount of the company's relevant linked liabilities at that time;

C is the amount of the company's relevant linked liabilities at the end of the accounting period for which the claim is made;

D is the amount at the end of that period of such of the company's relevant linked liabilities as are liabilities in respect of benefits to be determined by reference to the value of linked section 212 assets.

(6) Subject to subsection (7) below, subsection (9) below applies where—

(a) after the end of 1989 an insurance company exchanges section 212 assets ("the old assets") for other assets ("the new assets") to be held as assets of the long term business fund,

(b) the new assets are not section 212 assets but are assets on the disposal of which any gains accruing would be chargeable gains,

(c) both the old assets and the new assets are linked solely to basic life assurance and general annuity business, or both are neither linked solely to basic life assurance and general annuity business or pension business nor assets of the overseas life assurance fund, and

(d) the company makes a claim for the purpose within two years after the end of the accounting period in which the exchange occurs.

(7) Subsection (6) above shall have effect in relation to old assets only to the extent that their amount, when added to the amount of any assets to which subsection (9) below has already applied and which are assets of the same class, does not exceed the aggregate of—

(a) the amount of the assets of the same class included in the long term business fund at the beginning of 1990, other than assets linked solely to pension business and assets of the overseas life assurance fund, and

(b) 110 per cent. of the amount of the assets of that class which represents any subsequent increases in the company's relevant linked liabilities in respect of benefits to be determined by reference to the value of assets of that class.

(8) The reference in subsection (7)(b) above to a subsequent increase in liabilities is a reference to any amount by which the liabilities at the end of an accounting period ending after 31st December 1989 exceed those at the beginning of the period (or at the end of 1989 if that is later); and for the purposes of that provision the amount of assets which represents an increase in liabilities is the excess of—

(a) the amount of assets whose value at the later time is equivalent to the liabilities at that time, over

(b) the amount of assets whose value at the earlier time is equivalent to the liabilities at that time.

(9) Where this subsection applies, the insurance company (but not any other party to the exchange) shall be treated for the purposes of corporation tax on capital gains as if the exchange had not involved a disposal of the old

assets or an acquisition of the new, but as if the old and the new assets were the same assets acquired as the old assets were acquired.

(10) References in subsection (6) to (9) above to the exchange of assets include references to the case where the consideration obtained for the disposal of assets (otherwise than by way of an exchange within subsection (6)) is applied in acquiring other assets within six months after the disposal; and for the purposes of those subsections the time when an exchange occurs shall be taken to be the time when the old assets are disposed of.

(11) Where at any time after the end of 1989 there is a transfer of long term business of an insurance company ("the transferor") to another company ("the transferee") in accordance with a scheme sanctioned by a court under section 49 of the Insurance Companies Act 1982—

  (a) if the transfer is of the whole of the long term business of the transferor, subsections (1) to (10) above shall have effect in relation to the assets of the transferee as if that business had at all material times been carried on by him;

  (b) if the transfer is of part of the long term business of the transferor, those subsections shall have effect in relation to assets of the transferor and the transferee to such extent as is appropriate;

and any question arising as to the operation of paragraph (b) above shall be determined by the Special Commissioners who shall determine the question in the same manner as they determine appeals; but both the transferor and the transferee shall be entitled to appear and be heard or to make representations in writing.

GENERAL NOTE

This contains transitional provisions for the purposes of the charge under ss.212 and 213.

Assets held by a company linked to insurances made before April 1, 1990 are not chargeable provided that the company so claims, so long as there are linked liabilities, subject to a limitation by reference to the fraction in subs. (5).

Roll-over relief is available where assets chargeable under s.212 are exchanged for assets normally subject to tax, on a claim being made, subject to the limit provided by subs. (7). The relief applies to a disposal provided that the new assets are acquired within six months.

The relief under s.214 is also available to a transferee company.

CHAPTER IV

MISCELLANEOUS CASES

Building societies etc.

Disposal of assets on amalgamation of building societies etc.

215. If, in the course of or as part of an amalgamation of two or more building societies or a transfer of engagements from one building society to another, there is a disposal of an asset by one society to another, both shall be treated for the purposes of corporation tax on chargeable gains as if the asset were acquired from the one making the disposal for a consideration of such amount as would secure that on the disposal neither a gain nor a loss would accrue to the one making the disposal.

GENERAL NOTE

Transfers of assets on an amalgamation of building societies are dealt with on a no-gain/no-loss basis.

Assets transferred from society to company

216.—(1) This section and section 217 apply where there is a transfer of the whole of a building society's business to a company ("the successor company") in accordance with section 97 and the other applicable provisions of the Building Societies Act 1986.

(2) Where the society and the successor company are not members of the same group at the time of the transfer—
  (a) they shall be treated for the purposes of corporation tax on capital gains as if any asset disposed of as part of the transfer were acquired by the successor company for a consideration of such amount as would secure that on the disposal neither a gain nor a loss would accrue to the society, and
  (b) if because of the transfer any company ceases to be a member of the same group as the society, that event shall not cause section 178 or 179 to have effect as respects any asset acquired by the company from the society or any other member of the same group.
(3) Where the society and the successor company are members of the same group at the time of the transfer but later cease to be so, that later event shall not cause action 178 or 179 to have effect as respects—
  (a) any asset acquired by the successor company on or before the transfer from the society or any other member of the same group, or
  (b) any asset acquired from the society or any other member of the same group by any company other than the successor company which is a member of the same group at the time of the transfer.
(4) Subject to subsection (6) below, where a company which is a member of the same group as the society at the time of the transfer—
  (a) ceases to be a member of that group and becomes a member of the same group as the successor company, and
  (b) subsequently ceases to be a member of that group,
section 178 or 179 shall have effect on that later event as respects any relevant asset acquired by the company otherwise than from the successor company as if it had been acquired from the successor company.
(5) In subsection (4) above "relevant asset" means any asset acquired by the company—
  (a) from the society, or
  (b) from any other company which is a member of the same group at the time of the transfer,
when the company and the society, or the company, the society and the other company, were members of the same group.
(6) Subsection (4) above shall not apply if the company which acquired the asset and the company from which it was acquired (one being a 75 per cent. subsidiary of the other) cease simultaneously to be members of the same group as the successor company but continue to be members of the same group as one another.
(7) For the purposes of this section "group" shall be construed in accordance with section 170.

GENERAL NOTE
    Under the Building Societies Act 1986, building societies are given the option to convert themselves into public limited companies. This section and the following section, together with other provisions originally enacted by FA 1988, Sched. 12, are designed to prevent incidental tax charges which might inhibit such a decision.
    This section provides that there will be no charge to corporation tax on chargeable assets on the transfer, whether to a new company or an existing company.

Shares, and rights to shares, in successor company

217.—(1) Where, in connection with the transfer, there are conferred on members of the society—
  (a) any rights to acquire shares in the successor company in priority to other persons, or
  (b) any rights to acquire shares in that company for consideration of an amount or value lower than the market value of the shares, or

(c) any rights to free shares in that company,
any such right so conferred on a member shall be regarded for the purposes of tax on chargeable gains as an option (within the meaning of section 144) granted to, and acquired by, him for no consideration and having no value at the time of that grant and acquisition.

(2) Where, in connection with the transfer, shares in the successor company are issued by that company, or disposed of by the society, to a member of the society, those shares shall be regarded for the purposes of tax on chargeable gains—

(a) as acquired by the member for a consideration of an amount or value equal to the amount or value of any new consideration given by him for the shares (or, if no new consideration is given, as acquired for no consideration); and

(b) as having, at the time of their acquisition by the member, a value equal to the amount or value of the new consideration so given (or, if no new consideration is given, as having no value);

but this subsection is without prejudice to the operation of subsection (1) above, where applicable.

(3) Subsection (4) below applies in any case where—

(a) in connection with the transfer, shares in the successor company are issued by that company, or disposed of by the society, to trustees on terms which provide for the transfer of those shares to members of the society for no new consideration; and

(b) the circumstances are such that in the hands of the trustees the shares constitute settled property.

(4) Where this subsection applies, then, for the purposes of tax on chargeable gains—

(a) the shares shall be regarded as acquired by the trustees for no consideration;

(b) the interest of any member in the settled property constituted by the shares shall be regarded as acquired by him for no consideration and as having no value at the time of its acquisition;

(c) where a member becomes absolutely entitled as against the trustees to any of the settled property, both the trustees and the member shall be treated as if, on his becoming so entitled, the shares in question had been disposed of and immediately reacquired by the trustees, in their capacity as trustees within section 60(1), for a consideration of such an amount as would secure that on the disposal neither a gain nor a loss would accrue to the trustees (and accordingly section 71 shall not apply in relation to that occasion); and

(d) on the disposal by a member of an interest in the settled property, other than the disposal treated as occurring for the purposes of paragraph (c) above, any gain accruing shall be a chargeable gain (and accordingly section 76(1) shall not apply in relation to the disposal).

(5) Where, in connection with the transfer, the society disposes of any shares in the successor company, then, for the purposes of the Act, any gains arising on the disposal shall not be chargeable gains.

(6) In this section—

"free shares", in relation to a member of the society, means any shares issued by the successor company, or disposed of by the society, to that member in connection with the transfer but for no new consideration;

"member", in relation to the society, means a person who is or has been a member of it, in that capacity, and any reference to a member includes a reference to a member of any particular class or description;

"new consideration" means consideration other than—

    (a) consideration provided directly or indirectly out of the assets of the society; or

    (b) consideration derived from a member's shares or other rights in the society.

(7) References in this section to the case where a member becomes absolutely entitled to settled property as against the trustees shall be taken to include references to the case where he would become so entitled but for being an infant or otherwise under disability.

GENERAL NOTE

There will be no charge to C.G.T. on the conversion of members' share accounts into shares in the successor company, whether or not the members give consideration for the shares.

The Housing Corporation, Housing for Wales and housing associations

Disposals of land between the Housing Corporation, Housing for Wales or Scottish Homes and housing associations

218.—(1) Where—

(a) in accordance with a scheme approved under section 5 of the Housing Act 1964 or paragraph 5 of Schedule 7 to the Housing Associations Act 1985, the Housing Corporation acquires from a housing association the association's interest in all the land held by the association for carrying out its objects, or

(b) after the Housing Corporation has so acquired from a housing association all the land so held by it the Corporation disposes to a single housing association of the whole of that land (except any part previously disposed of or agreed to be disposed of otherwise than to a housing association), together with all related assets,

then both parties to the disposal of the land to or, as the case may be, by the Housing Corporation shall be treated for the purposes of corporation tax in respect of chargeable gains as if the land and any related assets disposed of therewith (and each part of that land and those assets) were acquired from the party making the disposal for a consideration of such an amount as would secure that on the disposal neither a gain nor a loss accrued to that party.

(2) In subsection (1) above, "housing association" has the same meaning as in the Housing Associations Act 1985, and "related assets" means, in relation to an acquisition of land by the Housing Corporation, assets acquired by the Corporation in accordance with the same scheme as that land, and in relation to a disposal of land by the Housing Corporation, assets held by the Corporation for the purposes of the same scheme as that land.

(3) This section shall also have effect with the substitution of the words "Housing for Wales" for the words "the Housing Corporation" and "the Corporation" in each place where they occur.

(4) This section shall also have effect with the substitution of the words "Scottish Homes" for the words "the Housing Corporation" and "the Corporation" in each place where they occur.

GENERAL NOTE

Disposals of land by housing associations to the Housing Corporation and subsequent disposals of land to a single housing association are dealt with on a no-gain/no-loss basis.

The same provisions apply to Housing for Wales and Scottish Homes.

Disposals by Housing Corporation, Housing for Wales, Scottish Homes and certain housing associations

219.—(1) In any case where—

(a) the Housing Corporation dispose of any land to a registered housing association, or

(b) a registered housing association disposes of any land to another registered housing association, or

(c) in pursuance of a direction of the Housing Corporation given under Part I of the Housing Associations Act 1985 requiring it to do so, a registered housing association disposes of any of its property, other than land, to another registered housing association, or

(d) a registered housing association or an unregistered self-build society disposes of any land to the Housing Corporation,

both parties to the disposal shall be treated for the purposes of tax on chargeable gains as if the land or property disposed of were acquired from the Housing Corporation, registered housing association or unregistered self-build society making the disposal for a consideration of such an amount as would secure that on the disposal neither a gain nor a loss accrued to the Corporation or, as the case may be, that association or society.

(2) Subsection (1) above shall also have effect with the substitution of the words "Housing for Wales" for the words "the Housing Corporation" and "the Corporation" in each place where they occur.

(3) Subsection (1) above shall also have effect with the substitution of the words "Scottish Homes" for the words "the Housing Corporation" and "the Corporation" in each place where they occur.

(4) In this section "registered housing association" and "unregistered self-build society" have the same meanings as in the Housing Associations Act 1985.

GENERAL NOTE

Provisions similar to s.218 apply to disposals between registered housing associations, unregistered self-build societies, and the Housing Corporation, Housing for Wales and Scottish Homes.

Disposals by Northern Ireland housing associations

220.—(1) In any case where—

(a) a registered Northern Ireland housing association disposes of any land to another such association, or

(b) in pursuance of a direction of the Department of the Environment for Northern Ireland given under Chapter II of Part VII of the Housing (Northern Ireland) Order 1981 requiring it to do so, a registered Northern Ireland housing association disposes of any of its property, other than land, to another such association,

both parties to the disposal shall be treated for the purposes of tax on chargeable gains as if the land or property disposed of were acquired from the association making the disposal for a consideration of such an amount as would secure that on the disposal neither a gain nor a loss accrued to that association.

(2) In subsection (1) above "registered Northern Ireland housing association" means a registered housing association within the meaning of Part VII of the Order referred to in paragraph (b) of that subsection.

GENERAL NOTE

Disposals between registered Northern Ireland housing associations are dealt with on a no-gain/no-loss basis.

Other bodies

Harbour authorities

221.—(1) For the purposes of this Act any asset transferred on the transfer of the trade shall be deemed to be for a consideration such that no gain or loss accrues to the transferor on its transfer; and for the purposes of Schedule 2 the transferee shall be treated as if the acquisition by the transferor of any asset so transferred had been the transferee's acquisition thereof.

(2) This section applies only where the trade transferred is transferred from any body corporate other than a limited liability company to a harbour

authority by or under a certified harbour reorganisation scheme (within the meaning of section 518 of the Taxes Act) which provides also for the dissolution of the transferor.

GENERAL NOTE

Assets transferred in pursuance of a certified harbour reorganisation scheme under the Harbours Act 1964, s.18, pass on a no-gain/no-loss basis and the transferee is treated as if the transferor's acquisition had been his.

PART VII

OTHER PROPERTY, BUSINESSES, INVESTMENTS ETC.

Private residences

Relief on disposal of private residence

222.—(1) This section applies to a gain accruing to an individual so far as attributable to the disposal of, or of an interest in—

(a) a dwelling-house or part of a dwelling-house which is, or has at any time in his period of ownership been, his only or main residence, or

(b) land which he has for his own occupation and enjoyment with that residence as its garden or grounds up to the permitted area.

(2) In this section "the permitted area" means, subject to subsections (3) and (4) below, an area (inclusive of the site of the dwelling-house) of 0.5 of a hectare.

(3) In any particular case the permitted area shall be such area, larger than 0.5 of a hectare, as the Commissioners concerned may determine if satisfied that, regard being had to the size and character of the dwelling-house, that larger area is required for the reasonable enjoyment of it (or of the part in question) as a residence.

(4) Where part of the land occupied with a residence is and part is not within subsection (1) above, then (up to the permitted area) that part shall be taken to be within subsection (1) above which, if the remainder were separately occupied, would be the most suitable for occupation and enjoyment with the residence.

(5) So far as it is necessary for the purposes of this section to determine which of two or more residences is an individual's main residence for any period—

(a) the individual may conclude that question by notice to the inspector given within two years from the beginning of that period but subject to a right to vary that notice by a further notice to the inspector as respects any period beginning not earlier than two years before the giving of the further notice,

(b) subject to paragraph (a) above, the question shall be concluded by the determination of the inspector, which may be as respects the whole or specified parts of the period of ownership in question,

and notice of any determination of the inspector under paragraph (b) above shall be given to the individual who may appeal to the General Commissioners or the Special Commissioners against that determination within 30 days of service of the notice.

(6) In the case of a man and his wife living with him—

(a) there can only be one residence or main residence for both, so long as living together and, where a notice under subsection (5)(a) above affects both the husband and the wife, it must be given by both, and

(b) any notice under subsection (5)(b) above which affects a residence owned by the husband and a residence owned by the wife shall be given to each and either may appeal under that subsection.

(7) In this section and sections 223 to 226, "the period of ownership" where the individual has had different interests at different times shall be

taken to begin from the first acquisition taken into account in arriving at the expenditure which under Chapter III of Part II is allowable as a deduction in the computation of the gain to which this section applies, and in the case of a man and his wife living with him—

(a) if the one disposes of, or of his or her interest in, the dwelling-house or part of a dwelling-house which is their only or main residence to the other, and in particular if it passes on death to the other as legatee, the other's period of ownership shall begin with the beginning of the period of ownership of the one making the disposal, and

(b) if paragraph (a) above applies, but the dwelling-house or part of a dwelling-house was not the only or main residence of both throughout the period of ownership of the one making the disposal, account shall be taken of any part of that period during which it was his only or main residence as if it was also that of the other.

(8) If at any time during an individual's period of ownership of a dwelling-house or part of a dwelling-house he—

(a) resides in living accommodation which is for him job-related within the meaning of section 356 of the Taxes Act, and

(b) intends in due course to occupy the dwelling-house or part of a dwelling-house as his only or main residence,

this section and sections 223 to 226 shall apply as if the dwelling-house or part of a dwelling-house were at that time occupied by him as a residence.

(9) Section 356(3)(b) and (5) of the Taxes Act shall apply for the purposes of subsection (8) above only in relation to residence on or after 6th April 1983 in living accommodation which is job-related within the meaning of that section.

(10) Apportionments of consideration shall be made wherever required by this section or sections 223 to 226 and, in particular, where a person disposes of a dwelling-house only part of which is his only or main residence.

GENERAL NOTE

Since his home will usually be the most important asset owned by an individual, the private residence exemption has great significance. The exemption applies to a dwelling-house or part thereof which is the individual's only or main residence or land which he has as garden or grounds up to the permitted area (originally one acre, increased to 0.5 of a hectare, approximately 1.2 acres, by FA 1991, s.93). The permitted area may be increased if the Commissioners concerned determine that a larger area is required for the reasonable enjoyment of the dwelling-house as a residence.

The application of the exemption has proved contentious in practice. It was held in *Varty* v. *Lynes* [1976] 1 W.L.R. 1091 that a disposal of the remainder of a garden following the disposal of the house and part of the garden was not protected by the exemption. In two contrasting decisions, *Makins* v. *Elson* (1976) 51 T.C. 437 and *Moore* v. *Thompson (Inspector of Taxes)* [1986] S.T.C. 170, a caravan was held in one case to be capable of being a dwelling-house and in the other not to be. The distinction would appear to be that in the second case the residence was occasional and sporadic.

Most of the reported cases have been at the other end of the scale. In *Green* v. *I.R.C.* (1982) 56 T.C. 10 the Court of Session held on slightly complicated facts that on the disposal of a renovated mansion-house the owner was entitled to relief on the main block and grounds extending to 15 acres, but not on two wings which were capable of separate occupation.

In England there are a number of authorities, commencing with *Batey* v. *Wakefield* [1982] 1 All E.R. 61. In that case the Court of Appeal held that a bungalow built in the grounds of a country house for the use of a caretaker/gardener was part of the dwelling-house which was the taxpayer's residence. This approach was followed in *Williams (Inspector of Taxes)* v. *Merrylees* [1987] 1 W.L.R. 1511 where a lodge 200 metres away from the main house was held to be part of the "entity which can sensibly be described as being a dwelling-house although split into different buildings performing different functions". However, in *Markey (Inspector of Taxes)* v. *Sanders* [1987] 1 W.L.R. 864, relief was denied in respect of a staff bungalow some 130 metres from the main house on the grounds that it was an important consideration that subsidiary buildings should be "very closely adjacent" to the main house.

The *Markey* v. *Sanders* approach has now been approved by the Court of Appeal in *Lewis* v. *Lady Rook* [1992] S.T.C. 171, in which it was held that any subsidiary building must be "within the curtilage of, and appurtenant to" the main building. This test has been applied in *Honour* v. *Norris* [1992] S.T.C. 304, in which the contention that a number of physically separate flats in a square could constitute a single dwelling-house was rejected.

The law in this area is obviously still in a state of development, but at the moment the trend of interpretation is restrictive.

Where an individual has two or more residences, he can conclude the question which is the main residence by notice to the inspector, subject to a right to vary the notice. Otherwise, the question may be determined by the inspector, subject to appeal.

Spouses living together can have only one main residence for both. Separate periods of ownership may be aggregated.

Where an individual lives in job-related accommodation within ICTA 1988, s.356, *e.g.* Number 10, Downing Street, he may maintain another property as his only or main residence.

Amount of relief

223.—(1) No part of a gain to which section 222 applies shall be a chargeable gain if the dwelling-house or part of a dwelling-house has been the individual's only or main residence throughout the period of ownership, or throughout the period of ownership except for all or any part of the last 36 months of that period.

(2) Where subsection (1) above does not apply, a fraction of the gain shall not be a chargeable gain, and that fraction shall be—

  (a) the length of the part or parts of the period of ownership during which the dwelling-house or the part of the dwelling-house was the individual's only or main residence, but inclusive of the last 36 months of the period of ownership in any event, divided by

  (b) the length of the period of ownership.

(3) For the purposes of subsections (1) and (2) above—

  (a) a period of absence not exceeding three years (or periods of absence which together did not exceed three years), and in addition

  (b) any period of absence throughout which the individual worked in an employment or office all the duties of which were performed outside the United Kingdom, and in addition

  (c) any period of absence not exceeding four years (or periods of absence which together did not exceed four years) throughout which the individual was prevented from residing in the dwelling-house or part of the dwelling-house in consequence of the situation of his place of work or in consequence of any condition imposed by his employer requiring him to reside elsewhere, being a condition reasonably imposed to secure the effective performance by the employee of his duties,

shall be treated as if in that period of absence the dwelling-house or the part of the dwelling-house was the individual's only or main residence if both before and after the period there was a time when the dwelling-house was the individual's only or main residence.

(4) Where a gain to which section 222 applies accrues to any individual and the dwelling-house in question or any part of it is or has at any time in his period of ownership been wholly or partly let by him as residential accommodation, the part of the gain, if any, which (apart from this subsection) would be a chargeable gain by reason of the letting, shall be such a gain only to the extent, if any, to which it exceeds whichever is the lesser of—

  (a) the part of the gain which is not a chargeable gain by virtue of the provisions of subsection (1) to (3) above or those provisions as applied by section 225; and

  (b) £40,000.

(5) Where at any time the number of months specified in subsections (1) and (2)(a) above is 36, the Treasury may by order amend those subsections by substituting references to 24 for the references to 36 in relation to disposals on or after such date as is specified in the order.

(6) Subsection (5) above shall also have effect as if 36 (in both places) read 24 and as if 24 read 36.

(7) In this section—

"period of absence" means a period during which the dwelling-house or the part of the dwelling-house was not the individual's only or main residence and throughout which he had no residence or main residence eligible for relief under this section; and

"period of ownership" does not include any period before 31st March 1982.

GENERAL NOTE

This restricts the *quantum* of relief in cases where the dwelling-house has not been the individual's only or main residence throughout the period of ownership. For this purpose, periods before March 31, 1982 and the last three years of ownership are ignored.

Periods of absence not exceeding three years, any period of absence in an employment overseas, and periods of absence not exceeding four years in which he was required to reside elsewhere by the exigencies of his work, are all ignored.

Subs. (4)

This provides that where part of the dwelling-house has been let as residential accommodation, the chargeable gain accruing on the disposal is reduced to the lesser of the gain qualifying for relief and £40,000. In *Owen* v. *Elliott (Inspector of Taxes)* [1990] Ch. 786, the Court of Appeal held that the relief applied to a boarding-house.

Subss. (5) and (6)

These allow the Treasury to vary by order the final period of ownership which is ignored up and down between two and three years.

Amount of relief: further provisions

224.—(1) If the gain accrues from the disposal of a dwelling-house or part of a dwelling-house part of which is used exclusively for the purpose of a trade or business, or of a profession or vocation, the gain shall be apportioned and section 223 shall apply in relation to the part of the gain apportioned to the part which is not exclusively used for those purposes.

(2) If at any time in the period of ownership there is a change in what is occupied as the individual's residence, whether on account of a reconstruction or conversion of a building or for any other reason, or there have been changes as regards the use of part of the dwelling-house for the purpose of a trade or business, or of a profession or vocation, or for any other purpose, the relief given by section 223 may be adjusted in such manner as the Commissioners concerned may consider to be just and reasonable.

(3) Section 223 shall not apply in relation to a gain if the acquisition of, or of the interest in, the dwelling-house or the part of a dwelling-house was made wholly or partly for the purpose of realising a gain from the disposal of it, and shall not apply in relation to a gain so far as attributable to any expenditure which was incurred after the beginning of the period of ownership and was incurred wholly or partly for the purpose of realising a gain from the disposal.

GENERAL NOTE

This contains further limiting provisions in relation to the private residence relief.

Subs. (1)

The gain is apportioned where part of the dwelling-house is used for business purposes.

Subs. (2)

The relief may be adjusted on a "just and reasonable" basis if there has been a change in what is occupied as the taxpayer's residence.

Subs. (3)

Relief is excluded in relation to acquisitions and subsequent expenditure wholly or partly for the purpose of realising a gain from the disposal.

Private residence occupied under terms of settlement

225. Sections 222 to 224 shall also apply in relation to a gain accruing to a trustee on a disposal of settled property being an asset within section 222(1) where, during the period of ownership of the trustee, the dwelling-house or part of the dwelling-house mentioned in that subsection has been the only or main residence of a person entitled to occupy it under the terms of the settlement, and in those sections as so applied—

(a) references to the individual shall be taken as references to the trustee except in relation to the occupation of the dwelling-house or part of the dwelling-house, and

(b) the notice which may be given to the inspector under section 222(5)(a) shall be a joint notice by the trustee and the person entitled to occupy the dwelling-house or part of the dwelling-house.

GENERAL NOTE

Gains on dwelling-houses held by trustees and occupied by beneficiaries entitled to them under the terms of a settlement are given relief. In *Sansom* v. *Peay* [1976] 1 W.L.R. 1073 it was held that occupation by virtue of a discretionary power exercised by trustees was covered by the exemption.

Private residence occupied by dependent relative before 6th April 1988

226.—(1) Subject to subsection (3) below, this section applies to a gain accruing to an individual so far as attributable to the disposal of, or of an interest in, a dwelling-house or part of a dwelling-house which, on 5th April 1988 or at any earlier time in his period of ownership, was the sole residence of a dependent relative of the individual, provided rent-free and without any other consideration.

(2) If the individual so claims, such relief shall be given in respect of it and its garden or grounds as would be given under sections 222 to 224 if the dwelling-house (or part of the dwelling-house) had been the individual's only or main residence in the period of residence by the dependent relative, and shall be so given in addition to any relief available under those sections apart from this section.

(3) If in a case within subsection (1) above the dwelling-house or part ceases, whether before 6th April 1988 or later, to be the sole residence (provided as mentioned above) of the dependent relative, any subsequent period of residence beginning on or after that date by that or any other dependent relative shall be disregarded for the purposes of subsection (2) above.

(4) Not more than one dwelling-house (or part of a dwelling-house) may qualify for relief as being the residence of a dependent relative of the claimant at any one time nor, in the case of a man and his wife living with him, as being the residence of a dependent relative of the claimant or of the claimant's husband or wife at any one time.

(5) The inspector, before allowing a claim, may require the claimant to show that the giving of the relief claimed will not under subsection (4) above preclude the giving of relief to the claimant's wife or husband or that a claim to any such relief has been relinquished.

(6) In this section "dependent relative" means, in relation to an individual—

(a) any relative of his or of his wife who is incapacitated by old age or infirmity from maintaining himself, or

(b) his or his wife's mother who, whether or not incapacitated, is either widowed, or living apart from her husband, or a single woman in consequence of dissolution or annulment of marriage.

(7) If the individual mentioned in subsection (6) above is a woman the references in that subsection to the individual's wife shall be construed as references to the individual's husband.

GENERAL NOTE
This useful relief, accorded to dwelling-houses occupied without consideration by a dependent relative (as defined in subs. (6)), was abolished in relation to disposals after April 6, 1988, by FA 1988, s.111. The relief is continued on a transitional basis where such an occupation existed on the abolition date.

Employee share ownership trusts

Conditions for roll-over relief

227.—(1) Relief is available under section 229(1) where each of the six conditions set out in subsections (2) to (7) below is fulfilled.

(2) The first condition is that a person ("the claimant") makes a disposal of shares, or his interest in shares, to the trustees of a trust which—

(a) is a qualifying employee share ownership trust at the time of the disposal, and

(b) was established by a company ("the founding company") which immediately after the disposal is a trading company or the holding company of a trading group.

(3) The second condition is that the shares—

(a) are shares in the founding company,

(b) form part of the ordinary share capital of the company,

(c) are fully paid up,

(d) are not redeemable, and

(e) are not subject to any restrictions other than restrictions which attach to all shares of the same class or a restriction authorised by paragraph 7(2) of Schedule 5 to the Finance Act 1989.

(4) The third condition is that, at any time in the entitlement period, the trustees—

(a) are beneficially entitled to not less than 10 per cent. of the ordinary share capital of the founding company,

(b) are beneficially entitled to not less than 10 per cent. of any profits available for distribution to equity holders of the founding company, and

(c) would be beneficially entitled to not less than 10 per cent. of any assets of the founding company available for distribution to its equity holders on a winding-up.

(5) The fourth condition is that the claimant obtains consideration for the disposal and, at any time in the acquisition period, all the amount or value of the consideration is applied by him in making an acquisition of assets or an interest in assets ("replacement assets") which—

(a) are, immediately after the time of the acquisition, chargeable assets in relation to the claimant, and

(b) are not shares in, or debentures issued by, the founding company or a company which is (at the time of the acquisition) in the same group as the founding company;

but the preceding provisions of this subsection shall have effect without the words ", at any time in the acquisition period," if the acquisition is made pursuant to an unconditional contract entered into in the acquisition period.

(6) The fifth condition is that, at all times in the proscribed period, there are no unauthorised arrangements under which the claimant or a person connected with him may be entitled to acquire any of the shares, or an interest in or right deriving from any of the shares, which are the subject of the disposal by the claimant.

(7) The sixth condition is that no chargeable event occurs in relation to the trustees in—

(a) the chargeable period in which the claimant makes the disposal,

(b) the chargeable period in which the claimant makes the acquisition, or

    (c) any chargeable period falling after that mentioned in paragraph (a) above and before that mentioned in paragraph (b) above.

GENERAL NOTE

During the 1980s there was a considerable increase in what were known as "management buy-outs", *i.e.* the acquisition of a company by its management and other employees. Such arrangements often involved the use of trusts. This section and the following sections introduced by FA 1990, ss.31–40, are designed to give roll-over relief to transfers of shares to employee share ownership trusts ("ESOTs"). The basic conditions for relief are set out in this section and s.228. The following conditions apply:

(1) the shares must be disposed of to a qualifying ESOT established by a trading company. For "qualifying ESOT", see FA 1989, Sched. 5, which applied for relief from corporation tax on contributions to ESOTs;

(2) the shares must be ordinary, paid-up, non-redeemable shares subject to no other restriction other than a requirement to dispose of the shares on leaving the company (FA 1989, Sched. 5, para. 7(2));

(3) the trustees must have a beneficial entitlement within a year to not less than 10 per cent. of the ordinary share capital, the equity profits and the assets on winding-up;

(4) the consideration for the disposal must be applied within six months of the disposal or, if later, the date on which condition (3) is satisfied on the acquisition of chargeable assets;

(5) there must be no unauthorised arrangement allowing for the repurchase of shares;

(6) no chargeable event occurs in relation to the trustees between the disposal and the acquisition by the claimant. For "chargeable event", see FA 1989, s.69.

Conditions for relief: supplementary

228.—(1) This section applies for the purposes of section 227.

(2) The entitlement period is the period beginning with the disposal and ending on the expiry of 12 months beginning with the date of the disposal.

(3) The acquisition period is the period beginning with the disposal and ending on the expiry of six months beginning with—

    (a) the date of the disposal, or

    (b) if later, the date on which the third condition (set out in section 227(4)) first becomes fulfilled.

(4) The proscribed period is the period beginning with the disposal, and ending on—

    (a) the date of the acquisition, or

    (b) if later, the date on which the third condition (set out in section 227(4)) first becomes fulfilled.

(5) All arrangements are unauthorised unless—

    (a) they arise wholly from a restriction authorised by paragraph 7(2) of Schedule 5 to the Finance Act 1989, or

    (b) they only allow one or both of the following as regards shares, interests or rights, namely, acquisition by a beneficiary under the trust and appropriation under an approved profit sharing scheme.

(6) An asset is a chargeable asset in relation to the claimant at a particular time if, were the asset to be disposed of at that time, any gain accruing to him on the disposal would be a chargeable gain, and either—

    (a) at that time he is resident or ordinarily resident in the United Kingdom, or

    (b) he would be chargeable to capital gains tax under section 10(1) in respect of the gain, or it would form part of his chargeable profits for corporation tax purposes by virtue of section 10(3),

unless (were he to dispose of the asset at that time) the claimant would fall to be regarded for the purposes of any double taxation relief arrangements as not liable in the United Kingdom to tax on any gains accruing to him on the disposal.

(7) The question whether a trust is at a particular time a qualifying employee share ownership trust shall be determined in accordance with Schedule 5 to the Finance Act 1989; and "chargeable event" in relation to trustees has the meaning given by section 69 of that Act.

(8) The expressions "holding company," "trading company" and "trading group" have the meanings given by paragraph 1 of Schedule 6; and "group" (except in the expression "trading group") shall be construed in accordance with section 170.

(9) "Ordinary share capital" in relation to the founding company means all the issued share capital (by whatever name called) of the company, other than capital the holders of which have a right to a dividend at a fixed rate but have no other right to share in the profits of the company.

(10) Schedule 18 to the Taxes Act (group relief: equity holders and profits or assets available for distribution) shall apply for the purposes of section 227(4) as if—
   (a) the trustees were a company,
   (b) the references to section 413(7) to (9) of that Act were references to section 227(4),
   (c) the reference in paragraph 7(1)(a) to section 413(7) of that Act were a reference to section 227(4), and
   (d) paragraph 7(1)(b) were omitted.

GENERAL NOTE
   This is a general definition section for the purposes of s.227.

The relief

229.—(1) In a case where relief is available under this subsection the claimant shall, on making a claim in the period of two years beginning with the acquisition, be treated for the purposes of this Act—
   (a) as if the consideration for the disposal were (if otherwise of a greater amount or value) of such amount as would secure that on the disposal neither a gain nor a loss accrued to him, and
   (b) as if the amount or value of the consideration for the acquisition were reduced by the excess of the amount or value of the actual consideration for the disposal over the amount of the consideration which the claimant is treated as receiving under paragraph (a) above.

(2) Relief is available under subsection (3) below where—
   (a) relief would be available under subsection (1) above but for the fact that part only of the amount or value mentioned in section 227(5) is applied as there mentioned, and
   (b) all the amount or value so mentioned except for a part which is less than the amount of the gain (whether all chargeable gain or not) accruing on the disposal is so applied.

(3) In a case where relief is available under this subsection the claimant shall, on making a claim in the period of two years beginning with the acquisition, be treated for the purposes of this Act—
   (a) as if the amount of the gain accruing on the disposal were reduced to the amount of the part mentioned in subsection (2)(b) above, and
   (b) as if the amount or value of the consideration for the acquisition were reduced by the amount by which the gain is reduced under paragraph (a) above.

(4) Nothing in subsection (1) or (3) above shall affect the treatment for the purposes of this Act of the other party to the disposal or of the other party to the acquisition.

(5) The provisions of this Act fixing the amount of the consideration deemed to be given for a disposal or acquisition shall be applied before the preceding provisions of this section are applied.

GENERAL NOTE
   This contains the roll-over relief on disposals qualifying under the preceding two sections. It is similar to the relief under s.152, save that the roll-over does not need to be into business assets, but into chargeable assets. A partial roll-over is dealt with on similar lines to s.153.

Dwelling-houses: special provision

230.—(1) Subsection (2) below applies where—
(a) a claim is made under section 229,
(b) immediately after the time of the acquisition mentioned in section 227(5) and apart from this section, any replacement asset was a chargeable asset in relation to the claimant,
(c) the asset is a dwelling-house or part of a dwelling-house or land, and
(d) there was a time in the period beginning with the acquisition and ending with the time when section 229(1) or (3) falls to be applied such that, if the asset (or an interest in it) were disposed of at that time, it would be within section 222(1) and the individual there mentioned would be the claimant or the claimant's spouse.

(2) In such a case the asset shall be treated as if, immediately after the time of the acquisition mentioned in section 227(5), it was not a chargeable asset in relation to the claimant.

(3) Subsection (4) below applies where—
(a) the provisions of section 229(1) or (3) have been applied,
(b) any replacement asset which, immediately after the time of the acquisition mentioned in section 227(5) and apart from this section, was a chargeable asset in relation to the claimant consists of a dwelling-house or part of a dwelling-house or land, and
(c) there is a time after section 229(1) or (3) has been applied such that, if the asset (or an interest in it) were disposed of at that time, it would be within section 222(1) and the individual there mentioned would be the claimant or the claimant's spouse.

(4) In such a case—
(a) the asset shall be treated as if, immediately after the time of the acquisition mentioned in section 227(5), it was not a chargeable asset in relation to the claimant and adjustments shall be made accordingly, but
(b) any gain treated as accruing in consequence of the application of paragraph (a) above shall be treated as accruing at the time mentioned in subsection (3)(c) above or, if there is more than one such time, at the earliest of them.

(5) Subsection (6) below applies where—
(a) a claim is made under section 229,
(b) immediately after the time of the acquisition mentioned in section 227(5) and apart from this section, any replacement asset was a chargeable asset in relation to the claimant,
(c) the asset was an option to acquire (or to acquire an interest in) a dwelling-house or part of a dwelling-house or land,
(d) the option has been exercised, and
(e) there was a time in the period beginning with the exercise of the option and ending with the time when section 229(1) or (3) falls to be applied such that, if the asset acquired on exercise of the option were disposed of at that time, it would be within section 222(1) and the individual there mentioned would be the claimant or the claimant's spouse.

(6) In such a case the option shall be treated as if, immediately after the time of the acquisition mentioned in section 227(5), it was not a chargeable asset in relation to the claimant.

(7) Subsection (8) below applies where—
(a) the provisions of section 229(1) or (3) have been applied,
(b) any replacement asset which, immediately after the time of the acquisition mentioned in section 227(5) and apart from this section, was a chargeable asset in relation to the claimant consisted of an option to acquire (or to acquire an interest in) a dwelling-house or part of a dwelling-house or land,

(c) the option has been exercised, and
(d) there is a time after section 229(1) or (3) has been applied such that, if the asset acquired on exercise of the option were disposed of at that time, it would be within section 222(1) and the individual there mentioned would be the claimant or the claimant's spouse.

(8) In such a case—
(a) the option shall be treated as if, immediately after the time of the acquisition mentioned in section 227(5), it was not a chargeable asset in relation to the claimant and adjustments shall be made accordingly, but
(b) any gain treated as accruing in consequence of the application of paragraph (a) above shall be treated as accruing at the time mentioned in subsection (7)(d) above or, if there is more than one such time, at the earliest of them.

(9) References in this section to an individual include references to a person entitled to occupy under the terms of a settlement.

GENERAL NOTE
This rather complex provision is designed to prevent a gain from a disposal of shares to an ESOT being rolled over into a dwelling-house, which could subsequently attract the private residence exemption. Accordingly, roll-over into such an asset does not qualify for relief.

The exclusion of relief also applies from the date when a dwelling-house becomes occupied as a private residence and to cases where the asset in question is an option to acquire a dwelling-house which is subsequently exercised and the house qualifies for private residence exemption.

Shares: special provision

231.—(1) Subsection (2) below applies where—
(a) a claim is made under section 229,
(b) immediately after the time of the acquisition mentioned in section 227(5) and apart from this section, any replacement asset was a chargeable asset in relation to the claimant,
(c) the asset consists of shares, and
(d) in the period beginning with the acquisition and ending when section 229(1) or (3) falls to be applied relief is claimed under Chapter III of Part VII of the Taxes Act (business expansion scheme) in respect of the asset.

(2) In such a case the asset shall be treated as if, immediately after the time of the acquisition mentioned in section 227(5), it was not a chargeable asset in relation to the claimant.

(3) Subsection (4) below applies where—
(a) the provisions of section 229(1) or (3) have been applied,
(b) any replacement asset which, immediately after the time of the acquisition mentioned in section 227(5) and apart from this section, was a chargeable asset in relation to the claimant consists of shares, and
(c) after section 229(1) or (3) has been applied relief is claimed under Chapter III of Part VII of the Taxes Act in respect of the asset.

(4) In such a case the asset shall be treated as if, immediately after the time of the acquisition mentioned in section 227(5), it was not a chargeable asset in relation to the claimant and adjustments shall be made accordingly.

(5) Subsection (4) above shall also apply where section 33(1) or (3) of the Finance Act 1990 has applied and the claimant acquired the replacement asset in a chargeable period beginning before 6th April 1992.

GENERAL NOTE
This section similarly precludes a roll-over into shares qualifying for relief under the Business Expansion Scheme (see s.150). The Business Expansion Scheme is due to be terminated at the end of 1993.

Chargeable event when replacement assets owned

232.—(1) Subsection (3) below applies where—

(a) the provisions of section 229(1) or (3) are applied,

(b) a chargeable event occurs in relation to the trustees on or after the date on which the disposal is made (and whether the event occurs before or after the provisions are applied),

(c) the claimant was neither an individual who died before the chargeable event occurs nor trustees of a settlement which ceased to exist before the chargeable event occurs, and

(d) the condition set out below is fulfilled.

(2) The condition is that, at the time the chargeable event occurs, the claimant or a person then connected with him is beneficially entitled to all the replacement assets.

(3) In a case where this subsection applies, the claimant or connected person (as the case may be) shall be deemed for all purposes of this Act—

(a) to have disposed of all the replacement assets immediately before the time when the chargeable event occurs, and

(b) immediately to have reacquired them,

at the relevant value.

(4) The relevant value is such value as secures on the deemed disposal a chargeable gain equal to—

(a) the amount by which the amount or value of the consideration mentioned in section 229(1)(b) was treated as reduced by virtue of that provision (where it applied), or

(b) the amount by which the amount or value of the consideration mentioned in section 229(3)(b) was treated as reduced by virtue of that provision (where it applied).

(5) In a case where subsection (3) above would apply if "all" read "any of" in subsection (2) above, subsection (3) shall nevertheless apply, but as if—

(a) in subsection (3)(a) "all the replacement assets" read "the replacement assets concerned," and

(b) the relevant value were reduced to whatever value is just and reasonable.

(6) Subsection (7) below applies where—

(a) subsection (3) above applies (whether or not by virtue of subsection (5) above), and

(b) before the time when the chargeable event occurs anything has happened as regards any of the replacement assets such that it can be said that a charge has accrued in respect of any of the gain carried forward by virtue of section 229(1) or (3).

(7) If in such a case it is just and reasonable for subsection (3) above to apply as follows, it shall apply as if—

(a) the relevant value were reduced (or further reduced) to whatever value is just and reasonable, or

(b) the relevant value were such value as secures that on the deemed disposal neither a gain nor a loss accrues (if that is just and reasonable);

but paragraph (a) above shall not apply so as to reduce the relevant value below that mentioned in paragraph (b) above.

(8) For the purposes of subsection (6)(b) above the gain carried forward by virtue of section 229(1) or (3) is the gain represented by the amount which by virtue of either of those provisions falls to be deducted from the expenditure allowable in computing a gain accruing on the disposal of replacement assets (that is, the amount found under subsection (4)(a) or (b) above, as the case may be).

(9) In this section "chargeable event" in relation to trustees has the meaning given by section 69 of the Finance Act 1989.

General Note

Together with the following two sections, this is designed to deal with the situation where an

ESOT ceases to qualify for relief on the occurrence of a chargeable event (as to which see FA 1989, s.69). In such a case a charge to C.G.T. crystallises on the disposal to the ESOT where the replacement assets are held by the claimant or persons connected with him. The charge is reduced where part of it has already crystallised.

Chargeable event when replacement property owned

233.—(1) Subsection (3) below applies where—
(a) paragraphs (a) to (c) of section 232(1) are fulfilled, and
(b) the condition set out below is fulfilled.
(2) The condition is that—
(a) before the time when the chargeable event occurs, all the gain carried forward by virtue of section 229(1) or (3) was in turn carried forward from all the replacement assets to other property on a replacement of business assets, and
(b) at the time the chargeable event occurs, the claimant or a person then connected with him is beneficially entitled to all the property.
(3) In a case where this subsection applies, the claimant or connected person (as the case may be) shall be deemed for all purposes of this Act—
(a) to have disposed of all the property immediately before the time when the chargeable event occurs, and
(b) immediately to have reacquired it,
at the relevant value.
(4) The relevant value is such value as secures on the deemed disposal a chargeable gain equal to—
(a) the amount by which the amount or value of the consideration mentioned in section 229(1)(b) was treated as reduced by virtue of that provision (where it applied), or
(b) the amount by which the amount or value of the consideration mentioned in section 229(3)(b) was treated as reduced by virtue of that provision (where it applied).
(5) In a case where subsection (3) above would apply if "all the" in subsection (2) above (in one or more places) read "any of the", subsection (3) shall nevertheless apply, but as if—
(a) in subsection (3)(a) "all the property" read "the property concerned", and
(b) the relevant value were reduced to whatever value is just and reasonable.
(6) Subsection (7) below applies where—
(a) subsection (3) above applies (whether or not by virtue of subsection (5) above), and
(b) before the time when the chargeable event occurs anything has happened as regards any of the replacement assets, or any other property, such that it can be said that a charge has accrued in respect of any of the gain carried forward by virtue of section 229(1) or (3).
(7) If in such a case it is just and reasonable for subsection (3) above to apply as follows, it shall apply as if—
(a) the relevant value were reduced (or further reduced) to whatever value is just and reasonable, or
(b) the relevant value were such value as secures that on the deemed disposal neither a gain nor a loss accrues (if that is just and reasonable);
but paragraph (a) above shall not apply so as to reduce the relevant value below that mentioned in paragraph (b) above.
(8) For the purposes of subsections (2) and (6)(b) above the gain carried forward by virtue of section 229(1) or (3) is the gain represented by the amount which by virtue of either of those provisions falls to be deducted from the expenditure allowable in computing a gain accruing on the disposal

of replacement assets (that is, the amount found under subsection (4)(a) or (b) above, as the case may be).

(9) For the purposes of subsection (2) above a gain is carried forward from assets to other property on a replacement of business assets if, by one or more claims under sections 152 to 158, the chargeable gain accruing on a disposal of the assets is reduced, and as a result an amount falls to be deducted from the expenditure allowable in computing a gain accruing on the disposal of the other property.

GENERAL NOTE

This applies the charge under s.232 where the assets acquired have been rolled over into assets qualifying for relief under ss.152–158 on the replacement of business assets.

Chargeable events when bonds owned

234.—(1) Subsection (3) below applies where—

(a) paragraphs (a) to (c) of section 232(1) are fulfilled, and

(b) the condition set out below is fulfilled.

(2) The condition is that—

(a) all the replacement assets were shares (new shares) in a company or companies,

(b) there has been a transaction to which section 116(10) applies and as regards which all the new shares constitute the old asset and qualifying corporate bonds constitute the new asset, and

(c) at the time the chargeable event occurs, the claimant or a person then connected with him is beneficially entitled to all the bonds.

(3) In a case where this subsection applies, a chargeable gain shall be deemed to have accrued to the claimant or connected person (as the case may be); and the gain shall be deemed to have accrued immediately before the time when the chargeable event occurs and to be of an amount equal to the relevant amount.

(4) The relevant amount is an amount equal to the lesser of—

(a) the first amount, and

(b) the second amount.

(5) The first amount is—

(a) the amount of the chargeable gain that would be deemed to accrue under 116(10)(b) if there were a disposal of all the bonds at the time the chargeable event occurs, or

(b) nil, if an allowable loss would be so deemed to accrue if there were such a disposal.

(6) The second amount is an amount equal to—

(a) the amount by which the amount or value of the consideration mentioned in section 229(1)(b) was treated as reduced by virtue of that provision (where it applied), or

(b) the amount by which the amount or value of the consideration mentioned in section 229(3)(b) was treated as reduced by virtue of that provision (where it applied).

(7) In a case where subsection (3) above would apply if "all the" in subsection (2) above (in one or more places) read "any of the", subsection (3) shall nevertheless apply, but as if—

(a) in subsection (5) above "all the bonds" read "the bonds concerned",

(b) the second amount were reduced to whatever amount is just and reasonable, and

(c) the relevant amount were reduced accordingly.

(8) Subsection (9) below applies where—

(a) subsection (3) above applies (whether or not by virtue of subsection (7) above), and

(b) before the time when the chargeable event occurs anything has happened as regards any of the new shares, or any of the bonds, such that it can be said that a charge has accrued in respect of any of the gain carried forward by virtue of section 229(1) or (3).

(9) If in such a case it is just and reasonable for subsection (3) above to apply as follows, it shall apply as if—

(a) the second amount were reduced (or further reduced) to whatever amount is just and reasonable, and

(b) the relevant amount were reduced (or further reduced) accordingly (if the second amount is less than the first amount),

but nothing in this subsection shall have the effect of reducing the second amount below nil.

(10) For the purposes of subsection (8)(b) above the gain carried forward by virtue of section 229(1) or (3) is the gain represented by the amount which by virtue of either of those provisions falls to be deducted from the expenditure allowable in computing a gain accruing on the disposal of replacement assets (that is, the amount found under subsection (6)(a) or (b) above, as the case may be).

GENERAL NOTE

This applies the charge under s.232 where the new assets acquired were shares and these have been rolled over into corporate bonds in circumstances qualifying for relief under s.116(10).

Information

235.—(1) An inspector may by notice require a return to be made by the trustees of an employee share ownership trust in a case where—

(a) a disposal of shares, or an interest in shares, has at any time been made to them, and

(b) a claim is made under section 229(1) or (3).

(2) Where he requires such a return to be made the inspector shall specify the information to be contained in it.

(3) The information which may be specified is information the inspector needs for the purposes of sections 232 to 234 and may include information about—

(a) expenditure incurred by the trustees;

(b) assets acquired by them;

(c) transfers of assets made by them.

(4) The information which may be required under subsection (3)(a) above may include the purpose of the expenditure and the persons receiving any sums.

(5) The information which may be required under subsection (3)(b) above may include the persons from whom the assets were acquired and the consideration furnished by the trustees.

(6) The information which may be required under subsection (3)(c) above may include the persons to whom assets were transferred and the consideration furnished by them.

(7) In a case where section 229(1) or (3) has been applied, the inspector shall send to the trustees of the employee share ownership trust concerned a certificate stating—

(a) that the provision concerned has been applied, and

(b) the effect of the provision on the consideration for the disposal or on the amount of the gain accruing on the disposal (as the case may be).

(8) For the purposes of this section, the question whether a trust is an employee share ownership trust shall be determined in accordance with Schedule 5 to the Finance Act 1989.

GENERAL NOTE

Where relief has been claimed under s.229, the Revenue are given powers to require information from the trustees of the ESOT regarding dealings by them.

Prevention of double charge

236.—(1) Where a charge can be said to accrue by virtue of section 232 or 233 in respect of any of the gain carried forward by virtue of section 229(1) or (3), so much of the gain charged shall not be capable of being carried forward (from assets to other property or from property to other property) under sections 152 to 158 on a replacement of business assets.

(2) For the purpose of construing subsection (1) above—

(a) what of the gain has been charged shall be found in accordance with what is just and reasonable;

(b) section 233(8) and (9) shall apply.

(3) In a case where—

(a) section 234 applies in the case of bonds,

(b) subsequently a disposal of the bonds occurs as mentioned in section 116(10)(b), and

(c) a chargeable gain is deemed to accrue under section 116(10)(b),

the chargeable gain shall be reduced by the relevant amount found under section 234 or (if the amount exceeds the gain) shall be reduced to nil.

(4) The relevant amount shall be apportioned where the subsequent disposal is of some of the bonds mentioned in subsection (3)(a) above; and subsection (3) shall apply accordingly.

GENERAL NOTE

Where a charge has occurred under ss.232–234, the amount of gain chargeable on a subsequent disposal of business assets or corporate bonds is appropriately adjusted.

Superannuation funds, profit sharing schemes, employee trusts etc.

Superannuation funds, annuities and annual payments

237. No chargeable gain shall accrue to any person on the disposal of a right to, or to any part of—

(a) any allowance, annuity or capital sum payable out of any superannuation fund, or under any superannuation scheme, established solely or mainly for persons employed in a profession, trade, undertaking or employment, and their dependants,

(b) an annuity granted otherwise than under a contract for a deferred annuity by a company as part of its business of granting annuities on human life, whether or not including instalments of capital, or an annuity granted or deemed to be granted under the Government Annuities Act 1929, or

(c) annual payments which are due under a covenant made by any person and which are not secured on any property.

GENERAL NOTE

This exempts the following from C.G.T.: (1) disposal of rights under pension schemes; (2) disposal of rights under annuities (other than a deferred annuity, as to which see s.210) granted by a company or the Government. Under FA 1962, s.33, annuities under the Government Annuities Act 1929 can now only arise in limited circumstances; (3) disposal of rights to annual payments due under an unsecured covenant. It was held in *Rank Xerox* v. *Lane* [1981] A.C. 269, H.L., that this relates to a unilateral promise enforceable in spite of the absence of consideration and was not apt to refer to a bilateral agreement in which the annual payments were consideration for some obligation undertaken by the payee. Also, "covenant" should be interpreted in accordance with the local law in England and Scotland.

Approved profit sharing and share option schemes

238.—(1) Notwithstanding anything in a profit sharing scheme approved under Schedule 9 of the Taxes Act or in paragraph 2(2) of that Schedule or in the trust instrument relating to that scheme, for the purposes of capital gains tax a person who is a participant in relation to that scheme shall be treated as absolutely entitled to his shares as against the trustees of the scheme.

(2) For the purposes of capital gains tax—

(a) no deduction shall be made from the consideration for the disposal of any shares by reason only that an amount determined under section 186 or 187 of or Schedule 9 or 10 to the Taxes Act is chargeable to income tax under section 186(3) or (4) of that Act;

(b) any charge to income tax by virtue of section 186(3) of that Act shall be disregarded in determining whether a distribution is a capital distribution within the meaning of section 122(5)(b);

(c) nothing in any provision of section 186 or 187 of or Schedule 9 or 10 to that Act with respect to—

(i) the order in which any of a participant's shares are to be treated as disposed of for the purposes of those provisions as they have effect in relation to profit sharing schemes, or

(ii) the shares in relation to which an event is to be treated as occurring for any such purpose,

shall affect the rules applicable to the computation of a gain accruing on a part disposal of a holding of shares or other securities which were acquired at different times; and

(d) a gain accruing on an appropriation of shares to which section 186(11) of that Act applies shall not be a chargeable gain.

(3) In this section "participant" and "the trust instrument" have the meanings given by section 187 of the Taxes Act.

(4) Where a right to acquire shares in a body corporate is released in consideration of the grant of a right to acquire shares in another body corporate in accordance with a provision included in a scheme pursuant to paragraph 15 of Schedule 9 to the Taxes Act, the transaction shall not be treated for the purposes of this Act as involving any disposal of the first-mentioned right but for those purposes the other right shall be treated as the same asset acquired as the first-mentioned right was acquired.

This subsection does not apply in relation to a savings-related share option scheme, within the meaning of section 187 of that Act, unless the first-mentioned right was acquired as mentioned in section 185(1) of that Act.

GENERAL NOTE

Employee share schemes conferring exemptions and reliefs from income tax were introduced in 1978, 1980 and 1984. The income tax provisions were codified in ICTA 1988, ss.185–187 and Scheds. 9 and 10. This section deals with consequential provisions for C.G.T.

Subs. (1)

Under profit-sharing schemes, participants must leave their shares in the hands of the trustees for a retention period. They are treated as absolutely entitled to the shares during this period.

Subs. (2)

This deals with various matters relating to profit-sharing schemes. Charges to income tax which may arise under s.186(3) and (4) are ignored in the computation for C.G.T. on a disposal or for determining whether a distribution is a capital distribution. The rules concerning appropriation of shares have no bearing for C.G.T. and do not occasion a charge to C.G.T.

Subs. (4)

Where the rules of a share option scheme permit the transfer of rights into shares of another company on the occasion of a take-over, the rights are rolled over for C.G.T. purposes.

Employee trusts

239.—(1) Where—

(a) a close company disposes of an asset to trustees in circumstances such that the disposal is a disposition which by virtue of section 13 of the Inheritance Tax Act 1984 (employee trusts) is not a transfer of value for the purposes of inheritance tax, or

(b) an individual disposes of an asset to trustees in circumstances such

that the disposal is an exempt transfer by virtue of section 28 of that Act (employee trusts: inheritance tax),
this Act shall have effect in relation to the disposal in accordance with subsection (2) and (3) below.

(2) Section 17(1) shall not apply to the disposal; and if the disposal is by way of gift or is for a consideration not exceeding the sums allowable as a deduction under section 38—

   (a) the disposal, and the acquisition by the trustees, shall be treated for the purposes of this Act as being made for such consideration as to secure that neither a gain nor a loss accrues on the disposal, and

   (b) where the trustees dispose of the asset, its acquisition by the company or individual shall be treated as its acquisition by the trustees.

Paragraph (b) above also applies where section 149(1) of the 1979 Act applied on the disposal of an asset to trustees who have not disposed of it before the coming into force of this section.

(3) Where the disposal is by a close company, section 125(1) shall apply to the disposal as if for the reference to market value there were substituted a reference to market value or the sums allowable as a deduction under section 38, whichever is the less.

(4) Subject to subsection (5) below, this Act shall also have effect in accordance with subsection (2) above in relation to any disposal made by a company other than a close company if—

   (a) the disposal is made to trustees otherwise than under a bargain made at arm's length, and

   (b) the property disposed of is to be held by them on trusts of the description specified in section 86(1) of the Inheritance Tax Act 1984 (that is to say, those in relation to which the said section 13 of that Act has effect) and the persons for whose benefit the trusts permit the property to be applied include all or most of either—

      (i) the persons employed by or holding office with the company, or

      (ii) the persons employed by or holding office with the company or any one or more subsidiaries of the company.

(5) Subsection (4) above does not apply if the trusts permit any of the property to be applied at any time (whether during any such period as is referred to in the said section 86(1) or later) for the benefit of—

   (a) a person who is a participator in the company ("the donor company"), or

   (b) any other person who is a participator in any other company that has made a disposal of property to be held on the same trusts as the property disposed of by the donor company, being a disposal in relation to which this Act has had effect in accordance with subsection (2) above, or

   (c) any other person who has been a participator in the donor company or any such company as is mentioned in paragraph (b) above at any time after, or during the 10 years before, the disposal made by that company, or

   (d) any person who is connected with a person within paragraph (a), (b) or (c) above.

(6) The participators in a company who are referred to in subsection (5) above do not include any participator who—

   (a) is not beneficially entitled to, or to rights entitling him to acquire, 5 per cent. or more of, or of any class of the shares comprised in, its issued share capital, and

   (b) on a winding-up of the company would not be entitled to 5 per cent. or more of its assets;

and in determining whether the trusts permit property to be applied as mentioned in that subsection, no account shall be taken—

(i) of any power to make a payment which is the income of any person for any of the purposes of income tax, or would be the income for any of those purposes of a person not resident in the United Kingdom if he were so resident, or

(ii) if the trusts are those of a profit sharing scheme approved under Schedule 9 to the Taxes Act of any power to appropriate shares in pursuance of the scheme.

(7) In subsection (4) above "subsidiary" has the meaning given by section 736 of the Companies Act 1985 and in subsections (5) and (6) above "participator" has the meaning given in section 417(1) of the Taxes Act, except that it does not include a loan creditor.

(8) In this section "close company" includes a company which, if resident in the United Kingdom, would be a close company as defined in section 288.

GENERAL NOTE
Under the Inheritance Act 1984, ss.13 and 28, transfers of value made by close companies and individuals to trusts for the benefit of employees under *ibid.*, s.86 are exempted from inheritance tax. This section deals with the consequences for C.G.T.

Subs. (2)
This disapplies the market-value rule under s.17 and allows a roll-over at not more than cost.

Subs. (3)
The provision regarding close companies' transferring assets at an undervalue is also disapplied.

Subss. (4)–(6)
These extend the exemption from C.G.T. to similar transfers made by companies which are not close companies, provided that certain conditions are met:

(1) the transfer must be to trusts qualifying under IHTA 1984, s.86, and must be for the benefit of all or most of the employees;

(2) the trusts must not permit any property to be applied for the benefit of a participator in the company or any other company which has made a similar disposal or to anyone connected with a participator. The timescale extends to 10 years before the disposal. "Participator" does not include anyone with less than a five per cent. interest. Payments of taxable income or profit-sharing schemes are not caught.

Leases

Leases of land and other assets

240. Schedule 8 shall have effect as respects leases of land and, to the extent specified in paragraph 9 of that Schedule, as respects leases of property other than land.

GENERAL NOTE
Leases, particularly of land, require special treatment, especially in relation to the rules for wasting assets under ss.44–47. See further the General Note to Sched. 8.

Furnished holiday lettings

241.—(1) The following provisions of this section shall have effect with respect to the treatment for the purposes of tax on chargeable gains of the commercial letting of furnished holiday accommodation in the United Kingdom.

(2) Section 504 of the Taxes Act (definitions relating to furnished holiday lettings) shall have effect for the purposes of this section as it has effect for the purposes of section 503 of that Act.

(3) Subject to subsections (4) to (9) below, for the purposes of sections 152 to 157, 165 and 253 and Schedule 6—

(a) the commercial letting of furnished holiday accommodation in respect of which the profits or gains are chargeable under Case VI of Schedule D shall be treated as a trade; and

(b) all such lettings made by a particular person or partnership or body of persons shall be treated as one trade.

(4) Subject to subsection (5) below, for the purposes of the sections mentioned in subsection (3) above as they apply by virtue of this section, where in any chargeable period a person makes a commercial letting of furnished holiday accommodation—

(a) the accommodation shall be taken to be used in that period only for the purposes of the trade of making such lettings; and

(b) that trade shall be taken to be carried on throughout that period.

(5) Subsection (4) above does not apply to any part of a chargeable period during which the accommodation is neither let commercially nor available to be so let unless it is prevented from being so let or available by any works of construction or repair.

(6) Where—

(a) a gain to which section 222 applies accrues to any individual on the disposal of an asset; and

(b) by virtue of subsection (3) above the amount or value of the consideration for the acquisition of the asset is treated as reduced under section 152 or 153,

the gain to which section 222 applies shall be reduced by the amount of the reduction mentioned in paragraph (b) above.

(7) Where there is a letting of accommodation only part of which is holiday accommodation such apportionments shall be made for the purposes of this section as appear to the inspector, or on appeal the Commissioners, to be just and reasonable.

(8) Where a person has been charged to tax in respect of chargeable gains otherwise than in accordance with the provisions of this section, such assessment, reduction or discharge of an assessment or, where a claim for repayment is made, such repayment, shall be made as may be necessary to give effect to those provisions.

GENERAL NOTE

This section, together with provisions now in ICTA 1988, ss.503 and 504, was introduced to correct the anomaly whereby the commercial letting of furnished holiday accommodation was not treated as a trade by the Inland Revenue. It is now treated as a trade for various purposes. The accommodation must be available for 140 days and be actually so occupied for 70 days, not normally in the same occupation for more than 31 days.

Where this applies, roll-over relief on replacement of business assets, relief for gifts of business assets, retirement relief and relief for loans to traders, will all be available. Appropriate apportionments are made where part of a dwelling-house is used for holiday accommodation and part as a private residence and also where only part of the letting ranks as holiday accommodation.

Part disposals

Small part disposals

242.—(1) This section applies to a transfer of land forming part only of a holding of land, where—

(a) the amount or value of the consideration for the transfer does not exceed one-fifth of the market value of the holding as it subsisted immediately before the transfer, and

(b) the transfer is not one which, by virtue of section 58 or 171(1), is treated as giving rise to neither a gain nor a loss.

(2) Subject to subsection (3) below, if the transferor so claims, the transfer shall not be treated for the purposes of this Act as a disposal, but all sums which, if it had been so treated, would have been brought into account as consideration for that disposal in the computation of the gain shall be deducted from any expenditure allowable under Chapter III of Part II as a deduction in computing a gain on any subsequent disposal of the holding.

(3) This section shall not apply—

(a) if the amount or value of the consideration for the transfer exceeds £20,000, or

(b) where in the year of assessment in which the transfer is made, the transferor made any other disposal of land, if the total amount or value of the consideration for all disposals of land made by the transferor in that year exceeds £20,000.

(4) No account shall be taken under subsection (3) above of any transfer of land to which section 243 applies.

(5) In relation to a transfer which is not for full consideration in money or money's worth "the amount or value of the consideration" in this section shall mean the market value of the land transferred.

(6) For the purposes of this section the holding of land shall comprise only the land in respect of which the expenditure allowable under paragraphs (a) and (b) of section 38(1) would be apportioned under section 42 if the transfer had been treated as a disposal (that is, as a part disposal of the holding).

(7) In this section references to a holding of land include references to any estate or interest in a holding of land, not being an estate or interest which is a wasting asset, and references to part of a holding shall be construed accordingly.

GENERAL NOTE

This section is designed to obviate a requirement to value land where there is a relatively small part-disposal. Where the disposal does not exceed one-fifth of the value of the entire holding and is not for more than £20,000, including other disposals in that year, the taxpayer may elect to have the consideration set against his base value for any other disposal of the rest of the land.

Part disposal to authority with compulsory powers

243.—(1) This section applies to a transfer of land forming part only of a holding of land to an authority exercising or having compulsory powers where—

(a) the amount or value of the consideration for the transfer, or if the transfer is not for full consideration in money or money's worth, the market value of the land transferred, is small, as compared with the market value of the holding as it subsisted immediately before the transfer, and

(b) the transferor had not taken any steps by advertising or otherwise to dispose of any part of the holding or to make his willingness to dispose of it known to the authority or others.

(2) If the transferor so claims, the transfer shall not be treated for the purposes of this Act as a disposal, but all sums which, if it had been so treated, would have been brought into account as consideration for that disposal in the computation of the gain shall be deducted from any expenditure allowable under Chapter III of Part II as a deduction in computing a gain on any subsequent disposal of the holding.

(3) For the purposes of this section the holding of land shall comprise only the land in respect of which the expenditure allowable under paragraphs (a) and (b) of section 38(1) would be apportioned under section 42 if the transfer had been treated as a disposal (that is, as a part disposal of the holding).

(4) In this section references to a holding of land include references to an estate or interest in a holding of land, not being an estate or interest which is a wasting asset, and references to part of a holding shall be construed accordingly.

(5) In this section "authority exercising or having compulsory powers" means, in relation to the land transferred, a person or body of persons acquiring it compulsorily or who has or had been, or could be, authorised to acquire it compulsorily for the purposes for which it is acquired, or for whom

another person or body of persons has or have been, or could be, authorised so to acquire it.

GENERAL NOTE
A provision similar to s.242 applies for small part-disposals of land to an authority with compulsory powers. The *quantum* is not specifically restricted as in s.242, but the transferor must not have taken any steps to dispose of the property by advertising or otherwise.

Part disposal: consideration exceeding allowable expenditure

244.—(1) The provisions of sections 242(2) and 243(2) shall have effect subject to this section.

(2) Where the allowable expenditure is less than the consideration for the part disposal (or is nil)—

(a) the said provisions shall not apply, and

(b) if the recipient so elects (and there is any allowable expenditure)—

(i) the consideration for the part disposal shall be reduced by the amount of the allowable expenditure, and,

(ii) none of that expenditure shall be allowable as a deduction in computing a gain accruing on the occasion of the part disposal or on any subsequent occasion.

In this subsection "allowable expenditure" means expenditure which, immediately before the part disposal, was attributable to the holding of land under paragraphs (a) and (b) of section 38(1).

GENERAL NOTE
This section applies where the consideration on a disposal under ss.242 and 243 exceeds the entire base cost. In such a case the taxpayer may elect instead to set the base cost against the consideration.

Compulsory acquisition

Compensation paid on compulsory acquisition

245.—(1) Where land or an interest in or right over land is acquired and the acquisition is, or could have been, made under compulsory powers, then in considering whether, under section 52(4), the purchase price or compensation or other consideration for the acquisition should be apportioned and treated in part as a capital sum within section 22(1)(a), whether as compensation for loss of goodwill or for disturbance or otherwise, or should be apportioned in any other way, the fact that the acquisition is or could have been made compulsorily, and any statutory provision treating the purchase price or compensation or other consideration as exclusively paid in respect of the land itself, shall be disregarded.

(2) In any case where land or an interest in land is acquired as mentioned in subsection (1) above from any person and the compensation or purchase price includes an amount in respect of severance of the land comprised in the acquisition or sale from other land in which that person is entitled in the same capacity to an interest, or in respect of that other land as being injuriously affected, there shall be deemed for the purposes of this Act to be a part disposal of that other land.

GENERAL NOTE
Where land is acquired under compulsory powers the statutory provisions dealing with the treatment of the consideration are ignored.
Where payments are made in respect of severance from or injurious affection to other land, these are treated as a part-disposal of that land.

Time of disposal and acquisition

246. Where an interest in land is acquired, otherwise than under a contract, by an authority possessing compulsory purchase powers, the time at which the disposal and acquisition is made is the time at which the compensation for the acquisition is agreed or otherwise determined (variations on appeal being disregarded for this purpose) or, if earlier (but after 20 April, 1971), the time when the authority enter on the land in pursuance of their powers.

GENERAL NOTE
  The time of disposal of land compulsorily acquired is the time at which compensation is agreed (ignoring variations on appeal) or the time when the authority enters on the land.

Roll-over relief on compulsory acquisition

247.—(1) This section applies where—
  (a) land ("the old land") is disposed of by any person ("the landowner") to an authority exercising or having compulsory powers; and
  (b) the landowner did not take any steps, by advertising or otherwise, to dispose of the old land or to make his willingness to dispose of it known to the authority or others; and
  (c) the consideration for the disposal is applied by the landowner in acquiring other land ("the new land") not being land excluded from this paragraph by section 248.
  (2) Subject to section 248, in a case where the whole of the consideration for the disposal was applied as mentioned in subsection (1)(c) above, the landowner, on making a claim as respects the consideration so applied, shall be treated for the purposes of this Act—
  (a) as if the consideration for the disposal of the old land were (if otherwise of a greater amount or value) of such amount as would secure that on the disposal neither a gain nor a loss accrues to him; and
  (b) as if the amount or value of the consideration for the acquisition of the new land were reduced by the excess of the amount or value of the actual consideration for the disposal of the old land over the amount of the consideration which he is treated as receiving under paragraph (a) above.
  (3) If part only of the consideration for the disposal of the old land was applied as mentioned in subsection (1)(c) above, then, subject to section 248, if the part of the consideration which was not so applied ("the unexpended consideration") is less than the amount of the gain (whether all chargeable gain or not) accruing on the disposal of the old land, the landowner, on making a claim as respects the consideration which was so applied, shall be treated for the purposes of this Act—
  (a) as if the amount of the gain so accruing were reduced to the amount of the unexpended consideration (and, if not all chargeable gain, with a proportionate reduction in the amount of the chargeable gain); and
  (b) as if the amount or value of the consideration for the acquisition of the new land were reduced by the amount by which the gain is reduced (or, as the case may be, the amount by which the chargeable gain is proportionately reduced) under paragraph (a) above.
  (4) Nothing in subsection (2) or subsection (3) above affects the treatment for the purposes of this Act of the authority by whom the old land was acquired or of the other party to the transaction involving the acquisition of the new land.
  (5) For the purposes of this section—
  (a) subsection (2) of section 152 shall apply in relation to subsection (2)(a) and subsection (2)(b) above as it applies in relation to subsection (1)(a) and subsection (1)(b) of that section; and
  (b) subsection (3) of that section shall apply as if any reference to the new assets were a reference to the new land, any reference to the old assets

were a reference to the old land and any reference to that section were a reference to this.

(6) Where this section applies, any such amount as is referred to in subsection (2) of section 245 shall be treated as forming part of the consideration for the disposal of the old land and, accordingly, so much of that subsection as provides for a deemed disposal of other land shall not apply.

(7) The provisions of this Act fixing the amount of the consideration deemed to be given for the acquisition or disposal of assets shall be applied before this section is applied.

(8) In this section—

"land" includes any interest in or right over land; and

"authority exercising or having compulsory powers" shall be construed in accordance with section 243(5).

GENERAL NOTE

This section, introduced in 1983, allows a roll-over relief similar to that under s.152 where the consideration for the compulsory acquisition of land is applied on the purchase of other land. The rules for s.152 generally apply.

Provisions supplementary to section 247

248.—(1) Land is excluded from paragraph (c) of subsection (1) of section 247 if—

(a) it is a dwelling-house or part of a dwelling-house (or an interest in or right over a dwelling-house), and

(b) by virtue of, or of any claim under, any provision of sections 222 to 226 the whole or any part of a gain accruing on a disposal of it by the landowner at a material time would not be a chargeable gain;

and for the purposes of this subsection "a material time" means any time during the period of six years beginning on the date of the acquisition referred to in the said paragraph (c).

(2) If, at any time during the period of six years referred to in subsection (1) above, land which at the beginning of that period was not excluded from section 247(1)(c) by virtue of that subsection becomes so excluded, the amount of any chargeable gain accruing on the disposal of the old land shall be redetermined without regard to any relief previously given under section 247 by reference to the amount or value of the consideration for the acquisition of that land; and all such adjustments of capital gains tax, whether by way of assessment or otherwise, may be made at any time, notwithstanding anything in section 34 of the Management Act (time limit for assessments).

This subsection also applies where the period of six years referred to above began before the commencement of this section (and accordingly the references to section 247 include references to section 111A of the 1979 Act).

(3) Where the new land is a depreciating asset, within the meaning of section 154, that section has effect as if—

(a) any reference in subsection (1) or subsection (4) to section 152 or 153 were a reference to subsection (2) or subsection (3) respectively of section 247; and

(b) para (b) of subsection (2) were omitted; and

(c) the reference in subsection (5) to section 152(3) were a reference to that provision as applied by section 247(5).

(4) No claim may be made under section 243 in relation to a transfer which constitutes a disposal in respect of which a claim is made under section 247.

(5) Expressions used in this section have the same meaning as in section 247.

GENERAL NOTE

The preceding section does not apply to the acquisition of an exempt dwelling-house, and an appropriate adjustment to tax may be made if property acquired becomes so exempt within six years. The relief will also be restricted if the new land is a depreciating asset within s.254. Also, claims may not be made under both s.247 and s.243.

Agricultural land and woodlands

Grants for giving up agricultural land

249. For the purposes of capital gains tax, a sum payable to an individual by virtue of a scheme under section 27 of the Agriculture Act 1967 (grants for relinquishing occupation of uncommercial agricultural units) shall not be treated as part of the consideration obtained by him for, or otherwise as accruing to him on, the disposal of any asset.

GENERAL NOTE
Payments under the Agriculture Act 1967, s.27, for relinquishing occupation of uncommercial units are exempt from C.G.T.

Woodlands

250.—(1) Consideration for the disposal of trees standing or felled or cut on woodlands managed by the occupier on a commercial basis and with a view to the realisation of profits shall be excluded from the computation of the gain if the person making the disposal is the occupier.

(2) Capital sums received under a policy of insurance in respect of the destruction of or damage or injury to trees by fire or other hazard on such woodlands shall be excluded from the computation of the gain if the person making the disposal is the occupier.

(3) Subsection (2) above has effect notwithstanding section 22(1).

(4) In the computation of the gain so much of the cost of woodland in the United Kingdom shall be disregarded as is attributable to trees growing on the land.

(5) In the computation of the gain accruing on a disposal of woodland in the United Kingdom so much of the consideration for the disposal as is attributable to trees growing on the land shall be excluded.

(6) References in this section to trees include references to saleable underwood.

GENERAL NOTE
The disposal of trees from woodlands managed on a commercial basis is exempt from C.G.T. So also are receipts from insurance policies on trees and from the disposal of woodlands, so far as this is attributable to trees growing on the land.

Debts

General provisions

251.—(1) Where a person incurs a debt to another, whether in sterling or in some other currency, no chargeable gain shall accrue to that (that is the original) creditor or his personal representative or legatee on a disposal of the debt, except in the case of the debt on a security (as defined in section 132).

(2) Subject to the provisions of sections 132 and 135 and subject to subsection (1) above, the satisfaction of a debt or part of it (including a debt on a security as defined in section 132) shall be treated as a disposal of the debt or of that part by the creditor made at the time when the debt or that part is satisfied.

(3) Where property is acquired by a creditor in satisfaction of his debt or part of it, then subject to the provisions of sections 132 and 135 the property shall not be treated as disposed of by the debtor or acquired by the creditor for a consideration greater than its market value at the time of the creditor's acquisition of it; but if under subsection (1) above (and in a case not falling

within either section 132 or 135) no chargeable gain is to accrue on a disposal of the debt by the creditor (that is the original creditor), and a chargeable gain accrues to him on a disposal by him of the property, the amount of the chargeable gain shall (where necessary) be reduced so as not to exceed the chargeable gain which would have accrued if he had acquired the property for a consideration equal to the amount of the debt or that part of it.

(4) A loss accruing on the disposal of a debt acquired by the person making the disposal from the original creditor or his personal representative or legatee at a time when the creditor or his personal representative or legatee is a person connected with the person making the disposal, and so acquired either directly or by one or more purchases through persons all of whom are connected with the person making the disposal, shall not be an allowable loss.

(5) Where the original creditor is a trustee and the debt, when created, is settled property, subsections (1) and (4) above shall apply as if for the references to the original creditor's personal representative or legatee there were substituted references to any person becoming absolutely entitled, as against the trustee, to the debt on its ceasing to be settled property, and to that person's personal representative or legatee.

GENERAL NOTE

The interpretation of this section has given some difficulty, particularly since s.21(1)(a) specifically brings debts within the scope of C.G.T. It was held in *Cleveleys Investment Trust Co.* v. *I.R.C.* (1971) 47 T.C. 300, C.S., that a loan to a trading company in anticipation of acquiring a controlling interest therein was not a debt, since the lender had acquired a "bundle of rights". A contingent liability is not a debt (*Marson* v. *Marriage* [1980] S.T.C. 177), nor is a right to receive deferred consideration on a disposal of shares, since if this were the case no charge to C.G.T. could ever arise where the person making the disposal did not receive immediate payment (*Marren* v. *Ingles* [1980] 1 W.L.R. 983, H.L.).

The expression "the debt on a security", which is excluded from the section, is also obscure. The definition of "security" in s.132 indicates that it can in fact be unsecured, but it is less certain what positive characteristics it must have. In *Aberdeen Construction Group* v. *I.R.C.* [1978] A.C. 885, H.L., Lord Wilberforce suggested that it was a debt "which has, if not a marketable character, at least such characteristics as enable it to be dealt in and if necessary converted into shares or other securities" (p. 895).

It is evident that the exclusion is intended to refer to ordinary trade debts.

Subs. (2)

The satisfaction of a debt is treated as the disposal of it.

Subs. (3)

Where property is acquired in satisfaction of a debt and subsequently disposed of, the base cost is not to be less than the amount of the debt.

Subs. (4)

Losses on debts acquired from the original creditor by connected persons (see s.286) are not allowable.

Subs. (5)

The section applies, *mutatis mutandis*, to debts held by trustees.

Foreign currency bank accounts

252.—(1) Subject to subsection (2) below, section 251(1) shall not apply to a debt owed by a bank which is not in sterling and which is represented by a sum standing to the credit of a person in an account in the bank.

(2) Subsection (1) above shall not apply to a sum in an individual's bank account representing currency acquired by the holder for the personal expenditure outside the United Kingdom of himself or his family or dependants (including expenditure on the provision or maintenance of any residence outside the United Kingdom).

Foreign currency bank accounts are within the scope of C.G.T., save for accounts held by individuals for personal expenditure outside the U.K., including provision or maintenance of a residence.

Relief for loans to traders

253.—(1) In this section "a qualifying loan" means a loan in the case of which—

(a) the money lent is used by the borrower wholly for the purposes of a trade carried on by him, not being a trade which consists of or includes the lending of money, and

(b) the borrower is resident in the United Kingdom, and

(c) the borrower's debt is not a debt on a security as defined in section 132;

and for the purposes of paragraph (a) above money used by the borrower for setting up a trade which is subsequently carried on by him shall be treated as used for the purposes of that trade.

(2) In subsection (1) above references to a trade include references to a profession or vocation; and where money lent to a company is lent by it to another company in the same group, being a trading company, that subsection shall apply to the money lent to the first-mentioned company as if it had used it for any purpose for which it is used by the other company while a member of the group.

(3) If, on a claim by a person who has made a qualifying loan, the inspector is satisfied that—

(a) any outstanding amount of the principal of the loan has become irrecoverable, and

(b) the claimant has not assigned his right to recover that amount, and

(c) the claimant and the borrower were not each other's spouses, or companies in the same group, when the loan was made or at any subsequent time,

this Act shall have effect as if an allowable loss equal to that amount had accrued to the claimant when the claim was made.

(4) If, on a claim by a person who has guaranteed the repayment of a loan which is, or but for subsection (1)(c) above would be, a qualifying loan, the inspector is satisfied that—

(a) any outstanding amount of, or of interest in respect of, the principal of the loan has become irrecoverable from the borrower, and

(b) the claimant has made a payment under the guarantee (whether to the lender or a co-guarantor) in respect of that amount, and

(c) the claimant has not assigned any right to recover that amount which has accrued to him (whether by operation of law or otherwise) in consequence of his having made the payment, and

(d) the lender and the borrower were not each other's spouses, or companies in the same group, when the loan was made or at any subsequent time and the claimant and the borrower were not each other's spouses, and the claimant and the lender were not companies in the same group, when the guarantee was given or at any subsequent time,

this Act shall have effect as if an allowable loss had accrued to the claimant when the payment was made; and the loss shall be equal to the payment made by him in respect of the amount mentioned in paragraph (a) above less any contribution payable to him by any co-guarantor in respect of the payment so made.

(5) Where an allowable loss has been treated under subsection (3) or (4) above as accruing to any person and the whole or any part of the outstanding amount mentioned in subsection (3)(a) or, as the case may be, subsection (4)(a) is at any time recovered by him, this Act shall have effect as if there

had accrued to him at that time a chargeable gain equal to so much of the allowable loss as corresponds to the amount recovered.

(6) Where—

(a) an allowable loss has been treated under subsection (4) above as accruing to any person, and

(b) the whole or any part of the amount of the payment mentioned in subsection (4)(b) is at any time recovered by him,

this Act shall have effect as if there had accrued to him at that time a chargeable gain equal to so much of the allowable loss as corresponds to the amount recovered.

(7) Where—

(a) an allowable loss has been treated under subsection (3) above as accruing to a company ("the first company"), and

(b) the whole or any part of the outstanding amount mentioned in subsection (3)(a) is at any time recovered by a company ("the second company") in the same group as the first company,

this Act shall have effect as if there had accrued to the second company at that time a chargeable gain equal to so much of the allowable loss as corresponds to the amount recovered.

(8) Where—

(a) an allowable loss has been treated under subsection (4) above as accruing to a company ("the first company"), and

(b) the whole or any part of the outstanding amount mentioned in subsection (4)(a), or the whole or any part of the amount of the payment mentioned in subsection (4)(b), is at any time recovered by a company ("the second company") in the same group as the first company,

this Act shall have effect as if there had accrued to the second company at that time a chargeable gain equal to so much of the allowable loss as corresponds to the amount recovered.

(9) For the purposes of subsections (5) to (8) above, a person shall be treated as recovering an amount if he (or any other person by his direction) receives any money or money's worth in satisfaction of his right to recover that amount or in consideration of his assignment of the right to recover it; and where a person assigns such a right otherwise than by way of a bargain made at arm's length he shall be treated as receiving money or money's worth equal to the market value of the right at the time of the assignment.

(10) No amount shall be treated under this section as giving rise to an allowable loss or chargeable gain in the case of any person if it falls to be taken into account in computing his income for the purposes of income tax or corporation tax.

(11) Where an allowable loss has been treated as accruing to a person under subsection (4) above by virtue of a payment made by him at any time under a guarantee—

(a) no chargeable gain shall accrue to him otherwise than under subsection (5) above, and

(b) no allowable loss shall accrue to him under this Act,

on his disposal of any rights that have accrued to him (whether by operation of law or otherwise) in consequence of his having made any payment under the guarantee at or after that time.

(12) References in this section to an amount having become irrecoverable do not include references to cases where the amount has become irrecoverable in consequence of the terms of the loan, of any arrangements of which the loan forms part, or of any act or omission by the lender or, in a case within subsection (4) above, the guarantor.

(13) For the purposes of subsections (7) and (8) above, 2 companies are in the same group if they were in the same group when the loan was made or have been in the same group at any subsequent time.

(14) In this section—

(a) "spouses" means spouses who are living together (construed in accordance with section 288(3)),

(b) "trading company" has the meaning given by paragraph 1 of Schedule 6, and

(c) "group" shall be construed in accordance with section 170.

(15) Subsection (3) above does not apply where the loan was made before 12th April, 1978 and subsection (4) above does not apply where the guarantee was given before that date.

GENERAL NOTE

This relief was introduced by FA 1978, s.49, during the business recession of the late 1970s and was amended by FA 1990, s.83, to tighten its operation. It covers losses on loans to traders which are not debts on a security, and so would not normally be allowable for C.G.T. Loss relief is available on a claim being made where the inspector is satisfied that the loan has become irrecoverable, there has been no assignment of the debt and that the lender and borrower were not spouses or companies in the same group (see s.170).

Subs. (4)

The relief is extended to cover payments under a guarantee of a loan (including a loan which is a debt on a security).

Subss. (5)–(8)

The loss relief is clawed back if there is a subsequent recovery, either by the claimant or by a company in the same group.

Subs. (9)

"Recovery" is defined to include the receipt of any money or money's worth and an assignment not by way of arm's length bargain is treated as made at market value.

Subs. (10)

Sums taken into account in computations of income are excluded from the section.

Subs. (11)

The rights of a guarantor subsequent to the loss are excluded from the operation of the section, except where he has made a recovery under subs. (5).

Subs. (12)

Losses arising from the terms of the loan, or default by the lender or guarantor, are excluded.

Relief for debts on qualifying corporate bonds

254.—(1) In this section "a qualifying loan" means a loan in the case of which—

(a) the borrower's debt is a debt on a security as defined in section 132,

(b) but for that fact, the loan would be a qualifying loan without the meaning of section 253, and

(c) the security is a qualifying corporate bond.

(2) If, on a claim by a person who has made a qualifying loan, the inspector is satisfied that one of the following 3 conditions is fulfilled, this Act shall have effect as if an allowable loss equal to the allowable amount had accrued to the claimant when the claim was made.

(3) The first condition is that—

(a) the value of the security has become negligible,

(b) the claimant has not assigned his right to recover any outstanding amount of the principal of the loan, and

(c) the claimant and the borrower are not companies which have been in the same group at any time after the loan was made.

(4) The second condition is that—

(a) the security's redemption date has passed,

(b) all the outstanding amount of the principal of the loan was irrecoverable (taking the facts existing on that date) or proved to be irrecoverable (taking the facts existing on a later date), and

(c) subsection (3)(b) and (c) above are fulfilled.

(5) The third condition is that—

(a) the security's redemption date has passed,

(b) part of the outstanding amount of the principal of the loan was irrecoverable (taking the facts existing on that date) or proved to be irrecoverable (taking the facts existing on a later date), and

(c) subsection (3)(b) and (c) above are fulfilled.

(6) In a case where the inspector is satisfied that the first or second condition is fulfilled, the allowable amount is the lesser of—

(a) the outstanding amount of the principal of the loan;

(b) the amount of the security's acquisition cost;

and if any amount of the principal of the loan has been recovered the amount of the security's acquisition cost shall for this purpose be treated as reduced (but not beyond nil) by the amount recovered.

(7) In a case where the inspector is satisfied that the third condition is fulfilled, then—

(a) if the security's acquisition cost exceeds the relevant amount, the allowable amount is an amount equal to the excess;

(b) if the security's acquisition cost is equal to or less than the relevant amount, the allowable amount is nil.

(8) For the purposes of subsection (7) above the relevant amount is the aggregate of—

(a) the amount (if any) of the principal of the loan which has been recovered, and

(b) the amount (if any) of the principal of the loan which has not been recovered but which in the inspector's opinion is recoverable.

(9) Where an allowable loss has been treated under subsection (2) above as accruing to any person and the whole or any part of the relevant outstanding amount is at any time recovered by him, this Act shall have effect as if there had accrued to him at that time a chargeable gain equal to so much of the allowable loss as corresponds to the amount recovered.

(10) Where—

(a) an allowable loss has been treated under subsection (2) above as accruing to a company ("the first company"), and

(b) the whole or any part of the relevant outstanding amount is at any time recovered by a company ("the second company") in the same group as the first company,

this Act shall have effect as if there had accrued to the second company at that time a chargeable gain equal to so much of the allowable loss as corresponds to the amount recovered.

(11) In subsections (9) and (10) above "the relevant outstanding amount" means—

(a) the amount of the principal of the loan outstanding when the claim was allowed, in a case where the inspector was satisfied that the first or second condition was fulfilled;

(b) the amount of the part (or the greater or greatest part) arrived at by the inspector under subsection (5)(b) above, in a case where he was satisfied that the third condition was fulfilled.

(12) This section does not apply if the security was issued before 15th March, 1989 and was not held on 15th March, 1989 by the person who made the loan.

GENERAL NOTE

This section, introduced by FA 1990, s.84, during the recession which began in the late 1980s, gives relief for losses on corporate bonds. Gains on such bonds are exempt from C.G.T. under s.115, and accordingly losses would not normally be allowable. This deterred lenders and accentuated the difficulty of businesses in raising finance. Accordingly, relief is given for losses on a loan which would qualify under s.253 but for being a debt on a security and which is a qualifying corporate bond (see s.117).

On a claim being made, the inspector must be satisfied that one out of three conditions is fulfilled:
(1) the value of the security has become negligible; (2) the redemption date has passed and the principal is irrecoverable; and (3) the redemption date has passed and part of the principal is irrecoverable.

Relief will be refused if the the debt has been assigned or the loan is between companies in the same group.

The *quantum* of relief is the lesser of the outstanding amount of principal and the acquisition cost, the latter being reduced by any principal recovered. In the case of partial loss, the acquisition cost is reduced by amounts of principal recovered or, in the inspector's opinion, recoverable.

The relief is clawed back on a recovery, either by the lender or by a company in the same group.

Provisions supplementary to section 254

255.—(1) For the purposes of section 254 a security's redemption date is the latest date on which, under the terms on which the security was issued, the company or body which issued it can be required to redeem it.

(2) For the purposes of section 254 a security's acquisition cost is the amount or value of the consideration in money or money's worth given, by or on behalf of the person who made the loan, wholly and exclusively for the acquisition of the security, together with the incidental costs to him of the acquisition.

(3) For the purposes of section 254(10) 2 companies are in the same group if they have been in the same group at any time after the loan was made.

(4) Section 253(9) shall apply for the purposes of section 254(6) and (8) to (10) as it applies for the purposes of section 253(5).

(5) Section 253(10), (12) and (14)(c) shall apply for the purposes of section 254 and of this section as they apply for the purposes of section 253, ignoring for this purpose the words following "lender" in section 253(12).

GENERAL NOTE
This provides supplementary definitions for s.254. Some of the terminology of s.253, particularly in relation to "recovery", is adopted for s.254.

Charities and gifts of non-business assets etc.

Charities

256.—(1) Subject to section 505(3) of the Taxes Act and subsection (2) below, a gain shall not be a chargeable gain if it accrues to a charity and is applicable and applied for charitable purposes.

(2) If property held on charitable trusts ceases to be subject to charitable trusts—
(a) the trustees shall be treated as if they had disposed of, and immediately reacquired, the property for a consideration equal to its market value, any gain on the disposal being treated as not accruing to a charity, and
(b) if and so far as any of that property represents, directly or indirectly, the consideration for the disposal of assets by the trustees, any gain accruing on that disposal shall be treated as not having accrued to a charity,
and an assessment to capital gains tax chargeable by virtue of paragraph (b) above may be made at any time not more than 3 years after the end of the year of assessment in which the property ceases to be subject to charitable trusts.

GENERAL NOTE
Gains accruing to a charity are exempt from C.G.T. The relief does not apply where the charity is not absolutely entitled to the property as against the trustees (*Prest* v. *Bettinson* (1980) 53 T.C. 437).

Following the decision in *I.R.C.* v. *Slater (Helen) Charitable Trust* [1982] Ch. 49, C.A., the exemption for charities was withdrawn in cases where a charity does not expend sufficient of its income and gains for charitable purposes: see ICTA 1988, ss.505(3), (5) and 506.

Where property ceases to be subject to charitable trusts there is a deemed disposal at market value and where the property represents the proceeds of a disposal by the trustees that gain also is deemed not to have accrued to a charity. An assessment in the latter case may be raised within three years after the end of charitable status.

Gifts to charities etc.

257.—(1) Subsection (2) below shall apply where a disposal of an asset is made otherwise than under a bargain at arm's length—

(a) to a charity, or

(b) to any bodies mentioned in Schedule 3 to the Inheritance Tax Act 1984 (gifts for national purposes, etc.).

(2) Sections 17(1) and 258(3) shall not apply; but if the disposal is by way of gift (including a gift in settlement) or for a consideration not exceeding the sums allowable as a deduction under section 38, then—

(a) the disposal and acquisition shall be treated for the purposes of this Act as being made for such consideration as to secure that neither a gain nor a loss accrues on the disposal, and

(b) where, after the disposal, the asset is disposed of by the person who acquired it under the disposal, its acquisition by the person making the earlier disposal shall be treated for the purposes of this Act as the acquisition of the person making the later disposal.

(3) Where—

(a) otherwise than on the termination of a life interest (within the meaning of section 72) by the death of the person entitled thereto, any assets or parts of any assets forming part of settled property are, under section 71, deemed to be disposed of and reacquired by the trustee, and

(b) the person becoming entitled as mentioned in section 71(1) is a charity, or a body mentioned in Schedule 3 to the Inheritance Tax Act 1984 (gifts for national purposes, etc.),

then, if no consideration is received by any person for or in connection with any transaction by virtue of which the charity or other body becomes so entitled, the disposal and reacquisition of the assets to which the charity or other body becomes so entitled shall, notwithstanding section 71, be treated for the purposes of this Act as made for such consideration as to secure that neither a gain nor a loss accrues on the disposal.

(4) In subsection (2)(b) above the first reference to a disposal includes a disposal to which section 146(2) of the 1979 Act applied where the person who acquired the asset on that disposal disposes of the asset after the coming into force of this section.

GENERAL NOTE

Gifts to charities or to the public bodies mentioned in IHTA 1984, Sched. 3, are exempt from C.G.T. Such gifts pass to the charity or public body on a no-gain/no-loss basis. The exemption applies to disposals by trustees.

Works of art etc.

258.—(1) A gain accruing on the disposal of an asset by way of gift shall not be a chargeable gain if the asset is property falling within subsection (2) of section 26 of the Inheritance Tax Act 1984 ("the 1984 Act") (gifts for public benefit) and the Board give a direction in relation to it under subsection (1) of that section.

(2) A gain shall not be a chargeable gain if it accrues on the disposal of an asset with respect to which an inheritance tax undertaking or an undertaking under the following provisions of this section has been given and—

    (a) the disposal is by way of sale by private treaty to a body mentioned in Schedule 3 to the 1984 Act (museums, etc.), or is to such a body otherwise than by sale, or

    (b) the disposal is to the Board in pursuance of section 230 of the 1984 Act or in accordance with directions given by the Treasury under section 50 or 51 of the Finance Act 1946 (acceptance of property in satisfaction of tax).

  (3) Subsection (4) below shall have effect in respect of the disposal of any asset which is property which has been or could be designated under section 31 of the 1984 Act, being—

    (a) a disposal by way of gift, including a gift in settlement, or

    (b) a disposal of settled property by the trustee on an occasion when, under section 71(1), the trustee is deemed to dispose of and immediately reacquire settled property (other than any disposal on which by virtue of section 73 no chargeable gain or allowable loss accrues to the trustee),

if the requisite undertaking described in section 31 of the 1984 Act (maintenance, preservation and access) is given by such person as the Board think appropriate in the circumstances of the case.

  (4) The person making a disposal to which subsection (3) above applies and the person acquiring the asset on the disposal shall be treated for all the purposes of this Act as if the asset was acquired from the one making the disposal for a consideration of such an amount as would secure that on the disposal neither a gain nor a loss would accrue to the one making the disposal.

  (5) If—

    (a) there is a sale of the asset and inheritance tax is chargeable under section 32 of the 1984 Act (or would be chargeable if an inheritance tax undertaking as well as an undertaking under this section had been given), or

    (b) the Board are satisfied that at any time during the period for which any such undertaking was given it has not been observed in a material respect,

the person selling that asset or as the case may be, the owner of the asset shall be treated for the purposes of this Act as having sold the asset for a consideration equal to its market value, and, in the case of a failure to comply with the undertaking, having immediately reacquired it for a consideration equal to its market value.

  (6) The period for which an undertaking under this section is given shall be until the person beneficially entitled to the asset dies or it is disposed of, whether by sale or gift or otherwise; and if the asset subject to the undertaking is disposed of—

    (a) otherwise than on sale, and

    (b) without a further undertaking being given under this section,

subsection (5) above shall apply as if the asset had been sold to an individual.

  References in this subsection to a disposal shall be construed without regard to any provision of this Act under which an asset is deemed to be disposed of.

  (7) Where under subsection (5) above a person is treated as having sold for a consideration equal to its market value any asset within section 31(1) (c), (d) or (e) of the 1984 Act, he shall also be treated as having sold and immediately reacquired for a consideration equal to its market value any asset associated with it; but the Board may direct that the preceding provisions of this subsection shall not have effect in any case in which it appears to them that the entity consisting of the asset and any assets associated with it has not been materially affected.

  For the purposes of this subsection 2 or more assets are associated with each other if one of them is a building falling within section 31(1)(c) of the

1984 Act and the other or others such land or objects as, in relation to that building, fall within section 31(1)(d) or (e) of the 1984 Act.

(8) If in pursuance of subsection (5) above a person is treated as having on any occasion sold an asset and inheritance tax becomes chargeable on the same occasion, then, in determining the value of the asset for the purposes of that tax, an allowance shall be made for the capital gains tax chargeable on any chargeable gain accruing on that occasion.

(9) In this section "inheritance tax undertaking" means an undertaking under Chapter II of Part II or section 78 of, or Schedule 5 to, the 1984 Act.

GENERAL NOTE

A gift of a wide range of national heritage property is exempt from inheritance tax by IHTA 1984, s.26, if the Inland Revenue so direct (see FA 1985, s.95). This exemption also applies for C.G.T. The exemption from C.G.T. also applies where there is a disposal to a public body or to the Revenue in satisfaction of an inheritance tax liability.

Where conditional exemption for national heritage property is accorded by IHTA 1984, s.31, this will also apply for C.G.T., subject to a charge when the condition ceases to be satisfied. Associated assets will be subject to a deemed disposal at market value.

Gifts to housing associations

259.—(1) Subsection (2) below shall apply where—
(a) a disposal of an estate or interest in land in the United Kingdom is made to a registered housing association otherwise than under a bargain at arm's length, and
(b) a claim for relief under this section is made by the transferor and the association.

(2) Section 17(1) shall not apply; but if the disposal is by way of gift or for a consideration not exceeding the sums allowable as a deduction under section 38, then—
(a) the disposal and acquisition shall be treated for the purposes of this Act as being made for such consideration as to secure that neither a gain nor a loss accrues on the disposal, and
(b) where, after the disposal, the estate or interest is disposed of by the association, its acquisition by the person making the earlier disposal shall be treated for the purposes of this Act as the acquisition of the association.

(3) In this section "registered housing association" means a registered housing association within the meaning of the Housing Associations Act 1985 or Part VII of the Housing (Northern Ireland) Order 1981.

(4) In subsection (2)(b) above the first reference to a disposal includes a disposal to which section 146A(2) of the 1979 Act applied where the association which acquired the estate or interest in land on that disposal disposes of it after the coming into force of this section.

GENERAL NOTE

This relief, introduced by FA 1989, s.125, exempts disposals of land to registered housing associations (see the Housing Associations Act 1985, s.3(2)).

Gifts on which inheritance tax is chargeable etc.

260.—(1) If—
(a) an individual or the trustees of a settlement ("the transferor") make a disposal within subsection (2) below of an asset,
(b) the asset is acquired by an individual or the trustees of a settlement ("the transferee"), and
(c) a claim for relief under this section is made by the transferor and the

transferee or, where the trustees of a settlement are the transferee, by the transferor alone,

then, subject to subsection (6) below and section 261, subsection (3) below shall apply in relation to the disposal.

(2) A disposal is within this subsection if it is made otherwise than under a bargain at arm's length and—

   (a) is a chargeable transfer within the meaning of the Inheritance Tax Act 1984 (or would be but for section 19 of that Act) and is not a potentially exempt transfer (within the meaning of that Act),

   (b) is an exempt transfer by virtue of—

      (i) section 24 of that Act (transfers to political parties),

      (ii) section 26 of that Act (transfers for public benefit),

      (iii) section 27 of that Act (transfers to maintenance funds for historic buildings etc.), or

      (iv) section 30 of that Act (transfers of designated property),

   (c) is a disposition to which section 57A of that Act applies and by which the property disposed of becomes held on trusts of the kind referred to in subsection (1)(b) of that section (maintenance funds for historic buildings etc.),

   (d) by virtue of subsection (4) of section 71 of that Act (accumulation and maintenance trusts) does not constitute an occasion on which inheritance tax is chargeable under that section,

   (e) by virtue of section 78(1) of that Act (transfers of works of art etc.) does not constitute an occasion on which tax is chargeable under Chapter III of Part III of that Act, or

   (f) is a disposal of an asset comprised in a settlement where, as a result of the asset or part of it becoming comprised in another settlement, there is no charge, or a reduced charge, to inheritance tax by virtue of paragraph 9, 16 or 17 of Schedule 4 to that Act (transfers to maintenance funds for historic buildings etc.).

(3) Where this subsection applies in relation to a disposal—

   (a) the amount of any chargeable gain which, apart from this section, would accrue to the transferor on the disposal, and

   (b) the amount of the consideration for which, apart from this section, the transferee would be regarded for the purposes of capital gains tax as having acquired the asset in question,

shall each be reduced by an amount equal to the held-over gain on the disposal.

(4) Subject to subsection (5) below, the reference in subsection (3) above to the held-over gain on a disposal is a reference to the chargeable gain which would have accrued on that disposal apart from this section.

(5) In any case where—

   (a) there is actual consideration (as opposed to the consideration equal to the market value which is deemed to be given by virtue of any provisions of this Act) for a disposal in respect of which a claim for relief is made under this section, and

   (b) that actual consideration exceeds the sums allowable as a deduction under section 38,

the held-over gain on the disposal shall be reduced by the excess referred to in paragraph (b) above or, if part of the gain on the disposal is relieved under Schedule 6, by so much, if any, of that excess as exceeds the part so relieved.

(6) Subsection (3) above does not apply in relation to a disposal of assets within section 115(1) on which a gain is deemed to accrue by virtue of section 116(10)(b).

(7) In the case of a disposal within subsection (2)(a) above there shall be allowed as a deduction in computing the chargeable gain accruing to the transferee on the disposal of the asset in question an amount equal to whichever is the lesser of—

(a) the inheritance tax attributable to the value of the asset; and

(b) the amount of the chargeable gain as computed apart from this subsection.

(8) Where an amount of inheritance tax is varied after it has been taken into account under subsection (7) above, all necessary adjustments shall be made, whether by the making of an assessment to capital gains tax or by the discharge or repayment of such tax.

(9) Where subsection (3) above applies in relation to a disposal which is deemed to occur by virtue of section 71(1) or 72(1), subsection (5) above shall not apply.

(10) Where a disposal is partly within subsection (2) above, or is a disposal within paragraph (f) of that subsection on which there is a reduced charge such as is mentioned in that paragraph, the preceding provisions of this section shall have effect in relation to an appropriate part of the disposal.

GENERAL NOTE

This relief, introduced in 1989 on the abolition of the general relief for gifts, gives a hold-over for C.G.T. on certain disposals on which inheritance tax is chargeable or not, as the case may be. The disposals include:

(1) chargeable transfers which are not potentially exempt transfers (broadly transfers to discretionary trusts);

(2) transfers within IHTA 1984, ss.24, 26, 27 and 30;

(3) transfers within *ibid.*, s.57A;

(4) the obtaining of an interest in possession in an accumulation and maintenance trust under *ibid.* s.71;

(5) transfers under *ibid.*, s.78;

(6) transfers under *ibid.*, Sched. 4, paras. 9, 16 or 17.

Where there is actual consideration for a disposal in excess of the base cost, the balance is deducted from the held-over gain. This does not apply to deemed disposals of settled property.

The relief does not apply to disposals caught by s.116(10)(b) *supra*.

On the disposal of an asset which was not the subject of a potentially exempt transfer, relief is given on the lower of the I.H.T. and the C.G.T. payable.

Section 260 relief: gifts to non-residents

261.—(1) Section 260(3) shall not apply where the transferee is neither resident nor ordinarily resident in the United Kingdom.

(2) Section 260(3) shall not apply where the transferee is an individual who—

(a) though resident or ordinarily resident in the United Kingdom, is regarded for the purposes of any double taxation relief arrangements as resident in a territory outside the United Kingdom, and

(b) by virtue of the arrangements would not be liable in the United Kingdom to tax on a gain arising on a disposal of the asset occurring immediately after its acquisition.

GENERAL NOTE

Relief under s.260 does not apply where the transferee is non-resident or is protected from C.G.T. by a double tax treaty.

Miscellaneous reliefs and exemptions

Chattel exemption

262.—(1) Subject to this section a gain accruing on a disposal of an asset which is tangible movable property shall not be a chargeable gain if the amount or value of the consideration for the disposal does not exceed £6,000.

(2) Where the amount or value of the consideration for the disposal of an asset which is tangible movable property exceeds £6,000, there shall be excluded from any chargeable gain accruing on the disposal so much of it as exceeds five-thirds of the difference between—

(a) the amount or value of the consideration, and

(b) £6,000.

(3) Subsections (1) and (2) above shall not affect the amount of an allowable loss accruing on the disposal of an asset, but for the purposes of computing under this Act the amount of a loss accruing on the disposal of tangible movable property the consideration for the disposal shall, if less than £6,000 be deemed to be £6,000 and the losses which are allowable losses shall be restricted accordingly.

(4) If two or more assets which have formed part of a set of articles of any description all owned at one time by one person are disposed of by that person, and—

(a) to the same person, or

(b) to persons who are acting in concert or who are connected persons, whether on the same or different occasions, the two or more transactions shall be treated as a single transaction disposing of a single asset, but with any necessary apportionments of the reductions in chargeable gains, and in allowable losses, under subsections (2) and (3) above.

(5) If the disposal is of a right or interest in or over tangible movable property—

(a) in the first instance subsections (1), (2) and (3) above shall be applied in relation to the asset as a whole, taking the consideration as including the market value of what remains undisposed of, in addition to the actual consideration,

(b) where the sum of the actual consideration and that market value exceeds £6,000, the part of any chargeable gain that is excluded from it under subsection (2) above shall be so much of the gain as exceeds five-thirds of the difference between that sum and £6,000 multiplied by the fraction equal to the actual consideration divided by the said sum, and

(c) where that sum is less than £6,000 any loss shall be restricted under subsection (3) above by deeming the consideration to be the actual consideration plus the said fraction of the difference between the said sum and £6,000.

(6) This section shall not apply—

(a) in relation to a disposal of commodities of any description by a person dealing on a terminal market or dealing with or through a person ordinarily engaged in dealing on a terminal market, or

(b) in relation to a disposal of currency of any description.

GENERAL NOTE

A relief from C.G.T. is given for a disposal of tangible movable property where the consideration does not exceed £6,000. Where it does exceed £6,000, marginal relief is given on the excess of the gain over five-thirds of the difference between the consideration and £6,000.

Subs. (3)

In the case of a loss, disposals for less than £6,000 are deemed to be £6,000.

Subs. (4)

Disposals of sets of articles to the same person or to persons acting in concert or connected are aggregated.

Subs. (5)

The relief is adjusted for disposals of rights or interests in or over tangible movable property.

Subs. (6)

The relief does not apply to commodities dealt with on terminal markets or currencies.

Passenger vehicles

263. A mechanically propelled road vehicle constructed or adapted for the carriage of passengers, except for a vehicle of a type not commonly used as a private vehicle and unsuitable to be so used, shall not be a chargeable asset; and accordingly no chargeable gain or allowable loss shall accrue on its disposal.

GENERAL NOTE
Cars generally are excluded from C.G.T. The exemption would appear to cover vintage passenger cars, but not racing cars.

Relief for local constituency associations of political parties on reorganisation of constituencies

264.—(1) In this section "relevant date" means the date of coming into operation of an Order in Council under the Parliamentary Constituencies Act 1986 (orders specifying new parliamentary constituences) and, in relation to any relevant date—

(a) "former parliamentary constituency" means an area which, for the purposes of parliamentary elections, was a constituency immediately before that date but is no longer such a constituency after that date; and

(b) "new parliamentary constituency" means an area which, for the purposes of parliamentary elections, is a constituency immediately after that date but was not such a constituency before that date.

(2) In this section "local constituency association" means an unincorporated association (whether described as an association, a branch or otherwise) whose primary purpose is to further the aims of a political party in an area which at any time is or was the same or substantially the same as the area of a parliamentary constituency or two or more parliamentary constituencies and, in relation to any relevant date—

(a) "existing association" means a local constituency association whose area was the same, or substantially the same, as the area of a former parliamentary constituency or two or more such constituencies; and

(b) "new association" means a local constituency association whose area is the same, or substantially the same, as the area of a new parliamentary constituency or two or more such constituencies.

(3) For the purposes of this section, a new association is a successor to an existing association if any part of the existing association's area is comprised in the new association's area.

(4) In any case where, before, on or after a relevant date—

(a) an existing association disposes of land to a new association which is a successor to the existing association, or

(b) an existing association disposes of land to a body (whether corporate or unincorporated) which is an organ of the political party concerned and, as soon as practicable thereafter, that body disposes of the land to a new association which is a successor to the existing association,

the parties to the disposal or, where paragraph (b) above applies, to each of the disposals, shall be treated for the purposes of tax on chargeable gains as if the land disposed of were acquired from the existing association or the body making the disposal for a consideration of such an amount as would secure that on the disposal neither a gain nor a loss accrued to that association or body.

(5) In a case falling within subsection (4) above, the new association shall be treated for the purposes of Schedule 2 as if the acquisition by the existing association of the land disposed of as mentioned in that subsection had been the new association's acquisition of it.

(6) In any case where—

(a) before, on or after a relevant date, an existing association disposes of any land which was used and occupied by it for the purposes of its functions, and

(b) the existing association transfers the whole or part of the proceeds of the disposal to a new association which is a successor to the existing association,

then, subject to subsection (7) below, this Act (and, in particular, the provisions of sections 152 to 158) shall have effect as if, since the time it was acquired by the existing association, the land disposed of had been the property of the new association and, accordingly, as if the disposal of it had been by the new association.

(7) If, in a case falling within subsection (6) above, only part of the proceeds of the disposal is transferred to the new association, that subsection shall apply—

(a) as if there existed in the land disposed of as mentioned in paragraph (a) of that subsection a separate asset in the form of a corresponding undivided share in that land, and subject to any necessary apportionments of consideration for an acquisition or disposal of, or of an interest in, that land; and

(b) as if the references in that subsection (other than paragraph (a) thereof) to the land disposed of and the disposal of it were references respectively to the corresponding undivided share referred to in paragraph (a) above and the disposal of that share;

and for this purpose a corresponding undivided share in the land disposed of is a share which bears to the whole of that land the same proportion as the part of the proceeds transferred bears to the whole of those proceeds.

(8) In this section "political party" means a political party which qualifies for exemption under section 24 of the Inheritance Tax Act 1984 (gifts to political parties).

GENERAL NOTE
  This section, introduced by F(No. 2)A 1983, s.7, confers exemption from C.G.T. on transfers of land by constituency associations of political parties due to the reorganisation of constituency boundaries. In such cases the transfer will be on a no-gain/no-loss basis. Political parties are defined by reference to IHTA 1984, s.24, which requires a party to obtain at least two seats or one seat and 150,000 votes at the preceding general election.

Designated international organisations

265.—(1) Where—
(a) the United Kingdom or any of the Communities is a member of an international organisation; and
(b) the agreement under which it became a member provides for exemption from tax, in relation to the organisation, of the kind for which provision is made by this section;

the Treasury may by order designate that organisation for the purposes of this section.

(2) The Treasury may by order designate any of the Communities or the European Investment Bank for the purposes of this section.

(3) Where an organisation has been designated for the purposes of this section, then any security issued by the organisation shall be taken, for the purposes of capital gains tax, to be situated outside the United Kingdom.

GENERAL NOTE
  Securities issued by organisations designated by the Treasury to which the U.K. or any of the Communities (see the European Communities Act 1972, s.1, Sched. 1 and the Interpretation Act 1978, Sched. 1) belong, including the Communities and the European Investment Bank, are treated as situated outside the U.K.

Inter-American Development Bank

266. A security issued by the Inter-American Development Bank shall be taken for the purposes of this Act to be situated outside the United Kingdom.

GENERAL NOTE
Securities issued by the Inter-American Development Bank are also treated as situated outside the U.K.

Sharing of transmission facilities

267.—(1) This section applies to any agreement relating to the sharing of transmission facilities—

(a) to which the parties are national broadcasting companies,

(b) which is entered into on or after 25th July 1991 (the date on which the Finance Act 1991 was passed) and before 1st January 1992 or such later date as may be specified for the purposes of this paragraph by the Secretary of State, and

(c) in relation to which the Secretary of State has certified that it is expedient that this section should apply.

(2) Where under an agreement to which this section applies one party to the agreement disposes of an asset to another party to the agreement, both parties shall be treated for the purposes of corporation tax on chargeable gains as if the asset acquired by the party to whom the disposal is made were acquired for a consideration of such amount as would secure that on the other's disposal neither a gain nor a loss would accrue to that other.

(3) Where under an agreement to which this section applies one party to the agreement disposes of an asset to another party to the agreement and the asset is one which the party making the disposal acquired on a part disposal by the party to whom the disposal under the agreement is made, then in applying subsection (2) above—

(a) section 42 shall be deemed to have had effect in relation to the part disposal with the omission of subsection (4),

(b) the amount or value of the consideration for the part disposal shall be taken to have been nil, and

(c) if the disposal under the agreement is one to which section 35(2) applies, the market value of the asset on 31st March 1982 shall be taken to have been nil.

(4) In this section "national broadcasting company" means a body corporate engaged in the broadcasting for general reception by means of wireless telegraphy of radio or television services or both on a national basis.

GENERAL NOTE

This section relates to the tax consequences of the reorganisation of shared transmission facilities prior to the privatisation of National Transcommunications Ltd. The transmission facilities of the Independent Broadcasting Authority were transferred, under the Broadcasting Act 1990, to a new company called National Transcommunications Ltd. The new company is to be sold, but before this, informal arrangements under which facilities are shared with other national broadcasters have to be replaced by formal commercial agreements. As part of this, assets and rights that one party has in relation to sites owned by the other are to be transferred to the site owner. Capital gains or losses which would otherwise arise on the termination of existing arrangements are deferred.

Decorations for valour or gallant conduct

268. A gain shall not be a chargeable gain if accruing on the disposal by any person of a decoration awarded for valour or gallant conduct which he acquired otherwise than for consideration in money or money's worth.

GENERAL NOTE

War decorations are exempt from C.G.T. unless they have been acquired for value.

Foreign currency for personal expenditure

269. A gain shall not be a chargeable gain if accruing on the disposal by an individual of currency of any description acquired by him for the personal expenditure outside the United Kingdom of himself or his family or dependants (including expenditure on the provision or maintenance of any residence outside the United Kingdom).

GENERAL NOTE
Foreign currency is exempt from C.G.T. on the same basis as foreign currency bank accounts (see s.252).

Chevening Estate

270. The enactments relating to capital gains tax (apart from this section) shall not apply in respect of property held on the trusts of the trust instrument set out in the Schedule to the Chevening Estate Act 1959.

GENERAL NOTE
Chevening House was settled by Earl Stanhope on trusts in favour of a person nominated by the Prime Minister from a limited class with certain gifts over and an ultimate reversion to the National Trust. It is presently the official residence of the Foreign Secretary.

Other miscellaneous exemptions

271.—(1) The following gains shall not be chargeable gains—
(a) gains accruing on the disposal of stock—
    (i) transferred to accounts in the books of the Bank of England in the name of the Treasury or the National Debt Commissioners in pursuance of any Act of Parliament; or
    (ii) belonging to the Crown, in whatever name it may stand in the books of the Bank of England;
(b) any gain accruing to a person from his acquisition and disposal of assets held by him as part of a fund mentioned in section 613(4) of the Taxes Act (Parliamentary pension funds) or of which income is exempt from income tax under section 614(1) of that Act (social security supplementary schemes);
(c) any gain accruing to a person from his acquisition and disposal of assets held by him as part of a fund mentioned in section 614(2) or paragraph (b), (c), (d), (f) or (g) of section 615(2) of the Taxes Act (India etc. pension funds) or as part of a fund to which subsection (3) of that section applies (pension funds for overseas employees);
(d) any gain accruing to a person from his acquisition and disposal of assets held by him as part of any fund maintained for the purpose mentioned in subsection (5)(b) of section 620 or subsection (5) of section 621 of the Taxes Act under a scheme for the time being approved under that subsection;
(e) any gain accruing on the disposal by the trustees of any settled property held on trusts in accordance with directions which are valid and effective under section 9 of the Superannuation and Trust Funds (Validation) Act 1927 (trust funds for the reduction of the National Debt);
(f) any gain accruing to a consular officer or employee, within the meaning of section 322 of the Taxes Act, of any foreign state to which that section applies on the disposal of assets which at the time of the disposal were situated outside the United Kingdom;
(g) any gain accruing to a person from his disposal of investments if, or to such extent as the Board are satisfied that, those investments were held by him or on his behalf for the purposes of a scheme which at the time of the disposal is an exempt approved scheme;
(h) any gain accruing to a person on his disposal of investments held by him for the purposes of an approved personal pension scheme;
(j) any gain accruing to a unit holder on his disposal of units in an

authorised unit trust which is also an approved personal pension scheme or is one to which section 592(10) of the Taxes Act applies.

In this subsection "exempt approved scheme" and "approved personal pension scheme" have the same meanings as in Part XIV of the Taxes Act.

(2) Where a claim is made in that behalf, a gain which accrues to a person on the disposal of investments shall not be a chargeable gain for the purposes of capital gains tax if, or to such extent as the Board are satisfied that, those investments were held by him or on his behalf for the purposes of a fund to which section 608 of the Taxes Act applies.

A claim under this subsection shall not be allowed unless the Board are satisfied that the terms on which benefits are payable from the fund have not been altered since 5th April, 1980.

(3) A local authority, a local authority association and a health service body shall be exempt from capital gains tax.

In this subsection "local authority association" and "health service body" have the meanings given by sections 519 and 519A of the Taxes Act respectively.

(4) Any bonus to which section 326 or 326A of the Taxes Act (certified contractual savings schemes and tax-exempt special savings accounts) applies shall be disregarded for all purposes of the enactments relating to capital gains tax.

In any case where there is a transfer to which section 216 applies, this subsection shall have effect in relation to any bonus payable after the transfer under a savings scheme which immediately before the transfer was a certified contractual savings scheme notwithstanding that it ceased to be such a scheme by reason of the transfer.

(5) A signatory to the Operating Agreement made pursuant to the Convention on the International Maritime Satellite Organisation which came into force on 16th July, 1979, other than a signatory designated for the purposes of the Agreement by the United Kingdom in accordance with the Convention, shall be exempt from capital gains tax in respect of any payment received by that signatory from the Organisation in accordance with the Agreement.

(6) The following shall, on a claim made in that behalf to the Board, be exempt from tax in respect of all chargeable gains—

(a) the Trustees of the British Museum and the Trustees of the British Museum (National History); and

(b) an Association within the meaning of section 508 of the Taxes Act (scientific research organisations).

(7) The Historic Buildings and Monuments Commission for England, the Trustees of the National Heritage Memorial Fund, the United Kingdom Atomic Energy Authority and the National Radiological Protection Board shall be exempt from tax in respect of chargeable gains; and for the purposes of this subsection gains accruing from investments or deposits held for the purposes of any pension scheme provided and maintained by the United Kingdom Atomic Energy Authority shall be treated as if those gains and investments and deposits belonged to the Authority.

(8) There shall be exempt from tax any chargeable gains accruing to the issue department of the Reserve Bank of India constituted under an Act of the Indian legislature called the Reserve Bank of India Act 1934, or to the issue department of the State Bank of Pakistan constituted under certain orders made under section 9 of the Indian Independence Act 1947.

(9) Any disposal and acquisition made in pursuance of an arrangement mentioned in subsection (1), (2) or (2A) of section 129 of the Taxes Act (stock lending) shall, subject to regulations under subsection (4) of that section, be disregarded for the purposes of capital gains tax.

(10) In subsections (1)(g) and (h) and (2) above "investments" includes futures contracts and options contracts; and paragraph 7(3)(d) of Schedule 22 to the Taxes Act shall be construed accordingly.

(11) For the purposes of subsection (10) above a contract is not prevented from being a futures contract or an options contract by the fact that any party is or may be entitled to receive or liable to make, or entitled to receive and liable to make, only a payment of a sum (as opposed to a transfer of assets other than money) in full settlement of all obligations.

GENERAL NOTE
This section groups together a number of miscellaneous exemptions from C.G.T. They relate mostly to public bodies and approved pension schemes.

PART VIII

SUPPLEMENTAL

Valuation: general

272.—(1) In this Act "market value" in relation to any assets means the price which those assets might reasonably be expected to fetch on a sale in the open market.

(2) In estimating the market value of any assets no reduction shall be made in the estimate on account of the estimate being made on the assumption that the whole of the assets is to be placed on the market at one and the same time.

(3) Subject to subsection (4) below, the market value of shares or securities listed in The Stock Exchange Daily Official List shall, except where in consequence of special circumstances prices quoted in that List are by themselves not a proper measure of market value, be as follows—

   (a) the lower of the two prices shown in the quotations for the shares or securities in The Stock Exchange Daily Official List on the relevant date plus one-quarter of the difference between those two figures, or

   (b) halfway between the highest and lowest prices at which bargains, other than bargains done at special prices, were recorded in the shares or securities for the relevant date,

choosing the amount under paragraph (a), if less than that under paragraph (b), or if no such bargains were recorded for the relevant date, and choosing the amount under paragraph (b) if less than that under paragraph (a).

(4) Subsection (3) shall not apply to shares or securities for which The Stock Exchange provides a more active market elsewhere than on the London trading floor; and, if the London trading floor is closed on the relevant date, the market value shall be ascertained by reference to the latest previous date or earliest subsequent date on which it is open, whichever affords the lower market value.

(5) In this Act "market value" in relation to any rights of unit holders in any unit trust scheme the buying and selling prices of which are published regularly by the managers of the scheme shall mean an amount equal to the buying price (that is the lower price) so published on the relevant date, or if none were published on that date, on the latest date before.

(6) The provisions of this section, with sections 273 and 274, have effect subject to Part I of Schedule 11.

GENERAL NOTE
This section contains the general rules for valuation of assets for C.G.T. The rule of market value without reduction for any hypothetical swamping of the market conforms with that for inheritance tax under IHTA 1984, s.160.

Stock exchange securities are valued on the basis of the Daily Official List unless special circumstances make the quoted prices not a proper measure of value. It was held that the fact that takeover negotiations were in progress at a relevant date was not a special circumstance, since directors often have confidential information which could affect the share price if made public (*Crabtree* v. *Hinchcliffe* [1972] A.C. 707, H.L.).

The reference to "trading floor" is now somewhat outdated with the advent of electronic trading.

Units in unit trusts are valued at the managers' buying price.
Part I of Schedule 11 relates to certain transitional provisions concerning valuation.

Unquoted shares and securities

273.—(1) The provisions of subsection (3) below shall have effect in any case where, in relation to an asset to which this section applies, there falls to be determined by virtue of section 272(1) the price which the asset might reasonably be expected to fetch on a sale in the open market.

(2) The assets to which this section applies are shares and securities which are not quoted on a recognised stock exchange at the time as at which their market value for the purposes of tax on chargeable gains falls to be determined.

(3) For the purposes of a determination falling within subsection (1) above, it shall be assumed that, in the open market which is postulated for the purposes of that determination, there is available to any prospective purchaser of the asset in question all the information which a prudent prospective purchaser of the asset might reasonably require if he were proposing to purchase it from a willing vendor by private treaty and at arm's length.

GENERAL NOTE
With respect to unquoted securities, for the purpose of establishing market value a prospective purchaser is to be deemed to have all the information which a prudent man might reasonably require on a purchase by private treaty.
This provision, which mirrors IHTA 1984, s.168, was inserted to reverse the House of Lords decision in *Lynall* v. *I.R.C.* [1972] A.C. 680, an estate duty case.

Value determined for inheritance tax

274. Where on the death of any person inheritance tax is chargeable on the value of his estate immediately before his death and the value of an asset forming part of that estate has been ascertained (whether in any proceedings or otherwise) for the purposes of that tax, the value so ascertained shall be taken for the purposes of this Act to be the market value of that asset at the date of the death.

GENERAL NOTE
Valuations determined on death for inheritance tax apply also for C.G.T. On death there is a deemed acquisition by personal representatives at market value, but no deemed disposal by the deceased (s.62).

Location of assets

275. For the purposes of this Act—
  (a) the situation of rights or interests (otherwise than by way of security) in or over immovable property is that of the immovable property.
  (b) subject to the following provisions of this subsection, the situation of rights or interests (otherwise than by way of security) in or over tangible movable property is that of the tangible movable property,
  (c) subject to the following provisions of this subsection, a debt, secured or unsecured, is situated in the United Kingdom if and only if the creditor is resident in the United Kingdom,
  (d) shares or securities issued by any municipal or governmental authority, or by any body created by such an authority, are situated in the country of that authority,
  (e) subject to paragraph (d) above, registered shares or securities are situated where they are registered and, if registered in more than one register, where the principal register is situated,
  (f) a ship or aircraft is situated in the United Kingdom if and only if the owner is then resident in the United Kingdom, and an interest or right

in or over a ship or aircraft is situated in the United Kingdom if and only if the person entitled to the interest or right is resident in the United Kingdom,

(g) the situation of good-will as a trade, business or professional asset is at the place where the trade, business or profession is carried on,

(h) patents, trade marks, service marks and registered designs are situated where they are registered, and if registered in more than one register, where each register is situated, and rights or licences to use a patent, trade mark, service mark or registered design are situated in the United Kingdom if they or any right derived from them are exercisable in the United Kingdom,

(j) copyright, design right and franchises, and rights or licences to use any copyright work or design in which design rights subsists, are situated in the United Kingdom if they or any right derived from them are exercisable in the United Kingdom,

(k) a judgment debt is situated where the judgment is recorded,

(l) a debt which—
(i) is owed by a bank, and
(ii) is not in sterling, and
(iii) is represented by a sum standing to the credit of an account in the bank of an individual who is not domiciled in the United Kingdom,
is situated in the United Kingdom if and only if that individual is resident in the United Kingdom and the branch or other place of business of the bank at which the account is maintained is itself situated in the United Kingdom.

GENERAL NOTE

This section provides rules for determining the *situs* of assets and follows generally the principles accepted in private international law: see textbooks such as Dicey & Morris, *Conflict of Laws*. It is of importance for C.G.T. because individuals resident but not domiciled in the U.K. are charged on a remittance basis on gains from the disposal of assets situated outside the U.K.

Para. (e)

It was held in *Young and Young* v. *Phillips (Inspector of Taxes)* (1984) 58 T.C. 232 that where rights under letters of allotment were renounced in the Channel Islands, the rights were to be taken as situated in the U.K., since that was where they could be enforced.

Para. (l) was added by FA 1984, s.69, to take out of charge foreign currency accounts of non-domiciled individuals with overseas branches of U.K. banks.

The territorial sea and the continental shelf

276.—(1) The territorial sea of the United Kingdom shall for all purposes of the taxation of chargeable gains (including the following provisions of this section) be deemed to be part of the United Kingdom.

(2) In this section—
(a) "exploration or exploitation activities" means activities carried on in connection with the exploration or exploitation of so much of the seabed and subsoil and their natural resources as is situated in the United Kingdom or a designated area; and

(b) "exploration or exploitation rights" means rights to assets to be produced by exploration or exploitation activities or to interests in or to the benefit of such assets; and

(c) references to the disposal of exploration or exploitation rights include references to the disposal of shares deriving their value or the greater part of their value directly or indirectly from such rights, other than shares quoted on a recognised stock exchange; and

(d) "shares" includes stock and any security as defined in section 254(1) of the Taxes Act; and

    (e) "designated area" means an area designated by Order in Council under section 1(7) of the Continental Shelf Act 1964.

    (3) Any gains accruing on the disposal of exploration or exploitation rights shall be treated for the purposes of this Act as gains accruing on the disposal of assets situated in the United Kingdom.

    (4) Gains accruing on the disposal of—

    (a) exploration or exploitation assets which are situated in a designated area, or

    (b) unquoted shares deriving their value or the greater part of their value directly or indirectly from exploration or exploitation assets situated in the United Kingdom or a designated area or from such assets and exploration or exploitation rights taken together,

shall be treated for the purposes of this Act as gains accruing on the disposal of assets situated in the United Kingdom.

    (5) For the purposes of this section, an asset disposed of is an exploration or exploitation asset if either—

    (a) it is not a mobile asset and it is being or has at some time been used in connection with exploration or exploitation activities carried on in the United Kingdom or a designated area; or

    (b) it is a mobile asset which has at some time been used in connection with exploration or exploitation activities so carried on and is dedicated to an oil field in which the person making the disposal, or a person connected with him, is or has been a participator;

and expressions used in paragraphs (a) and (b) above have the same meaning as if those paragraphs were included in Part I of the Oil Taxation Act 1975.

    (6) In subsection (4)(b) above "unquoted shares" means shares other than those which are quoted on a recognised stock exchange; and references in subsections (7) and (8) below to exploration or exploitation assets include references to unquoted shares falling within subsection (4)(b).

    (7) Gains accruing to a person not resident in the United Kingdom on the disposal of exploration or exploitation rights or of exploration or exploitation assets shall, for the purposes of capital gains tax or corporation tax on chargeable gains, be treated as gains accruing on the disposal of assets used for the purposes of a trade carried on by that person in the United Kingdom through a branch or agency.

    (8) In relation to exploration or exploitation rights or exploration or exploitation assets disposed of by a company resident in a territory outside the United Kingdom to a company resident in the same territory or in the United Kingdom, sections 171 to 174 and 178 to 181 shall apply as if in section 170 subsections (2)(a) and (9) were omitted.

GENERAL NOTE

This section is consolidated from FA 1973, s.38, and corresponds with ICTA 1988, s.830, which applies for income tax and corporation tax.

The territorial sea of the U.K., which is fairly limited in extent, is deemed to be part of the U.K. However, areas outside the territorial sea may be designated by Order in Council under the Continental Shelf Act 1964, s.1(7), passed in pursuance of the Geneva Convention on the High Seas 1958.

Subs. (3)

Gains on the disposal of exploration or exploitation rights are treated as accruing in the U.K.

Subs. (4)

Gains accruing on the disposal of exploration or exploitation assets situated in a designated area and of unquoted shares deriving their value from such assets are also treated as accruing in the U.K.

Subs. (5)

This defines "exploration or exploitation assets". Mobile assets are excluded unless they are dedicated to a field in which the taxpayer is a participator. See further the Oil Taxation Act 1975, Pt. I.

Subs. (7)
   Non-residents are treated for this purpose as carrying on a trade in the U.K. through a branch or agency.

Subs. (8)
   The provisions regarding groups of companies apply to non-resident companies for this purpose.
   For the general operation of the North Sea tax régime in the context of the P.A.Y.E. system, see *Clark* v. *Oceanic Contractors Inc.* (1982) 56 T.C. 183, H.L.

Double taxation relief

   277.—(1) For the purpose of giving relief from double taxation in relation to capital gains tax and tax on chargeable gains charged under the law of any country outside the United Kingdom, in Chapters I and II of Parts XVIII of the Taxes Act, as they apply for the purposes of income tax, for references to income there shall be substituted references to capital gains and for references to income tax there shall be substituted references to capital gains tax meaning, as the context may require, tax charged under the law of the United Kingdom or tax charged under the law of a country outside the United Kingdom.
   (2) Any arrangements set out in an order made under section 347 of the Income Tax Act 1952 before 5th August, 1965 (the date of the passing of the Finance Act 1965) shall so far as they provide (in whatever terms) for relief from tax chargeable in the United Kingdom on capital gains have effect in relation to capital gains tax.
   (3) So far as by virtue of this section capital gains tax charged under the law of a country outside the United Kingdom may be brought into account under the said Chapters I and II as applied by this section, that tax, whether relief is given by virtue of this section in respect of it or not, shall not be taken into account for the purposes of those Chapters as they apply apart from this section.
   (4) Section 816 of the Taxes Act (disclosure of information for purposes of double taxation) shall apply in relation to capital gains tax as it applies in relation to income tax.

GENERAL NOTE
   Double taxation relief is to be accorded for C.G.T. as it is for income tax, although in view of the many restrictions which now apply in relation to dual residence the ambit of this provision would appear to have been severely cut down.

Allowance for foreign tax

   278. Subject to section 277, the tax chargeable under the law of any country outside the United Kingdom on the disposal of an asset which is borne by the person making the disposal shall be allowable as a deduction in the computation of the gain.

GENERAL NOTE
   Foreign tax on a disposal not allowed under s.277 is allowed as a deduction for C.G.T.

Foreign assets: delayed remittances

   279.—(1) Subsection (2) below applies where—
   (a) chargeable gains accrue from the disposal of assets situated outside the United Kingdom, and
   (b) the person charged or chargeable makes a claim and shows that the conditions set out in subsection (3) below are, so far as applicable, satisfied as respects those gains ("the qualifying gains");

and subsection (2)(b) also applies where a claim has been made under section 13 of the 1979 Act.

(2) For the purposes of capital gains tax—

(a) the amount of the qualifying gains shall be deducted from the amounts on which the claimant is assessed to capital gains tax for the year in which the qualifying gains accrued to the claimant, but

(b) the amount so deducted shall be assessed to capital gains tax on the claimant (or his personal representatives) as if it were an amount of chargeable gains accruing in the year of assessment in which the conditions set out in subsection (3) below cease to be satisfied.

(3) The conditions are—

(a) that the claimant was unable to transfer the qualifying gains to the United Kingdom, and

(b) that that inability was due to the laws of the territory where the assets were situated at the time of the disposal, or to the executive action of its government, or to the impossibility of obtaining foreign currency in that territory, and

(c) that the inability was not due to any want of reasonable endeavours on the part of the claimant.

(4) Where under an agreement entered into under arrangements made by the Secretary of State in pursuance of section 1 of the Overseas Investment and Export Guarantees Act 1972 or section 11 of the Export Guarantees and Overseas Investment Act 1978 any payment is made by the Exports Credits Guarantee Department in respect of any gains which cannot be transferred to the United Kingdom, then, to the extent of the payment, the gains shall be treated as gains with respect to which the conditions mentioned in subsection (3) above are not satisfied (and accordingly cannot cease to be satisfied).

(5) No claim under this section shall be made in respect of any chargeable gain more than six years after the end of the year of assessment in which that gain accrues.

(6) The personal representatives of a deceased person may make any claim which he might have made under this section if he had not died.

(7) Where—

(a) a claim under this section is made (or has been made under section 13 of the 1979 Act) by a man in respect of chargeable gains accruing to his wife before 6th April, 1990, and

(b) by virtue of this section the amount of the gains falls to be assessed to capital gains tax as if it were an amount of gains accruing in the year 1992–93 or a subsequent year of assessment,

it shall be assessed not on the claimant (or his personal representatives) but on the person to whom the gains accrued (or her personal representatives).

(8) In relation to disposals before 19th March, 1991 subsection (3)(b) above shall have effect with the substitution of the words "income arose" for the words "assets were situated at the time of the disposal".

GENERAL NOTE

This provision, which corresponds to that for income tax in ICTA 1988, s.584, allows relief where the proceeds of the disposal of assets situated outside the U.K., cannot be remitted here because of the laws of the territory concerned or to Government action or to the impossibility of obtaining foreign exchange, and not for lack of reasonable endeavours on the taxpayer's part. The tax relieved, subject to a claim within six years, is clawed back when remittance becomes possible. It was held in *Van-Arkadie (Inspector of Taxes)* v. *Plunket* (1982) 56 T.C. 310 that the relief did not apply in respect of gains attributed to a member of a non-resident company under s.13.

Subs. (4)

Relief does not apply where payments have been made by the ECGD.

Subs. (7)
This follows from the introduction of the independent taxation of women.

Subs. (8)
This refers to an amendment made by F.A. 1991, s.97, to correct a patent error in the original drafting of the section.

Consideration payable by instalments

280. If the consideration, or part of the consideration, taken into account in the computation of the gain is payable by instalments over a period beginning not earlier than the time when the disposal is made, being a period exceeding 18 months, then, if the person making the disposal satisfies the Board that he would otherwise suffer undue hardship, the tax on a chargeable gain accruing on the disposal may, at his option, be paid by such instalments as the Board may allow over a period not exceeding eight years and ending not later than the time at which the last of the first-mentioned instalments is payable.

GENERAL NOTE
This gives the Revenue power to modify the general rule in s.48 ignoring the postponement of the receipt of consideration for a disposal, where the period involved exceeds 18 months. In such a case, if the taxpayer can demonstrate undue hardship, the tax may be paid by instalments over a period not exceeding eight years.

Payment by instalments of tax on gifts

281.—(1) Subsection (2) below applies where—
(a) the whole or any part of any assets to which this section applies is disposed of by way of gift or is deemed to be disposed of under section 71(1) or 72(1), and
(b) the disposal is one—
　　　(i) to which neither section 165(4) nor section 260(3) applies (or would apply if a claim were duly made), or
　　　(ii) to which either of those sections does apply but on which the held-over gain (within the meaning of the section applying) is less than the chargeable gain which would have accrued on that disposal apart from that section.
(2) Where this subsection applies, the capital gains tax chargeable on a gain accruing on the disposal may, if the person paying it by notice to the inspector so elects, be paid by 10 equal yearly instalments.
(3) The assets to which this section applies are—
(a) land or an estate or interest in land,
(b) any shares or securities of a company which, immediately before the disposal, gave control of the company to the person by whom the disposal was made or deemed to be made, and
(c) any shares or securities of a company not falling under paragraph (b) above and not quoted on a recognised stock exchange nor dealt in on the Unlisted Securities Market.
(4) Where tax is payable by instalments by virtue of this section, the first instalment shall be due on the day on which the tax would be payable apart from this section.
(5) Subject to the following provisions of this section—
(a) tax payable by instalments by virtue of this section shall carry interest in accordance with Part IX (except section 88) of the Management Act, and
(b) the interest on the unpaid portion of the tax shall be added to each instalment and paid accordingly.
(6) Tax payable by instalments by virtue of this section which is for the time being unpaid, with interest to the date of payment, may be paid at any time.

(7) Tax which apart from this subsection would be payable by instalments by virtue of this section and which is for the time being unpaid, with interest to the date of payment, shall become due and payable immediately if—
  (a) the disposal was by way of gift to a person connected with the donor or was deemed to be made under section 71(1) or 72(1), and
  (b) the assets are disposed of for valuable consideration under a subsequent disposal (whether or not the subsequent disposal is made by the person who acquired them under the first disposal).

GENERAL NOTE
The abolition of the general relief for gifts by FA 1989, s.124, meant that C.G.T might become payable in many cases where no funds to pay it were readily available. Accordingly, in such a case, where relief is not available under s.165 or s.260, the taxpayer may elect to pay the tax by 10 annual instalments.
The relief applies only to three classes of assets which might be regarded as especially illiquid—land, controlling interest in companies, and shares not quoted on the stock exchange not dealt in on the USM.
The instalments carry interest in accordance with TMA 1970, ss.86 and 89–92.
Where the gift is to a connected person or is a deemed gift under ss.71(1) or 72(1) and the asset is subsequently disposed of for valuable consideration, the charge crystallises.

Recovery of tax from donee

282.—(1) If in any year of assessment a chargeable gain accrues to any person on the disposal of an asset by way of gift and any amount of capital gains tax assessed on that person for that year of assessment is not paid within 12 months from the date when the tax becomes payable, the donee may, by an assessment made not later than two years from the date when the tax became payable, be assessed and charged (in the name of the donor) to capital gains tax on an amount not exceeding the amount of the chargeable gain so accruing, and not exceeding the grossed up amount of that capital gains tax unpaid at the time when he is so assessed, grossing up at the marginal rate of tax, that is to say, taking capital gains tax on a chargeable gain at the amount which would not have been chargeable but for that chargeable gain.

(2) A person paying any amount of tax in pursuance of this section shall be entitled to recover a sum of that amount from the donor.

(3) References in this section to a donor include, in the case of an individual who has died, references to his personal representatives.

(4) In this section references to a gift include references to any transaction otherwise than by way of a bargain made at arm's length so far as money or money's worth passes under the transaction without full consideration in money or money's worth, and "donor" and "donee" shall be construed accordingly; and this section shall apply in relation to a gift made by two or more donors with the necessary modifications and subject to any necessary apportionments.

GENERAL NOTE
Where a donor does not pay the tax due on a gift within 12 months of the date when the tax becomes payable, the donee may be assessed within two years of that date. The donee has a right of recovery from the donor.

Repayment supplements

283.—(1) Subject to the provisions of this section, where in the case of capital gains tax paid by or on behalf of an individual for a year of assessment for which he was resident in the United Kingdom, a repayment of that tax of not less than £25 is made by the Board or an inspector after the end of the 12 months following that year of assessment, the repayment shall be increased under this section by an amount ("a repayment supplement") equal to interest on the amount repaid at the rate applicable under section 178 of the

Finance Act 1989 for the period (if any) between the relevant time and the end of the tax month in which the order for the repayment is issued.

(2) For the purposes of subsection (1) above—

(a) if the repayment is of tax that was paid after the end of the 12 months following the year of assessment for which it was payable, the relevant time is the end of the year of assessment in which that tax was paid;

(b) in any other case, the relevant time is the end of the 12 months mentioned in that subsection;

and where a repayment to which subsection (1) above applies is of tax paid in two or more years of assessment, the repayment shall as far as possible be treated for the purposes of this subsection as a repayment of tax paid in a later rather than an earlier year among those years.

(3) A repayment supplement shall not be payable under this section in respect of a repayment or payment made in consequence of an order or judgment of a court having power to allow interest on the repayment or payment.

(4) Subsections (1) to (3) above shall apply in relation to a partnership or a United Kingdom trust (as defined in section 231(5) of the Taxes Act) or, in the case of a United Kingdom estate (as defined by section 701(9) of that Act), the personal representatives of a deceased person as such (within the meaning of section 701(4) of that Act) as they apply in relation to an individual.

(5) In this section "tax month" means the period beginning with the 6th day of any calendar month and ending with the 5th day of the following calendar month.

GENERAL NOTE

Repayment supplement (*i.e.* interest on repayments of tax overpaid) applies for the purposes of C.G.T. as it does for income tax. For the income tax provisions see ICTA 1988, ss.824 and 825.

The supplement applies to repayments of not less than £25 made more than a year after the end of the year of assessment concerned. The rate is fixed from time to time in accordance with a formula set out in The Taxes (Interest Rate) Regulations 1989, S.I. 1989 No. 1297, as amended, in accordance with powers under FA 1989, s.178.

Income tax decisions

284. Any assessment to income tax or decision on a claim under the Income Tax Acts, and any decision on an appeal under the Income Tax Acts against such an assessment or decision, shall be conclusive so far as, under any provision of this Act, liability to tax depends on the provisions of the Income Tax Acts.

GENERAL NOTE

Decisions or assessments, and any appeal decisions on these, in relation to income tax, are conclusive for questions concerning C.G.T., *e.g.* whether a gain is part of the profits of a trade.

Recognised investment exchanges

285. The Board may by regulations make provision securing that enactments relating to tax on chargeable gains and referring to The Stock Exchange have effect, for such purposes and subject to such modifications as may be prescribed by the regulations, in relation to all other recognised investment exchanges (within the meaning of the Financial Services Act 1986), or in relation to such of those exchanges as may be so prescribed.

GENERAL NOTE

The Revenue have power to extend provisions relating to the Stock Exchange to other recognised investment exchanges under the Financial Services Act, 1986.

Connected persons: interpretation

286.—(1) Any question whether a person is connected with another shall for the purposes of this Act be determined in accordance with the following subsections of this section (any provision that one person is connected with another being taken to mean that they are connected with one another).

(2) A person is connected with an individual if that person is the individual's husband or wife, or is a relative, or the husband or wife of a relative, of the individual or of the individual's husband or wife.

(3) A person, in his capacity as trustee of a settlement, is connected with any individual who in relation to the settlement is a settlor, with any person who is connected with such an individual and with a body corporate which, under section 681 of the Taxes Act, is deemed to be connected with that settlement ("settlement" and "settlor" having for the purposes of this subsection the meanings assigned to them by subsection (4) of the said section 681).

(4) Except in relation to acquisitions or disposals of partnership assets pursuant to bona fide commercial arrangements, a person is connected with any person with whom he is in partnership, and with the husband or wife or a relative of any individual with whom he is in partnership.

(5) A company is connected with another company—

(a) if the same person has control of both, or a person has control of one and persons connected with him, or he and persons connected with him, have control of the other, or

(b) if a group of two or more persons has control of each company, and the groups either consist of the same persons or could be regarded as consisting of the same persons by treating (in one or more cases) a member of either group as replaced by a person with whom he is connected.

(6) A company is connected with another person, if that person has control of it or if that person and persons connected with him together have control of it.

(7) Any two or more persons acting together to secure or exercise control of a company shall be treated in relation to that company as connected with one another and with any person acting on the directions of any of them to secure or exercise control of the company.

(8) In this section "relative" means brother, sister, ancestor or lineal descendant.

GENERAL NOTE

This contains the important definition of "connected persons". Under s.18, transactions between connected persons are deemed to be other than at arm's length, so that market value may be substituted for the actual consideration by s.17. Many other forms of relief and exemptions are restricted or excluded in the case of connected persons.

Orders and regulations made by the Treasury or the Board

287.—(1) Subject to subsection (2) below, any power of the Treasury or the Board to make any order or regulations under this Act or any other enactment relating to the taxation of chargeable gains passed after this Act shall be exercisable by statutory instrument.

(2) Subsection (1) above shall not apply in relation to any power conferred by section 288(6).

(3) Subject to subsection (4) below and to any other provision to the contrary, any statutory instrument to which subsection (1) above applies shall be subject to annulment in pursuance of a resolution of the House of Commons.

(4) Subsection (3) above shall not apply in relation to an order or regulations made under section 3(4) or 265 or paragraph 1 of Schedule 9, or—

(a) if any other Parliamentary procedure is expressly provided; or

(b) if the order in question is an order appointing a day for the purposes of any provision, being a day as from which the provision will have effect, with or without amendments, or will cease to have effect.

GENERAL NOTE
Powers to make orders or regulations are generally exercisable by statutory instrument, subject to annulment by the House of Commons.

Interpretation

288.—(1) In this Act, unless the context otherwise requires—
"the 1979 Act" means the Capital Gains Tax Act 1979;
"the 1990 Act" means the Capital Allowances Act 1990;
"allowable loss" shall be construed in accordance with sections 8(2) and 16;
"the Board" means the Commissioners of Inland Revenue;
"building society" has the same meaning as in the Building Societies Act 1986;
"chargeable period" means a year of assessment or an accounting period of a company for purposes of corporation tax;
"class", in relation to shares or securities, means a class of shares or securities of any one company;
"close company" has the meaning given by sections 414 and 415 of the Taxes Act;
"collective investment scheme" has the same meaning as in the Financial Services Act 1986;
"company" includes any body corporate or unincorporated association but does not include a partnership, and shall be construed in accordance with section 99;
"control" shall be construed in accordance with section 416 of the Taxes Act;
"double taxation relief arrangements" means, in relation to a company, arrangements having effect by virtue of section 788 of the Taxes Act and, in relation to any other person, means arrangements having effect by virtue of that section as extended to capital gains tax by section 277;
"dual resident investing company" has the meaning given by section 404 of the Taxes Act;
"inspector" means any inspector of taxes;
"investment trust" has the meaning given by section 842 of the Taxes Act;
"land" includes messuages, tenements, and hereditaments, houses and buildings of any tenure;
"local authority" has the meaning given by section 842A of the Taxes Act;
"the Management Act" means the Taxes Management Act 1970;
"notice" means notice in writing;
"personal representatives" has the meaning given by section 701(4) of the Taxes Act;
"recognised stock exchange" has the meaning given by section 841 of the Taxes Act;
"shares" includes stock;
"the Taxes Act" means the Income and Corporation Taxes Act 1988;
"trade" has the same meaning as in the Income Tax Acts;
"trading stock" has the meaning given by section 100(2) of the Taxes Act;
"wasting asset" has the meaning given by section 44 and paragraph 1 of Schedule 8;

"year of assessment" means, in relation to capital gains tax, a year beginning on 6th April and ending on 5th April in the following calendar year, and "1992–93" and so on indicate years of assessment as in the Income Tax Acts;

and any reference to a particular section, Part or Schedule is a reference to that section or Part of, or that Schedule to, this Act.

(2) In this Act "retail prices index" has the same meaning as in the Income Tax Acts and, accordingly, any reference in this Act to the retail prices index shall be construed in accordance with section 833(2) of the Taxes Act.

(3) References in this Act to a married woman living with her husband shall be construed in accordance with section 282 of the Taxes Act.

(4) References in this Act to quotation on a stock exchange in the United Kingdom or a recognised stock exchange in the United Kingdom shall be construed as references to listing in the Official List of The Stock Exchange.

(5) For the purposes of this Act, shares or debentures comprised in any letter of allotment or similar instrument shall be treated as issued unless the right to the shares or debentures thereby conferred remains provisional until accepted and there has been no acceptance.

(6) In this Act "recognised futures exchange" means the London International Financial Futures Exchange and any other futures exchange which is for the time being designated for the purposes of this Act by order made by the Board.

(7) An order made by the Board under subsection (6) above—

(a) may designate a futures exchange by name or by reference to any class or description of futures exchanges, including, in the case of futures exchanges in a country outside the United Kingdom, a class or description framed by reference to any authority or approval given in that country; and

(b) may contain such transitional and other supplemental provisions as appear to the Board to be necessary or expedient.

(8) The Table below indexes other general definitions in this Act.

Expression defined	*Reference*
"Absolutely entitled as against the trustee"	S.60(2)
"Authorised unit trust"	S.99
"Branch or agency"	S.10(6)
"Chargeable gain"	S.15(2)
"Connected", in references to persons being connected with one another	S.286
"Court investment fund"	S.100
"Gilt-edged securities"	Sch. 9
"Indexation allowance"	S.53
"Lease" and cognate expressions	Sch. 8, para. 10(1)
"Legatee"	S.64(2), (3)
"Market value"	S.272 to 274 and Sch. 11
"Part disposal"	S.21(2)
"Qualifying corporate bond"	S.117
"Relevant allowable expenditure"	S.53
"Resident" and "ordinarily resident"	S.9(1)
"Settled property"	S.68
"Unit trust scheme"	S.99

GENERAL NOTE

This is a general interpretation section.

Commencement

289.—(1) Except where the context otherwise requires, this Act has effect in relation to tax for the year 1992–93 and subsequent years of assessment, and tax for other chargeable periods beginning on or after 6th April 1992, and references to the coming into force of this Act or any provision in this Act shall be construed accordingly.

(2) The following provisions of this Act, that is—

(a) so much of any provision of this Act as authorises the making of any order or other instrument, and

(b) except where the tax concerned is all tax for chargeable periods to which this Act does not apply, so much of any provision of this Act as confers any power or imposes any duty the exercise or performance of which operates or may operate in relation to tax for more than one chargeable period.

shall come into force for all purposes of 6th April 1992 to the exclusion of the corresponding enactments repealed by this Act.

GENERAL NOTE
The Act comes into force as from April 6, 1992.

Savings, transitionals, consequential amendments and repeals

290.—(1) Schedules 10 (consequential amendments) and 11 (transitory provisions and savings) shall have effect.

(2) No letters patent granted or to be granted by the Crown to any person, city, borough or town corporate of any liberty, privilege, or exemption from subsidies, tolls, taxes, assessments or aids, and no statute which grants any salary, annuity or pension to any person free of any taxes, deductions or assessments, shall be construed or taken to exempt any person, city, borough or town corporate, or any inhabitant of the same, from tax chargeable in pursuance of this Act.

(3) Subject to Schedule 11, the enactments and instruments mentioned in Schedule 12 to this Act are hereby repealed to the extent specified in the third column of that Schedule (but Schedule 12 shall not have effect in relation to any enactment in so far as it has previously been repealed subject to a saving which still has effect on the coming into force of this section).

(4) The provisions of this Part of this Act are without prejudice to the provisions of the Interpretation Act 1978 as respects the effect of repeals.

GENERAL NOTE
Schedules 10, 11 and 12 contain consequential amendments, transitory provisions and repeals respectively.

Subs. (2)
This repeats an avoidance of exempting provisions contained in ICTA 1988, s.829(4).

Short title

291. This Act may be cited as the Taxation of Chargeable Gains Act 1992.

SCHEDULES

Section 3   SCHEDULE 1

APPLICATION OF EXEMPT AMOUNT IN CASES

INVOLVING SETTLED PROPERTY

1.—(1) For any year of assessment during the whole or part of which settled property is held on trusts which secure that, during the lifetime of a mentally disabled person or a person in receipt of attendance allowance or of a disability living allowance by virtue of entitlement to the care component at the highest or middle rate—

(a) not less than half of the property which is applied for the benefit of that person, and

(b) that person is entitled to not less than half of the income arising from the property, or no such income may be applied for the benefit of any other person,

section 3(1) to (6) shall apply to the trustees of the settlement as they apply to an individual.

(2) The trusts on which settled property is held shall not be treated as falling outside sub-paragraph (1) above by reason only of the powers conferred on the trustees by section 32 of the Trustee Act 1925 or section 33 of the Trustee Act (Northern Ireland) 1958 (powers of advancement); and the reference in that sub-paragraph to the lifetime of a person shall, where the income from the settled property is held for his benefit on trusts of the kind described in section 33 of the Trustee Act 1925 (protective trusts), be construed as a reference to the period during which the income is held on trust for him.

(3) In relation to a settlement which is one of two or more qualifying settlements comprised in a group, this paragraph shall have effect as if for the references in section 3 to the exempt amount for the year there were substituted references to one-tenth of that exempt amount or, if it is more, to such amount as results from dividing the exempt amount for the year by the number of settlements in the group.

(4) For the purposes of sub-paragraph (3) above—

(a) a qualifying settlement is any settlement (other than an excluded settlement) which is made on or after 10th March 1981 and to the trustees of which this paragraph applies for the year of assessment; and

(b) all qualifying settlements in relation to which the same person is the settlor constitute a group.

(5) If, in consequence of two or more persons being settlors in relation to it, a settlement is comprised in two or more groups comprising different numbers of settlements, sub-paragraph (3) above shall apply to it as if the number by which the exempt amount for the year is to be divided were the number of settlements in the largest group.

(6) In this paragraph—

"mentally disabled person" means a person who by reason of mental disorder within the meaning of the Mental Health Act 1983 is incapable of administering his property or managing his affairs;

"attendance allowance" means an allowance under section 64 of the Social Security Contributions and Benefits Act 1992 or section 64 of the Social Security Contributions and Benefits (Northern Ireland) Act 1992.

"disability living allowance" means a disability living allowance under section 71 of the Social Security Contributions and Benefits Act 1992 or section 71 of the Social Security Contributions and Benefits (Northern Ireland) Act 1992; and

"settlor" and "excluded settlement" have the same meanings as in paragraph 2 below.

(7) An inspector may by notice require any person, being a party to a settlement, to furnish him within such time as he may direct (not being less than 28 days) with such particulars as he thinks necessary for the purposes of this paragraph.

2.—(1) For any year of assessment during the whole or part of which any property is settled property, not being a year of assessment for which paragraph 1(1) above applies, section 3(1) to (6) shall apply to the trustees of a settlement as they apply to an individual but with the following modifications.

(2) In subsections (1) and (5) for "the exempt amount for the year" there shall be substituted "one-half of the exempt amount for the year".

(3) Section 3(6) shall apply only to the trustees of a settlement made before 7th June 1978 and, in relation to such trustees, shall have effect with the substitution for "the exempt amount for the year" and "twice the exempt amount for the year" of "one-half of the exempt amount for the year" and "the exempt amount for the year" respectively.

(4) In relation to a settlement which is one of two or more qualifying settlements comprised in a group, sub-paragraph (2) above shall have effect as if for the reference to one-half of the exempt amount for the year there were substituted a reference to one-tenth of that exempt amount or, if it is more, to such amount as results from dividing one-half of the exempt amount for the year by the number of settlements in the group.

(5) For the purposes of sub-paragraph (4) above—

(a) a qualifying settlement is any settlement (other than an excluded settlement) which is made after 6th June 1978 and to the trustees of which this paragraph applies for the year of assessment; and

(b) all qualifying settlements in relation to which the same person is the settlor constitute a group.

(6) If, in consequence of two or more persons being settlors in relation to it, a settlement is comprised in two or more groups comprising different numbers of settlements, sub-paragraph (4) above shall apply to it as if the number by which one-half of the exempt amount for the year is to be divided were the number of settlements in the largest group.

(7) In this paragraph "settlor" has the meaning given by section 681(4) of the Taxes Act and includes, in the case of a settlement arising under a will or intestacy, the testator or intestate and "excluded settlement" means—

(a) any settlement the trustees of which are not for the whole or any part of the year of assessment treated under section 69(1) as resident and ordinarily resident in the United Kingdom; and

(b) any settlement the property comprised in which—

> (i) is held for charitable purposes only and cannot become applicable for other purposes; or
>
> (ii) is held for the purposes of any such scheme or fund as is mentioned in sub-paragraph (8) below.

(8) The schemes and funds referred to in sub-paragraph (7)(b)(ii) above are funds to which section 615(3) of the Taxes Act applies, schemes and funds approved under section 620 or 621 of that Act, sponsored superannuation schemes as defined in section 624 of that Act and exempt approved schemes and statutory schemes as defined in Chapter I of Part XIV of that Act.

(9) An inspector may by notice require any person, being a party to a settlement, to furnish him within such time as he may direct (not being less than 28 days) with such particulars as he thinks necessary for the purposes of this paragraph.

GENERAL NOTE

The Schedule applies the annual exemption for individuals to trusts.

Para. 1

Trusts for mentally disabled persons or persons in receipt of an attendance allowance or persons with a disability living allowance at the highest or middle rate of care component, within the meaning of the relevant statutes, with entitlement to not less than one-half of the income, enjoy the full individual exemption. For multiple trusts the exemption is reduced to a maximum of one-tenth.

Para. 2

For all other trusts, one half of the individual exemption is applicable, and also one half of the reporting requirement under s.3(6).

Section 35   SCHEDULE 2

ASSETS HELD ON 6th APRIL 1965

PART I

QUOTED SECURITIES

Deemed acquisition at 6th April 1965 value

1.—(1) This paragraph applies—

(a) to shares and securities which on 6th April 1965 had quoted market values on a recognised stock exchange, or which had such quoted market values at any time in the period of six years ending on 6th April 1965, and

(b) to rights of unit holders in any unit trust scheme the prices of which are published regularly by the managers of the scheme.

(2) For the purposes of this Act it shall be assumed, wherever relevant, that any assets to which this paragraph applies were sold by the owner, and immediately reacquired by him, at their market value on 6th April 1965.

(3) This paragraph shall not apply in relation to a disposal of shares or securities of a company by a person to whom those shares or securities were issued as an employee either of the company or of some other person on terms which restrict his rights to dispose of them.

Restriction of gain or loss by reference to actual cost

2.—(1) Subject to paragraph 4 below and section 109(4), paragraph 1(2) above shall not apply in relation to a disposal of assets—

(a) if on the assumption in paragraph 1(2) a gain would accrue on that disposal to the person making the disposal and either a smaller gain or a loss would so accrue if paragraph 1(2) did not apply, or

(b) if on the assumption in paragraph 1(2) a loss would so accrue and either a smaller loss or a gain would accrue if paragraph 1(2) did not apply,

and accordingly the amount of the gain or loss accruing on the disposal shall be computed without regard to the preceding provisions of this Schedule except that in a case where this sub-paragraph would otherwise substitute a loss for a gain or a gain for a loss it shall be assumed, in relation to the disposal, that the relevant assets were sold by the owner, and immediately reacquired by him, for a consideration such that, on the disposal, neither a gain nor a loss accrued to the person making the disposal.

(2) For the purpose of—
(a) identifying shares or securities held on 6th April 1965 with shares or securities previously acquired, and
(b) identifying the shares or securities held on that date with shares or securities subsequently disposed of, and distinguishing them from shares or securities acquired subsequently,
so far as that identification is needed for the purposes of sub-paragraph (1) above, and so far as the shares or securities are of the same class, shares or securities acquired at a later time shall be deemed to be disposed of before shares or securities acquired at an earlier time.

(3) Sub-paragraph (2) above has effect subject to section 105.

3.—(1) Where—
(a) a disposal was made out of quoted securities before 20th March 1968, and
(b) by virtue of paragraph 2 of Schedule 7 to the Finance Act 1965 some of the quoted securities out of which the disposal was made were acquired before 6th April 1965 and some later,
then in computing the gain accruing on any disposal of quoted securities the question of what remained undisposed of on the earlier disposal shall be decided on the footing that paragraph 2 of that Schedule did not apply as respects that earlier disposal.

(2) The rules of identification in paragraph 2(2) above shall apply for the purposes of this paragraph as they apply for the purposes of that paragraph.

Election for pooling

4.—(1) This paragraph applies in relation to quoted securities as respects which an election under paragraphs 4 to 7 of Schedule 5 to the 1979 Act had not been made before the operative date, within the meaning of Part II of Schedule 13 to the Finance Act 1982, (so that they do not constitute a 1982 holding within the meaning of section 109), but does not apply in relation to relevant securities within the meaning of section 108.

(2) If a person so elects, quoted securities covered by the election shall be excluded from paragraph 2 above, so that paragraph 1(2) above is not excluded by that paragraph as respects those securities, and sub-paragraphs (3) to (7) (which re-enact section 65 of the 1979 Act) apply.

(3) Subject to section 105, any number of quoted securities of the same class held by one person in one capacity shall for the purposes of this Act be regarded as indistinguishable parts of a single asset (in this paragraph referred to as a holding) growing or diminishing on the occasions on which additional securities of the class in question are acquired, or some of the securities of the class in question are disposed of.

(4) Without prejudice to the generality of sub-paragraph (3) above, a disposal of quoted securities in a holding, other than the disposal outright of the entire holding, is a disposal of part of an asset and the provisions of this Act relating to the computation of a gain accruing on a disposal of part of an asset shall apply accordingly.

(5) Securities shall not be treated for the purposes of this paragraph as being of the same class unless they are so treated by the practice of a recognised stock exchange or would be so treated if dealt with on such a stock exchange, but shall be treated in accordance with this paragraph notwithstanding that they are identified in some other way by the disposal or by the transfer or delivery giving effect to it.

(6) This paragraph shall apply separately in relation to any securities held by a person to whom they were issued as an employee of the company or of any other person on terms which restrict his rights to dispose of them, so long as those terms are in force, and, while applying separately to any such securities, shall have effect as if the owner held them in a capacity other than that in which he holds any other securities of the same class.

(7) Nothing in this paragraph shall be taken as effecting the manner in which the market value of any asset is to be ascertained.

(8) An election made by any person under this paragraph shall be as respects all disposals made by him at any time, including disposals made before the election but after 19th March, 1968—
(a) of quoted securities of kinds other than fixed-interest securities and preference shares, or
(b) of fixed-interest securities and preference shares,
and references to the quoted securities covered by an election shall be construed accordingly.
Any person may make both of the elections.

(9) An election under this paragraph shall not cover quoted securities which the holder acquired on a disposal after 19th March 1968 in relation to which either section 58 or 171(1) applies, but this paragraph shall apply to the quoted securities so held if the person who made the original disposal (that is to say the wife or husband of the holder, or the other member of the group of companies) makes an election covering quoted securities of the kind in question.

For the purpose of identifying quoted securities disposed of by the holder with quoted securities acquired by him on a disposal in relation to which either section 58 or 171(1) applies, so far as they are of the same class, quoted securities acquired at an earlier time shall be deemed to be disposed of before quoted securities acquired at a later time.

(10) For the avoidance of doubt it is hereby declared—

(a) that where a person makes an election under this paragraph as respects quoted securities which he holds in one capacity, that election does not cover quoted securities which he holds in another capacity, and

(b) that an election under this paragraph is irrevocable.

(11) An election under this paragraph shall be made by notice to the inspector not later than the expiration of two years from the end of the year of assessment or accounting period of a company in which the first relevant disposal is made, or such further time as the Board may allow.

(12) Subject to paragraph 5 below, in this paragraph the "first relevant disposal", in relation to each of the elections referred to in sub-paragraph (8) of this paragraph, means the first disposal after 19th March 1968 by the person making the election of quoted securities of the kind covered by that election.

(13) All such adjustments shall be made, whether by way of discharge or repayment of tax, or the making of assessments or otherwise, as are required to give effect to an election under this paragraph.

Election by principal company of group

5.—(1) In the case of companies which at the relevant time are members of a group of companies—

(a) an election under paragraph 4 above by the company which at that time is the principal company of the group shall have effect also as an election by any other company which at that time is a member of the group, and

(b) no election under that paragraph may be made by any other company which at that time is a member of the group.

(2) In this paragraph "the relevant time", in relation to a group of companies, and in relation to each of the elections referred to in paragraph 4(8) above, is the first occasion after 19th March 1968 when any company which is then a member of a group disposes of quoted securities of a kind covered by that election, and for the purposes of paragraph 4(11) above that occasion is, in relation to the group, "the first relevant disposal".

(3) This paragraph shall not apply in relation to quoted securities of either kind referred to in paragraph 4(8) above which are owned by a company which, in some period after 19th March 1968 and before the relevant time, was not a member of the group if in that period it had made an election under paragraph 4 above in relation to securities of that kind (or was treated by virtue of this paragraph, in relation to another group, as having done so), or had made a disposal of quoted securities of that kind and did not make an election within the time limited by paragraph 4(11) above.

(4) This paragraph shall apply notwithstanding that a company ceases to be a member of the group at any time after the relevant time.

(5) In this paragraph "company" and "group" shall be construed in accordance with section 170(2) to (9).

Pooling at value on 6th April, 1965: exchange of securities etc.

6.—(1) Where a person who has made only one of the elections under paragraph 4 above disposes of quoted securities which, in accordance with Chapter II of Part IV, are to be regarded as being or forming part of a new holding, the election shall apply according to the nature of the quoted securities disposed of, notwithstanding that under that Chapter the new holding is to be regarded as the same asset as the original holding and that the election would apply differently to the original holding.

(2) Where the election does not cover the disposal out of the new holding but does cover quoted securities of the kind comprised in the original holding, then in computing the gain accruing on the disposal out of the new holding (in accordance with paragraph 3 above) the question of what remained undisposed of on any disposal out of the original holding shall be decided on the footing that paragraph 3 above applied to that earlier disposal.

(3) In the converse case (that is to say, where the election covers the disposal out of the new holding, but does not cover quoted securities of the kind comprised in the original holding) the question of how much of the new holding derives from quoted securities held on 6th April, 1965 and how much derives from other quoted securities, shall be decided as it is decided for the purposes of paragraph 3 above.

Underwriters

7. No election under paragraph 4 above shall cover quoted securities comprised in any underwriter's premiums trust fund, or premiums trust fund deposits, or personal reserves, being securities comprised in funds to which section 206 applies.

Interpretation of paragraphs 3 to 7

8.—(1) In paragraphs 3 to 7 above—
   "quoted securities" means assets to which paragraph 1 above applies,
   "fixed interest security" means any security as defined by section 132,
   "preference share" means any share the holder whereof has a right to a dividend at a fixed rate, but has no other right to share in the profits of the company.

(2) If and so far as the question whether at any particular time a share was a preference share depends on the rate of dividends payable on or before 5th April 1973, the reference in the definition of "preference share" in sub-paragraph (1) above to a dividend at a fixed rate includes a dividend at a rate fluctuating in accordance with the standard rate of income tax.

PART II

LAND REFLECTING DEVELOPMENT VALUE

9.—(1) Subject to paragraph 17(2) of Schedule 11, this Part of this Schedule shall apply in relation to a disposal of an asset which is an interest in land situated in the United Kingdom—
   (a) if, but for this paragraph, the expenditure allowable as a deduction in computing the gain accruing on the disposal would include any expenditure incurred before 6th April 1965, and
   (b) if the consideration for the asset acquired on the disposal exceeds the current use value of the asset at the time of the disposal, or if any material development of the land has been carried out after 17th December 1973 since the person making the disposal acquired the asset.

(2) For the purposes of this Act, it shall be assumed that, in relation to the disposal and, if it is a part disposal, in relation to any subsequent disposal of the asset which is an interest in land situated in the United Kingdom, that asset was sold by the person making the disposal, and immediately reacquired by him, at its market value on 6th April 1965.

(3) Sub-paragraph (2) above shall apply also in relation to any prior part disposal of the asset and, if tax has been charged, or relief allowed, by reference to that part disposal on a different footing, all such adjustments shall be made, whether by way of assessment or discharge or repayment of tax, as are required to give effect to the provisions of this sub-paragraph.

(4) Sub-paragraph (2) above shall not apply in relation to a disposal of assets—
   (a) on the assumption in that sub-paragraph a gain would accrue on that disposal to the person making the disposal and either a smaller gain or a loss would so accrue (computed in accordance with the provisions of this Act) if it did not apply, or
   (b) if on the assumption in sub-paragraph (2) a loss would so accrue and either a smaller loss or a gain would accrue if that sub-paragraph did not apply,
and accordingly the amount of the gain or loss accruing on the disposal shall be computed without regard to the provisions of this Schedule except that in a case where this sub-paragraph would otherwise substitute a loss for a gain or a gain for a loss it shall be assumed, in relation to the disposal, that the relevant assets were sold by the owner, and immediately reacquired by him, for a consideration such that, on the disposal, neither a gain nor a loss accrued to the person making the disposal.

(5) For the purposes of this Part of this Schedule—
   (a) "interest in land" means any estate or interest in land, any right in or over land or affecting the use or disposition of land, and any right to obtain such an estate, interest or right from another which is conditional on that other's ability to grant the estate, interest or right in question, except that it does not include the interest of a creditor (other than a creditor in respect of a rentcharge) whose debt is secured by way of a mortgage, an agreement for a mortgage or a charge of any kind over land, or, in Scotland, the interest of a creditor in a charge or security of any kind over land; and
   (b) "land" includes buildings.

10.—(1) For the purposes of this Part of this Schedule, the current use value of an interest in land shall be ascertained in accordance with the following provisions of this Part, and in this Part the time as at which current use value is to be ascertained is referred to as "the relevant time."

(2) Subject to the following provisions of this Part of this Schedule, the current use value of an interest in land at the relevant time is the market value of that interest at that time calculated on the assumption that it was at that time, and would continue to be, unlawful to carry out any material development of the land other than any material development thereof which, being authorised by planning permission in force at that time, was begun before that time.

In relation to any material development which was begun before 18th December 1973 this sub-paragraph shall have effect with the omission of the words from "other than" to "before that time."

(3) In this paragraph "planning permission" has the same meaning as in the Town and Country Planning Act 1990, or, in Scotland, the Town and Country Planning (Scotland) Act 1972, or, in Northern Ireland, the Planning (Northern Ireland) Order 1991, and in determining for the purposes of this paragraph what material development of any land was authorised by planning permission at a time when there was in force in respect of the land planning permission granted on an outline application (that is to say, an application for planning permission subject to subsequent approval on any matters), any such development of the land which at that time—

(a) was authorised by that permission without any requirement as to subsequent approval; or

(b) not being so authorised, had been approved in the manner applicable to that planning permission,

but no other material development, shall for those purposes be taken to have been authorised by that permission at that time.

(4) Where the value to be ascertained is the current use value of an interest in land which has been disposed of by way of a part disposal of an asset ("the relevant asset") consisting of an interest in land, the current use value at the relevant time of the interest disposed of shall be the relevant fraction of the current use value of the relevant asset at that time, calculated on the same assumptions as to the lawfulness or otherwise of any material development as fall to be made under this Part in calculating the current use value at that time of the interest disposed of.

(5) For the purposes of sub-paragraph (4) above "the relevant fraction" means that fraction of the sums mentioned in paragraph (6) below which under subsection (2) of section 42 is, or would but for subsection (4) of that section be, allowable as a deduction in computing the amount of the gain accruing on the part disposal.

(6) The sums referred to in sub-paragraph (5) above are the sums which, if the entire relevant asset had been disposed of at the time of the part disposal, would be allowable by virtue of section 38(1)(a) and (b) as a deduction in computing the gain accruing on that disposal of the relevant asset.

(7) Sub-paragraphs (4) to (6) above shall not apply—

(a) in the case of a disposal of an interest in land by way of a part disposal if, on making the disposal, the person doing so no longer has any interest in the land which is subject to that interest; or

(b) in a case to which the following provisions of this paragraph apply.

(8) In computing any gain accruing to a person on a part disposal of an interest in land resulting under subsection (1) of section 22 from the receipt as mentioned in paragraph (a), (c) or (d) of that subsection of a capital sum, the current use value at the relevant time of the interest out of which the part disposal was made shall be taken to be what it would have been at that time if the circumstances which caused the capital sum to be received had not arisen.

11.—(1) The current use value of an interest in land which is either—

(a) a freehold interest which is subject to a lease or an agreement for a lease, or

(b) an interest under a lease or agreement for a lease,

shall be ascertained without regard to any premium required under the lease or agreement for a lease or any sublease, or otherwise under the terms subject to which the lease or sublease was or is to be granted, but with regard to all other rights under the lease or prospective lease (and, for the current use value of an interest under a lease subject to a sublease, under the sublease).

(2) If under sub-paragraph (1) above an interest under a lease or agreement for a lease would have a negative value, the current use value of the interest shall be nil.

(3) If a lease is granted out of any interest in land after 17th December 1973, then, in computing any gain accruing on any disposal of the reversion on the lease made while the lease subsists, the current use value of the reversion at any time after the grant of the lease shall not exceed what would have been at that time the current use value of the interest in the land of the person then owning the reversion if that interest had not been subject to the lease.

(4) In the application of this paragraph to Scotland, "freehold" means the estate or interest of the proprietor of the dominium utile or, in the case of property other than feudal property, of the owner, and "reversion" means the interest of the landlord in property subject to a lease.

12. In computing any gain accruing to a person on a disposal of a lease which is a wasting asset, the current use value of the lease at the time of its acquisition by the person making the disposal shall be the fraction—

$$\frac{A}{B}$$

of what its current use value at that time would be apart from this paragraph, where—

A is equal to so much of the expenditure attributable to the lease under section 38(1)(a) and (b) as is not under paragraph 1 of Schedule 8 excluded therefrom for the purposes of the computation of the gain accruing on the disposal, and

B is equal to the whole of the expenditure which would be so attributable to the lease for those purposes apart from the said paragraph 1.

13.—(1) In this Part of this Schedule, "material development", in relation to any land, means the making of any change in the state, nature or use of the land, but the doing of any of the following things in the case of any land shall not be taken to involve material development of the land, that is to say—

(a) the carrying out of works for the maintenance, improvement, enlargement or other alteration of any building, so long as the cubic content of the original building is not exceeded by more than one-tenth;

(b) the carrying out of works for the rebuilding, as often as occasion may require, of any building which was in existence at the relevant time, or of any building which was in existence in the period of 10 years immediately preceding the day on which that time falls but was destroyed or demolished before the relevant time, so long as (in either case) the cubic content of the original building is not exceeded by more than one-tenth;

(c) the use of any land for the purposes of agriculture or forestry, the use for any of those purposes of any building occupied together with land so used, and the carrying out on any land so used of any building or other operations required for the purposes of that use;

(d) the carrying out of operations on land for, or the use of land for, the display of an advertisement, announcement or direction of any kind;

(e) the carrying out of operations for, or the use of the land for, car parking, provided that such use shall not exceed three years;

(f) in the case of a building or other land which at the relevant time was used for a purpose falling within any class specified in sub-paragraph (4) below or which, being unoccupied at that time, was last used for any such purpose, the use of that building or land for any other purpose falling within the same class;

(g) in the case of a building or other land which at the relevant time was in the occupation of a person by whom it was used as to part only for a particular purpose, the use for that purpose of any additional part of the building or land not exceeding one-tenth of the cubic content of the part of the building used for that purpose at the relevant time or, as the case may be, one-tenth of the area of the land so used at that time;

(h) in the case of land which at the relevant time was being temporarily used for a purpose other than the purpose for which it was normally used, the resumption of the use of the land for the last-mentioned purpose;

(i) in the case of land which was unoccupied at the relevant time, the use of the land for the purpose for which it was last used before that time.

References in this paragraph to the cubic content of a building are references to that content as ascertained by external measurement.

(2) For the purposes of sub-paragraph (1)(a) and (b)—

(a) where two or more buildings are included in a single development the whole of that development may be regarded as a single building, and where two or more buildings result from the redevelopment of a single building the new buildings may together be regarded as a single building, but two or more buildings shall not be treated as included in a single development unless they are or were comprised in the same curtilage; and

(b) in determining whether or not the cubic content of the original building has been exceeded by more than one-tenth, the cubic content of the building after the carrying out of the works in question shall be treated as reduced by the amount (if any) by which so much of that cubic content as is attributable to one or more of the matters mentioned in sub-paragraph (3) below exceeds so much of the cubic content of the original building as was attributable to one or more of the matters so mentioned.

(3) The matters referred to in sub-paragraph (2)(b) are the following, that is to say—

(a) means of escape in case of fire;

(b) car-parking or garage space;

(c) accommodation for plant providing heating, air-conditioning or similar facilities.

(4) The classes of purposes mentioned in sub-paragraph (1)(f) are the following—

Class A—Use as a dwelling-house or for the purpose of any activities which are wholly or mainly carried on otherwise than for profit, except use for a purpose falling within Class B, C or E.

Class B—Use as an office or retail shop.

Class C—Use as a hotel, boarding-house or guest-house, or as premises licensed for the sale of intoxicating liquors for consumption on the premises.

Class D—Use for the purpose of any activities wholly or mainly carried on for profit, except—

(a) use as a dwelling-house or for the purposes of agriculture or forestry; and

(b) use for a purpose falling within Class B, C or E.

Class E—Use for any of the following purposes, namely—

(a) the carrying on of any process for or incidental to any of the following purposes, namely—

(i) the making of any article or of any part of any article, or the production of any substance;

(ii) the altering, repairing, ornamenting, finishing, cleaning, washing, packing or canning, or adapting for sale, or breaking up or demolishing of any article; or

(iii) without prejudice to (i) or (ii) above, the getting, dressing or treatment of minerals,

being a process carried on in the course of a trade or business other than agriculture or forestry, but excluding any process carried on at a dwelling-house or retail shop;

(b) storage purposes (whether or not involving use as a warehouse or repository) other than storage purposes ancillary to a purpose falling within Class B or C.

14.—(1) For the purposes of this Part, material development shall be taken to be begun on the earliest date on which any specified operation comprised in the material development is begun.

(2) In this paragraph "specified operation" means any of the following, that is to say—

(a) any work of construction in the course of the erection of a building;

(b) the digging of a trench which is to contain the foundations, or part of the foundations, of a building;

(c) the laying of any underground main or pipe to the foundations, or part of the foundations, of a building or to any such trench as is mentioned in (b) above;

(d) any operation in the course of laying out or constructing a road or part of a road;

(e) any change in the use of any land.

(3) Subject to sub-paragraph (4) below, material development shall for the purposes of this Part of this Schedule not be treated as carried out after a particular date if it was begun on or before that date.

(4) If, in the case of any land—

(a) material development thereof was begun on or before 17th December, 1973 but was not completed on or before that date, and

(b) the development was on that date to any extent not authorised by planning permission (within the meaning of paragraph 10(3) above) then in force,

then, for the purposes of this Part of this Schedule, so much of the development carried out after that date as was not so authorised on that date shall be treated as begun on the earliest date after 17th December, 1973 on which any specified operation comprised therein is begun, and shall accordingly be treated as material development of the land carried out after 17th December, 1973.

15. In this Part of this Schedule, unless the context otherwise requires—

"agriculture" includes horticulture, fruit growing, seed growing, dairy farming, the keeping and breeding of livestock (including any creature kept for the production of food, wool, skins or fur, or for the purpose of its use in the farming of land), the use of land as grazing land, meadow land, osier land, market gardens and nursery grounds, and the use of land for woodlands where that use is ancillary to the farming of land for other agricultural purposes, and "agricultural" shall be construed accordingly;

"article" means an article of any description;

"building" includes part of a building and references to a building may include references to land occupied therewith and used for the same purposes;

"forestry" includes afforestation;

"minerals" includes all minerals and substances in or under land of a kind ordinarily worked for removal by underground or surface working;

"retail shop" includes any premises of a similar character where retail trade or business (including repair work) is carried on;

"substance" means any natural or artificial substance or material, whether in solid or liquid form or in the form of a gas or vapour.

PART III

OTHER ASSETS

Apportionment by reference to straightline growth of gain or loss over period of ownership

16.—(1) This paragraph applies subject to Parts I and II of this Schedule.

(2) On the disposal of assets by a person whose period of ownership began before 6th April 1965 only so much of any gain accruing on the disposal as is under this paragraph to be apportioned to the period beginning with 6th April 1965 shall be a chargeable gain.

(3) Subject to the following provisions of this Schedule, the gain shall be assumed to have grown at a uniform rate from nothing at the beginning of the period of ownership to its full amount at the time of the disposal so that, calling the part of that period before 6th April 1965, P, and the time beginning with 6th April 1965 and ending with the time of the disposal T, the fraction of the gain which is a chargeable gain is—

$$\frac{T}{P + T}$$

(4) If any of the expenditure which is allowable as a deduction in the computation of the gain is within section 38(1)(b)—

  (a) the gain shall be attributed to the expenditure, if any, allowable under section 38(1)(a) as one item of expenditure, and to the respective items of expenditure under section 38(1)(b) in proportion to the respective amounts of those items of expenditure.

  (b) sub-paragraph (3) of this paragraph shall apply to the part of the gain attributed to the expenditure under section 38(1)(a).

  (c) each part of the gain attributed to the items of expenditure under section 38(1)(b) shall be assumed to have grown at a uniform rate from nothing at the time when the relevant item of expenditure was first reflected in the value of the asset to the full amount of that part of the gain at the time of the disposal,

so that, calling the respective proportions of the gain $E(0)$, $E(1)$, $E(2)$ and so on (so that they add up to unity) and calling the respective periods from the times when the items under section 38(1)(b) were reflected in the value of the asset to 5th April 1965 $P(1)$, $P(2)$ and so on, and employing also the abbreviations in sub-paragraph (3) above, the fraction of the gain which is a chargeable gain is—

$$E(0)\ \frac{T}{P + T} + E(1)\ \frac{T}{P(1) + T} + E(2)\ \frac{T}{P(2) + T}\ \text{and so on.}$$

(5) In a case within sub-paragraph (4) above where there is no initial expenditure (that is no expenditure under section 38(1)(a)) or that initial expenditure is, compared with any item of expenditure under section 38(1)(b), disproportionately small having regard to the value of the asset immediately before the subsequent item of expenditure was incurred, the part of the gain which is not attributable to the enhancement of the value of the asset due to any item of expenditure under section 38(1)(b) shall be deemed to be attributed to expenditure incurred at the beginning of the period of ownership and allowable under section 38(1)(a), and the part or parts of the gain attributable to expenditure under section 38(1)(b) shall be reduced accordingly.

(6) The beginning of the period over which a gain, or part of a gain, is under sub-paragraphs (3) and (4) above to be treated as growing shall not be earlier than 6th April 1945 and this sub-paragraph shall have effect notwithstanding any provision in this Schedule or elsewhere in this Act.

(7) If in pursuance of section 42 an asset's market value at a date before 6th April 1965 is to be ascertained, sub-paragraphs (3) to (5) above shall have effect as if that asset had been on that date sold by the owner, and immediately reacquired by him, at that market value.

(8) If in pursuance of section 42 an asset's market value at a date on or after 6th April 1965 is to be ascertained sub-paragraphs (3) to (5) above shall have effect as if—

  (a) the asset on that date had been sold by the owner, and immediately reacquired by him, at that market value, and

  (b) accordingly, the computation of any gain on a subsequent disposal of that asset shall be computed—

      (i) by apportioning in accordance with this paragraph the gain or loss over a period ending on that date (the date on the part disposal), and

      (ii) by bringing into account the entire gain or loss over the period from the date of the part disposal to the date of subsequent disposal.

(9) For the purposes of this paragraph the period of ownership of an asset shall, where under section 43 account is to be taken of expenditure in respect of an asset from which the asset disposed of was derived, or where it would so apply if there were any relevant expenditure in respect of that other asset, include the period of ownership of that other asset.

(10) If under this paragraph part only of a gain is a chargeable gain, the fraction in section 223(2) shall be applied to that part instead of to the whole of the gain.

Election for valuation at 6th April 1965

17.—(1) If the person making a disposal so elects, paragraph 16 above shall not apply in relation to that disposal and it shall be assumed, both for the purposes of computing the gain accruing to that person on the disposal, and for all other purposes both in relation to that person and other persons, that the assets disposed of, and any assets of which account is to be taken in relation to the disposal under section 43, being assets which were in the ownership of that person on 6th April 1965, were on that date sold, and immediately reacquired, by him at their market value on 6th April 1965.

(2) Sub-paragraph (1) above shall not apply in relation to a disposal of assets if on the assumption in that sub-paragraph a loss would accrue on that disposal to the person making the disposal and either a smaller loss or a gain would accrue if sub-paragraph (1) did not apply, but in a case where this sub-paragraph would otherwise substitute a gain for a loss it shall be assumed, in relation to the disposal, that the relevant assets were sold by the owner, and immediately reacquired by him, for a consideration such that, on the disposal, neither a gain nor a loss accrued to the person making the disposal.

The displacement of sub-paragraph (1) above by this sub-paragraph shall not be taken as bringing paragraph 16 above into operation.

(3) An election under this paragraph shall be made by notice to the inspector given within two years from the end of the year of assessment or accounting period of a company in which the disposal is made or such further time as the Board may by notice allow.

(4) For the avoidance of doubt it is hereby declared that an election under this paragraph is irrevocable.

(5) An election may not be made under this paragraph as respects, or in relation to, an asset the market value of which at a date on or after 6th April 1965, and before the date of the disposal to which the election relates, is to be ascertained in pursuance of section 42.

Unquoted shares, commodities etc.

18.—(1) This paragraph has effect as respects shares held by any person on 6th April 1965 other than quoted securities within the meaning of paragraph 8 above and shares as respects which an election is made under paragraph 17 above.

(2) For the purpose of—
(a) identifying the shares so held on 6th April 1965 with shares previously acquired, and
(b) identifying the shares so held on that date with shares subsequently disposed of, and distinguishing them from shares acquired subsequently,
so far as the shares are of the same class, shares bought at a later time shall be deemed to have been disposed of before shares bought at an earlier time.

(3) Sub-paragraph (2) above has effect subject to section 105.

(4) Shares shall not be treated for the purposes of this paragraph as being of the same class unless if dealt with on a recognised stock exchange they would be so treated, but shall be treated in accordance with this paragraph notwithstanding that they are identified in a different way by a disposal or by the transfer or delivery giving effect to it.

(5) This paragraph, without sub-paragraph (4), shall apply in relation to any assets; other than shares, which are of a nature to be dealt with without identifying the particular assets disposed of or acquired.

Reorganisation of share capital, conversion of securities etc.

19.—(1) For the purposes of this Act, it shall be assumed that any shares or securities held by a person on 6th April 1965 (identified in accordance with paragraph 18 above) which, in accordance with Chapter II of Part IV, are to be regarded as being or forming part of a new holding were sold and immediately reacquired by him on 6th April 1965 at their market value on that date.

(2) If, at any time after 5th April 1965, a person comes to have, in accordance with Chapter II of Part IV, a new holding, paragraph 16(3) to (5) above shall have effect as if—
(a) the new holding had at that time been sold by the owner, and immediately reacquired by him, at its market value at that time, and

(b) accordingly, the amount of any gain on a disposal of the new holding or any part of it shall be computed—
    (i) by apportioning in accordance with paragraph 16 above the gain or loss over a period ending at that time, and
    (ii) by bringing into account the entire gain or loss over the period from that time to the date of the disposal.

(3) This paragraph shall not apply in relation to a reorganisation of a company's share capital if the new holding differs only from the original shares in being a different number, whether greater or less, of shares of the same class as the original shares.

PART IV

MISCELLANEOUS

Capital allowances

20. If under any provision in this Schedule it is to be assumed that any asset was on 6th April 1965 sold by the owner, and immediately reacquired by him, sections 41 and 47 shall apply in relation to any capital allowance or renewals allowance made in respect of the expenditure actually incurred by the owner in providing the asset, and so made for the year 1965–66 or for any subsequent year of assessment, as if it were made in respect of the expenditure which, on that assumption, was incurred by him in reacquiring the asset on 7th April 1965.

Assets transferred to close companies

21.—(1) This paragraph has effect where—
(a) at any time, including a time before 7th April 1965, any of the persons having control of a close company, or any person who is connected with a person having control of a close company, has transferred assets to the company, and
(b) paragraph 16 above applies in relation to a disposal by one of the persons having control of the company of shares or securities in the company, or in relation to a disposal by a person having, up to the time of disposal, a substantial holding of shares or securities in the company, being in either case a disposal after the transfer of the assets.

(2) So far as the gain accruing to the said person on the disposal of the shares is attributable to a profit on the assets so transferred, the period over which the gain is to be treated under paragraph 16 above as growing at a uniform rate shall begin with the time when the assets were transferred to the company, and accordingly a part of a gain attributable to a profit on assets transferred on or after 6th April 1965 shall all be a chargeable gain.

(3) This paragraph shall not apply where a loss, and not a gain, accrues on the disposal.

Husbands and wives

22. Where section 58 is applied in relation to a disposal of an asset by a man to his wife, or by a man's wife to him, then in relation to a subsequent disposal of the asset (not within that section) the one making the disposal shall be treated for the purposes of this Schedule as if the other's acquisition or provision of the asset had been his or her acquisition or provision of it.

Compensation and insurance money

23. Where section 23(4)(a) applies to exclude a gain which, in consequence of this Schedule, is not all chargeable gain, the amount of the reduction to be made under section 23(4)(b) shall be the amount of the chargeable gain and not the whole amount of the gain; and in section 23(5)(b) for the reference to the amount by which the gain is reduced under section 23(5)(a) there shall be substituted a reference to the amount by which the chargeable gain is proportionately reduced under section 23(5)(a).

GENERAL NOTE
The Schedule provides special rules for computing gains on assets held on April 6, 1965, the date when C.G.T. was originally introduced. Although the rebasing of the tax to March 31, 1982 will generally make these provisions redundant, there may be circumstances in which they will still apply (see s.35(3)) and accordingly they have been re-enacted, albeit with diminishing relevance.

Para. 1
This provides that quoted securities are to be deemed to have been acquired at their market value on April 6, 1965. The rule does not apply to securities acquired by an employee with a restriction on his right to dispose of them.

Para. 2
This restricts the operation of para. 1 in cases where it would produce an anomalous result. In such a case the gain or loss is restricted by reference to the historical cost of the asset, with a no-gain/no-loss rule where this would substitute a loss for a gain or a gain for a loss. A LIFO rule is used for identifying securities.

Para. 3
From March 19, 1968 the system of pooling for quoted securities held on April 6, 1965 ceased to apply unless the taxpayer so elected. In such cases the system does not apply to disposals between these dates. Instead, the LIFO rule applies.

Para. 4
This continues the pooling system up to its temporary abandonment in 1982 in cases where an election to do so had been made. In such a case, April 6, 1965 value must be adopted for securities entering the pool. Separate, irrevocable elections could be made in respect of equities and fixed-interest securities or preference shares.

Para. 5
Elections for a group are made by the principal company of the group (see s.170(3)(a)).

Para. 6
Where only a partial election has been made under para. 4, the election will not apply on an exchange of securities of different types.

Para. 7
A para. 4 election may not be made in relation to Lloyd's underwriters' funds (see s.206).

Para. 8
This provides rules for determining what is a fixed-interest security and a preference share.

Para. 9
Where land is disposed of for a consideration which exceeds its current use value, or where material development has been carried out after December 17, 1973 (the date of the introduction of the tax on development gains), the normal straight-line apportionment rule (see para. 16) does not apply. Instead, the land is deemed to have been acquired at its market value as at April 6, 1965.
For the interpretation of the provision prior to its amendment by FA 1974, s.48(3), see *Watkins* v. *Kidson* (1979) 53 T.C. 117, H.L. It applies even if no actual expenditure had been incurred before April 6, 1965, *e.g.* where the property was acquired by gift (*Mashiter (Inspector of Taxes)* v. *Pearmain* (1984) 58 T.C. 334, C.A.). Any "hope value" in the land as at April 6, 1965, is caught by the provision (*Morgan (Inspector of Taxes)* v. *Gibson* [1989] S.T.C. 568).

Para. 10
This provides rules for ascertaining the "current use value" of land.

Para. 11
This relates the foregoing to disposals of leases.

Para. 12
This provides for the apportionment of current use value where a lease is a wasting asset (see Sched. 8, para. 1).

Para. 13
This provides a definition of "material development".

Para. 14
This provides rules for ascertaining when "material development" has begun.

Para. 15
This contains sundry other definitions.

Para. 16
The general rule provided for all assets other than quoted securities and land is that the appreciation in value of assets held on April 6, 1965 is to be treated as accruing evenly over the period of ownership, except that any period before April 6, 1945, is to be disregarded.

Subsequent to the introduction of indexation in 1982 and prior to rebasing in 1988, there was a question whether indexation was to be applied against the entire gain, or only that part accruing after 1965. This issue was decided against the taxpayer in the High Court, but in her favour in the Court of Appeal (*Smith* v. *Schofield (Inspector of Taxes)* [1990] 1 W.L.R. 1447; [1992] S.T.C. 249).

Para. 17
   The rule in para. 16 may be displaced by an irrevocable election for the value as at April 6, 1965 within two years of a disposal, subject to exclusions under sub-para. (2).

Para. 18
   For unquoted shares and fungible assets in respect of which no para. 17 election has been made, disposals and acquisitions are matched on a LIFO basis.

Para. 19
   In the case of shares acquired under a reorganisation, these are deemed to have been disposed of and reacquired at the time of the reorganisation, and the subsequent apportioned gain is brought into charge.

Para. 20
   This applies the restriction of losses by reference to capital allowances under ss.41 and 47 to the deemed disposal and reacquisition of assets as at April 6, 1965.

Para. 21
   A possible means of avoiding C.G.T. would be for persons having control of a close company (see ICTA 1988, ss.414 and 415) to transfer assets to the company and subsequently sell their shares for a consideration reflecting the growth in value of the assets. In such a case, time apportionment under para. 16 is denied and the gain is treated as accruing from the time of the transfer.

Para. 22
   In the case of disposals between spouses, the acquiring spouse takes over the original acquisition date.

Para. 23
   When an election is made under s.23 to roll-over gains where insurance or compensation money is applied in replacement of assets, gains accruing before April 6, 1965 are left out of account in the set-off.

Section 35   SCHEDULE 3

ASSETS HELD ON 31st MARCH, 1982

Previous no gain/no loss disposals

1.—(1) Where—
(a) a person makes a disposal, not being a no gain/no loss disposal, of an asset which he acquired after 31st March 1982, and
(b) the disposal by which he acquired the asset and any previous disposal of the asset after 31st March 1982 was a no gain/no loss disposal,
he shall be treated for the purposes of section 35 as having held the asset on 31st March 1982.
   (2) For the purposes of this paragraph a no gain/no loss disposal is one on which by virtue of any of the enactments specified in section 35(3)(d) neither a gain nor a loss accrues to the person making the disposal.
   2.—(1) Sub-paragraph (2) below applies where a person makes a disposal of an asset acquired by him on or after 6th April 1988 in circumstances in which section 58 or 171 applied.
   (2) Where this sub-paragraph applies—
(a) an election under section 35(5) by the person making the disposal shall not cover the disposal, but
(b) the making of such an election by the person from whom the asset was acquired shall cause the disposal to fall outside subsection (3) of that section (so that subsection (2) of that section is not excluded by it) whether or not the person making the disposal makes such an election.

(3) Where the person from whom the asset was acquired by the person making the disposal himself acquired it on or after 6th April 1988 in circumstances in which section 58 or 171 applied, an election made by him shall not have the effect described in sub-paragraph (2)(b) above but an election made by—

(a) the last person by whom the asset was acquired after 5th April 1988 otherwise than in such circumstances, or

(b) if there was no such person, the person who held the asset on 5th April 1988,

shall have that effect.

Capital allowances

3. If under section 35 it is to be assumed that any asset was on 31st March 1982 sold by the person making the disposal and immediately reacquired by him, sections 41 and 47 shall apply in relation to any capital allowance or renewals allowance made in respect of the expenditure actually incurred by him in providing the asset as if it were made in respect of expenditure which, on that assumption, was incurred by him in reacquiring the asset on 31st March 1982.

Part disposals etc.

4.—(1) Where, in relation to a disposal to which section 35(2) applies, section 42 has effect by reason of an earlier disposal made after 31st March 1982 and before 6th April 1988, the sums to be apportioned under section 42 shall for the purposes of the later disposal be ascertained on the assumption stated in section 35(2).

(2) In any case where—

(a) subsection (2) of section 35 applies in relation to the disposal of an asset,

(b) if that subsection did not apply, section 23(2), 122(4), 133(4) or 244 would operate to disallow expenditure as a deduction in computing a gain accruing on the disposal, and

(c) the disallowance would be attributable to the reduction of the amount of the consideration for a disposal made after 31st March 1982 but before 6th April 1988,

the amount allowable as a deduction on the disposal shall be reduced by the amount which would be disallowed if section 35(2) did not apply.

Assets derived from other assets

5. Section 35 shall have effect with the necessary modifications in relation to a disposal of an asset which on 31st March 1982 was not itself held by the person making the disposal, if its value is derived from another asset of which account is to be taken in relation to the disposal under section 43.

Apportionment of pre-1965 gains and losses

6. In a case where because of paragraph 16 of Schedule 2 only part of a gain or loss is a chargeable gain or allowable loss, section 35(3)(a) and (b) shall have effect as if the amount of the gain or loss that would accrue if subsection (2) did not apply were equal to that part.

Elections under section 35(5): excluded disposals

7.—(1) An election under section 35(5) shall not cover disposals such as are specified in sub-paragraph (2) below.

(2) The disposals mentioned in sub-paragraph (1) above are disposals of, or of an interest in—

(a) plant or machinery,

(b) an asset which the person making the disposal has at any time held for the purposes of or in connection with—

　　(i) a trade consisting of the working of a source of mineral deposits, or

　　(ii) where a trade involves (but does not consist of) such working, the part of the trade which involves such working, or

(c) a licence under the Petroleum (Production) Act 1934 or the Petroleum (Production) Act (Northern Ireland) 1964; or

(d) shares which, on 31st March 1982, were unquoted and derived their value, or the greater part of their value, directly or indirectly from oil exploration or exploitation assets situated in the United Kingdom or a designated area or from such assets and oil exploration or exploitation rights taken together;

but a disposal does not fall within paragraph (a) or (b) above unless a capital allowance in respect of any expenditure attributable to the asset has been made to the person making the disposal or would have been made to him had he made a claim.

(3) For the purposes of sub-paragraph (2)(d) above—

(a) "shares" includes stock and any security, as defined in section 254(1) of the Taxes Act; and

(b) shares (as so defined) were unquoted on 31st March 1982 if, on that date, they were neither quoted on a recognised stock exchange nor dealt in on the Unlisted Securities Market;

but nothing in this paragraph affects the operation, in relation to such unquoted shares, of sections 126 to 130.

(4) In sub-paragraph (2)(d) above—

"designated area" means an area designated by Order in Council under section 1(7) of the Continental Shelf Act 1964;

"oil exploration or exploitation assets" shall be construed in accordance with sub-paragraphs (5) and (6) below; and

"oil exploration or exploitation rights" means rights to assets to be produced by oil exploration or exploitation activities (as defined in sub-paragraph (6) below) or to interests in or to the benefit of such assets.

(5) For the purposes of sub-paragraph (2)(d) above an asset is an oil exploration or exploitation asset if either—

(a) it is not a mobile asset and is being or has at some time been used in connection with oil exploration or exploitation activities carried on in the United Kingdom or a designated area; or

(b) it is a mobile asset which has at some time been used in connection with oil exploration or exploitation activities so carried on and is dedicated to an oil field in which the company whose shares are disposed of by the disposal, or a person connected with that company, is or has been a participator;

and, subject to sub-paragraph (6) below, expressions used in paragraphs (a) and (b) above have the same meaning as if those paragraphs were included in Part I of the Oil Taxation Act 1975.

(6) In the preceding provisions of this paragraph "oil exploration or exploitation activities" means activities carried on in connection with—

(a) the exploration of land (including the seabed and subsoil) in the United Kingdom or a designated area, as defined in sub-paragraph (4) above, with a view to searching for or winning oil; or

(b) the exploitation of oil found in any such land;

and in this sub-paragraph "oil" has the same meaning as in Part I of the Oil Taxation Act 1975.

(7) Where the person making the disposal acquired the asset on a no gain/no loss disposal, the references in sub-paragraph (2) above to that person are references to the person making the disposal, the person who last acquired the asset otherwise than on a no gain/no loss disposal or any person who subsequently acquired the asset on such a disposal.

(8) In this paragraph—

(a) "source of mineral deposits" shall be construed in accordance with section 121 of the 1990 Act, and

(b) references to a no gain/no loss disposal shall be construed in accordance with paragraph 1 above.

Elections under section 35(5): groups of companies

8.—(1) A company may not make an election under section 35(5) at a time when it is a member but not the principal company of a group unless the company did not become a member of the group until after the relevant time.

(2) Subject to sub-paragraph (3) below, an election under section 35(5) by a company which is the principal company of a group shall have effect also as an election by any other company which at the relevant time is a member of the group.

(3) Sub-paragraph (2) above shall not apply in relation to a company which, in some period after 5th April 1988 and before the relevant time, is not a member of the group if—

(a) during that period the company makes a disposal to which section 35 applies, and

(b) the period during which an election under subsection (5) of that section could be made expires without such an election having been made.

(4) Sub-paragraph (2) above shall apply in relation to a company notwithstanding that the company ceases to be a member of the group at any time after the relevant time except where—

(a) the company is an outgoing company in relation to the group, and

(b) the election relating to the group is made after the company ceases to be a member of the group.

(5) In relation to a company which is the principal company of a group the reference in section 35(6) to the first relevant disposal is a reference to the first disposal to which that section applies by a company which is—

(a) a member of the group but not an outgoing company in relation to the group, or

(b) an incoming company in relation to the group.

9.—(1) In paragraph 8 above "the relevant time", in relation to a group of companies, is—

(a) the first time when any company which is then a member of the group, and is not an outgoing company in relation to the group, makes a disposal to which section 35 applies,

(b) the time immediately following the first occasion when a company which is an incoming company in relation to the group becomes a member of the group,

(c) the time when an election is made by the principal company,

whichever is earliest.

(2) In paragraph 8 above and this paragraph—

"incoming company", in relation to a group of companies, means a company which—

(a) makes its first disposal to which section 35 applies at a time when it is not a member of the group, and

(b) becomes a member of the group before the end of the period during which an election under section 35(5) could be made in relation to it and at a time when no such election has been made, and

"outgoing company", in relation to a group of companies, means a company which ceases to be a member of the group before the end of the period during which an election under section 35(5) could be made in relation to it and at a time when no such election has been made.

(3) Section 170 shall have effect for the purposes of paragraph 8 above and this paragraph as for those of sections 170 to 181.

GENERAL NOTE

The Schedule contains a number of provisions consequent on the rebasing of C.G.T. to March 31, 1982.

Para. 1

This deals with the case where a person acquired assets after March 31, 1982 on a no-gain/no-loss basis (*e.g.* on a disposal between spouses). In such a case the acquirer is deemed to have held the asset on March 31, 1982. It does not cover cases of deferred charges on gains *before* March 31, 1982, as to which see Sched. 4.

Para. 2

In the case of a disposal between spouses or within a group of companies (see ss.58 and 171)· an election under s.35(5) for rebasing in relation to an asset acquired after April 5, 1988, must be made by the person from whom it was acquired.

Para. 3

The provisions under ss.41 and 47 restricting allowable losses where the deductible expenditure includes capital allowances and excluding the straightline restriction of allowable expenditure on wasting assets (see s.44) qualifying for capital allowances apply, notwithstanding the deemed reacquisition on March 31, 1982.

Para. 4

This deals with the situation where there was a part disposal between the introduction of indexation and the rebasing. In such a case apportionments are made using market value. Amounts which would have been disallowed under the provisions mentioned in sub-para. (2) will continue to be disallowed.

Para. 5

The provisions also apply to derived assets under s.43.

Para. 6

This applies the time apportionment rules for assets held before 1965, subject to the provisions precluding revaluation in certain cases.

Para. 7

The election for rebasing to 1982 does not apply in respect of certain classes of assets, including plant and machinery on which capital allowances can be claimed, assets held in connection with working mineral deposits or a petroleum licence and unquoted shares deriving their value from oil exploration or exploitation assets or rights.

Para. 8

This provides for elections in the case of a group of companies. Generally these are made by the principal company of a group (see s.170(3)), but special provision is made for incoming and outgoing companies at any relevant time.

Para. 9

This gives definitions for the purpose of para. 8.

Section 36   SCHEDULE 4

DEFERRED CHARGES ON GAINS BEFORE 31st MARCH 1982

Reduction of deduction or gain

1. Where this Schedule applies—
(a) in a case within paragraph 2 below, the amount of the deduction referred to in that paragraph, and
(b) in a case within paragraph 3 or 4 below, the amount of the gain referred to in that paragraph,
shall be one half of what it would be apart from this Schedule.

Charges rolled-over or held-over

2.—(1) Subject to sub-paragraphs (2) to (4) below, this Schedule applies on a disposal, not being a no gain/no loss disposal, of an asset if—
(a) the person making the disposal acquired the asset after 31st March 1982,
(b) a deduction falls to be made by virtue of any of the enactments specified in sub-paragraph (5) below from the expenditure which is allowable in computing the amount of any gain accruing on the disposal, and
(c) the deduction is attributable (whether directly or indirectly and whether in whole or in part) to a chargeable gain accruing on the disposal before 6th April 1988 of an asset acquired before 31st March 1982 by the person making that disposal.
(2) This Schedule does not apply where, by reason of the previous operation of this Schedule, the amount of the deduction is less than it otherwise would be.
(3) This Schedule does not apply if the amount of the deduction would have been less had relief by virtue of a previous application of this Schedule been duly claimed.
(4) Where—
(a) the asset was acquired on or after 19th March 1991,
(b) the deduction is partly attributable to a claim by virtue of section 154(4), and
(c) the claim applies to the asset,
this Schedule does not apply by virtue of this paragraph.
(5) The enactments referred to in sub-paragraph (1) above are sections 23(4) and (5), 152, 162, 165 and 247 of this Act and section 79 of the Finance Act 1980.

3.—(1) This paragraph applies where this Schedule would have applied on a disposal but for paragraph 2(4) above.
(2) This Schedule applies on the disposal if paragraph 4 below would have applied had—
(a) section 154(2) continued to apply to the gain carried forward as a result of the claim by virtue of section 154(4), and
(b) the time of the disposal been the time when that gain was treated as accruing by virtue of section 154(2).

Postponed charges

4.—(1) Subject to sub-paragraphs (3) to (5) below, this Schedule applies where—
(a) a gain is treated as accruing by virtue of any of the enactments specified in sub-paragraph (2) below, and
(b) that gain is attributable (whether directly or indirectly and whether in whole or in part) to the disposal before 6th April 1988 of an asset acquired before 31st March 1982 by the person making that disposal.
(2) The enactments referred to in sub-paragraph (1) above are sections 116(10) and (11), 134, 140, 154(2), 168 (as modified by section 67(6)), 178(3), 179(3) and 248(3).
(3) Where a gain is treated as accruing by virtue of section 178(3) or 179(3), this Schedule applies only if the asset was acquired by the chargeable company (within the meaning of section 178 or 179) before 6th April 1988.
(4) Where a gain is treated as accruing in consequence of an event, this Schedule does not apply if—
(a) the gain is attributable (whether directly or indirectly and whether in whole or part) to the disposal of an asset on or after 6th April 1988, or

(b) the amount of the gain would have been less had relief by virtue of a previous application of this Schedule been duly claimed.

(5) None of sections 134, 140(4), 154(2) and 248(3) shall apply in consequence of an event occurring on or after 6th April 1988 if its application would be directly attributable to the disposal of an asset on or before 31st March 1982.

Previous no gain/no loss disposals

5. Where—
(a) a person makes a disposal of an asset which he acquired on or after 31st March 1982, and
(b) the disposal by which he acquired the asset and any previous disposal of the asset on or after 31st March 1982 was a no gain/no loss disposal,
he shall be treated for the purposes of paragraphs 2(1)(c) and 4(1)(b) above as having acquired the asset before 31st March 1982.

6.—(1) Sub-paragraph (2) below applies where—
(a) a person makes a disposal of an asset which he acquired on or after 31st March 1982,
(b) the disposal by which he acquired the asset was a no gain/no loss disposal, and
(c) a deduction falling to be made as mentioned in paragraph (b) of sub-paragraph (1) of paragraph 2 above which was attributable as mentioned in paragraph (c) of that sub-paragraph was made—
  (i) on that disposal, or
  (ii) where one or more earlier no gain/no loss disposals of the asset have been made on or after 31st March 1982 and since the last disposal of the asset which was not a no gain/no loss disposal, on any such earlier disposal.

(2) Where this sub-paragraph applies the deduction shall be treated for the purposes of paragraph 2 above as falling to be made on the disposal mentioned in sub-paragraph (1)(a) above and not on the no gain/no loss disposal.

7. For the purposes of this Schedule a no gain/no loss disposal is one on which by virtue of any of the enactments specified in section 35(3)(d) neither a gain nor a loss accrues to the person making the disposal.

Assets derived from other assets

8. The references in paragraphs 2(1)(c) and 4(1)(b) above to the disposal of an asset acquired by a person before 31st March 1982 include references to the disposal of an asset which was not acquired by the person before that date if its value is derived from another asset which was so acquired and of which account is to be taken in relation to the disposal under section 43.

Claims

9.—(1) No relief shall be given under this Schedule unless a claim is made—
(a) in the case of a gain treated as accruing by virtue of section 178(3) or 179(3) to a company which ceases to be a member of a group, within the period of two years beginning at the end of the accounting period in which the company ceases to be a member of the group,
(b) in any other case, within the period of two years beginning at the end of the year of assessment or accounting period in which the disposal in question is made, or the gain in question is treated as accruing,
or within such longer period as the Board may by notice allow.

(2) A claim under sub-paragraph (1) above shall be supported by such particulars as the inspector may require for the purpose of establishing entitlement to relief under this Schedule and the amount of relief due.

GENERAL NOTE
The Schedule implements a relief in the case of assets acquired after March 31, 1982, where the acquisition cost was reduced as a result of holdover, rollover or other reliefs.

Para. 1
In cases where the relief applies, the amount of the relevant deduction or gain is reduced by one-half.

Para. 2
This deals with the more common cases of holdover and rollover relief.

Para. 3
This deals with holdover relief on depreciating assets under s.154(4).

Para. 4

This deals with cases where a gain is deferred but may be brought into charge on a subsequent event, *e.g.* where a company leaves a group.

Paras. 5–7

These preserve the relief where a person acquires an asset as the result of a no-gain/no-loss disposal.

Para. 8

This extends the relief to assets derived from other assets.

Para. 9

The relief is only available on a claim being made within two years of the end of the relevant period or year of assessment.

Section 86   SCHEDULE 5

ATTRIBUTION OF GAINS TO SETTLORS WITH INTEREST IN NON-RESIDENT OR DUAL RESIDENT SETTLEMENT

Construction of section 86(1)(e)

1.—(1) In construing section 86(1)(e) as regards a particular year of assessment, the effect of sections 3 and 77 to 79 shall be ignored.

(2) In construing section 86(1)(e) as regards a particular year of assessment—

(a) any deductions provided for by section 2(2) shall be made in respect of disposals of any of the settled property originating from the settlor, and

(b) section 16(3) shall be assumed not to prevent losses accruing to trustees in one year of assessment from being allowed as a deduction from chargeable gains accruing in a later year of assessment (so far as not previously set against gains).

(3) In a case where—

(a) the trustees hold shares in a company which originate from the settlor, and

(b) under section 13 gains or losses would be treated as accruing to the trustees in a particular year of assessment by virtue of the shares if the assumption as to residence specified in section 86(3) were made,

the gains or losses shall be taken into account in construing section 86(1)(e) as regards that year as if they had accrued by virtue of disposals of settled property originating from the settlor.

(4) Where, as regards a particular year of assessment, there would be an amount under section 86(1)(e) (apart from this sub-paragraph) and the trustees fall within section 86(2)(b), the following rules shall apply—

(a) assume that the references in section 86(1)(e) and sub-paragraphs (2)(a) and (3) above to settled property originating from the settlor were to such of it as constitutes protected assets;

(b) assume that the reference in sub-paragraph (3)(a) above to shares originating from the settlor were to such of them as constitute protected assets;

(c) find the amount (if any) which would be arrived at under section 86(1)(e) on those assumptions;

(d) if no amount is so found there shall be deemed to be no amount for the purposes of section 86(1)(e);

(e) if an amount is found under paragraph (c) above it must be compared with the amount arrived at under section 86(1)(e) apart from this sub-paragraph, and the smaller of the two shall be taken to be the amount arrived at under section 86(1)(e).

(5) Sub-paragraphs (2) to (4) above shall have effect subject to sub-paragraphs (6) and (7) below.

(6) The following rules shall apply in construing section 86(1)(e) as regards a particular year of assessment ("the year concerned") in a case where the trustees fall within section 86(2)(a)—

(a) if the conditions mentioned in section 86(1) are not fulfilled as regards the settlement in any year of assessment falling before the year concerned, no deductions shall be made in respect of losses accruing before the year concerned;

(b) if the conditions mentioned in section 86(1) are fulfilled as regards the settlement in any year or years of assessment falling before the year concerned, no deductions shall be made in respect of losses accruing before that year (or the first of those years) so falling,

but nothing in the preceding provisions of this sub-paragraph shall prevent deductions being made in respect of losses accruing in a year of assessment in which the conditions mentioned in section 86(1)(a) to (d) and (f) are fulfilled as regards the settlement.

(7) In construing section 86(1)(e) as regards a particular year of assessment and in relation to a settlement created before 19th March, 1991, no account shall be taken of disposals made

before 19th March, 1991 (whether for the purpose of arriving at gains or for the purpose of arriving at losses).

(8) For the purposes of sub-paragraph (4) above assets are protected assets if—

(a) they are of a description specified in the arrangements mentioned in section 86(2)(b), and

(b) were the trustees to dispose of them at any relevant time, the trustees would fall to be regarded for the purposes of the arrangements as not liable in the United Kingdom to tax on gains accruing to them on the disposal.

(9) For the purposes of sub-paragraph (8) above—

(a) the assumption as to residence specified in section 86(3) shall be ignored;

(b) a relevant time is any time, in the year of assessment concerned, when the trustees fall to be regarded for the purposes of the arrangements as resident in a territory outside the United Kingdom;

(c) if different assets are identified by reference to different relevant times, all of them are protected assets.

Test whether settlor has interest

2.—(1) For the purposes of section 86(1)(d) a settlor has an interest in a settlement if—

(a) any relevant property which is or may at any time be comprised in the settlement is, or will or may become, applicable for the benefit of or payable to a defined person in any circumstances whatever,

(b) any relevant income which arises or may arise under the settlement is, or will or may become, applicable for the benefit of or payable to a defined person in any circumstances whatever, or

(c) any defined person enjoys a benefit directly or indirectly from any relevant property which is comprised in the settlement or any relevant income arising under the settlement; but this sub-paragraph is subject to sub-paragraphs (4) to (6) below.

(2) For the purposes of sub-paragraph (1) above—

(a) relevant property is property originating from the settlor,

(b) relevant income is income originating from the settlor.

(3) For the purposes of sub-paragraph (1) above each of the following is a defined person—

(a) the settlor,

(b) the settlor's spouse;

(c) any child of the settlor or of the settlor's spouse;

(d) the spouse of any such child;

(e) a company controlled by a person or persons falling within paragraphs (a) to (d) above;

(f) a company associated with a company falling within paragraph (e) above.

(4) A settlor does not have an interest in a settlement by virtue of paragraph (a) of sub-paragraph (1) above at any time when none of the property concerned can become applicable or payable as mentioned in that paragraph except in the event of—

(a) the bankruptcy of some person who is or may become beneficially entitled to the property,

(b) any assignment of or charge on the property being made or given by some such person,

(c) in the case of a marriage settlement, the death of both parties to the marriage and of all or any of the children of the marriage, or

(d) the death under the age of 25 or some lower age of some person who would be beneficially entitled to the property on attaining that age.

(5) A settlor does not have an interest in a settlement by virtue of paragraph (a) of sub-paragraph (1) above at any time when some person is alive and under the age of 25 if during that person's life none of the property concerned can become applicable or payable as mentioned in that paragraph except in the event of that person becoming bankrupt or assigning or charging his interest in the property concerned.

(6) Sub-paragraphs (4) and (5) above apply for the purposes of paragraph (b) of sub-paragraph (1) above as they apply for the purposes of paragraph (a), reading "income" for "property".

(7) In sub-paragraph (3) above "child" includes a step-child.

(8) For the purposes of sub-paragraph (3) above the question whether a company is controlled by a person or persons shall be construed in accordance with section 416 of the Taxes Act; but in deciding that question for those purposes no rights or powers of (or attributed to) an associate or associates of a person shall be attributed to him under section 416(6) if he is not a participator in the company.

(9) For the purposes of sub-paragraph (3) above the question whether a company is associated with another shall be construed in accordance with section 416 of the Taxes Act; but where in deciding that question for those purposes it falls to be decided whether a company is

controlled by a person or persons, no rights or powers of (or attributed to) an associate or associates of a person shall be attributed to him under section 416(6) if he is not a participator in the company.

(10) In sub-paragraphs (8) and (9) "participator" has the meaning given by section 417(1) of the Taxes Act.

Exceptions from section 86

3. Section 86 does not apply if the settlor dies in the year.

4.—(1) This paragraph applies where for the purposes of section 86(1)(d) the settlor has no interest in the settlement at any time in the year except for one of the following reasons, namely, that—

    (a) property is, or will or may become, applicable for the benefit of or payable to one of the persons falling within paragraph 2(3)(b) to (d) above,

    (b) income is, or will or may become, applicable for the benefit of or payable to one of those persons, or

    (c) one of those persons enjoys a benefit from property or income.

(2) This paragraph also applies where sub-paragraph (1) above is fulfilled by virtue of two or all of paragraphs (a) to (c) being satisfied by reference to the same person.

(3) Where this paragraph applies, section 86 does not apply if the person concerned dies in the year.

(4) In a case where—

    (a) this paragraph applies, and

    (b) the person concerned falls within paragraph 2(3)(b) or (d) above,

section 86 does not apply if during the year the person concerned ceases to be married to the settlor or child concerned (as the case may be).

5.—(1) This paragraph applies where for the purposes of section 86(1)(d) the settlor has no interest in the settlement at any time in the year except for the reason that there are two or more persons, each of whom—

    (a) falls within paragraph 2(3)(b) to (d) above, and

    (b) stands to gain for the reason stated in sub-paragraph (2) below.

(2) The reason is that—

    (a) property is, or will or may become, applicable for his benefit or payable to him,

    (b) income is, or will or may become, applicable for his benefit or payable to him,

    (c) he enjoys a benefit from property or income, or

    (d) two or all of paragraphs (a) to (c) above apply in his case.

(3) Where this paragraph applies, section 86 does not apply if each of the persons concerned dies in the year.

Right of recovery

6.—(1) This paragraph applies where any tax becomes chargeable on, and is paid by, a person in respect of gains treated as accruing to him in a year under section 86(4).

(2) The person shall be entitled to recover the amount of the tax from any person who is a trustee of the settlement.

(3) For the purposes of recovering that amount, the person shall also be entitled to require an inspector to give him a certificate specifying—

    (a) the amount of the gains concerned, and

    (b) the amount of tax paid,

and any such certificate shall be conclusive evidence of the facts stated in it.

Meaning of "settlor"

7. For the purposes of section 86 of this Schedule, a person is a settlor in relation to a settlement if the settled property consists of or includes property originating from him.

Meaning of "originating"

8.—(1) References in section 86 and this Schedule to property originating from a person are references to—

    (a) property provided by that person;

    (b) property representing property falling within paragraph (a) above;

    (c) so much of any property representing both property falling within paragraph (a) above and other property as, on a just apportionment, can be taken to represent property so falling.

(2) References in this Schedule to income originating from a person are references to—

    (a) income from property originating from that person;

(b) income provided by that person.

(3) Where a person who is a settlor in relation to a settlement makes reciprocal arrangements with another person for the provision of property or income, for the purposes of this paragraph—

(a) property or income provided by the other person in pursuance of the arrangements shall be treated as provided by the settlor, but

(b) property or income provided by the settlor in pursuance of the arrangements shall be treated as provided by the other person (and not by the settlor).

(4) For the purposes of this paragraph—

(a) where property is provided by a qualifying company controlled by one person alone at the time it is provided, that person shall be taken to provide it;

(b) where property is provided by a qualifying company controlled by two or more persons (taking each one separately) at the time it is provided, those persons shall be taken to provide the property and each one shall be taken to provide an equal share of it;

(c) where property is provided by a qualifying company controlled by two or more persons (taking them together) at the time it is provided, the persons who are participators in the company at the time it is provided shall be taken to provide it and each one shall be taken to provide so much of it as is attributed to him on the basis of a just apportionment;

but where a person would be taken to provide less than one-twentieth of any property by virtue of paragraph (c) above and apart from this provision, he shall not be taken to provide any of it by virtue of that paragraph.

(5) For the purposes of sub-paragraph (4) above a qualifying company is a close company or a company which would be a close company if it were resident in the United Kingdom.

(6) For the purposes of this paragraph references to property representing other property include references to property representing accumulated income from that other property.

(7) For the purposes of this paragraph property or income is provided by a person if it is provided directly or indirectly by the person.

(8) For the purposes of this paragraph the question whether a company is controlled by a person or persons shall be construed in accordance with section 416 of the Taxes Act; but in deciding that question for those purposes no rights or powers of (or attributed to) an associate or associates of a person shall be attributed to him under section 416(6) if he is not a participator in the company.

(9) In this paragraph "participator" has the meaning given by section 417(1) of the Taxes Act.

(10) The preceding provisions of this paragraph shall apply to determine whether shares originate from the settlor for the purposes of paragraph 1(3)(a) above as they apply to determine whether property of any kind originates from a person.

Qualifying settlements, and commencement

9.—(1) A settlement created on or after 19th March 1991 is a qualifying settlement for the purposes of section 86 and this Schedule in—

(a) the year of assessment in which it is created, and

(b) subsequent years of assessment.

(2) A settlement created before 19th March 1991, and as regards which any of the four conditions set out in sub-paragraphs (3) to (6) below becomes fulfilled, is a qualifying settlement for the purposes of section 86 and this Schedule in—

(a) the year of assessment in which any of those conditions becomes fulfilled, and

(b) subsequent years of assessment.

(3) The first condition is that on or after 19th March 1991 property or income is provided directly or indirectly for the purposes of the settlement—

(a) otherwise than under a transaction entered into at arm's length, and

(b) otherwise than in pursuance of a liability incurred by any person before that date;

but if the settlement's expenses relating to administration and taxation for a year of assessment exceed its income for the year, property or income provided towards meeting those expenses shall be ignored for the purposes of this condition if the value of the property or income so provided does not exceed the difference between the amount of those expenses and the amount of the settlement's income for the year.

(4) The second condition is that—

(a) the trustees become on or after 19th March 1991 neither resident nor ordinarily resident in the United Kingdom, or

(b) the trustees, while continuing to be resident and ordinarily resident in the United Kingdom, become on or after 19th March 1991 trustees who fall to be regarded for the purposes of any double taxation relief arrangements as resident in a territory outside the United Kingdom.

(5) The third condition is that on or after 19th March 1991 the terms of the settlement are varied so that any person falling within sub-paragraph (7) below becomes for the first time a person who will or might benefit from the settlement.

(6) The fourth condition is that—

(a) on or after 19th March 1991 a person falling within sub-paragraph (7) below enjoys a benefit from the settlement for the first time, and

(b) the person concerned is not one who (looking only at the terms of the settlement immediately before 19th March 1991) would be capable of enjoying a benefit from the settlement on or after that date.

(7) Each of the following persons falls within this sub-paragraph—

(a) a settlor;

(b) the spouse of a settlor;

(c) any child of a settlor or of a settlor's spouse;

(d) the spouse of any such child;

(e) a company controlled by a person or persons falling within paragraphs (a) to (d) above;

(f) a company associated with a company falling within paragraph (e) above.

(8) In sub-paragraph (7) above "child" includes a step-child.

(9) For the purposes of sub-paragraph (7) above the question whether a company is controlled by a person or persons shall be construed in accordance with section 416 of the Taxes Act; but in deciding that question for those purposes no rights or powers of (or attributed to) an associate or associates of a person shall be attributed to him under section 416(6) if he is not a participator in the company.

(10) For the purposes of sub-paragraph (7) above the question whether one company is associated with another shall be construed in accordance with section 416 of the Taxes Act; but where in deciding that question for those purposes it falls to be decided whether a company is controlled by a person or persons, no rights or powers of (or attributed to) an associate or associates of a person shall be attributed to him under section 416(6) if he is not a participator in the company.

(11) In sub-paragraphs (9) and (10) "participator" has the meaning given by section 417(1) of the Taxes Act.

Information

10. An inspector may by notice require any person who is or has been a trustee of, a beneficiary under, or a settlor in relation to, a settlement to give him within such time as he may direct (which must not be less than 28 days beginning with the day the notice is given) such particulars as he thinks necessary for the purposes of section 86 and this Schedule and specifies in the notice.

11.—(1) This paragraph applies if—

(a) a settlement has been created before 19th March 1991,

(b) on or after that date a person transfers property to the trustees otherwise than under a transaction entered into at arm's length and otherwise than in pursuance of a liability incurred by any person before that date,

(c) the trustees are not resident or ordinarily resident in the United Kingdom at the time the property is transferred, and

(d) the transferor knows, or has reason to believe, that the trustees are not so resident or ordinarily resident.

(2) Before the expiry of the period of 12 months beginning with the relevant day, the transferor shall deliver to the Board a return which—

(a) identifies the settlement, and

(b) specifies the property transferred, the day on which the transfer was made, and the consideration (if any) for the transfer.

(3) For the purposes of sub-paragraph (2) above the relevant day is the later of—

(a) the day on which the transfer is made, and

(b) 25th July 1991 (the day on which the Finance Act 1991 was passed).

12.—(1) This paragraph applies if a settlement is created on or after 19th March 1991, and at the time it is created—

(a) the trustees are not resident or ordinarily resident in the United Kingdom, or

(b) the trustees are resident or ordinarily resident in the United Kingdom but fall to be regarded for the purposes of any double taxation relief arrangements as resident in a territory outside the United Kingdom.

(2) Any person who—

(a) is a settlor in relation to the settlement at the time it is created, and

(b) at that time fulfils the condition mentioned in sub-paragraph (4) below, shall, before the expiry of the period of three months beginning with the relevant day, deliver to the Board a return specifying the particulars mentioned in sub-paragraph (5) below.

(3) Any person who—
(a) is a settlor in relation to the settlement at the time it is created,
(b) at that time does not fulfil the condition mentioned in sub-paragraph (4) below, and
(c) fulfils that condition at a later time,

shall, before the expiry of the period of 12 months beginning with the relevant day, deliver to the Board a return specifying the particulars mentioned in sub-paragraph (5) below.

(4) The condition is that the person concerned is domiciled in the United Kingdom and is either resident or ordinarily resident in the United Kingdom.

(5) The particulars are—
(a) the day on which the settlement was created;
(b) the name and address of the person delivering the return;
(c) the names and addresses of the persons who are the trustees immediately before the delivery of the return.

(6) For the purposes of sub-paragraph (2) above the relevant day is the later of—
(a) the day on which the settlement is created, and
(b) 25th July 1991 (the day on which the Finance Act 1991 was passed).

(7) For the purposes of sub-paragraph (3) above the relevant day is the later of—
(a) the day on which the person first fulfils the condition after the settlement is created, and
(b) 25th July 1991 (the day on which the Finance Act 1991 was passed).

13.—(1) This paragraph applies if—
(a) the trustees of a settlement become at any time ("the relevant time") on or after 19th March 1991 neither resident nor ordinarily resident in the United Kingdom, or
(b) the trustees of a settlement, while continuing to be resident and ordinarily resident in the United Kingdom, become at any time ("the relevant time") on or after 19th March 1991 trustees who fall to be regarded for the purposes of any double taxation relief arrangements as resident in a territory outside the United Kingdom.

(2) Any person who was a trustee of the settlement immediately before the relevant time shall, before the expiry of the period of 12 months beginning with the relevant day, deliver to the Board a return specifying—
(a) the day on which the settlement was created,
(b) the name and address of each person who is a settlor in relation to the settlement immediately before the delivery of the return, and
(c) the names and addresses of the persons who are the trustees immediately before the delivery of the return.

(3) For the purposes of sub-paragraph (2) above the relevant day is the later of—
(a) the day when the relevant time falls, and
(b) 25th July 1991 (the day on which the Finance Act 1991 was passed).

14.—(1) Nothing in paragraph 11, 12 or 13 above shall require information to be contained in the return concerned to the extent that—
(a) before the expiry of the period concerned the information has been provided to the Board by any person in pursuance of the paragraph concerned or of any other provision, or
(b) after the expiry of the period concerned the information falls to be provided to the Board by any person in pursuance of any provision other than the paragraph concerned.

(2) Nothing in paragraph 11, 12 or 13 above shall require a return to be delivered if—
(a) before the expiry of the period concerned all the information concerned has been provided to the Board by any person in pursuance of the paragraph concerned or of any other provision, or
(b) after the expiry of the period concerned all the information concerned falls to be provided to the Board by any person in pursuance of any provision other than the paragraph concerned.

GENERAL NOTE

This Schedule provides detailed rules for the attribution of gains in non-resident or dual resident settlements to settlors with an interest in the settlement.

Para. 1

This defines the gains on which the settlor is chargeable. The annual exempt amount for individuals is ignored, as is the provision charging settlors with an interest in a resident settlement. Losses are allowable against gains. Gains may be attributed through a company. The charge in relation to dual resident settlements is confined to "protected assets" (see sub-para. (8)). In respect of non-resident settlements, losses incurred in years when they were resident may not be deducted.

The section does not operate for disposals before March 19, 1991.

Para. 2

This provides the test whether a settlor has an interest in the settlement. Where a benefit is or may be received from property or income originating from the settlor (see para. 8) by the settlor or a member of his family or by a company controlled by them or associated with such a company, he has an interest in it. This does not apply where the interest depends on contingencies such as bankruptcy, an assignment or charge, and the death of parties to a marriage settlement or of persons under 25 before attaining a beneficial interest. With relation to the provisions regarding companies, the definitions for close companies in ICTA 1988, ss.416 and 417, apply, except that rights of a person's associates are not to be attributed to him if he is not a participator.

Paras. 3–5

These set out three circumstances in which s.86 does not apply: (1) where the settlor dies during the year; (2) if the settlor's interest arises only through another beneficiary, and this connection is terminated by death or the cessation of a marriage; and (3) if the settlor's interest arises only through two or more other persons and each of them dies during the year.

Para. 6

The settlor has a right of recovery against the trustees.

Para. 7

This defines a settlor to include any person from whom property originates.

Para. 8

This enlarges on para. 7 by defining "originating", which is the all-important term for the purposes of para. 2. It is given a wide meaning to include the provision of property or income directly or indirectly, in particular through a controlled company.

Para. 9

The provisions may apply to any settlement created on or after March 19, 1991. Settlements created before that date may be caught if any of four conditions becomes applicable: (1) where property is gratuitously added to a settlement (except to meet a shortfall of income for administrative or fiscal expenses); (2) the settlement becomes non-resident or dual resident; (3) the terms of the settlement are varied to allow a benefit to the settlor, his family or controlled or associated companies; (4) one of the above persons actually receives such a benefit, when it does not appear that he could do so under the terms of the settlement as at March 19, 1991.

Paras. 10–14

It may be difficult for the Revenue to discover the facts necessary for raising an assessment under s.86. Accordingly, an inspector may require information from settlors, trustees and beneficiaries. A person transferring property into a non-resident settlement which was created before March 19, 1991 is obliged to apprise the Revenue of this. The settlor of a non-resident or dual resident trust on or after March 19, 1991 who is himself domiciled and either resident or ordinarily resident in the U.K. must also report the facts. The retiring trustees of a settlement which becomes non-resident or dual resident must also report this. None of this applies to the extent that the Revenue obtain the information from other sources.

These provisions are backed by the penalties in TMA 1970, s.98.

Sections 163, 164   SCHEDULE 6

RETIREMENT RELIEF ETC.

PART I

INTERPRETATION

1.—(1) This paragraph and paragraphs 2 and 3 below have effect for the purposes of this Schedule and sections 163 and 164.

(2) In the provisions referred to above—

"commercial association of companies" means a company together with such of its associated companies, within the meaning of section 416 of the Taxes Act, as carry on businesses which are of such a nature that the businesses of the company and the associated companies taken together may be reasonably considered to make up a single composite undertaking;

"family company" means, in relation to an individual, a company the voting rights in which are—

(i) as to not less than 25 per cent. exercisable by the individual, or

(ii) as to more than 50 per cent. exercisable by the individual or a member of his family and, as to not less than 5 per cent. exercisable by the individual himself;

"family" means, in relation to an individual, the husband or wife of the individual and a relative of the individual or of the individual's husband or wife and, for this purpose, "relative" means brother, sister, ancestor or lineal descendant;

"full-time working director", in relation to one or more companies, means a director who is required to devote substantially the whole of his time to the service of that company or, as the case may be, those companies taken together, in a managerial or technical capacity;

"group of companies" means a company which has one or more 51 per cent. subsidiaries, together with those subsidiaries;

"holding company" means a company whose business (disregarding any trade carried on by it) consists wholly or mainly of the holding of shares or securities of one or more companies which are its 51 per cent. subsidiaries;

"permitted period" means a period of one year or such longer period as the Board may, in any particular case, by notice allow;

"trade", profession", "vocation", "office" and "employment" have the same meaning as in the Income Tax Acts;

"trading company" means a company whose business consists wholly or mainly of the carrying on of a trade or trades;

"trading group" means a group of companies the business of whose members, taken together, consists wholly or mainly of the carrying on of a trade or trades.

(3) For the purposes of sub-paragraph (2) above, voting rights exercisable by trustees of a settlement are to be treated as voting rights exercisable by a member of the family of an individual if—

(a) the individual or any member of his family is a beneficiary under the settlement; and

(b) no one, other than the individual or a member of his family, is for the time being entitled under the settlement to receive any capital or income of the settled property; and

(c) the terms of the settlement are such that no one other than the individual or a member of his family can become entitled to capital or income except upon the failure (for whatever reason) of the individual or a member of his family to become so entitled.

(4) Any reference in sub-paragraph (3) above to a person being or becoming entitled to any capital or income of the settled property includes a reference to a person—

(a) whose entitlement is subject to a power which could be so exercised as to require all or any of the capital or income in question to be paid to some other person; or

(b) whose entitlement depends upon his exercising a power in his own favour.

2.—(1) For the purposes of the provisions referred to in paragraph 1(1) above, where, as part of a reorganisation, within the meaning of section 126, there is a disposal of shares or securities of a company and, apart from this sub-paragraph, the shares disposed of and the new holding (as defined in that section) would fall to be treated, by virtue of section 127, as the same asset, section 127 shall not apply if the individual concerned so elects or, in the case of a trustees' disposal, if the trustees and the individual concerned jointly so elect; and an election under this sub-paragraph shall be made by notice given to the Board not more than two years after the end of the year of assessment in which the disposal occurred.

(2) In sub-paragraph (1) above, the reference to a reorganisation, within the meaning of section 126, includes a reference to an exchange of shares or securities which is treated as such a reorganisation by virtue of section 135(3).

3.—(1) A person who has been concerned in the carrying on of a business shall be treated as having retired on ill-health grounds if, on production of such evidence as the Board may reasonably require, the Board are satisfied—

(a) that he has ceased to be engaged in and, by reason of ill-health, is incapable of engaging in work of the kind which he previously undertook in connection with that business; and

(b) that he is likely to remain permanently so incapable.

(2) In sub-paragraph (1) above, the reference to a person being concerned in the carrying on of a business is a reference to his being so concerned personally or as a member of a partnership carrying on the business; and the business which is relevant for the purposes of the provisions referred to in paragraph 1(1) above is that referred to—

    (a) in subsection (3) or subsection (4) of section 163 in relation to a material disposal of business assets;

    (b) in subsection (5) of section 164 in relation to a trustees' disposal; and

    (c) in subsection (7) of section 164 in relation to an associated disposal.

(3) A person who has been a full-time working director of a company or of two or more companies shall be treated as having retired on ill-health grounds if, on production of such evidence as the Board may reasonably require, the Board are satisfied—

    (a) that he has ceased to serve and, by reason of ill-health, is incapable of serving that company or, as the case may be, those companies in a managerial or technical capacity; and

    (b) that he is likely to remain permanently incapable of serving in such a capacity that company or those companies (as the case may be) or any other company engaged in business of a kind carried on by that company or those companies.

(4) In relation to an employee's disposal, a person who has been exercising any office or employment shall be treated as having retired on ill-health grounds if, on production of such evidence as the Board may reasonably require, the Board are satisfied—

    (a) that he has ceased to exercise and, by reason of ill-health, is incapable of exercising that office or employment; and

    (b) that he is likely to remain permanently so incapable.

4.—(1) In this Schedule—

    (a) "material disposal of business assets" has the same meaning as in section 163;

    (b) "employee's disposal" means a disposal falling within subsection (1) of section 164;

    (c) "trustees' disposal" means a disposal falling within subsection (3) of section 164 and, in relation to such a disposal, "the qualifying beneficiary" has the meaning assigned to it by paragraph (b) of that subsection;

    (d) "associated disposal" has the meaning assigned to it by section 164(7);

and "qualifying disposal" means any of the disposals referred to in paragraphs (a) to (d) above.

(2) Any reference in this Schedule to the qualifying period is a reference to the period of at least one year which—

    (a) in relation to a material disposal of business assets, is referred to in subsection (3), subsection (4)(a) or subsection (5) (as the case may require) of section 163;

    (b) in relation to an employee's disposal, is referred to in section 164(2)(a);

    (c) in relation to a trustees' disposal, is referred to in subsection (4) or subsection (5) (as the case may require) of section 164;

and, in relation to an associated disposal, any reference in this Schedule to the qualifying period is a reference to that period which is the qualifying period in relation to the material disposal of business assets with which the associated disposal is associated in accordance with section 164(7).

(3) In relation to a qualifying disposal, any reference in this Schedule to the amount available for relief is a reference to the amount determined in accordance with paragraphs 13 to 16 below.

PART II

THE OPERATION OF THE RELIEF

Disposals on which relief may be given

5.—(1) Relief in accordance with this Schedule shall not be given in respect of any disposal unless the qualifying period relating to that disposal ends on or after 6th April, 1985.

(2) Except in the case of a disposal which is made by an individual who has attained the age of 55, relief in accordance with this Schedule shall be given only on the making of a claim not later than two years after the end of the year of assessment in which the disposal occurred.

(3) In the case of a trustees' disposal, relief in accordance with this Schedule shall be given only on a claim made jointly by the trustees and the beneficiary concerned.

(4) Where a claim for relief in accordance with this Schedule is dependent upon an individual having retired on ill-health grounds below the age of 55, the claim shall be made to the Board.

Gains qualifying for relief

6. Subject to paragraphs 9 and 10 below, in the case of any qualifying disposal other than one of shares or securities of a company, the gains accruing to the individual or, in the case of a

trustees' disposal, the trustees on the disposal of chargeable business assets comprised in the qualifying disposal shall be aggregated, and only so much of that aggregate as exceeds the amount available for relief shall be chargeable gains (but not so as to affect liability in respect of gains accruing on the disposal of assets other than chargeable business assets).

7.—(1) Subject to paragraphs 9 to 11 below, in the case of a qualifying disposal of shares or securities of a trading company which is not a holding company—

(a) the gains which on the disposal accrue to the individual or, as the case may be, the trustees shall be aggregated, and

(b) of the appropriate proportion of the aggregated gains, only so much as exceeds the amount available for relief shall constitute chargeable gains (but not so as to affect liability in respect of gains representing the balance of the aggregated gains).

(2) For the purposes of sub-paragraph (1)(b) above, "the appropriate proportion" is that which that part of the value of the company's chargeable assets immediately before the end of the qualifying period which is attributable to the value of the company's chargeable business assets bears to the whole of that value, but, in the case of a company which has no chargeable assets, "the appropriate proportion" is the whole.

(3) For the purposes of this paragraph, every asset is a chargeable asset except one, on the disposal of which by the company immediately before the end of the qualifying period, no gain accruing to the company would be a chargeable gain.

8.—(1) Subject to paragraphs 9 to 11 below, in the case of a qualifying disposal of shares or securities of a holding company—

(a) the gains which on the disposal accrue to the individual or, as the case may be, the trustees shall be aggregated, and

(b) of the appropriate proportion of the aggregated gains, only so much as exceeds the amount available for relief shall constitute chargeable gains (but not so as to affect liability in respect of gains representing the balance of the aggregated gains).

(2) For the purposes of sub-paragraph (1)(b) above, "the appropriate proportion" is that which that part of the value of the trading group's chargeable assets immediately before the end of the qualifying period which is attributable to the value of the trading group's chargeable business assets bears to the whole of that value; but, in the case of a trading group which has no chargeable assets, "the appropriate proportion" is the whole.

(3) For the purposes of sub-paragraph (2) above—

(a) any reference to the trading group's chargeable assets or chargeable business assets is a reference to the chargeable assets or, as the case may be, chargeable business assets of every member of the trading group; and

(b) subject to paragraph (c) below, every asset is a chargeable asset except one, on the disposal of which by the member of the group concerned immediately before the end of the qualifying period no gain accruing to that member would be a chargeable gain; and

(c) a holding by one member of the trading group of the ordinary share capital of another member of the group is not a chargeable asset.

(4) Where the whole of the ordinary share capital of a 51 per cent. subsidiary of the holding company is not owned directly or indirectly by that company, then, for the purposes of sub-paragraph (2) above, the value of the chargeable assets and chargeable business assets of that subsidiary shall be taken to be reduced by multiplying it by a fraction of which the denominator is the whole of the ordinary share capital of the subsidiary and the numerator is the amount of that share capital owned, directly or indirectly, by the holding company.

(5) Expressions used in sub-paragraph (4) above have the same meaning as in section 838 of the Taxes Act (subsidiaries).

9.—(1) If, in the case of a trustees' disposal, there is, in addition to the qualifying beneficiary, at least one other beneficiary who, at the end of the qualifying period, has an interest in possession in the whole of the settled property or, as the case may be, in a part of it which consists of or includes the shares, securities or asset which is the subject matter of the disposal, only the relevant proportion of the gain which accrues to the trustees on the disposal shall be brought into account under paragraph 6, paragraph 7 or paragraph 8 above (as the case may require) and the balance of the gain shall, accordingly, be a chargeable gain.

(2) For the purposes of sub-paragraph (1) above, the relevant proportion is that which, at the end of the qualifying period, the qualifying beneficiary's interest in the income of the part of the settled property comprising the shares, securities or asset in question bears to the interests in that income of all the beneficiaries (including the qualifying beneficiary) who then have interests in possession in that part.

(3) The reference in sub-paragraph (2) above to the qualifying beneficiary's interest is a reference to the interest by virtue of which he is the qualifying beneficiary and not to any other interest he may hold.

10.—(1) If, in the case of an associated disposal—

(a) the asset in question was in use for the purposes of a business as mentioned in section

164(7)(c) for only part of the period in which it was in the ownership of the individual making the disposal, or

(b) for any part of the period in which the asset in question was in use for the purposes of a business as mentioned in section 164(7)(c), the individual making the disposal was not concerned in the carrying on of that business (whether personally, as a member of a partnership or as a full-time working director of any such company as is referred to in section 163(3)(b)), or

(c) for the whole or any part of the period in which the asset in question was in use for the purposes of a business as mentioned in section 164(7)(c), its availability for that use was dependent upon the payment of rent,

only such part of the gain which accrues on the disposal as appears to the Board to be just and reasonable shall be brought into account under paragraph 6, paragraph 7 or paragraph 8 above (as the case may require) and the balance of the gain shall, accordingly, be a chargeable gain.

(2) In determining how much of a gain it is just and reasonable to bring into account as mentioned in sub-paragraph (1) above, the Board shall have regard to the length of the period the asset was in use as mentioned in that sub-paragraph and the extent to which any rent paid was less than the amount which would have been payable in the open market for the use of the asset.

(3) In sub-paragraphs (1) and (2) above "rent" includes any form of consideration given for the use of the asset.

11.—(1) This paragraph applies where—

(a) there is a material disposal of business assets or a trustees' disposal which (in either case) consists of a disposal which the individual or trustees is or are treated as making by virtue of section 122 in consideration of a capital distribution; and

(b) the capital distribution consists wholly of chargeable business assets of the company or partly of such assets and partly of money or money's worth.

(2) Where the capital distribution consists wholly of chargeable business assets, no relief shall be given under this Schedule in respect of the gains accruing on the disposal.

(3) Where the capital distribution consists only partly of chargeable business assets, the gains accruing on the disposal (aggregated as mentioned in paragraph 7(1)(a) or paragraph 8(1)(a) above) shall be reduced for the purposes of this Schedule by multiplying them by the fraction—

$$\frac{A}{B}$$

where—

A is the part of the capital distribution which does not consist of chargeable business assets; and

B is the entire capital distribution;

and it shall be to that reduced amount of aggregated gains that, in accordance with sub-paragraph (1)(b) of paragraph 7 or, as the case may be, paragraph 8 above, the appropriate proportion determined under sub-paragraph (2) of that paragraph shall be applied.

(4) Any question whether or to what extent a capital distribution consists of chargeable business assets shall be determined by reference to the status of the assets immediately before the end of the qualifying period.

12.—(1) Subject to paragraphs 9 to 11 above, in arriving at the aggregate gains under any of paragraphs 6, 7(1) and 8(1) above—

(a) the respective amounts of the gains shall be computed in accordance with the provisions of this Act fixing the amount of chargeable gains, and

(b) any allowable loss which accrues on the qualifying disposal concerned shall be deducted,

and the provisions of this Schedule shall not affect the computation of the amount of any allowable loss.

(2) Subject to the following provisions of this paragraph, in paragraphs 6 to 11 above, "chargeable business asset" means an asset (including goodwill but not including shares or securities or other assets held as investments) which is, or is an interest in, an asset used for the purposes of a trade, profession, vocation, office or employment carried on by—

(a) the individual concerned; or

(b) that individual's family company; or

(c) a member of a trading group of which the holding company is that individual's family company; or

(d) a partnership of which the individual concerned is a member.

(3) An asset is not a chargeable business asset if, on the disposal of it, no gain which might accrue would be a chargeable gain.

(4) In relation to a trustees' disposal, references in sub-paragraph (2) above to the individual shall be construed as references to the beneficiary concerned.

(5) Sub-paragraph (6) below applies if—

(a) a qualifying disposal falling within paragraph 7 or paragraph 8 above is a disposal which the individual or trustees concerned is or are treated as making by virtue of section 122 in consideration of a capital distribution; and

(b) not later than two years after the end of the year of assessment in which the individual or the trustees received the capital distribution, the individual or trustees by notice to the inspector elects or elect that that sub-paragraph should apply.

(6) If, in a case where this sub-paragraph applies in relation to a qualifying disposal, any part of the assets of the company concerned consists, as at the end of the qualifying period, of the proceeds of the sale of an asset sold not more than six months before the end of that period, then, sub-paragraph (2) above and paragraph 7 or, as the case may be, paragraph 8 above shall have effect as if, at that time—

(a) the asset remained the property of the company and was in use for the purposes for which it was used before its sale; and

(b) the proceeds of sale of the asset did not form part of the assets of the company.

The amount available for relief: the basic rule

13.—(1) Subject to the following provisions of this Part of this Schedule, on a qualifying disposal by an individual the amount available for relief by virtue of sections 163 and 164 is an amount equal to the aggregate of—

(a) so much of the gains qualifying for relief as do not exceed the appropriate percentage of £150,000; and

(b) one half of so much of those gains as exceed the appropriate percentage of £150,000 but do not exceed that percentage of £600,000;

and for the purposes of this sub-paragraph "the appropriate percentage" is a percentage determined according to the length of the qualifying period which is appropriate to the disposal on a scale rising arithmetically from 10 per cent. where that period is precisely one year to 100 per cent. where it is 10 years.

(2) In sub-paragraph (1) above "the gains qualifying for relief" means, in relation to any qualifying disposal, so much of the gains accruing on that disposal (aggregated under paragraph 6, 7(1)(a) or 8(1)(a) above) as would, by virtue of this Schedule, not be chargeable gains if—

(a) sub-paragraph (1) above had specified as the amount available for relief a fixed sum in excess of those aggregate gains; and

(b) paragraphs 14 to 16 below were disregarded.

(3) The amount available for relief by virtue of section 164 on a trustees' disposal shall be determined, subject to sub-paragraph (4) below, in accordance with sub-paragraph (1) above on the assumption that the trustees' disposal is a qualifying disposal by the qualifying beneficiary.

(4) If, on the same day, there is both a trustees' disposal and a material disposal of business assets by the qualifying beneficiary, the amount available for relief shall be applied to the beneficiary's disposal in priority to the trustees' disposal.

Aggregation of earlier business periods

14.—(1) If, apart from this paragraph, the qualifying period appropriate to a qualifying disposal ("the original qualifying period") would be less than 10 years but throughout some period ("the earlier business period") which—

(a) ends not earlier than two years before the beginning of the original qualifying period, and

(b) falls, in whole or in part, within the period of 10 years ending at the end of the original qualifying period,

the individual making the disposal or, as the case may be, the relevant beneficiary was concerned in the carrying on of another business ("the previous business") then, for the purpose of determining the amount available for relief on the qualifying disposal, the length of the qualifying period appropriate to that disposal shall be redetermined on the assumptions and subject to the provisions set out below.

(2) For the purposes of the redetermination referred to in sub-paragraph (1) above, it shall be assumed that the previous business is the same business as the business at retirement and, in the first instance, any time between the end of the earlier business period and the beginning of the qualifying period shall be disregarded (so that those two periods shall be assumed to be one continuous period).

(3) The reference in sub-paragraph (1) above to a person being concerned in the carrying on of a business is a reference to his being so concerned personally or as a member of a partnership or, if the business was owned by a company, then as a full-time working director of that company or, as the case may be, of any member of the group or commercial association of which

it is a member; and the reference in sub-paragraph (2) above to the business at retirement is a reference to that business which, in relation to the qualifying disposal, is referred to—

(a) in subsection (3), subsection (4) or subsection (5) of section 163 where the qualifying disposal is a material disposal of business assets;

(b) in subsection (5) of section 164 where that disposal is a trustees' disposal; and

(c) in subsection (7) of section 164 where that disposal is an associated disposal.

(4) Any extended qualifying period resulting from the operation of sub-paragraph (2) above shall not begin earlier than the beginning of the period of 10 years referred to in sub-paragraph (1)(b) above.

(5) If the earlier business period ended before the beginning of the original qualifying period, any extended qualifying period which would otherwise result from the operation of the preceding provisions of this paragraph shall be reduced by deducting therefrom a period equal to that between the ending of the earlier business period and the beginning of the original qualifying period.

(6) Where there is more than one business which qualifies as the previous business and, accordingly, more than one period which qualifies as the earlier business period, this paragraph shall apply first in relation to that one of those businesses in which the individual in question was last concerned and shall then again apply (as if any extended qualifying period resulting from the first application were the original qualifying period) in relation to the next of those businesses and so on.

Relief given on earlier disposal

15.—(1) In any case where—

(a) an individual makes a qualifying disposal or is the qualifying beneficiary in relation to a trustees' disposal, and

(b) relief has been (or falls to be) given under this Schedule in respect of an earlier disposal which was either a qualifying disposal made by the individual or a trustees' disposal in respect of which he was the qualifying beneficiary,

the amount which, apart from this paragraph, would be the amount available for relief on the disposal mentioned in paragraph (a) above shall not exceed the limit in sub-paragraph (3) below.

(2) In the following provisions of this paragraph—

(a) the disposal falling within sub-paragraph (1)(a) above is referred to as "the later disposal"; and

(b) the disposal falling within sub-paragraph (1)(b) above or, if there is more than one such disposal, each of them is referred to as "the earlier disposal".

(3) The limit referred to in sub-paragraph (1) above is the difference between—

(a) the amount which would be available for relief on the later disposal—

(i) if the gains qualifying for relief on that disposal were increased by the amount of the underlying gains relieved on the earlier disposal (or the aggregate amount of the underlying gains relieved on all the earlier disposals, as the case may be); and

(ii) if the qualifying period appropriate to the later disposal (as redetermined where appropriate under paragraph 14 above) were extended by the addition of a period equal to so much (if any) of the qualifying period appropriate to the earlier disposal (or, as the case may be, to each of the earlier disposals) as does not already fall within the qualifying period appropriate to the later disposal; and

(b) the amount of relief given under this Schedule on the earlier disposal or, as the case may be, the aggregate of the relief so given on all the earlier disposals.

(4) Where there is only one earlier disposal, or where there are two or more such disposals but none of them took place on or after 6th April 1988, then, for the purposes of sub-paragraph (3)(a)(i) above—

(a) if the earlier disposal took place on or after 6th April 1988, the amount of the underlying gains relieved on that disposal is the aggregate of—

(i) so much of the gains qualifying for relief on that disposal as were, by virtue of paragraph 13(1)(a) above, not chargeable gains; and

(ii) twice the amount of so much of those gains as were, by virtue of paragraph 13(1)(b) above, not chargeable gains; and

(b) if the earlier disposal took place before 6th April 1988, the amount of the underlying gains relieved on that disposal (or on each such disposal) is so much of the gains qualifying for relief on that disposal as were, by virtue of paragraph 13 of Schedule 20 to the Finance Act 1985, not chargeable gains.

(5) Where there are two or more earlier disposals and at least one of them took place on or after 6th April 1988, then, for the purposes of sub-paragraph (3)(a)(i) above, the aggregate amount of the underlying gains relieved on all those disposals shall be determined as follows—

(a) it shall be assumed for the purposes of paragraph (b) below—

(i) that the amount which resulted from the calculation under sub-paragraph (3)(a) above on the last of those disposals ("the last disposal") was the amount of the gains qualifying for relief on that disposal which were, by virtue of this Schedule, not chargeable gains (the "gains actually relieved");

(ii) that the qualifying period appropriate to that disposal (as redetermined where appropriate under paragraph 14 above) was that period as extended in accordance with sub-paragraph (3)(a)(ii) above; and

(iii) that the last disposal was the only earlier disposal;

(b) there shall then be ascertained in accordance with paragraph 13(1) above (but on the assumptions in paragraph (a) above)—

(i) how much of the gains actually relieved would, by virtue of paragraph 13(1)(a) above, not have been chargeable gains; and

(ii) how much of those gains would, by virtue of paragraph 13(1)(b) above, not have been chargeable gains; and

(c) the aggregate amount of the underlying gains relieved on all the earlier disposals is the sum of—

(i) the amount ascertained under paragraph (b)(i) above; and

(ii) twice the amount ascertained under paragraph (b)(ii) above.

(6) In this paragraph "the gains qualifying for relief" has the meaning given by paragraph 13(2) above.

(7) References in this paragraph to relief given under this Schedule include references to relief given under section 34 of the Finance Act 1965 or section 124 of the 1979 Act; and—

(a) in relation to relief given under either of those sections, paragraph (b) of sub-paragraph (1) above shall have effect as if, for the words from "which was" onwards, there were substituted "made by the individual"; and

(b) for the purpose of determining the limit in sub-paragraph (3) above where the earlier disposal (or any of the earlier disposals) was a disposal in respect of which relief was given under either of those sections—

(i) the underlying gains relieved on that disposal shall (subject to sub-paragraph (5) above) be taken to be gains of an amount equal to the relief given under the section in question in respect of that disposal; and

(ii) the reference in sub-paragraph (3)(a)(ii) above to the qualifying period appropriate to the earlier disposal shall be taken to be a reference to the qualifying period within the meaning of the section in question.

Aggregation of spouse's interest in the business

16.—(1) In any case where—

(a) an individual makes a material disposal of business assets, and

(b) the subject matter of that disposal (whether business, assets or shares or securities) was acquired, in whole or in part, from that individual's spouse, and

(c) that acquisition was either under the will or intestacy of the spouse or by way of lifetime gift and in the year of assessment in which occurred the spouse's death or, as the case may be, the lifetime gift, the individual and his spouse were living together, and

(d) as a result of the acquisition the individual acquired the whole of the interest in the business, assets, shares or securities concerned which, immediately before the acquisition or, as the case may be, the spouse's death, was held by the spouse, and

(e) not later than two years after the end of the year of assessment in which the material disposal occurred, the individual elects that this paragraph should apply,

the period which, apart from this paragraph, would be the qualifying period appropriate to that disposal shall be extended by assuming that, in the conditions which under section 163 are the relevant conditions applicable to the disposal, any reference to the individual were a reference either to the individual or his spouse.

(2) An election under sub-paragraph (1)(e) above shall be made by notice to the inspector.

(3) Where the acquisition referred to in sub-paragraph (1)(c) above was by way of lifetime gift, the amount available for relief on the material disposal concerned, having regard to the extension of the qualifying period under sub-paragraph (1) above, shall not exceed the limit specified in sub-paragraph (4) below.

(4) The limit referred to in sub-paragraph (3) above is the amount which would have been available for relief on the material disposal if—

(a) the lifetime gift had not occurred; and
(b) the material disposal had been made by the spouse; and
(c) anything done by the individual in relation to the business concerned after the lifetime gift was in fact made had been done by the spouse.

GENERAL NOTE
The Schedule provides supplementary guidance for the interpretation and operation of retirement relief under ss.163 and 164.

Para. 1
This is the general definition provision.

Para. 2
Where there is a reorganisation of a company, an election may be made within two years not to have the provisions of ss.126 or 135 applying to it.

Para. 3
Ill health involves the likelihood of permanent incapacity.

Para. 4
This contains further explanatory references.

Para. 5
The relief in its present form runs from 1985 and, except in the case of a disposal by an individual over 55, must be claimed within two years.

Para. 6
Where the disposal is of chargeable business assets (see para. 12), the disposals are aggregated and only the amount above the limit (see para. 13) is taxable.

Para. 7
The same rule applies to disposals of shares of trading companies, subject to adjustment for assets which do not qualify for relief.

Para. 8
It also applies to disposals of shares of holding companies, subject to adjustment for assets within the group which do not qualify for relief.

Para. 9
In the case of a disposal by trustees where there is more than one beneficiary with an interest in possession, the relief is restricted to the proportion attributable to the beneficiary who is retiring.

Para. 10
In the case of an associated disposal (see s.164(7)) of an asset which does not wholly qualify for relief, an appropriate apportionment is made. The receipt of consideration for the use of the asset debars relief.

Para. 11
This paragraph covers the case where relief is sought in respect of a capital distribution from a company under s.122. Relief is only given to the extent that the distribution consists of chargeable business assets (see para. 12).

Para. 12
Where a multiple disposal includes losses as well as gains, the losses are set off against the gains.
An election may be made within two years of a disposal by virtue of a capital distribution not to have the proceeds of the sale of an asset sold not more than six months before the end of the qualifying period (see para. 4(2)) taken into account, but to have the asset treated as if it were still in use.

Para. 13
This contains the important provisions governing *quantum* of relief. Basically, gains of up to

£150,000 are wholly exempt from tax and there is also a marginal relief of half of the next £450,000. For periods of ownership under 10 years, the relief is scaled down by 10 per cent. per annum.

Para. 14

This allows earlier periods qualifying for relief within the 10-year timescale and ending not earlier than two years before the last period to be aggregated with it.

Para. 15

This governs the *quantum* of relief where there was an earlier disposal qualifying for relief. Relief on the later disposal is restricted to the difference between the relief that would have been available on that disposal on the basis of the same qualifying period, less the relief already given. Where the earlier disposal was after April 6, 1988, when the marginal relief was introduced, an adjustment is made of twice the amount qualifying for that relief.

Para. 16

Where an election to that effect is made within two years of a material disposal (see s.163(3)), interests acquired from spouses may be aggregated with individuals' interests, provided on a gift that the spouse would have qualified for relief.

SCHEDULE 7

RELIEF FOR GIFTS OF BUSINESS ASSETS

PART I

AGRICULTURAL PROPERTY AND SETTLED PROPERTY

Agricultural property

1.—(1) This paragraph applies where—
(a) there is a disposal of an asset which is, or is an interest in, agricultural property within the meaning of Chapter II of Part V of the Inheritance Tax Act 1984 (inheritance tax relief for agricultural property), and
(b) apart from this paragraph, the disposal would not fall within section 165(1) by reason only that the agricultural property is not used for the purposes of a trade carried on as mentioned in section 165(2)(a).

(2) Where this paragraph applies, section 165(1) shall apply in relation to the disposal if the circumstances are such that a reduction in respect of the asset—
(a) is made under Chapter II of Part V of the Inheritance Tax Act 1984 in relation to a chargeable transfer taking place on the occasion of the disposal, or
(b) would be so made if there were a chargeable transfer on that occasion, or
(c) would be so made but for section 124A of that Act (assuming, where there is no chargeable transfer on that occasion, that there were).

Settled property

2.—(1) If—
(a) the trustees of a settlement make a disposal otherwise than under a bargain at arm's length of an asset within sub-paragraph (2) below, and
(b) a claim for relief under section 165 is made by the trustees and the person who acquires the asset ("the transferee") or, where the trustees of a settlement are also the transferee, by the trustees making the disposal alone,

then, subject to sections 165(3), 166, 167 and 169, section 165(4) shall apply in relation to the disposal.

(2) An asset is within this sub-paragraph if—
(a) it is, or is an interest in, an asset used for the purposes of a trade, profession or vocation carried on by—
(i) the trustees making the disposal, or
(ii) a beneficiary who had an interest in possession in the settled property immediately before the disposal, or
(b) it consists of shares or securities of a trading company, or of the holding company of a trading group, where
(i) the shares or securities are neither quoted on a recognised stock exchange nor dealt in on the Unlisted Securities Market, or

(ii) not less than 25 per cent. of the voting rights exercisable by shareholders of the company in general meeting are exercisable by the trustees at the time of the disposal.

(3) Where section 165(4) applies by virtue of this paragraph, references to the trustees shall be substituted for the references in section 165(4)(a) to the transferor; and where it applies in relation to a disposal which is deemed to occur by virtue of section 71(1) or 72(1) section 165(7) shall not apply.

3.—(1) This paragraph applies where—

(a) there is a disposal of an asset which is, or is an interest in, agricultural property within the meaning of Chapter II of Part V of the Inheritance Tax Act 1984, and

(b) apart from this paragraph, the disposal would not fall within paragraph 2(1)(a) above by reason only that the agricultural property is not used for the purposes of a trade as mentioned in paragraph 2(2)(a) above.

(2) Where this paragraph applies paragraph 2(1) above shall apply in relation to the disposal if the circumstances are such that a reduction in respect of the asset—

(a) is made under Chapter II of Part V of the Inheritance Tax Act 1984 in relation to a chargeable transfer taking place on the occasion of the disposal, or

(b) would be so made if there were a chargeable transfer on that occasion, or

(c) would be so made but for section 124A of that Act (assuming, where there is no chargeable transfer on that occasion, that there were).

PART II

REDUCTIONS IN HELD-OVER GAIN

Application and interpretation

4.—(1) The provisions of this Part of this Schedule apply in cases where a claim for relief is made under section 165.

(2) In this Part of this Schedule—

(a) "the principal provision" means section 165(2), or, as the case may require, sub-paragraph (2) of paragraph 2 above,

(b) "shares" includes securities,

(c) "the transferor" has the same meaning as in section 165 except that, in a case where paragraph 2 above applies, it refers to the trustees mentioned in that paragraph, and

(d) "unrelieved gain", in relation to a disposal, has the same meaning as in section 165(7).

(3) In this Part of this Schedule—

(a) any reference to a disposal of an asset is a reference to a disposal which falls within subsection (1) of section 165 by virtue of subsection (2)(a) of that section or, as the case may be, falls within sub-paragraph (1) of paragraph 2 above by virtue of sub-paragraph (2)(a) of that paragraph, and

(b) any reference to a disposal of shares is a reference to a disposal which falls within subsection (1) of section 165 by virtue of subsection (2)(b) of that section or, as the case may be, falls within sub-paragraph (1) of paragraph 2 above by virtue of sub-paragraph (2)(b) of that paragraph.

(4) In relation to a disposal of an asset or of shares, any reference in the following provisions of this Part of this Schedule to the held-over gain is a reference to the held-over gain on that disposal as determined under subsection (6) or, where it applies, subsection (7) of section 165.

Reductions peculiar to disposals of assets

5.—(1) If, in the case of a disposal of an asset, the asset was not used for the purposes of the trade, profession or vocation referred to in paragraph (a) of the principal provision throughout the period of its ownership by the transferor, the amount of the held-over gain shall be reduced by multiplying it by the fraction—

$$\frac{A}{B}$$

where—

A is the number of days in that period of ownership during which the asset was so used, and

B is the number of days in that period.

(2) This paragraph shall not apply where the circumstances are such that a reduction in respect of the asset—

(a) is made under Chapter II of Part V of the Inheritance Tax Act 1984 in relation to a chargeable transfer taking place on the occasion of the disposal, or

(b) would be so made if there were a chargeable transfer on that occasion, or

(c) would be so made but for section 124A of that Act (assuming, where there is no chargeable transfer on that occasion, that there were).

6.—(1) If, in the case of a disposal of an asset, the asset is a building or structure and, over the period of its ownership by the transferor or any substantial part of that period, part of the building or structure was, and part was not, used for the purposes of the trade, profession or vocation referred to in paragraph (a) of the principal provision, there shall be determined the fraction of the unrelieved gain on the disposal which it is just and reasonable to apportion to the part of the asset which was so used, and the amount of the held-over gain (as reduced, if appropriate, under paragraph 5 above) shall be reduced by multiplying it by that fraction.

(2) This paragraph shall not apply where the circumstances are such that a reduction in respect of the asset—

(a) is made under Chapter II of Part V of the Inheritance Tax Act 1984 in relation to a chargeable transfer taking place on the occasion of the disposal, or

(b) would be so made if there were a chargeable transfer on that occasion, or

(c) would be so made but for section 124A of that Act (assuming, where there is no chargeable transfer on that occasion, that there were).

Reduction peculiar to disposal of shares

7.—(1) If in the case of a disposal of shares assets which are not business assets are included in the chargeable assets of the company whose shares are disposed of, or, where that company is the holding company of a trading group, in the group's chargeable assets, and either—

(a) at any time within the period of 12 months before the disposal not less than 25 per cent. of the voting rights exercisable by shareholders of the company in general meeting are exercisable by the transferor, or

(b) the transferor is an individual and, at any time within that period, the company is his family company,

the amount of the held-over gain shall be reduced by multiplying it by the fraction—

$$\frac{A}{B}$$

where—

A is the market value on the date of the disposal of those chargeable assets of the company or of the group which are business assets, and

B is the market value on that date of all the chargeable assets of the company, or as the case may be of the group.

(2) For the purposes of this paragraph—

(a) an asset is a business asset in relation to a company or a group if it is or is an interest in an asset used for the purposes of a trade, profession or vocation carried on by the company, or as the case may be by a member of the group; and

(b) an asset is a chargeable asset in relation to a company or a group at any time if, on a disposal at that time, a gain accruing to the company, or as the case may be to a member of the group, would be a chargeable gain.

(3) Where the shares disposed of are shares of the holding company of a trading group, then for the purposes of this paragraph—

(a) the holding by one member of the group of the ordinary share capital of another member shall not count as a chargeable asset, and

(b) if the whole of the ordinary share capital of a 51 per cent. subsidiary of the holding company is not owned directly or indirectly by that company, the value of the chargeable assets of the subsidiary shall be taken to be reduced by multiplying it by the fraction—

$$\frac{A}{B}$$

where—

A is the amount of the ordinary share capital of the subsidiary owned directly or indirectly by the holding company, and

B is the whole of that share capital.

(4) Expressions used in sub-paragraph (3) above have the same meanings as in section 838 of the Taxes Act.

Reduction where gain partly relieved by retirement relief

8.—(1) If, in the case of a disposal of an asset—

(a) the disposal is of a chargeable business asset and is comprised in a disposal of the whole or part of a business in respect of gains accruing on which the transferor is entitled to relief under Schedule 6, and

(b) apart from this paragraph, the held-over gain on the disposal (as reduced where appropriate, under the preceding provisions of this Part of this Schedule) would exceed the amount of the chargeable gain which, apart from section 165 would accrue on the disposal,

the amount of that held-over gain shall be reduced by the amount of the excess.

(2) In sub-paragraph (1) above "chargeable business asset" has the same meaning as in Schedule 6.

(3) If, in the case of a disposal of shares,—

(a) the disposal is or forms part of a disposal of shares in respect of the gains accruing on which the transferor is entitled to relief under Schedule 6, and

(b) apart from this paragraph, the held-over gain on the disposal (as reduced, where appropriate, under paragraph 7 above) would exceed an amount equal to the relevant proportion of the chargeable gain which, apart from section 165, would accrue on the disposal,

the amount of that held-over gain shall be reduced by the amount of the excess.

(4) In sub-paragraph (3) above "the relevant proportion", in relation to a disposal falling within paragraph (a) of that sub-paragraph, means the appropriate proportion determined under Schedule 6 in relation to the aggregate sum of the gains which accrue on that disposal.

GENERAL NOTE

This provides additional rules in relation to the relief for gifts of business assets under s.165.

Para. 1

The relief is extended to agricultural property as defined in IHTA 1984, s.115(2). This might not otherwise qualify as not being used for the purposes of a trade.

Para. 2

The relief is also extended to disposals by trustees where the relevant asset is used either by the trustees or by a beneficiary with an interest in possession for business purposes. Where the asset is shares, they must be either unquoted or held as to 25 per cent. by the trustees.

Para. 3

Agricultural property is also covered under para. 2.

Para. 4

The following provisions of the Schedule apply to reduce in certain cases the amount of the gain which may be held over.

Para. 5

In the case of an asset not used for business purposes throughout the period of ownership the relief is reduced on a *per diem* basis, except where it has qualified for relief under the agricultural property provisions of IHTA 1984.

Para. 6

For buildings partly used for business purposes and partly not so used, an apportionment is made on a "just and reasonable" basis, but again not where agricultural property relief for I.H.T. applies.

Para. 7

In the case of a disposal of shares, the held-over gain is reduced to the extent that the assets of the company are not business assets, allowance being made where a subsidiary is not wholly-owned.

Para. 8

Where retirement relief is also available, the held-over gain is appropriately reduced.

Section 240   SCHEDULE 8

LEASES

Leases of land as wasting assets: curved line restriction of allowable expenditure

1.—(1) A lease of land shall not be a wasting asset until the time when its duration does not exceed 50 years.

(2) If at the beginning of the period of ownership of a lease of land it is subject to a sublease not at a rackrent and the value of the lease at the end of the duration of the sublease, estimated as at the beginning of the period of ownership, exceeds the expenditure allowable under section 38(1)(a) in computing the gain accruing on a disposal of the lease, the lease shall not be a wasting asset until the end of the duration of the sublease.

(3) In the case of a wasting asset which is a lease of land the rate at which expenditure is assumed to be written off shall, instead of being a uniform rate as provided by section 46, be a rate fixed in accordance with the Table below.

(4) Accordingly, for the purposes of the computation of the gain accruing on a disposal of a lease, and given that—

   (a) the percentage derived from the Table for the duration of the lease at the beginning of the period of ownership is P(1),

   (b) the percentage so derived for the duration of the lease at the time when any item of expenditure attributable to the lease under section 38(1)(b) is first reflected in the nature of the lease is P(2), and

   (c) the percentage so derived for the duration of the lease at the time of the disposal is P(3). then—

      (i) there shall be excluded from the expenditure attributable to the lease under section 38(1)(a) a fraction equal to—

$$\frac{P(1) - P(3)}{P(1)},$$

and

      (ii) there shall be excluded from any item of expenditure attributable to the lease under section 38(1)(b) a fraction equal to—

$$\frac{P(2) - P(3)}{P(2)}.$$

(5) This paragraph applies notwithstanding that the period of ownership of the lease is a period exceeding 50 years and, accordingly, no expenditure shall be written off under this paragraph in respect of any period earlier than the time when the lease becomes a wasting asset.

(6) Section 47 shall apply in relation to this paragraph as it applies in relation to section 46.

TABLE

Years	Percentage	Years	Percentage
50 (or more).........	100	25	81.100
49...................	99.657	24	79.622
48...................	99.289	23	78.055
47...................	98.902	22	76.399
46...................	98.490	21	74.635
45...................	98.059	20	72.770
44...................	97.595	19	70.791
43...................	97.107	18	68.697
42...................	96.593	17	66.470
41...................	96.041	16	64.116
40...................	95.457	15	61.617
39...................	94.842	14	58.971
38...................	94.189	13	56.167
37...................	93.497	12	53.191
36...................	92.761	11	50.038
35...................	91.981	10	46.695
34...................	91.156	9	43.154
33...................	90.280	8	39.399
32...................	89.354	7	35.414
31...................	88.371	6	31.195
30...................	87.330	5	26.722
29...................	86.226	4	21.983
28...................	85.053	3	16.959
27...................	83.816	2	11.629
26...................	82.496	1	5.983
		0	0

If the duration of the lease is not an exact number of years the percentage to be derived from the Table above shall be the percentage for the whole number of years plus one-twelfth of the difference between that and the percentage for the next higher number of years for each odd month counting an odd 14 days or more as one month.

Premiums for leases

2.—(1) Subject to this Schedule where the payment of a premium is required under a lease of land, or otherwise under the terms subject to which a lease of land is granted, there is a part disposal of the freehold or other asset out of which the lease is granted.

(2) In applying section 42 to such a part disposal, the property which remains undisposed of includes a right to any rent or other payments, other than a premium, payable under the lease, and that right shall be valued as at the time of the part disposal.

3.—(1) This paragraph applies in relation to a lease of land.

(2) Where under the terms subject to which a lease is granted, a sum becomes payable by the tenant in lieu of the whole or part of the rent for any period, or as consideration for the surrender of the lease, the lease shall be deemed for the purposes of this Schedule to have required the payment of a premium to the landlord (in addition to any other premium) of the amount of that sum for the period in relation to which the sum is payable.

(3) Where, as consideration for the variation or waiver of any of the terms of a lease, a sum becomes payable by the tenant otherwise than by way of rent, the lease shall be deemed for the purposes of this Schedule to have required the payment of a premium to the landlord (in addition to any other premium) of the amount of that sum for the period from the time when the variation or wavier takes effect to the time when it ceases to have effect.

(4) If under sub-paragraph (2) or (3) above a premium is deemed to have been received by the landlord, otherwise than as consideration for the surrender of the lease, then subject to sub-paragraph (5) below, both the landlord and the tenant shall be treated as if that premium were, or were part of, the consideration for the grant of the lease due at the time when the lease was granted, and the gain accruing to the landlord on the disposal by way of grant of the lease shall be recomputed and any necessary adjustments of tax, whether by way of assessment for the year in which the premium is deemed to have been received, or by way of discharge or repayment of tax, made accordingly.

(5) If under sub-paragraph (2) or (3) above a premium is deemed to have been received by the landlord, otherwise than as consideration for the surrender of the lease, and the landlord is a tenant under a lease the duration of which does not exceed 50 years, this Schedule shall apply as if an amount equal to the amount of that premium deemed to have been received had been given by way of consideration for the grant of the part of the sublease covered by the period in respect of which the premium is deemed to have been paid as if that consideration were expenditure incurred by the sublessee and attributable to that part of the sublease under section 38(1)(b).

(6) Where under sub-paragraph (2) above a premium is deemed to have been received as consideration for the surrender of a lease the surrender of the lease shall not be the occasion of any recomputation of the gain accruing on the receipt of any other premium, and the premium which is consideration for the surrender of the lease shall be regarded as consideration for a separate transaction consisting of the disposal by the landlord of his interest in the lease.

(7) Sub-paragraph (3) above shall apply in relation to a transaction not at arm's length, and in particular in relation to a transaction entered into gratuitously, as if such sum had become payable by the tenant otherwise than by way of rent as might have been required of him if the transaction had been at arm's length.

Subleases out of short leases

4.—(1) In the computation of the gain accruing on the part disposal of a lease which is a wasting asset by way of the grant of a sublease for a premium the expenditure attributable to the lease under paragraphs (a) and (b) of section 38(1) shall be apportioned in accordance with this paragraph, and section 42 shall not apply.

(2) Out of each item of the expenditure attributable to the lease under paragraphs (a) and (b) of section 38(1) there shall be apportioned to what is disposed of—

(a) if the amount of the premium is not less than what would be obtainable by way of premium of the said sublease if the rent payable under that sublease were the same as the rent payable under the lease, the fraction which, under paragraph 1(3) of this Schedule, is to be written off over the period which is the duration of the sublease, and

(b) if the amount of the premium is less than the said amount so obtainable, the said fraction multiplied by a fraction equal to the amount of the said premium divided by the said amount so obtainable.

(3) If the sublease is a sublease of part only of the land comprised in the lease this paragraph shall apply only in relation of a proportion of the expenditure attributable to the lease under paragraphs (a) and (b) of section 38(1) which is the same as the proportion which the value of the land comprised in the sublease bears to the value of that and the other land comprised in the lease; and the remainder of that expenditure shall be apportioned to what remains undisposed of.

Exclusion of premiums taxed under Schedule A etc.

5.—(1) Where by reference to any premium income tax has become chargeable under section 34 of the Taxes Act on any amount, that amount out of the premium shall be excluded from the consideration brought into account in the computation of the gain accruing on the disposal for which the premium is consideration except where the consideration is taken into account in the denominator of the fraction by reference to which an apportionment is made under section 42.

(2) Where by reference to any premium in respect of a sublease granted out of a lease the duration of which (that is of the lease) does not, at the time of granting the lease, exceed 50 years, income tax has become chargeable under section 34 of the Taxes Act on any amount that amount shall be deducted from any gain accruing on the disposal for which the premium is consideration as computed in accordance with the provisions of this Act apart from this sub-paragraph, but not so as to convert the gain into a loss, or to increase any loss.

(3) Subject to subsection (4) below, where income tax has become chargeable under section 36 of the Taxes Act (sale of land with right of re-conveyance) on any amount a sum of that amount shall be excluded from the consideration brought into account in the computation of the gain accruing on the disposal of the estate or interest in respect of which income tax becomes so chargeable, except where the consideration is taken into account in the denominator of the fraction by reference to which an apportionment is made under section 42.

(4) If what is disposed of is the remainder of a lease or a sublease out of a lease the duration of which does not exceed 50 years, sub–paragraph (3) shall not apply but the amount there referred to shall be deducted from any gain accruing on the disposal as computed in accordance with the provisions of this Act apart from this sub-paragraph and sub-paragraph (3), but not so as to convert the gain into a loss, or to increase any loss.

(5) References in sub-paragraphs (1) and (2) above to a premium include references to a premium deemed to have been received under subsection (4) or (5) of section 34 of the Taxes Act (which correspond to paragraph 3(2) and (3) of this Schedule).

(6) Section 37 shall not be taken as authorising the exclusion of any amount from the consideration for a disposal of assets taken into account in the computation of the gain by reference to any amount chargeable to tax under section 348 or 349 of the Taxes Act.

6.—(1) If under section 37(4) of the Taxes Act (allowance where, by the grant of a sublease, a lessee has converted a capital amount into a right to income) a person is to be treated as paying additional rent in consequence of having granted a sublease, the amount of any loss accruing to him on the disposal by way of the grant of the sublease shall be reduced by the total amount of rent which he is thereby treated as paying over the term of the sublease (and without regard to whether relief is thereby effectively given over the term of the sublease), but not so as to convert the loss into a gain, or to increase any gain.

(2) Nothing in section 37 of this Act shall be taken as applying in relation to any amount on which tax is paid under section 35 of the Taxes Act (charge on assignment of lease granted at undervalue).

(3) If any adjustment is made under section 36(2)(b) of the Taxes Act on a claim under that paragraph, any necessary adjustment shall be made to give effect to the consequences of the claim on the operation of this paragraph or paragraph 5 above.

7. If under section 34(2) and (3) of the Taxes Act income tax is chargeable on any amount, as being a premium the payment of which is deemed to be required by the lease, the person so chargeable shall be treated for the purposes of the computation of any gain accruing to him as having incurred at the time the lease was granted expenditure of that amount (in addition to any other expenditure) attributable to the asset under section 38(1)(b).

Duration of leases

8.—(1) In ascertaining for the purposes of this Act the duration of a lease of land the following provisions shall have effect.

(2) Where the terms of the lease include provision for the determination of the lease by notice given by the landlord, the lease shall not be treated as granted for a term longer than one ending at the earliest date on which it could be determined by notice given by the landlord.

(3) Where any of the terms of the lease (whether relating to forfeiture or to any other matter) or any other circumstances render it unlikely that the lease will continue beyond a date falling

before the expiration of the term of the lease, the lease shall not be treated as having been granted for a term longer than one ending on that date.

(4) Sub-paragraph (3) applies in particular where the lease provides for the rent to go up after a given date, or for the tenant's obligations to become in any other respect more onerous after a given date, but includes provision for the determination of the lease on that date, by notice given by the tenant, and those provisions render it unlikely that the lease will continue beyond that date.

(5) Where the terms of the lease include provision for the extension of the lease beyond a given date by notice given by the tenant this paragraph shall apply as if the term of the lease extended for as long as it could be extended by the tenant, but subject to any right of the landlord by notice to determine the lease.

(6) It is hereby declared that the question what is the duration of a lease is to be decided, in relation to the grant or any disposal of the lease, by reference to the facts which were known or ascertainable at the time when the lease was acquired or created.

Leases of property other than land

9.—(1) Paragraphs 2, 3, 4 and 8 of this Schedule shall apply in relation to leases of property other than land as they apply to leases of land, but subject to any necessary modifications.

(2) Where by reference to any capital sum within the meaning of section 785 of the Taxes Act (leases of assets other than land) any person has been charged to income tax on any amount, that amount out of the capital sum shall be deducted from any gain accruing on the disposal for which that capital sum is consideration, as computed in accordance with the provisions of this Act apart from this sub-paragraph, but not so as to convert the gain into a loss, or increase any loss.

(3) In the case of a lease of a wasting asset which is movable property the lease shall be assumed to terminate not later than the end of the life of the wasting asset.

Interpretation

10.—(1) In this Act, unless the context otherwise requires "lease"—
(a) in relation to land, includes an underlease, sublease or any tenancy or licence, and any agreement for a lease, underlease, sublease or tenancy or licence and, in the case of land outside the United Kingdom, any interest corresponding to a lease as so defined,
(b) in relation to any description of property other than land, means any kind of agreement or arrangement under which payments are made for the use of, or otherwise in respect of, property,
and "lessor", "lessee" and "rent" shall be construed accordingly.

(2) In this Schedule "premium" includes any like sum, whether payable to the intermediate or a superior landlord, and for the purposes of this Schedule any sum (other than rent) paid on or in connection with the granting of a tenancy shall be presumed to have been paid by way of premium except in so far as the other sufficient consideration for the payment is shown to have been given.

(3) In the application of this Schedule to Scotland "premium" includes in particular a grassum payable to any landlord or intermediate landlord on the creation of a sublease.

GENERAL NOTE
This Schedule contains the rules pertaining to leases, in particular leases of land.

Para. 1
A lease of land is not a wasting asset until its duration does not exceed 50 years. This period may be reduced if the lease is subject to a sub-lease not at a rackrent and the value of the lease at the end of the sub-lease exceeds the acquisition cost.

The rate at which the value of a lease of land is assumed to erode is not the straightline formula provided by s.46 but is calculated in accordance with the Table.

For example, suppose a lease with 35 years to run is acquired for £2 m. and is sold for £6 m. when it has 17 years to run. The following percentage of the base cost will be written off:

$$\frac{91.981 - 66.470}{91.981} = 27.735$$

Accordingly, £554,700 is written off the acquisition cost of £2 m. and the resultant capital gain (ignoring indexation or other adjustments) will be £6 m. less £1,445,300, leaving a chargeable gain of £4,554,700.

The same principle is applied to expenditure incurred in enhancing the value of the asset.
The rule in s.47 for wasting assets qualifying for capital allowances applies to this paragraph.

Para. 2

Where a premium is required for a lease, this is treated as a part-disposal of the freehold and the computation under s.42 includes the capitalised value of the rents in the part undisposed of.

Para. 3

The provisions of para. 2 are applied *mutatis mutandis* to the grant of a sub-lease out of a head lease, and so on.

Para. 4

Where there is a part-disposal of a lease which is itself a wasting asset by way of the grant of a sub-lease for a premium, special rules apply. An apportionment is made to the sub-lease out of each item of expenditure attributable to the lease, either in accordance with the Table, or reduced if the sub-lease is on less favourable terms to the landlord. A further apportionment may be required if the sub-lease is only of part of the land.

Paras. 5–7

Where a premium is charged on the grant of a lease of land for less than 50 years, an income tax charge may arise under Case VI of Sched. D (ICTA 1988, ss.34–39). The amount of the premium taken into account for income tax will be excluded from the C.G.T. calculation, and the income tax will reduce any C.G.T., but not so as to create a loss.

Para. 8

The duration of a lease is to be determined by reference to known or ascertainable facts. In particular, it is not to be assumed to last longer than the date when the landlord could determine it or beyond which it is likely to continue in the light of prospective adjustments to rent or to other tenant's obligations. However, if the tenant may extend the lease, this is also taken into account.

Para. 9

The foregoing paras. 2–4 and 8 apply *mutatis mutandis* to leases of other assets besides land.

Para. 10

This provides definitions of "lease" and "premium". The definition of premium was considered in *Clarke* v. *United Real (Moorgate)* (1987) 61 T.C. 353. In that case it was held that expenditure reimbursed by a prospective tenant on the development of a site constituted a premium.

Section 288   SCHEDULE 9

GILT-EDGED SECURITIES

PART I

GENERAL

1. For the purposes of this Act "gilt-edged securities" means the securities specified in Part II of this Schedule, and such stocks and bonds issued under section 12 of the National Loans Act 1968, denominated in sterling and issued after 15th April 1969, as may be specified by order made by the Treasury.

2. The Treasury shall cause particulars of any order made under paragraph 1 above to be published in the London and Edinburgh Gazettes as soon as may be after the order is made.

3. Section 14(b) of the Interpretation Act 1978 (implied power to amend orders made by statutory instrument) shall not apply to the power of making orders under paragraph 1 above.

PART II

EXISTING GILT-EDGED SECURITIES

Stocks and bonds charged on the National Loans Fund

12¾%	Treasury Loan 1992
8 %	Treasury Loan 1992
10%	Treasury Stock 1992
3 %	Treasury Stock 1992

12¼%	Exchequer Stock 1992
13½%	Exchequer Stock 1992
10½%	Treasury Convertible Stock 1992
2 %	Index-linked Treasury Stock 1992
12½%	Treasury Loan 1993
6 %	Funding Loan 1993
13¾%	Treasury Loan 1993
10%	Treasury Loan 1993
8¼%	Treasury Stock 1993
14½%	Treasury Loan 1994
12½%	Exchequer Stock 1994
9 %	Treasury Loan 1994
10%	Treasury Loan 1994
13½%	Exchequer Stock 1994
8½%	Treasury Stock 1994
8½%	Treasury Stock 1994 "A"
2 %	Index-linked Treasury Stock 1994
3 %	Exchequer Gas Stock 1990–95
12%	Treasury Stock 1995
10¼%	Exchequer Stock 1995
12¾%	Treasury Loan 1995
9 %	Treasury Loan 1992–96
15¼%	Treasury Loan 1996
13¼%	Exchequer Loan 1996
14%	Treasury Stock 1996
2 %	Index-linked Treasury Stock 1996
10%	Conversion Stock 1996
13¼%	Treasury Loan 1997
10½%	Exchequer Stock 1997
8¾%	Treasury Loan 1997
8¾%	Treasury Loan 1997 "B"
8¾%	Treasury Loan 1997 "C"
15%	Exchequer Stock 1997
6¾%	Treasury Loan 1995–98
15½%	Treasury Loan 1998
12%	Exchequer Stock 1998
12%	Exchequer Stock 1998 "A"
9¾%	Exchequer Stock 1998
9¾%	Exchequer Stock 1998 "A"
9½%	Treasury Loan 1999
10½%	Treasury Stock 1999
12¼%	Exchequer Stock 1999
12¼%	Exchequer Stock 1999 "A"
12¼%	Exchequer Stock 1999 "B"
2½%	Index-linked Treasury Convertible Stock 1999
10¼%	Conversion Stock 1999
9 %	Conversion Stock 2000
9 %	Conversion Stock 2000 "A"
13%	Treasury Stock 2000
8½%	Treasury Loan 2000
14%	Treasury Stock 1998–2001
2½%	Index-linked Treasury Stock 2001
9¾%	Conversion Stock 2001
10%	Treasury Stock 2001
9½%	Conversion Loan 2001
12%	Exchequer Stock 1999–2002
12%	Exchequer Stock 1999–2002 "A"
9½%	Conversion Stock 2002
10%	Conversion Stock 2002
9 %	Exchequer Stock 2002
9¾%	Treasury Stock 2002
13¾%	Treasury Stock 2000–2003
13¾%	Treasury Stock 2000–2003 "A"
2½%	Index-linked Treasury Stock 2003
9¾%	Conversion Loan 2003

10%	Treasury Stock 2003
3½%	Funding Stock 1999–2004
11½%	Treasury Stock 2001–2004
9½%	Conversion Stock 2004
10%	Treasury Stock 2004
12½%	Treasury Stock 2003–2005
12½%	Treasury Stock 2003–2005 "A"
10½%	Exchequer Stock 2005
9½%	Conversion Stock 2005
9½%	Conversion Stock 2005 "A"
8 %	Treasury Loan 2002–2006
8 %	Treasury Loan 2002–2006 "A"
2 %	Index-linked Treasury Stock 2006
9¾%	Conversion Stock 2006
11¾%	Treasury Stock 2003–2007
11¾%	Treasury Stock 2003–2007 "A"
8½%	Treasury Loan 2007
13½%	Treasury Stock 2004–2008
9 %	Treasury Loan 2008
9 %	Treasury Loan 2008 "A"
2½%	Indexed-linked Treasury Stock 2009
8 %	Treasury Stock 2009
2½%	Index-linked Treasury Stock 2011
9 %	Conversion Loan 2011
5½%	Treasury Stock 2008–2012
2½%	Indexed-linked Treasury Stock 2013
7¾%	Treasury Loan 2012–2015
2½%	Treasury Stock 1986–2016
2½%	Index-linked Treasury Stock 2016
2½%	Index-linked Treasury Stock 2016 "A"
12%	Exchequer Stock 2013–2017
2½%	Index-linked Treasury Stock 2020
2½%	Index-linked Treasury Stock 2024
2½%	Annuities 1905 or after
2¾%	Annuities 1905 or after
2½%	Consolidated Stock 1923 or after
4 %	Consolidated Loan 1957 or after
3½%	Conversion Loan 1961 or after
2½%	Treasury Stock 1975 or after
3 %	Treasury Stock 1966 or after
3½%	War Loan 1952 or after
10%	Conversion Stock 1996 "A"
10%	Conversion Stock 1996 "B"
12%	Exchequer Stock 1998 "B"
9 %	Conversion Stock 2000 "B"
13%	Treasury Stock 2000 "A"
10%	Treasury Stock 2001 "A"
10%	Treasury Stock 2001 "B"
9¾%	Treasury Stock 2002 "A"
9¾%	Treasury Stock 2002 "B"
10%	Treasury Stock 2003 "A"
9½%	Conversion Stock 2004 "A"
9 %	Treasury Loan 2008 "B"
9 %	Treasury Loan 2008 "C"
9 %	Conversion Loan 2011 "A"

Securities issued by certain public corporations and guaranteed by the Treasury

3 %	North of Scotland Electricity Stock 1989–92

GENERAL NOTE

Gilt-edged securities are exempt from C.G.T. (s.115). Those extant at the time this Act came into force are listed in Pt. II. The Treasury has power under Pt. I to add to the list by order, published in the London and Edinburgh Gazettes.

SCHEDULE 10

CONSEQUENTIAL AMENDMENTS

Post Office Act 1969 c. 48

1. In section 74 of the Post Office Act 1969 for "Capital Gains Tax Act 1979" there shall be substituted "Taxation of Chargeable Gains Act 1992".

Taxes Management Act 1970 c. 9

2.—(1) The Taxes Management Act 1970 shall have effect subject to the following amendments.

(2) In sections 11(1)(b), 27(1), 47(1), 57(1)(a), 78(3)(b), 111 and 119(4) for "Capital Gains Tax Act 1979" there shall be substituted "1992 Act".

(3) In section 12(2)—

(a) for "Capital Gains Tax Act 1979" there shall be substituted "1992 Act";

(b) for "19(4)" there shall be substituted "51(1)";

(c) for "71" there shall be substituted "121";

(d) for "130, 131 or 133" there shall be substituted "263, 268 or 269";

(e) for "128(6)" there shall be substituted "262(6)".

(4) In section 25(9) for "sections 64, 93 and 155(1) of the Capital Gains Tax Act 1979" there shall be substituted "sections 99 and 288(1) of the 1992 Act."

(5) The following section shall be substituted for section 28—

28.—(1) A person holding shares or securities in a company which is not resident or ordinarily resident in the United Kingdom may be required by a notice by the Board to give such particulars as the Board may consider are required to determine whether the company falls within section 13 of the 1992 Act and whether any chargeable gains have accrued to that company in respect of which the person to whom the notice is given is liable to capital gains tax under that section.

(2) For the purposes of this section "company" and "shares" shall be construed in accordance with sections 99 and 288(1) of the 1992 Act.

(6) In section 30(2)(a) and (3)(a) for "47 of the Finance (No.2) Act 1975" there shall be substituted "283 of the 1992 Act".

(7) In section 31(3)(c) for "38 of the Finance Act 1973" there shall be substituted "276 of the 1992 Act".

(8) In section 86(4) for "7 of the Capital Gains Tax Act 1979" there shall be substituted "7 of the 1992 Act".

(9) In section 87A(3) for the words from "section 267(3C)" to "1979" there shall be substituted "137(4), 139(7) or 179(11) of the 1992 Act or section 96(8) of the Finance Act 1990".

This sub-paragraph shall come into force on the day appointed under section 95 of the Finance (No.2) Act 1987 for the purposes of section 85 of that Act.

(10) In section 98—

(a) in column 1 of the Table—

(i) for "149D of the Capital Gains Tax Act 1979" there shall be substituted "151 of the 1992 Act";

(ii) for "6(9) of Schedule 1 to the Capital Gains Tax Act 1979" there shall be substituted "2(9) of Schedule 1 to the 1992 Act";

(iii) for "84 of the Finance Act 1981" there shall be substituted "98 of the 1992 Act";

(iv) for "Paragraph 7(1) of Schedule 10 to the Finance Act 1988" there shall be substituted "Section 79(6) of the 1992 Act";

(v) for "39 of the Finance Act 1990" there shall be substituted "235 of the 1992 Act";

(vi) for "12 of Schedule 16 to the Finance Act 1991" there shall be substituted "10 of Schedule 5 to the 1992 Act"; and

(b) in column 2 of the Table—

(i) for "149D of the Capital Gains Tax Act 1979" there shall be substituted "151 of the 1992 Act"; and

(ii) for "13 to 16 of Schedule 16 to the Finance Act 1991" there shall be substituted "11 to 14 of Schedule 5 to the 1992 Act".

(11) In section 118(1)—

(a) in the definition of "chargeable gain" for "Capital Gains Tax Act 1979" there shall be substituted "1992 Act"; and

(b) in paragraph (b) of the definition of "the Taxes Acts" for "the Capital Gains Tax Act 1979" there shall be substituted "the Taxation of Chargeable Gains Act 1992" and

(c) immediately after that definition there shall be inserted—

"the 1992 Act" means the Taxation of Chargeable Gains Act 1992.

Finance Act 1973 c. 51

3.—(1) In section 38(2) of the Finance Act 1973 for "In this section and in Schedule 15 to this Act" there shall be substituted "Schedule 15 to this Act shall have effect and in that Schedule".

(2) In paragraphs 2 and 4 of Schedule 15 to that Act for "38 of this Act" there shall be substituted "276 of the Taxation of Chargeable Gains Act 1992".

British Aerospace Act 1980 c. 26

4. In section 12(2) of the British Aerospace Act 1980 for "272(5) of the Income and Corporation Taxes Act 1970" there shall be substituted "170(12) of the Taxation of Chargeable Gains Act 1992".

British Telecommunications Act 1981 c. 38

5. In section 82(1) for "Capital Gains Tax Act 1979" and "Schedule 5" there shall be substituted respectively "Taxation of Chargeable Gains Act 1992" and "Schedule 2".

Value Added Tax Act 1983 c. 55

6. In Group 11 of Schedule 6 to the Value Added Tax Act 1983 for "section 147(2) of the Capital Gains Tax Act 1979" there shall be substituted "section 258(2) of the Taxation of Chargeable Gains Act 1992".

Telecommunications Act 1984 c. 12

7. In section 72(2) of the Telecommunications Act 1984 for "272(5) of the Income and Corporation Taxes Act 1970" there shall be substituted "170(12) of the Taxation of Chargeable Gains Act 1992".

Inheritance Tax Act 1984 c. 51

8.—(1) The Inheritance Tax Act shall have effect subject to the following amendments.

(2) In section 31(4G)(b) for "147 of the Capital Gains Tax Act 1979" there shall be substituted "258 of the 1992 Act".

(3) In section 79(2) for "147 of the Capital Gains Tax Act" and "147" (where it secondly appears) there shall be substituted respectively "258 of the 1992 Act" and "258".

(4) In section 97—

(a) the amendments made by section 138(6) of the Finance Act 1989 shall continue to have effect notwithstanding the repeal by this Act of that provision; and

(b) for "273(1) of the Taxes Act 1970", "272 of the Taxes Act 1970" and "273 to 281" there shall be substituted respectively "171(1) of the 1992 Act", "170 of the 1992 Act" and "171 to 181".

(5) In sections 107(4), 113A(6) and 124A(6) for "77 to 86 of the Capital Gains Tax Act 1979" there shall be substituted "126 to 136 of the 1992 Act".

(6) In section 135 for "section 78 of the Capital Gains Tax Act 1979", "84", "77(1)", "82", "85", "86", "78", "93" and "77(1) of the Capital Gains Tax Act 1979" there shall be substituted respectively "127 of the 1992 Act", "134", "126(1)", "132", "135", "136", "127", "99" and "126(1)".

(7) In section 138 for "3 to the Capital Gains Tax Act 1979" there shall be substituted "8 to the 1992 Act".

(8) In section 165 for "Capital Gains Tax Act 1979" and "59" shall be substituted "1992 Act" and "282".

(9) In section 183 for "section 78 of the Capital Gains Tax Act 1979", "77(1)", "82", "85", "86", "78", "93" and "77(1) of the Capital Gains Tax Act 1979" there shall be substituted respectively "127 of the 1992 Act", "126(1)", "132", "135", "136", "127", "99" and "126(1)".

(10) In section 187 for "153 of the Capital Gains Tax Act 1979" shall be substituted "274 of the 1992 Act".

(11) In section 194 for "3 to the Capital Gains Tax Act 1979" there shall be substituted "8 to the 1992 Act".

(12) In section 270 for "Capital Gains Tax Act 1979" and "63" there shall be substituted "1992 Act" and "286".

(13) In section 272 at the end there shall be added 'and
"the 1992 Act" means the Taxation of Chargeable Gains Act 1992.'

Finance Act 1985 c. 54

9. In section 81 for "Capital Gains Tax Act 1979" there shall be substituted "Taxation of Chargeable Gains Act 1992".

Trustee Savings Bank Act 1985 c. 58

10.—(1) In paragraph 2 of Schedule 2 to the Trustee Savings Bank Act 1985—

(a) for "Capital Gains Tax Act 1979" there shall be substituted "1992 Act"; and

(b) for "5 to the Act of 1979" there shall be substituted "2 to the 1992 Act".

(2) In paragraph 3 of that Schedule—

(a) for "II of Part II of the Act of 1979" there shall be substituted "III of Part II of the 1992 Act"; and

(b) for "12 of Schedule 5 to the Act of 1979" there shall be substituted "16 of Schedule 2 to the 1992 Act".

(3) In paragraph 4 of that Schedule—

(a) for "Act of 1979" (in three places) there shall be substituted "1992 Act";

(b) for "134" and "26" there shall be substituted respectively "251" and "30"; and

(c) for "278 of the Taxes Act" (in both places) there shall be substituted "178 or 179 of the 1992 Act".

(4) In paragraph 9—

(a) at the end of sub-paragraph (1) there shall be added—

  ' "the 1992 Act" means the Taxation of Chargeable Gains Act 1992;' and

(b) in sub-paragraph (2) for "Capital Gains Tax Act 1979" there shall be substituted "1992 Act".

Transport Act 1985 c. 67

11. In section 130—

(a) in subsection (3) for "Capital Gains Tax Act 1979" and "5" there shall be substituted "Taxation of Chargeable Gains Act 1992" and "2"; and

(b) in subsection (4) for "278 of the Income and Corporation Taxes Act 1970" there shall be substituted "178 or 179 of the Taxation of Chargeable Gains Act 1992".

Airports Act 1986 c. 31

12. In section 77(2) of the Airports Act 1986 for "272(5) of the Income and Corporation Taxes Act 1970" there shall be substituted "170(12) of the Taxation of Chargeable Gains Act 1992".

Gas Act 1986 c. 44

13. In section 60(2) of the Gas Act 1986 for "272(5) of the Income and Corporation Taxes Act 1970" there shall be substituted "170(12) of the Taxation of Chargeable Gains Act 1992".

Income and Corporation Taxes Act 1988 c. 1

14.—(1) The Income and Corporation Taxes Act 1988 shall have effect subject to the following amendments.

(2) In section 11(2) for paragraph (b) there shall be substituted—

  (b) such chargeable gains as are, by virtue of section 10(3) of the 1992 Act, to be, or be included in, the company's chargeable profits,

(3) In section 56(5) for "82 of the 1979 Act" there shall be substituted "132 of the 1992 Act".

(4) In section 119(1) after "122" there shall be inserted "and section 201 of the 1992 Act".

(5) In section 122(4)(a) for "subsection (1)(b) above" there shall be substituted "section 201(1) of the 1992 Act".

(6) After section 126 there shall be inserted—

Charge to tax on appropriation of securities and bonds

126A.—(1) In any case where—

(a) any specified securities were held by a company in such circumstances that any gain or loss on their disposal would, apart from section 115 of the 1992 Act, have been taken into account in determining the company's liability to corporation tax on chargeable gains, and

(b) those securities are subsequently appropriated by the company in such circumstances that if they were disposed of after the appropriation, any profit accruing on their disposal would be brought into account in computing the company's income for corporation tax.

then for the purposes of corporation tax any loss incurred by the company on the disposal of those securities shall not exceed the loss which would have been incurred on that disposal if the amount or value of the consideration for the acquisition of the securities had been equal to their market value at the time of the appropriation.

(2) In any case where—

(a) any specified securities were held by a company in such circumstances that any profit accruing on their disposal would be brought into account in computing the company's income for corporation tax, and

(b) those securities are subsequently appropriated by the company in such circumstances that any gain accruing on their disposal would, by virtue of section 115 of the 1992 Act, be exempt from corporation tax on chargeable gains,

then for the purposes of corporation tax the company shall be treated as if, immediately before the appropriation, it had sold and repurchased the specified securities at their market value at the time of the appropriation.

(3) In this section "specified securities" means gilt-edged securities or qualifying corporate bonds.

(7) In section 128 for "72 of the Finance Act 1985" and "(2A)" there shall be substituted respectively "143 of the 1992 Act" and "(3)".

(8) In section 129(4) for "149B(9) of the 1979 Act" there shall be substituted "271(9) of the 1992 Act."

(9) In section 137(1)(b) and (2) for "1979" there shall be substituted "1992".

(10) In section 139(14) for "32A(4) of the 1979 Act" there shall be substituted "120(4) of the 1992 Act".

(11) In sections 140(3) and 162(10)(d) for "1979" and "150" there shall be substituted respectively "1992" and "272".

(12) In section 185—

(a) in subsection (3)(b) for "29A(1) of the 1979 Act" there shall be substituted "17(1) of the 1992 Act"; and

(b) in subsection (7) for "32(1)(a) of the 1979 Act" there shall be substituted 38(1)(a) of the 1992 Act".

(13) In section 187(2) for "1979 Act" (in the definition of "market value") and "77(1)(b) of the 1979 Act" (in the definition of "new holding") there shall be substituted respectively "1992 Act" and "126(1)(b) of the 1992 Act"

(14) In section 220 for "52 of the 1979 Act" (in subsection (2)) and "1979" (in subsection (9)) there shall be substituted respectively "69 of the 1992 Act" and "1992".

(15) In section 245B(1)(c) for "273(1) of the Taxes Act 1970" there shall be substituted "171(1) of the 1992 Act".

(16) In section 251 for "150(3) of the 1979 Act" and "152 of the 1979 Act" there shall be substituted respectively "272(3) of the 1992 Act" and "273 of the 1992 Act".

(17) In sections 299 and 305 for "77(2)(a) of the 1979 Act" and "78" there shall be substituted respectively "126(2)(a) of the 1992 Act" and "127".

(18) In section 312 for "86(1) of the 1979 Act" and "150 of the 1979 Act" there shall be substituted respectively "136(1) of the 1992 Act" and "272 of the 1992 Act".

(19) In section 399—

(a) in subsection (1) for "72(1) of the Finance Act 1985" there shall be substituted "143(1) of the 1992 Act", and

(b) in subsection (5) for "72 of the Finance Act 1985" and "(2A)" there shall be substituted "143 of the 1992 Act" and "143(3)" respectively.

(20) In section 400—

(a) in subsection (2)(e) for "345" there shall be substituted "8 of the 1992 Act"; and

(b) in subsection (6) for "42 of the 1979" there shall be substituted "50 of the 1992".

(21) In section 438(8) for "149B(1)(h) of the 1979 Act" there shall be substituted "271(1)(h) of the 1992 Act".

(22) In section 440—

(a) in subsection (3) for "273 or 274 of the 1970 Act" there shall be substituted "171 or 173 of the 1992 Act"; and

(b) in subsection (5) for "1979" there shall be substituted "1992".

(23) In section 404A—

(a) in subsection (5) for "66 of the 1979 Act" there shall be substituted "105 of the 1992 Act"; and

(b) for subsection (6) there shall be substituted—

(6) In this section—

"1982 holding" has the same meaning as in section 109 of the 1992 Act;

"new holding" has the same meaning as in section 104(3) of that Act; and

"securities" means shares, or securities of a company, and any other assets where they are of a nature to be dealt in without identifying the particular assets disposed of or acquired.

(24) In section 442 for "1979 Act" there shall be substituted "1992 Act".

(25) In section 444A(8) for "88 of the 1979 Act" there shall be substituted "138 of the 1992 Act".

(26) In section 450(6) for "31 or 33 of the 1979" there shall be substituted "37 or 39 of the 1992".

(27) In section 473—

(a) in subsections (2) and (5) for "77 to 86 of the 1979" and "84" there shall be substituted respectively "126 to 136 of the 1992" and "134";

(b) in subsection (6) for "82 of the 1979 Act", "86(7), 93 or 139" and "77 to 86" there shall be substituted respectively "132 of the 1992 Act", "136(3), 147 or 99" and "126 to 136";

(c) in subsection (7) for "85 or 86 of the 1979" and "87(1)" there shall be substituted "135 or 136 of the 1992" and "137(1)" respectively.

(28) In section 477B(5) for "64(3E) of the Finance Act 1984" there shall be substituted "117(4) of the 1992 Act".

(29) In section 484(2) for "270(4) of the 1970 Act" there shall be substituted "126A(1)".

(30) In subsection (1) of section 502 in the definition of "ring fence profits" for "same meaning as in section 79(5) of the Finance Act 1984" there shall be substituted "meaning given by subsection (1A) below" and at the end of that subsection there shall be inserted—

(1A) Where in accordance with section 197(3) of the 1992 Act a person has an aggregate gain for any chargeable period, that gain and his ring fence income (if any) for that period together constitute his ring fence profits for the purposes of this Chapter.

(31) In section 505(3), (5)(b) and (6) for "145 of the 1979 Act" there shall be substituted "256 of the 1992 Act".

(32) In section 513(3) for "272(5) of the 1970 Act" there shall be substituted "170(12) of the 1992 Act".

(33) In section 574(1) for "1979" there shall be substituted "1992".

(34) In section 575—

(a) in subsection (1)(c) for "22(2) of the 1979 Act" there shall be substituted "24(2) of the 1992 Act";

(b) in subsection (2) for "78 of the 1979 Act", in both places, there shall be substituted "127 of the 1992 Act"; and

(c) in subsection (3) for "85 or 86 of the 1979 Act" and "87" there shall be substituted "135 or 136 of the 1992 Act" and "137".

(35) In section 576—

(a) in subsection (2) for "26 of the 1979 Act' and "(4)" there shall be substituted "30 of the 1992 Act" and "(5)"; and

(b) in subsection (5)—

(i) for the definition of "holding" there shall be substituted—
"holding" means any number of shares of the same class held by one person in one capacity, growing or diminishing as shares of that class are acquired or disposed of, but shares shall not be treated as being of the same class unless they are so treated by the practice of a recognised stock exchange or would be so treated if dealt with on such a stock exchange, and subsection (4) of section 104 of the 1992 Act shall apply for the purposes of this definition as it applies for the purposes of subsection (1) of that section;

(ii) for "the first proviso to section 79(1) of the 1979 Act" there shall be substituted "paragraph (a) or (b) of section 128(2)"; and

(iii) for "155(2) of the 1979 Act" there shall be substituted "288(3) of the 1992 Act".

(36) In section 710—

(a) in subsection (2A) for "64(3E) of the Finance Act 1984" there shall be substituted "117(4) of the 1992 Act"; and

(b) in subsection (13) for "82 of the 1979" shall be substituted "132 of the 1992".

(37) In section 715(8) for "5(1) of Schedule 1 to the 1979", "12(3) of the 1979" and "18(4) of the 1979" there shall be substituted respectively "1(1) of Schedule 1 to the 1992", "10(6) of the 1992" and "275 of the 1992".

(38) In section 723(8) for "18(4) of the 1979" there shall be substituted "275 of the 1992".

(39) In section 727(2) for "149B(9) of the 1979" there shall be substituted "271(9) of the 1992".

(40) In section 731(4B) for "(9) of section 137 of the 1979 Act" there shall be substituted "(8) of section 144 of the 1992 Act".

(41) In section 734(2) for "72(5)(b) of the 1979 Act" there shall be substituted "122(5)(b) of the 1992 Act".

(42) In section 740(6)(a) for "80 or 81(2) of the Finance Act 1981" there shall be substituted "87 or 89(2) of the 1992 Act".

(43) In section 757—

(a) in subsection (1) for "78 of the 1979" there shall be substituted "127 of the 1992";

(b) in subsection (2) for "1979" there shall be substituted "1992";

(c) in subsections (3) and (4) for "49 of the 1979" there shall be substituted "62 of the 1992";

(d) in subsection (5) for "85", "1979" and "86" there shall be substituted respectively "135", "1992" and "136";

(e) in subsection (6) for "85(3) of the 1979" there shall be substituted "135(3) of the 1992"; and

(f) in subsection (7) for "Chapter II of Part II of the 1979" there shall be substituted "Chapter III of Part II of the 1992".

(44) In section 758—

(a) in subsection (5) for "78 of the 1979" there shall be substituted "127 of the 1992"; and

(b) in subsection (6) for "78 of the 1979", "85", "78 as " and "82" there shall be substituted respectively "127 of the 1992", "135", "127 as" and "132".

(45) In section 759(9) for "1979" and "150(4)" there shall be substituted "1992" and "272(5)".

(46) In section 760(4) for "78 of the 1979" there shall be substituted respectively "127 of the 1992".

(47) In section 761—

(a) in subsection (2) for "2 and 12 of the 1979 Act" there shall be substituted "2(1) and 10 of the 1992 Act";

(b) in subsection (3) for "12 of the 1979 Act" there shall be substituted "10 of the 1992 Act" and at the end of that subsection there shall be inserted 'and subsection (3) of that section (which makes similar provision in relation to corporation tax) shall have effect with the omission of the words "situated in the United Kingdom" ';

(c) in subsection (5) for "14 of the 1979 Act" there shall be substituted "12 of the 1992 Act";

(d) in subsections (6) and (7)(a) and (b) for "1979" there shall be substituted "1992".

(48) In section 762—

(a) in subsection (1) for "15 of the 1979 Act" there shall be substituted "13 of the 1992 Act";

(b) in subsection (2)—

(i) for "80 to 84 of the Finance Act 1981" there shall be substituted "87 to 90 and 96 to 98 of the 1992 Act";

(ii) in paragraph (a) for "80(5)" there shall be substituted "87(6)";

(iii) in paragraph (b) for the words from the beginning to "1979" there shall be substituted 'in section 87(2) of the 1992 Act for the words "tax under section 2(2)" ';

(iv) in paragraph (c) for "80(6)" there shall be substituted "87(7)"; and

(v) in paragraph (d) for "80(8) and 83(6)" there shall be substituted "87(10) and 97(6)";

(c) in subsection (3) for "80(5) of the Finance Act 1981" there shall be substituted "87(6) of the 1992 Act"; and

(d) in subsection (4) for "80 of the Finance Act 1981" there shall be substituted "87 of the 1992 Act".

(49) In section 763—

(a) for "the 1979 Act disposal", in each place, there shall be substituted "the 1992 Act disposal";

(b) in subsections (1) and (6) for "1979" there shall be substituted "1992";

(c) in subsection (2) for "31(1)" there shall be substituted "37(1)";

(d) in subsection (3) for "computation under Chapter II of Part II of the 1979 Act of any gain" there shall be substituted "computation of the gain";

(e) in subsection (4) for "35" there shall be substituted "42";

(f) in subsection (5) for "123" there shall be substituted "162"; and

(g) in subsection (6) for "79" there shall be substituted "128".

(50) In section 776(9) for "101 to 105 of the 1979" and "103(3)" there shall be substituted respectively "222 to 226 of the 1992" and "224(3)".

(51) In section 777 in subsections (11) and (12) for "122 of the 1979" and "31 and 33 of the 1979" there shall be substituted "161 of the 1992" and "37 and 39 of the 1992" respectively.

(52) In section 824(8) for "47 of the Finance (No. 2) Act 1975" there shall be substituted "283 of the 1992 Act".

(53) In section 831—

(a) at the end of subsection (3) there shall be inserted—

' "the 1992 Act" means the Taxation of Chargeable Gains Act 1992.'; and

(b) in subsection (5) for "1979"' there shall be substituted "1992".

(54) In section 832(1) in the definition of "chargeable gain" for "1979" there shall be substituted "1992".

(55) In section 842(4) for "64, 93 and 155(1) of the 1979 Act" there shall be substituted "99 and 288 of the 1990 Act".

(56) In section 843(2) for "10 of the 1979 Act" there shall be substituted "277 of the 1990 Act".

(57) In Schedule 4—

(a) in paragraphs 1(8), 19 and 20 for "1979" there shall be substituted "1992";

(b) in paragraph 2(4) for "82 of the 1979", "85(3) of the 1979" and "86(1)" there shall be substituted respectively "132 of the 1992", 135(3) of the 1992" and "136(1)";

(c) in paragraph 7 for "1979" (in both places) there shall be substituted "1992" and for "49(1)(b)", "82", "86(1)", "85(3)" and "78" there shall be substituted respectively "62(1)(b)", "132", "136(1)", "135(3)" and "127"; and

(d) in paragraph 12 for "88 of the Finance Act 1982" there shall be substituted "108 of the 1992 Act".

(58) In paragraph 5(7) of Schedule 10 for "1979" there shall be substituted "1992".

(59) In paragraph 12(2) of Schedule 20 for "145 of the 1979" there shall be substituted "256 of the 1992".

(60) In paragraph 7 of Schedule 22 for "149B(1)(g) of the 1979" there shall be substituted "271(1)(g) of the 1992".

(61) In Schedule 23A for "149B(9) of the 1979 Act" there shall be substituted "271(9) of the 1992 Act".

(62) In paragraph 3 of Schedule 26 for "II of Part II of the 1979" there shall be substituted "III of Part II of the 1992".

(63) In Schedule 28—

(a) in paragraph 2 for "1979" and "Chapter III of Part III of the Finance Act 1982" there shall be substituted respectively "1992" and "the 1992 Act";

(b) in paragraph 3—

(i) for "paragraph 2 of Schedule 13 to the Finance Act 1982" there shall be substituted "section 56(2) of the 1992 Act";

(ii) for "123 of the 1979 Act" there shall be substituted "162 of the 1992 Act";

(iii) in sub-paragraph (3) for the words from "section" to "shall" there shall be substituted "section 165 or 260 of the 1992 Act (relief for gifts) the claim shall";

(iv) for "31(1) of the 1979 Act" there shall be substituted "37(1) of the 1992 Act"; and

(v) for "29 of the 1979 Act" there shall be substituted "16 of the 1992 Act";

(c) in paragraphs 4(3)(b) and 8(3) for "86(5) of or Schedule 13 to the Finance Act 1982" and "86(5)(b) of or Schedule 13 to the Finance Act 1982" there shall be substituted "56, 57, 131 or 145 of the 1992 Act" and for "1979" there shall be substituted "1992".

British Steel Act 1988 c. 35

15. In section 11(2) of the British Steel Act 1988 for "272(5) of the Income and Corporation Taxes Act 1970" there shall be substituted "170(12) of the Taxation of Chargeable Gains Act 1992".

Finance Act 1988 c. 39

16.—(1) The Finance Act 1988 shall have effect subject to the following amendments.

(2) In section 50(4) for "3 to the Capital Gains Tax Act 1979" there shall be substituted "8 to the Taxation of Chargeable Gains Act 1992".

(3) In section 68(4) for "29A(1) of the Capital Gains Tax Act 1979" there shall be substituted "17(1) of the Taxation of Chargeable Gains Act 1992".

(4) In section 82(3)—

(a) for "78 to 81 of the Capital Gains Tax Act 1979" there shall be substituted "127 to 130 of the Taxation of Chargeable Gains Act 1992"; and

(b) for "78", "79(1)" and "79(2)" there shall be substituted respectively "127", "128(1) and (2)" and "128(3)".

(5) In section 84 for "32(1)(a) of the Capital Gains Tax Act 1979" there shall be substituted "38(1)(a) of the Taxation of Chargeable Gains Act 1992".

(6) In section 132(6) for "272 of the Taxes Act 1970" there shall be substituted "170 of the Taxation of Chargeable Gains Act 1992".

(7) In paragraph 6(2) of Schedule 12 for "72 of the Capital Gains Tax Act 1979" there shall be substituted "122 of the Taxation of Chargeable Gains Act 1992".

Health and Medicines Act 1988 c. 49

17. In section 6(2) of the Health and Medicines Act 1988 for "272(5) of the Income and Corporation Taxes Act 1970" there shall be substituted "170(12) of the Taxation of Chargeable Gains Act 1992".

Water Act 1989 c. 15

18. In section 95 of the Water Act 1989—

(a) in subsection (4) for "Capital Gains Tax Act 1979 ("the 1979 Act")" there shall be substituted "Taxation of Chargeable Gains Act 1992 ("the 1992 Act")";

(b) in subsection (5) for "1979" there shall be substituted "1992"; and

(c) in subsection (6) for "134 of the 1979" there shall be substituted "251 of the 1992".

Finance Act 1989 c. 26

19.—(1) In section 69(9) of the Finance Act 1989 for "85(1) of the Capital Gains Tax Act 1979" and "77" there shall be substituted "135(1) of the Taxation of Chargeable Gains Act 1992" and "126".

(2) In section 70(2) of that Act for "Capital Gains Tax Act 1979" and "32(1)(a)" there shall be substituted "Taxation of Chargeable Gains Act 1992" and "38(1)(a)".

(3) In section 158(2) of that Act in paragraph (a) for "section 47(1) of the Finance (No. 2) Act 1975" there shall be substituted "section 283(1) of the Taxation of Chargeable Gains Act 1992".

(4) In section 178(2) of that Act for paragraph (i) there shall be substituted—
          (i) section 283 of the Taxation of Chargeable Gains Act 1992;

(5) In Schedule 5 to that Act in paragraphs 8 and 11 for "85(1) of the Capital Gains Tax Act 1979" and "77" there shall be substituted "135(1) of the Taxation of Chargeable Gains Act 1992" and "126".

(6) In Schedule 11 to that Act—

(a) in paragraph 1(8)(c) for "Capital Gains Tax Act 1979" there shall be substituted "Taxation of Chargeable Gains Act 1992"; and

(b) in paragraph 19 for "88 of the Finance Act 1982" there shall be substituted "108 of the Taxation of Chargeable Gains Act 1992".

Electricity Act 1989 c. 29

20.—(1) In paragraph 2 of Schedule 11 to the Electricity Act 1989 for "278 of the Income and Corporation Taxes Act 1970" and "272 of the Income and Corporation Act 1970" there shall be substituted respectively "178 or 179 of the 1992 Act" and "170 of the 1992 Act"; and at the end of that paragraph there shall be added—
          2A. In this Schedule "the 1992 Act" means the Taxation of Chargeable Gains Act 1992.

(2) In paragraph 3 of that Schedule for "117 of the Capital Gains Tax Act 1979" and "117" (where it secondly appears) there shall be substituted "154 of the 1992 Act" and "154".

(3) In paragraphs 4 and 5 of that Schedule for "Capital Gains Tax Act 1979" (in each place) there shall be substituted "1992 Act".

Capital Allowances Act 1990 c. 1

21.—(1) The following section shall be inserted in the Capital Allowances Act 1990 after section 118—

Disposals of oil licences relating to undeveloped areas
          118A.—(1) If, at the time of the material disposal of a licence, the licence relates to an undeveloped area, then, to the extent that the consideration for the disposal consists of—
          (a) another licence which at that time relates to an undeveloped area or an interest in another such licence, or
          (b) an obligation to undertake exploration work or appraisal work in an area which is or forms part of the licensed area in relation to the licence disposed of,
the value of that consideration shall be treated as nil for the purposes of this Part and Part VII.

          (2) For the purposes of this section "material disposal" means a disposal (including a part disposal) other than a disposal in relation to which sections 157 and 158 of this Act have effect.

          (3) If a material disposal of a licence which, at the time of the disposal, relates to an undeveloped area is part of a larger transaction under which one party makes to another material disposals of two or more licences, each of which at the time of the disposal relates to an undeveloped area, the reference in subsection (1)(b) above to the licensed area in relation to the licence disposed of shall be construed as a reference to the totality of the licensed areas in relation to those two or more licences.

          (4) Expressions used in this section and in section 194 of the Taxation of Chargeable Gains Act 1992 have the same meaning in this section as they have in that.

(2) In section 138 of that Act the following subsection shall be inserted after subsection (7)—
          (7A) Where the relevant event is the material disposal of a licence for the purposes of section 118A, subsection (4) above shall have effect subject to that section.

Finance Act 1990 c. 29

22.—(1) The Finance Act 1990 shall have effect subject to the following amendments.

(2) In section 116(5) for "150(1) to (3) and 152 of the Capital Gains Tax Act 1979" there shall be substituted "272(1) to (4) and 273 of the Taxation of Chargeable Gains Act 1992."

(3) In section 120 for "27 of the Capital Gains Tax Act 1979" there shall be substituted "28 of the Taxation of Chargeable Gains Act 1992".

(4) In paragraph 24 of Schedule 10 for "88 of the Finance Act 1982" there shall be substituted "108 of the Taxation of Chargeable Gains Act 1992."

(5) In Schedule 12—
(a) in paragraph 12—
      (i) for "the Capital Gains Tax Act 1979 ("the 1979 Act")" there shall be substituted "the Taxation of Chargeable Gains Act 1992 ("the 1992 Act")";
      (ii) for "5" there shall be substituted "2"; and
      (iii) for "134 of the 1979" there shall be substituted "251 of the 1992";
(b) in paragraphs 4, 5 and 6 for "1979" there shall be substituted "1992";
(c) in paragraph 7 for "115 to 119 of the 1979" there shall be substituted "152 to 156 of the 1992"; and
(d) in paragraph 10 for the definition of "the 1979 Act" there shall be substituted—
"the 1992 Act" means the Taxation of Chargeable Gains Act 1992.

Finance Act 1991 c. 31

23. In section 72(4) of the Finance Act 1991 for "5(1) of the Capital Gains Tax Act 1979" there shall be substituted "3(1) of the Taxation of Chargeable Gains Act 1992".

Ports Act 1991 c. 52

24.—(1) In section 16 of the Ports Act 1991 for "Capital Gains Tax Act 1979" and "29A(1)" there shall be substituted respectively "1992 Act" and "17(1)".

(2) In section 17 of that Act—
(a) for "1979" (wherever it occurs) there shall be substituted "1992";
(b) in subsection (6) for "278(3) or (3C) of the Income and Corporation Taxes Act 1970" there shall be substituted "178(3) or (5) or 179(3) or (6) of the 1992 Act";
(c) in subsection (7)—
      (i) for paragraph (a) there shall be substituted—
'(a) "the relevant six-year limit" means in relation to section 178(3) or 179(3) the six year period mentioned in section 178(1) or 179(1) and in relation to section 178(5) or 179(6) the six year period mentioned in 178(5)(a) or 179(6)(a); and'; and
      (ii) in paragraph (b) for "278(3)", "278(3C)" and "subsection 3(D) of that section" there shall be substituted "178(3) or 179(3)", "178(5) or 179(6)" and "section 178(6) or 179(7)" respectively; and
(d) in subsection (13) for "272 to 281 of the Income and Corporation Taxes Act 1970", "(1E) and (1F) of section 272" and "(1E)" there shall be substituted "170 to 181 of the 1992 Act", "(7) and (8) of section 170" and "(7)" respectively.

(3) In section 18 of that Act—
(a) in subsections (2) and (8) for "1979" there shall be substituted "1992";
(b) in subsection (4) for "267(1) or 273(1) of the Income and Corporation Taxes Act 1970" there shall be substituted "139(1) or 171(1) of the 1992 Act".

(4) In section 20 of that Act for "27 of the Capital Gains Tax Act 1979" there shall be substituted "28 of the 1992 Act".

(5) In section 35 of that Act—
(a) in subsection (3) for "Capital Gains Tax Act 1979" there shall be substitute '1992 Act"; and
(b) in subsection (6) for "278 of the Income and Corporation Taxes Act 1970" and "273 to 281" there shall be substituted "178 or 179 of the 1992 Act" and "171 to 181".

(6) In section 40(1) of that Act there shall be added at the end 'and
"the 1992 Act" means the Taxation of Chargeable Gains Act 1992.'

British Technology Group Act 1991 c. 66

25. In section 12(2) of the British Technology Group Act 1991 for "345 of the Income and Corporation Taxes Act 1988" there shall be substituted "8 of the Taxation of Chargeable Gains Act 1992".

GENERAL NOTE

This contains consequential amendments to other statutes, where the predecessors to this Act are referred to.

SCHEDULE 11

TRANSITIONAL PROVISIONS AND SAVINGS

PART I

VALUATION

Preliminary

1.—(1) This Part of this Schedule has effect in cases where the market value of an asset at a time before the commencement of this Act is material to the computation of a gain under this Act; and in this Part any reference to an asset includes a reference to any part of an asset.

(2) Where sub-paragraph (1) above applies, the market value of an asset (or part of an asset) at any time before the commencement of this Act shall be determined in accordance with sections 272 to 274 but subject to the following provisions of this Part.

(3) In any case where section 274 applies in accordance with sub-paragraph (2) above the reference in that section to inheritance tax shall be construed as a reference to capital transfer tax.

Gifts and transactions between connected persons before 20th March, 1985

2.—(1) Where sub-paragraph (1) above applies for the purpose of determining the market value of any asset at any time before 20th March, 1985 (the date when section 71 of the Finance Act 1985, now section 19, replaced section 151 of the 1979 Act, which is reproduced below) sub-paragraphs (2) to (4) below shall apply.

(2) Except as provided by sub-paragraph (4) below section 19 shall not apply in relation to transactions occurring before 20th March, 1985.

(3) If a person is given, or acquires from one or more persons with whom he is connected, by way of two or more gifts or other transactions, assets of which the aggregate market value, when considered separately in relation to the separate gifts or other transactions, is less than their aggregate market value when considered together, then for the purposes of this Act their market value shall be taken to be the larger market value, to be apportioned rateably to the respective disposals.

(4) Where—
  (a) one or more transactions occurred on or before 19th March 1985 and one or more after that date, and
  (b) had all the transactions occurred before that date sub-paragraph (3) above would apply, and had all the transactions occurred after that date section 19 would have applied,
then those transactions which occurred on or before that date and not more than two years before the first of those which occurred after that date shall be treated as material transactions for the purposes of section 19.

Valuation of assets before 6th July 1973

3. Section 273 shall apply for the purposes of determining the market value of any asset any time before 6th July 1973 (the date when the provisions of section 51(1) to (3) of the Finance Act 1973, which are now contained in section 273, came into force) notwithstanding that the asset was acquired before that date or that the market value of the asset may have been fixed for the purposes of a contemporaneous disposal, and in paragraphs 4 and 5 below a "section 273 asset" is an asset to which section 273 applies.

4.—(1) This paragraph applies if, in a case where the market value of a section 273 asset at the time of its acquisition is material to the computation of any chargeable gain under this Act—
  (a) the acquisition took place on the occasion of a death occurring after 30th March 1971 and before 6th July 1973, and
  (b) by virtue of paragraph 9 below, the principal value of the asset for the purposes of estate duty on that death would, apart from this paragraph, be taken to be the market value of the asset at the date of the death for the purposes of this Act.

(2) If the principal value referred to in sub-paragraph (1)(b) above falls to be determined as mentioned in section 55 of the Finance Act 1940 or section 15 of the Finance (No. 2) Act (Northern Ireland) 1946 (certain controlling shareholdings to be valued on an assets basis), nothing in section 273 shall affect the operation of paragraph 9 below for the purpose of determining the market value of the asset at the date of the death.

(3) If sub-paragraph (2) above does not apply, paragraph 9 below shall not apply as mentioned in sub-paragraph (1)(b) above and the market value of the asset on its acquisition at the date of the death shall be determined in accordance with sections 272 (but with the same modifications as are made by paragraphs 7 and 8 below) and 273.

5.—(1) In any case where—
(a) before 6th July 1973 there has been a part disposal of a section 273 asset ("the earlier disposal"), and
(b) by virtue of any enactment, the acquisition of the asset or any part of it was deemed to be for a consideration equal to its market value, and
(c) on or after 6th July 1973 there is a disposal (including a part disposal) of the property which remained undisposed of immediately before that date ("the later disposal"),
sub-paragraph (2) below shall apply in computing any chargeable gain accruing on the later disposal.

(2) Where this sub-paragraph applies, the apportionment made by virtue of paragraph 7 of Schedule 6 to the Finance Act 1965 (corresponding to section 42 to this Act) on the occasion of the earlier disposal shall be recalculated on the basis that section 273(3) of this Act was in force at the time and applied for the purposes of the determination of—
(a) the market value referred to in sub-paragraph (1)(b) above, and
(b) the market value of the property which remained undisposed of after the earlier disposal, and
(c) if the consideration for the earlier disposal was, by virtue of any enactment, deemed to be equal to the market value of the property disposed of, that market value.

Valuation of assets on 6th April 1965

6.—(1) For the purpose of ascertaining the market value of any shares or securities in accordance with paragraph 1(2) of Schedule 2, section 272 shall have effect subject to the provisions of this paragraph.

(2) Subsection (3)(a) shall have effect as if for the words, "one-quarter" there were substituted the words "one-half", and as between the amount under paragraph (a) and the amount under paragraph (b) of that subsection the higher, and not the lower, amount shall be chosen.

(3) Subsection (5) shall have effect as if for the reference to an amount equal to the buying price there were substituted a reference to an amount halfway between the buying and selling prices.

(4) Where the market value of any shares or securities not within section 272(3) falls to be ascertained by reference to a pair of prices quoted on a stock exchange, an adjustment shall be made so as to increase the market value by an amount corresponding to that by which any market value is increased under sub-paragraph (2) above.

References to the London Stock Exchange before 25th March 1973 and Exchange Control restrictions before 13th December 1979

7.—(1) For the purposes of ascertaining the market value of an asset before 25th March 1973 section 272(3) and (4) shall have effect subject to the following modifications—
(a) for "listed in The Stock Exchange Daily Official List" and "quoted in that List" there shall be substituted respectively "quoted on the London Stock Exchange" and "so quoted";
(b) for "The Stock Exchange Daily Official List" there shall be substituted "the Stock Exchange Official Daily List";
(c) for "The Stock Exchange provides a more active market elsewhere than on the London trading floor" there shall be substituted "some other stock exchange in the United Kingdom affords a more active market"; and
(d) for "if the London trading floor is closed" there shall be substituted "if the London Stock Exchange is closed".

(2) For the purposes of ascertaining the market value of an asset before 13th December 1979 section 272 shall have effect as if the following subsection were inserted after subsection (5)—

(5A) In any case where the market value of an asset is to be determined at a time before 13th December 1979 and the asset is of a kind the sale of which was (at the time the market value is to be determined) subject to restrictions imposed under the Exchange Control Act 1947 such that part of what was paid by the purchaser was not retainable by the seller, the market value, as arrived at under subsection (1), (3), (4) or (5) above, shall be subject to such adjustment as is appropriate having regard to the difference between the amount payable by a purchaser and the amount receivable by a seller.

Depreciated valuations referable to deaths before 31st March 1973

8. In any case where this Part applies, section 272(2) shall have effect as if the following proviso were inserted at the end—

Provided that where capital gains tax is chargeable, or an allowable loss accrues, in consequence of a death before 31st March 1973 and the market value of any property on the date of death taken into account for the purposes of that tax or loss has been depreciated by reason of the death, the estimate of the market value shall take that depreciation into account.

Estate duty

9.—(1) Where estate duty (including estate duty leviable under the law of Northern Ireland) is chargeable in respect of any property passing on a death after 30th March 1971 and the principal value of an asset forming part of that property has been ascertained (whether in any proceedings or otherwise) for the purposes of that duty, the principal value so ascertained shall, subject to paragraph 4(3) above, be taken for the purposes of this Act to be the market value of that asset at the date of the death.

(2) Where the principal value has been reduced under section 35 of the Finance Act 1968 or section 1 of the Finance Act (Northern Ireland) 1968 (tapering relief for gifts inter vivos etc.), the reference in sub-paragraph (1) above to the principal value as ascertained for the purposes of estate duty is a reference to that value as so ascertained before the reduction.

Part II

Other Transitory Provisions

Value-shifting

10.—(1) Section 30 applies only where the reduction in value mentioned in subsection (1) of that section (or, in a case within subsection (9) of that section, the reduction or increase in value) is after 29th March 1977.

(2) No account shall be taken by virtue of section 31 of any reduction in the value of an asset attributable to the payment of a dividend before 14th March 1989.

(3) No account shall be taken by virtue of section 32 of any reduction in the value of an asset attributable to the disposal of another asset before 14th March 1989.

(4) Section 34 shall not apply where the reduction in value, by reason of which the amount referred to in subsection (1)(b) of that section falls to be calculated, occurred before 14th March 1989.

Assets acquired on disposal chargeable under Case VII of Schedule D

11.—(1) In this paragraph references to a disposal chargeable under Case VII are references to cases where the acquisition and disposal was in circumstances that the gain accruing on it was chargeable under Case VII of Schedule D, or where it would have been so chargeable if there were a gain so accruing.

(2) The amount or value of the consideration for the acquisition of an asset by the person acquiring it on a disposal chargeable under Case VII shall not under any provision of this Act be deemed to be an amount greater than the amount taken into account as consideration on that disposal for the purposes of Case VII.

(3) Any apportionment of consideration or expenditure falling to be made in relation to a disposal chargeable under Case VII in accordance with section 164(4) of the Income and Corporation Taxes Act 1970, and in particular in a case where section 164(6) of that Act (enhancement of value of land by acquisition of adjoining land) applied, shall be followed for the purposes of this Act both in relation to a disposal of the assets acquired on the disposal chargeable under Case VII and, where the disposal chargeable under Case VII was a part disposal, in relation to a disposal of what remains undisposed of.

(4) Sub-paragraph (3) above has effect notwithstanding section 52(4).

Unrelieved Case VII losses

12. Where no relief from income tax (for a year earlier than 1971–72) has been given in respect of a loss or part of a loss allowable under Case VII of Schedule D, the loss or part shall, notwithstanding that the loss accrued before that year, be an allowable loss for the purposes of capital gains tax, but subject to any restrictions imposed by section 18.

Devaluation of sterling: securities acquired with borrowed foreign currency

13.—(1) This paragraph applies where, in pursuance of permission granted under the Exchange Control Act 1947, currency other than sterling was borrowed before 19th November 1967 for the purpose of investing in foreign securities (and had not been repaid before that date), and it was a condition of the permission—

(a) that repayment of the borrowed currency should be made from the proceeds of the sale in foreign currency of the foreign securities so acquired or out of investment currency, and

(b) that the foreign securities so acquired should be kept in separate accounts to distinguish them from others in the same ownership,
and securities held in such a separate account on 19th November 1967 are in this paragraph referred to as "designated securities".

(2) In computing the gain accruing to the borrower on the disposal of any designated securities or on the disposal of any currency or amount standing in a bank account on 19th November 1967 and representing the loan, the sums allowable as a deduction under section 38(1)(a) shall, subject to sub-paragraph (3) below, be increased by multiplying them by seven-sixths.

(3) The total amount of the increases so made in computing all gains (and losses) which are referable to any one loan (made before 19th November 1967) shall not exceed one-sixth of the sterling parity value of that loan at the time it was made.

(4) Designated securities which on the commencement of this paragraph constitute a separate 1982 holding (within the meaning of section 109), shall continue to constitute a separate 1982 holding until such time as a disposal takes place on the occurrence of which sub-paragraph (3) above operates to limit the increases which would otherwise be made under sub-paragraph (2) in allowable deductions.

(5) In this paragraph and paragraph 14 below, "foreign securities" means securities expressed in a currency other than sterling, or shares having a nominal value expressed in a currency other than sterling, or the dividends on which are payable in a currency other than sterling.

Devaluation of sterling: foreign insurance funds

14.—(1) The sums allowable as a deduction under section 38(1)(a) in computing any gains to which this paragraph applies shall be increased by multiplying by seven-sixths.

(2) This paragraph applies to gains accruing—
(a) to any underwriting member of Lloyd's, or
(b) to any company engaged in the business of marine protection and indemnity insurance on a mutual basis,
on the disposal by that person after 18th November 1967 of any foreign securities which on that date formed part of a trust fund—
  (i) established by that person in any country or territory outside the United Kingdom, and
  (ii) representing premiums received in the course of that person's business, and
  (iii) wholly or mainly used for the purpose of meeting liabilities arising in that country or territory in respect of that business.

Gilt-edged securities past redemption date

15. So far as material for the purposes of this or any other Act, the definition of "gilt-edged securities" in Schedule 9 to this Act shall include any securities which were gilt-edged securities for the purposes of the 1979 Act, and the redemption date of which fell before 1st January 1992.

Qualifying corporate bonds, company reorganisations, share conversions etc.

16.—(1) Part IV of this Act has effect subject to the provisions of this paragraph.

(2) The substitution of Chapter II of that Part for the enactments repealed by this Act shall not alter the law applicable to any reorganisation or reduction of share capital, conversion of securities or company amalgamation taking place before the coming into force of this Act.

(3) Sub-paragraph (2) above applies in particular to the law determining whether or not any assets arising on an event mentioned in that sub-paragraph are to be treated as the same asset as the original holding of shares, securities or other assets.

(4) In relation to a disposal or exchange on or after 6th April 1992, the following amendments shall be regarded as always having had effect, that is to say, the amendments to section 64 of, or Schedule 13 to, the Finance Act 1984 made by section 139 of, or paragraph 6 of Schedule 14 to, the Finance Act 1989, paragraph 28 of Schedule 10 to the Finance Act 1990 or section 98 of, or paragraph 1 of Schedule 10 to, the Finance Act 1991, or by virtue of the amendments to paragraph 1 of Schedule 18 to the Taxes Act made by section 77 of the Finance Act 1991.

Land: allowance for betterment levy

17.—(1) Where betterment levy charged in the case of any land in respect of an act or event which fell within Case B or Case C or, if it was the renewal, extension or variation of a tenancy, Case F—
(a) has been paid, and
(b) has not been allowed as a deduction in computing the profits or gains or losses of a trade for the purposes of Case I of Schedule D;

then, if the person by whom the levy was paid disposes of the land or any part of it and so claims, the following provision of this paragraph shall have effect.

(2) Paragraph 9 of Schedule 2 shall apply where the condition stated in sub-paragraph (1)(a) of that paragraph is satisfied, notwithstanding that the condition in sub-paragraph (1)(b) of that paragraph is not satisfied.

(3) Subject to the following provisions of this paragraph, there shall be ascertained the excess, if any, of—
(a) the net development value ascertained for the purposes of the levy, over
(b) the increment specified in sub-paragraph (6) below;
and the amount of the excess shall be treated as an amount allowable under section 38(1)(b).

(4) Where the act or event in respect of which the levy was charged was a part disposal of the land, section 38 shall apply as if the part disposal had not taken place and sub-paragraph (5) below shall apply in lieu of sub-paragraph (3) above.

(5) The amount or value of the consideration for the disposal shall be treated as increased by the amount of any premium or like sum paid in respect of the part disposal, and there shall be ascertained the excess, if any, of —
(a) the aggregate specified in sub-paragraph (7) below, over
(b) the increment specified in sub-paragraph (6) below;
and the amount of the excess shall be treated as an amount allowable under section 38(1)(b).

(6) The increment referred to in sub-paragraphs (3)(b) and (5)(b) above is the excess, if any, of—
(a) the amount or value of the consideration brought into account under section 38(1)(a), over
(b) the base value ascertained for the purposes of the levy.

(7) The aggregate referred to in sub-paragraph (5)(a) above is the aggregate of—
(a) the net development value ascertained for the purposes of the levy, and
(b) the amount of any premium or like sum paid in respect of the part disposal, in so far as charged to tax under Schedule A (or, as the case may be, Case VIII of Schedule D), and
(c) the chargeable gain accruing on the part disposal.

(8) Where betterment levy in respect of more than one act or event has been charged and paid as mentioned in sub-paragraph (1) above, sub-paragraphs (2) to (7) above shall apply without modifications in relation to the betterment levy in respect of the first of them; but in relation to the other or others sub-paragraph (3) or, as the case may be, (5) above shall have effect as if the amounts to be treated thereunder as allowable under section 38(1)(b) were the net development value specified in sub-paragraph (3)(a) or, as the case may be, the aggregate referred to in sub-paragraph (5)(a) of this paragraph.

(9) Where the disposal is of part only of the land sub-paragraphs (2) to (8) above shall have effect subject to the appropriate apportionments.

(10) References in this paragraph to a premium include any sum payable as mentioned in section 34(4) or (5) of the Taxes Act (sums payable in lieu of rent or as consideration for the surrender of lease or for variation or waiver of term) and, in relation to Scotland, a grassum.

Non-resident trusts

18. Without prejudice to section 289 or Part III of this Schedule—
(a) any tax chargeable on a person which is postponed under subsection (4)(b) of section 17 of the 1979 Act shall continue to be postponed until that person becomes absolutely entitled to the part of the settled property concerned or disposes of the whole or part of his interest, as mentioned in that subsection; and
(b) section 70 of and Schedule 14 to the Finance Act 1984 shall continue to have effect in relation to amounts of tax which are postponed under that Schedule, and accordingly in paragraph 12 of that Schedule the references to section 80 of the Finance Act 1981 and to subsections (3) and (4) of that section include references to section 87 of this Act and subsections (4) and (5) of that section respectively.

Private residences

19. The reference in section 222(5)(a) to a notice given by any person within two years from the beginning of the period mentioned in section 222(5) includes a notice given before the end of the year 1966–67, if that was later.

Works of art etc.

20. The repeals made by this Act do not affect the continued operation of sections 31 and 32 of the Finance Act 1965, in the form in which they were before 13th March, 1975, in relation to estate duty in respect of deaths occurring before that date.

Disposal before acquisition

21. The substitution of this Act for the corresponding enactments repealed by this Act shall not alter the effect of any provision enacted before this Act (whether or not there is a corresponding provision in this Act) so far as it relates to an asset which—

(a) was disposed of before being acquired, and

(b) was disposed of before the commencement of this Act.

Estate duty

22. Nothing in the repeals made by this Act shall affect any enactment as it applies to the determination of any principal value for the purposes of estate duty.

Validity of subordinate legislation

23. So far as this Act re-enacts any provision contained in a statutory instrument made in exercise of powers conferred by any Act, it shall be without prejudice to the validity of that provision, and any question as to its validity shall be determined as if the re-enacted provision were contained in a statutory instrument made under those powers.

Amendments in other Acts

24.—(1) The repeal by this Act of the Income and Corporation Taxes Act 1970 does not affect—

(a) the amendment made by paragraph 3 of Schedule 15 of that Act to section 26 of the Finance Act 1956, or

(b) paragraph 10 of that Schedule so far it applies in relation to the Management Act.

(2) The repeal by this Act of Schedule 7 to the 1979 Act does not affect the amendments made by that Schedule to any enactment not repealed by this Act.

Saving for Part III of this Schedule

25. The provisions of this Part of this Schedule are without prejudice to the generality of Part III of this Schedule.

PART III

ASSETS ACQUIRED BEFORE COMMENCEMENT

26.—(1) The substitution of this Act for the enactments repealed by this Act shall not alter the effect of any provision enacted before this Act (whether or not there is a corresponding provision in this Act) so far as it determines—

(a) what amount the consideration is to be taken to be for the purpose of the computation under this Act of any chargeable gain; or

(b) whether and to what extent events in, or expenditure incurred in, or other amounts referable to, a period earlier than the chargeable periods to which this Act applies may be taken into account for any tax purposes in a chargeable period to which this Act applies.

(2) Without prejudice to sub-paragraph (1) above, the repeals made by this Act shall not affect—

(a) the enactments specified in Part V of Schedule 14 to the Finance Act 1971 (charge on death) so far as their operation before repeal falls to be taken into account in chargeable periods to which this Act applies,

(b) the application of the enactments repealed by the 1979 Act to events before 6th April, 1965 in accordance with paragraph 31 of Schedule 6 to the Finance Act 1965.

(3) This paragraph has no application to the law relating to the determination of the market value of assets.

27. Where the acquisition or provision of any asset by one person was, immediately before the commencement of this paragraph and by virtue of any enactment, to be taken for the purposes of Schedule 5 to the 1979 Act to be the acquisition or disposal of it by another person, then, notwithstanding the repeal by this Act of that enactment, Schedule 2 to this Act shall also have effect as if the acquisition or provision of the asset by the first-mentioned person had been the acquisition or provision of it by that other person.

PART IV

OTHER GENERAL SAVINGS

28. Where under any Act passed before this Act and relating to a country or territory outside the United Kingdom there is a power to affect Acts passed or in force before a particular time,

or instruments made or having effect under such Acts, and the power would, but for the passing of this Act, have included power to change the law which is reproduced in, or is made or has effect under, this Act, then that power shall include power to make such provision as will secure the like change in the law reproduced in, or made or having effect under, this Act notwithstanding that this Act is not an Act passed or in force before that time.

29.—(1) The continuity of the law relating to the taxation of chargeable gains shall not be affected by the substitution of this Act for the enactments repealed by this Act and earlier enactments repealed by and corresponding to any of those enactments ("the repealed enactments").

(2) Any reference, whether express or implied, in any enactment, instrument or document (including this Act or any Act amended by this Act) to, or to things done or falling to be done under or for the purposes of, any provision of this Act shall, if and so far as the nature of the reference permits, be construed as including, in relation to the times, years or periods, circumstances or purposes in relation to which the corresponding provision in the repealed enactments has or had effect, a reference to, or as the case may be, to things done or falling to be done under or for the purposes of, that corresponding provision.

(3) Any reference, whether express or implied, in any enactment, instrument or document (including the repealed enactments and enactments, instruments and documents passed or made after the passing of this Act) to, or to things done or falling to be done under or for the purposes of, any of the repealed enactments shall, if and so far as the nature of the reference permits, be construed as including, in relation to the times, years or periods, circumstances or purposes in relation to which the corresponding provision of this Act has effect, a reference to, or as the case may be to things done or falling to be done under or for the purposes of, that corresponding provision.

GENERAL NOTE
This contains transitional provisions, Pt. I in relation to valuation and Pt. II in relation to other matters. Parts III and IV make general savings required to preserve the continuity of the law.

Section 290   SCHEDULE 12

REPEALS

Chapter	Short title	Extent of repeal
1968 c. 48	International Organisations Act 1968	In Schedule 1, paragraph 24(b).
1970 c. 10	Income and Corporation Taxes Act 1970	The whole Act.
1970 c. 24	Finance Act 1970	Sections 27 and 28. Section 29(3), (5), (6), (7) and (9). Schedule 3. Schedule 6.
1971 c. 68	Finance Act 1971	Section 55.
1973 c. 51	Finance Act 1973	Section 38(1), (3) to (5) and (8).
1974 c. 30	Finance Act 1974	Section 29.
1974 c. 44	Housing Act 1974	Section 11.
1975 c. 45	Finance (No. 2) Act 1975	Section 47. Section 58.
1976 c. 40	Finance Act 1976	Section 54. In section 131(2) the words "and capital gains tax".
1977 c. 36	Finance Act 1977	Sections 41 and 42.
1979 c. 14	Capital Gains Tax Act 1979	The whole Act.
1979 c. 47	Finance (No. 2) Act 1979	Section 17.
1980 c. 48	Finance Act 1980	Section 61(2). Sections 77 to 84. Section 117. Schedule 18.
1981 c. 35	Finance Act 1981	Section 38(3) and (4). Sections 79 to 91. In section 135 the words "capital gains tax and".

Chapter	Short title	Extent of repeal
1982 c. 39	Finance Act 1982	Section 80. Sections 83 to 88. Section 148. Schedule 13.
1982 c. 53	Administration of Justice Act 1982	Section 46(2)(f).
1983 c. 20	Mental Health Act 1983	In Schedule 4 paragraph 49.
1983 c. 28	Finance Act 1983	Section 34. Schedule 6.
1983 c. 49	Finance (No. 2) Act 1983	Section 7.
1984 c. 32	London Regional Transport Act 1984	In Schedule 6 paragraphs 7 and 8.
1984 c. 43	Finance Act 1984	Section 44. Section 50. Section 56(3) and (4). Sections 63 to 71. Section 79 to 81. In section 126(3)(b) the words "and capital gains tax". Schedules 11, 13 and 14.
1984 c. 51	Inheritance Tax Act 1984	In Schedule 8 paragraphs 9 to 12 and 23.
1985 c. 54	Finance Act 1985	Sections 67 to 72. Section 95(1)(b). Schedules 19 to 21.
1985 c. 71	Housing (Consequential Provisions) Act 1985	In Schedule 2 paragraph 18.
1986 c. 41	Finance Act 1986	Sections 58, 59 and 60.
1986 c. 56	Parliamentary Constituencies Act 1986	In Schedule 3 paragraph 6.
1987 c. 16	Finance Act 1987	Section 40. Section 68(3).
1987 c. 51	Finance (No. 2) Act 1987	Section 64. Section 73. Sections 79, 80 and 81. In Schedule 6, paragraphs 2, 4 and 5.
1988 c. 1	Income and Corporation Taxes Act 1988	Section 122(1)(b) (and the word "and" immediately preceding it), (3) and (8). Sections 345 to 347. Section 761(4). In Schedule 28, paragraph 8(4) and (5). In Schedule 29, paragraphs 10(4)(b), 12 and 15 to 28; in the Table in paragraph 32, the entries relating to the Income and Corporation Taxes Act 1970, the Finance Act 1970, the Finance (No. 2) Act 1975, the Capital Gains Tax Act 1979, Schedule 18 to the Finance Act 1980, sections 83 and 84 of the Finance Act 1981, Schedule 6 to the Finance Act 1983, section 50 of the Finance Act 1984, sections 68, 71 and 72 of, and Schedules 19 and 20 to, the Finance Act 1985 and section 58 of the Finance Act 1986.
1988 c. 39	Finance Act 1988	Section 62 to 64. Sections 96 to 104. Section 105(1) to (5). Sections 106 to 116. Section 118. In Schedule 6, paragraph 6(5). Schedules 8 to 11. In Schedule 12, paragraphs 4, 5 and 7(b). In Schedule 13, paragraphs 16, 17 and 18.

Chapter	Short title	Extent of repeal
1988 c. 48	Copyright, Designs and Patents Act 1988	In Schedule 7 paragraph 26. Section 92(3) and in subsection (4) the words "the Capital gains Tax Act 1979 or any other enactment relating to capital gains tax". Section 96(3). Section 122. Section 123(1)(a). Section 124 to 141. Section 179(1)(a)(vi). In Schedule 12, paragraph 6. Schedules 14 and 15.
1989 c. 40	Companies Act 1989	In Schedule 18, paragraph 20.
1990 c. 1	Capital Allowances Act 1990	In Schedule 1, paragraphs 3 and 9(1) to (3).
1990 c. 29	Finance Act 1990	Section 28(3). Sections 31 to 40. Sections 46 and 47. Section 54. Sections 63 to 65. Section 70. Section 72. Section 81(3) and (6). Section 83 to 86. Section 127(2). In Schedule 6, paragraph 10. Schedule 8. In Schedule 9, paragraphs 1 and 2. In Schedule 10, paragraphs 28 and 29(2) and (3). In Schedule 12, paragraph 2(2). In Schedule 14, paragraphs 17, 18 and 19(2), (3) and (4). In Schedule 18, paragraph 3.
1991 c. 21	Disability Living Allowance and Disability Working Allowance Act 1991	In Schedule 2, paragraph 9.
1991 c. 31	Finance Act 1991	Section 57(4). Section 67. Section 77(2). Section 78(2), (3), (6) and (7). Sections 83 to 102. In Schedule 6, paragraph 6. In Schedule 7, paragraphs 14 and 15. In Schedule 10, paragraphs 1 and 4. Schedules 16 to 18.
1991 c. 52	Ports Act 1991	Section 18(8)(a).
1992 c. 6	Social Security (Consequential Provisions) Act 1992	In Schedule 2, paragraph 51.

Statutory Instruments

Number	Title	Extent of repeal
S.I. 1979/1231	Capital Gains Tax (Gilt-edged Securities) (No. 1) Order 1979	The whole Order.
S.I. 1979/1676	Capital Gains Tax (Gilt-edged Securities) (No. 2) Order 1979	The whole order

Number	Title	Extent of repeal
S.I. 1980/507	Capital Gains Tax (Gilt-edged Securities) (No. 1) Order 1980	The whole Order.
S.I. 1980/922	Capital Gains Tax (Gilt-edged Securities) (No. 2) Order 1980	The whole Order.
S.I. 1980/1910	Capital Gains Tax (Gilt-edged Securities) (No. 3) Order 1980	The whole Order.
S.I. 1981/615	Capital Gains Tax (Gilt-edged Securities) (No. 1) Order 1981	The whole Order.
S.I. 1981/1879	Capital Gains Tax (Gilt-edged Securities) (No. 2) Order 1981	The whole Order.
S.I. 1982/413	Capital Gains Tax (Gilt-edged Securities) (No. 1) Order 1982	The whole Order.
S.I. 1982/1774	Capital Gains Tax (Gilt-edged Securities) (No. 2) Order 1982	The whole Order.
S.I. 1983/1774	Capital Gains Tax (Gilt-edged Securities) Order 1983	The whole Order.
S.I. 1984/1966	Capital Gains Tax (Gilt-edged Securities) Order 1984	The whole Order.
S.I. 1986/12	Capital Gains Tax (Gilt-edged Securities) Order 1986	The whole Order.
S.I. 1987/259	Capital Gains Tax (Gilt-edged Securities) Order 1987	The whole Order.
S.I. 1988/360	Capital Gains Tax (Gilt-edged Securities) Order 1988	The whole Order.
S.I. 1989/944	Capital Gains Tax (Gilt-edged Securities) Order 1989	The whole Order.
S.I. 1991/2678	Capital Gains Tax (Gilt-edged Securities) Order 1991	The whole Order.

GENERAL NOTE

The major repeals effected are the remaining provisions of the Income and Corporation Taxes Act 1970, dealing with corporation tax on chargeable gains, and the whole of the Capital Gains Tax Act 1979.

TABLE OF DERIVATIONS

Note: The following abbreviations are used in this Table:

1970	=	Income and Corporation Taxes Act 1970 c. 10.
1970(F)	=	Finance Act 1970 c. 24.
1973	=	Finance Act 1973 c. 51.
HA 1974	=	Housing Act 1974 c. 44.
1975(2)	=	Finance (No. 2) Act 1975 c. 45.
1976	=	Finance Act 1976 c. 40.
1977	=	Finance Act 1977 c. 36.
1979	=	Capital Gains Tax Act 1979 c. 14.
1979(2)	=	Finance (No. 2) Act 1979 c. 47.

1980	= Finance Act 1980 c. 48.
1981	= Finance Act 1981 c. 35.
1982	= Finance Act 1982 c. 39.
AJA 1982	= Administration of Justice Act 1982 c. 53.
1983(2)	= Finance (No. 2) Act 1983 c. 49.
LRTA 1984	= London Regional Transport Act 1984 c. 32.
1984	= Finance Act 1984 c. 43.
ITA	= Inheritance Tax Act 1984 c. 51.
CCCPA	= Companies Consolidation (Consequential Provisions) Act 1985 c. 9.
1985	= Finance Act 1985 c.54.
HCPA	= Housing (Consequential Provisions) Act 1985 c. 71.
1986	= Finance Act 1986 c. 41.
PCA	= Parliamentary Constituencies Act 1986 c. 56.
1987	= Finance Act 1987 c. 16.
1987(2)	= Finance (No. 2) Act 1987 c. 51.
ICTA	= Income and Corporation Taxes Act 1988 c. 1.
1988	= Finance Act 1988 c. 39.
CDPA 1988	= Copyright, Designs and Patents Act 1988 c. 48.
HA 1988	= Housing Act 1988 c. 50.
1989	= Finance Act 1989 c. 26.
CAA	= Capital Allowances Act 1990 c. 1.
1990	= Finance Act 1900 c. 29.
DLA 1991	= Disability Living Allowance and Disability Working Allowance Act 1991 c. 21 Sch. 2 §9; Disability Living Allowance and Disability Working Allowance (Northern Ireland Consequential Amendments) Order 1991 Art. 2.
1991	= Finance Act 1991 c. 31.
SSCP	= Security Security (Consequential Provisions) Act 1992 c. 6; Security Security (Consequential Provisions) Act (Northern Ireland) 1992 c. 9.
SI 1988/744	= The Finance (No. 2) Act 1987 (Commencement) Order 1988.
SI 1989/1299	= The Income Tax (Stock Lending) Regulations 1989.
SI 1989/1788	= The Finance Act 1989 (Repeal of Tithe Redemption Enactments) (Appointed Day) Order 1989.
SI 1991/736	= Capital Gains (Annual Exempt Amount) Order 1991.

Provision of Bill	Derivation
1	1979 s.1.
2(1)	1979 s.2.
(2)	1979 s.4(1).
(3)	1979 s.29(5).
3(1)	1979 s.5(1); 1980 s.77(2); 1982 s.80(1).
(2)–(4)	1979 s.5(1A), (1B), (1C); 1982 s.80(2); S.I. 1991/736.
(5), (6)	1979 s.5(4), (5); 1982 s.80(1).
(7)	1979 Sch. 1 §4.
(8)	1979 s.5(6).
4	1988 s.98.
5	1988 s.100.
6	1988 s.102; 1991 Sch. 6 §6.
7	1979 s.7; 1980 s.61(2).
8	ICTA s.345, 834.
9	1979 s.18(1)–(3).
10(1)	1979 s.12(1).
(2)	1979 s.12(1A); 1989 s.128(2).
(3)	ICTA s.11(2)(b), 6(4).
(4)	1979 s.12(2).
(5)	1979 s.12(2A); 1989 s.126(2).
(6)	1979 s.12(3).
11	1979 s.18(5)–(8); ICTA Sch. 29 §16.
12	1979 s.14.
13(1)–(9)	1979 s.15(1)–(9).
(10)	1981 s.85.
(11)	1979 s.15(10).
14	1979 s.16.

Provision of Bill	Derivation
15	1979 s.28(1), (2), 30; 1982 s.86.
16	1979 s.29(1)–(4).
17	1979 s.29A(1), (2); 1981 s.90.
18	1979 s.62; 1981 s.90(3)(a), (b).
19	1985 s.71(1)–(4), (6), (7).
20	1985 Sch. 21.
21	1979 s.19(1), (2).
22	1979 s.20.
23	1979 s.21.
24	1979 s.22.
25	1989 s.127; 1990 Sch. 9 §2.
26	1979 s.23.
27	1979 s.24.
28	1979 s.27.
29	1979 s.25.
30(1)	1979 s.26(1); 1989 s.135(1).
(2)	1979 s.26(1A); 1989 s.135(1).
(3)–(7)	1979 s.26(2)–(6).
(8)	1979 s.26(7); 1989 s.135(2).
(9)	1979 s.26(8); 1989 s.135(3).
31	1979 s.26A; 1989 s.136.
32	1979 s.26B; 1989 s.136.
33	1979 s.26C; 1989 s.136.
34	1979 s.26D; 1989 s.137.
35	1988 s.96; Sch. 8 §1(3); 1989 Sch. 15 §4(2); 1990 s.70(7)(b), Sch. 12 §2(2); 1979 s.28(3); 1991 s.78(7).
36	1988 s.97.
37(1)–(3)	1979 s.31(1)–(3); CAA Sch. 1 §3.
(4)	1979 s.31(4); ICTA Sch. 29 §17.
38	1979 s.32.
39	1979 s.33; ICTA Sch. 29 §19.
40	1970 s.269; 1981 s.38(3), (4).
41	1979 s.34; 1988 Sch. 13 §16; CAA Sch. 1 §3.
42	1979 s.35.
43	1979 s.36.
44	1979 s.37.
45	1979 s.127.
46	1979 s.38.
47	1979 s.39.
48	1979 s.40(2).
49	1979 s.41.
50	1979 s.42.
51	1979 s.19(4), (5).
52	1979 s.43.
53	1982 s.86(2)–(4), (6); 1985 Sch. 19 §1.
54	1982 s.87; 1985 Sch. 19 §2.
55(1)	1985 s.68(4).
(2)	1985 s.68(5); 1988 Sch. 8 §11.
(3)	1985 s.68(5A); 1988 s.118.
(4)	1985 s.68(6).
(5)	1985 s.68(7), (7A): 1988 s.118; 1989 Sch. 15 §4; 1990 s.70(7); 1991 s.78(6), 99(1).
(6)	1985 s.68(8).
56(1)	1982 Sch. 13 §1; 1985 Sch. 19 §5(1).
(2)	1982 Sch. 13 §2; 1985 Sch. 19 §5(2)(b).
57	1982 Sch. 13 §4.
58	1979 s.44.
59	1979 s.60.
60	1979 s.46.
61	1979 s.99; AJA 1982 s.46(2)(f).
62	1979 s.49; 1981 s.90(3)(a).
63	1979 s.50.
64	1979 s.47.

Provision of Bill	Derivation
65	1979 s.48.
66	1979 s.61.
67	1980 s.79; 1979 s.56A; 1982 s.84; 1989 s.124(3).
68	1979 s.51.
69	1979 s.52.
70	1979 s.53; 1981 s.86.
71	1979 s.54; 1981 s.87.
72	1979 s.55(1), (3)–(6); 1982 s.84.
73(1)	1979 s.56(1); 1981 s.87.
(2), (3)	1979 s.56(1A), (1B); 1982 s.84(2).
74	1979 s.56A; 1982 s.84; 1989 Sch. 14 §6(1).
75	1979 s.57.
76	1979 s.58.
77	1988 Sch. 10 §1–4.
78(1), (2)	1988 Sch. 10 §5(1), (2).
(3)	1988 Sch. 10 §5(3); 1991 s.89(3).
79	1988 Sch. 10 §6–9.
80	1991 s.83.
81	1991 s.84.
82	1991 s.85.
83	1991 s.86.
84	1991 s.87.
85(1)	1981 s.88(1).
(2)–(9)	1991 s.88(1)–(8).
86(1)–(3)	1991 Sch. 16 §1(1)–(3).
(4)	1991 Sch. 16 §2.
(5)	—
87(1), (2)	1981 s.80(1), (2).
(3)	1980 s.80(2A); 1991 s.89(2).
(4)–(7)	1981 s.80(3)–(6).
(8)	1981 s.80(6A); 1991 Sch. 18 §1.
(9)	1981 s.80(7).
(10)	1981 s.80(1), (8); 1984 s.70(3).
88	1981 s.80A; 1991 Sch. 18 §2.
89	1981 s.81; 1991 Sch. 18 §3.
90	1981 s.82.
91	1991 Sch. 17 §4.
92(1)	1991 Sch. 17 §2(3).
(2)	1991 Sch. 17 §(2), (4), (5).
(3)	1991 Sch. 17 §3(1), (2).
(4)–(6)	1991 Sch. 17 §3(3)–(5).
93(1)	1991 Sch. 17 §5(1)(a), (b), (d), 6(1)(a), (b), (d).
(2)	1991 Sch. 17 §5(1)(c), (2), (3).
(3)	1991 Sch. 17 §6(1)(c), (2), (3).
(4)	1991 Sch. 17 §7.
94	1991 Sch. 17 §8.
95	1991 Sch. 17 §9.
96	1981 s.82A; 1991 Sch. 18 §4.
97(1)(a)	1981 s.83(1), (11); 1991 Sch. 17 §1(c), 18 §6(2).
(b)	1981 s.83(1A); 1991 Sch. 18 §6(3).
(2)–(6)	1981 s.83(2)–(6); 1990 Sch. 14 §18; 1991 Sch. 18 §6(4), (5).
(7)	1981 s.83(7); 1984 s.71; 1991 Sch. 18 §6(5).
(8)–(10)	1981 s.83(8)–(10); 1991 Sch. 18 §5.
98	1981 s.84.
99(1)	1979 s.93.
(2)	1979 s.92(1)(a), (b); 1987 s.40(3).
(3)	1979 s.92(2), (3)(a); 1987 s.40(4).
100(1)	1980 s.81(1).
(2)	1979 s.96.
(3)	1979 s.92(1)(d).
101	1979 s.98; 1980 s.81.
102	1989 s.140.

Provision of Bill	Derivation
103	1990 s.54.
104(1), (2)	1985 Sch. 19 §8, 9(1), 17(1).
(3)	1979 s.66(3), (4); 1985 s.68(9), (10), Sch. 19 §8(1)(c), 9(3).
(4)	1985 Sch. 19 §8(2).
(5)	1985 Sch. 19 §8(3).
(6)	1985 Sch. 19 §10.
105	1979 s.66(1), (2); 1985 Sch. 19 §17(2).
106	1975(2) s.58; 1979 Sch. 7.
107(1), (2)	1985 Sch. 19 §16(1), (2).
(3)–(6)	1985 Sch. 19 §18
(7)–(9)	1985 Sch. 19 §19.
108	1982 s.88; 1985 Sch. 19 §3.
109(1)–(3)	1982 Sch. 13 §6(1), (2), 7(1), 8(1), (2)(a), (3), 9, 10.
(4), (5)	1985 Sch. 19 §6(3), (4).
(6)	1985 Sch. 19 §7(2), (3).
110(1)–(3)	1985 Sch. 19 §11.
(4)	1985 Sch. 19 §12.
(5)–(9)	1985 Sch. 19 §13.
(10), (11)	1985 Sch. 19 §14.
111	1988 s.113.
112	1985 Sch. 19 §21(2), (3), 20.
113	1982 Sch. 13 §6, 1985 Sch. 19 §5(5).
114	1985 Sch. 19 §15.
115	1979 s.67; 1986 s.59.
116(1)	1984 s.64(7).
(2)–(4)	1984 Sch. 13 §7.
(5)–(8)	1984 Sch. 13 §8.
(9)	1984 Sch. 13 §9.
(10), (11)	1984 Sch. 13 §10; 1985 s.67(2)(c); 1989 s.139; 1990 s.70(6).
(12)–(14)	1984 Sch. 13 §11.
(15)	1984 Sch. 13 §12; 1990 s.85.
117(1)	1984 s.64(2)(b), (c), (2A); 1991 s.98.
(2)	1984 s.64(3).
(3)	1984 s.64(3A)–(3D); 1989 s.139; 1990 Sch. 10 §28.
(4)–(6)	1984 s.64(3E)–(3G); 1991 Sch. 10 §1.
(7), (8)	1984 s.64(4), (5); 1989 Sch. 14 §6(4).
(9)	1984 s.64(5A)–(5D); 1989 s.139; 1990 Sch. 10 §28.
(10)	1984 s.64(6); 1989 s.139.
(11)(a)	1984 s.64(8).
(11)(b), (12)	1984 s.64(9)–(11); 1991 Sch. 10 §1.
(13)	1991 Sch. 10 §1(5).
118	1979 s.132A; ICTA Sch. 29 §23; 1989 s.96(3).
119	1979 s.33A; ICTA Sch. 29 §20.
120(1)	1988 s.84.
(2)–(7)	1979 s.32A; ICTA Sch. 29 §18.
121	1979 s.71.
122	1979 s.72.
123	1979 s.73.
124	1979 s.74.
125	1979 s.75; 1988 Sch. 8 §7.
126	1979 s.77; 1982 Sch. 13 §5(3).
127	1979 s.78.
128(1)	1979 s.79(1).
(2)	1979 s.79(1), first and second provisos; 1981 s.91.
(3), (4)	1979 s.79(2), (3).
129	1979 s.80.
130	1979 s.81.
131	1982 Sch. 13 §5(1), (2).
132	1979 s.82; 1982 Sch. 13 §5(3).
133	1979 s.83.
134(1)	1979 s.84(1).
(2)	1979 s.84(2), (3).

Provision of Bill	Derivation
(3)	1979 s.84(4); 1985 s.67(2).
(4)–(6)	1979 s.84(5)–(7).
135	1979 s.85; 1982 Sch. 13 §5(3).
136	1979 s.86.
137	1979 s.87; 1987(2) Sch. 6 §5.
138	1979 s.88.
139(1), (2)	1970 s.267(1), (2); 238(4).
(3)	1970 s.267(2A); 1990 s.65(1).
(4)	1970 s.267(3); 1980 s.81(2).
(5)–(7)	1970 s.267(3A)–(3C); 1977 s.41.
(8)	1987(2) Sch. 6 §2.
(9)	1970 s.267(4).
140	1970 s.268A; 1977 s.42.
141	1979 s.89; 1981 s.91(2).
142	1979 s.90; 1981 s.90(3).
143(1), (2)	1985 s.72(1), (2); 1987(2) s.81(1), (2).
(3), (4)	1985 s.72(2A), (2B); 1987(2) s.81(3).
(5), (6)	1985 s.72(3), (4).
144(1)–(4)	1979 s.137(1)–(4); 1987(2) s.81.
(5)–(9)	1979 s.137(6)–(10); 1987(2) s.81.
145	1982 Sch. 13 §7.
146	1979 s.138; 1980 s.84(5), (6); 1987(2) s.81.
147	1979 s.139.
148	1991 s.102.
149	1991 Sch. 10 §4.
150	1979 s.149C; 1985 Sch. 19 §16(3); ICTA Sch. 29 §26; 1990 Sch. 14 §17; 1991 s.99(2).
151(1), (2)	1979 s.149D(1), (2); ICTA Sch. 29 §26.
(3)	1979 s.149D(2A); 1988 s.116.
152(1), (2)	1979 s.115(1), (2).
(3), (4)	1979 s.115(3).
(5)–(8)	1979 s.115(4)–(7).
(9)	1979 s.115(7A); 1988 Sch. 8 §9.
(10), (11)	1979 s.115(8), (9).
153	1979 s.116.
154(1), (2)	1979 s.117(1), (2); 1990 s.40(2).
(3), (4)	1979 s.117(2A), (3); 1990 s.40(3), (4).
(5)–(7)	1979 s.117(4)–(6).
155	1979 s.118; 1988 s.112.
156	1979 s.119.
157	1979 s.120; 1985 s.70(9).
158	1979 s.121.
159	1989 s.129.
160	1989 s.133.
161	1979 s.122.
162	1979 s.123.
163	1985 s.69; 1991 s.100.
164	1985 s.70(1)–(8); 1991 s.100.
165(1), (2)	1979 s.126(1), (1A); 1989 Sch. 14 §1.
(3)	1979 s.126(2); 1985 s.70(9); 1989 Sch. 14 §1(3).
(4)–(6)	1979 s.126(3)–(5).
(7)–(9)	1979 s.126(6)–(8); 1981 s.90(3)(a); 1985 s.70(9).
(10), (11)	1979 s.126(9), (10); 1989 Sch. 14 §1.
166	1979 s.126A; 1989 Sch. 14 §2.
167	1979 s.126B; 1989 Sch. 14 §2.
168	1981 s.79; 1989 Sch. 14 §6; 1991 s.92(2).
169	1986 s.58; 1989 Sch. 14 §6.
170(1)	1970 s.238(4); 1988 Sch. 14 Part V Note 3
(2)	1970 s.272(1); 1989 s.138(1); 1990 s.70(2).
(3)–(8)	1970 s.272(1A)–(1F); 1989 s.138(2); 1990 s.86.
(9)	1970 s.272(2); 1987(2) s.79; CCCPA Sch. 2.
(10), (11)	1970 s.272(3), (4): 1989 s.138(3), (4).

Provision of Bill	Derivation
(12), (13)	1970 s.272(5).
(14)	1970 s.272(6): LRTA 1984 Sch. 6 §7.
171(1)	1970 s.273(1).
(2)	1970 s.273(2); 1980 s.81(4); 1987(2) s.64(3); 1990 s.65(2).
(3)	1970 s.273(2A); 1988 s.115.
(4)	1970 s.273(3).
172	1970 s.273A; 1990 s.70.
173	1970 s.274.
174(1)–(3)	1970 s.275(1), (1A), (1B); 1990 s.70(3).
(4)	1970 s.275(2).
(5)	1970 s.275(3); 1980 s.81(5).
175(1)	1970 s.276(1); 1987(2) s.64(4).
(2)	1970 s.276(1A); 1987(2) s.64(4); 1990 s.65(3).
(3)	1970 s.276(2).
(4)	1990 s.65(6).
176	1970 s.280; CCCPA Sch. 2; 1988 Sch. 8 §6.
177	1970 s.281; 1990 s.70(4).
178(1)–(3)	1970 s.278(1)–(3).
(4)–(6)	1970 s.278(3B)–(3D); 1989 s.138(5).
(7)	1970 s.278(3F); 1989 s.138(5).
(8)–(10)	1970 s.278(4)–(6).
179(1)–(3)	1970 s.278(1)–(3); 1987(2) Sch. 6 §4(2).
(4)	1970 s.278(3A); 1987(2) Sch. 6 §4(2).
(5)–(9)	1970 s.278(3B)–(3F); 1989 s.138(5).
(10)	1970 s.278(4).
(11)	1970 s.278(5); 1987(2) Sch. 6 §4(3).
(12)	1970 s.278(5A); 1987(2) Sch. 6 §4(4).
(12)	1970 s.278(6).
180(1), (2)	1970 s.278(8); 1987(2) s.95(2); 1989 s.§138(7).
(3)–(7)	1989 s.138(8)–(12).
181	1970 s.278A; 1970(F) s.27.
182	1988 Sch. 11§1, 2.
183	1988 Sch. 11§3.
184	1988 Sch. 11§4, 5, 6; 1990 s.70(8).
185	1988 s.105(1)–(5).
186	1988 s.106.
187	1988 s.107.
188	1989 s.132.
189	ICTA s.346.
190	ICTA s.347.
191	1989 s.134.
192	1980 s.117, Sch. 18 §9, 10, 15, 23.
193	1987(2) s.80.
194	1988 s.62.
195	1988 s.63.
196	1988 s.64.
197	1984 s.79.
198	1984 s.80.
199	1989 s.131.
200	1990 s.64.
201(1), (2)	ICTAs. s.122(1).
(3)	ICTAs. s.122(3).
(4)	ICTAs. s.122(8).
202(1), (2)	1970(F) s.29(5), Sch. 6 §3.
(3), (4)	1970(F) Sch. 6 §4.
(5), (6)	1970(F) Sch. 6 §5.
(7), (8)	1970(F) Sch. 6 §6.
(9)–(11)	1970(F) Sch. 6 §7.
203	1970(F) s.29(6), (7), (9), Sch. 6 §8, 9.
204	1979 s.140, 149A(2).
205	1979 s.141.
206	1979 s.142; 1988, s.101.

Provision of Bill	Derivation
207(1)–(3)	1979 s.142A(1)–(3); ICTA Sch. 29 §24.
(4), (5)	1979 s.142A(4A), (4B); 1989 s.91; S.I. 1989/1299.
(6)	1979 s.142A(4).
208	1985 Sch. 19 §22, 23.
209	1979 s.142A(5–7); 1989 s.92.
210	1979 s.143.
211	1970 s.267A; 1990 Sch. 9 §1.
212	1990 s.46; 1991 Sch. 7 §14.
213	1990 s.47.
214	1990 Sch. 8; 1991 Sch. 7 §15.
215	1979 s.149A(1); ICTA Sch. 29 §26.
216	1988 Sch. 12 §1, 4.
217	1988 Sch. 12 §5.
218	1970 s.342; HCPA Sch. 2 §18; 1991 s.95, 96.
219	1970 s.342A; HA 1974 s.11; HCPA Sch. 2 §18; 1991 s.95, 96.
220	1970 s.342B; 1984 s.56(3).
221	1979 s.123A; ICTA Sch. 29 §22.
222	1979 s.101; ICTA Sch. 29 §21; 1991 s.93.
223(1)–(3)	1979 s.102(1)–(3); 1991 s.94.
(4)	1980 s.80(1); 1991 s.94.
(5), (6)	1979 s.102(5), (6); 1991 s.94.
(7)	1979 s.102(3), (4); 1988 Sch. 8 §8.
224	1979 s.103.
225	1979 s.104.
226(1), (2)	1979 s.105(1), (2); 1988 s.111(1), (2).
(3)	1988 s.111(3).
(4)–(7)	1979 s.105(3)–(6).
227	1990 s.31.
228	1990 s.32.
229	1990 s.33.
230	1990 s.34.
231	1990 s.35.
232	1990 s.36.
233	1990 s.37.
234	1990 s.38.
235	1990 s.39.
236	1990 s.40(5)–(8).
237	1979 s.144.
238	1979 s.144A; ICTA Sch. 29 §25.
239	1979 s.149; 1981 s.90(3); ITA Sch. 8 §11; CCCPA Sch. 2.
240	1979 s.106, 129.
241(1)	1984 s.50(1).
(2)	1984 s.50(2)–(9).
(3)	1984 Sch. 11 §1; 1985 s.70(10).
(4)–(8)	1984 Sch. 11 §4–7.
242	1979 s.107; 1984 s.63; 1986 s.60.
243	1979 s.108.
244	1979 s.109.
245	1979 s.110.
246	1979 s.111.
247	1979 s.111A; 1982 s.83.
248	1979 s.111B: 1982 s.83.
249	1979 s.112.
250	1979 s.113; 1988 Sch. 6 §6(5).
251	1979 s.134.
252	1979 s.135.
253(1)–(5)	1979 s.136(1)–(5).
(6)–(8)	1979 s.136(5A)–(5C); 1990 s.83.
(9)	1979 s.136(6); 1990 s.83.
(10)–(12)	1979 s.136(7)–(9).
(13)	1979 s.136(9A); 1990 s.83.
(14), (15)	1979 s.136(10), (11); 1989 Sch. 12 §6.

Provision of Bill	Derivation
254	1979 s.136A; 1990 s.84.
255	1979 s.136B; 1990 s.84.
256	1979 s.145.
257	1979 s.146; 1981 s.90; ITA Sch. 8 §9.
258	1979 s.147; ITA Sch. 8 §10; 1985 s.95(1)(b).
259	1979 s.146A; 1989 s.125.
260	1979 s.147A; 1989 Sch. 14 §4.
261	1979 s.147B; 1989 Sch. 14 §4.
262	1979 s.128; 1989 s.123.
263	1979 s.130.
264	1983(2) s.7; PCA Sch. 34 §6.
265	1984 s.126; 1985 s.96.
266	1976 s.131.
267	1991 s.78(1)–(3), (8).
268	1979 s.131.
269	1979 s.133.
270	1981 s.135.
271	1979 s.149B; ICTA Sch. 29 §26; 1988 Sch. 12 §7(b), Sch. 13 §17; 1990 s.28(3), 81, Sch. 18 §3; 1991 s.57(4).
272	1979 s.150(1)–(4), (6).
273	1979 s.152.
274	1979 s.153.
275	1979 s.18(4); 1984 s.69; CDPA 1988 Sch. 7 §26.
276(1)	1973 s.38(1); ICTA s.830(1).
(2), (3)	1973 s.38(2), (3).
(4)–(6)	1973 s.38(3A)–(3C); 1984 s.81(2); 1989 s.130(1).
(7)	1973 s.38(4); ICTA Sch. 29 §12.
(8)	1973 s.38(5); 1984 s.81.
277	1979 s.10.
278	1979 s.11.
279(1)–(6)	1979 s.13; 1991 s.97.
(7)	1988 s.104.
(8)	1991 s.97.
280	1979 s.40(1).
281	1979 s.7A; 1989 Sch. 14 §5.
282	1979 s.59.
283(1)	1975(2) s.47(1); 1989 s.179(1).
(2)	1975(2) s.47(4).
(3)	1975(2) s.47(8).
(4), (5)	1975(2) s.47(11), (12).
284	1979 s.154.
285	1987(2) s.73; ICTA s.841(3).
286	1979 s.63 ICTA Sch. 29 §15.
287	1979 s.5(1C), 92(3), 102(5), (7), 137(10), 142A(5), 149D(3), Sch. 2 §1; 1984 s.64(3F), (12), 126(1), (4); 1985 s.96(1), Sch. 19 §21(4); 1987(2) s.73, 81, 95(2), Sch. 6 §2, 4, 5; ICTA s.828, Sch. 29 §24, 26; 1989 s.92(6); 1990 s.46(9); 1991 s.94, Sch. 10 §1, Sch. 17 §4(8).
288	1979 s.155; 1979 s.64; 1984 s.64; 1985 s.72(6); ICTA Sch. 29 §27; 1988 Sch. 13 §18; 1989 Sch. 14 §6; 1990 s.127(2).
289	—
290	—
291	—
Sch. 1	
§1(1)	1979 Sch. 1 §5(1); 1980 s.77(4)(c); 1981 s.89(2); DLA 1991.
(2)	1979 Sch. 1 §5(1A); 1981 s.89(3).
(3)	1979 Sch. 1 §5(1B); 1981 s.89(3); 1982 s.80(3).
(4)	1979 Sch. 1 §5(1C); 1981 s.89(3).
(5)	1979 Sch. 1 §5(1D); 1981 s.89(3); 1982 s.80(3).
(6)	1979 Sch. 1 §5(2); Mental Health Act 1983 Sch. 4 §49; 1981 s.89(4); DLA 1991; SSCP.
(7)	1979 Sch. 1 §5(3), 1981 s.89(5).
2(1)	1979 Sch. 1 §6(1); 1980 s.78(2).

Provision of Bill	Derivation
(2)	1979 Sch. 1 §6(2); 1980 s.78(3); 1982 s.80(3)(b), (d).
(3)	1979 Sch. 1 §6(3); 1980 s.78(3); 1982 s.80(3)(e).
(4)	1979 Sch. 1 §6(4); 1980 s.78(3); 1982 s.80(3)(c), (d).
(5)	1979 Sch. 1 §6(5); 1980 s.78(3).
(6)	1979 Sch. 1 §6(6); 1980 s.78(3); 1982 s.80(3)(d).
(7)–(9)	1979 Sch. 1 §6(7)–(9); 1990 s.78(3).
Sch. 2	
§1–3	1979 Sch. 5 §1–3; 1982 Sch. 13 §11.
4(1)	—
(2)	1979 Sch; 5 §4(1).
(3)–(7)	1979 s.65.
(8)–(13)	1979 Sch. 5 §4(2)–(7).
5–8	1979 Sch. 5 §5–8.
9–15	1979 Sch. 5 §9, 10.
16	1979 Sch. 5 §11.
17	1979 Sch. 5 §12.
18	1979 Sch. 5 §13; 1982 Sch. 13 §11.
19–23	1979 Sch. 5 §14–18.
Sch. 3	
§1	1988 Sch. 8 §1; 1989 Sch. 15 §4(2); 1990 s.70(7)(b), Sch. 12 §2(2); 1991 s.78(7).
2	1988 Sch. 8 §2.
3	1988 Sch. 8 §3.
4	1988 Sch. 8 §4; 1989 Sch. 15 §3.
5	1988 Sch. 8 §5.
6	1988 Sch. 8 §10.
7	1988 Sch. 8 §12; 1990 s.63.
8	1988 Sch. 8 §13; 1989 Sch. 15 §5.
9	1988 Sch. 8 §14.
Sch. 4	
§1	1988 Sch. 9 §1; 1991 s.101(2).
2	1988 Sch. 9 §2; 1991 s.101(3), (4).
§3	1988 Sch. 9 §2A; 1991 s.101(5).
4(1)–(4)	1988 Sch. 9 §3; 1989 Sch. 15 §2; 1991 s.101(6)–(8).
(5)	1989 Sch. 15 §1.
5–8	1988 Sch. 9 §4–7.
9	1988 Sch. 9 §8; 1991 s.101(9).
Sch. 5	1991 Sch. 16 §3–16.
Sch. 6	
§1–12	1985 Sch. 20 §1–12; 1991 s.100.
13	1985 Sch. 20 §13; 1988 s.110; 1991 s.100.
14	1985 Sch. 20 §14.
15	1985 Sch. 20 §15; 1988 s.110.
16	1985 Sch. 20 §16; 1988 s.110.
Sch. 7	
§1	1979 Sch. 4 §1; ITA 1984 Sch. 8 §12; 1989 Sch. 14 §3(2).
2	1979 Sch. 4 §2; 1989 Sch. 14 §3(3).
3	1979 Sch. 4 §3; ITA 1984 Sch. 8 §12; 1989 Sch. 14 §3(4).
4	1979 Sch. 4 §4; 1989 Sch. 14 §3(5).
5, 6	1979 Sch. 4 §5, 6; 1989 Sch. 14 §3(6).
7	1979 Sch. 4 §7; 1989 Sch. 14 §3(7).
8	1979 Sch. 4 §8; 1985 s.70(9).
Sch. 8	1979 Sch. 3.
Sch. 9	
§1–3	1979 Sch. 2 §1–3.
Part II	1979 Sch. 2 Part II together with the securities specified in the Capital Gains Tax (Gilt-edged Securities) Orders 1979–1991 made under paragraph 1 of Schedule 2 to the 1979 Act; Gas Act 1986 (c. 44) s.50(3).

TABLE OF DESTINATIONS

Income and Corporation Taxes Act 1970
c.10

TABLE OF DESTINATIONS

FINANCE ACT 1976
c.40

1976	c.40
s.131	s.266

FINANCE ACT 1977
c.36

1977	c.36
s.41	s.139(5)–(7)
42	140

CAPITAL GAINS TAX ACT 1979
c.14

1979	c.14
s.1	s.1
2	2(1)
4(1)	2(2)
5(1)	3(1)
(1A)	3(2)–(4)
(1B)	3(2)–(4)
(1C)	3(2)–(4), 287
(4)	3(5)–(6)
(5)	3(5)–(6)
(6)	3(8)
7	7
7A	281
10	277
11	278
12(1)	10(1)
(1A)	10(2)
(2)	10(4)
(2A)	10(5)
(3)	10(6)
13	79(1)–(6)
14	12
15(1)	13(1)–(9)
(2)	13(1)–(9)
(3)	13(1)–(9)
(4)	13(1)–(9)
(5)	13(1)–(9)
(6)	13(1)–(9)
(7)	13(1)–(9)
(8)	13(1)–(9)
(9)	13(1)–(9)
(10)	13(11)
16	14
18(1)	9
(2)	9
(3)	9
(4)	275
(5)	11
(6)	11
(7)	11
(8)	11
19(1)	21
(2)	21
(4)	51
(5)	51
20	22
21	23
22	24
23	26
24	27
25	29
26(1)	30(1)

1979	c.14
s.26(1A)	30(2)
(2)	30(3)–(7)
(3)	30(3)–(7)
(4)	30(3)–(7)
(5)	30(3)–(7)
(6)	30(3)–(7)
(7)	30(8)
(8)	30(9)
26A	31
B	32
C	33
D	34
27	28
28(1)	15
(2)	15
(3)	35
29(1)	16
(2)	16
(3)	16
(4)	16
(5)	2(3)
29A(1)	17
(2)	17
30	15
31(1)	37(1)–(3)
(2)	37(1)–(3)
(3)	37(1)–(3)
(4)	37(4)
32	38
32A	120(2)–(7)
33	39
33A	119
34	41
35	42
36	43
37	44
38	46
39	47
40(1)	280
(2)	48
41	49
42	50
43	52
44	58
46	60
47	64
48	65
49	62
50	63
51	68
52	69

1979	c.14
s.53	70
54	71
55(1)	72
(3)	72
(4)	72
(5)	72
(6)	72
56A	67, 74
(1)	73(1)
(1A)	73(2), (3)
(1B)	73(2), (3)
57	75
58	76
59	282
60	59
61	60
62	18
63	286
64	288
65	Sched. 2, para. 4(3)–(7)
66(1)	105
(2)	105
(3)	104(3)
(4)	104(3)
67	115
71	121
72	122
73	123
74	124
75	125
77	126
78	127
79(1) (first and second provisos)	128(1) 128(2)
(2)	128(3), (4)
(3)	128(3), (4)
80	129
81	130
82	132
83	133
84(1)	134(1)
(2)	134(2)
(3)	134(2)
(4)	134(3)
(5)	134(4)–(6)
(6)	(4)–(6)
(7)	134(4)–(6)
85	135
86	136

TABLE OF DESTINATIONS

FINANCE ACT 1982
c.39

ADMINISTRATION OF JUSTICE ACT 1982
c.53

MENTAL HEALTH ACT 1983
c.20

FINANCE (No. 2) ACT 1983
c.49

LONDON REGIONAL TRANSPORT ACT 1984
c.32

TABLE OF DESTINATIONS

FINANCE ACT 1984
c.43

Housing (Consequential Provisions) Act 1985
c.71

Finance Act 1986
c.41

Gas Act 1986
c.44

Parliamentary Constituencies Act 1986
c.56

Finance Act 1987
c.16

Finance (No. 2) Act 1987
c.51

TABLE OF DESTINATIONS

INCOME AND CORPORATION TAXES ACT 1988
c.1

FINANCE ACT 1988
c.39

COPYRIGHT, DESIGNS AND PATENTS ACT 1988
c.48

FINANCE ACT 1989
c.26

THE INCOME TAX (STOCK LENDING) REGULATIONS 1989
No. 1299

CAPITAL ALLOWANCES ACT 1990
c.1

FINANCE ACT 1990
c.29

DISABILITY LIVING ALLOWANCE AND DISABILITY WORKING ALLOWANCE ACT 1991
c.21

TABLE OF DESTINATIONS

FINANCE ACT 1991
c.31

CAPITAL GAINS (ANNUAL EXEMPT AMOUNT) ORDER
No. 736

DISABILITY LIVING ALLOWANCE AND DISABILITY WORKING ALLOWANCE (NORTHERN IRELAND CONSEQUENTIAL AMENDMENTS) ORDER 1991
No. 2874

SOCIAL SECURITY (CONSEQUENTIAL PROVISIONS) ACT 1992
c.6

SOCIAL SECURITY (CONSEQUENTIAL PROVISIONS) (NORTHERN IRELAND) ACT 1992
c.9

INDEX

References are to sections and schedules

12–331

FURTHER AND HIGHER EDUCATION ACT 1992*

(1992 c. 13)

ARRANGEMENT OF SECTIONS

PART I

FURTHER EDUCATION

CHAPTER I

RESPONSIBILITY FOR FURTHER EDUCATION

The new funding councils

---

* Annotations by Professor J. Bell, University of Leeds.

Institutions in the higher education sector

General

PART III

MISCELLANEOUS AND GENERAL

An Act to make new provision about further and higher education.

[6th March 1992]

PARLIAMENTARY DEBATES
    Hansard, H.L. Vol. 532, col. 1021; Vol. 533, cols. 462, 557, 602, 667, 695, 875, 944, 1021, 1102; Vol. 534, cols. 122, 191, 358, 423, 633, 720; Vol. 535, cols. 10, 26; H.C. Vol. 203, cols. 828, 910; Vol. 205, col. 190.
    The Bill was discussed in Standing Committee F from February 18 to 26, 1992.

INTRODUCTION AND GENERAL NOTE
    According to the Government, the Act introduces "far-reaching reforms designed to provide a better deal for young people and adults and to increase still further participation in further and higher education" (Lord Belstead, Paymaster-General, *Hansard*, H.L. Vol. 532, col. 1022). The policy of expanding participation in education for those beyond compulsory school age was set out in three White Papers of May 1991: *Access and Opportunity: a Strategy for Education and Training* (Cm. 1530), *Education and Training for the 21st Century* (Cm. 1536), and *Higher Education: a New Framework* (Cm. 1541). This Act, together with the Further and Higher

Education (Scotland) Act 1992, implements the principal proposals of the last two of those White Papers.

This Act has two Parts. Part I deals with further education and Pt. II deals with higher education. The reforms introduced in relation to further education are more radical and far-reaching than those in relation to higher education, but they parallel the reforms introduced into this latter area by the Education Reform Act 1988 (hereafter "ERA 1988"). The ERA 1988 took polytechnics and higher education colleges out of the control of local education authorities and placed them under the direction of a separate central funding council (the Polytechnics and Colleges Funding Council: the "PCFC"). Part I of this Act takes colleges of further education and sixth-form colleges out of local authority control or grant-maintained status, and places them under the direction of a new central funding council, the Further Education Funding Council ("FEFC"). The purpose of this change is to give greater autonomy to further education and sixth-form colleges in deciding the provision of education they wish to make in relation to local needs: "Our aim is to give colleges much greater freedom to manage their own affairs and, through the funding régime, a powerful financial incentive to recruit additional students and thereby expand participation" (Paymaster-General, *Hansard*, H.L. Vol. 532, col. 1023; *ibid.* Vol. 533, col. 476). The reason for including sixth-form colleges in the new further education sector was to help to eradicate the dividing line between academic and vocational further education (White Paper, *Education and Training for the 21st Century*, Vol. 1, para. 4.8; Paymaster-General, *Hansard*, H.L. Vol. 534, col. 148). All institutions would be likely to offer a variety of academic and vocational courses as well as mixed courses.

The policy of Pt. II of the Act centres on the abolition of the "binary line" between universities, funded by the Universities Funding Council (the "UFC"), and polytechnics and colleges of higher education, funded by the PCFC. "The Government believes that the real key to achieving cost-effective expansion lies in greater competition for funds and students. That can best be achieved by breaking down the increasingly artificial and unhelpful barriers between the universities, and the polytechnics and colleges" (White Paper, *Higher Education: a New Framework*, para. 17). A single funding council, the Higher Education Funding Council ("HEFC"), will fund teaching and, to some extent, research in all those institutions. Polytechnics and colleges will have the opportunity to acquire the title "university" if they satisfy the Privy Council of their suitability.

In relation to both further education and higher education, there is a significant departure from the approach of ERA 1988 to funding councils. In that Act, the UFC and the PCFC covered the whole of Great Britain. This Act, together with the Further and Higher Education (Scotland) Act 1992, introduces a measure of territorial devolution. There are funding councils for both further education and higher education in England, Wales and Scotland. This enables the councils to meet the different educational systems and institutional structures in the different countries. All the same, "to ensure fair competition across territorial boundaries, the funding allocations by each territorial Secretary of State to the relevant body will be informed by the Government's general policy on higher education" (White Paper, *Higher Education: a New Framework*, para. 48).

The funding councils in the different countries will cooperate in the assessment of quality for both teaching and research in relation to the institutions which they fund. In all funded areas, the policy is that "responsibility for quality follows from responsibility for finance" (White Paper, *Education and Training for the 21st Century*, Vol. 1, para. 8.3). Responsibility for quality control over the quality of educational provision is primarily the responsibility of the institutions as providers. Quality audit is external scrutiny aimed at ensuring that institutions have suitable quality control mechanisms in place. Quality assessment involves external review of and judgments about the quality of teaching and learning in institutions. The funding councils have responsibility for this quality assessment. The provisions of this Act in relation to quality assessment form part of a policy also implemented by the Education (Schools) Act 1992.

The Scheme of the Act

Part I is divided into three chapters.

Chapter I begins with provisions (ss.1–9, together with Scheds. 1 and 2) creating Further Education Funding Councils for England and Wales and setting out their functions and the powers of the Secretary of State in relation to them.

Sections 10–14 then make adjustments in the functions and powers of local education authorities in relation to further education, as well as giving powers to schools to providing further education.

Chapter II makes provision for ways in which institutions might become part of the further education sector. Sections 15–27, together with Scheds. 3 and 4, provide for the creation of independent further education corporations out of local-authority-maintained colleges of further education and sixth-form colleges and of grant-maintained schools. These sections deal with the governing structures of these corporations and the transfer of property, rights and liabilities to them.

Sections 28–32 enable other institutions to become part of the further education sector by designation by the Secretary of State and provide for their governance and the transfer of property, rights and liabilities to them.

Sections 34–43 and 48–49 and Scheds. 5 and 7 make further provision in relation to the transfer of property, rights and liabilities, and employment relations to these new institutions within the further education sector.

Sections 44 and 45 make provision for collective worship and religious education in further education institutions other than former colleges of further education.

Section 46 enables trust deeds to be varied in connection with the creation of an institution within the further education sector.

Section 47 provides for the transfer of higher education institutions to the further education sector.

Sections 50, 51 and 53 make provision in relation to information, proposals and accounts of further education institutions.

Section 52 enables the FEFC to require education to be provided for named individuals.

Chapter III makes a number of general provisions in relation to this Part of the Act. Sections 54–57 set out the powers of the Secretary of State to obtain information, assure quality, and to intervene in the further education sector. Sections 58 and 59 make provision in relation to reorganisation in connection with the creation of further education institutions.

Sections 60 and 61 provide interpretations on the scope of the Act.

Part II of the Act deals with higher education.

Sections 62–70 create Higher Education Funding Councils for England and Wales and set out their functions and the powers of the Secretary of State in relation to them.

Sections 71–78 make provision for institutions to become part of the higher education sector. Sections 71–73, together with Sched. 6, introduce extensive amendments to Chapter II of Part II of the Education Reform Act 1988 in relation to higher education corporations. Sections 74 and 75 make provision on transfers of rights and liabilities and the variation of trust deeds consequential on institutions becoming part of this sector. Sections 76–78 enable polytechnics and colleges to obtain degree-awarding powers and be called "universities" and have their financial years aligned with existing, chartered universities.

Section 79 requires institutions to provide information to funding councils. Section 80 abolishes the Council for National Academic Awards which currently validates degrees of polytechnics and colleges, but which is no longer necessary because of s.76.

Section 81 sets out the powers of the Secretary of State to give directions in relation to the higher education sector.

Part III of the Act contains a number of general provisions.

Sections 82 and 83 provide for joint exercise of functions between the funding councils created by this Act and those created by the Further and Higher Education (Scotland) Act 1992.

Sections 84 and 86–88, together with Sched. 7, make further provision in relation to transfers of property, rights and liabilities and data which will occur under this Act.

Section 85 makes provision in relation to such further and higher education institutions which remain under local authority control.

Sections 89–92 make general provision on orders made under this Act and on interpretation. Section 92 is particularly useful in providing an index to definitions contained in this Act.

ABBREVIATIONS

Commencement No. 1 Order 1992	: Further and Higher Education Act 1992 (Commencement No. 1 and Transitional Provisions) Order 1992 (S.I. 1992 No. 831)
DES	: Department of Education and Science
EA	: Education Act. Each Act is identified by date, *e.g.* "EA 1944" means "Education Act 1944"
ERA 1988	: Education Reform Act 1988
FEFC	: Further Education Funding Council
HEFC	: Higher Education Funding Council
PCFC	: Polytechnics and Colleges Funding Council
TEC	: Training and Enterprise Council
UFC	: Universities' Funding Council
White Paper, *Education and Training*	: *Education and Training for the 21st Century* (Cm. 1536)
White Paper, *Higher Education*	: *Higher Education: a New Framework* (Cm. 1541)

PART I

FURTHER EDUCATION

CHAPTER I

RESPONSIBILITY FOR FURTHER EDUCATION

The new funding councils

The Further Education Funding Councils

1.—(1) There shall be established—

(a) a body corporate to be known as the Further Education Funding Council for England to exercise in relation to England the functions conferred on them, and

(b) a body corporate to be known as the Further Education Funding Council for Wales to exercise in relation to Wales the functions conferred on them.

(2) The Further Education Funding Council for England shall consist of not less than 12 nor more than 15 members appointed by the Secretary of State, of whom one shall be so appointed as chairman.

(3) The Further Education Funding Council for Wales shall consist of not less than eight nor more than 12 members appointed by the Secretary of State, of whom one shall be so appointed as chairman.

(4) In appointing the members of a council the Secretary of State—

(a) shall have regard to the desirability of including persons who appear to him to have experience of, and to have shown capacity in, the provision of education or to have held, and to have shown capacity in, any position carrying responsibility for the provision of education and, in appointing such persons, he shall have regard to the desirability of their being currently engaged in the provision of further education or in carrying responsibility for such provision, and

(b) shall have regard to the desirability of including persons who appear to him to have experience of, and to have shown capacity in, industrial, commercial or financial matters or the practice of any profession.

(5) In this Part of this Act any reference to a council is to a further education funding council.

(6) References in the Education Acts to the appropriate further education funding council, in relation to any educational institution—

(a) where the institution mainly serves the population of England, are to the Further Education Funding Council for England and, where the institution mainly serves the population of Wales, are to the Further Education Funding Council for Wales, and

(b) where the institution receives financial support from a further education funding council, are to that council also (if different).

(7) Any dispute as to whether any functions are exercisable by one of the councils shall be determined by the Secretary of State.

(8) Schedule 1 to this Act has effect with respect to each of the councils.

DEFINITIONS
  "council": subs. (5).
  "further education": s.14(1)–(4).

GENERAL NOTE
  The creation of a Further Education Funding Council (FEFC) for England and another for Wales moves responsibility for further education from local education authorities to independent funding bodies responsible to central Government working in parallel with equivalent bodies in higher education (see s.62). The creation of these FEFCs enables further education

and sixth-form colleges to be funded more directly by the Government, but mainly it enables them to be free to develop in their own individual ways in response to local demands from employers and students. The funding system is to provide incentives rather than directives for such developments (White Paper, *Education and Training*, Vol. 1, para. 9.3).

Subsection (1) creates the two FEFCs for England and Wales, and subs. (7) provides that the Secretary of State shall determine disputes as to the competence of the councils. Subsections (2) and (3) provide that the stipulated number of members shall be appointed by the relevant Secretary of State in each country. Subsection (4) sets out the criteria for appointing members to a FEFC. The criteria suggest particularly relevant considerations for choosing members, but in no way prescribe categories of members with particular qualifications as was done for the UFC and the PCFC under ERA 1988, ss.131 and 132. The Government was of the view that this was inappropriate in such small bodies: "The members will be appointed in a personal capacity. Funding Councils will be executive bodies. Executive bodies are not liable to function best when they are composed of persons appointed specifically to represent sectional interests" (Under-Secretary of State for Higher Education, *Hansard*, H.C. Standing Committee F, col. 125). The Government did anticipate that persons from the categories mentioned in subs. (4) would be appointed. As laid down in subs. (8), Sched. 1 has effect in setting out the structure and procedures of the councils.

This section came into force on May 6, 1992: see Commencement No. 1 Order 1992, para. 2 and Sched. 1.

Subs. (1)
Body corporate. This means a body of persons having perpetual succession as an artificial personality, and capable of holding land, entering contracts, suing and being sued. It has power to possess a seal for the purpose of executing deeds.

Subs. (2)
Secretary of State. Under s.90(5), the meaning of terms in this Act is the same as that in EA 1944. Thus reference to the Secretary of State is intended to be to the Secretary of State for Education and Science (see preamble to the Secretary of State for Education and Science Order 1964 (S.I. 1964 No. 490). This is without prejudice, however, to the general rule of interpretation that "Secretary of State" means one of Her Majesty's principal Secretaries of State (Interpretation Act 1978, Sched. 1), so that one may act for another (*Harrison* v. *Bush* (1855) 5 E. & B. 344 at 352). In this Act, "Secretary of State" means in England, Secretary of State for Education and Science and in Wales, Secretary of State for Wales, *e.g.* under subs. (3) (see Transfer of Functions (Wales) Order 1970 (S.I. 1970 No. 1536) and No. 2 Order 1978 (S.I. 1978 No. 274)).

Subs. (4)
Shall have regard to the desirability. The Government did not wish to be prescriptive about the membership of the councils. The Government wanted the Secretary of State to have regard primarily to the individual characteristics of candidates, rather than their ability to represent sectional interests, and for this flexibility in choice was required (Lord Cavendish of Furness, *Hansard*, H.L. Vol. 533, col. 545).

Experience of . . . the provision of education. It was established in *R.* v. *Croydon London Borough Council*, ex p. *Leney* (1987) 85 L.G.R. 466 that "persons of experience in education" may include those who do not hold a teaching qualification or have not had teaching experience. The form of words used here does not appear to exclude those whose experience is in the administration of education, rather than in teaching.

"Education" here includes all forms of education. The great majority of members of a local education authority would be eligible for appointment, as would a recently retired Her Majesty's Inspector or teacher (see *Hansard*, H.L. Vol. 533, col. 546, and *Hansard*, H.L. Vol. 534, cols. 151 and 153).

Currently engaged. This phrase includes both teachers and administrators of further education.

Carrying responsibility. This phrase includes those who are members of a governing body of a further education institution or of a local education authority with responsibility for further education under EA 1944, s.41, as redrafted by s.11 of this Act.

The new further education sector

Full-time education for 16 to 18 year-olds

2.—(1) It shall be the duty of each council to secure the provision for the population of their area of sufficient facilities for education to which this subsection applies, that is, full-time education suitable to the requirements of persons over compulsory school age who have not attained the age of 19 years.

(2) That duty extends to all persons among that population who may want such education and have not attained the age of 19 years.

(3) A council shall discharge that duty so as—

(a) to secure that the facilities are provided at such places, are of such character and are so equipped as to be sufficient to meet the reasonable needs of all persons to whom the duty extends, and

(b) to take account of the different abilities and aptitudes of such persons.

(4) A council may secure the provision of facilities for education to which subsection (1) above applies for persons to whom that duty does not extend.

(5) A council shall discharge their functions under this section so as to make the most effective use of the council's resources and, in particular, to avoid provision which might give rise to disproportionate expenditure.

(6) In discharging those functions a council shall have regard to any education to which subsection (1) above applies provided by schools maintained by local education authorities, grant-maintained schools, special schools not maintained by local education authorities, city technology colleges or city colleges for the technology of the arts.

DEFINITIONS

"city college for the technology of the arts": s.105(1) of ERA 1988.
"city technology college": s.105(1) of ERA 1988.
"council": s.1(5).
"compulsory school age": EA 1944, s.35.
"education": does not include higher education": s.14(4).
"grant-maintained school": s.52(3) of ERA 1988.
"school maintained by a local education authority": s.25(1) of ERA 1988.

GENERAL NOTE

This section transfers to the FEFC the duty of local education authorities to provide education for 16- to 18-year-olds. This duty is removed from local education authorities by amendments to the EA 1944, introduced by ss.10 and 11 of this Act.

The duty is to provide facilities for full-time education appropriate to the different abilities and aptitudes of the age-group, and to ensure that they are of a character and location sufficient to meet those needs (subs. 3). But, in carrying out this duty, the FEFC is to have regard to the provision made in the schools sector (subs. 6). The duty of the FEFC is to ensure adequate provision through the most efficient use of resources and to avoid disproportionate expenditure.

This section comes into force on April 1, 1993: see Commencement No. 1 Order 1992, para. 2 and Sched. 3.

Subs. (1)

The duty is limited to full-time education. Part-time education is dealt with by s.3. The provision of adult and leisure education remains the duty of the local education authority (ss.10 and 11).

Full-time education. Full-time education is not defined in this Act. It is, however, defined under regulations applicable to further education before the relevant provisions of this Act come into force: see para. 10, Education (Schools and Further Education) Regulations 1981 (S.I. 1981 No. 1086), as amended by the Education (Schools and Further Education) (Amendment) Regulations 1987 (S.I. 1987 No. 879).

Compulsory school age. This is defined in s.35 of the EA 1944 as any age between five and 16 years. The date at which a person over 16 can leave school is defined by s.7 of the EA 1962, but as soon as a person reaches 16, he or she is over compulsory school age. A person attains a particular age at the start of the anniversary of date of birth (s.9 of the Family Law Reform Act 1969).

Subs. (2)

The duty relates to the full-time education of all persons between 16 and 19, whether or not they are at school or are, for example, returning to full-time education after a period of full-time employment.

Subs. (3)

The duty relates to the location, character and resources of the facilities available for further education, as well as to the variety of learning needs and abilities within this age-group. On the issue of learning needs and abilities, see s.4.

Subs. (4)
Persons to whom that duty does not extend. This includes persons not from the area of the FEFC. It also enables the continuance of existing provision of education to prisoners by colleges at the invitation of the Home Office (Paymaster-General, *Hansard*, H.L. Vol. 533, col. 564).

Subs. (5)
Disproportionate expenditure. Under s.76 of the EA 1944, a local education authority has a duty to avoid "unreasonable expenditure". This provision has similar import. The Bill does not require the councils to avoid expensive provision, *e.g.* for those with learning difficulties, merely to avoid disproportionate expenditure (Lord Cavendish of Furness, *Hansard*, H.L. Vol. 533, col. 570; Lord Belstead, *ibid.* Vol. 534, col. 167; Under-Secretary of State for Higher Education, *Hansard*, H.C., Standing Committee F, col. 116).
   On the notion of proportionality, see especially J. Jowell and A. Lester, in *New Directions in Judicial Review* (Stevens, London 1988), pp. 51–72.

Subs. (6)
Local education authority. See ss.6 and 114(1) of the EA 1944. At the date on which this Act was passed, there were 116 local education authorities in England and Wales: 39 (shire) county councils in England, and eight in Wales; 36 metropolitan district councils; and 32 London borough councils and the Common Council of the City of London. This position is the result of the abolition of the Inner London Education Authority on April 1, 1990 under Pt. III of the ERA 1988. The situation is likely to change as a result of changes to county councils under the Local Government Act 1992.

Part-time education, and full-time education for those over 18

3.—(1) It shall be the duty of each council to secure the provision for the population of their area of adequate facilities for education to which this subsection applies, that is—
   (a) part-time education suitable to the requirements of persons of any age over compulsory school age, and
   (b) full-time education suitable to the requirements of persons who have attained the age of 19 years,
where the education is provided by means of a course of a description mentioned in Schedule 2 to this Act.
   (2) A council shall discharge that duty so as—
   (a) to secure that facilities are provided at such places, are of such character and are so equipped as to meet the reasonable need for education to which subsection (1) above applies, and
   (b) to take account of the different abilities and aptitudes of persons among that population.
   (3) A council may secure the provision of facilities for education to which subsection (1) above applies where they are not under a duty to do so.
   (4) A council shall discharge their functions under this section so as to make the most effective use of their resources and, in particular, to avoid provision which might give rise to disproportionate expenditure.
   (5) In discharging those functions a council shall have regard to any education to which subsection (1) above applies provided by institutions outside the further education sector or higher education sector.
   (6) The Secretary of State may by order amend Schedule 2 to this Act.

DEFINITIONS
   "council": s.1(5).
   "course": see Sched. 2.

GENERAL NOTE
   The purpose of this section is to impose a duty on the Funding Councils to provide further education other than that specified in s.2, *i.e.* part-time education and education for those over 18. The duty is similar in scope to that under s.2, but differs in that the FEFC only has to ensure provision through "courses" defined in Sched. 2, and it must have regard to the provision of

such education not only by schools, but also by other bodies, *e.g.* community colleges, long-term residential colleges, and adult education colleges.

This section comes into force on April 1, 1993: Commencement No. 1 Order 1992, para. 2 and Sched. 3.

Subs. (1)

The duty extends to securing the provision of courses defined in Sched. 2 of two kinds: part-time courses for any person over 16, and full-time courses for those over 18.

Course. This is taken to include a "programme of study" as well as separate subject units taken before commencing a programme of study (Paymaster-General, *Hansard*, H.L. Vol. 533, cols. 573–4). See further under Sched. 2.

Full-time education. See note to s.2(1).

Subs. (2)

See note to s.2(3).

Subs. (3)

See note to s.2(4).

Subs. (4)

See note to s.2(5).

Subs. (5)

Institutions outside the further education sector or higher education sector. These are defined in s.91(3) and (5) respectively. The importance of such institutions will be spelt out in guidance to the Funding Councils (*Hansard*, H.L. Vol. 533, cols. 578–9).

Subs. (6)

This provision enables changes to be made to the list of courses in Sched. 2. The Government considered that these were matters of detail. Any order under this subsection must be made by way of statutory instrument which is subject to a negative resolution (see s.89(1) and (3)).

Persons with learning difficulties

4.—(1) In exercising their functions under sections 2 and 3 of this Act, each council shall (subject to the provisions of those sections) do so in accordance with subsections (2) to (4) below.

(2) Each council shall have regard to the requirements of persons having learning difficulties.

(3) A council shall, if they are satisfied in the case of any person among the population of their area who has a learning difficulty and is over compulsory school age but has not attained the age of 25 years, that—

(a) the facilities available in institutions within the further education sector or the higher education sector are not adequate for him, and

(b) it is in his best interests to do so,

secure provision for him at an institution outside those sectors.

(4) A council shall, if they are satisfied that they cannot secure such provision for a person as they are required to secure under subsection (3) above unless they also secure the provision of boarding accommodation for him, secure the provision of boarding accommodation for him.

(5) In exercising their functions under sections 2 and 3 of this Act in the case of any person who has a learning difficulty and is over compulsory school age, a council may—

(a) if they are satisfied that the facilities available in institutions within the further education sector or the higher education sector are not adequate for him, secure provision for him at an institution outside those sectors, and

(b) secure the provision of boarding accommodation for him.

(6) Subject to subsection (7) below, for the purposes of this section a person has a "learning difficulty" if—

(a) he has a significantly greater difficulty in learning than the majority of persons of his age, or

(b) he has a disability which either prevents or hinders him from making use of facilities of a kind generally provided by institutions within the further education sector for persons of his age.

(7) A person is not to be taken as having a learning difficulty solely because the language (or form of the language) in which he is, or will be, taught is different from a language (or form of a language) which has at any time been spoken in his home.

DEFINITIONS
"compulsory school age": s.35 of the EA 1944.
"council": s.1(5).
"institution within the further education sector": s.91(3).
"institution within the higher education sector": s.91(5).
"learning difficulty": subss. (6) and (7).

GENERAL NOTE
This section was the subject of much debate in Parliament. Under s.2(1) of the EA 1981, a local education authority has a duty to have regard to provision for pupils with special educational needs. A pupil with special educational needs is defined under s.1(1) of that Act as a pupil with learning difficulties. This section imposes a similar duty on the FEFC to ensure continuity in provision for such persons over the age of 16. The duty under the EA 1981 was merely to "have regard" to provision for such persons, and the Government refused to make this stronger by imposing a duty on the FEFC to ensure provision for such persons. In the Government's view, a FEFC would have to make judgments on priorities in the context of resources, so it was appropriate to continue the existing wording of the duty (see Lord Cavendish of Furness, *Hansard*, H.L. Vol. 533, col. 635). There is no requirement that the FEFC or a local education authority conduct an assessment of the special needs of individuals with learning difficulties as is required for pupils of compulsory school age under EA 1981. However, where provision in institutions within the further or higher education sectors is inadequate and it is in the best interests of a person to do so, the FEFC does have a duty to secure provision of education for any person with learning difficulties aged between 18 and 25 at an institution outside those sectors. Subsection (4) imposes a duty to provide boarding accommodation for such a person, where it is necessary for providing education under subs. (3). A power to provide boarding accommodation is also granted under subs. (5) where the FEFC is performing its duties under ss.2 and 3. Subsection (6) defines "learning difficulty", but subs. (7) excludes from this definition the situation where a person has a difficulty merely because the language of instruction is different from that spoken at home.

Support services for persons with learning difficulties may be funded by the FEFC under s.5(5)(b), and by the HEFC under s.65(2)(d).

This section comes into force on April 1, 1993: see Commencement No. 1 Order 1992, para. 2 and Sched. 3.

Subs. (3)
This subsection imposes a duty to provide education, not just a power as under s.7(2) of the EA 1981. This change results from the experience of judicial review decisions in *Ex parte H.* (unreported, 1983) and *R.* v. *Secretary of State for Education and Science*, ex p. *Davis* [1989] 2 F.L.R. 190 (see *Hansard*, H.L. Vol. 534, cols. 207–8). In those decisions it was held that, on appeal, the Secretary of State could not require local authorities to make provision for the needs of a child, but could merely cause the local education authority to reconsider the issue.

Provision. This term includes the provision of transport. Duties to provide transport to an institution of further education or to an institution outside the further or higher education sectors are imposed on the local education authority under s.55 of the EA 1944, as amended by para. 5 of Sched. 8 to this Act.

Subs. (6)
Learning difficulty. The definition given here substantially follows s.1(2) of the EA 1981.

Subs. (7)
The qualification given here to the definition of "learning difficulty" in subs. (6) follows s.1(4) of the EA 1981.

Finance

Administration of funds by councils

5.—(1) A council may give financial support to the governing body of any institution within the further education sector or the higher education sector in respect of—

(a) the provision of facilities for further education, or

(b) the provision of facilities, and the carrying on of any activities, which the governing body of the institution consider necessary or desirable to be provided or carried on for the purpose of or in connection with the provision of facilities for further education.

(2) A council may give financial support to the governing body of any institution within the further education sector in respect of—

(a) the provision of facilities for higher education, or

(b) the provision of facilities, and the carrying on of any activities, which the governing body of the institution consider necessary or desirable to be provided or carried on for the purpose of or in connection with the provision of facilities for higher education.

(3) A council may give financial support to a further education corporation for the purposes of any educational institution to be conducted by the corporation, including the establishment of such an institution.

(4) For the purposes of section 4(3) to (5) of this Act, a council may give financial support to any person other than a local education authority, the governing body of a grant-maintained school or a person maintaining or carrying on a city technology college or city college for the technology of the arts.

(5) A council may give financial support to any person in respect of—

(a) the provision of training or advice, or

(b) the carrying on of research or other activities,

relevant to the provision of facilities for further education.

(6) Financial support under this section—

(a) shall take the form of grants, loans or other payments, and

(b) may be given on such terms and conditions as the council think fit.

(7) The terms and conditions on which a council make any grants, loans or other payments under this section may in particular—

(a) enable the council to require the repayment, in whole or in part, of sums paid by the council if any of the terms and conditions subject to which the sums were paid is not complied with, and

(b) require the payment of interest in respect of any period during which a sum due to the council in accordance with any of the terms and conditions remains unpaid,

but shall not relate to the application by the person to whom the financial support is given of any sums derived otherwise than from the council.

(8) A council may not give any financial support except in accordance with this section.

DEFINITIONS

"council": s.1(5).

"further education": s.14(1)–(4).

"further education corporation": s.17(1).

"governing body": s.90(1) and (2).

"higher education": s.90(1) and s.120(1) of and Sched. 6 to the ERA 1988.

"institution within the further education sector": s.91(3).

"institution within the higher education sector": ss.61(3)(a) and 91(5).

GENERAL NOTE

The FEFC receives funds from the Treasury and channels them to further education institutions or to other bodies providing courses of further education and ancillary activities. An FEFC is also empowered to make payments to individuals (subs. (5)). The FEFC may also make provision for higher education provided by such institutions. Deliberately, there is no funding formula in the Act, unlike in ss.139–147 of the ERA 1988. But, although there is no such statutory formula, it is expected that the FEFC will follow the pattern of the pre-Act UFC and the PCFC in adopting a funding formula of its own creation within guidance set by the Secretary of State (see White Paper, *Education and Training*, Vol. 2, para. 4.7).

Funding powers, notably the imposition of conditions on grants (subs. (7)) will enable the FEFC to determine the general character of the institution in receipt of funds, since it will only fund the kinds of education which it considers appropriate for that institution to provide (White Paper, *Education and Training*, Vol. 2, para. 4.14).

Subsections (1), (2) and (4) of this section only come into force when the FEFCs begin to fund institutions and courses on April 1, 1993. However, subs. (3) comes into force on September 30, 1992, and this enables the FEFC to provide funds for setting up institutions within the further education sector. Subsections (5), (6), (7) and (8) came into force on May 6, 1992. These commencement provisions are contained in the Commencement No. 1 Order 1992, para. 2 and, respectively, Scheds. 3, 2, and 1.

Subs. (1)
   Governing body. Following ss.131 and 132 of the ERA 1988, payments are made by the FEFC not to the institution, but to the governing body of the institution. Such an arrangement maintains the accountability of individuals for monies received.
   Facilities. Facilities for further education include the provision of such education in adult education colleges.

Subs. (2)
   This enables the FEFC to make funds available to further education institutions for the provision of higher education, *e.g.* by "access courses" or courses which are treated as contributing credits towards higher education qualifications.

Subs. (3)
   Institution. This includes both existing and future institutions which are conducted by the further education corporation.

Subs. (4)
   Grants to bodies other than further education corporations for the purposes of making provision for persons with learning difficulties are restricted to bodies which do not maintain part of the state school sector, for which separate provision already exists under the EA 1981.

Subs. (5)
   Any person. The White Paper *Education and Training*, Vol. 1, para. 4.5, envisages that the funding of the further education of individuals by an FEFC will be an exceptional measure. Normally such education is funded through institutions which provide courses of further education.
   This provision also enables the FEFC itself to appoint trainers, advisers, or researchers.

Subs. (6)
   Unlike ss.131(6) and 132(7) of the ERA 1988, the funding provided by the FEFC is not limited to grants, but may include loans or other payments. Like previous statutory provisions, the FEFC may impose such conditions as it sees fit, subject to subs. (7). It was envisaged that funding would be provided with elements related to (a) student enrolment numbers, (b) payments to colleges, and (c) staff training (Lord Cavendish of Furness, *Hansard*, H.L. Vol. 533, col. 671).

Subs. (7)
   This provision substantially reproduces s.134(3) of the ERA 1988, and enables the enforcement of conditions imposed under subs. (6). The proviso makes it clear that repayments may only be required from money received from the FEFC and not from other sources of income, *e.g.* grants from private bodies or from the European Communities.

Administration of funds: supplementary

6.—(1) Before exercising their discretion under section 5(1) to (4) of this Act with respect to the terms and conditions to be imposed in relation to any grants, loans or other payments, a council shall consult such of the following bodies as appear to the council to be appropriate to consult in the circumstances—
   (a) such bodies representing the interests of institutions within the further education sector as appear to the council to be concerned, and
   (b) the governing body of any particular institution within that sector which appears to the council to be concerned.

(2) In exercising their functions in relation to the provision of financial support under section 5 of this Act a council shall have regard to the desirability of not discouraging any institution in respect of which such support is given from maintaining or developing its funding from other sources.

(3) In exercising those functions a council shall have regard (so far as they think it appropriate to do so in the light of any other relevant considerations) to the desirability of maintaining what appears to them to be an appropriate balance in the support given by them as between institutions of a denominational character and other institutions.

(4) For the purposes of subsection (3) above an institution is an institution of a denominational character if it appears to the council that either—

(a) at least one quarter of the members of the governing body of the institution are persons appointed to represent the interests of a religion or religious denomination,

(b) any of the property held for the purposes of the institution is held upon trusts which provide that, in the event of the discontinuance of the institution, the property concerned shall be held for, or sold and the proceeds of sale applied for, the benefit of a religion or religious denomination, or

(c) any of the property held for the purposes of the institution is held upon trust for or in connection with—

(i) the provision of education, or
(ii) the conduct of an educational institution,

in accordance with the tenets of a religion or religious denomination.

(5) Where—

(a) the governing body of an institution within the further education sector to which this subsection applies ("the sponsoring body") receive from the governing body of an institution outside that sector ("the external institution") a request for the sponsoring body to apply to a council for financial support in respect of the provision of facilities for part-time, or adult, further education by the external institution in any academic year, and

(b) there are no arrangements for the provision in that year of any facilities of the kind specified in the application for the population of the sponsoring body's locality by any other institutions or the arrangements for such provision for that population in that year by other institutions are inadequate,

the sponsoring body shall apply to the council specified in the request for financial support to be given to the sponsoring body on terms requiring it to be applied in respect of the provision of the facilities specified in the application by the external institution in that year.

(6) In subsection (5) above—

(a) references to part-time, or adult, further education are to education provided by means of courses of any description mentioned in Schedule 2 to this Act, and

(b) references to the provision of facilities for such education by any institution in any academic year include the provision of facilities, and the carrying on of any activities, which the governing body of the institution consider necessary or desirable to be provided or carried on for the purpose of or in connection with the provision of facilities for such education by them in that year,

and that subsection applies to an institution within the further education sector if the institution is for the time being specified in an order, or for the time being falls within a description specified in an order, made by the Secretary of State.

<small>Definitions</small>
"council": s.1(5).
"courses": Sched. 2.

"external institution": subs. (5)(a).
"governing body": s.90(1) and (2).
"institution within the further education sector": s.91(3).
"institution of a denominational character": subs. (4).
"sponsoring body": subs. (5)(a).

GENERAL NOTE
    The arrangements for the operation of the FEFC reflect the pre-Act practices of the PCFC
and the UFC, *viz.* the consultation either of organisations representing institutions within the
sector or of the governing bodies of individual institutions. Among the considerations which the
FEFC has to keep in mind are the desirability that institutions obtain funding from other
sources (subs. (2)), and the proper balance between denominational and other institutions
within the sector (subs. (3)). In order to facilitate the orderly presentation of proposals, further
education colleges are to transmit to the FEFC requests for funding from institutions, such as
adult education colleges, which are not part of the further education sector (subss. (5) and (6)).
    This provision generally follows s.134(4) of the ERA 1988 and s.66 of this Act.
    Subsection (1) (the duty to consult) only comes into force when the FEFCs begin to fund
institutions and courses on April 1, 1993. Subsections (2), (3) and (4) came into force on May 6,
1992. Subsections (5) and (6) (external institutions) come into force on September 30, 1992, so
as to enable bids to be prepared before the FEFCs start their funding operations on April 1,
1993. These commencement provisions are contained in the Commencement No. 1 Order 1992,
para. 2 and, respectively, Scheds. 3, 1 and 2.

Subs. (1)
    Consult. Hodgson J. suggested in *R. v. Brent L.B.C.*, ex p. *Gunning* (1985) 84 L.G.R. 168,
that the duty to consult involves four elements: (i) it must take place at a time when proposals
are still at a formative stage; (ii) sufficient reasons must be given for any proposal to permit
intelligent consideration and response; (iii) adequate time must be given for consideration and
response; and (iv) the product of consultation must be conscientiously taken into account
before coming to the final decision. On requirements as to the manner and time needed for
consultation, see also *R. v. Secretary of State for Social Services*, ex p. *Association of Metropolitan Authorities* [1986] 1 W.L.R. 1, C. A.; *R. v. Secretary of State for Health*, ex p. *U.S. Tobacco
Industries* [1992] 1 All E.R. 212; *R. v. Coventry City Council*, ex p. *Newborne* (unreported,
September 26, 1985).

Subs. (2)
    Funding from other resources. This provision is in line with the policy of encouraging
institutions to seek support from outside bodies and to charge fees to students (White Paper,
Education and Training, Vol. 2, Chap. 6).

Subs. (4)
    Denominational character. Unlike the term as used in s.7(6)(b) of the ERA 1988, "denom-
inational character" is not confined to the Christian religion.

Subs. (5)
    External institution. This provision essentially covers adult education and community col-
leges. They do not make applications for funding directly to the FEFC, but must do so through
their local further education corporation. Ministers made it clear that such corporations have a
duty to forward appropriate requests for funding: "We believe that further education colleges
should have a formal rôle in determining adequacy [of submissions by adult education colleges],
in which process it would be necessary to confer with colleges making applications to it and the
local education authority as necessary" (Paymaster-General, *Hansard*, H.L. Vol. 534, col.
230). The further education college must forward the proposal of the external institution to the
FEFC where the provision in their area would not otherwise be adequate (Minister of State,
Hansard, H.C. Vol. 205, col. 256). In the event of default by the further education college, the
Secretary of State has powers to intervene under s.68 of the EA 1944, preserved by para. 9 of
Sched. 8 to this Act (Paymaster-General, *Hansard*, H.L. Vol. 534, col. 232). (On the exercise
of such powers, see *Secretary of State for Education and Science* v. *Tameside Metropolitan
Borough Council* [1977] A.C. 1014). The Government promised to issue guidance for institu-
tions about the procedure under this subsection: Secretary of State, *Hansard*, H.C. Vol. 205,
col. 204.

Subs. (6)
    Institution . . . specified in an order: see s.16.

Grants to councils

    7.—(1) The Secretary of State may make grants to each of the councils of
such amounts and subject to such terms and conditions as he may determine.

(2) The terms and conditions subject to which grants are made by the Secretary of State to either of the councils—

(a) may in particular impose requirements to be complied with in respect of every institution, or every institution falling within a class or description specified in the terms and conditions, being requirements to be complied with in the case of any institution to which the requirements apply before financial support of any amount or description so specified is provided by the council in respect of activities carried on by the institution, but

(b) shall not otherwise relate to the provision of financial support by the council in respect of activities carried on by any particular institution or institutions.

(3) Such terms and conditions may in particular—

(a) enable the Secretary of State to require the repayment, in whole or in part, of sums paid by him if any of the terms and conditions subject to which the sums were paid is not complied with, and

(b) require the payment of interest in respect of any period during which a sum due to the Secretary of State in accordance with any of the terms and conditions remains unpaid.

DEFINITIONS
"council": s.1(5).

GENERAL NOTE
The section is more detailed in specifying the powers of the Secretary of State in relation to monies made available to an FEFC than were ss.131(4) and 132(4) of the ERA 1988 in respect of the PCFC and the UFC. The section makes it clear that conditions may be attached to any grants made by the Secretary of State to an FEFC and clarifies what terms may be attached. The reasons for the greater detail are explained in the note to s.81 below. These powers are in addition to the power of the Secretary of State to issue directions under s.56.

Together with ss.56, 68 and 81, this section was one of the most controversial in Parliament. The original drafts of these sections were considered by opponents to empower the Secretary of State to interfere directly in relation to the operation of individual institutions. The Government's declared intention was to empower the Secretary of State to attach conditions which, while precluding him from favouring or harming an individual institution, might enable some classes of institution to be treated more favourably than others, *e.g.* by favouring sixth-form colleges over further education colleges (Paymaster-General, *Hansard*, H.L. Vol. 533, col. 684).

This section came into force on May 6, 1992: see Commencement No. 1 Order 1992, para. 2 and Sched. 1.

Subs. (1)
Secretary of State. See note to s.1(2).

Subs. (2)
The power of the Secretary of State to impose conditions on grants to the funding councils explicitly enables him to set out requirements which individual institutions must meet in order to qualify for funding from the FEFC. "[T]he power attaches general conditions which might have different impacts on institutions according to whether they meet the requirements specified. But it cannot involve making conditions, institution by institution" (Paymaster-General, *Hansard*, H.L. Vol. 535, col. 33). The prohibition on requirements relating to particular institutions parallels that in s.134(7) of the ERA 1988, but differs in some particulars from s.68 of this Act, governing the power of the Secretary of State to impose conditions on grants to the HEFC.

Activities. Unlike in s.5(1)(b) and (2)(b), "activities" are not expressly limited to activities connected with the provision of further or higher education.

Institution. This includes any institution receiving funds from the FEFC, whether it is an institution within the further education sector or not.

Subs. (3)
This provision parallels the powers of the FEFC in relation to the institutions which it funds (see s.5(7)).

Further functions

Supplementary functions

8.—(1) Each council—
  (a) shall provide the Secretary of State with such information or advice relating to the provision for the population of their area of further education as he may from time to time require, and
  (b) may provide the Secretary of State with such information or advice relating to such provision as they think fit,
and information and advice provided under this subsection shall be provided in such manner as the Secretary of State may from time to time determine.

(2) Each council shall keep under review the matters in respect of which they have power under this Part of this Act to give financial support.

(3) Where in the case of an institution within the further education sector or which provides any facilities for further education, the Secretary of State has, before the date on which the councils were established, made any grant, loan or other payment to the institution subject to any terms or conditions—
  (a) all the functions of the Secretary of State in relation to the grant, loan or other payment shall, if the Secretary of State so directs, be exercisable on his behalf by a council in accordance with such directions as he may give from time to time,
  (b) the council shall keep the Secretary of State informed of any action they take or propose to take in the exercise of those functions, and
  (c) the council shall immediately pay to the Secretary of State any sums received by them in the exercise of those functions.

(4) The Secretary of State may by order confer or impose on a council such supplementary functions relating to the provision of education as he thinks fit.

(5) For the purposes of subsection (4) above a function is a supplementary function in relation to a council if it is exercisable for the purposes of—
  (a) the exercise by the Secretary of State of functions of his under any enactment, or
  (b) the doing by the Secretary of State of anything he has power to do apart from any enactment,
and it is relevant to the provision of facilities for further education for the population of the council's area.

DEFINITIONS
"council": s.1(5).
"functions": s.61(1).
"further education": s.14(1)–(4).
"institution within the further education sector": s.91(3).

GENERAL NOTE
This section makes further provision about the relationship between the FEFC and the Secretary of State. The FEFC has a duty to provide the Secretary of State with such information relating to the provision of further education in its area as he may require, and has a power to provide him with such additional information as it thinks fit. Under subs. (2), the FEFC has a duty to keep under review matters over which it could exercise its funding powers. If the Secretary of State so directs, the FEFC may take over the administration of any loans made to an institution within the further education sector or for providing facilities for further education (subs. (3)). The Secretary of State may also confer on the FEFC such of his functions in relation to the provision of further education as he thinks fit.
    This section came into force on May 6, 1992: see Commencement No. 1 Order 1992, para. 2 and Sched. 1.

Subs. (1)
    The power to provide information under para. (b) parallels that granted to the UFC and the PCFC by ss.131(8)(b) and 132(10)(b) of the ERA 1988. The Secretary of State prescribes the form in which the information is given. There is no requirement that any information provided to the Secretary of State be published. In order to fulfil this rôle, the FEFC has power under s.54 to require institutions and local authorities to provide it with information. In addition, the

Secretary of State can require the publication of certain "performance indicators" by individual institutions (s.52).

Secretary of State. See note to s.1(2).

Subs. (2)
The duty to review parallels that of the UFC and the PCFC under ss.131(8)(a) and 132(10)(a) of the ERA 1988.

Subs. (3)
The powers of the Secretary of State to make loans is set out principally in s.3 of the Further Education Act 1985.

Subs. (4)
Such supplementary functions. Subsection (5) makes it clear that this subsection concerns only the transfer of existing powers of the Secretary of State and not the creation of additional powers.

Assessment of quality of education provided by institutions

9.—(1) Each council shall—
(a) secure that provision is made for assessing the quality of education provided in institutions within the further education sector, and
(b) establish a committee, to be known as the "Quality Assessment Committee", with the function of giving them advice on the discharge of their duty under paragraph (a) above and such other functions as may be conferred on the committee by the council.

(2) The majority of the members of the committee—
(a) shall be persons falling within subsection (3) below, and
(b) shall not be members of the council.

(3) Persons fall within this subsection if they appear to the council to have experience of, and to have shown capacity in, the provision of further education and, in appointing such persons, the council shall have regard to the desirability of their being currently engaged in the provision of further education or in carrying responsibility for such provision.

(4) Her Majesty's Chief Inspector of Schools in Wales shall, if asked to do so by the Further Education Funding Council for Wales, assess the quality of education provided in any institutions within the further education sector or any other institutions for which the council give, or are considering giving, financial support under this Part of this Act.

(5) Schedule 1 to this Act shall apply to a committee established under this section as it applies to committees established under paragraph 8 of that Schedule.

DEFINITIONS
"council": s.1(5).
"education": s.14(1).
"institution within the further education sector": s.91(3).

GENERAL NOTE
The monitoring of the quality of education has been a long-standing rôle of the Government in education. In relation to further education, this function has hitherto been performed by Her Majesty's Inspectors. Quality assessment involves external review of and judgements about the quality of teaching and learning in institutions (see further the note to s.70). This section establishes a Quality Assessment Committee within each FEFC to advise it on the assessment of quality within its sector, and to carry out such other functions as the FEFC requires. The quality of education is also subject to scrutiny as a result of the duty imposed on further education institutions by s.50 to publish information on the education they provide.

The membership of such a Committee is intended to be wider than that of those committees currently engaged in the provision of further education. Indeed, subs. (3) does not require that any member actually be currently engaged in further education, though the FEFC must have regard to the desirability of members with such experience when making nominations. All the same, the probable composition of such a Committee will include teachers, as well as representatives of industry and commerce.

With the exception of subs. (4), this section comes into force on April 1, 1993: see Commencement No. 1 Order 1992, para. 2 and Sched. 3.

Subs. (1)
   Education provided in institutions. Because of the breadth of the funding powers in s.5, the education subjected to quality assessment is not limited to further education, but includes any form of education funded by the FEFC or which it is considering funding.
   Although the Quality Assessment Committee has only advisory functions conferred upon it by the subsection, the committee may have powers to conduct an assessment conferred on it.

Subs. (3)
   Experience of . . . further education. It was established in *R. v. Croydon London Borough Council*, ex p. *Leney* (1987) 85 L.G.R. 466 that "persons of experience in education" may include those who do not hold a teaching qualification or have not had teaching experience. The form of words used here does not appear to exclude those whose experience is in the administration of education, rather than in teaching.

Subs. (4)
   Her Majesty's Chief Inspector of Schools in Wales. See s.5(1) of the Education (Schools) Act 1992. The power of the FEFC to request that quality assessment be conducted by Her Majesty's Chief Inspector of Schools in Wales enables the FEFC for Wales to avoid the need to appoint specialist assessors to its Quality Assessment Committee to conduct assessments.
   On other functions of Her Majesty's Inspectors, see s.55.

Subs. (5)
   The rules for the conduct of the Quality Assessment Committee are the same as for any other committee of the FEFC: see Sched. 1, para. 8.

Adjustment of local education authority sector

Functions of local education authorities in respect of secondary education

   10.—(1) In section 8 of the Education Act 1944 (duties of local education authorities) for subsection (1)(b) (secondary education) there is substituted—
>   "(b) for providing full-time education suitable to the requirements of pupils of compulsory school age, being either senior pupils or junior pupils who have attained the age of ten years and six months and whom it is expedient to educate together with senior pupils of compulsory school age."
   (2) After subsection (1) of that section there is inserted—
>   "(1A) A local education authority shall have power to secure the provision for their area of full-time education suitable to the requirements of persons over compulsory school age who have not attained the age of 19 years, including provision for persons from other areas."
   (3) In subsection (2) of that section (subsidiary obligations) for "fulfilling their duties" there is substituted "exercising their functions".

DEFINITIONS
   "compulsory school age": s.35 of the EA 1944.
   "local education authority": s.6 of the EA 1944.
   "pupil": s.14(6).

GENERAL NOTE
   This section makes adjustments to the duties of local education authorities consequent on the transfer of responsibility for further education to the FEFCs. The new s.8(1)(b) of the EA 1944 limits the duty of local authorities to providing full-time secondary education for pupils of compulsory school age. This does not preclude a local education authority from continuing sixth-form classes within their schools, which under s.14(2)(b) is deemed to be secondary education not further education. Under the new subs. (1A) to that section, local education authorities have a power to secure provision in their area for full-time education for those between 16 and 18. Such a power would include provision of such education within a school. This division of functions into duties and powers necessitates some rewording of s.8(2) of the EA 1944 (subs. (3)).
   This section comes into force on April 1, 1993: see Commencement No. 1 Order 1992, para. 2 and Sched. 3.

Subs. (1)
   Local education authority. See note to s.2(6).

Functions of local education authorities in respect of further education

11. For section 41 of the Education Act 1944 (functions of local education authorities in respect of further education) there is substituted—

"**Functions of local education authorities in respect of further education.**
41.—(1) It shall be the duty of every local education authority to secure the provision for their area of adequate facilities for further education.

(2) Subsection (1) above does not apply to education to which section 2(1) or 3(1) of the Further and Higher Education Act 1992 applies, but in respect of education to which section 3(1) of that Act applies a local education authority may—

(a) secure the provision for their area of such facilities as appear to them to be appropriate for meeting the needs of the population of their area; and

(b) do anything which appears to them to be necessary or expedient for the purposes of or in connection with such provision.

(3) Subject to subsection (4) below and section 14(1) to (4) of the Further and Higher Education Act 1992, in this Act "further education" means—

(a) full-time and part-time education suitable to the requirements of persons over compulsory school age (including vocational, social, physical and recreational training); and

(b) organized leisure-time occupation provided in connection with the provision of such education.

(4) In this Act "further education" does not include higher education or secondary education.

(5) In subsection (3)(b) above "organized leisure time occupation" means leisure-time occupation, in such organized cultural training and recreative activities as are suited to their requirements, for any persons over compulsory school age who are able and willing to profit by facilities provided for that purpose.

(6) A local education authority may secure the provision of further education for persons from other areas.

(7) In exercising their functions under this section a local education authority shall have regard to any educational facilities provided by institutions within the higher education sector or the further education sector, and other bodies, which are provided for, or available for use by persons in, their area.

(8) In exercising their functions under this section a local education authority shall also have regard to the requirements of persons over compulsory school age who have learning difficulties.

(9) Subject to subsection (10) below, for the purposes of subsection (8) above a person has a "learning difficulty" if—

(a) he has a significantly greater difficulty in learning than the majority of persons of his age; or

(b) he has a disability which either prevents or hinders him from making use of facilities of a kind generally provided in pursuance of the duty under subsection (1) above for persons of his age.

(10) A person is not to be taken as having a learning difficulty solely because the language (or form of the language) in which he is, or will be, taught is different from a language (or form of a language) which has at any time been spoken in his home.

(11) A local education authority may do anything which appears to them to be necessary or expedient for the purposes of or in connection with the exercise of their functions under this section."

DEFINITIONS
"further education": subss. (3) and (4); s.14(1) and (2).
"higher education": s.90(1); s.120(1) of and Sched. 6 to the ERA 1988.
"learning difficulties": subs. (10).
"local education authority": s.6 of the EA 1944.
"organised leisure-time occupation": subs. (5).
"secondary education": s.14(2)–(4).

GENERAL NOTE
This section enacts a revision of s.41 of the EA 1944, and sets out the reduced functions of local education authorities in respect of further education. In broad terms, the local education authority retains a duty only in respect of those aspects of further education which are not covered by the FEFC or by other sectors. The FEFC has exclusive duties to ensure the provision of full-time further education of those between 16 and 18 (s.2 of this Act), and has duties in respect of the full-time further education of others and part-time education (s.3). The general duty under the new s.41(1) of the EA 1944 that a local education authority must secure adequate facilities for further education in its area must be read as restricted by the duties of the FEFC. The new s.41(2) of the EA 1944 merely empowers the local education authority to secure the provision of facilities for further education appropriate to its population in relation to the full-time further education of those over 18 and part-time education. Given that the local education authority must have regard to what is already provided by others (subs. (7)), its scope for providing full-time further education for those over 18 and part-time education will be limited. The principal area for the local education authority's duty under s.41(1) of the EA 1944 will be the provision of adult and leisure education (subss. (3) and (5)). The White Paper *Education and Training* envisaged that funding through the FEFC for education for adults would be limited to "courses that can help them in their careers and in daily life" (Vol. 1, para. 9.11), and that local education authorities would provide other forms of adult education.
The Government resisted the inclusion of any explicit reference to youth services in the new s.41 of the EA 1944. Youth services are authorised both by s.41 and by s.53 of the EA 1944. "Youth services" is not a statutory term but combines two elements from the new s.41(3): vocational, social, physical and recreational training (para. (a)) and organised leisure-time occupation (para. (b)). Since the new s.41 does not differ from the original section in this respect, it was not considered necessary to include an explicit reference to youth services in the new version (see Paymaster-General, *Hansard*, H.L. Vol. 533, col. 703).
Special mention is made in subss. (8)–(10) of the new s.41 of the EA 1944 of the needs of persons with learning difficulties. This complements the duties of the FEFC under s.4.
This section comes into force on April 1, 1993: see Commencement No. 1 Order 1992, para. 2 and Sched. 3.

New s.41(1)
Local education authority. See note to s.2(6).
Further education. In this context, education provided at a school where full-time education of compulsory school age children takes place is secondary education, not further education (s.14(2)(b)).

New s.41(2)
Education to which section 2(1) or 3(1) . . . applies. In short, this refers to full-time education of those between 16 and 18 (s.2), and the full-time further education of those over 18, and part-time education (s.3). These are the province of the FEFC.

New s.41(3)
This provision encompasses adult education, leisure education and youth services. (On youth services see the General Note above).

New s.41(7)
Other bodies. These include community colleges and adult education institutions, as well as private sector providers.

New s.41(8), (9) and (10)
These provisions substantially reproduce s.4(1), (2), (6) and (7). For commentary see note to s.4.

Subs. (11)
Necessary and expedient. These and similar words (such as "it appears to . . . .") do not grant an unqualified discretion. The discretion must be exercised reasonably, on proper grounds and in good faith to achieve the purposes of the legislation (see H. W. R. Wade, *Administrative Law* (5th ed., Oxford 1988), pp. 445–54).

Provision of further education in schools

Provision of further education in maintained schools

12.—(1) At the end of section 9 of the Education Act 1944 (power of local authority to establish schools) there is added—

"(7) The powers conferred by subsection (1) of this section shall not extend to establishing a school to provide—
(a) part-time education suitable to the requirements of persons of any age over compulsory school age; or
(b) full-time education suitable to the requirements of persons who have attained the age of 19 years."

(2) In section 13 of the Education Act 1980 (requirement to publish proposal for alteration of voluntary school) after subsection (1) there is inserted—

"(1A) The reference in subsection (1) above to a change in the character of a school does not include a change in character resulting only from persons beginning or ceasing to be provided with—
(a) part-time education suitable to the requirements of persons of any age over compulsory school age; or
(b) full-time education suitable to the requirements of persons who have attained the age of 19 years;
and no proposals under this section by any persons that a school established or proposed to be established by them, or by persons whom they represent, should be maintained by a local education authority shall be approved by the Secretary of State if the school or proposed school is to provide education falling within paragraph (a) or (b) above."

(3) In Part III of the Education (No. 2) Act 1986 (conduct of county, voluntary and maintained special schools) after section 16 there is inserted—

"Provision of further education.

16A.—(1) The governing body of any county, voluntary or maintained special school shall be responsible for determining whether or not to provide—
(a) part-time education suitable to the requirements of persons of any age over compulsory school age; or
(b) full-time education suitable to the requirements of persons who have attained the age of 19 years,
but the governing body of a maintained special school shall not determine to provide, or to cease to provide, such education without the consent of the local education authority.

(2) It shall be the duty of the governing body of any such school which provides such education to secure that such education is not provided at any time in a room where pupils are at that time being taught except in such circumstances as may be prescribed."

(4) In section 9 of the Education Reform Act 1988 (exceptions, etc., relating to religious education for pupils) after subsection (1) there is inserted—

"(1A) It shall not be required, as a condition of any person attending any maintained school to receive further education, that he shall attend or abstain from attending any Sunday school or any place of religious worship."

(5) In section 33 of that Act (schemes for financing schools), in subsection (4)(a) (meaning of general schools budget) after "that authority" there is inserted "(other than expenditure in respect of the provision of part-time education suitable to the requirements of persons of any age over com-

pulsory school age or full-time education suitable to the requirements of persons who have attained the age of 19 years)".

(6) In section 36 of that Act (delegation to governing body of management of school's budget share), after subsection (5) (governing body entitled to spend sums for the purposes of the school) there is inserted—

"(5A) In subsection (5) above "the purposes of the school" does not include purposes wholly referable to the provision of—
  (a) part-time education suitable to the requirements of persons of any age over compulsory school age; or
  (b) full-time education suitable to the requirements of persons who have attained the age of 19 years."

(7) In section 38 of that Act (determination of budget share), after subsection (3) (matters that must or may be taken into account) there is inserted—

"(3A) The allocation formula under a scheme shall not include provision for taking into account persons provided with—
  (a) part-time education suitable to the requirements of persons of any age over compulsory school age; or
  (b) full-time education suitable to the requirements of persons who have attained the age of 19 years."

(8) In section 105 of that Act (city technology colleges etc.), in subsection (2)(b) (must provide education for pupils who have attained 11 but not 19 years) "but not the age of 19 years" is omitted.

(9) In section 106 of that Act (prohibition of charges), after subsection (1) (no charges for admission to maintained school) there is inserted—

"(1A) Subsection (1) above shall not apply to the admission of any person to any maintained school for the purpose of—
  (a) part-time education suitable to the requirements of persons of any age over compulsory school age; or
  (b) full-time education suitable to the requirements of persons who have attained the age of 19 years."

DEFINITIONS
  "city college for the technology of the arts": s.105(1) of the ERA 1988.
  "city technology college": s.105(1) of the ERA 1988.
  "compulsory school age": s.35 of the EA 1944.
  "county school": s.9(2) of the EA 1944.
  "governing body": s.90(1) and (2).
  "local authority": s.90(1).
  "maintained school": s.25(1) of the ERA 1988.
  "primary school": s.114 of the EA 1944, as amended by Sched. 8, para. 13 to this Act.
  "religious education": s.8(2) of the ERA 1988.
  "special school": s.9(5) of the EA 1944, as substituted by s.11(1) of the EA 1981.
  "voluntary school": s.9(2) of the EA 1944.

GENERAL NOTE
  This section alters the powers of a local education authority to establish institutions and make provision for further education. By an amendment to s.9 of the EA 1944 made by subs. (1), a local education authority may not establish institutions in this area for the part-time education of persons over 16, nor the full-time education of persons over 18. Under subs. (2), voluntary schools do not need to follow the procedure under s.13 of the EA 1980 when deciding to provide or cease to provide part-time education of persons over 16, nor the full-time education of persons over 18. It is for the governing body of the school in question to decide whether such education is to be provided by it (subs. (3)). City technology colleges are also empowered to provide such education (subs. (8)). Where provided in a school, such education is to be separated from that of pupils of compulsory school age (new s.16A (2) of the EA (No. 2) 1986). Such education is to be self-financing and provisions are made in subss. (5)–(7) to ensure that local authority budget allocations to schools observe this. A power for schools to make charges for such education is introduced by subs. (9).

The distinct status of those receiving further education in a school has as a consequence that they are to be exempted from the obligation to attend religious worship in a maintained school (subs. (4)). (Section 44 makes provision for collective worship in denominational schools).

This section comes into force on August 1, 1993: see Commencement No. 1 Order 1992, para. 2 and Sched. 4.

Subs. (2)

No proposals. This provision ensures that voluntary schools are only turned into further education institutions under the provisions of this Act.

Full-time education. See s.6(6) and note to s.2(1).

Subs. (3)

In a room where pupils . . . . The provision of further education in schools enabled by this section does not permit mixed classes. As Lord Cavendish explained, "Our aim is to protect pupils below compulsory school age from possible risk . . . . At the one end of the spectrum there is the risk of distraction and at the other the risk of child abuse in all its forms" (*Hansard*, H.L. Vol. 534, cols. 262–3). Further-education students may, however, attend classes alongside sixth-formers of the school. Family workshop teaching which involves parents and children undertaking classes together is not prohibited by this provision, where the courses are extra-curricular activities.

Subs. (4)

Religious worship in voluntary schools is covered by s.44. Under that section religious worship is optional for persons over compulsory school age in further education institutions. This provision ensures equivalent treatment where the further education is provided in a school.

Subs. (7)

This provision relates to budgets devolved from the local education authority to be administered by the governing body of the school as part of the local management of schools initiative under ss.38 and 39 of the ERA 1988.

Subs. (9)

This provision implements para. 4.12 of the White Paper, *Education and Training*. It is intended that schools will thereby be able to generate extra revenue and to use their resources more efficiently. As an indirect consequence, younger pupils will become accustomed to the idea that education is not just for children.

Provision of further education in grant-maintained schools

13.—(1) In section 57(5) of the Education Reform Act 1988 (provision by grant-maintained school of education which is neither primary nor secondary) after "provided that" there is inserted—

    "(a) it is part-time education suitable to the requirements of persons of any age over compulsory school age, or full-time education suitable to the requirements of persons who have attained the age of 19 years; or.

    (b) ."

(2) At the end of section 79 of that Act (grants to grant-maintained schools in respect of expenditure for the purposes of the school) there is added—

    "(13) In this section "the purposes of the school" do not include purposes wholly referable to the provision of—

        (a) part-time education suitable to the requirements of persons of any age over compulsory school age; or

        (b) full-time education suitable to the requirements of persons who have attained the age of 19 years."

(3) In section 89 of that Act (change of character of grant-maintained school) after subsection (1) there is inserted—

    "(1A) The reference in subsection (1) above to a change in the character of a school does not include a change in character resulting only from persons beginning or ceasing to be provided with part-time education suitable to the requirements of persons of any age over compulsory school age or full-time education suitable to the requirements of persons who have attained the age of 19 years, but it shall be the duty of the governing body of any grant-maintained school which provides such education to secure that it is not provided at any time in a room where pupils are at that time being taught except in such circumstances as may be prescribed."

DEFINITIONS
"grant-maintained school": s.52 of the ERA 1988.
"pupil": s.14(6).

GENERAL NOTE
This section empowers grant-maintained schools to provide further education in the same way, and under similar restrictions to those imposed upon schools maintained by a local education authority.

Subsection (1) amends s.57(5) of the ERA 1988 to empower grant-maintained schools to provide further education. Subsection (2) ensures that the education so provided is self-financing by preventing the Secretary of State from providing grants for that purpose. Subsection (3) ensures that the provision of such education does not amount to a change in character of the institution for the purposes of s.89 of the ERA 1988. Subsection (3) also introduces the restriction contained in s.12(9) that the education of pupils of compulsory school age and persons receiving further education should be kept distinct.

This section comes into force on August 1, 1993: see Commencement No. 1 Order 1992, para. 2 and Sched. 4.

Subs. (1)
Full-time education, part-time education. See s.6(6) and notes to s.2(1).

Subs. (3)
In a room. See note to s.12(9).

General

Meaning of "further education", "secondary education", "school" and "pupil"

14.—(1) Subject to subsection (2) below, for the purposes of the Education Acts education to which this subsection applies, that is, full-time education suitable to the requirements of persons over compulsory school age who have not attained the age of 19 years, is further education not secondary education.

(2) Subject to subsection (3) below, for the purposes of those Acts—
(a) education falling within section 8(1)(b) of the Education Act 1944 (full-time education suitable to the requirements of pupils of compulsory school age), and
(b) education to which subsection (1) above applies provided at a school where education falling within section 8(1)(b) of that Act is also provided,
is secondary education not further education.

(3) For the purposes of the Education Acts education provided for persons who have attained the age of 19 years is further education not secondary education; but where a person has begun a particular course of secondary education before attaining the age of 18 years, then, if he continues to attend that course, the education does not cease to be secondary education by reason of his having attained the age of 19 years.

(4) In subsections (1) to (3) above "education" does not include higher education.

(5) For the purposes of the Education Acts "school" means an educational institution not within the further education sector or the higher education sector, being an institution for providing any one or more of the following—
(a) primary education,
(b) education which is secondary education by virtue of subsection (2)(a) above, or
(c) education to which subsection (1) above applies,

whether or not the institution also provides further education or other secondary education.

(6) For the purposes of the Education Acts, and of any instrument made or having effect as if made under those Acts, "pupil" means a person for whom education is being provided at a school, other than—

(a) a person who has attained the age of 19 years for whom further education is being provided, or

(b) a person for whom part-time education suitable to the requirements of persons of any age over compulsory school age is being provided.

DEFINITIONS
"compulsory school age": s.35 of the EA 1944.
"education": subs. (4).
"Education Acts": ss.90(1) and 94(2).
"higher education": s.90(1).
"primary education": s.8 of the EA 1944, as amended by s.3 of the Education (Miscellaneous Provisions) Act 1948.
"pupil": subs. (6).
"secondary education": subs. (2).
"school": subs. (5).

GENERAL NOTE
This section provides definitions of "further education" and "secondary education". Full-time education of those over compulsory school age (16) and under 19 is defined as further education by subs. (1), as is the provision of education for those who are 19 and over (subs. (3)). Two exceptions are stated. Subsection (2) states that where full-time education for those between 16 and 18 is provided in a school where the education of pupils of compulsory school age takes place, then the education is deemed to be "secondary education". Subsection (3) provides that where a person began a course of secondary education before the age of 18, that education does not cease to be secondary education simply because he attains the age of 19.

Subsection (5) makes consequential amendments to the definition of a "school" within the Education Acts to cater for the fact that it may be providing further education.

Subsection (6) redefines "pupil" for the purposes of the Education Acts to exclude persons for whom further education within the meaning of subss. (1) and (2) is being provided.

Subsections (1) to (4) come into force on May 6, 1992, in relation to those provisions of this Act coming into force on that day, and on September 30, 1992, in relation to those provisions coming into force on that day. Subsections (1) to (5) come fully into force on April 1, 1993. Subsection (6) only comes into force on August 1, 1993. These commencement provisions are set out in the Commencement No. 1 Order 1992, para. 2 and Scheds. 1 to 4.

Subs. (6)
Pupil. Persons in receipt of further education in a school are not pupils and so are not subject to the same obligations as other pupils, *e.g.* in relation to religious worship (s.12(4)).

CHAPTER II

INSTITUTIONS WITHIN THE FURTHER EDUCATION SECTOR

The further education corporations

Initial incorporation of existing institutions

15.—(1) Before the appointed day the Secretary of State shall by order specify—

(a) each educational institution maintained by a local education authority which appears to him to fall within subsection (2) below, and

(b) each county school, controlled school or grant-maintained school which appears to him to fall within subsection (3) below.

(2) An institution falls within this subsection if on 1st November 1990 its enrolment number calculated in accordance with paragraph 1(1) of Schedule 3 to this Act was not less than 15 per cent. of its total enrolment number calculated in accordance with paragraph 1(2) of that Schedule.

(3) An institution falls within this subsection if on 17th January 1991 not less than 60 per cent. of the pupils at the institution were receiving full-time

education suitable to the requirements of persons over compulsory school age who have not attained the age of 19 years.

(4) On the appointed day a body corporate shall be established, for each institution so specified, for the purpose of conducting the institution as from the operative date.

(5) The name given in the order under subsection (1) above as the name of the institution shall be the initial name of the body corporate.

(6) Where an educational institution, being an institution maintained by a local education authority or a grant-maintained school, has been established since 1st November 1990 or, as the case may be, 17th January 1991 by a merger of two or more institutions existing on that date, the institution shall be treated as falling within subsection (2) or, as the case may be, subsection (3) above if it would have done so if the merger had taken place before that date.

(7) In this section "the appointed day" means the day appointed under section 94 of this Act for the commencement of subsection (4) above.

DEFINITIONS
"appointed day": subs. (7) and s.94(1).
"compulsory school age": s.35 of the EA 1944.
"controlled school": s.9(2) of the EA 1944.
"county school": s.9(2) of the EA 1944.
"enrolment number": Sched. 3, para. 1.
"grant-maintained school": s.52 of the ERA 1988.
"local education authority": s.6 of the EA 1944.
"school": s.14(5).
"total enrolment number": Sched. 3, para. 2.

GENERAL NOTE
This section defines one of four routes by which an institution can come within the further education sector. Under this section, the Secretary of State is required to specify certain existing institutions maintained by the local education authority or grant-maintained schools and these become further education corporations on the appointed day. This will be the principal route into the further education sector. The other routes are by later incorporation (s.16), designation (s.28) and transfer from the higher education sector (s.47).

This section requires the Secretary of State to specify bodies to become further education corporations on the appointed day which satisfy one of the two criteria set out in subss. (2) and (3). Under subs. (2), the first criterion is of "enrolment numbers" similar to "full-time equivalent enrolment number" under the original s.161(2) of and Sched. 9 to the ERA 1988. "Enrolment numbers" are calculated in accordance with Sched. 3 to this Act, and the multipliers set out there differ significantly from those in Sched. 9 of the ERA 1988. An institution qualifies to become a further education corporation under subs. (2) if the number of full-time, sandwich-course, block-release and day-release students on courses of further or higher education, as calculated in accordance with Sched. 3 (the "enrolment number"), was not less than 15 per cent. of the total number of further and higher education students of the institution, as calculated under that Schedule (the "total enrolment number") on November 1, 1990. The second criterion set out in subs. (3) relates to the age of the persons receiving education at an institution on January 17, 1991. If 60 per cent. of the pupils at an institution were receiving full-time education suitable for 16- to 18-year-olds on that date, then it should be designated as a further education corporation under subs. (1). This criterion typically identifies sixth-form colleges.

Provision is made in subs. (6) for new institutions or amalgamations of institutions after the qualifying dates specified in subss. (2) and (3), but before the appointed day for the commencement of this section.

The appointed day (subs. (7)) will be September 30, 1992 when subs. (4) comes into force: Commencement No. 1 Order 1992, para. 2 and Sched. 2. The rest of this section came into force on May 6, 1992: *ibid.*, Sched. 1.

Subs. (1)
This provision enables the Secretary of State to designate as further education corporations institutions maintained or controlled either by a local education authority or by the Secretary of State. Voluntary controlled schools, like other voluntary schools, will remain governed by their trust deed and become part of the further education sector by designation under s.28.
Secretary of State. See note to s.1(2).
Order. An order made under this section must be made by way of a statutory instrument which is subject to the negative resolution procedure in Parliament (s.89(1) and (3)).

Subs. (2)
   Body corporate. See note to s.1(1).

Subs. (4)
   Operative date. The operative date is the date specified by the Secretary of State in relation to each institution (s.17(2)).

Subs. (6)
   Merger. Merger involves the joinder of two institutions. This provision does not include a consortium of institutions.

Orders incorporating further institutions

16.—(1) The Secretary of State may by order make provision for the establishment of a body corporate—
   (a) for the purpose of establishing and conducting an educational institution, or
   (b) for the purpose of conducting an existing educational institution,
but shall not make an order in respect of an existing institution without the consent of the governing body.

   (2) Subsection (1) above does not apply to any educational institution maintained by a local education authority or any grant-maintained school; but if at any time it appears to the Secretary of State, in the case of any educational institution so maintained or any grant-maintained school—
   (a) that its enrolment number calculated in accordance with paragraph 1(1) of Schedule 3 to this Act was not less than 15 per cent. of its total enrolment number calculated in accordance with paragraph 1(2) of that Schedule, or
   (b) that it is principally concerned with the provision of full-time education suitable to the requirements of persons over compulsory school age who have not attained the age of 19 years.
he may by order make provision for the establishment of a body corporate for the purpose of conducting that institution.

   (3) If at any time a council proposes to the Secretary of State that a body corporate should be established for the purpose of conducting an educational institution which—
   (a) is maintained by a local education authority or is a grant-maintained school, and
   (b) is principally concerned with the provision of further or higher education or full-time education suitable to the requirements of persons over compulsory school age who have not attained the age of 19 years,
the Secretary of State may by order make provision for the establishment of a body corporate for that purpose.

   (4) The name given in the order under this section as the name of the institution shall be the initial name of the body corporate.

   (5) An order under this section shall provide for the institution to be conducted by the body corporate as from the operative date.

DEFINITIONS
   "compulsory school age": s.35 of the EA 1944.
   "council": s.1(5).
   "enrolment number": Sched. 3, para. 1(1).
   "governing body": s.90(1) and (2).
   "total enrolment number": Sched. 3, para. 1(2).

GENERAL NOTE
   This section empowers the Secretary of State to make an order at any time to incorporate as further education corporations institutions which do not fall within the criteria set out in s.15(2) and (3). Such a further education corporation may be incorporated to run either a new or an existing institution, provided that, in the latter case, the governing body consents. Subsection (2) allows for the incorporation of institutions mentioned in s.15(1), where they meet similar

criteria on "enrolment numbers" other than on the qualifying dates set out in s.15(2) and (3). Subsection (3) allows for the incorporation of institutions on the recommendation of the FEFC.

This section comes into effect on September 30, 1992: see Commencement No. 1 Order 1992, para. 2 and Sched. 2.

Subs. (1)
Secretary of State. See note to s.1(2).
Order. An order made under this section must be made by way of a statutory instrument which is subject to the negative resolution procedure in Parliament (s.89(1) and (3)).
Body corporate. See note to s.1(1).

Subs. (2)
Institutions which fail to qualify for incorporation as further education corporations under the criteria set out in s.15(2) and (3) because they do not meet them at the qualifying dates may nevertheless be incorporated if they satisfy one of two criteria. The first criterion on "enrolment numbers" is the same as under s.15(2). The second criterion, relating to the age of students, differs from s.15(3) in that there is no requirement that 60 per cent. of students be between 16 and 18, merely that the institution is "principally concerned" with the provision of education to such an age group (subs. (2)(b)).

Subs. (3)
The proposal of the FEFC that an institution be incorporated as a further education corporation must relate to an institution which satisfies qualifying criteria which are substantially the same as under s.16(2)(b) that it is maintained by a local authority or by the Secretary of State, and that it is principally concerned with the provision of education to 16- to 18-year-olds.
Order. See subs. (1) above. No order may be made without the consent of the governing body of the institution.

Subs. (5)
Operative date. The operative date is the date specified by the Secretary of State in relation to each institution s.17(2)).

"Further education corporation" and "operative date"

17.—(1) In this Act "further education corporation" means a body corporate established under section 15 or 16 of this Act.

(2) In this Part of this Act "operative date", in relation to a further education corporation and the institution, means—

   (a) in the case of a further education corporation established under section 15 of this Act, such date as the Secretary of State may by order appoint in relation to the corporations so established, and

   (b) in the case of a further education corporation established under section 16 of this Act, such date as the Secretary of State may by order appoint in relation to that corporation.

DEFINITIONS
"further education corporation": subs. (1).
"operative date": subs. (2).

GENERAL NOTE
This section provides definitions of "further education corporation" and "operative date", as this latter term is used in this Part of the Act. In relation to further education corporations created under ss.15 and 16, the operative date on which the corporation comes into existence is that specified by the Secretary of State in his order establishing it.

This section came into effect on May 6, 1992: see Commencement No. 1 Order 1992, para. 2 and Sched. 1.

Subs. (2)
Secretary of State. See note to s.1(2).

Principal powers of a further education corporation

18.—(1) A further education corporation may—
   (a) provide further and higher education, and
   (b) supply goods or services in connection with their provision of education,

and those powers are referred to in section 19 of this Act as the corporation's principal powers.

(2) For the purposes of subsection (1) above, goods are supplied in connection with the provision of education by a further education corporation if they result from—

    (a) their provision of education or anything done by them under this Act for the purpose of or in connection with their provision of education,

    (b) the use of their facilities or the expertise of persons employed by them in the fields in which they are so employed, or

    (c) ideas of a person employed by them, or of one of their students, arising out of their provision of education.

(3) For the purposes of that subsection, services are supplied in connection with the provision of education by a further education corporation if—

    (a) they result from their provision of education or anything done by them under this Act for the purpose of or in connection with their provision of education,

    (b) they are provided by making available their facilities or the expertise of persons employed by them in the fields in which they are so employed, or

    (c) they result from ideas of a person employed by them, or of one of their students, arising out of their provision of education.

DEFINITIONS
"further education": s.14(1) and (2).
"further education corporation": s.17(1).
"higher education": s.90(1); s.120(1) of and Sched. 6 to the ERA 1988.
"principal powers": subs. (1).

GENERAL NOTE
This section sets out the principal powers of a further education corporation. Under subs. (1), these principal powers are the provision of further and higher education, and the supply of goods and services relating to them. Subsection (2) sets out what is meant by the supply of goods and subs. (3) sets out what is meant by the supply of services. The provisions on the supply of goods and services substantially reproduce those contained in the Further Education Act 1985 (c.47), though the provider is no longer the local education authority.

This section comes into force on September 30, 1992: see Commencement No. 1 Order 1992, para. 2 and Sched. 2.

Subs. (2)
Supplied. Under the Supply of Goods and Services Act 1982, goods are supplied either by a contract for the transfer of goods (s.1) or a contract for the hire of goods (s.6).

Goods. This subsection makes it clear that goods supplied in connection with the provision of education include products arising from (a) the provision of education, *e.g.* course materials or the products of course work, (b) from the use of the facilities of a further education corporation or the expertise of its employees in their fields of work, or (c) from ideas generated by employees or students in the course of the provision of education.

Ideas. The ability of the institution to sell products of the ideas of employees and students was first contained in s.1(1)(c) of the Further Education Act 1985.

Subs. (3)
These provisions on services mirror those on the supply of goods in relation to the origin of the services. They substantially reproduce those contained in s.1(2) of the Further Education Act 1985.

Supplied. Under s.12(1) of the Supply of Goods and Services Act 1982, services are supplied when a person carries out a service.

Supplementary powers of a further education corporation

19.—(1) A further education corporation may do anything (including in particular the things referred to in subsections (2) to (4) below) which appears to the corporation to be necessary or expedient for the purpose of or in connection with the exercise of any of their principal powers.

(2) A further education corporation may conduct an educational institution for the purpose of carrying on activities undertaken in the exercise of

their powers to provide further or higher education and, in particular, may assume as from the operative date the conduct of the institution in respect of which the corporation is established.

(3) A further education corporation may provide facilities of any description appearing to the corporation to be necessary or desirable for the purposes of or in connection with carrying on any activities undertaken in the exercise of their principal powers (including boarding accommodation and recreational facilities for students and staff and facilities to meet the needs of students having learning difficulties within the meaning of section 4(6) of this Act).

(4) A further education corporation may—

(a) acquire and dispose of land and other property,

(b) enter into contracts, including in particular—

(i) contracts for the employment of teachers and other staff for the purposes of or in connection with carrying on any activities undertaken in the exercise of their principal powers, and

(ii) contracts with respect to the carrying on by the corporation of any such activities,

(c) borrow such sums as the corporation think fit for the purposes of carrying on any activities they have power to carry on or meeting any liability transferred to them under sections 23 to 27 of this Act and, in connection with such borrowing, may grant any mortgage, charge or other security in respect of any land or other property of the corporation,

(d) invest any sums not immediately required for the purposes of carrying on any activities they have power to carry on,

(e) accept gifts of money, land or other property and apply it, or hold and administer it on trust for, any of those purposes, and

(f) do anything incidental to the conduct of an educational institution providing further or higher education, including founding scholarships or exhibitions, making grants and giving prizes.

(5) The power conferred on a further education corporation by subsection (4)(c) above to borrow money may not be exercised without the consent of the appropriate council, and such consent may be given for particular borrowing or for borrowing of a particular class.

DEFINITIONS
"council": s.1(5).
"further education": s.14(1) and (2).
"further education corporation": s.17(1).
"higher education": s.90(1); s.120(1) of the ERA 1988.
"institution": s.91(6).
"land": s.90(1).
"operative date": s.17(2).
"principal powers": s.18(1).
"students having learning difficulties": s.4(3).

GENERAL NOTE
A further education corporation is given supplementary powers under this section to do anything necessary or expedient to the exercise of its principal powers. The supplementary powers include the power to run an educational institution (subs. (2)), to provide facilities, *e.g.* accommodation and sports facilities for staff and students (subs. (3)), and general powers in relation to property transactions, contracts, borrowing, investments, gifts, scholarships and prizes (subs. (4)). These powers follow closely those given to higher education corporations by s.124(2) of the ERA 1988. But a further education corporation does not have a power to form another body corporate, *e.g.* a company limited by guarantee, to carry on its activities (contrast s.124(2)(f) of the ERA 1988). Unlike a higher education corporation, its borrowing powers are subject to the consent of the FEFC (subs. (5)).

This section comes into force on September 30, 1992: see Commencement No. 1 Order 1992, para. 2 and Sched. 2.

Subs. (1)
Necessary or expedient. See note to s.11.

Subs. (2)
   Institution. This refers principally to the institution which has been transferred from the local authority to the further education corporation under the Act.

Subs. (3)
   Students with learning difficulties. See note to s.4(3). This phrase replaced "disabled student" (*cf.* s.124(2)(b) and (4) of the ERA 1988) in order to give consistency with the terminology used in the rest of this Act.

Constitution of corporation and conduct of the institution

   20.—(1) For every further education corporation established to conduct an educational institution there shall be—
   (a) an instrument providing for the constitution of the corporation (to be known as the instrument of government), and
   (b) an instrument in accordance with which the corporation, and the institution, are to be conducted (to be known as articles of government).
   (2) Instruments of government and articles of government—
   (a) shall comply with the requirements of Schedule 4 to this Act, and
   (b) may make any provision authorised to be made by that Schedule and such other provision as may be necessary or desirable.
   (3) The validity of any proceedings of a further education corporation, or of any committee of the corporation, shall not be affected by a vacancy amongst the members or by any defect in the appointment or nomination of a member.
   (4) Every document purporting to be an instrument made or issued by or on behalf of a further education corporation and to be duly executed under the seal of the corporation, or to be signed or executed by a person authorised by the corporation to act in that behalf, shall be received in evidence and be treated, without further proof, as being so made or issued unless the contrary is shown.

DEFINITIONS
   "articles of government": subs. (1)(b).
   "further education corporation": s.17(1).
   "instrument of government": subs. (1)(a).

GENERAL NOTE
   This section specifies the basic instruments which govern the constitution and conduct of the institution. The organisation of further education corporations, like that of higher education corporations under s.71, is more flexible than the higher education corporations established under the ERA 1988. For those bodies, s.123 of and Sched. 7 to the ERA 1988 set out a uniform set of rules for instruments of government. Subsection (2) follows a similar pattern for further education corporations by prescribing that all instruments and articles of government must comply with the requirements of Sched. 4. Unlike Sched. 7 to the ERA 1988, which contained 19 detailed paragraphs, Sched. 4 sets out in 12 short paragraphs the basic features which must appear either in the instrument of government or in the articles of government. The Act deliberately lightens the prescription of the past to provide further education corporations with greater flexibility in designing their own structures. In particular, there is no requirement that specific groups, staff, students, and local authorities, have any compulsory representation.
   This section comes into force on September 30, 1992: see Commencement No. 1 Order 1992, para. 2 and Sched. 2.

Subs. (1)
   Instrument. The initial instrument is created by order or by regulations as provided under s.21. Subsequent instruments are governed by the provisions of s.22.

Subs. (3)
   This provision reproduces Sched. 7, para. 14 to the ERA 1988.

Subs. (4)
   This provision reproduces Sched. 7, para. 17 to the ERA 1988.

Initial instruments and articles

21.—(1) As from the date on which a further education corporation is established, the instrument of government and articles of government—

   (a) in the case of an institution which was a grant-maintained school on that date, shall be such as is prescribed by the order in respect of the institution under section 15 or 16 of this Act, and

   (b) in any other case, shall be such as is prescribed by regulations.

(2) Such orders and regulations—

   (a) may provide for all or any of the persons who, on the date on which a corporation is established to conduct the grant-maintained school or other existing institution, are the members of the governing body of the institution to be the initial members of the corporation, and

   (b) may make such other provision in relation to grant-maintained schools or other existing institutions as appears to the Secretary of State necessary or desirable to secure continuity in their government.

(3) In the case of a further education corporation established to conduct an institution which, on the date the corporation was established, was a grant-maintained school, the governing body incorporated under Chapter IV of Part I of the Education Reform Act 1988 shall, on the operative date, be dissolved.

DEFINITIONS
   "articles of government": s.20(1)(b).
   "further education corporation": s.17(1).
   "grant-maintained school": s.52 of the ERA 1988.
   "instrument of government": s.20(1)(a).
   "operative date": s.17(2).

GENERAL NOTE
   This section makes provision for the initial instruments and articles of government of further education corporations created under ss.15 and 16.
   Among the new further education corporations, only grant-maintained schools already enjoy corporate status, by virtue of s.53 of the ERA 1988, and already have instruments and articles of government under ss.58 and 59 of that Act. The individual order specifying the institution as a further education corporation will give such schools their new instruments and articles of government. Their governing bodies are to be dissolved on the operative date for the incorporation of the school as a further education corporation (subs. (3)). In other cases, the body incorporated as a further education corporation will not yet have corporate status and will acquire instruments and articles of government by regulations, which are likely to be of general application. The general framework for these instruments and articles of government is set out in Sched. 4.
   Orders and regulations under this section may make provision to ensure continuity in the government of the institution by providing that all or any of its existing members shall be initial members of the corporation (subs. (2)).
   This section comes into force on September 30, 1992: see Commencement No. 1 Order 1992, para. 2 and Sched. 2.

Subs. (2)
   Secretary of State. See note to s.1(2).
   Order, regulation. An order or regulation made under this section must be made by way of a statutory instrument which is subject to the negative resolution procedure in Parliament (s.89(1) and (3)).

Subsequent instruments and articles

22.—(1) The Secretary of State may, after consulting the appropriate council—

   (a) if a further education corporation submits a draft of an instrument of government to have effect in place of their existing instrument, by order make a new instrument of government in terms of the draft or in such terms as he thinks fit, and

   (b) if such a corporation submits draft modifications of an instrument made under paragraph (a) above, by order modify the instrument in terms of the draft or in such terms as he thinks fit, but shall not make a new instrument otherwise than in terms of the draft, or modify the instrument otherwise than in terms of the draft, unless he has consulted the corporation.

(2) The Secretary of State may by order modify any instrument of government of any further education corporation.

(3) An order under subsection (2) above—

(a) may relate to all further education corporations, to any category of such corporations specified in the order or to any such corporation so specified, but

(b) shall not be made unless the Secretary of State has consulted the appropriate council and each further education corporation to which the order relates.

(4) A further education corporation may, with the consent of the Secretary of State—

(a) make new articles of government in place of their existing articles, or

(b) modify their existing articles.

(5) The Secretary of State may by a direction under this section require further education corporations, any class of such corporations specified in the direction or any particular further education corporation so specified—

(a) to modify their articles of government, or

(b) to secure that any rules or bye-laws made in pursuance of their articles of government are modified,

in any manner so specified.

(6) Before giving a direction under this section, the Secretary of State shall consult the further education corporation or (as the case may be) each further education corporation to which the direction applies.

DEFINITIONS

"articles of government": s.20(1)(b).
"further education corporation": s.17(1).
"grant-maintained school": s.52 of the ERA 1988.
"instrument of government": s.20(1)(a).
"modify": s.61(1).

GENERAL NOTE

This section empowers the Secretary of State to modify the existing instrument of government of a further education corporation or to make a new one by order. He may also approve modifications to the articles of government or direct that they be modified. Unlike in the case of higher education corporations under this Act (s.129A(7) of the ERA 1988 as introduced by s.73 of this Act), these powers reside in the Secretary of State, not in the Privy Council.

In so far as the instrument of government is concerned, under subs. (1), where a further education corporation submits a draft for a new instrument of government or for modifications to an existing instrument, the Secretary of State makes the modifications or a new instrument after consulting the FEFC and, if he wishes to change the draft, the corporation itself. Under subs. (2), the Secretary of State is given power to make an order modifying the instrument of government of one or more further education corporations, but he must consult all affected corporations before the order is made (subs. (3)).

As far as the articles of government are concerned, the further education corporation has power under subs. (4) to make or modify these, subject to the approval of the Secretary of State. Under subs. (5), the Secretary of State may give directions to the corporation (either individually or as part of a class of affected institutions) to modify their articles or rules and by-laws. No such directions may be made without first consulting the affected corporations (subs. (6)).

This section comes into force on September 30, 1992: see Commencement No. 1 Order 1992, para. 2 and Sched. 2.

Subs. (1)

Secretary of State. See note to s.1(2).

Consult. See note to s.6(1).

Order. Under s.89(2), orders under this section do not have to be made by statutory instrument.

Transfer of property, etc., to further education corporations

Transfer of property, etc.: institutions maintained by local education authorities

23.—(1) This section has effect in relation to a further education corporation established to conduct an institution which, on the date the corporation was established, was maintained by a local education authority.

(2) Subject to subsection (3) below and section 36 of this Act, on the operative date—

(a) all land or other property which, immediately before that date, was property of any local authority used or held for the purposes of the institution the corporation is established to conduct, and

(b) all rights and liabilities of any such authority subsisting immediately before that date which were acquired or incurred for those purposes,

shall be transferred to, and by virtue of this Act vest in, that corporation.

(3) Subsection (2) above shall not apply to—

(a) any liability of any such authority in respect of the principal of, or interest on, any loan, or

(b) any property, rights or liabilities excluded under subsections (4) or (5) below.

(4) If before the operative date—

(a) the governing body of the institution and the local authority have agreed in writing to exclude any land, and

(b) the Secretary of State has given his written approval of the agreement,

the land, and any rights or liabilities relating to it, shall be excluded.

(5) If in default of agreement under subsection (4) above—

(a) the governing body or the local authority have applied to the Secretary of State to exclude any land, and

(b) the Secretary of State has by order directed its exclusion,

the land, and any rights or liabilities relating to it, shall be excluded.

(6) An agreement under subsection (4) above may provide for the land to be used for the purposes of the institution on such terms as may be specified in or determined in accordance with the agreement; and directions under subsection (5) above—

(a) may confer any rights or impose any liabilities that could have been conferred or imposed by such an agreement, and

(b) shall have effect as if contained in such an agreement.

(7) References in subsections (4) and (5) above to anything done, other than the making of an order, include anything done before the passing of this Act.

(8) On the operative date—

(a) all land and other property which, immediately before that date, was property of the former governing body, and

(b) all rights and liabilities of that body subsisting immediately before that date,

shall be transferred to and, by virtue of this Act, vest in the corporation.

(9) In subsection (8) above "former governing body" in relation to an institution means the governing body of the institution immediately before the operative date.

DEFINITIONS
   "former governing body": subs. (9).
   "further education corporation": s.17(1).
   "land": s.90(1).
   "local education authority": s.6 of the EA 1944.
   "operative date": s.17(2).
   "rights and liabilities": s.61(2).

GENERAL NOTE

This section deals with transfers of property to the further education corporation where the institution it is to operate was maintained by a local education authority at the date of incorporation. Where the institution was previously a grant-maintained school, the transfer is governed by s.25. The provisions follow substantially those of s.126 of the ERA 1988 in relation to the creation of higher education corporations.

Under subs. (2), on the operative date, all property, rights and liabilities in relation to the institution are transferred from the local education authority to the further education corporation. Subsection (3) excludes from the transfer any liability to repay the principal or interest on a loan, and any land, rights and liabilities excluded by agreement between the governing body of the institution and the local education authority (subs. (4)), or, in default of such agreement, excluded by the Secretary of State (subs. (5)). Agreements made under subs. (4) require the approval of the Secretary of State. Agreements or orders under subss. (4) and (5) may make such provision for the use of land transferred for the purposes of the institution as are considered appropriate (subs. (6)), and may be made before the passing of the Act (subs. (7)).

The procedure for transfer is supervised by the Education Assets Board (see s.197 of the ERA 1988, as amended by para. 43 of Sched. 8 to this Act), and the construction of transfer agreements is governed by s.87 and Sched. 7. Controls on transfers are imposed by s.39. Where property is shared with another institution or the local education authority, the situation is governed by the provisions of s.36 and Sched. 5.

There is no provision for compensation to be paid to local authorities. These assets "were provided in order to secure further education for the local population. As the assets will continue to be available to serve that purpose, the Government does not propose to compensate local education authorities for the assets to be transferred to the new sector" (White Paper, *Education and Training*, Vol. 2, para. 7.2).

This section comes into force on September 30, 1992: see Commencement No. 1 Order 1992, para. 2 and Sched. 2.

Subs. (1)

Maintained by a local education authority. See s.25 of the ERA 1988.

Land. Special provision may be made in relation to land by an agreement under subs. (4) or an order under subs. (5) (see subs. (6)). Land includes any interest of the local education authority subsisting at the operative date which is used in relation to the institution (s.24(5)). Land also includes land which will cease to be used for a school under a plan for the reorganisation of schools (see s.58(2)).

Rights and liabilities. These include agreements to provide goods and services or the shares which a local education authority may hold in any body corporate under an agreement for the supply of goods (see s.24).

Subs. (2)

Used or held for the purposes of the institution. Where property is held for the purposes of more than one institution, it is to be apportioned under the provisions of Sched. 5 (see s.36(3)).

Operative date. Property here is transferred on the operative date and not on a date specified in the Act, unlike under ss.121(1) and 122(6) of the ERA 1988. The operative date is specified in relation to each institution by the order creating the further education corporation: see s.17(2).

Subs. (3)

Principal or interest on any loan. As under s.126(5)(b) of the ERA 1988, the new corporation is not to be burdened with the repayment of the principal or interest on loans taken out for the purposes of the institution by the local education authority. Historic debts thus remain with the local education authority. (It was considered too complex and time-consuming to identify and separate out charges relating to college property from the general mass of the local authority's historic debt: see White Paper, *Education and Training*, Vol. 2, para. 7.14). Provision is made in s.38 for the FEFC to make payments to a local authority in respect of such loan liabilities and provision may also be made by way of adjustments to the Revenue Support Grant paid by central government to local authorities under the Local Government Finance Act 1988.

Subs. (4)

Governing body of the institution. This refers to the governing body of the pre-incorporation institution, which will include representatives of the local education authority. Approval by the Secretary of State is seen as a safeguard. Such agreements are governed by s.84.

Agreed in writing. Such agreements to exclude property, rights and liabilities are made before the incorporation of the further education corporation, and may be made before the Act was passed (subs. (7)).

Secretary of State. See under s.1(2).

Subs. (5)
   Order. Although the application to the Secretary of State may be made before the passing of the Act, the order may not be (subs. (7)). The content of the order is such as the parties themselves could have made by agreement and has effect as if by agreement.

Subs. (7)
   This provision gives retrospective effect to any agreement or application to the Secretary of State made before March 6, 1992.

Provisions supplementary to section 23

24.—(1) Where in exercise of their powers under section 2 of the Further Education Act 1985 a local authority—
   (a) have entered into an agreement for the supply of goods or services or both through an educational institution, or
   (b) for the purposes of any agreement for such a supply through such an institution, hold shares in any body corporate,
and a further education corporation is established to conduct the institution, then, the rights and liabilities of the authority under or by virtue of the agreement or, as the case may be, the interest of the authority in the shares shall be treated as falling within section 23(2) of this Act.
   (2) Expressions used in subsection (1) above and in section 2 of that Act have the same meaning as in that section.
   (3) Where, immediately before the operative date in relation to a further education corporation, arrangements exist for the supply by a local authority of goods or services for the purposes of the institution in pursuance of a bid prepared under section 7 of the Local Government Act 1988 (restrictions on activities of local authorities), those arrangements shall have effect as from that date as if—
   (a) they were contained in an agreement made before that date between the local authority and the corporation on the terms specified in the bid, and
   (b) the agreement required the corporation or, as the case may be, the local authority to make payments corresponding to the provision made in the bid in pursuance of section 8(3) of that Act for items to be credited or, as the case may be, debited to any account.
   (4) Where such arrangements are for the supply to others as well as to the institution—
   (a) those arrangements shall have effect as mentioned in subsection (3) above only to the extent that they relate to the institution in question, and
   (b) the rights and liabilities arising under the agreement shall be such rights and liabilities as are properly required to give effect to the arrangements so far as relating to that institution.
   (5) Where at any time land is used for the purposes of such an institution, any interest of a local authority in the land subsisting at that time shall be taken for the purposes of section 23 of this Act to be land held for the purposes of that institution (whether or not it is by virtue of that interest that the land is so used).

DEFINITIONS
   "further education corporation": s.17(1).
   "institution": s.91(6).
   "interest in land": s.90(1).
   "land": s.90(1).
   "local authority": s.90(1).
   "operative date": s.17(2).
   "rights and liabilities": s.61(2).

GENERAL NOTE
This section provides interpretation in relation to the rights and liabilities to be transferred under s.23, especially in relation to goods and services. They are necessitated by the fact that the contracting party to agreements for goods and services under the Further Education Act 1985 was the local education authority.

Subsection (1) transfers to the further education corporation the rights and liabilities of the authority both in relation to agreements to supply goods and services and in relation to shares it holds in any body corporate for such supply through the institution, *e.g.* a commercial company for marketing products of the institution. Subsection (2) transfers to the further education corporation the rights and duties under a bid for goods or services to be provided for the institution which the local education authority was bound to put out to tender under s.7 of the Local Government Act 1988. Subsection (4) provides for the apportionment of such goods and services in the event of a bid to supply more than one institution or person. Subsection (5) makes provision in relation to the interests in land held by the local education authority for the purposes of the institution.

This section comes into force on September 30, 1992: see Commencement No. 1 Order 1992, para. 2, Sched. 2.

Subs. (4)
Arrangements for apportionment of rights and liabilities between institutions are governed additionally by s.36 and Sched. 5.

Subs. (5)
Interest of a local authority. This definition affects which interests in land are transferred under s.23.

Transfer of property, etc.: grant-maintained schools

25.—(1) This section has effect in relation to a further education corpora-tion established to conduct an institution which, on the date the corporation was established, was a grant-maintained school.

(2) On the operative date—

(a) all land or other property which, immediately before that date, was property of the governing body, and

(b) all rights and liabilities of that body subsisting immediately before that date,

shall be transferred to and, by virtue of this Act, vest in the corporation.

DEFINITIONS
"former governing body": subs. (9).
"further education corporation": s.17(1).
"grant-maintained school": s.52(3) of the ERA 1988.
"land": s.90(1).
"local education authority": s.6 of the EA 1944.
"operative date": s.17(2).
"rights and liabilities": s.61(2).

GENERAL NOTE
This section makes provision for the transfer of assets from a grant-maintained school to a further education corporation. Since the property of grant-maintained schools already belongs to a body corporate created under s.53 of the ERA 1988, the transfer of assets to the further education corporation under this section is easier than the transfers envisaged by s.23. Land and other property, rights and liabilities are all transferred without qualification.

The procedure for transfer is supervised by the Education Assets Board (see s.197 of the ERA 1988, as amended by para. 43 of Sched. 8 to this Act), and the construction of transfer agreements is governed by s.87 and Sched. 7. Controls on transfers are imposed by s.39. Where property is shared with another institution, the situation is governed by the provisions of s.36 and Sched. 5.

This section comes into force on September 30, 1992: see Commencement No. 1 Order 1992, para. 2, Sched. 2.

Transfer of staff to further education corporations

26.—(1) This section applies to any person who immediately before the operative date in relation to a further education corporation established to conduct an institution which, on the date the corporation was established, was maintained by a local education authority or was a grant-maintained school—

(a) is employed by the transferor to work solely at the institution the corporation is established to conduct, or

(b) is employed by the transferor to work at that institution and is designated for the purposes of this section by an order made by the Secretary of State.

(2) A contract of employment between a person to whom this section applies and the transferor shall have effect from the operative date as if originally made between that person and the corporation.

(3) Without prejudice to subsection (2) above—

(a) all the transferor's rights, powers, duties and liabilities under or in connection with a contract to which that subsection applies shall by virtue of this section be transferred to the corporation on the operative date, and

(b) anything done before that date by or in relation to the transferor in respect of that contract or the employee shall be deemed from that date to have been done by or in relation to the corporation.

(4) Subsections (2) and (3) above are without prejudice to any right of an employee to terminate his contract of employment if a substantial change is made to his detriment in his working conditions, but no such right shall arise by reason only of the change in employer effected by this section.

(5) An order under this section may designate a person either individually or as a member of a class or description of employees.

(6) References in this section, in relation to a further education corporation, to the transferor are—

(a) in relation to a corporation established to conduct an institution which, on the date on which it was established, was maintained by a local education authority, that authority,

(b) in relation to a corporation established to conduct an institution which, on that date, was a voluntary aided or special agreement school, the governing body of the school, and

(c) in relation to a corporation established to conduct an institution which, on that date, was a grant-maintained school, the governing body of the school.

(7) For the purposes of this section—

(a) a person employed by the transferor is to be regarded as employed to work at an institution if his employment with the transferor for the time being involves work at that institution, and

(b) subject to subsection (8) below, a person employed by the transferor is to be regarded as employed to work solely at an institution if his only employment with the transferor (disregarding any employment under a separate contract with the transferor) is for the time being at that institution.

(8) A person employed by the transferor in connection with the provision of meals shall not be regarded for the purposes of subsection (7)(b) above as employed to work solely at an institution unless the meals are provided solely for consumption by persons at the institution.

(9) This section is subject to section 48 of this Act.

DEFINITIONS
"contract of employment": s.90(1) and the Employment Protection Consolidation Act 1978, s.35.
"further education corporation": s.17(1).
"governing body": s.90(1) and (2).
"grant-maintained school": s.52(3) of the ERA 1988.

"liability": s.90(1).
"maintained by a local education authority": s.25 of the ERA 1988.
"operative date": s.17(2).
"order": subs. (5) and s.89(1).
"transferor": subs. (6).
"voluntary-aided school": s.15(2) of the EA 1944.

GENERAL NOTE

This section makes provision for the transfer of staff from existing institutions to the new further education corporations. The section deals only with individual contracts of employment. The Government considered that the new corporations should start with a clean sheet and should not be constrained by collective agreements made by those previously running the institution (see Paymaster-General, *Hansard*, H.L. Vol. 533, col. 970). Following the example of s.127 of the ERA 1988, subs. (1) transfers staff whose employment is solely or principally in the institution which is transferred to the further education corporation on the operative date. The employees in question are those who at the operative date worked at the institution and were solely employed there or fall within a class designated by an order of the Secretary of State. Transfers under this section preserve the continuity of employment through provisions in subss. (2) and (3). Continuity in relation to pay and conditions is also provided for in s.48 (see subs. (9)). Subsection (4) preserves the rights of the employee if the creation of the new further education corporation results in a substantial change in his working conditions. Subsection (6) defines who is to be treated as the "transferor" of employees, and subs. (7) defines those employees who are to be treated as falling within the classes to be transferred under subs. (1). Special provision is made in relation to those employed in the provision of meals by subs. (8). They are only transferred if the meals they provide are solely for consumption by persons within the institution. Those employed in a central catering service which happens to be located in a particular further education institution will not be transferred to the employment of the further education corporation unless an order under subs. (1)(b) so specifies.

To a significant extent, these provisions are similar to those under the Transfer of Undertakings (Protection of Employment) Regulations 1981 (S.I. 1981 No. 1794) as amended by the Transfer of Undertakings (Protection of Employment) (Amendment) Regulations 1987 (S.I. 1987 No. 442).

This section comes into force on September 30, 1992: see Commencement No. 1 Order 1992, para. 2 and Sched. 2.

Subs. (1)

Secretary of State. See note to s.1(2)

Order. Subsection (5) makes it clear that such an order may designate a person individually or collectively with others. Such an order has to be made by way of statutory instrument subject to a negative resolution in Parliament (s.89(1) and (3)).

Local education authority. See note to s.2(6).

Subs. (2)

As if originally made. The provisions of this subsection secure the continuity of employment rights and duties by treating the contract as if it had always been between the further education corporation and the employee. This provision should be read in the light of subss. (3) and (4) and s.48.

Subs. (3)

Rights, powers, duties and liabilities. For all purposes, the further education corporation is to replace the transferor in relation to the individual contract of employment. The deeming provision of para. (b) has the effect of making liability for breaches of contract by the transferor into the liability of the further education corporation, although it is primarily designed to ensure that any reorganisation of the institution commenced before the operative date can continue to have effect.

Subs. (4)

Substantial change . . . to his detriment in his working conditions. This is a matter of fact for an industrial tribunal to determine (see *Western Excavating (E.C.C.)* v. *Sharp* [1978] Q. B. 761 at 772).

Subs. (7)

Solely. This provision only applies where a person is employed by a single institution. Where an employee works at more than one institution, the transfer is effected to a designated institution by order under subs. (1)(b).

Subs. (9)

Section 48 makes provision in relation to the pay and conditions of schoolteachers who are transferred to institutions in the new sector.

Dissolution of further education corporations

Dissolution of further education corporations

27.—(1) Subject to the following provisions of this section, the Secretary of State may by order provide for the dissolution of any further education corporation and the transfer to any person mentioned in subsection (2) and (3) below of property, rights and liabilities of the corporation.

(2) Such property, rights and liabilities may be transferred to—

(a) any person appearing to the Secretary of State to be wholly or mainly engaged in the provision of educational facilities or services of any description, or

(b) any body corporate established for purposes which include the provision of such facilities or services,

with the consent of the person or body in question.

(3) Such property, rights and liabilities may be transferred to—

(a) a council, or

(b) a higher education funding council.

(4) Where the recipient of a transfer under any order under this section is not a charity established for charitable purposes which are exclusively educational purposes, any property transferred must be transferred on trust to be used for charitable purposes which are exclusively educational purposes.

(5) In subsection (4) above "charity" and "charitable purposes" have the same meanings as in the Charities Act 1960.

(6) An order under this section may apply section 26 of this Act with such modifications as the Secretary of State may consider necessary or desirable.

(7) Before making an order under this section in respect of a further education corporation the Secretary of State shall consult—

(a) the corporation, and

(b) the appropriate council, unless the order was made for the purpose of giving effect to a proposal of that council.

DEFINITIONS

"council": s.1(5).

"charitable purposes": s.46(1) of the Charities Act 1960.

"charity": s.45(1) of the Charities Act 1960.

"further education corporation": s.17(1).

"liability": s.90(1).

GENERAL NOTE

This section makes provision for the dissolution of further education corporations. Its provisions substantially follow s.128 of the ERA 1988. Subsection (1) empowers the Secretary of State, after consulting the persons mentioned in subs. (7), to make an order dissolving any further education corporation and transferring its property, rights and liabilities to persons mentioned in subs. (2) or (3), *viz.* to another body providing further education, or to the FEFC or the HEFC. Bodies mentioned in subs. (2) must consent to the transfer. Subsection (4) provides that where the transferee is not a charity established exclusively for educational charitable purposes, the transferred property, rights and liabilities must be transferred on trust for exclusively educational purposes. Subsection (6) provides that contracts of employment may be transferred if the Secretary of State by order applies s.26 of this Act with such modifications as he thinks desirable.

This section comes into force on September 30, 1992: see Commencement No. 1 Order 1992, para. 2 and Sched. 2.

Subs. (1)

Order. An order made under this section must be made by way of a statutory instrument which is subject to the negative resolution procedure in Parliament (s.89(1) and (3)). See note to s.15(1).

Secretary of State. See note to s.1(2).

Subs. (2)
Body corporate. See note to s.1(1). The principal body corporate envisaged here is a company limited by guarantee such as is envisaged in relation to higher education corporations by s.129B of the ERA 1988, as introduced by s.73 of this Act.

Subs. (3)
Since a further education corporation is an exempt charity by virtue of para. 69 of Sched. 8, this provision is effectively a form of *cy-près*.

Subs. (7)
Consult. See note to s.6(1).

Designation of institutions for funding by the councils

Designation of institutions

28.—(1) The Secretary of State may by order designate as eligible to receive support from funds administered by the councils any educational institution principally concerned with the provision of one or both of the following—
  (a) full-time education suitable to the requirements of persons over compulsory school age who have not attained the age of nineteen years, and
  (b) courses of further or higher education,
if the institution meets the requirements of subsection (2) below.
  (2) The institution must be one of the following—
  (a) a voluntary aided school,
  (b) an institution (other than a school) assisted by a local education authority, or
  (c) an institution which is grant-aided or eligible to receive aid by way of grant.
  (3) For the purposes of subsection (2)(c) above an institution is grant-aided or eligible to receive aid by way of grant if it is maintained by persons other than local education authorities who—
  (a) receive any grants under regulations made under section 100(1)(b) of the Education Act 1944, or
  (b) are eligible to receive such grants.
  (4) In this Part of this Act "designated institution" means an institution in relation to which a designation under this section has effect.

DEFINITIONS
  "compulsory school age": s.35 of the EA 1944.
  "council": s.1(5).
  "courses of further education": Sched. 4.
  "grant-aided": subs. (3).
  "voluntary aided school": s.15(2) of the EA 1944.

GENERAL NOTE
  This section provides an alternative route to ss.15 and 16 whereby an institution can become part of the further education sector. Instead of being incorporated as a further education corporation, an institution may be designated by the Secretary of State under this section as eligible to receive funding from the FEFC. To be eligible for such designation, subs. (1) stipulates that an educational institution must be principally concerned with the provision of either education for 16- to 18-year olds or courses of further or higher education. In addition, subs. (2) requires that the institution in question must be either a voluntary-aided school or an institution assisted by a local education authority or a grant-aided institution. The majority of such institutions are denominational sixth-form colleges or colleges of further education. In its White Paper *Education and Training* the Government announced its intention to designate the

Workers' Educational Association, seven long-term residential colleges (Coleg Harlech, the Cooperative College, Fircroft College, Hillcroft College, Norther College, Plater College and Ruskin College) as well as four London colleges (City Literary Institute, Mary Ward Centre, Morley College, and the Working Men's College), together with Cordwainers' College and the National Sea Training Trust and College of the Sea (see Vol. 2, paras. 2.7 and 2.8, confirmed by the Minister of State, *Hansard*, H. C., Standing Committee F, cols. 228–9 and 233). Many adult education and community colleges will not qualify for designation under this section, but will be supported by the FEFC by means of a proposal for funding made through a further education corporation under s.6(5).

This section came into force on May 6, 1992: see Commencement No. 1 Order 1992, para. 2 and Sched. 1.

Subs. (1)
   Secretary of State. See note to s.1(1).
   Order. An order made under this section must be made by way of a statutory instrument which is subject to the negative resolution procedure in Parliament (s.89(1) and (3)).
   Full-time education. See note to s.2(1).
   Courses of higher education. See Sched. 6 to the ERA 1988.

Subs. (2)
   Voluntary aided school. Such schools will typically be denominational sixth-form colleges. A proposal to include voluntary controlled schools was defeated in the House of Lords. Where a voluntary-aided school has already become grant-maintained before the commencement of this section, it will enter the further education sector under the provisions of s.15.

Subs. (3)
   Local education authority. See note to s.2(6).

Government and conduct of designated institutions

29.(1) This section has effect in relation to any designated institution, other than—
   (a) an institution conducted by a company, or
   (b) an institution conducted by an unincorporated association if the order designating the institution provides for its exemption.
   (2) For each institution in relation to which this section has effect there shall be—
   (a) an instrument providing for the constitution of a governing body of the institution (to be known as the instrument of government), and
   (b) an instrument in accordance with which the institution is to be conducted (to be known as the articles of government),
each of which meets the requirements of subsection (3) below.
   (3) Those requirements are that the instrument—
   (a) was in force when the designation took effect and is approved for the purposes of this section by the Secretary of State,
   (b) is made in pursuance of a power under a regulatory instrument, or is made under subsection (5) below, and is approved for the purposes of this section by the Secretary of State, or
   (c) is made under subsection (6) below.
   (4) In this section "regulatory instrument", in relation to an institution, means any instrument of government or articles of government and any other instrument relating to or regulating the institution.
   (5) Where there is no such power as is mentioned in subsection (3)(b) above to make the instrument, it may be made by the governing body of the institution and an instrument made by them under this subsection may replace wholly or partly any existing regulatory instrument.
   (6) The Secretary of State may by order make either of the instruments referred to in subsection (2) above and any instrument made by him under this subsection may replace wholly or partly any existing regulatory instrument.
   (7) If an instrument approved by the Secretary of State for the purposes of this section—

   (a) falls within subsection (3)(a) above or was made in pursuance of a
      power under a regulatory instrument and, apart from this section,
      there is no power to modify it, or
   (b) was made by the governing body of the institution,
the instrument may be modified by the governing body.

(8) The Secretary of State may by order modify either of the instruments
referred to in subsection (2) above and no instrument approved by him for
the purposes of this section may be modified by any other person without the
Secretary of State's consent.

(9) Before exercising any power under subsection (6) or (8) above in
relation to any instrument the Secretary of State shall consult—
   (a) the governing body of the institution, and
   (b) where there is such a power as is mentioned in subsection (3)(b)
      above to make or, as the case may be, modify the instrument and the
      persons having that power are different from the governing body of
      the institution, the persons having the power,
so far as it appears to him to be practicable to do so.

DEFINITIONS
   "articles of government": subs. (2).
   "designated institution": s.28(4).
   "governing body": s.90(1) and (2).
   "instrument of government": subs. (2).
   "regulatory instrument": subs. (4).

GENERAL NOTE
   This section provides for the government and conduct of institutions designated under s.28.
Although not a further education corporation, such an institution is required by subs. (2) to
have an instrument of government and articles of government approved or ordered by the
Secretary of State. Subsection (1) exempts from this requirement an institution conducted by a
company (which is governed by s.31) and an institution conducted by an unincorporated
association which the Secretary of State has so exempted in the designation order made under
s.28(1). The instruments mentioned in subs. (2) must satisfy the requirements as to their
making contained in subs. (3), *viz.* either that the Secretary of State has approved an existing
instrument or a new instrument made by the governing body of the institution or that the
Secretary of State makes such instruments by order under subs. (6). Subsection (5) empowers a
governing body to alter existing instruments or to make new ones for the purposes of subs.
(3)(b), even if there is no such power under any existing regulatory instrument governing the
conduct of the institution. Subsection (7) confers a similar power on the governing body to alter
an existing instrument approved under subs. (3)(a), even if there is no such power under the
regulatory instruments governing the conduct of the institution so approved. Such subsequent
alterations of instruments require the approval of the Secretary of State under subs. (8). That
subsection also empowers the Secretary of State to make orders modifying the instrument or
articles of government of an institution. Where the Secretary of State exercises a power to make
an order under subss. (6) or (8), subs. (9) requires that he must first consult the governing body
of the institution and any person having power to alter the instrument or articles of government.
   This section came into force on May 6, 1992: see Commencement No. 1 Order 1992, para. 2
and Sched. 1.

Subs. (1)
   Order designating the institution. This refers to an order made by the Secretary of State under
s.28(1).

Subs. (2)
   Instrument of government. A designated institution is thus to have a similar structure to a
further education corporation (see s.20), although there is to be greater flexibility as to its
content. In the case of voluntary-aided institutions, there are special restrictions on the content
of these instruments (see s.30). The structure parallels the memorandum and articles of
association of a company.

Subs. (3)
   Designation took effect. The date for the designation to take effect is specified in the order
note to s.28(1).

Secretary of State. See note to s.1(2).

Subs. (4)
Other instrument. This will include a trust deed.

Subs. (6) and (8)
Order. An order made under these subsections need not be made by way of a statutory instrument (s.89(2)).

Subs. (9)
Consult. See note to s.6(1).
Practicable. This cannot be construed as meaning "equitable", "fair", or "reasonable" (see *Farquhar, Re* [1943] 2 All E.R. 781 at p. 783, *per* Lord Greene M.R.).

Special provision for voluntary aided sixth form colleges

30. Notwithstanding anything in section 29 of this Act, the instrument of government of an institution which, when designated, was a voluntary aided school must provide—
(a) for the governing body of the institution to include persons appointed for the purpose of securing so far as practicable that the established character of the institution at the time of its designation is preserved and developed and, in particular, that the school is conducted in accordance with any trust deed relating to it, and
(b) for the majority of members of the governing body to be such governors.

DEFINITIONS
"governing body": s.90(1).
"instrument of government":s.20(1)(a).
"voluntary aided school": s.15(2) of the EA 1944.

GENERAL NOTE
This section makes provision concerning the instrument of government of a voluntary-aided school which is designated under s.28 to become part of the further education sector. This section preserves the established character of the school at the time of designation by ensuring that the majority of the members of the governing body are representative of that character. In the main, this provision deals with voluntary-aided sixth-form colleges. The provisions of this section derogate from those of s.29.
This section came into force on May 6, 1992: see Commencement No. 1 Order 1992, para. 2 and Sched. 1.
Voluntary aided school. See under s.28(2).

Designated institutions conducted by companies

31.—(1) This section has effect in relation to any designated institution conducted by a company.
(2) The articles of association of the company shall incorporate—
(a) provision with respect to the constitution of a governing body of the institution (to be known as the instrument of government of the institution), and
(b) provision with respect to the conduct of the institution (to be known as the articles of government of the institution).
(3) The Secretary of State may give to the persons who appear to him to have effective control over the company such directions as he thinks fit for securing that—
(a) the memorandum or articles of association of the company, or
(b) any rules or bye-laws made in pursuance of any power conferred by the articles of association of the company,
are amended in such manner as he may specify in the direction.
(4) No amendment of the memorandum or articles of association of the company (other than one required under subsection (3)(a) above) shall take

effect until it has been submitted to the Secretary of State for his approval and he has notified his approval to the company.

(5) Before giving any directions under subsection (3) above the Secretary of State shall consult the persons who appear to him to have effective control over the company.

DEFINITIONS
"articles of association": s.7(1) of the Companies Act 1985.
"designated institution": s.28(4).
"memorandum of association": s.2(1) of the Companies Act 1985.

GENERAL NOTE
This section deals with the instruments regulating the government and conduct of a company conducting an institution designated under s.28. Subsection (2) requires that the articles of association of the company shall incorporate both an instrument of government and articles of government for the institution (typically in similar form to those regulating a further education corporation). Subsection (3) empowers the Secretary of State to give directions to those having effective control over the company to secure that the relevant instruments regulating the company are altered to meet this requirement under subs. (2). This may involve changing the memorandum or articles of association, or rules or by-laws made thereunder. Before giving such directions, subs. (5) requires that the Secretary of State consult the persons to whom the direction may be addressed. Subsection (4) requires the Secretary of State to approve any change made in the memorandum or articles of the company for this purpose before it takes effect.
This section came into force on May 6, 1992: see Commencement No. 1 Order 1992, para. 2 and Sched. 1.

Subs. (3)
Persons . . . effective control over the company. These persons include majority shareholders and "shadow directors", persons under whose directions the board of directors is accustomed to act (s.741(2) of the Companies Act 1985).
Secretary of State. See note to s.1(2).
Directions. These may be revoked or varied at any time: see s.111 of the EA 1944, as applied by s.89(5) of this Act.

Transfer of property, etc., to designated institutions

32.—(1) This section has effect in relation to an institution designated under section 28 of this Act in any case where—
(a) the order designating the institution under that section so provides, and
(b) when designated the institution was a voluntary aided school or an institution (other than a school) assisted by a local education authority.
(2) Subject to subsection (4) below and section 36 of this Act, on the designation date—
(a) all land or other property which, immediately before that date, was property of a former assisting authority used or held for the purposes of the institution, and
(b) all rights and liabilities of that authority subsisting immediately before that date which were acquired or incurred for those purposes,
shall be transferred to and, by virtue of this Act, vest in the appropriate transferees.
(3) In this section and section 33 of this Act—
"appropriate transferees" means—
(a) in relation to an institution conducted by a company, the company, and
(b) in relation to an institution not so conducted, any persons specified in the order designating the institution as persons appearing to the Secretary of State to be trustees holding property for the purposes of that institution,

"designation date", in relation to a designated institution, means the date on which the designation takes effect, and

"former assisting authority" means—

(a) in relation to an institution which when designated was a voluntary aided school, the local education authority which maintained the school, and

(b) in relation to an institution which when designated was an institution (other than a school) assisted by a local education authority, that authority.

(4) Subsection (2) above shall not apply to—

(a) any liability of a former assisting authority in respect of the principal of, or interest on, any loan, or

(b) any property, rights or liabilities excluded under subsections (5) or (6) below.

(5) If before the designation date—

(a) the appropriate transferees and the former assisting authority have agreed in writing to exclude any land, and

(b) the Secretary of State has given his written approval of the agreement,

the land, and any rights or liabilities relating to it, shall be excluded.

(6) If in default of agreement under subsection (5) above—

(a) the appropriate transferees or the former assisting authority have applied to the Secretary of State to exclude any land, and

(b) the Secretary of State has by order directed its exclusion,

the land, and any rights or liabilities relating to it, shall be excluded.

(7) An agreement under subsection (5) above may provide for the land to be used for the purposes of the institution on such terms as may be specified in or determined in accordance with the agreement; and directions under subsection (6) above—

(a) may confer any rights or impose any liabilities that could have been conferred or imposed by such an agreement, and

(b) shall have effect as if contained in such an agreement.

(8) References in subsections (5) and (6) above to anything done, other than the making of an order, include anything done before the passing of this Act.

DEFINITIONS

"appropriate transferees": subs. (3).
"designation date": subs. (3).
"former assisting authority": subs. (3).
"land": s.90(1).
"liability": s.90(1).
"local education authority": s.90(1).
"voluntary aided school": s.15(2) of the EA 1944.

GENERAL NOTE

This section makes provision for the transfer of property to an institution from a local education authority which assisted a voluntary-aided school or institution before the date on which it was designated. Its provisions follow closely those of ss.23 and 130 of the ERA 1988. Subsection (2) provides for the transfer (subject to subs. (4), s.33 and Sched. 5) of the land or property of that former assisting authority used or held for the purposes of the assisted institution, as well as the rights and liabilities acquired or incurred for those purposes. As under s.23(3), subs. (4) provides that no liability to pay the principal or interest on a loan is transferred under this section. Any land, and rights and liabilities relating to it, can be excluded by agreement between the governing body of the institution and the local education authority (subs. (5)), or, in default of such agreement, excluded by the Secretary of State (subs. (6)). Agreements made under subs. (5) require the approval of the Secretary of State. Agreements or orders under subss. (5) and (6) may make such provision for the use of land transferred for the purposes of the institution as are considered appropriate (subs. (7)), and may be made before the passing of the Act (subs. (8)).

The procedure for transfer is supervised by the Education Assets Board (see s.197 of the ERA 1988, as amended by para. 43 of Sched. 8 to this Act), and the construction of transfer agreements is governed by s.87 and Sched. 7. Controls on transfers are imposed by s.39. Where property is shared with another institution or the local education authority, the situation is governed by the provisions of s.36 and Sched. 5.

There is no provision for compensation to be paid to local authorities. These assets "were provided in order to secure further education for the local population. As the assets will continue to be available to serve that purpose, the Government does not propose to compensate local education authorities for the assets to be transferred to the new sector" (White Paper, *Education and Training*, Vol. 2, para. 7.2).

This section came into force on May 6, 1992: see Commencement No. 1 Order 1992, para. 2 and Sched. 1.

Subs. (1)
Land. Special provision may be made in relation to land by an agreement under subs. (5) or an order under subs. (6) (see subs. (7)). Land includes any interest of the local education authority subsisting at the operative date which is used in relation to the institution (s.33(3)).
Voluntary aided school. See note to s.28(2).

Subs. (2)
Used or held for the purposes of the institution. Where property is held for the purposes of more than one institution, it is to be apportioned under the provisions of Sched. 5 (see s.36(3)).

Subs. (4)
Principal or interest on any loan. As under s.126(5)(b) of the ERA 1988, the new corporation is not to be burdened with the repayment of the principal or interest on loans taken out for the purposes of the institution by the local education authority. Historic debts thus remain with the local education authority. See further the note to s.23(3).

Subs. (5)
Governing body of the institution. This refers to the governing body of the pre-incorporation institution, which will include representatives of the local education authority. Approval by the Secretary of State is seen as a safeguard. For interpretation of "governing body" in this context, see further s.84.
Agreed in writing. Such agreements to exclude property, rights and liabilities are made before the incorporation of the further education corporation, and may be made before the Act was passed (subs. (8)).
Secretary of State. See note to s.1(2).

Subs. (6)
Order. Although the application to the Secretary of State may be made before the passing of the Act, the order may not be (subs. (8)). The content of the order is such as the parties themselves could have made by agreement and has effect as if by agreement.
An order made under this section must be made by way of a statutory instrument which is subject to the negative resolution procedure in Parliament (s.89(1) and (3)).

Subs. (8)
This provision gives retrospective effect to any agreement or application to the Secretary of State made before March 6, 1992.

Provisions supplementary to section 32

33.—(1) Subject to section 36(2) of this Act, where persons appearing to the Secretary of State to be trustees holding property for the purposes of the institution are the appropriate transferee, any land or other property or rights transferred to them under section 32 of this Act shall be held on the trusts applicable under such trust deed relating to or regulating that institution (if any) as may be specified in the order designating the institution or, if no such trust deed is so specified, on trust for the general purposes of the institution.

(2) Where persons so appearing to the Secretary of State are the appropriate transferee, they shall incur no personal liability by virtue of any liability so transferred but may apply any property held by them on trust for the purposes of the institution in meeting any such liability.

(3) Where at any time land is used for the purposes of an institution, any interest of a local authority in the land subsisting at that time shall be taken for the purposes of that section to be land held for the purposes of that institution (whether or not it is by virtue of that interest that the land is so used).

(4) References in this Part of this Act to the operative date, in relation to a designated institution, are to the designation date.

DEFINITIONS
"appropriate transferee": s.32(3).
"designated institution": s.28(4).
"designation date": s.32(3).
"liability": s.90(1).
"land": s.90(1).
"local authority": s.90(1).
"operative date": subs. (4).

GENERAL NOTE
This section ensures that trust property continues to be held on trust after a transfer made to a designated institution under s.32. Subsection (2) provides that, where such a transfer takes place, the trustees of the transferee institution incur no personal liability by virtue of the transfer. Should any liability arise, *e.g.* by way of constructive trust, the trustees may use any property of the transferee institution for meeting such liability (subs. (2)). Subsection (3) creates a presumption that, where land is used for the purposes of an institution, the interests of the local authority in it are held for the purposes of the institution, and may thus be the subject of a transfer under s.32.

The provisions of this section are subject to the apportionment provisions of s.36 and Sched. 5, and also the general provisions on transfers of land, property, rights and liabilities of s.87 and Sched. 7.

This section came into force on May 6, 1992: see Commencement No. 1 Order 1992, para. 2 and Sched. 1.

Subs. (2)
Secretary of State. See the note to s.1(2).

Property, rights and liabilities: general

Making additional property available for use

34.—(1) The Secretary of State may by order provide for any land or other property of a local authority to be made available for use by an institution within the further education sector (referred to in this section as the "new sector institution") if the requirements of subsection (2) below are satisfied.

(2) Those requirements are that in the opinion of the Secretary of State—
(a) the property—
    (i) either has within the preceding six months been used for the purpose of the provision of further education by an institution maintained by a local education authority but its use for that purpose has been discontinued or the local education authority intend its use for that purpose to be discontinued, or
    (ii) is being used for that purpose but the local education authority intend its use for that purpose to be discontinued, and
(b) it is necessary or desirable for the property to be available for use for the purposes of the new sector institution but the governing body of that institution have been unable to secure agreement with the local authority, on such terms as may reasonably be required, to secure that the property is so available.

(3) The Secretary of State shall not make an order under this section unless—
(a) the governing body of the new sector institution have applied to him, before the end of the period of three years beginning with the date

which is the operative date in relation to further education corporations established under section 15 of this Act, for such an order to be
made, and
(b) he has consulted the appropriate council, the local authority and the
Education Assets Board.
(4) For the purpose of making any property available for use for the
purposes of an institution, an order under this section may—
(a) transfer to, and vest in, the governing body—
(i) the property concerned, and
(ii) any rights or liabilities of the local authority acquired or
incurred for the purpose of the provision of further education
there, or
(b) confer any rights or impose any liabilities and, to the extent (if any)
that the order does so, it shall have effect as if contained in an
agreement between the local authority and the governing body.
(5) Subsection (4)(a)(ii) above shall not apply to any liability of the local
authority in respect of the principal of, or interest on, any loan.
(6) References in this section to use for the purpose of the provision of
further education are to use wholly or mainly for that purpose.

DEFINITIONS
"council": s.1(5).
"Education Assets Board": s.197 of the ERA 1988.
"employer": s.90(1).
"further education": s.14(1)–(4).
"governing body": s.90(1) and (2).
"institution within the further education sector": s.91(3).
"liability": s.90(1).
"land": s.90(1).
"local authority": s.90(1).
"new sector institution": subs. (1).
"operative date": s.17(2).
"redundancy payment": s.81(1) of the Employment Protection (Consolidation) Act 1978.

GENERAL NOTE
This section concerns land or other property the use of which for the provision of further
education has been discontinued in the six months prior to the order of the Secretary of State or
which the local education authority intends to discontinue. Such land or other property may
nevertheless be made available by order of the Secretary of State to an institution within the
further education sector, if he considers it necessary or desirable for the property to be made
available for the purposes of that institution. This provision applies where the institution has
failed to come to an agreement with the local education authority under s.23(4) or s.32(5) about
the property to be transferred (subs. (2)(b)), and the institution makes an application to the
Secretary of State within three years of the operative date established in relation to further
education corporations under s.15 (subs. (3)(a)). Subsection (3)(b) provides that the Secretary
of State must consult the FEFC, the local education authority, and the Education Assets Board
before making such an order. The order may either vest the property or rights and liabilities of
the local education authority in the institution or make an arrangment such as could have been
obtained by agreement between the authority and the governing body of the institution (subs.
(4)). Subsection (5) follows ss.23(3) and 32(4) in excluding the repayment of interest or
principal on a loan from such an order.
The provisions of this section are subject to the apportionment provisions of s.36 and Sched.
5, and the general provisions on transfers of land, property, rights and liabilities of s.87 and
Sched. 7.
This section comes into force on April 1, 1993: see Commencement No. 1 Order 1992, para. 2
and Sched. 3.

Subs. (1)
Secretary of State. See note to s.1(2).
Order. An order made under this section must be made by way of a statutory instrument
which is subject to the negative resolution procedure in Parliament (s.89(1) and (3)).

Subs. (2)
   Purpose of the provision of further education. Under subs. (6) this includes property wholly or mainly held for such a purpose.
   Agreement. See ss.23(4) and 32(5).

Subs. (3)
   Three years. The three years run from the date specified in an order under s.15(1) on which existing institutions maintained by local authorities or grant-maintained schools were created as further education corporations. This period applies even to institutions which were created after that date under s.16 or were designated at a later date under s.28.
   Education Assets Board. See note to s.36(5).
   Consult. See note to s.6(1).

Subs. (4)
   Rights and liabilities. For rights and liabilities under a contract of employment, see s.35.

Subs. (5)
   Loan. See note to s.23(3).

Voluntary transfers of staff in connection with section 34

   35.—(1) This section applies where—
   (a) for the purpose of making any property of a local authority available for use for the purposes of an institution within the further education sector, an order is made under section 34 of this Act,
   (b) at any time on or after such date as may be specified by the order a person employed by the local authority ceases to be so employed and is subsequently employed by the governing body of the institution, and
   (c) by virtue of section 84 of the Employment Protection (Consolidation) Act 1978 (renewal or re-engagement) that subsequent employment precludes his receiving any redundancy payment under Part VI of that Act.
   (2) Schedule 13 to that Act (computation of period of employment for the purposes of that Act) shall have effect in relation to that person as if it included the following provisions—
   (a) the period of employment of that person with the local authority shall count as a period of employment with the governing body, and
   (b) the change of employer shall not break the continuity of the period of employment.
   (3) The period of that person's employment with the local authority shall count as a period of employment with the governing body for the purposes of any provision of his contract of employment with the governing body which depends on his length of service with that employer.

DEFINITIONS
   "contract of employment": s.153(1) of the Employment Protection (Consolidation) Act 1978.
   "employer": s.90(1).
   "further education": s.14(1)–(4).
   "governing body": s.90(1) and (2).
   "institution within the further education sector": s.91(3).
   "local authority": s.90(1).
   "redundancy payment": s.81(1) of the Employment Protection (Consolidation) Act 1978.

GENERAL NOTE
   This section makes provision for the continuity of employment for the purposes of employment protection legislation in respect of a member of staff notwithstanding the transfer of the institution from the local education authority to an institution within the further education sector. These provisions complement those of s.26, which involve continuity in functions by the employee. This section deals with a situation where, following a transfer under s.34, an employee ceases to be employed by the local education authority and subsequently agrees to be

employed by the transferee institution, such that no redundancy payment is due (because of the operation of s.84 of the Employment Protection (Consolidation) Act 1978). In such a case, the period of employment with the transferee institution is deemed to include the period of employment with the transferor local authority.

This section comes into force on April 1, 1993: see Commencement No. 1 Order 1992, para. 2 and Sched. 3.

Subs. (1)
Order. An order under this section must be made by way of statutory instrument which is subject to a negative resolution in Parliament (see s.89(1) and (3)).

Redundancy payment. Under s.84 of the Employment Protection (Consolidation) Act 1978, an employee on a fixed-term or trial contract who is re-engaged at the end of it by the employer or by an associated employer within a period of no more than four weeks is not treated as having been dismissed by the employer, and so does not become entitled to a redundancy payment, where, as here, the original employer ceases to conduct the activity for which he was employed.

Subs. (2)
This subsection provides an interpretation of Sched. 13 of the Employment Protection (Consolidation) Act 1978 relating to the transfer made under s.34. It continues the calculation of period of employment for the purposes of rights in the case of unfair dismissal and redundancy.

Subs. (3)
This subsection provides for the continuity of rights of the employee arising specifically out of the contract of employment which confer benefits depending on the length of service, *e.g.* occupational pension rights.

General provisions about transfers under Chapter II

36.—(1) This section applies to any transfer under section 23 or 32 of this Act, and those sections are subject to Schedule 5 to this Act.

(2) Where any land or other property or rights—

(a) were immediately before the operative date in relation to any institution held on trust for any particular purposes, or (as the case may be) for the general purposes, of the institution, and

(b) fall to be transferred under any transfer to which this section applies, they shall continue to be so held by the transferee.

(3) Schedule 5 to this Act has effect for the purpose of—

(a) dividing and apportioning property, rights and liabilities which fall to be transferred under any transfer to which this section applies where that property has been used or held, or the rights or liabilities have been acquired or incurred, for the purposes of more than one educational institution,

(b) excluding from transfer in certain circumstances property, rights and liabilities which would otherwise fall to be transferred under any such transfer,

(c) providing for identifying and defining the property, rights and liabilities which fall to be so transferred, and

(d) making supplementary and consequential provisions in relation to transfers to which this section applies.

(4) Where arrangements for the supply by a local authority of goods or services for the purposes of an institution to be conducted by a further education corporation are to have effect as from the operative date in accordance with section 24(4)of this Act as if contained in an agreement made before that date between the local authority and the corporation, paragraphs 2 to 5 of Schedule 5 to this Act shall have effect as if the rights and liabilities of the corporation under the agreement were rights and liabilities of the local authority transferred to the corporation under a transfer to which this section applies.

(5) In carrying out the functions conferred or imposed on them by that Schedule, it shall be the duty of the Education Assets Board to secure that

each transfer to which this section applies is, so far as practicable, fully effective on the date on which it takes effect under this Act.

(6) Where in accordance with that Schedule anything falls to be or may be done by the Board for the purposes of or in connection with any such transfer—

(a) it may not be done by the transferee, and
(b) in doing it the Board shall be regarded as acting on behalf and in the name of the transferee,

and in a case where the transferee is a body corporate established under this Act paragraph (b) above applies both in relation to things done before and in relation to things done after that body is established under this Act.

(7) Not later than the end of the period of six months beginning with the operative date in relation to a further education corporation established under section 15 of this Act, the Board shall provide the appropriate council with a written statement giving such particulars of all property, rights and liabilities transferred to that corporation as are then available to the Board.

(8) If in any case within subsection (7) above full particulars of all property, rights and liabilities transferred to the corporation concerned are not given in the statement required under that subsection, the Board shall provide the appropriate council with a further written statement giving any such particulars omitted from the earlier statement as soon as it is possible for them to do so.

DEFINITIONS
   "council": s.1(5).
   "Education Assets Board": s.197 of the ERA 1988.
   "further education corporation": s.17(1).
   "governing body": s.90(1) and (2).
   "liability": s.90(1).
   "land": s.90(1).
   "local authority": s.90(1).
   "operative date": s.17(2).

GENERAL NOTE
   This section makes additional provision in relation to transfers made to a further education corporation or a designated institution under ss.23 and 32.
   Subsection (2) ensures that the property continues to be held on the same trusts as it was held before the transfer. Subsection (3) makes provision where land or property is shared between two institutions or between the transferee institution and the transferor local authority. The basic mechanisms for apportionment are set out in Sched. 5. Subsection (4) provides for the operation of Sched. 5 in relation to agreements for the supply of goods and services both to the institution and to another person. Subsection (5) confers on the Education Assets Board the duty to ensure that such transfers are effective. For the purposes of this section, the Education Assets Board is given power to perform certain acts on behalf of the transferee institution (subs. (6)). Subsection (7) imposes on it a duty to report to the FEFC at the end of six months after the operative date detailing the property rights and liabilities transferred to a further education corporation. Subsection (8) imposes a similar obligation in relation to details of such transfers which become available to the Board after that date. These provisions follow closely those of s.198 of the ERA 1988.
   This section comes into force on September 30, 1992: see Commencement No. 1 Order 1992, para. 2 and Sched. 2.

Subs. (3)
   Educational institution. This term includes a school, a further education corporation, or a higher education corporation.

Subs. (4)
   Goods and services. See note to s.24(4).

Subs. (5)
   Education Assets Board. This is a body corporate created by s.197 of the ERA 1988 whose members are appointed by the Secretary of State. Its principal functions were in relation to

transfers of property, rights and liabilities to grant-maintained schools and higher education corporations under the ERA 1988.

Under para. 43 of Sched. 8, new subss. (7A) and (7B) are inserted into s.197 of the ERA 1988 imposing on local authorities and institutions duties to provide the Education Assets Board with information which it requires for the purposes of its functions under this Act.

Subs. (6)
Body corporate. This means a further education corporation or a higher education corporation.

Attribution of surpluses and deficits

37.—(1) This section applies where, immediately before the date on which any educational institution becomes an institution within the further education sector—
   (a) it is maintained by a local education authority, or
   (b) it is a designated assisted institution dependent on assistance from a local education authority,
and in the financial year ending immediately before that date (referred to in this section as the "relevant financial year"), the institution was covered by a scheme under section 33 or 139 of the Education Reform Act 1988 (schemes for financing schools or institutions of further or higher education); and in this section, in relation to the institution, the scheme is referred to as the "applicable scheme" and the authority concerned as the "assisting authority".

(2) If the net expenditure of the institution for the relevant financial year is less than the net budget share of the institution for that year, the assisting authority shall pay to the new governing body of the institution a sum equal to the shortfall.

(3) If the net expenditure of the institution for the relevant financial year is greater than the net budget share of the institution for that year, the new governing body of the institution shall pay to the assisting authority a sum equal to the excess.

(4) In this section, in respect of any financial year of the institution—
   "net budget share" means the budget share—
      (i) less such amount as may be prescribed in respect of any earned income, and
      (ii) plus such amount as may be prescribed in respect of any surplus, and
   "net expenditure" means any expenditure, less such amount as may be prescribed in respect of earned income.

(5) Any sum payable under this section shall be paid in accordance with regulations, and the regulations may provide for sums to be payable by prescribed instalments and for sums to carry prescribed interest.

(6) Regulations may, in the case of any institution where the operative date falls within a financial year in which the institution was covered by such a scheme as is referred to in subsection (1) above, make provision for applying this section with modifications relating to the amounts that are to be taken for the purposes of this section to be the net budget share and the net expenditure of the institution for that year.

(7) In this section, in respect of any financial year of the institution—
   "budget share" means the amount which is that institution's budget share for the relevant financial year for the purposes of Chapter III of Part I or Chapter III of Part II of the Education Reform Act 1988,
   "earned income" means any sums, other than sums appropriated for the purposes of the institution by the assisting authority, received by the institution in respect of the relevant financial year which the institution is authorised under the applicable scheme to retain,

"expenditure" means such expenditure for the purposes of the institution incurred in the relevant financial year by the former governing body or the assisting authority as may be prescribed,

"financial year" has the same meaning as in the Education Reform Act 1988,

"former governing body" means the governing body of the institution immediately before the operative date and "new governing body" means the governing body of the institution on or after that date, and

"surplus" means the amount of any surplus which the institution is authorised under the applicable scheme to carry forward to the relevant financial year.

(8) In this section—

(a) references to a designated assisted institution are references to an institution designated by or under regulations made, or having effect as if made, under section 218(10)(b) of the Education Reform Act 1988 as an institution substantially dependent for its maintenance on assistance from local education authorities, and

(b) "prescribed" means prescribed by regulations.

(9) For the purposes of this section a designated assisted institution shall be regarded as dependent on assistance from a local education authority if it is assisted by that authority and either—

(a) it is not assisted by any other local education authority, or

(b) that authority provides a larger proportion than any other local education authority by whom the institution is assisted of the aggregate amount of the sums received by the governing body of the institution during any financial year by way of assistance from such authorities in respect of the expenses of maintaining the institution.

DEFINITIONS

"applicable scheme": subs. (1).
"assisting authority": subs. (1).
"budget share": subs. (7).
"council": s.1(5).
"designated assisted institution": subs. (8).
"earned income": subs. (7).
"expenditure": subs. (7).
"financial year": subs. (7).
"former governing body": subs. (7).
"governing body": s.90(1) and (2).
"institution within the further education sector": s.91(3).
"local education authority": s.6 of the EA 1944.
"net budget share": subs. (4).
"net expenditure": subs. (4).
"operative date": s.17(2).
"relevant financial year": subs. (1).
"surplus": subs. (7).

GENERAL NOTE

This section deals with the financial consequences of transfers under this Part of the Act during the course of a financial year.

Under ss.33 and 139 of the ERA 1988, schools and further education institutions had a budget defined by the local education authority which was managed by the institution. The budget was allocated by the local education authority in accordance with criteria established by regulations. Under this section, the balance remaining at the operative date of the institution's share of income and expenditure for the year is an asset to be transferred to the new further education corporation or designated institution (subss. (2) and (3)). Subsection (4) provides definitions of "net budget share" and "net expenditure" for these purposes. To assist in this process, the Secretary of State shall make regulations to determine such income and expenditure and to prescribe how this money is to be paid and the interest due thereon (subs. (5)). Subsection (6) enables regulations to be made modifying the calculations of the net budget share and net expenditure of an institution which is transferred partway through a financial year.

This section comes into force on April 1, 1993: see Commencement No. 1 Order 1992, para. 2 and Sched. 3.

Subs. (1)

Dependent on assistance from a local education authority. See subs. (9). On "local education authority", see note to s.2(6).

Subss. (5) and (8)

Regulations. These are to be made by way of statutory instrument which is subject to the negative resolution procedure in Parliament (s.89(1) and (3)).

Payments by council in respect of loan liabilities

38.—(1) This section applies to any excepted loan liability, that is, any liability of a local authority which—
- (a) in the case of a transfer by virtue of section 23 of this Act, would have been transferred but for subsection (3)(a) of that section,
- (b) in the case of a transfer by virtue of section 32 of this Act, would have been transferred but for subsection (4)(a) of that section, or
- (c) in the case of a transfer by virtue of section 34(4)(a) of this Act, could have been transferred but for subsection (5) of that section.

(2) A council may make payments, on such terms and conditions as the council may determine, to a local authority in respect of the principal of, and any interest on, any excepted loan liability of that authority.

(3) No payment shall be made under this section in respect of any excepted loan liability, where the class or classes of excepted loan liabilities in respect of which payments may be made are for the time being prescribed by an order of the Secretary of State, unless the liability falls within a prescribed class.

(4) The Secretary of State may by order provide for determining—
- (a) the amounts that may be paid under this section in respect of the principal of, and any interest on, any excepted loan liability,
- (b) the instalments by which any amounts may be paid, and
- (c) the rate at which interest may be paid on any outstanding amounts,

and, in the case of any payment to which such an order applies, no amount may be paid under this section in excess of any amount determined in accordance with the order.

DEFINITIONS
"council": s.1(5).
"excepted loan liability": subs. (1).
"local authority": s.90(1).

GENERAL NOTE
Under the provisions listed in subs. (1), local authorities are not able to transfer the liability to repay the interest or principal on loans taken out for the purposes of an institution to whom it is making a transfer of property rights and liabilities. This is called an "excepted loan liability". Subsection (2) empowers a FEFC to make payments to a local authority in respect of such a liability on such terms as it thinks fit, provided that that liability falls within a class prescribed under an order issued by the Secretary of State (subs. (3)). Subsection (4) sets out the powers of the Secretary of State to make such an order.

This section comes into force on April 1, 1993: see Commencement No. 1 Order 1992, para. 2 and Sched. 2.

Subs. (1)

Excepted loan liability. See note to s.23(3).

Subs. (4)

Order. An order made under this section does not have to be made by way of statutory instrument (s.89(2)).

Control of disposals of land

39.—(1) Subject to subsection (11) below, this section applies to any disposal during the controlled period—
  (a) of land which, immediately before the beginning of that period, was used or held for the purposes of any relevant institution, or
  (b) of land which was obtained before the beginning of that period for the purpose of being so used or held and had not before the beginning of that period been appropriated to any other use.

(2) For the purposes of this section and sections 41 and 43 of this Act, an institution is a relevant institution if—
  (a) it is an educational institution maintained by a local education authority and falls within section 15(2) of this Act,
  (b) it is a county school or controlled school and falls within section 15(3) of this Act, or
  (c) it is an educational institution such as is mentioned in section 28(1) of this Act and meets the requirements of subsection (2)(a) or (b) of that section.

(3) In this section "the controlled period" means the period beginning with 22nd March 1991 and ending with—
  (a) the operative date in relation to the institution in question or, if later, the date on which any matter relating to that land on which agreement is required to be reached under paragraph 2(1) of Schedule 5 to this Act is finally determined, or
  (b) in the case of an institution falling with paragraph (c) above, 21st March 1995 if earlier.

(4) Except with the consent of the Secretary of State, no local authority shall after the passing of this Act make a disposal to which this section applies.

(5) If at any time after 21st March 1991 and before the passing of this Act such an authority have made a disposal which would have been in contravention of the provisions of subsection (4) above if they had then been in force the same consequences shall follow as if those provisions had been contravened by that authority.

(6) Any consent for the purposes of this section may be given either in respect of a particular disposal or in respect of disposals of any class or description and either unconditionally or subject to conditions.

(7) Any signification of consent for the purposes of this section, or of such consent subject to conditions, given by the Secretary of State before the passing of this Act in respect of any disposal to which this section applies, shall be treated for the purposes of this section as a consent, or a consent subject to the conditions, given under this section.

(8) This section has effect notwithstanding anything in section 123 of the Local Government Act 1972 (general power to dispose of land) or in any other enactment: and the consent required by this section shall be in addition to any consent required by subsection (2) of that section or by any other enactment.

(9) A disposal shall not be invalid or, in the case of a disposal which consists of a contract, void by reason only that it has been made or entered into in contravention of this section; and (subject to the provisions of section 40 of this Act) a person acquiring land, or entering into a contract to acquire land, from a local authority shall not be concerned to enquire whether any consent required by this section has been given or any conditions have been complied with.

(10) In this section references to disposing of land include—
  (a) granting or disposing of any interest in land,

(b) entering into a contract to dispose of land or to grant or dispose of any such interest, and

(c) granting an option to acquire any land or any such interest.

(11) This section does not apply to a disposal falling within subsection (10)(a) above if it is made in pursuance of a contract entered into, or an option granted, on or before 21st March 1991.

(12) Where at any time land is used for the purposes of an institution, any interest of a local authority in the land subsisting at that time shall be taken for the purposes of subsection (1) above to be land held for the purposes of that institution (whether or not it is by virtue of that interest that the land is so used).

DEFINITIONS
"controlled school": s.9(2) of the EA 1944.
"controlled period": subs. (3).
"county school": s.9(2) of the EA 1944.
"disposal": subs. (10).
"interest in land": s.90(1).
"land": s.90(1).
"operative date": s.17(2).
"relevant institution": subs. (2).

GENERAL NOTE
Like s.137 of the ERA 1988, this section controls disposals of land from the date of the first Government announcement about the transfer of further education institutions from local education authorities until the end of the period within which this transfer is expected to be completed., *viz.* from March 22, 1991 to the operative date in respect of the individual institution, the date on which any agreement is made between the institution and the local education authority, or March 21, 1995 at the latest.

Subsection (1) defines the disposals which are controlled by this section. They are disposals of land which was held or acquired for the purposes of a "relevant institution" at the start of the controlled period. Subsection (2) defines the institutions which are to be treated as "relevant institutions" for the purposes of this section. These are institutions which are transferred to the further education sector under this Part of the Act. Subsection (3) defines the "controlled period". Subsection (10) defines what is meant by disposing of land. As a limitation on the general powers of local authorities (subs. (8)), subs. (4) requires that a local authority shall not dispose of any land so controlled without the consent of the Secretary of State. Subsection (5) applies this requirement to acts done before the passing of the Act on March 6, 1992, and subs. (7) deems any consent given before the passing of this Act to be given for the purposes of this section. Subsection (6) provides that consents may relate to particular institutions or classes of institution. Subsection (11) provides that this section does not prevent disposals under a contract or option made or granted before March 21, 1991. Subsection (9) preserves the rights of a person to whom a disposal has been made in breach of the provisions of this section, subject to the provisions of s.40.

This section came into force on May 6, 1992: see Commencement No. 1 Order 1992, para. 2 and Sched. 1.

Subs. (1)
Disposal. See subs. (10).

Subs. (3)
Controlled period. The period within which disposals of land are controlled began with the announcement of the proposed transfer of further education institutions from local authorities and finishes normally either with the date on which property is transferred by order of the Secretary of State under ss.15 or 16, or when an agreement is reached between the transferor and the Education Assets Board (on behalf of the transferee) under para. 2(1) of Sched. 5, whichever is later. At all events, the controlled period ends on March 21, 1995, even if there has been no such order or agreement.

Subs. (4)
Secretary of State. See note to s.1(2).

Subs. (8)
Consent. Consent is required under s.123(2) of the Local Government Act 1972 in relation to

the disposal, except by short lease, of an open space, *e.g.* recreation and sports facilities of a school or college.

Subs. (9)
Rather than making void a contract entered into in breach of this section, provisions are made for repudiation or compulsory purchase under s.40.

Wrongful disposals of land

40.—(1) This section applies where a local authority have made any disposal to which section 39 of this Act applies in contravention of that section (referred to below in this section as a wrongful disposal).

(2) Where a wrongful disposal consists in entering into a contract to dispose of any land or to grant or dispose of any interest in land, the Education Assets Board may by notice in writing served on the other party to the contract repudiate the contract at any time before the conveyance or grant of the land or interest in land to which it relates is completed or executed.

(3) Where a wrongful disposal consists in granting an option to acquire any land or any interest in land, the Education Assets Board may by notice in writing served on the option holder repudiate the option at any time before it is exercised.

(4) A repudiation under subsection (2) or (3) above shall have effect as if made by the local authority concerned.

(5) Where a wrongful disposal consists in granting or disposing of any interest in land (whether or not in pursuance of any earlier disposal of a description falling within subsection (2) or (3) above) the Education Assets Board may be authorised by the Secretary of State to purchase compulsorily the interest in land which was the subject of the disposal.

(6) The Acquisition of Land Act 1981 shall apply in relation to the compulsory purchase of land under subsection (5) above as if references in sections 12 and 13 of that Act to every owner of the land included references to the local authority concerned.

(7) On completion of a compulsory purchase under that subsection of any interest in land, the Education Assets Board shall convey that interest to the appropriate transferee.

(8) In subsection (7) above, "the appropriate transferee" means—
(a) where the interest disposed of, or the land in which the interest was granted, was—
   (i) used or held by the local authority concerned for the purposes of an institution to which section 39(2)(a) or (b) of this Act applies, or
   (ii) obtained by that authority for the purpose of being so used or held,
   the further education corporation established under this Act to conduct that institution, and
(b) where the interest disposed of, or the land in which the interest was granted, was—
   (i) so used or held for the purposes of an institution to which section 39(2)(c) of this Act applies, or
   (ii) obtained by the authority concerned for the purpose of being so used or held,
   the appropriate transferee within the meaning of section 32 of this Act in relation to that institution.

(9) Where the Education Assets Board acquire any interest in land by a compulsory purchase under subsection (5) above the Board shall be entitled to recover from the local authority concerned an amount equal to the aggregate of—
(a) the amount of compensation agreed or awarded in respect of that

purchase, together with any interest payable by the Board in respect of that compensation in accordance with section 11 of the Compulsory Purchase Act 1965 or section 52A of the Land Compensation Act 1973, and

(b) the amount of the costs and expenses incurred by the Board in connection with the making of the compulsory purchase order.

DEFINITIONS
"appropriate transferee": subs. (8).
"compulsory purchase": s.1(1) of the Acquisition of Land Act 1981.
"disposal": s.39(10).
"Education Assets Board": s.197 of the ERA 1988.
"interest in land": s.90(1).
"land": s.90(1).
"local authority": s.90(1).
"wrongful disposal": subs. (1).

GENERAL NOTE
This section makes provision in case of disposals of land in breach of the requirements of s.39(4) and (5). It follows the precedent of s.201 of the ERA 1988. Where a contract is made to dispose of land or any interest in land, the Education Assets Board may serve notice on the transferee to repudiate the contract before conveyance (subs. (2)). Similarly, it may repudiate options under subs. (3). Where the disposal has been completed, the Education Assets Board may be authorised by the Secretary of State to acquire the property by compulsory purchase (subs. (5)) and transfer it to the appropriate transferee (subs. (8)). Subsection (6) applies legislation on compulsory purchase procedures to acquisitions under subs. (5). Subsection (9) enables the Education Assets Board to recover from the local authority the sums paid out by way of compensation to the transferee for compulsory purchase and the expenses of the transaction.

This section came into force on May 6, 1992: see Commencement No. 1 Order 1992, para. 2 and Sched. 1.

Subs. (2)
Repudiate. Repudiation involves an intention no longer to be bound by the contract (G.H. Treitel, *The Law of Contract* (7th ed., 1987), p. 615). Such an anticipatory repudiation will normally amount to a breach of contract on the part of the local authority.

Education Assets Board. By virtue of subs. (4), the act of the Education Assets Board is the act of the local authority.

Subs. (5)
Compulsory purchase. Under Pt. II of the Acquisition of Land Act 1981, procedures are set out for the compulsory acquisition of land by a local authority or other public body. These procedures must be followed by the Education Assets Board in relation to acquisitions under this section. For these purposes, the Board is not acting on behalf of the local authority, and it may make representations against the compulsory purchase order.

Education Assets Board. See note to s.36(5).

Subs. (8)
Interest. The interest of a local authority is determined, *inter alia*, by s.23(5) in relation to para. (a) and s.33(3) in relation to para. (b).

Control of contracts

41.—(1) This section applies, subject to subsection (5) below, to any contract which, if a relevant institution were to become an institution within the further education sector, would or might on or after the operative date bind the governing body of the institution.

(2) Except with the appropriate consent, a local authority shall not after the passing of this Act enter into a contract to which this section applies.

(3) If at any time after 21st March 1991 and before the passing of this Act a local authority have entered into a contract which would have been in contravention of the provisions of subsection (2) above if they had then been in force, the same consequences shall follow as if those provisions had been contravened by the local authority.

(4) In relation to any contract the appropriate consent is—

(a) the consent of the existing governing body of the institution, and

(b) if (on the assumption in subsection (1) above) the contract will require the governing body of the institution to make payments on or after 1st April 1993 amounting in aggregate to £50,000 or more, the consent of the Secretary of State.

(5) This section does not apply to—

(a) a works contract (within the meaning of Part III of the Local Government, Planning and Land Act 1980) which is entered into in accordance with section 7 of that Act, or

(b) a works contract (within the meaning of Part I of the Local Government Act 1988) which is entered into in accordance with section 4 of that Act.

(6) Any consent for the purposes of this section may be given either in respect of a particular contract or in respect of contracts of any class or description and either unconditionally or subject to conditions.

(7) Any signification of consent for the purposes of this section, or of such consent subject to conditions, given by the governing body of an institution or the Secretary of State before the passing of this Act in respect of any contract to which this section applies shall be treated for the purposes of this section as a consent, or a consent subject to the conditions, given under this section.

(8) A contract shall not be void by reason only that it has been entered into in contravention of this section and (subject to section 42 of this Act) a person entering into a contract with a local authority shall not be concerned to enquire whether any consent required by this section has been given or any conditions of such a consent have been complied with.

(9) Where there is an obligation under a contract to which this section applies to provide any benefit other than money, subsection (4)(b) above shall apply as if the obligation were to pay a sum of money corresponding to the value of the benefit to the recipient.

(10) This section does not apply to a contract to dispose of land or to grant or dispose of any interest in land.

DEFINITIONS

"appropriate consent": subs. (4).
"governing body": s.90(1) and (2).
"institution within the further education sector": s.91(3).
"local authority": s.90(1).
"operative date": s.17(2).
"relevant institution": s.39(2).

GENERAL NOTE

The purpose of this section is to restrict the contracts made by local authorities that would bind the institution to which its rights and liabilities are transferred on or after the operative date under this Act. The section applies to all contracts made after March 21, 1991. No contract creating rights and liabilities after the operative date may be made unless it has the consent of the governing body of the institution. Where the sum potentially payable by an institution after April 1, 1993 exceeds £50,000, the Secretary of State must also consent to the contract (subs. (4)). Consent may be given to individual contracts or classes of contract (subs. (6)), and, under subs. (7), consent given before this Act was passed on March 6, 1992 is to be treated as consent for the purposes of this section. Exceptions are made for certain works contracts mentioned in subs. (5), and contracts for the disposal of land, which are governed by s.40. Under subs. (9), value is calculated in relation to obligations owed under the contract even if they are in kind. By virtue of subs. (8), as with breach of s.39, breach of the provisions of this section do not render a contract illegal and void, but render them liable to be repudiated by the Education Assets Board under s.42.

This section came into force on May 6, 1992: see Commencement No. 1 Order 1992, para. 2 and Sched. 1.

Subs. (1)
   Operative date. This section applies even if the operative date is later than April 1, 1993, and it affects the liabilities which an institution within the further education sector would acquire on the operative date by virtue of ss.23 or 32.

Subs. (2)
   Contract to which this section applies. See subss. (1), (5) and (10).

Subs. (3)
   Would have been a contravention. This means that it would have been a contravention if the appropriate consent under subs. (4) had not been obtained. This provision gives retrospective effect to the obligation to obtain such a consent.

Subs. (4)
   Existing governing body. See note to s.84.
   Secretary of State. See note to s.1(2).

Subs. (5)
   Works contract. For the purposes of the Local Government, Planning and Land Act 1980, a "works contract" is defined by s.5(1) of that Act as a contract for "construction and maintenance work", which term is defined in s.20(1) of the same Act. Section 7 of that Act requires that such contracts be entered into after a tender procedure.
   For the purposes of the Local Government Act 1988, a "works contract" is defined by s.3(2) of that Act. Under s.4 of that Act, such contracts must be entered into after a process of competitive tender or a public invitation to submit offers.
   The above procedures ensure the bona fides of the contracts which are made, and thus require no additional control such as imposed by the requirement of the appropriate consent under subs. (4).

Subs. (7)
   This subsection gives retrospective effect to the consents given. See further the note to s.23(7).

Wrongful contracts

   42.—(1) This section applies where a local authority have entered into a contract to which section 41 of this Act applies in contravention of that section.
   (2) The Education Assets Board may by notice in writing served on the other party to the contract repudiate the contract at any time before it is performed.
   (3) A repudiation under subsection (2) above shall have effect as if made by the local authority concerned.

DEFINITIONS
   "Education Assets Board": s.197 of the ERA 1988.
   "local authority": s.90(1).

GENERAL NOTE
   This section provides a sanction for contracts made in breach of the requirements of s.41 (called "wrongful contracts"). As under s.40 in relation to wrongful contracts to dispose of land, the Education Assets Board is empowered to repudiate the contract, acting in the name and in the place of the local authority.
   This section came into force on May 6, 1992: see Commencement No. 1 Order 1992, para. 2 and Sched. 1.

Subs. (2)
   Repudiate. See note to s.40(2).
   Education Assets Board. See note to s.36(5).

Remuneration of employees

   43.—(1) Where, in consequence of a determination by the local education authority or any other person of the rate of remuneration of any employees, the rate of remuneration of any relevant employees would, apart from this section, be increased as from a date (referred to in this section as the "proposed date of increase") falling after 1st September 1992, the authority—

(a) shall notify the Secretary of State in writing of the determination and the proposed date of increase, and

(b) shall not pay any relevant employee at the new rate unless the increase is authorised under this section by the Secretary of State.

(2) In this section "relevant employees" means persons who are employed at institutions which are relevant institutions by virtue of section 39(2)(a) or (b) of this Act.

(3) This section does not apply to remuneration determined in accordance with the scales and other provisions set out or referred to in a pay and conditions order (within the meaning of the School Teachers' Pay and Conditions Act 1991).

(4) Where the Secretary of State receives a notification under subsection (1) above, he shall, before the end of the period of four weeks beginning with the day on which he received the notification, either—

(a) authorise the increase resulting from the determination so far as it relates to relevant employees, or

(b) afford to the authority, and to such persons appearing to him to be representative of relevant employees affected by the determination as he considers appropriate, an opportunity of making representations to him in respect of the determination.

(5) After considering any representations made to him under subsection (4)(b) above, the Secretary of State shall—

(a) authorise the increase resulting from the determination, or

(b) refuse to authorise the increase,

so far as it relates to relevant employees.

(6) The Secretary of State shall give written notification of any decision under subsection (4)(a) or (5) above to the local education authority and, in the case of subsection (5) above, to any other persons who made representations to him under subsection (4)(b) above.

(7) Subsection (8) below applies where—

(a) by virtue of this section a relevant employee is not paid at the new rate on the proposed date of increase, but

(b) the Secretary of State authorises the increase after that date.

(8) Where this subsection applies, the employee concerned shall, for the purpose of determining the terms of any contract affected by section 26 of this Act, be regarded as having been entitled under his contract of employment to be paid by the local education authority at the new rate as from the proposed date of increase.

DEFINITIONS

"determination": subs. (1)(a).

"pay and conditions order": s.48(4).

"proposed date of increase": subs. (1).

"relevant employees": subs. (2).

"relevant institution": s.39(2)(a) and (b).

"school teacher": s.48(4).

GENERAL NOTE

The purpose of this section is to forestall possible excessive pay settlements made by local education authorities before the operative date on which responsibility for pay and conditions of staff is transferred to the institutions within the further education sector (Paymaster-General, *Hansard*, H.L. Vol. 533, col. 944). The Government intended that pay and conditions within the new sector should be settled through negotiation between employers and employees (White Paper, *Education and Training*, Vol. 2, para. 7.18). To safeguard the freedom of the new institutions to create their own conditions of service, subs. (1) requires that pay increases due after September 1, 1992 should be approved by the Secretary of State before they come into effect, with the exception of those salaries already approved by him under the School Teachers' Pay and Conditions Act 1991 (subs. (3)). This section applies by virtue of subs. (2) to all employees ("relevant employees") of institutions which are likely to become part of the further education sector on the operative date ("relevant institutions"). Before the Secretary of State refuses to authorise the increase within four weeks of notification of a proposed increase, he is obliged to give an opportunity to make representations to the local education authority and representatives of the employees affected (subs. (4)). Where approval for the increase comes after the proposed date of increase in salary defined in subs. (1), the local education authority remains liable to pay the increase retrospectively back to that date (subs. (8)).

This section came into force on May 6, 1992: see Commencement No. 1 Order 1992, para. 2 and Sched. 1.

Subs. (1)
   Secretary of State. See note to s.1(2).
   Local education authority. See note to s.2(6).

Subs. (3)
   Pay and conditions order. See note to s.48 for provisions relating to the remuneration of teachers subject to such an order.

Subs. (4)
   Opportunity of making representations. An opportunity to make representations involves "a fair opportunity to those who are parties to a controversy for correcting or contradicting anything prejudicial to their view" (Lord Loreburn, L.C., *Board of Education* v. *Rice* [1911] A.C. 179). In broad terms, this involves some indication of the opposing case, though this need not involve disclosure of all the arguments and evidence received (*R.* v. *Gaming Board for Great Britain*, ex p. *Benaim and Khaida* [1970] 2 Q.B. 417, *R.* v. *Monopolies and Mergers Commission*, ex p. *Brown (Matthew)* [1987] 1 W.L.R. 1235). There must also be adequate time to prepare a reply (see *R.* v. *Secretary of State for Social Services*, ex p. *Association of Metropolitan Authorities* [1986] 1 W.L.R. 1, C.A.; *R.* v. *Secretary of State for Health*, ex p. *U.S. Tobacco Industries* [1992] 1 All E.R. 212). On this, see generally H.W.R. Wade, *Administrative Law* (6th ed., Oxford 1988), pp. 538–44.

Miscellaneous

Collective worship

44.—(1) In this section "institution of voluntary origin" means a further education institution which, when it became a further education institution, was a voluntary school or a grant-maintained school which was a voluntary school before it became grant-maintained.

(2) The governing body of every further education institution except an institution which on the appointed day was a college of further education shall ensure that at an appropriate time on at least one day in each week during which the institution is open an act of collective worship is held at the institution which persons receiving education at the institution may attend.

(3) In an institution of voluntary origin such act of collective worship shall—

   (a) be in such forms as to comply with the provisions of any trust deed affecting the institution, and

   (b) reflect the religious traditions and practices of the institution before it became a further education institution.

(4) In all other further education institutions such act of collective worship shall be wholly or mainly of a broadly Christian character in that it shall reflect the broad traditions of Christian belief but need not be distinctive of any particular Christian denomination.

(5) If the governing body of a further education institution considers it appropriate to do so it may in addition to the act of collective worship referred to in subsection (3) or (4) provide for acts of worship which reflect the practices of some or all of the other religious traditions represented in Great Britain.

(6) In this section "the appointed day" means the day appointed under section 94 of this Act for the commencement of subsection (4) of section 15 of this Act.

DEFINITIONS
"appointed day": subs. (6).
"collective worship": s.6 of the ERA 1988.
"governing body": s.90(1) and (2).
"grant-maintained school": s.52 of the ERA 1988.
"institution of voluntary origin": subs. (1).
"voluntary aided school": s.15(2) of the EA 1944.

GENERAL NOTE
Sections 44 and 45 were amendments moved by the Bishop of Guildford and passed despite Government opposition in the House of Lords. They preserve some elements of the duty of sixth-form colleges and schools to make provision for collective worship and religious education under the Education Reform Act after they are transferred to the further education sector under the provisions of this Act.

Section 44 draws a distinction between the obligations of "institutions of voluntary origin" (typically voluntary-aided sixth-form colleges) and other institutions in respect of collective worship. All further education institutions, other than former further education colleges, are obliged to secure that there is an act of collective worship at least once a week (as opposed to each day under s.6 of the ERA 1988). There is no obligation on students to attend this collective worship. In institutions of voluntary origin, the act of collective worship complies with the trust deed and reflects the religious tradition of the institution before it became part of the further education sector. In other institutions, as under s.6 of the ERA 1988, subs. (4) provides that the worship will be of a broadly Christian character, though subs. (5) does empower the governing body of the institution to make alternative provision in a similar way to that permitted by s.7 of the ERA 1988.

This section comes into force on April 1, 1993, but only in respect of institutions which, before they became institutions within the further education sector, were schools maintained by a local education authority or were grant-maintained schools: see Commencement No. 1 Order 1992, para. 2 and Sched. 3.

Subs. (1)
Institution of voluntary origin. This concept includes two situations. On the one hand, a school or sixth-form college passes directly from being under the aegis of the local education authority to becoming a further education institution (usually by virtue of designation under s.28). On the other hand, such a school or college may have become first a grant-maintained school before the passing of the Act, and then becomes a further education corporation by virtue of s.15 or s.16 of this Act. Both kinds of institution are treated in the same way for the purposes of this section and s.45.

Further Education Institution
This phrase does not occur outside ss.44 and 45, but would not appear to differ in meaning from "institution within the further education sector": s.91(3).

Subs. (2)
On at least one day in each week. This contrasts with the daily worship required by s.6(1) of the ERA 1988.

Subs. (3)
Religious tradition. This covers institutions which have a particular religious or denominational character, *e.g.* Jewish or Catholic schools.

Subs. (4)
These provisions follow substantially the wording of s.7(1) and (2) of the ERA 1988.

Subs. (5)
Governing body. Under s.7(6) of the ERA 1988, it is necessary to obtain the advice of a standing advisory council before collective worship, other than of a broadly Christian character, is permitted. Under this subsection, the governing body of the institution can make such a decision without the need for such prior advice.

Religious education

45.—(1) In this section "institution of voluntary origin" means a further education institution which, when it became a further education institution, was a voluntary school or a grant-maintained school which was a voluntary school before it became grant-maintained.

(2) The governing body of every further education institution except an institution which on the appointed day was a college of further education shall ensure that religious education is provided at the institution for all persons attending the institution who wish to receive it.

(3) The governing body of a further education institution shall be deemed to be fulfilling its duty under this section if religious education is provided at a time or times at which it is convenient for the majority of full time students to attend.

(4) For the purposes of this section religious education may take the form of a course of lectures or classes or of single lectures or classes provided on a regular basis and may include a course of study leading to an examination or the award of a qualification.

(5) The form and content of religious education provided pursuant to this section shall be determined from time to time by the governing body of each further education institution and—

(a) in the case of an institution of voluntary origin—

(i) shall be in accordance with the provisions of any trust deed affecting the institution, and

(ii) shall not be contrary to the religious traditions of the institution before it became a further education institution;

(b) in the case of all further education institutions shall reflect the fact that the religious traditions in Great Britain are in the main Christian whilst taking account of the teaching and practices of the other principal religions represented in Great Britain.

(6) In this section "the appointed day" means the day appointed under section 94 of this Act for the commencement of subsection (4) of section 15 of this Act.

DEFINITIONS
"appointed day": subs. (6).
"governing body": s.90(1) and (2).
"grant-maintained school": s.52 of the ERA 1988.
"institution of voluntary origin": subs. (1).
"religious education": s.9(9)(b) of the ERA 1988.
"voluntary aided school": s.15(2) of the EA 1944.

GENERAL NOTE
In parallel with s.44, this section makes provision for further education institutions (other than former colleges of further education) to ensure that there is religious education available in their institution for students. Under s.8(3) of the ERA 1988, religious education relates to an agreed syllabus as part of the national curriculum, but under subs. (5), it is for the governing body of each institution to determine what shall be taught by way of religious education. In an institution of voluntary origin, this must conform to the trust deed and reflect the character of the institution before it became part of the further education sector. In other institutions, as under s.8(3) of the ERA 1988, religious education must reflect the fact that religious traditions in Great Britain are in the main Christian, though account is to be taken of other religious traditions. The religious education may take various forms, including courses leading to an examination or qualification (subs. (4)).

Under subs. (2), such religious education is entirely voluntary for students, but under subs. (3), it must be provided at a time or times which are convenient for the majority of full-time students to attend.

This section comes into force on April 1, 1993, but only in respect of institutions which, before they became institutions within the further education sector, were schools maintained by a local education authority or were grant-maintained schools: see Commencement No. 1 Order 1992, para. 2 and Sched. 3.

Further education institution. See note to s.44(1).

Subs. (5)
Religious tradition. This covers institutions which have a particular religious or denomin-ational character, *e.g.* Jewish or Catholic schools.
Governing body. Under s.8 of the ERA 1988, there was no provision for "opting out" of the national curriculum on religious education except by individual pupils under s.9 of the ERA 1988. Here religious education is truly voluntary, but a similar character of religious education must be provided to that previously undertaken by the institution in relation to the national curriculum, since the education must continue to be of a broadly Christian character. The character of the education is now determined by the governing body without any imposed external curriculum (see subs. (4)).

Variation of trust deeds

46.—(1) The Secretary of State may by order make such modifications as he thinks fit in any trust deed or other instrument—

(a) relating to or regulating an institution within the further education sector, or

(b) relating to any land or other property held by any person for the purposes of such an institution.

(2) Before making any modifications under subsection (1) above of any trust deed or other instrument the Secretary of State shall so far as it appears to him to be practicable to do so consult—

(a) the governing body of the institution,

(b) where that deed or instrument, or any other instrument relating to or regulating the institution concerned, confers power on any other persons to modify or replace that deed or instrument, those persons, and

(c) where the instrument to be modified is a trust deed and the trustees are different from the persons mentioned in paragraphs (a) and (b) above, the trustees.

DEFINITIONS
"governing body": s.90(1) and (2).
"institution within the further education sector": s.91(3).
"land": s.90(1).
"modifications": s.61(1).

GENERAL NOTE
This section empowers the Secretary of State to vary any trust deeds or instruments as he thinks fit. This power is principally to enable certain voluntary institutions to enter the further education sector, typically by designation under s.28. Such modifications may relate to the institution itself or to the land or property held for its purposes.
Subsection (2) imposes duties on the Secretary of State to consult the governing body of the institution and the trustees or other persons with power to modify the trust deed or instrument.
An equivalent provision exists under s.75 in relation to institutions within the higher education sector.
This section comes into force on April 1, 1993: see Commencement No. 1 Order 1992, para. 2 and Sched. 3.

Subs. (1)
Secretary of State. See note to s.1(2).
Order. An order made under this section need not be made by way of a statutory instrument (s.89(2)).

Subs. (2)
Consult. See note to s.6(1).

Transfer of higher education institutions to further education sector

47.—(1) The Secretary of State may by order provide for the transfer of a higher education corporation to the further education sector.

(2) Where an order is made under this section in respect of a higher education corporation, sections 20 and 21 of this Act shall have effect as if, on the date the order has effect, the corporation were established as a further education corporation; and the order may make any provision that may be made by an order under section 15 of this Act specifying a grant-maintained school.

(3) On such date as may be specified in the order the corporation shall cease to be a higher education corporation and become a further education corporation.

(4) An order under section 28 of this Act in respect of any institution may revoke any order in respect of that institution under section 129 of the Education Reform Act 1988 (designation of institutions).

DEFINITIONS
"further education corporation": s.17(1).
"higher education corporation": s.90(1).
"institution within the further education sector": s.91(3).
"institution within the higher education sector": s.91(5).

GENERAL NOTE
This section permits the rationalisation of the further and higher education sectors. The Secretary of State is empowered to order the transfer of a higher education corporation to the further education sector (subs. (1)) and it will thereby be established as a further education corporation (subs. (2)). An order made under this section overrides any designation order made in respect of the institution under s.129 of the ERA 1988. This provision has its counterpart in s.74, which provides for the transfer of further education institutions to the higher education sector.

This section comes into force on April 1, 1993: see Commencement No. 1 Order 1992, para. 2 and Sched. 3.

Subs. (1)
Secretary of State. See note to s.1(2).
Order. An order made under this section must be made by way of a statutory instrument which is subject to the negative resolution procedure in Parliament (s.89(1) and (3)).

Statutory conditions of employment

48.—(1) This section applies where—
(a) an educational institution at which a school teacher is employed by a local education authority, or by the governing body of a voluntary or grant-maintained school, becomes an institution within the further education sector, and
(b) immediately before the operative date, any of the terms and conditions of his employment have effect by virtue of a pay and conditions order.

(2) as from the operative date the person's contract of employment shall have effect—
(a) in relation to him and to the governing body of the institution as it had effect immediately before that date in relation to school teachers and to local education authorities or governing bodies of voluntary or grant-maintained schools, and
(b) as if the contract required any remuneration determined in accordance with the scales and other provisions set out or referred to in the relevant pay and conditions order to be paid to him by the governing body of the institution.

(3) Nothing in this section affects any right to vary the terms of any contract of employment.

(4) In this section—
(a) "pay and conditions order" and "school teacher" have the same meaning as in the School Teachers' Pay and Conditions Act 1991, and
(b) "relevant pay and conditions order", in relation to any person, means

the pay and conditions order having effect in relation to him immediately before the operative date or, if that order is no longer in force,
the pay and conditions order which would have had effect in relation
to him if the institution at which he is employed had not become an
institution within the further education sector.

DEFINITIONS
"contract of employment": s.5(1) of the School Teachers' Pay and Conditions Act 1991.
"governing body": s.90(1) and (2).
"grant-maintained school": s.52 of the ERA 1988.
"institution within the further education sector": s.91(3).
"pay and conditions order": s.2(3) of the School Teachers' Pay and Conditions Act 1991.
"relevant pay and conditions order": subs. (4)(b).
"school teacher": s.5(1) of the School Teachers' Pay and Conditions Act 1991.
"voluntary school": s.9(2) of the EA 1944.

GENERAL NOTE
This section continues the terms and conditions of employment of schoolteachers working in
institutions which have become institutions within the further education sector and thus fall
outside the School Teachers' Pay and Conditions Act 1991. Under that Act, the salaries of
schoolteachers are determined by order of the Secretary of State upon the recommendation of
the teachers' pay review body. This section ensures that the provisions of such an order shall
continue to have effect in relation to a teacher's contract of employment despite the change in
the employing institution effected by this Act.
Subsection (1) sets out the basic conditions for the application of this section, *viz.* that the
employee is a schoolteacher, subject to a pay and conditions order. Subsection (2) provides that
the employee's contract of employment shall have effect from the operative date as it did in
relation to his employing institution prior to that date and subject to the terms set out in the
relevant pay and conditions order. Subsection (4) defines such an order as one which did apply
at the operative date, or which would have applied but for the transfer of the institution to the
further education sector. Subsection (3) notes that nothing in this section prevents a new
institution from varying the terms and conditions of employment so inherited. As the
Paymaster-General put it, "contracts are not set in stone and can be varied subsequently"
(*Hansard*, H.L. Vol. 534, col. 433).
This section comes into force on April 1, 1993: see Commencement No. 1 Order 1992, para. 2
and Sched. 3.

Subs. (4)
Pay and Conditions Order. For the purpose of ascertaining whether a pay and conditions
order has effect in relation to a person, no account is to be taken of the amendments made by
this Act to the definitions of "secondary education" and "further education" in relation to the
definition of "school teacher" in s.5 of the School Teachers' Pay and Conditions Act 1991: see
Commencement No. 1 Order 1992, para. 5.

Avoidance of certain contractual terms

49.—(1) This section applies to any contract made between the governing
body of an institution within the further education sector and any person
employed by them, not being a contract made in contemplation of the
employee's pending dismissal by reason of redundancy.
(2) In so far as a contract to which this section applies provides that the
employee—
  (a) shall not be dismissed by reason of redundancy, or
  (b) if he is so dismissed, shall be paid a sum in excess of the sum which the
      employer is liable to pay to him under section 81 of the Employment
      Protection (Consolidation) Act 1978,
the contract shall be void and of no effect.

DEFINITIONS
"dismissal by reason of redundancy": s.83 of the Employment Protection (Consolidation)
Act 1978.
"governing body": s.90(1) and (2).
"institution within the further education sector": s.91(3).

GENERAL NOTE

This section renders void certain contracts between the governing body of an institution within the further education sector and an employee. The contracts affected are those which provide that he will not be dismissed at some future date or that, if he is, he will receive a payment in excess of the statutory entitlement to redundancy payment (subs. (2)). Such a prohibition does not affect contracts made in contemplation of the imminent dismissal of an employee by reason of redundancy (subs. (1)).

Unlike ss.40 and 42, this section primarily concerns agreements made by a new further education sector institution with its employees. This preservation of managerial freedom follows s.221 of the ERA 1988.

This section comes into force on April 1, 1993: see Commencement No. 1 Order 1992, para. 2 and Sched. 3.

Subs. (1)

Institution within the further education sector. This term covers only institutions created under this Act. Any contract of employment which contains any clause prohibited under this section and which is made by a local education authority will be treated by virtue of s.26(3)(b) as having been made by the further education corporation. Therefore, this section will also apply to such a contract.

Dismissal by reason of redundancy. The right to claim that a substantial change in working conditions constitutes constructive dismissal by reason of redundancy is preserved by s.26(4).

Information with respect to institutions within the further education sector

50.—(1) The Secretary of State may by regulation require the governing body of any institution within the further education sector to publish such information as may be prescribed about—

(a) the education provision made or proposed to be made for their students,

(b) the educational achievements of their students on entry to the institution and the educational achievements of their students while at the institution (including in each case the results of examinations, tests and other assessments),

(c) the financial and other resources of the institution and the effectiveness of the use made of such resources, and

(d) the careers of their students after completing any course or leaving the institution.

(2) For the purposes of subsection (1)(d) above, a person's career includes any education, training, employment or occupation; and the regulations may in particular require the published information to show—

(a) the numbers of students not undertaking any career, and

(b) the persons providing students with education, training or employment.

(3) The information shall be published in such form and manner and at such times as may be prescribed.

(4) The published information shall not name any student to whom it relates.

(5) In this section "prescribed" means prescribed by regulations.

DEFINITIONS

"governing body": s.90(1) and (2).

"institution within the further education sector": s.91(3).

GENERAL NOTE

This section makes it possible for the Secretary of State to prescribe that certain information about the educational provision and resources of an institution or the achievement of its students shall be published by it. The White Paper *Education and Training*, Vol. 1, para. 4.11, stated that, just as schools already have to publish results of their pupils in a standard format that is easily understood, further education institutions should do the same. That paragraph envisaged that the publication of results would initially be voluntary, but that formal regulations would be produced to help ensure comparability and comprehensibility of information. The proposed information includes both information for students, parents, sponsors and employers about what is provided and how well students perform, and information on the "value-added element", the effective use of resources (Lord Cavendish of Furness, *Hansard*, H.L. Vol. 534, col. 434). On this last element, the Government rejected the inclusion of data relating to the achievements of students prior to their entry on to the course (Lord Cavendish of Furness, *Hansard*, H.L. Vol. 533, col. 950). The subsequent careers of students (as defined in subs. (2)) is, however, taken as a measure of success in education (subs. (1)(d)).

Subsection (3) provides that regulations shall determine the form and manner of the publication of information required under subs. (1). Subsection (4) makes it clear that any data published shall not name individual students.

This section comes into force on April 1, 1993: see Commencement No. 1 Order 1992, para. 2 and Sched. 3.

Subs. (1)
Prescribed. Under subs. (3), the rules are prescribed by regulations, which must be in the form of a statutory instrument subject to the negative resolution procedure in Parliament (s.89(1) and (3)). Such regulations are made by the Secretary of State (s.61(1)).

Educational achievements. Similar information is already required of schools under the Education (Information on School Examination Results) (England) Regulations 1991 (S.I. 1991 No. 1265) and DES Circular 9/91. These regulations were issued under powers given to the Secretary of State by s.8 of the EA 1980 and s.22 of the ERA 1988.

Secretary of State. See note to s.1(2).

Subs. (5)
Regulations. Regulations made under this section must be made by way of a statutory instrument which is subject to the negative resolution procedure in Parliament (s.89(1) and (3)).

Publication of proposals

51.—(1) A council shall not make a proposal for—
  (a) the establishment by the Secretary of State of a body corporate under section 16(1) of this Act,
  (b) the establishment by the Secretary of State of a body corporate under subsection (3) of that section, or
  (c) the dissolution of any further education corporation by the Secretary of State under section 27 of this Act,
unless the following conditions have been complied with.
  (2) The conditions are that—
  (a) a draft of the proposal, or of a proposal in substantially the same form, giving such information as may be prescribed has been published by such time and in such manner as may be prescribed,
  (b) the council have considered any representations about the draft made to them within the prescribed period, and
  (c) copies of the draft and of any such representations have been sent to the Secretary of State.
  (3) The Secretary of State shall not make—
  (a) an order under section 16(1) of this Act, other than an order made for the purpose of giving effect to a proposal by a council, or
  (b) an order under section 16(2) of this Act,
unless he has published a draft of the proposed order, or of an order in substantially the same form, by such time and in such manner as may be prescribed.
  (4) In this section "prescribed" means prescribed by regulations.

DEFINITIONS
  "council": s.90(1).
  "further education corporation": s.17(1).

GENERAL NOTE
  This section requires that an FEFC publish proposals and consider representations before it makes proposals for the establishment of a further education corporation under s.16(1) or (3), or for the dissolution of such a corporation under s.27. Similar duties are imposed on the

Secretary of State in relation to orders creating a further education corporation in other cases under s.16(1) or (2). In particular, this section concerns proposals to convert an existing institution maintained by a local education authority or a grant-maintained school into a further education corporation under s.16(2) or (3).

Under subs. (2) of this section, an FEFC must publish a draft, consider representations within the prescribed period and send copies of the draft and representations to the Secretary of State. Similarly, under subs. (3), the Secretary of State must publish a draft order within a specified time period. Since such an order is subject to annulment in Parliament (s.89(3)), there is some opportunity for objections to be made to the order.

This section comes into force on September 30, 1992: see Commencement No. 1 Order 1992, para. 2 and Sched. 2.

Subs. (1)
    Body corporate. This means a further education corporation.
    Prescribed. See note to s.50(1).
    Secretary of State. See note to s.1(2).

Subs. (2)
    Representations. See "consult" in the note to s.6(1).

Duty to provide for named individuals

52.—(1) This section applies where an institution within the further education sector provides full-time education suitable to the requirements of persons over compulsory school age who have not attained the age of nineteen years.

(2) A council may by notice given to the governing body of such an institution—

    (a) require them to provide for such individuals as may be specified in the notice such education falling within subsection (1) above as is appropriate to their abilities and aptitudes, or

    (b) withdraw such a requirement.

(3) The governing body of such an institution shall, for any academic year in respect of which they receive financial support from a council, secure compliance with any requirement in respect of any individual who has not attained the age of nineteen years which is or has been imposed by that council under subsection (2) above and has not been withdrawn.

DEFINITIONS
    "compulsory school age": s.35 of the EA 1944.
    "council": s.90(1).
    "further education corporation": s.17(1).
    "governing body": s.90(1) and (2).

GENERAL NOTE
The power of an FEFC under this section to require that a particular institution provide further education for a named individual is intended as an exceptional measure (Lord Cavendish of Furness, *Hansard*, H.L. Vol. 533, col. 955). The principal kind of person for whom such a requirement is envisaged is a person with learning difficulties or other special needs for whom special arrangements are necessary.

Subsection (1) specifies that this section only applies to an individual between 16 and 18 for whom a full-time place at an institution within the further education sector is required. Subsection (2) empowers an FEFC to require that such an institution provide appropriate further education to such a named individual and to withdraw this requirement at any time. Subsection (3) requires that the institution in question comply with the requirement and provide such education for every year in which they receive financial support from the FEFC. Guidance will be issued by the Secretary of State as to the exercise of this power.

This section comes into force on April 1, 1993: see Commencement No. 1 Order 1992, para. 2 and Sched. 3.

Subs. (1)
    Compulsory school age. See note to s.2(1).

Full-time education. See note to s.2(1).

Subs. (3)
   Academic year. The academic year is not defined in this Act. It is, however, defined under regulations applicable to further education before the relevant provisions of this Act come into force (see para. 10(7) of the Education (Schools and Further Education) Regulations 1981 (S.I. 1981 No. 1086), as amended by the Education (Schools and Further Education) (Amendment) Regulations 1990 (S.I. 1990 No. 2259)).
   Financial support. The obligation to comply with the requirement under subs. (2) applies even though no financial support is earmarked for the education of the person named in the notice under subs. (2)(a). The FEFC does, however, have power to provide financial support to any individual under s.5(5).

Inspection of accounts

53.—(1) The accounts of—
   (a) any further education corporation, and
   (b) any designated institution,
shall be open to the inspection of the Comptroller and Auditor General.
   (2) In the case of any such corporation or institution—
   (a) the power conferred by subsection (1) above, and
   (b) the powers under sections 6 and 8 of the National Audit Act 1983
       (examinations into the economy, efficiency and effectiveness of cer-
       tain bodies and access to documents and information) conferred on
       the Comptroller and Auditor General by virtue of section 6(3)(c) of
       that Act,
shall be exercisable only in, or in relation to accounts or other documents which relate to, any financial year in which expenditure is incurred by the corporation, or by the governing body of the institution in question, in respect of which grants, loans or other payments are made to them under this Part of this Act.

DEFINITIONS
   "designated institution": s.28(4).
   "financial year": Sched. 4, para. 8.
   "further education corporation": s.17(1).

GENERAL NOTE
   This section deals with accountability for spending by institutions within the further educa-
tion sector. Like s.135 of the ERA 1988 in relation to universities and higher education corporations, this section provides that the accounts of further education corporations and designated institutions shall be open to inspection by the Comptroller and Auditor General. This is to enable the National Audit Office to examine both the accounts and the economy, efficiency and effectiveness of these institutions in performance of its functions under s.6 of the National Audit Act 1983. It can require further information under s.8 of that Act. The jurisdiction of the National Audit Office arises because more than half the income of such institutions will come from public funds (s.7(1) of that Act). Under s.220 of the ERA 1988, as amended by para. 51 of Sched. 8 to this Act, the Audit Commission is given competence to conduct efficiency studies in relation to the FEFC and to institutions within the further education sector. The rôle of the Audit Commission in relation to efficiency studies serves to assist the principal functions on this matter of the relevant FEFC in relation to institutions within its area under s.83. Under subs. (2), the obligation to open accounts to inspection relates only to financial years in which the institution was in receipt of funds under this Part of the Act. In other words, such accountability only arises as a result of the receipt of public funds and is to ensure that these are properly and efficiently spent. All the same, the power of the Comptroller and Auditor General under subs. (1) relates to all accounts of the institution funded from whatever source.
   This section comes into force on September 30, 1992: see Commencement No. 1 Order 1992, para. 2 and Sched. 2.

CHAPTER III

GENERAL

Duty to give information

54.—(1) Each of the following shall give a council such information as they may require for the purposes of the exercise of any of their functions under this Part of this Act—

(a) a local education authority,

(b) the governing body of any institution maintained by a local education authority, grant-maintained school, city technology college or city college for the technology of the arts,

(c) the governing body of any institution within the further education sector or the higher education sector, and

(d) the governing body of any institution which is receiving or has received financial support under section 5 of this Act.

(2) Such information relating to the provision which has been made by a local education authority in respect of any pupil at an institution as the authority may require for the purposes of claiming any amount in respect of the pupil from another authority under section 51 of the Education (No. 2) Act 1986 or by virtue of regulation under section 52 of that Act shall, where the institution becomes an institution within the further education sector, be provided to the authority by the governing body of the institution.

DEFINITIONS

"city college for technology and the arts": s.105(1)(a) of the ERA 1988.

"city technology college": s.105(1)(a) of the ERA 1988.

"council": s.90(1).

"functions": s.61(1).

"further education corporation": s.17(1).

"governing body": s.90(1) and (2).

"institution within the further education sector": s.91(3).

"institution within the higher education sector": s.91(5).

"pupil": s.114 of the EA 1944, as amended by para. 13 of Sched. 8 to this Act.

GENERAL NOTE

This section imposes a duty on both certain bodies receiving funding from an FEFC and certain bodies providing education in related sectors to provide information to the FEFC for the purposes of the exercise of its functions (including providing information to the Secretary of State under s.8(1)). Subsection (1) sets out the power of an FEFC to require information to be provided and the bodies which must comply. Subsection (2) states that where a local authority has provided education and wishes to recoup the money so expended under ss.51 or 52 of the Education (No. 2) Act 1986, it shall be the duty of the governing body of the institution at which the education was provided to provide the local education authority with the necessary information, even though that institution is no longer under the control of that authority.

Subsection (1) came into force on May 6, 1992, but subs. (2) only comes into force on April 1, 1993: see Commencement No. 1 Order 1992, para. 2 and, respectively, Scheds. 1 and 3.

Subs. (2)

The purposes of claiming any amount. Where one local education authority provides education for a person for whom another education authority is responsible, ss.51 and 52 of the Education (No. 2) Act 1986 provide that the former can recover payment from the latter for the education so provided. The obligation of the institution to provide information is to enable the provider authority to draw up its bill.

Inspection etc. of local education authority institutions, other than schools, and advice to Secretary of State

55.—(1) The chief inspector shall have the general duty of keeping the Secretary of State informed about—

(a) the quality of education provided in local education authority institutions,

(b) the educational standards achieved in such institutions, and

(c) whether the financial resources made available to such institutions are managed efficiently.

(2) When asked to do so by the Secretary of State, the chief inspector shall—

(a) give advice to the Secretary of State on such matters relating to local education authority institutions, and on such other matters relating to further education, as may be specified in the Secretary of State's request, and

(b) inspect and report on any such local education authority institution, or any such class of local education authority institution, as may be so specified.

(3) In connection with the duties imposed on the chief inspector under this section, his powers, and those of his inspectors, in relation to the inspection of schools under any enactment shall extend to the inspection of institutions under this section.

(4) In relation to any local education authority institution maintained or assisted by them, a local education authority—

(a) shall keep under review the quality of education provided, the educational standards achieved and whether the financial resources made available are managed efficiently, and

(b) may cause an inspection to be made by persons authorised by them.

(5) A local education authority shall not authorise any person to inspect any institution under this section unless they are satisfied that he is suitably qualified to do so.

(6) A person who wilfully obstructs any person authorised to inspect an institution under or by virtue of this section in the exercise of his functions shall be guilty of an offence and liable on summary conviction to a fine not exceeding level 4 on the standard scale.

(7) In this section—

(a) in relation to institutions in England, "chief inspector" means Her Majesty's Chief Inspector of Schools in England and "his inspectors" means Her Majesty's Inspectors of Schools in England,

(b) in relation to institutions in Wales, "chief inspector" means Her Majesty's Chief Inspector of Schools in Wales and "his inspectors" means Her Majesty's Inspectors of Schools in Wales, and

(c) "local education authority institution" means and educational institution, other than a school, maintained or assisted by a local education authority.

DEFINITIONS
"assisted": s.234 of the ERA 1988.
"Chief Inspector": subs. (7).
"his inspectors": subs. (7).
"local education authority institution": subs. (7).

GENERAL NOTE
This section provides that Her Majesty's Chief Inspector shall continue to have the duty of monitoring the quality, educational standards and efficient use of financial resources in institutions remaining as local authority institutions. Under subss. (1) and (2), the Chief Inspector's duty is to keep the Secretary of State informed on these matters, to advise him on them or on any other further education matter he requests, and to inspect such institutions. Subsection (3) provides that the powers of Her Majesty's Inspectors in this respect are the same as in relation to the inspection of schools. The rôle of Her Majesty's Inspectors in relation to local authority institutions is paralleled by that of the Quality Assessment Committee of the FEFC in relation to institutions within the further education sector under s.9.

Subsection (4) imposes a duty on the local education authority to engage in the quality assurance of the education provided in institutions maintained or assisted by it, and to cause them to be inspected by persons appointed by it. Subsection (5) provides that such inspectors must be suitably qualified. (These provisions parallel those in relation to the inspection of schools under the Education (Schools) Act 1992). This approach to quality assurance and assessment by the provider of education reduces the importance of quality assessment by Her Majesty's inspectors under subs. (2).

Subsection (6) creates the offence of wilful obstruction of an inspection either by Her Majesty's Inspectors or by inspectors appointed by the local authority under subs. (4).

This section replaces the provision for the inspection of such establishments under s.77 of the EA 1944 (Sched. 8, para. 10 to this Act), and confers on Her Majesty's inspectors broadly similar powers to those they will possess under the Education (Schools) Act 1992.

Subsections (1) to (3) come into force on April 1, 1993, in respect of England only: see Commencement No. 1 Order 1992, para. 2 and Sched. 3. Subsections (4) to (6) and (7)(a) and (c) also come into force on that date, *ibid.*

Subss. (1) and (2)
These provisions follow ss.2(1) and (2), and 6(1) and (2) of the Education (Schools) Act 1992. *Secretary of State.* See note to s.1(2).

Subs. (4)
These provisions on inspection differ from those for the inspection of schools. Under s.9 of the Education (Schools) Act 1992, Her Majesty's Chief Inspector of Schools appoints the inspectors for schools following the tender procedure set out in Sched. 2, para. 2 of that Act. Under this subsection, it is the local education authority which authorises persons to conduct the inspection of its establishments.

Subs. (5)
Under s.10 of the Education (Schools) Act 1992, the inspector for a school has to be chosen from persons registered for this purpose. This provision is wider because no register is to be maintained of such inspectors for further education.

Subs. (6)
This provision parallels ss.3(4) and (5), and 7(4) and (5) of the Education (Schools) Act 1992.

Subs. (7)
Her Majesty's Chief Inspector of Schools. See ss.1(1) and 5(1) of the Education (Schools) Act 1992.

Directions

56.—(1) In exercising their functions under this Part of this Act, each council shall comply with any directions contained in an order made by the Secretary of State.

(2) Directions under this section may be general or special, and special directions may, in particular, relate to the provision of financial support by the council in respect of activities carried on by any particular institution or institutions.

DEFINITIONS
"council": s.1(5).
"functions": s.61(1).

GENERAL NOTE
According to the Paymaster-General, this section "is founded on the proposition that the Secretary of State needs a longstop power of intervention in order to protect taxpayers' interests in the considerable sums of public money that do flow and will flow into further education in the form of grant to the funding councils" (*Hansard*, H.L. Vol. 535, col. 77). As a result of concern about the effect of such a power on the academic freedom of individual institutions, amendments were introduced in the House of Lords to divide the power of the Secretary of State to intervene into a power to issue general directions to the FEFC (this section) and powers to intervene in individual institutions in the event of mismanagement or breach of duty (s.57).

The power to issue general directions under this section closely follows s.134(8) and (9) of the ERA 1988, but with the addition of the clarification that such directions may relate to the provision of financial support in respect of activities carried on by any particular institution or institutions. In this respect, the wording of this section differs also from that of s.81, which contains no such clarification in respect of the power of the Secretary of State to issue directions to the HEFC. The reason for such differences in wording within this Act had more to do with the timetable for the discussion of these two sections in Parliament than with any difference in policy between them.

Directions under this section may relate to any aspect of the work of the councils and would enable the Secretary of State to initiate policy developments in further education. The power under this section supplements the power of the Secretary of State under s.7(1) to attach conditions to grants, a power which is more circumscribed in its application to individual institutions than is this power.

This section came into force on May 6, 1992: see Commencement No. 1 Order 1992, para. 2 and Sched. 1.

Subs. (1)
Order. An order made under this section must be made by way of a statutory instrument which is subject to the negative resolution procedure in Parliament (s.89(1) and (3)).
Secretary of State. See note to s.1(2).

Subs. (2)
Directions. These may be revoked or varied at any time (see s.111 of the EA 1944, as applied by s.89(5) of this Act).

Intervention in the event of mismanagement or breach of duty

57.—(1) If the Secretary of State is satisfied that the affairs of any institution within the further education sector have been or are being mismanaged, he may on the recommendation of the appropriate council by order—

(a) remove all or any of the members of the governing body of the institution and appoint new members in their places, and

(b) make such modifications of the instrument of government of the institution as he thinks fit.

(2) An appointment of a member of a governing body of an institution under subsection (1) above shall have effect as if made in accordance with the instrument of government and articles of government of the institution.

(3) If the Secretary of State is satisfied, either upon complaint by any person interested or otherwise, that—

(a) a council, or

(b) the governing body of any institution within the further education sector,

have failed to discharge any duty imposed on them by or for the purposes of the Education Acts, he may make an order under this subsection.

(4) An order under subsection (3) above shall declare the council or the governing body, as the case may be, to be in default in respect of that duty, and may give such directions for the purpose of enforcing the execution of that duty as appear to the Secretary of State to be expedient.

(5) A council or governing body in respect of which an order is made under subsection (3) above shall comply with any directions contained in the order.

(6) Section 93 of the Education Act 1944 (power to hold local inquiries) applies for the purposes of the Secretary of State's functions under this section as it applies for the purposes of his functions under that Act.

DEFINITIONS
"articles of government": ss.20(1)(b), 29(2)(b) and 31(2)(b).
"council": s.1(5).
"Education Acts": s.90(1).
"further education corporation": s.17(1).
"governing body": s.90(1) and (2).
"institution within the further education sector": s.91(3).
"institution within the higher education sector": s.91(5).
"instrument of government": ss.20(1)(a), 29(2)(a) and 31(2)(a).
"modification": s.61(1).

GENERAL NOTE

This section was produced by the Government in order to define more precisely the powers of the Secretary of State to intervene in the operation of individual institutions. Under this section, the Secretary of State may intervene either on the ground of mismanagement (subs. (1)), or on the ground of breach of duty (subs. (3)). In the case of mismanagement by an individual institution, subs. (1) provides that the Secretary of State makes an order on the recommendation of the relevant FEFC. Under that subsection, such an order may remove all or any members of the governing body of the institution and appoint new members to replace them, as well as modify the instrument of government. Subsection (2) provides that any nomination of new members of the governing body in an order made under subs. (1) has effect as if it were made under the instrument of government. Under subss. (3) and (4), where the Secretary of State receives a complaint that either the FEFC or an individual institution within the further education sector has failed to discharge any duty under the Education Acts, he may make an order declaring the council or institution in default and giving directions for the execution of the duty. The council or institution must comply with the directions in the order.

This section is in addition to the general powers of the Secretary of State under s.68 of the EA 1944 to prevent the unreasonable exercise of functions by an FEFC or by the governing body of an institution within the further education sector (see Sched. 8, para. 9).

Subsections (3) to (6) came into force on May 6, 1992, insofar as they apply to an FEFC: Commencement No. 1 Order 1992, para. 2 and Sched. 1. The rest of this section comes into force on April 1, 1993: *ibid.*, para. 2 and Sched. 3.

Subs. (1)

Secretary of State. See note to s.1(2).

Instrument of government. This means an instrument required to be made by a further education corporation under s.20(1) or by a designated institution under s.29(2) or included in the articles of association of a company conducting a further education institution under s.31(2).

Mismanagement. This term is not defined, but would appear to include incompetence as well as wilful default or fraud. The term is used in s.81(3) and has a precedent in s.150 of the ERA 1988 in relation to the management of devolved budgets by the governing bodies of schools.

Order. An order made under this section need not be made by way of a statutory instrument (s.89(2)).

Subs. (6)

Local inquiries. These may be held at the order of the Secretary of State into the functions of individual local education authorities or institutions under s.93 of the EA 1944.

Reorganisations of schools involving establishment of further education corporation

58.—(1) Subsection (2) below applies where, in connection with a reorganisation of schools maintained by a local education authority, any land used for the purposes of one or more of the schools affected by the reorganisation or, as the case may be, the school so affected—

(a) is to cease to be so used or is to continue to be so used for a limited period, and

(b) while it is so used, or after it has ceased to be so used, is to be used for the purposes of an institution conducted by a further education corporation;

and in that subsection that land is referred to as "the land to be transferred".

(2) If the land to be transferred is land of the local authority, the land and any other property of the local authority used for the purposes of the school on that land shall be treated for the purposes of section 23 of this Act as used for the purposes of the educational institution conducted by the corporation.

(3) For the purposes of this section there is a reorganisation of schools maintained by a local education authority if, in the case of each of the schools affected by the reorganisation or (if there is only one) the school so affected—

(a) the local education authority cease to maintain the school, or

(b) a significant change is made in the character of the school or the premises of the school are significantly enlarged, whether or not the reorganisation also involves the establishment of one or more new schools.

DEFINITIONS
"land": s.90(1).
"land to be transferred": subs. (1).
"local education authority": ss.6 and 118 of the EA 1944.
"school": s.14(3).

GENERAL NOTE
This section makes provision in the case where land ceases to be used for the purposes of a school as a result of a reorganisation of schools involving the establishment of a further education corporation, typically a sixth-form college. This section provides for the transfer of that land to the newly established further education corporation.
Subsection (1) defines "the land to be transferred" as land used for the purposes of one or more schools which will cease to be used for that purpose now, or after a limited period, and is intended to be used for the purpose of an institution conducted by a further education corporation. Subsection (2) provides that such land shall be transferred to the further education corporation under s.23. Subsection (3) defines a reorganisation of schools.
This section comes into force on September 30, 1992: see Commencement No. 1 Order 1992, para. 2 and Sched. 2.

Subs. (1)
Limited period. This term has no statutory definition.
Local education authority. See note to s.2(6).

Subs. (2)
Treated ... as used for the purposes of the educational institution. This has the effect of including the land and property used for the purposes of the school among the land or property which is to be transferred to the further education corporation under s.23(2).

Subs. (3)
Reorganisation. A reorganisation of schools is subject to procedures under s.14 of the EA 1944 and ss.12–14 of the Education Act 1980, as restricted by s.59.

Reorganisations, affecting provision for further education, of schools

59.—(1) This subsection applies where—
(a) the governors of a school maintained by a local education authority as a voluntary school intend to discontinue the school, and
(b) the intention arises in connection with a proposal by a council, or by the Secretary of State, for the establishment under section 16 of this Act of a further education corporation to conduct an educational institution in the same area.
(2) Where subsection (1) above applies—
(a) section 14 of the Education Act 1944 (restrictions on discontinuance) shall not apply,
(b) section 13 of the Education Act 1980 (establishment and alteration of voluntary schools) and, so far as relating to that section, section 16(1) to (3B) of that Act, shall apply as they would apply if the intention were to make a significant change in the character of the school, and
(c) if the school is discontinued the duty of the local education authority to maintain the school as a voluntary school shall be extinguished.
(3) Where—
(a) a local education authority intend to cease to maintain any county school or (except as provided by section 14 of the Education Act 1944) voluntary school or to make any significant change in the character of a county school, or
(b) the governors of a school maintained by a local education authority as a voluntary school intend to discontinue the school or to make any significant change in the character of the school,

and ceasing to maintain or discontinuing the school, or the change, will affect the facilities for full-time education suitable to the requirements of persons over compulsory school age who have not attained the age of 19 years, they shall, before they publish notice of their proposals in pursuance of section 12 or 13 of the Education Act 1980 or serve notice under section 14 of the Education Act 1944, consult the appropriate council.

(4) In subsection (3) above, references to any significant change in the character of a school include a significant enlargement of its premises.

(5) Where—

(a) a local education authority propose to make any change in any arrangements for any special school as to the pupils for whom provision is made or the special educational provision made for them or propose to cease to maintain any special school, and

(b) the change, or ceasing to maintain the school, will affect the facilities for full-time education suitable to the requirements of persons over compulsory school age who have not attained the age of nineteen years,

they shall, before they give written notice of the proposed change to the Secretary of State in pursuance of regulations under section 12 of the Education Act 1981 (approval of special schools) or serve notice of their proposals under section 14 of that Act (discontinuance of maintained special school), consult the appropriate council.

DEFINITIONS
"compulsory school age": s.35 of the EA 1944.
"council": s.1(5).
"county school": s.9(2) of the EA 1944.
"further education corporation": s.17(1).
"local education authority": ss.6 and 118 of the EA 1944.
"significant change in the character": subs. (4).
"voluntary school": s.9(2) of the EA 1944.

GENERAL NOTE
Parallel to s.58, this section makes provision in the case where the governors of a voluntary school decide to discontinue it in connection with proposals for the establishment under s.16 of a further education corporation in the same geographical area. In such a case, the normal substantive restrictions on such discontinuance do not apply, but the procedure under s.13 of the EA 1980 must still be followed (subs. (2)). Where the decision to discontinue the school goes ahead, subs. (2) provides that the duty of the local education authority to maintain it thereby ceases.

Subsection (3) concerns both decisions by a local education authority to cease to maintain a county school or voluntary school or to make a significant change in the character of a county school, and decisions by the governors of a voluntary school to discontinue it or to make a significant change in its character. Where such decisions affect the facilities available for the full-time education of those between 16 and 18, the decision-maker must consult the FEFC before commencing the statutory procedures to give effect to the decision. Subsection (4) defines "significant change in the character" of the school for these purposes.

A similar obligation to consult the FEFC is imposed by subs. (5) where a local education authority proposes to change or cease to maintain a special school and this would affect the facilities available for the full-time education of those between 16 and 18 years of age. Such consultation must take place before the local education authority serves a notice on the Secretary of State to give effect to its decision.

Subsections (3), (4) and (5) came into force on May 6, 1992: see Commencement No. 1 Order 1992, para. 2 and Sched. 1. Subsections (1) and (2) come into force on September 30, 1992: *ibid.*, para. 2 and Sched. 2.

Subs. (1)
Secretary of State. See note to s.1(2).

Subs. (3)
Consult. See under s.6(1). Duties to consult under ss.12–14 of the Education Act 1980 and its predecessor, s.13 of the EA 1944, have been subject to judicial interpretation, notably in *Legg*

v. *Inner London Education Authority* [1972] 1 W.L.R. 1245; *R.* v. *Secretary of State for Wales and Clwyd County Council*, ex p. *Russell* (unreported, June 28, 1983); and *R.* v. *Brent London Borough Council*, ex p. *Gunning* (1985) 84 L.G.R. 891.

Saving as to persons detained by order of a court

60. No function conferred or imposed by this Act on a further education funding council shall be construed as relating to any person who is detained, otherwise than at a school, in pursuance of an order made by a court or of an order of recall made by the Secretary of State.

DEFINITIONS
  "further education funding council": s.1(5).
  "school": s.14(5).

GENERAL NOTE
  This section excludes from the remit of the FEFC responsibility for the education of those who are detained in a Borstal or prison. Responsibility for such persons remains the responsibility of the Home Office, which may arrange the provision of their education by contract with an institution within the further education sector (see note to s.2(4)).
  This section comes into force on April 1, 1993: see Commencement No. 1 Order 1992, para. 2 and Sched. 3.
  Secretary of State. In this case the Secretary of State for the Home Department is meant.
  Detained otherwise than at a school. This includes detention in a Borstal or prison.

Interpretation of Part I

61.—(1) In this Part of this Act—
    "functions" includes powers and duties,
    "modifications" includes additions, alterations and omissions and "modify" shall be construed accordingly, and
    "regulations" means regulations made by the Secretary of State.
  (2) References in the Part of this Act, except section 26, to the transfer of any person's rights or liabilities do not include—
    (a) rights or liabilities under a contract of employment, or
    (b) liabilities of that person in respect of compensation for premature retirement of any person formerly employed by him.
  (3) In relation to any time before the commencement of section 65 of this Act, references in this Part of this Act and, so far as relating to this Part, Part III of this Act—
    (a) to institutions within the higher education sector are to universities, to institutions within the PCFC funding sector and to higher education institutions which receive, or are maintained by persons who receive, grants under regulations made under section 100(1)(b) of the Education Act 1944, and
    (b) to a higher education funding council are to the Universities Funding Council established under section 131 of the Education Reform Act 1988 and to the Polytechnics and Colleges Funding Council established under section 132 of that Act.

DEFINITIONS
  "contract of employment": s.90(1).
  "functions": subs. (1).
  "institution within the further education sector": s.91(3).
  "institution within the PCFC sector": s.132(6) of the ERA 1988.
  "modifications": subs. (1).
  "regulations": subs. (1).
  "university": s.90(3).

GENERAL NOTE
  Subsections (1) and (2) provide definitions for the purposes of this Part of the Act. Subsection (3) is a transitional provision until the commencement of s.65 of this Act. For the purposes of

Pt. I and related provisions of Pt. III of this Act, "institution within the higher education sector" and "higher education funding council" are to be interpreted as equivalent to certain terms in the ERA 1988.

This section came into force on May 6, 1992: see Commencement No. 1 Order 1992, para. 2 and Sched. 1.

PART II

HIGHER EDUCATION

The new funding councils

The Higher Education Funding Councils

62.—(1) There shall be established—
(a) a body corporate to be known as the Higher Education Funding Council for England to exercise in relation to England the functions conferred on them, and
(b) a body corporate to be known as the Higher Education Funding Council for Wales to exercise in relation to Wales the functions conferred to them.

(2) The Higher Education Funding Council for England shall consist of not less than 12 nor more than 15 members appointed by the Secretary of State, of whom one shall be so appointed as chairman.

(3) The Higher Education Funding Council for Wales shall consist of not less than eight nor more than 12 members appointed by the Secretary of State, of whom one shall be so appointed as chairman.

(4) In appointing the members of a council the Secretary of State—
(a) shall have regard to the desirability of including persons who appear to him to have experience of, and to have shown capacity in, the provision of higher education or to have held, and to have shown capacity in, any position carrying responsibility for the provision of higher education and, in appointing such persons, he shall have regard to the desirability of their being currently engaged in the provision of higher education or in carrying responsibility for such provision, and
(b) shall have regard to the desirability of including persons who appear to him to have experience of, and to have shown capacity in, industrial, commercial or financial matters or the practice of any profession.

(5) In this Part of this Act any reference to a council is to a higher education funding council.

(6) In the Education Acts any reference to a higher education funding council—
(a) in relation to matters falling within the responsibility of the Higher Education Funding Council for England or to educational institutions in England, is to that council, and
(b) in relation to matters falling within the responsibility of the Higher Education Funding Council for Wales or to educational institutions in Wales, is to that council.

(7) In this Part of this Act references to institutions in England or institutions in Wales—
(a) are to institutions whose activities are carried on, or principally carried on, in England or, as the case may be, Wales, but
(b) include, in both cases, the Open University.

(8) Any dispute as to whether any functions are exercisable by one of the councils shall be determined by the Secretary of State.

(9) Schedule 1 to this Act has effect with respect to each of the councils.

DEFINITIONS

"Education Acts": s.90(1).

"higher education": s.90(1); s.120 of and Sched. 6 to the ERA 1988.

GENERAL NOTE

As a consequence of the abolition of the "binary line" dividing polytechnics and universities (see especially s.77), this section amalgamates the functions of the UFC and the PCFC created by ss.131 and 132 of the ERA 1988 into a single funding council for England and another for Wales. Like the FEFC created in s.1, the HEFC is envisaged as an executive body administering funding and monitoring institutions within the higher education sector. Therefore, its members are to be chosen for their personal qualities, rather than as representatives of sectional interests (Paymaster-General, *Hansard*, H.L. Vol. 533, col. 982). This principle on the membership of the funding councils leads to a departure in subs. (4) from the equivalent provisions in ss.131(3) and 132(3) of the ERA 1988. Like an FEFC, an HEFC is a body corporate. Disputes between the funding councils as to their functions are determined by the Secretary of State (subs. (8)). The provisions on the organisation, procedure, accounts and tenure of membership of the HEFC are the same as for the FEFC and are set out in Sched. 1.

This section came into force on May 6, 1992: see Commencement No. 1 Order 1992, para. 2 and Sched. 1.

Subs. (2) and (3)

The size of the two funding councils will be typically smaller than either the UFC or the PCFC (see ss.131(2) and 132(2) of the ERA 1988). The Government envisaged them as executive bodies and did not wish to increase their size to ensure representation from persons with particular interests. (See further the note to s.1(2)).

Secretary of State. See note to s.1(2).

Subs. (4)

Sections 131(3) and 132(3) of the ERA 1988 required that between six and nine of the 15 members of the UFC and the PCFC should be drawn from those having experience of the provision of higher education and currently engaged in it. Paragraph (a) reduces such qualifications from requirements to considerations to the desirability of which the Secretary of State shall have regard.

Experience of ... higher education. See note to s.1(4). It is clear from the wording of this provision that it includes not only those who teach in higher education, but also those who administer it.

Paragraph (b) reproduces the relevant wording of ss.131(3) and 132(3) of the ERA 1988.

Dissolution of existing councils

63.—(1) On the appointed day—
  (a) the Universities Funding Council and the Polytechnics and Colleges Funding Council (referred to in this section as the "existing councils") shall be dissolved, and
  (b) all property, rights and liabilities to which either of the existing councils were entitled or subject immediately before that date shall become by virtue of this section property, rights and liabilities of the Higher Education Funding Council for England,
but this subsection does not apply to rights or liabilities under a contract of employment.

  (2) Where—
  (a) immediately before the appointed day, a person (referred to below as "the employee") is employed by an existing council (referred to below as "the existing employer") under a contract of employment which would have continued but for the dissolution of the existing employer, and
  (b) the employee is designated for the purposes of this section by an order made by the Secretary of State,
the contract of employment shall not be terminated by that dissolution but shall have effect as from the appointed day as if originally made between the employee and the new employer.

(3) In this section "the new employer", in relation to the employee, means such higher education funding council as may be specified in relation to the employee by the order designating him for the purposes of this section; and in this subsection "higher education funding council" includes the Scottish Higher Education Funding Council.

(4) Without prejudice to subsection (2) above, where that subsection applies—

(a) all the existing employer's rights, powers, duties and liabilities under or in connection with the contract of employment shall by virtue of this section be transferred on the appointed day to the new employer, and

(b) anything done before that date by or in relation to the existing employer in respect of that contract or the employee shall as from that date be treated as having been done by or in relation to the new employer.

(5) Subsections (2) and (4) above are without prejudice to any right of the employee to terminate his contract of employment if a substantial change is made to his detriment in his working conditions, but no such right shall arise by reason only of the change in employer effected by this section.

(6) An order under this section may designate a person either individually or as a member of a class of description of employees.

(7) In this section "the appointed day" means the day appointed under section 94 of this Act for the commencement of this section.

DEFINITIONS
"appointed day": subs. (7).
"contract of employment": s.90(1).
"employee": subs. (2)(a) and s.90(1).
"existing employer": subs. (2)(a).
"liability": s.90(1).
"new employer": subs. (3).
"Polytechnics and Colleges Funding Council": s.132 of the ERA 1988.
"Universities Funding Council": s.131 of the ERA 1988.

GENERAL NOTE
The appointed day for the commencement of this section will be April 1, 1993 (Commencement No. 1 Order 1992, para. 2 and Sched. 3). On that day, the HEFC for England and that for Wales (as well as the Scottish Higher Education Funding council) will take over the functions of the UFC and the PCFC. Subsection (1) provides for the transfer of property, rights and liabilities of the UFC and PCFC which is regulated by subss. (2) to (6). It is provided that, where the Secretary of State designates an employee by order, the contract of employment with the existing funding council is continued with the new funding council to the service of which the employee is designated. Where, however, a substantial change in working conditions occurs, the employee preserves his rights to terminate his employment (subs. (5)).

Subs. (1)
This provision envisages the complete transfer of property, rights and liabilities on the appointed day, other than those arising under a contract of employment. Actions to enforce such rights or liabilities must thus be brought by or against the HEFC for England after that date.

Subss. (2) and (4)
The provisions on transfer of employment follow closely those of s.127 of the ERA 1988. Subsection (2) is substantially the same as s.127(1) and (2) of the ERA 1988. Subsection (4) is substantially the same as s.127(3) of the ERA 1988. See generally under s.26(2) and (3).
Secretary of State. See note to s.1(2).

Subs. (5)
This provision is substantially the same as s.127(4) of the ERA 1988.
Substantial change ... conditions. See note to s.26(4).

Subs. (6)

This provision is substantially the same as s.127(5) of the ERA 1988.

Order. An order made under this section must be made by way of a statutory instrument which is subject to the negative resolution procedure in Parliament (s.89(1) and (3)).

Transitional arrangements

64.—(1) Until the commencement of section 65 of this Act, any institution which is a university and was at any time the PCFC funding sector shall be treated for the purposes of Chapter II of Part II of the Education Reform Act 1988 (reorganisation and provision of funding of higher education) as if it were within that sector and were not a university.

(2) Until their dissolution the Universities Funding Council shall give to the higher education funding councils and the Scottish Higher Education Funding Council all such assistance as those councils may reasonably require for the purpose of enabling them to exercise their functions on and after the commencement of section 65 of this Act or, as the case may be, the corresponding provisions of the Further and Higher Education (Scotland) Act 1992.

(3) Until their dissolution the Polytechnics and Colleges Funding Council shall give to the higher education funding councils all such assistance as those councils may reasonably require for the purpose of enabling them to exercise their functions on and after the commencement of section 65 of this Act.

(4) The Higher Education Funding Council for England shall discharge any duty under paragraph 17 of Schedule 8 to the Education Reform Act 1988 (accounts) in respect of any period ending before the dissolution of the Universities Funding Council and the Polytechnics and Colleges Funding Council under section 63 of this Act which would have fallen to be discharged by those councils after the dissolution or fell to be so discharged before the dissolution but has not been discharged.

DEFINITIONS

"commencement": s.94(6).

"higher education funding council": s.62(6).

"Polytechnics and Colleges Funding Council": s.132 of the ERA 1988.

"Universities Funding Council": s.131 of the ERA 1988.

"university": s.90(3).

GENERAL NOTE

This section deals with the transition between the current rôle of the UFC and the PCFC and the creation of the HEFCs. Under s.65 the HEFCs will commence work on April 1, 1993.

During the period between the passage of the Act and the commencement of the work of HEFC, no transfer of institutions between the two existing funding sectors is permitted. Thus, even if an institution becomes a "university" during that period, it will remain for funding purposes within the PCFC funding sector (subs. (1)).

Since s.62 commenced on May 6, 1992, and its members were appointed thereafter, the HEFC will exist in some form before it begins operations once s.65 commences. The UFC and PCFC are under a duty to assist the HEFC so as to enable it to take up its functions (subss. (2) and (3)). Because its jurisdiction includes Scottish universities, the UFC has duties also to assist the Scottish Higher Education Funding Council (subs. (2)). The HEFC will have the duty of producing accounts for the final year of operation of the UFC and PCFC (subs. (4)).

This section came into force on May 6, 1992: see Commencement No. 1 Order 1992, para. 2 and Sched. 1.

Subs. (1)

PCFC funding sector. Bodies eligible to receive funds from the PCFC are defined as institutions within the PCFC funding sector (see ss.132(6) and 156(1) of the ERA 1988).

University. A university is an institution so created by Royal Charter. Under s.77, a new method of granting university status is created and that came into force on May 6, 1992. It is likely that the Privy Council will exercise its power under that section to grant the status of university to a number of erstwhile polytechnics and colleges of higher education before the HEFC commences its funding operations under s.65 on April 1, 1993. Under s.90(3), the term includes a university college, or college in a university.

This subsection preserves the rôle of the PCFC in relation to a body from its sector which becomes a university before the HEFC comes into operation.

Scottish Higher Education Funding Council. This is a body equivalent to the HEFC for England and the HEFC for Wales set up under s.37 of the Further and Higher Education (Scotland) Act 1992.

Subs. (4)

Under para. 17 of Sched. 8 to the ERA 1988, the UFC and PCFC have a duty to provide accounts for the year ending March 31, 1993.

Funds

Administration of funds by councils

65.—(1) Each council shall be responsible, subject to the provisions of this Part of this Act, for administering funds made available to the council by the Secretary of State and others for the purposes of providing financial support for activities eligible for funding under this section.

(2) The activities eligible for funding under this section are—

(a) the provision of education and the undertaking of research by higher education institutions in the council's area,

(b) the provision of any facilities, and the carrying on of any other activities, by higher education institutions in their area which the governing bodies of those institutions consider it necessary or desirable to provide or carry on for the purpose of or in connection with education or research,

(c) the provision—

(i) by institutions in their area maintained or assisted by local education authorities, or

(ii) by such institutions in their area as are within the further education sector,

of prescribed courses of higher education, and

(d) the provision by any person of services for the purposes of, or in connection with, the provision of education or the undertaking of research by institutions within the higher education sector.

(3) A council may—

(a) make grants, loans or other payments to the governing body of any higher education institution in respect of expenditure incurred or to be incurred by them for the purposes of any activities eligible for funding under this section by virtue of subsection (2)(a) or (b) above, and

(b) make grants, loans or other payments to any persons in respect of expenditure incurred or to be incurred by them for the purposes of the provision as mentioned in subsection (2)(c) above of prescribed courses of higher education or the provision of services as mentioned in subsection (2)(d) above,

subject in each case to such terms and conditions as the council think fit.

(4) The terms and conditions on which a council may make any grants, loans or other payments under this section may in particular—

(a) enable the council to require the repayment, in whole or in part, of sums paid by the council if any of the terms and conditions subject to which the sums were paid is not complied with, and

(b) require the payment of interest in respect of any period during which a sum due to the council in accordance with any of the terms and conditions remains unpaid, but shall not relate to the application by the body to whom the grants or other payments are made of any sums derived otherwise than from the council.

(5) In this section and section 66 of this Act "higher education institution" means a university, an institution conducted by a higher education corporation or a designated institution.

DEFINITIONS

"council": s.62(5).
"governing body": s.90(1) and (2).
"higher education": s.90(1); s.120(1) of and Sched. 6 to the ERA 1988.
"higher education institution": subs. (5).
"institution within the further education sector": s.91(3).
"institution within the higher education sector": ss.61(3)(a) and 91(5).

GENERAL NOTE

Like s.5 in relation to the FEFC, this section sets out the basic powers of the HEFC in terms of its funding rôle. Its primary responsibility is to administer funds made available to it by the Secretary of State or others (subs. (1)).

The activities eligible for funding are the provision of education and research (as well as connected facilities and services) by higher education institutions, and the provision of higher education courses by institutions either maintained by local education authorities (*e.g.* adult education colleges) or within the further education sector. The mention of the provision of prescribed courses of higher education in para. (c) and the provision of services by any person in para. (d) are additional to the list of activities to be funded in s.131(5) of the ERA 1988 relating to the UFC, but follow s.132(5) relating to the PCFC. In this way, the diversity of provision of higher education and ancillary services is recognised.

The HEFC provides funding by way of grant, loan or other payment which may be subject to such terms and conditions as the council thinks fit (subs. (3)). Subsection (4) enables the HEFC to prescribe that monies shall be repaid (with interest) if the terms and conditions are not met. This provision on repayment reproduces s.134(3) of the ERA 1988.

This section comes into force on April 1, 1993: see Commencement No. 1 Order 1992, para. 2 and Sched. 3.

Subs. (1)

Secretary of State. See note to s.1(2).

Subs. (2)

Education. Although not formally limited in para. (a) to higher education (as in para. (c)), it is envisaged that funding given to higher education institutions will be so directed.

Research. Like the UFC and PCFC under ss.131(5) and 132(5) of the ERA 1988, the HEFC maintains a responsibility for research funding as well as funding for teaching. This implements the proposal in the White Paper *Higher Education*, para. 43, that funding for teaching and general research should flow through the same channel, and that this should exist alongside the funding of research by the Research Councils.

Provision by any person of services. This provision was not contained in s.132(5) of the ERA 1988, but deals with the situation of an autonomous provider of educational or research services.

Subs. (3)

Governing body. As under ss.131(6) and 132(6) of the ERA 1988, loans and grants are made to the governing body of an institution (see note to s.5(4)). Among the recipients of funding, the provision distinguishes between the education, research and ancillary facilities and activities conducted by the higher education institution within paras. (a) and (b) of subs. (2), and other persons who provide the courses or services within paras. (c) and (d).

Loans or other payments. This power to make loans or other payments is new. Under ss.131(6) and 132(7) of the ERA 1988, the UFC and the PCFC were only empowered to make grants.

Subs. (4)

The proviso to this subsection prevents a higher education institution being required to repay a loan or grant out of monies provided from another source, *e.g.* a research council grant (see note to s.5(7)).

Administration of funds: supplementary

66.—(1) Before exercising their discretion under section 65(3)(a) of this Act with respect to the terms and conditions to be imposed in relation to any grants, loans or other payments, a council shall consult such of the following bodies as appear to the council to be appropriate to consult in the circumstances—

    (a) such bodies representing the interests of higher education institutions as appear to the council to be concerned, and

    (b) the governing body of any particular higher education institution which appears to the council to be concerned.

(2) In exercising their functions in relation to the provision of financial support for activities eligible for funding under section 65 of this Act a council shall have regard to the desirability of not discouraging any institution for whose activities financial support is provided under that section from maintaining or developing its funding from other sources.

(3) In exercising those functions a council shall have regard (so far as they think it appropriate to do so in the light of any other relevant considerations) to the desirability of maintaining—

    (a) what appears to them to be an appropriate balance in the support given by them as between institutions which are of a denominational character and other institutions, and

    (b) any distinctive characteristics of any institution within the higher education sector for whose activities financial support is provided under that section.

(4) For the purposes of subsection (3) above an institution is an institution of a denominational character if it appears to the council that either—

    (a) at least one quarter of the members of the governing body of the institution are persons appointed to represent the interests of a religion or religious denomination,

    (b) any of the property held for the purposes of the institution is held upon trusts which provide that, in the event of the discontinuance of the institution, the property concerned shall be held for, or sold and the proceeds of sale applied for, the benefit of a religion or religious denomination, or

    (c) any of the property held for the purposes of the institution is held on trust for or in connection with—

        (i) the provision of education, or

        (ii) the conduct of an educational institution,

    in accordance with the tenets of a religion or religious denomination.

DEFINITIONS

    "council": s.62(5).

    "governing body": s.90(1) and (2).

    "higher education institution": s.65(5).

    "institution of a denominational character": subs. (4).

    "institution within the higher education sector": ss.61(3)(a) and 91(5).

GENERAL NOTE

    The arrangements for the operation of the HEFC reproduce the practices of the UFC and PCFC, and parallel those of the FEFC set out in s.6 of this Act. Before imposing terms and conditions on loans or grants it must consult either organisations representing institutions within the sector (currently the Committee of Vice-Chancellors and Principals and the Committee of Polytechnic Directors) or the governing bodies of any affected institutions (subs. (1)). Like the UFC and PCFC, the HEFC has to have regard to the desirability of not discouraging institutions from seeking outside funding for their activities (subs. (2)). The policy is stated more clearly in the White Paper *Higher Education*, para. 14: "The Government believes that it is in the interests of universities, polytechnics and colleges to continue to look for increased levels of funding from private sources, in particular from industry and commerce, from benefactors and alumni, and from present sources of fee income". Another consideration to which the HEFC shall have regard is the appropriate balance between denominational and other institutions within the sector (subs. (3)). Such institutions exist currently as affiliated colleges or colleges in their own right.

This section comes into force on April 1, 1993: see Commencement No. 1 Order 1992, para. 2 and Sched. 3.

Subs. (1)
   Consult. See note to s.6(1).
   This provision substantially reproduces s.134(4) of the ERA 1988.

Subs. (2)
   This provision substantially reproduces ss.131(7) and 132(8) of the ERA 1988.

Subs. (3)
   This provision follows s.132(9) of the ERA 1988, but adds that the HEFC shall have regard to the desirability of maintaining the distinctive characteristics of a denominational institution, lest its specific contribution to the sector be lost.

Subs. (4)
   Denominational character. Unlike in s.132 of the ERA 1988, a definition of an institution of a denominational character is provided. The definition is the same as under s.6(4) of this Act. Unlike the term as used in s.7(6)(b) of the ERA 1988, "denominational character" is not confined to the Christian religion: see note to s.44(4).

Payments in respect of persons employed in provision of higher or further education

67.—(1) In section 133 of the Education Reform Act 1988 (payments by PCFC in respect of persons employed in the provision of higher or further education) for subsection (1) there is substituted—

   "(1) A higher education funding council shall have power to make payments, subject to such terms and conditions as the council think fit, to—
    (a) any local education authority in their area;
    (b) the London Residuary Body;
    (c) the London Pensions Fund Authority; and
    (d) the governing body of any institution designated under section 129 of this Act, as originally enacted;
   in respect of relevant expenditure incurred or to be incurred by that authority or body of any class or description prescribed for the purposes of this section."

   (2) In subsection (2)(a) of that section (meaning of relevant expenditure) after "education authority" there is inserted "the London Residuary Body or the London Pensions Fund Authority".

   (3) At the end of subsection (3) of that section (meaning of references to higher and further education) there is added "and in any other case the reference to further education shall be read as a reference to further education within the meaning of section 41 of the 1944 Act as that section had effect on that date".

   (4) In subsection (4) of that section (duty to give information) after paragraph (a) there is inserted—
    "(aa) the London Residuary Body;
    (ab) the London Pensions Fund Authority".

   (5) That section as originally enacted shall have effect, or be treated as having had effect, as if—
    (a) in subsection (1), in relation to anything done before regulations for the purposes of that subsection were in force, the words "of any class or description prescribed for the purposes of this section" were omitted, and
    (b) in subsections (1) and (2) the references to a local education authority included the London Residuary Body and the London Pensions Fund Authority.

DEFINITIONS
    "governing body": s.90(1) and (2).
    "London Pensions Fund Authority": para. 2 of the London Government Reorganisation (Pensions etc.) Order 1989 (S.I. 1985 No. 1815).
    "London Residuary Body": s.57(6) of the Local Government Act 1985.

GENERAL NOTE
    Section 133 of the ERA 1988 empowered the PCFC to reimburse local education authorities and governing bodies of bodies designated as within the PCFC sector under s.129 of that Act for liabilities to former and serving staff of polytechnics and other institutions. These functions are now transferred to the HEFC by subs. (1). Because of the abolition of the Inner London Education Authority following Pt. III of the ERA 1988, a number of consequential amendments are made to the persons who may be reimbursed. The London Residuary Body was given duties in respect of the payment of pensions which would have been paid to former employees by the Inner London Education Authority (s.178 of the ERA 1988) and some of these duties have now been transferred to the London Pensions Funds Authority under the London Government Reorganisation (Pensions etc.) Order 1989 (S.I. 1989 No. 1815) and the London Government Reorganisation (Pensions etc.) (Amendment) Order 1990 (S.I. 1990 No. 118). Subsection (5) disapplies the requirement in s.133(1) of the ERA 1988 that only expenditure specified in regulations may be reimbursed for the period before such regulations came into force.
    Subsections (2) to (5) came into force on May 6, 1992: see Commencement No. 1 Order 1992, para. 2 and Sched. 1, but subs. (1) only comes into force on April 1, 1993: *ibid.*, para. 2 and Sched. 3.

Subs. (1)
    Local education authority. See note to s.10(1).
    Any institution designated under section 129. Such institutions were polytechnics and colleges designated by the Secretary of State as eligible to receive funding from the PCFC. Typical payments under this section will now relate to retired employees.

Subs. (5)
    Be treated as having had effect. This phrase ensures that the revision of s.133 shall have retrospective effect.

Grants to councils

    68.—(1) The Secretary of State may make grants to each of the councils of such amounts and subject to such terms and conditions as he may determine.
    (2) The terms and conditions subject to which grants are made by the Secretary of State to either of the councils—
    (a) may in particular impose requirements to be complied with in respect of every institution, or every institution falling within a class or description specified in the terms and conditions, being requirements to be complied with in the case of any institution to which the requirements apply before financial support of any amount or description so specified is provided by the council in respect of activities carried on by the institution, but
    (b) shall not otherwise relate to the provision of financial support by the council in respect of activities carried on by any particular institution or institutions.
    (3) Such terms and conditions may not be framed by reference to particular courses of study or programmes of research (including the contents of such courses or programmes and the manner in which they are taught, supervised or assessed) or to the criteria for the selection and appointment of academic staff and for the admission of students.
    (4) Such terms and conditions may in particular—
    (a) enable the Secretary of State to require the repayment, in whole or in part, of sums paid by him if any of the terms and conditions subject to which the sums were paid is not complied with, and
    (b) require the payment of interest in respect of any period during which

a sum due to the Secretary of State in accordance with any of the terms and conditions remains unpaid.

DEFINITIONS
"council": s.62(5).
"institution": s.91(6).

GENERAL NOTE
This section grants powers to the Secretary of State in relation to grants to funding councils substantially similar to those continued in s.134(6) and (7) of the ERA 1988, which concerned grants made by him to the UFC and PCFC. Under those provisions, grants could be made subject to terms and conditions, provided that they did relate to the making of grants by a funding council to any specified institution. This proviso, carried against the Government by an amendment in the House of Lords, is strengthened by subs. (3) of this section, again introduced by an amendment in the House of Lords and carried against the Government. Subsection (3) provides that terms and conditions may not relate to particular courses of study or programmes of research or to the criteria for selecting staff or students. This restriction was introduced to preserve and reinforce the academic freedom of institutions (see Lord Beloff, *Hansard*, H.L. Vol. 535, col. 99 *et seq.*). The Government itself had always intended that this section empower the Secretary of State to impose general conditions and not ones relating to specific institutions (see Paymaster-General, *Hansard*, H.L. Vol. 533, col. 1035; Vol. 535, col. 95). The power to impose conditions is to enable the Secretary of State to promote policy developments in higher education (*ibid. Hansard*, H.L. Vol. 534, col. 638).

Subsection (2) clarifies the form which terms and conditions may take in the light of judicial interpretation of s.134(6) of the ERA 1988. Subsection (4) makes it clear that the terms and conditions may require the repayment by an HEFC of all or part of the grant if they are not fulfilled, and that interest is payable. Subsections (1), (2) and (4) reproduce the wording of s.7(1), (2) and (3) in relation to the FEFC, but subs. (3) is specific to grants made to the HEFC.

This section came into force on May 6, 1992: see Commencement No. 1 Order 1992, para. 2 and Sched. 1.

Subs. (1)
    Secretary of State. See note to s.1(2).
    As he may determine. See note to s.7(1).

Subs. (2)
    This subsection enables the Secretary of State to impose conditions which must be met before individual institutions qualify for funding from the HEFC. The conditions may relate to all institutions or to classes of institutions. This clarification of the power in subs. (1) was rendered necessary by the interpretation given to its predecessor, s.134(6) of the ERA 1988, by Simon Brown J. in *R.* v. *Secretary of State for Education and Science*, ex p. *Association of Polytechnic and College Teachers*, *The Independent*, August 9, 1991. In his view, that subsection did not entitle the Secretary of State to make payment of part of the annual grant to the PCFC conditional upon a satisfactory pay settlement with academic staff.

    Paragraph (b) substantially reproduces s.134(7) of the ERA 1988 in its prohibition on conditions relating to particular institutions.

    Activities. Unlike in s.65(2), activities here include all activities carried on by an institution, whether or not they are eligible for funding from the HEFC.

Subs. (3)
    This subsection expands on subs. (2) by prohibiting terms and conditions relating to particular courses of study or programmes of research, including their teaching, supervision and assessment, as well as to criteria for selecting staff or admitting students. For example, this would preclude a condition preventing institutions from running architecture courses of seven years' duration, a condition which the Secretary of State had suggested would be a proper use of the power under subs. (1) (see interview in *The Higher*, December 13, 1991, p. 3). The wording of this subsection does, however, give effect to an assurance made by the Government in the House of Lords (see Paymaster-General, *Hansard*, H.L. Vol. 533, col. 1035).

    Course. See note to s.3(1).

Subs. (4)
    The powers of the Secretary of State to "claw back" money mirrors that of the HEFC in relation to individual institutions under s.65(4). Similar powers exist in relation to the FEFC under s.7(3).

Further functions

Supplementary functions

69.—(1) Each council—
(a) shall provide the Secretary of State with such information or advice relating to the provision for their area of higher education as he may from time to time require, and
(b) may provide the Secretary of State with such information or advice relating to such provision as they think fit,
and information and advice provided under this subsection shall be provided in such manner as the Secretary of State may from time to time determine.

(2) Each council shall keep under review activities eligible for funding under section 65 of this Act.

(3) A council may provide, on such terms as may be agreed, such advisory services as the Department of Education for Northern Ireland or the Department of Agriculture for Northern Ireland may require in connection with the discharge of the department's functions relating to higher education in Northern Ireland.

(4) Where—
(a) any land or other property is or was used or held for the purposes of an institution, and
(b) the Secretary of State is entitled to any right or interest in respect of the property, or would be so entitled on the occurrence of any event,
then, if the institution is within the higher education sector, the Secretary of State may direct that all or any of his functions in respect of the property shall be exercisable on his behalf by the council, and the functions shall be so exercised in accordance with such directions as he may give from time to time.

(5) The Secretary of State may by order confer or impose on a council such supplementary functions relating to the provision of education as he thinks fit.

(6) For the purposes of subsection (5) above a function is a supplementary function in relation to a council if it is exercisable for the purposes of—
(a) the exercise by the Secretary of State of functions of his under any enactment, or
(b) the doing by the Secretary of State of anything he has power to do apart from any enactment,
and it relates to, or to the activities of, any institution mentioned in subsection (7) below.

(7) Those institutions are—
(a) institutions within the higher education sector, or
(b) institutions within the further education sector, or maintained or assisted by local education authorities, at which prescribed courses of higher education are currently provided.

DEFINITIONS
"assisted by a local education authority": s.114(2) of the EA 1944, as amended by s.234(2) of the ERA 1988.
"council": s.62(5).
"higher education": s.90(1); s.120(1) of and Sched. 6 to the ERA 1988.
"institutions within the further education sector": s.91(3).
"institutions within the higher education sector": s.91(3)
"supplementary functions": subss. (6) and (7).

GENERAL NOTE
This section makes provision for the relationship between the HEFC and the Secretary of State other than the administration of funds provided by the latter. The HEFC has a duty to provide the Secretary of State with such information relating to the provision of higher education in its area as he may require, and to provide him with such additional information as it

thinks fit (subs. (1)). It has a general brief to review activities eligible for funding (subs. (2)). It may also provide assistance by way of advice in relation to higher education in Northern Ireland, which is not to have its own funding council. The HEFC may also be given further functions by the Secretary of State in relation to his rights or interests in property used or held for the purposes of a higher education institution (subs. (4)) or in relation to the provision of education (subs. (5)).

This section came into force on May 6, 1992: see Commencement No. 1 Order 1992, para. 2 and Sched. 1.

Subs. (1)
This provision adds to the parallel provisions in ss.131(8)(b) and 132(10)(b) of the ERA 1988, by imposing on the HEFC a duty to provide information and advice as the Secretary of State requires. The Secretary of State prescribes the form in which information or advice is tendered. There is no requirement that such information or advice be published nor is there a power to make public of its own initiative any report on the higher education sector (see Paymaster-General, *Hansard*, H.L. Vol. 533, cols. 1070–1).

The HEFC has power to obtain information from others in order to perform its functions by virtue of s.79.
Secretary of State. See note to s.1(2).

Subs. (2)
This provision reproduces ss.131(8)(a) and 132(10)(a) of the ERA 1988.

Subs. (3)
This provision reproduces ss.131(8)(c) and 132(10)(c) of the ERA 1988.

Subs. (4)
Directions. These may be revoked or varied at any time (s.111 of the EA 1944, as applied by s.89(5) of this Act).

Subs. (5)
This provision reproduces s.134(1) of the ERA 1988, and is qualified by subss. (6) and (7) to make it clear that only functions under existing enactments may be transferred to the HEFC. The Secretary of State has no power to create new functions.

Subs. (7)
For the powers of further education institutions to provide higher education, see s.18(1)(a).
Local education authority. See note to s.10(1).

Assessment of quality of education provided by institutions

70.—(1) Each council shall—

(a) secure that provision is made for assessing the quality of education provided in institutions for whose activities they provide, or are considering providing, financial support under this Part of this Act, and

(b) establish a committee, to be known as the "Quality Assessment Committee", with the function of giving them advice on the discharge of their duty under paragraph (a) above and such other functions as may be conferred on the committee by the council.

(2) The majority of the members of the committee—

(a) shall be persons falling within subsection (3) below, and

(b) shall not be members of the council.

(3) Persons fall within this subsection if they appear to the council to have experience of, and to have shown capacity in, the provision of higher education in institutions within the higher education sector and, in appointing such persons, the council shall have regard to the desirability of their being currently engaged in the provision of higher education or in carrying responsibility for such provision.

(4) Schedule 1 to this Act shall apply to a committee established under this section as it applies to committees established under paragraph 8 of that Schedule.

DEFINITIONS
"council": s.62(5).
"institution within the higher education sector": ss.61(3)(a) and 91(5).

GENERAL NOTE
This section establishes the mechanisms for implementing the policy on quality assurance set out in the White Paper *Higher Education*, Chap. 5. That chapter identifies a number of quality assurance mechanisms. *Quality control* involves the institution providing education having mechanisms for maintaining and enhancing its provision. *Quality audit* involves external scrutiny aimed at securing that institutions do have such mechanisms of quality control in place. These are currently operated by the Academic Audit Unit of the Committee of Vice-Chancellors and Principals. The Secretary of State is empowered by s.82(2) to direct that the English, Welsh and Scottish HEFCs establish their own arrangements for academic audit: see note to that subsection. *Quality assessment* involves "external review of, and judgments about, the quality of teaching and learning in institutions" (White Paper *Higher Education*, para. 60). The subjection of institutions to quality assessment is seen as a mechanism for ensuring their accountability for the public funds they receive (*ibid.* para. 58).

Subsection (1) does not require the HEFC to conduct the quality assessment itself, merely to ensure that such assessment occurs. It could, thus, rely on procedures set up by another body. The HEFC does, however, have to establish a Quality Assessment Committee with at least an advisory rôle on quality assessment (subs. (1)(b)). This is to be an independent body of persons with experience providing higher education. It was envisaged in the White Paper *Higher Education* that such a Committee would have responsibility for conducting quality assessment (*ibid.* para. 82). Subsections (2) and (3) make provision about the membership of the Committee and subs. (4) subjects its proceedings and membership to the rules on committees of funding councils set out in Sched. 1, para. 8.

This section came into force on May 6, 1992: see Commencement No. 1 Order 1992, para. 2 and Sched. 1.

Subs. (1)
Assessing. The White Paper *Higher Education*, paras. 80 and 81, stated that quality assessment could be developed in two ways: by identifying quantifiable outcomes (performance indicators and measures of "value added") and by external judgments based on direct observation. Both are provided for by this provision. As Lord Belstead put it, "Higher education institutions educate students, and it is right that performance indicators should include data showing how well they do it" (Paymaster-General, *Hansard*, H.L. Vol. 535, col. 678).
Functions. The functions mentioned here are any functions of the HEFC, but notably those in respect of quality assessment under s.70(1)(a).

Subs. (3)
It is envisaged that the persons initially recruited to this Committee will be in part from staff with responsibility for higher education in Her Majesty's Inspectorate, of which a proportion will have a background in university education (White Paper *Higher Education*, para. 82; Under-Secretary of State, *Hansard*, H.C. Vol. 203, col. 90). The majority of members will be representatives of institutions within the higher education sector (Lord Cavendish, *Hansard*, H.L. Vol. 533, col. 11). There is nothing to prevent students from being appointed to the Committee (Under-Secretary of State, *Hansard*, H. C., Standing Committee F, col. 401).
Experience . . . of higher education. See note to s.1(3).

Institutions in the higher education sector

Higher education corporations: constitution and conduct

71.—(1) After section 124 of the Education Reform Act 1988 there is inserted—

"Constitution and conduct of corporations

124A.—(1) For each higher education corporation established on or after the appointed day there shall be an instrument (to be known as the instrument of government) providing for the constitution of the corporation and making such other provision as is required under this section.

(2) The initial instrument of government of a higher education corporation established on or after that day shall be such as is prescribed by an order of the Privy Council.

(3) An order of the Privy Council may—

(a) make an instrument of government of any higher education corporation with respect to which Schedule 7 to this Act has effect or make a new instrument of government of any higher education corporation in place of the instrument prescribed under subsection (2) above; or

(b) modify an instrument made in pursuance of this subsection.

(4) An instrument of government of a higher education corporation—

(a) shall comply with the requirements of Schedule 7A to this Act; and

(b) may make any provision authorised to be made by that Schedule and such other provision as may be necessary or desirable.

(5) An order under subsection (2) or (3) above may make such provisions as appears to the Privy Council necessary or desirable to secure continuity in the government of the institution or institutions to which it relates.

(6) The validity of any proceedings of a higher education corporation for which an instrument of government has effect, or of any committee of such a corporation, shall not be affected by a vacancy amongst the members or by any defect in the appointment or nomination of a member.

(7) Every document purporting to be an instrument made or issued by or on behalf of a higher education corporation for which an instrument of government has effect and to be duly executed under the seal of the corporation, or to be signed or executed by a person authorised by the corporation to act in that behalf, shall be received in evidence and be treated, without further proof, as being so made or issued unless the contrary is shown.

(8) In relation to a higher education corporation for which an instrument of government has effect the members of the corporation for the time being shall be known as the board of governors of the institution conducted by the corporation.

(9) The Secretary of State may by order amend or repeal any of paragraphs 3 to 5 and 11 of Schedule 7A to this Act.

(10) In this section and section 124C "the appointed day" means the day appointed under section 94 of the Further and Higher Education Act 1992 for the commencement of section 71 of that Act.

Accounts

124B.—(1) It shall be the duty of each corporation—

(a) to keep proper accounts and proper records in relation to the accounts; and

(b) to prepare in respect of each financial year of the corporation a statement of accounts.

(2) The statement shall—

(a) give a true and fair account of the state of the corporation's affairs at the end of the financial year and of the corporation's income and expenditure in the financial year; and

(b) comply with any directions given by the higher education funding council as to the information to be contained in the statement, the manner in which the information is to be presented or the methods and principles according to which the statement is to be prepared.

(3) The corporation shall supply a copy of the statement to any person who asks for it and, if the corporation so requires, pays a fee of

such amount not exceeding the cost of supply as the corporation thinks fit.

(4) The accounts (including any statement prepared under this section) shall be audited by persons appointed in respect of each financial year by the corporation.

(5) The corporation shall consult, and take into account any advice given by, the Audit Commission for Local Authorities and the National Health Service in England and Wales before appointing any auditor under subsection (4) above in respect of their first financial year.

(6) No person shall be qualified to be appointed auditor under that subsection except—

(a) an individual, or firm, eligible for appointment as a company auditor under section 25 of the Companies Act 1989;

(b) a member of the Chartered Institute of Public Finance and Accountancy; or

(c) a firm each of the members of which is a member of that institute.

(7) In this section, in relation to a corporation—

"the first financial year" means the period commencing with the date on which the corporation is established and ending with the second 31st March following that date; and

"financial year" means that period and each successive period of 12 months.

Initial and transitional arrangements

124C.—(1) The Secretary of State shall be the appointing authority in relation to the appointment of the first members of a corporation established on or after the appointed day and, in determining the number of members to appoint within each variable category of members, he shall secure that at least half of all the members of the corporation as first constituted are independent members.

(2) In subsection (1) above "variable category of members" and "independent members" have the same meaning as in Schedule 7A to this Act.

(3) The following provisions apply where an instrument of government is made under section 124A of this Act for a higher education corporation with respect to which Schedule 7 to this Act has effect.

(4) The instrument shall apply, subject to subsection (5) below, as if the persons who, immediately before its coming into effect, were the members of the corporation had been appointed in accordance with the instrument for the residue of the term of their then subsisting appointment.

(5) Any local authority nominee, teacher nominee, general staff nominee or student nominee (within the meaning, in each case, of Schedule 7 to this Act) shall cease to hold office.

Exercise of Powers by Privy Council

124D.—(1) This section applies in relation to the exercise of powers for the purposes of this Part of this Act.

(2) A power vested in the Privy Council may be exercised by any two or more of the lords and others of the Council.

(3) An act of the Privy Council shall be sufficiently signified by an instrument signed by the clerk of the Council.

(4) An order or act signified by an instrument purporting to be signed by the clerk of the Council shall be deemed to have been duly made or done by the Privy Council.

(5) An instrument so signed shall be received in evidence in all courts and proceedings without proof of the authority or signature of the clerk of the Council or other proof."

(2) In section 125 of that Act (articles of government) for "the Secretary of State" (in each place where it appears) there is substituted "the Privy Council"; but nothing in this subsection requires further approval to be given for anything approved by the Secretary of State under that section before the commencement of this subsection.

(3) In Schedule 7 to that Act (constitution of higher education corporations)—

(a) at the end of paragraph 7 (appointments) there is added—

"(8) If the number of independent members of the corporation falls below the number needed in accordance with its articles of government for a quorum, the Secretary of State is the appointing authority in relation to the appointment of such number of independent members as is required for a quorum", and

(b) in paragraph 18 (accounts) after sub-paragraph (2) there is inserted—

"(2A) The corporation shall supply a copy of the statement to any person who asks for it and, if the corporation so requires, pays a fee of such amount not exceeding the cost of supply as the corporation thinks fit."

(4) After that Schedule there is inserted the Schedule set out in Schedule 6 to this Act.

DEFINITIONS

"appointed day": s.124A(10) of the ERA 1988, added by subs. (1) of this section.
"articles of government": s.125(1) of the ERA 1988.
"board of governors": s.124A(8) of the ERA 1988, added by subs. (1) of this section.
"financial year": s.124B(7) of the ERA 1988, added by subs. (1) of this section.
"first financial year": s.124B(7) of the ERA 1988, added by subs. (1) of this section.
"higher education corporation": s.123(1) of the ERA 1988.
"independent members": Sched. 7A, para. 3(2)(a) of the ERA 1988, added by Sched. 6 to this Act.
"Secretary of State": see under s.1(1).
"variable category of members": Sched. 7A, para. 11 of the ERA 1988, added by Sched. 6 to this Act.

GENERAL NOTE

In consequence of the abolition of the "binary" line between universities and polytechnics and higher education colleges, and in anticipation that most of the latter will adopt the title "university" under s.77, this section brings arrangements for the constitutions of such institutions broadly into line with those of the existing, chartered universities. Polytechnics and higher education colleges were transferred from the control of local education authorities and constituted as independent "higher education corporations" under ss.121 and 122 of the ERA 1988. By s.123(3) of the ERA 1988, the initial instrument of government of a higher education corporation was effectively laid down in Sched. 7 to that Act. Under s.125 of the ERA 1988, the articles of government were to be made by corporation with the approval of the Secretary of State. The Secretary of State had the power to approve or direct changes to the articles of government of a higher education or corporation or to direct changes in its by-laws (s.125(5) and (6)).

This section transfers the powers of the Secretary of State to the Privy Council from the appointed date. In a new s.124A of the ERA 1988 the powers of the Privy Council are specified and it is provided that higher education corporations shall have new instruments of government. The rules governing the proof of instruments (s.124A(7)) and the proceedings under such an instrument of government (s.124A(6)) are to be the same as under Sched. 7 to the ERA 1988.

The rules for accounts under the new s.124B follow those set out in Sched. 7, para. 18 to the ERA 1988, with the addition of a requirement under subs. (3) that the corporation supply a copy of a statement of accounts to any person who asks for it.

As under Sched. 7, para. 5 to the ERA 1988, the new s.124C specifies that the Secretary of State shall be the appointing authority for any new higher education corporation created under s.122 of the ERA 1988 after the appointed day. The transitional provisions for any higher education corporation for whom a new instrument of government is made under s.124A are that the existing members continue until the expiry of their current term of office (subs. (4)), but that local authority, teacher, general staff and student nominees cease to hold office (subs. (5)). The reason for this provision and the abolition of mandatory categories of members under the new Sched. 7A, para. 3 to the ERA 1988 (Sched. 6 to this Act) is to ensure greater flexibility in choice of members by reducing prescription (Lord Cavendish of Furness, *Hansard*, H.L. Vol. 533, col. 1131).

The new s.124D of the ERA makes provision for the exercise of powers by the Privy Council.

Subsections (2) and (3) of this section make consequential amendments to s.125 of and Sched. 7 to the ERA 1988.

This section came into force on May 6, 1992: see Commencement No. 1 Order 1992, para. 2 and Sched. 1.

Subs. (1)

S.124A Instrument of government. Under Sched. 7 to the ERA 1988, a basic form of government was set out for all higher education corporations and under s.125, the corporation adopted articles of government. These are now to be replaced by the instrument of government required by s.124A. Such an instrument is made and amended by the Privy Council (s.124A(2), (3)).

The content is determined in outline by Sched. 7A to the ERA 1988 (Sched. 6 to this Act). The Privy Council shall have regard to the continuity of the institutions (s.124A(5)).

Validity of proceedings. This provision reproduces the provisions of Sched. 7, para. 14 to the ERA. It is of some significance in that an unpublished survey by N. A. Bastin of the Department of Law, Huddersfield Polytechnic suggests that most higher education corporations were in default on the nomination of independent members to their boards of governors by the deadline of August 20, 1991.

Every document purporting . . . . Section 124A(7) reproduces Sched. 7, para. 17 to the ERA 1988.

Board of governors. Section 124A(8) retains the name given to the governing body of a higher education corporation by Sched. 7, para. 3(3) to the ERA 1988.

Secretary of State. See note to s.1(2).

The powers of the Secretary of State are now reduced to amending the rules for the instruments of government contained in Sched. 7A to the ERA 1988 (Sched. 6 to this Act), but only in relation to the size and membership of the corporation and to the interpretation of that Schedule (s.124A(9)).

Order. An order made under this section must be made by way of a statutory instrument which is subject to the negative resolution procedure in Parliament (s.232(1) and (4) of the ERA 1988).

S.124B Accounts. The accounts of a higher education corporation must be prepared annually for the period ending March 31, as was required by Sched. 7, para. 17 to the ERA 1988. The financial year may be changed by the Secretary of State under s.78 of this Act.

Unlike that paragraph, s.124B provides that the accounts shall be independently audited by persons appointed by the corporation, not by the Comptroller and Auditor General as under para. 17(2) of Sched. 7 to the ERA 1988. The manner and form of accounts is now to be specified by the HEFC and not by the Secretary of State (s.124B(2)(b)).

Auditors. The auditor is chosen by the corporation. In relation to the first financial year, it is necessary for the corporation to consult the Audit Commission about the auditor (s.124B(5)), but thereafter the only restriction on choice is that the person or firm appointed must be a company auditor or a member of CIPFA (s.124B(6)).

Copy of statement. The duty under s.124B(3) to supply a copy of the statement of accounts to any person who asks for it maintains the public accountability of the higher education corporation which previously had to supply copies of its accounts to the Secretary of State and the Comptroller and Auditor General (Sched. 7, para. 17(1)(c) to the ERA 1988).

S.124C Independent members. Section 124(1)(c) preserves the obligation of the Secretary of State under Sched. 7, para. 5(2) to the ERA 1988 to ensure that at least half the members of the corporation are independent members.

Variable category of members. This "variable category" in s.124(1) replaces the prescribed list of nominees under Sched. 7, para. 4(1) to the ERA 1988 under which representatives of local authorities, teachers, staff and students were all guaranteed fixed numbers of places on board of governors of the corporation. These nominees will cease to hold office under s.124C(5). Members of such categories may be reappointed, not as representatives, but for their personal capabilities, as co-opted members (Sched. 7A, para. 3(4) to the ERA 1988, added by Sched. 6 of this Act.)

S.124D Privy Council. This provision sets out the procedure whereby the powers granted to the Privy Council under ss.124A and 125 of the ERA 1988 shall be exercised. Orders under this section do not have to be made by way of statutory instrument. For a discussion of the powers and procedures of the Privy Council in related matters see *Halsbury's Laws of England* (4th edn.), vol. 8, paras. 1150–51.

Subs. (2)
This provision removes the power of the Secretary of State to approve and alter or direct the alteration of articles of government. His powers are transferred to the Privy Council.

Subs. (3)
Independent members. This provision introduces a power for the Secretary of State to appoint independent members to the corporation, where the corporation itself has failed to exercise its powers to make such appointments under Sched. 7, para. 7(5) to the ERA 1988 (*cf.* the Bastin survey mentioned above) or where the number has fallen below the quorum for any reason.
Copy of the statement. The new para. 18(2A) of Sched. 7 merely replicates the provision on accessibility of accounts of a higher education corporation to the public introduced by s.124B(3) of the ERA 1988 by subs.(1).

Further power of designation

72.—(1) In section 129 of the Education Reform Act 1988 (designation of institutions)—
    (a) for subsections (1) and (2) there is substituted—
      "(1) The Secretary of State may by order designate as an institution eligible to receive support from funds administered by a higher education funding council—
        (a) any institution which appears to him to fall within subsection (2) below; and
        (b) any institution which is, or is to be, conducted by a successor company to a higher education corporation.
    (2) An institution falls within this subsection if its full-time equivalent enrolment number for courses of higher education exceeds 55 per cent. of its total full-time equivalent enrolment number", and
    (b) subsections (3) and (4) of that section are omitted.
    (2) An order in force immediately before the commencement of subsection (1) above designating an institution as falling within subsection (3) of that section shall have effect as if made under that section as amended by subsection (1) above.
    (3) In this Part of this Act "designated institution" means an institution in relation to which a designation made, or having effect as if made, under section 129 of that Act has effect.

DEFINITIONS
"courses of higher education": s.235(2)(e) of and Sched. 6 to the ERA 1988.
"designated institution": subs. (3).
"full-time equivalent enrolment number": s.161(2) and (3) of the ERA 1988.
"higher education corporation": s.123(1) of the ERA 1988.
"successor company": s.129(5) of the ERA 1988.

GENERAL NOTE
This section makes consequential amendments to s.129 of the ERA 1988. The Secretary of State is to continue to have the power to designate institutions as eligible for funding now from the HEFC rather than from the PCFC. Subsection (1) retains the basic qualification of the original s.129(1) of the ERA 1988 to meet the new funding context. Subsection (2) retains the basic qualification criterion that 55 per cent. of its full-time equivalent enrolment number be enrolled on courses of higher education, but omits any reference to how the institution is currently funded (*cf.* s.129(2)(b)). The original subss. (3) and (4) of s.129 are now repealed by subs. (1)(b), since they set out eligibility criteria by reference to past dates which are no longer relevant to funding decisions. Subsection (2) makes provision to ensure the continuing validity of an order made under the original s.129(3) after the commencement of subs. (1) of this section. Subsection (3) provides a definition of "designated institution" for the purposes of this Part of the Act.

This section came into force on May 6, 1992: see Commencement No. 1 Order 1992, para. 2 and Sched. 1.

Subs. (1)
    Secretary of State. See under s.1(2).
    Order. Such an order is made by a statutory instrument subject to a negative resolution in Parliament (see s.232 of the ERA 1988).
    Successor company. The provision in s.129(1)(b) of the ERA 1988 was introduced to enable polytechnics to adopt the form of a company limited by guarantee rather than a higher education corporation.
    Full-time equivalent enrolment number. The total full-time equivalent enrolment number is the aggregate of all such enrolment numbers for all courses of all descriptions offered by an institution (s.161(2) of the ERA 1988). The full-time equivalent enrolment number for any individual course is calculated by reference to Sched. 9 to the ERA 1988 (s.161(3) of that Act).

Subs. (2)
    Commencement. Subsection (1) commenced on May 6, 1992, see General Note above.
    Order in force. This means an order made under s.129(1) as originally drafted.

Government and conduct of designated institutions

    73.—(1) After section 129 of the Education Reform Act 1988 there is inserted—

> **"Government and conduct of designated institutions**
>   **129A.**—(1) The section has effect in relation to any designated institution, other than an institution conducted by a company.
>   (2) For each such institution there shall be—
>   (a) an instrument providing for the constitution of a governing body of the institution (to be known as the instrument of government); and
>   (b) an instrument in accordance with which the institution is to be conducted (to be known as the articles of government),
> each of which meets the requirements of subsection (3) below.
>   (3) Those requirements are that the instrument—
>   (a) was in force when the designation took effect; or
>   (b) is made in pursuance of a power under a regulatory instrument, or is made under subsection (5) below,
> and is approved for the purposes of this section by the Privy Council.
>   (4) In this section "regulatory instrument", in relation to an institution, means any instrument of government or articles of government and any other instrument relating to or regulating the institution.
>   (5) Where there is no such power as is mentioned in subsection (3)(b) above to make the instrument, it may be made by the body of persons responsible for the management of the institution and an instrument made by them under this subsection may replace wholly or partly any existing regulatory instrument.
>   (6) If an instrument approved by the Privy Council for the purposes of this section—
>   (a) falls within subsection (3)(a) above or was made in pursuance of a power under a regulatory instrument and, apart from this section, there is no power to modify it; or
>   (b) was made by the body of persons responsible for the management of the institution,
> the instrument may be modified by those persons.
>   (7) Either of the instruments referred to in subsection (2) above may be modified by order of the Privy Council and no instrument approved by the Privy Council for the purposes of this section may be modified by any other person without the Privy Council's consent.
>   (8) Before exercising any power under subsection (7) above in relation to any instrument the Privy Council shall consult—

(a) the governing body of the institution, and
(b) where there is such a power as is mentioned in subsection (3)(b) above to modify the instrument and the persons having that power are different from the governing body of the institution, the persons having the power,
so far as it appears to them to be practicable to do so.

(9) Nothing in this section requires further approval for any instrument approved by the Secretary of State for the purposes of section 156 of the Act, and references in this section to instruments approved by the Privy Council for the purposes of this section include instruments so approved by the Secretary of State.

(10) In this section and section 129B "designated institution" means an institution in relation to which a designation made, or having effect as if made, under section 129 of this Act has effect but does not include any institution established by Royal Charter.

Designated institutions conducted by companies

129B.—(1) This section has effect in relation to any designated institution conducted by a company.

(2) The articles of association of the company shall incorporate—
(a) provision with respect to the constitution of a governing body of the institution (to be known as the instrument of government of the institution); and
(b) provision with respect to the conduct of the institution (to be known as the articles of government of the institution).

(3) The Privy Council may give to the persons who appear to them to have effective control over the company such directions as they think fit for securing that—
(a) the memorandum of articles of association of the company; or
(b) any rules or bye-laws made in pursuance of any power conferred by the articles of association of the company,
are amended in such manner as they may specify in the direction.

(4) No amendment of the memorandum or articles of association of the company (other than one required under subsection (3)(a) above) shall take effect until it has been submitted to the Privy Council for their approval and they have notified their approval to the company.

(5) Before giving any directions under subsection (3) above the Privy Council shall consult the persons who appear to them to have effective control over the company."

(2) Section 156 of that Act (government and conduct of certain further and higher education institutions) shall cease to have effect in relation to designated institutions.

DEFINITIONS
"articles of government": s.129A(2)(b) of the ERA 1988, as introduced by subs. (1).
"designated institution": s.72(3) and s.129A(10) of the ERA 1988, as introduced by subs. (1) of this section.
"governing body": s.161(1)(d) of the ERA 1988.
"instrument of government": s.129A(2)(a) of the ERA 1988, as introduced by subs. (1).
"regulatory instrument": s.129A(4) of the ERA 1988, as introduced by subs. (1).

GENERAL NOTE
This section makes provision for the government and conduct of institutions designated as eligible for funding from the HEFC under s.129 (as amended). Under s.156(6)–(11) of the ERA 1988 the Secretary of State had power to approve or amend the instrument of government and articles of government of such an institution (where it is not conducted by a company). The new s.129A of the ERA 1988 transfers that power to the Privy Council and makes consequential adjustments to the approval procedure for such regulatory instruments. Where the designated institution is conducted by a company, s.156(2)–(5) of the ERA 1988 gave certain powers to the Secretary of State to require changes in the memorandum, articles or other rules of the

company. These powers are now transferred to the Privy Council by a new s.129B of the ERA 1988.

Subsection (2) provides that s.156 of the ERA 1988 is no longer of effect in relation to designated institutions.

This section came into force on May 6, 1992: see Commencement No. 1 Order 1992, para. 2 and Sched. 1.

Subs. (1)

S.129A

As under s.156(7) of the ERA 1988, the instrument of government and articles of government are to be made by the responsible authority of the institution but are now to be approved by the Privy Council, not by the Secretary of State (s.129A(9)). The instrument in question is either the existing instrument or one made for the purpose by the responsible authority (s.129A(3)). Where the existing instrument does not provide a power to make such a new instrument, then a power to do so is conferred by s.129A(5). Once made and approved by the Privy Council, the persons responsible for the management of the institution may amend it, whether or not an express power of amendment is conferred on them by that instrument (s.129A(6)).

Parallel to the power of the Secretary of State under s.156(10) of the ERA 1988, s.129A(7) empowers the Privy Council to modify an approved instrument by order. A duty to consult the governing body and those who have power to amend the instrument is imposed before the power is exercised (s.129A(8), following s.156(11) of the ERA 1988).

Consult. See note to s.6(1).

Order. Under s.232(2) of the ERA 1988, orders made by the Secretary of State under s.156(10) did not have to be exercised by statutory instrument. The orders are now made by the Privy Council under the procedure laid down in s.124D of the ERA 1988, introduced by s.71(1) of this Act.

Secretary of State. See note to s.1(2).

Institution established by Royal Charter. This refers to institutions called "universities" before the Act, which were exempted from the designation powers under the original s.129(1) of the ERA 1988.

S.129B

Like the provisions of s.156(2)–(4) of the ERA 1988, this section requires that the articles of association of a designated institution conducted by a company shall incorporate the instrument and articles of government required under s.124A of the ERA 1988, as introduced by s.71 of this Act. Similar to the case of s.129A, the Privy Council may issue directions to secure changes in the memorandum and articles of the company after consulting persons appearing to the Privy Council to have effective control over the company. The Privy Council must approve all changes to the memorandum or articles of association (s.129B(4)).

Direction. This may be revoked or varied under s.111 of the EA 1944 (see s.89(5)).

Consult. See note to s.6(1).

Transfer of further education institutions to higher education sector

74.—(1) After section 122 of the Education Reform Act 1988 (orders incorporating higher education institutions maintained by local education authorities) there is inserted—

"Orders transferring further education corporations to higher education sector

122A.—(1) The Secretary of State may by order provide for the transfer of a further education corporation to the higher education sector if it appears to him that the full-time equivalent enrolment number of the institution conducted by the corporation for courses of higher education exceeds 55 per cent. of its total full-time equivalent enrolment number.

(2) Where an order under this section is made in respect of a further education corporation, sections 124A and 125 of the Act shall have effect as if—

(a) on the date the order has effect, the corporation were established as a higher education corporation, and

(b) the Secretary of State were the appointing authority in relation to the first members of the higher education corporation.

(3) In determining in pursuance of subsection (2)(b) above the number of members to appoint within each variable category of members, the Secretary of State shall secure that at least half of all the members of the higher education corporation as first constituted are independent members; and in this subsection "variable category of members" and "independent members" have the same meaning as in Schedule 7A to this Act.

(4) On such date as may be specified in the order the corporation shall cease to be a further education corporation and become a higher education corporation and any member of the further education corporation who is not re-appointed by the Secretary of State in pursuance of subsection (2)b) above shall cease to hold office on that date."

(2) An order under section 129 of the Education Reform Act 1988 (designation of institutions for the purposes of the higher education sector) in respect of any institution may revoke any order in respect of that institution under section 28 of this Act.

DEFINITIONS
"course of higher education": s.235(2)(c) of and Sched. 6 to the ERA 1988.
"full-time equivalent enrolment number": s.161(2) and (3) of the ERA 1988.
"further education corporation": s.17(1).
"higher education corporation": s.123(1) of the ERA 1988.
"independent members": Sched. 7A, para. 3(2)(a), as introduced by Sched. 6 to this Act.
"institution": s.91(6).
"variable category of members": Sched. 7A, para. 11, as introduced by Sched. 6 to this Act.

GENERAL NOTE
This section creates a new s.122A of the ERA 1988 and empowers the Secretary of State to rationalise the place of institutions within the funding structure established by the Act and to transfer a further education corporation to the higher education sector. (This is the mirror of the transfer of higher education institutions to the further education sector empowered by s.47). The trigger level of full-time enrolment numbers on higher education courses under s.122A(1) is the same as that under s.129(2).

Where such an order for the transfer of an institution is made, the provisions as to its governance under ss.124A and 125 of the ERA 1988 operate and the Secretary of State is the appointing authority for the first members of the new higher education corporation (s.122A(2) of the ERA 1988). In making such appointments the Secretary of State has the duty to ensure that at least half the members are independent members (s.122A(2) of s.124(1) of the ERA 1988, introduced by s.71(1)). Members of the corporation who are not appointed as one of the first members of the new higher education corporation cease to be members on the date on which the corporation ceases to be a further education corporation.

Subsection (2) provides that a designation order under s.129 of the ERA 1988 revokes any designation order of an institution as part of the further education sector under s.28 of this Act.

This section comes into force on April 1, 1992: see Commencement No. 1 Order 1992, para. 2 and Sched. 1.

Subs. (1)
Order. An order is made by statutory instrument, subject to a negative resolution in Parliament (s.232(1) and (4) of the ERA 1988 and s.89(1) and (3) of this Act).
Full-time enrolment numbers. See note to s.72(1).
Independent members and *variable category members.* See note to s.71(1) (s.124C of the ERA 1988).

Subs. (2)
Order ... under s.28. See s.28(1).

Variation of trust deeds

75. In section 157 of the Education Reform Act 1988 (variation of trust deeds, etc.) for subsections (1) to (3) (variations by Secretary of State in connection with institutions in the higher education sector or designated assisted institutions) there is substituted—

> "(1) An order of the Privy Council may modify any trust deed or other instrument—
>> (a) relating to or regulating any such institution as is mentioned in subsection (2) below; or
>> (b) relating to any land or other property held by any person for the purposes of any such institution.
>
> (2) The institutions referred to in subsection (1) above are—
>> (a) any institution conducted by a higher education corporation; and
>> (b) any institution in relation to which a designation made, or having effect as if made, under section 129 of this Act has effect, other than an institution established by Royal Charter.
>
> (3) Before making any modifications under subsection (1) above of any trust deed or other instrument the Privy Council shall so far as it appears to them to be practicable to do so consult—
>> (a) the governing body of the institution;
>> (b) where that deed or instrument, or any other instrument relating to or regulating the institution concerned, confers power on any other persons to modify or replace that deed or instrument, those persons; and
>> (c) where the instrument to be modified is a trust deed and the trustees are different from the persons mentioned in paragraphs (a) and (b) above, the trustees."

DEFINITIONS
"higher education corporation": s.123(1) of the ERA 1988.
"institution in the higher education sector": s.91(5).
"land": s.90(1); s.235(1) of the ERA 1988.
"governing body": s.90(1); s.161(1)(d) of the ERA 1988.

GENERAL NOTE
Section 157 of the ERA 1988 empowered the Secretary of State to modify trust deeds and other instruments in relation to institutions conducted by a higher education corporation, or any designated assisted institution under s.139(6) of the ERA 1988, or an institution designated under s.129 of the ERA 1988. This section re-enacts s.157(1) and (3) and transfers these powers to the Privy Council. Subsection (3) imposes the same duties of consultation on the Privy Council as were imposed on the Secretary of State under the original s.157. A parallel provision for institutions in the further education sector exists in s.46.
This section came into force on May 6, 1992: see Commencement No. 1 Order 1992, para. 2 and Sched. 1.

S.157(1)
Order. See s.124D, introduced by s.71(1) of this Act.

S.157(2)
This omits reference to a "designated assisted institution" found in the original s.157(2) since such institutions have been transferred to the further education sector.

Power to award degrees, etc.

76.—(1) The Privy Council may by order specify any institution which provides higher education as competent to grant in pursuance of this section either or both of the kinds of award mentioned in subsection (2)(a) and (b) below.

(2) The kinds of award referred to in subsection (1) above are—
(a) awards granted to persons who complete an appropriate course of study and satisfy an appropriate assessment, and
(b) awards granted to persons who complete an appropriate programme of supervised research and satisfy an appropriate assessment,

and in this section "award" means any degree, diploma, certificate or other academic award or distinction and "assessment" includes examination and test.

(3) An institution for the time being specified in such an order may grant any award of a kind mentioned in subsection (2)(a) or (b) above which it is competent to grant by virtue of the order to persons who complete the appropriate course of study or, as the case may be, programme of supervised research on or after the date specified in the order.

(4) An institution specified in such an order may also—

(a) grant honorary degrees, and

(b) grant degrees to members of the academic and other staff of the institution.

(5) Any power conferred on an institution to grant awards in pursuance of this section includes power—

(a) to authorise other institutions to do so on behalf of the institution,

(b) to do so jointly with another institution, and

(c) to deprive any person of any award granted to him by or on behalf of the institution in pursuance of this section (or, in the case of an award granted to him by the institution and another institution jointly, to do so jointly with the other institution).

(6) It shall be for the institution to determine in accordance with any relevant provisions of the instruments relating to or regulating the institution the courses of study or programmes of research, and the assessments, which are appropriate for the grant of any award and the terms and conditions on which any of the powers conferred under this section may be exercised.

(7) Section 124D of the Education Reform Act 1988 applies in relation to orders under subsection (1) above as it applies in relation to the exercise of powers for the purposes of Part II of that Act.

DEFINITIONS

"assessment": subs. (2).

"award": subs. (2).

"higher education": s.90(1); s.120 of and Sched. 6 to the ERA 1988.

"institution": s.91(5).

GENERAL NOTE

The awarding of degrees is seen as one of the hallmarks of a "university" (see *St David's College, Lampeter* v. *Minister of Education* [1951] 1 All E.R. 559 at p. 561, *per* Vaisey J.). Only recognised bodies are empowered to award degrees (see s.216 of the ERA 1988). A list of such recognised bodies is to be found in the Education (Listed Bodies) Order 1988 (S.I. 1988 No. 2034). Non-recognised bodies have to provide degree courses under the auspices of a recognised body. Prior to this Act, degrees were only awarded by chartered universities and by the Council for National Academic Awards (CNAA). This section empowers the Privy Council to grant this power to other institutions, a development which will lead to polytechnics (typically renamed "universities" under s.77) awarding their own degrees. The CNAA is dissolved by s.80. Instead, and following the White Paper *Higher Education*, para. 65, the power to award degrees is extended not only to polytechnics, but also to other higher education institutions which satisfy the Privy Council that it is appropriate for them to have such a power. The White Paper *Higher Education*, paras. 65 and 66, stressed that such institutions would have to demonstrate effective internal validation and review processes, as well as other criteria. No such criteria are mentioned in this section. In a written answer of December 16, 1991, the Secretary of State did suggest that the principal criterion would be, in general terms, "for taught-course degrees, an institution needs to be a self-critical, cohesive academic community with a proven commitment to quality assurance supported by effective assurance and enhancement systems" (*Hansard*, H.C. Vol. 201, *Written Answers*, col. 31). The necessary characteristics to demonstrate that an institution satisfies this criterion are: "(a) a commitment to quality assurance and a demonstrably successful system for defining objectives and safeguarding standards...; (b) systems for the identification and transmission of good practice...; (c) appropriate external academic and professional points of reference so that standards were judged against those of the wider academic world . . .; (d) suitable administrative systems supporting an institution's academic work" (*ibid*. col. 32).

The White Paper *Higher Education*, para. 62, was of the view that it would be too restrictive to give degree-awarding powers only to those institutions which were accredited by the CNAA for both taught-course and research degrees, as the CNAA had itself suggested. Subsection (1) enables the Privy Council by order to grant an institution power to grant either taught-course awards or supervised research awards, or both, from a specified date. Subsection (2) specifies what is meant by these two categories of award. Subsection (3) empowers an institution given such a power to confer an award on persons who have completed the appropriate course of study or supervised research after the date specified in the Privy Council's order. Subsection (4) makes provision for honorary degrees. Subsection (5) enables an institution to authorise another institution to make awards or to make awards jointly with another institution. It also empowers the institution to revoke an award. Subsection (6) makes it clear that it is for the institution itself to determine the courses of study or programmes of research which qualify a person for an award. Subsection (7) applies the procedure of s.124D of the ERA 1988 (as introduced by s.71(1) of this Act) to the orders made by the Privy Council under subs. (1).

This section came into force on May 6, 1992: see Commencement No. 1 Order 1992, para. 2 and Sched. 1.

Subs. (1)

Institution which provides higher education. This phrase is broader than an institution within the higher education sector, since a further education corporation may provide higher education (see s.18(1)(a)). Nevertheless, it is clear from the White Paper *Higher Education* that only higher education institutions are intended to be given degree-awarding powers.

Order. See s.124D of the ERA 1988, under the note to s.71 of this Act.

Subs. (2)

Course of study. This phrase is intended to cover undergraduate and postgraduate taught courses, both degree courses and courses of a lower standard or shorter duration, such as certificates or diplomas.

Supervised research. A research degree is defined here as supervised research which is subjected to assessment, as opposed to independent research which a person may undertake. This would seem to preclude the award of higher doctorates which are degrees conferred as the result of unsupervised research of a distinguished character. Subsection (4)(b) might, however, permit higher doctorates to be awarded to staff of the institution, though not to distinguished alumni.

Subs. (3)

This provision enables an institution to confer awards on those who *complete* their course or research after the date on which it is empowered to grant such awards. This enables an institution to grant awards even where the course was begun under the accreditation of the CNAA (see note under s.80).

Subs. (4)

Honorary degrees. No restriction is made as to the level of such degrees. Thus, in principle, an institution empowered only to grant taught-course awards may confer a honorary degree at doctorate level. However, an order of the Privy Council will make provision as to which honorary degree titles may be awarded by a particular institution.

Subs. (5)

Other institutions. This provision enables an institution empowered to grant awards under subs. (1) to validate the awards of other institutions. With the dissolution of the CNAA, it will be necessary for institutions without degree-awarding powers to have their courses validated by another institution. It will be for the non-degree-awarding institution to choose its own validating body, be it an existing chartered university or an institution given degree-awarding powers under subs. (1) (White Paper *Higher Education*, para. 72). It is expected that such validation arrangements will be in place by September 1992 (see *Hansard*, H.L. Vol. 533, col. 1174; *Hansard*, H.C. Vol. 201, *Written Answers*, col. 33).

Subs. (6)

Instruments. The instruments regulating the institution include the instrument of government and the articles of government (see s.73(4)).

Use of "university" in title of institution

77.—(1) Where—
(a) power is conferred by any enactment or instrument to change the name of any educational institution or any body corporate carrying on such an institution, and
(b) the educational institution is within the higher education sector,

then, if the power is exercisable with the consent of the Privy Council, it may (whether or not the institution would apart from this section be a university) be exercised with the consent of the Privy Council so as to include the word "university" in the name of the institution and, if it is carried on by a body corporate, in the name of the body.

(2) The reference in subsection (1) above to a power to change the name of an institution or body includes any power (however expressed and whether or not subject to any conditions or restrictions) in the exercise of which the name of the institution or body may be changed; but the power as extended by that subsection has effect subject to any such conditions or restrictions.

(3) In exercising any power exercisable by virtue of this section to consent to a change in any name the Privy Council shall have regard to the need to avoid names which are or may be confusing.

(4) Any educational institution whose name includes the word "university" by virtue of the exercise of any power as extended by subsection (1) above is to be treated as a university for all purposes.

DEFINITIONS
"institution within the higher education sector": s.91(5).
"university": s.90(3).

GENERAL NOTE
This section confirms the end of the "binary line" between polytechnics and universities by permitting educational institutions within the higher education sector to become "universities" with the consent of the Privy Council. This major change was welcomed by all political parties and by both sides of the "binary line".

The term "university" is not a term of art, but is currently used to describe institutions which have powers to award degrees in a wide range of areas under a royal charter (see *St David's College, Lampeter* v. *Minister of Education* [1951] 1 All E.R. 559). Royal Charters are granted by the Privy Council under the College Charters Act 1871.

The Secretary of State set out in a written answer of January 15, 1992 the final criteria for extending the title "university" beyond the existing polytechnics. These are to be (1) that at least 300 full-time equivalent higher education students are in a majority of the PCFC's nine academic programmes; (2) that there should be a higher education enrolment of at least 4,000 full-time equivalent students; (3) that at least 3,000 full-time equivalent students should be on degree-level courses; and (4) that such institutions should have the power to award their own taught-course and research degrees (*Hansard*, H.C. Vol. 201, *Written Answers*, col. 582). The last of these criteria matches the criterion set out in a letter of December 16, 1991 from the Secretary of State for Education and Science stating that to acquire university status a polytechnic would be required to have a full range of degree-awarding powers. Powers to award taught-course degrees would not be enough, though it might justify the status of "polytechnic" (*Hansard*, H.C. Vol. 201, *Written Answers*, col. 32, para. 16).

Subsection (1) enables the name of an institution within the higher education sector to be changed to that of "university" where a power to do so with the consent of the Privy Council exists. Subsection (2) preserves any restrictions which may exist on changes of name under any enactment or instrument relating to the institution. Subsection (3) requires the Privy Council to have regard to the need to avoid names which may be confusing, *e.g.* where there is already a university in the same city. Subsection (4) provides that where an institution does become a "university" under subs. (1), it becomes a university for all purposes.

This section came into force on May 6, 1992: see Commencement No. 1 Order 1992, para. 2 and Sched. 1.

Subs. (1)
Power ... *conferred by any enactment or instrument.* The principal power is contained in

para. 1 of Sched. 7A to the ERA 1988, introduced by Sched. 6 to this Act, with which the instrument of government of any higher education corporation must comply under s.124A(4) of the ERA 1988 (introduced by s.71(1) of this Act). Paragraph 59 of Sched. 8 makes a parallel change to para. 1(4) of Sched. 7 to the ERA 1988, governing the power of a higher education corporation to change its name before s.124A comes into force. For higher education institutions conducted by a company, the instrument of government will contain similar provisions to those in Sched. 7A to the ERA 1988 by virtue of an order by the Secretary of State under s.31 of this Act, but the name of the company would be subject to change only under the provisions of the Companies Act 1985, s.28.

Subs. (2)
This subsection covers indirect powers to change the name of an institution, but preserves any restrictions on its exercise which may be contained in the empowering statute or instrument.

Subs. (3)
This provision is similar to the powers of the Secretary of State to avoid misleading names for companies under ss.28(2) and 31 of the Companies Act 1985.

Financial years of higher education corporations

78.—(1) If the Secretary of State directs that any financial year specified in the direction of the higher education corporations, and subsequent financial years, are to begin with a date specified in the direction, then—
  (a) the financial year of the corporations immediately preceding the year specified in the direction shall end immediately before the date specified in the direction, and
  (b) the financial year specified in the direction and subsequent financial years shall be each successive period of 12 months.
  (2) Section 124B(7) of, and paragraph 18 of Schedule 7 to, the Education Reform Act 1988 (financial years) shall have effect subject to this section.

DEFINITIONS
"higher education corporation": s.123(1) of the ERA 1988.

GENERAL NOTE
This section empowers the Secretary of State to direct that the financial year of a higher education corporation shall begin on a date other than April 1, which is the date specified for financial years (other than the first financial year of the corporation's existence) by para. 18(6) of Sched. 7 to the ERA 1988 and s.124B(7) of the ERA 1988, as introduced by s.71(1) of this Act. The purpose is to enable the Secretary of State to bring the financial year of higher education institutions into line with other parts of the higher education sector. (Universities, for example, operate a financial year beginning on August 1). Where such a direction is given, subs. (1) makes provision for the end of the first and subsequent financial years of the new arrangement. Subsection (2) establishes the priority over the conflicting provisions on financial years contained in s.124B(7) of and para. 18(6) to Sched. 7 to the ERA 1988.
This section came into force on May 6, 1992: see Commencement No. 1 Order 1992, para. 2 and Sched. 1.

Subs. (1)
Secretary of State. See note to s.1(2).
Directs. Any direction may be revoked or varied by the Secretary of State under s.111 of the EA 1944 (see s.89(5) of this Act).
Financial year . . . immediately preceding. The financial year prior to the date specified in the direction will be either that specified under s.124B(7) of the ERA 1988, as introduced by s.71(1), or, if the direction is made before the day appointed for the commencement of s.71, that specified under para. 18(6) of Sched. 7 to the ERA 1988.

General

Duty to give information to the funding councils

79. Each of the following shall give a council such information as they may require for the purposes of the exercise of any of their functions under the Education Acts—

(a) a local education authority,

(b) the governing body of any institution within the higher education sector, and

(c) the governing body of any institution at which prescribed courses of higher education are currently or have at any time been provided.

DEFINITIONS

"council": s.62(5).

"courses of higher education": s.235(2)(e) of and Sched. 6 to the ERA 1988.

"Education Acts": ss.90(1) and 94(2).

"governing body": s.90(1) and (2).

"institution within the higher education sector": s.91(5).

"local education authority": ss.6 and 118 of the EA 1944.

GENERAL NOTE

This section imposes a duty on certain persons to provide information to an HEFC which it requires for the performance of its functions. As the funder of students by way of student awards under the Education (Fees and Awards) Act 1983 and as persons responsible for certain provisions within the further education sector, local education authorities are required to provide information to an HEFC under para. (a). Past or present providers of higher education are also required to provide information, whether they are institutions within the higher education sector (para. (b)) or merely providers of courses of higher education (para. (c)).

This section came into force on May 6, 1992; see Commencement No. 1 Order 1992, para. 2: and Sched. 1.

Functions. These include the function of providing information to the Secretary of State under s.69.

Courses of higher education ... are provided. This provision enables an HEFC to obtain information, in particular, from further education corporations which exercise their power under s.18(1)(a) to provide higher education.

Dissolution of Council for National Academic Awards

80.—(1) The Secretary of State may by order provide—

(a) for the dissolution of the Council for National Academic Awards, and

(b) for all property, rights and liabilities to which the Council is entitled or subject immediately before the order comes into force to become property, rights and liabilities of such person as may be specified in the order.

(2) If the order so provides the person so specified shall discharge any duty relating to accounts and records under the statutes of the Council for National Academic Awards in respect of any period ending before the dissolution of the council which would have fallen to be discharged by the council after the dissolution or fell to be so discharged before the dissolution but has not been discharged.

GENERAL NOTE

This section provides for the dissolution of the Council for National Academic Awards and the transfer of its property rights and liabilities. These provisions implement the White Paper *Higher Education*, para. 73, which no longer saw a rôle for the CNAA, and transferring its property, rights and liabilities to another person (probably the HEFC for England). Subsection (2) provides for the discharge of any duties, such as those relating to accounts and records, which the CNAA did not discharge before its dissolution.

This section came into force on May 6, 1992: see Commencement No. 1 Order 1992, para. 2 and Sched. 1.

Subs. (1)

Secretary of State. See note to s.1(2).

Order. An order made under this section must be made by way of a statutory instrument which is subject to the negative resolution procedure in Parliament (s.89(1) and (3)).

Council for National Academic Awards. It was not considered practicable to keep the CNAA in existence for those students who had commenced courses under CNAA validation. They will have the validation of their awards transferred either to an existing chartered university or to an institution with degree-awarding powers under s.76 (see *Hansard*, H.L. Vol. 533, col. 1174).

It is envisaged that the CNAA will continue in operation until September 30, 1992 and will wind up its activities in March 1993 (Secretary of State, *Hansard*, H.C. Vol. 201, *Written Answers*, col. 33).

Directions

81.—(1) In exercising their functions under this Part of this Act, each council shall comply with any directions under this section, and such directions shall be contained in an order made by the Secretary of State.

(2) The Secretary of State may give general directions to a council about the exercise of their functions.

(3) If it appears to the Secretary of State that the financial affairs of any institution within the higher education sector have been or are being mismanaged he may, after consulting the council and the institution, give such directions to the council about the provision of financial support in respect of the activities carried on by the institution as he considers are necessary or expedient by reason of the mismanagement.

DEFINITIONS
"council": s.62(5).
"institution within the higher education sector": s.91(5).

GENERAL NOTE
This section empowers the Secretary of State to give directions to the HEFC and obliges the HEFC to comply with them. This section was the subject of considerable controversy because its original draft, which did not contain subs. (3), was thought to be too wide and thereby constituted a threat to academic freedom.

The power of the Secretary of State under subs. (2) to issue general directions by an order to the HEFC as to its functions is broadly similar to his power in relation to the UFC and PCFC under s.134(8) and (9) of the ERA 1988. The duty of the funding council to comply under subs. (1) follows the wording of s.134(8) of the ERA 1988. Subsection (3) represents a very restricted version of the original Bill, which empowered the Secretary of State to give directions which could relate to individual institutions. This was described as a "long-stop protection" (Paymaster-General, *Hansard*, H.L. Vol. 533, col. 1036; Vol. 534, col. 638) designed to protect the taxpayers' interests in the use of public monies in higher education. The present subs. (3) was introduced by the Government at the Third Reading in the House of Lords and focuses solely on the question of financial mismanagement by an institution. It empowers the Secretary of State to give directions to the HEFC about funding arrangements in consequence of financial mismanagement by an individual institution within the higher education sector.

The Secretary of State no longer has powers to intervene under s.68 of the EA 1944 where an institution or the Council has acted unreasonably (Sched. 8, para. 50).

This section came into force on May 6, 1992: see Commencement No. 1 Order 1992, para. 2 and Sched. 1.

Subs. (1)
Directions. There is no prescribed form or control for such directions. These may be revoked at any time (s.111 of the EA 1944 and s.89(4) of this Act).
Secretary of State. See note to s.1(2).
Order. This order is to be made by statutory instrument, subject to a negative resolution in Parliament: see s.89(1) and (3).
Functions. The principal functions of the HEFC are the administration of funds (s.65), the provision of information, and the review of the higher education sector (s.69), and quality assessment (s.70).

Subs. (3)
Mismanagement. This term is not defined but would appear to include incompetence as well as wilful default or fraud.
Necessary or expedient. See note to s.11.

PART III

MISCELLANEOUS AND GENERAL

Joint exercise of functions

82.—(1) Any two or more councils may exercise jointly any of their functions where it appears to them that to do so—
(a) will be more efficient, or
(b) will enable them more effectively to discharge any of their functions.
(2) Any two or more councils shall, if directed to do so by the Secretary of State, jointly make provision for the assessment by a person appointed by them of matters relating to the arrangements made by each institution in Great Britain which is within the higher education sector for maintaining academic standards in the institution.
(3) In this section—
(a) "council" means a higher education funding council, a further education funding council or the Scottish Higher Education Funding Council, and
(b) references to institutions within the higher education sector include institutions within the higher education sector within the meaning of Part II of the Further and Higher Education (Scotland) Act 1992.

DEFINITIONS
"council": subs. (3)(a).
"institution within the higher education sector": subs. (3)(b) and s.91(5).

GENERAL NOTE
This section provides for the collaboration between any of the further education funding councils or higher education funding councils created under this Act or between any of them and the Scottish Higher Education Funding Council created under s.31(1) of the Further and Higher Education (Scotland) Act 1992. For example, there is likely to be collaboration on standards and practices for quality assessment conducted by Quality Assessment Committees of the funding councils under ss.9 and 70 of this Act and s.39 of the Further and Higher Education (Scotland) Act 1992. Subsection (2) enables a central quality audit unit to be created by the funding councils to ensure that individual institutions have appropriate quality control mechanisms in place. It is envisaged, however, that quality audit will be conducted by a central organisation set up by the institutions themselves and this will cover the whole of Great Britain (see Paymaster-General, *Hansard*, H.L. Vol. 534, col. 715). In which case, a collaborative arrangement between the funding councils will be needed to approve and support its work but the Secretary of State will not have to exercise his power under subs. (2) to require the funding councils to create their own quality audit unit (Under-Secretary of State, *Hansard*, H.C., Standing Committee F, col. 397).
Subsection (1) empowers any two such councils to exercise any of their functions jointly where this would be more efficient or effective. Subsection (2) makes specific provision for collaboration on quality assessment. The Secretary of State is empowered to direct councils to make joint provision for quality assessment of institutions within Great Britain. This was seen as necessary to make best use of the expertise available in this area.
This section came into force on May 6, 1992: see Commencement No. 1 Order 1992, para. 2 and Sched. 1.

Subs. (2)
Assessment. This does not refer to the functions of the FEFC and the HEFC to secure that provision is made for the assessment of the quality of education provided in institutions within their sector (see ss.9 and 70). In this context, it refers to the review of quality control mechanisms in individual institutions involved in the concept of quality audit (on this see further General Note to s.70).
Secretary of State. See note to s.1(2).
Directed. See note to s.81.
This power to direct the councils was seen as a reserve power (*Hansard*, H.L. Vol. 534, col. 715).

Efficiency studies

83.—(1) A further education funding council or a higher education funding council may arrange for the promotion or carrying out by any person of studies designed to improve economy, efficiency and effectiveness in the management or operations of an institution within the further education sector or, as the case may be, the higher education sector.

(2) A person promoting or carrying out such studies at the request of a council may require the governing body of the institution concerned—

(a) to furnish the person, or any person authorised by him, with such information, and

(b) to make available to him, or any person so authorised, for inspection their accounts and such other documents,

as the person may reasonably require for that purpose.

DEFINITIONS
"council": s.1(5).
"further education corporation": s.17(1).
"governing body": s.90(1) and (2).
"institution within the further education sector": s.91(3).
"institution within the higher education sector": s.91(5).

GENERAL NOTE
This section empowers the FEFC and the HEFC to arrange for efficiency studies to be conducted into the management of institutions. The purpose of this section is to enable the funding councils "to arrange studies whose principal purpose is to assist institutions in improving the efficiency with which they manage their finances" (Paymaster-General, *Hansard*, H.L. Vol. 534, col. 716). The councils are thus to perform a rôle similar to that of the Audit Commission, which conducts such studies in relation to various public bodies, and which, under s.220 of the ERA 1988 (as amended by para. 51 of Sched. 8 to this Act) has such functions in relation to both the councils themselves and the institutions within their sectors. This section expands the scope of para. 19 of Sched. 7 to the ERA 1988, which empowered the PCFC to conduct such efficiency studies in relation to higher education corporations.

Subsection (1) empowers the councils to appoint persons to conduct such efficiency studies for any institution within their sector. Subsection (2) empowers the person conducting such a study to require information, documents, or accounts from the institution concerned.

This section came into force on May 6, 1992: see Commencement No. 1 Order 1992, para. 2 and Sched. 1.

Subs. (1)
Economy, efficiency and effectiveness. These terms reproduce those in s.26 of the Local Government Finance Act 1982 in relation to the Audit Commission's powers regarding local government and other public bodies. None of these terms has a statutory definition. "Economic" was discussed in *Bromley London Borough Council* v. *Greater London Council* [1983] 1 A.C. 768. "Efficiency" is generally seen in terms of "value for money" (see T. Byrne, *Local Government in Britain* (5th ed., London 1990), pp. 255–6).

Effect of agreements made before date of transfer

84.—(1) This section applies where—

(a) (apart from this section) any land or other property of a local authority would on any date ("the date of transfer") be transferred under Part I of this Act or Part II of the Education Reform Act 1988 to the governing body of an institution within the further education sector or the higher education sector, and

(b) at any time before that date the authority, the governing body of the institution and the governing body of any other institution which will on that date be an institution within the further education sector or the higher education sector have agreed in writing that the land or property should be transferred on that or a subsequent date to the governing body of that other institution.

(2) If the Secretary of State has approved the agreement at any time before the date of transfer, Part I of this Act or, as the case may be, Part II of

the Education Report Act 1988 shall have effect as if they required the property to be transferred in accordance with the agreement.

(3) References in this section to anything done include anything done before the passing of this Act.

DEFINITIONS
"date of transfer"; s.84(1)(a).
"governing body": s.90(1) and (2).
"institution within the further education sector": s.91(3).
"institution within the higher education sector": s.91(5).
"land": s.90(1).
"local authority": s.90(1).

GENERAL NOTE
This section provides that the land or property of a local authority which would be transferred to an institution within the further or higher education sector under the provisions of Pt. I of this Act or Pt. II of the ERA 1988, may be transferred instead to another institution in either sector. Such an arrangement is made by way of an agreement in writing between the three parties (subs. (1)), approved by the Secretary of State before the date of transfer (subs. (2)). The effect of such an approved agreement is to supersede the provisions of Pt. I of this Act or Pt. II of the ERA 1988 as to the destination of the land or property. Subsection (3) makes it clear that the provisions apply to validate agreements and approvals made before the Act was passed.

This section came into force on May 6, 1992: see Commencement No. 1 Order 1992, para. 2 and Sched. 1.

Subs. (1)
Part I of this Act. This refers to transfers of property from a local education authority to a further education corporation under s.23 or to a designated institution under s.32, both of which are subject to the provisions of s.36 and Sched. 5.
Part II of the Education Reform Act 1988. This refers to transfers of property from a local education authority to a higher education corporation under s.126 of the ERA 1988 or to a designated institution under s.130, both of which are subject to the provisions of s.138 and Sched. 10 to the ERA 1988.
That date. This refers to the date of transfer in subs. (1)(a).

Subs. (2)
Shall have effect as if . . . agreement. This deeming provision ensures that the terms of the agreement prevail over the statutory provisions mentioned in relation to the destination of the property.
Secretary of State. See note to s.1(2).

Finance and government of locally funded further and higher education

85.—(1) Chapter III of Part II of the Education Reform Act 1988 (finance and government of locally funded further and higher education) shall cease to have effect; and section 156 of that Act (government and conduct of certain further and higher education institutions) shall cease to have effect in relation to designated assisted institutions.

(2) A local education authority shall have the following powers in relation to any institution, not within the further education sector or the higher education sector, which is maintained by them in the exercise of their further or higher education functions.

(3) The authority may—
(a) make such provision as they think fit in respect of the government of the institution (including replacing any instrument of government or articles of government of the institution made under that Chapter or that section), and
(b) delegate to the governing body of the institution such functions relating to the management of the finances of the institution, and such other functions relating to the management of the institution (including the appointment and dismissal of staff), as the authority may determine.

DEFINITIONS
"articles of government": s.151(1)(b) of the ERA 1988.
"designated assisted institution": s.139(6) of the ERA 1988 and s.27 of the EA 1980.
"further education": s.90(1); s.120(1) of and Sched. 6 to the ERA 1988.
"institution not within the further education sector": s.91(3).
"institution not within the higher education sector": s.91(5).
"instrument of government": s.151(1)(a) of the ERA 1988.

GENERAL NOTE
This section repeals provisions in Chapter III of Pt. II and s.156 of the ERA 1988. Under Chapter III of Pt. II of the ERA 1988, local education authorities were obliged to draw up funding schemes for locally funded further and higher education institutions. The central feature of such schemes were that the institutions were to be responsible for the management of budgets devolved to them under the schemes (see ss.139, 142, 144 and 146 of the ERA 1988). These funding schemes required by those provisions of the ERA 1988 are now in place and thus the provisions have served their purpose. Furthermore, they have been overtaken by the provisions of Pt. I of this Act in relation to further education. Only a small number of institutions or courses of further and higher education will remain funded by local education authorities. Section 156 of the ERA 1988 made provision, *inter alia*, in relation to the government of such locally funded institutions, called "designated assisted institutions" in s.139 of the ERA 1988. This is now repealed by subs. (1), and the powers of the local education authority in relation to such institutions are set out in subs. (3). Under subs. (3), the local authority may make such provision for the government of the institution as it thinks fit. The Secretary of State no longer has any power to order an amendment to the instrument or articles of government of the institution, as under ss.153(2) and 156(10) of the ERA 1988. The local education authority may also delegate functions relating to the finances and management of the institution to the governing body as it determines. The requirements as to delegation of the management of finances under s.144 of the ERA 1988 and those relating to staff management under s.148 no longer apply. In practice this will make little difference as many institutions remaining under local authority control did not satisfy the test of enrolment numbers under s.144(2) of the ERA 1988. All the same, local authorities are left freer to administer the institutions remaining within their control.
This section comes into force on April 1, 1993: see Commencement No. 1 Order 1992, para. 2 and Sched. 3.

Subs. (1)
Designated assisted institutions. These are institutions which substantially depend for their maintenance on assistance from local authorities. As a consequence of Pt. I of this Act, the institutions in question are those which provide full-time further education for those over 18 and part-time education, typically adult education and community colleges (see General Note to s.11 and note to s.11(2)). Other institutions which were "designated assisted institutions" within s.139 of the ERA 1988 will become under this Act institutions within the further or higher education sector.
Local education authority. See under s.2(6).

Subs. (3)
Government of the institution. Under s.153 of the ERA 1988, the Secretary of State made regulations for the government of all institutions providing full-time education as designated assisted institutions.
Management of finances. Section 144 of the ERA 1988 required the delegation of management of finances under a funding scheme where there are at least 200 full-time equivalent students.
Appointment and dismissal of staff. For previous powers see s.148(2), (3) and (4) of the ERA 1988.

Temporary exclusion of section 5 of Data Protection Act 1984 in relation to data transferred to new bodies

86.—(1) Where personal data are transferred under any provision of this Act to a body corporate established under this Act, section 5(1) of the Data Protection Act 1984 (prohibition of unregistered holding, etc, of personal data) shall not apply in relation to the holding by that body corporate of the data so transferred or any data of the same description as the data so transferred until the end of the period of six months beginning—

(a) in the case of a body established to conduct an educational institution, the date on which the body begins to conduct the institution, and
(b) in any other case, when the body is established.
(2) Expressions used in subsection (1) above and in that Act have the same meaning in that subsection as in that Act.

DEFINITIONS
"personal data": s.1(3) of the Data Protection Act 1984.

GENERAL NOTE
This section provides protection for personal data transferred to a body corporate established under this Act for six months after the date on which the body was established or began to conduct the institution. This protection applies as an exception to the provisions of s.5(1) of the Data Protection Act 1984, which prohibits such holding of data unless the holder is registered. This enables data to be transferred efficiently by computer between the local authority and the new further and higher education corporations without the need for registration by the transferee. This provision follows that in s.223 of the ERA 1988.
This section came into force on May 6, 1992: see Commencement No. 1 Order 1992, para. 2 and Sched. 1.

Subs. (1)
Personal data. See s.1(3) of the Data Protection Act 1984. Records of staff and students held on computers clearly fall within this category.
Body established to conduct an educational institution. This means a further education corporation or a higher education corporation.

Transfers of property, etc.: supplementary provision

87. Schedule 7 to this Act has effect to supplement the provisions of this Act relating to the transfer of property, rights and liabilities.

GENERAL NOTE
This section gives effect to Sched. 7 to this Act. That schedule makes provision for the proof of title to property, the construction of agreements, the transfer of rights, remedies and the continuity of applications and legal actions pending at the time of transfer. The powers of the Education Assets Board in relation to such transfers should be read together with s.197 of and Sched. 10 to the ERA 1988, as amended by paras. 43 and 61–65 of Sched. 8 to this Act.
This section comes into force on September 30, 1992: Commencement No. 1 Order 1992, para. 2 and Sched. 2.

Stamp duty

88.—(1) Subject to subsection (2) below, stamp duty shall not be chargeable in respect of any transfer effected under or by virtue of any of the following sections of this Act: 23, 25, 27, 32, 34, 40(5) and (7), 63 and 80.
(2) No instrument (other than a statutory instrument) made or executed under or in pursuance of any of the provisions mentioned in subsection (1) shall be treated as duly stamped unless it is stamped with the duty to which it would, but for this section (and, if applicable, section 129 of the Finance Act 1982), be liable or it has, in accordance with the provisions of section 12 of the Stamp Act 1891, been stamped with a particular stamp denoting that it is not chargeable with any duty or that it has been duly stamped.

DEFINITIONS
"statutory instrument": s.1 of the Statutory Instruments Act 1946.

GENERAL NOTE
This section gives a general exemption from payment of stamp duty for transfers under the Act, subject to the procedure under subs. (2) which requires that instruments of transfer, other than statutory instruments, are to be stamped so as to show the duty to which they would otherwise have been liable or that duty is not chargeable. This provision follows s.130 of the ERA 1988.
This section came into force on May 6, 1992: see Commencement No. 1 Order 1992, para. 2 and Sched. 1.

Section 129 of the Finance Act 1982. This exempts from stamp duty transfers to charities. A further education corporation is an exempt charity by virtue of para. 69 of Sched. 8. A higher education corporation is an exempt charity by virtue of para. 64 of Sched. 12 to the ERA 1988.

Instrument. This refers to a contract or other document transferring or agreeing to transfer land or other property liable to stamp duty.

Orders, regulations and directions

89.—(1) Any power of the Secretary of State to make orders or regulations under this Act (other than under any of the excepted provisions) shall be exercised by statutory instrument.

(2) For the purposes of subsection (1) above the excepted provisions are sections 22, 29(6) and (8), 38, 46 and 57; but section 14 of the Interpretation Act 1978 (implied power to amend) applies to orders made under those sections as it applies to orders made by statutory instrument.

(3) A statutory instrument containing any order or regulations under this Act, other than an order under section 94, shall be subject to annulment in pursuance of a resolution of either House of Parliament.

(4) Orders or regulations under this Act may make different provision for different cases, circumstances or areas and may contain such incidental, supplemental, saving or transitional provisions as the Secretary of State thinks fit.

(5) Section 111 of the Education Act 1944 (revocation and variation) applies to directions given under this Act as it applies to directions given under that Act.

DEFINITIONS
"statutory instrument": s.1 of the Statutory Instruments Act 1946.

GENERAL NOTE
Subsection (1) provides that the Secretary of State shall make orders or regulations under this Act by way of statutory instrument, except when exercising powers under the sections mentioned in subs. (2). The exceptions listed in subs. (2) relate to the powers of the Secretary of State exercisable in relation to an individual institution, modifying its instrument of government or its trust deed, making provision in respect of loans or mismanagement in the institution. Apart from commencement orders under s.94(3), statutory instruments made under this Act are subject to the negative resolution procedure in Parliament (subs. (3)). Subsection (4) confirms that orders or regulations under the Act need not be of universal application, but may make different provisions for different cases, as well as other incidental, saving or transitional provisions. Subsection (5) provides that directions made under this Act are subject to s.111 of the EA 1944 and thus may be revoked by the Secretary of State at any time.

This section came into force on May 6, 1992: see Commencement No. 1 Order 1992, para. 2 and Sched. 1.

Subs. (1)
Secretary of State. See note to s.1(2).

Subs. (2)
Implied powers to amend. Section 14 of the Interpretation Act 1978 provides that, unless the contrary intention appears, a power to make orders and regulations includes a power to amend and revoke them in the same manner.

Subs. (5)
Directions. See note to s.81.

Interpretation

90.—(1) In this Act—
   "contract of employment", "employee" and "employer" have the same meaning as in the Employment Protection (Consolidation) Act 1978, and "employed" means employed under a contract of employment,

"the Education Acts" means the Education Acts 1944 to 1992,
"governing body", in relation to an institution, means, subject to subsection (2) below—
    (a) in the case of an institution conducted by a further educa-
    tion corporation or a higher education corporation, the
    corporation,
    (b) in the case of a university not falling within paragraph (a)
    above, the executive governing body which has responsibility for
    the management and administration of its revenue and property
    and the conduct of its affairs,
    (c) in the case of any other institution not falling within para-
    graph (a) or (b) above for which there is an instrument of
    government providing for the constitution of a governing body,
    the governing body so provided for, and
    (d) in any other case, any board of governors of the institution
    or any persons responsible for the management of the institu-
    tion, whether or not formally constituted as a governing body or
    board of governors,
"higher education" has the same meaning as in the Education Reform
    Act 1988,
"higher education corporation" means a body corporate established
    under section 121 or 122 of the Education Reform Act 1988,
    including those sections as applied by section 227(4) of that Act
    (application to Wales), or a body corporate which has become a
    higher education corporation by virtue of section 122A of that Act,
"interest in land" includes any easement, right to charge in, to or over
    land,
"land" includes buildings and other structures, land covered with water
    and any interest in land,
"liability" includes obligation, and
"local authority" means a county council, a district council, a London
    borough council or (in their capacity as a local authority) the
    Common Council of the City of London.
(2) The Secretary of State may by order provide for any reference in the
Education Acts to the governing body of an institution, in relation to an
institution which is—
(a) a designated institution for the purposes of Part I or Part II of this Act,
    and
(b) conducted by a company,
to be read as a reference to the governing body provided for in the instrument of government, or to the company or to both.
(3) In this Act "university" includes a university college and any college,
or institution in the nature of a college, in a university; but where a college or
institution would not, apart from this subsection, fall to be treated separately it shall not be so treated for the purpose of determining whether any
institution is in England or in Wales.
(4) References in this Act to institutions within the PCFC funding sector
are to be construed in accordance with section 132(6) of the Education
Reform Act 1988.
(5) Subject to the provisions of this Act, expressions used in this Act and
in the Education Act 1944 have the same meaning in this Act as in that Act.

DEFINITIONS
    "designated institution": s.28(4).
    "instrument of government": ss.20(1), 29(2) of this Act; s.129A(2) of the ERA 1988 (as
introduced by s.73 of this Act).

GENERAL NOTE
    Subsection (1) provides a number of definitions of terms used in this Act. Subsection (2)

empowers the Secretary of State to make an order providing for reference in the Education Acts to a governing body to be read as a reference to the governing body provided for in the instrument of government or to the company running the institution. Subsection (3) defines "university". Subsections (4) and (5) make further provisions on interpretation of this Act.

This section came into force on May 6, 1992: see Commencement No. 1 Order 1992, para. 2 and Sched. 1.

Subs. (2)
    Company. See s.31 of this Act and s.129B of the ERA 1988, as introduced by s.73 of this Act.

Subs. (3)
    This subsection reproduces the relevant part of s.235(1) of the ERA 1988 with an additional rider that concerns the division of institutions between the English and Welsh HEFCs.
    University college. The Secretary of State has indicated that he does not consider that "university college" should be used except to designate a constituent part of a university (*Hansard*, H.C. Vol. 201, *Written Answers*, col. 583). For a discussion of the status of a chartered college in this context, see *St David's College, Lampeter* v. *Minister of Education* [1951] 1 All E.R. 559).

Interpretation of Education Acts

91.—(1) This section applies for the interpretation of the Education Acts.
    (2) References to a further education funding council are to a council established under section 1 of this Act.
    (3) References to institutions within the further education sector are to—
    (a) institutions conducted by further education corporations, and
    (b) designated institutions for the purposes of Part I of this Act (defined in section 28(4) of this Act),
and references to institutions outside the further education sector are to be read accordingly.
    (4) References to a higher education funding council are to a council established under section 62 of this Act, subject to subsection (6) of that section.
    (5) References to institutions within the higher education sector are to—
    (a) universities receiving financial support under section 65 of this Act,
    (b) institutions conducted by higher education corporations, and
    (c) designated institutions for the purposes of Part II of this Act (defined in section 72(3) of this Act),
and references to institutions outside the higher education sector are to be read accordingly.
    (6) References, in relation to a further education corporation or higher education corporation, to the institution—
    (a) in relation to any time before the operative date for the purposes of Part I of this Act (defined in section 17 of this Act) or, as the case may be, the transfer date for the purposes of the Education Reform Act 1988 (defined in section 123 of that Act), are to the institution the corporation is established to conduct, and
    (b) in relation to any later time or to any corporation which is a further education corporation by virtue of section 47 of this Act or a higher education corporation by virtue of section 122A of that Act, are to any institution for the time being conducted by the corporation in the exercise of their powers under this or that Act.

GENERAL NOTE
    This section provides definitions of terms in relation to the Education Acts defined in ss.90(1) and 94(2). The terms defined are the FEFC and the HEFC and the institutions within their sectors.
    This section came into force on May 6, 1992: see Commencement No. 1 Order 1992, para. 2 and Sched. 1.

Index

92. The expressions listed in the left-hand column below are respectively defined by or (as the case may be) are to be interpreted in accordance with the provisions of this Act listed in the right-hand column in relation to those expressions.

Expression	Relevant provision
appropriate further education funding council	section 1(6)
contract of employment, etc.	section 90(1)
council (in Part I), or further education funding council	sections 1(5) and 91(2)
council (in Part II), or higher education funding council	sections 61(3)(b), 62(5) and (6) and 91(4)
designated institution (in Part I)	section 28(4)
designation institution (in Part II)	section 72(3)
the Education Acts	section 90(1)
functions	section 61(1)
further education	section 14(1) to (4)
further education corporation	section 17(1)
governing body	section 90(1) and (2)
higher education	section 90(1)
higher education corporation	section 90(1)
institution in England or in Wales (in relation to higher education funding councils)	section 62(7)
institutions within or outside the further education sector	section 91(3)
institutions within or outside the higher education sector	sections 61(3)(a) and 91(5)
institutions within the PCFC funding sector	section 90(4)
interest in land	section 90(1)
land	section 90(1)
liability	section 90(1)
local authority	section 90(1)
modification	section 61(1)
operative date	sections 17 and 33(4)
pupil	section 14(6)
regulations	section 61(1)
secondary education	section 14(2) to (4)
school	section 14(5)
transfer of rights or liabilities	section 61(2)
university	section 90(3)

GENERAL NOTE

This is a rather innovatory (and welcome) summary of the location of definitions within this Act.

This section came into force on May 6, 1992: see Commencement No. 1 Order 1992, para. 2 and Sched. 1.

Amendments and repeals

93.—(1) Schedule 8 (which makes minor and consequential amendments) shall have effect.

(2) The enactments mentioned in Schedule 9 to this Act are repealed to the extent mentioned in the third column.

GENERAL NOTE

The various paragraphs of Sched. 8 come into force on different dates set out in the Commencement No. 1 Order 1992, para. 2 and Scheds. 1–3. Section 93(1) comes into force in relation to those paragraphs set out in that Order.

The various repeals in Sched. 9 come into effect on either May 6, 1992 or April 1, 1993, as provided by the Commencement No. 1 Order 1992, para. 2 and Scheds. 1 and 3 (and the annex thereto). Section 93(2) comes into force in relation to those repeals on the dates set out in that Order.

Short title, commencement, etc.

94.—(1) This Act may be cited as the Further and Higher Education Act 1992.

(2) The Education Acts 1944 to 1990, the School Teachers' Pay and Conditions Act 1991 and this Act may be cited together as the Education Acts 1944 to 1992.

(3) This Act shall come into force on such day as the Secretary of State may by order appoint and different days may be appointed for different provisions and for different purposes.

(4) Subject to the following provisions of this section, this Act extends to England and Wales only.

(5) Sections 63, 64 and 82 of this Act extend also to Scotland.

(6) Section 80 extends also to Scotland and Northern Ireland.

(7) The amendment by this Act of an enactment which extends to Scotland or Northern Ireland extends also to Scotland, or, as the case may be, Northern Ireland.

GENERAL NOTE

This section came into force on May 6, 1992: see Commencement No. 1 Order 1992, para. 2 and Sched. 1.

SCHEDULES

Sections 1, 9, 62 and 70   SCHEDULE 1

THE FURTHER AND HIGHER EDUCATION FUNDING COUNCILS

Supplementary powers

1.—(1) Subject to sub-paragraph (2) below, the council may do anything which appears to them to be necessary or expedient for the purpose of or in connection with the discharge of their functions, including in particular—

(a) acquiring and disposing of land and other property,

(b) entering into contracts,

(c) investing sums not immediately required for the purpose of the discharge of their functions, and

(d) accepting gifts of money, land or other property.

(2) The council shall not borrow money.

Chief officer

2.—(1) One of the members of the council shall be the chief officer.

(2) The first chief officer shall be appointed as such by the Secretary of State and shall hold and vacate office in accordance with the terms of his appointment.

(3) Each subsequent chief officer shall be appointed by the council with the approval of the Secretary of State on such terms and conditions (including terms with respect to tenure and vacation of office) as the council may with the approval of the Secretary of State determine.

(4) On approval by the Secretary of State of the person to be appointed on any occasion as chief officer of the council and the terms and conditions of his appointment, the Secretary of State shall—

(a) if that person is not already a member of the council, appoint him as a member for the same term as the term of his appointment as chief officer, or

(b) if he is already such a member but his term of appointment as such ends before the term of his appointment as chief officer ends, extend his term of appointment as a member so that it ends at the same time as the term of his appointment as chief officer.

Tenure of members of councils

3.—(1) A person shall hold and vacate office as a member or as chairman or chief officer of the council in accordance with the terms of his appointment and shall, on ceasing to be a member, be eligible for re-appointment.

(2) A person may at any time by notice in writing to the Secretary of State resign his office as a member or as chairman of the council.

4. If the Secretary of State is satisfied that a member of the council—

(a) has been absent from meetings of the council for a period longer than six consecutive months without the permission of the council, or

(b) is unable or unfit to discharge the functions of a member,

the Secretary of State may by notice in writing to that member remove him from office and thereupon the office shall become vacant.

Salaries, allowances and pensions

5.—(1) The council—

(a) shall pay to their members such salaries or fees, and such travelling, subsistence or other allowances, as the Secretary of State may determine, and

(b) shall, as regards any member in whose case the Secretary of State may so determine, pay or make provision for the payment of such sums by way of pension, allowances and gratuities to or in respect of him as the Secretary of State may determine.

(2) If a person ceases to be a member of the council and it appears to the Secretary of State that there are special circumstances which make it right that he should receive compensation, the Secretary of State may direct the council to make to that person a payment of such amount as the Secretary of State may determine.

(3) The council shall pay to the members of any of their committees who are not members of the council such travelling, subsistence and other allowances as the Secretary of State may determine.

(4) A determination or direction of the Secretary of State under this paragraph requires the approval of the Treasury.

House of Commons disqualification

6. In Part III of Schedule 1 to the House of Commons Disqualification Act 1975 (disqualifying offices) there are inserted at the appropriate places—

"Any member of the Further Education Funding Council for England in receipt of remuneration.

Any member of the Further Education Funding Council for Wales in receipt of remuneration.

Any member of the Higher Education Funding Council for England in receipt of remuneration.

Any member of the Higher Education Funding Council for Wales in receipt of remuneration."

Staff

7.—(1) The council may appoint such employees as they think fit.

(2) The council shall pay to their employees such remuneration and allowances as the council may determine.

(3) The employees shall be appointed on such other terms and conditions as the council may determine.

(4) A determination under sub-paragraph (2) or (3) above requires the approval of the Secretary of State given with the consent of the Treasury.

(5) Employment with the council shall be included among the kinds of employment to which a scheme under section 1 of the Superannuation Act 1972 can apply, and accordingly in Schedule 1 to that Act (in which those kinds of employment are listed), at the end of the list of "Other Bodies" there is inserted—

"Further Education Funding Council for England.

Further Education Funding Council for Wales.

Higher Education Funding Council for England.

Higher Education Funding Council for Wales."

(6) The council shall pay to the Treasury, at such times as the Treasury may direct, such sums as the Treasury may determine in respect of the increase attributable to sub-paragraph (5) above in the sums payable out of money provided by Parliament under that Act.

(7) Where an employee of the council is, by reference to that employment, a participant in a scheme under section 1 of that Act and is also a member of the council, the Treasury may determine that his service as such a member shall be treated for the purposes of the scheme as service as an employee of the council (whether or not any benefits are payable to or in respect of him by virtue of paragraph 5 above).

Committees

8.—(1) The council may establish a committee for any purpose.

(2) The number of the members of a committee established under this paragraph, and the terms on which they are to hold and vacate office, shall be fixed by the council.

(3) Such a committee may include persons who are not members of the council.

(4) The council shall keep under review the structure of committees established under this paragraph and the scope of each committee's activities.

Further Education Funding Council for England: regional committees

9.—(1) There shall be established for each region of England determined by the Secretary of State a committee of the Further Education Funding Council for England to advise the council on such matters relating to the facilities for the population of the region—
(a) for further education, or
(b) for full-time education (other than further education) suitable to the requirements of persons over compulsory school age who have not attained the age of 19 years,
as the council may from time to time require.

(2) The number of the members of a committee established under this paragraph shall be determined by the Secretary of State and he shall appoint the members of the committee.

(3) Paragraphs 3 and 4 above apply to members of a committee established under this paragraph as they apply to members of a council.

Delegation of Functions

10. The council may authorise the chairman, the chief officer or any committee established under paragraph 8 above to exercise such of their functions as they may determine.

Proceedings

11. Without prejudice to any other rights the Secretary of State may require to be accorded to him as a condition of any grants made to the council under this Act—
(a) a representative of the Secretary of State shall be entitled to attend and take part in any deliberations (but not in decisions) at meetings of the council or of any committee of the council, and
(b) the council shall provide the Secretary of State with such copies of any documents distributed to members of the council or of any such committee as he may require.

12. The validity of any proceedings of the council or of any committee of the council shall not be affected by a vacancy among the members or by any defect in the appointment of a member.

13. Subject to the preceding provisions of this Schedule, the council may regulate their own procedure and that of any of their committees.

Application of seal and proof of instruments

14. The application of the seal of the council shall be authenticated by the signature—
(a) of the chairman or of some other person authorised either generally or specially by the council to act for that purpose, and
(b) of one other member.

15. Every document purporting to be an instrument made or issued by or on behalf of the council and to be duly executed under the seal of the council, or to be signed or executed by a person authorised by the council to act in that behalf, shall be received in evidence and be treated, without further proof, as being so made or issued unless the contrary is shown.

Accounts

16.—(1) It shall be the duty of the council—
(a) to keep proper accounts and proper records in relation to the accounts,
(b) to prepare in respect of each financial year of the council a statement of accounts, and
(c) to send copies of the statement to the Secretary of State and to the Comptroller and

Auditor General before the end of the month of August next following the financial year
to which the statement relates.

(2) The statement of accounts shall comply with any directions given by the Secretary of State
with the approval of the Treasury as to—

(a) the information to be contained in it,

(b) the manner in which the information contained in it is to be presented, or

(c) the methods and principles according to which the statement is to be prepared,

and shall contain such additional information as the Secretary of State may with the approval of
the Treasury require to be provided for the information of Parliament.

(3) The Comptroller and Auditor General shall examine, certify and report on each statement received by him in pursuance of this paragraph and shall lay copies of each statement and
of his report before each House of Parliament.

(4) In this paragraph "financial year" means the period beginning with the date on which the
council is established and ending with the second 31st March following that date, and each
successive period of 12 months.

Status of council

17. The council shall not be regarded as the servant or agent of the Crown or as enjoying any
status, immunity or privilege of the Crown; and the property of the council shall not be regarded
as property of, or property held on behalf of, the Crown.

DEFINITIONS
"council": s.19(5) or s.62(5).
"employee": s.90(1).
"financial year": para. 16(4).
"functions": s.61(1).
"land": s.90(1).
"months": Sched. 1 of the Interpretation Act 1978.

GENERAL NOTE
This Schedule sets out the institutional structure of an FEFC or HEFC. Its provisions follow
closely those of Sched. 8 to the ERA 1988 on the UFC and PCFC. The councils are envisaged as
executive bodies responsible to the Secretary of State. The Secretary of State appoints the first
chief officer and approves subsequent appointments, as well as the terms and conditions of his
or her tenure (para. 2). The other members are appointed by the Secretary of State (ss.1(2) and
62(2)) and may be removed by him for absence or incapacity (para. 4). The Secretary of State
also issues determinations and directions in relation to the salaries, allowances and pensions of
members (para. 5). The Secretary of State is also empowered to require that his representative
be entitled to attend all meetings of a council and that he should be provided with all papers
distributed for any meeting of the council or its committees (para. 11).

This Schedule came into force on May 6, 1992: see Commencement No. 1 Order 1992, para. 2
and Sched. 1.

Para. 1
This paragraph provides that the council has the usual ancillary powers of property ownership, contracting, investing and receiving gifts of a body corporate. It is prohibited by sub-para.
(2) from borrowing money.

Para. 2
First chief officer. Proposed appointments of the first chief officers were announced before
the Act was passed (see *The Higher*, January 24, 1992).

Para. 5
Determination or direction. Directions made may be revoked or varied at any time (see s.111
of the EA 1944, as applied by s.89(5) of this Act). No such determination or direction requires
to be in any particular form, nor is any form prescribed for Treasury approval under sub-para.
(4).

Para. 7
Although the council may appoint its staff, the terms and conditions of employment (including pay) require approval of the Secretary of State and Treasury consent. Sub-paragraph (5)
enables staff to be admitted to the Principal Civil Service Pension Scheme but not to the
exclusion of other arrangements.

Para. 8
Committee. Such committees must include a quality assessment committee (ss.9(1)(b) and 70(1)(b)).

Para. 9
Committee. Unlike for committees established under para. 8, the Secretary of State both determines the number of members of regional committees of the FEFC and appoints its members. The function of the committees will be to replace the local authorities in determining local needs for further education and to reduce their effectiveness in this area.

Regional advisory committees of the Ministry of Education (now the DES) were set up by ministerial circular in 1947 to disseminate good practice. The Government wanted by this provision to give greater flexibility in the operation of further education in the regions and to leave colleges to adjust to student and employer demands, rather than to any pre-determined regional plan. It is expected that the regional committees will liaise with local education authorities and Training and Enterprise Councils (TECs) (*Hansard*, H.L. Vol. 533, col. 490). The Government intends to nominate representatives of the TECs to regional committees, but did not wish to be prescriptive about the involvement of any particular local organisation (*ibid.* col. 521, and White Paper, *Education and Training*, Vol. 2, para. 4.2).

Para. 16
The financial year of the funding councils is currently matched by that of further education corporations and higher education corporations, but the financial years of higher education corporations may be altered by order of the Secretary of State (see s.78).

Para. 17
Servant or agent of the Crown. This provision follows s.134 of the ERA 1988 and ensures that the Council can sue and be sued like any ordinary public body. It does perform public functions and will be subject to judicial review.

Sections 3 and 6   SCHEDULE 2

COURSES OF FURTHER EDUCATION

The descriptions of courses of further education referred to in section 3(1) of this Act are the following—
  (a) a course which prepares students to obtain a vocational qualification which is, or falls within a class, for the time being approved for the purposes of this sub-paragraph by the Secretary of State,
  (b) a course which prepares students to qualify for—
        (i) the General Certificate of Secondary Education, or
        (ii) the General Certificate of Education at Advanced Level or Advanced Supplementary Level (including Special Papers),
  (c) a course for the time being approved for the purposes of this sub-paragraph by the Secretary of State which prepares students for entry to a course of higher education,
  (d) a course which prepares students for entry to another course falling within paragraphs (a) to (c) above,
  (e) a course for basic literacy in English,
  (f) a course to improve the knowledge of English of those for whom English is not the language spoken at home,
  (g) a course to teach the basic principles of mathematics,
  (h) in relation to Wales, a course for proficiency or literacy in Welsh,
  (j) a course to teach independent living and communication skills to persons having learning difficulties which prepares them for entry to another course falling within paragraphs (d) to (h) above.

DEFINITIONS
"persons having learning difficulties": s.4(6).

GENERAL NOTE
This Schedule provides a definition of courses of further education, a term used to determine the education funded by an FEFC under ss.5 and 7 and the powers of a local education authority under s.41 of the EA 1944 (as replaced by s.11 of this Act). Neither statute nor regulations have previously provided a definition of courses of further education. The list covers two types of course—those leading to a formal qualification or preparation for such a course (paras. (a) and

(d)) and those offering basic skills for everyday living (paras. (e)–(j)). Special attention is given to the needs of persons with learning difficulties, and the inclusion of courses for independent living for such persons was the result of an amendment in the House of Lords introduced by the Government.

Section 3(6) empowers the Secretary of State to amend this Schedule by order.

This Schedule comes into force on September 30, 1992: see Commencement No. 1 Order 1992, para. 2 and Sched. 2.

Courses. A "course" in this Schedule can be taken to include a "programme of study" including a separate subject studied before embarking on the main programme (see Paymaster-General, *Hansard,* H.L. Vol. 533, cols. 573–4).

Sections 15 and 16 SCHEDULE 3

CALCULATION OF ENROLMENT NUMBERS

Enrolment numbers

1.—(1) The enrolment number for any institution at any time is the aggregate of—
(a) the number of full-time students enrolled at that institution at that time to follow courses of further or higher education, and
(b) the numbers arrived at under sub-paragraph (3) below for each mode of attendance at such courses specified in the first three entries in column 1 of the table in paragraph 2 below.

(2) The total enrolment number for any institution at any time is the aggregate of—
(a) the number of full-time students enrolled at that institution at that time to follow courses of further or higher education, and
(b) the numbers arrived at under sub-paragraph (3) below for each mode of attendance at such courses specified in column 1 of the table in paragraph 2 below.

(3) The number for any mode of attendance at a course is that arrived at by multiplying by the appropriate multiplier the number of students enrolled at the institution at the time in question to follow the course by that mode of attendance.

(4) In sub-paragraph (3) above "the appropriate multiplier" means, in relation to a mode of attendance, the figure given in relation to that mode of attendance in column 2 of the table.

Table for calculating enrolment numbers for sandwich courses, etc.

2. The following table applies for the purpose of determining the numbers mentioned in paragraph 1(1)(b) and (2)(b) above—

(1) Mode of attendance	(2) Multiplier
1. Sandwich course	0.7
2. Block release	1.0
3. Day release	0.3
4. Part-time (other than day release but including some day-time study)	0.2
5. Part-time (evening only study)	0.1
6. Open or distance learning	0.075

Interpretation of paragraphs 1 and 2

3.—(1) For the purposes of paragraph 1(1)(a) and (2)(a) above a student is a full-time student in relation to a course of any description if all his studies for the purposes of that course are full-time studies.

(2) For the purposes of paragraph 2 above—
(a) a student's mode of attendance at a course of any description is by way of a sandwich course if—
   (i) in following that course, he engages in periods of full-time study for the purposes of the course alternating with periods of full-time work experience which form part of that course, and
   (ii) his average period of full-time study for the purposes of the course for each academic year included in the course is 19 weeks or more,
(b) a student's mode of attendance at a course of any description is by way of block release if—

(i) the course involves a period of full-time study interrupted by a period of industrial training or employment (whether or not it also includes study on one or two days a week during any other period), and

(ii) his average period of full-time study for the purposes of the course for each academic year included in the course is less than 19 weeks,

(c) a student's mode of attendance at a course of any description is by way of day release if—

(i) he is in employment, and

(ii) he is released by his employer to follow that course during any part of the working week, and

(d) a student's mode of attendance at a course of any description is by way of open or distance learning if—

(i) he is provided for the purposes of the course with learning material for private study, and

(ii) his written work for the purposes of the course is subject to a marking and comment service provided for students following the course by private study (whether or not any additional advisory or teaching services are also provided for such students as part of the course).

Amendment of paragraphs 1 to 3

4. The Secretary of State may by order amend paragraphs 1 to 3 above except so far as they apply for calculating an institution's enrolment number, or total enrolment number, on 1st November 1990.

Exclusion of non-EEC students

5. For the purpose of calculating under those paragraphs any enrolment number at any time of any institution, any student enrolled at the institution whose ordinary place of residence then was or is in a country or territory other than a member State shall be disregarded.

GENERAL NOTE

The purpose of using enrolment numbers calculated under paras. 1 and 2 of this Schedule is to equate the amount of time and expenditure devoted to students with a different mode of attendance. The calculations and definitions used follow those used in the further Education Statistical Record, compiled annually by the Department of Education and Science. In some significant respects, the mode of calculation and the multipliers differ from those laid down in Sched. 9 to the ERA 1988.

This Schedule came into force on May 6, 1992: see Commencement No. 1 Order 1992, para. 2 and Sched. 1.

Para. 4

This follows para. 4 of Sched. 9 to the ERA 1988 in empowering the Secretary of State by order to amend paras. 1–3. Unlike under para. 4 of Sched. 9 to the ERA 1988, such orders must be made by statutory instrument subject to a negative resolution in Parliament (see s.89(1) and (3)).

Secretary of State. See under s.1(2).

Para. 5

This excludes from calculations "overseas students", students who are ordinarily resident outside the European Economic Community. "Ordinary residence" means, in this context, habitual and normal residence from choice and for a settled purpose (including education) apart from temporary or occasional absences (*Akborali* v. *Brent London Borough Council* [1983] 2 A.C. 309).

Section 20   SCHEDULE 4

INSTRUMENTS AND ARTICLES OF GOVERNMENT FOR FURTHER EDUCATION CORPORATIONS

1. References in this Schedule to an instrument are to an instrument of government or articles of government.

2.—(1) An instrument shall provide for the number of members of the further education corporation, the eligibility of persons for membership and the appointment of members.

(2) An instrument may provide for the nomination of any person for membership by another, including by a body nominated by the Secretary of State.

3. An instrument shall provide for one or more officers to be chosen from among the members.

4. An instrument may provide for the corporation to establish committees and permit such committees to include persons who are not members of the corporation.

5. An instrument may provide for the delegation of functions of the corporation to officers or committees.

6. An instrument may provide for the corporation to pay allowances to its members.

7. An instrument shall provide for the authentication of the application of the seal of the corporation.

8. An instrument shall require the corporation to keep proper accounts and proper records in relation to the accounts and to prepare in respect of each financial year of the corporation a statement of accounts.

9. An instrument shall provide for the appointment of a principal of the institution and determine which functions exercisable in relation to the institution are to be exercised by the corporation, its officers or committees and which by the principal of the institution.

10. An instrument shall make provision about the procedures of the corporation and of the institution.

11. An instrument shall provide—

(a) for the appointment, promotion, suspension and dismissal of staff, and

(b) for the admission, suspension and expulsion of students.

12. An instrument may make provision authorising the corporation to make rules or bye-laws for the government and conduct of the institution, including in particular rules or bye-laws about the conduct of students, staff or both.

DEFINITIONS

"articles of government": s.20(1)(b) or s.29(2)(b).
"instrument of government": s.20(1)(a) or s.29(2)(a).

GENERAL NOTE

This Schedule sets out a list of provisions with which the instruments and articles of government of a further education corporation or a designated institution must comply by virtue of ss.20 and 29 of this Act. In essence, the Schedule is a list of topics on which those instruments and articles must have provisions. Such institutions will typically already have an instrument of government and articles of government by virtue of s.151 of the ERA 1988. The requirements of Sched. 4 are fewer than those under s.152 of the ERA 1988, which previously regulated such institutions, or Sched. 7A of the ERA 1988 (as introduced by Sched. 6 to this Act), regulating higher education corporations. This was a deliberate policy by the Government to give the corporations greater flexibility in the structure of their government. The consequence is that no provision is made in this Schedule regarding the size of the governing body or its composition. Guidance on the matter will be issued by the Secretary of State. No representation is required for staff, students or any interested party, *e.g.* a local authority or representative of those with special needs. It is, however, anticipated that the further education corporations will include representatives of staff and students on their governing bodies (Lord Cavendish of Furness, *Hansard*, H.L. Vol. 533, cols. 892–93). The Government announced that model instruments of government for further education institutions will provide for the membership of a further education corporation to include a student representative as well as a representative of the local Training and Enterprise Council, and up to two local authority representatives may be co-opted (Lord Cavendish of Furness, *Hansard*, H.L. Vol. 534, cols. 397, 400, 401; White Paper, *Education and Training*, Vol. 1, para. 9.7; Vol. 2, paras. 5.5–5.9).

This Schedule comes into force on September 30, 1992: see Commencement No. 1 Order 1992, para. 2 and Sched. 2.

Section 36   SCHEDULE 5

IDENTIFICATION AND APPORTIONMENT, ETC., OF PROPERTY

Division and apportionment of property etc.

1.—(1) Any property, rights and liabilities of a transferor authority held or used, or subsisting—

(a) for the purposes of more than one relevant institution, or

(b) partly for the purposes of one or more relevant institutions and partly for other purposes of the transferor authority,

shall, where the nature of the property, right or liability permits, be divided or apportioned between the transferees, or (as the case may be) between the transferor authority and the transferee or transferees, in such proportions as may be appropriate.

(2) Where any estate or interest in land falls to be so divided—

(a) any rent payable under a lease in respect of that estate or interest, and

(b) any rent charged on that estate or interest,

shall be correspondingly divided or apportioned so that each part is payable in respect of, or charged on, only one part of the estate or interest and the other part or parts are payable in respect of, or charged on, only the other part or parts of the estate or interest.

(3) Any property, right or liability held or used, or subsisting, as mentioned in sub-paragraph (1) above the nature of which does not permit its division or apportionment as so mentioned shall be transferred to the transferee (or to one or other of the transferees) or retained by the transferor authority according to—

(a) in the case of an estate or interest in land, whether on the operative date the transferor authority or the transferee (or one or other of the transferees) appears to be in greater need of the security afforded by that estate or interest or, where none of them appears to be in greater need of that security, which of them appears on that date to be likely to make use of the land to the greater extent, or

(b) in the case of any other property or any right or liability, which of them appears on the operative date to be likely to make use of the property or (as the case may be) to be affected by the right or liability to the greater extent,

subject (in either case) to such arrangements for the protection of the other person or persons concerned as may be agreed between the transferor authority and the Education Assets Board or determined by the Board under paragraph 3 below.

(4) In this paragraph—

(a) references to a relevant institution are references to—

(i) any institution a body corporate is established under this Act to conduct, and

(ii) any institution in relation to which section 32 of this Act has effect, and

(b) references to a transferor authority are references to a local authority who are the transferor for the purposes of any transfer to which this Schedule applies.

Identification of property, rights and liabilities

2.—(1) It shall be the duty of the transferor and the Education Assets Board, whether before or after the operative date, so far as practicable to arrive at such written agreements, and to execute such other instruments, as are necessary or expedient to identify or define the property, rights and liabilities transferred to the transferee or retained by the transferor or for making any such arrangements as are mentioned in paragraph 1(3) above and as will—

(a) afford to the transferor and the transferee as against one another such rights and safeguards as they may require for the proper discharge of their respective functions, and

(b) make as from such date, not being earlier than the operative date, as may be specified in the agreement or instrument such clarifications and modifications of the effect of the provision of this Act under which the transfer is required on the property, rights and liabilities of the transferor as will best serve the proper discharge of the respective functions of the transferor and the transferee.

(2) Any such agreement or instrument shall provide so far as it is expedient—

(a) for the granting of leases and for the creation of other liabilities and rights over land whether amounting in law to interests in land or not, and whether involving the surrender of any existing interest or the creation of a new interest or not,

(b) for the granting of indemnities in connection with the severance of leases and other matters,

(c) for responsibility for registration of any matter in any description of statutory register.

3.—(1) The Education Assets Board may, in the case of any matter on which agreement is required to be reached under paragraph 2(1) above—

(a) if it appears to them that it is unlikely that such an agreement will be reached, or

(b) if such an agreement has not been reached within such period as may be prescribed by regulations,

give a direction determining that matter, and may include in the direction any provision which might have been included in an agreement under paragraph 2(1).

(2) A direction under sub-paragraph (1) above may be given before or after the operative date.

(3) Any property, rights or liabilities required by a direction under this paragraph to be transferred to the transferee shall be regarded as having been transferred to, and by virtue of this Act vested in, the transferee accordingly.

(4) The Board shall, before giving a direction under this paragraph, give the transferor and the transferee such opportunity as may be prescribed by regulations to make written representations.

4.—(1) The transferor or transferee, if dissatisfied with a determination under paragraph 3 above, may appeal to the Secretary of State.

(2) An appeal under this paragraph shall be made in accordance with regulations.

(3) The Secretary of State shall, before determining an appeal under this paragraph, give the appellant and the respondent such opportunity as may be prescribed by regulations to make written representations.

(4) On an appeal under this paragraph the Secretary of State may—

(a) allow or dismiss the appeal or vary the determination of the Board, and

(b) give a direction accordingly under paragraph 3 above.

5.—(1) Regulations may prescribe the procedure to be followed in making any determination under paragraphs 3 and 4 above.

(2) The regulations may in particular—

(a) provide for a time limit within which written representations and any supporting documents must be submitted,

(b) empower the determining authority to proceed to a determination taking into account only such written representations and supporting documents as were submitted within the time limit, and

(c) empower the determining authority to proceed to a determination, after giving the transferor and the transferee or, as the case may be, the appellant and the respondent written notice of their intention to do so, notwithstanding that no written representations were made within the time limit, if it appears to the determining authority that they have sufficient material before them to enable them to make a determination.

(3) In sub-paragraph (2) above the "determining authority" means the Board or the Secretary of State, as the case may be.

Documents of title

6.—(1) Where a transfer to which this Schedule applies relates to registered land, it shall be the duty of the transferor to execute any such instrument under the Land Registration Acts 1925 to 1986, to deliver any such certificate under those Acts and to do such other things under those Acts as he would be required to execute, deliver or do in the case of a transfer by agreement between the transferor and the transferee.

(2) Where on any transfer to which this Schedule applies the transferor is entitled to retain possession of any documents relating in part to the title to any land or other property transferred to the transferee, the transferor shall be treated as having given to the transferee an acknowledgment in writing of the right of the transferee to production of that document and to delivery of copies of it; and section 64 of the Law of Property Act 1925 shall have effect accordingly, and on the basis that the acknowledgment did not contain any such expression of contrary intention as is mentioned in that section.

Third parties affected by vesting provisions

7.—(1) Without prejudice to the generality of paragraphs 2 to 4 of Schedule 7 to this Act, any transaction effected between a transferor and a transferee in pursuance of paragraph 2(1) or of a direction under paragraph 3 above shall be binding on all other persons, and notwithstanding that it would, apart from this sub-paragraph, have required the consent or concurrence of any person other than the transferor and the transferee.

(2) If as a result of any such transaction any person's rights or liabilities become enforceable as to part by or against the transferor and as to part by or against the transferee, the Education Assets Board shall give that person written notification of that fact.

(3) If in consequence of a transfer to which this Schedule applies or of anything done in pursuance of the provisions of this Schedule—

(a) the rights or liabilities of any person other than the transferor or the transferee which were enforceable against or by the transferor become enforceable as to part against or by the transferor and as to part against or by the transferee, and

(b) the value of any property or interest of that person is thereby diminished,

such compensation as may be just shall be paid to that person by the transferor, the transferee or both.

(4) Any dispute as to whether and if so how much compensation is payable under sub-paragraph (3) above, or as to the person to whom it shall be paid, shall be referred to and determined by an arbitrator appointed by the Lord Chancellor.

(5) Where the transferor or the transferee under a transfer to which this Schedule applies purports by any conveyance or transfer to transfer to some person other than the transferor or the transferee for consideration any land or other property which before the operative date belonged to the transferor, or which is an interest in property which before that date belonged to the transferor, the conveyance or transfer shall be as effective as if both the transferor and the

transferee had been parties to it and had thereby conveyed or transferred all their interest in the property conveyed or transferred.

(6) A court shall have the power set out in sub-paragraph (7) below if at any stage in proceedings before it to which the transferor or transferee under a transfer to which this Schedule applies and a person other than the transferor or the transferee are parties it appears to it that the issues in the proceedings—

  (a) depend on the identification or definition of any of the property, rights or liabilities transferred which the transferor and the Education Assets Board have not yet effected, or

  (b) raise a question of construction on the relevant provisions of this Act which would not arise if the transferor and the transferee constituted a single person.

(7) In any such case the court may, if it thinks fit on the application of a party to the proceedings other than the transferor or the transferee, hear and determine the proceedings on the footing that such one of the transferor and the transferee as is a party to the proceedings represents and is answerable for the other of them, and that the transferor and the transferee constitute a single person.

(8) Any judgment or order given by a court in proceedings determined on that footing shall bind both the transferor and the transferee accordingly.

(9) It shall be the duty of the transferor and of the Education Assets Board to keep one another informed of any case where the transferor or the transferee under a transfer to which this Schedule applies may be prejudiced by sub-paragraph (5) above or any judgment or order given by virtue of sub-paragraph (8) above.

(10) If either the transferor or the transferee claims that he has been so prejudiced and that the other of them ought to indemnify or make a payment to him on that account and has unreasonably failed to meet that claim, he may refer the matter to the Secretary of State for determination by the Secretary of State.

Delivery of documents to transferee

8. When it appears to the Education Assets Board, in the case of any transfer, that any agreements and instruments required to be made or executed in pursuance of paragraph 2(1) above or in pursuance of a direction under paragraph 3 above have been made or executed, the Board shall deliver those agreements and instruments (if any) to the transferee.

DEFINITIONS
  "determining authority": para. 5(3).
  "interest in land": s.90(1).
  "land": s.90(1).
  "liability": s.90(1).
  "local authority": s.90(1).
  "modification": s.61(1).
  "operative date": ss.17 and 33(4).
  "person": Sched. 1 to the Interpretation Act 1978.
  "relevant institution": para. 4(a).
  "transferor authority": para. 1(4)(b).

GENERAL NOTE
  This Schedule makes supplementary provisions for the transfers of land, property, rights and liabilities from a local authority to a further education corporation or to an institution designated as part of the further education sector under s.28. These provisions of this Schedule are given effect by s.36(1) of this Act in relation to transfers under ss.23 and 32, and relate to the apportionment of property, rights and liabilities between institutions.
  This Schedule is modelled on Sched. 10 to the ERA 1988, which in turn was modelled on Sched. 4 to the Transport Act 1968, as amended for the Transport Act 1985, with some additions from the British Telecommunications Act 1981. The transfers under s.23 will be of grant-maintained schools and of further education colleges and sixth-form colleges maintained by a local education authority. The transfers under s.32 will principally be of voluntary-aided colleges.
  This Schedule comes into force on September 30, 1992: see Commencement No. 1 Order 1992, para. 2 and Sched. 2.

Para. 1
  This provides for the division of land, property, rights and liabilities which are shared

between more than one relevant institution (as defined in sub-para. (4)) or partly between the relevant institution and the transferor authority.

Education Assets Board. This is a body created under s.197 of the ERA 1988 to administer the transfer of property mainly in relation to the creation of higher education corporations under that Act (see further the note to s.36(5)).

Relevant institution. The definition in sub-para. (4) refers to further education corporations created under ss.15 or 16 and to institutions designated under s.28.

Para. 2

This requires the Education Assets Board (on behalf of transferee institutions) and the transferor authority to enter into written agreements (a) to allocate property rights and liabilities so as to enable the transferor and the transferees properly to discharge their respective functions, and (b) to provide, so far as is expedient, for the granting of leases and the creation of other rights and liabilities over land, any indemnities and any necessary statutory registration.

Para. 3

This paragraph, unlike para. 3 of Sched. 10 to the ERA 1988, empowers the Education Assets Board to give directions where agreement has not been reached or is unlikely to be reached, and these operate to transfer the relevant property, rights and liabilities to the transferee (sub-para. (3)). Before exercising this power, the Education Assets Board is required to afford the parties an opportunity to make written representations. (Under Sched. 10 to the ERA 1988, equivalent powers were granted to the Secretary of State).

Regulations. These may be made under para. 5. They must be made by way of statutory instrument and are subject to a negative resolution in Parliament (see s.89(1) and (3)).

Written representations. The requirement of affording an opportunity for written representations is preferred to that of consultation imposed by Sched. 10, para. 3(4) to the ERA 1988. In practice, very little difference will be involved, as both procedures involve giving a hearing, though the requirement here is that both parties are heard. On the requirements of a duty to hear representations, see *"Consult"* in the note to s.6(1).

Para. 4

This provides that a transferor or transferee dissatisfied with a determination by the Education Assets Board under para. 3 may appeal to the Secretary of State. Again, opportunity must be given for written representations on both sides.

Secretary of State. See note to s.1(2).

Para. 5

This enables regulations to be made governing the making of determinations under paras. 3 and 4, especially in relation to time limits.

Para. 6

This makes provision in relation to documents of title and conveyancing procedures.

Para. 7

This follows para. 9 of Sched. 10 to the ERA 1988. It establishes the position of third parties in relation to vesting provisions. Sub-paragraph (1) provides that they are bound by transactions under paras. 2 and 3: the Education Assets Board shall notify them where their rights or liabilities become enforceable, partly against or by the transferor and partly against or by the transferee (sub-para. (2)). Where transfers under this Schedule diminish the value of the property or interests of a third party, compensation is payable under sub-paras. (3) and (4). The title to property transferred to third parties is safeguarded by sub-para. (5). In certain circumstances specified in sub-para. (6) where the definition of property rights or liabilities transferred under this Act is in question, a third party may apply to a court under sub-para. (7), and it may make a determination binding on both the transferor and transferee (under sub-para. (8)). Sub-paragraph (9) provides for the transferor and the Education Assets Board to keep each other informed of where the transferor or transferee may be prejudiced by sub-para. (5) or under sub-para. (8). Sub-paragraph (10) enables the Secretary of State to settle disputes of either the transferor or transferee's claim to have been so prejudiced.

SCHEDULE 6

New Schedule 7A to the Education Reform Act 1988

"Schedule 7A

Instruments of government made by Privy Council

Name of corporation

1. The instrument shall empower the corporation to change their name with the consent of the Privy Council.

Membership

2. The instrument shall make provision for the membership of the corporation which meets all the requirements of paragraphs 3 to 5 below.

3.—(1) The corporation shall consist of—

(a) not less than 12 and not more than 24 members appointed in accordance with the following provisions; and

(b) the person who is for the time being the principal of the institution, unless he chooses not to be a member.

(2) Of the appointed members—

(a) up to 13 (referred to below in this Schedule as the "independent members") shall be persons appearing to the appointing authority to have experience of, and to have shown capacity in, industrial, commercial or employment matters or the practice of any profession;

(b) up to two may be teachers at the institution nominated by the academic board and up to two may be students at the institution nominated by the students at the institution; and

(c) at least one and not more than nine (referred to below in this Schedule as the "co-opted members") shall be persons nominated by the members of the corporation who are not co-opted members.

(3) The co-opted member required by sub-paragraph (2)(c) above shall be a person who has experience in the provision of education.

(4) A person (other than a person appointed in pursuance of sub-paragraph (2)(b) above) who is—

(a) employed at the institution (whether or not as a teacher);

(b) a full-time student at the institution; or

(c) an elected member of any local authority,

is not eligible for appointment as a member of the corporation otherwise than as a co-opted member.

(5) For the purposes of this paragraph, a person who is not for the time being enrolled as a student at the institution shall be treated as such a student during any period when he has been granted leave of absence from the institution for the purposes of study or travel or for carrying out the duties of any office held by him in the student union at the institution.

(6) It shall be for the appointing authority to determine any question as to whether any person is qualified in accordance with the preceding provisions of this paragraph for appointment as a member of the corporation of any description or category.

Numbers

4.—(1) The corporation shall make a determination with respect to their membership numbers.

(2) Such a determination shall fix the number of members of each variable category of which the corporation are to consist, subject to the limits applicable in relation to that category in accordance with paragraph 3 above.

(3) In making such a determination, the corporation shall secure that at least half of all the members of the corporation, when constituted in accordance with the determination, will be independent members.

(4) Such a determination shall not have effect so as to terminate the appointment of any person who is a member of the corporation at the time when it takes effect.

(5) Such a determination may be varied by a subsequent determination.

Appointments

5.—(1) Subject to section 124C of this Act, no appointment of members of the corporation may be made before the first determination of the corporation in accordance with paragraph 4 above takes effect.

(2) Subject to that section, the corporation are the appointing authority in relation to the appointment of any member of the corporation other than an independent member.

(3) Where an appointment of an additional independent member of the corporation falls to be made in consequence of a determination in accordance with paragraph 4 above, the appointing authority in relation to the appointment—

(a) shall be the corporation if the appointment is made within the period of three months beginning with the date of the determination; or

(b) if the appointment is not made within that period, shall be the current independent members of the corporation.

(4) Where a vacancy in the office of an independent member of the corporation arises on any existing independent member ceasing to hold office on the expiry of his term of office—

(a) his successor shall not be appointed more than six months before the expiry of that term; and

(b) the appointing authority in relation to the appointment of his successor—

(i) shall be the corporation if the appointment is made not less than three months before the expiry of that term; or

(ii) if the appointment is not so made, shall be the current independent members of the corporation.

(5) Where a vacancy in the office of an independent member of the corporation arises on the death of any such member or on any such member ceasing to hold office in accordance with the instrument, the appointing authority in relation to the appointment of his successor—

(a) shall be the corporation if the appointment is made within the period of three months beginning with the date of death or the date on which the office becomes vacant (as the case may be); or

(b) if the appointment is not made within that period, shall be the current independent members of the corporation.

(6) No appointment of an independent member of the corporation by the corporation in accordance with sub-paragraph (3)(a), (4)(b)(i) or (5)(a) above shall be made unless the appointment has been approved by the current independent members of the corporation.

(7) If the number of independent members of the corporation falls below the number needed in accordance with its articles of government for a quorum, the Secretary of State is the appointing authority in relation to the appointment of such number of independent members as is required for a quorum.

Tenure of office etc.

6. Subject to any other requirements of this Act, the instrument may provide for the eligibility of persons for membership of the corporation and shall provide for their period of office and the circumstances in which they are to cease to hold office.

Officers

7. The instrument shall provide for one or more officers to be chosen from among the members.

Committees

8. The instrument may provide for the corporation to establish committees and permit such committees to include persons who are not members of the corporation.

Allowances

9. The instrument may provide for the corporation to pay allowances to its members.

Seal of corporation

10. The instrument shall provide for the authentication of the application of the seal of the corporation.

Interpretation

11. References in this Schedule, in relation to a corporation, to a variable category of members are references to any category of members in relation to which the number applicable in accordance with paragraph 3 above is subject to variation."

Definitions
 "corporation": s.123(1) of the ERA 1988.

"institution": s.91(6).
"local authority": s.90(1).

GENERAL NOTE

This Schedule replaces Sched. 7 to the ERA 1988 in relation to higher education corporations when s.124A(4) of the ERA 1988 (as introduced by s.71(1) of this Act) comes into operation. In general, this Schedule is less prescriptive than its predecessor, in line with the Government's policy of allowing greater flexibility to individual institutions. This Schedule came into force on May 6, 1992: see Commencement No. 1 Order 1992, para. 2 and Sched. 1.

The principal differences from Sched. 7 to the ERA 1988 are as follows.

Para 1

This introduces a power for a higher education corporation to change its own name with the consent of the Privy Council, rather than this being the act of the Secretary of State. (A similar provision is introduced into Sched. 7 to the ERA 1988 by para. 59(a) of Sched. 8).

Para. 3(2)(b)

This provides that a corporation is no longer required to have any members as nominees from the categories of a local education authority, students, teachers, and general staff, as well as academic nominees. It merely provides for a maximum number for any teachers and students who may be appointed to the governing body. The category of "teachers" now is equivalent to the "academic nominees" under Sched. 7 to the ERA 1988, since they are nominated by the academic board, rather than by the body of teaching members of staff. Consequently, there are more persons in the co-opted category.

Para. 5(7)

This empowers the Secretary of State to appoint such independent members as are necessary to restore a quorum. For the reasons for this, see note to s.71(1) under *Validity of proceedings*.

Para. 6

This is much reduced in detail compared with paras. 8 and 9 of Sched. 7 to the ERA 1988 in respect of the tenure of office and eligibility for membership of the governing body.

Para. 7

This has much less detail and is broader in scope than para. 12 of Sched. 7 to the ERA 1988 on the chairman of the governors.

Paras. 8 and 9

These merely reword provisions on committees.

Para. 10

This is shorter than paras. 16 and 17 of Sched. 7 to the ERA 1988.

Two provisions of Sched. 7 to the ERA 1988 are now found in the body of this Act. Paragraph 18 (accounts) is now s.124B of the ERA 1988, introduced by s.71(1) of this Act. Paragraph 19 on efficiency studies is now covered by s.83 of this Act.

Section 87   SCHEDULE 7

TRANSFERS: SUPPLEMENTARY PROVISIONS

Proof of title by certificate

1. The Education Assets Board may issue a certificate stating that any property specified in the certificate, or any such interest in or right over any such property as may be so specified, or any right or liability so specified, was or was not transferred by virtue of this Act to any body corporate or persons so specified; and any such certificate shall be conclusive evidence for all purposes of that fact.

Construction of agreements

2.—(1) Where any rights or liabilities transferred by virtue of this Act are rights or liabilities under an agreement to which the transferor was a party immediately before the date on which the transfer took effect (referred to in this Schedule as the "transfer date"), the agreement shall, unless the context otherwise requires, have effect on and after the transfer date as if—

(a) the transferee had been a party to the agreement,
(b) for any reference (whether express or implied and, if express, however worded) to the transferor there were substituted, as respects anything falling to be done on or after the transfer date, a reference to the transferee,
(c) any reference (whether express or implied and, if express, however worded) to a specified officer of the transferor or a person employed by the transferor in a specified capacity were, as respects anything falling to be done on or after the transfer date, a reference to such person as the transferee may appoint or, in default of appointment, to an officer or employee of the transferee who corresponds as closely as possible to the person referred to in the agreement,
(d) where the agreement refers to property, rights or liabilities which fall to be apportioned or divided between the transferor and the transferee, the agreement constituted two separate agreements separately enforceable by and against the transferor and the transferee as regards the part of the property, rights or liabilities retained by the transferor or (as the case may be) the part vesting in the transferee, and not as regards the other part,

and paragraph (d) above shall apply in particular to the covenants, stipulations and conditions of any lease by or to the transferor.

(2) This paragraph applies to any agreement whether in writing or not and whether or not of such a nature that rights and liabilities under it could be assigned by the transferor.

3.—(1) Without prejudice to the generality of paragraph 2 above, the transferee under a transfer made by virtue of this Act and any other person shall, as from the transfer date, have the same rights, powers and remedies (and in particular the same rights and powers as to the taking or resisting of legal proceedings or the making or resisting of applications to any authority) for ascertaining, perfecting or enforcing any right or liability transferred to and vested in the transferee by virtue of this Act as he would have had if that right or liability had at all times been a right or liability of the transferee.

(2) Any legal proceedings or applications to any authority pending on the transfer date by or against the transferor, in so far as they relate to any property, right or liability transferred to the transferee by virtue of this Act, or to any agreement relating to any such property, right or liability, shall be continued by or against the transferee to the exclusion of the transferor.

4. The provisions of paragraphs 2 and 3 above shall have effect for the interpretation of agreements subject to the context, and shall not apply where the context otherwise requires.

DEFINITIONS
"Education Assets Board": s.197 of the ERA 1988.
"rights and liabilities": s.61(2).
"transfer date": para. 2(1).

GENERAL NOTE
This Schedule makes certain common provisions in relation to transfers made under this Act and is given effect by s.87. It follows closely Sched. 10, paras. 5 to 8 to the ERA 1988. The principal transfers covered by these provisions are those under ss.23, 25, 27, 32, and 36.

This Schedule comes into force on September 30, 1992: see Commencement No. 1 Order 1992, para. 2 and Sched. 2.

Para. 1
This provides that a certificate issued by the Education Assets Board will constitute conclusive evidence of title.
Education Assets Board. See note to s.36(5).

Paras. 2, 3 and 4
These relate to rights and liabilities under agreements which are transferred under this Act.
Paragraph 2 makes provision for the interpretation of agreements which are the subject of transfer between parties (usually a transfer from a local education authority to an institution within the further education sector). The transfer operates essentially as by way of assignment. The transferee is treated as a party to the agreement, and references to the transferor and officers of the transferor are to be interpreted as referring to the transferee and the nearest equivalent officer of the transferee. In the case of rights and liabilities which are apportioned, the transferee is to be party to the assigned aspects of the agreement, and the transferor remains party in respect of the others. Sub-paragraph (2) makes it clear that such transfers of rights and liabilities have effect, even if they were not assignable.
Paragraph 3 provides for the complete substitution of the transferee for the transferor in respect of all rights, powers and remedies under any transferred agreement, and that the transferee shall succeed to any legal proceedings or applications pending at the transfer date.

Transferor. In transfers under ss.23 and 24, the transferor is the local education authority. Under s.25, it is the governing body of a grant-maintained school. Under s.27, it is a further education corporation. Under ss.32 and 33, it is the former assisting authority defined in s.32(3).

Transfer date. In transfers under ss.23, 24, and 25, the transfer date is the operative date defined under s.17(2). Under s.27, it is the date mentioned in the order under s.27(1). In transfers under ss.32 and 33, the transfer date is the designation date defined in s.32(3) and is as stated in the designation order made by the Secretary of State under s.28(1).

Section 93

SCHEDULE 8

Minor and Consequential Amendments

Part I

Amendments of the Education Acts

The Education Act 1944 (c. 31)

1. The Education Act 1944 is amended as follows.
2. The duty imposed on local education authorities by section 7 (stages and purposes of statutory system of education) does not extend to matters in respect of which the higher education funding councils or the further education funding councils have a duty.
3. Section 8(3) is omitted.
4. In section 9(1) for "duties" there is substituted "functions".
5. In section 55 (provision of transport and other facilities)—
(a) for subsection (1) there is substituted—
   "(1) A local education authority shall make such arrangements for the provision of transport and otherwise as they consider necessary or as the Secretary of State may direct for the purpose of facilitating the attendance of persons receiving education—
   (a) at schools,
   (b) at any institution maintained or assisted by them which provides higher education or further education (or both),
   (c) at any institution within the further education sector, or
   (d) at any institution outside the further education sector and higher education sector, where a further education funding council has secured provision for those persons at the institution under section 4(3) or (5) of the Further and Higher Education Act 1992;
   and any transport provided in pursuance of such arrangements shall be provided free of charge."
(b) in subsection (2) for "pupil in attendance" there is substituted "person receiving education",
(c) in subsection (3) for "pupil", in each place, there is substituted "person",
(d) for subsection (4) there is substituted—
   "(4) Arrangements made by a local education authority under subsection (1) above shall make provision—
   (a) for pupils at grant-maintained schools which is no less favourable than the provision made in pursuance of the arrangements for pupils at schools maintained by a local education authority,
   (b) for persons receiving full-time education at any institution within the further education sector which is no less favourable than the provision made in pursuance of the arrangements for pupils of the same age at schools maintained by a local education authority, and
   (c) for persons receiving full-time education at institutions mentioned in subsection (1)(d) above which is no less favourable than the provision made in pursuance of the arrangements—
      (i) for persons of the same age with learning difficulties (within the meaning of section 41(9) of this Act) at schools maintained by a local education authority, or
      (ii) where there are no such arrangements, for such persons for whom the authority secures the provision of education at any other institution.", and
(e) after subsection (4) there is added—
   "(5) Regulations under section 8(5) of the Education Act 1980 may require publication, within the meaning of that section, by every local education authority of such information as may be required by the regulations with respect to the authority's policy and arrange-

ments for provision under this section for persons attending institutions mentioned in subsection (1)(c) or (d) above who are over compulsory school age and who have not attained the age of nineteen years."

6. At the end of section 56 (power to provide primary and secondary education otherwise than at school) (which becomes subsection (1)) there is added—

"(2) In this section "secondary education" includes any full-time education suitable to the requirements of persons over compulsory school age who have not attained the age of nineteen years and, for the purposes of the Education Acts 1944 to 1992—

(a) any such education, or education similar in other respects but less than full-time, provided in pursuance of this section is to be treated as secondary education; and

(b) any person for whom education is provided in pursuance of this section is to be treated as a pupil."

7. In section 62(1) (duties of Secretary of State and of local education authorities as to the training of teachers), after "grant-maintained schools" there is inserted "institutions within the further education sector".

8. Section 67(4A) (determination of disputes and questions—part-time senior education and post-school age education) is omitted.

9. Section 68 (power of Secretary of State to prevent unreasonable exercise of functions) shall apply in relation to a further education funding council or the governing body of an institution within the further education sector as it applies in relation to a local education authority or, as the case may be, the governors of a county or voluntary school.

10. Section 77 (inspection of educational establishments) shall cease to have effect in relation to any institution other than a school.

11. In section 81 (power of local education authorities to give assistance by means of scholarships and otherwise)—

(a) for "pupils" (where it first appears) there is substituted "persons", and

(b) in paragraph (c)—

(i) for "pupils" (where it first appears) there is substituted "persons", and

(ii) the words from "including" to the end are omitted.

12. In section 85(2) and (3) (power of local education authorities to accept gifts for educational purposes), the words "for providing primary or secondary education" are omitted.

13.—(1) Section 114 (interpretation) is amended as follows.

(2) In subsection (1)—

(a) in the definition of "further education", after "section 41 of this Act" there is added "as read with section 14 of the Further and Higher Education Act 1992",

(b) the definitions of "part-time senior education" and "post-school age education" are omitted,

(c) for the definition of "primary school" there is substituted—

" "Primary school" means, subject to regulations under section 1 of the Education Act 1964, a school for providing primary education, whether or not it also provides further education",

(d) for the definition of "pupil" there is substituted—

" "Pupil" has the meaning assigned to it by section 14(6) of the Further and Higher Education Act 1992",

(e) for the definition of "school" there is substituted—

" "School" has the meaning assigned to it by section 14(5) of the Further and Higher Education Act 1992",

(f) in the definition of "secondary education", for "eight of this Act" there is substituted "14 of the Further and Higher Education Act 1992", and

(g) for the definition of "secondary school" there is substituted—

" "Secondary school" means, subject to regulations under section 1 of the Education Act 1964, a school for providing secondary education, whether or not it also provides primary or further education."

(3) Subsections (1A), (1B) and (1C) are omitted.

(4) In subsection (2A)—

(a) for "PCFC funding sector" there is substituted "higher education sector other than a university", and

(b) after "any institution" there is inserted "within the further education sector or".

The Education Act 1946 (c. 50)

14. In the First Schedule to the Education Act 1946 (maintenance of voluntary schools) after paragraph 8 there is added—

"9. Paragraph 8 of this Schedule shall not apply in the case of an institution which is or has at any time been within the further education sector."

The Education (Miscellaneous Provisions) Act 1948 (c. 40)

15. Section 3(3) of the Education (Miscellaneous Provisions) Act 1948 (allocation between primary and secondary education of children between 10 and a half and 12 years old—definition of secondary education) is omitted.

16. In section 5(3) of that Act (amendment and consolidation of enactments as to provision of clothing) after paragraph (a) there is inserted—

"(aa) for persons who have not attained the age of 19 years and who are receiving education at an institution within the further education sector."

The Education Act 1980 (c. 20)

17. After section 22(3A) of the Education Act 1980 (school meals—England and Wales) there is inserted—

"(3B) Subsection (1) above applies in relation to persons, other than pupils, who receive education at a school maintained by a local education authority or a grant-maintained school, and in relation to the authority maintaining the school or the governing body of the grant-maintained school, as it applies in relation to pupils at a school maintained by a local education authority and the authority maintaining the school; and an authority or governing body must charge for anything so provided and must charge every such person the same price for the same quantity of the same item."

The Education Act 1981 (c. 60)

18. In section 14(2) of the Education Act 1981 (discontinuance of maintained special schools—notice) after paragraph (a) there is inserted—

"(aa) the appropriate further education funding council."

The Education (Fees and Awards) Act 1983 (c. 40)

19. In section 1(3) of the Education (Fees and Awards) Act 1983 (fees at universities and further education establishments)—

(a) for paragraph (b) there is substituted—

"(b) any institution within the higher education sector," and

(b) after paragraph (c) there is inserted—

"(ca) any institution within the further education sector."

The Further Education Act 1985 (c. 47)

20. At the end of section 1 of the Further Education Act 1985 (supply of goods and service through further education establishments) there is added—

"(4) In this Act "institution" does not include a school."

21.—(1) In section 2(2) of that Act (power of LEAs to lend money for those purposes) for paragraphs (a) to (d) there is substituted—

"(a) to a higher education corporation or further education corporation (within the meaning of the Further and Higher Education Act 1992);

(b) in the case of the following institutions—

(i) an institution within the higher education sector which is not conducted by a higher education corporation;

(ii) an institution within the further education sector which is not conducted by a further education corporation; or

(iii) an institution which provides higher education or further education and is assisted by a local education authority,

to the governing body of the institution or, if it is conducted by a company, to the company; or

(c) to a body corporate in which such a corporation or company as is mentioned in paragraph (a) or (b) above has a holding such as is mentioned in subsection (8) below."

(2) In subsection (8) of that section for "(2)(d)" there is substituted "(2)(c)".

The Education (No. 2) Act 1986 (c. 61)

22. In section 43 of the Education (No. 2) Act 1986 (freedom of speech in universities, etc.)—

(a) in subsection (5)—

(i) for paragraph (aa) there is substituted—

"(aa) any institution other than a university within the higher education sector,"

(ii) after paragraph (b) there is inserted—

"(ba) any institution within the further education sector," and

(iii) paragraph (c) is omitted, and
(b) in subsection (7) paragraph (b) and "or authorities maintaining or (as the case may be) assisting the establishment" are omitted.
23. In section 49(3) of that Act (appraisal of performance of teachers)—
(a) paragraphs (d) and (da) are omitted,
(b) after paragraph (da) there is inserted—
"(db) at any institution within the further education sector," and
(c) in paragraph (e) for "(da)" there is substituted "(db)".
24. In section 51 of that Act (recoupment)—
(a) in subsection (2)(b) the words from "made" to the end are omitted,
(b) subsections (5) and (6) are omitted,
(c) in subsection (8) for "(1) to (6)" there is substituted "(1) and (2)", and
(d) after subsection (12) there is added—
"(13) References in this section to a pupil, in relation to any school or other institution, include any person who receives education at the school or institution."
25. In section 52(1)(a) and (3) of that Act (recoupment: cross-border provisions) for "pupil", in each place, there is substituted "person".
26. In section 58 of that Act (travelling and subsistence allowances for governors of schools and establishments of further education)—
(a) subsections (3), (4) and (5)(a) are omitted, and
(b) in subsection (5)(ab) "and are not designated establishments of higher or further education" is omitted.

The Education Reform Act 1988 (c. 40)

27. The Education Reform Act 1988 is amended as follows.
28. In section 24(1)(b) (extension of certain provisions)—
(a) for the words from "a reference" to second "and" there is substituted "except in relation to a local education authority, a reference to",
(b) in sub-paragraph (ii) after "a university" there is inserted "or an institution within the higher education sector", and
(c) after that sub-paragraph there is added—
"and
(iii) any institution within the further education sector."
29. In section 100 (provision of benefits and services for pupils by local education authorities), after subsection (1) there is inserted—
"(1A) Where—
(a) a local education authority are under a duty, or have power, to provide any benefits or services for persons, other than pupils, receiving education at a school; and
(b) the duty is to be performed, or the power may be exercised, both in relation to such persons at schools maintained by a local education authority and in relation to such persons at grant-maintained schools;
the authority shall in performing the duty, or in exercising the power, treat such persons at grant-maintained schools no less favourably (whether as to the benefits or services provided or as to the terms on which they are provided) than such persons at schools maintained by a local education authority."
30. In section 120 (functions of local education authorities with respect to higher and further education)—
(a) subsection (2) is omitted,
(b) in subsection (3)(b) for "living outside their area" there is substituted "from other areas",
(c) in subsection (4)—
(i) for "universities, institutions within the PCFC funding sector" there is substituted "institutions within the higher education sector", and
(ii) after "sector" there is inserted "or the further education sector", and
(d) subsections (6), (7), (8), (9)(a)(ii) and (9)(b) are omitted.
31. In section 122 (orders incorporating higher education institutions maintained by local education authorities) subsections (2) to (5) are omitted.
32. In section 123 (provisions supplementary to sections 121 and 122)—
(a) at the end of subsection (1) there is added "or which has become a higher education corporation by virtue of section 122A of this Act", and
(b) for subsection (3) there is substituted—
"(3) Schedule 7 to this Act has effect with respect to each higher education corporation established before the appointed day (within the meaning of section 124A of this Act) unless an instrument of government for the corporation made under that section has effect.

(4) A higher education corporation established under section 122 of this Act on or after that day for the purpose of conducting any institution shall be established initially under the name given in the order under that section establishing the corporation."

33. In section 124 (powers of a higher education corporation)—

(a) in subsection (2)(b) for "disabled students" there is substituted "students having learning difficulties within the meaning of section 41(9) of the Education Act 1944", and

(b) subsection (4) is omitted.

34. In section 128 (dissolution of higher education corporations)—

(a) a subsection (1)(b)—

(i) for sub-paragraphs (iii) and (iv) there is substituted—

"(iii) a higher education funding council," and

(ii) after those sub-paragraphs there is inserted—

"(v) a further education funding council,"

(b) for subsection (4)(b) there is substituted—

"(b) the higher education funding council," and

(c) after subsection (5) there is added—

"(6) An order under this section may apply section 127 of this Act with such modifications as the Secretary of State may consider necessary or desirable."

35. Sections 131, 132 and 134 (Universities Funding Council and Polytechnics and Colleges Funding Council) are omitted.

36. In section 135 (inspection of accounts)—

(a) for subsection (1)(c) there is substituted—

"(c) any designated institution within the meaning of section 129A of this Act," and

(b) in subsection (2) for the words from "grants" to the end there is substituted "financial support has been given to them under section 65 of the Further and Higher Education Act 1992".

37. In section 136 (transfer to Polytechnics and Colleges Funding Council of property and staff of National Advisory Body for Public Sector Higher Education)—

(a) in subsection (2) for "Polytechnics and Colleges Funding Council" there is substituted "Higher Education Funding Council for England", and

(b) subsections (3) to (7) are omitted.

38. In section 137(2) (control of disposals of land) "or 129(3)" is omitted.

39. In section 157 (construction of instruments providing for institution ceasing to be maintained or assisted by local education authority)—

(a) in subsection (4)—

(i) the words "or assisted" in both places are omitted,

(ii) after "becomes" there is inserted "an institution within the further education sector", and

(iii) for "the PCFC funding sector" there is substituted "the higher education sector",

(b) subsection (5)(b) is omitted, and

(c) in subsection (6)—

(i) at the beginning of paragraph (b) there is inserted "an institution within the further education sector or", and

(ii) in that paragraph for "the PCFC funding sector" there is substituted "the higher education sector".

40. In section 158(2) (reports and returns) paragraphs (a)(i) and (iii) and (b) are omitted.

41. Section 159(2)(b) (information with respect to educational provision in institutions providing further or higher education—designated assisted institutions) is omitted.

42. In section 161 (interpretation of Part II) subsection (1)(c) is omitted.

43. In section 197 (Education Assets Board)—

(a) in subsection (4) after "this Act" there is inserted "and section 36 of and Schedule 5 to the Further and Higher Education Act 1992",

(b) in subsection (6) for "this Act" there is substituted "the Education Acts 1944 to 1992", and

(c) after subsection (7) there is inserted—

"(7A) A local education authority shall give the Board, within such reasonable time as the Board may specify, such information as the Board may require for the purposes of the exercise of any of their functions under the Further and Higher Education Act 1992 or under section 126 or 130 of this Act.

(7B) The governing body of any institution within the further education sector or the higher education sector shall give the Board, within such reasonable time as the Board may specify, such information as the Board may require for the purpose of the exercise of any of their functions under the Education Acts 1944 to 1992."

44. In section 198(5) (transfers under Parts I and II) for "the Polytechnics and Colleges Funding Council" there is substituted "the higher education funding council".

45. In section 205 (procedure for exercise of University Commissioners' powers)—
(a) for subsection (2)(d) there is substituted—
   "(d) the higher education funding council," and
(b) subsection (6) is omitted.
46. In section 210 (grants for the education of travellers and displaced persons), after "local education authorities" (in subsections (1) and (3)(d)) there is inserted "or institutions within the further education sector".
47. In section 211 (grants in respect of special provision for immigrants)—
(a) after paragraph (b) there is inserted—
   "(ba) the governing body of an institution within the further education sector," and
(b) paragraph (c) is omitted.
48. In section 214(2)(a) (unrecognised degrees) after "Royal Charter or" there is inserted "by or under".
49. In section 218 (school and further and higher education regulations)—
(a) in subsection (1)(f) for "pupils" there is substituted "persons receiving education",
(b) in subsection (7)(b) for "pupils attending" there is substituted "persons receiving education at",
(c) in subsection (10)—
      (i) after paragraph (a) there is inserted—
   "(aa) it is within the further education sector," and
      (ii) paragraph (b) is omitted, and
(d) in subsection (11) for "the PCFC funding sector" there is substituted "the higher education sector in receipt of financial support under section 65 of the Further and Higher Education Act 1992".
50. In section 219 (powers of Secretary of State in relation to certain educational institutions) subsections (1)(b), (2)(d) and (e) and (3)(c)(ii) are omitted.
51.—(1) Section 220 (extension of functions of Audit Commission) is amended as follows.
(2) In subsection (1)—
(a) for "the Polytechnics and Colleges Funding Council, a higher education corporation" there is substituted—
   "(a) a higher education funding council or the governing body of an institution within the higher education sector,"
(b) for "the governing body" there is substituted—
   "(b) a further education funding council or the governing body of an institution within the further education sector, or
   (c) the governing body."
(3) In subsection (2)—
(a) for paragraphs (a) and (b) there is substituted—
   "(a) with respect to studies relating to a higher education funding council, the council;
   (b) with respect to studies relating to the governing body of an institution within the higher education sector, the higher education funding council or the governing body," and
(b) after those paragraphs there is inserted—
   "(ba) with respect to studies relating to a further education funding council, the council;
   (bb) with respect to studies relating to the governing body of an institution within the further education sector, the appropriate further education funding council or the governing body."
(4) For subsection (3) there is substituted—
   "(3) The Commission may, at the request of a higher education funding council or a further education funding council, give the council advice in connection with the discharge of the council's functions under section 124B(2)(b) or paragraph 18(2)(b) of Schedule 7 to this Act.
(5) In subsection (4) after "a higher education corporation" there is inserted "a further education corporation".
52. In section 221 (avoidance of certain contractual terms) subsection (1)(c) and, in subsection (3), the definition of "relevant institution" are omitted.
53. In section 222 (application of employment law during financial delegation) subsection (2)(b) and, in subsection (3)(c), "or institutions required to be covered by schemes under section 139 of this Act" are omitted.
54. In section 227 (application to Wales) subsections (2) to (4) are omitted.
55. In section 230 (stamp duty)—
(a) in subsection (1) "section 136(2)" is omitted, and
(b) in subsection (3)—
      (i) for paragraph (b) there is substituted—
   "(b) an institution within the higher education sector,"

(ii) paragraph (c)(ii) is omitted, and

(iii) after paragraph (c) there is inserted—

"(ca) an institution within the further education sector."

56. In section 232 (orders and regulations)—

(a) in subsection (2) "140(1), 141(6), 145(6), 151(4), 156(10)" is omitted,

(b) in subsection (3) "or 227" is omitted, and

(c) in subsection (4)(b) "227" is omitted.

57. In section 234 (meaning of "assisted" for the purposes of the 1944 Act and Acts construed as one with it)—

(a) in subsection (1) for "the PCFC funding sector" there is substituted "the higher education sector other than a university", and

(b) subsection (2)(b) is omitted.

58. In section 235 (general interpretation) subsection (2)(a) and (h) are omitted.

59. In Schedule 7 (Higher Education Corporations)—

(a) for paragraph 1(4) there is substituted—

"(4) A corporation may change their name with the consent of the Privy Council.",

(b) in paragraph 18—

(i) in sub-paragraph (2)(b) for "the Polytechnics and Colleges Funding Council" there is substituted "the higher education funding council", and

(ii) for sub-paragraph (5) there is substituted—

"(5) No person shall be qualified to be appointed auditor under that sub-paragraph except—

(a) an individual, or firm, eligible for appointment as a company auditor under section 25 of the Companies Act 1989;

(b) a member of the Chartered Institute of Public Finance and Accountancy; or

(c) a firm each of the members of which is a member of that institute.", and

(c) paragraph 19 is omitted.

60. Schedule 8 (the funding councils and the assets board) shall cease to have effect so far as it relates to the Universities Funding Council and the Polytechnics and Colleges Funding Council.

61. Paragraphs 62 to 64 below shall have effect, in place of paragraph 3 of Schedule 10 (supplementary provisions with respect to transfers) in the case of any transfer by virtue of section 126 or 130 and in such a case references to that paragraph of Schedule 10 shall be construed as references to paragraphs 62 to 64 below.

62.—(1) The Education Assets Board may, in the case of any matter on which agreement is required to be reached under paragraph 2(1) of that Schedule—

(a) if it appears to them that it is unlikely that such an agreement will be reached, or

(b) if such an agreement has not been reached within such period as may be prescribed by regulations,

give a direction determining that matter, and may include in the direction any provision which might have been included in an agreement under that paragraph.

(2) A direction under sub-paragraph (1) above may be given before or after the transfer date.

(3) Any property, rights or liabilities required by a direction under this paragraph to be transferred to the transferee shall be regarded as having been transferred to, and by virtue of this Act vested in, the transferee accordingly.

(4) The Board shall, before giving a direction under this paragraph, give the transferor and the transferee such opportunity as may be prescribed by regulations to make representations.

63.—(1) The transferor or transferee, if dissatisfied with a determination under paragraph 62 above, may appeal to the Secretary of State.

(2) An appeal under this paragraph shall be made in accordance with regulations.

(3) The Secretary of State shall, before determining an appeal under this paragraph, give the appellant and the respondent such opportunity as may be prescribed by regulations to make representations.

(4) On an appeal under this paragraph the Secretary of State may—

(a) allow or dismiss the appeal or vary the determination of the Board, and

(b) give a direction accordingly under paragraph 62 above.

64.—(1) Regulations may prescribe the procedure to be followed in making any determination under paragraphs 62 and 63 above.

(2) The regulations may in particular—

(a) provide for a time limit within which representations and any supporting documents must be submitted,

(b) empower the determining authority to proceed to a determination taking into account only such written representations and supporting documents as were submitted within the time limit, and

(c) empower the determining authority to proceed to a determination, after giving the transferor and the transferee or, as the case may be, the appellant and the respondent written notice of their intention to do so, notwithstanding that no written representations were made within the time limit, if it appears to the determining authority that they have sufficient material before them to enable them to make a determination.

(3) In sub-paragraph (2) above the "determining authority" means the Board or the Secretary of State, as the case may be.

(4) In this paragraph and paragraphs 62 and 63 above "regulations" means regulations made by the Secretary of State.

65. In paragraph 4 of that Schedule at the beginning there is inserted—

"(1) Where a transfer by virtue of section 126 or 130 relates to registered land, it shall be the duty of the transferor to execute any such instrument under the Land Registration Acts 1925 to 1986, to deliver any such certificate under those Acts and to do such other things under those Acts as he would be required to execute, deliver or do in the case of a transfer by agreement between the transferor and the transferee.

(2)".

66. In Schedule 12 (minor and consequential amendments) paragraphs 68, 69(2), 70, 100(2) and 101(4) are omitted.

The Education (Student Loans) Act 1990 (c. 6)

67. In section 1(3)(a) of the Education (Student Loans) Act 1990 (loans for students)—
(a) for "131 or 132 of the Education Reform Act 1988" there is substituted "65 of the Further and Higher Education Act 1992", and
(b) for the words from "institutions designated" to "local education authorities" there is substituted "institutions receiving recurrent grants towards their costs from a further education funding council".

PART II

AMENDMENTS OF OTHER ACTS

The Public Records Act 1958 (c. 51)

68. In Schedule 1 to the Public Records Act 1958 (definition of public records), in Part II of the Table at the end of paragraph 3 (organisations whose records are public records) there is inserted in the appropriate place—

"Further Education Funding Council for England.
Further Education Funding Council for Wales.
Higher Education Funding Council for England.
Higher Education Funding Council for Wales."

The Charities Act 1960 (c. 58)

69.—(1) A further education corporation shall be an exempt charity for the purposes of the Charities Act 1960.

(2) Paragraph (e) of Schedule 2 to that Act (institutions connected with institutions which are exempt charities for the purposes of that Act by virtue of the preceding provisions of that Schedule) shall apply in relation to an institution conducted by a further education corporation as it applies in relation to an institution included in that Schedule above that paragraph.

The Veterinary Surgeons Act 1966 (c. 36)

70. In Schedule 3 to the Veterinary Surgeons Act 1966 (exemptions from restrictions on practice of veterinary surgery), in the definition of "recognised institution" after paragraph (a)(i) there is inserted—

"(iA) an institution within the further education sector within the meaning of section 91(3) of the Further and Higher Education Act 1992."

The Local Authorities (Goods and Services) Act 1970 (c. 39)

71.—(1) Subject to sub-paragraph (2) below, in the Local Authorities (Goods and Services) Act 1970 (supply of goods and services by local authorities to public bodies) "public body" shall include any institution within the further education sector or the higher education sector.

(2) The provisions of sub-paragraph (1) above shall have effect as if made by an order under section 1(5) of that Act (power to provide that a person or description of persons shall be a public body for the purposes of that Act).

(3) An order under that section may accordingly vary or revoke the provisions of sub-paragraph (1) above as they apply to an institution within the further education sector or the higher education sector specified in the order.

The Chronically Sick and Disabled Persons Act 1970 (c. 44)

72. In section 8(2) of the Chronically Sick and Disabled Persons Act 1970 (access to, and facilities at, university and school buildings)—
(a) for paragraph (aa) there is substituted—
"(aa) institutions within the higher education sector within the meaning of section 91(5) of the Further and Higher Education Act 1992," and
(b) after paragraph (b) there is inserted—
"(ba) institutions within the further education sector within the meaning of section 91(3) of the Further and Higher Education Act 1992."

The Superannuation Act 1972 (c. 11)

73. In Schedule 1 to the Superannuation Act 1972 the entries relating to the Universities Funding Council and the Polytechnics and Colleges Funding Council are omitted.

The House of Commons Disqualification Act 1975 (c. 24)

74. In Part III of Schedule 1 to the House of Commons Disqualification Act 1975 the entries relating to the Polytechnics and Colleges Funding Council and the Universities Funding Council are omitted.

The Sex Discrimination Act 1975 (c. 65)

75. The Sex Discrimination Act 1975 is amended as follows.
76.—(1) The Table in section 22 (discrimination by bodies in charge of educational establishments) is amended as follows.
(2) After paragraph 3A there is inserted—

"3B. Institution within the further education sector (within the meaning of section 91(3) of the Further and Higher Education Act 1992).	Governing body."

(3) For paragraph 4A there is substituted—

"4A. Institution, other than a university, within the higher education sector (within the meaning of section 91(5) of the Further and Higher Education Act 1992).	Governing body."

(4) In paragraph 5 for "to 4" there is substituted "to 4A."
77. After that section there is inserted—

"Meaning of pupil in section 22
22A. For the purposes of section 22, "pupil" includes, in England and Wales, any person who receives education at a school or institution to which that section applies."
78. After section 23 (other discrimination by local education authorities) there is inserted—

"Discrimination by Further Education and Higher Education Funding Councils
23A. It is unlawful for the Further Education Funding Council for England, the Further Education Funding Council for Wales, the Higher Education Funding Council for England or the Higher Education Funding Council for Wales in carrying out their functions under the Education Acts 1944 to 1992, to do any act which constitutes sex discrimination."
79.—(1) In section 25(6) (general duty in public sector of education)—
(a) in paragraph (c)(i), for "4A" there is substituted "3B", and
(b) after paragraph (c) there is added—
"(d) the Further Education Funding Council for England and the Further Education Funding Council for Wales."
(2) In relation to a further education corporation or a Further Education Funding Council the reference in section 25(2) to section 99 of the Education Act 1944 is to be read as a reference to section 57(3) of the Further and Higher Education Act 1992.
80. After section 26(3) (exception for single-sex establishments) there is added—
"(4) In this section, as it applies to an establishment in England and Wales, "pupil" includes any person who receives education at that establishment."

81. After section 27(5) (exception for single-sex establishments turning co-educational) there is added—

"(6) In this section, as it applies to an establishment in England and Wales, "pupil" includes any person who receives education at that establishment."

82. In section 82(1) (general interpretation provisions) in the definition of "further education", for "section 41(2)(a) of the Education Act 1944" there is substituted "section 41(3) of the Education Act 1944 as read with section 14 of the Further and Higher Education Act 1992".

83. For paragraph 4 of Schedule 2 (transitional exemption orders for education admissions) there is substituted—

"4. Regulations under section 218 of the Education Reform Act 1988 may provide for the submission to the Secretary of State of an application for the making by him of a transitional exemption order in relation to any school or institution to which that section, or any part of that section, applies and which does not fall within paragraph 3 above, and for the making by him of the order."

The Race Relations Act 1976 (c. 74)

84. The Race Relations Act 1976 is amended as follows.

85.—(1) The Table in section 17 (discrimination by bodies in charge of educational establishments) is amended as follows.

(2) After paragraph 3A there is inserted—

"3B. Institution within the further education sector (within the meaning of section 91(3) of the Further and Higher Education Act 1992).	Governing body."

(3) For paragraph 4A there is substituted—

"4A. Institution, other than a university, within the higher education sector (within the meaning of section 91(5) of the Further and Higher Education Act 1992).	Governing body."

(4) In paragraph 5 for "to 4" there is substituted "to 4A".

86. After that section there is inserted—

"Meaning of pupil in section 17

17A. For the purposes of section 17, "pupil" includes in England and Wales, any person who receives education at a school or institution to which that section applies".

87. After section 18 (other discrimination by local education authorities) there is inserted—

"Discrimination by Further Education and Higher Education Funding Councils

18A. It is unlawful for the Further Education Funding Council for England, the Further Education Funding Council for Wales, the Higher Education Funding Council for England or the Higher Education Funding Council for Wales in carrying out their functions under the Education Acts 1944 to 1992, to do any act which constitutes racial discrimination."

88.—(1) In section 19(6) (general duty in public sector of education)—

(a) in paragraph (c)(i), for "4A" there is substituted "3B", and

(b) after paragraph (c) there is added—

"(d) the Further Education Funding Council for England and the Further Education Funding Council for Wales."

(2) In relation to a further education corporation or a Further Education Funding Council the reference in section 19(2) to section 99 of the Education Act 1944 is to be read as a reference to section 57(3) of the Further and Higher Education Act 1992.

The Employment Protection (Consolidation) Act 1978 (c. 44)

89. In section 29(1) of the Employment Protection (Consolidation) Act 1978 (persons holding certain offices to be allowed time off for public duties), in paragraph (ef) after "governing body of a" there is inserted "further education corporation or".

The Public Passenger Vehicles Act 1981 (c. 14)

90. In section 46(3) of the Public Passenger Vehicles Act 1981 (fare-paying passengers on

school buses) in the definition of "free school transport" for "pupils" there is substituted "persons".

The Disabled Persons (Services, Consultation and Representation) Act 1986 (c. 33)

91.—(1) Section 5 of the Disabled Persons (Services, Consultation and Representation) Act 1986 disabled persons leaving special education) is amended as follows.

(2) for subsections (3) and (4) there is substituted—

"(3) In the following provisions of this section and in section 6 a person in respect of whom the appropriate officer has given his opinion that he is a disabled person is referred to as a "disabled student".

(3A) The responsible authority shall give to the appropriate officer written notification for the purposes of subsection (5) of the date on which any disabled student will cease to be of compulsory school age, and the notification shall state—

    (a) his name and address; and

    (b) whether or not he intends to remain in full-time education and, if he does, the name of the school or other institution at which the education will be received;

and shall be given not earlier than twelve months, nor later than eight months, before that date.

(3B) Where, in the case of a disabled student over compulsory school age who is receiving relevant full-time education, that is—

    (a) full-time education at a school; or

    (b) full-time further or higher education at an institution other than a school;

it appears to the responsible authority that the student will cease to receive relevant full-time education on a date ("the leaving date") on which he will be under the age of 19 years and eight months, the responsible authority shall give written notification for the purposes of subsection (5) to the appropriate officer.

(3C) That notification shall state—

    (a) his name and address; and

    (b) the leaving date;

and shall be given not earlier than 12 months, nor later than eight months, before the leaving date.

(4) If at any time it appears to the responsible authority—

    (a) that a disabled student has ceased to receive relevant full-time education or will cease to do so on a date less than eight months after that time, and

    (b) that no notification has been given under subsection (3B), but

    (c) that, had the responsible authority for the time being been aware of his intentions eight months or more before that date, they would have been required to give notification under that subsection with respect to him,

that authority shall, as soon as is reasonably practicable, give written notification for the purposes of subsection (5) to the appropriate officer of his name and address and of the date on which he ceased to receive, or will cease to receive, that education."

(3) In subsection (5)—

(a) for "any person under subsection (3)" there is substituted "a student under subsection (3A) that he does not intend to remain in full-time education or under subsection (3B)", and

(b) for "notification under subsection (3)" there is substituted "notification under subsection (3A) or (3B)".

(4) In subsection (6)—

(a) for "(3)" in both places there is substituted "(3A) that he does not intend to remain in full-time education or under subsection (3B)", and

(b) for the words from "a local education authority" to "establishment of further or higher education" there is substituted "the responsible authority that the person will be receiving relevant full-time education".

(5) In subsection (9) (interpretation)—

(a) in the definition of "child" after "school or" there is inserted "as a student at",

(b) in the definition of "the responsible authority" for paragraph (b) there is substituted—

    "(b) in relation to a person receiving full-time further education or higher education at an institution within the further education sector or the higher education sector, means the governing body of the institution; and

    (c) in relation to a person for whom a further education funding council has secured full-time further education at an institution (other than a school) outside the further education sector or the higher education sector, the council,"

(c) after "the Education Act 1944" there is inserted "or the Further and Higher Education Act 1922", and

(d) for "that Act" there is substituted "those Acts".

92. For section 6(1) of that Act (review of expected leaving dates from full-time education of disabled persons) there is substituted—

"6.—(1) The responsible authority shall for the purposes of section 5 above keep under review the date when any disabled student is expected to cease to receive relevant full-time education."

The Employment Act 1989 (c. 38)

93. In section 5(6) of the Employment Act 1989 (exemption for discrimination in connection with certain education appointments)—
(a) after paragraph (b) there is inserted—
"(ba) any institution designated by order under section 28 of the Further and Higher Education Act 1992," and
(b) for paragraph (c) there is substituted—
"(c) any institution designated by order made or having effect as if made under section 129 of the Education Reform Act 1988."

The Town and Country Planning Act 1990 (c. 8)

94. In section 76(1) of the Town and Country Planning Act 1990 (duty to draw attention to certain provisions for benefit of disabled)—
(a) in paragraph (d) for "the PCFC funding sector" there is substituted "the higher education sector within the meaning of section 91(5) of the Further and Higher Education Act 1992", and
(b) after paragraph (e) there is inserted—
"(f) of a building intended for the purposes of an institution within the further education sector within the meaning of section 91(3) of the Further and Higher Education Act 1992."

The Environmental Protection Act 1990 (c. 43)

95. In section 98(2) of the Environmental Protection Act 1990 (definitions)—
(a) paragraph (a) is omitted,
(b) for paragraph (d) there is substituted—
"(d) any institution within the higher education sector within the meaning of section 91(5) of the Further and Higher Education Act 1992," and
(c) after paragraph (d) there is inserted—
"(da) any institution within the further education sector within the meaning of section 91(3) of the Further and Higher Education Act 1992."

DEFINITIONS
"further education": s.14(1)–(4).
"higher education": s.90(1); s.120(1) of and Sched. 6 to the ERA 1988.
"pupil": s.14(6).
"school": s.14(5).

GENERAL NOTE
This Schedule mainly makes consequential changes to existing Acts of Parliament. In Pt. I, amendments are made to the Education Acts as defined in s.90(1). In Pt. II, changes are made to other legislation.

The various paragraphs of this Schedule have different commencement dates as provided by the Commencement No. 1 Order 1992. Under para. 2 and Sched. 1 of that Order, the following paragraphs came into force on May 6, 1992: paras. 1, 9, 13(1) and 2(a) (but only in relation to references to "further education" in provisions of the Act as they are brought into force), 18, 27, 31, 32(b), 34, 36(a), 37(b), 38, 43, 48, 50 (only insofar as it relates to s.219(2)(e) of the ERA 1988), 51, 54, 56(b) and (c), 59, 61 to 65, 68, 75, 76, 78, 79, 84, 85, 87, 88 and 93(b). Under para. 2 and Sched. 2 of that Order, the following provisions come into force on September 30, 1992: paras. 21, 69 and 89. Under para. 2 and Sched. 3 of that Order, the following provisions come into force on April 1, 1993: paras. 2, 3, 4, 5, 6, 7, 8, 11, 12, 13 (so far as not already in force and with the exception of sub-para. 2(d)), 14, 15, 16, 19, 20, 22, 23, 24 (which is not retrospective in relation to sub-para. (a)), 25, 26, 28, 30, 32(a), 33, 35, 36(b), 37(a), 39, 40, 41, 42, 44, 45, 46, 47, 49, 50 (so far as not already in force), 52, 53, 55, 56(a), 57, 58, 60, 66, 67, 70, 71, 72, 73, 74, 81, 82, 83, 90, 91, 92, 93(a), 94 and 95.
Among noteworthy amendments in Pt. I are the following.

Para. 5

A duty is laid on local education authorities to provide transport to facilitate attendance not only at institutions which they maintain or assist, but also at any institution within the further education sector or an institution to which a person with learning difficulties is to be sent under s.4(3) or (5) of this Act.

Para. 9

This continues the power of the Secretary of State to intervene under s.68 of the EA 1944 in the case of unreasonable exercise of functions by an FEFC or an institution within the further education sector. By virtue of para. 50, the Secretary of State has no comparable power in the higher education sector.

Para. 10

This comes into force on September 1, 1992, in relation to institutions within the PCFC funding sector, and otherwise on April 1, 1993 (though these commencement provisions do not relate to Wales): see Commencement No. 1 Order 1992, para. 3.

Para. 13

This revises a number of definitions in the main EA 1944, which are used in other Acts. One revision is that primary and secondary education are no longer rigidly demarcated in consequence of amendments made in para. 15.

Para. 29

This amends s.100 of the ERA 1988 to ensure equal treatment by local education authorities between students other than pupils (*i.e.* further education students) in schools which they maintain and those in grant-maintained schools.

Para. 32

This ensures that Sched. 7 to the ERA 1988 continues to apply to higher education corporations until an instrument of government under s.124A of the ERA 1988 (as introduced by s.71(1) of this Act) is in place.

Para. 50

This removes the power of the Secretary of State to intervene under s.68 of the EA 1944 in the case of unreasonable exercise of functions by a higher education corporation by amending s.219 of the ERA 1988.

Para. 51

This extends the powers of the Audit Commission under s.220 of the ERA 1988 to both the further education sector and the higher education sector, including universities, and enables both institutions and funding councils to request that the Audit Commission conduct studies designed to improve the economy, efficiency and effectiveness of their management or operations. This is additional to the powers of the funding councils to conduct such studies in relation to individual institutions in their sector under s.83.

Para. 59

This amends Sched. 7 to the ERA 1988 to empower higher education corporations to change their own name with the consent of the Privy Council, rather than that of the Secretary of State. This relates to the change of name of such institutions to "university" under s.77 of this Act.

Paras. 61–65

These paragraphs make changes to the powers and procedures of the Education Assets Board. In brief, they provide that the Education Assets Board may issue directions of its own initiative in relation to transfers under this Act (para. 62), and that these are susceptible to appeal to the Secretary of State under para. 63. Previously, under Sched. 10, para. 3 to the ERA 1988, the decision was taken by the Secretary of State after notification of lack of agreement by the Education Assets Board.

Although these paragraphs came into force on May 6, 1992, they have no application to matters notified to the Secretary of State by the Education Assets Board prior to that date.

Para. 69

This provides that a further education corporation will be an exempt charity, a status which a higher education corporation enjoys by virtue of the ERA 1988. See further note to s.88.

Paras. 91 and 92

These paragraphs make amendments in connection with notifications necessary when a disabled student is over compulsory school age.

Section 93   SCHEDULE 9

REPEALS

Chapter	Short title	Extent of repeal
1944 c. 31.	The Education Act 1944.	Section 8(3). Section 67(4A). In section 85(2) and (3) "for providing primary or secondary education". In section 114(1), the definitions of "part-time senior education" and "post-school age education". Section 114(1A), (1B) and (1C).
1948 c. 40.	The Education (Miscellaneous Provisions) Act 1948.	Section 3(3).
1972 c. 11.	The Superannuation Act 1972.	In Schedule 1 the entries relating to the Universities Funding Council and the Polytechnics and Colleges Funding Council.
1975 c. 24.	The House of Commons Disqualification Act 1975.	In Part III of Schedule 1 the entries relating to the Polytechnics and Colleges Funding Council and the Universities Funding Council.
1986 c. 61.	The Education (No. 2) Act 1986.	Section 43(5)(c) and, in subsection (7), paragraph (b) and "or authorities maintaining or (as the case may be) assisting the establishment". Section 49(3)(d) and (da). In section 51, in subsection (2)(b) the words from "made" to the end and subsections (5) and (6). Section 58(3), (4) and (5)(a) and in subsection (5)(ab) "and are not designated establishments of higher or further education".
1988 c. 40.	The Education Reform Act 1988.	In section 105(2)(b) "but not the age of nineteen years". Section 120(2), (6), (7), (8), (9)(a)(ii) and (9)(b). Section 122(2) to (5). Section 124(4). Section 129(3) and (4). Sections 131 and 132. Section 134. Section 136(3) to (7). In section 137(2) "or 129(3)". Chapter III or Part II. Section 156. In section 157 the words "or assisted" in both places in subsection (4) and subsection (5)(b). Section 158(2)(a)(i) and (iii) and (b). Section 159(2)(b). Section 161(1)(c). Section 205(6). Section 211(c). Section 218(10)(b).

Chapter	Short title	Extent of repeal
		Section 219(1)(b), (2)(d) and (e) and (3)(c)(ii).
		In section 221, subsection (1)(c) and, in sub-section (3), the definition of "relevant institution".
		In section 222, subsection (2)(b) and, in subsection (3)(c), "or institutions required to be covered by schemes under section 139 of this Act".
		Section 227(2) to (4).
		In section 230, in subsection (1) "section 136(2)" and subsection (3)(c)(ii).
		In section 232, in subsection (2) "140(1), 141(6), 145(6), 151(4), 156(10)", in sub-section (3) "or 227" and in subsection (4)(b) "227".
		Section 234(2)(b).
		Section 235(2)(a) and (h).
		Paragraph 19 of Schedule 7.
		Paragraphs 68, 69(2), 70, 100(2) and 101(4) of Schedule 12.
1990 c. 43.	The Environmental Protection Act 1990.	Section 98(2)(a).

GENERAL NOTE

The provisions concerning the commencement dates for these repeals are set out in the Commencement No. 1 Order 1992, para. 2 and Scheds. 1 and 3 (and the appendix thereto). The respective commencement dates are May 6, 1992, for provisions listed in Sched. 1 and April 1, 1993, for those listed in the appendix to Sched. 3 of that Order.

INDEX

References are to sections and schedules

LOCAL GOVERNMENT FINANCE ACT 1992*

(1992 c. 14)

ARRANGEMENT OF SECTIONS

PART I

COUNCIL TAX: ENGLAND AND WALES

CHAPTER I

MAIN PROVISIONS

Preliminary

CHAPTER II

VALUATION LISTS

Preliminary

*Annotations by Colin Crawford, Senior Lecturer, Faculty of Law, University of Birmingham.

An Act to provide for certain local authorities to levy and collect a new tax, to be called council tax; to abolish community charges; to make further provision with respect to local government finance (including provision with respect to certain grants by local authorities); and for connected purposes.   [6th March 1992]

PARLIAMENTARY DEBATES
Hansard, H.C. Vol. 198, cols. 783, 917, 1005; Vol. 201, cols. 22, 155; Vol. 203, col. 136; Vol. 205, cols. 324, 345; H.L. Vol. 533, col. 1574; Vol. 534, cols. 479, 730, 954, 975, 1017, 1060, 1170, 1258, 1428, 1497; Vol. 535, cols. 159, 731, 992, 1057, 1093, 1117, 1368; Vol. 536, col. 368.
The Bill was discussed in Standing Committee A from November 19 to December 18, 1991.

ABBREVIATIONS
"the 1987 Act": the Abolition of Domestic Rates Etc. (Scotland) Act 1987
"the 1988 Act": the Local Government Finance Act 1988

INTRODUCTORY NOTE
This Act will bring into effect another system of local government finance, to replace that established by the 1987 Act in Scotland and the 1988 Act for England and Wales.

Those Acts had radically altered the system of local taxation, by abolishing the rating system as it then applied to domestic property, and amending it in regard to non-domestic property. The existing system was replaced by a system which retained rates for non-domestic property but placed this under central control. In regard to domestic property, the basic principle was that there was to be no taxation on the property itself, only on the residents. The three community charges, personal, standard or collective, were designed to tax individuals or second homes, and were not related to ability to pay in that the charge was a flat-rate charge for any individual authority, subject only to a reduction to 20 per cent. for certain groups. The community charge, or "poll tax" proved to be both very unpopular and difficult to collect in that, apart from political objections to such a regressive tax, persons, unlike property, are mobile, and the registration and enforcement proceedings proved very complicated, expensive and emotive. The tax was perceived to be an electoral liability, and dissatisfaction with it played its part in the downfall of the Prime Minister, Mrs Thatcher, with whom it was closely associated.

The basic system of local finance which these Acts introduced is based on three elements. First, the income received from the non-domestic rate, which is now fixed nationally and was to be increased only in line with the retail prices index. By means of a pooling exercise, the Secretary of State redistributes the sums to local authorities. This, therefore, is a relatively fixed element in the income of local authorities, and subject to little discretion on the part of either the Secretary of State or the local authority. The second element is the contribution from grants, of which the crucial element is the revenue support grant, as opposed to special grants. This is subject to very wide Ministerial discretion and is both complex and uncertain. The theory is that the combination of these first two items brings all authorities to a common base, before the third element is calculated. Under the changes introduced by this Act, these two elements must be dealt with each year by a Local Government Finance Order, subject to the affirmative resolution procedure of the House of Commons. The third element is the tax raised locally by the authority, over which it does have some discretion. Under the previous system that was the community charge. Under the new system, introduced by this Act, it will be the council tax.

The proportion of the income of local authorities over which they have control has declined dramatically. From the position under the rating system where the locally determined rates provided in excess of 50 per cent. of the income of authorities, the system under the 1987 and 1988 Acts reduced this to provide approximately 20 per cent. of their revenue. When this change was linked to the change in regard to the various systems of "capping" of expenditure or tax, it resulted in the claims by many commentators that a constitutional change had taken place. That situation has been compounded by the further reduction of the amount raised locally. The unpopularity of the community charge resulted in a reduction of the amounts by £140 per chargepayer, under the Community Charges (General Reduction) Act 1991, and paid for by means of an increase in the centrally controlled value added tax. This has now reduced the contribution of locally raised tax to approximately 11 per cent. of revenue. Local authorities' discretion in raising expenditure is now severely curtailed both from the legal point of view with a "capping" régime in operation, and also politically in that an increase of expenditure of 10 per cent. in the total budget would have to be translated into a rise in the local tax of up to 100 per cent.

This main purpose of this Act is therefore to abolish the community charges from the financial year 1993–94 and establish the new system of council tax in regard to the third element of local government finance. However, it also amends in a more minor fashion the law relating to the first two elements, non-domestic rates and the grant system, together with other minor provisions.

The Act received the Royal Assent shortly before the dissolution of Parliament before the 1992 General Election. In order that it could be passed before the election and to meet the aim of having the new system in place by April 1993, the Bill passed through its various legislative stages at record speed and, perhaps not surprisingly, relatively free from amendment. There was much criticism of the inability of Parliament, and outside pressure groups, to have sufficient time to respond to the Bill. Only two new sections were added to the Act, both relating to the existing community charge system in order to solve problems raised in practice, and few other amendments were accepted. The opposition parties were committed to replace the Act by another system, whether based on a property tax or income tax, but in the event, with the return of a Conservative government, the Act has survived.

The basic structure of the Act therefore remains as it did in the original Bill. Liability for the new council tax falls on a daily basis on a dwelling which is not exempt. The extensive, if crude, valuation exercise places all residential property into one of eight bands, different for England, Wales, and Scotland respectively, on the basis of capital value in 1991. The proportion to be paid by each band is specified in a manner which means that the properties in the highest band will be liable to pay only three times the tax payable by those in the lowest band.

It is not, however, simply a property tax like the domestic rating system, based on limited capital banding. It is assumed that each dwelling will be occupied by two eligible adults and liability is calculated accordingly. Where there is only one eligible adult resident a discount of 25 per cent. will operate. In this way the tax retains some personal element, as in the community charge. Spouses, defined as those who are married or living together as husband and wife, are jointly and severally liable for the tax. Unlike the previous system, where discretion was given to all authorities, discounts are provided for second homes, although discretion is to remain for Welsh authorities only to vary this.

There has been much criticism of the tax. By combining both elements of a property tax and a personal tax, it is open to debate as to whether it combines the virtues or the demerits of each. In regard to the property element, there has been much criticism of the crude valuation exercise; of the relatively limited differentiation of the bands; and of its lack of sensitivity to differences in regional property prices. In regard to the personal element it has been dubbed "son of Poll Tax" in that fears are expressed about the continuing disincentive raised by the discount system for persons to disclose where they live by registering for electoral purposes; about the need for a limited system of recording the residences of individuals; about the problems of joint and several liability; and about the difficulties of enforcement and the levying of distress.

In keeping with its predecessor, the Act includes extensive provisions relating to the setting of the tax, precepts, and limitation or "capping" of the tax. Throughout the Act extensive regulation-making powers have been given to the Secretary of State. This now seems to be a permanent feature of legislation on local government. In regard to the 1988 Act, Lord Rippon warned that such powers allowed central government "to make a new law virtually as they go along" and that such powers were "inherently dangerous and have to be monitored". No doubt, however, the experience of the community charge strengthens the belief that such complex systems can be introduced quickly only by using such powers. There is little in this new Act that the Secretary of State cannot change by regulation. While it is possible to change the banding values and proportions, and the discounts for unoccupied property or second homes, this can be done only by an affirmative resolution of the House of Commons.

Part I

Council Tax: England and Wales

Chapter I

Main Provisions

Preliminary

Council tax in respect of dwellings

1.—(1) As regards the financial year beginning in 1993 and subsequent financial years, each billing authority shall, in accordance with this Part, levy and collect a tax, to be called council tax, which shall be payable in respect of dwellings situated in its area.

(2) In this Part "billing authority" means a district or London borough council, the Common Council or the Council of the Isles of Scilly.

(3) For the purposes of this Part the Secretary of State may make regulations containing rules for treating a dwelling as situated in a billing authority's area if part only of the dwelling falls within the area.

Definitions
  "billing authority": subs. (2) and s.69(1).
  "Common Council": s.69(1) and (3).
  "council tax": subs. (1).
  "dwelling": ss.3 and 69(1).
  "financial year": ss.69(1) and 116(1).
  "levy": s.69(1).

General Note
  This section establishes the new tax, to be known as the council tax, to be introduced from the financial year commencing April 1993. This will replace the previous local personal taxation system and, by s.100 of this Act, the community charges established by the 1988 Act will be abolished at the end of March 1993. Unlike its predecessor, the new tax is to be payable in respect of dwellings. However, like the community charges, it also includes a personal element in that 50 per cent. of the tax is based on the assumption that each dwelling includes two eligible residents and s.11 provides for a discount of 25 per cent. for dwellings occupied by only one eligible resident. This section places a duty on each billing authority to levy and collect the council tax in respect of dwellings within its area. This duty commences with the financial year 1993/94 and continues for subsequent years. The billing authority is defined by subs. (2) as a metropolitan or non-metropolitan district council, London borough, the Common Council of the City of London, or the Council of the Isles of Scilly. By subs. (3), the Secretary of State is permitted to make regulations to deal with the situation where the dwelling is situated in more than one authority's area, by treating it as situated in only one of the areas. For the regulations, see the Council Tax (Situation and Valuation of Dwellings) Regulations 1992 (S.I. 1992 No. 550), which place the dwelling in the area of the authority in which falls the greater part of the dwelling, as ascertained by the superficial extent of the building. Where it is impossible to ascertain this, the allocation shall be by agreement between the authorities where the dwelling falls within the area of more than one, and by the authority where it falls within different areas of the same authority.

Liability to tax determined on a daily basis

2.—(1) Liability to pay council tax shall be determined on a daily basis.

(2) For the purposes of determining for any day—
(a) whether any property is a chargeable dwelling;
(b) which valuation band is shown in the billing authority's valuation list as applicable to any chargeable dwelling;
(c) the person liable to pay council tax in respect of any such dwelling; or
(d) whether any amount of council tax is subject to a discount and (if so) the amount of the discount,
it shall be assumed that any state of affairs subsisting at the end of the day had subsisted throughout the day.

DEFINITIONS
"billing authority": ss.1(2) and 69(1).
"chargeable dwelling": s.4(2).
"council tax": s.1(1).
"dwelling": ss.3 and 69(1).
"valuation band": s.5(2) and (3).
"valuation list": s.22.

GENERAL NOTE
This section establishes that, like the community charge, liability for the appropriate council tax is to be determined on a daily basis. It is anticipated that since the tax is levied primarily on property, this will not cause such difficulties for registration and collection as the previous system. However, since the new tax does incorporate a personal element, the Opposition anticipated that difficulties would still arise in relation to non-disclosure of residency, non-registration on the electoral register, etc. A number of factors specified by this Act affect the liability to pay the council tax and, for each of these, this subsection specifies that the situation which exists at the end of the day shall be deemed to have existed throughout the day. The factors are, whether the property is a dwelling subject to the tax, as defined by ss.3 and 4; what valuation band is shown as applicable to the dwelling, as established by s.5; the person liable to pay the tax in respect of the dwelling, as defined by ss.6–9; and any discount applicable to the dwelling, as authorised by s.11.

Chargeable dwellings

Meaning of "dwelling"

3.—(1) This section has effect for determining what is a dwelling for the purposes of this Part.
(2) Subject to the following provisions of this section, a dwelling is any property which—
(a) by virtue of the definition of hereditament in section 115(1) of the General Rate Act 1967, would have been a hereditament for the purposes of that Act if that Act remained in force; and
(b) is not for the time being shown or required to be shown in a local or a central non-domestic rating list in force at that time; and
(c) is not for the time being exempt from local non-domestic rating for the purposes of Part III of the Local Government Finance Act 1988 ("the 1988 Act");
and in applying paragraphs (b) and (c) above no account shall be taken of any rules as to Crown exemption.
(3) A hereditament which—
(a) is a composite hereditament for the purposes of Part III of the 1988 Act; and
(b) would still be such a hereditament if paragraphs (b) to (d) of section 66(1) of that Act (domestic property) were omitted,
is also, subject to subsection (6) below, a dwelling for the purposes of this Part.
(4) Subject to subsection (6) below, none of the following property, namely—
(a) a yard, garden, outhouse or other appurtenance belonging to or

enjoyed with property used wholly for the purposes of living accommodation; or

(b) a private garage which either has a floor area of not more than 25 square metres or is used wholly or mainly for the accommodation of a private motor vehicle; or

(c) private storage premises used wholly or mainly for the storage of articles of domestic use,

is a dwelling except in so far as it forms part of a larger property which is itself a dwelling by virtue of subsection (2) above.

(5) The Secretary of State may by order provide that in such cases as may be prescribed by or determined under the order—

(a) anything which would (apart from the order) be one dwelling shall be treated as two or more dwellings; and

(b) anything which would (apart from the order) be two or more dwellings shall be treated as one dwelling.

(6) The Secretary of State may by order amend any definition of "dwelling" which is for the time being effective for the purposes of this Part.

DEFINITIONS

"central non-domestic rating list": s.52(1) of the 1988 Act.
"composite hereditament": s.64(9) of the 1988 Act.
"domestic property": s.66 of the 1988 Act.
"dwelling": ss.3 and 69(1).
"hereditament": ss.64 and 67 of the 1988 Act.
"local non-domestic rating list": s.41(1) of the 1988 Act.
"prescribed": s.116(1).

GENERAL NOTE

This section establishes the basis of liability, namely for a "dwelling" other than those which are exempt. The definition of a dwelling is therefore provided. By subs. (2), a dwelling is defined, essentially negatively, as any property which would have been included within the relevant definition under the old rating system under the General Rate 1967, but which has neither been incorporated into the new non-domestic rating system, nor exempted from such under the 1988 Act. For the properties which would otherwise be exempt because of Crown exemption, these shall be included in the definition of "dwelling", on which see also s.19. More positively, subs. (3) includes composite hereditaments together with any hereditament which is used wholly for the purposes of living accommodation. However, excluded from the definition, by subs. (4), are types of premises which are considered as a dwelling only if they form part of a larger property which is itself a dwelling by subs. (2). Thus yards, garden outhouses, garages of up to 25 square metres used primarily in relation to a private car, or private storage premises for domestic goods are excluded in themselves, but they will be incorporated as part of a dwelling if associated with another property which is already within the definition of a dwelling. Wide powers are given to the Secretary of State to make regulations to amend the definition. Under subs. (5), to deal with subdivision and incorporation of property, he may prescribe that certain single dwellings be classed as two or more dwellings, or that two or more dwellings be classed as a single dwelling. This has been invoked in the Council Tax (Chargeable Dwellings) Order 1992 (S.I. 1992 No. 549). More importantly, under subs. (6), the Secretary of State has the general power to amend by regulation the definition of dwelling given by this section. Under s.113, this power of amendment is subject to the negative resolution procedure of the House of Commons only.

Dwellings chargeable to council tax

4.—(1) Council tax shall be payable in respect of any dwelling which is not an exempt dwelling.

(2) In this Chapter—

"chargeable dwelling" means any dwelling in respect of which council tax is payable;

"exempt dwelling" means any dwelling of a class prescribed by an order made by the Secretary of State.

(3) For the purposes of subsection (2) above, a class of dwellings may be prescribed by reference to such factors as the Secretary of State sees fit.

(4) Without prejudice to the generality of subsection (3) above, a class of dwellings may be prescribed by reference to one or more of the following factors—
  (a) the physical characteristics of dwellings;
  (b) the fact that dwellings are unoccupied or are occupied for prescribed purposes or are occupied or owned by persons of prescribed descriptions.

DEFINITIONS
"billing authority": subs. (2) and s.69(1).
"chargeable dwelling": subs. (2).
"council tax": s.1(1).
"dwelling": ss.3 and 69(1).
"exempt dwelling": subs. (2).
"prescribed": s.116(1).

GENERAL NOTE
This establishes the basis of liability, namely for a "dwelling" other than those which are exempt. A "dwelling" is defined by s.3. Under this section, the Secretary of State may also exempt specified classes of dwellings from liability for the council tax. The relevant regulations are contained in the Council Tax (Exempt Dwellings) Order 1992 (S.I. 1992 No. 558).

Subs. (1)
This subsection provides that council tax is payable on all dwellings, other than those which are exempt by virtue of regulations made under the authority of this section.

Subs. (2)
The term "dwelling", as established by s.3 of this Act, is divided into two classes, which are defined by this subsection. The first, that of "chargeable dwelling", is defined as those dwellings subject to the council tax. The second class, that of "exempt dwelling", is defined as those which are exempt by being of a class specified by the Secretary of State in regulations made under the authority of this section.

Subs. (3)
The Secretary of State is given a general power to prescribe the classes of dwellings to be exempt from council tax, by reference to such factors as he thinks fit. While not reducing the wide discretion given by this power, subs. (4) provides further indications of the factors which may be taken into account.

Subs. (4)
While confirming the width of the discretion of the Secretary of State under subs. (3), this subsection makes it clear that some of the factors may be the physical characteristics of the dwelling; that the dwelling may be unoccupied; that it is occupied for prescribed purposes and that it is occupied or owned by persons of prescribed descriptions. This has been used in the Council Tax (Exempt Dwellings) Order 1992 (S.I. 1992 No. 558) to prescribe 10 classes, which are dwellings which have been recently erected or to which works have been carried out; which have been unoccupied for less than six months; which are the homes of people living elsewhere or detained in specified circumstances; where someone has died; where occupation is prohibited; which are kept for ministers of religion; which are the homes of people resident elsewhere to take care of others; which are the homes of people resident elsewhere for the purpose of their studies; which are in the possession of a mortgagee; and which is a hall of residence wholly occupied by students, or part of armed forces accommodation.

Different amounts for dwellings in different valuation bands

5.—(1) The amounts of council tax payable in respect of dwellings situated in the same billing authority's area (or the same part of such an area) and listed in different valuation bands shall be in the proportion—
          6: 7: 8: 9: 11: 13: 15: 18
where 6 is for dwellings listed in valuation band A, 7 is for dwellings listed in valuation band B, and so on.
  (2) The valuation bands for dwellings in England are set out in the following Table—

Range of values	*Valuation band*
Values not exceeding £40,000	A
Values exceeding £40,000 but not exceeding £52,000	B
Values exceeding £52,000 but not exceeding £68,000	C
Values exceeding £68,000 but not exceeding £88,000	D
Values exceeding £88,000 but not exceeding £120,000	E
Values exceeding £120,000 but not exceeding £160,000	F
Values exceeding £160,000 but not exceeding £320,000	G
Values exceeding £320,000	H

(3) The valuation bands for dwellings in Wales are set out in the following Table—

Range of values	*Valuation band*
Values not exceeding £30,000	A
Values exceeding £30,000 but not exceeding £39,000	B
Values exceeding £39,000 but not exceeding £51,000	C
Values exceeding £51,000 but not exceeding £66,000	D
Values exceeding £66,000 but not exceeding £90,000	E
Values exceeding £90,000 but not exceeding £120,000	F
Values exceeding £120,000 but not exceeding £240,000	G
Values exceeding £240,000	H

(4) The Secretary of State may by order, as regards financial years beginning on or after such date as is specified in the order—

   (a) substitute another proportion for that which is for the time being effective for the purposes of subsection (1) above;

   (b) substitute other valuation bands for those which are for the time being effective for the purposes of subsection (2) or (3) above.

(5) No order under subsection (4) above shall be made unless a draft of the order has been laid before and approved by resolution of the House of Commons.

(6) Any reference in this Part to dwellings listed in a particular valuation band shall be construed as a reference to dwellings to which that valuation band is shown as applicable in the billing authority's valuation list.

DEFINITIONS
   "billing authority": ss.1(2) and 69(1).
   "council tax": s.1(1).
   "dwelling": ss.3 and 69(1).
   "financial year": ss.69(1) and 116(1).
   "valuation band": subss. (2) and (3).
   "valuation list": s.22(1).

GENERAL NOTE
   A banding system for the value of dwellings is established by this section, which also prescribes the proportions to be paid by each band. Separate bands are provided for England and Wales. While these are included in the primary Act, either or both aspects may be altered by the Secretary of State by regulation, but only with the positive approval of the House of Commons.

Subs. (1)
   This subsection specifies the proportions of council tax to be paid by each band. Thus, dwellings in the highest band will be liable to pay three times that paid by the lowest band. While going some way to meet the criticism that the community charge was flat-rate and thus regressive, there has been much criticism of these proportions on the ground that they are not sufficiently differentiated.

Subs. (2)
   Eight valuation bands are provided for England, as originally provided for in Pt. I of the

Schedule to the Domestic Property (Valuation) Regulations 1991 (S.I. 1991 No. 1934), which gave the initial legal authority for the creation of the valuation lists. Again, while going some way to meet the criticism that the community charge was flat-rate and thus regressive, there has been much criticism of these bands on the ground that they are not sufficiently differentiated.

Subs. (3)

Eight valuation bands are provided for Wales. These bands are as originally provided for in Pt. I of the Schedule to the Domestic Property (Valuation) Regulations 1991, which gave the initial legal authority for the creation of the valuation lists. Again, while going some way to meet the criticism that the community charge was flat-rate and thus regressive, there has been much criticism of these bands on the ground that they are not sufficiently differentiated.

Subs. (4)

Under the authority of this subsection, the Secretary of State may alter either or both of the proportions and the bands, as established by subs. (1) and subss. (2) and (3) respectively. This will therefore allow the system to be modified to meet any continuing objections to the limited banding or narrow proportions. Including further bands could be used to provide for a revaluation.

Subs. (5)

Where the Secretary of State replaces either or both of the proportions and the bands, under subs. (4), this must be approved by positive resolution of the House of Commons.

Subs. (6)

Despite s.69 being a separate interpretation section for Pt. I of the Act, this subsection provides a definition, for the purposes of Pt. I, of the phrase "dwellings listed in a particular valuation band". This is defined as all dwellings shown in the billing authority's valuation list, as established by s.22.

Liability to tax

Persons liable to pay council tax

6.—(1) The person who is liable to pay council tax in respect of any chargeable dwelling and any day is the person who falls within the first paragraph of subsection (2) below to apply, taking paragraph (a) of that subsection first, paragraph (b) next, and so on.

(2) A person falls within this subsection in relation to any chargeable dwelling and any day if, on that day—

(a) he is a resident of the dwelling and has a freehold interest in the whole or any part of it;

(b) he is such a resident and has a leasehold interest in the whole or any part of the dwelling which is not inferior to another such interest held by another such resident;

(c) he is both such a resident and a statutory or secure tenant of the whole or any part of the dwelling;

(d) he is such a resident and has a contractual licence to occupy the whole or any part of the dwelling;

(e) he is such a resident; or

(f) he is the owner of the dwelling.

(3) Where, in relation to any chargeable dwelling and any day, two or more persons fall within the first paragraph of subsection (2) above to apply, they shall each be jointly and severally liable to pay the council tax in respect of the dwelling and that day.

(4) Subsection (3) above shall not apply as respects any day on which one or more of the persons there mentioned fall to be disregarded for the purposes of discount by virtue of paragraph 2 of Schedule 1 to this Act (the severely mentally impaired) and one or more of them do not; and liability to pay the council tax in respect of the dwelling and that day shall be determined as follows—

(a) if only one of those persons does not fall to be so disregarded, he shall be solely liable;

(b) if two or more of those persons do not fall to be so disregarded, they shall each be jointly and severally liable.

(5) In this Part, unless the context otherwise requires—

"owner", in relation to any dwelling, means the person as regards whom the following conditions are fulfilled—

   (a) he has a material interest in the whole or any part of the dwelling; and

   (b) at least part of the dwelling or, as the case may be, of the part concerned is not subject to a material interest inferior to his interest;

"resident", in relation to any dwelling, means an individual who has attained the age of 18 years and has his sole or main residence in the dwelling.

(6) In this section—

"material interest" means a freehold interest or a leasehold interest which was granted for a term of six months or more;

"secure tenant" means a tenant under a secure tenancy within the meaning of Part IV of the Housing Act 1985;

"statutory tenant" means a statutory tenant within the meaning of the Rent Act 1977 or the Rent (Agriculture) Act 1976.

DEFINITIONS
   "chargeable dwelling": s.4(2).
   "council tax": s.1(1).
   "dwelling": ss.3 and 69(1).
   "owner": subs. (5) and s.69(1).
   "resident": subs. (5) and s.69(1).
   "secure tenant": subs. (5).
   "statutory tenant": subs. (5).

GENERAL NOTE
   This section establishes the persons liable to pay the council tax for a chargeable dwelling on any particular day.

Subs. (1)
   This rather clumsy construction simply establishes that the person who is liable to pay council tax for any chargeable dwelling is the person who falls within the first of the categories in subs. (2) to apply, taking each in sequence. This hierarchy in subs. (2) is composed of six categories which must be examined in turn. Thus if a person falls within subs. (2)(a), that person will be the person liable. If, however, no person falls within subs. (2)(a) or (b), but one does fall within subs. (2)(c), then that person will be the person liable. This process continues until liability is established.

Subs. (2)
   This subsection provides the list of categories to establish the person liable to pay the council tax. That person is the one who falls within the first of the categories to apply, taking each in sequence. The categories are based on two elements, namely residency and legal interest. The top category in the hierarchy is the person who is both a resident of the building and has a freehold interest in whole or part of it. The hierarchy then progresses through a variety of categories of legal interest, namely leasehold, tenancy and contractual licence, but all linked to residency, and then to one where there is residency but no legal interest. Where there is no residency, then the final category of ownership establishes liability.

Subs. (3)
   Where two or more persons fall within the same category for any day, as established by subs. (2), then they will be jointly and severally liable to pay the council tax for every such day.

Subs. (4)
   This subsection was included on amendment following pressure to accommodate the problems of the mentally impaired.

Subs. (5)
   Despite s.69 being a separate interpretation section for Pt. I of the Act, this subsection

provides definitions, for the purposes of Pt. I, of the terms "owner" and "resident". These terms are crucial to establishing liability to pay the council tax.

"Owner" is defined as the person entitled to possession of all or part of the dwelling.

"Resident", as the first of the qualifying classes, is defined as an individual who both is 18 years of age and occupies the dwelling as the sole or main residence. Since it is a daily tax, an individual becomes liable from the day on which the age of 18 is attained. As with the community charge, the term "sole or main residence" is crucial to establishing liability. As with the 1988 Act, this Act does not define the term "sole or main residence", and its interpretation in this context will be influenced by the interpretation adopted in other areas of law. The general approach of the courts has been that the phrase should be considered in its ordinary meaning and as a matter of fact and degree (see *Akbarali* v. *Brent London Borough Council*; *Abdullah* v. *Shropshire County Council*; *Shabpar* v. *Barnet London Borough Council*; *Shah (Jitendra)* v. *Barnet London Borough Council*; *Barnet London Borough Council* v. *Shah* [1983] 2 A.C. 309; *Hipperson* v. *Electoral Registration Officer for the District of Newbury* [1985] Q.B. 1060). In *Bradford City Metropolitan Council* v. *Anderton* 89 L.G.R. 681, it was held that the house where a merchant seaman spent only 90 days per year, the rest of the year being spent on a ship, was his sole residence. The argument that it was not his main residence was rejected on the basis that a merchant ship could not constitute a residence.

Thus, while it is accepted that a person can have more than one residence (*Fox* v. *Stirk and Bristol Electoral Registration Officer*; *Ricketts* v. *Cambridge City Electoral Registration Officer* [1970] 2 Q.B. 463), a number of factors will be taken into account when determining which is the main residence. However, although both the subjective opinion of the individual and objective factors, such as where most of the personal belongings are kept, will be relevant, it is likely that most weight will be attached to the time spent at each dwelling, since the charge is considered to be a charge for the services provided. In *Bradford City Metropolitan Council* v. *Anderton*, above, in determining that a merchant seaman had his residence in a house where he spent only 90 days of the year, Hutchinson J. held that apart from time, other factors in determining residence were the subjective view of what the individual regarded as his home, the fact that it was where his wife lived, and that he had a legal interest in the house. However, in *Stevenson* v. *Rodgers*, unreported, February 15, 1991, the Inner House of the Court of Session indicated that time was not simply one factor among others but the most important of the criteria. Thus where a person worked and slept during the week in Liverpool, but his wife and children lived in Edinburgh, where he spent most weekends, the number of nights spent in each place was not evenly balanced. Only where the numbers were more evenly balanced should the other factors be considered as providing a contrary indication of residence. Differing views were expressed by the three judges as to the relevance of a legal interest in the house, where the person was registered with a GP, where the person appeared on the electoral register, and where the rest of the family was living.

Subs. (6)

For the purposes of this section, the terms relating to the specific legal interest are defined.

Liability in respect of caravans and boats

7.—(1) Subsections (2) to (4) below shall have effect in substitution for section 6 above in relation to any chargeable dwelling which consists of a pitch occupied by a caravan, or a mooring occupied by a boat.

(2) Where on any day the owner of the caravan or boat is not, but some other person is, a resident of the dwelling, that other person shall be liable to pay the council tax in respect of the dwelling and that day.

(3) Where on any day subsection (2) above does not apply, the owner of the caravan or boat shall be liable to pay the council tax in respect of the dwelling and that day.

(4) Where on any day two or more persons fall within subsection (2) or (3) above, they shall each be jointly and severally liable to pay the council tax in respect of the dwelling and that day.

(5) Subsection (4) of section 6 above shall apply for the purposes of subsection (4) above as it applies for the purposes of subsection (3) of that section.

(6) In this section "caravan" shall be construed in accordance with Part I of the Caravan Sites and Control of Development Act 1960.

(7) Any reference in this section to the owner of a caravan or boat shall be construed—

(a) in relation to a caravan or boat which is subject to an agreement for hire-purchase or conditional sale, as a reference to the person in possession under the agreement;

(b) in relation to a caravan or boat which is subject to a bill of sale or mortgage, as a reference to the person entitled to the property in it apart from the bill or mortgage.

DEFINITIONS
"caravan": subs. (5).
"chargeable dwelling": s.4(2).
"council tax": s.1(1).
"dwelling": ss.3 and 69(1).
"owner": subs. (6); ss.6(5) and 69(1).
"resident": ss.6(5) and 69(1).

GENERAL NOTE
This section provides additional rules in regard to the liability of a person where the chargeable dwelling is a caravan or boat.

Subs. (1)
The normal rules as regards liability of a person to pay the council tax, as laid down in s.6, are displaced and replaced by the provisions contained in subss. (2)–(4) of this section in regard to a pitch occupied by a caravan or a mooring occupied by a boat.

Subs. (2)
Where a person resides in the caravan or boat, as their sole or main residence, and is not the owner, then it is that person, rather than the owner, who is liable to pay the council tax.

Subs. (3)
Where there is no person resident, or the owner is resident, then it is the owner who is liable to pay the council tax.

Subs. (4)
Where two or more persons are liable by virtue of subss. (2) or (3), either as joint owners or by having the caravan or boat as their sole or main residence, then they are jointly and severally liable to pay the council tax.

Subs. (5)
For the purposes of this section, a "caravan" is defined in accordance with Pt. I of the Caravan Sites and Development Act 1960. See also, for the purpose of the application of s.1 where the dwelling falls within more than one area, the definition of the "superficial extent" of a caravan or houseboat in the Council Tax (Situation and Valuation of Dwellings) Regulations 1992 (S.I. 1992, No. 550).

Subs. (6)
Given the different nature of caravans and boats as opposed to other dwellings, the definition of "owner" by ss.6(5) and 69(1) has been modified to meet two special cases. Thus the "owner" is any person entitled to possession where there is a hire-purchase or conditional sale agreement or the person entitled to it apart from a bill of sale or mortgage.

Liability in prescribed cases

8.—(1) Subsections (3) and (4) below shall have effect in substitution for section 6 or (as the case may be) section 7 above in relation to any chargeable dwelling of a class prescribed for the purposes of this subsection.

(2) Subsections (3) and (4) below shall have effect in substitution for section 6 or (as the case may be) section 7 above in relation to any chargeable dwelling of a class prescribed for the purposes of this subsection, if the billing authority so determines in relation to all dwellings of that class which are situated in its area.

(3) Where on any day this subsection has effect in relation to a dwelling, the owner of the dwelling shall be liable to pay the council tax in respect of the dwelling and that day.

(4) Where on any day two or more persons fall within subsection (3) above, they shall each be jointly and severally liable to pay the council tax in respect of the dwelling and that day.

(5) Subsection (4) of section 6 above shall apply for the purposes of subsection (4) above as it applies for the purposes of subsection (3) of that section.

(6) Regulations prescribing a class of chargeable dwellings for the purposes of subsection (1) or (2) above may provide that, in relation to any dwelling of that class, subsection (3) above shall have effect as if for the reference to the owner of the dwelling there were substituted a reference to the person falling within such description as may be prescribed.

(7) Subsections (3) and (4) of section 4 above shall apply for the purposes of subsections (1) and (2) above as they apply for the purposes of subsection (2) of that section.

DEFINITIONS
"billing authority": ss.1(2) and 69(1).
"chargeable dwelling": s.4(2).
"council tax": s.1(1).
"dwelling": ss.3 and 69(1).
"owner": ss.6(5), 7(6) and 69(1).

GENERAL NOTE
This section provides additional rules in regard to the liability of an owner where the chargeable dwelling, including a caravan or boat, has been prescribed in regulation. The aim is to ensure that the owner, as opposed to any resident, pays the council tax. Thus, in situations like hostels, where the residents may be short-term and difficult to trace, this will ensure payment. In this way the system is similar to, and replaces, the collective community charge. Under this section, see the Council Tax (Liability for Owners) Regulations 1992 (S.I. 1992 No. 551).

Subs. (1)
Where any class of chargeable dwelling has been prescribed in regulation under this subsection, then the provisions of s.6, or s.7, for caravans or boats, are displaced and replaced by the provisions contained in subss. (3) and (4). The Council Tax (Liability for Owners) Regulations 1992 (S.I. 1992 No. 551) have prescribed that the classes are nursing-homes and other similar homes; houses of religious communities; houses in multiple occupation; residences of staff who live in houses occasionally occupied by an employer; and residences of ministers of religion.

Subs. (2)
The purpose of this subsection is to allow the Secretary of State to prescribe classes of chargeable dwellings, including pitches for caravans and moorings for boats, for which the billing authority will retain discretion to make the owner rather than the resident liable to pay the council tax. Where any class of chargeable dwelling has been prescribed in regulation under this subsection and the authority decides to exercise its discretion, then the provisions of s.6, or s.7 for caravans or boats, are displaced and replaced by the provisions contained in subss. (3) and (4). Where, however, the billing authority does decide to exercise that discretion in relation to a particular class, then it must be applied to the owners of all dwellings within that class, there being no discretion to apply it within the class.

Subs. (3)
This makes clear that when this subsection has effect, it is the owner and not the resident who is liable to pay the council tax for any chargeable day. Thus, the hierarchy of liability established in s.6 is displaced.

Subs. (4)
Where two or more persons are liable by virtue of subs. (3), then they are jointly and severally liable to pay the council tax.

Subs. (5)
This subsection was included to give effect to the policy underlying the amendment to s.6 whereby the problems of the mentally impaired were taken into account.

Subs. (6)
In order to further clarify liability, any regulations made under subss. (1) or (2) may also make provision for determining who is to be considered as the owner of any dwelling in that class. Given the wording of ss.6(5), 7(6) and 69(1), this will allow the Secretary of State to prescribe new definitions of "owner" for such classes.

Subs. (7)
By applying s.4(3) and (4) to subss. (1) and (2) of this section, any dwellings prescribed under this section by the Secretary of State may be prescribed by reference to such factors as he thinks fit. While not reducing the wide discretion given by this power, further indications of the factors which may be taken into account are provided. Thus some of the factors may be the physical characteristics of the dwelling; that the dwelling may be unoccupied; that it is occupied for prescribed purposes and that it is occupied or owned by persons of prescribed descriptions.

Liability of spouses

9.—(1) Where—
(a) a person who is liable to pay council tax in respect of any chargeable dwelling of which he is a resident and any day is married to another person; and
(b) that other person is also a resident of the dwelling on that day but would not, apart from this section, be so liable,
those persons shall each be jointly and severally liable to pay the council tax in respect of the dwelling and that day.
(2) Subsection (1) above shall not apply as respects any day on which the other person there mentioned falls to be disregarded for the purposes of discount by virtue of paragraph 2 of Schedule 1 to this Act (the severely mentally impaired).
(3) For the purposes of this section two persons are married to each other if they are a man and a woman—
(a) who are married to each other; or
(b) who are not married to each other but are living together as husband and wife.

DEFINITIONS
"chargeable dwelling": s.4(2).
"council tax": s.1(1).
"dwelling": ss.3 and 69(1).
"resident": ss.6(5) and 69(1).

GENERAL NOTE
This section is intended to ensure that married couples are jointly and severally liable to pay the council tax, notwithstanding that joint and several liability has not been created by the other preceding sections.

Subs. (1)
Where two people are married to each other and, while both are resident in the dwelling, one would not otherwise be liable to pay the council tax, then they shall be jointly and severally liable for the council tax.

Subs. (2)
This subsection was included to give effect to the policy underlying the amendment to s.6 whereby the problems of the mentally impaired were taken into account.

Subs. (3)
For the purpose of establishing joint and several liability under this section, two persons are deemed to be married to each other not only if they are a man and a woman and are actually married to each other, but also if they are a man and a woman living together as husband and wife.

Amounts of tax payable

Basic amounts payable

10.—(1) Subject to sections 11 to 13 below, a person who is liable to pay council tax in respect of any chargeable dwelling and any day shall, as respects the dwelling and the day, pay to the billing authority for the area in which the dwelling is situated an amount calculated in accordance with the formula—

$$\frac{A}{D}$$

where—

> A is the amount which, for the financial year in which the day falls and for dwellings in the valuation band listed for the dwelling, has been set by the authority for its area or (as the case may be) the part of its area in which the dwelling is situated;
> D is the number of days in the financial year.

(2) For the purposes of this Part the Secretary of State may make regulations containing rules for ascertaining in what part of a billing authority's area a dwelling is situated (whether situated in the area in fact or by virtue of regulations made under section 1(3) above).

DEFINITIONS
"billing authority": ss.1(2) and 69(1).
"chargeable dwelling": s.4(2).
"council tax": s.1(1).
"dwelling": ss.3 and 69(1).
"dwelling listed in a valuation band": s.5(6).
"financial year": ss.69(1) and 116(1).

GENERAL NOTE
The basic formula by which the amount to be paid by any person liable to pay the council tax is to be calculated is provided by this section.

Subs. (1)
Working from the position that liability for a particular dwelling is calculated on a daily basis, the formula for calculating the amount to be paid is the sum set by the billing authority for dwellings in that valuation band divided by the number of days in the financial year. The amount set for the valuation band may be for the whole or part of the area. From this starting point, the amount may be reduced either by discounts established under the authority of ss.11 or 12, or in accordance with regulations made under s.13 by the Secretary of State. Thus, the amount to be paid may vary during the year, depending on the circumstances existing on any particular day.

Subs. (2)
Rules for ascertaining within what part of an authority's area the dwelling is situated may be made by regulation by the Secretary of State. This will accommodate the setting of different amounts of council tax because of different precepts, or special expenses for different parts of the area. The dwelling need not be actually situated within the area but may be deemed to be so by virtue of regulations made under s.1(3). For the regulations, see the Council Tax (Situation and Valuation of Dwellings) Regulations 1992 (S.I. 1992 No. 550), which place the dwelling in the area of the authority in which the greater part of the dwelling falls, as ascertained by the superficial extent of the building. Where it is impossible to ascertain this, the allocation shall be by agreement between the authorities where the dwelling falls within the area of more than one, and by the authority where it falls within different areas of the same authority.

Discounts

11.—(1) The amount of council tax payable in respect of any chargeable dwelling and any day shall be subject to a discount equal to the appropriate percentage of that amount if on that day—

(a) there is only one resident of the dwelling and he does not fall to be disregarded for the purposes of discount; or

(b) there are two or more residents of the dwelling and each of them except one falls to be disregarded for those purposes.

(2) Subject to section 12 below, the amount of council tax payable in respect of any chargeable dwelling and any day shall be subject to a discount equal to twice the appropriate percentage of that amount if on that day—

(a) there is no resident of the dwelling; or

(b) there are one or more residents of the dwelling and each of them falls to be disregarded for the purposes of discount.

(3) In this section and section 12 below "the appropriate percentage" means 25 per cent. or, if the Secretary of State by order so provides in relation to the financial year in which the day falls, such other percentage as is specified in the order.

(4) No order under subsection (3) above shall be made unless a draft of the order has been laid before and approved by resolution of the House of Commons.

(5) Schedule 1 to this Act shall have effect for determining who shall be disregarded for the purposes of discount.

DEFINITIONS
"appropriate percentage": subs. (3).
"chargeable dwelling": s.4(2).
"council tax": s.1(1).
"dwelling": ss.3 and 69(1).
"resident": ss.6(5) and 69(1).

GENERAL NOTE
The council tax is not simply a property-based tax like the rating system, but includes a personal element as in the community charge. For that element, it has been assumed that any dwelling will be occupied by two or more residents, and the amount is calculated accordingly. This section therefore provides for discounts to be made available where this is not the situation, and the dwelling has only one resident or includes residents who are to be considered exempt from the personal element. While the conditions for, and levels of, discount are provided by the section, they may be varied by an order which has been positively approved by the House of Commons. Under this section, discounts of 25 per cent. are granted where there is only one resident or only one who is not to be disregarded for this purpose, and 50 per cent. where there is no resident or all the residents are to be disregarded for this purpose. The classes of persons who are to be so disregarded are provided by Sched. 1; see also the annotations to that Schedule.

Subs. (1)
This subsection provides that in two circumstances a discount of 25 per cent., as the "appropriate percentage" defined by subs. (3), will be granted. The first is where there is only one resident, who does not fall within the classes of persons to be disregarded listed in Sched. 1. The second is where there are two or more residents, but only one does not fall within the classes of persons to be disregarded listed in Sched. 1.

Subs. (2)
This subsection provides that in two circumstances a discount of 50 per cent., as twice the "appropriate percentage" defined by subs. (3), will be granted. The first is where there is no resident of the dwelling. The second is where there are one or more residents, all of whom fall within the classes of persons to be disregarded listed in Sched. 1. Additional provision is made by s.12 for Wales, where authorities are given discretion to vary the discount on dwellings with no residents. Despite pleas within Parliament for this discretion to be given to other areas, the Government considered Wales to be a special case.

Subss. (3) and (4)
The "appropriate percentage" is set at 25 per cent. This is the unit of discount which is incorporated into subs. (1) to provide 25 per cent. discount, and subs. (2) to provide 50 per cent. discount, where the conditions are met. The Secretary of State may alter the "appropriate percentage" by order, but any such alteration must be for the whole of a financial year, and must be approved by the affirmative resolution procedure of the House of Commons.

Subs. (5)

The classes of those to be disregarded, or "invisible", for the purposes of liability for the personal element of the council tax are provided by Sched. 1. The main classes in the schedule are: persons in detention; the severely mentally impaired; persons in respect of whom child benefit is payable; students; hospital patients; patients in homes; care workers; and residents of hostels or similar accommodation for the homeless or itinerant. The Secretary of State may amend these classes, or add to the classes, by order. This has been done in the Council Tax (Additional Provisions for Discounts Disregards) Order 1992 (S.I. 1992 No. 552), reg. 3, which establishes three further classes: members of international headquarters and defence organisations; members of religious communities; and school-leavers.

Discounts: special provision for Wales

12.—(1) Where any class of dwellings in Wales is prescribed for the purposes of this section for any financial year, a Welsh billing authority may determine that for the year subsection (2) or (3) below shall have effect in substitution for section 11(2)(a) above in relation to all dwellings of that class which are situated in its area.

(2) Where this subsection has effect for any year in relation to any class of dwellings, the amount of council tax payable in respect of—

(a) any chargeable dwelling of that class; and

(b) any day in the year on which there is no resident of the dwelling,

shall be subject to a discount equal to the appropriate percentage of that amount.

(3) Where this subsection has effect for any year in relation to any class of dwellings, the amount of council tax payable in respect of—

(a) any chargeable dwelling of that class; and

(b) any day in the year on which there is no resident of the dwelling,

shall not be subject to a discount.

(4) A determination under subsection (1) above for a financial year may be varied or revoked at any time before the year begins.

(5) Subsections (3) and (4) of section 4 above shall apply for the purposes of subsection (1) above as they apply for the purposes of subsection (2) of that section.

(6) A billing authority which has made a determination under subsection (1) above shall, before the end of the period of 21 days beginning with the day of doing so, publish a notice of the determination in at least one newspaper circulating in the authority's area.

(7) Failure to comply with subsection (6) above does not make the making of the determination invalid.

DEFINITIONS

"appropriate percentage": s.11(3).

"billing authority": ss.1(2) and 69(1).

"chargeable dwelling": s.4(2).

"council tax": s.1(1).

"dwelling": ss.3 and 69(1).

"financial year": ss.69(1) and 116(1).

"prescribed": s.116(1).

"resident": ss.6(5) and 69(1).

GENERAL NOTE

The purpose of this section is to introduce further provisions for dwellings in Wales where there is no resident. The issue of second or holiday homes in Wales is more controversial politically than elsewhere in Britain, and this section is designed to allow the local authorities in Wales some discretion to take a different approach to discounts in regard to such dwellings, by either reducing the discount from 50 per cent. to 25 per cent., or giving no discount at all.

Subs. (1)

A Welsh billing authority may make a determination amending the discount which would apply to a dwelling if a number of conditions are satisfied. First, the dwelling must have no residents, and so be eligible for a discount under s.11(2)(a). Secondly, it must fall within a class of dwellings prescribed by the Secretary of State for any financial year. Thirdly, the determination must invoke either subs. (2), which reduces the discount from 50 per cent. to 25 per cent., or subs. (4), which gives no discount. Any such determination must be made by the authority, in accordance with s.67. In addition, the determination may not be questioned in any proceedings other than by an application for judicial review.

Subs. (2)

A determination made under subs. (1) to invoke this subsection in relation to a prescribed class of dwelling will reduce the discount from 50 per cent. to 25 per cent. for each day on which there is no resident of the dwelling.

Subs. (3)

A determination made under subs. (1) to invoke this subsection in relation to a prescribed class of dwelling will mean that no discount is given for each day on which there is no resident of the dwelling.

Subs. (4)

A determination by the billing authority under subs. (1) may be revoked or varied for any financial year before that year begins.

Subs. (5)

By applying s.4(3) and (4) to subs. (1) of this section, any dwellings prescribed under this section may be prescribed by reference to such factors as the Secretary of State thinks fit. While not reducing the wide discretion given by this power, further indications of the factors which may be taken into account are provided. Thus some of the factors may be the physical characteristics of the dwelling; that the dwelling may be unoccupied; that it is occupied for prescribed purposes; and that it is occupied or owned by persons of prescribed descriptions.

Subs. (6)

A billing authority is required to publicise any decision to alter the discount for a class of dwelling, by publishing a notice of its determination in at least one newspaper circulating in the area of the authority. This must be done within 21 days of the determination's being made. The power under subs. (4) to vary or revoke the determination could then be used in the light of the public response.

Subs. (7)

Although there is a duty under subs. (6) to publish the notice, a failure to do so will not invalidate the determination to alter the discount for that class of dwelling.

Reduced amounts

13.—(1) The Secretary of State may make regulations as regards any case where—

   (a) a person is liable to pay an amount to a billing authority in respect of council tax for any financial year which is prescribed; and
   (b) prescribed conditions are fulfilled.
   (2) The regulations may provide that the amount he is liable to pay shall be an amount which—
   (a) is less than the amount it would be apart from the regulations; and
   (b) is determined in accordance with prescribed rules.
   (3) This section applies whether the amount mentioned in subsection (1) above is determined under section 10 above or under that section read with section 11 or 12 above.
   (4) The conditions mentioned in subsection (1) above may be prescribed by reference to such factors as the Secretary of State thinks fit; and in particular such factors may include the making of an application by the person concerned and all or any of—
   (a) the factors mentioned in subsection (5) below; or
   (b) the factors mentioned in subsection (6) below.
   (5) The factors referred to in subsection (4)(a) above are—
   (a) community charges for a period before 1st April 1993;
   (b) the circumstances of, or other matters relating to, the person concerned;

    (c) an amount relating to the authority concerned and specified, or to be specified, for the purposes of the regulations in a report laid, or to be laid, before the House of Commons;

    (d) such other amounts as may be prescribed or arrived at in a prescribed manner.

  (6) The factors referred to in subsection (4)(b) above are—

    (a) a disabled person having his sole or main residence in the dwelling concerned;

    (b) the circumstances of, or other matters relating to, that person;

    (c) the physical characteristics of, or other matters relating to, that dwelling.

  (7) The rules mentioned in subsection (2) above may be prescribed by reference to such factors as the Secretary of State thinks fit; and in particular such factors may include all or any of the factors mentioned in subsection (5) or subsection (6)(b) or (c) above.

  (8) Without prejudice to the generality of section 113(2) below, regulations under this section may include—

    (a) provision requiring the Secretary of State to specify in a report, for the purposes of the regulations, an amount in relation to each billing authority;

    (b) provision requiring him to lay the report before the House of Commons;

    (c) provision for the review of any prescribed decision of a billing authority relating to the application or operation of the regulations;

    (d) provision that no appeal may be made to a valuation tribunal in respect of such a decision, notwithstanding section 16(1) below.

  (9) To the extent that he would not have power to do so apart from this subsection, the Secretary of State may—

    (a) include in regulations under this section such amendments of any social security instrument as he thinks expedient in consequence of the regulations under this section;

    (b) include in any social security instrument such provision as he thinks expedient in consequence of regulations under this section.

  (10) In subsection (9) above "social security instrument" means an order or regulations made, or falling to be made, by the Secretary of State under the Social Security Acts, that is to say, the Social Security Contributions and Benefits Act 1992 and the Social Security Administration Act 1992.

DEFINITIONS

    "billing authority": ss.1(2) and 69(1).
    "community charge": s.1 of the 1988 Act.
    "council tax": s.1(1).
    "dwelling": ss.3 and 69(1).
    "financial year": ss.69(1) and 116(1).
    "prescribed": s.116(1).
    "social security instrument": subs. (10).
    "valuation tribunal": ss.15(1) and 69(1).

GENERAL NOTE

    In the consultation paper on the council tax, *A New Tax For Local Government*, it was stated that the intention was to phase in the full amount of council-tax bills in order to mitigate the effect of any high increases (para. 8.1). This section allows that undertaking to be implemented by giving the Secretary of State the power to make regulations reducing the amount to be paid in certain circumstances. The cost of this may be met by a grant to the authority, as authorised by para. 18 of Sched. 10, which inserts a new s.88A of the Local Government Finance Act 1988, but only with consent of the Treasury.

Subs. (1)

    This provides the Secretary of State with the authority to make regulations in regard to the liability of council taxpayers where the conditions specified in the regulations are met. See the Council Tax (Reductions for Disabilities) Regulations 1992 (S.I. 1992 No. 554).

Subs. (2)
The regulations made under the authority of subs. (1) may reduce the amount that the council taxpayer would otherwise be liable to pay, provided that the new amount is in accordance with the prescribed rules.

Subs. (3)
The regulations made under the authority of subs. (1) may apply irrespective of entitlement to any discounts under s.11.

Subss. (4), (5) and (6)
Without prejudice to the generality of the ability of the Secretary of State to prescribe, by reference to such factors as he thinks fit, the conditions which permit the reduction of the amount of council tax to which a taxpayer is liable, this section specifies a number of such factors. The first is whether an application for such a reduction has been made. Four more, drawn from subs. (5), are the community charge before the council tax was introduced; the circumstances of the taxpayer concerned; amounts relating to the authority concerned, provided that the amount is specified in a report which will be laid before the House of Commons; and such other amounts as may be prescribed or calculated in accordance with the regulations. Another three, drawn from subs. (6), are whether the dwelling is the sole or main residence of a disabled person; the circumstances of that person; and the physical characteristics or other matters relating to that dwelling.

Subs. (7)
Without prejudice to the generality of the ability of the Secretary of State to prescribe the rules relating to the amount of any reduction of council tax by reference to such factors as he thinks fit, this section specifies a number of such factors. These factors are some, but not all of the factors which may be taken into account in prescribing the conditions under subs. (1). Four, drawn from subs. (5), are the community charge before the council tax was introduced; the circumstances of the taxpayer concerned; amounts relating to the authority concerned, provided that the amount is specified in a report which will be laid before the House of Commons; and such other amounts as may be prescribed or calculated in accordance with the regulations. Another two, drawn from subs. (6), are the circumstances of a disabled person, and the physical characteristics or other matters relating to that dwelling. This difference between the factors which may be taken into account in prescribing the conditions for reductions and the rules specifying the amount of the reduction must be seen in the light of the fact that neither prejudices the discretion of the Secretary of State to prescribe both according to such factors as he sees fit.

Subs. (8)
Without prejudice to s.113(2), which gives the Secretary of State the wide power to make such incidental, consequential or supplementary provisions to any regulations as he thinks necessary or expedient, this subsection makes it clear that regulations made under this section may include four specific factors. First, a requirement that the Secretary of State specify in a report an amount in relation to each billing authority and, secondly, that the report be laid before the House of Commons. Thirdly, the regulations may contain provisions for reviewing a decision of the billing authority in relation to the regulations, thus permitting some type of appeal system. However, the final factor permits the Secretary of State to provide that such appeals should not be made to the valuation tribunal.

Subs. (9)
This makes it clear that the Secretary of State may amend any "social security instrument", namely any social security order or regulation as defined by subs. (10), either directly to take account of regulations made under this section, or indirectly by regulations made under this section.

Subs. (10)
This subsection provides the necessary definition of "social security instrument" for the purposes of making or amending regulations under subs. (9).

Administration and appeals

Administration, penalties and enforcement

14.—(1) Schedule 2 to this Act (which contains provisions about administration, including collection) shall have effect.

(2) Schedule 3 to this Act (which contains provisions about civil penalties) shall have effect.

(3) Schedule 4 to this Act (which contains provisions about the recovery of sums due, including sums due as penalties) shall have effect.

GENERAL NOTE

This section simply brings into effect Scheds. 2, 3 and 4 of this Act which deal with administration and collection, penalties, and enforcement respectively. For an explanation of these provisions, see the notes to those schedules. See also the Council Tax (Administration and Enforcement) Regulations 1992 (S.I. 1992 No. 613), in regard to each Schedule.

Valuation tribunals

15.—(1) Valuation and community charge tribunals established under Schedule 11 to the 1988 Act shall be known as valuation tribunals.

(2) Such tribunals shall exercise, in addition to the jurisdiction conferred on them by or under the 1988 Act, the jurisdiction conferred on them by—
 (a) section 16 below;
 (b) regulations made under section 24 below; and
 (c) paragraph 3 of Schedule 3 to this Act.

DEFINITIONS

"valuation and community charge tribunal": s.136 of and Sched. 11 to the 1988 Act.
"valuation tribunal": subs. (1) and s.69(1).

GENERAL NOTE

The valuation and community charge tribunals established under the Local Government Finance Act 1988 are now renamed as the valuation tribunals, and the jurisdiction is extended to cover appeals made under s.16 of this Act in relation to the designation of a dwelling as chargeable, or an individual as liable to the council tax, or the amount of council tax determined by the billing authority as the amount due. In addition, the jurisdiction will also include appeals under s.24 against the alteration of a valuation list and, under para. 3 of Sched. 3, against the imposition of a penalty by the billing authority for failing to notify or supply information which is required by the authority, or knowingly supplying such information which is materially inaccurate.

Appeals: general

16.—(1) A person may appeal to a valuation tribunal if he is aggrieved by—
 (a) any decision of a billing authority that a dwelling is a chargeable dwelling, or that he is liable to pay council tax in respect of such a dwelling; or
 (b) any calculation made by such an authority of an amount which he is liable to pay to the authority in respect of council tax.

(2) In subsection (1) above the reference to any calculation of an amount includes a reference to any estimate of the amount.

(3) Subsection (1) above shall not apply where the grounds on which the person concerned is aggrieved fall within such category or categories as may be prescribed.

(4) No appeal may be made under subsection (1) above unless—
 (a) the aggrieved person serves a written notice under this subsection; and
 (b) one of the conditions mentioned in subsection (7) below is fulfilled.

(5) A notice under subsection (4) above must be served on the billing authority concerned.

(6) A notice under subsection (4) above must state the matter by which and the grounds on which the person is aggrieved.

(7) The conditions are that—

(a) the aggrieved person is notified in writing, by the authority on which he served the notice, that the authority believes the grievance is not well founded, but the person is still aggrieved;

(b) the aggrieved person is notified in writing, by the authority on which he served the notice, that steps have been taken to deal with the grievance, but the person is still aggrieved;

(c) the period of two months, beginning with the date of service of the aggrieved person's notice, has ended without his being notified under paragraph (a) or (b) above.

(8) Where a notice under subsection (4) above is served on an authority, the authority shall—

(a) consider the matter to which the notice relates;

(b) include in any notification under subsection (7)(a) above the reasons for the belief concerned;

(c) include in any notification under subsection (7)(b) above a statement of the steps taken.

DEFINITIONS
"billing authority": ss.1(2) and 69(1).
"chargeable dwelling": s.4(2).
"council tax": s.1(1).
"dwelling": ss.3 and 69(1).
"prescribed": s.116(1).
"valuation tribunal": ss.15(1) and 69(1).

GENERAL NOTE
This section establishes the right of appeal to the valuation tribunal in regard to certain matters, although appeals on these matters may be prohibited if the grounds of appeal fall within categories prescribed by regulation. In order to try to resolve as many matters as possible without the need for an appeal, before the appeal can be made the person aggrieved must serve a notice on the billing authority and remain dissatisfied after the response from the authority is received, or have received no response within two months. To facilitate the speedy resolution of the matter, and to simplify the appeal procedure, the authority is also charged with the duty of considering the matters raised by such a notice and with supplying reasons for their decision and any steps taken to deal with the grievance contained in the notice.

Subs. (1)
The right to appeal to a valuation tribunal is given in three circumstances. First, if the person is not satisfied with the designation of a dwelling as a chargeable dwelling, under s.4; secondly, if the person is not satisfied with the decision of the billing authority that he is liable to pay council tax in respect of a chargeable dwelling, under ss.6–9; thirdly, if the person is not satisfied with the decision of the billing authority as to any calculation of the amount of council tax which he is liable to pay. This right of appeal may be restricted if the ground of appeal is one which falls within any category prescribed by the Secretary of State, under subs. (3), and, before the appeal can be made, the procedures laid down in subs. (4) must be met.

Subs. (2)
Since a bill for council tax will usually be issued in advance of the actual liability, which is on a daily basis, this provision makes it clear that the reference in subs. (1) to any calculation of the amount of council tax to which the person is liable includes an estimate of that amount.

Subs. (3)
The grounds on which appeals can be raised concerning the matters in subs. (1) may be restricted by regulations made under this subsection. It has been stated that it is envisaged that the jurisdiction of the valuation tribunals will be taken away from matters concerning discounts and benefits.

Subs. (4)
Before an appeal can be made, two requirements must be satisfied. First, the aggrieved person must have served a written notice on the billing authority. Subsections (5) and (6) lay down that such a notice must be served on the billing authority concerned and must state the

matter and grounds by which the person is aggrieved. Secondly, one of three conditions specified in subs. (7) must be met. These are that, having notified the authority, the person must remain dissatisfied after a written explanation from the authority as to why the grievance is not well founded; or remain dissatisfied after a written explanation of the steps which the authority proposes to take to meet the grievance; or the person has received no written notification of either result within two months commencing with the date of service of the written statement of the grievance.

Subs. (5)

The notice which is required to be served under subs. (4) before an appeal can be made must be served on the billing authority concerned.

Subs. (6)

The notice which is required to be served under subs. (4) before an appeal can be made must state the matter by which the person is aggrieved and the ground of that grievance. The restriction in subs. (3) as to the grounds of appeal which are prescribed by the Secretary of State apply only to the appeal stage so a person aggrieved is not precluded from raising such matters with the authority.

Subs. (7)

The second of the requirements specified in subs. (4) which must be satisfied before an appeal can be made is dealt with by this subsection. Having notified the authority, the person must remain dissatisfied after a written explanation from the authority as to why the grievance is not well founded; or remain dissatisfied after a written explanation of the steps which the authority proposes to take to meet the grievance; or the person has received no written notification of either result within two months commencing with the date of service of the written statement of the grievance.

Subs. (8)

When the billing authority receives a written notice under subs. (4) it is placed under a duty to consider the matter to which the notice relates and then, if of the opinion that the grievance is not well founded, state the reasons for this in the notification to the person concerned or, if taking steps to deal with the grievance, specify the steps in the notification to the person concerned. This is an attempt to allow as many grievances to be resolved as soon as possible without the need for an appeal, and to clarify matters for any subsequent appeal.

Miscellaneous

Completion of new dwellings

17.—(1) Subject to the provisions of this section, Schedule 4A to the 1988 Act (which makes provision with respect to the determination of a day as the completion day in relation to a new building) shall, with the exception of paragraph 6, apply for the purposes of this Part as it applies for the purposes of Part III of that Act.

(2) Any reference in this section to the Schedule is a reference to Schedule 4A to the 1988 Act as it applies for the purposes of this Part.

(3) Where—

(a) a completion notice is served under the Schedule; and

(b) the building to which the notice relates is not completed on or before the relevant day,

any dwelling in which the building or any part of it will be comprised shall be deemed for the purposes of this Part to have come into existence on that day.

(4) For the purposes of subsection (3) above the relevant day in relation to a completion notice is—

(a) where an appeal against the notice is brought under paragraph 4 of the Schedule, the day stated in the notice; and

(b) where no appeal against the notice is brought under that paragraph, the day determined under the Schedule as the completion day in relation to the building to which the notice relates.

(5) Where—

(a) a day is determined under the Schedule as the completion day in relation to a new building; and

(b) the building is one produced by the structural alteration of a building which is comprised in one or more existing dwellings,
the existing dwelling or dwellings shall be deemed for the purposes of this Part to have ceased to exist on that day.

(6) Any reference in this section or the Schedule to a new building includes a reference to a building produced by the structural alteration of an existing building where—

(a) the existing building or any part of it is comprised in a dwelling which, by virtue of the alteration, becomes, or becomes part of, a different dwelling or different dwellings; or

(b) neither the existing building nor any part of it is, except by virtue of the alteration, comprised in any dwelling.

(7) Any reference in this section to a building includes a reference to a part of a building; and any reference in the Schedule to the valuation officer shall be construed as a reference to the listing officer.

DEFINITIONS
"building": subs. (7).
"completion notice": Sched. 4A, para. 1(6) of the 1988 Act, as enacted by s.139 and Sched. 5 of the 1989 Act.
"dwelling": ss.3 and 69(1).
"listing officer": ss.20 and 69(1).
"new building": subs. (6).
"valuation officer": s.67(2) of the 1988 Act, as amended by subs. (7) of this section.

GENERAL NOTE
The system of completion notices established to allow the local authority to serve a notice on new buildings in order to establish their rateable value for non-domestic rates is extended to dwellings by this section in relation to the council tax. Much of the drafting reflects that found in s.46A of the 1988 Act. This system is similar to that found previously in the General Rate Act 1967.

Subs. (1)
The system of completion notices and completion days contained in Sched. 4A to the 1988 Act, as enacted by s.139 of and Sched. 5 to the 1989 Act, is applied by this section for council-tax purposes. The exception to this is the exclusion of para. 6 of Sched. 4A, which deals with the position pending appeals. This section allows a completion notice to be served in respect of new buildings which comprise the whole or part of a dwelling. This notice establishes the date from which liability to the council tax in regard to that dwelling begins.

Subs. (2)
This makes it clear that any reference to "the Schedule" within this section is a reference to Sched. 4A of the 1988 Act, excluding para. 6, as it applies for council-tax purposes.

Subs. (3)
Where a completion notice is served on a building which is not yet complete, the notice specifies a "completion day", which is to be not more than three months after service of the notice. This date may be altered on appeal to the valuation tribunal. This subsection provides that even if the dwelling is not completed by that date, the "relevant date", it is nevertheless deemed to have been completed for the purpose of liability to council tax.

Subs. (4)
The definition of the "relevant date", for the purposes of subs. (3) is clarified as either of the date confirmed or substituted by the valuation tribunal on appeal, or the original date in the notice where there is no appeal.

Subs. (5)
Where a new building is created by means of a structural alteration of one or more existing buildings, then the existing buildings are deemed to cease to exist on the "completion day", as defined by the Schedule. This will entail a revaluation of any remaining separate buildings.

Subs. (6)
This subsection makes clear that a "new building", for the purposes of this section, includes

the alteration of an existing building, whether or not the existing building was a dwelling. Thus two circumstances are specified: first, where the existing building is a dwelling and becomes a different dwelling, or becomes part of a different dwelling, by virtue of the alteration; and secondly, where no part of the existing building was a dwelling.

Subs. (7)

For clarification, this provides that a reference to a "building" includes part of a building, and it also updates the language of Sched. 4A to the 1988 Act by substituting "listing officer" for "valuation officer" for the purpose of council-tax valuation lists.

Death of persons liable

18.—(1) The Secretary of State may make such regulations as he thinks fit to deal with any case where a person dies and at any time before his death—

(a) he was (or is alleged to have been) liable to pay council tax under section 6, 7 or 8 above;

(b) he was (or is alleged to have been) so liable, as spouse, under section 9 above; or

(c) a penalty was imposed on him under paragraph 1 of Schedule 3 to this Act.

(2) Nothing in the following provisions of this section shall prejudice the generality of subsection (1) above.

(3) The regulations may provide that where before his death a sum has become payable by the deceased but has not been paid his executor or administrator shall be liable to pay the sum and may deduct out of the assets and effects of the deceased any payments made (or to be made).

(4) The regulations may provide that where before his death a sum in excess of his liability has been paid (whether the excess arises because of his death or otherwise) and has not been repaid or credited his executor or administrator shall be entitled to the sum.

(5) The regulations may provide for the recovery of any sum which is payable under the regulations and is not paid.

(6) The regulations may provide that proceedings (whether by way of appeal or otherwise) may be instituted, continued or withdrawn by the deceased's executor or administrator.

DEFINITIONS

"council tax": s.1(1).

GENERAL NOTE

This section provides the authority for the Secretary of State to make regulations relating to the consequences of the death of a person liable to pay council tax, or a penalty imposed in relation to the tax. While the section is essentially a general enabling section, without prejudicing the discretion of the Secretary of State a number of particular examples of what the regulations may contain are provided.

Subs. (1)

This provides the general authority for the Secretary of State to make such regulations as he sees fit in regard to the death of a person who was, or was alleged to be, liable to pay council tax either directly under ss.6, 7 or 8, or jointly or severally for a spouse under s.9, or on whom a penalty under Sched. 3 had been imposed.

Subs. (2)

Despite the remaining parts of the section giving examples of what the regulations may be expected to contain, this makes it clear that the provision of these does not prejudice the discretion of the Secretary of State in formulating the regulations.

Subs. (3)

The regulations may provide that the executor or administrator of the estate of the deceased shall be liable for any outstanding sums, and that any such sum may be deducted from the assets and effects of the deceased.

Subs. (4)
The regulations may provide that the executor or administrator of the estate of the deceased shall be entitled to any outstanding sums owed to the deceased, such as sums paid before liability has arisen.

Subs. (5)
The regulations may provide for the recovery of any sums due under the regulations.

Subs. (6)
The regulations may give to the executor or administrator the powers to institute, continue or withdraw appeals on behalf of the deceased.

Exclusion of Crown exemption in certain cases

19.—(1) Subsection (2) below applies in the case of a dwelling provided and maintained by an authority mentioned in subsection (3) below for purposes connected with the administration of justice, police purposes or other Crown purposes.

(2) Any rules as to Crown exemption which would have applied apart from this subsection shall not prevent—
  (a) the dwelling being a chargeable dwelling; or
  (b) any person being liable to pay council tax in respect of the dwelling.
(3) The authorities are—
  (a) a billing authority other than the Council of the Isles of Scilly;
  (b) a county council;
  (c) a metropolitan county police authority;
  (d) the Northumbria Police Authority;
  (e) the Receiver for the Metropolitan Police District; and
  (f) a combined police authority as defined in section 144 of the 1988 Act.
(4) The Secretary of State may by order provide that subsection (2) above shall also apply in relation to any dwelling of a class prescribed by the order.
(5) Subsections (3) and (4) of section 4 above shall apply for the purposes of subsection (4) above as they apply for the purposes of subsection (2) of that section.

DEFINITIONS
  "billing authority": ss.1(2) and 69(1).
  "chargeable dwelling": s.4(2).
  "council tax": s.1(1).
  "dwelling": ss.3 and 69(1).

GENERAL NOTE
This section is designed to remove immunity from liability, on the basis of Crown status, from certain dwellings. It is a general principle of law that the Crown is not bound by statute unless expressly stated to be so (*Lord Advocate* v. *Dumbarton District Council* [1990] 2 A.C. 580). Historically, because the Crown was not mentioned in the Statute of Elizabeth, Crown properties were not rateable. Premises occupied by the departments of state and the fighting services clearly came within this category, such as Government offices, army barracks, prisons and hospitals under the control of area health authorities. The Crown exemption is extended to properties occupied for the purposes of the Crown in the carrying out of functions of central government, even though the occupants are not strictly the servants of the Crown, so that exemption had been afforded to police stations (*Coomber* v. *Berkshire J.J.* (1882) 2 App.Cas. 61). However, under s.64(5) of the 1988 Act, all hereditaments provided and maintained for purposes connected with the administration of justice, police purposes and other Crown purposes by a specified authority were excluded from this exemption, and such properties must be entered in the rating list. This section extends that approach to the council-tax system for properties which fall within the classes specified. Power is also given to the Secretary of State to extend the classes by means of regulations.

Subs. (1)
This establishes that where a dwelling is provided and maintained by one of the authorities listed in subs. (3), for purposes connected with the administration of justice, police purposes and other Crown purposes, then subs. (2), which removes Crown exemption, will apply.

Subs. (2)

Where this subsection is deemed to apply, Crown exemption is removed from dwellings and the person who would otherwise be liable to pay the council tax for a chargeable dwelling shall be so liable.

Subs. (3)

Where a dwelling is provided and maintained for purposes connected with the administration of justice, police purposes and other Crown purposes by one of the authorities listed in this subsection, then Crown exemption is removed from liability to pay the council tax.

Subs. (4)

Power is given to the Secretary of State to extend, by means of regulation, the classes of dwelling from which Crown exemption will be removed.

Subs. (5)

By applying s.4(3) and (4) to subs. (4) of this section, any dwellings prescribed under this section may be prescribed by reference to such factors as the Secretary of State thinks fit. While not reducing the wide discretion given by this power, further indications of the factors which may be taken into account are provided. Thus some of the factors may be the physical characteristics of the dwelling; that the dwelling may be unoccupied; that it is occupied for prescribed purposes; and that it is occupied or owned by persons of prescribed descriptions.

CHAPTER II

VALUATION LISTS

Preliminary

Listing officers

20.—(1) The Commissioners of Inland Revenue shall appoint a listing officer for each billing authority.

(2) The remuneration of, and any expenses incurred by, listing officers in carrying out their functions (including the remuneration and expenses of persons, whether or not in the service of the Crown, to assist them) shall be paid out of money provided by Parliament.

(3) Any reference in this Chapter to a listing officer's or the Commissioners' functions is a reference to the functions imposed or conferred on him or them by or under this Chapter.

DEFINITIONS

"billing authority": ss.1(2) and 69(1).
"listing officer": ss.20 and 69(1).

GENERAL NOTE

Listing officers are to be appointed for each billing authority by the Commissioners of Inland Revenue, and shall be Crown servants paid out of central funds, rather than by the authority. The functions of the listing officer and the Commissioners are defined as those duties or powers contained within Chapter II of this Part of the Act.

The lists

Valuations for purposes of lists

21.—(1) The Commissioners of Inland Revenue shall—
(a) carry out such valuations of dwellings in England and Wales;
(b) furnish listing officers with such information obtained in carrying out the valuations or in the exercise of the powers conferred by section 27 below; and
(c) disclose to such officers such contents of particulars delivered documents,
as they consider necessary or expedient for the purpose of facilitating the compilation and maintenance by those officers of valuation lists in accordance with this Chapter.

(2) The valuations shall be carried out by reference to 1st April 1991 and on such assumptions and in accordance with such principles as may be prescribed.

(3) Without prejudice to the generality of their powers, the Commissioners of Inland Revenue may appoint persons who are not in the service of the Crown to assist them in carrying out the valuations.

(4) For the purposes of the valuations the Commissioners of Inland Revenue may disclose to a person appointed under subsection (3) above—

(a) any survey report obtained for any purpose of rating, including non-domestic rating; and

(b) any information obtained in the exercise of the powers conferred by section 27 below.

(5) If any person to whom any report or information is disclosed by virtue of subsection (4) above uses or discloses the report or information, in whole or in part, otherwise than for the purposes of the valuations, he shall be liable—

(a) on conviction on indictment, to imprisonment for a term not exceeding two years or a fine or both; and

(b) on summary conviction, to imprisonment for a term not exceeding six months or a fine not exceeding the statutory maximum or both.

(6) Except as provided by subsection (4) above, nothing in this section permits the disclosure to any person appointed under subsection (3) above of information which is subject to the rules of confidentiality applicable to the Commissioners of Inland Revenue.

DEFINITIONS
"dwelling": ss.3 and 69(1).
"information": s.116(1).
"listing officer": ss.20 and 69(1).
"particulars delivered documents": s.69(1).
"prescribed": s.116(1).
"valuation list": s.22(1).

GENERAL NOTE
The initial legal authority for the valuation of domestic properties for council-tax purposes was provided by s.3 of the Local Government Finance and Valuation Act 1991. That Act is now repealed by the present Act and the provisions relating to valuation are now included in amended form in this section. It places a duty on the Commissioners of Inland Revenue to carry out valuations to assist listing officers in compiling the valuation list. They are empowered to appoint persons not in the service to assist in this process, and in practice much of the work has been undertaken by estate agents. It also makes provision for the disclosure of information to such appointees but with restrictions on its use.

Subs. (1)
The Commissioners of Inland Revenue are required to carry out such valuations as they consider necessary or expedient for facilitating the compilation and maintenance of the valuation lists. They are also to supply, as they consider necessary or expedient, information obtained in the valuation exercise, or from community charge officers or others by virtue of the powers conferred by s.27, or relevant information from particulars delivered documents in the possession of the Commissioners of Inland Revenue.

Subs. (2)
The value of a dwelling is to be taken to be that on April 1, 1991, based on market capital value. The Secretary of State is also empowered to prescribe further assumptions and principles for the valuation exercise. For the regulations, see the Council Tax (Situation and Valuation of Dwellings) Regulations 1992 (S.I. 1992 No. 550), which provides that the principle is that the value at that is that which it might reasonably have been expected to realise if it had been sold in the open market by a willing vendor. The assumptions on which that is based are that the sale was with vacant possession; that the interest was freehold or a lease of 99 years at a nominal rent; that it was sold free of any rent charge or other incumbrance; that it was in a state of reasonable repair, and that where there are common parts that they were in a similar state, but that the costs of maintenance of the common parts could be taken into account; that fixtures are

not included in the dwelling; that it would be permanently restricted to use as a dwelling; and that it had no development value other than value attributable to permitted development. Where, under s.24, it is alleged that there has been a material reduction in the value it shall be assumed that the physical state of the locality of the dwelling was the same as on the date from which the alteration of the list would have effect; and the size, layout and character of the dwelling the same as on the date from which the alteration would take place.

Subs. (3)
This makes it clear that the Commissioners of Inland Revenue can appoint persons not in their service to undertake the work. Given the scale of the task of valuing every dwelling, this was essential and a significant proportion of the initial valuation was carried out by estate agents through contracts.

Subs. (4)
The disclosure by the Commissioners of Inland Revenue of certain information to any person appointed to carry out valuations is authorised by this subsection. The information may be a survey report obtained for rating purposes under the old system of rating or from the more recent non-domestic rating system. They may also disclose any information obtained under the authority of s.27 about specific dwellings from a community charges officer or any other person prescribed by regulation. Such information would normally be subject to confidentiality, so in order to safeguard the interests of those about whom information is disclosed, subs. (5) prohibits its use for any purpose other than valuation.

Subs. (5)
In order to protect the interests of those about whom information is disclosed under subs. (4), it will be an offence to use or disclose further the information for any purpose other than valuation. The penalty for this offence is, on indictment, up to two years' imprisonment or a fine, or both. On summary conviction, the penalty is up to six months' imprisonment or a fine up to the statutory maximum, or both.

Subs. (6)
For the avoidance of doubt, it is provided that no information which is subject to the rules on confidentiality should be disclosed to those appointed to conduct valuations other than as authorised explicitly by subs. (4).

Compilation and maintenance of lists

22.—(1) In accordance with this Chapter, the listing officer for a billing authority shall compile, and then maintain, a list for the authority (to be called its valuation list).

(2) The list must be compiled on 1st April 1993 and shall come into force on that day.

(3) Before the list is compiled the listing officer must take such steps as are reasonably practicable in the time available to ensure that it is accurately compiled on 1st April 1993.

(4) Any valuation of a dwelling carried out by the listing officer in pursuance of subsection (3) above shall be carried out in accordance with section 21(2) above.

(5) At the following times, namely—
   (a) not later than 1st September 1992; and
   (b) not earlier than 15th November 1992 and not later than 1st December 1992,
the listing officer shall send to the billing authority a copy of the list which he proposes (on the information then before him) to compile.

(6) As soon as reasonably practicable after receiving the copy under subsection (5)(b) above the authority shall deposit it at its principal office and take such steps as it thinks most suitable for giving notice of it.

(7) As soon as reasonably practicable after compiling a list the listing officer shall send a copy of it to the authority.

(8) As soon as reasonably practicable after receiving the copy under subsection (7) above the authority shall deposit it at its principal office.

(9) The list must be maintained for so long as is necessary for the purposes of this Part.

DEFINITIONS
"billing authority": ss.1(2) and 69(1).
"dwelling": ss.3 and 69(1).
"listing officer": ss.20 and 69(1).
"valuation list": subs. (1).

GENERAL NOTE
Each listing officer for a billing authority must compile and maintain a valuation list, which is technically to be "compiled" on April 1, 1993 and come into force on that day. Prior to that, a number of stages must be gone through in order to allow public scrutiny of the draft list and corrections to be made.

Subs. (1)
A duty is placed on the listing officer for a billing authority to compile and maintain a valuation list for all dwellings in the area.

Subs. (2)
The valuation list is technically to be "compiled" on April 1, 1993 and come into force on that day.

Subs. (3)
A general duty is placed on the listing officer to ensure that the list is as accurate as reasonably possible prior to its being "compiled". That the short time-scale available for such a large exercise will restrict what is possible is recognised by the explicit qualification of "reasonably practicable in the time available". During the Parliamentary proceedings, a number of amendments to the effect that the introduction should be delayed a year to allow the process to proceed more accurately failed to find success. The intention in the exercise is to take account of the physical characteristics and external environment of the property as at April 1, 1993, but the value placed is that which would have prevailed in relation to those characteristics on April 1, 1991. Within this general duty and constraint, further specific requirements are laid down by subss. (5)–(8).

Subs. (4)
This subsection confirms that the introduction of what is "reasonably possible in the time available" does not alter the duty imposed on the listing officer by s.21(2) to carry out the valuation on such assumptions and principles as are laid down in regulations.

Subs. (5)
At two stages in the process leading up to the formal compilation of the valuation list, the listing officer must send to the billing authority a copy of the proposed list. The first date is set as not later than September 1, 1992, and the second has to be within the period November 15–December 1. This will allow the billing authority to make comments.

Subs. (6)
Following receipt of the second proposed valuation list, publicity must be given to the list by the billing authority. The precise form of the publicity is left to the discretion of the authority, but a copy of the list must be deposited at the principal office of the authority for public scrutiny.

Subs. (7)
Soon after April 1, 1993, when the list is formally "compiled", the listing officer must send a copy to the billing authority. Again, this duty is qualified as being as soon as is "reasonably practicable".

Subs. (8)
When the final copy of the valuation list is received, the billing authority is required to deposit it at its principal office. At this stage, there is no need for further publicity.

Subs. (9)
The duty to maintain the valuation list is a continuing one.

Contents of lists

23.—(1) A valuation list must show, for each day for which it is in force, each dwelling which is situated in the billing authority's area.

(2) For each day on which a dwelling is shown in a list, the list must also show which of the valuation bands is applicable to the dwelling.

(3) A list must also contain such information about dwellings shown in it as may be prescribed.

(4) The omission from a list of any matter required to be included in it shall not of itself render the list invalid.

(5) Any rules as to Crown exemption which would have applied apart from this subsection shall not prevent a list showing a dwelling, showing the valuation band applicable to a dwelling and containing any prescribed information about a dwelling.

DEFINITIONS
"billing authority": ss.1(2) and 69(1).
"dwelling": ss.3 and 69(1).
"prescribed": s.116(1).
"valuation band": s.5(2) and (3).
"valuation list": s.22(1).

GENERAL NOTE
This section establishes the minimum contents of a valuation list and gives the Secretary of State the power to make regulations further specifying the contents.

Subss. (1) and (2)
Each dwelling in the billing authority's area must be shown in the valuation list for each day for which it is in force, together with the valuation band applicable. Exclusion from the valuation list does not affect the status of the dwelling as "chargeable dwelling", but the amount of tax payable could not be calculated in accordance with s.10, so no tax could be demanded in relation to a dwelling not shown in the valuation list for that day.

Subs. (3)
The Secretary of State may make regulations requiring the valuation list to show additional information. This has been used in the Council Tax (Contents of Valuation Lists) Regulations 1992 (S.I. 1992 No. 553) to require that the lists show a reference number for each dwelling, and indicate if the property is a composite hereditament. In addition, where the list has been altered, it must show the period for which or the date from which the alteration is to take effect, and whether the alteration was made in compliance with an order of the valuation tribunal or the High Court.

Subs. (4)
The validity of the valuation list itself, as opposed to validity in regard to the item, will not be automatically affected by the omission of any matter which should have been included by virtue of this section and any regulations made under it. Should the defects be sufficiently grave, however, it would be open to the court to decide that the list was void.

Subs. (5)
Any dwelling which would otherwise be exempt from liability to be shown in the list by virtue of Crown exemption shall be included in the list, together with the applicable band and any other information required by regulation. This does not, however, mean that council tax will be required to be paid. Only those dwellings which would have had Crown exemption but for s.19 will be required to pay council tax. The custom whereby the Crown may nevertheless make a contribution in aid may continue, although there is no provision in this Act similar to s.59 of the 1988 Act recognising this practice.

Alteration of lists

24.—(1) The Secretary of State may make regulations about the alteration by listing officers of valuation lists which have been compiled under this Chapter; and subsections (2) to (10) below shall apply for the purposes of this subsection.

(2) The regulations may include provision that where a listing officer intends to alter the list with a view to its being accurately maintained, he shall not alter it unless prescribed conditions (as to notice or otherwise) are fulfilled.

(3) The regulations may include provision that any valuation of a dwelling carried out in connection with a proposal for the alteration of the list shall be carried out in accordance with section 21(2) above.

(4) The regulations may include provision that no alteration shall be made of a valuation band shown in the list as applicable to any dwelling unless—

  (a) since the valuation band was first shown in the list as applicable to the dwelling—

      (i) there has been a material increase in the value of the dwelling and a relevant transaction has been subsequently carried out in relation to the whole or any part of it;

      (ii) there has been a material reduction in the value of the dwelling;

      (iii) the dwelling has become or ceased to be a composite hereditament for the purposes of Part III of the 1988 Act; or

      (iv) in the case of a dwelling which continues to be such a hereditament, there has been an increase or reduction in its domestic use,

    and (in any case) prescribed conditions are fulfilled;

  (b) the listing officer is satisfied that—

      (i) a different valuation band should have been determined by him as applicable to the dwelling; or

      (ii) the valuation band shown in the list is not that determined by him as so applicable; or

  (c) an order of a valuation tribunal or of the High Court requires the alteration to be made.

(5) The regulations may include provision—

  (a) as to who (other than a listing officer) may make a proposal for the alteration of the list with a view to its being accurately maintained;

  (b) as to the manner and circumstances in which a proposal may be made and the information to be included in a proposal;

  (c) as to the period within which a proposal must be made;

  (d) as to the procedure for and subsequent to the making of a proposal;

  (e) as to the circumstances in which and the conditions upon which a proposal may be withdrawn; and

  (f) requiring the listing officer to inform other prescribed persons of the proposal in a prescribed manner.

(6) The regulations may include provision that, where there is a disagreement between the listing officer and another person making a proposal for the alteration of a list—

  (a) about the validity of the proposal; or

  (b) about the accuracy of the list,

an appeal may be made to a valuation tribunal.

(7) The regulations may include—

  (a) provision as to the period for which or day from which an alteration of a list is to have effect (including provision that it is to have retrospective effect);

  (b) provision requiring a list to be altered so as to indicate the effect (retrospective or otherwise) of the alteration;

  (c) provision requiring the listing officer to inform prescribed persons of an alteration within a prescribed period;

  (d) provision requiring the listing officer to keep for a prescribed period a record of the state of the list before the alteration was made.

(8) The regulations may include provision as to financial adjustments to be made as a result of alterations, including—

(a) provision requiring payments or repayments to be made; and

(b) provision as to the recovery (by deduction or otherwise) of sums due.

(9) The regulations may include provision that where—

(a) the listing officer for a billing authority has informed the authority of an alteration of the list; and

(b) a copy of the list has been deposited by the authority under section 22(8) above,

the authority must alter the copy accordingly.

(10) In this section—

"domestic use", in relation to a dwelling, means use in such a manner as to constitute it domestic property for the purposes of Part III of the 1988 Act;

"material increase", in relation to the value of a dwelling, means any increase which is caused (in whole or in part) by any building, engineering or other operation carried out in relation to the dwelling, whether or not constituting development for which planning permission is required;

"material reduction", in relation to the value of a dwelling, means any reduction which is caused (in whole or in part) by the demolition of any part of the dwelling, any change in the physical state of the dwelling's locality or any adaptation of the dwelling to make it suitable for use by a physically disabled person;

"relevant transaction" means a transfer on sale of the fee simple, a grant of a lease for a term of seven years or more or a transfer on sale of such a lease.

DEFINITIONS

"composite hereditament": s.64(9) of the 1988 Act.

"domestic use": subs. (10); s.66 of the 1988 Act.

"dwelling": ss.3 and 69(1).

"listing officer": ss.20 and 69(1).

"material increase": subs. (10).

"material reduction": subs. (10).

"prescribed": s.116(1).

"relevant transaction": subs. (10).

"valuation band": s.5(2) and (3).

"valuation list": s.22(1).

"valuation tribunal": ss.15(1) and 69(1).

GENERAL NOTE

This section provides the Secretary of State with a wide power to make regulations regarding the amendment of the valuation lists. Indications of what the regulations may contain are given by a number of the subsections.

Subs. (1)

The Secretary of State is given a general power to make regulations concerning the alteration of valuation lists by listing officers, subject to the clarification and elaboration in the remainder of the section.

Subs. (2)

This makes it clear that before a listing officer is able to alter a valuation list, any conditions in the regulations must be fulfilled. The scope of the conditions is not limited by the subsection, but may concern periods of notice.

Subs. (3)

As would be expected, the regulations should include provision for applying the same assumptions and principles of valuation as the original valuation exercise, as established by s.21(2).

Subs. (4)

This subsection is not drafted as clearly as it could be, despite amendment during the legislative process. It would appear that the intention is that before an alteration can be made to the valuation band, shown as applicable to a particular dwelling, one of three factors must have changed from the time of the original compilation of the valuation list. The first of these, in para. (a), relates to extent of domestic use and the value of the dwelling; the second, in para. (b), to the opinion of the listing officer as to the value; and the third, in para. (c), to an order of the valuation tribunal or High Court. The lack of clarity in the drafting relates to the relationship between the three factors.

Para. (a). The first factor, namely the extent of domestic use and the value of the dwelling, is in turn divided into four components, one of which must be present to satisfy the requirement. The first two are relatively straightforward and deal with an increase or reduction in the value of the property. Where the value has increased, the valuation band can be altered only where there has also been a "relevant transaction" in regard to all or some of the dwelling, that is, a sale of the property or the grant, or transfer on sale, of a lease of seven years or longer. Where the value has decreased, that fact alone will not be sufficient to meet the requirement of para. (a). The reduction must have been due in whole or in part to demolition of part of the dwelling, some physical change in the locality of the property, or adaptation to meet the needs of the disabled. The third and fourth components relate to a "composite hereditament", that is, a property only part of which is domestic, with the rest non-domestic and thus subject to the non-domestic rating system. If a dwelling has become, or ceased to be, a composite hereditament, then, as the third component, the valuation band may be altered. The fourth component would allow the valuation band to be altered where, in relation to an existing composite hereditament, there is a change in the proportion of the domestic use. However, in regard to all four components of the first factor, the Secretary of State may prescribe additional conditions which must be fulfilled.

Para. (b). The second factor is the opinion of the listing officer as to the value of the dwelling. It is envisaged that two different situations could occur, both of which appear to concern errors and would allow the valuation band to be changed. The first deals with a situation where the wrong valuation has been made, and the listing officer is of the opinion that a different valuation band should have been determined by him for the dwelling. The second appears to deal with the situation where a mistake occurs over the actual entry, and the valuation band shown in the list is not that actually determined by him at that time as applicable to the dwelling. It is open to interpretation as to whether that allows for a subsequent determination different from that shown in the list, but where that shown in the list was not initially incorrect.

Para. (c). The third factor is the order of a valuation tribunal or the High Court requiring the alteration to the valuation list to be made.

The lack of clarity in the drafting relates to the relationship between the three factors and the difficulty of interpretation of para. (b). On the original drafting of the Bill, no provision was made for composite hereditaments or that the original determination of the band by the listing officer could be wrong. Under para. (a) therefore the band could be altered only if the value had increased or reduced, and under para. (b) if the "valuation band shown in the list is not the valuation band determined by the listing officer as applicable to the dwelling". The relationship between para. (b) and para. (c) is clear in both versions. These are alternatives and clearly both do not have to be present. The problem is the relationship between para. (a) and the other two. On the original drafting, since there was no connecting link from para. (a) to (b), but there was between paras. (b) and (c), it appeared to be the intention that there had to be a change in the value *and* either the listing officer had to consider that the valuation band shown in the list was no longer appropriate or the valuation tribunal or High Court ordered the alteration to be made. It would appear that the intention of the revised drafting is that it is not necessary for both paras. (a) *and* (b) or (c) to be present. Such a connection is possible, but not necessary. Had the drafting included "; or" at the end of para. (a) this would have been clearer, and would require it to be read as allowing mistakes in the valuation to be corrected. Indeed, that formulation is used in the equivalent power in relation to Scotland, under s.87 of this Act.

Subs. (5)

Matters concerning initiation and making of proposals for alteration, the relevant time periods and procedures for dealing with proposals, and publicity for and withdrawal of the proposals may be provided for by regulation. As with all regulations made under this Act, the regulations may contain such incidental, consequential and supplementary provisions as the Secretary of State or Treasury think necessary or expedient.

Subs. (6)

This permits the regulations to provide that, where there is a disagreement between the listing officer and another person about the validity of a proposal to alter the list, or about the accuracy of the list, then an appeal may be considered by a valuation tribunal.

Subs. (7)

Where a list is to be altered, the regulations may contain provisions relating to the date or period from which the alteration is to have effect; the effect of the alteration to the list, including whether it is to operate retrospectively; requirements for the listing officer to inform any persons; and requirements as to the keeping of a record of the list prior to the alteration.

Subs. (8)

Where a list is to be altered, the regulations may contain provisions requiring payments or repayments to be made, and for the recovery of sums due.

Subs. (9)

This subsection allows for the billing authority to be required to alter its copy of the list upon notification of the change by the listing officer.

Subs. (10)

This provides additional definitions for this section, relating to subs. (4).

Compilation and maintenance of new lists

25.—(1) This section applies where the Secretary of State makes an order under subsection (4)(b) of section 5 above providing that, as regards financial years beginning on or after such date as is specified in the order, valuation bands so specified shall be substituted for those for the time being effective for the purposes of subsection (2) or (3) of that section.

(2) For the purpose of—

(a) requiring listing officers to compile, and then maintain, new valuation lists for those financial years; and

(b) facilitating the compilation and maintenance by those officers of those lists,

the provisions of this Chapter shall have effect with the modifications mentioned in subsection (3) below.

(3) The modifications are—

(a) for the date specified in section 22(2) and (3) above there shall be substituted the date specified in the order; and

(b) for the dates specified in sections 21(2) and 22(5) above there shall be substituted such dates as are specified in an order made by the Secretary of State under this subsection.

DEFINITIONS

"financial year": s.69(1).
"listing officer": ss.20 and 69(1).
"valuation band": s.5(2) and (3).
"valuation list": s.22(1).

GENERAL NOTE

This section makes provision for the implementation of any decision of the Secretary of State, under s.5(4), to alter the valuation bands. Listing officers will be required to compile and maintain new valuation lists in accordance with the general provisions in relation to the lists, subject to certain modifications. The modifications are the date on which the list was compiled; the date by reference to which the valuations are to be treated as having been carried out; and the dates by which the listing officer must supply the billing authority with an advance copy of the new list.

Supplemental

Powers of entry

26.—(1) If a valuation officer needs to value a dwelling for the purpose of carrying out any of his functions, he and any servant of the Crown authorised by him in writing may enter on, survey and value the dwelling if subsections (2) and (3) below are fulfilled.

(2) At least three clear days' notice in writing of the proposed exercise of the power must be given; and there shall be disregarded for this purpose any day which is—

(a) a Saturday, a Sunday, Christmas Day or Good Friday; or

(b) a day which is a bank holiday under the Banking and Financial Dealings Act 1971 in England and Wales.

(3) In a case where a person authorised by a valuation officer proposes to exercise the power, that person must if required produce his authority.

(4) If a person intentionally delays or obstructs a person in the exercise of a power under this section, he shall be liable on summary conviction to a fine not exceeding level 2 on the standard scale.

(5) In this section and section 27 below "valuation officer" means any listing officer and any other officer of the Commissioners of Inland Revenue who is for the time being appointed by them to carry out any of their functions.

DEFINITIONS
"dwelling": ss.3 and 69(1).
"valuation officer": subs. (5).

GENERAL NOTE
By this section, authorised officers are entitled to enter upon property in order to carry out their functions in regard to the valuation of property for the purposes of compilation and maintenance of the valuation lists. A minimum period of notice before entry is prescribed, and the offence of obstructing the exercise of this power is created.

Subs. (1)
A valuation officer, as defined by subs. (5), may enter a dwelling in order to survey and value it, provided that the conditions in subss. (2) and (3) are met. The wording of this section means that the valuation officer has no right to enter property for the purpose of valuing another property. The valuation officer may also authorise any other servant of the Crown, such as valuers, to enter the property for the purpose of valuing that property, provided that the authorisation is in writing. The drafting in regard to this last aspect may have been improved by the use of the phrase "he or any servant of the Crown". The use of the phrase "he *and* any servant of the Crown" gives the impression that the valuation officer must accompany the other servant of the Crown. However, this interpretation would make subs. (3) below redundant.

Subs. (2)
The first condition to be met before the valuation officer may enter a property for the purpose of valuing that property is that adequate notice in writing must be given. This is defined as three clear days' notice, excluding Saturday or Sunday, Christmas Day or Good Friday, and any other bank holiday. The period of notice was increased from a simple 24 hours' notice as proposed in the original Bill.

Subs. (3)
Where the entry to the property is to be carried out by a servant of the Crown authorised by the valuation officer under subs. (1) above, then that person must produce written authority if requested.

Subs. (4)
This section makes it an offence to delay or obstruct deliberately the exercise of the power of entry. On summary conviction the penalty shall not exceed level 2 on the standard scale.

Subs. (5)
For the purposes of this section and s.27, the valuation officer is not simply the listing officer but includes any other officer appointed by the Commissioners of Inland Revenue to carry out any of their functions under this Act.

Information about properties

27.—(1) In any case where—

(a) a notice is served by a listing officer or the Commissioners of Inland

Revenue on a charging or billing authority, a community charges registration officer or any other person prescribed for the purposes of this subsection;

(b) the notice requests the supply of information of a description specified in the notice; and

(c) the information relates to property and is information which the listing officer or the Commissioners reasonably believe will assist him or them in carrying out any of his or their functions,

the authority, officer or other person shall supply the information requested, and shall do so in such form and manner and at such time as the listing officer or the Commissioners specify in the notice.

(2) For the purpose of carrying out any of his functions, a valuation officer may serve on a person who is or has been an owner or occupier of any dwelling a notice—

(a) requesting him to supply to the officer information which is of a description specified in the notice; and

(b) stating that the officer believes the information requested will assist him in carrying out his functions.

(3) A person on whom a notice is served under subsection (2) above shall supply the information requested if it is in his possession or control, and shall do so in such form and manner as is specified in the notice and within the period of 21 days beginning with the day on which the notice is served.

(4) If a person on whom a notice has been served under subsection (2) above fails without reasonable excuse to comply with subsection (3) above, he shall be liable on summary conviction to a fine not exceeding level 2 on the standard scale.

(5) If, in supplying information in purported compliance with subsection (3) above, a person on whom a notice has been served under subsection (2) above—

(a) makes a statement which he knows to be false in a material particular; or

(b) recklessly makes a statement which is false in a material particular,

he shall be liable on summary conviction to imprisonment for a term not exceeding three months or a fine not exceeding level 3 on the standard scale or both.

(6) If in the course of the exercise of its functions any information comes to the notice of a charging or billing authority which it considers would assist a listing officer in carrying out any of his functions, it shall be the authority's duty to inform the listing officer.

(7) In carrying out any of his or their functions, a listing officer or the Commissioners of Inland Revenue may also take into account any other information available to him or them, whatever its source and whether or not obtained under a provision contained in or made under this or any other Act.

(8) In this section—

"charging authority" shall be construed in accordance with section 144(1) of the 1988 Act;

"community charges registration officer" shall be construed in accordance with section 26 of that Act.

<small>Definitions</small>
  "billing authority": ss.1(2) and 69(1).
  "charging authority": subs. (8); s.144(1) of the 1988 Act.
  "community charges registration officer": subs. (8); s.26 of the 1988 Act.
  "dwelling": ss.3 and 69(1).
  "information": s.116(1).
  "listing officer": ss.20 and 69(1).
  "owner": ss.6(5) and 69(1).
  "valuation officer": s.26(5).

GENERAL NOTE

This section permits a listing officer or the Commissioners of Inland Revenue to require information about properties to be made available from a number of sources. Duties are placed on authorities and other persons to comply with the terms of the notice requiring the information to be supplied. It also provides for associated offences and makes clear the breadth of the ability of the listing officer or the Commissioners of Inland Revenue to take into account information received.

Subs. (1)

This subsection deals with information sought by the listing officer or Commissioners of Inland Revenue from "official" sources. Information may be obtained by means of a notice which must conform to the requirements of this subsection. The notice may be served on a charging or billing authority, a community charges registration officer, or any other person prescribed in regulations made for the purposes of this section. The information must relate to property, but this is likely to be interpreted to include information about persons in that property. There is no attempt in the section to further specify the type of information, but there is provided a limitation that the listing officer or Commissioners of Inland Revenue must reasonably believe that the information will assist them in carrying out their functions. The notice must also specify the information sought, and the manner, form and timing of the reply. Where a notice is served which conforms to these requirements, then it is the duty of those on whom the notice is served to supply the information in such manner, form and time as is specified in the notice.

Subs. (2)

This subsection deals with information sought by the listing officer or Commissioners of Inland Revenue from "unofficial" sources. Information may be obtained by means of a notice which must conform to the requirements of this subsection. The notice may be served on an owner or occupier of any dwelling. The information required must be specified in the notice. There is no attempt in the section to further specify the type of information, but there is provided a limitation that the listing officer or Commissioners of Inland Revenue must state in the notice that they believe that the information will assist them in carrying out their functions.

Subs. (3)

Where a notice is served under subs. (2), the notice must also specify the manner and form of the reply. Where a notice is served which conforms to these requirements, then it is the duty of those on whom the notice is served to supply the information in the manner and form requested within 21 days from the date of service of the notice. Subsection (4) below makes it an offence to fail to comply with this requirement, but this subsection provides the defence of reasonable excuse, such as that the information was not within the recipient's possession or control.

Subs. (4)

It is an offence to fail to comply with the requirement, imposed by subs. (3), to supply the information requested by a notice, served under subs. (2), in the manner and form requested within 21 days from the date of service of the notice. On summary conviction the maximum fine shall not exceed level 2 on the standard scale. There is provided the defence of "reasonable excuse", and in this regard subs. (3) provides a defence that the information was not within the recipient's possession or control.

Subs. (5)

Where the recipient does provide information in response to a notice served under subs. (2), but thereby either knowingly or recklessly makes a statement which is false, then he is guilty of an offence. On summary conviction for this offence the maximum punishment is a term of imprisonment not exceeding three months, a fine not exceeding level 3 on the standard scale, or both.

Subs. (6)

This subsection places a further duty upon the charging or billing authority to provide information to the listing officer. For the duty to operate, the following two criteria must be satisfied. First, the information must have been obtained in the exercise of the functions of the charging or billing authority. Secondly, the authority must be of the opinion that the information would assist the listing officer in carrying out his functions.

Subs. (7)

This subsection is intended to ensure that the listing officer or the Commissioners of Inland

Revenue are not to be limited unduly in the information which may be taken into account in exercising their functions. Thus it is provided that they may take into account not merely information obtained under the provisions of this Act, but also any other information available, whatever its source. This, presumably, should be interpreted to mean available lawfully and not, for example, supplied in breach of the Data Protection Act 1984. It should also be noted that this formulation is wider than the equivalent power in relation to Scotland, under s.90 of this Act, which restricts the relevant officer to any other information available under other enactments relating to valuation, community charges or electoral registration.

Subs. (8)
The necessary definitions in relation to obtaining information from community charge sources is provided by this subsection.

Information about lists

28.—(1) A person may require a listing officer to give him access to such information as will enable him to establish what is the state of a list, or has been its state at any time since it came into force, if—
    (a) the officer is maintaining the list; and
    (b) the list is in force or has been in force at any time in the preceding five years.

(2) A person may require a billing authority to give him access to such information as will enable him to establish what is the state of a copy of a list, or has been its state at any time since it was deposited, if—
    (a) the authority has deposited the copy under section 22(8) above; and
    (b) the list is in force or has been in force at any time in the preceding five years.

(3) A person may require a billing authority to give him access to such information as will enable him to establish what is the state of a copy of a proposed list if—
    (a) the authority has deposited the copy under section 22(6) above; and
    (b) the list itself is not yet in force.

(4) A requirement under subsection (1), (2) or (3) above must be complied with at a reasonable time and place and without payment being sought; but the information may be in documentary or other form, as the person or authority of whom the requirement is made thinks fit.

(5) Where access is given under this section to information in documentary form the person to whom access is given may—
    (a) make copies of (or of extracts from) the document;
    (b) require a person having custody of the document to supply to him a photographic copy of (or of extracts from) the document.

(6) Where access is given under this section to information in a form which is not documentary the person to whom access is given may—
    (a) make transcripts of (or of extracts from) the information;
    (b) require a person having control of access to the information to supply to him a copy in documentary form of (or of extracts from) the information.

(7) If a reasonable charge is required for a facility under subsection (5) or (6) above, the subsection concerned shall not apply unless the person seeking to avail himself of the facility pays the charge.

(8) If without reasonable excuse a person having custody of a document containing, or having control of access to, information access to which is sought under this section—
    (a) intentionally obstructs a person in exercising a right under subsection (1), (2), (3), (5)(a) or (6)(a) above; or
    (b) refuses to comply with a requirement under subsection (5)(b) or (6)(b) above,
he shall be liable on summary conviction to a fine not exceeding level 2 on the standard scale.

DEFINITIONS
"billing authority": ss.1(2) and 69(1).
"information": s.116(1).
"listing officer": ss.20 and 69(1).

GENERAL NOTE
The aim of this section is to ensure that public access to the information contained in the valuation lists is protected. Information about the present and historic state of the list must be made available at reasonable times and free of charge, although relevant photocopies may be charged for. Obstruction of rights of access, or failure to comply with the requirements of this section, is made an offence.

Subs. (1)
Where the listing officer is maintaining a valuation list which is in force, or has been at any time in the previous five years, then any person may require the officer to give access to such information as will enable him to establish the state of the list, either currently or at any time since it came into force. This is subject to the limitation that the duty to maintain the information on a list falls five years after the list ceases to be in force.

Subs. (2)
Where the billing authority has deposited a copy of a compiled list at its principal office, under s.22(8) of this Act, and the list is in force, or has been at any time in the previous five years, then any person may require the billing authority to give access to such information as will enable him to establish the state of the copy of the list, either currently or at any time since it was deposited.

Subs. (3)
Where the billing authority has deposited at its principal office, under s.22(6) of this Act, a copy of a list which the listing officer proposes to compile, and the list is not in force, then any person may require the billing authority to give access to such information as will enable him to establish the state of the copy of the proposed list. This will allow the public to inspect the proposed list when issued between November 15 and December 1, 1992.

Subs. (4)
The requirement to allow access under subss. (1), (2) and (3) operates only at a reasonable time and place, and the requirement may be met by making available the information in whatever form the person on whom the requirement is placed thinks fit. The information may therefore be in documentary or some other form, such as a computer database. No charge may be made for such access.

Subs. (5)
Where the information is provided in documentary form, then the person seeking the information is entitled to copy all or some of the document and the listing officer or billing authority may be required by that person to supply a photocopy. In the latter event, the authority may make a reasonable charge under the authority of subs. (7).

Subs. (6)
Where the information is not provided in documentary form, then the person seeking the information is entitled to make transcripts of all or some of the document and the person having control of access to the information may be required by that person to supply a documentary copy of all or part of the information. In the latter event, the authority may make a reasonable charge under the authority of subs. (7).

Subs. (7)
This permits the relevant authority to make a charge for the supply of photocopies or documents under subss. (5) and (6). Indeed, if a charge is demanded and not paid, then the right of the person to invoke the relevant subsection is taken away.

Subs. (8)
Where any person having control of information, whether documentary or otherwise, intentionally obstructs the exercise of a right of access to information, or the making of copies of transcripts, or fails to comply with a request for a photocopy or documentary copy, then he shall be guilty of an offence and liable on summary conviction to a fine not exceeding level 2 on the standard scale. The defence of "reasonable excuse" is provided.

Information about proposals and appeals

29.—(1) A person may, at a reasonable time and without making payment, inspect any proposal made or notice of appeal given under regulations made under section 24 above, if made or given as regards a list which is in force when inspection is sought or has been in force at any time in the preceding five years.

(2) A person may—

(a) make copies of (or of extracts from) a document mentioned in subsection (1) above; or

(b) require a person having custody of such a document to supply to him a photographic copy of (or of extracts from) the document.

(3) If a reasonable charge is required for a facility under subsection (2) above, that subsection shall not apply unless the person seeking to avail himself of the facility pays the charge.

(4) If without reasonable excuse a person having custody of a document mentioned in subsection (1) above—

(a) intentionally obstructs a person in exercising a right under subsection (1) or (2)(a) above; or

(b) refuses to supply a copy to a person entitled to it under subsection (2)(b) above,

he shall be liable on summary conviction to a fine not exceeding level 2 on the standard scale.

GENERAL NOTE

The aim of this section is to ensure that protection is given to public access to any proposal made to alter a valuation list or to a notice of appeal given under any regulations made in relation to s.24. Information about such a proposal or appeal, in relation to a list which is current or has been in force at any time during the previous five years, must be made available at reasonable times and free of charge, although relevant photocopies may be charged for. Obstruction of this right of access, or failure to comply with the requirements to supply a copy, is made an offence.

Subs. (1)

Access must be granted to any person wishing to inspect any proposal made to alter a valuation list, or notice of appeal given under any regulations made in relation to s.24. Information about such a proposal or appeal in relation to a list, which is either current or has been in force at any time during the previous five years, must be made available at reasonable time and free of charge.

Subs. (2)

The person seeking the information is entitled to copy all or some of the relevant document and the person having custody of such a document may be required by that person to supply a photocopy of all or part of the document. In the latter event, a reasonable charge may be made under the authority of subs. (3).

Subs. (3)

This permits a charge to be made for the supply of photocopies or documents under subs. (2). Indeed, if a charge is demanded and not paid, then the right of the person to invoke the right of inspection is taken away.

Subs. (4)

Where any person having custody of a document relevant to the right of inspection under subs. (1) intentionally obstructs the exercise of a right of access to information, or the making of copies of transcripts, or fails to comply with a request for a photocopy or documentary copy, then he shall be guilty of an offence and liable on summary conviction to a fine not exceeding level 2 on the standard scale. The defence of "reasonable excuse" is provided.

CHAPTER III

SETTING OF COUNCIL TAX

Setting of amounts

Amounts for different categories of dwellings

30.—(1) For each financial year and each category of dwellings in its area, a billing authority shall, in accordance with subsection (2) below, set an amount of council tax.

(2) An amount so set shall be calculated by taking the aggregate of—

(a) the amount which, in relation to the year and the category of dwellings, has been calculated (or last calculated) by the authority in accordance with sections 32 to 36 below; and

(b) any amounts which, in relation to the year and the category of dwellings, have been calculated in accordance with sections 43 to 47 below and have been stated (or last stated) in accordance with section 40 below in precepts issued to the authority by major precepting authorities.

(3) Where the aggregate amount given by subsection (2) above is a negative amount, the amount set shall be nil.

(4) Dwellings fall within different categories for the purposes of subsections (1) and (2) above according as different calculations have been made in relation to them in accordance with sections 32 to 36 below or sections 43 to 47 below or both.

(5) A billing authority shall assume for the purposes of subsections (1) and (2) above that each of the valuation bands is shown in its valuation list as applicable to one or more dwellings situated in its area or (as the case may be) each part of its area as respects which different calculations have been so made.

(6) Any amount must be set before 11th March in the financial year preceding that for which it is set, but is not invalid merely because it is set on or after that date.

(7) No amount may be set before the earlier of the following—

(a) 1st March in the financial year preceding that for which the amount is set;

(b) the date of the issue to the authority of the last precept capable of being issued to it (otherwise than by way of substitute) by a major precepting authority for the financial year for which the amount is set.

(8) No amount may be set unless the authority has made in relation to the year the calculations required by this Chapter.

(9) A purported setting of an amount, if done in contravention of subsection (7) or (8) above, shall be treated as not having occurred.

DEFINITIONS
   "billing authority": ss.1(2) and 69(1).
   "council tax": s.1(1).
   "dwelling": ss.3 and 69(1).
   "financial year": s.69(1).
   "major precepting authority": ss.39(1) and 69(1).
   "valuation band": s.5(2) and (3).
   "valuation list": s.22(1).

GENERAL NOTE
   This section requires the billing authority to set for each financial year an amount of council tax payable for each category of dwellings in its area. Provision is made for both the timing of this process and the requirement to incorporate the system of precepting.

Subs. (1)
   A basic duty is imposed on the billing authority to set for each financial year an amount of

council tax payable for each category of dwellings in its area. This duty must be carried out in conformity with the requirements of subs. (2).

Subs. (2)

The amount to be set under subs. (1) must be calculated by aggregating two sums: first, the amount which has been calculated for each category of dwelling, under ss.32–36, by the billing authority as necessary for its own purposes; and secondly, the amount which has been calculated for each category of dwelling, under ss.43–47, by the billing authority as necessary for its own purposes, and which has been issued to the billing authority in accordance with the requirements of s.40.

Subs. (3)

If the result of the process of aggregation under subs. (2) is to produce a negative sum, then the amount set for each category of dwelling is to be nil.

Subs. (4)

This makes it clear that the categories of dwelling for the purposes of the setting of the appropriate amount of council tax are to be in accordance with the amounts set in relation to the calculations of the billing authority and major precepting authority under the provisions of ss.32–36 and 43–47 respectively.

Subs. (5)

In setting the amount of council tax, under subss. (1) and (2), for each category of dwellings, the billing authority must assume that there are one or more dwellings from each of the valuation bands in its valuation list. Thus even if there are no dwellings in a particular band, the billing authority must set an amount of council tax which would have applied to that band.

Subs. (6)

This sets the first element of the time limits applicable to setting the amount of the council tax. The billing authority is required to set the amounts of council tax applicable for any financial year before March 11 in the preceding financial year. This duty is, however, directory only and failure to comply will not result in the invalidity of an amount set on or after that date. This therefore avoids the problem which had arisen in relation to the old system of domestic rates, where it was argued that the failure to set the rate within the time limit made any subsequent determination void and of no legal effect, thus depriving the authority of the right to set the rate. This may be compared with the effect of a failure to comply with the requirements of subss. (7) and (8) below, in relation to which subs. (9) provides that the purported setting of the amount of council tax will be void.

Subs. (7)

This sets the second element of the time limits applicable to setting the amount of the council tax. The billing authority may not set the amounts of council tax applicable for any financial year before the earlier of two dates. The relevant dates are March 1 in the preceding financial year, and the date of issue to the billing authority of the precept from the major precepting authority. That precept must be the final one possible, other than by way of the process of substitution under s.42. The effect of a failure to meet this requirement is dealt with by subs. (9).

Subs. (8)

A duty is placed on the billing authority to comply with the calculations required by the provisions of Chapter III of the Act. If these requirements are not followed, then no amount of council tax may be set. The effect of a failure to meet this requirement is dealt with by subs. (9).

Subs. (9)

A setting of an amount of council tax payable will be void and of no legal effect if it fails to meet the requirement of subss. (7) or (8). Thus, a failure to comply with either the time limit before which an amount may not be set, or the requirement that the amount of the council tax is to be calculated in accordance with the calculations required by the provisions of Chapter III of the Act, will mean that any sum set will merely be "purported" to have been set, but will have no legal status whatsoever.

Substituted amounts

31.—(1) Where a billing authority has set amounts for a financial year under section 30 above and at any later time—

(a) it makes substitute calculations under section 37 or 60 below; or

(b) it is issued with a precept for the year (originally or by way of substitute) by a major precepting authority,

it shall as soon as reasonably practicable after that time set amounts in substitution so as to give effect to those calculations or that precept.

(2) Any amount set in substitution under subsection (1) above must be set in accordance with section 30 above, but subsection (6) of that section shall be ignored for this purpose.

(3) Where a billing authority sets any amount in substitution under subsection (1) above (a new amount), anything paid to it by reference to the amount for which it is substituted (the old amount) shall be treated as paid by reference to the new amount.

(4) If the old amount exceeds the new amount, the following shall apply as regards anything paid if it would not have been paid had the old amount been the same as the new amount—

(a) it shall be repaid if the person by whom it was paid so requires;

(b) in any other case it shall (as the billing authority determines) either be repaid or be credited against any subsequent liability of the person to pay in respect of any council tax set by the authority in accordance with section 30 above.

(5) Where an authority sets amounts in substitution under subsection (1)(b) above, it may recover from the major precepting authority administrative expenses incurred by it in, or in consequence of, so doing.

DEFINITIONS
"billing authority": ss.1(2) and 69(1).
"financial year": s.69(1).
"major precepting authority": ss.39(1) and 69(1).

GENERAL NOTE
This section requires the billing authority to set substituted amounts of council tax in two situations. First, where the billing authority has been required to make a substitute calculation in regard to its own budget requirements. Secondly, where the major precepting authority has issued an original or substitute precept. Provision is made for the manner of calculation of such a substituted amount, for dealing with payments already made in relation to the original amount set, and for the recovery of expenses from the major precepting authority.

Subs. (1)
The billing authority is required to set substituted amounts of council tax in two situations: first, where the billing authority has been required to make a substitute calculation in regard to its own budget requirements, under the provisions of ss.37 or 60; and secondly, where the major precepting authority has issued a precept, whether original, if this is after March 1 in the preceding financial year, or substitute. This duty must be complied with as soon as reasonably practicable after the new calculation is made or the precept issued.

Subs. (2)
The amount of council tax set in substitution must be calculated in accordance with the principles applicable, under s.30, to the setting of the original amount set, with the exception that there is no requirement to set it before March 11 in the preceding financial year.

Subs. (3)
Where payments have already been made to the billing authority on the basis of the original amount set, then those sums shall be treated as having been paid in relation to the new amount set. This general approach is clarified by subs. (4).

Subs. (4)
This covers the situation where two factors are present. First, the original amount set is higher than the substituted amount. Secondly, payments have already been made to the billing authority on the basis of the original amount and the sums paid are greater than would have been paid in relation to the substituted amount. In this situation, the taxpayer has the right to require a repayment. If the taxpayer does not make such a request, then it is within the

discretion of the billing authority whether to repay the overpayment or to credit the sum against liability of that person for a future financial year.

Subs. (5)

Where the substituted amount is necessary because of a late or substituted precept, then the authority may recover from the major precepting authority the administrative costs of substituting a new amount.

The requisite calculations

Calculation of budget requirement

32.—(1) In relation to each financial year a billing authority shall make the calculations required by this section.

(2) The authority must calculate the aggregate of—

(a) the expenditure which the authority estimates it will incur in the year in performing its functions and will charge to a revenue account for the year;

(b) such allowance as the authority estimates will be appropriate for contingencies in relation to expenditure to be charged to a revenue account for the year;

(c) the financial reserves which the authority estimates it will be appropriate to raise in the year for meeting its estimated future expenditure;

(d) such financial reserves as are sufficient to meet so much of the amount estimated by the authority to be a revenue account deficit for any earlier financial year as has not already been provided for; and

(e) any amounts which it estimates will be transferred from its general fund to its collection fund pursuant to a direction under section 98(5) of the 1988 Act and charged to a revenue account for the year.

(3) The authority must calculate the aggregate of—

(a) the sums which it estimates will be payable for the year into its general fund and in respect of which amounts will be credited to a revenue account for the year, other than sums which it estimates will be so payable in respect of redistributed non-domestic rates, revenue support grant or additional grant;

(b) any amounts which it estimates will be transferred from its collection fund to its general fund pursuant to a direction under section 98(4) of the 1988 Act and credited to a revenue account for the year; and

(c) the amount of the financial reserves which the authority estimates that it will use in order to provide for the items mentioned in paragraphs (a), (b) and (e) of subsection (2) above.

(4) If the aggregate calculated under subsection (2) above exceeds that calculated under subsection (3) above, the authority must calculate the amount equal to the difference; and the amount so calculated shall be its budget requirement for the year.

(5) In making the calculation under subsection (2) above the authority must ignore—

(a) payments which must be met from its collection fund under section 90(2) of the 1988 Act or from a trust fund; and

(b) subject to subsection (2)(e) above, sums which have been or are to be transferred from its general fund to its collection fund.

(6) In estimating under subsection (2)(a) above the authority shall take into account—

(a) the amount of any precept issued to it for the year by a local precepting authority; and

(b) the amount of any levy or special levy issued to it for the year;

but (except as provided by regulations under section 41 below or regulations under section 74 or 75 of the 1988 Act) shall not anticipate a precept, levy or special levy not issued.

(7) For the purposes of subsection (2)(c) above an authority's estimated future expenditure is—

(a) that which the authority estimates it will incur in the financial year following the year in question, will charge to a revenue account for the year and will have to defray in the year before the following sums are sufficiently available, namely—

   (i) sums which will be payable for the year into its general fund and in respect of which amounts will be credited to a revenue account for the year; and

   (ii) sums which will be transferred as regards the year from its collection fund to its general fund; and

(b) that which the authority estimates it will incur in the financial year referred to in paragraph (a) above or any subsequent financial year in performing its functions and which will be charged to a revenue account for that or any other year.

(8) In making the calculation under subsection (3) above the authority must ignore, subject to paragraph (b) of that subsection, sums which have been or are to be transferred from its collection fund to its general fund.

(9) The Secretary of State may by regulations do one or both of the following—

(a) alter the constituents of any calculation to be made under subsection (2) or (3) above (whether by adding, deleting or amending items);

(b) alter the rules governing the making of any calculation under subsection (2) or (3) above (whether by deleting or amending subsections (5) to (8) above, or any of them, or by adding other provisions, or by a combination of those methods).

(10) Calculations to be made in relation to a particular financial year under this section must be made before 11th March in the preceding financial year, but they are not invalid merely because they are made on or after that date.

(11) References in this section to expenditure incurred by an authority shall be construed in accordance with section 41(3) of the Local Government and Housing Act 1989.

DEFINITIONS

"additional grant": s.69(1); s.85(2) of the 1988 Act.
"billing authority": ss.1(2) and 69(1).
"collection fund": s.89(1) of the 1988 Act.
"estimated future expenditure": subs. (7).
"financial year": ss.69(1) and 116(1).
"general fund": s.91 of the 1988 Act.
"levy": s.69(1).
"local precepting authority": ss.39(2) and 69(1).
"redistributed non-domestic rates": s.69(1); Sched. 8 to the 1988 Act.
"revenue support grant": s.69(1); s.78(1) of the 1988 Act.
"special levy": s.69(1); s.75 of the 1988 Act.

GENERAL NOTE

A duty is imposed upon a billing authority to calculate its "budget requirement" for each financial year, defined as the difference between its expenditure and income as defined by this section. The "budget requirement" is a figure which it is necessary to calculate before proceeding to the calculation, under s.33, of the basic amount of council tax for any financial year. The items which are to be taken into account in calculating the budget requirement, and the method of this calculation, are specified by the section, but the Secretary of State is given power to amend these by regulation. The date by which the calculations are to be made is also specified.

Subs. (1)

The basic duty upon a billing authority to calculate its budget requirements for each financial year in accordance with the rest of the section is imposed by this subsection.

Subs. (2)

In order to produce the figure for the expenditure requirement of the authority, the billing authority is required to calculate the aggregate of five sums. These are the estimate of revenue expenditure for the year; allowances for contingencies in relation to the revenue expenditure; the reserves to be raised in the year in regard to meeting estimated future expenditure; estimated reserves to meet any outstanding revenue deficit for an earlier financial year; and any estimated amounts which will be transferred from its general fund to its collection fund as a result of a direction by the Secretary of State under s.98(5) of the 1988 Act, which allows the Secretary of State to override the normal rules as to transfers between accounts. The definition of "expenditure" to be applied, by subs. (11) below, is that given by s.41(3) of the 1989 Act.

Subs. (3)

In order to produce the figure for the income element of the authority, the billing authority is required to calculate the aggregate of three sums. These are the sums which it estimates will be payable for the year into its general fund and in respect of which amounts are to be credited to a revenue account for the year, other than from non-domestic rates, general grant or additional grants, which are taken into account in the calculation under s.33; any amount transferred from its collection fund to its general fund as a result of a direction by the Secretary of State under s.98(4) of the 1988 Act, which allows the Secretary of State to override the normal rules as to transfers between accounts; and the amount of the financial reserves which the authority estimated to be necessary to use to meet estimated expenditure and contingencies in relation to its functions for the year, and for balancing the movements from general fund to collection fund in accordance with a direction under s.8(5) of the 1988 Act.

Subs. (4)

Where the "income" produced by aggregating the items specified in subs. (3) is less than the sum of the "expenditure" produced by the aggregation of the items specified in subs. (2), then that difference is defined as the budget requirement for the year.

Subs. (5)

In making the "expenditure" calculation, the billing authority must ignore two types of payment. The first of these is payments made from the collection fund as required by s.90(2) of the 1988 Act, or from a trust fund. Section 90(2) covers precepts and interest; payments to the Secretary of State, including balancing payments for non-domestic rates or repayment of revenue support grant; payments to other authorities, including any direction from the Secretary of State to pay all or some of additional grant to another authority; repayments of excess receipts in regard to non-domestic rates or community charge and interest payments on the excess non-domestic rate receipts; or any other payment specified by the Secretary of State. The second type of payment which must be ignored is any sum which, subject to the ability of the Secretary of State under s.98(5) of the 1988 Act to direct such a transfer, has been or will be transferred from the general fund to the collection fund.

Subs. (6)

In calculating the estimate of the expenditure on performing its functions for the financial year, for the purpose of calculating the aggregate under subs. (2), the billing authority must take into account two factors: first, the amount of any precept issued to it by a local precepting authority; and, secondly, the amount of any levy or special levy issued to it by a "levying body", as defined by s.74(1) of the 1988 Act. Any levy issued to a precepting body will have been included in the precept issued to the billing authority. However, the billing authority is permitted to include in the calculation only a levy or special levy already actually issued. An anticipated levy or special levy may not be included, no matter how likely it is to be issued, except in accordance with any regulations made under s.41 of this Act, and ss.74 and 75 of the 1988 Act.

Subs. (7)

In calculating the estimate of the reserves which it is appropriate to raise in relation to estimated future expenditure, for the purpose of calculating the aggregate under subs. (2), the billing authority must take into account the definition of "future expenditure". This is defined in two parts: first, the sums which the authority estimates it will incur in the following financial year and will have to charge to a revenue account before that account has available to it sufficient sums from those paid to the general account in that year and sums which will be transferred to the general account from the collection fund (this deals with the "cash-flow" problems); and secondly, the sums which the authority estimates it will incur in the following or any subsequent financial year, and which will be charged to that or any other year. This allows for forward planning in relation to exceptional expenditure.

Subs. (8)

In calculating the "income" aggregate, under subs. (3), the billing authority is required to ignore any sums which have been or are to be transferred from the collection fund to the general fund, other than those which have been required by a direction from the Secretary of State under s.98(4) of the 1988 Act.

Subs. (9)

The requirements as to the calculation of the budget requirement may be altered by the Secretary of State, both as regards the items to be taken into account, under subss. (2) and (3), and the more specific methods of calculation, under subss. (5)–(8). Thus the items may be added to, deleted or amended, and the specific methods of calculation may be deleted, amended or added to, singly or in combination.

Subs. (10)

The billing authority is under a duty to carry out the calculations required by this section before March 11 in the financial year preceding that for which the calculation is made. However, this duty is directory only and failure to comply with this time limit will not invalidate a late calculation.

Subs. (11)

The definition of "expenditure" to be applied in this section is that given by s.41(3) of the 1989 Act. On the basis that local government finance is to be conducted on an annual basis (*R.* v. *Greater London Council*, ex p. *Westminster City Council* [1986] A.C. 668), s.41 of the 1989 Act prescribed what expenditure is to be charged to a revenue account, although s.42 also prescribed what expenditure was excluded from this requirement. Section 41(3) of the 1989 Act provides that expenditure incurred by a local authority in any financial year includes any amount which is not part of the capital receipts and which is set aside to meet credit liabilities, and also any amount set aside for the year to meet any liability or loss for which, although likely or certain to be incurred, the amount is still uncertain.

Calculation of basic amount of tax

33.—(1) In relation to each financial year a billing authority shall calculate the basic amount of its council tax by applying the formula—

$$\frac{R - P}{T}$$

where—
> R is the amount calculated (or last calculated) by the authority under section 32(4) above as its budget requirement for the year;
>
> P is the aggregate of the sums which the authority estimates will be payable for the year into its general fund in respect of redistributed non-domestic rates, revenue support grant or additional grant;
>
> T is the amount which is calculated by the authority as its council tax base for the year and, where one or more major precepting authorities have power to issue precepts to it, is notified by it to those authorities ("the major precepting authorities concerned") within the prescribed period.

(2) Where the aggregate calculated (or last calculated) by the authority for the year under subsection (2) of section 32 above does not exceed that so calculated under subsection (3) of that section, the amount for item R in subsection (1) above shall be nil.

(3) The aggregate of the sums mentioned in item P in subsection (1) above shall be—
> (a) increased by the amount of any sum which the authority estimates will be transferred in the year from its collection fund to its general fund in accordance with subsection (3) of section 97 of the 1988 Act; or

(b) reduced by the amount of any sum which the authority estimates will be transferred in the year from its general fund to its collection fund in accordance with subsection (4) of that section.

(4) Regulations under section 32(9) above may make such consequential alterations of the constituents of any calculation required by item P in subsection (1) above or subsection (3) above (whether by adding, deleting or amending items) as appear to the Secretary of State to be necessary or expedient.

(5) The Secretary of State shall make regulations containing rules for making for any year the calculation required by item T in subsection (1) above; and a billing authority shall make the calculation for any year in accordance with the rules for the time being effective (as regards the year) under the regulations.

(6) Regulations prescribing a period for the purposes of item T in subsection (1) above may provide that, in any case where a billing authority fails to notify its calculation to the major precepting authorities concerned within that period, that item shall be determined in the prescribed manner by such authority or authorities as may be prescribed.

DEFINITIONS
"additional grant": s.69(1); s.85(2) of the 1988 Act.
"billing authority": ss.1(2) and 69(1).
"budget requirement": s.32(4).
"collection fund": s.89(1) of the 1988 Act.
"council tax": s.1(1).
"financial year": ss.69(1) and 116(1).
"general fund": s.91 of the 1988 Act.
"major precepting authority": ss.39(1) and 69(1).
"prescribed": s.116(1).
"redistributed non-domestic rates": s.69(1); Sched. 8 to the 1988 Act.
"revenue support grant": s.69(1); s.78(1) of the 1988 Act.

GENERAL NOTE
This section provides the formula for the calculation of the basic amount of council tax for each financial year. The items to be taken into account in this calculation are specified, although power is given to the Secretary of State to issue further regulations amending these.

Subs. (1)
The calculation of the basic amount of council tax is to be determined by dividing the sum required to be raised through the council tax, by the council tax base. The first of these, the sum required to be raised through the council tax, is to be calculated by subtracting from the budget requirement (R), as determined by the calculation under s.32(4), amounts which the authority will receive from central government (P). These amounts relate to the authority's share of non-domestic rates, its revenue support grant and additional grants. The council-tax base figure (T) is that calculated by the billing authority, incorporating any relevant figures from a major precepting authority which has been communicated within a prescribed period.

Subs. (2)
If, as calculated in accordance with s.32(2), the "expenditure" element of the budget requirement is equal to or less than the amount of "income", calculated in accordance with s.32(3), then the element R in the calculation of the basic amount of council tax, under subs. (1) above, could in principle be a negative sum. However, this provision makes clear that, in such circumstances, the element R, the budget requirement under s.32(4), will be treated as £0.

Subs. (3)
The element P, in the calculation of the basic amount of council tax, under subs. (1) above, which is the aggregate of the grants and non-domestic rates payable to the authority, shall be amended to incorporate any transfers between the general and collection funds in accordance with s.97 of the 1988 Act. That original section has been replaced by a new s.97, as enacted by s.104 of and Sched. 10, para. 22 to this Act. Under the new s.97(3), where there is a surplus in the collection fund for the preceding year, then the authority shall transfer to the general fund the appropriate share of the surplus. Under the new s.97(3), where there is a deficit in the

collection fund for the preceding year, then the authority shall transfer from the general fund the amount equal to the appropriate share of the deficit, as determined in accordance with regulations.

Subs. (4)

This power is given to the Secretary of State, as appears to him to be necessary or expedient, to alter the method of calculation of element P, in the calculation of the basic amount of council tax, under subss. (1) or (3) above. It may be altered, whether by addition, deletion or other amendment, by regulations made under the authority of s.32(9) above.

Subs. (5)

This provides the legal authority for the regulations necessary to prescribe the calculation of element T, in the determination of the basic amount of council tax, under subs. (1) above, including the prescribed periods for notification by the major precepting authorities, and it places a duty on the Secretary of State to make these regulations. In relation to this element, the billing authority is placed under a duty to make the calculation in accordance with the regulations.

Subs. (6)

In relation to element T, in the determination of the basic amount of council tax, under subs. (1) above, the regulations which prescribe the period in which T has to be calculated may also provide for the element to be determined by another authority if the billing authority fails to notify the calculation to the major precepting authorities within the prescribed time. The regulations may prescribe which authority or authorities may carry out this calculation, and determine the manner in which it should be carried out. The effect of this is that the process will not be able to be frustrated by the billing authority's failing to comply with the relevant time limits.

Additional calculations where special items relate to part only of area

34.—(1) This section applies where for any financial year an item mentioned in section 35(1) below relates to a part only of a billing authority's area; and in this section "special item" means any such item which so relates and "the relevant part", in relation to such an item, means the part concerned.

(2) The authority shall calculate the basic amount of its council tax for dwellings in a part of its area to which no special item relates by applying the formula—

$$B - \frac{A}{T}$$

where—

   B is the amount calculated (or last calculated) by the authority under section 33(1) above as the basic amount of its council tax;

   A is the aggregate amount of all special items;

   T is the amount determined for item T in section 33(1) above.

(3) The authority shall calculate the basic amount of its council tax for dwellings in a part of its area to which one or more special items relate by adding to the amount given by the formula in subsection (2) above the aggregate of the amounts which, in relation to each of those special items, are given by the formula—

$$\frac{S}{TP}$$

where—

   S is (in each case) the amount of the special item;

   TP is (in each case) the amount of the authority's council tax base for the relevant part as calculated by it for the year.

(4) The Secretary of State shall make regulations containing rules for making for any year any calculation required by item TP in subsection (3) above; and a billing authority shall make the calculation for any year in accordance with the rules for the time being effective (as regards the year) under the regulations.

DEFINITIONS
 "billing authority": ss.1(2) and 69(1).
 "council tax": s.1(1).
 "dwelling": ss.3 and 69(1).
 "financial year": ss.69(1) and 116(1).
 "relevant part": subs. (1).
 "special item": subs. (1).

GENERAL NOTE
 This section makes provision for the situation where "special items", as defined by s.35, relate to part only of the area of the billing authority. The billing authority must make additional calculations, in accordance with the formulae set out in this section, to recover the sums in relation to the special items from the areas to which they relate. Power is also given to the Secretary of State to prescribe by regulation the rules for calculating one of the items to be taken into account in this process. See the Local Authorities (Calculation of Council Tax Base) Regulations 1992 (S.I. 1992 No. 612).

Subs. (1)
 The provisions of this section are triggered where any item, specified in s.35(1), applies for any financial year to a part only of the billing authority's area. The necessary definitions are given for this section, with the term "special item" meaning any such item which triggers the provisions of this section, and "the relevant part" is defined as that part of the billing authority's area to which the special item relates.

Subs. (2)
 Where there are special items relating to some part or parts of the area of the billing authority, then the method of calculation of the basic amount of council tax for a particular area to which no special items relate is provided for by this subsection. The principle is that the basic amount is calculated by subtracting an appropriate amount from the sum calculated, under s.33(1), as the basic amount of council tax (B) payable before special items are taken into account. The sum to be subtracted is the quotient of the aggregate amount of all special items (A) divided by the council-tax base (T). The council-tax base (T) is calculated by the billing authority, under s.33(1), incorporating any relevant figures from a major precepting authority which has been communicated within a prescribed period or, in default, by another authority under the regulations made under s.33(6).

Subs. (3)
 Where there are special items relating to some part or parts of the area of the billing authority, then the method of calculation of the basic amount of council tax for a particular area to which a special item relates is provided for by this subsection. The principle is that the basic amount for dwellings in the area to which the special item relates is calculated by adding an appropriate amount to the sum calculated, under subs. (2), as the sum payable in regard to a dwelling in an area to which no special item relates. The sum to be added is determined for each special item by dividing the amount of the special item (S) by the amount of the billing authority's council-tax base for that area for that year (TP).

Subs. (4)
 This provides the legal authority for the regulations necessary to prescribe the calculation of element TP, in relation to the calculation to be made under subs. (3) above, and it places a duty on the Secretary of State to make these regulations. In relation to this element, the billing authority is placed under a duty to make the calculation in accordance with the regulations.

Special items for purposes of section 34

 35.—(1) The items referred to in section 34(1) above are—
 (a) any precept issued to or anticipated by the authority which is or is believed to be applicable to a part of its area and was taken into account by it in making the calculation (or last calculation) in relation to the year under section 32(2) above; and
 (b) any expenses of the authority which are its special expenses and were taken into account by it in making that calculation.
 (2) For the purposes of subsection (1) above—
 (a) provided a resolution of a billing authority to the following effect is in

force, the expenses of meeting a levy or special levy issued to or anticipated by it are its special expenses or (if the resolution relates to some only of those expenses) those to which the resolution relates are its special expenses;

(b) any expenses which a billing authority believes will have to be met out of amounts transferred or to be transferred from its collection fund to its general fund, and which arise out of its possession of property held in trust for a part of its area, are its special expenses;

(c) any expenses which a billing authority believes will have to be met out of amounts transferred or to be transferred from its collection fund to its general fund, and which relate to a part of its area, are its special expenses provided that expenses of the same kind which relate to another part of its area are to be met out of property held in trust for that part;

(d) any expenses incurred by a billing authority in performing in a part of its area a function performed elsewhere in its area by the sub-treasurer of the Inner Temple, the under-treasurer of the Middle Temple, a parish or community council or the chairman of a parish meeting are the authority's special expenses unless a resolution of the authority to the contrary effect is in force; and

(e) provided a resolution of a billing authority to the following effect is in force, the expenses incurred by it in performing in a part of its area a function performed elsewhere in its area by a body with power to issue a levy or special levy to it are its special expenses or (if the resolution relates to some only of those expenses) those to which the resolution relates are its special expenses.

(3) The following rules shall apply to the making of a resolution under subsection (2)(e) above by a billing authority—

(a) no such resolution may be made unless the body mentioned in subsection (2)(e) above is one in relation to which the billing authority has made under subsection (2)(a) above a resolution which is in force;

(b) the resolution under subsection (2)(e) above may not be made so as to be in force at any time when that under subsection (2)(a) above is not in force;

(c) the fact that the resolution under subsection (2)(a) above relates to all the expenses concerned does not mean that the resolution under subsection (2)(e) above must relate to all the expenses concerned; and

(d) the fact that the resolution under subsection (2)(a) above relates to part of the expenses concerned does not mean that the resolution under subsection (2)(e) above must relate to part, or any particular part, of the expenses concerned.

Definitions
"billing authority": ss.1(2) and 69(1).
"collection fund": s.89(1) of the 1988 Act.
"general fund": s.91 of the 1988 Act.
"levy": s.69(1); s.74 of the 1988 Act.
"special expenses": subs. (2) of this section.
"special levy": s.69(1); s.75 of the 1988 Act.

General Note
This section specifies those items which are to be treated as "special items" for the purposes of the calculation of the amount of council tax, under s.34(1). These are defined within two broad categories as, first, a precept relating to part only of the billing authority's area and, second, any "special expenses", as defined by subs. (2), and operated in accordance with subs. (3).

Subs. (1)
For the purposes of the calculation of council tax to be made under s.34(1), a "special item" is

defined as one of two categories. First, a precept relating to part only of the billing authority's area. This may be a precept actually issued or one which it is anticipated will be made. It must also have already been taken into account in the most recent calculation, under s.32(2), of the "expenditure" element in the calculation of the budget requirement. The second category is composed of any "special expenses", as defined by subs. (2). Again, it must also have been taken into account in the most recent calculation, under s.32(2), of the "expenditure" element in the calculation of the budget requirement.

Subs. (2)
"Special expenses" in turn fall into a number of different categories. The first category relates to a levy or special levy, and may be incurred in two ways: first, as the expenses in meeting a levy or special levy; and secondly, by undertaking directly the function performed elsewhere in the area by a body which may issue a levy or special levy. These are defined as a special expense by subs. (2)(a) and (e) respectively. However, in regard to both, a resolution of the billing authority must be in force, and the relationship between these resolutions is governed by subs. (3). The second category relates to transfers from the collection to the general funds. Such a transfer, whether actual or prospective, is deemed to be a special expense if it is incurred in relation to the possession by the authority of a property held in trust for part of its area. Equally, it is a special expense if it relates to part of the area only and is met by such a payment, while expenses of the same kind are incurred in relation to another part of the area but met from property held in trust for that part. The third category relates to expenses incurred by the billing authority in performing a function in part of its area when another authority performs the same function in another part. The major application of this is in relation to functions carried out by parish or community councils, but in addition, the functions of the sub-treasurer of the Inner Temple and the under-treasurer of the Middle Temple are included. This category will not apply, however, where the billing authority has in force a resolution to the contrary effect.

Subs. (3)
The relationship between resolutions made under subs. (2)(a) and (e) respectively is governed by subs. (3). However, in regard to both, a resolution of the billing authority must be in force to trigger the operation of the subsection. The billing authority must first make a resolution under subs. (2)(a) in relation to the expenses of meeting the levy or special levy. Thereafter a further resolution, under subs. (2)(e) may be made relating to the performance of the function directly, but this may not be made to be in force at the same time as the resolution under subs. (2)(a). There is no need for the resolutions to be identical in relation to the particular expenses. It is possible for the resolution under para. (e) to be concerned with part of the expenses covered by a resolution under para. (a). Equally, where a resolution under para. (a) covers part of the expenses only, the resolution under para. (e) is not restricted and must relate to part only, or any particular part, of the total expenses.

Calculation of tax for different valuation bands

36.—(1) The amount to be taken into account under section 30(2)(a) above for any financial year in respect of a category of dwellings listed in a particular valuation band shall be calculated by applying the formula—

$$A \times \frac{N}{D}$$

where—
> A is the amount calculated (or last calculated) by the billing authority for that year under section 33(1) above or, where section 34 above applies, the amount calculated (or last calculated) by it for that year under subsection (2) or (3) of that section in relation to that category of dwellings;
> N is the number which, in the proportion set out in section 5(1) above, is applicable to dwellings listed in that valuation band;
> D is the number which, in that proportion, is applicable to dwellings listed in valuation band D.

(2) Dwellings fall within different categories for the purposes of this section according as different calculations have been made in relation to them under section 34 above.

DEFINITIONS
"billing authority": ss.1(2) and 69(1).

"dwelling": ss.3 and 69(1).
"financial year": ss.69(1) and 116(1).
"valuation band": s.5(2) and (3).

GENERAL NOTE
Having calculated the basic amount of council tax, and taken account of any special items, the billing authority must then calculate the amount of council tax payable for the financial year by dwellings in each of the valuation bands, for each of the areas for which it has calculated a different amount of basic tax. This section sets out the formula for this calculation.

Subs. (1)
The amount of council tax payable for the financial year by dwellings in each of the valuation bands is calculated by multiplying the basic amount of council tax, applicable to the whole or part of the area of the billing authority, by the appropriate factor. The basic amount of council tax (A) is that calculated under s.33(1) or, where special items apply, under s.34(2) or (3). The factor is the quotient of the number applicable to dwellings in that valuation band (N), divided by the number applicable to dwellings in valuation band D (D). Both numbers are established by s.5(1). Thus dwellings in valuation band D will pay the basic amount of council tax while those in higher or lower bands will pay an amount which is proportionately more or less, according to the ratio established by s.5(1).

Subs. (2)
This makes it clear that the category of dwelling to which this section applies is defined not only by the valuation band itself, but also by whether different calculations have been made, under s.34, to take account of special items. Thus different basic amounts of council tax may be produced for dwellings within the same valuation band but within different areas of the billing authority.

Substitute calculations

37.—(1) An authority which has made calculations in accordance with sections 32 to 36 above in relation to a financial year (originally or by way of substitute) may make calculations in substitution in relation to the year in accordance with those sections, ignoring section 32(10) above for this purpose.

(2) None of the substitute calculations shall have any effect if—
 (a) the amount calculated under section 32(4) above, or any amount calculated under section 33(1) or 34(2) or (3) above as the basic amount of council tax applicable to any dwelling, would exceed that so calculated in the previous calculations; or
 (b) the billing authority fails to comply with subsection (3) below in making the substitute calculations.

(3) In making substitute calculations under section 33(1) or 34(3) above, the billing authority must use any amount determined in the previous calculations for item P or T in section 33(1) above or item TP in section 34(3) above.

(4) For the purposes of subsection (2)(a) above, one negative amount shall be taken to exceed another if it is closer to nil (so that minus £1 shall be taken to exceed minus £2).

(5) For the purposes of subsection (3) above, the billing authority may treat any amount determined in the previous calculations for item P in section 33(1) above as increased by the amount of any sum which —
 (a) it estimates will be payable for the year into its general fund in respect of additional grant; and
 (b) was not taken into account by it in making those calculations.

(6) Subsections (2) and (3) above shall not apply if the previous calculations have been quashed because of a failure to comply with sections 32 to 36 above in making the calculations.

DEFINITIONS
 "additional grant": s.69(1); s.85(2) of the 1988 Act.
 "billing authority": ss.1(2) and 69(1).

"council tax": s.1(1).
"dwelling": ss.3 and 69(1).
"financial year": ss.69(1) and 116(1).
"general fund": s.91 of the 1988 Act.

GENERAL NOTE

Provided that the rules established by this section are complied with, it will be possible for a billing authority, having already made calculations as to its budget requirement and council tax, to make a substitute calculation. However, the rules establish a number of limitations, not least of which is that the substitute basic amount of council tax may not be greater than the original amount.

Subs. (1)

This establishes that it is possible for a billing authority, having already made calculations as to its budget requirement and council tax, under ss.32–36, to make a substitute calculation, and thereafter be able to make further substitute calculations for that financial year. In doing so, the authority must, as with the original calculation, comply with the provisions of ss.32–36, with the exception of the time limit of March 11 in the preceding financial year, established by s.32(10).

Subs. (2)

A purported substitute calculation will have no legal effect in two situations: first, if either the budget requirement, calculated under s.32(4), or the basic amount of council tax, calculated under ss.33(1) or 34(2) or (3), is greater than that in the previous calculation; and secondly, if the billing authority fails to comply with the requirement in subs. (3) to use the same amounts for the items specified in that subsection.

Subs. (3)

In calculating the revised amount of council tax, the billing authority must, in principle, use the same amount as determined in the previous calculations for three items. First, in relation to the calculation under s.33(1), the aggregate of redistributed non-domestic rates, revenue support and additional grants payable to the general fund (P). This is, however, subject to the qualification, introduced by subs. (5), that the amount of the aggregate may be increased if it is a result of an increase in the amount of additional grant which was not taken into account in the original calculation. Secondly, again in relation to the calculation under s.33(1), the amount of the council-tax base for the year (T). Thirdly, in relation to a calculation under s.34(3), the amount of the council-tax base for the year for part of the area where special items apply (TP). The effect of this is that a change in the amount of funds received from central government through these sources, or of the council-tax base, will not be allowed to lead to a recalculation of the council tax payable.

Subs. (4)

For the avoidance of doubt, this makes clear that in applying the rule against an increase in the substituted amount, a negative amount may still exceed another negative amount. Thus although a minus sum (*e.g.* £1) remains a negative figure, it will be taken to exceed another negative figure which is a larger minus sum (*e.g.* £2).

Subs. (5)

This establishes the qualification to subs. (3) that the amount of the aggregate of redistributed non-domestic rates, revenue support and additional grants payable to the general fund (P), under s.33(1) may be increased if it is a result of an increase in the amount of additional grant which was not taken into account in the original calculation.

Subs. (6)

This makes clear that the limitations in subss. (2) and (3) will not apply when the previous calculation has been quashed for a failure to comply with the provisions of ss.32–36. In those circumstances, the amount of the budget requirement or the basic amount of council tax may be higher than the original calculation, and the amounts relating to the council-tax base (T and TP) and aggregate of redistributed non-domestic rates, revenue support and additional grants payable to the general fund (P) may be varied.

Supplemental

Information for purposes of Chapter III

38.—(1) If the Secretary of State so requires by regulations, a precepting authority shall supply prescribed information within a prescribed period to any billing authority to which it has power to issue a precept.

(2) A billing authority which has set amounts in accordance with section 30 above (originally or by way of substitute) shall, before the end of the period of 21 days beginning with the day of doing so, publish a notice of the amounts in at least one newspaper circulating in the authority's area.

(3) Failure to comply with subsection (2) above does not make the setting of amounts invalid.

DEFINITIONS
"billing authority": ss.1(2) and 69(1).
"information": subs. (1) and s.116(1).
"precepting authority": ss.39 and 69(1).
"prescribed": s.116(1).

GENERAL NOTE
This section imposes duties on authorities to supply or publish information in two ways. First, a precepting authority may be required to supply information to a billing authority. Secondly, a billing authority must publish information regarding the different amounts of council tax for dwellings in a local newspaper.

Subs. (1)
A precepting authority may be required, by regulations to be made by the Secretary of State, to supply information to a billing authority, to which it has power to issue a precept. The information may be such as is prescribed in the regulations, and it is to be supplied within such period as the regulations prescribe.

Subss. (2) and (3)
Once the billing authority has, under s.30, set an amount of council tax for each category of dwellings in its area, then, within 21 days from the date of setting the amounts, it must publicise the amounts by means of a notice in a newspaper circulating in the authority's area. As is made clear in subs. (3), this duty is directory only, and failure to comply with the duty will not result in the setting of the amounts being invalid.

CHAPTER IV

PRECEPTS

Preliminary

Precepting and precepted authorities

39.—(1) Each of the following is a major precepting authority for the purposes of this Part, namely—
(a) a county council;
(b) a metropolitan county police authority;
(c) the Northumbria Police Authority;
(d) a metropolitan county fire and civil defence authority;
(e) the London Fire and Civil Defence Authority; and
(f) the Receiver for the Metropolitan Police District.
(2) Each of the following is a local precepting authority for the purposes of this Part, namely—
(a) the sub-treasurer of the Inner Temple;
(b) the under-treasurer of the Middle Temple;
(c) a parish or community council;
(d) the chairman of a parish meeting; and
(e) charter trustees.
(3) A precept may only be issued to an appropriate billing authority.
(4) If the whole or part of a billing authority's area falls within a precepting authority's area, it is an appropriate billing authority in relation to the precepting authority to the extent of the area which so falls.

GENERAL NOTE
Major and local precepting authorities are defined by this section. In addition, it is provided that a precept from a major or local precepting authority may only be issued to an appropriate billing authority. This is in turn defined as one where the whole or part of its area falls within the area of the precepting authority, but it is the appropriate billing authority only for that part of the area.

Issue of precepts

Issue of precepts by major precepting authorities

40.—(1) For each financial year a major precepting authority shall issue a precept or precepts in accordance with this section.

(2) A precept issued to a billing authority under this section must state—

(a) the amount which, in relation to the year and each category of dwellings in the billing authority's area, has been calculated (or last calculated) by the precepting authority in accordance with sections 43 to 47 below; and

(b) the amount which has been calculated (or last calculated) by the precepting authority in accordance with section 48 below as the amount payable by the billing authority for the year.

(3) Dwellings fall within different categories for the purposes of subsection (2) above according as different calculations have been made in relation to them in accordance with sections 43 to 47 below.

(4) A major precepting authority shall assume for the purposes of subsection (2) above that each of the valuation bands is shown in the billing authority's valuation list as applicable to one or more dwellings situated in its area or (as the case may be) each part of its area as respects which different calculations have been so made.

(5) A precept under this section must be issued before 1st March in the financial year preceding that for which it is issued, but is not invalid merely because it is issued on or after that date.

(6) No such precept may be issued to a billing authority before the earlier of the following—

(a) the earliest date on which, for the financial year for which the precept is issued, each of the periods prescribed for the purposes of item T in section 33(1) above, item T in section 44(1) below and item TP in section 45(3) below has expired;

(b) the earliest date on which, for that year, each billing authority has notified its calculations for the purposes of those items to the precepting authority.

(7) No such precept may be issued unless the precepting authority has made in relation to the year the calculations required by this Chapter.

(8) A purported issue of such a precept, if done in contravention of subsection (6) or (7) above, shall be treated as not having occurred.

GENERAL NOTE

A major precepting authority is required to issue a precept for each financial year in accordance with the provisions of this section. The precept must state the amount of council tax which the precepting authority calculates is applicable to each category of dwellings in the area of the billing authority. It must also state the amount which the precepting authority calculates is the amount payable by the billing authority in respect of the precept for that financial year.

Subs. (1)

A duty is placed upon a major precepting authority to issue a precept in accordance with the requirements of this section.

Subs. (2)

The precept issued to the billing authority, under the duty imposed by subs. (1), must state two things: first, the amount of council tax which the precepting authority calculates, in accordance with ss.43–47, is applicable to each category of dwellings in the area of the billing authority for that financial year; and secondly, the amount which the precepting authority calculates, in accordance with s.48, is the amount payable by the billing authority in respect of the precept for that financial year.

Subs. (3)

The categories into which the dwellings fall are those according to which the calculations have been made under ss.43–47.

Subs. (4)

To meet the requirement imposed by subs. (2) of stating the amount of council tax which the precepting authority calculates is applicable to each category of dwellings in the area of the billing authority, it shall be assumed that there is one or more dwellings in each of the valuation bands for each relevant part of the area, whether or not this is the case in fact. Thus a sum for each of the valuation bands must be shown in relation to each part of the area for which a different basic amount of council tax is payable.

Subs. (5)

A duty is placed on the precepting authority to issue a precept for any financial year before March 1 in the preceding financial year. However, this duty is directory only and a precept issued later than that will not be invalid solely for that reason.

Subs. (6)

The precept may not be issued until either the prescribed period for notification of the tax base, as required by ss.33(1), 44(1), and 45(3), must have expired, or the billing authority has actually notified the precepting authority of its calculations in relation to that tax base.

Subs. (7)

This reinforces the requirement implicit in subs. (1) that all the calculations demanded by this chapter of the Act must have been made before a precept may be issued for any financial year.

Subs. (8)

Any purported precept which has been issued without the necessary calculations having been undertaken, or which has been issued before the tax base has been notified or the period for notification has expired, as required by subss. (6) and (7), will have no legal effect.

Issue of precepts by local precepting authorities

41.—(1) For each financial year a local precepting authority may issue a precept in accordance with this section.

(2) A precept issued to a billing authority under this section must state, as the amount payable by that authority for the year, the amount which has been calculated (or last calculated) by the precepting authority under section 50 below as its budget requirement for the year.

(3) The Secretary of State may by regulations make provision that a billing authority making calculations in accordance with section 32 above (originally or by way of substitute) may anticipate a precept under this section; and the regulations may include provision as to—

(a) the amounts which may be anticipated by billing authorities in pursuance of the regulations;

(b) the sums (if any) to be paid by such authorities in respect of amounts anticipated by them; and

(c) the sums (if any) to be paid by such authorities in respect of amounts not anticipated by them.

(4) A precept under this section must be issued before 1st March in the financial year preceding that for which it is issued, but is not invalid merely because it is issued on or after that date.

DEFINITIONS
"billing authority": ss.1(2) and 69(1).
"financial year": ss.69(1) and 116(1).
"local precepting authority": ss.39(2) and 69(1).
"precepting authority": ss.39 and 69(1).

GENERAL NOTE
A local precepting authority has the discretion to issue a precept for each financial year in accordance with the provisions of this section. The precept must state the precepting authority's budget requirement for the year and it is that amount which is payable by the billing authority in respect of the precept for that financial year. Although there is a duty to issue any such precept for a financial year before March 1 in the preceding financial year, power is given to the Secretary of State to make regulations to allow the billing authority to anticipate the issue of such a precept, when determining their own budget requirement.

Subs. (1)
A local precepting authority has the discretion to issue a precept for each financial year in accordance with the provisions of this section.

Subs. (2)
The local precepting authority must state in any precept issued what the sum payable by the billing authority is to be. That amount must be the sum calculated by the precepting authority as the budget requirement for that financial year, in accordance with the requirements of s.50.

Subs. (3)
This provides a general power for the Secretary of State to make regulations to allow the billing authority to anticipate the issue of such a precept when determining its own budget requirement under s.32. Without prejudice to the generality of that power, the regulations may include provision as to the amounts which may be so anticipated, and the sums to be paid in respect of those amounts, whether anticipated or unanticipated.

Subs. (4)
A duty is placed on the precepting authority to issue a precept for any financial year before March 1 in the preceding financial year. However, this duty is directory only and a precept issued later than that will not be invalid solely for that reason.

Substituted precepts

42.—(1) Where—

(a) a precepting authority has issued a precept or precepts for a financial year (originally or by way of substitute); and

(b) at any later time it makes substitute calculations under section 49 or 61 or (as the case may be) section 51 below,

it shall as soon as reasonably practicable after that time issue a precept or precepts in substitution so as to give effect to those calculations.

(2) Any precept issued in substitution under subsection (1) above must be issued in accordance with section 40 or (as the case may be) section 41 above, but subsection (5) of section 40 and subsection (4) of section 41 shall be ignored for this purpose.

(3) Where a precepting authority issues a precept in substitution (a new precept) anything paid to it by reference to the precept for which it is substituted (the old precept) shall be treated as paid by reference to the new precept.

(4) If the amount stated in the old precept exceeds that of the new precept, the following shall apply as regards anything paid if it would not have been paid had the amount of the old precept been the same as that of the new precept—

(a) it shall be repaid if the billing authority by whom it was paid so requires;

(b) in any other case it shall (as the precepting authority determines) either be repaid or be credited against any subsequent liability of the billing authority in respect of any precept of the precepting authority.

(5) Any reference in subsection (4) above to the amount stated in a precept shall be construed, in relation to a precept issued by a major precepting authority, as a reference to the amount stated in the precept in accordance with section 40(2)(b) above.

DEFINITIONS
"billing authority": ss.1(2) and 69(1).
"financial year": ss.69(1) and 116(1).
"precepting authority": ss.39 and 69(1).

GENERAL NOTE
Where a precepting authority has made a substitute calculation after a precept has already been issued, then it is under a duty to issue a substitute precept as soon as reasonably practicable thereafter. The section also makes provision as to the amount payable in respect of a substitute precept.

Subs. (1)
Where a precepting authority has made a substitute calculation under ss.49, 51, or 61 after a precept has already been issued, then it is under a duty to issue a substitute precept as soon as reasonably practicable after the substitute calculation. This applies whether the precept already issued is the original precept or is another substitute precept.

Subs. (2)
Any substitute precept must comply with the requirements which apply to the original precept, under s.40, with the exception that there is no requirement to set it by March 1 in the preceding financial year.

Subs. (3)
Where payments have already been made to the billing authority on the basis of the original amount set, then those sums shall be treated as having been paid in relation to the new amount set. This general approach is clarified by subs. (4).

Subs. (4)
This covers the situation where two factors are present. First, the original amount of the precept is higher than the substituted precept. Secondly, payments have already been made to the precepting authority on the basis of the original precept and the sums paid are greater than would have been paid in relation to the substituted precept. In this situation, the billing authority has the right to require a repayment. If the billing authority does not make such a request, then it is within the discretion of the precepting authority whether to repay the overpayment or to credit the sum against liability of the billing authority in regard to a precept for a future financial year.

Subs. (5)
Where the original precept has been issued by a major precepting authority, then, in applying subs. (4), the amount shall be taken to be the sum stated in the original precept, as required by s.40(2), as the amount which the precepting authority calculates, in accordance with s.48, is the total amount payable by the billing authority in respect of the precept for that financial year.

Calculations by major precepting authorities

Calculation of budget requirement

43.—(1) In relation to each financial year a major precepting authority shall make the calculations required by this section.

(2) The authority must calculate the aggregate of—

(a) the expenditure the authority estimates it will incur in the year in performing its functions and will charge to a revenue account for the year, other than expenditure which it estimates will be so incurred in pursuance of regulations under section 99(3) of the 1988 Act;

(b) such allowance as the authority estimates will be appropriate for contingencies in relation to expenditure to be charged to a revenue account for the year;

(c) the financial reserves which the authority estimates it will be appropriate to raise in the year for meeting its estimated future expenditure; and

(d) such financial reserves as are sufficient to meet so much of the amount estimated by the authority to be a revenue account deficit for any earlier financial year as has not already been provided for.

(3) The authority must calculate the aggregate of—

(a) the sums which it estimates will be payable to it for the year and in respect of which amounts will be credited to a revenue account for the year, other than sums which it estimates will be so payable in respect of redistributed non-domestic rates, revenue support grant or additional grant or any precept issued by it, or in pursuance of regulations under section 99(3) of the 1988 Act; and

(b) the amount of the financial reserves which the authority estimates that it will use in order to provide for the items mentioned in paragraphs (a) and (b) of subsection (2) above.

(4) If the aggregate calculated under subsection (2) above exceeds that calculated under subsection (3) above, the authority must calculate the amount equal to the difference; and the amount so calculated shall be its budget requirement for the year.

(5) In estimating under subsection (2)(a) above an authority which is a county council shall take into account the amount of any levy issued to it for the year but (except as provided by regulations under section 74 of the 1988 Act) shall not anticipate a levy not issued.

(6) For the purposes of subsection (2)(c) above an authority's estimated future expenditure is—

(a) that which the authority estimates it will incur in the financial year following the year in question, will charge to a revenue account for the year and will have to defray in the year before the following sums are sufficiently available, namely, sums—

(i) which will be payable to it for the year; and

(ii) in respect of which amounts will be credited to a revenue account for the year; and

(b) that which the authority estimates it will incur in the financial year referred to in paragraph (a) above or any subsequent financial year in performing its functions and which will be charged to a revenue account for that or any other year.

(7) The Secretary of State may by regulations do one or both of the following—

(a) alter the constituents of any calculation to be made under subsection (2) or (3) above (whether by adding, deleting or amending items);

(b) alter the rules governing the making of any calculation under subsection (2) or (3) above (whether by deleting or amending subsections (5) and (6) above, or either of them, or by adding other provisions, or by a combination of those methods).

(8) References in this section to expenditure incurred by an authority shall be construed in accordance with section 41(3) of the Local Government and Housing Act 1989.

DEFINITIONS

"additional grant": s.69(1); s.85(2) of the 1988 Act.

"estimated future expenditure": subs. (6).
"expenditure": subs. (8).
"financial year": ss.69(1) and 116(1).
"major precepting authority": ss.39(1) and 69(1).
"redistributed non-domestic rates": s.69(1); Sched. 8 to the 1988 Act.
"revenue support grant": s.69(1); s.78(1) of the 1988 Act.

GENERAL NOTE

A duty is imposed upon a major precepting authority to calculate its "budget requirement" for each financial year, defined as the difference between its expenditure and income as defined by this section. The "budget requirement" is a figure which it is necessary to calculate before proceeding to the calculation, under s.44, of the basic amount of its council tax for any financial year. The items which are to be taken into account in calculating the budget requirement, and the method of this calculation, are specified by the section, but the Secretary of State is given power to amend these by regulation.

Subs. (1)

The basic duty upon a major precepting authority to calculate its budget requirements for each financial year in accordance with the rest of the section is imposed by this subsection.

Subs. (2)

In order to produce the figure for the expenditure requirement of the authority, the major precepting authority is required to calculate the aggregate of four sums. First, the estimate of revenue expenditure for the year, other than expenditure which it estimates will be incurred in relation to regulations made under s.99(3) of the 1988 Act, as amended by s.104 of and Sched. 10 to this Act, dealing with deficits and surpluses on collection funds. Secondly, allowances for contingencies in relation to the revenue expenditure. Thirdly, the reserves to be raised in the year in regard to meeting estimated future expenditure and, fourthly, estimated reserves to meet any outstanding revenue deficit for an earlier financial year. The definition of "expenditure" to be applied, by subs. (8) below, is that given by s.41(3) of the 1989 Act.

Subs. (3)

In order to produce the figure for the income element of the authority, the major precepting authority is required to calculate the aggregate of two sums. The first sum is that which it estimates will be payable to it for the year and which will be credited to a revenue account, other than from the sources of non-domestic rates, general grant or additional grants, which are taken into account in the calculation under s.44. The second is the amount of the financial reserves which the authority estimated to be necessary to use to meet estimated expenditure and contingencies in relation to its functions for the year.

Subs. (4)

Where the "income" produced by aggregating the items specified in subs. (3) is less than the sum of the "expenditure" produced by the aggregation of the items specified in subs. (2), then that difference is defined as the budget requirement for the year.

Subs. (5)

In calculating the estimate of the expenditure on performing its functions for the financial year, for the purpose of calculating the aggregate under subs. (2), the major precepting authority must take into account the amount of any levy issued to it. However, the authority is permitted to include in the calculation only a levy already actually issued. An anticipated levy may not be included, no matter how likely it is to be issued, except in accordance with any regulations made under s.74 of the 1988 Act.

Subs. (6)

In calculating the estimate of the reserves which it is appropriate to raise in relation to estimated future expenditure, for the purpose of calculating the aggregate under subs. (2), the major precepting authority must take into account the definition of "future expenditure". This is defined in two parts. First, the sums which the authority estimates it will incur in the following financial year and will have to charge to a revenue account before that account has available to it sufficient sums from those payable to it. This deals with the "cash-flow" problems. Secondly, the sums which the authority estimates it will incur in the following or any subsequent financial year, and which will be charged to that or any other year. This allows for forward planning in relation to exceptional expenditure.

Subs. (7)

The requirements as to the calculation of the budget requirement may be altered by the

Secretary of State, both as regards the items to be taken into account, under subss. (2) and (3), and the more specific methods of calculation, under subss. (5) and (6). Thus the items may be added to, deleted, or amended, and the specific methods of calculation may be deleted, amended or added to, singly or in combination.

Subs. (8)
The definition of "expenditure" to be applied in this section is that which was given by s.41(3) of the 1989 Act. On the basis that local government finance is to be conducted on an annual basis (*R. v. Greater London Council*, ex p. *Westminster City Council* [1986] A.C. 668), s.41 of the 1989 Act prescribed what expenditure is to be charged to a revenue account, although s.42 also prescribed what expenditure was excluded from this requirement. Section 41(3) of the 1989 Act provides that expenditure incurred by a local authority in any financial year includes any amount which is not part of the capital receipts and which is set aside to meet credit liabilities, and also any amount set aside for the year to meet any liability or loss for which, although likely or certain to be incurred, the amount is still uncertain.

Calculation of basic amount of tax

44.—(1) In relation to each financial year a major precepting authority shall calculate the basic amount of its council tax by applying the formula—

$$\frac{R - P}{T}$$

where—
>   R is the amount calculated (or last calculated) by the authority under section 43(4) above as its budget requirement for the year;
>   P is the aggregate of the sums which the authority estimates will be payable to it for the year in respect of redistributed non-domestic rates, revenue support grant or additional grant;
>   T is the aggregate of the amounts which are calculated by the billing authorities to which the authority issues precepts ("the billing authorities concerned") as their council tax bases for the year for their areas, or (as the case may require) for the parts of their areas falling within the authority's area, and are notified by them to the authority within the prescribed period.

(2) Where the aggregate calculated (or last calculated) by the authority for the year under subsection (2) of section 43 above does not exceed that so calculated under subsection (3) of that section, the amount for item R in subsection (1) above shall be nil.

(3) The aggregate of the sums mentioned in item P in subsection (1) above shall be—
>   (a) increased by the aggregate amount of any sums which the authority estimates will be paid to it in the year by billing authorities in accordance with regulations under section 99(3) of the 1988 Act; and
>   (b) reduced by the aggregate amount of any sums which the authority estimates will be paid by it in the year to billing authorities in accordance with such regulations.

(4) Regulations under section 43(7) above may make such consequential alterations of the constituents of any calculation required by item P in subsection (1) above or subsection (3) above (whether by adding, deleting or amending items) as appear to the Secretary of State to be necessary or expedient.

(5) The Secretary of State shall make regulations containing rules for making for any year the calculations required by item T in subsection (1) above; and the billing authorities concerned shall make the calculations for any year in accordance with the rules for the time being effective (as regards the year) under the regulations.

(6) Regulations prescribing a period for the purposes of item T in subsection (1) above may provide that, in any case where a billing authority fails to notify its calculation to the precepting authority within that period, that

item shall be determined in the prescribed manner by such authority or authorities as may be prescribed.

(7) Any negative amount given by a calculation under subsection (1) above shall be assumed to be nil for the purposes of this Chapter.

DEFINITIONS
"additional grant": s.69(1); s.85(2) of the 1988 Act.
"billing authority": ss.1(2) and 69(1).
"budget requirement": s.43(4).
"council tax": s.1(1).
"financial year": ss.69(1) and 116(1).
"major precepting authority": ss.39(1) and 69(1).
"precepting authority": ss.39 and 69(1).
"prescribed": s.116(1).
"redistributed non-domestic rates": s.69(1); Sched. 8 to the 1988 Act.
"revenue support grant": s.69(1); s.78(1) of the 1988 Act.

GENERAL NOTE
This section provides the formula for the calculation of the basic amount of council tax for each financial year for a major precepting authority. The items to be taken into account in this calculation are specified, although power is given to the Secretary of State to issue further regulations amending these. See the Local Authorities (Calculation of Council Tax Base) Regulations 1992 (S.I. 1992 No. 612).

Subs. (1)
The calculation of the basic amount of council tax for a precepting authority is to be determined by dividing the sum required to be raised through the council tax by the council-tax base. The first of these, the sum required to be raised through the council tax, is to be calculated by subtracting from the budget requirement (R), as determined by the calculation under s.43(4), amounts which the authority will receive from central government (P). These amounts relate to the authority's share of non-domestic rates, its revenue support grant and additional grants. The council-tax base figure (T) is that calculated by the billing authority, and communicated within the prescribed period, as being the tax base for its area, or parts of the area.

Subs. (2)
If, as calculated in accordance with s.43(2), the "expenditure" element of the budget requirement is equal to or less than the amount of "income", calculated in accordance with s.43(3), then the element R in the calculation of the basic amount of council tax, under subs. (1) above, could in principle be a negative sum. However, this provision makes it clear that, in such circumstances, the element R, the budget requirement under s.43(4), will be treated as £0.

Subs. (3)
The element P, in the calculation of the basic amount of council tax, under subs. (1) above, which is the aggregate of the grants and non-domestic rates payable to the authority, shall be amended to incorporate any transfers between the major precepting authority and the billing authority in accordance with regulations made under s.99(3) of the 1988 Act. That original section has been replaced by a new s.99, as enacted by s.104 of and Sched. 10, para. 24 to this Act. Under the new s.99(3), where there is a surplus in the collection fund for the preceding year, then the billing authority shall transfer to the major precepting authority the appropriate share of the surplus, as determined in accordance with regulations. Under the new s.99(3), where there is a deficit in the collection fund for the preceding year, then the major precepting authority must bear the amount equal to the appropriate share of the deficit, as determined in accordance with regulations.

Subs. (4)
This power is given to the Secretary of State, as appears to him to be necessary or expedient, to alter the method of calculation of element P, in the calculation of the basic amount of council tax, under subss. (1) or (3) above. It may be altered, whether by addition, deletion or other amendment, by regulations made under the authority of s.43(7) above.

Subs. (5)
This provides the legal authority for the regulations necessary to prescribe the calculation of element T, in the determination of the basic amount of council tax, under subs. (1) above, including the prescribed periods for notification by the major precepting authorities, and it

places a duty on the Secretary of State to make these regulations. In relation to this element, the billing authority is placed under a duty to make the calculation in accordance with the regulations.

Subs. (6)

In relation to element T, in the determination of the basic amount of council tax, under subs. (1) above, the regulations which prescribe the period in which T has to be calculated may also provide for the element to be determined by another authority if the billing authority fails to notify the calculation to the major precepting authorities within the prescribed time. The regulations may prescribe which authority or authorities may carry out this calculation, and determine the manner in which it should be carried out. The effect of this is that the process will not be able to be frustrated by the billing authority's failing to comply with the relevant time limits.

Subs. (7)

Any negative amount produced by the calculation of the basic amount of council tax for a precepting authority shall be assumed to be nil for the purposes of further calculations by the billing authority of the council tax due. In this way, the major precepting authority will not be required to pay any sums to the billing authority because it has a surplus of "income" over "expenditure" as calculated in accordance with these provisions.

Additional calculations where special items relate to part only of area

45.—(1) This section applies where for any financial year an item mentioned in section 46(1) below relates to a part only of a major precepting authority's area; and in this section "special item" means any such item which so relates and "the relevant part", in relation to such an item, means the part concerned.

(2) The authority shall calculate the basic amount of its council tax for dwellings in a part of its area to which no special item relates by applying the formula—

$$B - \frac{A}{T}$$

where—
> B is the amount calculated (or last calculated) by the authority under section 44(1) above as the basic amount of its council tax;
> A is the aggregate amount of all special items;
> T is the amount determined for item T in section 44(1) above.

(3) The authority shall calculate the basic amount of its council tax for dwellings in a part of its area to which one or more special items relate by adding to the amount given by the formula in subsection (2) above the aggregate of the amounts which, in relation to each of those special items, are given by the formula—

$$\frac{S}{TP}$$

where—
> S is (in each case) the amount of the special item;
> TP is (in each case) the aggregate of the amounts which are calculated by the billing authorities to which the authority has power to issue precepts as respects the special item ("the billing authorities concerned") as their council tax bases for the year for their areas, or (as the case may require) for the parts of their areas falling within the relevant part, and are notified by them to the authority within the prescribed period.

(4) The Secretary of State shall make regulations containing rules for making for any year the calculations required by item TP in subsection (3) above; and the billing authorities concerned shall make the calculations for any year in accordance with the rules for the time being effective (as regards the year) under the regulations.

(5) Regulations prescribing a period for the purposes of item TP in subsection (3) above may provide that, in any case where a billing authority fails to notify its calculation to the precepting authority within that period, that item shall be determined in the prescribed manner by such authority or authorities as may be prescribed.

(6) Any negative amount given by a calculation under subsection (2) or (3) above shall be assumed to be nil for the purposes of this Chapter.

DEFINITIONS
   "billing authority": ss.1(2) and 69(1).
   "council tax": s.1(1).
   "dwelling": ss.3 and 69(1).
   "financial year": ss.69(1) and 116(1).
   "major precepting authority": ss.39(1) and 69(1).
   "prescribed": s.116(1).
   "relevant part": subs. (1).
   "special item": subs. (1).

GENERAL NOTE
   This section makes provision for the situation where "special items", as defined by s.46, relate to part only of the area of the major precepting authority. The major precepting authority must make additional calculations, in accordance with the formulae set out in this section, to recover the sums in relation to the special items from the areas to which they relate. Power is also given to the Secretary of State to prescribe by regulation the rules for calculating one of the items to be taken into account in this process. See the Local Authorities (Calculation of Council Tax Base) Regulations 1992 (S.I. 1992 No. 612).

Subs. (1)
   The provisions of this section are triggered where any item, specified in s.46(1), applies for any financial year to a part only of the major precepting authority's area. The necessary definitions are given for this section, with the term "special item" meaning any such item which triggers the provisions of this section, and "the relevant part" is defined as that part of the major precepting authority's area to which the special item relates.

Subs. (2)
   Where there are special items relating to some part or parts of the area of the major precepting authority, then the method of calculation of the basic amount of its council tax for a particular area to which no special items relate is provided for by this subsection. The principle is that the basic amount is calculated by subtracting an appropriate amount from the sum calculated, under s.44(1), as the basic amount of council tax (B) payable before special items are taken into account. The sum to be subtracted is the quotient of the aggregate amount of all special items (A) divided by the council-tax base (T). The council-tax base (T) for the area or areas of the major precepting authority is calculated by the billing authority, under s.44(1), and notified within the prescribed period, or, in default, by another authority under the regulations made under s.44(6).

Subs. (3)
   Where there are special items relating to some part or parts of the area of the major precepting authority, then the method of calculation of the basic amount of its council tax for a particular area to which a special item relates is provided for by this subsection. The principle is that the basic amount for dwellings in the area to which the special item relates is calculated by adding an appropriate amount to the sum calculated, under subs. (2), as the sum payable in regard to a dwelling in an area to which no special item relates. The sum to be added is determined for each special item by dividing the amount of the special item (S) by the amount of the billing authority's council-tax base for that area for that year (TP).

Subs. (4)
   This provides the legal authority for the regulations necessary to prescribe the calculation of element TP, in relation to the calculation to be made under subs. (3) above, and it places a duty on the Secretary of State to make these regulations. In relation to this element, the billing authority is placed under a duty to make the calculation in accordance with the regulations.

Subs. (5)
   In relation to element TP, in the determination of the basic amount of council tax for the

major precepting authority where special items apply, under subs. (3) above, the regulations which prescribe the period in which TP has to be calculated may also provide for the element to be determined by another authority if the billing authority fails to notify the calculation to the major precepting authorities within the prescribed time. The regulations may prescribe which authority or authorities may carry out this calculation, and determine the manner in which it should be carried out. The effect of this is that the process will not be able to be frustrated by the billing authority's failing to comply with the relevant time limits.

Subs. (6)

Any negative amount produced by the calculation of the basic amount of council tax for a precepting authority where special items apply shall be assumed to be nil for the purposes of further calculations by the billing authority of the council tax due. In this way, the major precepting authority will not be required to pay any sums to the billing authority because it has a surplus of "income" over "expenditure" as calculated in accordance with these provisions.

Special items for purposes of section 45

46.—(1) The items referred to in section 45(1) above are any expenses of the major precepting authority which are its special expenses and were taken into account by it in making the calculation in relation to the year under section 43(2) above.

(2) For the purposes of subsection (1) above—

(a) if a county council is the police authority for part only of its area, its expenses as police authority are special expenses provided a resolution of the council to that effect is in force;

(b) provided a resolution of a county council to the following effect is in force, the expenses of meeting a levy issued to or anticipated by it are its special expenses or (if the resolution relates to some only of those expenses) those to which the resolution relates are its special expenses;

(c) if the library area of a Welsh county council consists of part of its administrative area, its expenses in exercising its functions as library authority in its library area are its special expenses; and

(d) the expenses of the Receiver for the Metropolitan Police District relating to the magistrates' courts in the inner London area and the probation service in that area are his special expenses.

(3) For the purposes of section 45(1) above—

(a) expenses which are special by virtue of a resolution under subsection (2)(a) above relate to the part of the council's area for which it is the police authority;

(b) expenses which are special by virtue of a resolution under subsection (2)(b) above relate to the part of the council's area in which the levying body carries out functions;

(c) expenses which are special by virtue of subsection (2)(c) above relate to the part of the council's administrative area which consists of its library area; and

(d) expenses which are special by virtue of subsection (2)(d) above relate to the inner London area.

(4) In this section—

"inner London area" has the same meaning as in the Justices of the Peace Act 1979;

"library area" shall be construed in accordance with the Public Libraries and Museums Act 1964;

and any reference to magistrates' courts in the inner London area includes references to domestic courts and to youth courts for that area and the City.

DEFINITIONS

"inner London area": subs. (4).

"library area": subs. (4).

"major precepting authority": ss.39(1) and 69(1).

GENERAL NOTE
   This section specifies those items which are to be treated as "special items" for the purposes of the calculation of the amount of council tax for a major precepting authority, under s.45(1). These are defined as any "special expenses", as defined by subs. (2), and are operated in accordance with subs. (3).

Subs. (1)
   For the purposes of the calculation of council tax to be made under s.45(1), a "special item" is defined as any "special expenses", as defined by subs. (2), and which were taken into account in making the calculation, under s.43(2), of the "expenditure" element in the calculation of the budget requirement.

Subs. (2)
   "Special expenses" in turn fall into four categories. First, the expenses of a county council as police authority, if it is the police authority for part only of its area. If it is police authority for the whole of the area it is of course a general function, not a special expense. Secondly, the expenses of a county council in meeting a levy or anticipated levy, or parts of such levies. For both of these categories, there must be a resolution of the county council in force to this effect. Thirdly, the expenses of a county council as library authority, where its library area consists of part of its general area. Fourthly, the expenses of the Receiver for the Metropolitan Police District in relation to the costs of the magistrates' courts and probation service in inner London. These categories are clarified further by subs. (3), which makes it clear that such special expenses relate only to those parts of the area to which the appropriate resolution relates or where the function is carried out.

Subs. (3)
   This makes it clear that such special expenses, as defined in subs. (2) relate only to those parts of the area to which the appropriate resolution relates or where the function is carried out.

Subs. (4)
   This provides the necessary additional definitions for this section.

Calculation of tax for different valuation bands

   47.—(1) The amount to be stated under section 40(2)(a) above for any financial year in respect of any category of dwellings listed in a particular valuation band shall be calculated by applying the formula—

$$A \times \frac{N}{D}$$

where—
   A is the amount calculated (or last calculated) by the major precepting authority for that year under section 44(1) above or, where section 45 above applies, the amount calculated (or last calculated) by it for that year under subsection (2) or (3) of that section in relation to that category of dwellings.
   N is the number which, in the proportion set out in section 5(1) above, is applicable to dwellings listed in that valuation band;
   D is the number which, in that proportion, is applicable to dwellings listed in valuation band D.
   (2) Dwellings fall within different categories for the purposes of this section according as different calculations have been made in relation to them under section 45 above.

DEFINITIONS
   "dwelling": ss.3 and 69(1).
   "financial year": ss.69(1) and 116(1).
   "major precepting authority": ss.39(1) and 69(1).
   "valuation band": s.5(2) and (3).

GENERAL NOTE
   Having calculated the basic amount of its council tax, and taken account of any special items, the major precepting authority must then calculate the amount of council tax payable for the

financial year by dwellings in each of the valuation bands, for each of the areas for which it has calculated a different amount of basic tax. This section sets out the formula for this calculation.

Subs. (1)
The amount of council tax in relation to the major precepting authority payable for the financial year by dwellings in each of the valuation bands is calculated by the formula in this subsection. The sum is arrived at by multiplying the basic amount of council tax, applicable to the whole or part of the area of the major precepting authority, by the appropriate factor. The basic amount of council tax (A) is that calculated under s.44(1) or, where special items apply, under s.45(2) or (3). The factor is the quotient of the number applicable to dwellings in that valuation band (N), divided by the number applicable to dwellings in valuation band D (D). Both numbers are established by s.5(1). Thus dwellings in valuation band D will pay the basic amount of council tax while those in higher or lower bands will pay an amount which is proportionately more or less, according to the ratio established by s.5(1).

Subs. (2)
This makes it clear that the category of dwelling to which this section applies is defined not only by the valuation band itself, but also by whether different calculations have been made, under s.34, to take account of special items. Thus different basic amounts of council tax may be produced for dwellings within the same valuation band but within different areas of the billing authority.

Calculation of amount payable by each billing authority

48.—(1) This section makes provision for calculating the amount required by section 40(2)(b) above to be stated in a precept as the amount payable by a billing authority for any financial year.

(2) Where an amount calculated (or last calculated) for the year under section 44(1) or 45(2) or (3) above applies to dwellings in the whole of the billing authority's area, the amount payable by that authority shall be calculated by applying the formula—

$$C \times T$$

where—
    C is the amount so calculated;
    T is the amount which, in relation to the billing authority, is determined
        for item T in section 33(1) above.

(3) Where an amount calculated (or last calculated) for the year under section 44(1) or 45(2) or (3) above applies to dwellings in a part of the billing authority's area, the amount payable by that authority shall be calculated by applying the formula—

$$CP \times TP$$

where—
    CP is the amount so calculated;
    TP is the amount which is calculated by the billing authority as its
        council tax base for the year for the part of its area concerned and is
        notified by it to the major precepting authority within the pre-
        scribed period.

(4) Where different amounts calculated (or last calculated) for the year under section 45(2) or (3) above apply to dwellings in different parts of the billing authority's area, the amount payable by that authority shall be the aggregate of the amounts which, in relation to each of the amounts so calculated, are given by the formula—

$$CP \times TP$$

where—
    CP is (in each case) the amount so calculated;
    TP is (in each case) the amount which is calculated by the billing
        authority as its council tax base for the year for the part of its area
        concerned and is notified by it to the major precepting authority
        within the prescribed period.

(5) The Secretary of State shall make regulations containing rules for making for any year the calculations required by item TP in subsection (3) or (4) above; and the billing authority shall make the calculations for any year in accordance with the rules for the time being effective (as regards the year) under the regulations.

(6) Regulations prescribing a period for the purposes of item TP in subsection (3) or (4) above may provide that, in any case where the billing authority fails to notify its calculation to the precepting authority within that period, that item shall be determined in the prescribed manner by such authority or authorities as may be prescribed.

DEFINITIONS
"billing authority": ss.1(2) and 69(1).
"dwelling": ss.3 and 69(1).
"financial year": ss.69(1) and 116(1).
"major precepting authority": ss.39(1) and 69(1).
"prescribed": s.116(1).

GENERAL NOTE
This section provides the method of calculation of the amount payable by each billing authority to the major precepting authority, as required to be stated in the precept to the billing authority, under s.40(2)(b). Different formulae apply in relation to whether the council tax of the major precepting authority applies to the whole or only part of the area of the billing authority. Power is also given to the Secretary of State to make regulations prescribing rules for items in this calculation. See the Local Authorities (Calculation of Council Tax Base) Regulations 1992 (S.I. 1992 No. 612).

Subs. (1)
This simply provides that the rest of the sections gives the method of calculation of the amount payable by each billing authority to the major precepting authority, as required to be stated in the precept to the billing authority, under s.40(2)(b).

Subs. (2)
This formula governs the situation where the basic amount of council tax for the major precepting authority applies to the whole of the area of the billing authority. In that situation, the amount payable by the billing authority is calculated by multiplying two sums. First, the basic amount of council tax for the major precepting authority (C), whether under s.44(1) or taking account of special items under s.45(2) or (3). Secondly, the amount calculated by the billing authority, under s.33(1), as its council-tax base for the year (T) and notified to the major precepting authority within the prescribed period, or as calculated in default by another authority under s.33(6). The product of these sums is the amount payable by the billing authority.

Subs. (3)
This formula governs the situation where the basic amount of council tax for the major precepting authority applies to the part only of the area of the billing authority. In that situation, the amount payable by the billing authority is calculated by multiplying two sums. First, the basic amount of council tax for the major precepting authority for that area (CP), whether under s.44(1) or taking account of special items under s.45(2) or (3). Secondly, the amount calculated by the billing authority as its council-tax base for the year for that part of its area (TP), and notified to the major precepting authority within the prescribed period or as calculated in default by another authority under s.33(6). The product of these sums is the amount payable by the billing authority.

Subs. (4)
This formula governs the situation where the basic amount of council tax for the major precepting authority applies to different parts of the area of the billing authority. In that situation, the amount payable by the billing authority is calculated by multiplying two sums. First, the basic amount of council tax for the major precepting authority for each area (CP), whether under s.44(1) or taking account of special items under s.45(2) or (3). Secondly, the amount calculated by the billing authority as its council-tax base for the year for each part of its area (TP), and notified to the major precepting authority within the prescribed period or as calculated in default by another authority under s.33(6). The product of these sums is the amount payable by the billing authority.

Subs. (5)

This provides the legal authority for the regulations necessary to prescribe the calculation of element TP, in relation to the calculation to be made under subss. (3) and (4) above as to the amount payable by the billing authority to the major precepting authority, and it places a duty on the Secretary of State to make these regulations. In relation to this element, the billing authority is placed under a duty to make the calculation in accordance with the regulations.

Subs. (6)

In relation to element TP, as regards to the calculation to be made under subss. (3) and (4) above as to the amount payable by the billing authority to the major precepting authority (subs. (3) above), the regulations which prescribe the period in which TP has to be calculated may also provide for the element to be determined by another authority if the billing authority fails to notify the calculation to the major precepting authorities within the prescribed time. The regulations may prescribe which authority or authorities may carry out this calculation, and determine the manner in which it should be carried out. The effect of this is that the process will not be able to be frustrated by the billing authority's failing to comply with the relevant time limits.

Substitute calculations

49.—(1) A major precepting authority which has made calculations in accordance with sections 43 to 48 above in relation to a financial year (originally or by way of substitute) may make calculations in substitution in relation to the year in accordance with those sections.

(2) None of the substitute calculations shall have any effect if—

(a) the amount calculated under section 43(4) above, or any amount calculated under section 44(1) or 45(2) or (3) above as the basic amount of council tax applicable to any dwelling, would exceed that so calculated in the previous calculations; or

(b) the authority fails to comply with subsection (3) below in making the substitute calculations.

(3) In making substitute calculations under section 44(1) or 45(3) above, the authority must use any amount determined in the previous calculations for item P or T in section 44(1) above or item TP in section 45(3) above.

(4) For the purposes of subsection (3) above, the authority may treat any amount determined in the previous calculations for item P in section 44(1) above as increased by the amount of any sum which—

(a) it estimates will be payable to it for the year in respect of additional grant; and

(b) was not taken into account by it in making those calculations.

(5) Subsections (2) and (3) above shall not apply if the previous calculations have been quashed because of a failure to comply with sections 43 to 48 above in making the calculations.

DEFINITIONS

"additional grant": s.69(1); s.85(2) of the 1988 Act.
"dwelling": ss.3 and 69(1).
"financial year": ss.69(1) and 116(1).
"major precepting authority": ss.39(1) and 69(1).

GENERAL NOTE

Provided that the rules established by this section are complied with, it will be possible for a major precepting authority, having already made calculations as to its budget requirement and council tax, to make a substitute calculation. However, the rules establish a number of limitations, not least of which is that the substitute basic amount of council tax may not be greater than the original amount.

Subs. (1)

This establishes that it is possible for a major precepting authority, having already made calculations as to its budget requirement and council tax under ss.43–48, to make a substitute calculation, and thereafter be able to make further substitute calculations for that financial year. In doing so, the authority must, as with the original calculation, comply with the provisions of ss.43–48.

Subs. (2)

A purported substitute calculation will have no legal effect in two situations: first, if either the budget requirement, calculated under s.43(4), or the basic amount of council tax, calculated under s.44(1) or s.45(2) or (3), is greater than that in the previous calculation; and secondly, if the major precepting authority fails to comply with the requirement in subs. (3) to use the same amounts for the items specified in that subsection.

Subs. (3)

In calculating the revised amount of council tax, the major precepting authority must, in principle, use the same amount as determined in the previous calculations for three items. First, in relation to the calculation under s.44(1), the aggregate of redistributed non-domestic rates, revenue support and additional grants payable to the general fund (P). This is, however, subject to the qualification, introduced by subs. (4), that the amount of the aggregate may be increased if it is a result of an increase in the amount of additional grant which was not taken into account in the original calculation. Secondly, again in relation to the calculation under s.44(1), the amount of the council-tax base for the year (T). Thirdly, in relation to a calculation under s.45(3), the amount of the council-tax base for the year for part of the area where special items apply (TP). The effect of this is that a change in the amount of funds received from central government through these sources, or of the council-tax base, will not be allowed to lead to a recalculation of the council tax payable.

Subs. (4)

This establishes the qualification to subs. (3) that the amount of the aggregate of redistributed non-domestic rates, revenue support and additional grants payable to the major precepting authority (P) under s.44(1) may be increased if it is a result of an increase in the amount of additional grant which was not taken into account in the original calculation.

Subs. (5)

This makes clear that the limitations in subss. (2) and (3) will not apply when the previous calculation has been quashed for a failure to comply with the provisions of ss.43–48. In those circumstances, the amount of the budget requirement or the basic amount of council tax may be higher than the original calculation, and the amounts relating to the council-tax base (T and TP) and aggregate of redistributed non-domestic rates, revenue support and additional grants payable to the general fund (P) may be varied.

Calculations by local precepting authorities

Calculation of budget requirement

50.—(1) In relation to each financial year a local precepting authority shall make the calculations required by this section.

(2) The authority must calculate the aggregate of—

(a) the expenditure the authority estimates it will incur in the year in performing its functions and will charge to a revenue account for the year;

(b) such allowance as the authority estimates will be appropriate for contingencies in relation to expenditure to be charged to a revenue account for the year;

(c) the financial reserves which the authority estimates it will be appropriate to raise in the year for meeting its estimated future expenditure; and

(d) such financial reserves as are sufficient to meet so much of the amount estimated by the authority to be a revenue account deficit for any earlier financial year as has not already been provided for.

(3) The authority must calculate the aggregate of—

(a) the sums which it estimates will be payable to it for the year and in respect of which amounts will be credited to a revenue account for the year, other than sums which it estimates will be so payable in respect of any precept issued by it; and

(b) the amount of the financial reserves which the authority estimates that it will use in order to provide for the items mentioned in paragraphs (a) and (b) of subsection (2) above.

(4) If the aggregate calculated under subsection (2) above exceeds that calculated under subsection (3) above, the authority must calculate the amount equal to the difference; and the amount so calculated shall be its budget requirement for the year.

(5) For the purposes of subsection (2)(c) above an authority's estimated future expenditure is—

(a) that which the authority estimates it will incur in the financial year following the year in question, will charge to a revenue account for the year and will have to defray in the year before the following sums are sufficiently available, namely, sums—

(i) which will be payable to it for the year; and

(ii) in respect of which amounts will be credited to a revenue account for the year; and

(b) that which the authority estimates it will incur in the financial year referred to in paragraph (a) above or any subsequent financial year in performing its functions and which will be charged to a revenue account for that or any other year.

(6) References in this section to expenditure incurred by an authority shall be construed in accordance with section 41(3) of the Local Government and Housing Act 1989.

DEFINITIONS
"estimated future expenditure": s.32(7).
"expenditure": subs. (6).
"financial year": ss.69(1) and 116(1).
"local precepting authority": ss.39(2) and 69(1).

GENERAL NOTE
A duty is imposed upon a local precepting authority to calculate its "budget requirement" for each financial year, defined as the difference between its expenditure and income as defined by this section. The items which are to be taken into account in calculating the budget requirement, and the method of this calculation, are specified by the section.

Subs. (1)
The basic duty upon a local precepting authority to calculate its budget requirements for each financial year in accordance with the rest of the section is imposed by this subsection.

Subs. (2)
In order to produce the figure for the expenditure requirement of the authority, the local precepting authority is required to calculate the aggregate of four sums: first, the estimate of revenue expenditure for the year; secondly, allowances for contingencies in relation to the revenue expenditure; thirdly, the reserves to be raised in the year in regard to meeting estimated future expenditure; and, fourthly, estimated reserves to meet any outstanding revenue deficit for an earlier financial year. The definition of "expenditure" to be applied, by subs. (8) below, is that given by s.41(3) of the 1989 Act.

Subs. (3)
In order to produce the figure for the income element of the authority, the local precepting authority is required to calculate the aggregate of two sums. The first sum is that which it estimates will be payable to it for the year and which will be credited to a revenue account, other than sums payable to it in respect of a precept issued by it. The second is the amount of the financial reserves which the authority estimated to be necessary to use to meet estimated expenditure and contingencies in relation to its functions for the year.

Subs. (4)
Where the "income" produced by aggregating the items specified in subs. (3) is less than the sum of the "expenditure" produced by the aggregation of the items specified in subs. (2), then that difference is defined as the budget requirement for the year.

Subs. (5)
In calculating the estimate of the reserves which it is appropriate to raise in relation to estimated future expenditure, for the purpose of calculating the aggregate under subs. (2), the

local precepting authority must take into account the definition of "future expenditure". This is defined in two parts. First, the sums which the authority estimates it will incur in the following financial year and will have to charge to a revenue account before that account has available to it sufficient sums from those payable to it. This deals with the "cash-flow" problems. Secondly, the sums which the authority estimates it will incur in the following or any subsequent financial year, and which will be charged to that or any other year. This allows for forward planning in relation to exceptional expenditure.

Subs. (6)
The definition of "expenditure" to be applied in this section is that which was given by s.41(3) of the 1989 Act. On the basis that local government finance is to be conducted on an annual basis (*R.* v. *Greater London Council*, ex p. *Westminster City Council* [1986] A.C. 668), s.41 of the 1989 Act prescribes what expenditure is to be charged to a revenue account, although s.42 also prescribes what expenditure is excluded from this requirement. Section 41(3) of the 1989 Act provides that expenditure incurred by a local authority in any financial year. It includes any amount which is not part of the capital receipts and which is set aside to meet credit liabilities, and also any amount set aside for the year to meet any liability or loss for which, although likely or certain to be incurred, the amount is still uncertain.

Substitute calculations

51.—(1) A local precepting authority which has made calculations in accordance with section 50 above in relation to a financial year (originally or by way of substitute) may make calculations in substitution in relation to the year in accordance with that section.

(2) None of the substitute calculations shall have any effect if the amount calculated under section 50(4) above would exceed that so calculated in the previous calculations.

(3) Subsection (2) above shall not apply if the previous calculation under subsection (4) of section 50 above has been quashed because of a failure to comply with that section in making the calculation.

DEFINITIONS
"financial year": ss.69(1) and 116(1).
"local precepting authority": ss.39(2) and 69(1).

GENERAL NOTE
Provided that the rules established by this section are complied with, it will be possible for a local precepting authority, having already made calculations as to its budget requirement, to make a substitute calculation. However, the section establishes a limitation that the substitute basic amount of council tax may not be greater than the original amount, unless the original amount has been quashed for a failure to comply with the requirements of s.50.

Subs. (1)
This establishes that it is possible for a local precepting authority, having already made calculations as to its budget requirement under s.50, to make a substitute calculation and thereafter be able to make further substitute calculations for that financial year. In doing so, the authority must, as with the original calculation, comply with the provisions of s.50.

Subs. (2)
A purported substitute calculation will have no legal effect if the budget requirement calculated under s.50(4) is greater than that in the previous calculation.

Subs. (3)
This makes it clear that the limitation in subs. (2) will not apply when the previous calculation has been quashed for a failure to comply with the provisions of s.50. In those circumstances, the amount of the budget requirement may be higher than the original calculation.

Supplemental

Information for purposes of Chapter IV

52. If the Secretary of State so requires by regulations, a billing authority shall supply prescribed information within a prescribed period to any pre-cepting authority which has power to issue a precept to the billing authority.

DEFINITIONS
"billing authority": ss.1(2) and 69(1).
"information": subs. (1) and s.116(1).
"precepting authority": ss.39 and 69(1).
"prescribed": s.116(1).

GENERAL NOTE
A billing authority may be required, by regulations to be made by the Secretary of State, to supply information to a precepting authority, which it has power to issue a precept to. The information may be such as is prescribed in the regulations, and it is to be supplied within such period as the regulations prescribe.

CHAPTER V

LIMITATION OF COUNCIL TAX AND PRECEPTS

Preliminary

Authorities subject to designation

53.—(1) In this Chapter any reference to an authority is a reference to a billing authority or a relevant precepting authority, that is, a major precept-ing authority other than the Receiver for the Metropolitan Police District.

(2) In this Chapter any reference to the amount calculated by an authority as its budget requirement for a financial year is a reference to the amount calculated by it in relation to the year—

(a) in the case of a billing authority, under section 32(4) above;

(b) in the case of a relevant precepting authority, under section 43(4) above.

DEFINITIONS
"authority": subs. (1).
"billing authority": ss.1(2) and 69(1).
"relevant precepting authority": subs. (1).

GENERAL NOTE
This section establishes the authorities which may be subject to council tax or precept limitation. These are all billing authorities and all major precepting authorities with the exception of the receiver for the Metropolitan Police District. It also defines the budget requirement for the purposes of this process as being the sum calculated for the purpose of setting the tax, under s.32(4) and s.43(4) for a billing authority and major precepting authority respectively.

The system of "capping" the council tax or precept continues that which had been in existence in relation to the community charge, under Pt. VII of the 1988 Act. That in turn had built upon the system introduced by the Rates Act 1984, and the Scottish system under the Local Government (Scotland) Act 1966, as amended by the Local Government and Planning (Scotland) Act 1982. The new system includes some amendments and simplifications to the system.

Designation

Power to designate authorities

54.—(1) As regards a financial year the Secretary of State may designate an authority if in his opinion—

(a) the amount calculated by it as its budget requirement for the year is excessive; or

(b) there is an excessive increase in the amount so calculated over the amount calculated by it as its budget requirement for the preceding financial year.

(2) A decision whether to designate an authority shall be made in accordance with principles determined by the Secretary of State and, in the case of an authority falling within any of the classes specified in subsection (3) below, those principles shall be the same either—

(a) for all authorities falling within that class; or

(b) for all of them which respectively have and have not been designated under this Chapter, or (as the case may be) Part VII of the 1988 Act, as regards the preceding financial year.

(3) The classes are—

(a) councils of metropolitan districts;

(b) councils of non-metropolitan districts;

(c) councils of inner London boroughs;

(d) councils of outer London boroughs;

(e) county councils;

(f) metropolitan county police authorities and the Northumbria Police Authority; and

(g) metropolitan county fire and civil defence authorities.

(4) Subject to subsection (6) below, any reference in subsection (1) above to the amount calculated by a billing authority as its budget requirement for a financial year shall be construed as a reference to the amount so calculated less the aggregate amount for the year of any precepts—

(a) issued to it by local precepting authorities; or

(b) anticipated by it in pursuance of regulations under section 41 above, which were taken into account by it in making the calculation under section 32(2) above.

(5) In construing subsection (1) above any calculation for which another has been substituted at the time designation is proposed shall be ignored.

(6) The Secretary of State may by order provide that subsection (4) above shall not apply in relation to—

(a) any financial year specified in the order; or

(b) any other financial year in so far as it provides the basis of comparison for the purposes of subsection (1)(b) above in relation to a year so specified.

(7) A statutory instrument containing an order under this section shall be subject to annulment in pursuance of a resolution of the House of Commons.

DEFINITIONS

"authority": s.53(1).

"billing authority": ss.1(2) and 69(1).

"budget requirement": ss.32(4), 43(4) and 53(2).

"financial year": ss.69(1) and 116(1).

"local precepting authority": ss.39(2) and 69(1).

GENERAL NOTE

This section provides the authority, for any financial year from 1993, for the Secretary of State to designate an authority for "capping" of the council tax or precept, if in his opinion its budget requirement is excessive or if there is an excessive increase over the previous year. In the basic framework, powers and criteria to be applied, this section substantially follows ss.100–102 of the 1988 Act. However, unlike the original scheme under s.101(1) of the 1988 Act, there is now no financial threshold before this power to designate is triggered in relation to English authorities. That requirement had been repealed for the community charge system by s.1(1) of the Local Government and Valuation Act 1991, with effect from April 1, 1992. The legislative framework for the criteria for designation remain the same, leaving the power with the Secretary of State to make the necessary regulations.

Subs. (1)

An authority may be designated by the Secretary of State on one of two criteria. First, the excessiveness of the budget requirement in itself. Secondly, the excessiveness of the increase in budget requirement in relation to the budget requirement in the preceding financial year.

However, this broad power is modified by the requirement under subs. (2) to apply to each authority the same principles as apply to others in the same class, or in relation to those which have or have not been designated previously, whether under this Act or under the 1988 Act. In addition, under s.55, there is special provision made for the first year of operation of the power, where the budget requirement is to be compared with the "relevant notional amount".

Subs. (2)

The broad power to designate, under subs. (1), is modified by the requirement to apply to each authority the same principles as apply to others in the same class, or in relation to those which have or have not been designated previously, whether under this Act or under the 1988 Act. However, as has been pointed out, this leaves a great deal of discretion to the Secretary of State and it is possible for the principles to apply in a manner which may appear somewhat arbitrary, given that the underlying philosophy or criteria need not be made clear. On this, see *R.* v. *Secretary of State for the Environment,* ex p. *Brent London Borough Council* [1982] Q.B. 593; *R.* v. *Secretary of State for the Environment,* ex p. *Hackney London Borough Council* (unreported, 1985); and *R.* v. *Secretary of State for the Environment,* ex p. *Hammersmith and Fulham London Borough Council* [1991] 1 A.C. 521.

Subs. (3)

These classes replicate those established by s.100(5) of the 1988 Act.

Subs. (4)

In determining the budget requirement of a billing authority, in relation to the power under subs. (1) to designate for capping, the amount shall be reduced by the aggregate amount of any precepts issued by a local precepting authority, or any precept anticipated in accordance with s.41. This is designed to allow the capping procedure to concentrate on the expenditure requirements of the billing authority itself. However, under subs. (6), the Secretary of State is empowered to override by order the application of this subsection in two ways: first, generally in relation to any specified financial year; and secondly, to any other financial year if so doing facilitates comparison of budget requirements in relation to the factor, established by subs. (1)(b), of the excessiveness of the increase over the preceding financial year.

Subs. (5)

This power replicates that which applied to the community charge system, under s.100(6) and (7) of the 1988 Act. It simply makes it clear that the capping process is to be applied only to the later or latest calculation of the budget requirement where there has been a substitute calculation.

Subs. (6)

Under subs. (4), when determining the budget requirement of a billing authority, in relation to the power under subs. (1) to designate for capping, the amount is normally to be reduced by the aggregate amount of any precepts issued by a local precepting authority, or any precept anticipated in accordance with s.41. This would normally allow the capping procedure to concentrate on the expenditure requirements of the billing authority itself, without the distortion of these other amounts. However, by this subsection, the Secretary of State is empowered to override by order the application of subs. (4) in two ways: first, generally in relation to any specified financial year; and, secondly, to any other financial year if so doing facilitates comparison of budget requirements in relation to the factor, established by subs. (1)(b), of the excessiveness of the increase over the preceding financial year.

Subs. (7)

An order under the authority of this section will be subject to the negative resolution procedure only.

Special transitional provisions

55.—(1) The Secretary of State may specify in a report—
 (a) as regards the financial year beginning in 1993 and any authority; or
 (b) as regards any subsequent financial year and any authority whose boundaries or functions have changed or will change at any time during the period consisting of that year and the preceding financial year,

the relevant notional amount, that is, the amount which in his opinion should be used as the basis of comparison for the purposes of section 54(1)(b) above in place of the basis of comparison there referred to.

(2) A report under this section—

(a) shall contain such explanation as the Secretary of State considers desirable of the calculation by him of the relevant notional amount; and

(b) shall be laid before the House of Commons.

(3) A report under this section may relate to two or more authorities and may be amended by a subsequent report under this section.

(4) If a report under this section is approved by resolution of the House of Commons, section 54(1)(b) above shall have effect, as regards the year and any authority to which the report relates, as if the relevant notional amount were the basis of comparison there referred to.

DEFINITIONS

"authority": s.53(1).

"financial year": ss.69(1) and 116(1).

"relevant notional amount": subs. (1).

GENERAL NOTE

In the first year of the new system of council tax there would be no possibility of designating an authority for capping by applying, under s.54(1)(b), the test of the excessiveness of the increase in the budget requirement over that for the preceding financial year. Equally, there would be a problem in applying this in future years where the boundaries or functions of the authority have changed so that there is no direct comparison between financial years. However, this section allows the Secretary of State to bring into effect a figure, known as the "relevant notional amount", which will operate as the yardstick for the preceding financial year against which the budget requirement in 1993, or in future years where there has been a change in boundaries or functions, will be measured. In regard to the first year of operation of the new system, similar provision was made by s.103 of the 1988 Act in regard to the community charge. The provision in regard to changing boundaries and functions is, however, new and will accommodate changes brought in as a result of the activities of the Local Government Commission. Limited restrictions as to the procedure for implementing this power are provided.

Subs. (1)

In relation to two situations, the Secretary of State may specify in a report a sum known as the relevant notional amount, which is to be used as the basis of comparison for the budget requirement of an authority, under s.54(1)(b): first, for the budget requirement in 1993 where there is a preceding financial year against which the budget requirement may be measured; and secondly, for future years where there has been a change in boundaries or functions of the authority, where there would also otherwise be a difficulty in direct comparison.

Subs. (2)

A report made under subs. (1) must be laid before the House of Commons, which will facilitate some scrutiny, and to assist in that it must contain such explanation of the calculation as the Secretary of State considers desirable. On the basis of the analogy with the principles of designation, it is unlikely that the courts would force the Secretary of State to disclose the underlying philosophy or to make clear the criteria (see *R. v. Secretary of State for the Environment,* ex p. *Brent London Borough Council* [1982] Q.B. 593; *R. v. Secretary of State for the Environment,* ex p. *Hackney London Borough Council* (unreported, 1985); and *R. v. Secretary of State for the Environment,* ex p. *Hammersmith and Fulham London Borough Council* [1991] A.C. 521.

Subs. (3)

A report under subs. (1) may not relate to one authority only. The minimum number is two, but given that a subsequent report is allowed to amend an earlier report, this may effectively allow the Secretary of State to develop a report for one authority only.

Subs. (4)

The report will only have effect as the basis of comparison under s.54(1)(b) if approved by positive resolution of the House of Commons.

Designation of authorities

56.—(1) If the Secretary of State decides under section 54 above to designate an authority he shall notify it in writing of—

(a) his decision;

(b) the principles determined under subsection (2) of that section in relation to it; and

(c) the amount which he proposes should be the maximum for the amount calculated by it as its budget requirement for the year.

(2) A designation—

(a) is invalid unless subsection (1) above is complied with; and

(b) shall be treated as made at the beginning of the day on which the authority receives a notification under that subsection.

(3) Where—

(a) an authority has been designated under this section; and

(b) after the designation is made the authority makes substitute calculations in relation to the year,

the substitute calculations shall be invalid unless they are made in accordance with section 60 or (as the case may be) section 61 below.

(4) Before the end of the period of 28 days beginning with the day it receives a notification under this section, an authority may inform the Secretary of State by notice in writing that—

(a) for reasons stated in the notice, it believes the maximum amount stated under subsection (1)(c) above should be such as the authority states in its notice; or

(b) it accepts the maximum amount stated under subsection (1)(c) above.

(5) References in the following provisions of this Chapter to a designated authority are to an authority designated under this section.

DEFINITIONS
"authority": s.53(1).
"budget requirement": ss.32(4), 43(4), and 53(2).
"designated authority": subs. (5).

GENERAL NOTE
Once the decision to designate an authority has been taken, under s.54(1), this section places certain requirements on the Secretary of State as to the manner in which this is to be communicated to the authority, including notifying the authority of its proposed maximum budget requirement for that year. In response to that communication, the authority may either accept the maximum amount or within 28 days state reasons for a higher amount, in a notice to the Secretary of State. If it adopts the latter course, the provisions of s.57 come into play, which involve a process of reopening the original decision with the ability to take new information into account and the Secretary of State may increase or reduce the figure previously suggested as a maximum. This section effectively follows that which operated, under s.102 of the 1988 Act, in relation to the capping of the community charge, and the process renegotiation of that under s.104.

Subs. (1)
Following the decision to designate the authority for capping under s.54, the Secretary of State must inform the authority in writing of his decision and the principles on which it was based, although it is unlikely that this will need to be very detailed. In addition, he must include his proposal for the maximum amount of the budget requirement as the basis for future action. Failure to comply with these requirements will result in the designation being invalid, as established by subs. (2).

Subs. (2)
Failure to comply with the requirements of subs. (1) in relation to notification of the decision to designate for capping will result in the designation being invalid. In addition, the relevant date for the designation having been made is fixed as the date on which the authority receives notification. Thus, for the purposes of the response to the Secretary of State, under subs. (4) and s.57, the period of 28 days will run from that date.

Subs. (3)
Having received notification of designation for capping, one option for the authority is to accept this and make a substitute calculation. This makes it clear that in doing so, the authority must comply with the provisions of s.60, if a billing authority, or s.61 if a precepting authority. Among other requirements, this ensures that the budget requirement should not be calculated to be above that notified to the authority or that the amount of council tax should not exceed that set in regard to the previous budget requirement.

Subs. (4)
Within 28 days from receiving the notification of the designation the authority must reply to the Secretary of State. In the reply, it must be stated whether the maximum amount of budget requirement proposed in the notification is accepted. If not, the authority must suggest another amount and the reasons for this. If the latter course is adopted, the provisions of s.57 come into play, which involve a process of reopening the original decision with the ability of the Secretary of State to take new information into account and the figure previously suggested as a maximum may be increased or reduced. There is thus a disincentive for the authority to "appeal" since the budget requirement may be reduced further.

Subs. (5)
The definition of "designated authority" is provided.

Maximum amounts

Challenge of maximum amount

57.—(1) This section applies where a designated authority informs the Secretary of State by notice in writing under section 56(4)(a) above.

(2) After considering any information he thinks is relevant the Secretary of State shall (subject to subsection (5) below) make an order stating the amount which the amount calculated by the authority as its budget requirement for the year is not to exceed.

(3) Subject to subsection (4) below, the amount stated under subsection (2) above may be the same as, or greater or smaller than, that stated in the notice under section 56(1)(c) above.

(4) The amount stated under subsection (2) above may not exceed the amount already calculated by the authority as its budget requirement for the year unless, in the Secretary of State's opinion, the authority failed to comply with section 32 or (as the case may be) section 43 above in making the calculation.

(5) No order under this section shall be made unless a draft of it has been laid before and approved by resolution of the House of Commons.

(6) An order under this section may relate to two or more authorities.

(7) As soon as is reasonably practicable after an order under this section is made the Secretary of State shall serve on the authority (or each authority) a notice stating the amount stated in the case of the authority in the order.

(8) When he serves a notice under subsection (7) above on a precepting authority the Secretary of State shall also serve a copy of it on each billing authority to which the precepting authority has power to issue a precept.

(9) In construing subsection (4) above any calculation for which another has been substituted at the time of designation shall be ignored.

DEFINITIONS
"authority": s.53(1).
"billing authority": ss.1(2) and 69(1).
"budget requirement": ss.32(4), 43(4) and 53(2).
"designated authority": s.56(5).
"information": ss.64 and 116(1).
"precepting authority": ss.39 and 69(1).

GENERAL NOTE
This section applies where, under s.56(4), the authority has decided to challenge the maximum amount of budget requirement proposed to it under s.56(1)(c). It involves a process

of reopening the original decision with the Secretary of State able to take new information into account and increase or reduce the figure previously suggested as a maximum. He may also increase the amount beyond that which was originally calculated by the authority, but only if it is his opinion that the authority failed to comply with the duty under s.32, for the billing authority, or s.43 for a major precepting authority. This section effectively follows that which operated under s.104 of the 1988 Act.

Subs. (1)

This section applies where, under s.56(4), the authority which has been designated for capping has informed the Secretary of State that it wishes to challenge the proposed maximum amount of budget requirement notified to it under s.56(1)(c).

Subs. (2)

In considering the representations of the designated authority that the budget requirement should be other than proposed by the Secretary of State in the notification of the designation for capping, the Secretary of State is permitted to consider any information which he thinks is relevant, not merely the information which has been taken into account in the previous calculations. The content of the information is not restricted by the statutory definition, given in s.116(1) for other parts of the Act, of information being simply accounts estimates and returns. Instead, s.64(4) permits the Secretary of State to require the authority to supply such information as he specifies in relation to his functions. The authority is under a duty, by s.64(5), to comply with this request, provided that the information is in its possession or control. Having assessed the information, the Secretary of State may then make an order stating the amount of the budget requirement which the designated authority may not then exceed. The content of the order and procedure for bringing it into effect are governed by the remainder of this section.

Subs. (3)

Any order under subs. (2) is not tied to the previous levels of budget requirement proposed by the Secretary of State in the notice of designation under s.56(1)(c). While it may be the same as that in the notice of designation, the amount specified in such an order may also be higher or lower.

Subs. (4)

Any order under subs. (2) is, however, tied to the immediately previous levels of budget requirement set by the designated authority. It may not normally exceed the amount specified already by the authority. As is made clear by subs. (9), where there has been a substitute calculation by the authority, the relevant amount is that set in relation to the later or latest calculations and not the original calculation. However, if the Secretary of State is of the opinion that the calculation by the authority did not accord with the requirements of s.32, for the billing authority, or s.43 for a major precepting authority, then he may allow the budget requirement to be increased. This may provide an alternative route to having the budget requirement quashed because the requirements of s.32 or s.43 have not been complied with.

Subs. (5)

Any order made under subs. (2) is subject to the affirmative resolution procedure of the House of Commons.

Subs. (6)

An order under subs. (2) is not restricted to dealing with one authority only, but may relate to two or more authorities. Any ambiguity in the wording, which may also be read as meaning that the order may relate to two or more authorities only, is resolved not only implicitly by the fact that only one authority may invoke the procedure, but also explicitly by subs. (7), which recognises that the order may apply to one authority only.

Subs. (7)

The Secretary of State is under a duty to serve notice of its maximum budget requirement on the authority, or authorities, concerned as soon as is reasonably practicable after the order is made following the resolution of the House of Commons.

Subs. (8)

If the authority which is designated and has "appealed" is a precepting authority, then the Secretary of State must also serve a copy of the maximum budget requirement on the relevant billing authority or authorities.

Subs. (9)
Where an original calculation of the budget requirement by the designated authority has been substituted, then it is only the substituted amount which, in accordance with subs. (4), provides the reference point for the maximum amount for the budget requirement.

Acceptance of maximum amount

58.—(1) This section applies where a designated authority informs the Secretary of State by notice in writing under section 56(4)(b) above.

(2) As soon as is reasonably practicable after he receives the notice the Secretary of State shall serve on the authority a notice stating the amount which the amount calculated by it as its budget requirement for the year is not to exceed; and the amount stated shall be that stated in the notice under section 56(1)(c) above.

(3) When he serves a notice under subsection (2) above on a precepting authority, the Secretary of State shall also serve a copy of it on each billing authority to which the precepting authority has power to issue a precept.

DEFINITIONS
"authority": s.53(1).
"billing authority": ss.1(2) and 69(1).
"budget requirement": ss.32(4), 43(4) and 53(2).
"designated authority": s.56(5).
"precepting authority": ss.39 and 69(1).

GENERAL NOTE
This section provides for the formal confirmation of the amount of the budget requirement where the authority which has been designated for capping has accepted the proposal by the Secretary of State. When the authority has notified the Secretary of State, under s.56(4)(b), of its acceptance, the Secretary of State is under a duty to serve on the authority, as soon as reasonably practicable after the receipt of the acceptance, a notice stating the maximum amount. That figure will be the same as the proposed amount notified under s.56(1)(c). In this event, there is no need for approval by the House of Commons. If the authority which is designated is a precepting authority, then the Secretary of State must also serve a copy of the maximum budget requirement on the relevant billing authority or authorities. This follows the provisions of s.105 of the 1988 Act in relation to the community charge.

No challenge or acceptance

59.—(1) This section applies where the period mentioned in subsection (4) of section 56 above ends without a designated authority informing the Secretary of State by notice in writing under paragraph (a) or (b) of that subsection.

(2) As soon as is reasonably practicable after the period ends the Secretary of State shall (subject to subsection (3) below) make an order stating the amount which the amount calculated by the authority as its budget requirement for the year is not to exceed; and the amount stated shall be that stated in the notice under section 56(1)(c) above.

(3) No order under this section shall be made unless a draft of it has been laid before and approved by resolution of the House of Commons.

(4) An order under this section may relate to two or more authorities.

(5) As soon as is reasonably practicable after an order under this section is made the Secretary of State shall serve on the authority (or each authority) a notice stating the amount stated in the case of the authority in the order.

(6) When he serves a notice under subsection (5) above on a precepting authority, the Secretary of State shall also serve a copy of it on each billing authority to which the precepting authority has power to issue a precept.

DEFINITIONS
"authority": s.53(1).
"billing authority": ss.1(2) and 69(1).
"budget requirement": ss.32(4), 43(4) and 53(2).

"designated authority": s.56(5).
"precepting authority": ss.39 and 69(1).

GENERAL NOTE

This section provides for the formal confirmation of the amount of the budget requirement where the authority which has been designated for capping has neither accepted nor challenged the proposal by the Secretary of State. In this event there is need for approval by the House of Commons through the affirmative resolution procedure. If the authority which is designated is a precepting authority, then the Secretary of State must also serve a copy of the maximum budget requirement on the relevant billing authority or authorities. This follows the provisions of s.106 of the 1988 Act in relation to the community charge.

Subs. (1)

This section applies where the authority which has been designated for capping has not informed the Secretary of State, under s.56(4), that it either wishes to challenge, or that it accepts, the proposed maximum amount of budget requirement notified to it under s.56(1)(c).

Subs. (2)

When the period of 28 days for notification to the Secretary of State, under s.56(4), has expired, then the Secretary of State is under a duty to serve on the authority, as soon as reasonably practicable, a notice stating the maximum amount. That figure will be the same as the proposed amount notified under s.56(1)(c).

Subs. (3)

Any order made under subs. (2) is subject to the affirmative resolution procedure of the House of Commons.

Subs. (4)

An order under subs. (2) is not restricted to dealing with one authority only, but may relate to two or more authorities. Any ambiguity in the wording, which may also be read as meaning that the order may relate to two or more authorities only, is resolved not only implicitly by the fact that only one authority may invoke the procedure, but also explicitly by subs. (5), which recognises that the order may apply to one authority only.

Subs. (5)

The Secretary of State is under a duty to serve notice of its maximum budget requirement on the authority or authorities concerned as soon as is reasonably practicable after the order is made following the resolution of the House of Commons.

Subs. (6)

If the authority which is designated is a precepting authority, then the Secretary of State must also serve a copy of the maximum budget requirement on the relevant billing authority or authorities.

Substitute calculations

Duty of designated billing authority

60.—(1) Where a billing authority has received a notice under section 57(7), 58(2) or 59(5) above, it shall make substitute calculations in relation to the year in accordance with sections 32 to 36 above, ignoring section 32(10) above for this purpose.

(2) The substitute calculations shall be made so as to secure—

(a) that the amount calculated by the authority as its budget requirement for the year does not exceed that stated in the notice; and

(b) subject to subsection (3) below, that any amount calculated under section 33(1) or 34(2) or (3) above as the basic amount of council tax applicable to any dwelling does not exceed that so calculated in the previous calculations.

(3) Subsection (2)(b) above does not apply in any case where the amount stated in the notice exceeds that already calculated by the authority as its budget requirement for the year.

(4) In making substitute calculations under section 33(1) or 34(3) above, the authority must use any amount determined in the previous calculations for item P or T in section 33(1) above or item TP in section 34(3) above.

(5) For the purposes of subsection (4) above, the authority may treat any amount determined in the previous calculations for item P in section 33(1) above as increased by the amount of any sum which—

    (a) it estimates will be payable for the year into its general fund in respect of additional grant; and

    (b) was not taken into account by it in making those calculations.

DEFINITIONS
"additional grant": ss.69(1); s.85(2) of the 1988 Act.
"authority": s.53(1).
"billing authority": ss.1(2) and 69(1).
"budget requirement": ss.32(4), 43(4) and 53(2).
"council tax": s.1(1).
"dwelling": ss.3 and 69(1).
"general fund": s.91 of the 1988 Act.

GENERAL NOTE
Where a billing authority has received a notice either confirming or imposing a new maximum budget requirement, it is under a duty imposed by this section to make a substitute calculation in accordance with the general principles applicable under ss.32–36 and conforming to the new maximum. In addition, the amount of council tax must be no higher than that set in relation to the preceding budget requirement. This follows in part s.107 of the 1988 Act in relation to the community charge.

Subs. (1)
This establishes the duty on a billing authority, having already received a notice either confirming or imposing a new maximum budget requirement, to make substitute calculation of its budget requirement. In doing so, the authority must, as with the original calculation, comply with the provisions of ss.32–36, with the exception of the time limit of March 11 in the preceding financial year, established by s.32(10).

Subs. (2)
A substitute calculation must ensure two things: first, that the budget requirement, calculated under s.32(4), does not exceed that stated in the notice; and secondly, that the basic amount of council tax, calculated under s.33(1) or s.34(2) or (3), is no greater than that in the previous calculation.

Subs. (3)
The requirement in subs. (2)(b) that the basic amount of council tax is to be no greater than that in the previous calculation does not apply when the Secretary of State has exercised his discretion, under s.57(4), where the calculation by the authority did not accord with the requirements of s.32, to allow the budget requirement to be increased.

Subs. (4)
In calculating the revised amount of council tax, the billing authority must, in principle, use the same amount as determined in the previous calculations for three items. First, in relation to the calculation under s.33(1), the aggregate of redistributed non-domestic rates, revenue support and additional grants payable to the general fund (P). This is, however, subject to the qualification, introduced by subs. (5), that the amount of the aggregate may be increased if it is a result of an increase in the amount of additional grant which was not taken into account in the original calculation. Secondly, again in relation to the calculation under s.33(1), the amount of the council-tax base for the year (T). Thirdly, in relation to a calculation under s.34(3), the amount of the council-tax base for the year for part of the area where special items apply (TP). The effect of this is that a change in the amount of funds received from central government through these sources, or of the council-tax base, will not be allowed to lead to a recalculation of the council tax payable.

Subs. (5)
This establishes the qualification to subs. (4), that the amount of the aggregate of redistributed non-domestic rates, revenue support and additional grants payable to the general fund

(P), under s.33(1), may be increased if it is a result of an increase in the amount of additional grant which was not taken into account in the original calculation.

Duty of designated precepting authority

61.—(1) Where a relevant precepting authority has received a notice under section 57(7), 58(2) or 59(5) above, it shall make substitute calculations in relation to the year in accordance with sections 43 to 48 above.

(2) The substitute calculations shall be made so as to secure—

(a) that the amount calculated by the authority as its budget requirement for the year does not exceed that stated in the notice; and

(b) subject to subsection (3) below, that any amount calculated under section 44(1) or 45(2) or (3) above as the basic amount of council tax applicable to any dwelling does not exceed that so calculated in the previous calculations.

(3) Subsection (2)(b) above does not apply in any case where the amount stated in the notice exceeds that already calculated by the authority as its budget requirement for the year.

(4) In making substitute calculations under section 44(1) or 45(3) above, the authority must use any amount determined in the previous calculations for item P or T in section 44(1) above or item TP in section 45(3) above.

(5) For the purposes of subsection (4) above, the authority may treat any amount determined in the previous calculations for item P in section 44(1) above as increased by the amount of any sum which—

(a) it estimates will be payable to it for the year in respect of additional grant; and

(b) was not taken into account by it in making those calculations.

DEFINITIONS
   "additional grant": s.69(1); s.85(2) of the 1988 Act.
   "authority": s.53(1).
   "budget requirement": ss.32(4), 43(4) and 53(2).
   "dwelling": ss.3 and 69(1).
   "general fund": s.91 of the 1988 Act.
   "relevant precepting authority": s.53(1).

GENERAL NOTE
   Where a precepting authority has received a notice either confirming or imposing a new maximum budget requirement then it is under a duty imposed by this section to make a substitute calculation in accordance with the general principles applicable under ss.43–48 and conforming to the new maximum. In addition, the amount of council tax must be no higher than that set in relation to the preceding budget requirement. This follows in part s.107 of the 1988 Act in relation to the community charge.

Subs. (1)
   This establishes the duty on a precepting authority, having already received a notice either confirming or imposing a new maximum budget requirement, to make a substitute calculation of its budget requirement. In doing so, the authority must, as with the original calculation, comply with the provisions of ss.43–48.

Subs. (2)
   A substitute calculation must ensure two things: first, that the budget requirement, calculated under s.43(4), does not exceed that stated in the notice; and secondly, that the basic amount of council tax, calculated under s.44(1) or s.45(2) or (3), is no greater than that in the previous calculation.

Subs. (3)
   The requirement in subs. (2)(b) that the basic amount of council tax is to be no greater than that in the previous calculation does not apply when the Secretary of State has exercised his discretion, under s.57(4), where the calculation by the authority did not accord with the requirements of s.43, to allow the budget requirement to be increased.

Subs. (4)

In calculating the revised amount of council tax, the precepting authority must, in principle, use the same amount as determined in the previous calculations for three items. First, in relation to the calculation under s.44(1), the aggregate of redistributed non-domestic rates, revenue support and additional grants payable to the general fund (P). This is, however, subject to the qualification, introduced by subs. (5), that the amount of the aggregate may be increased if it is a result of an increase in the amount of additional grant which was not taken into account in the original calculation. Secondly, again in relation to the calculation under s.44(1), the amount of the council-tax base for the year (T). Thirdly, in relation to a calculation under s.45(3), the amount of the council-tax base for the year for part of the area where special items apply (TP). The effect of this is that a change in the amount of funds received from central government through these sources, or of the council-tax base, will not be allowed to lead to a recalculation of the council tax payable.

Subs. (5)

This establishes the qualification to subs. (4), that the amount of the aggregate of redistributed non-domestic rates, revenue support and additional grants payable to the general fund (P), under s.44(1) may be increased if it is a result of an increase in the amount of additional grant which was not taken into account in the original calculation.

Failure to substitute

62.—(1) This section applies if an authority which has received a notice under section 57(7), 58(2) or 59(5) above fails to comply with section 60 or (as the case may be) section 61 above before the end of the period of 21 days beginning with the day on which it receives the notice.

(2) In the case of a billing authority, it shall have no power during the period of restriction to transfer any amount from its collection fund to its general fund and sections 97 and 98 of the 1988 Act (transfers between funds) shall have effect accordingly.

(3) In the case of a relevant precepting authority, any authority to which it has power to issue a precept shall have no power during the period of restriction to pay anything in respect of a precept issued by it for the year.

(4) For the purposes of this section the period of restriction is the period which—

(a) begins at the end of the period mentioned in subsection (1) above; and

(b) ends at the time (if any) when the authority complies with section 60 or 61 above.

DEFINITIONS

  "authority": s.53(1).
  "billing authority": ss.1(2) and 69(1).
  "collection fund": s.89(1) of the 1988 Act.
  "general fund": s.91 of the 1988 Act.
  "relevant precepting authority": s.53(1).

GENERAL NOTE

This section applies where an authority refuses to comply, within 21 days, with the duty to make a substitute calculation of the budget requirement and council tax, after receiving a notice stating a new maximum budget requirement. The sanctions which are imposed mean that the collection fund is closed off to the authority, leaving it effectively insolvent. This provides a similar power to that which existed in relation to the community charge under s.108 of the 1988 Act.

Subs. (1)

This section applies where an authority refuses to comply with the duty imposed on a billing authority by s.60 and on a precepting authority by s.61. That duty is to make a substitute calculation of the budget requirement and council tax within 21 days of receiving the notice stating a new maximum budget requirement.

Subs. (2)

Where the authority which does not comply with the duty to make a substitute calculation is a billing authority, the sanction is that the authority will have no power to transfer funds from its collection fund to its general fund. It will thus have no access to its income. Under subs. (4), this prohibition continues until the authority complies with its duty to make a substitute calculation under s.60.

Subs. (3)

Where the authority which does not comply with the duty to make a substitute calculation is a precepting authority, the sanction is that the billing authority will have no power to transfer funds from its collection fund to the precepting authority. It will thus have no access to its income. Under subs. (4), this prohibition continues until the authority complies with its duty to make a substitute calculation under s.61.

Subs. (4)

The starting point for the period of restricting access to the income of the authority, under subss. (2) or (3), is at the end of the 21-day period from the date when the notification from the Secretary of State of the new maximum budget requirement is received by the authority. The end point will only be when the authority complies with its duty to make a substitute calculation under s.60 or s.61 as appropriate.

Supplemental

Separate administration in England and Wales

63.—(1) This Chapter shall be read as applying separately, and be administered separately, in England and Wales.

(2) In particular, for England and Wales respectively separate principles shall be determined under section 54(2) above.

(3) This Chapter shall be construed accordingly so that (for instance) references to authorities shall be read as references to those in England or Wales, as the case may be.

DEFINITIONS
"authority": s.53(1).

GENERAL NOTE
This section establishes that the administration of the capping régime shall be different in England and Wales. This is particularly important in regard to the principles for designation of an authority for capping, where subs. (2) stresses that the principles shall be different. This continues the position which existed in regard to the community charge under ss.101 and 140 of the 1988 Act.

Information for purposes of Chapter V

64.—(1) An authority shall notify the Secretary of State in writing of any amount calculated by it as its budget requirement for a financial year, whether originally or by way of substitute.

(2) A billing authority shall also notify the Secretary of State in writing of the aggregate amount for any financial year of any precepts—
  (a) issued to it by local precepting authorities; or
  (b) anticipated by it in pursuance of regulations under section 41 above, which were taken into account by it in making a calculation in relation to the year under section 32(2) above.

(3) A notification under subsection (1) or (2) above must be given before the end of the period of seven days beginning with the day on which the calculation was made.

(4) The Secretary of State may serve on an authority a notice requiring it to supply to him such other information as is specified in the notice and required by him for the purpose of deciding whether to exercise his powers, and how to perform his functions, under this Chapter.

(5) The authority shall supply the information required if it is in its possession or control, and shall do so in such form and manner, and at such time, as the Secretary of State specifies in the notice.

(6) An authority may be required under subsection (4) above to supply information at the same time as it gives a notification under subsection (1) or (2) above or at some other time.

(7) If an authority fails to comply with subsection (1) or (2) above, or with subsection (5) above, the Secretary of State may decide whether to exercise his powers, and how to perform his functions, under this Chapter on the basis of such assumptions and estimates as he sees fit.

(8) In deciding whether to exercise his powers, and how to perform his functions, under this Chapter the Secretary of State may also take into account any other information available to him, whatever its source and whether or not obtained under a provision contained in or made under this or any other Act.

DEFINITIONS
"authority": s.53(1).
"billing authority": ss.1(2) and 69(1).
"budget requirement": ss.32(4), 43(4) and 53(2).
"financial year": ss.69(1) and 116(1).
"information": ss.64 and 116(1).
"local precepting authority": ss.39(2) and 69(1).

GENERAL NOTE
This section gives to the Secretary of State the right to obtain information from a local authority to enable him to exercise his functions in regard to capping the budget requirement. It establishes duties in regard to different authorities to supply specified information, and allows the Secretary of State in default to apply his own assumptions for the purposes of capping. This reflects the situation which existed in relation to the community charge under s.110 of the 1988 Act.

Subs. (1)
A specific duty is imposed on an authority to notify its budget requirement to the Secretary of State in writing each year. This duty applies to a substitute amount in addition to the original calculation.

Subs. (2)
In regard to a billing authority only, a specific duty is imposed to notify to the Secretary of State, in writing each year, the aggregate amount of precepts which the authority has built into its calculation of the budget requirement. This duty applies to precepts issued by local precepting authorities and those anticipated under s.41.

Subs. (3)
In regard to the duties imposed by subss. (1) and (2), this must be complied with within seven days of the authority's making the relevant calculation of the budget requirement.

Subs. (4)
This less specific, but wide, power allows the Secretary of State to demand from the authority other information which is required by him to decide whether, and how, to perform the designation and capping functions. It would appear that the definition of "information" is not here restricted to the narrow one provided in s.116, namely "accounts, estimates and returns", since, together with subs. (8), it seems clear that the context and application to this Chapter require a wider definition. The Secretary of State is thus free to demand whatever information is objectively required by him, provided that it is stated in a notice to the authority issued under this subsection (*R. v. Secretary of State for the Environment, ex p. Greater London Council and Inner London Education Authority* (Court of Appeal, March 1, 1985, unreported)).

Subs. (5)
The authority is placed under a duty to supply the information required by a notice issued under subs. (4). This must be in such form and manner and within such time limits as is specified by the Secretary of State in the notice. It is, however, a justification for the authority to fail to supply the information if it is not in its possession or control. This last point is important in relation to when it is legitimate for the Secretary of State, under subs. (7), to act in default of an authority supplying information, and act on the basis of such assumptions and estimates as he sees fit.

Subs. (6)

This makes it clear what is implicit in the above subsections, namely that the duty to supply information may be exercised in conjunction with the requirements to supply information under subss. (1) or (2) or at any other time.

Subs. (7)

Where the authority fails to comply with the duty to provide information, whether under subs. (1), subs. (2) or subs. (5), it is legitimate for the Secretary of State to act in default on the basis of such assumptions and estimates as he sees fit. In *R.* v. *Secretary of State for the Environment,* ex p. *Greater London Council and Inner London Education Authority* (Court of Appeal, March 1, 1985, unreported) it was held that a challenge to the Secretary of State's discretion, under s.110 of the 1988 Act, had to be directed to the objective reasonableness of the decision, not to a subjective examination of it.

Subs. (8)

This makes it clear that in addition to the information supplied by the authority, the Secretary of State may take into account any other information. It would appear that the definition of "information" is not here restricted to the narrow one provided in s.116, namely "accounts, estimates and returns", since, together with subs. (4), it seems clear that the context and application to this chapter requires a wider definition.

CHAPTER VI

MISCELLANEOUS AND SUPPLEMENTAL

Duty to consult ratepayers

65.—(1) A relevant authority shall consult under this section persons or bodies appearing to it to be representative of persons subject to non-domestic rates under sections 43 and 45 of the 1988 Act as regards hereditaments situated in the authority's area.

(2) Consultations must be made as to each financial year, and must be about the authority's proposals for expenditure (including capital expenditure) in that financial year; and the Secretary of State may by regulations prescribe matters which are to be treated as expenditure for this purpose.

(3) In this section "relevant authority" means a billing authority or a major precepting authority other than the Receiver for the Metropolitan Police District.

(4) The duty to consult as to a financial year shall be performed—

(a) where the authority is a billing authority, before it makes calculations (otherwise than by way of substitute) in relation to the financial year under section 32 above;

(b) where the authority is a precepting authority, before it issues the first precept to be issued by it for the financial year.

(5) In performing the duty to consult, an authority shall have regard to any guidance issued by the Secretary of State concerning—

(a) persons or bodies to be regarded for the purposes of this section as representative of persons subject to non-domestic rates under sections 43 and 45 of the 1988 Act as regards hereditaments situated in the authority's area; and

(b) the timing and manner of consultations under this section.

(6) An authority shall make available to persons or bodies it proposes to consult under this section such information as may be prescribed and is in its possession or control; and it shall do so in such form and manner, and at such time, as may be prescribed.

DEFINITIONS

"authority": s.53(1).
"billing authority": ss.1(2) and 69(1).
"financial year": ss.69(1) and 116(1).
"hereditament": s.64 of the 1988 Act.

"information": subs. (6) and s.116(1).
"precepting authority": ss.39 and 69(1).
"prescribed": s.116(1).
"relevant authority": subs. (3).

GENERAL NOTE
   This reproduces the substance of the duty to consult ratepayers in regard to the community charge, under s.134 of the 1988 Act. That in turn had followed the duty to consult in regard to the rates first imposed under the Rates Act 1984. Despite the fact that the non-domestic ratepayer now has no direct interest in the level of charge or council tax, it was the Government view that such consultation would enhance the relationship between local government and business. The section requires the billing authorities and major precepting authorities to consult representatives of non-domestic ratepayers in regard to their expenditure for each financial year.

Subs. (1)
   A duty is placed on each relevant authority to consult representatives of non-domestic ratepayers in their area. A relevant authority is defined by subs. (3) as the billing authorities and major precepting authorities, with the exception of the Receiver for the Metropolitan Police District. A discretion is left to the authority to choose those persons or bodies who appear to be representative of non-domestic ratepayers, but this is modified by subs. (5), which requires the authority to have regard to any guidance issued by the Secretary of State as to whom should be considered representative.

Subs. (2)
   This specifies that the consultation required by subs. (1) must take place in regard to each financial year and in relation to the expenditure, both revenue and capital. In relation to what is to be counted as expenditure, power is given to the Secretary of State to make regulations for this purpose.

Subs. (3)
   A relevant authority, for the purposes of the duty to consult under subs. (1), is defined as the billing authorities and major precepting authorities, with the exception of the Receiver for the Metropolitan Police District.

Subs. (4)
   The duty to consult under subs. (1) must be performed before the authority issues a precept or, for a billing authority, before its budget requirement is calculated. Under subs. (5) the authority is also required to have regard to any guidance issued by the Secretary of State as to the timing or manner of the consultation.

Subs. (5)
   The basic duties imposed by this section in regard to the bodies to be consulted, timing and manner of the consultation are modified to the extent that the authority is also required to have regard to any guidance issued by the Secretary of State as to whom should be considered representative for this purpose, and the timing or manner of the consultation.

Subs. (6)
   The authority is also placed under a duty to provide information to those it proposes to consult under subs. (1). The type of information, and the manner, form and timing of the giving of information, may be prescribed by regulation.

Judicial review

   66.—(1) The matters mentioned in subsection (2) below shall not be questioned except by an application for judicial review.
   (2) The matters are—
   (a) the specification of a class of "exempt dwelling" in an order of the Secretary of State under section 4(2) above;
   (b) a determination made under section 8(2) or 12(1) above;
   (c) a calculation made in accordance with any of sections 32 to 37 or section 60 or any of sections 43 to 51 or section 61 above, whether originally or by way of substitute;

    (d) the setting under Chapter III of this Part of an amount of council tax for a financial year, whether originally or by way of substitute; and

    (e) a precept issued under Chapter IV of this Part, whether originally or by way of substitute.

    (3) If on an application for judicial review the court decides to grant relief in respect of any of the matters mentioned in subsection (2)(b) to (e) above, it shall quash the determination, calculation, setting or precept (as the case may be).

GENERAL NOTE
    The intention of this section is to ensure that certain matters cannot be raised in a collateral challenge, but only through judicial review. Thus the matters specified may not be challenged in, for example, any proceedings for recovery of the tax. The matters specified, by subs. (2) are the designation of "exempt dwellings" by the Secretary of State; determinations as to discounts or liability in prescribed cases; a calculation of the budget requirement; and the setting of the council tax or precept, whether original or by substitute. With the exception of the designation of a class of "exempt dwellings", where the matter of the remedy is left to the discretion of the court, it is provided by subs. (3) that in all matters to be dealt with exclusively by judicial review the court must quash the relevant determination, calculation or setting of the amount, if it decides to grant relief.

Functions to be discharged only by authority

    67.—(1) Subject to subsection (3) below, each of the functions of an authority mentioned in subsection (2) below shall be discharged only by the authority.

    (2) The functions are—

    (a) making a determination under section 8(2) or 12(1) above;

    (b) making a calculation in accordance with any of sections 32 to 37 or section 60 or any of sections 43 to 51 or section 61 above, whether originally or by way of substitute;

    (c) setting an amount of council tax for a financial year under Chapter III of this Part, whether originally or by way of substitute; and

    (d) issuing a precept under Chapter IV of this Part, whether originally or by way of substitute.

    (3) The functions of an authority mentioned in subsection (2)(c) above may, if the authority so directs, be exercised by a committee of the authority appointed by it for that purpose; and as respects a committee so appointed—

    (a) the number of members and their term of office shall be fixed by the authority; and

    (b) each member shall be a member of the authority.

    (4) Part VA (access to meetings and documents of certain authorities, committees and sub-committees) of the Local Government Act 1972 shall apply in relation to a committee appointed under subsection (3) above as it applies in relation to a committee appointed under section 102 of that Act.

GENERAL NOTE
    This section modifies the general rule of local government law, under s.101 of the Local Government Act 1972, that the authority may discharge its function through a committee, sub-committee, or an officer of the authority. The purpose of this section, by subs. (1), is to ensure that certain of the functions under this Act are to be discharged only by the authority itself or, by subs. (3), by the authority or a committee only. The functions under subs. (2) which may be discharged only by the authority itself are determinations as to discounts or liability in prescribed cases, and the setting of the council tax or precept, whether original or by substitute.

The function which, by subss. (2) and (3), may be discharged by the authority or a committee only is a calculation of the budget requirement.

Where it is decided to discharge the function of the calculation of the budget requirement by a committee, it is also provided by subs. (3) that the committee composition must be regulated other than simply in accordance with the normal rules applicable to committees. First, the authority itself, not the committee, must specify the number of members of the committee and fix the terms of office. This is intended to stop any "packing" of the committee by changing its composition in the light of voting intentions, thus avoiding the situation in *R.* v. *Greenwich London Borough Council,* ex p. *Lovelace; Same* v. *Same,* ex p. *Fay* [1990] 1 W.L.R. 18, where it was held that in order to ensure that council policy was followed, a councillor who opposed the policy could be replaced (affirmed [1991] 1 W.L.R. 506). Secondly, the members of the committee must all be members of the authority and not co-opted outsiders. The final restriction, under subs. (4), is that the provision in relation to access to meetings and documents, under Pt. VA of the Local Government Act 1972, applies as it does to committees set up under s.102 of that Act.

Information required by Secretary of State

68.—(1) Subsection (2) below applies where—
(a) the Secretary of State serves a notice on a relevant authority or relevant officer requiring it or him to supply to the Secretary of State information specified in the notice;
(b) the information is required by the Secretary of State for the purpose of deciding whether to exercise his powers, and how to perform his functions, under this Part; and
(c) the information is not personal information.
(2) The authority or officer shall supply the information required, and shall do so in such form and manner and at such time as the Secretary of State specifies in the notice.
(3) If an authority or officer fails to comply with subsection (2) above the Secretary of State may assume the information required to be such as he sees fit; and in such a case the Secretary of State may decide in accordance with the assumption whether to exercise his powers, and how to perform his functions, under this Part.
(4) In deciding whether to exercise his powers, and how to perform his functions, under this Part the Secretary of State may also take into account any other information available to him, whatever its source and whether or not obtained under a provision contained in or made under this Part or any other enactment.
(5) In this section—
"relevant authority" means a billing authority or a precepting authority;
"relevant officer" means a proper officer (within the meaning of the Local Government Act 1972) of such an authority.
(6) For the purposes of this section personal information—
(a) is information which relates to an individual (living or dead) who can be identified from that information or from that and other information supplied to any person by the authority or officer concerned; and
(b) includes any expression of opinion about the individual and any indication of the intentions of any person in respect of the individual.

DEFINITIONS
"authority": s.53(1).
"billing authority": ss.1(2) and 69(1).
"information": ss.68 and 116(1).
"personal information": subs. (6).
"precepting authority": ss.39 and 69(1).
"relevant authority": subs. (5).
"relevant officer": subs. (5).

GENERAL NOTE

This section gives to the Secretary of State the right to obtain information from a local authority to enable him to exercise his functions in regard to the whole of Pt. I of the Act. It thus overlaps to some extent with the more wider aspects of the generally more specific power, under s.64, in relation to capping. It establishes duties in regard to different authorities and officers to supply specified information, and allows the Secretary of State in default to apply his own assumptions for the purposes of capping.

Subs. (1)

This wide power allows the Secretary of State to demand from the authority or officer information which is required by him to decide whether, and how, to perform his functions under this Part of the Act. It would appear that the definition of "information" is not here restricted to the narrow one provided in s.116, namely "accounts, estimates and returns", since it seems clear that the context and application to this Part require a wider definition, not least since there would have been no need to include the limitation in subs. (1)(c). The Secretary of State is thus free to demand whatever information is objectively required by him, provided that it is stated in a notice to the authority issued under this subsection (*R.* v. *Secretary of State for the Environment*, ex p. *Greater London Council and Inner London Education Authority* (Court of Appeal, March 1, 1985, unreported)). However, that wide discretion is limited by the express exclusion, in subs. (1)(c), of personal information from this. Personal information is defined by subs. (6).

Subs. (2)

The authority or officer is placed under a duty to supply the information required by a notice issued under subs. (1). This must be in such form and manner and within such time limits as is specified by the Secretary of State in the notice. It is not, however, as with s.64(5), a justification to fail to supply the information if it is not in the authority's or officer's possession or control. This last point is important in relation to when it is legitimate for the Secretary of State, under subs. (3), to act in default of an authority supplying information, and act on the basis of such assumptions and estimates as he sees fit.

Subs. (3)

Where the authority or officer fails to comply with the duty to provide information under subs. (2), it is legitimate for the Secretary of State to act in default on the basis of such assumptions and estimates as he sees fit. In *R.* v. *Secretary of State for the Environment,* ex p. *Greater London Council and Inner London Education Authority* (Court of Appeal, March 1, 1985, unreported) it was held that a challenge to the Secretary of State's discretion, under s.110 of the 1988 Act, had to be directed to the objective reasonableness of the decision, not to a subjective examination of it. This may well similarly apply in this instance.

Subs. (4)

This makes it clear that in addition to the information supplied by the authority, the Secretary of State may take into account any other information. It would appear that the definition of "information" is not here restricted to the narrow one provided in s.116, namely "accounts, estimates and returns", since it seems clear that the context and application to this Part require a wider definition.

Subs. (6)

Personal information, as defined by this subsection, is excluded from the information which it is legitimate for the Secretary of State to seek from a relevant authority or officer, under subs. (1).

Interpretation etc.

69.—(1) In this Part, unless the context otherwise requires—
"additional grant" has the meaning given by section 85(2) of the 1988 Act;
"billing authority" has the meaning given by section 1(2) above;
"the City" means the City of London;
"the Common Council" means the Common Council of the City;
"dwelling" has the meaning given by section 3 above;
"financial year", except in references to earlier or preceding financial years, does not include the financial year beginning in 1992 or earlier financial years;

"levy" means a levy under regulations made under section 74 of the
   1988 Act;
"listing officer" shall be construed in accordance with section 20 above;
"local precepting authority" has the meaning given by section 39(2)
   above;
"major precepting authority" has the meaning given by section 39(1)
   above;
"owner" has the meaning given by section 6(5) above;
"particulars delivered document" means any document which, having
   been (whether before or after the passing of this Act)—
         (a) produced to the Commissioners of Inland Revenue in
   pursuance of section 28 of the Finance Act 1931; or
         (b) furnished to them in pursuance of Schedule 2 to that Act,
   is for the time being in their possession or under their control;
"precepting authority" means a major precepting authority or a local
   precepting authority;
"redistributed non-domestic rates" means any sums payable by the
   Secretary of State under paragraph 12 or 15 of Schedule 8 to the
   1988 Act;
"resident" has the meaning given by section 6(5) above;
"revenue support grant" has the meaning given by section 78(1) of the
   1988 Act;
"special levy" means a special levy under regulations made under
   section 75 of the 1988 Act;
"valuation tribunal" shall be construed in accordance with section 15
   above.
(2) In this Part—
(a) any reference to dwellings listed in a particular valuation band shall
   be construed in accordance with section 5(6) above;
(b) any reference to an amount payable in respect of council tax for any
   financial year includes a reference to an amount payable in respect of
   council tax for any period falling within that year; and
(c) any reference to a billing authority's general fund shall be construed
   in relation to the Common Council as a reference to the City fund.
(3) For the purposes of this Part the Inner Temple and the Middle Temple
shall be taken to fall within the area of the Common Council.
(4) No provision of this Part which provides an express remedy shall
prejudice any remedy available to a person (apart from that provision) in
respect of a failure to observe a provision of this Part; and references in this
subsection to this Part include references to instruments made under it.

PART II

COUNCIL TAX: SCOTLAND

Preliminary

Council tax in respect of dwellings

70.—(1) In respect of the financial year 1993–94 and each subsequent
financial year, each local authority in Scotland shall impose a tax
which—
(a) shall be known as—
         (i) the regional council tax;
         (ii) the islands council tax; or
         (iii) the district council tax,
   depending upon which local authority impose it; and
(b) shall be payable in respect of dwellings situated in that authority's
   area.
(2) The expenses of a local authority in discharging functions under any
public general Act, so far as not met otherwise or so far as not otherwise

provided for in any such Act, shall be met out of the council tax imposed by the local authority under this Part.

"district council tax": subs. (1).
"dwelling": s.72(2).
"financial year": s.116(1).
"islands council tax": subs. (1).
"local authority": s.99(1).
"regional council tax": subs. (1).

GENERAL NOTE
This section establishes the new tax to be introduced from the financial year commencing April 1993. This will replace the previous local personal taxation system and, by s.100 of this Act, the community charges established by the 1987 Act will be abolished at the end of March 1993. Unlike its predecessor, the new tax is to be payable in respect of dwellings. However, like the community charges, it also includes a personal element in that 50 per cent. of the tax is based on the assumption that each dwelling includes two eligible residents and s.79 provides for a discount of 25 per cent. for dwellings occupied by only one eligible resident. The new tax will be known as the regional council tax, the district council tax, or the islands council tax, depending on which authority imposes it. This section places a duty on each authority to impose the appropriate tax in respect of dwellings within its area. This duty commences with the financial year 1993–94 and continues for subsequent years. In addition, subs. (2) provides that the authority's council tax must meet the expenses of the authority in discharging its functions, other than in regard to private Acts or common good powers, except in so far as those expenses are met through other means.

Liability to be determined on a daily basis

71.—(1) Liability to pay council tax shall be determined on a daily basis.
(2) For the purposes of determining for any day—
(a) whether any property is a chargeable dwelling;
(b) which valuation band is shown in a valuation list as applicable to any chargeable dwelling;
(c) the person liable to pay council tax in respect of any such dwelling; or
(d) whether any amount of council tax is subject to a discount and (if so) the amount of the discount,
it shall be assumed that any state of affairs subsisting at the end of the day had subsisted throughout the day.

DEFINITIONS
"chargeable dwelling": s.72(6).
"council tax": s.99(1).
"dwelling": s.72(2).
"valuation band": s.74(2) and (3).
"valuation list": s.84(1).

GENERAL NOTE
This section establishes that, like the community charge, liability for the appropriate council tax is to be determined on a daily basis. It is anticipated that since the tax is levied primarily on property, this will not cause such difficulties for registration and collection as the previous system did. However, since the new tax does incorporate a personal element, the Opposition warned that difficulties would still arise in relation to non-disclosure of residency, non-registration on the electoral register, etc. A number of factors specified by this Act affect the liability to pay the council tax and, for each of these, this subsection specifies that the situation which exists at the end of the day shall be deemed to have existed throughout the day. The factors are whether the property is a dwelling subject to the tax, as defined by ss.72 and 73; what valuation band is shown as applicable to the dwelling, as established by s.74; the person liable to pay the tax in respect of the dwelling, as defined by ss.75–77; and any discount applicable to the dwelling, as authorised by s.79.

Chargeable dwellings

Dwellings chargeable to council tax

72.—(1) Council tax shall be payable in respect of any dwelling which is not an exempt dwelling.

(2) In this Part, "dwelling"—

(a) means any lands and heritages—

(i) which consist of one or more dwelling houses with any garden, yard, garage, outhouse or pertinent belonging to and occupied with such dwelling house or dwelling houses; and

(ii) which would, but for the provisions of section 73(1) below, be entered separately in the valuation roll;

(b) includes—

(i) the residential part of part residential subjects; and

(ii) that part of any premises which has, in terms of section 45 of the 1980 Act, been apportioned as at 1st April 1989, as a dwelling house; and

(c) does not include a caravan which is not a person's sole or main residence.

(3) For the purposes of subsection (2) above "caravan" has the same meaning as it has in Part I of the Caravan Sites and Control of Development Act 1960.

(4) The Secretary of State may vary the definition of dwelling in subsection (2) above by including or excluding such lands and heritages or parts thereof or such class or classes of lands and heritages or parts thereof as may be prescribed.

(5) The Secretary of State may by order provide that in such cases as may be prescribed by or determined under the order—

(a) anything which would (apart from the order) be one dwelling shall be treated as two or more dwellings; and

(b) anything which would (apart from the order) be two or more dwellings shall be treated as one dwelling.

(6) In this Part—

"chargeable dwelling" means any dwelling in respect of which council tax is payable;

"exempt dwelling" means any dwelling of a class prescribed by an order made by the Secretary of State.

(7) For the purposes of subsection (6) above, a class of dwelling may be prescribed by reference to—

(a) the physical characteristics of dwellings;

(b) the fact that dwellings are unoccupied or are occupied for prescribed purposes or are occupied or owned by persons of prescribed descriptions; or

(c) such other factors as the Secretary of State thinks fit.

(8) Schedule 5 to this Act shall have effect in relation to part residential subjects.

DEFINITIONS

"caravan": s.72(3); Pt. I of the Caravan Sites and Control of Development Act 1960.

"chargeable dwelling": subs. (6).

"council tax": s.99(1).

"dwelling": s.72(2).

"exempt dwelling": subs. (6).

"part residential subjects": s.99(1).

"prescribed": s.116(1).

"valuation roll": s.1 of the Local Government (Scotland) Act 1975.

GENERAL NOTE

This section establishes the basis of liability, namely for a "dwelling" other than those which are exempt. The definition of a dwelling is therefore provided. In addition, wide powers are given to the Secretary of State to amend the definition by regulation. Under s.113, this power of amendment is subject to the negative resolution procedure of the House of Commons only. Part residential subjects are dealt with by Sched. 5.

Subs. (1)
This establishes the basis of liability, namely for a "dwelling" other than those which are exempt. A "dwelling" is defined by subs. (2).

Subs. (2)
A dwelling in regard to liability for council tax in Scotland is defined similarly to that of "domestic subjects" under the 1987 Act. It includes the residential parts of part residential subjects and parts of premises which have been apportioned as dwelling-houses under the Water (Scotland) Act 1980. It does not include a caravan, unless that caravan is a person's sole or main residence. Any differences in the definitions under this section and the 1987 Act which may be created are accommodated by s.73(2) and (3) in regard to the valuation roll, by inclusion or deletion of these.

Subs. (3)
For the purposes of subs. (2) the definition of caravan is given.

Subs. (4)
A wide power is given to the Secretary of State to amend the definition of "dwelling" by regulation. He may exclude all or part of a class of land or heritage, and part of that land or heritage itself. See the Council Tax (Dwellings) (Scotland) Regulations 1992 (S.I. 1992 No. 1334) for a variation of that definition. Under s.113, this power of amendment is subject to the negative resolution procedure of the House of Commons only.

Subs. (5)
To deal with subdivision and incorporation of property, the Secretary of State may prescribe that certain single dwellings be classed as two or more dwellings, or that two or more dwellings be classed as a single dwelling. Again, under s.113, regulations made under this power are subject to the negative resolution procedure of the House of Commons only.

Subs. (6)
The term "dwelling", as established by s.3 of this Act, is divided into two classes, which are defined by this subsection. The first, that of "chargeable dwelling", is defined as those dwellings subject to the council tax. The second class, that of "exempt dwelling", is defined as those which are exempt by being of a class specified by the Secretary of State in regulations made under the authority of this section. The Secretary of State may thus exempt dwellings by regulation, in accordance with subs. (7). See the Council Tax (Exempt Dwellings) (Scotland) Order 1992 (S.I. 1992 No. 1333) for further qualification of the term "exempt dwelling". Again, under s.113, regulations made under this power are subject to the negative resolution procedure of the House of Commons only.

Subs. (7)
The discretion given to the Secretary of State under subs. (6) to exempt dwellings from liability to council tax is wide. While not undermining the width of the discretion, this subsection makes it clear that some of the factors which he may take into account in implementing this power may be the physical characteristics of the dwelling; that the dwelling may be unoccupied; that it is occupied for prescribed purposes and that it is occupied or owned by persons of prescribed descriptions.

Subs. (8)
This subsection gives effect to Sched. 5 in regard to part residential properties. For the effect of this, see the annotations to that Schedule.

Alterations to valuation roll

73.—(1) Subject to subsection (7) below, dwellings shall not be entered in the valuation roll in respect of the financial year 1993–94 or any subsequent financial year.

(2) Dwellings in respect of which there is an entry in the valuation roll immediately before 1st April 1993 shall be deleted from the roll with effect from that date.

(3) Lands and heritages—

(a) in respect of which there is, by reason of the fact that they constitute domestic subjects within the meaning of section 2(3) of the Abolition of Domestic Rates Etc. (Scotland) Act 1987 ("the 1987 Act"), no entry on the roll immediately before 1st April 1993; and

(b) which are not dwellings within the meaning of section 72(2) above, shall be entered on the valuation roll with effect from that date.

(4) Where, after 1st April 1993, any lands and heritages (including a caravan which constitutes a person's sole or main residence) or any parts of lands and heritages cease to be a dwelling, they shall be entered in the valuation roll with effect from the date on which they so cease.

(5) Where after 1st April 1993, by virtue of regulations made under section 72(4) above, any lands and heritages or any parts of lands and heritages—

(a) cease to be dwellings, they shall be entered in the valuation roll;

(b) become dwellings, any entry in the valuation roll in respect of such lands and heritages shall be deleted,

with effect from such date as may be prescribed by such regulations.

(6) Where a part of any lands and heritages falls within a class prescribed under section 72(4) above—

(a) the part so affected and the remainder shall be treated for the purposes of the Valuation Acts as separate lands and heritages, and

(b) the part of those lands and heritages which does not constitute a dwelling shall be entered in the valuation roll accordingly.

(7) Nothing in this section affects the entering in the valuation roll of part residential subjects.

DEFINITIONS

"caravan": s.72(3); Pt. I of the Caravan Sites and Control of Development Act 1960.
"domestic subjects": s.2(3) of the 1987 Act.
"dwelling": s.72(2).
"financial year": s.116(1).
"part residential subjects": s.99(1).
"prescribed": s.116(1).
"Valuation Acts": s.99(1).
"valuation roll": s.1 of the Local Government (Scotland) Act 1975.

GENERAL NOTE

This section provides for alterations to the valuation roll to reflect the fact that dwellings, apart from part residential subjects, shall not be entered in the valuation roll after the financial year commencing 1993–94. Provision is made for the alteration of the valuation roll in respect of the whole or part of any lands and heritages which cease to be dwellings, or become dwellings.

Subs. (1)

Starting from April 1993, dwellings are not to be entered in the valuation roll. Under s.2 of the 1987 Act domestic subjects were not to be entered in this.

Subs. (2)

Any property which now falls within the meaning of "dwelling", and which was included in the valuation roll before April 1, 1993, shall be deleted from the roll.

Subs. (3)

As the opposite to subs. (2), any property which previously constituted domestic subjects under the 1987 Act, and thus was not included in the valuation roll under s.2 of that Act, but which does not fall within the meaning of dwelling under this Act, shall be included in the valuation roll from April 1, 1993.

Subs. (4)

Once the new system is in operation, from April 1, 1993, then any property or part of it which ceases to be a dwelling, including a caravan if it was a person's sole or main residence, shall be entered in the valuation roll, with effect from the date of the change.

Subs. (5)

Similarly to subs. (4), if any regulation made under s.72(4) has the effect of excluding any property from the definition of dwelling, the property shall be entered in the valuation roll from such date as the regulations prescribe. Equally, if the effect of the regulation is to include the property within the definition of dwelling, it shall be entered in the valuation roll from such date as the regulations prescribe. See the Council Tax (Dwellings) (Scotland) Regulations 1992 (S.I. 1992 No. 1334).

Subs. (6)

Where any change in the definition of dwelling under s.72(4) has the effect of treating part property differently in regard to the definition of dwelling, then the resulting parts shall be treated as different lands and heritages, and the part which does not fall within the definition of dwelling shall be entered in the valuation roll. The section is silent in regard to the effective date. In the absence of the relevant regulation specifying the effective date, then it must be presumed to be the date from which the change in status takes place.

Subs. (7)

For the avoidance of doubt, this section does not alter the requirement that part residential subjects shall be included in the valuation roll.

Different amounts for dwellings in different valuation bands

74.—(1) The amounts of regional, islands or district council tax payable in respect of dwellings situated in any local authority's area and listed in different valuation bands shall be in the proportion—

6: 7: 8: 9: 11: 13: 15: 18

where 6 is for dwellings listed in valuation band A, 7 is for dwellings listed in valuation band B, and so on.

(2) The valuation bands for dwellings are set out in the following Table—

Range of values	*Valuation band*
Values not exceeding £27,000	A
Values exceeding £27,000 but not exceeding £35,000	B
Values exceeding £35,000 but not exceeding £45,000	C
Values exceeding £45,000 but not exceeding £58,000	D
Values exceeding £58,000 but not exceeding £80,000	E
Values exceeding £80,000 but not exceeding £106,000	F
Values exceeding £106,000 but not exceeding £212,000	G
Values exceeding £212,000	H

(3) The Secretary of State may by order, as regards financial years beginning on or after such date as is specified in the order—

(a) substitute another proportion for that which is for the time being effective for the purposes of subsection (1) above;

(b) substitute other valuation bands for those which are for the time being effective for the purposes of subsection (2) above.

(4) No order under subsection (3) above shall be made unless a draft of the order has been laid before and approved by resolution of the House of Commons.

(5) Any reference in this Part to dwellings listed in a particular valuation band shall be construed as a reference to dwellings to which that valuation band is shown as applicable in the valuation list.

DEFINITIONS

"district council tax": s.70(1).
"dwelling": s.72(2).
"dwelling listed in a particular valuation band": s.99(3).
"financial year": s.116(1).
"islands council tax": s.70(1).
"local authority": s.99(1).
"regional council tax": s.70(1).
"valuation band": subss. (2) and (3).
"valuation list": s.84(1).

GENERAL NOTE

A banding system for the value of dwellings is established by this section, which also prescribes the proportions to be paid by each band. While these are included in the primary Act, either or both aspects may be altered by the Secretary of State by regulation, but only with the positive approval of the House of Commons.

Subs. (1)

This subsection specifies the proportions of council tax to be paid by each band. Thus, dwellings in the highest band will be liable to pay three times that paid by the lowest band. While going some way to meet the criticism that the community charge was flat-rate and thus regressive, there has been much criticism of these proportions on the ground that they are not sufficiently differentiated.

Subs. (2)

Eight valuation bands are provided, as originally provided for in the Schedule to the Domestic Property (Valuation) (Scotland) Regulations 1991 (S.I. 1991 No. 2022), which gave the initial legal authority for the creation of the valuation lists. Again, while going some way to meet the criticism that the community charge was flat-rate and thus regressive, there has been much criticism of these bands on the ground that they are not sufficiently differentiated.

Subs. (3)

Under the authority of this subsection, the Secretary of State may alter either or both of the proportions and the bands, as established by subs. (2). This will therefore allow the system to be modified to meet any continuing objections to the limited banding or narrow proportions. The inclusion of further bands could be used to provide for a revaluation.

Subs. (4)

Where the Secretary of State replaces either or both of the proportions and the bands, under subs. (3), this must be approved by the affirmative resolution procedure of the House of Commons.

Subs. (5)

This subsection provides a definition, for the purposes of Pt. II relating to Scotland, of the phrase "dwellings listed in a particular valuation band". This is defined as all dwellings shown in the billing authority's valuation list, as established by s.84.

Liability to tax

Persons liable to pay council tax

75.—(1) The person who is liable to pay council tax in respect of any chargeable dwelling and any day is the person who falls within the first paragraph of subsection (2) below to apply, taking paragraph (a) of that subsection first, paragraph (b) next, and so on.

(2) A person falls within this subsection in relation to any chargeable dwelling and any day if, on that day—

(a) he is the resident owner of the whole or any part of the dwelling;

(b) he is a resident tenant of the whole or any part of the dwelling;

(c) he is a resident statutory tenant, resident statutory assured tenant or resident secure tenant of the whole or any part of the dwelling;

(d) he is a resident sub-tenant of the whole or any part of the dwelling;

(e) he is a resident of the dwelling; or

(f) he is any of the following—

(i) the sub-tenant of the whole or any part of the dwelling under a sub-lease granted for a term of 6 months or more;

(ii) the tenant, under a lease granted for a term of 6 months or more, of any part of the dwelling which is not subject to a sub-lease granted for a term of 6 months or more;

(iii) the owner of any part of the dwelling which is not subject to a lease granted for a term of 6 months or more.

(3) Where, in relation to any chargeable dwelling and any day, two or more persons fall within the first paragraph of subsection (2) above to apply,

they shall be jointly and severally liable to pay the council tax payable in respect of the dwelling and that day.

(4) Subsection (3) above shall not apply as respects any day on which one or more of the persons there mentioned fall to be disregarded for the purposes of discount by virtue of paragraph 2 of Schedule 1 to this Act (the severely mentally impaired) and one or more of them do not; and liability to pay the council tax in respect of the dwelling and that day shall be determined as follows—

   (a) if only one of those persons does not fall to be so disregarded, he shall be solely liable;
   (b) if two or more of those persons do not fall to be so disregarded, they shall be jointly and severally liable.

(5) In this section—

   "secure tenant" means a tenant under a secure tenancy within the meaning of Part III of the Housing (Scotland) Act 1987;

   "statutory tenant" means a statutory tenant within the meaning of the Rent (Scotland) Act 1984;

   "statutory assured tenant" means a statutory assured tenant within the meaning of the Housing (Scotland) Act 1988.

DEFINITIONS
   "chargeable dwelling": s.72(6).
   "council tax": s.99(1).
   "dwelling": s.72(2).
   "secure tenant": subs. (5).
   "statutory assured tenant": subs. (5).
   "statutory tenant": subs. (5).

GENERAL NOTE
   This section establishes the persons liable to pay the council tax for a chargeable dwelling on any particular day.

Subs. (1)
   This rather clumsy construction simply establishes that the person who is liable to pay council tax for any chargeable dwelling is the person who falls within the first of the categories in subs. (2) to apply, taking each in sequence. This hierarchy in subs. (2) is composed of six categories, which must be examined in turn. Thus if a person falls within subs. (2)(a) that person will be the person liable. If, however, no person falls within subs. (2)(a) or (b), but one does fall within subs. (2)(c), then that person will be the person liable. This process continues until liability is established.

Subs. (2)
   This subsection provides the list of categories to establish the person liable to pay the council tax. That person is the one who falls within the first of the categories to apply, taking each in sequence. The categories are based on two elements, namely residency and legal interest. The top category in the hierarchy is the person who is both a resident of the building and the owner of whole or part of it. The hierarchy then progresses through a variety of categories of legal interest, but all linked to residency, and then to one where there is residency but no legal interest. Where there is no residency, then the final category of ownership establishes liability.

   Unlike the equivalent provision in regard to England and Wales, under s.6 of this Act, no statutory definition of residency is attempted. In that section, "resident" is defined as an individual who is both 18 years of age and occupies the dwelling as his sole or main residence. Since it is a daily tax, an individual becomes liable from the day on which the age of 18 is attained. As with the community charge, the term "sole or main residence" is crucial to establishing liability. However, as with the Local Government Finance Act 1988, this Act does not define the term "sole or main residence", and its interpretation in this context will be influenced by the interpretation adopted in other areas of law. Thus the attempt to provide a statutory definition for England and Wales does little to help the problem of interpretation.

   The general approach of the courts has been that the phrase should be considered in its ordinary meaning and as a matter of fact and degree. Thus, while it is accepted that a person can have more than one residence (*Fox* v. *Stirk and Bristol Electoral Registration Officer*; *Ricketts* v. *Cambridge City Electoral Registration Officer* [1970] 2 Q.B. 463), a number of factors will be taken into account into determining which is the main residence. However, although both the subjective opinion of the individual and objective factors, such as where most of the personal belongings are kept, will be relevant, it is likely that most weight will be attached to the time spent at each dwelling since, like the community charge, the council tax will be considered to be a charge for the services provided. Thus, similar to the approach in *Frost* v. *Feltham* [1981] 1 W.L.R. 452, in *Bradford Metropolitan City Council* v. *Anderton* 89 L.G.R. 681, in determining that a merchant seaman had his residence in a house where he spent only 90 days of the year, Hutchinson J. held that apart from time, other factors in determining residence were the subjective view of what the individual regarded as his home, that it was where his wife lived, and that he had a legal interest in the house. However, in *Stevenson* v. *Rodgers* (unreported), February 15, 1991, the Inner House of the Court of Session indicated that time was not simply one factor among others but the most important of the criteria. Thus where a person worked and slept during the week in Liverpool, but his wife and children lived in Edinburgh, where he spent most weekends, the number of nights spent in each place was not evenly balanced. Only where the numbers were more evenly balanced should the other factors be considered as providing a contrary indication of residence. Differing views were expressed by the three judges as to the relevance of a legal interest in the house, where the person was registered with a GP, where the person appeared on the electoral register, and where the rest of the family was living.

Subs. (3)
   Where two or more persons fall within the same category for any day, as established by subs. (2), then they will be jointly and severally liable to pay the council tax for every such day.

Subs. (4)
   This subsection was included on amendment following pressure to accommodate the problems of the mentally impaired.

Subs. (5)
   For the purposes of this section, the terms relating to the specific legal interest are defined.

Liability in prescribed cases

   76.—(1) Subsections (3) and (4) below shall have effect in substitution for section 75 above in relation to any chargeable dwelling of a class prescribed for the purposes of this subsection.
   (2) Subsections (3) and (4) below shall have effect in substitution for section 75 above in relation to any chargeable dwelling of a class prescribed for the purposes of this subsection, if the levying authority so determines in relation to all dwellings of that class which are situated in its area.
   (3) Where on any day this subsection has effect in relation to a dwelling, the owner of the dwelling shall be liable to pay the council tax in respect of the dwelling and that day.
   (4) Where on any day two or more persons fall within subsection (3) above, they shall each be jointly and severally liable to pay the council tax in respect of the dwelling and that day.
   (5) Subsection (4) of section 75 above shall apply for the purposes of subsection (4) above as it applies for the purposes of subsection (3) of that section.
   (6) Regulations prescribing a class of chargeable dwellings for the purposes of subsection (1) or (2) above may provide that, in relation to any dwelling of that class, subsection (3) above shall have effect as if for the reference to the owner of the dwelling there were substituted a reference to the person falling within such description as may be prescribed.
   (7) Subsection (7) of section 72 above shall apply for the purposes of subsections (1) and (2) above as it applies for the purposes of subsection (6) of that section.

DEFINITIONS
   "chargeable dwelling": s.72(6).
   "council tax": s.99(1).
   "dwelling": s.72(2).
   "levying authority": s.99(1).
   "prescribed": s.116(1).

GENERAL NOTE

This section provides additional rules in regard to the liability of an owner where the chargeable dwelling has been prescribed in regulation. The aim is to ensure that the owner pays the council tax as opposed to any resident. Thus, in situations like hostels, where the residents may be short-term and difficult to trace, this will ensure payment. In this way the system is similar to, and replaces, the collective community charge. Under this section, see the Council Tax (Liability of Owners) (Scotland) Regulations 1992 (S.I. 1992 No. 1331).

Subs. (1)

Where any class of chargeable dwelling has been prescribed in regulation under this subsection, then the provisions of s.75 are displaced and replaced by the provisions contained in subss. (3) and (4) of this section. The Council Tax (Liability of Owners) (Scotland) Regulations 1992 (S.I. 1992 No. 1331) have prescribed that the classes are residential care homes; houses of religious communities; houses in multiple occupation; residences of staff who live in houses occasionally occupied by an employer; and residences of ministers of religion.

Subs. (2)

The purpose of this subsection is to allow the Secretary of State to prescribe classes of chargeable dwellings for which the levying authority will retain discretion to make the owner rather than the resident liable to pay the council tax. Where any class of chargeable dwelling has been prescribed in regulation under this subsection and the authority decides to exercise its discretion, then the provisions of s.75 are displaced and replaced by the provisions contained in subss. (3) and (4) of this section. Where, however, the levying authority does decide to exercise that discretion in relation to a particular class, then it must be applied to the owners of all dwellings within that class, there being no discretion to apply it within the class.

Subs. (3)

This makes it clear that when this subsection has effect, it is the owner and not the resident who is liable to pay the council tax for any chargeable day. Thus, the hierarchy of liability established in s.75 is displaced.

Subs. (4)

Where two or more persons are liable by virtue of subs. (3), then they are jointly and severally liable to pay the council tax.

Subs. (5)

This subsection was included to give effect to the policy underlying the amendment to s.75 whereby the problems of the mentally impaired were taken into account.

Subs. (6)

In order to further clarify liability, any regulations made under subs. (1) or subs. (2) may also make provision for determining who is to be considered as the owner of any dwelling in that class. See S.I. 1992 No. 1331 for further details.

Subs. (7)

By applying subs. (7) of s.72 to subss. (1) and (2) of this section, any dwellings prescribed under this section by the Secretary of State may be prescribed by reference to such factors as he thinks fit. While not reducing the wide discretion given by this power, further indications of the factors which may be taken into account are provided. Thus some of the factors may be the physical characteristics of the dwelling; that the dwelling may be unoccupied; that it is occupied for prescribed purposes and that it is occupied or owned by persons of prescribed descriptions.

Liability of spouses

77.—(1) Where—

(a) a person who is liable to pay council tax in respect of any chargeable dwelling and any day is married to another person; and

(b) that other person is also a resident of the dwelling on that day but would not, apart from this section, be so liable,

those persons shall be jointly and severally liable to pay the council tax payable in respect of that dwelling and that day.

(2) Subsection (1) above shall not apply as respects any day on which the other person there mentioned falls to be disregarded for the purposes of discount by virtue of paragraph 2 of Schedule 1 to this Act (the severely mentally impaired).

(3) For the purposes of this section two persons are married to each other if they are a man and a woman—
(a) who are married to each other; or
(b) who are not married to each other but are living together as husband and wife.

DEFINITIONS
  "chargeable dwelling": s.72(6).
  "council tax": s.99(1).
  "dwelling": s.72(2).

GENERAL NOTE
  This section is intended to ensure that married couples are jointly and severally liable to pay the council tax, notwithstanding that joint and several liability has not been created by the other preceding sections.

Subs. (1)
  Where two people are married to each other and, while both are resident in the dwelling, one would not otherwise be liable to pay the council tax, then they shall be jointly and severally liable for the council tax.

Subs. (2)
  This subsection was included to give effect to the policy whereby the problems of the mentally impaired were taken into account.

Subs. (3)
  For the purpose of establishing joint and several liability under this section, two persons are deemed to be married to each other not only if they are a man and a woman and are actually married to each other, but also if they are a man and a woman living together as husband and wife.

Amounts of tax payable

Basic amounts payable

78. Subject to sections 79 and 80 below, a person who is liable to pay council tax in respect of any chargeable dwelling and any day shall, as respects the dwelling and the day, pay to the levying authority for the area in which the dwelling is situated an amount calculated in accordance with the formula—

$$\frac{A}{D}$$

where—
  A is the amount or, as the case may be, the aggregate of the amounts which, for the financial year in which the day falls and for dwellings in the valuation band listed for the dwelling, has or have been imposed by the local authority or authorities in whose area or areas the dwelling is situated;
  D is the number of days in the financial year.

DEFINITIONS
  "chargeable dwelling": s.72(6).
  "council tax": s.99(1).
  "dwelling": s.72(2).
  "dwelling listed in a valuation band": ss.74(5) and 99(3).
  "financial year": s.116(1).
  "levying authority": s.99(1).
  "local authority": s.99(1).

GENERAL NOTE
  The basic formula by which the amount to be paid by any person liable to pay the council tax is to be calculated is provided by this section. Working from the position that liability for a

particular dwelling is calculated on a daily basis, the formula for calculating the amount to be paid is the sum set by the billing authority for dwellings in that valuation band divided by the number of days in the financial year. From this starting point, the amount may be reduced either by discounts established under the authority of s.79, or in accordance with regulations made under s.80 by the Secretary of State. Thus, the amount to be paid may vary during the year, depending on the circumstances existing on any particular day.

Discounts

79.—(1) The amount of council tax payable in respect of a chargeable dwelling and any day shall be subject to a discount equal to the appropriate percentage of that amount if on that day—
  (a) there is only one resident of the dwelling and he does not fall to be disregarded for the purposes of discount; or
  (b) there are two or more residents of the dwelling and each of them except one falls to be disregarded for those purposes.

(2) The amount of council tax payable in respect of a chargeable dwelling and any day shall be subject to a discount equal to twice the appropriate percentage of that amount if on that day—
  (a) there is no resident of the dwelling; or
  (b) there are one or more residents of the dwelling and each of them falls to be disregarded for the purposes of discount.

(3) In this section "the appropriate percentage" means 25 per cent. or, if the Secretary of State by order so provides in respect of the financial year in which the day falls, such other percentage as is specified in the order.

(4) No order under subsection (3) above shall be made unless a draft of the order has been laid before and approved by resolution of the House of Commons.

(5) Schedule 1 to this Act shall have effect for determining who shall be disregarded for the purposes of discount.

DEFINITIONS
  "appropriate percentage": subs. (3).
  "chargeable dwelling": s.72(6).
  "council tax": s.99(1).
  "dwelling": s.72(2).
  "financial year": s.116(1).

GENERAL NOTE
  The council tax is not simply a property-based tax like the rating system, but includes a personal element as in the community charge. For that element, it has been assumed that any dwelling will be occupied by two or more residents, and the amount is calculated accordingly. This section therefore provides for discounts to be made available where this is not the situation, and the dwelling has only one resident or includes residents who are to be considered exempt from the personal element. While the conditions for, and levels of, discount are provided by the section, they may be varied by an order which has been positively approved by the House of Commons. Under this section, discounts of 25 per cent. are granted where there is only one resident or only one who is not to be disregarded for this purpose, and 50 per cent. where there is no resident or all the residents are to be disregarded for this purpose. The classes of persons who are to be so disregarded are provided by Sched. 1; see also the annotations to that Schedule.

Subs. (1)
  This subsection provides that in two circumstances a discount of 25 per cent., as the "appropriate percentage" defined by subs. (3), will be granted. The first is where there is only one resident, who does not fall within the classes of persons to be disregarded listed in Sched. 1. The second is where there are two or more residents, but only one does not fall within the classes of persons to be disregarded listed in Sched. 1.

Subs. (2)
  This subsection provides that in two circumstances a discount of 50 per cent., as twice the "appropriate percentage" defined by subs. (3), will be granted. The first is where there is no

resident of the dwelling. The second is where there are one or more residents, all of whom fall within the classes of persons to be disregarded listed in Sched. 1.

Subs. (3)

The "appropriate percentage" is set at 25 per cent. This is the unit of discount which is incorporated into subs. (1) to provide 25 per cent. discount, and subs. (2) to provide 50 per cent. discount, where the conditions are met. The Secretary of State may alter the "appropriate percentage" by order, but any such alteration must be for the whole of a financial year.

Subs. (4)

Any alteration by the Secretary of State of the "appropriate percentage", by means of an order under subs. (3), must be approved by the affirmative resolution procedure of the House of Commons.

Subs. (5)

The classes of those to be disregarded, or "invisible", for the purposes of liability for the personal element of the council tax are provided by Sched. 1. The main classes in the schedule are: persons in detention; the severely mentally impaired; persons in respect of whom child benefit is payable; students; hospital patients; patients in homes; care workers; and residents of hostels or similar accommodation for the homeless or itinerant. The Secretary of State may amend these classes, or add to the classes, by order.

Reduced amounts

80.—(1) The Secretary of State may make regulations as regards any case where—

(a) a person is liable to pay an amount to a levying authority in respect of council tax for any financial year which is prescribed; and

(b) prescribed conditions are fulfilled.

(2) The regulations may provide that the amount he is liable to pay shall be an amount which—

(a) is less than the amount it would be apart from the regulations; and

(b) is determined in accordance with prescribed rules.

(3) This section applies whether the amount mentioned in subsection (1) above is determined under section 78 above or under that section read with section 79 above.

(4) The conditions mentioned in subsection (1) above may be prescribed by reference to such factors as the Secretary of State thinks fit; and in particular such factors may include the making of an application by the person concerned and all or any of—

(a) the factors mentioned in subsection (5) below; or

(b) the factors mentioned in subsection (6) below.

(5) The factors mentioned in subsection (4)(a) above are—

(a) community charges for a period before 1st April 1993;

(b) the circumstances of, or other matters relating to, the person concerned;

(c) an amount—

(i) relating to any local authority whose council tax constitutes all or part of the amount referred to in subsection (1) above; and

(ii) which is specified, or is to be specified, in a report laid, or to be laid, before the House of Commons;

(d) such other amounts as may be prescribed or arrived at in a prescribed manner.

(6) The factors referred to in subsection (4)(b) above are—

(a) a disabled person having his sole or main residence in the dwelling concerned;

(b) the circumstances of, or other matters relating to, that person;

(c) the physical characteristics of, or other matters relating to, that dwelling.

(7) The rules mentioned in subsection (2) above may be prescribed by reference to such factors as the Secretary of State thinks fit; and in particular

such factors may include all or any of the factors mentioned in subsection (5) or subsection (6)(b) or (c) above.

(8) Without prejudice to the generality of section 113(2) below, regulations under this section may include—

(a) provision requiring the Secretary of State to specify in a report, for the purposes of the regulations, an amount in relation to each local authority;

(b) provision requiring him to lay the report before the House of Commons;

(c) provision for the review of any prescribed decision of a levying authority relating to the application or operation of the regulations;

(d) provision that no appeal may be made to a valuation appeal committee in respect of such a decision, nothwithstanding section 81(1) below.

(9) To the extent that he would not have power to do so apart from this subsection, the Secretary of State may—

(a) include in regulations under this section such amendments of any social security instrument as he thinks expedient in consequence of the regulations under this section;

(b) include in any social security instrument such provision as he thinks expedient in consequence of regulations under this section.

(10) In subsection (9) above "social security instrument" means an order or regulations made, or falling to be made, by the Secretary of State under the Social Security Acts.

DEFINITIONS
"community charge": s.26(1); s.7 of the 1987 Act.
"council tax": s.99(1).
"dwelling": s.72(2).
"financial year": s.116(1).
"levying authority": s.99(1).
"local authority": s.99(1).
"prescribed": s.116(1).
"social security instrument": subs. (10).
"valuation appeal committee": s.99(1).

GENERAL NOTE
In the consultation paper on the council tax, *A New Tax For Local Government*, it was stated that the intention was to phase in the full amount of council-tax bills in order to mitigate the effect of any high increases (para. 8.1). This section allows that undertaking to be implemented by giving the Secretary of State the power to make regulations reducing the amount to be paid in certain circumstances. Under this section see the Council Tax (Reductions for Disabilities) (Scotland) Regulations 1992 (S.I. 1992 No. 1335).

Subs. (1)
This provides the Secretary of State with the authority to make regulations in regard to the liability of council taxpayers where the conditions specified in the regulations are met.

Subs. (2)
The regulations made under the authority of subs. (1) may reduce the amount that the council taxpayer would otherwise be liable to pay, provided that the new amount is in accordance with the prescribed rules.

Subs. (3)
The regulations made under the authority of subs. (1) may apply irrespective of entitlement to any discounts under s.79.

Subss. (4), (5) and (6)
Without prejudice to the generality of the ability of the Secretary of State to prescribe, by reference to such factors as he thinks fit, the conditions which permit the reduction of the amount of council tax to which a taxpayer is liable, this section specifies a number of such factors. The first is whether an application for such a reduction has been made. Four more, drawn from subs. (5), are the community charge before the council tax was introduced; the

circumstances of the taxpayer concerned; amounts relating to the authority if its council tax constitutes all or part of the amount to which the person is liable, provided that the amount is specified in a report which will be laid before the House of Commons; and such other amounts as may be prescribed or calculated in accordance with the regulations. Another three, drawn from subs. (6), are whether the dwelling is the sole or main residence of a disabled person; the circumstances of that person; and the physical characteristics or other matters relating to that dwelling.

Subs. (7)
Without prejudice to the generality of the ability of the Secretary of State to prescribe the rules relating to the amount of any reduction of council tax by reference to such factors as he thinks fit, this section specifies a number of such factors. These factors are some, but not all the factors which may be taken into account in prescribing the conditions under subs. (1). Four, drawn from subs. (5), are the community charge before the council tax was introduced; the circumstances of the taxpayer concerned; amounts relating to the authority concerned, provided that the amount is specified in a report which will be laid before the House of Commons; and such other amounts as may be prescribed or calculated in accordance with the regulations. Another two, drawn from subs. (6), are the circumstances of a disabled person and the physical characteristics or other matters relating to that dwelling. This difference between the factors which may be taken into account in prescribing the conditions for reductions and the rules specifying the amount of the reduction must be seen in the light of the fact that neither prejudices the discretion of the Secretary of State to prescribe both according to such factors as he sees fit.

Subs. (8)
Without prejudice to s.113(2), which gives the Secretary of State the wide power to make such incidental, consequential or supplementary provisions to any regulations as he thinks necessary or expedient, this subsection makes it clear that regulations made under this section may include four specific factors. First, a requirement that the Secretary of State specify in a report an amount in relation to each local authority and, secondly, that the report be laid before the House of Commons. Thirdly, the regulations may contain provisions for reviewing a decision of the levying authority in relation to the regulations, thus permitting some type of appeal system. However, the final factor permits the Secretary of State to provide that such appeals should not be made to the valuation appeal committee.

Subs. (9)
This makes it clear that the Secretary of State may amend any "social security instrument", namely any social security order or regulation as defined by subs. (10), either directly to take account of regulations made under this section, or indirectly by regulations made under this section.

Subs. (10)
This subsection provides the necessary definition of "social security instrument" for the purposes of making or amending regulations under subs. (9).

Appeals

Appeal to valuation appeal committee

81.—(1) A person may appeal to a valuation appeal committee if he is aggrieved by—
    (a) any decision of a levying authority that a dwelling is a chargeable dwelling, or that he is liable to pay council tax in respect of such a dwelling; or
    (b) any calculation made by a levying authority of an amount which he is liable to pay to the authority in respect of council tax,
and the committee shall make such decision as they think just.
    (2) In subsection (1) above the reference to any calculation of an amount includes a reference to any estimate of the amount.
    (3) Subsection (1) above shall not apply where the grounds on which the person concerned is aggrieved fall within such category or categories as may be prescribed.
    (4) No appeal may be made under subsection (1) above unless—

(a) the aggrieved person serves a written notice under this subsection; and

(b) one of the conditions mentioned in subsection (7) below is fulfilled.

(5) A notice under subsection (4) above must be served on the levying authority concerned.

(6) A notice under subsection (4) above must state the matter by which and the grounds on which the person is aggrieved.

(7) The conditions are that—

(a) the aggrieved person is notified in writing, by the authority on which he served the notice, that the authority believes the grievance is not well founded, but the person is still aggrieved;

(b) the aggrieved person is notified in writing, by the authority on which he served the notice, that steps have been taken to deal with the grievance, but the person is still aggrieved;

(c) the period of two months, beginning with the date of service of the aggrieved person's notice, has ended without his being notified under paragraph (a) or (b) above.

(8) Where a notice under subsection (4) above is served on an authority, the authority shall—

(a) consider the matter to which the notice relates;

(b) include in any notification under subsection (7)(a) above the reasons for the belief concerned;

(c) include in any notification under subsection (7)(b) above a statement of the steps taken.

DEFINITIONS

"chargeable dwelling": s.72(6).
"council tax": s.99(1).
"dwelling": s.72(2).
"levying authority": s.99(1).
"valuation appeal committee": s.99(1).

GENERAL NOTE

This section establishes the right of appeal to the valuation appeal committee in regard to certain matters, although appeals on these matters may be prohibited if the grounds of appeal fall within categories prescribed by regulation. In order to try to resolve as many matters as possible without the need for an appeal, before the appeal can be made the person aggrieved must serve a notice on the levying authority and remain dissatisfied after the response from the authority is received, or have received no response within two months. To facilitate the speedy resolution of the matter, and to simplify the appeal procedure, the authority is also charged with the duty of considering the matters raised by such a notice and supplying reasons for their decision and any steps taken to deal with the grievance contained in the notice.

Subs. (1)

The right to appeal to a valuation appeal committee is given in three circumstances. First, if the person is not satisfied with the designation of a dwelling as a chargeable dwelling, under s.72. Secondly, if the person is not satisfied with the decision of the levying authority that he is liable to pay council tax in respect of a chargeable dwelling, under ss.75–77. Thirdly, if the person is not satisfied with the decision of the levying authority as to any calculation of the amount of council tax which he is liable to pay. This right of appeal may be restricted if the ground of appeal is one which falls within any category prescribed by the Secretary of State, under subs. (3), and, before the appeal can be made, the procedures laid down in subs. (4) must be met.

Subs. (2)

Since a bill for council tax will usually be issued in advance of the actual liability, which is on a daily basis, this provision makes it clear that the reference in subs. (1) to any calculation of the amount of council tax to which the person is liable includes an estimate of that amount.

Subs. (3)

The grounds on which appeals can be raised concerning the matters in subs. (1) may be restricted by regulations made under this subsection. It has been stated that it is envisaged that the jurisdiction of the valuation appeal committees will be taken away from matters concerning discounts and benefits.

Subs. (4)

Before an appeal can be made, two requirements must be satisfied. First, the aggrieved person must have served a written notice on the levying authority. Subsections (5) and (6) lay down that such a notice must be served on the levying authority concerned and must state the matter and grounds by which the person is aggrieved. Secondly, one of three conditions specified in subs. (7) must be met. These are that, having notified the authority, the person must remain dissatisfied after a written explanation from the authority as to why the grievance is not well founded; or remain dissatisfied after a written explanation of the steps which the authority proposes to take to meet the grievance; or the person has received no written notification of either result within two months commencing with the date of service of the written statement of the grievance.

Subs. (5)

The notice which is required to be served under subs. (4) before an appeal can be made must be served on the levying authority concerned.

Subs. (6)

The notice which is required to be served under subs. (4) before an appeal can be made must state the matter by which the person is aggrieved and the ground of that grievance. The restriction in subs. (3) as to the grounds of appeal which are prescribed by the Secretary of State applies only to the appeal stage, so a person aggrieved is not precluded from raising such matters with the authority.

Subs. (7)

The second of the requirements specified in subs. (4) which must be satisfied before an appeal can be made is dealt with by this subsection. Having notified the authority, the person must remain dissatisfied after a written explanation from the authority as to why the grievance is not well founded; or remain dissatisfied after a written explanation of the steps which the authority proposes to take to meet the grievance; or the person has received no written notification of either result within two months commencing with the date of service of the written statement of the grievance.

Subs. (8)

When the levying authority receives a written notice under subs. (4) it is placed under a duty to consider the matter to which the notice relates and then, if of the opinion that the grievance is not well founded, to state the reasons for this in the notification to the person concerned or, if taking steps to deal with the grievance, specify the steps in the notification to the person concerned. This is an attempt to allow as many grievances as possible to be resolved as soon as possible without the need for an appeal, and to clarify matters for any subsequent appeal.

Appeal procedure

82.—(1) The Secretary of State may by regulations make provision for the procedure to be followed in appeals under this Part to a valuation appeal committee.

(2) Regulations under this section may include provision—

(a) as to the time within which any proceedings before the committee are to be instituted;

(b) for requiring persons to attend to give evidence and produce documents and for granting to any person such recovery of documents as might be granted by the Court of Session; and

(c) as to the manner in which any decision of the committee is to be implemented.

(3) Any person who fails to comply with any requirement imposed by regulations under paragraph (b) of subsection (2) above shall be guilty of an offence and liable on summary conviction to a fine not exceeding level 1 on the standard scale.

(4) Any party to an appeal under this Part may appeal against a decision of the valuation appeal committee on a point of law to the Court of Session.

(5) Neither section 1(3A) of the Lands Tribunal Act 1949 nor section 15 of the Local Government (Financial Provisions) (Scotland) Act 1963 shall apply to appeals to or from a valuation appeal committee under this Part.

(6) It shall be a defence for a person charged with an offence under subsection (3) above to prove that he had a reasonable excuse for acting as he did.

DEFINITIONS
"valuation appeal committee": s.99(1).

GENERAL NOTE
This section allows for the procedure in appeals to the valuation appeal committee, under s.81, to be prescribed. It also provides for appeals to the Court of Session on a point of law.

Subss. (1) and (2)
The procedure for appeals to the valuation appeal committee, under s.81, may be prescribed by regulation under subs. (1). Without restricting the wide power available in regard to such regulations, under s.113, the regulations may include provisions relating to time limits; attendance, evidence, recovery of documents; and the manner of implementation of the decision of a valuation appeal committee.

Subs. (3)
A person who fails to comply with any regulations made in regard to attendance to give evidence or for recovery of documents shall be guilty of an offence. On summary conviction, liability may not exceed level 1 on the standard scale. This is, however, subject to the defence of reasonable excuse, under subs. (6).

Subs. (4)
Any party to an appeal to the valuation appeal committee may appeal on a point of law to the Court of Session.

Subs. (5)
The two other provisions relating to proceedings in appeals specified here shall not apply to appeals in relation to the council tax.

Subs. (6)
The defence of reasonable excuse is provided to the offence, under subs. (3), of failing to comply with any regulations made in regard to attendance to give evidence or for recovery of documents, under subs. (1).

New dwellings

Completion of new dwellings

83.—(1) Schedule 6 to this Act (which makes provision with respect to the determination of a day as the completion day in relation to a new building which, or any part of which, will constitute or constitutes a dwelling) shall have effect.

(2) A dwelling in a new building shall be deemed for the purposes of this Part to have come into existence on the day determined under that Schedule as the completion day in respect of that building, whether or not the building is completed on that day.

(3) Where—

(a) a day is determined under that Schedule as the completion day in relation to a new building; and

(b) the building is one produced by the structural alteration of a building which consists of one or more existing dwellings,

the existing dwelling or dwellings shall be deemed for the purposes of this Part to have ceased to exist on that day.

(4) Any reference in this section or that Schedule to a new building includes a reference to a building produced by the structural alteration of an existing building where—

(a) the existing building constitutes a dwelling which, by virtue of the alteration, becomes, or becomes part of, a different dwelling or different dwellings; or

(b) the existing building does not, except by virtue of the alteration, constitute a dwelling.

(5) Any reference in this section or that Schedule to a building includes a reference to a part of a building.

DEFINITIONS
"building": subs. (5).
"dwelling": s.72(2).
"new building": subs. (4).

GENERAL NOTE
This section allows the local assessor to serve a completion notice in respect of new buildings which comprise the whole or part of a dwelling. This notice establishes the date from which liability to the council tax in regard to that dwelling begins.

Subs. (1)
This section brings into effect Sched. 6, which specifies the procedures to be followed in relation to the issue of completion notices. See further the notes to that Schedule.

Subs. (2)
This subsection provides that even if the dwelling is not completed by the date prescribed by Sched. 6, the "relevant date", it is nevertheless deemed to have been completed for the purpose of liability to council tax.

Subs. (3)
Where a new building is created by means of a structural alteration to one or more existing buildings, the existing buildings are deemed to cease to exist on that day. This will entail a revaluation of any remaining separate buildings.

Subs. (4)
This subsection makes clear that a "new building" for the purposes of this section includes the alteration of an existing building, whether or not the existing building was a dwelling. Thus two circumstances are specified: first, where the existing building is a dwelling and becomes a different dwelling, or becomes part of a different dwelling, by virtue of the alteration; and secondly, where no part of the existing building was a dwelling.

Valuation lists

Compilation and maintenance of valuation lists

84.—(1) In accordance with this Part, the local assessor for each regional and islands council shall compile, and then maintain, a list for that council (to be known as the "valuation list").

(2) A valuation list must show, for each day for which it is in force—

(a) each dwelling which is situated in the regional or islands council's area; and

(b) which of the valuation bands mentioned in section 74(2) above is applicable to the dwelling.

(3) A list must also contain such information about dwellings shown in it as may be prescribed.

(4) The omission from a list of any matter required to be included in it shall not of itself render the list invalid, so far as any other matter contained in it is concerned.

(5) Any rules as to Crown exemption which would have applied apart from this subsection shall not prevent a list showing a dwelling, showing the valuation band applicable to a dwelling and containing any prescribed information about a dwelling.

(6) A list must be compiled on 1st April 1993 and shall come into force on that day.

(7) Before a list is compiled the local assessor must take such steps as are reasonably practicable in the time available to ensure that it is accurately compiled on 1st April 1993.

(8) Any valuation of a dwelling carried out by the local assessor in pursuance of subsection (7) above shall be carried out in accordance with section 86(2) below.

(9) The local assessor shall maintain the valuation list for so long as is necessary for the purposes of this Part.

(10) In this Part "local assessor" means the assessor appointed under section 116(2) or (5) (appointment of assessors) of the 1973 Act for each region and islands area; and any depute assessor appointed under the said section 116(2) or (5) shall have all the functions of a local assessor under this Part.

DEFINITIONS
"dwelling": s.72(2).
"information": s.116(1).
"local assessor": subs. (10).
"prescribed": s.116(1).
"valuation band": s.74(2) and (3).
"valuation list": subs. (1).

GENERAL NOTE
This section provides for the compilation and maintenance, by the local assessor, of a valuation list for each regional and islands authority. The list is to be compiled, and to come into effect, on April 1, 1993, the commencement date for the operation of the council-tax system. The contents of the list are prescribed by this section, requiring it to show each dwelling in the area of the authority and the valuation band to which the dwelling has been allocated. Crown property which would otherwise be exempt must be shown in the list. Any error in compilation which results in an omission from the list will not of itself invalidate the list. However, it remains possible for the list to be so fundamentally flawed that it is void. Under this section, see the Council Tax (Contents of Valuation Lists) (Scotland) Regulations 1992 (S.I. 1992 No. 1330).

Subs. (1)
A duty is placed on the local assessor for a regional or islands authority to compile and maintain a valuation list for all dwellings in the area.

Subs. (2)
Each dwelling in the authority's area must be shown in the valuation list for each day for which it is in force, together with the valuation band applicable. Exclusion from the valuation list does not affect the status of the dwelling as "chargeable dwelling", but the amount of tax payable could not be calculated in accordance with s.178, so no tax could be demanded in relation to a dwelling not shown in the valuation list for that day.

Subs. (3)
The Secretary of State is empowered to make regulations requiring the valuation list to show additional information. See the Council Tax (Contents of Valuation Lists) (Scotland) Regulations 1992 (S.I. 1992 No. 1330).

Subs. (4)
The validity of the valuation list itself, as opposed to validity in regard to the item, will not be automatically affected by the omission of any matter which should have been included by virtue of this section and any regulations made under it. Should the defects be sufficiently grave, however, it would be open to the court to decide that the list was void.

Subs. (5)
Any dwelling which would otherwise be exempt from liability to be shown in the list by virtue of Crown exemption shall be included in the list, together with the applicable band and any other information required by regulation.

Subs. (6)
The valuation list is technically to be "compiled" on April 1, 1993 and come into force on that day.

Subs. (7)
A general duty is placed on the local assessor to ensure that the list is as accurate as

reasonably possible prior to its being "compiled". That the short time-scale available for such a large exercise will restrict what is possible is recognised by the explicit qualification of "reasonably practicable in the time available". During the Parliamentary proceedings, a number of amendments to the effect that the introduction should be delayed a year to allow the process to proceed more accurately failed to find success. The intention in the exercise is to take account of the physical characteristics and external environment of the property as at April 1, 1993, but the value placed is that which would have prevailed in relation to those characteristics on April 1, 1991. Within this general duty and constraint, further specific requirements are laid down by subss. (5)–(8).

Subs. (8)
This subsection confirms that the introduction of what is "reasonably possible in the time available" does not alter the duty imposed on the local assessor by s.86(2) to carry out the valuation on such assumptions and principles as are laid down in regulation.

Subs. (9)
The duty to maintain the valuation list is a continuing one.

Subs. (10)
The definition of local assessor is provided, and provides that the depute assessor shall have the same powers as the assessor in regard to the provisions of this Act.

Distribution of lists

85.—(1) At the following times, namely—
  (a) not later than 1st September 1992; and
  (b) not earlier than 15th November 1992 and not later than 1st December 1992,
the local assessor shall send to each council for which he has been appointed to act as local assessor a copy of the list which he proposes (on the information then before him) to compile for that council's area.

(2) At the same time as he sends a copy of the valuation list to a council under subsection (1) above, the local assessor for a regional council shall send to each district council in the region a copy of so much of the regional valuation list as relates to dwellings in the area of that district.

(3) As soon as reasonably practicable after receiving a copy of a list under subsection (1)(b) above the regional or islands council shall deposit it at their principal office and take such steps as they think fit for giving notice of it.

(4) As soon as reasonably practicable after compiling a list the local assessor shall—
  (a) send to each council for which he has been appointed to act as local assessor a copy of the list compiled for that council's area; and
  (b) in the case of a regional council, send to each district council in the region a copy of so much of the list as relates to dwellings in the area of that district.

(5) As soon as reasonably practicable after receiving a copy of a list under subsection (4) above the regional or islands council shall deposit it at their principal office.

(6) The local assessor shall, as soon as is reasonably practicable after 1st April in each year, send a copy of the valuation list as in force on that date to the Keeper of the Records of Scotland for preservation by him.

DEFINITIONS
  "dwelling": s.72(2).
  "information": s.116(1).
  "local assessor": s.84(10).
  "valuation list": s.84(1).

GENERAL NOTE
  Prior to formal compilation of the valuation list, a number of stages must be gone through in order to allow public scrutiny of the draft list and corrections to be made. The local assessor is to provide to his authority copies of the list which he proposes to compile, at two stages. In

addition, for the regional authorities, another copy in regard to the dwellings in the area of the district council must be sent to the district council. Further provision is made for drawing the provisional list to the attention of the public.

Subs. (1)

At two stages in the process leading up to the formal compilation of the valuation list, the local assessor must send to the relevant regional or islands authority a copy of the proposed list. The first date is set as not later than September 1, 1992, and the second has to be within the period November 15–December 1. This will allow the authority to make comments.

Subs. (2)

At two stages in the process leading up to the formal compilation of the valuation list, the local assessor must send to the relevant district authority a copy of the proposed list in so far as it relates to dwellings within the area of that council. The first date is set as not later than September 1, 1992, and the second has to be within the period November 15–December 1. This will allow the authority to make comments.

Subs. (3)

Following receipt of the second proposed valuation list, publicity must be given to the list by the authority. The precise form of the publicity is left to the discretion of the authority, but a copy of the list must be deposited at the principal office of the authority for public scrutiny.

Subs. (4)

As soon as possible after April 1, 1993, when the list is formally "compiled", the local assessor must send a copy to the relevant regional or islands authority and, for the regional authorities, another copy in regard to the dwellings in the area of the district council must be sent to the district council. Again, this duty is qualified as being as soon as is "reasonably practicable".

Subs. (5)

When the final copy of the valuation list is received, the regional or islands authority is required to deposit it at its principal office. At this stage, there is no need for further publicity.

Subs. (6)

As soon as possible after April 1, 1993, when the list is formally "compiled", and in each subsequent year, the local assessor must send a copy of the list which is currently in force to the Keeper of the Records of Scotland, who will preserve it. Again, this duty is qualified as being as soon as is "reasonably practicable".

Valuation of dwellings

86.—(1) In order to enable him to compile a valuation list for his area under section 84 above, a local assessor shall, in accordance with the provisions of this Part, carry out a valuation of such of the dwellings in his area as he considers necessary or expedient for the purpose of determining which of the valuation bands mentioned in section 74(2) above applies to each dwelling in his area.

(2) The valuation shall be carried out by reference to 1st April 1991 and on such assumptions and in accordance with such principles as may be prescribed.

(3) Where it appears to a local assessor that, having regard to the assumptions and principles mentioned in subsection (2) above, and to any directions given under subsection (5) below, a dwelling falls clearly within a particular valuation band, he need not carry out an individual valuation of that dwelling.

(4) Subject to subsection (5) below, the local assessor shall carry out the valuation in the region or islands area for which he has been appointed as assessor.

(5) A local assessor shall comply with such directions as may be given in relation to the valuation by the Commissioners of Inland Revenue.

(6) The Commissioners of Inland Revenue may, for the purpose of preparing any directions under subsection (5) above, make such investigations and set up such facilities in Scotland as appear to them to be appropriate.

(7) A local assessor may appoint persons to assist him.

(8) A local assessor may disclose to a person appointed by him under subsection (7) above any information available to him or obtained by him in the exercise of the powers conferred by section 90 below.

(9) If any person to whom any information is disclosed by virtue of subsection (8) above uses or discloses the information, in whole or in part, otherwise than for the purposes of the valuation, he shall be guilty of an offence and liable—

(a) on conviction on indictment, to imprisonment for a term not exceeding two years or a fine or both; and

(b) on summary conviction, to imprisonment for a term not exceeding six months or a fine not exceeding the statutory maximum or both.

(10) A regional or islands council shall secure the provision of sufficient staff, accommodation and other resources (including sums for the payment of persons appointed by the local assessor to assist him) to enable the local assessor to carry out his functions.

(11) The Secretary of State may, with the consent of the Treasury, make grants of such amounts as he may, with such consent, determine to regional or islands councils towards such of their expenditure under this section as he considers to have been reasonably incurred.

DEFINITIONS
   "dwelling": s.72(2).
   "information": s.116(1).
   "local assessor": s.84(10).
   "valuation band": s.74(2) and (3).
   "valuation list": s.84(1).

GENERAL NOTE
   The initial legal authority for the valuation of domestic properties for council-tax purposes was provided by s.3 of the Local Government Finance and Valuation Act 1991. This section provides for the local assessor to undertake valuations for the purpose of assigning dwellings to valuation bands. The assessor is required to comply with any directions, in regard to the valuation, given by the Commissioners of Inland Revenue. The assessor is also empowered to appoint persons to assist in the work, and those persons may have disclosed to them any information obtained by the assessor under s.90, which would otherwise be subject to non-disclosure under the provisions of that section. Under this section see the Council Tax (Valuation of Dwellings) (Scotland) Regulations 1992 (S.I. 1992 No. 1329).

Subs. (1)
   The local assessor is empowered to carry out such valuations of dwellings as are necessary to assign valuation bands to each dwelling in the area.

Subs. (2)
   The value of a dwelling is to be taken to be that on April 1, 1991, based on market capital value. The Secretary of State is also empowered to prescribe further assumptions and principles for the valuation exercise. See the Council Tax (Valuation of Dwellings) (Scotland) Regulations 1992 (S.I. 1992 No. 1329).

Subs. (3)
   Individual valuation of property is not necessary where, having regard to the assumptions and principles laid down in the regulations and any directions given by the Commissioners of Inland Revenue, it appears to the assessor that the dwelling falls clearly within a particular valuation band. This process has been subject to much criticism as being too crude a valuation exercise.

Subs. (4)
   A somewhat redundant provision, this makes it clear that the local assessor is charged with the duty to carry out the valuation exercise for the area for which he has been appointed as assessor, subject to any directions given under the authority of subs. (5).

Subss. (5) and (6)
   The local assessor is charged with the duty of carrying out the valuation exercise for the area for which he has been appointed as assessor, subject to any directions in regard to the valuation,

given by the Commissioners of Inland Revenue. In order to allow the Commissioners to prepare such directions, subs. (6) gives them a wide discretion to set up facilities and undertake investigations in Scotland.

Subs. (7)

This makes it clear that the local assessor can appoint persons such as private-sector valuers to undertake the work. Given the scale of the task of valuing every dwelling, this was considered essential, although there was much criticism of the process in general.

Subs. (8)

The disclosure by the local assessor of certain information to any person appointed to carry out valuations is authorised by this subsection. He may disclose any information obtained under the authority of s.90. Such information would normally be subject to confidentiality, so in order to safeguard the interests of those about whom information is disclosed, subs. (9) prohibits its use for any purpose other than valuation.

Subs. (9)

In order to protect the interests of those about whom information is disclosed under subs. (8), it will be an offence to use or disclose further the information for any purpose other than valuation. The penalty for this offence is, on indictment, up to two years' imprisonment or a fine, or both. On summary conviction, the penalty is up to six months' imprisonment or a fine up to the statutory maximum, or both.

Subss. (10) and (11)

The regional or islands authority is placed under a duty to provide sufficient staff, accommodation and financial and other resources to allow the local assessor to carry out his functions. This was included to ensure that the authority could not frustrate the introduction of the new system and, in order to meet some or all of the additional costs, subs. (11) permits the Secretary of State to give a grant toward these costs, but only with the consent of the Treasury.

Alteration of lists

87.—(1) The Secretary of State may make regulations about the alteration by local assessors of valuation lists which have been compiled under this Part; and subsections (2) to (10) below shall apply for the purposes of this subsection.

(2) The regulations may include provision that where a local assessor intends to alter the list with a view to its being accurately maintained, he shall not alter it unless prescribed conditions (as to notice or otherwise) are fulfilled.

(3) The regulations may include provision that any valuation of a dwelling carried out in connection with a proposal for the alteration of the list shall be carried out in accordance with section 86(2) above.

(4) The regulations may include provision that no alteration shall be made of a valuation band shown in the list as applicable to any dwelling unless—
- (a) since the valuation band was first shown in the list as applicable to the dwelling—
  - (i) there has been a material increase in the value of the dwelling and it, or any part of it, has subsequently been sold; or
  - (ii) there has been a material reduction in the value of the dwelling,
  - and (in either case) prescribed conditions are fulfilled; or
- (b) the local assessor is satisfied that—
  - (i) a different valuation band should have been determined by him as applicable to the dwelling; or
  - (ii) the valuation band shown in the list is not that determined by him as so applicable; or
- (c) the assessor has, under Schedule 5 to this Act, added, amended or deleted an apportionment note relating to any lands and heritages included in the valuation roll; or
- (d) there has been a successful appeal under this Act against the valuation band shown in the list.

(5) The regulations may include provision—
(a) as to who (other than a local assessor) may make a proposal for the alteration of the list with a view to its being accurately maintained;
(b) as to the manner and circumstances in which a proposal may be made and the information to be included in a proposal;
(c) as to the period within which a proposal must be made;
(d) as to the procedure for and subsequent to the making of a proposal;
(e) as to the circumstances within which and the conditions upon which a proposal may be withdrawn; and
(f) requiring the local assessor to inform other prescribed persons of the proposal in a prescribed manner.

(6) The regulations may include provision that, where there is a disagreement between the local assessor and another person making a proposal for the alteration of a list—
(a) about the validity of the proposal; or
(b) about the accuracy of the list,
an appeal may be made to a valuation appeal committee.

(7) The regulations may include—
(a) provision as to the period for which or day from which an alteration of a list is to have effect (including provision that it is to have retrospective effect);
(b) provision requiring a list to be altered so as to indicate the effect (retrospective or otherwise) of the alteration;
(c) provision requiring the local assessor to inform prescribed persons of an alteration within a prescribed period;
(d) provision requiring the local assessor to keep for a prescribed period a record of the state of the list before the alteration was made.

(8) The regulations may include provision as to financial adjustments to be made as a result of alterations, including—
(a) provision requiring payments or repayments to be made; and
(b) provision as to the recovery (by deduction or otherwise) of sums due.

(9) The regulations may include provision that where—
(a) a local assessor has informed a regional or islands council of an alteration to a list; and
(b) a copy of the list has been deposited by that authority under section 85(5) above,
the authority must alter the copy accordingly.

(10) In this section—
"material increase", in relation to the value of a dwelling, means any increase which is caused (in whole or in part) by any building, engineering or other operation carried out in relation to the dwelling, whether or not constituting development for which planning permission is required;
"material reduction", in relation to the value of a dwelling, means any reduction which is caused (in whole or in part) by the demolition of any part of the dwelling, any change in the physical state of the dwelling's locality or any adaptation of the dwelling to make it suitable for use by a physically disabled person.

DEFINITIONS
"apportionment note": s.99(1).
"dwelling": s.72(2).
"local assessor": s.84(10).
"material increase": subs. (10).
"material reduction": subs. (10).
"prescribed": s.116(1).
"valuation appeal committee": s.99(1).
"valuation band": s.74(2) and (3).
"valuation list": s.84(1).
"valuation roll": s.1 of the Local Government (Scotland) Act 1975.

GENERAL NOTE

This section provides the Secretary of State with a wide power to make regulations regarding the amendment of the valuation lists. Indications of what the regulations may contain are given by a number of the subsections.

Subs. (1)

The Secretary of State is given a general power to make regulations concerning the alteration of valuation lists by local assessors, subject to the clarification and elaboration in the remainder of the section.

Subs. (2)

This makes clear that before a local assessor is able to alter a valuation list, any conditions in the regulations must be fulfilled. The scope of the conditions is not limited by the subsection, but may concern periods of notice.

Subs. (3)

As would be expected, the regulations should include provision for applying the same assumptions and principles of valuation as the original valuation exercise, as established by s.86(2).

Subs. (4)

This subsection was subject to amendment during the legislative process. The intention is that before an alteration can be made to the valuation band, shown as applicable to a particular dwelling, one of four factors must have changed from the time of the original compilation of the valuation list. The first of these, in para. (a), relates to extent of domestic use and the value of the dwelling; the second, in para. (b), to the opinion of the listing officer as to the value; the third, in para. (c), to the fact that the property has been changed in regard to its status as a part residential subject; and the fourth, in para. (d), that there has been a successful appeal. The lack of clarity in the drafting of the equivalent English provision, under s.24, relating to the relationship between these factors, is absent in regard to clearer drafting of this section.

The first factor, namely the extent of domestic use and the value of the dwelling, is in turn divided into four components, one of which must be present to satisfy the requirement. The first two are relatively straightforward and deal with an increase or reduction in the value of the property. Where the value has increased, the valuation band can be altered only where the dwelling has been sold. Where the value has decreased, that fact alone will not be sufficient to meet the requirement of para. (a). The reduction must have been due, in whole or in part by demolition of part of the dwelling, to some physical change in the locality of the property, or adaptation to meet the needs of the disabled. However, in regard to both components of this first factor, the Secretary of State may prescribe additional conditions which must be fulfilled.

The second factor is the opinion of the local assessor as to the value of the dwelling. It is envisaged that two different situations could occur, both of which appear to concern errors and would allow the valuation band to be changed. The first deals with a situation where the wrong valuation has been made, and the listing officer is of the opinion that a different valuation band should have been determined by him for the dwelling. The second appears to deal with the situation where a mistake occurs over the actual entry, and the valuation band shown in the list is not that actually determined by him at that time as applicable to the dwelling. It is open to interpretation whether that allows for a subsequent determination different from that shown in the list, but where that shown in the list was not initially incorrect.

The third factor is that there has been a change in relation to the status of the dwelling as part residential subjects, as regulated by Sched. 5. The fourth factor is that there has been an order of a valuation appeal committee or the Court of Session requiring the alteration to the valuation list to be made.

Subs. (5)

Matters concerning initiation and making of proposals for alteration, the relevant time periods and procedures for dealing with proposals, and publicity for and withdrawal of the proposals may be provided for by regulation. As with all regulations made under this Act, the regulations may contain such incidental, consequential and supplementary provisions as the Secretary of State or the Treasury think necessary or expedient.

Subs. (6)

This permits the regulations to provide that, where there is a disagreement between the local assessor and another person about the validity of a proposal to alter the list, or about the accuracy of the list, an appeal may be considered by a valuation appeal committee.

Subs. (7)
Where a list is to be altered, the regulations may contain provisions relating to the date or period from which the alteration is to have effect; the effect of the alteration to the list, including whether it is to operate retrospectively; requirements for the local assessor to inform any persons; and requirements as to the keeping of a record of the list prior to the alteration.

Subs. (8)
Where a list is to be altered, the regulations may contain provisions requiring payments or repayments to be made, and for the recovery of sums due.

Subs. (9)
This subsection allows for the relevant regional or islands authority to be required to alter its copy of the list upon notification of the change by the listing officer.

Subs. (10)
This provides additional definitions for this section, relating to subs. (4).

Compilation and maintenance of new lists

88.—(1) This section applies where the Secretary of State makes an order under subsection (3)(b) of section 74 above providing that, as regards financial years beginning on or after such date as is specified in the order, valuation bands so specified shall be substituted for those for the time being effective for the purposes of subsection (2) of that section.
(2) For the purpose of—
(a) requiring local assessors to compile, and then maintain, new valuation lists for those financial years; and
(b) facilitating the compilation and maintenance by the local assessors of those lists,
the provisions of this Part shall have effect with the modifications mentioned in subsection (3) below.
(3) The modifications are—
(a) for the date specified in section 84(6) and (7) above there shall be substituted the date specified in the order; and
(b) for the dates specified in sections 85(1) and 86(2) above there shall be substituted such dates as are specified in an order made by the Secretary of State under this subsection.

DEFINITIONS
"financial year": s.116(1).
"local assessor": s.84(10).
"valuation band": s.74(2) and (3).
"valuation list": s.84(1).

GENERAL NOTE
This section makes provision for the implementation of any decision of the Secretary of State, under s.74(3), to alter the valuation bands. Local assessors will be required to compile and maintain new valuation lists in accordance with the general provisions in relation to the lists, subject to certain modifications.

Subs. (1)
Where the Secretary of State makes an alteration to the valuation bands under s.74(3)(b), then the provisions of the remainder of this section shall have effect.

Subs. (2)
The provisions which apply to the original valuation list are also to apply to any amended lists, subject to the modifications introduced by subs. (3) of this section.

Subs. (3)
The modifications referred to in subs. (2) are the date on which the list was compiled, the date

by reference to which the valuations are to be treated as having been carried out, and the dates by which the local assessor must supply the billing authority with an advance copy of the new list.

Valuation lists: supplemental

Powers of entry

89.—(1) Subject to subsection (2) below, if a local assessor needs to value a property for the purpose of carrying out any functions conferred or imposed on him by or under this Part, he may enter on, survey and value the property.

(2) At least three clear days' notice in writing of the proposed exercise of the power must be given to the occupier; and there shall be disregarded for this purpose any day which is—

(a) a Saturday, a Sunday, Christmas Day or Good Friday; or

(b) a day which is a bank holiday under the Banking and Financial Dealings Act 1971 in Scotland.

(3) Any person who wilfully delays or obstructs a person in the exercise of a power under this section shall be guilty of an offence and liable on summary conviction to a fine not exceeding level 2 on the standard scale.

DEFINITIONS
"local assessor": s.84(10).

GENERAL NOTE
By this section, local assessors are entitled to enter upon property in order to carry out their functions in regard to the valuation of property for the purposes of compilation and maintenance of the valuation lists. A minimum period of notice before entry is prescribed, and the offence of obstructing the exercise of this power is created.

Subs. (1)
A local assessor may enter a dwelling in order to survey and value it, provided that the condition in subs. (2) is met. The wording of this section means that the valuation officer has no right to enter property for the purpose of valuing another property.

Subs. (2)
The first condition to be met before the valuation officer may enter a property for the purpose of valuing that property is that adequate notice in writing must be given. This is defined as three clear days' notice, excluding Saturday or Sunday, Christmas Day or Good Friday, and any other bank holiday. The period of notice was increased from a simple 24 hours' notice as proposed in the original Bill.

Subs. (3)
This section makes it an offence to delay or obstruct deliberately the exercise of the power of entry. On summary conviction the penalty shall not exceed level 2 on the standard scale.

Information about properties

90.—(1) This section makes provision in relation to the carrying out by the local assessor of any functions conferred or imposed on him by or under this Part.

(2) The local assessor shall have access to and the use of any information available to—

(a) the assessor for the purposes of the Valuation Acts;

(b) the community charges registration officer; or

(c) the electoral registration officer,

for his area.

(3) In any case where—

(a) a notice is served by a local assessor on a regional, islands or district council, a housing body or on any other person prescribed for the purposes of this section; and

(b) the notice requests the supply of information of a description specified in the notice; and

(c) the information relates to property and is information which the local assessor reasonably believes will assist him in carrying out any of his functions under this Part,

the council or other person shall supply the information requested, and shall do so in such form and manner and at such time as the local assessor specifies in the notice.

(4) For the purpose of carrying out any of his functions under this Part, a local assessor may serve on a person who is or has been an owner or occupier of any dwelling in his area a notice—

(a) requesting him to supply to the local assessor information which is of a description specified in the notice; and

(b) stating that the local assessor believes the information requested will assist him in carrying out those functions.

(5) A person on whom a notice is served under subsection (4) above shall supply the information requested if it is in his possession or control, and shall do so in such form and manner as is specified in the notice and within the period of 21 days beginning with the day on which the notice is served.

(6) If a person on whom a notice has been served under subsection (4) above fails to comply with subsection (5) above, he shall be guilty of an offence and liable on summary conviction to a fine not exceeding level 2 on the standard scale.

(7) If, in supplying information in purported compliance with subsection (5) above, a person on whom a notice has been served under subsection (4) above—

(a) makes a statement which he knows to be false in a material particular; or

(b) recklessly makes a statement which is false in a material particular,

he shall be guilty of an offence and liable on summary conviction to imprisonment for a term not exceeding 3 months or a fine not exceeding level 3 on the standard scale or both.

(8) If in the course of the exercise of their functions any information comes to the notice of a levying authority which they consider would assist the local assessor in carrying out any of his functions under this Part, they shall give him that information.

(9) It shall be a defence for a person charged with an offence under subsection (6) above to prove that he had a reasonable excuse for acting as he did.

DEFINITIONS
"community charges registration officer": s.26(1); s.12 of the 1987 Act.
"dwelling": s.72(2).
"housing body": s.99(1).
"information": s.116(1).
"levying authority": s.99(1).
"local assessor": s.84(10).
"Valuation Acts": s.99(1).

GENERAL NOTE
This section permits a local assessor to require information about properties to be made available from a number of sources. Duties are placed on levying authorities and other persons to comply with the terms of the notice. It also provides for associated offences and makes clear the breadth of the ability of the local assessor to take into account information received.

Subs. (1)
This somewhat redundant subsection simply establishes that the remainder of the section gives further powers to the local assessor in relation to his functions under this Act.

Subs. (2)

This subsection is intended to ensure that the local assessor is not to be limited unduly in the information which may be taken into account in exercising his functions. Thus it is provided that he may take into account not merely information obtained under the provisions of this Act, but also any other information available under other enactments relating to valuation, community charges or electoral registration. This is a narrower formulation than the equivalent provision relating to England and Wales, under s.27(7), where the listing officer or Commissioners of Inland Revenue are empowered to take into account other information, whatever its source.

Subs. (3)

This subsection deals with information sought by the local assessor from "official" sources. Information may be obtained by means of a notice which must conform to the requirements of this subsection. The notice may be served on a regional, district or islands authority, a housing body, or any other person prescribed in regulations made for the purposes of this section. The information must relate to property, but this is likely to be interpreted to include information about persons in that property. There is no attempt in the section to specify further the type of information, but there is provided a limitation that the local assessor must reasonably believe that the information will assist in carrying out his functions. The notice must also specify the information sought, and the manner, form and timing of the reply. Where a notice is served which conforms to these requirements, then it is the duty of those on whom the notice is served to supply the information in such manner, form and time as is specified in the notice.

Subs. (4)

This subsection deals with information sought by the local assessor from "unofficial" sources. Information may be obtained by means of a notice which must conform to the requirements of this subsection. The notice may be served on an owner or occupier of any dwelling. The information required must be specified in the notice. There is no attempt in the section to specify further the type of information, but there is provided a limitation that the local assessor must state in the notice that he believes that the information will assist in carrying out his functions.

Subs. (5)

Where a notice is served under subs. (4), the notice must also specify the manner and form of the reply. Where a notice is served which conforms to these requirements, it is the duty of those on whom the notice is served to supply the information in the manner and form requested within 21 days from the date of service of the notice. Subsection (6) below makes it an offence to fail to comply with this requirement, but subs. (9) provides the defence of reasonable excuse, such as that the information was not within the recipient's possession or control.

Subs. (6)

It is an offence to fail to comply with the requirement imposed by subs. (5) to supply the information requested by a notice served under subs. (4) in the manner and form requested within 21 days from the date of service of the notice. On summary conviction the maximum fine shall not exceed level 2 on the standard scale. There is provided the defence of "reasonable excuse", and in this regard subs. (5) provides a defence that the information was not within the recipient's possession or control.

Subs. (7)

Where the recipient does provide information in response to a notice served under subs. (4), but thereby either knowingly or recklessly makes a statement which is false, then he is guilty of an offence. On summary conviction for this offence the maximum punishment is a term of imprisonment not exceeding three months, a fine not exceeding level 3 on the standard scale, or both.

Subs. (8)

This subsection places a further duty upon the levying authority to provide information to the local assessor. For the duty to operate, the following two criteria must be satisfied. First, the information must have been obtained in the exercise of the functions of the authority. Secondly, the authority must be of the opinion that the information would assist the local assessor in carrying out his functions.

Subs. (9)

This provides the defence of reasonable excuse in regard to the offence under subs. (6). In this regard subs. (5) provides a defence that the information was not within the recipient's possession or control.

Information about lists

91.—(1) A person may require a local assessor to give him access to such information as will enable him to establish what is the state of a list, or has been its state at any time since it came into force, if—

(a) the local assessor is maintaining the list; and

(b) the list is in force or has been in force at any time in the preceding 5 years.

(2) A person may require a levying authority to give him access to such information as will enable him to establish what is the state of a copy of a list, or has been its state at any time since it was deposited, if—

(a) the authority has deposited the copy under section 85(5) above; and

(b) the list is in force or has been in force at any time in the preceding 5 years.

(3) A person may require a levying authority to give him access to such information as will enable him to establish what is the state of a copy of a proposed list if—

(a) the authority has deposited the copy under section 85(3) above; and

(b) the list itself is not yet in force.

(4) A requirement under subsection (1), (2) or (3) above must be complied with at a reasonable time and place and without payment being sought; but the information may be in documentary or other form, as the person or authority of whom the requirement is made thinks fit.

(5) Where access is given under this section to information in documentary form the person to whom access is given may—

(a) make copies of (or of extracts from) the document;

(b) require a person having custody of the document to supply to him a photographic copy of (or of extracts from) the document.

(6) Where access is given under this section to information in a form which is not documentary the person to whom access is given may—

(a) make transcripts of (or of extracts from) the information;

(b) require a person having control of access to the information to supply to him a copy in documentary form of (or of extracts from) the information.

(7) If a reasonable charge is required for a facility under subsection (5) or (6) above, the subsection concerned shall not apply unless the person seeking to avail himself of the facility pays the charge.

(8) If a person having custody of a document containing, or having control of access to, information access to which is sought under this section—

(a) intentionally obstructs a person in exercising a right under subsection (1), (2), (3), (5)(a) or (6)(a) above; or

(b) refuses to comply with a requirement under subsection (5)(b) or (6)(b) above,

he shall be guilty of an offence and liable on summary conviction to a fine not exceeding level 2 on the standard scale.

(9) It shall be a defence for a person charged with an offence under subsection (8) above to prove that he had a reasonable excuse for acting as he did.

DEFINITIONS

"information": s.116(1).

"levying authority": s.99(1).

"local assessor": s.84(10).

"valuation list": s.84(1).

GENERAL NOTE

The aim of this section is to ensure that public access to the information contained in the valuation lists is protected. Information about the present and historic state of the list must be made available at reasonable times and free of charge, although relevant photocopies may be charged for. Obstruction of rights of access, or failure to comply with the requirements of this section, is made an offence.

Subs. (1)
Where the local assessor is maintaining a valuation list which is in force, or has been at any time in the previous five years, then any person may require the assessor to give access to such information as will enable him to establish the state of the list, either currently or at any time since it came into force. This is subject to the limitation that the duty to maintain the information on a list falls five years after the list ceases to be in force.

Subs. (2)
Where the levying authority has deposited a copy of a compiled list at its principal office, under s.85(5) of this Act, and the list is in force, or has been at any time in the previous five years, then any person may require the levying authority to give access to such information as will enable him to establish the state of the copy of the list, either currently or at any time since it was deposited.

Subs. (3)
Where the levying authority has deposited at its principal office, under s.85(3) of this Act, a copy of a list which the local assessor proposes to compile, and the list is not in force, then any person may require the levying authority to give access to such information as will enable him to establish the state of the copy of the proposed list. This will allow the public to inspect the proposed list when issued between November 15 and December 1, 1992.

Subs. (4)
The requirement to allow access under subss. (1), (2) and (3) operates only at a reasonable time and place, and the requirement may be met by making available the information in whatever form the person on whom the requirement is placed thinks fit. The information may therefore be in documentary or some other form, such as a computer database. No charge may be made for such access.

Subs. (5)
Where the information is provided in documentary form, then the person seeking the information is entitled to copy all or some of the document and the local assessor or levying authority may be required by that person to supply a photocopy. In the latter event, the authority may make a reasonable charge under the authority of subs. (7).

Subs. (6)
Where the information is not provided in documentary form, the person seeking the information is entitled to make transcripts of all or some of the document and the person having control of access to the information may be required by that person to supply a documentary copy of all or part of the information. In the latter event, the authority may make a reasonable charge under the authority of subs. (7).

Subs. (7)
This permits the relevant authority to make a charge for the supply of photocopies or documents under subss. (5) and (6). Indeed, if a charge is demanded and not paid, then the right of the person to invoke the relevant subsection is taken away.

Subss. (8) and (9)
Where any person having control of information, whether documentary or otherwise, intentionally obstructs the exercise of a right of access to information, or the making of copies of transcripts, or fails to comply with a request for a photocopy or documentary copy, then he shall be guilty of an offence and liable on summary conviction to a fine not exceeding level 2 on the standard scale. The defence of "reasonable excuse" is provided.

Information about proposals and appeals

92.—(1) A person may, at a reasonable time and without making payment, inspect any proposal made or notice of appeal given under regulations made under section 87 above, if made or given as regards a list which is in force when inspection is sought or has been in force at any time in the preceding five years.
(2) A person may—

(a) make copies of (or of extracts from) a document mentioned in sub-section (1) above; or

(b) require a person having custody of such a document to supply to him a photographic copy of (or of extracts from) the document.

(3) If a reasonable charge is required for a facility under subsection (2) above, that subsection shall not apply unless the person seeking to avail himself of the facility pays the charge.

(4) If a person having custody of a document mentioned in subsection (1) above—

(a) intentionally obstructs a person in exercising a right under subsection (1) or (2)(a) above; or

(b) refuses to supply a copy to a person entitled to it under subsection (2)(b) above,

he shall be guilty of an offence and liable on summary conviction to a fine not exceeding level 2 on the standard scale.

(5) It shall be a defence for a person charged with an offence under subsection (4) above to prove that he had a reasonable excuse for acting as he did.

DEFINITIONS
"valuation list": s.84(1).

GENERAL NOTE
The aim of this section is to ensure that protection is given to public access to any proposal made to alter a valuation list or to a notice of appeal given under any regulations made in relation to s.87. Information about such a proposal or appeal, in relation to a list which is current or has been in force at any time during the previous five years, must be made available at reasonable times and free of charge, although relevant photocopies may be charged for. Obstruction of this right of access, or failure to comply with the requirements to supply a copy, is made an offence.

Subs. (1)
Access must be granted to any person wishing to inspect any proposal made to alter a valuation list, or notice of appeal given under any regulations made in relation to s.87. Information about such a proposal or appeal in relation to a list which is either current or has been in force at any time during the previous five years must be made available at reasonable times and free of charge.

Subs. (2)
The person seeking the information is entitled to copy all or some of the relevant document and the person having custody of such a document may be required by that person to supply a photocopy of all or part of the document. In the latter event, a reasonable charge may be made under the authority of subs. (3).

Subs. (3)
This permits a charge to be made for the supply of photocopies or documents under subs. (2). Indeed, if a charge is demanded and not paid, the right of the person to invoke the right of inspection is taken away.

Subss. (4) and (5)
Where any person having custody of a document relevant to the right of inspection under subs. (1) intentionally obstructs the exercise of a right of access to information, or the making of copies of transcripts, or fails to comply with a request for a photocopy or documentary copy, then he shall be guilty of an offence and liable on summary conviction to a fine not exceeding level 2 on the standard scale. The defence of "reasonable excuse" is provided.

Setting of the tax

Setting of council tax

93.—(1) In respect of the financial year 1993–94 and each subsequent financial year, a local authority shall—

(a) set an amount of regional, islands or district council tax, as appropriate, to be paid in respect of a chargeable dwelling in their area listed in valuation band D (whether or not there is such a dwelling in their area) as specified in section 74(2) above;

(b) determine the amount of council tax to be paid in respect of a chargeable dwelling in each of the other valuation bands specified in that section in accordance with the proportion mentioned in subsection (1) of that section,

and references in this Part to the setting of a council tax or of an amount of council tax shall be construed as references to the setting of the amount mentioned in paragraph (a) above.

(2) A local authority shall set its council tax before 11th March in the financial year preceding that for which it is set but it is not invalid merely because it is set on or after that date.

(3) The amounts mentioned in paragraphs (a) and (b) of subsection (1) above shall be such as will provide sufficient money to meet such part of the total estimated expenses to be incurred by that authority during the financial year in respect of which the amount is set as falls to be met out of their council tax, together with such additional sum as is, in their opinion, required—

(a) to cover expenses previously incurred;

(b) to meet contingencies;

(c) to meet any expenses which may fall to be met before the money to be received in respect of their council tax for the next following financial year will become available.

(4) In calculating, for the purposes of subsection (3) above, such part of the total estimated expenses to be incurred by a local authority as falls to be met out of council tax, account shall be taken of any means by which those expenses may otherwise be met or provided for.

DEFINITIONS
"amount of council tax": subs. (1).
"council tax": s.99(1).
"district council tax": s.70(1).
"financial year": s.116(1).
"islands council tax": s.70(1).
"local authority": s.99(1).
"regional council tax": s.70(1).
"valuation band": s.74(2) and (3).

GENERAL NOTE
This section imposes a duty on the relevant local authorities, from the financial year 1993–94 onwards, to set an amount for its council tax for a chargeable dwelling in each valuation band. It is a requirement that the amounts must be sufficient to meet four items: first, the expenses of the authority which are required to be met from council tax; secondly, any deficits; thirdly, sums to meet contingencies; and fourthly, other expenses which fall to be met before the revenue from the council tax for the following financial year will be received.

Subs. (1)
A duty is placed on the relevant local authorities, from the financial year 1993–94 onwards, to set an amount for their regional, district or islands council tax as appropriate. This is to be done by first setting an amount for a chargeable dwelling in band D, under s.74(2), whether or not any dwellings in the areas have been placed in that valuation band. Thereafter the authority must determine the amount for each valuation band in accordance with the proportions prescribed in that subsection.

Subs. (2)
This sets the time limit applicable to setting the amount of the council tax. The authority is required to set the amounts of its council tax, applicable for any financial year, before March 11 in the preceding financial year. This duty is, however, directory only and failure to comply will not result in the invalidity of an amount set on or after that date. This therefore avoids the

problem which had arisen in relation to the old system of domestic rates where it was argued that the failure to set the rate within the time limit made any subsequent determination void and of no legal effect, thus depriving the authority of the right to set the rate.

Subs. (3)
It is a requirement that the amounts of council tax set under subs. (1) must be sufficient to meet four items. First, the expenses of the authority which are required to be met from council tax, and not met from other sources. Secondly, such amounts as in its opinion are required to meet any expenses previously incurred or deficits. Thirdly, such amounts as in its opinion are required to meet any contingencies. Fourthly, such amounts as in its opinion are required to meet any other expenses which fall to be met before the revenue from the council tax for the following financial year will be received.

Subs. (4)
This makes it clear that the authority in determining the expenses of the authority which are required to be met from council tax, under subs. (3), must take account of expenses which may be met from other sources.

Substituted and reduced settings

94.—(1) Subject to subsection (3) below, a local authority may set, in substitution for an amount of council tax already set or deemed to have been set, a lesser amount of council tax for the same financial year.

(2) Schedule 7 to this Act has effect for the purpose of making provision as to the reduction of council tax where the Secretary of State is satisfied, in accordance with that Schedule, that the total estimated expenses mentioned in section 93(3) above of a local authority are excessive or that an increase in those expenses is excessive.

(3) A local authority may not set a substitute amount of council tax during the period between the approval by the House of Commons of a report in respect of that authority made by the Secretary of State under paragraph 1 of that Schedule and the setting or deemed setting of a reduced amount of council tax under paragraph 3 of that Schedule.

(4) Section 93(2) above shall not apply for the purposes of this section.

(5) A local authority who, in respect of any financial year, set (or are deemed to have set) a substituted or reduced council tax shall neither wholly nor partially offset the difference between—
  (a) the amount produced by that substituted or reduced setting; and
  (b) the amount which would have been produced had they not substituted or reduced their setting,
with sums advanced from their loans fund established under Schedule 3 to the 1975 Act:
  Provided that such offsetting may nevertheless be permitted by the Secretary of State in any case on such terms and conditions as he considers appropriate.

(6) If the Secretary of State is of the opinion that subsection (5) above, or any term or condition imposed under the proviso thereto, has been contravened, the local authority shall, on such opinion being intimated to them, reimburse their loans fund forthwith or within such time as the Secretary of State may allow.

(7) Anything paid by reference to one setting of council tax shall be treated as paid by reference to a substitute setting under subsection (1) above or a reduced setting or deemed setting by virtue of paragraph 3 of Schedule 7 to this Act.

(8) Where a person has paid by reference to one setting of council tax more than is due under a substituted or reduced setting—
  (a) the balance shall be repaid to the person if he so requires;
  (b) in any other case the balance shall (as the levying authority determine) either be repaid to the person or be credited against any

subsequent liability of the person to pay in respect of any council tax due to the authority.

(9) Where—

(a) a substitute amount of council tax has been set under subsection (1) above; or

(b) a reduced amount of council tax has been set or been deemed to have been set under paragraph 3 of that Schedule,

the regional council shall levy and collect that substituted or reduced amount in place of the previous amount of council tax and may recover from the district council any administrative expenses incurred in so doing in relation to a substituted or reduced amount of district council tax.

DEFINITIONS

"amount of council tax": subs. (1).

"council tax": s.99(1).

"financial year": s.116(1).

"local authority": s.99(1).

GENERAL NOTE

This provides the framework within which "capping" of an authority's council tax takes place. It re-enacts s.2 of the 1987 Act, as amended by s.2 of the Local Government Finance and Valuation Act 1991, by providing that the Secretary of State may lay before the House of Commons a report proposing the reduction of an authority's council tax where he considers that the total estimated expenditure of that authority is excessive, or where there is an excessive increase over the expenditure for the previous financial year.

Subs. (1)

Subject to the restriction on timing imposed by subs. (3), a local authority is hereby permitted to set a substituted amount of council tax for that already set for the same financial year. This discretion must be seen in the light of subs. (2), which brings into effect Sched. 7, which has the effect of requiring the authority to reduce its council tax after a report from the Secretary of State is confirmed by the House of Commons. See further the note to Sched. 7.

Subs. (2)

This brings into effect Sched. 7, which has the effect of requiring the authority to reduce its council tax after a report from the Secretary of State is confirmed by the House of Commons. The Secretary of State may make a proposal for the reduction of the council tax of the authority where he considers that the total estimated expenditure of that authority is excessive, or where there is an excessive increase over the expenditure for the previous financial year. See further the note to Sched. 7.

Subs. (3)

The local authority may not make a substituted amount of council tax in the period between the House of Commons approving the report of the Secretary of State and the time at which the authority is required to comply with that report under para. 3 of Sched. 7. This is designed to stop public "posturing" and the issue of too many amounts of council tax.

Subs. (4)

Not unrealistically, although the other requirements of s.93 would apply to the setting of the substituted or reduced amounts of council tax, the requirement in s.93(2) that this must be done before March 11 in the preceding financial year does not apply.

Subs. (5)

This prohibits a local authority from using money from its loans fund to meet the difference from the revenue which would have been raised by the original amounts of council tax and that which will result from the revised amounts of council tax. However, a residual discretion is given to the Secretary of State to allow this on whatever terms he thinks appropriate. This continues the very wide discretion given to the Secretary of State in this field.

Subs. (6)

Where there has, in the opinion of the Secretary of State, been a breach of subs. (5) then he may order the reimbursement of the loans fund. The perceived breach may be either in terms of the offsetting of revenue reduction from the loans fund, or the breach of a condition attached to the consent issued by the Secretary of State.

Subs. (7)

Where sums have been paid to the authority in regard to the original amount of council tax set, then those sums are to be treated as paid toward the revised amount. Where the sum already paid is greater than that demanded by the revised amount, subs. (8) operates.

Subs. (8)

Where the sum already paid in regard to the original amount of council tax set is greater than that demanded by the revised amount, then if the taxpayer requests this, the levying authority is under a duty to repay the balance. If there is no such request from the taxpayer, then the discretion is given to the levying authority to either repay the sum or credit it to any subsequent liability of the taxpayer for the next financial year.

Subs. (9)

Where a district council has set a revised district council tax, it is the regional authority which will levy and collect the new amounts, in accordance with s.97. However, the regional authority may recover the administrative costs of this revised council tax collection from the district council.

District council tax: setting and collection

95.—(1) In relation to each financial year, a regional council shall estimate the amount which would be produced by each of the district council taxes for that year in each district in their region as that amount falls to be ascertained in pursuance of regulations made under subsection (6) below.

(2) For the purpose of making the estimate mentioned in subsection (1) above, the regional council shall assume that in respect of the financial year concerned both the regional council and the district council set £1, or such other amount as may be prescribed, as the amount mentioned in section 93(1)(a) above.

(3) The regional council shall, before such date as may be prescribed in relation to each financial year, notify the council of each district in their region of the estimate made under subsection (1) above in relation to that district for that financial year.

(4) In respect of the financial year 1993–94 and each subsequent financial year, every district council shall, within two days of the date mentioned in section 93(2) above, intimate to the regional council within whose region their district falls—

(a) the amount of district council tax they have set; and

(b) such further information with respect to the district council tax as may reasonably be needed by the regional council for the purpose of issuing notices in accordance with regulations made under paragraph 2 of Schedule 2 to this Act.

(5) A regional council shall be liable to pay to the council of each district in their region, in respect of the district council tax for any financial year, the amount produced in the district by that tax; and shall, in accordance with such arrangements as may be prescribed, make payments to the district council on account of that liability.

(6) For the purposes of subsection (5) above, the amount produced in a district by the district council tax for a financial year shall, subject to subsection (7) below, be ascertained after the end of that year in such manner as may be prescribed, and—

(a) if that amount exceeds the aggregate amount of payments on account made under subsection (5) above, the balance shall be paid by the regional council to the district council; and

(b) if that amount is less than the said aggregate amount, the balance shall be set off against payments on account under subsection (5) above in respect of the next following financial year.

(7) The Secretary of State may prescribe what deductions are to be made in estimating and ascertaining the amount produced by each of the regional and district council taxes levied by a regional council.

(8) There shall be taken into account, in the calculation of the amount which a regional council are liable, under subsection (5) above, to pay to a district council, the amount of any council tax and council water charge which has been collected by the district council under paragraph 19 of Schedule 2 to this Act and is due but has not been paid to the regional council.

(9) The amount which a regional council are liable to pay under subsection (5) above to a district council shall, if not paid by such date as may be prescribed, attract interest at such rate as may be prescribed.

DEFINITIONS

"amount of council tax": subs. (1).
"council tax": s.99(1).
"council water charge": s.99(1).
"district council tax": s.70(1).
"financial year": s.116(1).
"information": s.116(1).
"prescribed": s.116(1).

GENERAL NOTE

The regional authority, in the light of the valuations of the local assessor, must estimate the product for each district of a £1 council tax. This will then allow the district council to set the amounts of its council tax for each valuation band, which must in turn be notified to the regional authority which becomes responsible for paying to the district council the amount produced by the district council tax.

Subss. (1) and (2)

The regional authority is placed under a duty, in regard to each financial year, to estimate the product for each district of its district council tax, on the assumption that a council tax of £1 is set for dwellings in valuation band D.

Subs. (3)

The appropriate calculation made under subs. (1) must be communicated to the relevant district council by a date to be prescribed.

Subs. (4)

Having set its council tax by March 11 in the preceding financial year, the district council is then under a duty to communicate this within two days of that date to the regional council. This must be accompanied by such other information as is required by the regional council for the purposes of issuing notices under Sched. 2 to this Act.

Subs. (5)

This establishes the general duty of the regional council to pay to the district council the amount produced by the district council tax. The payment of this amount must be made in accordance with regulations which may be made to deal with payments on account. The general duty is, however, modified by subss. (6)–(9).

Subs. (6)

At the end of any financial year, the final amount raised in relation to the district council tax shall be calculated in accordance with regulations to be made under this section. If the amount of the aggregate payments on account to the district council is less than the final sum due, then the regional council must pay the balance to the district council. If, however, the amount of the aggregate payments on account to the district council exceeds the final sum due, then the balance shall be set off against payments to be made in relation to the following financial year.

Subs. (7)

Power is given to the Secretary of State to prescribe the deductions made in ascertaining the amount produced by the regional and district council taxes. This will accommodate, among other items, the allocation of the administrative costs of collection.

Subs. (8)

In calculating the amount which a regional council is liable to pay to a district council under subs. (5), account must be taken of any sums collected by the district council in relation to council tax or council water charge. Such sums may be collected under arrangements with the regional council, under para. 17 of Sched. 2 to this Act, by virtue of the district council's being a housing body.

Subs. (9)
Any overdue payments from the regional to the district council attract interest at a prescribed rate.

Information

96.—(1) Within 21 days after setting a council tax, a local authority shall publish in at least one newspaper circulating in their area a notice of—
(a) the provision of this Act under which the council tax has been set; and
(b) the amounts payable in respect of chargeable dwellings in each valuation band.
(2) Failure to comply with subsection (1) above does not make the setting of an amount invalid.

DEFINITIONS
"amount of council tax": subs. (1).
"chargeable dwelling": s.72(6).
"council tax": s.99(1).
"local authority": s.99(1).
"valuation band": s.74(2) and (3).

GENERAL NOTE
This section imposes duties on authorities to supply or publish information in relation to the council tax. The local authority, having set an amount of council tax for each category of dwellings in its area, must then, within 21 days from the date of setting the amounts, publicise the amounts by means of a notice in a newspaper circulating in the authority's area. It must also publicise whether the tax has been set as an original or substitute council tax. As is made clear in subs. (2), this duty is directory only and does not make invalid the setting of the council tax.

Levying and collection of the tax

Levying and collection of council tax

97.—(1) An islands authority shall levy and collect the islands council tax set by them in respect of their area.
(2) A regional authority shall levy and collect—
(a) the regional council tax set by them in respect of their area; and
(b) the district council tax set by each district in their area.
(3) Schedule 2 to this Act (which contains provisions about administration, including collection) shall have effect.
(4) Schedule 3 to this Act (which contains provisions about civil penalties) shall have effect.
(5) Schedule 8 to this Act (which contains provisions about the recovery of sums due, including sums due as penalties) shall have effect.

DEFINITIONS
"district council tax": s.70(1).
"islands council tax": s.70(1).
"regional council tax": s.70(1).

GENERAL NOTE
This section establishes that the council tax shall be collected by the island authority for the islands council tax, and by the regional authority from the regional and district council taxes, for their respective areas. In addition, Scheds. 2, 3 and 8 are brought into effect by this section. For an explanation of these schedules see the notes to these.

Miscellaneous and supplemental

Information required by Secretary of State

98.—(1) Subsection (2) below applies where—

(a) the Secretary of State serves a notice on a levying authority requiring them to supply to the Secretary of State information specified in the notice;

(b) the information is in the possession or control of the authority and was obtained by them for the purpose of carrying out their functions under this Act; and

(c) the information is not personal information.

(2) The authority shall supply the information required, and shall do so in such form and manner and at such time as the Secretary of State specifies in the notice.

(3) Personal information is information which relates to an individual (living or dead) who can be identified from that information or from that and other information supplied by the authority; and personal information includes any expression of opinion about the individual and any indication of the intentions of any person in respect of the individual.

DEFINITIONS
"information": s.116(1).
"levying authority": s.99(1).
"personal information": subs. (3).

GENERAL NOTE
Under this section, the Secretary of State may obtain information from the levying authority. The information is not restricted to the definition in s.116(1), namely accounts, estimates and returns, but may be such as is specified in a notice to the authority from the Secretary of State. However, it must be within the possession or control of the authority and have been obtained in the course of carrying out any of its functions under this Act. The Secretary of State may not obtain personal information as defined by subs. (3).

Interpretation of Part II

99.—(1) In this Part and in sections 107 to 112 below, unless the context otherwise requires—

"the 1947 Act" means the Local Government (Scotland) Act 1947;
"the 1956 Act" means the Valuation and Rating (Scotland) Act 1956;
"the 1968 Act" means the Sewerage (Scotland) Act 1968;
"the 1973 Act" means the Local Government (Scotland) Act 1973;
"the 1975 Act" means the Local Government (Scotland) Act 1975;
"the 1980 Act" means the Water (Scotland) Act 1980;
"the Valuation Acts" means the Lands Valuation (Scotland) Act 1854, the Acts amending that Act, and any other enactment relating to valuation;
"apportionment note" has the meaning assigned to it in paragraph 1 of Schedule 5 to this Act;
"council tax" shall be construed in accordance with the provisions of section 70(1) above;
"council water charge" shall be construed in accordance with the provisions of paragraph 6 of Schedule 11 to this Act;
"levying authority" means a regional or islands council;
"local authority", except in Schedule 11, means a regional, islands or district council;
"housing body" means—
     (a) a district council;
     (b) a development corporation (within the meaning of the New Towns (Scotland) Act 1968); or
     (c) Scottish Homes;
"part residential subjects" means lands and heritages which are used partly as the sole or main residence of any person, other than—
     (a) dwellings (except the residential part of part residential subjects);

     (b) such other class or classes of lands and heritages as may be prescribed;

"public sewage treatment works" has the meaning assigned to it in section 59(1) of the 1968 Act;

"public sewer" has the meaning assigned to it in section 59(1) of the 1968 Act;

"rateable value" shall be construed in accordance with the provisions of section 6 of the 1956 Act;

"resident", in relation to any dwelling, means an individual who has attained the age of 18 years and has his sole or main residence in the dwelling; and cognate expressions shall be construed accordingly;

"valuation appeal committee" means a valuation appeal committee established under section 4 of the 1975 Act;

"water authority" has the meaning assigned to it in section 3 of the 1980 Act.

(2) In this Part and sections 107 to 112 below and in any other enactment, whether passed or made before or after the passing of this Act, and unless the context otherwise requires—

    (a) the word "rate" shall mean—
        (i) the non-domestic rate;
        (ii) the non-domestic water rate; and
        (iii) the non-domestic sewerage rate;
    (b) the expression "non-domestic rate" shall be construed in accordance with the provisions of section 37 of the 1975 Act;
    (c) the expression "non-domestic water rate" shall be construed in accordance with the provisions of section 40 of the 1980 Act; and
    (d) the expression "non-domestic sewerage rate" shall be construed in accordance with the provisions of paragraph 19 of Schedule 11 to this Act,

and cognate expressions shall be construed accordingly.

(3) In this Part—

    (a) any reference to dwellings listed in a particular valuation band shall be construed in accordance with section 74(5) above; and
    (b) any reference to an amount payable in respect of council tax for any financial year includes a reference to an amount payable in respect of council tax for any period falling within that year.

PART III

COMMUNITY CHARGES

Abolition of community charges

100.—(1) No person shall be subject to a community charge in respect of any day falling after 31st March 1993.

(2) In this section "community charge" means—

    (a) in relation to England and Wales, any community charge provided for by the 1988 Act;
    (b) in relation to Scotland, any community charge or community water charge provided for by the 1987 Act.

DEFINITIONS
   "community charge": subs. (2).

GENERAL NOTE
   For England, Wales and Scotland, this section abolishes the community charge from March

31, 1993 in so far as no liability can be incurred from that date. However, that does not affect liability for previous years for which the collection and enforcement provisions remain.

Transitory exemption for school leavers

101.—(1) After paragraph 5 of Schedule 1 to the 1988 Act (personal community charge: exemption) there shall be inserted the following paragraph—

"School leavers

5A. A person is an exempt individual on a particular day if—
(a) he is aged under 20 on the day,
(b) the day falls within the period of 6 months beginning with 1 May 1992,
(c) immediately before that date he was undertaking a qualifying course of education, and
(d) the course was not undertaken in consequence of an office or employment held by him."

(2) After sub-paragraph (1) of paragraph 6A of Schedule 1A to the 1987 Act (personal community charge: exemption) there shall be inserted the following sub-paragraph—

"(1A) If such a person as is mentioned in sub-paragraph (1) above ceases to undertake such a course of education on or after 30th April 1992, he shall continue to be exempt until the start of the earlier of the following days—
(a) 1st November 1992,
(b) his twentieth birthday."

DEFINITIONS
"qualifying course of education": s.30 of the 1988 Act, as amended by s.139 of and Sched. 5 to the Local Government and Housing Act 1989.

GENERAL NOTE
This amendment to the original Bill granted a concession in relation to liability for students, by extending the period for exemption in relation to school-leavers and students.

Transitory enforcement provisions for England and Wales

102.—(1) Schedule 4 to the 1988 Act (community charges: enforcement) shall be amended as follows.

(2) In paragraph 7 (distress), after sub-paragraph (3) there shall be inserted the following sub-paragraph—
"(3A) The regulations may include provision that—
(a) no person shall make a distress unless he is an officer of the authority concerned, or he is a person of a prescribed description and any prescribed conditions are fulfilled;
(b) no person making a distress shall seize goods of a prescribed description."

(3) In paragraph 8 (commitment to prison), in sub-paragraph (1)(a), for the words "it appears to the authority that no (or insufficient) goods of the debtor can be found" there shall be substituted the words "the person making the distress reports to the authority that he was unable (for whatever reason) to find any or sufficient goods of the debtor".

(4) After paragraph 13 there shall be inserted the following paragraph—

"Admissibility of evidence

13A.—(1) Regulations under this Schedule may include provision that, in any proceedings before a magistrates' court under any provision included by virtue of the preceding provisions of this Part of this Schedule—

  (a) a statement contained in a document of record shall be admissible as evidence of any fact stated in it of which direct oral evidence would be admissible; and

  (b) a certificate which is made with respect to a document of record produced by a computer and purports to be signed by a responsible person shall be admissible as evidence of anything which is stated in it to the best of his information and belief.

(2) In this paragraph—

  'document of record' means a document constituting or forming part of a record compiled by the authority concerned;

  'responsible person' means a person occupying a responsible position in relation to the operation of the computer;

  'statement' includes any representation of fact, whether made in words or otherwise."

(5) In paragraph 15 (joint and several liability), in sub-paragraph (3), for the words "it appears to the authority concerned that no (or insufficient) goods of that person can be found" there shall be substituted the words "the person making the distress reports to the authority that he was unable (for whatever reason) to find any or sufficient goods of the chargeable person".

DEFINITIONS
"community charge": s.1 of the 1988 Act.

GENERAL NOTE
A number of practical problems arose in relation to the enforcement of the community charge, governed by s.22 of and Sched. 4 to the 1988 Act. This section provides some limited reform of the system to overcome some of the difficulties. First, under subs. (2), the rules are amended to allow only officers of the authority or other prescribed persons to levy distress. In addition, it will be possible to prescribe certain goods which should not be seized, thus avoiding the criticism that essential items were being taken. Secondly, under subs. (3), there is introduced a change to one of the tests in relation to the conditions which must exist before commitment to prison. Instead of the authority itself having to be satisfied that insufficient goods can be found, it is simply that the person who attempts to make the distress must have reported to the authority that he was unable to find any or sufficient goods. This is an easier test to satisfy than the previous one. It also applies, under subs. (5), to matters concerning joint and several liability. Thirdly, problems of proof had arisen in relation to the issuing of a liability order. The evidence produced for the amount of charge unpaid was usually in the form of computer records. In *R.* v. *Coventry Justices,* ex p. *Bullard* [1992] RA 79 it was held that this evidence amounted to hearsay only since the information, although in mechanical form, was generated by human input. Under subs. (4), the practical problem caused by this decision has now been resolved by permitting a statement, contained in a document of record compiled by the authority, to be admissible as evidence of any fact stated in it of which direct oral evidence would be admissible. A certificate made in respect of such a document of record produced by a computer and purported to be signed by a person occupying a responsible position in relation to the operation of the computer shall be admissible as evidence of anything which is stated in it to the best of his information and belief (see also the Community Charges and Non-Domestic Rating (Miscellaneous Provisions) Regulations 1992 (S.I. 1992 No. 474)). It has been made clear by these regulations that where the amount outstanding cannot be levied by distress, the authority may apply for the issue of a warrant, irrespective of the reason for the failure of the attempt to levy.

PART IV

MISCELLANEOUS

Social security

Council tax benefit

103. Schedule 9 to this Act (which amends the Social Security Acts so as to make provision for benefit in respect of council tax in Great Britain) shall have effect.

GENERAL NOTE

This section gives effect to Sched. 9, which amends the Social Security Acts. For an explanation of these changes see the notes to that Schedule.

English and Welsh provisions

Non-domestic rating, grants and funds

104. Schedule 10 to this Act (which amends the provisions of the 1988 Act relating to non-domestic rating, grants and funds) shall have effect.

GENERAL NOTE

This section gives effect to Sched. 10, which amends the 1988 Act in relation to non-domestic rating, grants and funds. For an explanation of these changes see the notes to that Schedule.

Grants to voluntary organisations

105. In section 48 of the Local Government Act 1985 (grants to voluntary organisations), after subsection (4) there shall be inserted the following subsection—

"(4A) The Secretary of State may by order provide that if—
(a) a scheme requires the total expenditure to be incurred under the scheme in any financial year—
(i) in the making of grants; and
(ii) in the discharging by the designated council of its functions under the scheme,
to be approved in accordance with the scheme by some or all of the constituent councils; and
(b) the total expenditure to be incurred in any financial year is not approved as required by the scheme before such date as may be specified in relation to that financial year in the order,
the constituent councils shall be deemed, subject to any order which has been or may be made under subsection (5) below, all to have given their approval for that financial year to total expenditure of an amount equal to the amount that was approved or, as the case may be, deemed to have been approved for the preceding financial year."

DEFINITIONS

"financial year": s.105(2) of the Local Government Act 1985 and s.270(1) of the Local Government Act 1972.

GENERAL NOTE

The consultation paper on the *Structure of Local Government in England* acknowledged that for some services, such as grants to the voluntary sector, the joint arrangements in London and the metropolitan counties had not worked as well as was hoped. Provision for such joint arrangements is made in s.48 of the Local Government Act 1985. This provides that a simple majority of councils in Greater London or the area of a metropolitan county can establish a scheme to make grants to voluntary organisations whose activities bring benefit, either direct or indirect, to the whole of the area or to the area of more than one borough or district. Schemes have been set up in all such areas, with the exception of South Yorkshire and Merseyside, where other arrangements have been made. In London the London Boroughs Grants Scheme required a two-thirds majority to set the budget but there had been real difficulty in achieving this. It was, therefore, decided in the light of the responses to the consultation paper to amend s.48 to provide a mechanism to ensure the timely setting of the annual budget for schemes set up under that section.

This section does not amend the basic provisions of s.48 as to how a scheme should be set up and run, its scope and the basis on which contributions to expenditure are made. It does, however, insert a new subs. (4A) into s.48 of the 1985 Act. Under this subsection the Secretary of State is given a power to make an order to provide that the constituent councils will be deemed to have approved expenditure equal to that approved, or deemed to have been approved, for the previous year. This will only be triggered, however, if two conditions are met. First, if a scheme set up under s.48 includes the requirement for some or all of the constituent councils to approve the total expenditure on the making of grants and administration of the scheme by the lead authority in any financial year. Secondly, that total expenditure has not been approved by a date which the Secretary of State has specified in the order.

Section 103 of the Local Government Act 1985 provides that such orders will be subject to the negative resolution procedure. It also allows the order-making power to make different provision for different cases, including different areas. It was stated to be the Secretary of State's intention that initially the new order-making power would only need to be applied in London.

Council tax and community charges: restrictions on voting

106.—(1) This section applies at any time to a member of a local authority, or a member of a committee of a local authority or of a joint committee of two or more local authorities (including in either case a sub-committee), if at that time—

(a) a sum falling within paragraph 1(1)(a) of Schedule 4 to this Act; or

(b) a sum falling within paragraph 1(1)(a), (b), (d) or (ee) of Schedule 4 to the 1988 Act (corresponding provisions with respect to community charges),

has become payable by him and has remained unpaid for at least two months.

(2) Subject to subsection (5) below, if a member to whom this section applies is present at a meeting of the authority or committee at which any of the following matters is the subject of consideration, namely—

(a) any calculation required by Chapter III, IV or V of Part I of this Act;

(b) any recommendation, resolution or other decision which might affect the making of any such calculation; or

(c) the exercise of any functions under Schedules 2 to 4 to this Act or Schedules 2 to 4 to the 1988 Act (corresponding provisions with respect to community charges),

he shall at the meeting and as soon as practicable after its commencement disclose the fact that this section applies to him and shall not vote on any question with respect to the matter.

(3) If a person fails to comply with subsection (2) above, he shall for each offence be liable on summary conviction to a fine not exceeding level 3 on the standard scale, unless he proves that he did not know—

(a) that this section applied to him at the time of the meeting; or

(b) that the matter in question was the subject of consideration at the meeting.

(4) A prosecution for an offence under this section shall not be instituted except by or on behalf of the Director of Public Prosecutions.

(5) Subsections (1) to (3) of section 97 of the Local Government Act 1972 (removal or exclusion of liability etc.) shall apply in relation to this section and any disability imposed by it as they apply in relation to section 94 of that Act and any disability imposed by that section.

(6) In this section "local authority" has the same meaning as in sections 94 and 97 of the Local Government Act 1972.

DEFINITIONS
"community charge": s.1 of the 1988 Act.
"local authority": subs. (6).

GENERAL NOTE
This section prevents certain members of a local authority or a committee, joint committee of two or more local authorities, or a sub-committee from voting at meetings on any matters affecting the level of council tax or the arrangements for administering either the community charge or council tax. It does not, however, remove their right to speak at such meetings. The restriction applies to members of local authorities and their committees, joint committees and

sub-committees, who have not paid an amount due in respect of their community charge or council tax for at least two months after it became payable. Those members must, at the meeting where any matter defined in subs. (2) is discussed, and as soon as practicable after its commencement, make it known that the restriction applies to them and not vote on any question concerning the above matters. Failure to do so is an offence, under subs. (3). For each offence the member will be liable to a fine not exceeding level 3 on the standard scale. It is a defence to prove that he did not know that he was two months in arrears, or that the matter in question was for consideration at the meeting. Prosecutions in relation to such alleged offences are, by subs. (3), to be instituted only by or on behalf of the Director of Public Prosecutions. A member to whom the restriction applies is able, under subs. (5), to apply for a dispensation to permit voting at meetings. The restrictions under this section may be removed by a district council in the case of a parish or community council member, and by the Secretary of State in any other case. These provisions apply to county councils, district councils, London borough councils, the Isles of Scilly, joint authorities and parish or community councils. In Scotland, under s.112 of this Act, the relevant period for unpaid arrears is three months.

Scottish provisions

Water and sewerage charges

107.—(1) Parts I to III of Schedule 11 to this Act shall have effect in relation to water and sewerage charges in respect of the financial year 1993–94 and subsequent financial years.

(2) The 1980 Act shall have effect subject to the amendments made in Part IV of that Schedule.

DEFINITIONS
"financial year": s.116(1).

GENERAL NOTE
This section brings into effect Sched. 11 to this Act, which relates to water and sewerage charges from 1993–94 onwards and amends the Water (Scotland) Act 1960. This will replace the provisions of Sched. 5 to the 1987 Act.

Payments to local authorities by Secretary of State

108.—(1) The Secretary of State may, in respect of the financial year 1993–94 and each subsequent financial year—
  (a) make grants, (to be known as "reve: ue support grants") to local authorities; and
  (b) distribute among local authorities the money recovered by way of non-domestic rates ("non-domestic-rate income") in that financial year.

(2) Schedule 12 to this Act has effect in relation to revenue support grant and the recovery and distribution of non-domestic rate income.

DEFINITIONS
"financial year": s.116(1).
"local authority": s.99(1).
"non-domestic rate": s.99(2).
"revenue support grant": subs. (1).

GENERAL NOTE
This section re-enacts the provisions of s.23(2) of the 1987 Act in respect of revenue support grants. It also combines the provisions for revenue support grant with a new provision dealing with the distribution to local authorities of money recovered by way of non-domestic rates. The provisions of this section, together with Sched. 12 to this Act, bring Scotland into line with England and Wales so that the income from non-domestic rates will be transferred by levying authorities to the Secretary of State and then redistributed to local authorities in such a manner as the Secretary of State prescribes. The new arrangements would take effect from the financial year 1993–94.

Subs. (1)
  This re-enacts s.23(2) of the 1987 Act in relation to revenue support grant. By subs. (1)(b) the

Secretary of State is empowered to distribute the money recovered by way of non-domestic rates among local authorities. Previously, non-domestic rate income was retained by the levying authorities and the district proportion distributed to the districts by those authorities in proportion to their rate poundages. Nothing in subs. (1)(b) alters the Secretary of State's powers to determine non-domestic rate poundages which are covered in s.110 of this Act.

Subs. (2)
By this subsection Sched. 12, which contains detailed provisions relating to revenue support grant and non-domestic rate income contributions and distribution, is brought into effect. See further the notes to that Schedule.

Council tax grants

109.—(1) If regulations under section 80 above have effect in respect of a financial year the Secretary of State may, with the consent of the Treasury, pay a grant to a levying authority as regards that financial year.

(2) The amount of the grant shall be such as the Secretary of State may with the consent of the Treasury determine.

(3) A grant under this section shall be paid at such time, or in instalments of such amounts and at such times, as the Secretary of State may with the consent of the Treasury determine.

(4) In making any payment of grant under this section the Secretary of State may impose such conditions as he may with the consent of the Treasury determine; and the conditions may relate to the repayment in specified circumstances of all or part of the amount paid.

(5) In deciding whether to pay a grant under this section, and in determining the amount of any such grant, the Secretary of State shall have regard to his estimate of any amount which, in consequence of the regulations, the authority might reasonably be expected to lose, or to have lost, by way of payments in respect of council tax as it has effect for the financial year concerned.

DEFINITIONS
"council tax": s.99(1).
"financial year": s.116(1).
"levying authority": s.99(1).

GENERAL NOTE
This section provides for the Secretary of State, where regulations under s.80 have effect, to pay grant to a levying authority, having regard to the expected or actual loss in council-tax revenue caused to the authority in consequence of the regulations. Treasury consent is needed before the Secretary of State may implement this power.

Subss. (1) and (2)
Where regulations under s.80 which reduce the amount of council tax for which a person is liable have effect for a financial year, the Secretary of State may pay a grant to a levying authority for that financial year. The decision to give a grant and its amount require Treasury consent.

Subs. (3)
Any grant, under subs. (1), shall be paid at such time, or in instalments at such times, as the Secretary of State may determine. Again the consent of the Treasury is required.

Subs. (4)
In paying grant under subs. (1), the Secretary of State may impose such conditions as he determines, including repayment in specified circumstances in whole or part. Again the consent of the Treasury is required.

Subs. (5)
In deciding whether and how much to pay in grant under subs. (1), the Secretary of State shall take account of his estimate of any amount of council-tax payments the authority might reasonably be expected to lose, or to have lost, in consequence of the regulations.

Amendments to the 1975 Act in relation to non-domestic rates

110.—(1) After section 7 of the 1975 Act there shall be inserted the following section—

"Provisions as to setting of non-domestic rates

7A.—(1) The Secretary of State shall, in respect of the financial year 1993–94 and each subsequent financial year, prescribe for each local authority a rate which shall be their non-domestic rate in respect of that year.

(2) Non-domestic rates shall be levied in accordance with section 7 of this Act by each rating authority in respect of lands and heritages—

    (a) which are subjects (other than part residential subjects) in respect of which there is an entry in the valuation roll, according to their rateable value or, where a rateable value has been prescribed or determined in respect of the lands and heritages under section 128 of the Local Government Finance Act 1988, according to that rateable value; or

    (b) which are part residential subjects, according to that part of their rateable value which is shown in the apportionment note as relating to the non-residential use of those subjects or, where a rateable value has been prescribed or determined in respect of the lands and heritages under section 128 of the Local Government Finance Act 1988, according to that part of that rateable value which is so shown in the apportionment note.

(3) The rates prescribed under subsection (1) above shall be known—

    (a) in the case of the regional council, as the non-domestic regional rate;

    (b) in the case of the district council, as the non-domestic district rate; and

    (c) in the case of the islands council, as the non-domestic islands rate.

(4) References (however expressed) in any enactment to the non-domestic rate determined by a local authority shall be construed as references to the non-domestic rate prescribed for the local authority under this section.

(5) A statutory instrument containing any order under this section shall be subject to annulment in pursuance of a resolution of either House of Parliament."

(2) For section 7A of the 1975 Act there shall be substituted the following section—

"Provisions as to setting of non-domestic rates

7B.—(1) The Secretary of State shall, in respect of the financial year following that in which this subsection comes into force and each subsequent financial year, prescribe a rate which shall be the non-domestic rate to be levied throughout Scotland in respect of that financial year.

(2) Subject to subsection (3) below, non-domestic rates shall be levied in accordance with section 7 of this Act by each rating authority in respect of lands and heritages in their area, being lands and heritages—

    (a) which are subjects (other than part residential subjects) in respect of which there is an entry in the valuation roll, according to their rateable value or, where a rateable value has been prescribed or determined in respect of the lands and heritages under section 128 of the Local Government Finance Act 1988, according to that rateable value; or

    (b) which are part residential subjects, according to that part of their rateable value which is shown in the apportionment note as relating to the non-residential use of those subjects or, where a rateable value has been prescribed or determined in respect of the lands and heritages under section 128 of the Local Government Finance Act 1988, according to that part of that rateable value which is so shown in the apportionment note.

(3) In the application of section 7 of this Act to the levying of the non-domestic rate prescribed under this section, for the words 'to which the rate relates' in each of subsections (1) and (2) of that section there shall be substituted the words 'of the rating authority'.

(4) References (however expressed) in any enactment to the non-domestic rate determined by a local authority shall be construed as references to the non-domestic rate prescribed under this section.

(5) A statutory instrument containing any order under this section shall be subject to annulment in pursuance of a resolution of either House of Parliament."

(3) In section 37 (interpretation) of the 1975 Act, in the definition of "non-domestic rate", for "section 7A" there shall be substituted "section 7B".

(4) For section 9A of the 1975 Act (as inserted by paragraph 13 of Schedule 12 to the 1988 Act) there shall be substituted the following section—

"Interest on rates paid in error

9A.—(1) Subject to regulations made under this section—

(a) where any amount has been paid to a rating authority in respect of rates either—

(i) in error; or

(ii) in consequence of the entry on to the valuation roll of a valuation which is subsequently reduced,

and the rating authority repay the amount, the authority shall also pay to the person to whom the repayment is made interest on the amount; and

(b) where any amount has been repaid to any person by a rating authority either—

(i) in error; or

(ii) in consequence of the entry on to the valuation roll of a valuation which is subsequently increased,

and the rating authority recover the amount, the authority may also recover from that person any interest paid on that amount.

(2) The Secretary of State may by regulations make provision as to—

(a) the circumstances in which interest is to be payable or recoverable by a rating authority;

(b) the rate at which any interest is to be paid, or the manner in which such rate is to be determined; and

(c) the date or dates from which, or by reference to which, any payment of interest is to run.

(3) This section applies to any payments such as are mentioned in subsection (1) which were made—

(a) after 1st April 1990; and

(b) before the coming into force of this section,

as it applies to such payments made after the coming into force of this section; but does not entitle any person to receive any payment of interest in respect of any such payment made before 1st April 1990.

(4) Regulations made under this section may provide for the deduction from any sum paid by way of interest under or by virtue of this section of any sum previously paid under or by virtue of any other enactment by way of interest in respect of the same payment.

(5) Regulations under this section—

(a) may make different provision in relation to different cases or descriptions of case;

(b) may include such transitional provisions as appear to the Secretary of State to be necessary or expedient; and

(c) shall be made by statutory instrument subject to annulment in pursuance of a resolution of either House of Parliament."

DEFINITIONS

"apportionment note": s.99(1).

"council tax": s.99(1).

"financial year": s.116(1).

"levying authority": s.99(1).

"local authority": s.99(1).

"non-domestic district rate": subs. (3).

"non-domestic islands rate": subs. (3).

"non-domestic rate": subs. (4) and s.99(2).

"non-domestic regional rate": subs. (3).

"part residential subjects": s.99(1).

"prescribed": s.116(1).

"rateable value": s.99(1).

"valuation roll": s.1 of the Local Government (Scotland) Act 1975.

GENERAL NOTE

This section inserts two new sections into, and further amends, the Local Government (Scotland) Act 1975. The main purpose is to enact provisions similar to those presently in ss.3A and 3B of the 1987 Act, which allows the Secretary of State to prescribe the non-domestic rate for each rating area. The new provision will apply in respect of the year 1993–94 and subsequent years until all the non-domestic rates in Scotland have been brought to a common level. At that time, subs. (2) will be brought into effect to allow the Secretary of State to prescribe a single non-domestic rate for Scotland.

Subs. (1)

This inserts into the 1975 Act a new s.7A covering the following matters:

Subsection (1) of the new s.7A empowers the Secretary of State to prescribe the non-domestic rate for each rating area.

Subsection (2) of the new s.7A provides that the rates prescribed by the Secretary of State should be levied by the rating authorities according to the existing legislation.

Subsection (3) of the new s.7A provides for the rates prescribed under subs. (1) of the new s.7A to be known as the regional, district or islands non-domestic rates, as appropriate.

Subsection (4) provides that references in any previous enactment to the non-domestic rate determined by a local authority shall be construed as a reference to the non-domestic rate prescribed for the local authority under the new s.7A.

Subsection (5) subjects any order by the Secretary of State under the new s.7A, prescribing level of non-domestic rates, to the negative resolution procedure of either House of Parliament.

Subs. (2)

Once the non-domestic rates in Scotland have been brought to a common level, s.7A will be replaced by a new s.7B, covering the following matters:

Subsection (1) empowers the Secretary of State to prescribe the non-domestic rate to be levied throughout Scotland.

Subsection (2) provides that the non-domestic rate prescribed by the Secretary of State should be levied by the rating authorities according to the existing legislation.

Subsection (3) amends for these purposes the wording of s.7 of the 1975 Act in line with the prescription of a single rate for the whole of Scotland rather than individual rate poundages for each authority.

Subsection (4) provides that references in any previous enactment to the non-domestic rate determined by a local authority shall be construed as a reference to the non-domestic rate prescribed for the local authority under the new s.7B.

Subsection (5) subjects any order by the Secretary of State under the new s.7B, prescribing level of non-domestic rates, to the negative resolution procedure of either House of Parliament.

Subs. (3)
A consequential amendment in s.37 of the 1975 Act is to be brought into force when the new s.7B is substituted for the new s.7A.

Subs. (4)
This subsection deletes the existing s.9A of the Local Government (Scotland) Act 1975, as inserted by para. 13 of Sched. 12 to the Local Government Finance Act 1988, and replaces it with a new s.9A to allow, as far as is practicable, harmonisation between Scotland and England/Wales in the method of payment of interest by local authorities on rates repaid by them to ratepayers. The existing powers available to the Secretary of State under s.9A enabled local authorities to pay interest in order to compensate ratepayers who have overpaid rates by reason of an error or who are successful in having their rateable values reduced on appeal following revaluation, but they were more restrictive than those available in England and Wales. This meant that the Secretary of State could not ensure that payments of interest were made on the same basis as between Scotland and England/Wales. The new s.9A is therefore designed to bring the Scottish legislation into line with that of England and Wales with retrospective effect from April 1, 1990, which was the date of implementation in England and Wales.

The new s.9A covers the following matters:

Subsection (1)(a) provides for the payment of interest by a rating authority where, either as a result of an error, or as a result of a reduction in rateable value, an amount falls to be repaid to the ratepayer concerned. A statutory power to repay rates paid in error is contained in s.20 of the Local Government (Financial Provisions) (Scotland) Act 1963.

Subsection (1)(b) provides for the recovery by a rating authority of interest paid by it where, either as a result of an error, or as a result of an increase in rateable value, an amount falls to be recovered by the rating authority from the ratepayer concerned. An example of the latter is where on second appeal the rateable value is increased from that determined on the initial appeal.

Subsection (2) enables the Secretary of State to prescribe the circumstances in which interest is to be payable, or recoverable by a rating authority; the rate at which any interest is to be paid, or the manner in which such rate is to be determined; and the period for which any payment of interest is to run. This mirrors the provisions in England and Wales. Subsection (3) is a retrospective provision and applies to any payments, described in subs. (1), made after April 1, 1990 and before the coming into force of this section in the same way as it applies to payments made after the coming into force of the section. It excludes entitlement to interest in respect of payments made before April 1, 1990.

Subsection (4) gives power to adjust the interest payable to take account of payments made since August 1, 1991 under the old s.9A. The effect of this is to allow a set-off of the amount of interest paid under the Local Government (Interest on Repayment of Rates) (Scotland) Order 1991 (S.I. 1991 No. 1780).

Subsection (5) gives the flexibility that already exists in England and Wales and provides for regulations under this section to make different provision in relation to different cases or descriptions of case and to include such transitional provisions as appear to the Secretary of State to be necessary or expedient. It also provides for the regulations to be made by statutory instrument subject to the negative resolution procedure of either House of Parliament.

Statutory and other references to rateable values etc.

111.—(1) Where—
(a) in any deed relating to heritable property executed before 1st April 1989 there is any provision which apportions any liability according to the assessed rental or, as the case may be, the gross annual, net annual or rateable value of any properties; and
(b) all the properties involved in the apportionment appear in the valuation roll in force immediately before 1st April 1989; and
(c) one or more of the properties constitute dwellings,
then, with effect from 1st April 1989, any reference to the assessed rental or, as the case may be, to any of those values in any such deed shall, unless the context otherwise requires, be construed as a reference to the net annual value or, as the case may be, to the gross annual, net annual or rateable value which appears in relation to any of those properties in the valuation roll in force immediately before that date.

(2) Where in any document executed before 1st April 1989 there is a reference to the assessed rental or, as the case may be, to the gross annual, net annual or rateable value of any property which—

(a) constitutes a dwelling; and

(b) appears in the valuation roll in force immediately before 1st April 1989,

then, with effect from that date that reference shall, unless the context otherwise requires, be construed as a reference to the net annual value or, as the case may be, to the gross annual, net annual or rateable value which appears in relation to that property in the valuation roll in force immediately before that date.

(3) Subject to subsection (4) below, where in any enactment (including an enactment contained in a subordinate instrument) there is a reference to the gross annual value, net annual value or rateable value of any property which constitutes a dwelling, then, with effect from 1st April 1989, that reference shall, unless the context otherwise requires, be construed as a reference to the gross annual value, net annual value or rateable value—

(a) subject to subsection (6) below, which appears in relation to that property in the valuation roll in force immediately before that date; or

(b) subject to subsection (7) below, in the case of such property which does not come into existence or occupancy as a dwelling until after that date, which would have appeared in the roll in respect of it had it been in existence or occupancy as such immediately before that date.

(4) Where in any enactment (including an enactment contained in a subordinate instrument or an enactment which falls to be construed in accordance with subsection (3) above) there is a reference to a rate or rateable value or to any factor connected with rating, or valuation for rating, the Secretary of State may make regulations providing that the reference shall instead be such as is prescribed.

(5) Regulations may provide as mentioned in subsection (4) above—

(a) as regards such enactment, or enactments of such description, as may be prescribed;

(b) in such way as the Secretary of State thinks fit (whether by amending enactments or otherwise).

(6) Where, before or after 1st April 1989, there is a material change of circumstances, within the meaning of section 37(1) of the 1975 Act—

(a) in relation to any such property as is mentioned in subsection (3)(a) above; and

(b) in respect of which no alteration has been made to the valuation roll in force immediately before that date,

references in that subsection to the gross annual, net annual or rateable value of that property which appears in the roll in force immediately before that date shall be construed as references to the gross annual, net annual or rateable value which would have so appeared had that roll been altered to take account of that material change of circumstances.

(7) Where there is a material change of circumstances, within the meaning of section 37(1) of the 1975 Act, in relation to any such property as is mentioned in subsection (3)(b) above, references in that subsection to the gross annual, net annual or rateable value of that property which would have appeared in respect of it in the roll in force immediately before 1st April 1989 shall be construed as references to the gross annual, net annual or rateable value which would have so appeared had that material change of circumstances been taken into account.

(8) The assessor shall, at the request of any person and on payment of such fee as may be prescribed, certify—

(a) what would have appeared in the valuation roll in force immediately before 1st April 1989 as the gross annual value, net annual value or rateable value of any such property as is mentioned in subsection (3)(b) above; or

(b) what would have appeared in that roll as the gross annual value, net annual value or rateable value of any such property as is mentioned in subsection (3) above had that roll been altered to take account of any material change of circumstances, within the meaning of section 37(1) of the 1975 Act, occurring before or after that date.

(9) An appeal shall lie—

(a) against any certificate issued by the assessor under subsection (8) above; or

(b) against any refusal by the assessor to issue a certificate under that subsection,

and the provisions of the Valuation Acts in regards to appeals and complaints shall apply, subject to such modifications and adaptations as may be prescribed, for the purposes of this subsection.

(10) Without prejudice to section 35 of the Lands Valuation (Scotland) Act 1854 (which relates to the preservation of valuation rolls by the Keeper of the Records of Scotland), the assessor for each valuation area shall retain a copy of the valuation roll in force immediately before 1st April 1989 for the purposes of this Act; and the copy so retained shall be made available for public inspection at the assessor's offices during ordinary business hours.

(11) Where the net annual value of any property does not appear, or would not have appeared, in the valuation roll in force immediately before 1st April 1989, references in this section to the appearance in that roll of the net annual value of that property shall be taken as references to the appearance of its rateable value.

(12) For the purposes of this section "gross annual value", "net annual value" and "rateable value" shall continue to be construed in accordance with the provisions of section 6 of the 1956 Act as those provisions had effect immediately before 1st April 1989.

DEFINITIONS
"dwelling": s.72(2).
"gross annual value": subs. (12).
"local assessor": s.84(10).
"net annual value": subs. (12).
"prescribed": s.116(1).
"rateable value": subs. (12) and s.99(1).
"Valuation Acts": s.99(1).
"valuation roll": s.1 of the Local Government (Scotland) Act 1975.

GENERAL NOTE
This section re-enacts in the context of the council tax the provisions of s.5 of the 1987 Act, as amended by the Local Government Finance Act 1988, changing references, where appropriate, from "domestic subjects" to a "dwelling". The purpose is to ensure that where deeds relating to heritable property, other documents, or enactments contain provisions referring to the gross annual value, net annual value, or rateable value of that or other property, they will remain valid notwithstanding the deletion from the valuation roll from April 1, 1989 of entries relating to domestic subjects and from April 1, 1993 of entries relating to dwellings. The principal effect of the section is that, with effect from April 1989, such references are construed as references to the respective values which appeared in the valuation roll in relation to the properties in question immediately before April 1, 1989. As regards references to gross annual value, net annual value, and rateable value in enactments, the section also creates a new procedure to deal with cases where there was no such value for a property immediately prior to April 1, 1989, and also where the value of a property would have been altered as a result of a material change of circumstances, had it remained on the valuation roll. Under this procedure the assessor is required to certify what the value, or the alteration in value, would have been. A right of appeal against the assessor's certificate is also created.

The rateable values of properties were used primarily for the purposes of the rating system in the calculation of the amount of rates leviable in respect of the properties to which the rateable values related. But, in addition, rateable values, and also gross annual value and net annual value, were used for a range of other purposes which had no connection with the assessment of rates. These uses are generally termed "secondary uses". Such secondary uses frequently arise in contracts, and in conveyances or leases of tenement property where values are used to determine the basis of apportionment of liability among individual flats, shops or offices of expenditure on matters relating to the burdens of common ownership such as repairs to the roof, stairs, common drainage system and so on. Secondary uses are also authorised by a number of Acts of Parliament, most commonly in the fields of land compensation and housing.

Subs. (1)

This subsection applies to deeds relating to heritable property which contain provisions apportioning any liability according to gross annual value, net annual value or rateable value and which were executed before April 1, 1989. It provides that if all the properties involved in the apportionment appeared in the valuation roll in force immediately before April 1, 1989, and one or more of the properties constitute a dwelling, then references in such deeds to gross annual value, net annual value or rateable value shall, unless the context otherwise requires, be construed from April 1, 1989 as references to the value which appears in relation to any of those properties in the valuation roll in force immediately before that date.

Subs. (2)

Similarly to subs. (1), this makes provision as regards documents executed before April 1, 1989 which contain a reference to the gross annual value, net annual value or rateable value of properties which are dwellings and appeared in the valuation roll in force immediately before April 1, 1989. It requires that such a reference shall, unless the context otherwise requires, be construed with effect from that date as a reference to the gross annual value, net annual value or rateable value which appears in relation to that property in the valuation roll in force immediately before that date.

Subs. (3)

Where there are references in other enactments to the gross annual value, net annual value or rateable value of property which constitutes a dwelling, then, subject to subs. (4), from April 1, 1989 such a reference shall mean one of two things. First, unless the context otherwise requires, it shall be construed as a reference to the gross annual value, net annual value or rateable value which appeared in the valuation roll in force immediately before April 1, 1989 in relation to the property. Secondly, if the property did not come into existence or occupancy as a dwelling until after that date, it shall be construed as a reference to the gross annual value, net annual value or rateable value which would have appeared in the valuation roll had it been in existence or occupancy as a dwelling-house immediately before that date.

Subs. (4)

References in primary or subordinate legislation to a rate, rateable value or factor concerned with rating or valuation for rating can be changed in such a way as the Secretary of State prescribes.

Subs. (5)

Without prejudice to the width of subs. (4), this describes what the regulations under that subsection may provide.

Subs. (6)

This clarifies the operation of subs. (3) and makes provision as regards property in the valuation roll in force immediately before April 1, 1989. Thus, cases covered by subs. (3)(a) where, as a result of a material change of circumstances, as defined in s.37(1) of the Local Government (Scotland) Act 1975 and which occurred before or after April 1, 1989, the gross annual value, net annual value or rateable value would have been liable to be altered by the assessor.

Subs. (7)

Similarly to subs. (6), this makes corresponding provision as regards property which comes into existence or occupancy as a dwelling only after April 1, 1989, namely cases covered by subs. (3)(b).

Subs. (8)

Under subs. (8)(a), upon the request of any person and on payment of such fee as may be prescribed, the assessor is to certify, for property covered by subs. (3)(b) which comes into existence or occupancy as a dwelling only after April 1, 1989, what would have been its gross annual value, net annual value or rateable value immediately before that date. Under subs. (8)(b), he is required to certify for dwellings covered by subs. (3) what their gross annual value, net annual value or rateable value would have been after taking into account any material change of circumstances which occurred before or after that date.

Subs. (9)

An appeal shall lie against a certificate issued under subs. (8)(a) or a refusal by an assessor to issue such a certificate under subs. (8)(b). The provisions of the Valuation Acts regarding appeals and complaints are to apply, subject to any modifications and adaptations which the Secretary of State may prescribe.

Subs. (10)

The assessor is under a duty to retain a copy of the valuation roll in force immediately before April 1, 1989 for the purposes of the Act, and the copy retained must be made available for public inspection at the assessor's offices during ordinary business hours. This does not alter s.35 of the Lands Valuation (Scotland) Act 1954 which, as replaced by para. 4 of Pt. II of Sched. 6 to the Local Government (Scotland) Act 1975, requires the assessor, as soon as is reasonably practicable after the valuation roll has ceased to be in force, to transmit the roll to the Keeper of the Records of Scotland for preservation.

Subs. (11)

Where the net annual value of a property was not included in the valuation roll in force immediately before April 1, 1989, for the purposes of this section the net annual value shall be taken to be the rateable value.

Subs. (12)

The definitions of the terms "gross annual value", "net annual value" and "rateable value" for the purposes of this section are provided.

Council tax and community charges: restrictions on voting

112.—(1) This section applies at any time to a member of a local authority, or a member of a committee of a local authority or of a joint committee of two or more local authorities (including in either case a sub-committee), if at that time—

(a) a sum falling within paragraph 1(1)(a) of Schedule 8 to this Act (including a sum falling within that paragraph by virtue of paragraph 11 of Schedule 11 to this Act) has become payable by him and has remained unpaid for at least two months; or

(b) a sum falling within paragraph—

(i) 4 or 5 of Schedule 2 (collection etc. of community charges); or

(ii) 11 of Schedule 5 (as read with the said paragraphs 4 and 5),

to the 1987 Act has become payable by him and has remained unpaid for at least three months.

(2) Subject to subsection (4) below, if a member to whom this section applies is present at a meeting of the authority or committee at which any of the following matters is the subject of consideration, namely—

(a) the setting of council tax under section 93(1)(a) above;

(b) the substitute setting of council tax under section 94(1) above;

(c) a reduced or deemed setting under paragraph 3 of Schedule 7 to this Act;

(d) the setting of council water charge under paragraph 9(a) of Schedule 11 to this Act; or

(e) the exercise of any functions under Schedule 2, 3 or 8 or paragraph 11 of Schedule 11 to this Act, or Schedule 2 or paragraph 11 of Schedule 5 to the 1987 Act,

he shall at the meeting and as soon as practicable after its commencement disclose the fact that this section applies to him and shall not vote on any question with respect to the matter.

(3) If a person fails to comply with subsection (2) above, he shall be guilty of an offence, and shall for each offence be liable on summary conviction to a fine not exceeding level 3 on the standard scale, unless he proves that he did not know—

(a) that this section applied to him at the time of the meeting; or

(b) that the matter in question was the subject of consideration at the meeting.

(4) Subsections (1) to (3) of section 41 (removal or exclusion of disability) of the 1973 Act shall apply in relation to this section and any disability imposed by it as they apply in relation to section 38 (provision as to disability of members of authorities from voting) of that Act and any disability imposed by that section.

DEFINITIONS
    "community charge": s.26 of the 1987 Act.
    "council tax": s.99(1).
    "council water charge": s.99(1).
    "local authority": s.99(1).

GENERAL NOTE
    This section prevents certain members of a local authority or a committee, joint committee of two or more local authorities, or a subcommittee, from voting at meetings on any matters affecting the level of council tax or the arrangements for administering either the community charge or council tax. It does not, however, remove their right to speak at such meetings. The restriction applies to members of local authorities and their committees, joint committees and subcommittees who have not paid an amount due in respect of their community charge or council tax for at least three months after it became payable. The three-month limit was substituted for the originally proposed two-month period, which operates for England and Wales. Those members must, at the meeting where any matter defined in subs. (2) is discussed, and as soon as practicable after its commencement, make it known that the restriction applies to them and not vote on any question concerning the above matters. Failure to do so is an offence, under subs. (3). For each offence the member will be liable to a fine not exceeding level 3 on the standard scale. It is a defence to prove that he did not know that he was three months in arrears, or that the matter in question was for consideration at the meeting. A member to whom the restriction applies is able, under subs. (4), to apply for a dispensation to permit voting at meetings, and the restriction may be removed by the Secretary of State.

PART V

SUPPLEMENTAL

Orders and regulations

    113.—(1) Any power of the Secretary of State or the Treasury under this Act to make orders or regulations (other than the power to make orders under section 54(6) above) may be so exercised as to make different provision for different cases or descriptions of case, including different provision for different areas or for different authorities.

    (2) Any power of the Secretary of State or the Treasury under this Act to make orders or regulations includes power to make such incidental, consequential, transitional or supplementary provision as he or they think necessary or expedient.

    (3) Any power of the Secretary of State or the Treasury under this Act to make orders or regulations shall be exercisable by statutory instrument which, except in the case of orders under—
    (a) section 5(4), 11(3), 54(6), 57(2), 59(2), 74(3) or 79(3) above;
    (b) section 119(2) below; or
    (c) paragraph 1 of Schedule 12 to this Act,
shall be subject to annulment in pursuance of a resolution of either House of Parliament.

GENERAL NOTE
    In relation to all the powers given by this Act to the Secretary of State or the Treasury, with the exception of the power to designate an authority for council-tax capping, it is made clear not only that the regulation may as normal contain such further incidental, consequential, and transitional provisions as thought necessary, but also that the regulations may be made expressly to differentiate between areas and/or authorities. It is further provided that with the exception of those listed, all powers to make orders must be exercised in accordance with the negative resolution procedure of the House of Commons. Those exceptions fall into two

groups: those listed in subs. (3)(a) are required to be exercised in accordance with the positive resolution procedure of the House of Commons, whereas others need only be laid or not laid at all.

For orders made under this section for Scotland see the Council Tax (Valuation of Dwellings) (Scotland) Regulations 1992 (S.I. 1992 No. 1329), the Council Tax (Contents of Valuation Lists) (Scotland) Regulations 1992 (S.I. 1992 No. 1330), the Council Tax (Administration and Enforcement) (Scotland) Regulations 1992 (S.I. 1992 No. 1332), the Council Tax (Discounts) (Scotland) Order 1992 (S.I. 1992 No. 1408) and the Council Tax (Discounts) (Scotland) Regulations 1992 (S.I. 1992 No. 1409).

Power to make supplementary provision

114.—(1) The Secretary of State may at any time by order make such supplementary, incidental, consequential or transitional provision as appears to him to be necessary or expedient for the general purposes or any particular purposes of this Act or in consequence of any of its provisions or for giving full effect to it.

(2) An order under this section may in particular make provision for amending, repealing or revoking (with or without savings) any provision of an Act passed before or in the same session as this Act, or of an instrument made under an Act before the passing of this Act, and for making savings or additional savings from the effect of any amendment or repeal made by this Act.

(3) Any provision that may be made under this section shall be in addition and without prejudice to any other provision of this Act.

(4) No other provision of this Act shall be construed as prejudicing the generality of the powers conferred by this section.

(5) In this section "Act" includes a private or local Act.

GENERAL NOTE
In addition to the wide powers under s.113 to make regulations and supplementary provision, it is made clear that other regulations may be made to deal with the situation where it subsequently transpires that another provision of another Act, whether public or private, is in conflict with the provisions of this Act.

Financial provisions

115.—(1) There shall be paid out of money provided by Parliament—
(a) any sums required to enable valuations to be carried out in accordance with Part I or II of this Act;
(b) any expenses of the Secretary of State incurred in consequence of this Act; and
(c) any increase attributable to this Act in the sums payable out of money so provided under any other enactment.
(2) There shall be paid into the Consolidated Fund—
(a) any sums received by the Secretary of State in consequence of this Act; and
(b) any increase attributable to this Act in the sums payable into that Fund under any other enactment.

Interpretation: general

116.—(1) In this Act, unless the context otherwise requires—
"the 1987 Act" means the Abolition of Domestic Rates Etc. (Scotland) Act 1987;
"the 1988 Act" means the Local Government Finance Act 1988;
"the Social Security Acts" means the Social Security Contributions and Benefits Act 1992 and the Social Security Administration Act 1992;
"financial year" means any period of twelve months beginning with 1st April;
"information" includes accounts, estimates and returns;
"prescribed" means prescribed by regulations made by the Secretary of State.

(2) Nothing in any private or local Act (whenever passed) shall in any way affect the operation of this Act or of anything done under it.

Minor and consequential amendments and repeals

117.—(1) The enactments mentioned in Schedule 13 to this Act shall have effect subject to the amendments there specified (being minor amendments and amendments consequential on the provisions of this Act).

(2) The enactments mentioned in Schedule 14 to this Act (which include some that are spent or no longer of practical utility) are hereby repealed to the extent specified in the third column of that Schedule.

GENERAL NOTE

This section gives effect to Scheds. 13 and 14. For an explanation of these changes, see the notes to those schedules.

Savings and transitional provisions

118.—(1) Nothing in this Act (except sections 101 and 102) shall affect the operation of the 1988 Act in relation to any community charge in respect of a day falling before 1st April 1993; and nothing in this Act (except paragraphs 1 to 4 and 6(11) of Schedule 10) shall affect the operation of that Act in relation to any financial year beginning before that date.

(2) Nothing in this Act (except section 101) shall affect the operation of the 1987 Act in relation to any community charge in respect of a day falling before 1st April 1993.

(3) The repeal by this Act of the 1987 Act shall not affect any amendment made by that Act to any other enactment; and the repeal by this Act of any enactment amending that Act shall not affect any amendment so made to that Act.

(4) Nothing in this Act shall affect the operation of the Social Security Acts in relation to any community charge benefit in respect of a day falling before 1st April 1993.

(5) In relation to any time before the commencement of the Social Security Acts, this Act and the repealed enactments shall have effect as if—

(a) any reference in this Act to those Acts were a reference to those enactments;

(b) any reference in this Act (except paragraph 4 of Schedule 9) to either of those Acts, or to any provision of those Acts, were a reference to the corresponding provisions or provision of those enactments;

(c) subsections (1) to (7) of the section set out in paragraph 4 of Schedule 9 to this Act were substituted for subsections (8A), (8AA) and (8B) to (8F), and subsection (11) of that section were substituted for subsections (8G) and (8H), of section 20 of the Social Security Act 1986; and

(d) subsections (8) and (9) of the section so set out were substituted for subsections (5A) and (5B), and paragraphs (a) and (b) of subsection (10) of that section were substituted for paragraph (c) of subsection (6), of section 21 of that Act.

(6) The provisions of any regulations or orders relating to council tax benefit which—

(a) are made before the commencement of the Social Security Acts; and

(b) are expressed to come into force after that commencement,

may refer to any relevant provisions of those Acts rather than to the corresponding provisions of the repealed enactments.

(7) In this section—

"community charge" has the same meaning as in section 100 above;

"the repealed enactments" means the enactments repealed by the Social Security (Consequential Provisions) Act 1992;

and any reference to an enactment includes a reference to any regulations or orders made (or having effect as if made) under that enactment.

Short title, commencement and extent

119.—(1) This Act may be cited as the Local Government Finance Act 1992.

(2) The following provisions of this Act, namely—

(a) sections 99(2), 110 and 111;

(b) paragraphs 1 to 4 of Schedule 10;

(c) paragraphs 29(a), 30, 31(b), 32 to 37 and 38(a), (b), (c) and (e) of Schedule 11;

(d) Schedule 13 except paragraphs 15 to 25, 31, 42, 44(c), 45 to 47, 59 to 74, 76 to 88, 92, 99 and 100; and

(e) Schedule 14 except the repeals in the 1988 Act (other than the repeals in Schedule 12) and the repeals in the Social Security Acts,

shall not come into force until such day as the Secretary of State may by order appoint; and different days may be appointed for different provisions or for different purposes.

(3) Part I of this Act, sections 102 and 104 to 106 above and Schedule 10 to this Act extend to England and Wales only.

(4) Part II of this Act, sections 107 to 112 above and Schedules 11 and 12 to this Act extend to Scotland only.

(5) This Act does not extend to Northern Ireland.

SCHEDULES

SCHEDULE 1

PERSONS DISREGARDED FOR PURPOSES OF DISCOUNT

Persons in detention

1.—(1) A person shall be disregarded for the purposes of discount on a particular day if on the day—

(a) he is detained in a prison, a hospital or any other place by virtue of an order of a court to which sub-paragraph (2) below applies;

(b) he is detained under paragraph 2 of Schedule 3 to the Immigration Act 1971 (deportation);

(c) he is detained under Part II or section 46, 47, 48 or 136 of the Mental Health Act 1983; or

(d) he is detained under Part V or section 69, 70, 71 or 118 of the Mental Health (Scotland) Act 1984.

(2) This sub-paragraph applies to the following courts—

(a) a court in the United Kingdom; and

(b) a Standing Civilian Court established under the Armed Forces Act 1976.

(3) If a person—

(a) is temporarily discharged under section 28 of the Prison Act 1952, or temporarily released under rules under section 47(5) of that Act; or

(b) is temporarily discharged under section 27 of the Prisons (Scotland) Act 1989, or temporarily released under rules under section 39(6) of that Act,

for the purposes of sub-paragraph (1) above he shall be treated as detained.

(4) Sub-paragraph (1) above does not apply where the person—

(a) is detained under regulations made under paragraph 8 of Schedule 4 to this Act;

(b) is detained under section 76 of the Magistrates' Courts Act 1980, or section 9 of the Criminal Justice Act 1982, for default in payment of a fine; or

(c) is detained only under section 407 of the Criminal Procedure (Scotland) Act 1975.

(5) In sub-paragraph (1) above "order" includes a sentence, direction, warrant or other means of giving effect to the decision of the court concerned.

(6) The Secretary of State may by order provide that a person shall be disregarded for the purposes of discount on a particular day if—

(a) on the day he is imprisoned, detained or in custody under the Army Act 1955, the Air Force Act 1955 or the Naval Discipline Act 1957; and

(b) such conditions as may be prescribed by the order are fulfilled.

The severely mentally impaired

2.—(1) A person shall be disregarded for the purposes of discount on a particular day if—

(a) on the day he is severely mentally impaired;
(b) as regards any period which includes the day he is stated in a certificate of a registered medical practitioner to have been or to be likely to be severely mentally impaired; and
(c) as regards the day he fulfils such conditions as may be prescribed by order made by the Secretary of State.

(2) For the purposes of this paragraph a person is severely mentally impaired if he has a severe impairment of intelligence and social functioning (however caused) which appears to be permanent.

(3) The Secretary of State may by order substitute another definition for the definition in sub-paragraph (2) above as for the time being effective for the purposes of this paragraph.

Persons in respect of whom child benefit is payable

3.—(1) A person shall be disregarded for the purposes of discount on a particular day if on the day he—
(a) has attained the age of 18 years; but
(b) is a person in respect of whom another person is entitled to child benefit, or would be so entitled but for paragraph 1(c) of Schedule 9 to the Social Security Contributions and Benefits Act 1992.

(2) The Secretary of State may by order substitute another provision for subparagraph (1)(b) above as for the time being effective for the purposes of this paragraph.

Students etc.

4.—(1) A person shall be disregarded for the purposes of discount on a particular day if—
(a) on the day he is a student, student nurse, apprentice or youth training trainee; and
(b) such conditions as may be prescribed by order made by the Secretary of State are fulfilled.

(2) In this paragraph "apprentice", "student", "student nurse" and "youth training trainee" having the meanings for the time being assigned to them by order made by the Secretary of State.

5.—(1) An institution shall, on request, supply a certificate under this paragraph to any person who is following or, subject to sub-paragraph (3) below, has followed a course of education at that institution as a student or student nurse.

(2) A certificate under this paragraph shall contain such information about the person to whom it refers as may be prescribed by order made by the Secretary of State.

(3) An institution may refuse to comply with a request made more than one year after the person making it has ceased to follow a course of education at that institution.

(4) In this paragraph—
"institution" means any such educational establishment or other body as may be prescribed by order made by the Secretary of State; and
"student" and "student nurse" have the same meanings as in paragraph 4 above.

Hospital patients

6.—(1) A person shall be disregarded for the purposes of discount on a particular day if on the day he is a patient who has his sole or main residence in a hospital.

(2) In this paragraph "hospital" means—
(a) a health service hospital within the meaning of the National Health Service Act 1977 or section 108(1) (interpretation) of the National Health Service (Scotland) Act 1978; and
(b) a military, air-force or naval unit or establishment at or in which medical or surgical treatment is provided for persons subject to military law, air-force law or the Naval Discipline Act 1957.

(3) The Secretary of State may by order substitute another definition for the definition in sub-paragraph (2) above as for the time being effective for the purposes of this paragraph.

Patients in homes in England and Wales

7.—(1) A person shall be disregarded for the purposes of discount on a particular day if on the day—
(a) he has his sole or main residence in a residential care home, nursing home, mental nursing home or hostel in England and Wales; and
(b) he is receiving care or treatment (or both) in the home or hostel.

(2) In this paragraph—
"hostel" means anything which falls within any definition of hostel for the time being prescribed by order made by the Secretary of State under this sub-paragraph;

"mental nursing home" means anything which is a mental nursing home within the meaning of the Registered Homes Act 1984;

"nursing home" means anything which is a nursing home within the meaning of the Registered Homes Act 1984 or would be but for section 21(3)(a) of that Act;

"residential care home" means—

    (a) an establishment in respect of which registration is required under Part I of the Registered Homes Act 1984 or would be so required but for section 1(4) or 5(j) of that Act; or

    (b) a building or part of a building in which residential accommodation is provided under section 21 of the National Assistance Act 1948.

(3) The Secretary of State may by order substitute another definition for any definition of "mental nursing home", "nursing home" or "residential care home" for the time being effective for the purposes of this paragraph.

Patients in homes in Scotland

8.—(1) A person shall be disregarded for the purposes of discount on a particular day if on the day—

(a) he has as his sole or main residence a residential care home, nursing home, private hospital or hostel in Scotland; and

(b) he is receiving care or treatment (or both) in the home, hospital or hostel.

(2) In this paragraph—

"hostel" means anything which falls within any definition of hostel for the time being prescribed by order made by the Secretary of State under this sub-paragraph;

"nursing home" means—

    (a) a nursing home within the meaning of section 10(2) of the Nursing Homes Registration (Scotland) Act 1938 in respect of which a person is registered; or

    (b) any premises in respect of which an exemption has been granted under section 6 or 7 of that Act;

"private hospital" means a private hospital within the meaning of section 12 (registration of private hospitals) of the Mental Health (Scotland) Act 1984;

"residential care home" means—

    (a) a residential establishment provided and maintained by a local authority in respect of their functions under section 13B (provision of care and after-care) of the Social Work (Scotland) Act 1968; or

    (b) a residential establishment to which Part IV of the said Act of 1968 applies; or

    (c) residential accommodation provided and maintained by a local authority under section 7 (functions of local authorities) of the Mental Health (Scotland) Act 1984,

where the sole or main function of the establishment or accommodation is to provide personal care or support, combined with board, to persons who are solely or mainly resident in the establishment or accommodation.

(3) In the definition of "residential care home" in sub-paragraph (2) above—

"personal care" includes the provision of appropriate help with physical and social needs; and

"support" means counselling or other help provided as part of a planned programme of care.

(4) The Secretary of State may by order substitute another definition for any definition of "nursing home", "private hospital" or "residential care home" for the time being effective for the purposes of this paragraph.

Care workers

9.—(1) A person shall be disregarded for the purposes of discount on a particular day if—

(a) on the day he is engaged in providing care or support (or both) to another person or other persons; and

(b) such conditions as may be prescribed are fulfilled.

(2) Without prejudice to the generality of sub-paragraph (1)(b) above the conditions may—

(a) require the care or support (or both) to be provided on behalf of a charity or a person fulfilling some other description;

(b) relate to the period for which the person is engaged in providing care or support (or both);

(c) require his income for a prescribed period (which contains the day concerned) not to exceed a prescribed amount;

(d) require his capital not to exceed a prescribed amount;

(e) require him to be resident in prescribed premises;

(f) require him not to exceed a prescribed age;
(g) require the other person or persons to fulfil a prescribed description (whether relating to age, disablement or otherwise).

Residents of certain dwellings

10.—(1) A person shall be disregarded for the purposes of discount on a particular day if on the day he has his sole or main residence in a dwelling to which sub-paragraph (2) below applies.
(2) This sub-paragraph applies to any dwelling if—
(a) it is for the time being providing residential accommodation, whether as a hostel or night shelter or otherwise; and
(b) the accommodation is predominantly provided—
  (i) otherwise than in separate and self-contained sets of premises;
  (ii) for persons of no fixed abode and no settled way of life; and
  (iii) under licences to occupy which do not constitute tenancies.

Persons of other descriptions

11. A person shall be disregarded for the purposes of discount on a particular day if—
(a) on the day he falls within such description as may be prescribed; and
(b) such conditions as may be prescribed are fulfilled.

GENERAL NOTE
The purpose of this schedule is to define those persons who are to be disregarded for the purposes of discount. It applies to England, Wales and Scotland, although there are separate paragraphs in relation to patients in homes, for the jurisdictions of England and Wales, and Scotland, respectively. In addition, the provisions of para. 5, which in the original Bill applied to Scotland only, have also been applied to England and Wales.
If a person is disregarded for the purposes of discount it means that he is not taken into account in determining, under ss.11 or 79, how many residents there are in the dwelling, and so whether the council tax payable in respect of that dwelling is subject to a discount and, if so, how much. Eight identifiable groups are specified: persons in detention; the severely mentally impaired; persons in respect of whom child benefit is payable; students; hospital patients; patients in homes; care workers; and persons in hostels and night-shelters. In addition, under para. 11, the Secretary of State is empowered to make regulations specifying further categories of persons to be disregarded, and may prescribe conditions to be fulfilled. See the Council Tax (Discounts Disregards) Order 1992 (S.I. 1992 No. 548) and the Council Tax (Additional Provisions for Discounts Disregards) Order 1992 (S.I. 1992 No. 552). For Scotland see the Council Tax (Discounts) (Scotland) Order 1992 (S.I. 1992 No. 1408) and the Council Tax (Discounts) (Scotland) Regulations 1992 (S.I. 1992 No. 1409).

Para. 1
This provides that certain detained persons are to be disregarded for the purposes of discount. These are defined as persons detained (1) by an order of a court, as defined in para. 1(2); (2) under provisions of the Immigration Act 1971; and (3) under provisions of the Mental Health Acts of 1983 and 1984. Temporary discharge or release does not alter this designation. Paragraph 1(4) provides that being detained for non-payment of the council tax, under para. 8 of Sched. 4 to this Act, or for default in payment of a fine, under s.76 of the Magistrates' Courts Act 1980 or s.9 of the Criminal Justice Act 1982, or under s.407 of the Criminal Procedure (Scotland) Act 1975, will not be disregarded for the purposes of discount. Under para. 1(6) the Secretary of State can, by order, provide that any person detained, imprisoned or held in custody under the Army Act 1955, the Air Force Act 1955 or the Naval Discipline Act 1957, will be disregarded, provided that that person fulfils any conditions which may be imposed by the order. In this regard see the Council Tax (Discounts Disregards) Order 1992 (S.I. 1992 No. 548), art. 2. For Scotland see the Council Tax (Discounts) (Scotland) Order 1992 (S.I. 1992 No. 1408).

Para. 2
Persons who are severely mentally impaired are to be disregarded for the purposes of discount. A severely mentally impaired person will be disregarded if on any day he has a relevant medical certificate and fulfils any conditions which the Secretary of State may prescribe in an order made under para. 2(1). Paragraph 2(2) defines a person as severely mentally impaired if he has a severe impairment of intelligence and social functioning, however caused, which appears to be permanent. Under para. 2(3) the Secretary of State is empowered to change the definition of "severely mentally impaired" by order. In this regard see the Council Tax (Discounts Disregards) Order 1992 (S.I. 1992 No. 548), art. 3. For Scotland see the Council Tax (Discounts) (Scotland) Regulations 1992 (S.I. 1992 No. 1409).

Para. 3
Persons in respect of whom child benefit is payable are to be disregarded for the purpose of

discount. This applies to any person who has attained the age of 18 and is someone in respect of whom another person is entitled to receive child benefit, or would be but for the provisions of para. 1(c) of Sched. 9 to the Social Security Contributions and Benefits Act 1992, which excludes persons from entitlement to child benefit in respect of certain categories of children, such as foster children. Under para. 3(2) the Secretary of State is empowered to change, by order, the provisions relating to this category of persons.

Paras. 4 and 5

Those falling within the definitions of "students", "student nurses", "apprentices" and "youth training trainees" are to be disregarded for the purposes of discount. The meaning of these terms may be prescribed by the Secretary of State. In this regard see the Council Tax (Discounts Disregards) Order 1992 (S.I. 1992 No. 548), art. 4. The order may also specify conditions to be fulfilled before a person can be disregarded. Paragraph 5 provides for certification procedures for present or past students or student nurses at institutions. An institution must supply, on request, a certificate to any person who is following, or who has followed, a course of instruction at that institution as a student or student nurse, and the certificate must contain such information about the person to whom it refers as may be prescribed in regulations. In this regard see the Council Tax (Discounts Disregards) Order 1992 (S.I. 1992 No. 548), art. 5. An institution may refuse to provide a certificate if the person requesting it does so more than one year after ending his or her course at that institution.

For Scotland see the Council Tax (Discounts) (Scotland) Order 1992 (S.I. 1992 No. 1408).

Para. 6

Certain hospital patients are to be disregarded for the purposes of discount, if on any particular day they are patients who have their sole or main residence in a hospital. Under para. 6(3) the Secretary of State is empowered to change the definition of "hospital" by order.

Para. 7

Certain patients living in homes in England and Wales are to be disregarded for the purposes of discount, if they have their sole or main residence, and are receiving care and/or treatment, in a residential care home, nursing-home, mental nursing-home or hostel. The definitions of "mental nursing-home", "nursing-home" and "residential care home" are provided but the definition of "hostel" is left to regulation. The Secretary of State may change any of those definitions by order. In this regard see the Council Tax (Discounts Disregards) Order 1992 (S.I. 1992 No. 548), art. 6.

Para. 8

Certain patients living in homes in Scotland are to be disregarded for the purposes of discount. A person must have his sole or main residence, and be receiving care and/or treatment, in a residential care home, nursing-home, private hospital or hostel in Scotland. Paragraph 8(2) provides that "hostel" shall be defined by the Secretary of State by order, and defines "nursing-home", "private hospital" and "residential care home", while para. 8(3) defines the terms "personal care" and "support", which are used in the definition of residential care home. The Secretary of State is empowered to change any of the definitions of nursing-home, private hospital or residential care home, by order. See the Council Tax (Discounts) (Scotland) Order 1992 (S.I. 1992 No. 1408).

Para. 9

Care workers are to be disregarded for the purposes of discount, if on any day they are engaged in providing care and/or support to another person or persons, and they fulfil any conditions which the Secretary of State may prescribe by order. While not providing a definition, para. 9(2) lists some of the factors which may be taken into account in the regulations. In this regard see the Council Tax (Additional Provisions for Discounts Disregards) Order 1992 (S.I. 1992 No. 552), reg. 2 and the Council Tax (Discounts) (Scotland) Regulations 1992 (S.I. 1992 No. 1409).

Para. 10

Residents of certain dwellings are to be disregarded for the purposes of discount. A person must have his sole or main residence in a dwelling which fulfils two conditions. First, it is for the time being providing residential accommodation, for example as a hostel or night-shelter. Secondly, it is predominantly providing accommodation in other than separate and self-contained units for persons of no fixed abode and no settled way of life and under licences to occupy which are not tenancies.

Para. 11

The Secretary of State is empowered to make regulations specifying other categories of persons to be disregarded, and may prescribe conditions to be fulfilled. In this regard see the

Council Tax (Additional Provisions for Discounts Disregards) Order 1992 (S.I. 1992 No. 552), reg. 3, which establishes three further classes: members of international headquarters and defence organisations; members of religious communities; and school-leavers. For Scotland see the Council Tax (Discounts) (Scotland) Regulations 1992 (S.I. 1992 No. 1409).

Sections 14(1) and 97(3)   SCHEDULE 2

ADMINISTRATION

Introduction

1.—(1) The Secretary of State may make regulations containing such provision as he thinks fit in relation to—

(a) the collection of amounts persons are liable to pay in respect of council tax; and

(b) other aspects of administration as regards council tax.

(2) Any reference in this Schedule to an authority is a reference to a billing authority or a levying authority.

Collection of council tax

2.—(1) In the following provisions of this paragraph—

(a) any reference to the liable person is a reference to a person who is solely liable to pay to an authority, in respect of a particular dwelling, an amount in respect of council tax for a financial year, and includes, unless the context otherwise requires, a reference to a person who in the opinion of the authority will be so liable; and

(b) any reference to the chargeable amount is a reference to the amount the liable person is or will be liable to pay.

(2) Regulations under this Schedule may include provision—

(a) that the liable person is to make payments on account of the chargeable amount, which may include payments during the course of the financial year concerned;

(b) that payments on account must be made in accordance with an agreement between the liable person and the authority or a prescribed scheme for payment by instalments or a scheme or such payment made by the authority in accordance with prescribed rules;

(c) that in prescribed circumstances payments on account must be calculated by reference to an estimate of the chargeable amount; and

(d) that an estimate must be made on prescribed assumptions.

(3) Regulations under this Schedule may include provision—

(a) that any person appearing to an authority to be a resident, owner or managing agent of a particular dwelling shall supply to the authority such information as fulfils the following conditions—

(i) it is in the possession or control of the person concerned;

(ii) the authority requests the person concerned to supply it; and

(iii) it is requested by the authority for the purpose of identifying the person who, in respect of any period specified in the request, is or will be the liable person in relation to the dwelling;

(b) that the information is to be supplied within a prescribed period of the request being made and, if the authority so requires, in a form specified in the request; and

(c) that a request may be served on the person concerned either by name or by such description as may be prescribed.

(4) Regulations under this Schedule may include provision—

(a) that the authority must serve a notice or notices on the liable person stating the chargeable amount or its estimated amount and what payment or payments he is required to make (by way of instalment or otherwise);

(b) that no payment on account of the chargeable amount need be made unless a notice requires it;

(c) that a notice may be served on the liable person either by name or by such description as may be prescribed;

(d) that a notice must be in a prescribed form;

(e) that a notice must contain prescribed matters;

(f) that a notice must not contain other prescribed matters;

(g) that where a notice is invalid because it does not comply with regulations under paragraph (d) or (e) above, and the circumstances are such as may be prescribed, a requirement contained in the notice by virtue of regulations under paragraph (a) or (b) above shall nevertheless have effect as if the notice were valid;

(h) that where a notice is invalid because it does not comply with regulations under paragraph (d) above, and a requirement has effect by virtue of regulations under paragraph (g) above, the authority must take prescribed steps to issue to the liable person a document in the form which the notice would have taken had it complied with regulations under paragraph (d) above;

(i) that where a notice is invalid because it does not comply with regulations under paragraph (e) above, and a requirement has effect by virtue of regulations under paragraph (g) above, the authority must take prescribed steps to inform the liable person of such of the matters prescribed under paragraph (e) above as were not contained in the notice; and

(j) that the authority must supply prescribed information to the liable person when it serves a notice.

(5) Regulations under this Schedule may include provision—

(a) that if the liable person fails to pay an instalment in accordance with the regulations, the unpaid balance of the chargeable amount or its estimated amount it to be payable on the day after the end of a prescribed period which begins with the day of the failure; and

(b) that any amount paid by the liable person in excess of his liability (whether the excess arises because an estimate turns out to be wrong or otherwise) must be repaid or credited against any subsequent liability.

3.—(1) Regulations under this Schedule may include provision as to the collection of amounts persons are jointly and severally liable to pay in respect of council tax.

(2) The regulations may include provision equivalent to that included under paragraph 2 above subject to any modifications the Secretary of State thinks fit.

(3) The regulations may include rules for determining whether any payment made by a person jointly and severally liable as to a fraction of an amount is (or is not) made towards satisfaction of his liability as to that fraction.

Discounts

4.—(1) In the following provisions of this paragraph—

(a) any reference to the chargeable amount is a reference to an amount which, in respect of a particular dwelling, a person is solely liable to pay to an authority in respect of council tax for a financial year, and includes, unless the context otherwise requires, an amount which in the opinion of the authority a person will be so liable to pay; and

(b) any reference to any calculation of the chargeable amount includes a reference to any estimate of the amount.

(2) Regulations under this Schedule may include provision that, before making any calculation of the chargeable amount for the purposes of regulations under this Schedule, the authority shall take reasonable steps to ascertain whether that amount is subject to any discount, and if so, the amount of that discount.

(3) The regulations may include provision that—

(a) where (having taken such steps) the authority has no reason to believe that the chargeable amount is subject to a discount, it shall assume, in making any calculation of the chargeable amount for the purposes of regulations under this Schedule, that the chargeable amount is not subject to any discount; and

(b) where (having taken such steps) the authority has reason to believe that the chargeable amount is subject to a discount of a particular amount, it shall assume, in making any such calculation, that the chargeable amount is subject to a discount of that amount.

(4) The regulations may include provision that the authority must inform the person who is or will be liable to pay the chargeable amount of that assumption.

(5) The regulations may include provision that where—

(a) in accordance with any provision included under sub-paragraph (4) above the authority informs the person concerned that it has assumed that the chargeable amount is subject to a discount of a particular amount; and

(b) at any time before the end of the financial year following the financial year concerned, the person has reason to believe that the chargeable amount is not in fact subject to any discount, or is subject to a discount of a smaller amount,

the person shall, within such period as may be prescribed, notify the authority of his belief.

(6) In construing the reference in sub-paragraph (5)(b) above to the chargeable amount, the fact that the person concerned has wholly or partly discharged his liability to pay the amount shall be ignored.

5. Regulations under this Schedule may include, as regards a case where persons are or will be jointly and severally liable to pay to an authority, in respect of a particular dwelling, an amount in respect of council tax for a financial year, provision equivalent to that included under paragraph 4 above subject to any modifications the Secretary of State thinks fit.

Reductions for lump sum payment etc.

6.—(1) Regulations under this Schedule may include provision empowering an authority, subject to such conditions as may be prescribed, to accept, in such cases as the authority may determine and in satisfaction of a person's sole liability to pay in respect of a dwelling an amount ("the chargeable amount") in respect of council tax for a financial year, an amount which—

(a) is determined by the authority; and

(b) is payable in a single lump sum; and

(c) is less than the authority's estimate of the chargeable amount.

(2) The regulations may include provision empowering or requiring the authority to make such adjustments (whether by way of an additional sum due to the authority or by way of repayment or credit by the authority or otherwise) as may be prescribed where the chargeable amount is subsequently estimated to be or proves to be greater or less than the amount originally (or last) estimated.

(3) The regulations may include, as regards a case where persons are jointly and severally liable to pay the chargeable amount, provision equivalent to that included under sub-paragraphs (1) and (2) above subject to any modifications the Secretary of State thinks fit.

(4) The regulations may include provision that, in a case where an authority has made provision by virtue of any of sub-paragraphs (1) to (3) above, any provision which is included in regulations under this Schedule by virtue of paragraph 2 or 3 above and is prescribed under this sub-paragraph shall not apply.

7.—(1) Regulations under this Schedule may include provision that where—

(a) a person has sole liability to pay to an authority a sum on account in respect of council tax;

(b) a sum smaller than that sum is paid; and

(c) such conditions as may be prescribed are fulfilled;

the authority may accept the smaller sum in satisfaction of the liability to pay the sum on account.

(2) The regulations may include provision that—

(a) for prescribed purposes the sum on account shall be treated as having been paid in full;

(b) for other prescribed purposes for the fact that only the smaller sum has been paid shall be taken into account.

(3) The regulations may include, as regards a case where persons are jointly and severally liable to pay to an authority a sum on account in respect of council tax, provision equivalent to that included under sub-paragraphs (1) and (2) above subject to any modifications the Secretary of State thinks fit.

Exempt dwellings etc.

8.—(1) Regulations under this Schedule may include provision that an authority which has received a copy of a proposed list sent to it under section 22(5)(b) or 85(1)(b) of this Act shall, as respects each dwelling shown in the copy which in the opinion of the authority will be a relevant dwelling on the day when the list comes into force, notify the person concerned of such matters relating to the dwelling's entry in the copy as may be prescribed.

(2) Regulations under this Schedule may include provision that in any case where—

(a) a dwelling is not shown in the copy of a proposed list sent to an authority under section 22(5)(b) or 85(1)(b) of this Act but is shown in the copy of the list sent to the authority under section 22(7) or 85(4) of this Act; and

(b) in the opinion of the authority the dwelling was a relevant dwelling on the day when the list came into force,

the authority shall notify the person concerned of such matters relating to the dwelling's entry in the copy of the list sent to the authority under section 22(7) or 85(4) of this Act as may be prescribed.

(3) Regulations under this Schedule may include provision that in any case where—

(a) the valuation band shown as applicable to a dwelling in the copy of a proposed list sent to an authority under section 22(5)(b) or 85(1)(b) of this Act is different from that shown as applicable to it in the copy of the list sent to the authority under section 22(7) or 85(4) of this Act; and

(b) in the opinion of the authority the dwelling was a relevant dwelling on the day when the list came into force,

the authority shall notify the person concerned of such matters relating to the dwelling's entry in the copy of the list sent to the authority under section 22(7) or 85(4) of this Act as may be prescribed.

(4) The regulations may include provision—

(a) as to the period within which or time at which any notification must be given;

(b) prescribing additional information which the notification must contain;

(c) that if at the time when a person is notified under any provision included in regulations under sub-paragraph (2) or (3) above the authority has not yet given him a notification under any provision included in regulations under sub-paragraph (1) above, the authority shall not be required to give him such a notification.

(5) For the purposes of this paragraph a dwelling is a relevant dwelling on any day if—

(a) on the day the dwelling is an exempt dwelling; or

(b) in respect of the financial year in which the day falls and the dwelling, the amount set under section 30 or 93 of this Act or, where the authority is a regional council, each amount set under section 93 of this Act is nil.

(6) In this paragraph any reference to the person concerned is a reference to a person who, in respect of the particular dwelling, would be solely liable to pay to the authority an amount in respect of council tax for the particular day if the dwelling were not or had not been a relevant dwelling on that day.

9.—(1) Regulations under this Schedule may include provision that, as regards each financial year, an authority shall take reasonable steps to ascertain whether any dwellings will be or were exempt dwellings for any period during the year.

(2) The regulations may include provision that—

(a) where (having taken such steps) the authority has no reason to believe that a particular dwelling will be or was an exempt dwelling for any period during the year, it shall assume, for the purposes of regulations under this Schedule, that the dwelling will be or was a chargeable dwelling for that period; and

(b) where (having taken such steps) the authority has reason to believe that a particular dwelling will be or was an exempt dwelling for any period during the year, it shall assume, for those purposes, that the dwelling will be or was an exempt dwelling for that period.

(3) The regulations may include provision—

(a) that the authority must inform the relevant person of that assumption;

(b) prescribing additional information which the authority must give to that person;

(c) as to the period within which or time at which any information must be given.

(4) The regulations may include provision that where—

(a) in accordance with any provision included under sub-paragraph (3) above the authority informs the relevant person that it has assumed that the dwelling will be or was an exempt dwelling for a particular period during the year; and

(b) at any time before the end of the following financial year, the person has reason to believe that in fact the dwelling will not be or was not an exempt dwelling for that period, or will be or was an exempt dwelling for a shorter period,

the person shall, within such period as may be prescribed, notify the authority of his belief.

(5) Regulations under this Schedule may include provision—

(a) that any person appearing to an authority to be a resident, owner or managing agent of a particular dwelling shall supply to the authority such information as fulfils the following conditions—

(i) it is in the possession or control of the person concerned;

(ii) the authority requests the person concerned to supply it; and

(iii) it is requested by the authority for the purpose of identifying the person who, in respect of any period specified in the request, is or will be the relevant person in relation to the dwelling;

(b) that the information is to be supplied within a prescribed period of the request being made and, if the authority so requires, in a form specified in the request; and

(c) that a request may be served on the person concerned either by name or by such description as may be prescribed.

(6) In this paragraph any reference to the relevant person is a reference to a person who, in respect of the particular dwelling—

(a) is or will be solely liable to pay to the authority an amount in respect of council tax for the period to which the assumption relates; or

(b) would be so liable if the dwelling were not or had not been an exempt dwelling for that period.

10.—(1) Regulations under this Schedule may include, as regards a case where, in respect of a particular dwelling, persons would be jointly and severally liable to pay to an authority an amount in respect of council tax for a particular day if the dwelling were not or had not been on the day a relevant dwelling for the purposes of paragraph 8 above, provision equivalent to that included under that paragraph subject to any modifications the Secretary of State thinks fit.

(2) Regulations under this Schedule may include, as regards a case where, in respect of a particular dwelling, persons—

(a) are or will be jointly and severally liable to pay to an authority an amount in respect of council tax for a particular period; or

(b) would be so liable if the dwelling were not or had not been an exempt dwelling for that period,

provision equivalent to that included under paragraph 9 above subject to any modifications the Secretary of State thinks fit.

Supply of information to authorities

11.—(1) Regulations under this Schedule may include provision that any person mentioned in sub-paragraph (2) below shall supply to a billing authority such information as fulfils the following conditions—

(a) it is in the possession or control of the person concerned;

(b) the authority requests the person concerned to supply it;

(c) it is requested by the authority for the purpose of carrying out its functions under Part I of this Act; and

(d) it does not fall within any prescribed description of information which need not be supplied.

(2) The persons referred to in sub-paragraph (1) above are—

(a) any other authority;

(b) any precepting authority;

(c) the electoral registration officer for any area in Great Britain; and

(d) any community charges registration officer.

(3) The regulations may include provision that the information is to be supplied in a prescribed form and within a prescribed period of the request being made.

(4) In this paragraph and paragraph 12 below references to any community charges registration officer shall be construed—

(a) in relation to such officers in England or Wales, in accordance with section 26 of the 1988 Act; and

(b) in relation to such officers in Scotland, in accordance with section 12 of the 1987 Act.

12.—(1) Regulations under this Schedule may include provision that any person mentioned in sub-paragraph (2) below shall supply to a levying authority such information as fulfils the following conditions—

(a) it is in the possession or control of the person concerned;

(b) the authority request the person concerned to supply it;

(c) it is requested by the authority for the purpose of carrying out their functions under Part II of this Act; and

(d) it does not fall within any prescribed description of information which need not be supplied.

(2) The persons referred to in sub-paragraph (1) above are—

(a) any other authority;

(b) any district council;

(c) the electoral registration officer for any area in Great Britain;

(d) any community charges registration officer;

(e) the local assessor for the levying authority's area; and

(f) any housing body operating in the levying authority's area.

(3) The regulations may include provision that the information is to be supplied in a prescribed form and within a prescribed period of the request being made.

13.—(1) Regulations under this Schedule may include provision that—

(a) a registrar of births and deaths in England and Wales shall supply to any appropriate billing authority which is prescribed such particulars of such deaths as may be prescribed;

(b) the Registrar General for England and Wales shall supply to any billing authority which is prescribed such particulars of such deaths as may be prescribed.

(2) Regulations under this Schedule may include provision that—

(a) a district registrar in Scotland shall supply to any appropriate levying authority which is prescribed such particulars of such deaths as may be prescribed;

(b) the Registrar General for Scotland shall supply to any levying authority which is prescribed such particulars of such deaths as may be prescribed.

(3) The regulations may include provision as to the times at which and the manner in which the particulars are to be supplied.

(4) For the purposes of this paragraph—

(a) an appropriate billing authority, in relation to a registrar of births and deaths, is a billing authority whose area includes all or part of, or falls within, the registrar's sub-district;

(b) an appropriate levying authority, in relation to a district registrar, is a levying authority whose area includes all or part of, or falls within, the registrar's registration district.

14.—(1) Where regulations under this Schedule impose a duty on a billing authority to supply information to any person, they may also require—

(a) the Secretary of State;

(b) any appropriate precepting authority; or

(c) any appropriate levying body,

to supply the billing authority with prescribed information if the Secretary of State considers it to be information the billing authority needs in order to fulfil its duty.

(2) Where regulations under the Schedule contain provision about the contents or form of a notice to be served by a billing authority, they may also require the Secretary of State or any appropriate precepting authority to supply the billing authority with prescribed information if the Secretary of State considers it to be information the billing authority needs to ensure that the provision is met.

(3) Where any person other than the Secretary of State fails to supply information to a billing authority in accordance with regulations made by virtue of sub-paragraph (1) or (2) above, he shall be liable to indemnify the authority against any loss or damage which the authority sustains in consequence of the failure.

(4) For the purposes of sub-paragraph (1) or (2) above an authority is an appropriate precepting authority in relation to a billing authority if it has power to issue a precept to the billing authority.

(5) For the purposes of sub-paragraph (1) above a body is an appropriate levying body in relation to a billing authority if—

(a) it has power to issue a levy or special levy to the billing authority; or

(b) it has power to issue a levy to a county council which has power to issue a precept to the billing authority.

15.—(1) Regulations under this Schedule may include provision that no duty of confidentiality shall prevent the Secretary of State from disclosing relevant information to an authority.

(2) For the purposes of this paragraph information is relevant information if—

(a) it was obtained by the Secretary of State in exercising his functions under the Social Security Acts;

(b) the Secretary of State believes it would be useful to the authority in exercising its functions under Part I or II of this Act; and

(c) it falls within a prescribed description.

Supply of information by authorities

16.—(1) Regulations under this Schedule may include provision that (so far as it does not have power to do so apart from the regulations) an authority may supply relevant information to another authority, even if it is not requested to supply the information.

(2) For the purposes of this paragraph information is relevant information if—

(a) it was obtained by the first-mentioned authority in exercising its functions under Part I or II of this Act;

(b) it believes it would be useful to the other authority in exercising its functions under either of those Parts; and

(c) it does not fall within any prescribed description of information which is not to be supplied.

17.—(1) Regulations under this Schedule may include provision that an authority—

(a) may supply relevant information to any person who requests it for a purpose not relating to Part I or II of this Act; and

(b) may charge a prescribed fee for supplying the information.

(2) For the purposes of sub-paragraph (1) above information is relevant information if—

(a) it was obtained by the authority for the purpose of carrying out its functions under Part I or II of this Act; and

(b) it is not personal information.

(3) For the purposes of sub-paragraph (2) above personal information is information which relates to an individual (living or dead) who can be identified from that information or from that and other information supplied to any person by the authority; and personal information includes any expression of opinion about the individual and any indication of the intentions of any person in respect of the individual.

Use of information by authorities

18. Regulations under this Schedule may include provision that, in carrying out its functions under Part I or II of this Act, an authority may use information which—

(a) is obtained under any other enactment; and

(b) does not fall within any prescribed description of information which cannot be used.

Arrangements with Scottish housing bodies

19.—(1) Subject to sub-paragraph (3) below, a levying authority may make arrangements with a housing body for the exercise by that body on behalf of the authority of any of—

(a) the authority's functions under or by virtue of this Schedule or Schedule 3 or 8 to this Act; or

(b) the authority's responsibilities as regards council tax benefit in pursuance of Part VII of the Social Security Contributions and Benefits Act 1992.

(2) Arrangements under sub-paragraph (1) above may, without prejudice to the generality of that sub-paragraph—

(a) provide that a housing body may accept service of a notice under section 81(4) of this Act on behalf of a levying authority and may exercise the functions of that authority under subsections (7) and (8) of that section:

(b) provide as to the term upon which, instalments by which and manner in which council tax is to be payable to and collected and recovered by the body.

(3) Arrangements under this paragraph for the exercise of functions under paragraph 2(1)(a) of Schedule 8 to this Act may be made only with a district council.

(4) Every person by whom council tax is payable to a housing body under arrangements under this paragraph shall pay it to the body in accordance with those arrangements.

(5) Arrangements under sub-paragraph (1) above shall be on such terms as may be agreed between the levying authority and the housing body or, failing agreement, as may be determined by the Secretary of State.

(6) Where the Secretary of State is satisfied that a levying authority wish to make arrangements under sub-paragraph (1) above with a housing body but that body has not agreed to enter into them, he may, by regulations made after consultation with the authority and the body, require the body to do so.

(7) No document issued by a housing body in pursuance of an arrangement made under this paragraph to a person liable to pay council tax or any instalment of council tax shall contain or refer to arrangements for any payment other than—

(a) the payment of any council tax instalment;

(b) the payment of any council water charge; or

(c) the payment of any council tax benefit in pursuance of Part VII of the Social Security Contributions and Benefits Act 1992.

Supplemental

20. In this Schedule—

(a) any reference to a payment on account of an amount, however expressed, is to any payment (whether interim, final or sole) in respect of the amount; and

(b) any reference to a managing agent, in relation to a dwelling, is to a person authorised to arrange lettings of the dwelling.

GENERAL NOTE

This schedule enables the Secretary of State to make regulations relating to the collection of council tax, and other aspects of administration. See also the Council Tax (Administration and Enforcement) Regulations 1992 (S.I. 1992 No. 613). For Scotland see the Council Tax (Administration and Enforcement) (Scotland) Regulations 1992 (S.I. 1992 No. 1332).

Para. 1

The Secretary of State is empowered to make regulations relating to the collection of amounts payable by way of council tax, and to other administrative matters. For these purposes the relevant authority is the billing authority or levying authority.

Paras. 2 and 3

This provides that regulations may be made in relation to payments on account of the chargeable amount; payments by instalments, calculations by reference to estimate and the making of estimates on the basis of assumptions. Regulations may be made concerning the obtaining of information from the owner, resident or managing agent of a dwelling, and concerning other notices and information. Under para. 2(4), regulations may be made to provide for payment of the unpaid balance of the chargeable amount to become due where a person fails to pay an instalment in accordance with the regulations, and for repayments or credits where too much has been paid. Paragraph 3 enables regulations to make provision for the case where persons are jointly and severally liable to make payments in respect of council tax. Such provision may be equivalent to that where a person is solely liable, but with whatever modifications the Secretary of State thinks fit. The regulations may include rules for the purpose of establishing whether a payment made by a person who is jointly and severally liable for only part of an amount is or is not made towards meeting that liability.

Paras. 4 and 5

Regulations may require billing and levying authorities, before making calculations, to take reasonable steps to ascertain whether or not the chargeable amount is subject to any discount, and if so, its amount; to require billing and levying authorities which have taken reasonable steps to ascertain discount entitlements, to make assumptions that the chargeable amount is or is not subject to discount, depending whether the authority has reason to believe that it is or is not so subject; to require billing and levying authorities to inform the liable person of any discount assumptions which it has made; and to require a person in whose case an assumption as to discount entitlement has been made, and who has been informed of that assumption, to notify the authority concerned where he has reason to believe that the chargeable amount is not in fact subject to a discount or is subject to a discount *less* than that assumed. The last requirement to notify applies until the end of the financial year after that in respect of which the assumption was made, and is to apply notwithstanding that the chargeable amount in question has been wholly or partly paid. Paragraph 5 allows the Secretary of State to include in regulations provision equivalent to that included under para. 4, subject to modifications, for cases of joint and several liability.

Paras. 6 and 7
Regulations may be made to allow an authority, subject to conditions, to accept single lump-sum payments of an amount determined by the authority which is less than its estimate of the chargeable amount; to permit or require an authority to make financial adjustments where it has accepted a lump sum and the chargeable amount turns out to be different from that estimated when the lump sum was accepted; to make equivalent provision in cases of joint and several liability; and to disapply other collection provisions made under paras. 2 or 3 where an authority accepts lump-sum payments. Paragraph 7 provides that regulations may allow authorities to accept reduced amounts in other prescribed circumstances, and that the payment of a reduced amount is to be treated as payment of the full amount for purposes to be specified in the regulations. For other prescribed purposes, account is to be taken of the smaller sum actually paid. Equivalent provision is permitted to be made in cases of joint and several liability.

Para. 8
Regulations may require an authority which has received a copy of a proposed list sent to it by the listing officer or local assessor to notify the owner of a dwelling shown in that copy of certain matters relating to the relevant entry, where the dwelling is one which, in the authority's opinion, will be an exempt dwelling on the day when the list comes into force. Provision may also be made for the notification of owners in cases where a dwelling not shown in the copy of the proposed list sent to the authority is shown in a subsequent copy of the list sent to the authority, and, in the authority's opinion, the dwelling was exempt on the day on which the list came into force. An authority may be required to notify the owner of an exempt dwelling of matters relating to its entry in a list where the valuation band differs from that shown in an earlier proposed list. Further provision may be made about notifications including provision as to timing and the giving of additional information. Under para. 9 the authority is placed under a duty to take reasonable steps to ascertain whether dwellings were exempt for all or part of the financial year, and provision is made for notification and the obtaining of information. Paragraph 10 makes provision for joint and several liability.

Paras. 11–15
Regulations may provide for the supply of certain information relevant to Pts. I and II of the Act. Information may be requested from other billing authorities, levying authorities, precepting authorities, electoral registration officers, local assessors, housing bodies, and community charges registration officers. The regulations may make provision as to the form in which and time within which information is to be supplied. The regulations may also provide for the supply of particulars about deaths to billing authorities and levying authorities. The persons from whom particulars may be obtained are registrars of births and deaths in England and Wales, the Registrar General for England and Wales, and district registrars in Scotland. The regulations may make provision to how and when particulars are to be supplied. Where regulations require a billing authority to supply information to a person, they may also require the Secretary of State, appropriate precepting authorities and appropriate levying bodies to supply the billing authority with prescribed information, if the Secretary of State considers that the authority needs that information to fulfil its duty and, where regulations require a billing authority to serve a notice in a prescribed form, or containing prescribed matters, they may also require the Secretary of State and appropriate precepting authorities to supply the billing authority with prescribed information deemed necessary by the Secretary of State to ensure that the provision is met. Failure on the part of a person other than the Secretary of State to supply a billing authority with information in accordance with these provisions renders him liable to indemnify the authority against loss or damage sustained by it as a result of that failure. The regulations may provide that the Secretary of State is not prevented by any duty of confidentiality from disclosing relevant information to a billing or levying authority.

Paras. 16 and 17
Regulations may provide for the supply of relevant information between billing and levying

authorities, whether or not in response to any request, and may allow an authority to supply, and charge a fee for relevant information, other than personal information, to a person who requests it for a purpose unrelated to Pts. I or II of the Bill.

Para. 18

Regulations may provide that in carrying out its functions under Pts. I or II of the Bill an authority may use information obtained under any other legislation, unless it is of a description prescribed which cannot be used.

Para. 19

This provides for the collection by housing bodies in Scotland of the council tax, acting as agents of levying authorities, and specifies the arrangements to be made between levying authorities and housing bodies. The provisions contain arrangements broadly similar to those made in relation to rates under s.10 of the Local Government (Scotland) Act 1975, and in relation to community charge under para. 5 of Sched. 2 to the 1987 Act. A levying authority may enter an arrangement with a housing body whereby that body will carry out certain of the levying authority's functions on its behalf. The functions in question are those under Sched. 2 on Administration, Sched. 3 on Penalties, Sched. 8 on Enforcement, and also the administration of council tax benefit arrangements. A housing body acting under such an arrangement can accept service of notices which s.81 requires to be served on a levying authority as part of the appeals process. It can also carry out the functions relating to a response to such a notice. It also provides for the arrangements to include terms for the payment, collection and recovery of council tax to or by the housing body. Arrangements for the recovery of sums under summary warrant can only be made where the housing body is a district council. Where an arrangement exists for council tax to be paid to a housing body a person is required to pay it to the body in accordance with the arrangements. The terms of such arrangements are to be a matter for agreement between the levying and the housing body but, where there has been a failure to agree terms, the Secretary of State may determine these. Where the levying authority wishes to make arrangements, but the housing body has not agreed to enter into them, then the Secretary of State, after consulting both parties, may make regulations requiring the housing body to enter into arrangements. Documents issued by the housing body in pursuance of an arrangement shall refer only to payments of any council-tax instalment, payment of the council water charge or payment of council tax benefit.

Sections 14(2) and 97(4)   SCHEDULE 3

PENALTIES

Failure to supply information to or notify billing authority

1.—(1) Where a person is requested by a billing authority to supply information under any provision included in regulations under paragraph 2, 3, 9 or 10(2) of Schedule 2 to this Act, the authority may impose a penalty of £50 on him if—
   (a) he fails to supply the information in accordance with the provision; or
   (b) in purported compliance with the provision he knowingly supplies information which is inaccurate in a material particular.
(2) In any case where—
   (a) a person is required by any provision included in regulations under paragraph 4, 5, 9 or 10(2) of Schedule 2 to this Act to notify a billing authority; and
   (b) he fails without reasonable excuse to notify the authority in accordance with the provision,
the authority may impose a penalty of £50 on him.
(3) Where a penalty has been imposed on a person under sub-paragraph (1) above and he is requested by the authority again to supply the same information under the same provision, the authority may impose a further penalty of £200 on him if—
   (a) he fails to supply the information in accordance with the provision; or
   (b) in purported compliance with the provision he knowingly supplies information which is inaccurate in a material particular.
(4) Sub-paragraph (3) above applies each time the authority repeats a request.
(5) A penalty under this paragraph shall be paid to the authority imposing it.
(6) An authority may quash a penalty imposed by it under this paragraph.

Failure to supply information to or notify levying authority

2.—(1) Where a person is requested by a levying authority to supply information under any provision included in regulations under paragraph 2, 3, 9 or 10(2) of Schedule 2 or paragraph 5 of Schedule 8 to this Act, the authority may impose a penalty of £50 on him if—

(a) he fails to supply the information in accordance with the provision; or

(b) in purported compliance with the provision he knowingly supplies information which is inaccurate in a material particular.

(2) In any case where—

(a) a person is required by any provision included in regulations under paragraph 4, 5, 9 or 10(2) of Schedule 2 to this Act to notify a levying authority; and

(b) he fails to notify the authority in accordance with the provision,

the authority may impose a penalty of £50 on him.

(3) Where a penalty has been imposed on a person under sub-paragraph (1) above and he is requested by the authority again to supply the same information under the same provision, the authority may impose a further penalty of £200 on him if—

(a) he fails to supply the information in accordance with the provision; or

(b) in purported compliance with the provision he knowingly supplies information which is inaccurate in a material particular.

(4) Sub-paragraph (3) above applies each time the authority repeats a request.

(5) A penalty under this paragraph shall be paid to the authority imposing it.

(6) If, after the imposition of a penalty under this paragraph but before the making of an appeal under paragraph 3 below against that imposition, the levying authority are satisfied that the person upon whom the penalty was imposed had a reasonable excuse for his failure, they may revoke the imposition of the penalty.

General

3.—(1) A person may appeal to a valuation tribunal if he is aggrieved by the imposition on him of a penalty under paragraph 1 above.

(2) A person may appeal to a valuation appeal committee if he is aggrieved by the imposition on him of a penalty under paragraph 2 above.

(3) Where a penalty is imposed on a person under paragraph 1 or 2 above, and he alleges that there is no power in the case concerned to impose a penalty of the amount imposed, he may appeal under sub-paragraph (1) or (2) above against the imposition.

4. Where a person is convicted of an offence, the conduct by reason of which he is convicted shall not also allow a penalty to be imposed under paragraph 1 or 2 above.

5.—(1) If it appears to the Treasury that there has been a change in the value of money since the passing of this Act or (as the case may be) the last occasion when the power conferred by this paragraph was exercised, they may by order substitute for any sum for the time being specified in paragraph 1 or 2 above such other sum as appears to them to be justified by the change.

(2) An order under this paragraph shall not apply in relation to any failure which began or anything done before the date on which the order comes into force.

6.—(1) The Secretary of State may make regulations containing provision as to the collection of amounts payable as penalties under paragraph 1 or 2 above.

(2) The regulations may include provision for the collection of such amounts (including provision about instalments and notices) which is equivalent to that made in regulations under paragraphs 2 and 3 of Schedule 2 to this Act for the collection of amounts persons are liable to pay in respect of council tax subject to any modifications the Secretary of State thinks fit.

(3) The regulations may include provision that, where the imposition of a penalty is subject to an appeal, no amount shall be payable in respect of the penalty while the appeal is outstanding.

(4) The regulations may include rules for ascertaining whether an imposition is subject to an appeal, and whether an appeal is outstanding; and the regulations may treat an appeal as outstanding unless it is finally disposed of or abandoned or fails for non-prosecution.

(5) The regulations may include provisions dealing with any case where a penalty under paragraph 1 or 2 above is quashed or revoked, and may in particular provide for the repayment of an amount or the allowance of an amount by way of deduction against a sum due.

(6) In the application of this paragraph to England and Wales, any reference to an appeal includes a reference to an arbitration in pursuance of regulations made under paragraph 4 of Schedule 11 to the 1988 Act (valuation tribunals).

GENERAL NOTE

This schedule relates to the imposition of penalties by a billing authority or levying authority on persons failing to comply with certain duties under the Act, or knowingly supplying inaccurate information. See also the Council Tax (Administration and Enforcement) Regulations 1992 (S.I. 1992 No. 613). For Scotland see the Council Tax (Administration and Enforcement) (Scotland) Regulations 1992 (S.I. 1992 No. 1332).

Paras. 1 and 2

Where regulations impose a duty on a person to notify or provide information to a billing authority or levying authority and he fails to do so or supplies information which he knows to be inaccurate, the authority may impose a penalty of £50. For further offences in regard to the same information the fine rises to £200. A penalty so imposed is to be paid to the authority which imposed it, and a billing authority which has imposed a penalty may quash it. For the levying authority in Scotland, the penalty may be revoked but only before an appeal, under para. 3, is heard and if the authority is satisfied that the person had reasonable excuse.

Para. 3

A person may appeal to a valuation tribunal or valuation appeal committee as appropriate if he is aggrieved by the imposition of a penalty under paras. 1 or 2. This may be against either the imposition of a penalty or in regard to an allegation that there was no power to impose the penalty in the case concerned.

Para. 4

This prevents the imposition of a penalty in respect of conduct which has led to a person's conviction of an offence.

Para. 5

The Treasury may make an order substituting some other value for the level of fines specified in paras. 1 and 2 if it appears to it that there has been a change in the value of money, provided that where such an order is made a penalty of the new amount may not be imposed in respect of a failure which began before the order came into force.

Para. 6

The Secretary of State may make regulations to provide for the collection of penalties to include provision equivalent to that contained in regulations made under paras. 2 and 3 of Sched. 2 for the collection of council tax, subject to such modifications as the Secretary of State thinks fit. It may be provided that a penalty need not be paid while an appeal is outstanding. The regulations may contain rules for determining whether a penalty is subject to appeal; whether an appeal is outstanding; and for treating an appeal as outstanding until it is finally disposed of, or abandoned, or fails for non-prosecution. The regulations may also provide for financial adjustments in cases where a penalty has been quashed or revoked. Any reference to an appeal includes, in relation to England and Wales, a reference to arbitration pursuant to regulations under para. 4 of Sched. 11 to the 1988 Act. Regulations under that provision allow matters within the jurisdiction of valuation tribunals to be referred to arbitration where the relevant parties agree to that course.

For Scotland see the Council Tax (Administration and Enforcement) (Scotland) Regulations 1992 (S.I. 1992 No. 1332).

Section 14(3)   SCHEDULE 4

ENFORCEMENT: ENGLAND AND WALES

Regulations for recovery of sums payable

1.—(1) The Secretary of State may make regulations in relation to the recovery of any sum which has become payable to a billing authority under any provision included in regulations under—

(a) paragraph 2, 3 or 6(2) or (3) of Schedule 2 to this Act; or

(b) paragraph 6 of Schedule 3 to this Act,

and has not been paid.

(2) The Secretary of State may also make regulations in relation to the recovery of any sum which has become payable (by way of repayment) to a person other than a billing authority under any provision included in regulations under paragraph 2, 3 or 6(2) or (3) of Schedule 2 to this Act and has not been paid.

(3) References in sub-paragraphs (1) and (2) above to a sum which has become payable and has not been paid include references to a sum forming part of a larger sum which has become payable and the other part of which has been paid.

Provision which may be made

2.—(1) Regulations under sub-paragraph (1) of paragraph 1 above may make, in relation to the recovery of any sum falling within that sub-paragraph which a person is solely liable to pay, any such provision as is authorised by the following paragraphs of this Schedule.

(2) Regulations under that sub-paragraph may make, in relation to any sum falling within that sub-paragraph which persons are jointly and severally liable to pay, provision equivalent to any so authorised subject to any modifications the Secretary of State thinks fit.

(3) Regulations under sub-paragraph (2) of that paragraph may provide that any sum falling within that sub-paragraph shall be recoverable in a court of competent jurisdiction.

Liability orders

3.—(1) Regulations under paragraph 1(1) above may provide that—

(a) the authority concerned may apply to a magistrates' court for an order (a "liability order") against the person by whom the sum is payable;

(b) the magistrates' court shall make the order if it is satisfied that the sum has become payable by the person concerned and has not been paid.

(2) The regulations may include provision that the order shall be made in respect of an amount equal to the aggregate of—

(a) the sum payable; and

(b) a sum (of a prescribed amount or an amount determined in accordance with prescribed rules) in respect of the costs incurred in obtaining the order.

(3) The regulations may include provision that, where the sum payable is paid after the order has been applied for but before it is made, the magistrates' court shall nonetheless make the order in respect of a sum (of a prescribed amount or an amount determined in accordance with prescribed rules) in respect of the costs incurred in applying for it.

(4) The regulations may include—

(a) provision prescribing steps to be taken before an application may be made;

(b) provision that no application may be made after a prescribed period has expired;

(c) provision prescribing the procedure to be followed for the initiation of an application (which may include provision as to form);

(d) provision prescribing the procedure to be followed in dealing with an application;

(e) provision prescribing the form and contents of an order.

Information

4.—(1) Regulations under paragraph 1(1) above may provide that where a magistrates' court has made a liability order against a person ("the debtor") he shall, during such time as the amount in respect of which the order was made remains wholly or partly unpaid, be under a duty to supply relevant information to the authority concerned.

(2) For the purposes of this paragraph relevant information is such information as fulfils the following conditions—

(a) it is in the debtor's possession or control;

(b) the authority requests him to supply it; and

(c) it falls within a prescribed description of information.

(3) The regulations may include provision that the information is to be supplied in a prescribed form and within a prescribed period of the request being made.

Attachment of earnings etc.

5.—(1) Regulations under paragraph 1(1) above may provide that where a magistrates' court has made a liability order against a person ("the debtor") and the debtor is an individual—

(a) the authority concerned may make an order (an "attachment of earnings order") to secure the payment of any such outstanding sum which is or forms part of the amount in respect of which the liability order was made;

(b) such an order shall be expressed to be directed to a person who has the debtor in his employment, and shall operate as an instruction to such a person to make deductions from the debtor's earnings and to pay the amounts deducted to the authority;

(c) the authority may serve a copy of the order on a person who appears to the authority to have the debtor in his employment; and

(d) a person who has the debtor in his employment shall comply with the order if a copy of it is served on him.

(2) The regulations may include—

(a) provision allowing an attachment of earnings order to be varied;

(b) provision requiring a person who has the debtor in his employment to comply with the order as varied if a copy of the order as varied is served on him;

(c) provision requiring an order to be in a prescribed form;

(d) provision requiring an order to specify the sum to which the order relates, the rate at which the debtor's earnings are to be applied to meet the sum, and such other particulars as may be prescribed;

(e) rules about the rate which may be so specified;

(f) provision allowing the person who deducts and pays amounts under the order to deduct from the debtor's earnings prescribed sums, or sums determined in accordance with prescribed rules, towards his administrative costs;

(g) provision requiring the person who deducts and pays amounts under the order to notify the debtor, in a prescribed manner and at any prescribed time, of the total amount of sums (including sums towards administrative costs) deducted up to the time of the notification or of the total amount of sums (including sums towards such costs) that will fall to be deducted after that time;

(h) provision requiring any person on whom a copy of the order is served to notify the authority in a prescribed manner and within a prescribed period if he does not have, or subsequently ceases to have, the debtor in his employment;

(i) provision that, where the whole amount to which the order relates has been paid, the authority shall give notice of that fact to any person who appears to it to have the debtor in his employment and who has been served with a copy of the order;

(j) provision allowing or requiring an order to be discharged.

(3) The regulations may include provision that while an attachment of earnings order is in force—

(a) the debtor shall from time to time notify the authority concerned, in a prescribed manner and within a prescribed period, of each occasion when he leaves any employment or becomes employed or re-employed, and shall include in such a notification a statement of his earnings and expected earnings from the employment concerned and of such other matters as may be prescribed;

(b) any person who becomes the debtor's employer and knows that the order is in force and by what authority it was made shall notify the authority concerned, in a prescribed manner and within a prescribed period, that he is the debtor's employer, and shall include in such a notification a statement of the debtor's earnings and expected earnings from the employment concerned and of such other matters as may be prescribed.

(4) The regulations may include provision with respect to the priority to be accorded as between—

(a) two or more orders made under the regulations;

(b) orders made under the regulations and orders made under the Attachment of Earnings Act 1971 or the Child Support Act 1991.

(5) The regulations may include provision that a person may appeal to a magistrates' court if he is aggrieved by the making or the terms of an attachment of earnings order, or there is a dispute whether payments constitute earnings or as to any other prescribed matter relating to the order.

(6) The regulations may include—

(a) provision prescribing the procedure to be followed for initiating an appeal;

(b) provision prescribing the procedure to be followed in dealing with an appeal;

(c) provision as to the powers of the court (which may include provision as to the quashing of an attachment of earnings order or the variation of the terms of such an order).

(7) The provisions of this paragraph (except sub-paragraphs (3) and (4)(b) above) shall apply to elected members of billing authorities or relevant precepting authorities as they apply to persons in employment; and for the purposes of the application of those provisions in relation to any such members—

(a) any reference to a person having the debtor in his employment shall be construed as a reference to such an authority having the debtor as an elected member; and

(b) any reference to the debtor's earnings shall be construed as a reference to allowances payable to the debtor by such an authority.

(8) For the purposes of sub-paragraph (7) above—

(a) a relevant precepting authority is a major precepting authority other than the Receiver for the Metropolitan Police District; and

(b) a person is an elected member of a relevant precepting authority other than a county council if he is appointed to the authority by a constituent council of which he is an elected member.

Deductions from income support

6.—(1) Regulations under paragraph 1(1) above may provide that where a magistrates' court has made a liability order against a person ("the debtor") and the debtor is entitled to income support within the meaning of the Social Security Contributions and Benefits Act 1992—

(a) the authority concerned may apply to the Secretary of State asking him to deduct sums from any amounts payable to the debtor by way of income support, in order to secure the payment of any outstanding sum which is or forms part of the amount in respect of which the liability order was made; and

(b) the Secretary of State may deduct such sums and pay them to the authority towards satisfaction of any such outstanding sum.

(2) The regulations may include—

(a) provision allowing or requiring adjudication as regards an application, and provision as to appeals and reviews;

(b) a scheme containing provision as to the circumstances and manner in which and times at which sums are to be deducted and paid, provision about the calculation of such sums (which may include provision to secure that amounts payable to the debtor by way of income support do not fall below prescribed figures), and provision as to the circumstances in which the Secretary of State is to cease making deductions;

(c) provision requiring the Secretary of State to notify the debtor, in a prescribed manner and at any prescribed time, of the total amount of sums deducted up to the time of the notification;

(d) provision that, where the whole amount to which the application relates has been paid, the authority shall give notice of that fact to the Secretary of State.

Distress

7.—(1) Regulations under paragraph 1(1) above may provide that where a magistrates' court has made a liability order against a person ("the debtor") the authority concerned may levy the appropriate amount by distress and sale of the debtor's goods.

(2) For the purposes of this paragraph the appropriate amount is the aggregate of—

(a) an amount equal to any outstanding sum which is or forms part of the amount in respect of which the liability order was made; and

(b) a sum (of a prescribed amount or an amount determined in accordance with prescribed rules) in respect of the charges connected with the distress.

(3) The regulations may include provision that—

(a) a distress may be made anywhere in England and Wales;

(b) a distress shall not be deemed unlawful on account of any defect or want of form in the liability order and no person making a distress shall be deemed a trespasser on that account;

(c) no person making a distress shall be deemed a trespasser from the beginning on account of any subsequent irregularity in making the distress, but a person sustaining special damage by reason of the irregularity may recover full satisfaction for the special damage (and no more) by proceedings in trespass or otherwise.

(4) The regulations may include provision that—

(a) no person shall make a distress unless he is an officer of the authority concerned, or he is a person of a prescribed description and any prescribed conditions are fulfilled;

(b) no person making a distress shall seize goods of a prescribed description.

(5) The regulations may include provision that a person may appeal to a magistrates' court if he is aggrieved by the levy of, or an attempt to levy, a distress.

(6) The regulations may include—

(a) provision prescribing the procedure to be followed for initiating an appeal;

(b) provision prescribing the procedure to be followed in dealing with an appeal;

(c) provision as to the powers of the court (which may include provision as to the discharge of goods distrained or the payment of compensation in respect of goods distrained and sold).

Commitment to prison

8.—(1) Regulations under paragraph 1(1) above may provide that—

(a) where an authority has sought to levy an amount by distress under any provision included by virtue of paragraph 7 above, the debtor is an individual who has attained the age of 18 years, and the person making the distress reports to the authority that he was unable (for whatever reason) to find any or sufficient goods of the debtor on which to levy the amount, the authority may apply to a magistrates' court for the issue of a warrant committing the debtor to prison;

(b) on such application being made the court shall (in the debtor's presence) inquire as to his means and inquire whether the failure to pay which has led to the application is due to his wilful refusal or culpable neglect;

(c) if (and only if) the court is of opinion that his failure is due to his wilful refusal or culpable neglect it may if it thinks fit issue a warrant of commitment against the debtor, or fix a term of imprisonment and postpone the issue of the warrant until such time and on such conditions (if any) as the court thinks just;

(d) the warrant shall be made in respect of the relevant amount (within the meaning given by sub-paragraph (2) below);

(e) the warrant shall state that amount;

(f) the order in the warrant shall be that the debtor be imprisoned for a time specified in the warrant (which shall not exceed three months), unless the amount stated in the warrant is sooner paid;

(g) the period of imprisonment shall be reduced by a prescribed amount in respect of part payment in prescribed circumstances;

(h) a warrant may be directed to the authority concerned and to such other persons (if any) as the court issuing it thinks fit;

(i) a warrant may be executed anywhere in England and Wales by any person to whom it is directed.

(2) For the purposes of sub-paragraph (1) above the relevant amount is the aggregate of—

(a) an amount equal to the appropriate amount within the meaning of paragraph 7 above or (as the case may be) to so much of it as remains outstanding; and

(b) a sum (of a prescribed amount or an amount determined in accordance with prescribed rules) in respect of the costs of commitment.

(3) The regulations may include—

(a) provision that a single warrant shall not be issued, under any provision included under this paragraph, against more than one person;

(b) provision as to the form of a warrant;

(c) provision allowing remission of payment where no warrant is issued or term of imprisonment fixed;

(d) provision allowing an application to be renewed where no warrant is issued or term of imprisonment fixed;

(e) provision that a statement in writing to the effect that wages of any amount have been paid to the debtor during any period, purporting to be signed by or on behalf of his employer, shall be evidence of the facts there stated;

(f) provision that, for the purpose of enabling inquiry to be made as to the debtor's conduct and means, a justice of the peace may issue a summons to him to appear before a magistrates' court and (if he does not obey the summons) may issue a warrant for his arrest;

(g) provision that, for the purpose of enabling such inquiry, a justice of the peace may issue a warrant for the debtor's arrest without issuing a summons;

(h) provision as to the execution of a warrant for arrest (which may include provision allowing it to be executed anywhere in England and Wales).

Bankruptcy

9.—(1) Regulations under paragraph 1(1) above may provide that where a magistrates' court has made a liability order against a person ("the debtor") and the debtor is an individual, the amount due shall be deemed to be a debt for the purposes of section 267 of the Insolvency Act 1986 (grounds of creditor's petition).

(2) The amount due is an amount equal to any outstanding sum which is or forms part of the amount in respect of which the liability order was made.

Winding up

10.—(1) Regulations under paragraph 1(1) above may provide that where a magistrates' court has made a liability order against a person ("the debtor") and the debtor is a company, the amount due shall be deemed to be a debt for the purposes of section 122(1)(f) of the Insolvency Act 1986 (winding up of companies by the court) or, as the case may be, section 221(5)(b) of that Act (winding up of unregistered companies).

(2) The amount due is an amount equal to any outstanding sum which is or forms part of the amount in respect of which the liability order was made.

Charging orders

11.—(1) Regulations under paragraph 1(1)(a) above may provide that where a magistrates' court has made a liability order against a person ("the debtor") and prescribed conditions are fulfilled—

(a) the authority concerned may apply to a court for an order (a "charging order") imposing, on any interest held by the debtor beneficially in the relevant dwelling, a charge for securing the due amount; and

(b) a charge imposed by a charging order shall have the like effect and shall be enforceable in the same courts and in the same manner as an equitable charge created by the debtor by writing under his hand.

(2) For the purposes of sub-paragraph (1) above the relevant dwelling is the dwelling in respect of which, at the time the application for the liability order was made, the debtor was liable to pay the sum falling within paragraph 1(1)(a) above.

(3) For the purposes of sub-paragraph (1) above the due amount is the aggregate of—
  (a) an amount equal to any outstanding sum which is or forms part of the amount in respect of which the liability order was made; and
  (b) a sum (of a prescribed amount or an amount determined in accordance with prescribed rules) in respect of costs connected with the charging order.
(4) The regulations may include provision—
  (a) as to the court to which an application may be made (which may be the High Court or a county court);
  (b) as to the factors to be considered by the court in deciding whether to make a charging order;
  (c) requiring an order to specify the dwelling and interest concerned, and such other matters as may be prescribed;
  (d) requiring an order to be in a prescribed form;
  (e) allowing an order to be made absolutely or subject to conditions;
  (f) as to the discharge or variation of an order.

Relationship between remedies

12.—(1) As regards a case where a magistrates' court has made a liability order, regulations under paragraph 1(1) above may include provision that—
  (a) attachment of earnings may be resorted to more than once;
  (b) deductions from income support may be resorted to more than once;
  (c) distress may be resorted to more than once;
  (d) attachment of earnings, deductions from income support and distress (or any two of them) may be resorted to in any order or alternately (or both);
  (e) steps by way of attachment, deduction, distress, commitment, bankruptcy, winding up or charging may not be taken while steps by way of another of those methods are being taken;
  (f) where a warrant of commitment is issued against (or a term of imprisonment is fixed in the case of) the person concerned no steps, or no further steps, by way of attachment, deduction, distress, bankruptcy or charging may be taken.
(2) Any reference in this paragraph to attachment of earnings includes a reference to attachment of allowances.

Magistrates and justices

13. Regulations under paragraph 1(1) above may include—
  (a) provision for determining what justices and magistrates' courts are to have jurisdiction in cases provided for by the regulations;
  (b) provision as to the composition of magistrates' courts in cases provided for by the regulations.

Admissibility of evidence

14.—(1) Regulations under paragraph 1(1) above may include provision that, in any proceedings before a magistrates' court under any provision included by virtue of the preceding provisions of this Schedule—
  (a) a statement contained in a document of record shall be admissible as evidence of any fact stated in it of which direct oral evidence would be admissible; and
  (b) a certificate which is made with respect to a document of record produced by a computer and purports to be signed by a responsible person shall be admissible as evidence of anything which is stated in it to the best of his information and belief.
(2) In this paragraph—
  "document of record" means a document constituting or forming part of a record compiled by the authority concerned;
  "responsible person" means a person occupying a responsible position in relation to the operation of the computer;
  "statement" includes any representation of fact, whether made in words or otherwise.

Exclusion of certain matters

15. Regulations under paragraph 1(1) above may provide that any matter which could be the subject of an appeal under section 16 of this Act, or regulations under section 24 of this Act, may not be raised in proceedings under the regulations.

Costs

16. Regulations under paragraph 1(1) above may provide that where an authority has

received in proceedings under the regulations an amount by way of costs it shall pay a prescribed amount, or an amount determined in accordance with prescribed rules, to a prescribed person for the benefit of such court as is identified in accordance with prescribed rules.

Termination of proceedings

17.—(1) Regulations under paragraph 1(1) above may provide that in a case where—
  (a) proceedings under the regulations have been taken as regards the recovery of any sum mentioned in paragraph 1(1) above; and
  (b) the outstanding amount is paid or tendered to the authority to which it is payable;
the authority shall accept the amount, no further steps shall be taken as regards its recovery, and any person committed to prison in pursuance of the proceedings shall be released.

(2) The outstanding amount is an amount equal to the sum concerned or to so much of it as remains outstanding (as the case may be).

(3) In a case where costs and charges are relevant the outstanding amount shall be treated as augmented by a sum (of a prescribed amount or an amount determined in accordance with prescribed rules) in respect of costs and charges incurred in the proceedings up to the time of payment or tender.

Offences

18.—(1) Regulations under paragraph 1(1) above may provide that a person shall be guilty of an offence if he is required by any provision included by virtue of paragraph 4 above to supply information and—
  (a) he fails without reasonable excuse to supply the information in accordance with the provision; or
  (b) in supplying information in purported compliance with the provision he makes a statement which he knows to be false in a material particular or recklessly makes a statement which is false in a material particular.

(2) Regulations under paragraph 1(1) above may provide that—
  (a) a person shall be guilty of an offence if he is required by any provision included by virtue of paragraph 5(1)(d) or (2)(b) above to comply with an attachment of earnings order and fails to do so;
  (b) it shall be a defence for a person charged with such an offence to prove that he took all reasonable steps to comply with the order.

(3) Regulations under paragraph 1(1) above may provide that a person shall be guilty of an offence if he is required by any provision included by virtue of paragraph 5(2)(g) or (h) or (3)(a) or (b) above to notify another person and—
  (a) he fails without reasonable excuse to notify the other person in accordance with the provision; or
  (b) in notifying the other person in purported compliance with the provision he makes a statement which he knows to be false in a material particular or recklessly makes a statement which is false in a material particular.

(4) Regulations under paragraph 1(1) above may provide that a person guilty of an offence under any provision included by virtue of sub-paragraphs (1) to (3) above shall be liable on summary conviction to a fine not exceeding—
  (a) level 2 on the standard scale (where the provision is included by virtue of sub-paragraph (1)(a) or (3)(a) above); or
  (b) level 3 on the standard scale (where the provision is included by virtue of sub-paragraph (1)(b), (2) or (3)(b) above).

Other enactments

19.—(1) Regulations under paragraph 1(1) above may apply any provision contained in or made under a relevant enactment, or may apply any such provision subject to prescribed modifications, or may contain provision equivalent to any such provision (whether or not subject to prescribed modifications).

(2) For the purposes of sub-paragraph (1) above relevant enactments are the Attachment of Earnings Act 1971, the Charging Orders Act 1979, Part II of the Social Security Administration Act 1992, and any enactment applied by any of those enactments.

(3) Regulations under paragraph 1(1) above may exclude any provision contained in the Distress (Costs) Act 1817 or the Distress (Costs) Act 1827 (which make provision as to the costs and expenses chargeable in respect of the levying of certain distresses).

GENERAL NOTE
  This schedule provides for the recovery of sums due by way of council tax which have not
been paid, and for the recovery of penalties imposed under Sched. 3. These follow the system
applicable to the community charge under the 1988 Act. See also the Council Tax (Administration and Enforcement) Regulations 1992 (S.I. 1992 No. 613).

Paras. 1 and 2
  The Secretary of State may make regulations governing the recovery of sums due by way of
unpaid council tax which arises either through sole liability or joint and several liability, and
whether in respect of a full amount or one which has been reduced through incentives to pay by
lump sum, etc.; and for the recovery of penalties. Regulations may also be made in respect of
the recovery of such sums which have become payable by way of repayment to a person other
than an authority. Provision for such repayments is referred to in Sched. 2, where a person pays
an amount in excess of his liability. Further provision is made in para. 2(2). The recovery
provisions apply not only where the whole of the sum is unpaid, but also where the unpaid sum
forms part of a larger sum, the other part of which has been paid. Regulations under para. 1(1)
may make such provisions as are authorised by the remainder of the schedule, and they shall
apply to liability incurred in relation to joint and several liability subject to any modification the
Secretary of State thinks fit. Regulations under para. 1(2) for the recovery of unpaid repayments may provide for recovery in a court of competent jurisdiction.

Para. 3
  Regulations may provide that the authority may apply to a magistrates' court for a liability
order against the person by whom the sum is payable, and that the court is to grant such an order
if it is satisfied that the sum has become payable by the person concerned and has not been paid.
The regulations may also provide that the sum specified in the liability order is to be the
aggregate of the sum payable and an amount in respect of the costs incurred in obtaining the
order, which may be either a prescribed amount, or determined in accordance with prescribed
rules. In addition, they may include provision that where the sum is paid after the authority has
applied to the court, but before a liability order has been made, the court may make an order in
respect of the costs incurred in applying for the order, which again may be either a prescribed
amount, or determined in accordance with prescribed rules. Finally, the regulations may
specify the steps to be taken before a liability order may be applied for; that no application may
be made after a prescribed period has expired; the requirement for the initiation of an
application, including the form; the procedure to be followed in dealing with it; and the form
and contents of a liability order.

Para. 4
  Regulations may provide that a person against whom a liability order has been made is to be
under a duty to supply information to the authority while the unpaid sum, or any part of it,
remains unpaid, provided that the information which the authority has asked him to supply is in
the possession or control of the debtor, and falls within a prescribed description. The regulations may include provision that the information is to be supplied in a prescribed form and
within a prescribed period of the request's being made.

Para. 5
  Regulations may be made which provide that, where a liability order has been made against
an individual, the authority may make an attachment-of-earnings order to secure the payment
of all or part of the sum which is the subject of the liability order; that an attachment-of-earnings
order is to be directed to the debtor's employer instructing him to make deductions from the
debtor's earnings and to pay the amount deducted to the authority; that the authority may serve
a copy of an attachment-of-earnings order on any person who appears to have the debtor in his
employment; and that a person who has the debtor in his employment is to comply with an
attachment order if it is served on him. The regulations may include provisions allowing an
attachment-of-earnings order to be varied; for an employer to comply with a varied order if it is
served on him; for an order to be in a prescribed form; for an order to specify the sum to which it
relates, the rate of deduction, and other particulars as may be prescribed; for rules about the
rate of deduction; allowing the employer to make deductions in respect of his administrative
costs in complying with the order, of sums which may be prescribed or determined in accordance with prescribed rules; requiring the employer to notify the debtor in a prescribed manner
and at a prescribed time of the sums which have been deducted, or of the sums which remain to
be deducted, including sums by way of costs; requiring anyone on whom an attachment-of-
earnings order is served to notify the authority if he does not have the debtor in his employment,
or if the debtor ceases to be in his employment; that where the sum to which an attachment-of-

earnings order relates has been paid the authority is to give notice of the fact to an employer on whom the order has been served; and allowing or requiring an order to be discharged.

Provision may also be made requiring the debtor, in a prescribed manner and within a prescribed period, to notify the authority if he leaves any employment, or becomes employed, or re-employed, and to include in his notification a statement of his earnings and expected earnings, and other prescribed matters. Any person who becomes the debtor's employer, and who knows that the order is in force, is obliged to notify the authority that he is the debtor's employer and may also be required to provide a statement of his earnings or expected earnings, and other prescribed information.

Provision may be made for determining the priority between two different attachment-of-earnings orders made under these provisions, or orders made under these provisions and those made under the Attachment of Earnings Act 1971 or the Child Support Act 1991.

An appeal may be allowed to a magistrates' court if the person is aggrieved by the making or terms of an attachment-of-earnings order, or if there is any dispute whether payments constitute earnings, or about any other matter which may be prescribed. Where this is permitted, the regulations may make provisions prescribing the procedure for initiating an appeal and the procedure for dealing with it, and provisions relating to the powers of the court, including quashing or varying an attachment-of-earnings order.

Under para. 5(7), elected members of authorities may have the provision of this paragraph applied to their allowances as if those were their earnings.

Para. 6

Where a liability order has been made against a debtor who is in receipt of income support, the regulations may permit the authority to apply to the Secretary of State for Social Security for deductions to be made from his income support to secure the payment of all or part of the sum in respect of which the order was made, and the Secretary of State may then deduct such sums and pay them to the authority. Where such an application for deductions has been made, the regulations may include provision for allowing or requiring adjudication, and provision for appeals and reviews; a scheme for the making of deductions, and their calculation, which may include provision for ensuring that the debtor's income support does not fall below a prescribed amount; provision for circumstances in which deductions are to cease; provision for the notification of the debtor of the sums deducted from his income support; and provision for the authority to notify the Secretary of State when the whole amount to which the deductions relate has been paid.

Para. 7

An authority which has obtained a liability order against a debtor may be permitted to levy the appropriate amount by distress and sale of his goods. The appropriate amount is defined as the aggregate of the outstanding sum in respect of which the liability order was made, or part of it, and an amount in respect of the charges connected with the distress, which may be either a prescribed amount or determined in accordance with prescribed rules. The regulations make provision that a distress may be made anywhere in England and Wales; that distress is not to be deemed unlawful if there is a defect or want of form in the liability order, and that no person is to be deemed a trespasser on that account; that no person making a distress is to be deemed a trespasser from the beginning on account of any subsequent irregularity in making the distress; but that where a person suffers special damage by reason of the irregularity he may recover full satisfaction for the special damage by proceedings in trespass or otherwise. In line with the changes to the community-charge system, introduced by s.102 of this Act, the regulations may require the distress to be carried out by an officer of the authority or otherwise prescribed, and prohibit the seizing of specified goods.

A person may be permitted to appeal to a magistrates' court if he is aggrieved by the levy of, or an attempt to levy, a distress. If so, the regulations may prescribe the procedure for initiating an appeal, the procedure for dealing with it, and provision relating to the powers of the court, including provision as to the discharge of goods distrained or the payment of compensation in respect of goods distrained and sold.

Para. 8

The regulations may provide that where an authority has sought to levy distress against an individual and it appears that no or insufficient goods can be found on which to levy the amount, it may apply to the magistrates' court for a warrant committing the debtor to prison. Where such an application is made the court is to enquire into the debtor's means in his presence, and enquire whether the failure to pay is due to wilful refusal or culpable neglect. If the court is of the opinion that the failure is due to wilful refusal or culpable neglect it may issue a warrant of commitment against the debtor, or fix a term of imprisonment and postpone the issue of the warrant until such time, or on such conditions, as it thinks just. The warrant is to be made in respect of, and must state, the relevant amount, as defined in para. 8(2), as the aggregate of the outstanding sum in respect of which the liability order was made, or part of it, and an amount in respect of the charges connected with distress which may be either a prescribed amount or determined in accordance with prescribed rules, to which is to be added a sum in respect of the costs of commitment, which also may be either a prescribed sum or a sum determined in accordance with prescribed rules. The order in the warrant is to be for the debtor to be imprisoned for a term specified in the warrant, which is not to exceed three months, unless the amount stated in the warrant is paid sooner, and the period of imprisonment is to be reduced if part payment is made, with power given to the Secretary of State to prescribe the reduction and the circumstances in which it applies. A warrant may be directed to the authority and to any other person the court thinks fit, and be executed anywhere in England and Wales by any person to whom it is directed.

The regulations may specify that a single warrant may not be issued against more than one person; the form of a warrant; remission of payment where the court neither issues a warrant nor fixes a term of imprisonment; that an application is to be renewed in those circumstances; that a settlement in writing from the debtor's employer that wages have been paid is to be evidence of the facts there stated; that summonses and arrest warrants be issued to ensure the debtor's presence at a means inquiry and that a justice of the peace may issue an arrest warrant without issuing a summons; and the execution of an arrest warrant.

Para. 9
Where a liability order has been issued against an individual the amount due is to be deemed to be a debt for the purposes of s.267 of the Insolvency Act 1986, which specifies the grounds of creditor's petition.

Para. 10
Where a liability order has been made against a company the amount due is to be deemed to be a debt for the purposes of s.122(1)(f) of the Insolvency Act 1986, which deals with the winding-up of companies by the court, or, as the case may be, s.221(5)(b), which deals with the winding-up of unregistered companies.

Para. 11
Where a liability order has been issued against a debtor the authority may be permitted to apply to a court for a charging order. This places a charge on the debtor's beneficial interest in the relevant dwelling for securing the due amount. Such a charging order is to have the same effect, and be enforceable in the same courts, as an equitable charge created by the debtor in writing under his own hand. The regulations may make provision as to the court to which an application for a charging order may be made, which may be the High Court or a county court; for the factors to be considered by the court in deciding whether to make an order; requiring an order to specify the dwelling and interest concerned, such other matters as may be prescribed, and to be in a prescribed form; and allowing an order to be made either absolutely or subject to conditions, and provision for the discharge or variation of an order.

Paras. 12
The regulations may make provision that attachment of earnings, deductions from income support and distress may be resorted to more than once in any case where a liability order has been made. They may also provide that these three remedies, or any two of them, may be resorted to in any order, or alternately, or both. They may provide that steps by way of these three remedies, commitment to prison, bankruptcy, winding-up or charging, may not be taken while steps by way of another of them are being taken. Finally, they may provide that no steps by way of any other remedy may be taken once a court has either issued a warrant of commitment or fixed a term of imprisonment.

Para. 13
The regulations may determine what justices and magistrates' courts are to have jurisdiction in the enforcement matters provided for in the regulations, and provide for the composition of magistrates' courts in such cases.

Para. 14
In line with the changes to the community-charge system, introduced by s.102 of this Act, the regulations may provide for the problems of proof arising in relation to the issuing of a liability order. The evidence produced for the amount of charge unpaid was usually in the form of computer records. In *R.* v. *Coventry Justices,* ex p. *Bullard* [1992] RA 79, it was held that this

evidence amounted to hearsay only since the information, although in mechanical form, was generated by human input. The practical problem caused by this decision is resolved by permitting a statement, contained in a document of record compiled by the authority, to be admissible as evidence of any fact stated in it of which direct oral evidence would be admissible. A certificate made in respect of such a document of record produced by a computer and purported to be signed by a person occupying a responsible position in relation to the operation of the computer shall be admissible as evidence of anything which is stated in it to the best of his information and belief.

Para. 15
    It will be possible to exclude a matter which could be the subject of a general appeal under s.16 of this Act or in regard to the regulations under s.24 relating to alteration of lists from proceedings under the regulations.

Para. 16
    Where an authority has received an amount by way of costs, the regulations may require payment to the court, according to prescribed rules.

Para. 17
    Where, following proceedings under the regulations, the outstanding sum is paid or tendered to the person to whom it is payable, it is to be accepted, and all proceedings for its recovery stopped; and any person committed to prison on account of it is to be released. Where costs and charges are relevant, the outstanding amount is to be augmented by a sum in respect of any costs and charges incurred up to the time of the payment or tender, which may be either a prescribed amount, or determined in accordance with prescribed rules.

Para. 18
    Various offences may be created. Under para. 18(1) a person may be guilty of an offence if he fails without reasonable excuse to provide information which he is required to provide, or knowingly or recklessly provides information which is false in a material particular. Under para. 18(2) a person may be guilty of an offence if he is an employer who is required to comply with an attachment-of-earnings order and fails to do so. It is, however, to be a defence to prove that he took all reasonable steps to comply with the order. Under para. 18(3), an employer who is required to notify a debtor about the deductions which have been, or remain to be, made under an attachment-of-earnings order, and who fails to do so without reasonable excuse, or knowingly or recklessly makes a statement which is false in a material particular; an employer who is required to notify an authority when a debtor leaves his employment, and who acts similarly; a debtor who is required to notify an authority about changes in his employment, and who acts similarly; and an employer who is required to notify an authority that he has become a debtor's employer, and who acts similarly, may all be deemed to be guilty of an offence. For all offences under this paragraph, the maximum level of penalty will be level 2 on the standard scale for debtors who fail to supply information and employers who fail to notify debtors about deductions, and level 3 on the standard scale for debtors and employers who knowingly or recklessly provide false information, and employers who fail to comply with an attachment-of-earnings order.

Para. 19
    Regulations may apply any provision, whether in a modified form or in a form equivalent to the provision, of the Attachment of Earnings Act 1971, the Charging Orders Act 1979, Pt. II of the Social Security Act 1992, and any enactment applied by them. The regulations may also exclude any provisions of the Distress (Costs) Acts of 1817 and 1827, which cover the costs and expenses chargeable in respect of the levying of certain distresses.

Section 72(8)   SCHEDULE 5

PART RESIDENTIAL SUBJECTS: SCOTLAND

Addition, deletion or amendment of apportionment notes

    1. Where, on or after 1st April 1993, the assessor alters the valuation roll by entering therein lands and heritages which are part residential subjects, he shall apportion the net annual value and the rateable value of those lands and heritages as between the residential and non-residential use made of them and shall include in the entry an apportionment note.
    2. Subject to paragraph 6 below, where, on or after 1st April 1993—
    (a) lands and heritages included in the valuation roll become or cease to be part residential subjects; or

(b) there is such a change as between the residential and non-residential use of lands and heritages that the apportionments of the net annual value and the rateable value shown in the valuation roll are incorrect,

the assessor shall apportion or, as the case may be, re-apportion the net annual value and the rateable value of those lands and heritages as between the residential and non-residential use made of them, and shall alter the roll by adding an apportionment note to the entry in respect of those lands and heritages or, as the case may be, by deleting or amending the existing note.

3. Subject to paragraph 6 below, where, under any of the provisions of section 2(1) of the 1975 Act (which provides for the alteration of the valuation roll in certain circumstances), the assessor alters the net annual value and the rateable value of any lands and heritages which are part residential subjects, he shall apportion the new net annual value and the new rateable value as between the residential and the non-residential use of the subjects, and shall amend the apportionment note accordingly.

Date of coming into effect of addition, deletion or amendment of apportionment note

4. Where an apportionment note is included under paragraph 1 above as part of an entry relating to any land and heritages in the valuation roll, the note shall take effect from—
  (a) the date when the lands and heritages to which the entry relates come into existence or occupancy; or
  (b) the beginning of the financial year in which the entry is made,
whichever is the later.

5. Subject to paragraph 6 below, where the valuation roll is altered by the addition or deletion of, or by an amendment to, an apportionment note under paragraph 2 above, or by an amendment to an apportionment note under paragraph 3 above, the alteration shall take effect from—
  (a) the date of the event by reason of which the addition, deletion or amendment is made, or
  (b) the beginning of the financial year in which the addition, deletion or amendment is made,
whichever is the later.

6. No alteration to the valuation roll consisting of an amendment to an apportionment note shall be made or take effect until three months, or such other period as may be prescribed, after the date when that apportionment note is made or takes effect, whichever is the later.

Revaluation

7. Where the assessor makes up a valuation roll in respect of a financial year which is a year of revaluation within the meaning of section 37(1) of the 1975 Act (which defines terms used in that Act), he shall apportion the new net annual value and the new rateable value of any lands and heritages which are part residential subjects as between the residential and non-residential use of the subjects, and shall include in the entry relating to those lands and heritages a new apportionment note.

General

8. For the purposes of this Schedule the extent to which subjects are used residentially shall be determined by reference to the use made of the subjects as the sole or main residence of any person, and criteria may be prescribed by reference to which any apportionment or re-apportionment of net annual values and rateable values under this Schedule is to be carried out.

9. No rates shall be leviable in respect of such part of their rateable value as relates to the residential use of any lands and heritages which are part residential subjects.

Noting of date on which alterations take effect

10. Where the assessor has altered the entry in the valuation roll relating to any lands and heritages by adding, deleting or amending an apportionment note, he shall also alter the entry by adding thereto a note of the date on which the alteration takes effect.

Notification of addition, deletion or alteration of apportionment notes

11. Section 3 of the 1975 Act (which requires the assessor to notify the rating authority and other persons affected of any alterations in the roll, and provides for a right of appeal against any such alterations) shall apply to any addition, deletion or amendment of apportionment notes made under this Schedule as it applies to deletions and alterations made under section 1 or 2 of that Act.

GENERAL NOTE

This schedule re-enacts Pts. I and II of Sched. 1 to the 1987 Act in the context of the council tax. Part residential subjects are defined in s.99(1) and this schedule requires an apportionment to be made between the residential and non-residential use of such subjects in the valuation roll entry relative to them. It is recognised that this apportionment will already have been made in many cases in the context of the 1987 Act and makes provision relating to the addition, deletion or amendment of apportionment notes.

Para. 1
   Where, on or after April 1, 1993, the assessor alters the valuation roll by entering lands and heritages which are part residential subjects, he is under a duty to apportion the net annual value and the rateable value of the lands and heritages as between the residential and non-residential use made of them, and to include in the entry an apportionment note.

Para. 2
   Where, on and after April 1, 1993, lands and heritages included in the valuation roll become or cease to be part residential subjects, or there is such a change as between the residential and non-residential use of the lands and heritages that the apportionments of the net annual value and rateable value shown in the valuation roll are incorrect, the assessor is required to apportion or reapportion the relevant value and to alter the valuation roll by adding an apportionment note, or by deleting or amending the existing apportionment note. This is, however, subject to para. 6 of this schedule.

Para. 3
   Where the assessor, under s.2(1) of the Local Government (Scotland) Act 1975, alters the net annual value and rateable value of lands and heritages which are part residential subjects, he is required to apportion the new values as between the residential and non-residential use of the subjects and to amend the apportionment note accordingly. This is, however, subject to para. 6 of this schedule.

Para. 4
   A new apportionment note, under para. 1, is to take effect from whichever is the later of (1) the date when the lands and heritages to which the entry relates come into existence or occupancy or (2) the beginning of the financial year in which the entry is made.

Para. 5
   Alterations to the valuation roll, under paras. 2 or 3, are to take effect from the later of (1) the date of the event by reason of which the addition, deletion or amendment of the apportionment note is made, or (2) the beginning of the year in which the addition, deletion or amendment of the apportionment note is made. This is, however, subject to para. 6 of this schedule.

Para. 6
   No alteration to the valuation roll consisting of an amendment to an apportionment note is to be made or take effect until three months, or such other period as may be prescribed, after the date when that apportionment note is made or takes effect, whichever is later.

Para. 7
   This sets out the duties of the assessor regarding apportionment notes when he is making up a new valuation roll in a year which is a year of revaluation within the meaning of s.37(1) of the Local Government (Scotland) Act 1975. It requires him to apportion the new net annual value and the new rateable value as between the residential and non-residential use of the subjects and to include in the entry relating to those lands and heritages a new apportionment note.

Paras. 8 and 9
   The extent of residential use is to be determined by reference to the use made of the subjects as the sole or main residence of any person. The Secretary of State may prescribe criteria by reference to which any apportionment or reapportionment of net annual values and rateable values is to be carried out. No rates are to be levied in respect of the residential use.

Para. 10
   Where the assessor has altered the entry in the valuation roll relating to any lands and heritages by adding, deleting and amending an apportionment note, he is under a duty to alter the entry by adding to it a note of the date on which the alteration takes effect.

Para. 11
   Section 3 of the Local Government (Scotland) Act 1975 is to apply to such additions,

deletions or amendments of apportionment notes, made under the schedule, requiring the assessor to notify the rating authority and other persons affected of any deletions or alterations to the valuation roll, and a right of appeal against such alterations is provided.

Section 83(1)   SCHEDULE 6

COMPLETION OF NEW BUILDINGS: SCOTLAND

1.—(1) Where a local assessor is of the opinion—

(a) that the erection of a building has been completed; or

(b) that the work remaining to be done on a building is such that its erection can reasonably be expected to be completed within three months,

and that the building constitutes, or when completed will constitute, a dwelling, the local assessor may serve on the owner of the building a notice (referred to as "a completion notice") stating that the erection of the building is to be treated for the purposes of this Schedule as completed on the date of service of the notice or on such later date as may be specified by the notice; and the local assessor shall along with the completion notice send to the owner a notice of his right of appeal by virtue of paragraph 2 below.

(2) If a person on whom a completion notice is served agrees in writing that the erection of the building to which the notice relates shall be treated for the purposes of this Schedule as completed on a date specified by the agreement, it shall be treated for those purposes as completed on that day and the notice shall be deemed to be withdrawn.

(3) Where a completion notice has been served on any person, the local assessor may withdraw the notice by a subsequent notice served on that person; and a notice under this sub-paragraph may be served—

(a) at any time before an appeal under paragraph 2 below is brought against the completion notice; and

(b) with the agreement of that person, at any time thereafter and before the appeal is determined.

2.—(1) A person on whom a completion noticed is served may, during the period of twenty-one days beginning with the date of service of the notice, appeal to the valuation appeal committee against the notice on the ground that the erection of the building to which the notice relates has not been, or, as the case may be, cannot reasonably be expected to be, completed by the date specified by the notice.

(2) If a completion notice served in respect of a building is not withdrawn and no appeal is brought under this paragraph against the notice or such an appeal is abandoned or dismissed, the erection of the building shall be treated for the purposes of this Schedule as completed on the date specified by the notice; and if such an appeal is brought and is not abandoned or dismissed and the completion notice in question is not withdrawn, the erection of the building shall be treated for those purposes as completed on such date as the valuation appeal committee shall determine.

3.—(1) Subject to subparagraph (2) below, section 192 (service of notices by local authority) of the 1973 Act shall apply to the service of notices under this Schedule as it applies to the service of notices under that Act.

(2) In the application of the said section 192 to the service of notices under this Schedule, any reference to sending a notice by post shall be construed as a reference to sending it by registered post or by the recorded delivery service.

4. In the case of a building to which work remains to be done of a kind which is customarily done to a building of the type in question after the erection of the building has been substantially completed, it shall be assumed for the purposes of this Schedule that the erection of the building has been or can reasonably be expected to be completed at the expiration of such period, beginning with the date of its completion apart from the work, as is reasonably required for carrying out the work.

GENERAL NOTE

This provides for the determination of a day as the completion day in relation to a new building which will constitute, in whole or in part, a dwelling. Where a local assessor considers that the erection of a building is complete, or can reasonably be expected to be completed within three months, the local assessor may serve a completion notice on the building's owner. This notice will state that the building is to be treated as completed on the date of service of the notice, or a later date specified by the notice. With the completion notice the owner will also be sent a notice of his appeal rights under para. 2 of the schedule. Upon receipt, if the person on whom a completion notice is served agrees in writing then the erection of the building shall be treated as completed on a date specified by the agreement and the notice shall be deemed to be withdrawn. The local assessor may also withdraw the completion notice by service of a subsequent notice either before an appeal under para. 2 is brought or, with the agreement of that person, at any time thereafter and before the appeal is determined. The erection of the building shall be treated as completed on the date specified by the notice if the notice is not withdrawn and no appeal is brought under para. 2.

Under para. 2, a person on whom a completion notice is served may appeal against it. This appeal must be made within 21 days from the date of service of the notice, and the appeal is to a valuation appeal committee. The appeal may be on the grounds that the erection of the building has not been, or cannot reasonably be expected to be, completed by the date specified by the notice. The erection of the building shall be treated as completed on the date specified by the notice if such an appeal is abandoned or dismissed. If such an appeal is brought and is not abandoned or dismissed and the notice is not withdrawn, then the erection of the building shall be treated for those purposes as completed on such a date as the valuation appeal committee shall determine.

Section 192 of the Local Government (Scotland) Act 1973 is to apply to the service of notices under this schedule, and any reference to sending a notice by post shall mean that it must be sent by registered post or by recorded delivery service. In the case of a building to which work remains to be done of the kind which is customarily done to a building of that type after the erection of the building has been substantially completed, then it shall be assumed that the erection of the building has been or can reasonably be expected to be completed after a period such as is reasonably required for carrying out the work and which begins with the date of its completion apart from the work.

Section 94(2)   SCHEDULE 7

REDUCTION OF COUNCIL TAX: SCOTLAND

Parliamentary proceedings for reduction of council tax

1.—(1) If the Secretary of State is satisfied that the total estimated expenses mentioned in section 93(3) of this Act of a local authority in respect of any financial year are excessive or that there is an excessive increase in those expenses over the total estimated expenses there mentioned of the local authority in respect of the financial year preceding that year, he may make and cause to be laid before the House of Commons a report proposing a reduction in the council tax set by the authority in respect of that year and stating—

(a) the amount of the reduction so proposed; and

(b) his reasons for proposing that reduction.

(2) A report under sub-paragraph (1) above shall set out any representations made by the local authority to which it relates with respect to the matters referred to in the report or a summary of these representations.

(3) In determining, for the purposes of sub-paragraph (1) above, whether, in relation to any financial year, the total estimated expenses of a local authority are excessive or that any increase in those expenses is excessive, the Secretary of State—

(a) may leave out of account such categories of estimated expenses as he thinks fit; and

(b) shall have regard to such principles as he may determine in respect of that year.

(4) Different principles may be determined under sub-paragraph (3) above for different classes of local authority and the Secretary of State may classify local authorities for the purposes of this sub-paragraph by reference to such factors as he thinks fit.

(5) In determining what amount to state under sub-paragraph (1)(a) above, the Secretary of State may have regard to any balances in the general fund of the local authority.

(6) In the financial year 1993–94, the Secretary of State may consider an increase in expenses excessive when comparing the total estimated expenses mentioned in section 93(3) of this Act with the total estimated expenses to be met by the local authority during the financial year 1992–93.

Procedure prior to Parliamentary proceedings

2. The Secretary of State shall not make and cause to be laid a report under paragraph 1 above without having afforded to the local authority to which the report relates an opportunity of making representations on—

(a) whether the total estimated expenses of the authority are excessive or, as the case may be, whether the increase in those expenses is excessive;

(b) the amount of the reduction proposed in the council tax; and

(c) his reasons for proposing that reduction,

but need not afford them such an opportunity where he has, in proposing the reduction, taken account of representations made by the authority in relation to a reduction previously proposed by him in that council tax.

Effect of approval of report

3.—(1) If a report under paragraph 1 above is approved by the House of Commons, the local authority to which it relates shall forthwith set under this sub-paragraph a new council tax less, by the amount of the reduction proposed in the report or by such smaller amount as the Secretary of State may agree, than the council tax set by them under section 93 or 94 of this Act.

(2) Where, for any reason whatsoever, by the twenty-eighth day after the House of Commons approve a report, the local authority to whom the report relates have not made a setting required by sub-paragraph (1) above, the authority shall be deemed to have set on that day a council tax under sub-paragraph (1) above such that the reduction proposed in the report is effected.

(3) Where an authority is deemed to have set a council tax under sub-paragraph (2) above, paragraph (1)(b) of section 93 of this Act shall apply as if that tax had been set by the authority.

Supplementary

4.—(1) A report under paragraph 1 above may relate to more than one local authority and, if a report so relating is approved by a resolution of the House of Commons, paragraph 3 above shall apply in relation to each of the authorities to which the report relates.

(2) Any reference in this Act (except in paragraph 3 above) and in any other enactment, whether passed before or after the passing of this Act, to such council tax as is set under section 93 or 94 of this Act shall be construed as including a reference to such council tax as has been set, or is deemed to have been set, under paragraph 3 above.

(3) In sub-paragraph (2) above "enactment" includes an enactment contained in a statutory order.

(4) Paragraph 5 of Schedule 12 to this Act shall apply for the purposes of the Secretary of State's functions under this Schedule as it applies under that paragraph for the purposes of his functions in relation to revenue support grants or non-domestic rate income.

GENERAL NOTE

This schedule contains the detailed provisions relating to the reduction of council tax, or "capping", where the Secretary of State is satisfied that the total estimated expenditure of a local authority is excessive increase in its total estimated expenditure compared with that for the previous financial year.

Para. 1

This permits the Secretary of State to lay before the House of Commons a report proposing a reduction in an authority's council tax, if he is satisfied that the authority's total estimated expenses under s.93(3) are excessive, or where there has been an excessive increase in those expenses over the previous financial year. In determining this he may have regard to the balances in the general fund of the authority. The report must state the amount of the proposed reduction and the Secretary of State's reasons for proposing it. The Secretary of State must include in the report any representations made by the authority about the proposed reduction or a summary of those representations. Otherwise, the Secretary of State has very wide discretion and, in deciding whether to propose a reduction in council tax, he may leave out of account such categories of estimated expenses as he thinks fit. Equally, he may have regard to such principles as he may determine, and apply different principles for different classes of authority. The Secretary of State will be able to determine, and publicise, these principles in advance of local authority budgeting, but there is no such legal requirement. Transitional arrangements for 1993–94 are covered by para. 1(6), which allows a comparison to be made between the total estimated expenses under s.93(3) for the financial year 1993–94 and the total estimated expenses to be met by the local authority during the financial year 1992–93.

Para. 2

The Secretary of State must give an authority the opportunity to make representations on his proposal before making and laying the report. The authority must have an opportunity to comment on whether its total estimated expenses are excessive or whether the increase in these expenses is excessive; on the amount of the reduction proposed in its council tax; and on the Secretary of State's reasons for proposing that reduction. The Secretary of State does not have to give an authority the opportunity to make representations where he is proposing a reduction which takes account of representations made by the authority on a previous proposal to reduce its council tax for the year in question.

Para. 3

After the report has been approved by the House of Commons, the local authority must lower its council tax either by the amount in the report, or by a smaller amount if the Secretary of State agrees. If an authority has not lowered the council tax within 28 days after the approval of the report, then it is deemed to have made the reduction proposed in the report. When there has been a deemed reduction, s.93 will operate in respect of dwellings in all the different valuation bands.

Para. 4

The Secretary of State may lay a report relating to more than one authority. In addition, para. 5 of Sched. 12 applies to the Secretary of State's functions in respect of proposed reductions in the council tax. This means that the Secretary of State may make his own estimates in respect of the information he requires from a local authority for the purposes of a reduction in council tax if the authority has failed to give him that information timeously.

Section 97(5)   SCHEDULE 8

ENFORCEMENT: SCOTLAND

1.—(1) This Schedule applies to any sum which has become payable to a levying authority under any provision included in regulations under—

(a) paragraph 2, 3, 6(2) or (3) of Schedule 2 to this Act; or

(b) paragraph 6 of Schedule 3 to this Act,

and has not been paid.

(2) References in sub-paragraph (1) above to a sum which has become payable and has not been paid include references to a sum forming part of a larger sum which has become payable and the other part of which has been paid.

2.—(1) Subject to sub-paragraphs (4) and (5) below, any sum to which this Schedule applies may be recovered by the levying authority by diligence—

(a) authorised by a summary warrant granted under sub-paragraph (2) below; or

(b) in pursuance of a decree granted in an action of payment.

(2) The sheriff, on an application by the authority accompanied by a certificate from them containing such particulars as may be prescribed, shall grant a summary warrant in a form provided for by Act of Sederunt authorising the recovery, by any of the diligences mentioned in sub-paragraph (3) below, of the amount of the sum remaining due and unpaid along with a surcharge of 10 per cent. of that amount.

(3) The diligences referred to in sub-paragraph (2) above are—

(a) a poinding and sale in accordance with Schedule 5 to the Debtors (Scotland) Act 1987;

(b) an earnings arrestment;

(c) an arrestment and action of furthcoming or sale.

(4) It shall be incompetent for the sheriff to grant a summary warrant under sub-paragraph (2) above in respect of any sum to which this Schedule applies if an action has already been raised for the recovery of that sum; and, without prejudice to sub-paragraph (5) below, on the raising of an action for the recovery of any such sum, any existing summary warrant in so far as it relates to the recovery of that sum shall cease to have effect.

(5) It shall be incompetent to raise an action in Scotland for the recovery of any sum to which this Schedule applies if, in pursuance of a summary warrant, any of the diligences mentioned in sub-paragraph (3) above for the recovery of that sum has been executed.

(6) The Secretary of State may by order substitute another percentage for the percentage which is for the time being mentioned in sub-paragraph (2) above.

3.—(1) In any proceedings for the recovery of any sum to which this Schedule applies, whether by summary warrant or otherwise, no person shall be entitled to found upon failure by the levying authority or any other authority or body to comply with any provision included in regulations made under the provisions specified in paragraph 1 above relating to the date by which something shall be done.

(2) No misnomer or inaccurate description of any person or place or mistake or informality in any notice or other document or communication relating to the levy or collection of any council tax or council water charge or in any proceedings for the payment thereof shall prejudice the recovery thereof.

4.—(1) Subject to sub-paragraph (2) below and without prejudice to paragraphs 25 to 34 of Schedule 5 to the Debtors (Scotland) Act 1987, the sheriff officer's fees, together with the outlays necessarily incurred by him, in connection with the execution of a summary warrant under paragraph 2 above shall be chargeable against the debtor.

(2) No fees shall be chargeable by the sheriff officer against the debtor for collecting, and accounting to the levying authority for, the sums paid to him by the debtor in satisfaction of an amount owing to the authority by way of council tax or council water charge.

5.—(1) Regulations under this Schedule may provide that where a summary warrant or a decree in an action for payment has been granted against a person ("the debtor") he shall, during such time as the amount in respect of which the warrant or decree was granted remains wholly or partly unpaid, be under a duty to supply relevant information to the authority concerned.

(2) Relevant information is such information as fulfils the following conditions—

(a) it is in the debtor's possession or control;

(b) the authority request him to supply it; and

(c) it falls within a prescribed description of information.

(3) The regulations may include provision that the information is to be supplied in a prescribed form and within a prescribed period of the request being made.

6.—(1) Regulations made under this paragraph may provide that where a levying authority has obtained a summary warrant or a decree against a person (the debtor) in respect of arrears of sums payable under paragraph 1(1) above and the debtor is entitled to income support within the meaning of the Social Security Contributions and Benefits Act 1992—

(a) the levying authority may, without prejudice to their right to pursue any other means of recovering such arrears, apply to the Secretary of State asking him to deduct sums from any amounts payable to the debtor by way of income support in order to secure the payment of any outstanding sum which is or forms part of the amount in respect of which the summary warrant or decree was granted; and

(b) the Secretary of State may deduct such sums and pay them to the authority towards satisfaction of any such outstanding sum.

(2) Regulations made under this paragraph may include—

(a) provision allowing or requiring adjudication as regards an application and provision as to appeals and reviews;

(b) a scheme containing provision as to the circumstances and manner in which and times at which sums are to be deducted and paid, provision about the calculation of such sums (which may include provision to secure that amounts payable to the debtor by way of income support do not fall below prescribed figures), and provision as to the circumstances in which the Secretary of State is to cease making deductions;

(c) provision requiring the Secretary of State to notify the debtor, in a prescribed manner and at any prescribed time, of the total amount of sums deducted up to the time of the notification;

(d) provision that, where the whole amount to which the application relates has been paid, the authority shall give notice of that fact to the Secretary of State.

GENERAL NOTE

This schedule makes provision for the recovery of arrears of council tax and council water charge either by various means under the summary warrant procedure or by the raising of an action in court. See the Council Tax (Administration and Enforcement) (Scotland) Regulations 1992 (S.I. 1992 No. 1332).

Para. 1

The enforcement provisions apply to any unpaid sum, which becomes payable to a levying authority under the relevant provisions relating to amounts of council tax or amounts due in respect of civil penalties, and apply to an unpaid part of a larger sum the other part of which has been paid.

Para. 2

The levying authority is given the choice to recover sums by summary warrant or in pursuance of a decree granted in an action of payment where a court action has been raised. The levying authority may submit an application to the sheriff accompanied by a certificate containing such particulars as may be prescribed. On such an application the sheriff is to grant a summary warrant authorising the recovery of the sum outstanding, along with a surcharge of 10 per cent. of that amount. The Secretary of State may vary by regulations the percentage surcharge. Recovery is to be achieved by any of the following diligences: a poinding and sale, by which a debtor's goods are attached, brought within the control of the court and sold, and the proceeds used to pay off the debt; an earnings arrestment, by which a creditor attaches the debtor's earnings; and an arrestment and action of forthcoming or sale, by which a creditor attaches property owed to the debtor in the hands of a third party, *e.g.* bank accounts or goods. The sheriff is not to grant a summary warrant if a court action has already been raised for recovery of sums under this schedule, and the raising of such an action will render ineffective any existing summary warrant so far as it relates to the sum concerned. This is, however, without prejudice to para. 2(5), which provides that it is to be incompetent to raise a court action in Scotland for recovery of sums under this schedule if a summary warrant has been granted in respect of those sums and the stage of execution of any of the diligences mentioned above has been reached.

Para. 3

Defects in the notices or procedures are not to prejudice the recovery of sums due. Thus, any person in any proceedings for recovery of sums under this schedule is prevented from founding upon failure by the levying authority or any other authority or body to comply with any provision included in regulations, made under the provisions specified in para. 1, relating to the date by which something shall be done. Equally, misnomers, inaccuracies, mistakes or informalities in notices or other documents or communications relating to the levy or collection of any council tax or council water charge or in any proceedings for payment are not to prejudice recovery.

Para. 4

The sheriff officer's fees, together with the outlays necessarily incurred by him in connection with executing a summary warrant, shall be charged to the debtor. This is without prejudice to paras. 25–34 of Sched. 5 to the Debtors (Scotland) Act 1987. However, no fees shall be chargeable by the sheriff officer against the debtor for collecting, and accounting to the levying authority for, the sums paid to him by the debtor in regard to an amount owing for council tax or council water charge for which no warrant has been issued.

Para. 5

While an unpaid sum, or any part of it, remains outstanding, the regulations may provide that a person against whom a summary warrant or a decree in an action for payment has been granted is under a duty to supply relevant information to the levying authority, provided that the information which the authority has asked him to supply is in the possession or control of the debtor, and falls within a prescribed description. The regulations include provision that the information is to be supplied in a prescribed form and within a prescribed period of the request being made. The penalty for failure to supply information, provided by para. 2 of Sched. 3, is £50 for a first refusal, and £200 for continued refusals after the imposition of the first penalty.

Para. 6

Where a levying authority has obtained a summary warrant or a decree against the debtor for sums payable under para. 1 and the debtor is entitled to income support, then the regulations may permit the levying authority, without prejudice to other means of recovery, to apply to the Secretary of State to make deductions from the debtor's income support and pay these to the authority towards satisfaction of the debt. In this regard, the regulations may include provisions allowing or requiring adjudication as regards an application and provision as to appeals and reviews; a scheme containing provision on how and when sums are to be deducted and paid, the calculation of sums, and circumstances in which deductions shall stop; provisions requiring the Secretary of State to notify the debtor of total deductions to date; and provisions that when the debt is paid the authority shall notify the Secretary of State accordingly.

Section 103   SCHEDULE 9

SOCIAL SECURITY: COUNCIL TAX BENEFIT

Social Security Contributions and Benefits Act 1992 (c. 4)

1.—(1) In subsection (1) of section 123 of the Social Security Contributions and Benefits Act 1992 (income-related benefits), for paragraph (e) there shall be substituted the following paragraph—

"(e) council tax benefit."

(2) For subsections (4) to (6) of that section there shall be substituted the following subsection—

"(4) Each billing or levying authority—

(a) shall take such steps as appear to it appropriate for the purpose of securing that any person who may be entitled to council tax benefit in respect of council tax payable to the authority becomes aware that he may be entitled to it; and

(b) shall make copies of the council tax benefit scheme, with any modifications adopted by it under the Administration Act, available for public inspection at its principal office at all reasonable hours without payment."

2. In subsection (2)(a) of section 129 of that Act (disability working allowance), for the words "community charge benefit" there shall be substituted the words "council tax benefit".

3. In subsection (2) of section 130 of that Act (housing benefit), for the words from "mortgage payments" to the end there shall be substituted the following paragraphs—

"(a) payments to a billing or levying authority in respect of council tax; or
(b) mortgage payments, or, in relation to Scotland, payments under heritable securities."
4. For section 131 of that Act there shall be substituted the following section—

"Council tax benefit

Council tax benefit
131.—(1) A person is entitled to council tax benefit in respect of a particular day falling after 31st March 1993 if the following are fulfilled, namely, the condition set out in subsection (3) below and either—
(a) each of the two conditions set out in subsections (4) and (5) below; or
(b) the condition set out in subsection (6) below.
(2) Council tax benefit—
(a) shall not be allowed to a person in respect of any day falling before the day on which his entitlement is to be regarded as commencing for that purpose by virtue of paragraph (1) of section 6(1) of the Administration Act; but
(b) may be allowed to him in respect of not more than 6 days immediately following the day on which his period of entitlement would otherwise come to an end, if his entitlement is to be regarded by virtue of that paragraph as not having ended for that purpose.
(3) The main condition for the purposes of subsection (1) above is that the person concerned—
(a) is for the day liable to pay council tax in respect of a dwelling of which he is a resident; and
(b) is not a prescribed person or a person of a prescribed class.
(4) The first condition for the purposes of subsection (1)(a) above is that there is an appropriate maximum council tax benefit in the case of the person concerned.
(5) The second condition for the purposes of subsection (1)(a) above is that—
(a) the day falls within a week in respect of which the person concerned has no income;
(b) the day falls within a week in respect of which his income does not exceed that applicable amount; or
(c) neither paragraph (a) nor paragraph (b) above is fulfilled in his case but amount A exceeds amount B where—
    (i) amount A is the appropriate maximum council tax benefit in his case; and
    (ii) amount B is a prescribed percentage of the difference between his income in respect of the week in which the day falls and the applicable amount.
(6) The condition for the purposes of subsection (1)(b) above is that—
(a) no other resident of the dwelling is liable to pay rent to the person concerned in respect of the dwelling; and
(b) there is an alternative maximum council tax benefit in the case of that person which is derived from the income or aggregate incomes of one or more residents to whom this subsection applies.
(7) Subsection (6) above applies to any other resident of the dwelling who—
(a) is not a person who, in accordance with Schedule 1 to the Local Government Finance Act 1992, falls to be disregarded for the purposes of discount; and
(b) is not a prescribed person or a person of a prescribed class.
(8) Subject to subsection (9) below, where a person is entitled to council tax benefit in respect of a day, the amount to which he is entitled shall be—
(a) if subsection (5)(a) or (b) above applies, the amount which is the appropriate maximum council tax benefit in his case;
(b) if subsection (5)(c) above applies, the amount found by deducting amount B from amount A, where "amount A" and "amount B" have the meanings given by that subsection; and
(c) if subsection (6) above applies, the amount which is the alternative maximum council tax benefit in his case.
(9) Where a person is entitled to council tax benefit in respect of a day, and both subsection (5) and subsection (6) above apply, the amount to which he is entitled shall be whichever is the greater of—
(a) the amount given by paragraph (a) or, as the case may be, paragraph (b) of subsection (8) above; and
(b) the amount given by paragraph (c) of that subsection.
(10) Regulations shall prescribe the manner in which—
(a) the appropriate maximum council tax benefit;
(b) the alternative maximum council tax benefit,

are to be determined in any case.

(11) In this section 'dwelling' and 'resident' have the same meanings as in Part I or II of the Local Government Finance Act 1992."

5.—(1) In subsection (1) of section 132 of that Act (couples), for the words "a community charge benefit" there shall be substituted the words "council tax benefit".

(2) In subsection (5) of that section, for the words "and the appropriate maximum community charge benefit" there shall be substituted the words "the appropriate maximum council tax benefit and the alternative maximum council tax benefit".

(3) In subsection (7) of that section, for the word "first", in both places where it occurs, there shall be substituted the word "main".

(4) In subsection (9) of that section, for paragraph (b) there shall be substituted the following paragraph—

> "(b) references to the main condition are references to the condition mentioned in section 131(3) above."

6. In subsection (3) of section 133 of that Act (polygamous marriages), for the words "a community charge benefit" there shall be substituted the words "council tax benefit".

7. Subsection (3) of section 134 (exclusion of benefit) of that Act shall cease to have effect.

8. In subsection (5) of section 135 (the applicable amount) of that Act, for the words "any community charge benefit" there shall be substituted the words "council tax benefit".

9. In subsection (1) of section 137 (interpretation of Part VII) of that Act—

(a) for the definition of "charging authority" there shall be substituted the following definition—

> " 'billing authority' has the same meaning as in Part I of the Local Government Finance Act 1992;";

(b) the definitions of "contribution period", "the 1987 Act" and "the 1988 Act" shall cease to have effect;

(c) for the definition of "levying authority" there shall be substituted the following definition—

> " 'levying authority' has the same meaning as in Part II of the Local Government Finance Act 1992;"; and

(d) in the definition of "week", for the words "community charge benefits" there shall be substituted the words "council tax benefit".

10. In subsection (6) of section 175 of that Act (regulations, orders and schemes), for the words "community charge benefits" there shall be substituted the words "council tax benefit".

11. A statutory instrument containing (alone or with other provisions) regulations relating to council tax benefit and made by virtue of section 123 or sections 131 to 137 of that Act shall not be made before 1st April 1993 unless a draft of the instrument has been laid before and has been approved by a resolution of each House of Parliament.

Social Security Administration Act 1992 (c. 5)

12.—(1) In subsection (1) of section 6 of the Social Security Administration Act 1992 (regulations about community charge benefits administration)—

(a) for the words "any community charge benefit" there shall be substituted the words "council tax benefit";

(b) in paragraph (d), the words "or a consequential reduction" shall cease to have effect; and

(c) in paragraphs (j), (n), (o), (r), (s) and (t), the words "or consequential reduction", in each place where they occur, shall cease to have effect.

(2) In subsection (2) of that section, for the words from "provision" to "shall not apply" there shall be substituted the words "provision in relation to council tax benefit that prescribed provisions shall apply instead of prescribed provisions of Part I or II of the Local Government Finance Act 1992, or that prescribed provisions of either of those Parts shall not apply".

(3) For subsection (3) of that section there shall be substituted the following subsection—

"(3) References in subsection (2) above to either of the Parts there mentioned include references to regulations made under the Part concerned".

13. In subsection (3) of section 7 of that Act (relationship between community charge benefits and other benefits), for the words "any community charge benefit" there shall be substituted the words "council tax benefit".

14.—(1) In subsection (1) of section 63 of that Act (adjudication) for paragraphs (b) and (c) there shall be substituted the following paragraph—

"(b) council tax benefit,".

(2) In subsection (3) of that section, for the words "community charge benefits" there shall be substituted the words "council tax benefit".

15.—(1) In subsection (1) of section 76 of that Act (excess benefits), for the words "charging authority" there shall be substituted the words "billing authority" and for the words "a community charge benefit" there shall be substituted the words "council tax benefit".

(2) In subsection (2) of that section, the words "As regards any case where the benefit is in respect of a personal community charge" shall cease to have effect.

(3) In subsection (3) of that section, for the words "the charge concerned" there shall be substituted the words "council tax".

(4) Subsections (4), (5) and (7) of that section shall cease to have effect.

16.—(1) In subsection (1) of section 77 of that Act (shortfall in benefits), for the words "charging authority" there shall be substituted the words "billing authority" and for the words "a community charge benefit" there shall be substituted the words "council tax benefit".

(2) Subsections (2) and (3) of that section shall cease to have effect.

17.—(1) In subsection (2) of section 116 of that Act (legal proceedings), for the words "community charge benefits", in both places where they occur, there shall be substituted the words "council tax benefit".

(2) In subsection (5) of that section, for the words "community charge benefits" there shall be substituted the words "council tax benefit".

18.—(1) In subsection (1) of section 128 of that Act (information for purposes of community charge benefits), for the words "charging authorities" there shall be substituted the words "billing authorities" and for the words "community charge benefits" there shall be substituted the words "council tax benefit".

(2) In subsection (2) of that section, for the words "Charging authorities" there shall be substituted the words "Billing authorities" and for the words "community charge benefits" there shall be substituted the words "council tax benefit".

(3) In subsection (3) of that section—

(a) for the words "charging authority" there shall be substituted the words "billing authority";

(b) for the words "community charge benefits", in both places where they occur, there shall be substituted the words "council tax benefit"; and

(c) for the words "community charge benefit subsidy" there shall be substituted the words "council tax benefit subsidy".

19.—(1) For subsections (1) and (2) of section 138 of that Act (nature of benefits) there shall be substituted the following subsection—

"(1) Regulations shall provide that where a person is entitled to council tax benefit in respect of council tax payable to a billing authority or levying authority the benefit shall take such of the following forms as is prescribed in the case of the person—

(a) a payment or payments by the authority to the person;

(b) a reduction in the amount the person is or becomes liable to pay to the authority in respect of the tax for the relevant or any subsequent financial year;

(c) both such payment or payments and such reduction."

(2) Subsections (3) and (4) of that section shall cease to have effect.

(3) In subsection (5) of that section, for the words "subsections (1) and (2)" there shall be substituted the words "subsection (1)" and for the words "chargeable financial year", in both places where they occur, there shall be substituted the words "financial year".

(4) Subsections (6) to (8) of that section shall cease to have effect.

(5) In subsection (9) of that section, the words "or (2) or (3)" shall cease to have effect and for the words "the 1987 Act or the 1988 Act" there shall be substituted the words "Part I or II of the Local Government Finance Act 1992".

20.—(1) In subsection (1) of section 139 of that Act (arrangements for community charge benefits), for the words "Any community charge benefit" there shall be substituted the words "Council tax benefit" and for the words "community charge benefit scheme" there shall be substituted the words "council tax benefit scheme".

(2) For subsections (2) and (3) of that section there shall be substituted the following subsection—

"(2) For the purposes of this section the appropriate authority is the billing authority or levying authority which levied the council tax as regards which a person is entitled to the benefit."

(3) In subsection (4) of that section, for the words "Charging authorities" there shall be substituted the words "Billing authorities" and for the words "community charge benefits" there shall be substituted the words "council tax benefit".

(4) In subsection (5) of that section, for the words "community charge benefits" there shall be substituted the words "council tax benefit".

(5) In subsection (6) of that section, for the words "charging authority" there shall be substituted the words "billing authority" and for the words "community charge benefit scheme" there shall be substituted the words "council tax benefit scheme".

(6) In subsection (7) of that section, for the word "benefits", in both places where it occurs, there shall be substituted the word "benefit".

(7) In subsection (9) of that section—

(a) for the words "community charge benefit scheme" there shall be substituted the words "council tax benefit scheme";

(b) for the words "community charge benefits" there shall be substituted the words "council tax benefit"; and

(c) for the word "benefits", in the second and third places where it occurs, there shall be substituted the word "benefit".

(8) In subsection (10) of that section, for the word "benefits" there shall be substituted the word "benefit".

21.—(1) In subsection (1) of section 140 of that Act (community charge benefit finance), for the words "community charge benefit subsidy" there shall be substituted the words "council tax benefit subsidy" and for the words "charging authority" there shall be substituted the words "billing authority".

(2) In subsection (2) of that section, for the words "community charge benefit subsidy to be paid to a charging authority" there shall be substituted the words "council tax benefit subsidy to be paid to a billing authority".

(3) In subsection (3) of that section, for the words "community charge benefits" there shall be substituted the words "council tax benefit".

(4) In subsection (4) of that section, for the words "to a charging or levying authority by way of community charge benefit subsidy" there shall be substituted the words "to a billing or levying authority by way of council tax benefit subsidy".

(5) In subsection (5) of that section, for the words "community charge benefit subsidy" there shall be substituted the words "council tax benefit subsidy" and for the words "community charge benefits" there shall be substituted the words "council tax benefit".

(6) In subsection (6) of that section, for the words "community charge benefits" there shall be substituted the words "council tax benefit".

(7) In subsection (7) of that section, for the words "charging authority" there shall be substituted the words "billing authority".

22. In subsection (2)(d) of section 163 of that Act (general financial arrangements), for the words "community charge benefit subsidy" there shall be substituted the words "council tax benefit subsidy".

23. In subsection (1) of section 176 of that Act (consultation with representative organisations), for the words "community charge benefits" there shall be substituted the words "council tax benefit".

24. In subsection (7) of section 189 of that Act (regulations and orders: general), for the words "community charge benefits" there shall be substituted the words "council tax benefit".

25. In section 191 of that Act (interpretation: general)—

(a) for the definitions of "chargeable financial year" and "charging authority" there shall be substituted the following definition—

" 'billing authority' has the same meaning as in Part I of the Local Government Finance Act 1992;";

(b) after the definition of "dwelling" there shall be inserted the following definition—

" 'financial year' has the same meaning as in the Local Government Finance Act 1992;";

(c) in the definition of "income-related benefit", for paragraph (e) there shall be substituted the following paragraph—

"(e) council tax benefit."; and

(d) for the definition of "levying authority" there shall be substituted the following definition—

" 'levying authority' has the same meaning as in Part II of the Local Government Finance Act 1992;".

26. A statutory instrument containing (alone or with other provisions) regulations or an order relating to council tax benefit and made by virtue of section 6, 7, 63, 76, 77, 128, 138 or 139 of that Act shall not be made before 1st April 1993 unless a draft of the instrument has been laid before and has been approved by a resolution of each House of Parliament.

GENERAL NOTE

This schedule makes amendments to the Social Security Contributions and Benefits Act 1992 and the Social Security Administration Act 1992. It amends these Acts to provide a new income-related benefit for the council tax to replace community charge benefit from April 1, 1993. It also makes consequential amendments to the Child Support Act 1991. Paragraphs 1–11 amend the Social Security Contributions and Benefits Act 1992, while paras. 12–26 amend the Social Security Administration Act 1992.

Para. 1
This amends the Social Security Contributions and Benefits Act 1992 to replace community charge benefit with council tax benefit. It also places local authorities under a duty to inform the public about council tax benefit.

Para. 2
This entitles a person to disability working allowance in prescribed circumstances if he has been in receipt of council tax benefit for one or more of the 56 days preceding a claim for disability working allowance.

Para. 3
This amends s.130(2) of the Social Security Contributions and Benefits Act 1992 to preclude council-tax payments made to billing or levying authorities from treatment as "payments in respect of a dwelling" so that such payments cannot qualify a claimant for an award of housing benefit.

Para. 4
This specifies the entitlement conditions for council tax benefit and replaces s.131 of the Social Security Contributions and Benefits Act 1992 with a new s.131.

Para. 5
This amends s.132 of the Social Security Contributions and Benefits Act 1992, which deals with the treatment of couples, to accommodate the introduction of the council tax.

Para. 6
This amends s.133(3) of the Social Security Contributions and Benefits Act 1992 to provide the power to make separate regulations prescribing both the conditions and the amount of entitlement to council tax benefit for a member of a polygamous marriage.

Para. 7
This repeals s.134(3) of the Social Security Contributions and Benefits Act 1992, which permitted more than one community charge benefit to be allowed in respect of members of the same family.

Para. 8
This amends s.135(5) of the Social Security Contributions and Benefits Act 1992 to provide that the applicable amount of council tax benefit for a severely disabled person shall include a premium in respect of that person's disability.

Para. 9
This amends s.137(1) of the Social Security Contributions and Benefits Act 1992 to incorporate definitions relevant to council tax benefit.

Para. 10
This amends s.175(6) of the Social Security Contributions and Benefits Act 1992 to provide that there is power to make council tax benefit regulations or orders which include different provisions for different areas.

Para. 11
This provides that regulations relating to council tax benefit made before April 1, 1993 shall be subject to the affirmative resolution procedure of both Houses of Parliament.

Para. 12
This amends s.6 of the Social Security Administration Act 1992, which concerns the regulation-making powers governing the administration of community charge benefit, so that it applies to council tax benefit.

Para. 13
This amends s.7(3) of the Social Security Administration Act 1992 to provide the power to prescribe in regulations the relationship between council tax benefit and other benefits. Regulations can therefore provide that a claim for council tax benefit may be treated as a claim for any other prescribed benefit and that a claim for any other prescribed benefit may be treated as a claim for council tax benefit and for payments on account of one benefit to be treated as payments on account of another.

Para. 14
This amends s.63 of the Social Security Administration Act 1992 governing benefit determinations and adjudication so as to apply to council tax benefit.

Para. 15
This amends s.76 of the Social Security Administration Act 1992 which specifies the conditions governing the recovery of excess benefit awarded to a claimant to which he was not entitled so that it applies to the recovery of excess council tax benefit.

Para. 16
This amends s.77 of the Social Security Administration Act 1992 to provide powers to deal with a shortfall in an award of council tax benefit.

Para. 17
This amends s.116 of the Social Security Administration Act 1992 to prescribe how, and by whom, legal proceedings may be taken for an offence relating to council tax benefit.

Para. 18
This amends s.128 of the Social Security Administration Act 1992 to provide for the supply of information necessary for the administration of council tax benefit.

Para. 19
This amends s.138 of the Social Security Administration Act 1992 to prescribe when and how council tax benefit will be paid.

Para. 20
This amends s.139 of the Social Security Administration Act 1992 to provide arrangements for the administration of council tax benefit.

Para. 21
This amends s.140 of the Social Security Administration Act 1992 to require that an annual council tax benefit subsidy will be paid to the billing and levying authorities by the Secretary of State.

Para. 22
This amends s.163(2)(d) of the Social Security Administration Act 1992 to require that Parliament shall provide the funds for council tax benefit subsidy.

Para. 23
This amends subs. 176(1) of the Social Security Administration Act 1992 to require the Secretary of State to consult with representative organisations before council-tax regulations are made, except where such regulations increase amounts specified in previous regulations. Consultation may be waived if the representative organisations agree or if the Secretary of State considers that the urgent need for regulations so dictates.

Para. 24
This amends s.189(7) of the Social Security Administration Act 1992 to provide the power to make different council-tax regulations for different areas.

Para. 25
This amends s.191 of the Social Security Administration Act 1992 to incorporate definitions relevant to council tax benefit.

Para. 26
This provides that regulations relating to council tax benefit which are made before April 1, 1993 shall be subject to the affirmative resolution procedure of both Houses of Parliament.

SCHEDULE 10

LOCAL GOVERNMENT FINANCE: ENGLAND AND WALES

PART I

NON-DOMESTIC RATING

Alteration of lists

1. In section 55 of the 1988 Act (alteration of lists), in subsection (7), for paragraphs (a) and (b) there shall be substituted the following paragraph—

"(a) provision requiring payments or repayments to be made, with or without interest, and."

Multiple moorings

2.—(1) In section 64 of the 1988 Act (hereditaments), after subsection (3) there shall be inserted the following subsections—

"(3A) The Secretary of State may make regulations providing that where on any land there are two or more moorings which—

(a) are owned by the same person,

(b) are not domestic property, and

(c) are separately occupied, or available for separate occupation, by persons other than that person,

a valuation officer may determine that, for the purposes of the compilation or alteration of a local non-domestic rating list, all or any of the moorings, or all or any of them together with any adjacent moorings or land owned and occupied by that person, shall be treated as one hereditament.

(3B) Regulations under subsection (3A) above may provide that—

(a) where a valuation officer makes a determination as mentioned in that subsection, he shall, if prescribed conditions are fulfilled, supply prescribed persons with prescribed information;

(b) while such a determination is in force—

(i) the person who on any day is the owner of the moorings (or the moorings and land) which constitute the hereditament shall be treated for the purposes of sections 43, 44A and 45 above as being in occupation of all of the hereditament on that day; and

(ii) no other person shall be treated for those purposes as being in occupation of all or any part of the hereditament on that day."

(2) After subsection (11) of that section there shall be inserted the following subsection—

"(12) In subsections (3A) and (3B) above 'owner', in relation to a mooring, means the person who (if the mooring is let) is entitled to receive rent, whether on his own account or as agent or trustee for any other person, or (if the mooring is not let) would be so entitled if the mooring were let, and 'owned' shall be construed accordingly."

Places of religious worship etc.

3. In Schedule 5 to the 1988 Act (non-domestic rating: exemption), in paragraph 11, for sub-paragraph (2) there shall be substituted the following sub-paragraphs—

"(2) A hereditament is exempt to the extent that it is occupied by an organisation responsible for the conduct of public religious worship in a place falling within sub-paragraph (1)(a) above and—

(a) is used for carrying out administrative or other activities relating to the organisation of the conduct of public religious worship in such a place; or

(b) is used as an office or for office purposes, or for purposes ancillary to its use as an office or for office purposes.

(3) In this paragraph 'office purposes' include administration, clerical work and handling money; and 'clerical work' includes writing, bookkeeping, sorting papers or information, filing, typing, duplicating, calculating (by whatever means), drawing and the editorial preparation of matter for publication."

Valuation

4. In Schedule 6 to the 1988 Act (non-domestic rating: valuation), in paragraph 2, for sub-paragraph (6A) there shall be substituted the following sub-paragraph—

"(6A) For the purposes of sub-paragraph (6) above the material day shall be such day as is determined in accordance with rules prescribed by regulations made by the Secretary of State."

Special authorities' multipliers

5. In Part II of Schedule 7 to the 1988 Act (non-domestic rating: special authorities' multipliers), in paragraph 9, for sub-paragraphs (3) and (4) there shall be substituted the following sub-paragraphs—

"(3) The multiplier must be not greater than the required maximum for the year.

(4) The required maximum for the year shall be calculated in accordance with the formula—

$$A + \frac{B\ (C - D)}{E \times F}$$

where—

A is the non-domestic rating multiplier for the year determined in accordance with Part I of this Schedule,

B is a percentage prescribed for the year by order made by the Secretary of State,

C is the amount calculated (or last calculated) for the year by the authority under section 32(4) of the Local Government Finance Act 1992,

D is an amount determined by the Secretary of State for the year and notified by him to the authority before 1 March in the preceding financial year,

E is the total of the rateable values shown in the authority's local non-domestic rating list on 31 December in the preceding financial year, and

F is a factor determined by the Secretary of State for the year and notified by him to the authority before 1 March in the preceding financial year.

(5) An order under sub-paragraph (4) above in its application to a particular financial year (including an order amending or revoking another) shall not be effective unless it comes into force before 1 March in the preceding financial year."

Contributions

6.—(1) Part II of Schedule 8 to the 1988 Act (non-domestic rating contributions) shall be amended as follows.

(2) In sub-paragraph (1) of paragraph 4, for the words "charging authority" there shall be substituted the words "billing authority".

(3) In sub-paragraph (3)(a) of that paragraph, for the words "required minimum for the year" there shall be substituted the words "non-domestic rating multiplier for the year determined in accordance with Part I of Schedule 7 above".

(4) Sub-paragraph (4) of that paragraph shall cease to have effect.

(5) After sub-paragraph (5) of that paragraph there shall be inserted the following sub-paragraph—

"(5A) The Secretary of State may also incorporate in the rules provision for the deduction, in the case of a special authority, of an amount determined by him for the year in relation to that authority; and sub-paragraph (3) above shall have effect subject to this."

(6) In sub-paragraph (2) of paragraph 5, for the words "charging authority" there shall be substituted the words "billing authority".

(7) In sub-paragraph (6) of that paragraph, for paragraphs (b) and (c) there shall be substituted the following paragraphs—

"(b) notify the amount so calculated to the Secretary of State, and

(c) arrange for the calculation and the amount to be certified under arrangements made by the Audit Commission for Local Authorities in England and Wales (the Commission)."

(8) After that sub-paragraph there shall be inserted the following sub-paragraph—

"(6A) The Commission shall send a copy of the certification of the calculation and the amount to the Secretary of State."

(9) In sub-paragraphs (8) and (9) of that paragraph, for the words "sub-paragraph (6)(c) above" there shall be substituted the words "sub-paragraph (6)(b) above".

(10) For sub-paragraph (10) of that paragraph there shall be substituted the following sub-paragraphs—

"(10) If the amount notified under sub-paragraph (6)(b) above is less than the provisional amount, the Secretary of State shall—

(a) if he believes that the amount so notified is not likely to have been calculated in accordance with the regulations under paragraph 4 above, inform the authority of his reasons for that belief;

(b) if he is not of that belief, pay to the authority, at such time as he decides with the Treasury's approval, an amount equal to the difference between the amount so notified and the provisional amount.

(11) Sub-paragraph (12) below applies where—

(a) at any time after the year ends the Secretary of State has received both a notification from an authority under sub-paragraph (6)(b) above and a copy of a certification sent to him in relation to the authority under sub-paragraph (6A) above, and

(b) the amount which is certified by the certification to be the authority's non-domestic rating contribution for the year (the certified amount) is different from the amount notified to the Secretary of State under sub-paragraph (6)(b) above.

(12) Where this sub-paragraph applies the Secretary of State shall—

(a) calculate the amount of the difference (if any) between the certified amount and the provisional amount, and

(b) if there is a difference, inform the authority of the amount of the difference.

(13) If at the time the Secretary of State makes the calculation required by sub-paragraph (12) above no payment has been made under sub-paragraph (9) or (10) above in relation to the amount notified under sub-paragraph (6)(b) above—

(a) sub-paragraphs (9) and (10) above shall not apply in relation to that amount, and

(b) sub-paragraph (14) below shall apply.

(14) Where this sub-paragraph applies—

(a) if the certified amount exceeds the provisional amount the authority shall pay an amount equal to the difference to the Secretary of State at such time as he may direct, and

(b) if the certified amount is less than the provisional amount the Secretary of State shall pay an amount equal to the difference to the authority, and the amount shall be paid at such time as he decides with the Treasury's approval.

(15) Regulations under this sub-paragraph may make provision for financial adjustments to be made where at the time the Secretary of State makes the calculation required by sub-paragraph (12) above a payment has already been made under sub-paragraph (9) or (10) above in relation to the amount notified under sub-paragraph (6)(b) above; and the regulations may include provision—

(a) for the making of payments by the Secretary of State or the authority, and

(b) as to the time at which any such payment must be made."

(11) For sub-paragraph (2) of paragraph 6 there shall be substituted the following sub-paragraph—

"(2) Such a calculation shall be made on the basis of the information before the person making the calculation at the time he makes it; but the Secretary of State may make regulations—

(a) requiring a calculation under paragraph 5(2) or (3) above to be made on the basis of that information read subject to prescribed assumptions;

(b) enabling a calculation under paragraph 5(6) above to be made without taking into account any information as regards which the following conditions are satisfied—

　(i) it is not reasonably practicable for the person making the calculation to take it into account; and

　(ii) it was received by the authority after a prescribed date (which may be before or after the end of the year in question)."

Pooling

7. For Part III of Schedule 8 to the 1988 Act (non-domestic rating: pooling) there shall be substituted the following Part—

"Part III

Distribution

Interpretation

8.—(1) For the purposes of this Part of this Schedule a receiving authority is any billing authority or major precepting authority.

(2) Any reference in this Part of this Schedule to a local government finance report is a reference to a report made under section 78A above.

Distributable amount

9.—(1) Before a financial year begins the Secretary of State shall estimate—

(a) the aggregate of the items of account which will be credited to the account kept for the year; and

(b) the aggregate of the items of account which will be debited to the account kept for the year under paragraphs 2(2)(a) and 3(3)(b) above.

(2) In making any estimate under sub-paragraph (1) above the Secretary of State may make such assumptions as he sees fit.

(3) If the aggregate estimated under sub-paragraph (1)(a) above exceeds the aggregate estimated under sub-paragraph (1)(b) above the Secretary of State shall calculate the amount equal to the difference.

(4) In the local government finance report for the year the Secretary of State shall specify the amount arrived at under this paragraph (the distributable amount for the year).

Distribution: local government finance reports

10.—(1) A local government finance report for a financial year shall specify the basis (the basis of distribution) on which the Secretary of State proposes to distribute among receiving authorities the distributable amount for the year.

(2) Before making the report the Secretary of State shall notify to such representatives of local government as appear to him to be appropriate the general nature of the basis of distribution.

11.—(1) This paragraph applies where—

(a) in relation to a financial year, the distributable amount for the year has been calculated and specified in a report in accordance with paragraph 9 above; and

(b) the report has been laid before the House of Commons.

(2) If the report is approved by resolution of the House of Commons, the distributable amount for the year shall be distributed among and paid to receiving authorities in accordance with this paragraph and paragraph 12 below.

(3) As soon as is reasonably practicable after the report has been so approved, the Secretary of State shall calculate what sum falls to be paid to each receiving authority as its share of the distributable amount for the year in accordance with the basis of distribution specified in the report as so approved.

(4) Subject to sub-paragraph (5) below, after making a calculation under sub-paragraph (3) above, the Secretary of State may, at any time before the end of the financial year following the financial year to which the report relates, make one further calculation of what sum falls to be paid to each receiving authority as its share of the distributable amount for the year in accordance with the basis of distribution so specified.

(5) The power to make a calculation under sub-paragraph (4) above shall not be exercisable after the approval by resolution of the House of Commons of any amending report made under paragraph 13 below in relation to the local government finance report.

(6) If the Secretary of State decides that he will leave out of account information received by him after a particular date in making a calculation under sub-paragraph (3) or (4) above, the calculation shall be made accordingly, and he may decide different dates for different kinds of information.

(7) Sub-paragraph (6) above applies only if the Secretary of State informs each receiving authority in writing of his decision and of the date (or the dates and kinds of information) concerned; but he may do this at any time before the calculation is made under this paragraph (whether before or after the distributable amount for the year is calculated under paragraph 9 above).

(8) As soon as is reasonably practicable after making a calculation under sub-paragraph (3) or (4) above, the Secretary of State shall inform each receiving authority of the sum he calculates falls to be paid to it as its share of the distributable amount for the year.

12.—(1) Where a calculation is made under paragraph 11(3) above the Secretary of State shall pay to each receiving authority any sum calculated as falling to be paid to it.

(2) The sum shall be paid in instalments of such amounts, and at such times in the financial year to which the report relates (the financial year concerned), as the Secretary of State determines with the Treasury's consent.

(3) Where a calculation is made under paragraph 11(4) above and the sum it shows as falling to be paid to a receiving authority exceeds that shown as falling to be paid to it by the calculation for the financial year concerned under paragraph 11(3) above, the Secretary of State shall pay to the authority a sum equal to the difference.

(4) The sum shall be paid at such time, or in instalments of such amounts and at such times, as the Secretary of State determines with the Treasury's consent; but any such time must fall after the end of the financial year concerned.

(5) Where a calculation is made under paragraph 11(4) above and the sum it shows as falling to be paid to a receiving authority is less than that shown as falling to be paid to it by the calculation for the financial year concerned under paragraph 11(3) above, a sum equal to the difference shall be paid by the authority to the Secretary of State.

(6) The sum shall be paid on such day after the end of the financial year concerned as the Secretary of State may specify; and if it is not paid on or before that day it shall be recoverable in a court of competent jurisdiction.

Distribution: amending reports

13.—(1) Subject to sub-paragraph (6) below, after a local government finance report has been made the Secretary of State may, at any time before the end of the financial year following the financial year concerned, make in relation to the report one or more amending reports under this paragraph.

(2) An amending report under this paragraph shall contain amendments to the basis of distribution specified in the local government finance report.

(3) Before making the report the Secretary of State shall notify to such representatives of local government as appear to him to be appropriate the general nature of the amendments which he proposes to make.

(4) The report shall be laid before the House of Commons.

(5) As soon as is reasonably practicable after the report is laid before the House of Commons, the Secretary of State shall send a copy of it to each receiving authority.

(6) Where an amending report under this paragraph has been approved by resolution of the House of Commons, the Secretary of State may not make a subsequent amending report under this paragraph in relation to the same local government finance report.

14.—(1) As soon as is reasonably practicable after an amending report made under paragraph 13 above has been approved by resolution of the House of Commons, the Secretary of State shall calculate what sum falls to be paid to each receiving authority as its share of the distributable amount for the year in accordance with the basis of distribution specified in the local government finance report as amended by the amending report.

(2) Subject to sub-paragraph (3) below, after making a calculation under sub-paragraph (1) above the Secretary of State may make one further calculation of what sum falls to be paid to each receiving authority as its share of the distributable amount for the year in accordance with that basis of distribution.

(3) A calculation may not be made under sub-paragraph (2) above after whichever is the later of—

(a) the end of the financial year following the financial year concerned, and

(b) the end of the period of three months beginning with the day on which the amending report is approved by resolution of the House of Commons.

(4) Sub-paragraphs (6) to (8) of paragraph 11 above apply in relation to calculations made under sub-paragraphs (1) and (2) above as they apply in relation to calculations made under sub-paragraphs (3) and (4) of that paragraph.

15.—(1) This paragraph applies where a calculation (the relevant calculation) is made under paragraph 14(1) or (2) above in relation to an amending report.

(2) Where the sum shown by the relevant calculation as falling to be paid to a receiving authority for the financial year concerned exceeds that shown as falling to be paid to it by the relevant previous calculation, the Secretary of State shall pay to the authority a sum equal to the difference.

(3) The sum shall be paid at such times, or in instalments of such amounts and at such times, as the Secretary of State determines with the Treasury's consent; but any such time must fall after the end of the financial year in which the amending report was made.

(4) Where the sum shown by the relevant calculation as falling to be paid to a receiving authority for the financial year concerned is less than that shown as falling to be paid to it by the relevant previous calculation, a sum equal to the difference shall be paid by the authority to the Secretary of State.

(5) The sum shall be paid on such day after the end of the financial year in which the amending report was made as the Secretary of State may specify; and if it is not paid on or before that day it shall be recoverable in a court of competent jurisdiction.

(6) In this paragraph 'the relevant previous calculation' means—

(a) in relation to a calculation made under paragraph 14(1) above, the calculation under paragraph 11(3) above or, where a further calculation has been made under paragraph 11(4) above, that further calculation;

(b) in relation to a calculation made under paragraph 14(2) above, the calculation made under paragraph 14(1) above."

PART II

GRANTS

8. In section 76 of the 1988 Act (interpretation), for subsections (2) and (3) there shall be substituted the following subsection—

"(2) A receiving authority is any billing authority or major precepting authority."

9. In section 78 of the 1988 Act (revenue support grant), subsections (6) and (7) shall cease to have effect.

10. After section 78 of the 1988 Act there shall be inserted the following section—

"Local government finance reports

78A.—(1) A determination under section 78 above shall be specified in a report (to be called a local government finance report).

(2) A local government finance report shall also specify the basis (the basis of distribution) on which the Secretary of State proposes to distribute among receiving authorities the amount of revenue support grant which under this Part falls to be paid to such authorities for the financial year to which the report relates (the financial year concerned).

(3) Before making the report the Secretary of State shall notify to such representatives of local government as appear to him to be appropriate the general nature of the basis of distribution.

(4) The report shall be laid before the House of Commons.

(5) As soon as is reasonably practicable after the report is laid before the House of Commons, the Secretary of State shall send a copy of it to each receiving authority."

11.—(1) In subsection (1) of section 79 of the 1988 Act (effect of report's approval), for the words "section 78" there shall be substituted the words "sections 78 and 78A".

(2) In subsection (4) of that section, for the words "sections 80 to 83 below or sections 80 to 84 below (as the case may be)" there shall be substituted the words "sections 82 and 83 below".

12. Sections 80 and 81 of the 1988 Act (distribution reports and their effect) shall cease to have effect.

13. For section 82 of the 1988 Act there shall be substituted the following section—

"Calculation of sums payable

82.—(1) As soon as is reasonably practicable after a local government finance report for a financial year has been approved by resolution of the House of Commons, the Secretary of State shall calculate what sum, if any, falls to be paid to each receiving authority by way of revenue support grant for the year in accordance with the basis of distribution specified in the report as so approved.

(2) Subject to subsection (3) below, after making a calculation under subsection (1) above the Secretary of State may, at any time before the end of the financial year following the financial year concerned, make one further calculation of what sum, if any, falls to be paid to each receiving authority by way of revenue support grant for the year in accordance with the basis of distribution so specified.

(3) The power to make a calculation under subsection (2) above shall not be exercisable after the approval by resolution of the House of Commons of any amending report made under section 84A below in relation to the local government finance report.

(4) If the Secretary of State decides that he will leave out of account information received by him after a particular date in making a calculation under subsection (1) or (2) above the calculation shall be made accordingly, and he may decide different dates for different kinds of information.

(5) Subsection (4) above applies only if the Secretary of State informs each receiving authority in writing of his decision and of the date (or the dates and kinds of information) concerned; but he may do this at any time before the calculation is made under this section (whether before or after a determination is made for the year under section 78 above).

(6) As soon as is reasonably practicable after making a calculation under subsection (1) or (2) above the Secretary of State shall, subject to subsection (7) below, inform each receiving authority of the sum he calculates falls to be paid to it by way of revenue support grant for the year.

(7) If the Secretary of State calculates in the case of a particular receiving authority that no sum falls to be paid to it as mentioned in subsection (6) above, he shall inform the receiving authority of that fact."

14. Section 84 of the 1988 Act (special provision for transitional years) shall cease to have effect.

15. Immediately before section 85 of the 1988 Act there shall be inserted the following sections—

"Revenue support grant: amending reports

Amending reports

84A.—(1) Subject to subsection (6) below, after a local government finance report has been made the Secretary of State may, at any time before the end of the financial year following the financial year concerned, make in relation to the report one or more amending reports under this section.

(2) An amending report under this section shall contain amendments to the basis of distribution specified in the local government finance report.

(3) Before making the report the Secretary of State shall notify to such representatives of local government as appear to him to be appropriate the general nature of the amendments which he proposes to make.

(4) The report shall be laid before the House of Commons.

(5) As soon as is reasonably practicable after the report is laid before the House of Commons, the Secretary of State shall send a copy of it to each receiving authority.

(6) Where an amending report under this section has been approved by resolution of the House of Commons, the Secretary of State may not make a subsequent amending report under this section in relation to the same local government finance report.

Calculation of sums payable under amending reports

84B.—(1) As soon as is reasonably practicable after an amending report made under section 84A above has been approved by resolution of the House of Commons, the Secretary of State shall calculate what sum, if any, falls to be paid to each receiving authority by way of revenue support grant for the financial year concerned in accordance with the basis of distribution specified in the local government finance report as amended by the amending report.

(2) Subject to subsection (3) below, after making a calculation under subsection (1) above the Secretary of State may make one further calculation of what sum, if any, falls to be paid to each receiving authority by way of revenue support grant for the year in accordance with that basis of distribution.

(3) A calculation may not be made under subsection (2) above after whichever is the later of—

(a) the end of the financial year following the financial year concerned, and

(b) the end of the period of three months beginning with the day on which the amending report is approved by resolution of the House of Commons.

(4) Subsections (4) to (7) of section 82 above apply in relation to calculations made under subsections (1) and (2) above as they apply in relation to calculations made under subsections (1) and (2) of that section.

Payment of sums under amending reports

84C.—(1) This section applies where a calculation (the relevant calculation) is made under section 84B(1) or (2) above in relation to an amending report.

(2) Where the sum shown by the relevant calculation as falling to be paid to a receiving authority for the financial year concerned exceeds that shown as falling to be paid to it by the relevant previous calculation, the Secretary of State shall pay to the authority a sum equal to the difference.

(3) The sum shall be paid at such times, or in instalments of such amounts and at such times, as the Secretary of State determines with the Treasury's consent; but any such time must fall after the end of the financial year in which the amending report was made.

(4) Where the sum shown by the relevant calculation as falling to be paid to a receiving authority for the financial year concerned is less than that shown as falling to be paid to it by the relevant previous calculation, a sum equal to the difference shall be paid by the authority to the Secretary of State.

(5) The sum shall be paid on such day after the end of the financial year in which the amending report was made as the Secretary of State may specify; and if it is not paid on or before that day it shall be recoverable in a court of competent jurisdiction.

(6) In this section 'the relevant previous calculation' means—

(a) in relation to a calculation made under section 84B(1) above, the calculation under section 82(1) above or, where a further calculation has been made under section 82(2) above, that further calculation;

(b) in relation to a calculation made under section 84B(2) above, the calculation made under section 84B(1) above."

16.—(1) In subsection (1) of section 85 of the 1988 Act (additional grant), for the words "revenue support grant report" there shall be substituted the words "local government finance report".

(2) In subsection (7) of that section, for the words "notifiable authority" there shall be substituted the words "receiving authority".

17. In section 86 of the 1988 Act (effect of report's approval), subsections (4) to (6) shall cease to have effect.

18. For section 88A of the 1988 Act there shall be substituted the following sections—

"Other grants

Council tax grants

88A.—(1) If regulations under section 13 of the Local Government Finance Act 1992 (reduced amounts of tax) have effect as regards a financial year the Secretary of State may, with the consent of the Treasury, pay a grant to a billing authority as regards that financial year.

(2) The amount of the grant shall be such as the Secretary of State may with the consent of the Treasury determine.

(3) A grant under this section shall be paid at such time, or in instalments of such amounts and at such times, as the Secretary of State may with the consent of the Treasury determine.

(4) In making any payment of grant under this section the Secretary of State may impose such conditions as he may with the consent of the Treasury determine; and the conditions may relate to the repayment in specified circumstances of all or part of the amount paid, or otherwise.

(5) In deciding whether to pay a grant under this section, and in determining the amount of any such grant, the Secretary of State shall have regard to his estimate of any amount which, in consequence of the regulations, the authority might reasonably be expected to lose, or to have lost, by way of payments in respect of the council tax set by it for the financial year concerned.

Special grants

88B.—(1) The Secretary of State may, with the consent of the Treasury, pay a grant (in this section referred to as a special grant) in accordance with this section to a relevant authority.

(2) Where the Secretary of State proposes to make one special grant he shall, before making the grant, make a determination stating with respect to the grant—
    (a) to which authority it is to be paid,
    (b) the purpose for which it is to be paid, and
    (c) the amount of the grant or the manner in which the amount is to be calculated.

(3) Where the Secretary of State proposes to make two or more special grants to different authorities he shall, before making the grants, make a determination stating with respect to the grants—
    (a) to which authorities they are to be paid,
    (b) the purpose for which they are to be paid, and
    (c) either—
        (i) the amount of the grant which he proposes to pay to each authority or the manner in which the amount is to be calculated; or
        (ii) the total amount which he proposes to distribute among the authorities by way of special grants and the basis on which he proposes to distribute that amount.

(4) A determination under subsection (2) or (3) above shall be made with the consent of the Treasury and shall be specified in a report (to be called a special grant report) which shall contain such explanation as the Secretary of State considers desirable of the main features of the determination.

(5) A special grant report shall be laid before the House of Commons and, as soon as is reasonably practicable after the report has been so laid, the Secretary of State shall send a copy of it to any relevant authority to whom a special grant is proposed to be paid in accordance with the determination in the report.

(6) No special grant shall be paid unless the special grant report containing the determination relating to the grant has been approved by a resolution of the House of Commons.

(7) A special grant report may specify conditions which the Secretary of State, with the consent of the Treasury, intends to impose on the payment of (or of any instalment of) any special grant to which the report relates; and the conditions may—

(a) require the provision of returns or other information before a payment is made to the relevant authority concerned, or

(b) relate to the use of the amount paid, or to the repayment in specified circumstances of all or part of the amount paid, or otherwise.

(8) Without prejudice to compliance with any conditions imposed as mentioned in subsection (7) above, a special grant shall be paid at such time or in instalments of such amounts and at such times as the Secretary of State may, with the consent of the Treasury, determine.

(9) For the purposes of this section each of the following is a relevant authority—

(a) a receiving authority;

(b) a metropolitan county passenger transport authority established by section 28 of the Local Government Act 1985."

PART III

FUNDS

19. In subsection (1) of section 89 of the 1988 Act (collection funds), for the words "charging authority" there shall be substituted the words "billing authority".

20. For section 90 of the 1988 Act there shall be substituted the following section—

"Payments to and from collection funds

90.—(1) The following shall be paid into the collection fund of a billing authority—

(a) sums received by the authority in respect of council tax set by it in accordance with section 30 of the Local Government Finance Act 1992 (but not sums received by way of penalty),

(b) sums received by the authority from any major precepting authority under regulations made under section 99(3) below,

(c) sums received by the authority in respect of any non-domestic rate under this Act,

(d) sums received by the authority under paragraph 5(10) or (14) of Schedule 8 below or regulations made under paragraph 5(15) or 6(5) of that Schedule, and

(e) any other sums which the Secretary of State specifies are to be paid into a billing authority's collection fund.

(2) The following payments shall be met from the collection fund of a billing authority—

(a) payments to be made by the authority in respect of the amount of any precept issued by a major precepting authority under Part I of the Local Government Finance Act 1992 (but not payments to be so made in respect of interest on such an amount),

(b) payments to be made by the authority to any major precepting authority under regulations made under section 99(3) below,

(c) payments to be made by the authority to the Secretary of State under paragraph 5 of Schedule 8 below or regulations made under sub-paragraph (15) of that paragraph,

(d) payments to be made by the authority to another person in repaying, under regulations under this Act or Part I of the Local Government Finance Act 1992, excess receipts by way of non-domestic rates or of council tax, and

(e) any other payments which are to be made by the authority to another person and which the Secretary of State specifies are to be met from a billing authority's collection fund.

(3) The power to specify under this section—

(a) includes power to revoke or amend a specification made under the power;

(b) may be exercised differently in relation to different authorities."

21. Sections 95 and 96 of the 1988 Act (calculations and substitute calculations to be made by authorities) shall cease to have effect.

22. For section 97 of the 1988 Act there shall be substituted the following section—

"Principal transfers between funds

97.—(1) Subject to subsection (2) below, a billing authority which has made calculations in accordance with sections 32 to 36 of the Local Government Finance Act 1992 (originally or by way of substitute) shall transfer from its collection fund to its general fund an amount which shall be calculated by applying the formula—

$$B \times T$$

where—

B is the amount calculated (or last calculated) by the authority under section 33(1) of that Act as the basic amount of its council tax;

T is the amount determined for item T in section 33(1) of that Act.

(2) Where the amount given by subsection (1) above is a negative amount, the authority shall transfer the equivalent positive amount from its general fund to its collection fund.

(3) Where in accordance with regulations under section 99(3) below a billing authority has estimated that there is a surplus in its collection fund for the preceding year, it shall transfer from its collection fund to its general fund an amount equal to so much of the surplus as, in accordance with the regulations, the authority calculates to be its share.

(4) Where in accordance with regulations under section 99(3) below a billing authority has estimated that there is a deficit in its collection fund for the preceding year, it shall transfer from its general fund to its collection fund an amount equal to so much of the deficit as, in accordance with the regulations, the authority calculates must be borne by it.

(5) In this section and sections 98 and 99 below, any reference to a billing authority's general fund shall be construed in relation to the Common Council as a reference to the City fund."

23.—(1) In section 98 of the 1988 Act (other transfers between funds), the following shall cease to have effect, namely—

(a) subsections (1) and (2);
(b) in subsection (3), in paragraph (a), the words "or to the City fund (as the case may be)", in paragraph (c), the words "or from the City fund (as the case may be)", and paragraph (d);
(c) in subsection (4), the words "or to the City fund (as the case may be)"; and
(d) in subsection (5), the words "or from the City fund (as the case may be)".

(2) In subsections (4) and (5) of that section, for the words "charging authority" there shall be substituted the words "billing authority".

(3) In subsection (6) of that section, for the words "subsection (1), (4) or (5)" there shall be substituted the words "subsection (4) or (5)".

24. For section 99 of the 1988 Act there shall be substituted the following section—

"Regulations about funds

99.—(1) The Secretary of State may make regulations about the discharge of the following liabilities of a billing authority—

(a) the liability to pay anything from its collection fund or its general fund in respect of any precept issued by a major or local precepting authority under Part I of the Local Government Finance Act 1992;
(b) the liability to transfer anything from its collection fund under section 97(1) or (3) above; and
(c) the liability to transfer anything from its general fund under section 97(2) or (4) above.

(2) The regulations may include provision—

(a) that anything falling to be paid or transferred must be paid or transferred within a prescribed period;
(b) that anything falling to be paid or transferred must be paid or transferred in instalments of such amounts, and at such times, as are determined by the billing authority in accordance with prescribed rules;
(c) that the billing authority must inform any precepting authorities when instalments will be paid and how they are to be calculated;
(d) that if an instalment is not paid to a precepting authority in accordance with the regulations, it is to be entitled to interest on the amount of the instalment;
(e) as to the circumstances in which the billing authority is to be treated as having discharged the liabilities mentioned in subsection (1) above;
(f) as to the recovery (by deduction or otherwise) of any excess amount paid by the billing authority to any precepting authority in purported discharge of the liability mentioned in subsection (1)(a) above; and
(g) as to the transfer back of any excess amount transferred by the billing authority in purported discharge of the liability mentioned in subsection (1)(b) or (c) above.

(3) The Secretary of State may by regulations make provision as regards any financial year—

(a) that a billing authority must estimate at a prescribed time in the preceding financial year and in accordance with prescribed rules whether there is a deficit or surplus in its collection fund for that year and, if so, the amount of the deficit or surplus;
(b) that any surplus or deficit so estimated shall in the financial year concerned—
    (i) be shared among, or be borne between, the billing authority and major precepting authorities in accordance with prescribed rules; or
    (ii) in the case of the financial year beginning in 1993, belong solely to, or be borne solely by, the billing authority;

(c) that the billing authority must within a prescribed period inform any major precepting authorities of the effects of any estimates and rules mentioned in paragraphs (a) and (b) above;

(d) as to the manner in which any payments which fall to be made by a billing authority or a major precepting authority by virtue of any provision included in regulations under paragraph (a) or (b) above must be made;

(e) as to the period within which, or time or times at which, any such payments or instalments of such payments must be made; and

(f) as to the recovery (by deduction or otherwise) of any excess amount paid by a major precepting authority or a billing authority in purported discharge of any liability arising by virtue of any provision included in regulations under paragraph (a) or (b) above.

(4) The Secretary of State may make regulations requiring transfers between funds, or adjustments or assumptions, to be made to take account of any substitute calculation under section 32(4) of the Local Government Finance Act 1992.

(5) The Secretary of State may make regulations providing that sums standing to the credit of a billing authority's collection fund at any time in a financial year must not exceed a total to be calculated in such manner as may be prescribed.

(6) Regulations under subsection (5) above in their application to a particular financial year (including regulations amending others) shall not be effective unless they come into force before 1 January in the preceding financial year; but this does not affect regulations which merely revoke others."

GENERAL NOTE
This schedule amends the 1988 Act in relation to non-domestic rating, grants and funds.

Part I: Non-Domestic Rating

Para. 1
This enables regulations about the alteration of these lists to include provision for payments or repayments to be made with or without interest.

Para. 2
This empowers the Secretary of State to make regulations to permit valuation officers in certain circumstances to treat groups of moorings as one hereditament in the occupation of the owner rather than as a number of separately occupied hereditaments.

Para. 3
This extends exemption from non-domestic rating to premises used as offices connected with an organisation responsible for the conduct of public worship.

Para. 4
This enables the Secretary of State to provide for the determination of the "material day" in relation to non-domestic rating. It is a substitute for para. 6A of Sched. 6 to the 1988 Act, which contains the present definition. The Act provides that certain circumstances which affect the valuation of a property are to be taken to be as they are assumed to be on the material day. The definition is used for valuations made with a view to altering a non-domestic rating list. The new provision authorises the determination in accordance with rules set out in regulations.

Para. 5
This establishes new provisions for the determination by a special authority of its non-domestic rating multiplier for a year. It substitutes new provisions for para. 9(3) and (4) of Sched. 7 to the 1988 Act, which determine the limits within which a special authority can set its non-domestic multiplier. The multiplier must not be greater than the required maximum. The existing provision, which also provides that the multiplier must be not less than a required minimum, is removed. The maximum multiplier is to be calculated in accordance with a formula which links it to the national non-domestic multiplier. The formula requires the application of a prescribed percentage to an amount calculated by reference to the difference between the authority's budget requirement and an amount notified to the authority by March 1 in the preceding financial year. The percentage must be set, and can be amended, by order made by the Secretary of State. In order to be effective, the order prescribing the percentage must come into force before March 1 in the year preceding the financial year in respect of which it is first to have effect.

Para. 6

This amends the rules governing the payment by charging authorities of their contributions into the non-domestic rating pool. It amends provisions governing the calculation by a special authority of its payments into the pool and the adjustment of the contributions made by charging authorities into the pool after the end of the financial year. In addition, it includes changes consequential on the change of name of charging authorities to billing authorities.

In the case of a special authority, the rules governing the calculation of the authority's non-domestic rating contribution for a year must be framed so that the amount calculated under them in relation to the authority is broadly the same as the total which would be payable to it in respect of the year under ss.43 and 45 of the Act, in regard to occupied and unoccupied property rates, if the authority's multiplier was equal to the national non-domestic rating multiplier, rather than the required minimum multiplier, and the authority acted diligently. By virtue of para. 4(5) of Sched. 8, this rule is subject to the Secretary of State's power to incorporate in the rules provision for certain deductions which will include a new allowance for a special authority. The Secretary of State is empowered to incorporate in the rules which govern the calculation of an authority's contribution into the non-domestic rate pool provision for the deduction, in the case of a special authority, of an amount determined by him in relation to that authority.

In regard to the notification and certification of the amount calculated by charging authorities after the end of the year of their final contribution into the pool, authorities are required to notify the calculated amount to the Secretary of State. They must arrange for the calculation and the amount to be certified under arrangements made by the Audit Commission for Local Authorities to send the Secretary of State a copy of the certification of the calculation, and the amount is replaced by a duty on the Audit Commission to forward a copy of the certification and the amount to the Secretary of State.

Where the Secretary of State has received both a notification from an authority and a copy of the Audit Commission's certification, and the certified amount differs from the notified amount, then he must calculate the amount of any difference between the certified amount and the provisional amount calculated and inform the authority of the difference. If, at the time the Secretary of State makes the previous calculation, no adjusting payment has been made on the basis of the amount notified, those adjustments should not be made. Instead, the difference between the certified amount and the provisional amount must be paid by the authority to the Secretary of State, if the certified amount is greater, or by the Secretary of State to the authority, if the certified amount is less. The Secretary of State is empowered to make regulations covering financial adjustments in cases where, at the time the Secretary of State makes the calculation of the difference between the certified amount and the provisional amount, an adjustment has already been made on the basis of the amount notified.

Para. 7

This substitutes a new Pt. III of Sched. 8 to the 1988 Act. The new part provides for the distribution of the distributable amount of non-domestic rates to be set out in a local government finance report, for that report to be amended by means of amending reports, and for the payment of sums in respect of the distributable amount.

New para. 9 of Sched. 8 to the 1988 Act

Before a financial year begins the Secretary of State shall estimate, on the basis of such assumptions as he sees fit, the aggregate of items which will be credited and the aggregate of those to be debited to the account for the year. If the aggregate of items to be credited exceeds the aggregate of items to be debited, then the Secretary of State shall calculate the amount equal to the difference, and the amount arrived at, the distributable amount, shall be specified in the local government finance report for the year.

New para. 10 of Sched. 8 to the 1988 Act

The local government finance report for a financial year must set out the basis of distribution of the distributable amount to receiving authorities, and a duty is placed on the Secretary of State to notify appropriate representatives of local government of the general nature of the basis of distribution.

New para. 11 of Sched. 8 to the 1988 Act

This deals with the calculation of the share of the distributable amount to be paid to each authority.

Once the distributable amount for the year has been calculated and specified in the local government finance report for the year the report is laid before the House of Commons. If the report is approved by resolution of the House of Commons, the distributable amount for the year shall be distributed and paid to receiving authorities, and the Secretary of State is to calculate the share of the distributable amount to be paid to each authority in accordance with the basis of distribution set out in the local government finance report, as soon as possible after the report is approved by the House of Commons. After making this calculation, the Secretary of State may, before the end of the financial year following the financial year to which the report relates, make one further calculation of the share of the distributable amount for the year to be paid to receiving authorities in accordance with the basis of distribution so specified. However, a further calculation may not be made after approval by the House of Commons of any amending report made under the new para. 13 in relation to the local government finance report. In making either an original or further calculation, the Secretary of State may decide not to take into account information received after a particular date. The date may differ for different kinds of information, but this applies only if the Secretary of State informs each receiving authority in writing of the date and kind of information concerned, which he may do at any time before making the calculation, whether before or after the distributable amount for the year is calculated. As soon as possible after making a calculation, the Secretary of State shall inform each receiving authority of the share of the distributable amount for the year to be paid to it.

New para. 12 of Sched. 8 to the 1988 Act
   This deals with payment of sums to authorities. Where an original calculation has been made under new para. 11(3), then the Secretary of State shall pay to each receiving authority any sum calculated as falling to be paid to it. The sum shall be paid in such instalments and at such times in the financial year concerned as the Secretary of State determines with Treasury consent. Where a further calculation is made and the sum shown to be payable to a receiving authority exceeds that shown as falling to be paid to it by the original calculation, the Secretary of State shall pay the authority a sum equal to the difference. The sum shall be paid at such time, or in instalments of such amounts and at such times, as the Secretary of State determines with Treasury consent, but any such time must fall after the end of the financial year concerned. Where, however, a further calculation is made and the sum thereby payable to a receiving authority is less than that shown as falling to be paid to it by the original calculation, the authority shall pay the Secretary of State a sum equal to the difference. Again, the sum shall be paid on such day after the end of the financial year as the Secretary of State shall specify, and if it is not paid on or before that day it shall be recoverable in a court of competent jurisdiction.

New para. 13 of Sched. 8 to the 1988 Act
   This deals with the making of amending reports to the local government finance report. After a local government finance report has been made, the Secretary of State may make amending reports at any time before the end of the financial year following the year concerned, provided that where an amending report under this power has been approved by the House of Commons, the Secretary of State may not make a subsequent amending report relating to the same local government finance report. An amending report shall amend the basis of distribution set out in the local government finance report. The Secretary of State must notify appropriate representatives of local government of the general nature of the amendments he intends to make, and the amending report shall be laid before the House of Commons. As soon as reasonably practicable after the report has been laid before the House, the Secretary of State shall send a copy to each receiving authority.

New para. 14 of Sched. 8 to the 1988 Act
   This deals with further calculations under an amendment report. As soon as reasonably practicable after the approval by the House of an amending report, the Secretary of State is under a duty to calculate what sum falls to be paid to each receiving authority on the basis of the distribution specified in the local government finance report, as amended by the amending report. Thereafter, the Secretary of State may make one further calculation of the sum to be paid to each receiving authority as its share of the distributable amount for the year in accordance with that basis of distribution, but not after the end of the financial year following the financial year concerned or the end of the period of three months beginning with the day on which the House approved the amending report, whichever is the later. Otherwise, the rules apply in relation to calculations made here as they apply in relation to the original.

New para. 15 of Sched. 8 to the 1988 Act
   This deals with payments to and from authorities as a result of an amending report. When a calculation is made in relation to an amending report, and the sum shown by the relevant calculation as falling to be paid to a receiving authority for the financial year concerned is greater than that under the relevant previous calculation, then the Secretary of State shall pay the difference to the receiving authority. The amount shall be paid at such times or in

instalments of such amounts and at such times as the Secretary of State determines with the Treasury's consent, but any such time or times must fall after the end of the financial year in which the amending report was made. However, when the sum shown by the relevant calculation as falling to be paid to a receiving authority for the financial year concerned is less than that under the relevant previous calculation, then the authority shall pay the difference to the Secretary of State. The sum shall be paid on such a day after the end of the financial year in which the amending report was made as the Secretary of State may specify, and if not paid on or before that day it shall be recoverable in a court of competent jurisdiction.

Part II: Grants

Para. 8
   This replaces the definitions of receiving authorities and notifiable authorities in s.76 of the 1988 Act with a new definition of receiving authorities. The new definition allows grant to be paid to billing authorities and major preceptors.

Para. 9
   This repeals subss. (6) and (7) of s.78 of the 1988 Act, which provide for determinations of revenue support grant to be set out in a revenue support grant report.

Para. 10
   This inserts a new s.78A into the 1988 Act which provides for local government finance reports. Revenue support grant determinations are to be set out in a local government finance report, which will set out the basis of distribution of the amount of revenue support grant falling to be paid to receiving authorities for the financial year to which the report relates. The Secretary of State, before making the report, must notify the local government representatives of the general nature of the basis of distribution, and the report must be laid before the House of Commons. After being laid before the House the report shall be sent to each receiving authority.

Para. 11
   This makes minor consequential amendments to s.79 on the effect of the report's approval.

Para. 12
   This provides that s.80, on distribution reports, and s.81, on the effect of distribution reports, of the 1988 Act shall no longer have effect.

Para. 13
   This substitutes a new s.82 in the 1988 Act, in regard to the calculation of sums payable. The Secretary of State is to calculate the amount of grant payable to each authority in accordance with the basis of distribution set out in the local government finance report, as soon as reasonably practicable after the report is approved by the House of Commons. He may make a second calculation of grant before the end of the financial year following the year to which the report relates, but not a second calculation of grant under the original report if the House has approved an amending report for the financial year concerned. In making a calculation under s.82(1) or (2) the Secretary of State may decide not to take into account information received after a particular date. The date may differ for different kinds of information, but this only applies if the Secretary of State informs each receiving authority in writing of the date and kind of information concerned. He may do this at any time before making the calculation, whether before or after the determination is made for the year under s.78. As soon as reasonably possible after making a calculation, the Secretary of State shall inform each receiving authority of the grant to be paid to it. Where the Secretary of State calculates that no sum is payable, he shall inform the authority of that fact.

Para. 14
   This provides that s.84 of the 1988 Act, dealing with special provision for transitional years, shall no longer have effect.

Para. 15
   This inserts new ss.84A, 84B and 84C into the 1988 Act, which provide for amending reports, and calculation and payment of sums due under amending reports.
   Section 84 provides that after a local government finance report has been made the Secretary of State may make amending reports at any time before the end of the financial year following the year concerned, subject to where an amending report under s.84A has been approved by

the House of Commons, when the Secretary of State may not make a subsequent amending report relating to the same local government finance report. An amending report under s.84A shall amend the basis of distribution of revenue support grant set out in a local government finance report. A duty is placed on the Secretary of State to notify appropriate representatives of local government of the general nature of the amendments he intends to make, and the report shall be laid before the House of Commons. As soon as reasonably practicable after the report has been laid before the House, the Secretary of State shall send a copy to each receiving authority.

Section 84B provides that as soon as practicable after the approval of the amending report under s.84A, the Secretary of State shall calculate what sum, if any, falls to be paid to each receiving authority on the basis of the distribution specified in the local government finance report as amended by the amending report. After making this calculation the Secretary of State may make one further calculation of the sum to be paid to each receiving authority by way of revenue support grant for the year in accordance with that basis of distribution, but the further calculation may not be made after the end of the financial year following the financial year concerned, or the end of the period of three months beginning with the day on which the House approved the amending report, whichever is the later. The provisions in s.82 relating to the calculation of sums payable apply also in relation to calculations made under s.84B.

Section 84C provides that it applies when a calculation is made under s.84B(1), the first calculation under an amending report, or s.84B(2), the further calculation under an amending report. Where either of these calculations is made and the sum falling to be paid to a receiving authority for the financial year concerned is greater than that under the relevant previous calculation, then the Secretary of State shall pay the difference to the receiving authority. The amount shall be paid at such times or in instalments of such amounts and at such times as the Secretary of State determines with the Treasury's consent. But any such time must fall after the end of the financial year in which the amending report was made. When either of the calculations is made and the sum falling to be paid to a receiving authority for the financial year concerned is less than that under the relevant previous calculation, then the authority shall pay the difference to the Secretary of State. The sum shall be paid on such a day after the end of the financial year in which the amending report was made as the Secretary of State may specify. If not paid on or before that day it shall be recoverable in a court of competent jurisdiction.

Para. 16

In consequence of the above changes, this substitutes "local government finance report" for "revenue support grant report" in s.85(1) of the 1988 Act, and "receiving authority" for "notifiable authority" in subs. (7) of that section.

Para. 17

This repeals subss. (4)–(6) of s.86 of the 1988 Act, dealing with the effect of the report's approval.

Para. 18

This substitutes two new sections, ss.88A and 88B, on council tax grants and special grants respectively, for the existing s.88A of the 1988 Act.

New s.88A

The Secretary of State may, with the consent of the Treasury as to the amount, pay grant to a billing authority if regulations under s.13 of this Act, dealing with reduced amounts of council tax, have effect for that financial year. The grant is to be paid at such times, or in such instalments, as the Secretary of State may, with the Treasury's consent, determine, and the Secretary of State, again with Treasury consent, may impose conditions on the payment of grant. The conditions may relate to the repayment of grant in specified circumstances. In determining the amount of any grant the Secretary of State shall have regard to any amount which authorities may have lost, or be expected to lose, by way of payments in respect of council tax for the financial year concerned, in consequence of the regulations under s.13.

New s.88B

The Secretary of State may pay special grants to relevant authorities with the Treasury's consent. These are required to be specified in a special grant report which shall contain such explanation of the main features of the grant as the Secretary of State sees fit, and must be laid before the House of Commons and sent to any relevant authority which it is proposed should receive a special grant. The report must also contain a number of items. For a report paying grant to one authority, it must set out the authority to which it is to be paid; the purpose of the grant; and either the amount of the grant or the manner in which the amount is to be calculated.

For a report dealing with more than one authority, it must also include either: the amount of the grant to be paid to each authority or the manner in which the amount to be paid to each authority is to be calculated; or the total amount to be distributed as special grants and the basis of its distribution. No special grant shall be paid unless the related special grant report is approved by the House. A special grant report may specify conditions that the Secretary of State, with Treasury consent, intends to impose on the payment of grant or instalments of grant to which the report relates. The conditions may require returns or information from authorities before payment is made; or relate to the use of the amount paid, or to the repayment of all or part of the amount paid, or otherwise. Without prejudice to any special conditions imposed, a special grant shall be paid at such times or in such instalments as the Secretary of State may determine. The relevant authorities, for the purposes of this section, are receiving authorities and metropolitan county passenger transport authorities.

Part III: Funds

GENERAL NOTE
These amendments to the 1988 Act deal with the collection fund and the general fund. Certain provisions in the 1988 Act relating to calculations by charging authorities are also repealed.

Para. 19
The new s.89 requires a billing authority, rather than the old charging authority, to establish and then maintain a collection fund.

Para. 20
This substitutes a new s.90, which makes provision as to the sums to be paid into and defrayed from the collection fund of billing authorities in England and Wales. These are specified, but the Secretary of State is given the power to amend by regulation. This power to specify includes power to revoke or amend a specification made under the power, and may be exercised differently in relation to different authorities.

Para. 21
The requirement on a charging authority to make certain calculations for all financial years from April 1, 1990 in connection with its estimated expenditure and income for the year, and the provisions for the making of substitute calculations, ceases to have effect.

Para. 22
This substitutes a new s.97, which requires a billing authority which has made calculations in accordance with ss.32–36 of the Act, whether originally or by way of substitute, to make such transfer between its collection fund and its general fund as is found to be required by the application of the formula set out in the section. It also makes provision for transfers between a billing authority's collection fund and its general fund pursuant to regulations made under s.99(3), dealing with surpluses or deficits on a collection fund.

Para. 23
Section 98 makes provision for an English charging authority to transfer from its collection fund to its general fund an amount in respect of additional grant. Sums receivable by way of additional grant will no longer be included among amounts payable into the collection fund of a billing authority as a result of the amendment to s.90. They will be paid direct to all receiving authorities. There are other consequential amendments.

Para. 24
Section 99 of the 1988 Act provided for the Secretary of State to make regulations about the discharge of liabilities to pay anything in respect of any precept or to transfer anything under s.97 from a collection fund. This is a new section which makes similar provisions with regard to liabilities in respect of precepts and transfers between funds. It also makes provision for the Secretary of State to make regulation for the estimation by billing authorities of surpluses and deficits on collection funds and for the treatment of such estimated amounts.

SCHEDULE 11

WATER AND SEWERAGE CHARGES: SCOTLAND

PART I

CHARGES FOR WATER SERVICES

1. Subject to the provisions of this Part of this Schedule, the expenditure incurred by the council of a region or islands area (in this Schedule referred to as a "local authority") in meeting any requisition under Part IV or VIII of the 1980 Act and in the exercise of any of their functions under any enactment (within the meaning of section 109(1) of that Act) in relation to water supply in their area shall, insofar as not otherwise met, be met out of—
    (a) the charges (hereinafter in this Schedule referred to as "direct charges") made under section 49 (payment of water supplies by meter) of the 1980 Act;
    (b) the council water charge mentioned in paragraph 6 below; and
    (c) the non-domestic water rate mentioned in paragraph 12 below.

Estimation and apportionment of expenditure

2. In respect of the financial year 1993–94 and each subsequent financial year, each local authority shall, before such date as may be prescribed in relation to each of those years—
    (a) subject to paragraph 3 below, estimate the amount of the expenditure mentioned in paragraph 1 above which they will incur in respect of that year; and
    (b) subject to paragraph 4 below, determine what proportion of that expenditure is to be met from each of the sources mentioned in sub-paragraphs (a) to (c) of paragraph 1 above.
3. In estimating the expenditure mentioned in paragraph 1 above which they will incur in respect of any financial year a local authority shall take into account—
    (a) such additional sum as is in their opinion required—
        (i) to cover expenses previously incurred;
        (ii) to meet contingencies; and
        (iii) to meet any expenses which may fall to be met before the money to be received from the sources mentioned in paragraph 1 above in respect of the next following financial year will become available; and
    (b) any means by which any part of that expenditure may otherwise be met or provided for.
4. A local authority may apportion their estimated expenditure under paragraph 2 above on whatever basis they consider appropriate, but they shall ensure that the apportionment is not such as to show undue preference to, or discriminate unduly against, any class or classes of person liable to pay—
    (a) the direct charges;
    (b) the council water charge; or
    (c) the non-domestic water rate,
respectively.

Direct charges

5. After a local authority have, under paragraph 2 above, determined what proportion of their estimated expenditure in respect of a particular financial year is to be met out of direct charges, they shall, before such date as may be prescribed in relation to that year, determine such rate or rates of direct charges in respect of that year as will, when calculated in accordance with the provisions of section 49 (payment for water supplied by meter) of the 1980 Act, produce sufficient money to meet the said proportion; and different rates of direct charges may be determined for different circumstances.

Council water charge

6. Each local authority shall impose a water charge, which—
    (a) shall be known as the regional council water charge or the islands council water charge, depending upon which authority impose it; and
    (b) shall be payable in respect of dwellings situated in that authority's area.

Liability to pay council water charge

7.—(1) The council water charge shall be payable in respect of any dwelling which is not an exempt dwelling and in respect of which the qualifying conditions are met.
    (2) For the purposes of this Schedule—
        "dwelling" has the meaning assigned to it by section 72(2) of this Act;

"chargeable dwelling" means any dwelling in respect of which council water charge is payable; and

"exempt dwelling" means any dwelling of a class prescribed by an order made by the Secretary of State.

(3) For the purposes of sub-paragraph (2) above, a class of dwelling may be prescribed by reference to—

(a) the physical characteristics of dwellings;

(b) the fact that dwellings are unoccupied or are occupied for prescribed purposes or are occupied or owned by persons of prescribed descriptions; or

(c) such other factors as the Secretary of State thinks fit.

8. The qualifying conditions for the purposes of paragraph 7 above are—

(a) that a water authority provide a supply of water to that dwelling;

(b) that the water is not supplied wholly by meter; and

(c) that the supply is not one which the water authority—

(i) were, immediately before 16th May 1949; and

(ii) continue to be,

under an obligation to provide free of charge.

Setting of council water charge

9. After a local authority have, under paragraph 2 above, determined what proportion of their estimated expenditure in respect of a particular financial year is to be met out of the council water charge, they shall, before such date as may be prescribed in relation to that year—

(a) set an amount of regional council water charge or islands council water charge, as appropriate, to be paid for that year in respect of a chargeable dwelling in their area listed in valuation band D (whether or not there is such a dwelling in their area) as specified in section 74(2) of this Act;

(b) determine the amount of council water charge to be paid in respect of a chargeable dwelling in each of the other valuation bands specified in that section in accordance with the proportion mentioned in subsection (1) of that section,

and references in this Schedule to the setting of an amount of council water charge shall be construed as references to the setting of the amount mentioned in paragraph (a) above.

10. The amounts mentioned in paragraph 9(a) and (b) above shall be such as will provide sufficient money to meet such proportion of the authority's estimated expenditure for that year as they have determined under paragraph 2 above is to be met out of the council water charge.

Application of provisions relating to council tax

11. The provisions of sections 71, 75 to 81, 96, 97 and 99(3) of this Act shall have effect, subject to such adaptations, exceptions and modifications as may be prescribed, in relation to the council water charge as they have effect in relation to the council tax.

Non-domestic water rate

12. The provisions of section 40 of the 1980 Act shall continue to have effect in relation to the non-domestic water rate.

PART II

CHARGES FOR SEWERAGE SERVICES

13. The expenditure incurred by a local authority in carrying out any of their functions under the 1968 Act shall, insofar as not otherwise met, be met out of—

(a) the council tax; and

(b) the non-domestic sewerage rate described in paragraphs 19 to 22 below.

Estimation and apportionment of expenditure

14. In respect of the financial year 1993–94 and each subsequent financial year, each local authority shall, before such date as may be prescribed in relation to each of those years—

(a) subject to paragraph 15 below, estimate the amount of the expenditure mentioned in paragraph 13 above which they will incur in respect of that year; and

(b) subject to paragraphs 16 and 17 below, determine what proportion of that expenditure is to be met out of—

(i) the council tax; and

(ii) the said non-domestic sewerage rate,

respectively.

15. In estimating the expenditure mentioned in paragraph 13 above which they will incur in respect of any financial year a local authority shall take into account—
  (a) such additional sum as is in their opinion required—
          (i) to cover expenses previously incurred;
          (ii) to meet contingencies; and
          (iii) to meet any expenses which may fall to be met before the money to be received from the sources mentioned in paragraph 13 above in respect of the next following financial year will become available; and
  (b) any means by which any part of that expenditure may otherwise be met or provided for.

16. The proportion of the expenditure mentioned in paragraph 13 above which is to be met out of the council tax shall be such proportion as the local authority consider to be reasonably attributable to the provision by them of the sewerage services mentioned in section 1(1) of the 1968 Act to dwellings in their area, and no part of that proportion shall be met out of any other charge or rate leviable by the local authority.

17. Subject to paragraph 16 above, a local authority may apportion their estimated expenditure mentioned in paragraph 14(a) above on whatever basis they consider appropriate, but they shall ensure that the apportionment is not such as to show undue preference to, or discriminate unduly against, any class or classes of person liable to pay—
  (a) the council tax; or
  (b) the non-domestic sewerage rate,
respectively.

18. Where a local authority have determined in respect of any financial year what proportion of their estimated expenditure under the 1968 Act falls to be met out of the council tax, that amount shall form part of the total estimated expenses in respect of that year which are mentioned in section 93(3) of this Act.

Non-domestic sewerage rate

19. Each local authority shall, in respect of the financial year 1993–94 and each subsequent financial year, determine, before such date as may be prescribed in relation to each of those years, such amount of the non-domestic sewerage rate as will provide sufficient money to meet the proportion of their estimated expenditure under the 1968 Act for that year which they have determined under paragraph 14 above is to be met out of that rate.

20. Subject to paragraphs 21 and 23 below, the non-domestic sewerage rate shall be levied in respect of lands and heritages whose drains or private sewers are connected with public sewers or public sewage treatment works and which are—
  (a) subjects (other than part residential subjects) in respect of which there is an entry in the valuation roll, according to the rateable value of those subjects; or
  (b) part residential subjects, according to that part of their rateable value which is shown in the apportionment note as relating to the non-residential use of those subjects.

21.—(1) Where, in respect of a financial year, the non-domestic sewerage rate is leviable under paragraph 20 above in respect of lands and heritages which are both—
  (a) church or charity premises; and
  (b) premises to which, by virtue of subsection (4) of section 41 of the 1980 Act, that section applies, whether or not they are premises in respect of which the non-domestic water rate is leviable,
the non-domestic sewerage rate shall be levied not according to the rateable value of those lands and heritages or that part thereof which is shown in the apportionment note as relating to their non-residential use but instead in accordance with sub-paragraph (2) below.
  (2) Where—
  (a) the water authority, in a resolution under subsection (1) of the said section 41, made with respect to the lands and heritages mentioned in sub-paragraph (1) above or to a class of premises which includes those lands and heritages, have specified for the purposes of that subsection in respect of that year a fraction of net annual value smaller than one half, then the non-domestic sewerage rate shall be levied according to that smaller fraction of the rateable value of those lands and heritages or, as the case may be, that part thereof; and
  (b) the water authority have not so specified a smaller fraction, then the non-domestic sewerage rate shall be levied according to one half of the rateable value of those lands and heritages or, as the case may be, that part thereof.
  (3) In sub-paragraph (1) above "church or charity premises" means—
  (a) premises to the extent to which, under section 22(1) of the 1956 Act (exemption from non-domestic rates of church premises etc.), no non-domestic rate is leviable on them in respect of the financial year; or
  (b) lands and heritages in respect of which relief in respect of the non-domestic rate is given

in respect of the financial year under subsection (2) of section 4 of the Local Government (Financial Provisions etc.) (Scotland) Act 1962 (relief for premises occupied by charities); or

(c) lands and heritages in respect of which a reduction of or remission from the non-domestic rate has effect in respect of the financial year under subsection (5) of the said section 4.

22. The person who is liable to pay the non-domestic sewerage rate in respect of any premises shall be the person who is liable to pay the non-domestic rate in respect of those premises, or who would be liable to pay the non-domestic rate but for any enactment which exempts those premises from that rate or by or under which relief or remission from liability for that rate is given.

23. The provisions of—
(a) Part XI of the 1947 Act;
(b) Part VII of the 1973 Act; and
(c) sections 7, 8, 9 and 10 of the 1975 Act,

(all of which relate to rating) shall apply, subject to such adaptations and modifications as may be prescribed, to the levying, collection and recovery of the non-domestic sewerage rate.

PART III

MISCELLANEOUS PROVISIONS

Accounts

24. Without prejudice to section 96(1) of the 1973 Act (which relates to the keeping of accounts by local authorities), each local authority shall prepare and maintain separate accounts in respect of its functions under the 1968 and 1980 Acts respectively.

25. The provisions of sections 96(2) to (4) (which impose requirements as to the accounts mentioned in section 96(1)) and 105(1) (which empowers the Secretary of State to make regulations as to the said accounts) of the 1973 Act shall apply in relation to the accounts mentioned in paragraph 24 above as they apply to the accounts mentioned in the said section 96(1).

Tariff of charges

26. Each local authority shall, in respect of the financial year 1993–94 and each subsequent financial year, and before such date as may be prescribed in relation to each of those years, prepare a statement, to be known as a tariff of charges, indicating—
(a) the basis upon which they have apportioned their estimated expenditure under paragraph 2 above as between—
    (i) the direct charges,
    (ii) the council water charge, and
    (iii) the non-domestic water rate;
(b) the amount determined or set by them in respect of that year as—
    (i) the rate or rates of the direct charges under paragraph 5 above,
    (ii) the council water charge under paragraph 9 above, and
    (iii) the non-domestic water rate under section 40 of the 1980 Act;
(c) the basis upon which they have apportioned their estimated expenditure for that year under paragraph 14 above as between—
    (i) the council tax, and
    (ii) the non-domestic sewerage rate; and
(d) the amount determined by them for that year as the non-domestic sewerage rate.

27. Each local authority shall make their tariff of charges available for public inspection at all reasonable hours at such places within their area as they may determine, and shall send a copy of the tariff to the Secretary of State.

PART IV

AMENDMENTS TO THE 1980 ACT

28. The 1980 Act shall be amended in accordance with the following provisions of this Part.
29. In section 9A (which relates to the exemption from charges of water for fire fighting)—
(a) for the words "community water charges" there shall be substituted the words "council water charge"; and

(b) for paragraphs (a) and (b) there shall be substituted the following paragraphs—
   "(a) water taken for the purpose of extinguishing fires or taken by a fire authority for any other emergency purposes;
   (b) water taken for the purpose of testing apparatus installed or equipment used for extinguishing fires or for the purpose of training persons for fire-fighting; or
   (c) the availability of water for any purpose mentioned in paragraph (a) or (b) above:".

30. In section 35 (which relates to the power to supply water fittings)—
(a) in subsection (1) the words "by way either of sale or hire" shall cease to have effect;
(b) in subsection (2), for the words "let for hire" there shall be substituted the words "supplied otherwise than by sale"; and
(c) for subsection (5) there shall be substituted the following subsection—
   "(5) If any person—
   (a) so interferes with a meter used by the authority in determining the amount of any charges fixed in relation to any premises as intentionally or recklessly to prevent the meter from showing, or from accurately showing, the volume of water supplied to those premises; or
   (b) carries out, without the consent of the water authority, any works which he knows are likely to affect the operation of such a meter or which require the disconnection of such a meter; or
   (c) otherwise wilfully or negligently injures or suffers to be injured any water fitting belonging to the authority,
he shall be guilty of an offence and liable on summary conviction to a fine not exceeding level 3 on the standard scale."

31. In section 40 (which provides for liability to the non-domestic water rate)—
(a) in subsection (2)(a), for the words "the water authority" there shall be substituted the words "a water authority"; and
(b) in subsection (4), for the words "5 to the Abolition of Domestic Rates Etc. (Scotland) Act 1987" there shall be substituted the words "11 to the 1992 Act".

32. After section 41 there shall be inserted—

"Supply of water by meter

41A.—(1) Where premises to which water is supplied are premises in respect of which there is an entry on the valuation roll, the occupier shall have the option of taking the supply by meter.
(2) Where premises to which water is supplied constitute a dwelling within the meaning of section 72(2) of the 1992 Act—
   (a) the owner of the dwelling; or
   (b) the person or persons who, in terms of section 75 of that Act—
      (i) are liable to pay council tax on the dwelling; or
      (ii) would have been so liable had the building not been exempt from council tax under section 72(6) of that Act,
shall have the option of taking the supply by meter.
(3) Neither of the parties mentioned in paragraph (a) or (b) of subsection (2) above may exercise the option mentioned in that subsection without the consent of the other.
(4) The exercise of the option mentioned in subsections (1) and (2) above is subject to—
   (a) the payment by the person exercising the option of any reasonable charges made by the authority under section 35 of this Act; and
   (b) the acceptance by him of such reasonable terms and conditions as may be published by the authority under section 55(1) of this Act,
and any question as to whether any such charges or terms and conditions are reasonable shall, in default of agreement, be referred to the Secretary of State who may determine it himself or, if he thinks fit, refer it for arbitration."

33. In section 46(2) (which relates to transport hereditaments), for the words "community water charge" there shall be substituted the words "council water charge".

34. For section 49 (which relates to payment for water supplied by meter) there shall be substituted—

"Payment for supplies by meter

49.—(1) Subject to the provisions of this section, where water is supplied by meter by a water authority, they may make—
   (a) such a standing charge as they may from time to time consider appropriate, irrespective of whether any water is consumed on the premises; and
   (b) charges calculated on the amount of water, if any, actually so consumed.

(2) Charges payable under this section shall be payable—

(a) in the case of premises (other than premises constituting the residential part of part residential subjects) in respect of which there is an entry on the valuation roll, by the occupier of the premises in respect of which they are due; or

(b) in the case of a dwelling within the meaning of section 72(2) of the 1992 Act, by the person or persons who—

(i) are liable to pay council tax on the dwelling; or

(ii) would have been so liable had the building not been exempt from council tax under section 72(6) of that Act.

(3) Charges payable under this section, including charges for any meter supplied by the authority, shall be recoverable in the manner in which non-domestic rates are recoverable.

(4) No charges shall be made under this section in relation to any lands and heritages such as are mentioned in section 5 (rebates for institutions in Scotland for the disabled) of the Rating (Disabled Persons) Act 1978 during any rebate period (within the meaning of section 6(2) of that Act)."

35. After section 56 there shall be inserted—

"Regulations as to meters

56A. The Secretary of State may make regulations under this Act as to the installation, connection, use, maintenance, authentication and testing of meters, and as to any related matters."

36. In section 58(3) (which relates to the termination of the right to the supply of water on special terms), for the words "community water charge" there shall be substituted the words "council water charge".

37. In section 61(1)(b) (which relates to the calculation of the amount to be requisitioned by water authorities), for the words "community water charges" there shall be substituted the words "the council water charge".

38. In section 109(1) (which defines terms used in the Act)—

(a) before the definition of "agricultural lands and heritages" there shall be inserted—

" 'the 1992 Act' means the Local Government Finance Act 1992;

(b) in the definition of "apportionment note", for the words "2 of Schedule 1 to the Abolition of Domestic Rates Etc. (Scotland) Act 1987" there shall be substituted the words "1 of Schedule 5 to the 1992 Act";

(c) after the definition of "contributing authority" there shall be inserted—

" 'council water charge' shall be construed in accordance with the provisions of paragraph 6 of Schedule 11 to the 1992 Act:";

(d) after the definition of "enactment" there shall be inserted—

" 'fire authority' has the same meaning as in the Fire Services Act 1947;";

(e) in the definition of "part residential subjects" for the words from "section" to the end there shall be substituted the words "section 99 (interpretation of Part II etc.) of the 1992 Act;"; and

(f) in the definition of "prescribed", after "prescribed by" there shall be inserted the words "or determined under".

Part I: Charges for Water Services

GENERAL NOTE

This makes provision for the three main sources of income from which a local authority, whether a regional or islands council, will meet its expenditure on water-supply services. It sets out the procedure and makes provision for the timetable to be followed by a local authority in estimating its annual expenditure on water services and in apportioning that fairly between classes of consumer; it describes the arrangements to be followed by a local authority in setting the rate(s) of direct charges which will bring in sufficient income to the proportion of its estimated expenditure for the year which it has determined is to be met out of those charges; it introduces the council water charge which shall be payable in respect of dwellings situated in each authority's area; it provides for the council water charge to be payable in respect of any dwelling which is not an exempt dwelling and in respect of which qualifying conditions are met; it makes provision as to how a local authority will determine the amount of the council water charge, and how the charges are to be collected by an authority; it applies various provisions of the Act to the council water charge as they apply to council tax; it provides for the arrangements relating to liability for the non-domestic water rate to continue; and it makes provision as to how a local authority is to meet its expenditure on sewerage services under the Sewerage (Scotland) Act 1968.

A local authority meets expenditure on water services in three main ways:

(a) direct charges made under s.49 of the Water (Scotland) Act 1980, which are based on the volume of water used as measured by meter;

(b) the community water charges; and

(c) the non-domestic water rate.

Expenditure is also met by charges for water supplied for special purposes and by grants-in-aid, but the contribution to overall income from these sources is very small. The Act does not provide for changes to these arrangements.

Procedurally, the arrangements in the Water (Scotland) Act 1980 for estimating expenditure on, or setting charges for, water services were replaced by provisions in the 1987 Act and, for the first time, provision was made for the apportioning of expenditure between classes of consumer. This principle remains in replacing the community water charges by the council water charge.

For direct charges, s.49 of the Water (Scotland) Act 1980 provides that, where water is supplied to premises by meter from the public supply, the charge for the supply is to be based on the volume of water consumed on the premises. The authority may determine and impose a fixed minimum charge for such supplies. For non-domestic water rate, all consumers of water in non-domestic premises are liable to pay the non-domestic water rate if they receive a public water supply otherwise than by a direct metered supply. The provisions relating to liability for the non-domestic water rate are set out in s.40 of the Water (Scotland) Act 1980 and are not changed by this Schedule. Expenditure on sewerage services has been met from the community charges and the non-domestic sewerage rate. Trade effluent charges under the Sewerage (Scotland) Act 1968 may also require to be paid separately by non-domestic consumers but these charges are not affected by the Act.

Para. 1

This retains the existing arrangements for recovery of expenditure on water supply services by direct "metered" charges under s.49 of the 1980 Act and the non-domestic water rate, but community water charges are replaced by the council water charge. These charges and the non-domestic water rate and their related provisions are dealt with in paras. 5–12 and 26 of the schedule. The balance of a local authority's expenditure, after allowing for income from other sources, on its functions relating to the supply of water and in making payments for water services supplied to it by other local authorities or by water development boards, is to be met out of the direct charges under s.49 of the 1980 Act: the council water charge and the non-domestic water rate.

Para. 2

For each financial year from 1993–94 the local authority must estimate its expenditure on water services and determine the proportion of its expenditure to be met from direct charges, the council water charge and the non-domestic water rate respectively. The date by which the local authority must make its estimate and determine its apportionment will be prescribed by the Secretary of State.

Para. 3

In estimating its expenditure for a financial year the local authority should take into account such additional sums as it considers necessary to meet current expenses already incurred, contingencies, and expenses relating to the following financial year before the income from that year is available. The local authority must also take into account any other means by which the estimated expenditure may be met.

Para. 4

The local authority remains free to determine an appropriate basis on which its estimated expenditure is to be apportioned, provided that in doing so it does not favour unduly or discriminate unduly against any class of persons liable to make payment in respect of water services by way of direct charges, the council water charge or the non-domestic water rate.

Para. 5

For each financial year, the local authority must determine the rate or rates of direct charges in accordance with s.49 of the 1980 Act. An authority may determine different rates of direct charges for different circumstances. The rate(s) determined must produce sufficient income to meet the proportion of estimated expenditure which the local authority have determined is to be met out of direct charges. The rate(s) of direct charges must be fixed by a date to be prescribed by the Secretary of State. Note that para. 34 of the schedule makes other amendments to the terms of s.49 of the 1980 Act.

Para. 6
Each local authority must impose a water charge to be known as the regional council water charge, or the islands council water charge. These charges are to be payable in respect of dwellings situated in that authority's area.

Para. 7
The council water charge shall be payable in respect of any dwelling which is not an exempt dwelling and in respect of which the qualifying conditions are met. It defines "dwelling", "chargeable dwelling" and "exempt dwelling" and enables the Secretary of State to prescribe classes of dwelling as exempt by reference to certain specific factors or such other factors as he thinks fit. For Scotland, see the Council Tax (Exempt Dwellings) (Scotland) Order 1992 (S.I. 1992 No. 1333).

Para. 8
This sets out the qualifying conditions for liability to pay the council water charge. An occupier of a dwelling is liable to pay the charge if a water authority supplies the dwelling with a supply of water; if the water is not supplied wholly by meter; and if the supply is not one which the water authority is under an obligation to provide free of charge.

Para. 9
For each financial year from 1993–94 onwards, each local authority will determine the amount of council water charge to be paid for that financial year in respect of a chargeable dwelling in its area listed in valuation Band D and then determine the amount of council water charge to be paid in respect of a chargeable dwelling in each of the other valuation bands specified in accordance with the proportion mentioned in s.74. The amount of the charge must be set before a date to be prescribed by the Secretary of State.

Para. 10
The amount of the council water charge must deliver sufficient income to meet that part of the local authority's expenses on water services which is to be met by the council water charge. The expenses to be covered by this income are to be the proportion of the estimated expenditure on water services which falls to be met from the council water charge, as determined under para. 2 of this schedule.

Para. 11
This applies to the council water charge the provisions of the Act relating to liability, basic amounts payable and discounts, and interpretation. The Secretary of State is empowered to make adaptations, exceptions and modifications to these provisions as they apply to the council water charge. See the Council Water Charge (Scotland) Regulations 1992 (S.I. 1992 No. 1203), the Council Tax (Liability of Owners) (Scotland) Regulations 1992 (S.I. 1992 No. 1331), the Council Tax (Administration and Enforcement) (Scotland) Regulations 1992 (S.I. 1992 No. 1332), the Council Tax (Reductions for Disabilities) (Scotland) Regulations 1992 (S.I. 1992 No. 1335), the Council Tax (Discounts) (Scotland) Order 1992 (S.I. 1992 No. 1408) and the Council Tax (Discounts) (Scotland) Regulations 1992 (S.I. 1992 No. 1409).

Para. 12
The provisions relating to the non-domestic water rate, contained in s.40 of the 1980 Act, as replaced by para. 29 of Sched. 5 to the 1987 Act, continue to have effect.

Para. 13
A local authority's expenditure, net of income from trade effluent charges, etc., on the provision of sewerage services under the 1968 Act shall be met from the council tax, and the non-domestic sewerage rate under paras. 19–22 of this schedule.

Part II: Charges for Sewerage Services

GENERAL NOTE
This sets out the procedures and makes provision for the timetable to be followed by a local authority in estimating its annual expenditure on sewerage services and in apportioning it fairly among classes of persons liable to pay for the service. It also prescribes the premises in respect of which, and the circumstances in which, liability for the non-domestic sewerage rate arise, and the persons liable to pay the rate. It provides the procedure for determining the amount of the non-domestic sewerage rate and the expenses which it is to meet, and makes provision for the application of certain other Acts for the levying, collection and recovery of the rate.

Para. 14
For each financial year from 1993–94 onward each local authority must estimate its expenditure on sewerage services and determine the proportion of its expenditure to be met from the

council tax and the non-domestic sewerage rate respectively. The date by which the local authority must makes its estimate and determine the apportionment of its expenditure will be prescribed by the Secretary of State.

Para. 15
In estimating its expenditure for a financial year the local authority should take into account such additional sums as it considers necessary to cover expenses already incurred; meet contingencies; and meet expenses relating to the following financial year before the income from that year is available. The local authority must also take into account any other means by which the estimated expenditure may be met.

Para. 16
The proportion of expenditure on sewerage services to be met out of the council tax is to be such proportion as the local authority considers to be reasonably attributable to the services provided under s.1(1) of the Sewerage (Scotland) Act 1968 to dwellings in the authority's area. The proportion of expenditure to be met from the council tax is to be met from the council tax only and from no other source. Thus it cannot be supplemented by any of the local authority's other rates or charges.

Para. 17
The local authority remains free to determine an appropriation basis on which its estimated expenditure is to be apportioned, provided that in doing so it does not favour unduly, or discriminate unduly against, any class or classes of persons liable to pay for sewerage services by way of the council tax or the non-domestic sewerage rate.

Para. 18
The total estimated expenses of the local authority are to include the proportion of the authority's estimated expenditure on sewerage services.

Para. 19
For each financial year from 1993–94 onwards, each local authority will determine the amount of its non-domestic sewerage rate. The amount of the rate must provide sufficient income to meet that part of its expenses on sewerage services which the local authority has determined under para. 14 should be met by the non-domestic sewerage rate. The amount of the rate must be set before a date to be prescribed by the Secretary of State. The expenses to be covered by this income are to be the proportion of the estimated expenditure which falls to be met from the non-domestic sewerage rate as the authority has determined.

Para. 20
The non-domestic sewerage rate should be levied if lands and heritages are connected to "public sewers" or "public sewage treatment works", as defined in s.59(1) of the Sewerage (Scotland) Act 1968. The rate is levied in respect of those lands and heritages which are not part residential subjects according to the rateable value shown in the valuation roll. Where the lands and heritages are part residential subjects, the rate is levied according to that part of the rateable value of the subjects which the apportionment note shows as relating to their non-residential use.

Para. 21
The non-domestic sewerage rate levied in respect of lands and heritages which are both church or charity premises and premises to which s.41(4) of the Water (Scotland) Act 1980 applies shall be levied at a reduced level. That rate shall be levied according to one-half of the rateable value of the premises, or, if the water authority has specified a smaller fraction under s.41(1) of the 1980 Act for the purposes of relief from the non-domestic water rate, the rate will be levied according to that smaller function.

Para. 22
The person who is liable to pay the non-domestic sewerage rate for any premises will be the same person who is liable to pay the non-domestic rate in respect of those premises.

Para. 23
This applies to the non-domestic sewerage rate the provisions relating to the levying, collection and recovery of non-domestic rates, subject to any adaptations and modifications prescribed by the Secretary of State.

Part III: Miscellaneous Provisions

GENERAL NOTE
This requires local authorities to prepare and maintain separate accounts in respect of their

sewerage and water functions. It also provides that certain sections of the Local Government (Scotland) Act 1973, relating to accounts of local authorities generally, shall apply to accounts for water and sewerage. It introduces a requirement for a local authority to prepare a statement, to be known as a tariff of charges, giving details of the apportionment of its estimated expenditure on, and the rates and charges for, water and sewerage services; and it provides for public access to the statement.

Local authorities have a general statutory duty under s.96(1) of the 1973 Act to keep accounts of all transactions relating to all funds of the authority. Section 96(2)–(4) of the 1973 Act imposes requirements as to those accounts, and s.105(1) empowers the Secretary of State to make such regulations regarding the accounts as appear to him to be necessary. In regard to the tariff of charges, the provisions in Sched. 5 to the 1987 Act require a local authority to publish a similar statement of its estimated expenditure on water and sewerage services, and the basis on which it apportions expenditure in providing water and sewerage services among differing classes of persons liable to pay for those services.

Para. 24
Without prejudice to s.96(1) of the 1973 Act, each local authority must prepare and maintain separate accounts in respect of its sewerage functions under the Sewerage (Scotland) Act 1968 and its water functions under the Water (Scotland) Act 1980.

Para. 25
Section 96(2)–(4) of the 1973 Act, which imposes requirements relating to the making up, preparation of abstracts and auditing of accounts, together with s.105(1) of the 1973 Act, which empowers the Secretary of State to make regulations regarding such accounts, also applies to the water and sewerage accounts.

Para. 26
For each financial year from 1993–94 onwards, a local authority must prepare a statement, to be known as a tariff of charges, including the basis upon which it has apportioned its estimated expenditure on water services between direct charges, and the council water charge and the non-domestic water rate. It must also include the amount determined as the rate or rates of the direct charges, as the council water charge and as the non-domestic water rate under s.40 of the Water (Scotland) Act 1980. In regard to sewerage matters the statement must include the basis of the apportionment of its estimated expenditure on sewerage services as between the council tax and the non-domestic sewerage rate, and the amount it has determined to be the non-domestic sewerage rate. This statement is to be prepared before such date as the Secretary of State may prescribe.

Para. 27
The local authority must make its tariff of charges available for inspection by the public at all reasonable hours and at such places within its area as it determines. The local authority is also required to send a copy of its tariff to the Secretary of State.

Part IV: Amendments to the Water (Scotland) Act 1980

GENERAL NOTE
This makes various amendments to provisions in the Water (Scotland) Act 1980, some merely consequential.

Para. 29
This extends the present exemptions from charges for water used for extinguishing fires to cover water taken for other emergency purposes; provision is made for exemption from charges of water used in fire-fighting training. The existing provision on exemption from charges for the availability for water for any of the purposes specified is retained.

Para. 30
This extends s.35(1) to allow the supply of water fittings other than by sale or hire. The new s.35(5) re-enacts the existing offence of wilfully or negligently injuring water fittings belonging to a water authority and creates new offences relative to tampering with water meters. The penalty on summary conviction for such offences is to be a fine not exceeding level 3 on the standard scale, as opposed to the previous penalty of a fine not exceeding level 1 on the standard scale.

Para. 31
This corrects one drafting error and provides one consequential amendment.

Para. 32
The new s.41A provides for the option to be given to all consumers of having their water supplied by meter. The consumers who can exercise the option concerned are the occupier of premises for which there is an entry on the valuation roll and, in the case of a dwelling, the owner or the person or persons liable, or who would be liable but for an exemption, to pay the council tax on the dwelling. If the owner and the liable person are different, both must agree to exercise the option. The person exercising the meter option shall be liable for any reasonable charges made by the authority of the 1980 Act and shall be required to accept such reasonable terms and conditions as the authority may publish. The Secretary of State shall, if required, settle any disagreement over whether such charges or terms and conditions are reasonable either himself or by reference to arbitration.

Para. 34
The new s.49 allows for a standing charge, determined by the water authority, to be made in respect of metered supplies in addition to charges for the water actually consumed. Charges are to be payable by occupiers of premises, other than premises which constitute the residential part of a part residential subject, for which there is a valuation roll entry, or, in the case of a dwelling, by the person or persons liable for the council tax, or who would be liable but for an exemption. Charges are to continue to be recoverable in the same way as non-domestic rates are recoverable. Provision is made for exemption from metered charges of lands and heritages mentioned in s.5 of the Rating (Disabled Persons) Act 1978 during any rebate period.

Para. 35
The Secretary of State is empowered to make regulations under the 1980 Act as to the installation, connection, use, maintenance, authentication and testing of meters, and for related matters.

Para. 38
Consequential amendments are made to s.109(1). The definition of "prescribed" is expanded to allow for matters not only to be prescribed in regulations made under the 1980 Act but also to be prescribed under such regulations.

Section 108   SCHEDULE 12

PAYMENTS TO LOCAL AUTHORITIES BY SECRETARY OF STATE: SCOTLAND

PART I

PAYMENTS TO LOCAL AUTHORITIES

General

1.—(1) The local authorities—
(a) to which revenue support grant is payable; and
(b) among whom the distributable amount (within the meaning of paragraph 9 below) of non-domestic rate income is distributed,
in respect of a financial year shall be such local authorities as are specified in an order made by the Secretary of State; and different provision may be made for the purposes of sub-paragraphs (a) and (b) of this paragraph in respect of the same authority.

(2) The amount of revenue support grant payable in respect of a financial year to a local authority so specified shall be such amount as is determined in relation to that authority by order made by the Secretary of State.

(3) The amount of non-domestic rate income distributed in respect of a financial year to a local authority so specified shall be such part of the distributable amount for that year as is determined in relation to that authority by order made by the Secretary of State.

(4) Subject to paragraph 4 below, the Secretary of State may at any time by order—
(a) make such amendments as he thinks fit to; or
(b) revoke; or
(c) revoke and replace with a different order,
any order made under this paragraph; and any amount of revenue support grant or non-domestic rate income which has been paid and which, in consequence of anything done under this paragraph, falls to be repaid may be recovered by the Secretary of State whenever and however he thinks fit.

(5) An order under this paragraph shall be known as a local government finance order.

2.—(1) A local government finance order shall be made only with the consent of the Treasury.

(2) Before making a local government finance order the Secretary of State shall consult such associations of local authorities as appear to him to be appropriate.

(3) A local government finance order together with a report of the considerations which led to its provisions shall be laid before the House of Commons but shall have no effect until approved by a resolution of that House.

Payment of revenue support grant and non-domestic rate income

3. Revenue support grant and non-domestic rate income shall be paid to a local authority in such instalments and at such times as the Secretary of State may, with the consent of the Treasury, determine.

4. The Secretary of State may determine that the amount of revenue support grant or non-domestic rate income which has been paid to a local authority in respect of a financial year shall be final and, where he does so, he shall have no power to redetermine that amount.

Secretary of State's power on local authority's failure to provide information

5. Where under section 199 of the 1973 Act (which provides for reports and returns being made by local authorities and others) the Secretary of State requires a local authority to give information for the purposes of his functions in relation to revenue support grants or non-domestic rate income payable for the financial year 1993–94 or for any subsequent financial year, but that information is not given timeously—

(a) he may make an estimate as regards any element of the required information; and

(b) without prejudice to section 211 of that Act (which makes general provision concerning failure by a local authority to do what is required of them), for the said purposes any such estimate shall be deemed to be information given by the local authority.

PART II

NON-DOMESTIC RATING ACCOUNTS

The accounts

6.—(1) In accordance with this Part of this Schedule the Secretary of State shall keep, in respect of the financial year 1993–94 and each subsequent financial year, an account (to be called a non-domestic rating account).

(2) The Secretary of State—

(a) shall keep each account in such form as the Treasury may direct; and

(b) shall at such time as the Treasury may direct send copies of each account to the Comptroller and Auditor General.

(3) The Comptroller and Auditor General shall examine, certify and report on any account of which copies are sent to him under sub-paragraph (2) above and shall lay copies of the account and of his report before each House of Parliament.

Credits and debits

7.—(1) For each financial year there shall be credited (as items of account) to the account kept for the year any sums received by the Secretary of State in the year under paragraph 11 below.

(2) Any amounts of non-domestic rate income distributed by the Secretary of State in a financial year under—

(a) paragraph 3 above;

(b) paragraph 11(9) and (10) below; or

(c) regulations made under paragraph 12(5) below,

shall be debited (as items of account) to the account kept for the year.

8.—(1) As soon as is reasonably practicable after the end of each financial year the Secretary of State shall calculate the following—

(a) the aggregate of the items of account credited to the account kept for the year; and

(b) the aggregate of the items of account debited to the account kept for the year.

(2) If the aggregate mentioned in sub-paragraph (1)(a) above exceeds that mentioned in sub-paragraph (1)(b) above, a sum equal to the excess shall be—

(a) debited (as an item of account) to the account kept for the year; and

(b) credited (as an item of account) to the account kept for the next financial year.

(3) If the aggregate mentioned in sub-paragraph (1)(b) above exceeds that mentioned in sub-paragraph (1)(a) above, a sum equal to the excess shall be—

(a) credited (as an item of account) to the account kept for the year; and
(b) debited (as an item of account) to the account kept for the next financial year.

Distributable amount

9.—(1) Before a financial year begins the Secretary of State shall estimate—
(a) the aggregate of the items of account which will be credited to the account kept for that year; and
(b) the aggregate of the items of account which will be debited to the account kept for that year under paragraphs 7(2)(b) and (c) and 8(3)(b) above.

(2) In making any estimate under sub-paragraph (1) above the Secretary of State may make such assumptions as he thinks fit.

(3) If the aggregate estimated under sub-paragraph (1)(a) above exceeds the aggregate estimated under sub-paragraph (1)(b) above the Secretary of State shall calculate the amount equal to the difference.

(4) In any local government finance order in respect of that year the Secretary of State shall specify the amount arrived at under this paragraph (the distributable amount for the year).

PART III

CONTRIBUTION

Non-domestic rating contributions

10.—(1) The Secretary of State may make regulations containing rules for the calculation of an amount for a financial year in relation to each levying authority (to be called its non-domestic rating contribution for the year).

(2) Subject to sub-paragraph (3) below, the rules shall be so framed that the amount calculated under them in relation to an authority is broadly the same as the total which would be payable to that authority if there were added—
(a) any sum paid to them by way of a contribution in aid made in respect of lands and heritages which, but for any rule of law relating to Crown exemption, would be liable to non-domestic rates; and
(b) the sum which, if the authority acted diligently, would be payable to them in respect of non-domestic rates for that year.

(3) The Secretary of State may incorporate in the rules provision for deductions (of such extent (if any) as he thinks fit) as regards—
(a) the operation of—
    (i) section 243A (relief of rates in respect of lands and heritages occupied only for a short time) of the 1947 Act;
    (ii) section 244 (remission of rates on account of poverty) of the 1947 Act; and
    (iii) section 4(5) (reduction and remission of rates payable by charitable and other organisations) of the Local Government (Financial Provisions) (Scotland) Act 1962;
(b) the costs of collection and recovery; and
(c) such other matters (if any) as he thinks fit.

(4) Regulations under this paragraph in their application to a particular financial year (including regulations amending or revoking others) shall not be effective unless they come into force before 1st January in the preceding financial year.

11.—(1) This paragraph applies where regulations under paragraph 10 above are in force in respect of a financial year, and has effect subject to any such regulations.

(2) Before the beginning of the relevant financial year, the Secretary of State shall calculate the amount of each levying authority's non-domestic rating contribution for that year, and shall inform each authority of the amount so calculated in respect of them.

(3) The authority shall be liable to pay to the Secretary of State an amount (the "provisional amount") equal to that calculated and notified to them under sub-paragraph (2) above.

(4) The authority shall pay the provisional amount during the course of the year, in such instalments and at such times as the Secretary of State may with the consent of the Treasury direct.

(5) Within such period after the year ends as the Secretary of State may direct the authority shall—
(a) calculate, in such manner as may be prescribed, the amount of its non-domestic rating contribution for the year;
(b) notify the amount so calculated to the Secretary of State; and
(c) arrange for the calculation and the amount to be certified under arrangements made by the Commission for Local Authority Accounts in Scotland.

(6) The Commission shall send a copy of the certification of the calculation and the amount to the Secretary of State.

(7) When the Secretary of State receives notification from an authority under sub-paragraph (5)(b) above he shall—

(a) calculate the amount of the difference (if any) between that amount (the "notified amount") and the provisional amount; and

(b) if there is a difference, inform the authority of the amount of the difference.

(8) If the notified amount exceeds the provisional amount the authority shall pay an amount equal to the difference to the Secretary of State at such time as he may direct.

(9) If the notified amount is less than the provisional amount the Secretary of State shall pay an amount equal to the difference to the authority; and the amount shall be paid at such time as he decides with the Treasury's approval.

(10) When the Secretary of State receives notification of the certified amount from the Commission under sub-paragraph (6) above he shall inform the authority of the amount of any difference between the certified amount and the notified amount, and sub-paragraphs (8) and (9) above shall apply in relation to differences between the certified amount and the notified amount as they apply in relation to differences between the provisional amount and the notified amount.

(11) If the authority fail to comply with sub-paragraph (5) above the Secretary of State may suspend payments which would otherwise fall to be made to the authority under—

(a) paragraph 3 above;

(b) sub-paragraph (9) or (10) above; or

(c) regulations made under paragraph 12(5) below,

but if the authority then comply with the sub-paragraph he shall resume payments falling to be made to the authority under those provisions and make payments to them equal to those suspended.

(12) Where the Secretary of State has suspended payments under sub-paragraph (9) above by reason of the authority's failure to make the calculation required under sub-paragraph (5)(a) above in the manner prescribed, for the purposes of sub-paragraph (10) above sub-paragraphs (8) and (9) above shall apply to differences between the provisional amount and the certified amount as they apply to differences between the provisional amount and the notified amount.

12.—(1) Any calculation under paragraph 11 above of the amount of an authority's non-domestic rating contribution for a year shall be made on the basis of the information before the person making the calculation at the time he makes it; but regulations under paragraph 10 above may include provision—

(a) requiring a calculation under paragraph 11(2) above to be made on the basis of that information read subject to prescribed assumptions;

(b) enabling a calculation under paragraph 11(5)(a) above to be made without taking into account any information as regards which the following conditions are satisfied—

(i) it is not reasonably practicable for the person making the calculation to take it into account; and

(ii) it was received by the authority after a prescribed date (which may be before or after the end of the year in question).

(2) Regulations under paragraph 10 above may incorporate in the rules provision for adjustments to be made in the calculation of the amount of an authority's non-domestic rating contribution under paragraph 11(2) or (5) above, being adjustments to take account of relevant changes affecting the amount of the authority's non-domestic rating contribution for an earlier year.

(3) For the purposes of sub-paragraph (2) above, a change is a relevant change if it results from a decision, determination or other matter which (whether by reason of the time at which it was taken, made or occurred or otherwise) was not taken into account by the authority in the calculation under paragraph 11(5) above of the amount of their non-domestic rating contribution for the earlier year in question.

(4) The power to give directions under paragraph 11 above—

(a) includes power to revoke or amend a direction given under the power;

(b) may be exercised differently for different authorities.

(5) The Secretary of State may make regulations providing that, once the provisional amount has been arrived at under paragraph 11 above as regards an authority for a financial year and if prescribed conditions are fulfilled, the provisional amount is to be treated for the purposes of that paragraph as being an amount smaller than it would otherwise be.

(6) Regulations under sub-paragraph (5) above may include—

(a) provision as to the re-calculation of the provisional amount, including provision for the procedure to be adopted for re-calculation if the prescribed conditions are fulfilled;

(b) provision as to financial adjustments to be made as a result of any re-calculation, including provision for the making of reduced payments under paragraph 11 above or of repayments.

GENERAL NOTE

This re-enacts the substance of Sched. 4 to the 1987 Act in relation to revenue support grant and makes new provision for the payment to the Secretary of State of non-domestic rate pooling contributions and the distribution by him of the amounts received. A single Local Government Finance Order, subject to affirmative resolution of the House of Commons, will provide for the amounts of payments by the Secretary of State both of revenue support grant and non-domestic rate income. Any rules for the calculation of the amounts, both of revenue support grant and non-domestic rate income contributions and payments, are set out in the schedule.

Part I: Payments to Local Authorities

Para. 1

This establishes the local authorities to which revenue support grant and the distributable amount of non-domestic rate income are payable, and how they are determined. The provisions made for revenue support grant may differ from those made for non-domestic rate income in respect of the same authority. The order dealing with non-domestic rate income or revenue support grant is to be termed the "Local Government Finance Order". Previously only revenue support grant was covered by such an Order and the new terminology encompasses both revenue support grant and non-domestic rate income. The Secretary of State is given powers to make regulations to determine, amend, revoke and replace the amount of such payments. It also gives the Secretary of State the power to recover from local authorities any amount due to him as a consequence of the amendment, revocation or replacement of an order.

Para. 2

The Local Government Finance Order requires the consent of the Treasury and before making it the Secretary of State must consult local authority associations. The order should be accompanied by a report setting out the considerations leading to the provisions in the order, and it shall have no effect until approved under the affirmative resolution procedure of the House of Commons.

Para. 3

The Secretary of State is empowered to determine the times at which instalments both of revenue support grant and non-domestic rate income shall be paid to local authorities, subject to Treasury consent.

Para. 4

The Secretary of State may declare the amount of revenue support grant or non-domestic rate income for a financial year final. He has no power to redetermine these.

Para. 5

This general power allows the Secretary of State to make estimates in any case where a local authority has failed to supply information required under s.199 of the 1973 Local Government (Scotland) Act and to use them for the purposes of this functions in relation to the revenue support grants or non-domestic income payable for the financial year 1993–94 or later years. It was stated that it is unlikely that the provisions will be used except in exceptional circumstances, as in the past there had been no great difficulty arising from local authorities' refusing to provide information. However, since there had been instances of them being very late in providing material, it was considered that the provision was therefore necessary.

Part II: Non-Domestic Rating Accounts

Para. 6

This provides for the keeping of a non-domestic rating account by the Secretary of State from the year 1993–94 and specifies the Treasury's rôle in determining the form of the accounts and the rôle of the Controller and Auditor General in certifying the accounts. This is similar to the provisions for England and Wales under para. 1 of Sched. 8 of the Local Government Finance Act 1988.

Para. 7

The sums which are to be credited and debited to the account are defined respectively as those received from the local authorities as contributions of non-domestic rate income to be made by levying authorities to the Secretary of State, and the amounts of non-domestic rate income to be distributed by the Secretary of State. These latter amounts are the main distributable amount paid to authorities, in-year adjustments to that amount, and adjustments arising after the end of the year.

Para. 8

This regulates the finalisation of the accounts after the year end and the procedures to be adopted in rolling forward any credit or debit balance to the following year's accounts. As soon as is reasonably practicable after the year-end the Secretary of State must calculate the aggregate of the debit and credit amounts applying to the account during that year. If the credits to the account during the year exceed the debits to the account, then the account shall be debited with the amount of the excess and that the credit amount shall be rolled forward to the account kept for the following financial year. If the amounts debited to the account during the year exceed the credits, then the accounts are required to be credited with the amount of the deficit and the deficit itself shall be carried forward as a debit to the account kept for the following financial year.

Para. 9

The definition of the "distributable amount" to be paid to authorities parallels the provisions for England and Wales in para. 9 of Sched. 8 to the Local Government Finance Act 1988, as replaced by para. 6 of Sched. 10 to this Act. Before the beginning of the financial year, the Secretary of State must estimate the amount of income likely to be credited to the account during the year from the levying of the non-domestic rate. This includes contributions arising from the levying of the rate for that financial year, together with any foreseen adjustments and any additional credits arising from adjustments to earlier financial years. He is also required to estimate the debits to the account arising from debits rolled forward from the previous year, payments to authorities whose contributions in the previous year were in excess of the amount collected and foreseeable reductions to the local authorities' contributions for the year for which the accounts are being kept. In making these estimates, the Secretary of State may make such assumptions as he thinks fit. The Secretary of State is to deduct the aggregate of credits from the total of debits, and the amount calculated, which will be the amount to be distributed as non-domestic rates from the pool to local authorities in the forthcoming year, is to be specified in the Local Government Finance Order. It will be known as the "distributable amount" for the year.

Part III: Non-Domestic Rating Contributions

Para. 10

The Secretary of State is empowered to make the necessary regulations to define the non-domestic rating contributions for the year for each levying authority. The rules must be framed so that the amount of non-domestic rating contribution by each authority will be broadly the same as it would have collected in non-domestic rates for the year, together with the sums which are received in respect of Crown properties as contributions in lieu of non-domestic rates. Contributions in lieu by Crown properties will operate in the same way under pooling as they did previously, in that the contributions will be made to the levying authority relative to the rate poundage being charged by that authority and no payments will be made direct on behalf of Crown properties to the Secretary of State. The Secretary of State may incorporate into the rules special deductions in relation to loss of income through discretionary reliefs already operating. He may also take into consideration such other matters as he thinks fit, thus giving him the option to include as deductions the cost of collection and recovery of non-domestic rates. The regulations will be ineffective unless in force before January 1 of the preceding financial year.

Para. 11

This provides the mechanism for payments of non-domestic rating contributions to the Secretary of State by levying authorities. The Secretary of State must make an initial estimate of the amount of each levying authority's non-domestic rating contribution for the year and inform the authority of the amount before the beginning of the financial year in question, and the levying authority is required to pay an amount equal to that calculated as the "provisional amount". The Secretary of State, with the consent of the Treasury, may set the amounts of the instalments and the dates of payment. After the end of the financial year but before a date which the Secretary of State may direct, the levying authorities are required to calculate the actual amount of their non-domestic rating contribution and to notify the amount to the Secretary of State. They must also arrange to have the amount certified by the auditor appointed by the Commission for Local Authority Accounts in Scotland, and the Commission must send a copy of the certified calculation to the Secretary of State. On receipt of the notification from an authority of the notified amount, the Secretary of State should compare it with the provisional amount which has been contributed by the authority during the year and inform the authority of any difference between the amounts. In the event of the notified amount's exceeding the provisional amount, the authority is required to pay the difference to the Secretary of State, as directed. If the notified amount is less than the provisional amount, the Secretary of State must pay an amount equal to the difference to the authority. The Treasury's approval is required to the timing of the payment. Where the auditor finds it necessary to alter the amount previously notified by the authority to the Secretary of State, the payment is to be adjusted to take account of the certified rather than the notified amount. The Secretary of State is empowered, in the event of the local authority failing to provide timeously a calculation of the "notified amount", to withhold payments which are due to the authority as regular distributions of non-domestic rate income or which result from adjustments which have been made to the non-domestic rating account.

Para. 12

In regard to the calculation of the non-domestic rating contribution made by the local authority, the regulations provide for the incorporation of adjustments relating to the non-domestic rating contribution for an earlier year. The regulations may allow the provisional amount to be altered to a smaller figure during the course of the year, thus dealing with the loss, during the year, of rate income resulting from such occurrences as the closure of a large rating unit or a successful valuation appeal.

Section 117(1)   SCHEDULE 13

MINOR AND CONSEQUENTIAL AMENDMENTS

Forged Transfers Act 1891 (c. 43)

1. In section 2 of the Forged Transfers Act 1891 (definitions), for paragraph (a) there shall be substituted the following paragraphs—
    "(a) a billing authority or a precepting authority, as defined in section 69 of the Local Government Finance Act 1992;
    (aa) a regional, islands or district council within the meaning of the Local Government (Scotland) Act 1973;
    (ab) a combined police authority or a combined fire authority, as defined in section 144 of the Local Government Finance Act 1988;".

Public Health (Scotland) Act 1897 (c. 38)

2. In section 3 of the Public Health (Scotland) Act 1897, for the definition of "ratepayer" (which was inserted by paragraph 1 of Schedule 15 to the Environmental Protection Act 1990) there shall be substituted the following definition—
    "The word 'ratepayer' means a person who is either liable to pay any council tax imposed under the Local Government Finance Act 1992 (or would be so liable but for any enactment or anything provided or done under any enactment) or a non-domestic ratepayer."

Public Health Acts Amendment Act 1907 (c. 53)

3. In section 21 of the Public Health Acts Amendment Act 1907 (power to alter names of streets), for the words from "and persons" to "community charge" there shall be substituted the words "and persons who are liable to pay an amount in respect of council tax".

Small Holdings and Allotments Act 1908 (c. 36)

4. In section 23 of the Small Holdings and Allotments Act 1908 (duty of certain councils to provide allotments), in subsection (2), for the words from "persons" to "community charge" there shall be substituted the words "persons who are liable to pay an amount in respect of council tax".

5. In section 29 of that Act (management of allotments), in subsection (1), for the words from "liable" to the end of the subsection there shall be substituted the words "liable to pay to the district or London borough council in whose area the land is situated an amount in respect of council tax".

Civil Defence Act 1939 (c. 31)

6. In section 62 of the Civil Defence Act 1939 (power of local authorities and public utility undertakers to appropriate lands and buildings for purposes of civil defence), in subsection (1A)(a), for the words from "charging authority" to "Local Government Finance Act 1988" there shall be substituted the words "billing authority or precepting authority, as defined in section 69 of the Local Government Finance Act 1992".

Statutory Orders (Special Procedure) Act 1945 (c. 18)

7. In section 11 of the Statutory Orders (Special Procedure) Act 1945 (interpretation), in subsection (1), for paragraph (a) there shall be substituted the following paragraphs—
"(a) a billing authority or a precepting authority, as defined in section 69 of the Local Government Finance Act 1992;
(aa) a combined police authority or a combined fire authority, as defined in section 144 of the Local Government Finance Act 1988;".

Civil Defence Act 1948 (c. 5)

8. In section 9 of the Civil Defence Act 1948 (interpretation), in subsection (1), in the definition of "local authority", for paragraph (a) there shall be substituted the following paragraphs—
"(a) a billing authority or a precepting authority, as defined in section 69 of the Local Government Finance Act 1992;
(aa) a combined police authority or a combined fire authority, as defined in section 144 of the Local Government Finance Act 1988;".

Valuation and Rating (Scotland) Act 1956 (c. 60)

9. After section 20 of the 1956 Act there shall be inserted—

"Contributions by police authorities
20A.—(1) The police authority of any police area may incur expenses in the making of contributions in aid of council tax in respect of dwellings, whether in the police area or elsewhere, which are occupied for the purposes of the police force for that area, being dwellings in respect of which no council tax is paid.
(2) A contribution under this section shall be treated as money paid as council tax."
10. For section 22 of that Act there shall be substituted the following section—

"Exemption of churches, etc. from rates
22.—(1) No non-domestic rate shall be levied on any premises to the extent that they consist of—
(a) a building occupied by a religious body and used for the purpose of religious worship;
(b) a church hall, chapel hall or similar premises used in connection with a building such as is referred to in paragraph (a) above for the purposes of the religious body which occupies that building; or
(c) any premises occupied by a religious body and used by it—
(i) for carrying out administrative or other activities relating to the organisation of the conduct of religious worship in a building such as is referred to in paragraph (a) above; or
(ii) as an office or for office purposes, or for purposes ancillary to its use as an office or for office purposes.
(2) Where any such premises as are mentioned in subsection (1) above form part of other lands and heritages and are not entered separately in the valuation roll, the net annual value of those lands and heritages shall be apportioned between the said premises and the remainder of the lands and heritages, and the net annual values of such premises and of the remainder shall be shown separately in the valuation roll.
(3) The provisions of the Valuation Acts (including, without prejudice to the foregoing generality, the provisions with respect to persons whose property is valued and with respect to appeals and complaints) shall apply with regard to any matter required by subsection (2) above to be shown in the valuation roll.
(4) In subsection (1)(c) above—
" 'office purposes' " includes administration, clerical work and handling money; and
" 'clerical work' " includes writing, book-keeping, sorting papers or information, filing, typing, duplicating, calculating (by whatever means), drawing and the editorial preparation of matter for publication."

Local Government (Financial Provisions etc.) (Scotland) Act 1962 (c. 9)

11. In subsection (9) of section 4 of the Local Government (Financial Provisions etc.) (Scotland) Act 1962 (exemption from relief under that section of premises exempt under section 22 of the Valuation and Rating (Scotland) Act 1956), the words "paragraph (a) or (b) or (c) of" shall be omitted.

Stock Transfer Act 1963 (c. 18)

12. In section 4 of the Stock Transfer Act 1963 (interpretation), in subsection (1), in the definition of "local authority", for paragraph (a) there shall be substituted the following paragraphs—

"(a) a billing authority or a precepting authority, as defined in section 69 of the Local Government Finance Act 1992;

(aa) a combined police authority or a combined fire authority, as defined in section 144 of the Local Government Finance Act 1988;".

Industrial and Provident Societies Act 1965 (c. 12)

13. In section 31 of the Industrial and Provident Societies Act 1965 (investments), in paragraph (a), for sub-paragraph (i) there shall be substituted the following sub-paragraphs—

"(i) a billing authority or a precepting authority, as defined in section 69 of the Local Government Finance Act 1992;

(ia) a combined police authority or a combined fire authority, as defined in section 144 of the Local Government Finance Act 1988;".

Public Works Loans Act 1965 (c. 63)

14. In section 2 of the Public Works Loans Act 1965 (new form of local loan and automatic charge for securing it), in subsection (1)(a), for sub-paragraph (i) there shall be substituted the following sub-paragraphs—

"(i) a billing authority or a precepting authority, as defined in section 69 of the Local Government Finance Act 1992;

(ia) a combined police authority or a combined fire authority, as defined in section 144 of the Local Government Finance Act 1988;".

General Rate Act 1967 (c. 9)

15. In section 70 of the General Rate Act 1967 (provision for objections to proposals), in subsection (5), for the words "valuation and community charge tribunal" there shall be substituted the words "valuation tribunal".

16. In section 72 of that Act (agreed alterations after proposals), in subsection (1), for the words "valuation and community charge tribunal" there shall be substituted the words "valuation tribunal".

17. In section 73 of that Act (opposed proposals), in subsections (1) and (2)(b), for the words "valuation and community charge tribunal" there shall be substituted the words "valuation tribunal".

18. In section 74 of that Act (proposals objected to by valuation officer), in subsections (2) and (3), for the words "valuation and community charge tribunal", in each place where they occur, there shall be substituted the words "valuation tribunal".

19. In section 75 of that Act (two or more proposals in respect of the same hereditament), in paragraph (b), for the words "valuation and community charge tribunal" there shall be substituted the words "valuation tribunal".

20. In section 76 of that Act (appeals against objections to proposals), in subsections (1), (2), (2B), (3) and (4), for the words "valuation and community charge tribunal" there shall be substituted the words "valuation tribunal".

21. In section 77 of that Act (appeal to Lands Tribunal), for the words "valuation and community charge tribunal" there shall be substituted the words "valuation tribunal".

22. In section 78 of that Act (arbitration with respect to proposals), in subsection (1), for the words "before a valuation and community charge tribunal" there shall be substituted the words "before a valuation tribunal".

23. In section 83 of that Act (use of returns as evidence), in subsections (8) and (9), for the words "a valuation and community charge tribunal" there shall be substituted the words "a valuation tribunal".

24. In section 93 of that Act (membership of local authority etc. not to be a disqualification in certain cases), in subsection (1), for the words "a valuation and community charge tribunal" there shall be substituted the words "a valuation tribunal".

25. In section 108 of that Act (inspection of documents), in subsection (1)(c), for the words "valuation and community charge tribunal" there shall be substituted the words "valuation tribunal".

National Loans Act 1968 (c. 13)

26. In Schedule 4 to the National Loans Act 1968 (local loans), in paragraph 1(a), for sub-paragraph (i) there shall be substituted the following sub-paragraphs—

"(i) a billing authority or a precepting authority, as defined in section 69 of the Local Government Finance Act 1992;
(ia) a combined police authority or a combined fire authority, as defined in section 144 of the Local Government Finance Act 1988;".

International Organisations Act 1968 (c. 48)

27. In section 2 of the International Organisations Act 1968 (specialised agencies of United Nations), in subsection (2)(aa), for the words from "subject to" to "collective community charge" there shall be substituted the words "liable to pay anything in respect of council tax".

28. In Part II of Schedule 1 to that Act (privileges and immunities of representatives, members of subordinate bodies, high officers, experts and persons on missions), in paragraph 9B, for the words from "subject to" to "collective community charge" there shall be substituted the words "liable to pay anything in respect of council tax".

Development of Tourism Act 1969 (c. 51)

29. In section 14 of the Development of Tourism Act 1969 (general restrictions on the making of grants and loans), in subsection (2)(a), for sub-paragraph (i) there shall be substituted the following sub-paragraphs—
"(i) a billing authority or a precepting authority, as defined in section 69 of the Local Government Finance Act 1992;
(ia) a combined police authority or a combined fire authority, as defined in section 144 of the Local Government Finance Act 1988;".

Pensions (Increase) Act 1971 (c. 56)

30. In Schedule 3 to the Pensions (Increase) Act 1971 (administrative, incidental and consequential provisions) in paragraph 6(1)(a), for sub-paragraph (i) there shall be substituted the following sub-paragraphs—
"(i) a billing authority or a precepting authority, as defined in section 69 of the Local Government Finance Act 1992;
(ia) a combined police authority or a combined fire authority, as defined in section 144 of the Local Government Finance Act 1988;".

Tribunals and Inquiries Act 1971 (c. 62)

31. In Part I of Schedule 1 to the Tribunals and Inquiries Act 1971 (tribunals under direct supervision of Council on Tribunals), in paragraph 12A, for the words "Valuation and community charge tribunals" there shall be substituted the words "Valuation tribunals".

Local Government Act 1972 (c. 70)

32. In section 97 of the Local Government Act 1972 (removal or exclusion of disability etc.), in subsection (4), for the words from "under the Local Government Finance Act 1988" to "community charge" there shall be substituted the words "to pay an amount in respect of any community charge or in respect of council tax".

33. In section 150 of that Act (expenses of parish and community councils), in the proviso to subsection (1), for the words from "section 33(4)(d)" to "charging authority)" there shall be substituted the words "section 35(2)(d) of the Local Government Finance Act 1992 (special expenses of a billing authority)".

34.—(1) In subsection (1)(b) of section 168 of that Act (local financial returns)—
(a) for the words "charging authority" there shall be substituted the words "billing authority"; and
(b) in sub-paragraph (i), for the words from "personal community charge" to "collective community charge" there shall be substituted the words "council tax".
(2) In subsection (5) of that section, for paragraph (a) there shall be substituted the following paragraphs—
"(a) a billing authority or a precepting authority, as defined in section 69 of the Local Government Finance Act 1992;
(aa) a combined police authority or a combined fire authority, as defined in section 144 of the Local Government Finance Act 1988;".

Local Government (Scotland) Act 1973 (c. 65)

35. In section 41(4) of the Local Government (Scotland) Act 1973 (exclusion from voting disability), after "1987" there shall be inserted the words "or any council tax or council water charge imposed under the Local Government Finance Act 1992".

36. In section 56 of that Act (arrangements for discharge of functions by local authorities), for subsection (6) there shall be substituted the following subsection—

"(6) A local authority's functions with respect to—

(a) determining a rate;

(b) setting an amount of council tax in accordance with section 93(1) of the Local Government Finance Act 1992, or setting a reduced amount of council tax under section 94 of that Act or paragraph 3 of Schedule 7 to that Act;

(c) setting an amount of council water charge in accordance with paragraph 9 of Schedule 11 to the Local Government Finance Act 1992; or

(d) borrowing money,

shall be discharged only by the authority."

37.—(1) In subsection (1) of section 109 of that Act (rating authorities), for paragraphs (a) and (b) there shall be substituted the following paragraph—

"(a) in the case of the non-domestic rate prescribed under section 7B of the Local Government (Scotland) Act 1975, the regional council and the islands council;".

(2) In subsection (2) of that section, for the words from "falls" onwards there shall be substituted the words "falls, such information as may reasonably be required for the preparation of demand notes for the purposes of levying the non-domestic rate".

38. Sections 110 and 110A of that Act (which make provision as to the distribution of non-domestic rate income) shall cease to have effect.

39. In section 111 of that Act (power to make regulations as to certain matters connected with non-domestic rates), subsection (1)(a), (b) and (d) shall cease to have effect.

40. In subsection (1) of section 118 of that Act (local financial returns), the words "district council in respect of the non-domestic district rate and to any" shall cease to have effect.

Local Government (Scotland) Act 1975 (c. 30)

41. In section 2 of the Local Government (Scotland) Act 1975 (alterations to valuation roll which is in force), in subsection (1)(e) for the words "section 10(2) of the Local Government (Financial Provisions) (Scotland) Act 1963 or" there shall be substituted the word "under".

42. In section 6 of that Act (valuation by formula of certain lands and heritages), at the end of subsection (1) there shall be inserted "and, for the purposes of this subsection, "class or description" of lands and heritages includes lands and heritages, or classes of lands and heritages, falling within such geographical area may be prescribed."

43. In section 37 of that Act (general interpretation)—

(a) after the definition of "the Assessor" there shall be inserted the following definition—

" 'apportionment note' shall be construed in accordance with the provisions of paragraph 1 of Schedule 5 to the Local Government Finance Act 1992;";

(b) after the definition of "material change of circumstances" there shall be inserted the following definitions—

" 'non-domestic rate' shall be construed in accordance with the provisions of section 7A of this Act;

'part residential subjects' shall be construed in accordance with the provisions of section 99(1) of the Local Government Finance Act 1992;"; and

(c) in the definition of "prescribed", after the words "Secretary of State" there shall be inserted the words ", and cognate expressions shall be construed accordingly".

44. In Schedule 3 to that Act (which relates to borrowing and lending by local authorities)—

(a) in paragraph 6(2)(a), for the words "the community charges and the community water charges" there shall be substituted the words "the council tax and the council water charge";

(b) in paragraph 20(2), for the words "the community charges and the community water charges" there shall be substituted the words "the council tax and the council water charge";

(c) in paragraph 22(2), after the words "incurred by the authority for the purposes of" there shall be inserted—

"(a) their functions under any enactment (within the meaning of section 109(1) of the Water (Scotland) Act 1980) in relation to water supply in their area; or

(b) under the Sewerage (Scotland) Act 1968; or

(c)"; and

(d) in paragraph 31, after the definition of "borrowing account" there shall be inserted the following definitions—

" 'council tax' shall be construed in accordance with the provisions of section 70(1) of the Local Government Finance Act 1992;

'council water charge' shall be construed in accordance with the provisions of paragraph 6 to Schedule 11 to the Local Government Finance Act 1992;";

and the definitions of "community charges" and "community water charges" shall cease to have effect.

Local Government (Miscellaneous Provisions) Act 1976 (c. 57)

45. The power conferred by section 16 of the Local Government (Miscellaneous Provisions) Act 1976 (power of local authorities to obtain particulars of persons interested in land) shall not be exercisable with a view to performing any functions under Part I of this Act.

Rating (Disabled Persons) Act 1978 (c. 40)

46. In section 2 of the Rating (Disabled Persons) Act 1978 (rebates for institutions for the disabled), in subsections (5B) and (5C), for the words "valuation and community charge tribunal", in each place where they occur, there shall be substituted the words "valuation tribunal".

47. In Schedule 1 to that Act (amount of rebate under section 1 of that Act), in paragraph 11, in sub-paragraphs (2) and (3), for the words "valuation and community charge tribunal", in each place where they occur, there shall be substituted the words "valuation tribunal".

Justices of the Peace Act 1979 (c. 55)

48. In section 65 of the Justices of the Peace Act 1979 (justices not disqualified by reason of being rate-payers etc.)—
   (a) after the words "charging authority" there shall be inserted the words "council tax set by a billing authority"; and
   (b) after the words "such community charges" there shall be inserted the words "such council tax".

Local Government, Planning and Land Act 1980 (c. 65)

49. In section 2(7)(aa) of the Local Government, Planning and Land Act 1980 (manner in which local authorities are required to publish information), for sub-paragraph (ii) there shall be substituted the following sub-paragraph—
   "(ii) a notice given by virtue of regulations made under paragraph 2 of Schedule 2 to the Local Government Finance Act 1992".

Highways Act 1980 (c. 66)

50. In Part I of Schedule 6 to the Highways Act 1980 (procedure for making and confirming certain orders relating to footpaths and bridleways), in paragraph 3(3)(a), for sub-paragraph (i) there shall be substituted the following sub-paragraphs—
   "(i) a billing authority or a precepting authority, as defined in section 69 of the Local Government Finance Act 1992;
   (ia) a combined police authority or a combined fire authority, as defined in section 144 of the Local Government Finance Act 1988;".

New Towns Act 1981 (c. 64)

51. In section 80 of the New Towns Act 1981 (general interpretation provisions), in sub-section (1), in the definition of "local authority", for paragraph (a) there shall be substituted the following paragraphs—
   "(a) a billing authority or a precepting authority, as defined in section 69 of the Local Government Finance Act 1992;
   (aa) a combined police authority or a combined fire authority, as defined in section 144 of the Local Government Finance Act 1988;".

Acquisition of Land Act 1981 (c. 67)

52. In section 7 of the Acquisition of Land Act 1981 (interpretation), in subsection (1), in the definition of "local authority", for paragraph (a) there shall be substituted the following paragraphs—
   "(a) a billing authority or a precepting authority, as defined in section 69 of the Local Government Finance Act 1992;
   (aa) a combined police authority or a combined fire authority, as defined in section 144 of the Local Government Finance Act 1988;".

Debtors (Scotland) Act 1987 (c. 18)

53.—(1) In subsection (5) of section 1 of the Debtors (Scotland) Act 1987 (which relates to time to pay directions), for paragraphs (e) and (ee) there shall be substituted the following paragraph—

"(e) in an action by or on behalf of—

(i) a rating authority for payment of rates;

(ii) a regional or islands council for the payment of any community charge, community water charge, council tax or council water charge; or

(iii) a regional or islands council for payment of any amount payable as a civil penalty within the meaning of subsection (9) below."

(2) At the end of that section there shall be inserted the following subsection—

"(9) In paragraph (e) of subsection (5) above—

'community charge' and 'community water charge' have the meanings assigned to them in section 26 of the Abolition of Domestic Rates Etc. (Scotland) Act 1987 and the reference in that paragraph to payments of these charges includes reference to any amount payable under section 18(3) of that Act (payment of charges in respect of backdated period);

'council tax' and 'council water charge' have the meanings assigned to them by section 99(1) of the Local Government Finance Act 1992; and

'civil penalty' means a penalty under section 17(10) or (11) of that Act of 1987 or under paragraph 2 of Schedule 3 to that Act of 1992."

54.—(1) In subsection (4) of section 5 of that Act (which relates to time to pay orders), for paragraphs (e) and (ee) there shall be substituted the following paragraph—

"(e) in relation to a debt including any sum due to—

(i) a rating authority for payment of rates;

(ii) a regional or islands council for the payment of any community charge, community water charge, council tax or council water charge; or

(iii) a regional or islands council for payment of any amount payable as a civil penalty within the meaning of subsection (9) below."

(2) At the end of that section there shall be inserted the following subsection—

"(9) In paragraph (e) of subsection (4) above—

'community charge' and 'community water charge' have the meanings assigned to them in section 26 of the Abolition of Domestic Rates Etc. (Scotland) Act 1987 and the reference in that paragraph to payments of these charges includes reference to any amount payable under section 18(3) of that Act (payment of charges in respect of backdated period);

'council tax' and 'council water charge' have the meanings assigned to them by section 99(1) of the Local Government Finance Act 1992; and

'civil penalty' means a penalty under section 17(10) or (11) of that Act of 1987 or under paragraph 2 of Schedule 3 to that Act of 1992."

55. In section 106 of that Act (interpretation)—

(a) the definition of "levying authority" shall cease to have effect; and

(b) in the definition of "summary warrant", for the word "or" there shall be substituted the words ", paragraph 2 of Schedule 8 to the Local Government Finance Act 1992 or".

56. In paragraph 35 of Schedule 5 to that Act, in the definition of "creditor" there shall be inserted at the end—

"(e) for the purposes of paragraph 2 of Schedule 8 to the Local Government Finance Act 1992, the levying authority."

Income and Corporation Taxes Act 1988 (c. 1)

57. In section 842A of the Income and Corporation Taxes Act 1988 (local authorities), in subsection (2), for paragraphs (a) to (c) there shall be substituted the following paragraphs—

"(a) a billing authority as defined in section 69 of the Local Government Finance Act 1992;

(b) a precepting authority as defined in that section;

(c) a body having power by virtue of regulations under section 74 of the Local Government Finance Act 1988 to issue a levy;".

Education Reform Act 1988 (c. 40)

58.—(1) At the end of subsection (8)(b) of section 81 of the Education Reform Act 1988 (recovery from local funds of sums in respect of maintenance grant) there shall be added the words "or from any amount payable by him to the authority under Part III of Schedule 8 to the Local Government Finance Act 1988 (which makes provision in respect of redistributed non-domestic rates)".

(2) Subsection (8A) of that section shall cease to have effect.

Local Government Finance Act 1988 (c. 41)

59. In section 41 of the 1988 Act (local rating lists), in subsection (1), for the words "charging authority" there shall be substituted the words "billing authority".

60. In section 43 of that Act (occupied hereditaments: liability), in subsection (7), for the words "charging authority" there shall be substituted the words "billing authority".

61. In section 44 of that Act (occupied hereditaments: supplementary), in subsection (5), for the words "charging authority" there shall be substituted the words "billing authority".

62.—(1) In subsection (1) of section 44A of that Act (partly occupied hereditaments), for the words "charging authority's" there shall be substituted the words "billing authority's".

(2) In subsections (6)(a) and (8)(a) of that section, for the words "charging authority" there shall be substituted the words "billing authority".

63. In section 45 of that Act (unoccupied hereditaments: liability), in subsection (7), for the words "charging authority" there shall be substituted the words "billing authority".

64. In section 46 of that Act (unoccupied hereditaments: supplementary), in subsection (4), for the words "charging authority" there shall be substituted the words "billing authority".

65.—(1) In subsections (1)(a) and (3) of section 47 of that Act (discretionary relief in respect of local non-domestic rates), for the words "charging authority" there shall be substituted the words "billing authority".

(2) In subsection (9) of that section, for the words from "a charging authority" to the end there shall be substituted the following paragraphs—

"(a) a billing authority; or

(b) a precepting authority, other than the Receiver for the Metropolitan Police District or charter trustees."

66.—(1) In subsection (1) of section 49 of that Act (reduction or remission of liability in respect of local non-domestic rates), for the words "charging authority" there shall be substituted the words "billing authority".

(2) In subsection (2)(b) of that section, for the words "subject to its community charges" there shall be substituted the words "liable to pay council tax set by it".

67.—(1) In subsection (1)(a) of section 55 of that Act (alteration of lists), for the words "charging authority" there shall be substituted the words "billing authority".

(2) In subsection (5) of that section, for the words "valuation and community charge tribunal" there shall be substituted the words "valuation tribunal".

(3) In subsection (7A)(a) of that section, for the words "charging authority" there shall be substituted the words "billing authority".

68. In section 58 of that Act (special provision for 1995 onwards), in subsection (9), for the words "charging authorities" there shall be substituted the words "billing authorities".

69. In section 61 of that Act (valuation officers), in subsection (1)(a), for the words "charging authority" there shall be substituted the words "billing authority".

70.—(1) In subsection (2D) of section 66 of that Act (domestic property), the words from "other than" to the end shall cease to have effect.

(2) In subsections (3)(b) and (4) of that section, the words "(construing sole or main residence in accordance with section 2 above)" shall cease to have effect.

71. In section 67 of that Act (interpretation), in subsection (2), for the words "charging authorities" there shall be substituted the words "billing authorities".

72.—(1) In subsection (4) of section 74 of that Act (levies), for paragraphs (a) and (b) there shall be substituted the following paragraphs—

"(a) that a billing authority making calculations in accordance with section 32 of the Local Government Finance Act 1992 (originally or by way of substitute) may anticipate a levy;

(b) that a county council making calculations in accordance with section 43 of that Act (originally or by way of substitute) may anticipate a levy;".

(2) For subsection (5) of that section there shall be substituted the following subsection—

"(5) The regulations may include—

(a) provision equivalent to anything in Chapter III or IV of Part I of the Local Government Finance Act 1992 or regulations made under either Chapter (subject to such modifications as the Secretary of State thinks fit);

(b) provision amending or adapting any provision of that Act in consequence of any provision included under subsection (4) above."

73.—(1) In subsection (2) of section 75 of that Act (special levies)—

(a) in paragraph (a), for the words "charging authority" there shall be substituted the words "billing authority"; and

(b) in paragraph (b), for the words "charging authorities" there shall be substituted the words "billing authorities".

(2) In subsections (4)(c) and (5) of that section, for the words "charging authority" there shall be substituted the words "billing authority".

(3) In subsection (6) of that section, for paragraph (a) there shall be substituted the following paragraph—

"(a) that a billing authority making calculations in accordance with section 32 of the Local Government Finance Act 1992 (originally or by way of substitute) may anticipate a special levy;".

(4) For subsection (7) of that section there shall be substituted the following subsection—

"(7) The regulations may include—

(a) provision equivalent to anything in Chapter III or IV of Part I of the Local Government Finance Act 1992 or regulations made under either Chapter (subject to such modifications as the appropriate Minister thinks fit);

(b) provision amending or adapting any provision of that Act in consequence of any provision included under subsection (6) above."

74. In section 118 of that Act (rates: power to abolish or modify), in subsection (1)(c), for the words "charging authority" there shall be substituted the words "billing authority".

75. In section 128(1C) of that Act (levying of rates after 1 April 1990), for the words "Abolition of Domestic Rates Etc. (Scotland) Act 1987" there shall be substituted the words "Local Government Finance Act 1992".

76.—(1) In subsection (2) of section 138 of that Act (judicial review), paragraphs (a) to (d) and (g) shall cease to have effect.

(2) For subsection (3) of that section there shall be substituted the following subsection—

"(3) If on an application for judicial review the court decides to grant relief in respect of any of the matters mentioned in subsection (2)(e) or (f) or (h) to (j) above, it shall quash the levy, special levy, specification or setting (as the case may be)."

77.—(1) In subsection (5)(a) of section 139A of that Act (information), for the words "charging authority" there shall be substituted the words "billing authority".

(2) For subsection (6) of that section there shall be substituted the following subsection—

"(6) A proper officer (within the meaning of the Local Government Act 1972) of a relevant authority is a relevant officer."

(3) After subsection (7) of that section there shall be inserted the following subsection—

"(7A) A community charges registration officer shall supply to a billing authority such information as fulfils the following conditions—

(a) it is in his possession or control;

(b) the authority requests him to supply it; and

(c) it is requested by the authority for the purpose of complying with subsection (2) above;

and the reference in this subsection to a community charges registration officer shall be construed in accordance with section 26 above."

(4) Subsection (8) of that section shall cease to have effect.

78.—(1) In subsection (1) of section 140 of that Act (separate administration for England and Wales), for the words from "Parts III" to "Schedule 12A below" there shall be substituted the words "Parts III and V".

(2) In subsection (2) of that section, for paragraphs (d) to (g) there shall be substituted the following paragraphs—

"(d) separate local government finance reports shall be made, and

(e) separate amending reports under section 84A above or paragraph 13 of Schedule 8 below shall be made."

(3) In subsection (3) of that section, for the words from "Parts III" to "Schedule 12A below" there shall be substituted the words "Parts III and V".

79.—(1) For subsections (6) to (8) of section 141 of that Act (payments to and from authorities) there shall be substituted the following subsections—

"(6) Each of the following is a receiving authority—

(a) a billing authority, and

(b) a major precepting authority.

(7) The first relevant provisions are sections 83, 84C and 86 above, paragraph 5(10) and (14) of Schedule 8 below, regulations made under paragraph 5(15) or 6(5) of that Schedule, paragraphs 12 and 15 of that Schedule and section 4 of the Community Charges (General Reduction) Act 1991.

(8) The second relevant provisions are sections 83 and 84C above, paragraph 5 of Schedule 8 below, regulations made under sub-paragraph (15) of that paragraph and paragraphs 12 and 15 of that Schedule."

(2) Subsection (9) of that section shall cease to have effect.

80.—(1) In subsection (3) of section 143 of that Act (orders and regulations), for the word "(9B)" there shall be substituted the word "(9A)".

(2) In subsection (6) of that section, the words "section 101(1) or (2) above or" shall cease to have effect.

(3) Subsections (7) and (9B) of that section shall cease to have effect.

81.—(1) For subsection (2) of section 144 of that Act (interpretation: authorities) there shall be substituted the following subsection—

"(2) 'Billing authority', 'precepting authority', 'major precepting authority' and 'local precepting authority' have the same meaning as in Part I of the Local Government Finance Act 1992."

(2) In subsection (6) of that section, for the words "charging authority" there shall be substituted the words "billing authority".

82. In section 146 of that Act (interpretation: other provisions), subsection (1) shall cease to have effect.

83.—(1) In paragraph 1 of Schedule 4A to that Act (non-domestic rating: completion days for new buildings), in sub-paragraphs (1) to (3) for the words "charging authority" there shall be substituted the words "billing authority".

(2) In paragraph 4(1) of that Schedule, for the words "valuation and community charge tribunal" there shall be substituted the words "valuation tribunal".

(3) In paragraph 6(3) of that Schedule, for paragraphs (a) and (b) there shall be substituted the following paragraph—

"(a) provision requiring payments or repayments to be made, with or without interest; and".

(4) In paragraph 7 of that Schedule, in sub-paragraphs (1) to (3), for the words "charging authority" there shall be substituted the words "billing authority".

(5) In paragraph 10(2) of that Schedule, in the paragraph beginning "references to the valuation officer", for the words "charging authority" there shall be substituted the words "billing authority".

84.—(1) In Schedule 7 to that Act (non-domestic rating multipliers), in paragraph 5(13), for the words "revenue support grant report" there shall be substituted the words "local government finance report".

(2) In paragraph 6 of that Schedule—
(a) in sub-paragraph (1), for the words "charging authority" there shall be substituted the words "billing authority"; and
(b) in sub-paragraph (4)(a), for the words "revenue support grant report" there shall be substituted the words "local government finance report".

85. In Schedule 7A to that Act (non-domestic rating: 1990–95), in paragraph 5(9), for the words "charging authorities" there shall be substituted the words "billing authorities".

86.—(1) In sub-paragraph (1)(c) of paragraph 2 of Schedule 8 to that Act (non-domestic rating: pooling), after the words "paragraph 5 below" there shall be added the words "or regulations made under sub-paragraph (15) of that paragraph".

(2) In sub-paragraph (2) of that paragraph—
(a) in paragraph (a), for the words from "under paragraph 5(10) below" to "paragraph 6(5) below" there shall be substituted the words "under paragraph 5(10) or (14) below or under regulations made under paragraph 5(15) or 6(5) below"; and
(b) in paragraph (b), for the words "paragraph 9, 12, or 13 below (as the case may be)" there shall be substituted the words "paragraph 12 or 15 below".

(3) In paragraph 6 of that Schedule, in sub-paragraph (7)(c), for the words "paragraphs 9, 12 and 13 below" there shall be substituted the words "paragraphs 12 and 15 below".

87.—(1) In paragraph 2(1)(c) of Schedule 9 to that Act (non-domestic rating: administration), for the words "charging authority" there shall be substituted the words "billing authority".

(2) In paragraph 3 of that Schedule—
(a) in sub-paragraph (1), for the words "charging authority" there shall be substituted the words "billing authority"; and
(b) in sub-paragraph (3), for the words "included under Parts II and VIII of Schedule 4 above" there shall be substituted the words "provision included in regulations made under paragraph 1(1) of Schedule 4 to the Local Government Finance Act 1992".

(3) In paragraphs 4(1)(b) and 4A(1) of that Schedule, for the words "charging authority" there shall be substituted the words "billing authority".

(4) In paragraph 6 of that Schedule, in sub-paragraphs (1) and (1A), for the words "charging authority" there shall be substituted the words "billing authority".

(5) After paragraph 6 of that Schedule there shall be inserted the following paragraph—

"6A.—(1) Where regulations under this Schedule impose a duty on a billing authority to supply information to any person, they may also require—
(a) the Secretary of State;
(b) any appropriate precepting authority; or
(c) any appropriate levying body,
to supply the billing authority with prescribed information if the Secretary of State considers it to be information the billing authority needs in order to fulfil its duty.

(2) Where regulations under this Schedule contain provision about the contents or form of a notice to be served by a billing authority, they may also require the Secretary of State or any appropriate precepting authority to supply the billing authority with prescribed information if the Secretary of State considers it to be information the billing authority needs to ensure that the provision is met.

(3) Where any person other than the Secretary of State fails to supply information to a billing authority in accordance with regulations made by virtue of sub-paragraph (1) or (2) above, he shall be liable to indemnify the authority against any loss or damage which the authority sustains in consequence of the failure.

(4) For the purposes of sub-paragraph (1) or (2) above an authority is an appropriate precepting authority in relation to a billing authority if it has power to issue a precept to the billing authority under Part I of the Local Government Finance Act 1992.

(5) For the purposes of sub-paragraph (1) above a body is an appropriate levying body in relation to a billing authority if—

   (a) it has power to issue a levy or special levy to the billing authority; or

   (b) it has power to issue a levy to a county council which has power to issue a precept to the billing authority under Part I of the Local Government Finance Act 1992."

(6) In paragraph 8 of the Schedule, in sub-paragraphs (2) and (4), for the words "charging authority" there shall be substituted the words "billing authority".

88.—(1) In paragraph 1(1) of Schedule 11 to that Act (tribunals), for the words "valuation and community charge tribunals" there shall be substituted the words "valuation tribunals".

(2) In paragraph 2 of that Schedule, after paragraph (c) there shall be added the following paragraphs—

   "(d) section 16 of the 1992 Act;

   (e) regulations under section 24 of that Act;

   (f) paragraph 3 of Schedule 3 to that Act."

(3) In paragraph 5 of that Schedule, in sub-paragraph (1)(p), for the words "as may be prescribed" there shall be substituted the words "as the Secretary of State may, with the approval of the Treasury, from time to time determine".

(4) In sub-paragraph (4) of paragraph 6 of that Schedule, for the words "valuation and community charge tribunal" there shall be substituted the words "valuation tribunal".

(5) Sub-paragraph (6) of that paragraph shall cease to have effect.

(6) In sub-paragraph (3) of paragraph 8 of that Schedule, for paragraph (e) there shall be substituted the following paragraphs—

   "(e) that no rule of confidentiality applicable to the Commissioners of Inland Revenue shall prevent the disclosure for the purposes of the appeal of particulars delivered documents (within the meaning of Part I of the 1992 Act);

  (ea) as to evidence generally (whether written evidence or oral evidence given under oath or affirmation) and, in particular, as to the use as evidence of particulars delivered documents or of information supplied under—

    (i) Schedule 9 above;

    (ii) regulations under Schedule 2 above;

    (iii) section 82 of the 1967 Act; or

    (iv) regulations under Schedule 2 to the 1992 Act;".

(7) In sub-paragraph (4) of that paragraph, for paragraph (f) there shall be substituted the following paragraphs—

   "(f) that an order may require a register or list to be altered (prospectively or retrospectively);

  (fa) that an order may require the designation of an individual as a responsible individual or as a certification officer, or a designation under section 5 above, to be revoked;

  (fb) that an order may require an estimate to be quashed or altered;

  (fc) that an order may require a penalty to be quashed;

  (fd) that an order may require a decision of a billing authority to be reversed;

  (fe) that an order may require a calculation (other than an estimate) of an amount to be quashed and may require the amount to be recalculated;".

(8) In paragraph 9 of that Schedule, in sub-paragraph (1), for paragraphs (a) to (c) there shall be substituted the following paragraphs—

   "(a) the community charges registration officer for a charging authority to alter the authority's community charges register,

   (b) the valuation officer for a billing authority to alter a local non-domestic rating list of the authority,

   (c) the central valuation officer to alter a central non-domestic rating list, or

   (d) the listing officer for a billing authority to alter the authority's valuation list."

(9) After paragraph 10 of that Schedule there shall be inserted the following paragraph—

"10A.—(1) This paragraph applies where a tribunal orders a billing authority—

(a) to reverse a decision that a particular dwelling is a chargeable dwelling for the purposes of Chapter I of Part I of the 1992 Act, or that a particular person is liable to pay council tax in respect of such a dwelling,

(b) to quash or alter an estimate of an amount which a person is liable to pay to the authority in respect of council tax,

(c) to quash a calculation (other than an estimate) of such an amount, or to recalculate the amount, or

(d) to quash a penalty imposed by the authority under Schedule 3 to the 1992 Act.

(2) If the order is recorded in accordance with any provision included in regulations under paragraph 1 above, the authority ordered shall—

(a) reverse the decision, quash or alter the estimate, quash the calculation, recalculate the amount or quash the penalty accordingly; and

(b) attend to any ancillary matter provided for in the order (such as the repayment of an amount, or the allowance of an amount by way of deduction against a sum due)."

(10) In sub-paragraph (1) of paragraph 11 of that Schedule—

(a) at the end of paragraph (a) there shall be added the words "section 16 of the 1992 Act, paragraph 3 of Schedule 3 to that Act or regulations under section 24 of that Act"; and

(b) in paragraph (b), for the words "regulations under section 55 above" there shall be substituted the words "paragraph 4 of Schedule 4A above or regulations under section 55 above".

(11) In sub-paragraph (2) of that paragraph, for paragraph (d) there shall be substituted the following paragraph—

"(d) provision requiring a charging authority, the community charges registration officer for a charging authority, a billing authority, the valuation officer or listing officer for a billing authority, or the central valuation officer, to act in accordance with any order made by the High Court or the Lands Tribunal, and provision that paragraph 9, 10 or 10A above is to have effect subject to such a requirement."

(12) In paragraph 14 of that Schedule—

(a) paragraph (a) shall cease to have effect; and

(b) in paragraphs (b) and (c), for the words "valuation and community charge tribunal" there shall be substituted the words "valuation tribunal".

(13) In paragraph 15 of that Schedule, in paragraph (b), for the words "valuation and community charge tribunal" there shall be substituted the words "valuation tribunal".

(14) In paragraph 16 of that Schedule, in sub-paragraph (1)—

(a) for the words "valuation and community charge tribunals" there shall be substituted the words "valuation tribunals"; and

(b) at the end there shall be added the words "or the 1992 Act".

(15) For paragraph 18 of that Schedule there shall be substituted the following paragraph—

"18. In this Schedule—

'the 1967 Act' means the General Rate Act 1967; and

'the 1992 Act' means the Local Government Finance Act 1992."

89. Paragraph 5 of Schedule 12 to that Act shall cease to have effect.

Local Government and Housing Act 1989 (c. 42)

90. In section 39 of the Local Government and Housing Act 1989 (application of Part IV of that Act), in subsection (3), for paragraphs (c) and (d) there shall be substituted the following paragraphs—

"(c) a body to which section 118 of that Act applies;

(d) a local precepting authority, as defined in section 69 of the Local Government Finance Act 1992; or

(e) the Receiver for the Metropolitan Police District."

Town and Country Planning Act 1990 (c. 8)

91. In section 336 of the Town and Country Planning Act 1990 (interpretation), in subsection (1), in the definition of "local authority", for paragraph (a) there shall be substituted the following paragraphs—

"(a) a billing authority or a precepting authority (except the Receiver for the Metropolitan Police District), as defined in section 69 of the Local Government Finance Act 1992;

(aa) a combined police authority or a combined fire authority, as defined in section 144 of the Local Government Finance Act 1988;".

Caldey Island Act 1990 (c. 44)

92. In section 2 of the Caldey Island Act 1990, after the words "to the community charge" there shall be inserted the words "to council tax".

Natural Heritage (Scotland) Act 1991 (c. 28)

93. In paragraph 6 of Schedule 7 to the Natural Heritage (Scotland) Act 1991 (provisions regarding drought orders), for the words from "community water charge" to the end there shall be substituted the words "council water charge imposed under Part I of Schedule 11 to the Local Government Finance Act 1992".

Child Support Act 1991 (c. 48)

94. In Schedule 2 to the Child Support Act 1991 (provision of information to Secretary of State), in paragraph 2—
  (a) in sub-paragraph (2), for the words "community charge benefit" there shall be substituted the words "council tax benefit"; and
  (b) in sub-paragraph (4), in paragraph (b) of the definition of "appropriate authority", for the words "community charge benefit, the charging authority" there shall be substituted the words "council tax benefit, the billing authority".

Water Resources Act 1991 (c. 57)

95.—(1) In subsection (5) of section 11 of the Water Resources Act 1991 (change of composition of regional flood defence committee)—
  (a) for paragraph (b) there shall be substituted the following paragraph—
    "(b) the relevant Minister considers it necessary or expedient to make an order under this subsection,"; and
  (b) the words "in relation to times after the coming into force of the variation, rules or regulations or alteration" shall cease to have effect.
  (2) After that subsection there shall be inserted the following subsection—
    "(5A) An order under subsection (5) above shall relate—
    (a) where paragraph (a) of that subsection applies, to times after the coming into force of the variation; and
    (b) where paragraph (b) of that subsection applies, to such times as are specified in the order."
  (3) In subsection (7) of that section, for paragraphs (a) and (b) there shall be substituted the words—
    "(a) if he considers it to be inappropriate that that council should appoint a member of the committee; or
    (b) if he considers that one or more members should be appointed jointly by that council and one or more other constituent councils,
    may include provision to that effect in the order."
  (4) In subsection (8) of that section, the definitions of "relevant area" and "relevant population" shall cease to have effect.
  96.—(1) In subsection (2) of section 135 of that Act (amount, assessment etc. of general drainage charge), the words "determined in accordance with section 136 below" shall cease to have effect.
  (2) In subsection (3)(a) of that section, the words "determined under section 136 below" shall cease to have effect.
  (3) After subsection (6) of that section there shall be added the following subsection—
    "(7) In this section 'relevant quotient' means a quotient determined for the year concerned in accordance with rules contained in regulations made by either of the Ministers."
  97. Section 136 of that Act (determination of the relevant quotient) shall cease to have effect.
  98. In Schedule 15 to that Act (supplemental provisions with respect to drainage charges), in paragraph 12(1), for the words "charging authority" there shall be substituted the words "billing authority".

Land Drainage Act 1991 (c. 59)

99. In section 45 of the Land Drainage Act 1991 (appeals against determinations of annual value), in subsections (6) and (7)(a), for the words "valuation and community charge tribunal" there shall be substituted the words "valuation tribunal".
  100.—(1) In subsections (1), (3) and (4) of section 46 of that Act (hearing and determination of appeals under section 45 of that Act), for the words "valuation and community charge tribunal" there shall be substituted the words "valuation tribunal".

(2) In subsection (6) of that section—
  (a) for the words "valuation and community charge tribunals" there shall be substituted the words "valuation tribunals"; and
  (b) for the words "valuation and community charge tribunal" there shall be substituted the words "valuation tribunal".

GENERAL NOTE

This Schedule deals with minor and consequential amendments. Many of the amendments fall into one of the following categories:
  (a) amendments substituting for relevant parts of existing definitions of "local authority" words which reflect the terminology of the Act, in particular "billing authority" and "precepting authority", which are defined in s.69(1);
  (b) amendments which reflect s.15(1), which provides for existing valuation and community-charge tribunals to be known as valuation tribunals;
  (c) amendments which reflect the proposed abolition of community charges by substituting references to council tax and billing authorities for references to community charge and charging authorities.

Section 117(2)   SCHEDULE 14

REPEALS

Chapter	Short title	Extent of repeal
1963 c. 12.	Local Government (Financial Provisions) (Scotland) Act 1963.	Section 10.
1965 c. 49.	Registration of Births, Deaths and Marriages (Scotland) Act 1965.	Section 28B.
1966 c. 51.	Local Government (Scotland) Act 1966.	In Part I of Schedule 1, paragraph 2A.
1973 c. 65.	Local Government (Scotland) Act 1973.	Sections 110 and 110A. In section 111(1), paragraphs (a), (b) and (d). In section 118(1)(b), the words from "district council" to "to any".
1975 c. 30.	Local Government (Scotland) Act 1975.	In section 37(1), the definition of "rate". In Schedule 3, in paragraph 31, the definitions of "community charges" and "community water charges".
1980 c.45.	Water (Scotland) Act 1980.	Section 9(6). Section 41(2) and (2A). In section 54(3)(b), the words "in respect of the premises supplied". In section 109(1), the definition of "community water charges".
1980 c. 65.	Local Government, Planning and Land Act 1980.	Section 46.
1982 c. 27.	Civil Jurisdiction and Judgements Act 1982.	In Schedule 8, in paragraph 4(1)(c), the words "(other than proceedings under section 16 of the Abolition of Domestic Rates Etc. (Scotland) Act 1987)".
1987 c. 18.	Debtors (Scotland) Act 1987.	In section 106, the definition of "levying authority".
1987 c. 47.	Abolition of Domestic Rates Etc. (Scotland) Act 1987.	The whole Act.
1988 c. 40.	Education Reform Act 1988.	Section 81(8A).

Chapter	Short title	Extent of repeal
1988 c. 41.	Local Government Finance Act 1988.	Parts I and II. In section 66, in subsection (2D), the words from "other than" to the end, and in subsections (3) and (4), the words "(construing sole or main residence in accordance with section 2 above)". Sections 68 to 73. Section 74A. Section 75A. In section 78, subsections (6) and (7). Sections 80 and 81. Section 84. In section 86, subsections (4) to (6). Sections 95 and 96. In section 98, subsections (1) and (2), and in subsection (3), in paragraph (a), the words "or to the City fund (as the case may be)", in paragraph (c), the words "or from the City fund (as the case may be)", and paragraph (d), in subsection (4), the words "or to the City fund (as the case may be)" and in subsection (5), the words "or from the City fund (as the case may be)". Part VII. Section 129. Sections 133 and 134. In section 138, in subsection (2), paragraphs (a) to (d) and (g). In section 139(2), paragraphs (a) to (c). Section 139A(8). Section 141(9). Sections 141A and 141B. In section 143, in subsection (6), the words "section 101(1) or (2) above or", and subsections (7) and (9B). Section 145A. Section 146(1). In Schedule 8, paragraph 4(4). In Schedule 11, paragraphs 6(6) and 14(a). In Schedule 12, paragraphs 5, 8, 10, 13, 15, 17 to 36 and 38. Schedule 12A.
1989 c. 42.	Local Government and Housing Act 1989.	Sections 140 to 144. Section 146. In Schedule 5, paragraphs 2 to 18, 30(4), 43, 49 to 54, 55(3), 56, 58, 59, 61, 63 to 65, 70, 71, 73, 74, 76(3), 77 and 78. In Schedule 6, paragraphs 8, 10 to 15, 20 to 22, and 24 to 29. In Schedule 11, paragraph 98.
1990 c. 43.	Environmental Protection Act 1990.	In Schedule 15, paragraph 1.
1991 c. 2.	Caravans (Standard Community Charge and Rating) Act 1991.	Section 2.
1991 c. 8.	Community Charges (Substitute Setting) Act 1991.	The whole Act.
1991 c. 51.	Local Government Finance and Valuation Act 1991.	The whole Act.

Chapter	Short title	Extent of repeal
1991 c. 57.	Water Resources Act 1991.	In section 11, in subsection (5), the words "in relation to times after the coming into force of the variation, rules or regulations or alteration" and in subsection (8), the definitions of "relevant area" and "relevant population". In section 135, in subsection (2), the words "determined in accordance with section136 below", and in subsection (3), the words "determined under section 136 below". Section 136.
1992 c. 4.	Social Security Contributions and Benefits Act 1992.	Section 134(3). In section 137(1), the definitions of "contribution period", "the 1987 Act" and "the 1988 Act".
1992 c. 5.	Social Security Administration Act 1992.	In section 6(1), in paragraph (d), the words "or a consequential reduction" and in paragraphs (j), (n), (o), (r), (s) and (t), the words "or consequential reduction", in each place where they occur. In section 76, in subsection (2), the words "As regards any care where the benefit is in respect of a personal community charge", and subsections (4), (5) and (7). In section 77, subsections (2) and (3). In section 138, subsections (3), (4) and (6) to (8), and in subsection (9), the words "or (2) or (3)".

INDEX

References are to section numbers

OFFSHORE SAFETY ACT 1992*

(1992 c. 15)

ARRANGEMENT OF SECTIONS

SECT.
1. Application of Part I of 1974 Act for offshore purposes.
2. Application of Part I for other purposes.
3. Provisions consequential on sections 1 and 2.
4. Increased penalties under Part I.
5. Directions for preserving security of petroleum and petroleum products.
6. Corresponding provisions for Northern Ireland.
7. Short title, repeals, commencement and extent.

SCHEDULES:
   Schedule 1—Model Clauses Referred to in Section 3(2).
   Schedule 2—Repeals.

An Act to extend the application of Part I of the Health and Safety at Work etc. Act 1974; to increase the penalties for certain offences under that Part; to confer powers for preserving the security of supplies of petroleum and petroleum products; and for connected purposes.

[6th March 1992]

PARLIAMENTARY DEBATES
   Hansard, H.L. Vol. 532, cols. 148, 658, 1419; Vol. 533, col. 935; H.C. Vol. 203, col. 679; Vol. 205, col. 379.
   The Bill was discussed in Standing Committee E on February 18, 1992.

INTRODUCTION AND GENERAL NOTE

The Piper Alpha Disaster
   On July 6, 1988 a series of explosions occurred on board the Piper Alpha oil platform in the North Sea. As a result, 165 of the 226 persons on board died, along with two of the crew from the fast rescue craft of the standby vessel *Sandhaven*. It was the world's worst offshore disaster. In addition to the terrible loss of life, the insurance industry faced massive claims initially estimated at between $1 and $1.5 billion, with the insured value of the platform alone being around $800 million (see Lloyd's List, July 9, 1988). The costs of implementing new safety measures have been estimated at between £850 million to £5 billion (see *Government response to the Cullen Report*, below).
   An official inquiry held by Lord Cullen (see *The Cullen Inquiry*, below) made a large number of criticisms of current law and offshore practice and produced many recommendations for reform (see *The Public Inquiry into the Piper Alpha Disaster*, Department of Energy (Cm. 1310, HMSO, 1990), hereafter the Cullen Report). The Offshore Safety Act 1992 is a direct result of the tragedy and the Cullen Report and can only be understood in that context. The 1992 Act does not purport to solve all of the problems of offshore safety that have arisen and is but a part of the Government's response (see further, *Government response to the Cullen Report*, below).

The regulatory régime for offshore safety
   A main focus of attention after the disaster was on the effectiveness of the regulatory régime, in general, and of the Department of Energy (DEn), in particular. There were questions about whether there were conflicts of interest between its rôle in promoting economic development offshore, while at the same time regulating safety standards.
   The DEn was involved with safety on Piper Alpha through its administration of the statutory framework provided by the Mineral Workings (Offshore Installations) Act 1971 and the Health and Safety at Work etc. Act 1974 (HSWA 1974): see generally the Cullen Report (chapter 16), below. In addition, exploration and production licences issued by the DEn were subject to model clauses prescribed by regulations issued under the Petroleum Production Act 1934 (and see the General Note to s.3, below). These clauses contained health and safety requirements,

---

* Annotations by Nicholas Gaskell, Reader in Maritime Law, Institute of Maritime Law, Faculty of Law, University of Southampton.

but were clearly of less practical significance than the Mineral Workings (Offshore Installations) Act 1971, which had been passed after investigations following the collapse of the exploration rig *Sea Gem* in 1965.

The Mineral Workings (Offshore Installations) Act 1971 required offshore installations to be certified as fit and for safety, health and welfare regulations to be made for persons on them. A number of regulations had been issued under it, including the Offshore Installations (Inspectors and Casualties) Regulations 1973 (S.I. 1973 No. 1842), the Offshore Installations (Construction and Survey) Regulations 1974 (S.I. 1974 No. 289), the Offshore Installations (Operational Safety, Health and Welfare) Regulations 1976 (S.I. 1976 No. 1019), the Offshore Installations (Emergency Procedures) Regulations 1976 (S.I. 1976 No. 1542), the Offshore Installations (Life-saving Appliances) Regulations 1977 (S.I. 1977 No. 486), the Offshore Installations (Fire-fighting Equipment) Regulations 1978 (S.I. 1978 No. 611) and the Offshore Installations (Well Control) Regulations 1980 (S.I. 1980 No. 1759).

A separate regulatory régime existed for the construction and use of offshore pipelines, under the Petroleum and Submarine Pipe-lines Act 1975. Regulations had been issued under it, for example the Submarine Pipe-lines (Diving Operations) Regulations 1976 (S.I. 1976 No. 923) and the Submarine Pipe-lines Safety Regulations 1982 (S.I. 1982 No. 1513).

Similarly, separate rules issued by the Department of Transport (DTp) under the Merchant Shipping Acts apply generally in relation to vessels (see the Merchant Shipping (Health and Safety: General Duties) Regulations 1984 (S.I. 1984 No. 408) and the Merchant Shipping (Diving Operations) Regulations 1975 (S.I. 1975 No. 116), relating to the use of submersible or supporting apparatus). The DTp would apply the ordinary maritime principles, *e.g.* allowing regulation of safety by the flag state except where a foreign vessel was in U.K. waters. It has issued, for example, the Merchant Shipping (Code of Safe Practices) Regulations 1980 (S.I. 1980 No. 686) and in 1991 issued a revised Code of Safe Working Practices for Merchant Seamen. Chapter 30 of the Code specifically applies to ships serving offshore installations. The Code refers to specific merchant shipping regulations that would be relevant to safety, for example, the Merchant Shipping (Protective Equipment and Clothing) Regulations 1985 (S.I. 1985 No. 1664) and the Merchant Shipping (Hatches and Lifting Plant) Regulations 1985 (S.I. 1985 No. 1639).

Finally, the HSWA 1974 was passed after the Robens Report (Report of the Committee on Safety and Health at Work 1970–1972, Cmnd. 5034), which had concluded that there was far too much technical law on safety and that a new safety culture was required, along with a modern regulatory structure to support it (see also *"Existing statutory provisions"*, General Note to s.1, below). Sections 10 and 11 of the 1974 Act established a Health and Safety Commission (HSC) to effect the general purposes of the Act (as set out in s.2), with a Health and Safety Executive (HSE) to administer the Act on behalf of the HSC, particularly with regard to enforcement. Under s.84, the 1974 Act could only be extended outside Great Britain by Order. This was first done by Order in 1977 (see the Health and Safety at Work etc. Act 1974 (Application Outside Great Britain) Order 1977 (S.I. 1977 No. 1232), as amended, now superseded by the Health and Safety at Work etc. Act 1974 (Application Outside Great Britain) Order 1989 (S.I. 1989 No. 840)). The 1989 Order extended the relevant parts of the HSWA 1974 (ss.1–59, 80–82), (i) to offshore installations outside Great Britain, and (ii) to pipelines within territorial waters (see the Territorial Sea Act 1987) or areas designated under s.1(7) of the Continental Shelf Act 1964). However, s.15(9) of the HSWA 1974 provided that any Order in Council could not apply to health and safety regulations offshore unless those regulations *expressly* so provided. In fact, by the time of the Cullen Report the only HSWA 1974 regulations that had been applied offshore were the Offshore Installations and Pipeline Works (First Aid) Regulations 1989 (S.I. 1989 No. 1671).

However, it was agreed in 1976 by the Government that the main administrative responsibility should be assumed by the Safety Directorate which was part of the Petroleum Engineering Division (PED) of the DEn. The HSC accordingly exercised its powers under s.13(1)(a) of the HSWA 1974 by making an agreement with the Secretary of State for Energy whereby the latter undertook responsibility for the enforcement offshore of the HSWA 1974 and regulations made under it. In 1978 the Government appointed a Committee to examine, *inter alia*, the rôle offshore of the DEn. The Burgoyne Report 1980 (*Report of the Committee on Offshore Safety*, March 1980, chaired by Dr J. Burgoyne, Cmnd. 7866) by a majority recommended that the DEn should continue in its supervisory rôle. A minority of the Committee considered that the HSE should be the sole regulatory body for health and safety, onshore and offshore. The Government accepted the majority recommendations and in 1981 transferred ministerial responsibility under the HSWA 1974 from the Secretary of State for Employment to the Secretary of State for Energy. The latter was to be advised by the HSC, in turn relying on the PED. The PED was to assume full enforcement responsibility for the various regulations (taking over some functions from the Factory Inspectorate) and the PED, HSC and HSE were also to co-operate closely on diving operations. A new agency agreement was created in 1981 to give effect to the increased co-operation between the three bodies. The adequacy of fire-fighting equipment, life-saving appliances and navigational aids was achieved by surveys conducted by the DTp on behalf of the DEn. Offshore installations were also to be certified periodically by certifying authorities such as Lloyd's Register of Shipping.

The Cullen Inquiry

On July 13, 1988, one week after the Piper Alpha disaster, the Secretary of State for Energy, Cecil Parkinson, set up a Public Inquiry under the Offshore Installations (Public Inquiries) Regulations 1974 (S.I. 1974 No. 338), as authorised by the Mineral Workings (Offshore Installations) Act 1971. Lord Cullen, a Senator of the College of Justice in Scotland, was appointed to hold the inquiry and he reported on October 19, 1990. His two-volume report was presented to Parliament in November 1990, after an enormous amount of work had been undertaken and several million pounds expended. It was widely praised as being thorough, clear and decisive and can be commended as being a model of its type.

Lord Cullen sought the answers to two questions: what were the causes and circumstances of the disaster on the Piper Alpha platform on July 6, 1988; and what should be recommended with a view to the preservation of life and the avoidance of similar accidents in the future?

The analysis, below, of the answers to these questions is taken in part from the Cullen Report itself (to which due acknowledgment is made) and shows the context in which the Offshore Safety Act 1992 was passed.

The Cullen Report: findings

Causes of the disaster. An initial explosion occurred on the Piper Alpha platform at about 22.00 on July 6, 1988, in gas compression C Module (one of its four production modules). It was due to the ignition of a low-lying cloud of condensate which had leaked as a result of steps taken by night-shift personnel with a view to restarting a pump which had been shut down for maintenance. Unknown to them, a pressure safety valve had been removed from the relief line of that pump. A blank flange assembly which had been fitted at the site of the valve was not leak-tight. The lack of awareness of the removal of the valve resulted from failures in the communication of information at shift handover earlier in the evening and failure in the operation of a "permit to work" system (under which supervisory staff should have been aware of all work in progress) in connection with the work which had entailed its removal.

The initial explosion caused extensive damage. It led immediately to a large crude oil fire in B Module, the oil separation module, which engulfed the north end of the platform in dense black smoke. This fire, which extended into C Module, was fed by oil from the platform and by a leak from the main oil line to the shore, to which pipelines from the Claymore and Tartan platforms were connected. At about 22.20 there was a second major explosion, which caused a massive intensification of the fire. This was due to the rupture of the riser on the gas pipeline from Tartan as a result of the concentration and high temperature of the crude oil fire. It is probable that this rupture would have been delayed if oil production on the other platforms had been shut down earlier than it was. The fire was further intensified by the ruptures of risers on the gas pipeline to the Frigg disposal system and the gas pipeline connecting Piper with Claymore at about 22.50 and 23.20 respectively. The timing of the start of depressurisation of the gas pipelines could not have had any material effect on the fire at Piper. The Offshore Installation Managers (OIMs) on Claymore and Tartan were ill-prepared for an emergency on another platform with which their own platform was connected.

The initial explosion also put the main power supplies and the Control Room at Piper out of action. It appears that the emergency shutdown system was activated and the emergency shutdown valves on the gas pipeline risers probably closed, although there was probably a failure of the valve on the Claymore riser to close fully. The other emergency systems of the platform failed immediately or within a short period of the initial explosion. In particular the fire-water system was rendered inoperative, due to either physical damage or loss of power. However, at the time of the initial explosion the diesel fire pumps were on manual mode, so that, even if they had not been disabled, they would have required manual intervention in order to start them. Of the 226 men on the platform, 62 were on night-shift duty; the great majority of the remainder were in the accommodation, where many survivors who were on duty made their way. At no stage was there a systematic attempt to lead men to escape from the accommodation. To remain in the accommodation meant certain death.

Many organisations, vessels and aircraft were involved in the rescue and subsequent treatment of survivors. There was some initial delay and confusion onshore due to the lack of accurate information. However, this did not affect the toll of death and injury. The events demonstrated the value of fast rescue craft and the bravery of their crews in getting close to the platform even where the fire was raging at its fiercest. They also demonstrated the shortcomings of the type of standby vessel which was in attendance at Piper, often converted trawlers with limited manoeuvrability.

The principal cause of death in 109 cases (including 79 recovered from the accommodation) was inhalation of smoke and fire. 14 apparently died during an attempt to escape from the platform. Few died of burns.

Defects in procedures, equipment, training and management. The failure in the operation of the formal "permit-to-work" system was not an isolated mistake but there were a number of respects in which the laid-down procedure was not adhered to and unsafe practices were followed. One particular danger, which was relevant to the disaster, was the need to prevent the inadvertent or unauthorised recommissioning of equipment which was still under maintenance and not in a state in which it could safely be put into service. The evidence also indicated dissatisfaction with the standard of information which was communicated at shift handover. This had been the subject of criticism in the light of a fatality in September 1987.

As regards the fire-water system, the practice of keeping the diesel fire pumps on manual mode during periods of diving was peculiar to Piper and in spite of an audit recommendation that it should be changed.

Evidence as to training for emergencies showed that the induction was cursory and, in regard to demonstrating lifeboats and life-rafts, not consistently given. Muster drills and the training of persons with special duties in an emergency did not take place with the frequency laid down in the procedures of Occidental (the operator). The OIMs and platform management did not show the necessary determination to ensure that regularity was achieved.

Occidental management should have been more aware of the need for a high standard of incident prevention and fire-fighting. They were too easily satisfied that the permit-to-work system was being operated correctly. They failed to provide the training required to ensure that an effective permit-to-work system was operated in practice. They adopted a superficial attitude to the assessment of the risk of major hazard. They failed to ensure that emergency training was being provided as they intended. The platform personnel and management were not prepared for a major emergency as they should have been. The safety policies and procedures were in place: the practice was deficient.

Defects in the regulatory system. Installations such as Piper Alpha were subject to regular PED inspections to assess the adequacy of the safety of the installation as a whole. Piper was inspected in June 1987 and June 1988. The latter visit was also used to follow up what Occidental had done in the light of the fatality, which was in part due to failures in the operation of the permit-to-work system and the communication of information at shift handover. Even after making allowance for the fact that the inspections were based on sampling, it was clear that they were "superficial to the point of being of little use" as a test of safety on the platform and did not reveal obvious deficiencies. While the effectiveness of inspections had been affected by persistent under-manning and inadequate guidance, the evidence led Lord Cullen to question whether the type of inspection practised by the DEn could be an effective means of assessing or monitoring the management of safety by operators.

The Cullen Report: recommendations

General recommendations. Lord Cullen made no fewer than 106 recommendations (see the Cullen Report, Chapter 23). These covered detailed technical issues, for instance the availability of emergency control facilities, means of escape, the standard of standby vessels and the provision of personal survival suits. They also addressed matters such as emergency training. However, it would be fair to say that most of the recommendations related to the *management* of offshore facilities, both by the operators themselves and by the U.K. regulatory authorities. The Cullen Report showed that there were serious inadequacies in the whole management of safety offshore and in the regulatory framework that applied to it. The criticisms about management practices were echoed by Sheriff Principal Ireland in November 1991 in his determination about a fatality that occurred aboard the oil rig *Ocean Odyssey* in September 1988 (see Lloyd's List, November 9, 1991).

The Safety Case. The disaster involved an explosion following a hydrocarbon leak leading to the failure of gas pipes which added fuel to the fire. Although such remote, but potentially hazardous, events had been envisaged, Occidental did not require them to be assessed systematically, nor did the offshore safety régime require this. Lord Cullen was satisfied that operators of installations should be required by regulation to carry out a formal safety assessment of major hazards. The purpose of the formal safety assessment would be to demonstrate that the potential major hazards of the installation and the risks to personnel thereon have been identified and appropriate controls provided. He specifically recommended that the formal safety assessment should apply to all installations, both fixed and mobile and both planned and existing (see para. 17.41). It is not quite clear which mobile installations he had in mind (see also the General Note to s.1, below), but he would certainly have included jack-up oil rigs and their like. The presentation of the formal safety assessment was to be in the form of a *Safety Case*, which would be updated at regular intervals and on major changes of circumstances. The Safety Case procedure was one which derived from the HSE's CIMAH regulations (the Control of Major Industrial Hazards Regulations 1984 (S.I. 1984 No. 1902). Lord Cullen noted that it was valuable in imposing a discipline on operators to show that they had identified the major hazards and had created appropriate controls (Cullen Report, para. 22.16).

The existence of a temporary safe refuge for personnel ought to be a central feature of the Safety Case. The Safety Case should deal with the passability of escape routes, the integrity of embarkation points and lifeboats and the safe evacuation, escape and rescue of personnel.

Each operator should be required in the Safety Case to demonstrate that the safety management system of the company and that of the installation was adequate to ensure that the design and operation of the installation and its equipment were safe. The safety management system of the company should set out the safety objectives, the system by which those objectives are to be achieved, the performance standards which are to be met and the means by which adherence to those standards is to be monitored.

Regulatory supervision

Lord Cullen thought it inappropriate and impracticable for the regulatory body to undertake the detailed auditing of an operator's compliance with a safety management system. Operators should therefore be required to satisfy *themselves* by means of regular audits that the system was being adhered to. On the other hand, the regulatory body should be required to review the operator's audits on a selective basis and itself to carry out such further audits as it thinks fit and by regular inspection verify that the output of the system is satisfactory.

All this involved a completely new approach to regulation in the U.K. offshore safety régime. However, it was totally consistent with the HSWA 1974 and the concept of self-regulation. It represented a logical development from the requirement of a Safety Case for each installation (see also the General Note to s.1, below).

Responsibility for regulation

The main regulatory recommendation was that there should be a single regulatory body which would discharge the Government's responsibilities to set standards and ensure their achievement (see para. 21.62). Developments in regulatory techniques, experience of the capabilities and approach of offshore and onshore regulators and the imminence of major changes in the offshore safety régime caused Lord Cullen to raise the question as to which body should be responsible. The choice as a practical matter lay between the DEn and the HSE, in either case being suitably strengthened. He came to the conclusion that the balance of advantage lay in favour of the transfer of responsibility to the HSE. The decisive considerations arose from the differences in approach between these two bodies to the development and enforcement of regulatory control.

The HSE has the general responsibility concerning safety onshore in the U.K. and there are clear benefits in integrating the work of the offshore safety regulator with the specialist functions of the HSE. It has always been rather anomalous that its remit did not fully extend offshore. In 1980 the majority report of the Burgoyne Committee had concluded that the DEn was capable of handling regulatory matters, taking advice, where appropriate, from other bodies such as the DTp, the Department of Trade and the HSE. The Cullen Report noted that there was no reason why the DTp should not continue to act as an agent of the DEn in regard to the certification of fire-fighting equipment and life-saving appliances (except where the Merchant Shipping Acts applied). It was still clearly preferable to use the HSE instead of the DEn, even if the latter was given a higher level of manning with greater in-house expertise. Moreover, the major legislative changes recommended were ones which were in line with the philosophy which the HSE has followed. In effect, the minority (trade union) report of the 1980 Burgoyne Committee was finally vindicated.

Legislative recommendations

Lord Cullen thought many existing safety regulations were unduly restrictive in that they were of the type which imposed "solutions" rather than "objectives" and were out of date in relation to technological advances. Guidance notes were expressed, or at any rate lent themselves to interpretation, in such a way as to discourage alternatives. The principal regulations should therefore take the form of requiring stated objectives to be met. Guidance notes should give non-mandatory advice.

It may be helpful to set out here the recommendations as to legislation made by the Cullen Report, although it is recommendation 18, below, with which the Offshore Safety Act 1992 is primarily concerned.

"Legislation—General

17. (i) The principal regulations in regard to offshore safety should take the form of requiring that stated objectives are to be met (referred to as "goal-setting regulations") rather than prescribing that detailed measures are to be taken (para. 21.67).

(ii) In relation to goal-setting regulations, guidance notes should give non-mandatory advice on one or more methods of achieving such objectives without prescribing any particular method as a minimum or as the measure to be taken in default of an acceptable alternative (para. 21.67).

(iii) However, there will be a continuing need for some regulations which prescribe detailed measures (para. 21.67).

18. The provisions of the Mineral Workings (Offshore Installations) Act 1971 and the Petroleum and Submarine Pipe-lines Act 1975 which have the same general purposes as those of Part I of the Health and Safety at Work etc. Act 1974 (HSWA), and the regulations made under such provisions, should be made relevant statutory provisions for the purposes of the HSWA (para. 21.68).

19. The Construction and Survey Regulations, the Fire Fighting Equipment Regulations, the Life-Saving Appliances Regulations and the Emergency Procedures Regulations should be revoked and replaced by—

(i) Construction Regulations, covering, *inter alia*, the structure and layout of the installation and its accommodation.

(ii) Plant and Equipment Regulations, covering, *inter alia*, plant and equipment on the installation and in particular those handling hydrocarbons.

(iii) Fire and Explosion Protection Regulations, covering, *inter alia*, both active and passive fire protection and explosion protection, and

(iv) Evacuation, Escape and Rescue Regulations, covering, *inter alia*, emergency procedures, life-saving appliances, evacuation, escape and rescue.

Each of the above sets of regulations should include goal-setting regulations as their main or primary provisions and should be supported by guidance notes giving advice which is non-mandatory in the sense set out in paragraph (ii) of recommendation 17 (para. 21.69).

20. Operators should be encouraged to specify the standards which they will use to comply with goal-setting regulations. For a given installation, compliance may be demonstrated by reference to such standards, the terms of guidance notes and what is shown by a safety assessment, or a combination of one or more of such methods (paras. 17.66 and 21.70).

21. As regards existing guidance notes the regulatory body should consider whether and to what extent they should be treated without replacement or modification as giving non-mandatory advice in the sense set out in paragraph (ii) of recommendation 17; and should inform the industry accordingly (para. 21.71).

22. In connection with the preparation of guidance notes the regulatory body should review the procedures for consultation so as to ensure that the views of the representatives of employers and employees involved in work offshore are adequately taken into account (para. 21.72)."

Government response to the Cullen Report

The Government reaction to the Cullen Report was to accept all of the 106 recommendations and the Offshore Safety Act 1992 is part of its response. At the Second Reading Debate in the Commons, the Secretary of State for Employment, Michael Howard, outlined some other changes that had already been made (see *Hansard*, H.C. Vol. 203, col. 679). On April 1, 1991, responsibility for offshore safety was finally transferred to the Secretary of State for Employment from the Secretary of State for Energy (see also Lloyd's List, January 3, 1991). The responsibility was now being administered on the former's behalf by the HSC and the HSE.

One of the criticisms of the Cullen Report concerned the resources devoted to offshore safety. It was noted that in a number of areas the work of the Safety Directorate of the PED had been "hampered by persistent undermanning" (Cullen Report, para. 22.11). This was also a feature that had been noted by the Burgoyne Committee in 1980 (para. 4.14). Lord Cullen also considered that the inspectors were "inadequately trained, guided and led" (Cullen Report, para. 15.49). In 1991 the Select Committee on Energy also noted the need for there to be a proper training scheme for the new offshore inspectorate of the HSE and that secondment from oil companies should only be a temporary measure (see the Seventh Report of the Energy Committee on "Offshore Safety Management", July 17, 1991, H.C. 343, 1990–1991). The

Government has now increased the resources made available to the HSC and HSE from £12 million in 1990–1991 to £20 million in 1991–1992. The budget is planned to rise progressively to £35 million by 1994–1995. It was stated that the increased resources would allow a fourfold increase in the number of HSE personnel working on offshore safety. The Select Committee on Energy was given evidence that new safety expenditure arising from the Cullen Report was £850 million and that future expenditure could rise to £1.7–£5 billion over the next 10–15 years (Seventh Report, above, para. 13, and see Lloyd's List, January 3, 1991). Apparently, 70 to 80 per cent. of that expenditure will come from the Exchequer, in the sense that there will be offsets against petroleum revenue tax.

A second example of Government action on the Cullen Report was the production, in July 1991, of a revised code of practice for the assessment of the suitability of standby vessels (see *Assessment of the suitability of standby vessels attending offshore installations: Instructions for the guidance of surveyors*, HMSO, Rev. ed. 1991). The Code was published jointly by the HSE and the DTp and came into operation on July 16, 1991. By December 31, 1992 all vessels must comply fully with its requirements. The Code incorporates improvements in the design and provision of equipment on the standby vessels that are required to be within five nautical miles of every offshore installation to assist in emergencies (see the Offshore Installations (Emergency Procedures) Regulations 1976 (S.I. 1976 No. 1542), reg. 10, made under the Mineral Workings (Offshore Installations) Act 1971). The Cullen Report recognised that it was appropriate for the DTp to carry out certain surveying functions on behalf of the HSE and the revised Code is an example of cooperation between the two bodies. Compliance with the Code would be evidence of fulfilment of the general duties under the HSWA 1974 (for example, under s.2). However, it appears that the Code is voluntary in nature, in that it cannot impose direct obligations on the owners of the vessels (see also Cullen Report, para. 20.37). The existing 1976 Regulations, and those to be made under the powers granted by s.1 of the Offshore Safety Act 1992 (below), are mainly intended to create duties on the part of the operators and owners of installations. The owners and operators can demonstrate compliance with the Regulations by showing that they have contractual undertakings with owners whose vessels comply with the Code. To that extent the Code is not mandatory, in contrast with the general safety standards applied by the Merchant Shipping legislation. (See also *Application to craft operating offshore*, in the General Note to s.1, below, for difficulties about introducing regulations directly affecting vessels generally).

A number of new regulations were issued in the aftermath of the Cullen Report: see the Offshore Installations (Emergency Pipe-line Valve) Regulations 1989 (S.I. 1989 No. 1029) and the Offshore Installations (Included Apparatus or Works) Order 1989 (S.I. 1989 No. 978). Most of the detailed changes recommended by Lord Cullen will come about through new regulations and Codes of Practice issued by the HSE rather than by primary legislation such as the Offshore Safety Act 1992. The HSC was said to be urgently preparing regulations and accompanying guidance in order to give effect to the Cullen recommendations concerning the production of "Safety Cases". This action had been strongly urged by the Select Committee on Energy in 1981 (Seventh Report, above, para. 9). The draft Offshore Safety (Safety Case) Regulations were issued in February 1992, while the Bill was still in the Commons, with the intention that the regulations would be implemented progressively for new and existing installations from 1993. There will need to be a safety case for each installation. As there are presently over 200 installations in the North Sea (and 40–60 more expected in the next few years), it may take some time to develop and process them (Seventh Report, above, Minutes of Evidence, p. 99).

Many changes will not need legislative action at all. Thus, the United Kingdom Offshore Operators Association (UKOOA) has already issued revised guidance on offshore emergency training and the Oil Industry Advisory Committee of the HSE has published guidance on work permit systems. In July 1989, the police prepared a booklet, approved by the UKOOA, dealing with emergency communications and procedures. Other changes will require preliminary research, as accepted by the Cullen Report.

Industrial relations and offshore safety

Trade union recognition
One of the more controversial issues concerning offshore safety is industrial relations, in general, and the extent to which trade unions should be involved, in particular. Onshore, s.2 of the HSWA 1974 allowed regulations to be made whereby recognised trade unions can appoint safety representatives whom employers must consult. These provisions were implemented by the Safety Representatives and Safety Committees Regulations 1977 (S.I. 1977 No. 500). There is only a limited recognition of unions on offshore installations and the operators opposed its extension to the offshore area, especially as the Offshore Installations (Safety Representatives and Safety Committees) Regulations 1989 (S.I. 1989 No. 971) had only been operating for a

short time. Lord Cullen did not recommend the extension of the 1977 Regulations, but did recommend further study (Cullen Report, para. 21.84). The HSE has appointed consultants from Aberdeen University to undertake an in-depth study of the workings of the 1989 Regulations. The Government did accept the recommendation (Cullen Report, para. 21.87) that the 1989 Regulations should be modified so that the training of safety representatives should be paid for by the operator of the installation where the safety representatives work and not by their employers (who might be different). As already noted, the overall review of the 1989 Regulations is expected to be completed by Spring 1993. In the meantime, the Government has shown no inclination to extend the 1977 Regulations offshore (and see also the annotations to the Offshore Safety (Protection Against Victimisation) Act 1992 (c.24), below).

Victimisation. Lord Cullen responded to trade union concerns about victimisation of workers who complained about health and safety by stating that it was appropriate for the type of protection provided in the case of trade union activities under s.58(1)(b) of the Employment Protection (Consolidation) Act 1978 to be afforded to the activities of an employee as a safety representative (Cullen Report, para. 21.86).

There is little doubt that the Government and the operators had little sympathy for an increase in trade union activities offshore. Yet it may be arguable that low safety standards are easier to maintain where there is little union influence. The extension of s.58 of the Employment Protection (Consolidation) Act 1978 would mean that a claimant would be able to sue for unfair dismissal and would not be faced by the two-year qualification period before a claim can be made. The protection would be immediate.

At Second Reading in the Commons, the Secretary of State for Employment explained that the victimisation recommendation of Lord Cullen was not being implemented in the Offshore Safety Act 1992 as the Act was dealing with *safety* and not *employment* issues. It was intended to introduce a provision "as soon as a suitable legislative vehicle becomes available" (*Hansard*, H.C. Vol. 213, col. 682).

It does seem that the Government was dragging its feet and it is hard to see why a suitable section could not have been included in the 1992 Act. Lord Cullen made his recommendation specifically to improve safety, being conscious that he did *not* want to become involved in general employment issues. It therefore seems rather lame to say that nothing can be done because the amendment relates to employment: the fact is that it relates to both employment *and* safety. The Government was no doubt aware that the introduction of employment issues into the Bill might have delayed its passage, at a time when much legislation was being rushed through Parliament before the onset of a general election. Still, the Opposition were willing to give undertakings not to cause procedural difficulties, for example, if the Government had wanted to alter the long and short titles of the Bill.

However, on January 20, 1992 a private member's Bill, the Offshore Safety (Protection Against Victimisation) Bill 1992, was introduced in the House of Lords by Baroness Turner of Camden, specifically to deal with victimisation. After initial uncertainty, the Government agreed to support the general aims of the Bill and extended and improved upon it. Accordingly, victimisation is now dealt with in the Offshore Safety (Protection Against Victimisation) Act 1992 (c.24) (annotated by N.J.J. Gaskell in Current Law Statutes Annotated 1992).

The European dimension. In 1989 the E.C. produced, under Art. 118a of the Treaty of Rome, what has been known as the "Framework Directive" 89/391 on the safety and health of workers (the Council Directive of June 12, 1989 on the introduction of measures to encourage improvements in the safety and health of workers at work, O.J. L/183, March 29, 1989). This has to be given effect by national Governments by December 31, 1992. It sets out broad principles relating to the obligations of employers and workers and, in particular, gives rights to individual workers. For example, it creates rights to stop work and to complain to safety inspectors and not to be victimised (see *Victimisation*, above, and the annotations to the Offshore Safety (Protection Against Victimisation) Act 1992 (c.24), by N.J.J. Gaskell, Current Law Statutes Annotated 1992). It seems clear that further Government legislative action will be needed during the course of 1992 if there is to be compliance with the Framework Directive.

The European Commission has also produced a draft E.C. Council Directive concerning the minimum requirements for improving the safety and health of workers in the extractive industries (see Com. (91) 493 final, December 20, 1991). The proposals, sent to the E.C. Council on January 13, 1992 (as amended, Council Document 4126/92), state that they have been specifically amended to take account of Lord Cullen's Report on the Piper Alpha disaster. The Government stated in debates that the Offshore Safety Act 1992 was utterly compatible with the draft directive (see, for example, *Hansard*, H.C. Vol. 213, col. 729). There had been concerns that the E.C. drafts were rather prescriptive by nature and contrary to the "goal-setting" approach of the HSWA 1974, as endorsed by the Cullen Report (see the Seventh Report of the Energy Committee, above, para. 6). A reading of the draft does lend some support to these fears. There are a number of articles setting out general principles, but Art. 10 requires compliance with a detailed 31-page Annex.

Legal aftermath of the Piper Alpha disaster
The families and friends of those injured naturally sought compensation from, amongst others, the operator of the Piper Alpha platform, Occidental Petroleum (Caledonia) Ltd. The prospect of suit in the U.S.A. was considered, but the jurisdictional features of the case always suggested a Scottish venue (and see T.M. Kolman, "The Piper Alpha Oil Rig Disaster" [1988] S.L.T. 293). It has been reported that claims on behalf of the families of the deceased have been settled.
Most of the public focus was upon the claims of the families that the oil company should be prosecuted in respect of the disaster. Similar pressure has been exerted following other transport disasters, such as the Zeebrugge disaster in 1987 and that involving the Marchioness in 1989. The Lord Advocate, Lord Fraser of Carmyllie, decided not to prosecute the company (Occidental) for culpable homicide (manslaughter) or any other offence under the legislation then applicable (see Lloyd's List, July 25, 1991). Nevertheless, the Piper Alpha Families' and Survivors' Association considered the possibility of bringing a private prosecution for culpable homicide. The procedure for doing so in Scotland appears to be more difficult than in England and few successful private prosecutions have been recorded. In January 1992 it was reported that the Association had decided not to proceed, partly in view of the expense involved, but also as the company had been sold, key staff had changed, vital evidence was no longer available and witnesses had disappeared (see *New L.J.*, January 31, 1992, 115).

Outline of the Offshore Safety Act 1992
The purpose of the Offshore Safety Act 1992 was to pave the way for the reform of the existing mass of safety regulations affecting the offshore industry. The Act does not itself deal with all the detailed changes to law and practice recommended in the Cullen Report (see also *Legislative recommendations*, above). Most of that detail will be provided later in new regulations, directions and guidance notes to be issued by the HSE. The 1992 Act provides for the introduction of a "goal-setting" regulatory framework along the lines of the HSWA 1974 which will allow for the progressive replacement of the existing regulations (s.1). It establishes a framework for the regulation of security on offshore platforms and inshore terminals or refineries (s.5). It also deals with certain onshore works (s.2) and provides for increased penalties for a number of health and safety offences.

ABBREVIATIONS

Burgoyne Report	:	*Report of the Committee on Offshore Safety 1980* (Cmnd. 7866)
CIMAH	:	Control of Major Industrial Hazards Regulations 1984 (S.I. 1984 No. 1902)
COSHH	:	Control of Substances Hazardous to Health Regulations 1988 (S.I. 1988 No. 1657)
Cullen Report	:	*The Public Inquiry into the Piper Alpha Disaster*, Department of Energy, (Cmnd. 1310, HMSO, 1990)
DEn	:	Department of Energy
DTp	:	Department of Transport
HSC	:	Health and Safety Commission
HSE	:	Health and Safety Executive
HSWA 1974	:	Health and Safety at Work etc. Act 1974
OIM	:	Offshore Installation Manager
PED	:	Petroleum Engineering Division
Robens Report	:	Report of the Committee on Safety and Health at Work 1970–1972 (Cmnd. 5034)
UKOOA	:	United Kingdom Offshore Operators Association

Application of Part I of 1974 Act for offshore purposes

1.—(1) The general purposes of Part I of the Health and Safety at Work etc. Act 1974 ("the 1974 Act") shall include—
  (a) securing the safety, health and welfare of persons on offshore installations or engaged on pipe-line works;
  (b) securing the safety of such installations and preventing accidents on or near them;
  (c) securing the proper construction and safe operation of pipe-lines and preventing damage to them; and
  (d) securing the safe dismantling, removal and disposal of offshore installations and pipe-lines;

and that Part shall have effect as if the provisions mentioned in subsection (3) below were existing statutory provisions within the meaning of that Part and, in the case of the enactments there mentioned, were specified in the third column of Schedule 1 to that Act.

(2) Without prejudice to the generality of subsection (1) of section 15 of the 1974 Act (health and safety regulations), regulations under that section may—

(a) repeal or modify any of the provisions mentioned in subsection (3) below; and

(b) make any provision which, but for any such repeal or modification, could be made by regulations or orders made under any enactment there mentioned.

(3) The provisions referred to in subsections (1) and (2) above are—

(a) the Mineral Workings (Offshore Installations) Act 1971;

(b) sections 26, 27 and 32 (safety, inspectors and regulations) of the Petroleum and Submarine Pipe-lines Act 1975;

(c) in the Petroleum Act 1987, section 11(2)(a) (regulations) so far as relating to safety requirements and sections 21 to 24 (safety zones); and

(d) the provisions of any regulations or orders made or having effect under any enactment mentioned in the foregoing paragraphs.

(4) In this section—

"offshore installation" means any installation which is an offshore installation within the meaning of the Mineral Workings (Offshore Installations) Act 1971, or is to be taken to be an installation for the purposes of sections 21 to 23 of the Petroleum Act 1987;

"pipe-line" and "pipe-line works" have the same meanings as in section 26(1) of the Petroleum and Submarine Pipe-lines Act 1975.

(5) The provisions mentioned in subsection (3) above and the definitions in subsection (4) above shall have effect as if any reference in—

(a) section 1(4) of the Mineral Workings (Offshore Installations) Act 1971;

(b) section 20(2) of the Petroleum and Submarine Pipe-lines Act 1975; or

(c) section 16(1) or 21(7) of the Petroleum Act 1987,

to tidal waters and parts of the sea in or adjacent to the United Kingdom, or to the territorial sea adjacent to the United Kingdom, were a reference to tidal waters and parts of the sea in or adjacent to Great Britain, or to the territorial sea adjacent to Great Britain.

DEFINITIONS

"the existing statutory provisions": HSWA 1974, s.53 and Sched. 1.
"general purposes": HSWA 1974, s.1(4).
"offshore installation": subs. (4).
"person": Interpretation Act 1978, Sched. 1.
"pipe-line": subs. (4).
"pipe-line works": subs. (4).
"United Kingdom": Interpretation Act 1978, Sched. 1.

GENERAL NOTE

As already noted, transfer of responsibility for offshore safety from the DEn to the Department of Employment has already been effected by administrative means from April 1, 1991. Section 1 adds legislative support to the recommendation of the Cullen Report that the HSE should become the single body regulating safety on offshore platforms, taking over functions from the DEn (see *Responsibility for Regulation*, above). It does so by extending the general purposes of the HSWA 1974 to cover most offshore activities, and thus gives effect to recommendation 18 of the Cullen Report (see *Legislative Recommendations*, above).

General purposes. Section 1(4) of the HSWA 1974 states that references to the "general purposes" of Pt. I of that Act are to be taken as references to those purposes mentioned in s.1(1) of the HSWA 1974. That section lists four broad objectives: (a) securing the health, safety and welfare of persons at work; (b) protecting persons other than workers (such as visitors) who might be affected by work-created risks; (c) controlling the storage and use of explosive, highly flammable or other dangerous substances; (d) controlling emissions into the atmosphere of noxious or offensive substances. It can be seen that s.1(1) of the Offshore Safety Act 1992 mirrors these 1974 objectives in the context of the type of activities likely on offshore platforms.

The remit of the HSE will therefore cover securing the health and welfare of persons on board oil platforms such as Piper Alpha. The HSE will also be concerned to secure the safety of seafarers who may happen to be nearby, to the extent that they might be harmed by events on a platform itself.

Offshore activities affected. The subsection refers to "offshore installation", "pipe-line" and "pipe-line works" in relation to the extension of the HSWA 1974. These are defined in subs. (4) by reference to existing legislation (and see *Application to craft operating offshore*, below). In essence, the HSE powers will extend not only to oil platforms, such as Piper Alpha, but also to associated works, such as the pipe-lines that connect the various platforms in a field together and to the shore. Thus the Piper Alpha platform was connected by gas pipelines to the Claymore, Tartan and MCP-01 platforms in the Piper Field, which covered 12 square miles. It was also connected by 128 miles of oil pipeline to Flotta in the Orkney Isles. The 1992 Act extends the HSWA 1974 powers in respect of all these works. Accordingly, control can be exercised over pipe-line maintenance occurring well away from platforms. Moreover, specific mention is made of the need to secure the safe dismantling or removal and disposal of platforms and pipe-lines, as this can be a particularly hazardous activity in the weather conditions prevailing in the North Sea. '

Subsection 1(c) refers specifically to the construction of pipe-lines. This raises the question of whether the HSWA 1974 will be applied to the construction, tow-out and commissioning of *oil platforms*. The generality of paras. (a) and (b) might have extended to such activities, but the particularity of para. (c) could raise the inference that it is excluded. It would seem a curious omission, as the operation of *dismantling* a platform is covered by para. (d). In theory the powers of the HSE under the latter might extend to the operations of towing a platform back to land—an activity that might more naturally fall within the expertise of the DTp. Construction of a platform at an onshore site would already be covered by existing HSE powers, but if the initial tow-out of a new platform, and its erection on site, are indeed excluded there appears to be a large gap in the intended regulatory régime. At the Committee stage in the Commons the Minister, Eric Forth, was asked specifically about the construction, repair and dismantling of platforms. In his rather ambiguous reply, he assured the Committee that the health and safety general duties applied to the construction of offshore installations and would apply whether or not they were on dry land, just inshore or in deep sea (see Standing Committee E, February 18, 1992, col. 12). Tow-out, construction and commissioning might be dealt with at the design stage, but (at the very least) the wording of the Offshore Safety Act 1992 can only add to the doubts. It would have been preferable if the point had been clarified. Further, in 1980 the Burgoyne Report (para. 5.6) noted that the HSWA 1974 and its Order did not (and should not) apply to offshore installations during tow-out or transit, nor to the transport of employees by air or sea. It is interesting to note that the Annex to the draft E.C. Directive deals specifically with movements offshore, including towing and stability (see *The European dimension*, Introduction and General Note to the Act, above).

Application to craft operating offshore. There is also a lack of clarity as to the extent to which the HSE will be entitled generally to regulate activities aboard vessels and other craft operating offshore; for example, supply vessels or heavy lift vessels.

Under the Offshore Safety Act 1992 the HSE can clearly regulate activities aboard anything categorised as an "offshore installation". The Mineral Workings (Offshore Installations) Act 1971 did not define the concept particularly clearly (although the Offshore Installations (Registration) Regulations 1972 (S.I. 1972 No. 702) purported to clarify matters in respect of "mobile installations"). The present version of the 1971 Act resulted from amendments produced by the Oil and Gas (Enterprise) Act 1982, s.24, and the Territorial Sea Act 1987, ss.1 and 3. Section 1(4) of the Mineral Workings (Offshore Installations) Act 1971 now defines an offshore installation as "any installation [including under s.1(5), any floating structure or device maintained on station by whatever means] which is or has been maintained, or is intended to be established, for the carrying on of any activity to which the Act applies". The activities to which the 1971 Act applies are listed in s.1(2) to include "(a) the exploration or exploitation of mineral resources . . . (b) the storage of gas . . . (c) the conveyance of things by means of a pipe-line . . . (d) the provision of accommodation for persons who work on or from an installation . . .". This definition of offshore installation would extend to jack-up oil rigs, semi-submersible rigs and drilling ships (and see M. Summerskill, *Oil Rigs: Law and Insurance* (1979), at p. 52). It would also extend to "flotels" (floating platforms used as hotels), such as the *Safe Supporter*, from which workers were being transferred to Cormorant Alpha by the helicopter which crashed with the loss of 11 lives on March 14, 1992 (see *The Independent*, March 16, 1992). The Offshore Safety Act 1992 would clearly give the HSE the powers to require Safety Cases for mobile installations brought into U.K. controlled waters (and see the Cullen Report, para. 17.41). However, attendant vessels, such as tugs, supply vessels and heavy lift submersibles, are probably not covered by the definition of offshore installation in the Mineral Workings (Offshore Installations) Act 1971 and there is no express reference to them in the Offshore Safety Act 1992. In 1980 the Burgoyne Report had recommended that U.K. law be applied to pipeline laying vessels "and that the problem of attending vessels be thoroughly examined" (see para. 5.8). The question of attending vessels was only addressed by the Cullen Report in the context of standby vessels, although it is not always clear whether Lord Cullen was recommending the imposition of higher standards on the installation operators who would hire the standby vessels (through the Safety Case procedure), or directly on the owners of the vessels themselves (*cf.* paras. 20.39 and 20.42).

The point is important, especially where the HSE may seek to regulate standards aboard attending vessels which are foreign-flagged and purporting to exercise rights of navigation on the high seas, outside U.K. territorial waters, but within its continental shelf (see generally, I. Shearer (ed.), *D. O'Connell, The International Law of the Sea* (1982), Vol. 1, Chapter 13). The matter is governed internationally by the Convention on the Continental Shelf 1958 (for similar provisions see Pt. VI of the UN Convention on the Law of the Sea 1982). It may be a difficult question as to whether the imposition by a state of standards for attending foreign-flag vessels are "reasonable measures for the exploration of the continental shelf" (within Art. 4) or are "an unjustifiable interference with navigation" (within Art. 5). Article 5 of the Convention does allow states to create safety zones around platforms and "to take in those zones measures necessary for their protection". The U.K. has exercised the right to create safety zones in ss.21–24 of the Petroleum Act 1987. It is arguable that a state could impose safety standards for the attending foreign-flag vessels if they wish to enter a safety zone, although it would be difficult to impose the standards in respect of the vessels' general navigation to and from the offshore installation which they are attending.

It is apparently intended that the *general* words of s.1(1) of the Offshore Safety Act 1992 would extend not only to the platforms themselves, but also, more widely, to activities which might be connected with them. Specific mention was made of divers and diving operations and to the crews of standby vessels (see *Hansard*, H.C. Vol. 203, col. 680). At the Committee Stage in the Commons the Government resisted an attempt to add *expressly* to s.1(1)(a) the words "or on vessels providing support and standby services". The reasons for this refusal are not readily apparent and it may be argued that specific reference ought to have been made to the problem of attending vessels, certainly where powers are claimed over foreign-flag vessels exercising rights of navigation in international waters over the continental shelf. It was said that the general safety of crews is provided for by the merchant shipping legislation, which applies to standby vessels. The HSWA 1974 may to some extent already have been extended to the crews of supply vessels and standby vessels, as regards their *activities* relating to offshore installations, by the Health and Safety at Work etc. Act 1974 (Application Outside Great Britain) Order 1989 (S.I. 1989 No. 840). During emergency operations, standby vessels carry out functions in relation to the "safety, health and welfare of persons on offshore installations", within s.1(1)(a) of the Offshore Safety Act 1992, and to that extent could be covered by the HSWA 1974 as extended. The standby vessel code will deal with questions as to the fitness of such vessels (see the *Government response to the Cullen Report*, above). But, as already noted, the Code only applies voluntarily at present, although UKOOA had given the HSE an assurance that its members would not charter any vessel that had not been certificated to the Code's standards (see *Hansard*, H.C. Standing Committee E, February 18, 1992, col. 10). The Safety Case procedure, when introduced, will be relevant (*ibid.*), as the HSE will see, in each operator's safety case, how far it has made arrangements for standby vessels.

So far as helicopters are concerned, the safety of air crews and passengers is covered by the Civil Aviation Authority (CAA), although loading and unloading at installations are covered by the HSWA 1974 and the safety case could make provision for helicopter crashes. As noted above, the Burgoyne Report had recommended that the HSWA 1974 should not apply to transit by air. Thus, it would seem to be the primary responsibility of the CAA, not the HSE, to insist that helicopters be fitted with a Health and Usage Monitoring System (HUMS). The helicopter that crashed into the North Sea on March 14, 1992 was apparently not fitted with such a system, as the CAA had not made its fitting compulsory (see *The Independent*, March 16, 1992). The HSE might, under the HSWA 1974, be able to produce regulations forbidding such aircraft from landing. It might also require operators of installations to provide search and rescue (SAR) helicopter facilities (*cf.* Lloyd's List, March 17, 1992).

There is a real area of uncertainty concerning the interlinking of the various safety régimes. The Offshore Safety Act 1992, although giving extended powers to the HSE, does not clearly define the boundaries between the various responsibilities to be exercised by the HSE, the CAA and the DTp. It is accepted that the Merchant Shipping (Code of Safe Practices) Regulations 1980 (S.I. 1980 No. 686) apply to merchant ships. Chapter 30 of the 1991 revised edition of the DTp's *Code of Safe Working Practices for Merchant Seamen* specifically applies to ships servicing offshore installations. Moreover, detailed regulations deal with specific aspects of safety on board (see, for example, Merchant Shipping (Protective Clothing and Equipment) Regulations 1985 (S.I. 1985 No. 1664) and the Merchant Shipping (Hatches and Lifting Plant) Regulations 1988 (S.I. 1988 No. 1639)). Appropriate maritime authorities abroad will have powers to create similar obligations in respect of vessels having their nationality. To what extent can the HSE issue regulations governing what happens on board vessels working with an offshore installation? Where and when exactly can powers be exercised in respect of "securing the safety, health and welfare of persons on offshore installations" or "preventing accidents on *or near them*" (emphasis added)? The emphasised words might seem to indicate that the HSE's powers could extend to vessels near the installations (as opposed to applying to activities on the installations likely to harm those who might happen to be near). There seems little doubt that the HSE could issue regulations dealing with loading and discharge *operations* (whether from helicopters or attending vessels) which involve an installation. Perhaps it might be said that the power would extend not to the attending vessel itself, but to some of the operations undertaken by it. The problem is more than one involving the jurisdiction of several Government departments, as foreign companies exercising international legal rights might also be concerned. Most of the offshore installation legislation is expressly designed to apply to such bodies, as part of the internationally accepted exercise of rights over the continental shelf (see for example, the Mineral Workings (Offshore Installations) Act 1971, s.12(4)). Where foreign ships service installations they would already be subject to regulation by their own maritime authority under accepted principles of international maritime law. It is difficult to see how the HSE could require, for example, that supply ships or heavy lift vessels should themselves be subject to the full safety case procedure (with its attendant penalty system), except in so far as they come within the 500-metre safety zone created by the Petroleum Act 1987.

Existing statutory provisions. Subsection (1) adds the provisions listed in subs. (3) to those contained in Sched. 1 of the HSWA 1974. The purpose of the listing of statutory provisions in that Schedule was to allow the then newly created HSE progressively to replace a large number of existing statutes (and subsidiary legislation made under them) relating to health and safety with a new system of regulations and approved codes of practice conforming with the general philosophy of the HSWA 1974. One idea was to infuse the replacement provisions with some of the principles recommended by the Robens Committee on Safety and Health at Work 1970–1972 (Cmnd. 5034), upon which the HSWA 1974 drew heavily. These included the idea of creating a climate whereby there would be greater and better self-regulation in industry (see generally R.C. Simpson's annotation of the HSWA 1974 in Current Law Statutes Annotated 1974). The Cullen Report, paras. 16.32–16.39, noted with apparent approval the emphasis of the HSC on specifying principles rather than solutions. This approach was compared favourably with that of the DEn, which was categorised as over-conservative and insular, failing to take into account modern approaches to the regulation of industrial safety (Cullen Report, paras. 22.20, 22.21). One important *caveat* was made by s.1(2) of the HSWA 1974, and that was designed to make it clear that any replacement provisions should "maintain or improve the standards of health, safety and welfare" established by the existing legislation.

An advantage of having a progressive replacement of existing (onshore) legislation was that of regularising the statute book by having all provisions created under a single enabling statute. The Cullen Report (para. 16.36) noted that 143 sets of safety regulations had already been replaced (under s.15) by 35 "packages" of regulations based on modern principles. These were backed by approved codes of practice (under s.16) and guidance, where appropriate. One advantage of the use of codes of practice was that their non-mandatory nature and ease of production (avoiding lengthy Parliamentary processes) enabled speedy changes to be made which reflected modern technology.

Accordingly, it was necessary to enable the HSE (under s.15 of the HSWA 1974) progressively to replace the existing web of statutes and regulations relating to health and safety offshore. This is achieved by the combination of subss. (1) and (3) of s.1 of the Offshore Safety Act 1992. These add to Sched. 1 to the HSWA 1974 the following: the whole of the Mineral Workings (Offshore Installations) Act 1971; ss.26, 27 and 32 of the Petroleum and Submarine Pipe-lines Act 1975; and ss.11(2)(a), 21–24 of the Petroleum Act 1987. Also added are any regulations or orders made under these Acts. The replacements can naturally make use of the new purposes listed in s.1(1), paras. (a)–(d).

For application to Northern Ireland, note subs. (5) and ss.6 and 7(4), below.

Application of Part I for other purposes

2.—(1) The general purposes of Part I of the 1974 Act shall include—

  (a) securing the proper construction and safe operation of pipe-lines and preventing damage to them;

(b) securing that, in the event of the accidental escape or ignition of anything in a pipe-line, immediate notice of the event is given to persons who will or may have to discharge duties or take steps in consequence of the happening of the event; and

(c) protecting the public from personal injury, fire, explosions and other dangers arising from the transmission, distribution, supply or use of gas;

and that Part shall have effect as if the provisions mentioned in subsection (3) below were existing statutory provisions within the meaning of that Part and, in the case of the enactments there mentioned, were specified in the third column of Schedule 1 to that Act.

(2) Without prejudice to the generality of subsection (1) of section 15 of the 1974 Act (health and safety regulations), regulations under that section may—

(a) repeal or modify any of the provisions mentioned in subsection (3) below; and

(b) make any provision which, but for any such repeal or modification, could be made by regulations made under any enactment mentioned in paragraph (b) of that subsection.

(3) The provisions referred to in subsections (1) and (2) above are—

(a) sections 27 to 32 and 37 (avoidance of damage to pipe-lines and notification of accidents etc.) of the Pipe-lines Act 1962;

(b) in the Gas Act 1986, section 16 (standards of quality) so far as relating to standards affecting safety and section 47(3) and (4) (provision which may be made by regulations) so far as relating to regulations under section 16 so far as so relating; and

(c) the provisions of any regulations made or having effect under any enactment mentioned in paragraph (b) above.

(4) In this section—

"gas" means any substance which is or (if it were in a gaseous state) would be gas within the meaning of Part I of the Gas Act 1986;

"pipe-line" has the same meaning as in the Pipe-lines Act 1962.

DEFINITIONS
"the existing statutory provisions": subs. (1); HSWA 1974, s.53 and Sched. 1.
"gas": subs. (4).
"person": Interpretation Act 1978, Sched. 1.
"pipe-line": subs. (4).

GENERAL NOTE
General purposes. See the General Note to s.1, above. This section aims to achieve a similar effect to that achieved by s.1, above, but by extending the general purposes of the HSWA 1974, s.1, to cover pipelines onshore. The purposes will now include the proper construction and safe operation of such pipelines; the giving of notice to appropriate bodies, such as the emergency services, of accidental releases or fires of substances, such as oil, in the pipeline. These matters in s.2(1)(a) and (b) were not covered in the existing HSWA 1974.

Gas. Since February 1, 1984 the HSE has been responsible for most of the consumer gas safety law. The Secretary of State for Energy retained the power to prescribe certain standards of pressure, purity and odour of gas. These standards are set out in the Gas Quality Regulations 1983 (S.I. 1983 No. 363), which have effect as if made under s.16 of the Gas Act 1986. The standards are really safety standards, for example where it is important to retain pressure to prevent pilot lights in appliances going out, with the risk that a subsequent increase in pressure might create a risk of explosion. The opportunity has now been taken through subss. (1) and (3)(b) to transfer responsibility for these safety standards to the HSE. Further, the existing general purposes of the HSWA 1974 cover only gas supplied through pipes. Liquid petroleum gas (LPG) is supplied to many users in the form of refillable or replaceable tanks and cylinders kept, for instance, at home. These are not covered consistently by existing regulations which protect consumers from incompetent gas installation work. Section 2(1)(c) therefore extends the general purposes of the HSWA 1974 to cover protection of the public from the dangers arising generally from the transmission, distribution, supply or use of gas. The purposes would include accidents to gas pipe-lines and to LPG cylinders. The extension to LPG is made by the new definition of gas given in subs. (4). Again, the effect of subss. (1) and (2) is that the HSE can repeal or modify any of the regulations covering the new extended general purposes. See also the consequential provisions in s.3(3), below.

Toxic substances. One of the criticisms of the Cullen Report (para. 22.19) was that in 1985 the DEn had advised against the offshore application of the COSHH Regulations (Control of Substances Hazardous to Health Regulations 1988 (S.I. 1988 No. 1657)). Yet these represented a major change onshore, aiming to ensure that where employees might be exposed to toxic substances there would be formal procedures to ensure that their exposure was minimised and in any event kept below the maximum exposure level. There was no evidence that the COSHH Regulations were unsuitable for offshore use and s.2(1)(b) and (c) would now appear to allow that extension.

Existing statutory provisions. See the General Note to s.1, above. Subsections (1) and (3) add to the list in Sched. 1 to the HSWA 1974 the relevant safety legislation relating to *onshore* pipe-lines, so that the HSE can fulfil its functions of replacing the existing web of rules with a coherent set of regulations and codes of practice conforming to the general principles of the HSWA 1974. The relevant legislation is set out in subs. (3) and consists of the Pipe-lines Act 1962, ss.27–32 and 37, and the safety-related parts of the Gas Act 1986, ss.16, 47. Also included are regulations and orders made under those provisions.

Provisions consequential on sections 1 and 2

3.—(1) In consequence of the provision made or authorised to be made by section 1 above, the following shall cease to have effect, namely—
  (a) section 1(4) of the Continental Shelf Act 1964 (model clauses to include provision for the safety, health and welfare of persons employed on offshore operations);
  (b) section 84(5) of the 1974 Act (inspectors not to institute proceedings for offences under Part I committed outside Great Britain);
  (c) in the Petroleum and Submarine Pipe-lines Act 1975, section 28(2)(b) (notices with respect to unsafe works) and, so far as relating to proceedings for offences created by regulations under section 26 or 27, section 29(2) (institution of proceedings);
  (d) in the Oil and Gas (Enterprise) Act 1982, section 27(3) (prosecutions) so far as relating to prosecutions for offences under the Mineral Workings (Offshore Installations) Act 1971 or section 23 of the Petroleum Act 1987; and
  (e) in the Petroleum (Production) (Seaward Areas) Regulations 1988, clause 26 of the model clauses set out in Schedule 4 and clause 11 of the model clauses set out in Schedule 5.
(2) Also in consequence of that provision—
  (a) any incorporation in a licence of a model clause specified in Schedule 1 to this Act shall cease to have effect;
  (b) any functions of the Secretary of State under a licence, or under section 2 of the Petroleum (Production) Act 1934, may be exercised without regard to safety considerations; and
  (c) nothing done in the exercise of any such functions shall prejudice or affect the operation of the relevant statutory provisions within the meaning of Part I of the 1974 Act or any requirements imposed under those provisions.
(3) In consequence of the provision made by section 2 above, in the Gas Act 1986—
  (a) section 18(1) (safety regulations) shall cease to have effect;
  (b) section 47(5) (restriction on institution of proceedings) shall cease to have effect so far as relating to proceedings for offences created by regulations made or having effect under section 16 so far as relating to standards affecting safety;
  (c) in sub-paragraph (2) of paragraph 6 of Schedule 8 (savings), for the words "the general purpose mentioned in section 18(1) of this Act" there shall be substituted the words "the general purpose of protecting the public from personal injury, fire, explosions and other dangers

arising from the transmission or distribution of gas through pipes, or from the use of gas supplied through pipes"; and
(d) after that sub-paragraph there shall be inserted the following sub-paragraph—
"(2A) In sub-paragraph (2) above 'gas' has the same meaning as in Part I of this Act."
(4) In this "licence" means a licence granted under section 2 of the Petroleum (Production) Act 1934, whether before or after the commencement of this section.

DEFINITIONS
"gas": subs. (3)(d).
"licence": subs. (4).
"Secretary of State": Interpretation Act 1978, Sched. 1.

GENERAL NOTE
This section contains provisions which are consequential on the enactment of ss.1 and 2, above. In many existing provisions there are requirements connecting certain model clauses, relating to the health and safety of persons employed offshore, to various licensing functions exercised, for instance, by the Secretary of State for Energy. Examples of the legislation would be s.1(4) of the Continental Shelf Act 1964 and the Petroleum (Production) (Seaward Areas) Regulations 1988 (S.I. 1988 No. 1213) (made under the Petroleum Production Act 1934). Now that the HSE has the overall control of safety it will presumably set out its own standards in due course. At that stage, the model clauses in licences will no longer be necessary. Accordingly, s.7(3) allows the relevant parts of s.3 to be brought into force by statutory instrument. Subsection (2)(a) and Sched. 1 will ensure that model clauses in existing licences will cease to have effect. Section 3 will repeal the requirements for the insertion of model clauses in licences, so that the Secretary of State for Energy will not be obliged to exercise licensing functions with regard to safety considerations. The Secretary of State for Employment will have overall responsibility for safety offshore, although it will be administered by the HSE. In effect, there will be a "clean break" between the licensing régime for petroleum exploration and development, as administered by the Secretary of State for Energy, and the health and safety régime, as now to be administered by the Secretary of State for Employment. In future, the granting of licences can be made solely on the basis of the economic development of petroleum resources. At the Committee stage in the Commons, the Parliamentary Under-Secretary of State for Employment, Eric Forth, appeared to backtrack slightly, in that he appeared to leave open the possibility of the Secretary of State for Energy taking into account an operator's safety record before issuing a licence (see *Hansard*, H.C. Standing Committee E, February 18, 1992, col. 21). The necessary revocations will not take place by order under s.7(3) until the new safety case regulations and the new "goal-setting" régime is in place (see *Safety recommendations*, in *Cullen Report: recommendations*, in the Introduction and General Note to the Act, above). It may be more appropriate for the HSE to exercise its powers under the safety case régime to ensure that an operator acts safely than for the Secretary of State for Energy to exercise a veto at an early stage.

The section also repeals various statutory provisions, thus removing restrictions on the institution of certain criminal proceedings. An example is s.84(5) of the HSWA 1974, which would have prevented health and safety inspectors bringing prosecutions for offences committed outside Great Britain. Section 28(2)(b) of the Petroleum and Submarine Pipe-lines Act 1975 is repealed because it is made unnecessary by s.1 of the Offshore Safety Act 1992, above. Section 18(1) of the Gas Act 1986 has been superseded by s.2 of the Offshore Safety Act 1992 (see *Gas* in the General Note to s.2, above). Subsection (3) amends Sched. 8, para. 6(2), to the Gas Act 1986 to ensure that the scope of the Gas Safety (Installation and Use) Regulations 1984 (S.I. 1984 No. 1358) will not be automatically extended to certain LPG systems before new regulations can be put in place.

Increased penalties under Part I

4.—(1) In subsection (6) of section 15 of the 1974 Act (health and safety regulations), after paragraph (d) there shall be inserted the following paragraph—
"(e) in the case of regulations made for any purpose mentioned in section 1(1) of the Offshore Safety Act 1992, may provide that any offence consisting of a contravention of the regulations, or

of any requirement or prohibition imposed by or under them, shall be punishable on conviction on indictment by imprisonment for a term not exceeding two years, or a fine, or both."

(2) After subsection (1) of section 33 of that Act (offences under Part I) there shall be inserted the following subsection—

"(1A) Subject to any provision made by virtue of section 15(6)(d), a person guilty of an offence under subsection (1)(a) above consisting of failing to discharge a duty to which he is subject by virtue of sections 2 to 6 shall be liable—

    (a) on summary conviction, to a fine not exceeding £20,000;

    (b) on conviction on indictment, to a fine."

(3) After subsection (2) of that section there shall be inserted the following subsection—

"(2A) A person guilty of an offence under subsection (1)(g) or (o) above shall be liable—

    (a) on summary conviction, to imprisonment for a term not exceeding six months, or a fine not exceeding £20,000, or both;

    (b) on conviction on indictment, to imprisonment for a term not exceeding two years, or a fine, or both."

(4) In subsection (3) of that section—

    (a) after the words "section 15(6)(d)" there shall be inserted the words "or (e)"; and

    (b) for the words "an offence under any paragraph of subsection (1) above not mentioned in the preceding subsection, or of an offence under subsection (1)(e) above not falling within the preceding subsection" there shall be substituted the words "an offence under subsection (1) above not falling within subsection (1A), (2) or (2A) above".

(5) Subsections (4)(d) and (5) of that section shall cease to have effect.

(6) This section does not affect the punishment for any offence committed before the commencement of this section.

DEFINITIONS
"person": Interpretation Act 1978, Sched. 1.

GENERAL NOTE
The purpose of s.4 is to lay down the maximum penalties that may be imposed in regulations relating to offshore safety and also to increase some of the penalties that may already be imposed under the HSWA 1974. In 1989–1990 the average fine for all health and safety cases taken by the HSE in any court was £732, increased to £881 in the following year. The existing maximum fine in a magistrates' court is £2,000, with an unlimited fine on indictment. The Government considered that there must be increases in the maximum penalties for certain health and safety offences. This object was partly achieved by the Criminal Justice Act 1991, Pt. I of which will have the effect of increasing the maximum fine in magistrates' courts to £5,000 from October 1992 for all health and safety offences. This section provides for further general increases, in subss. (2) and (3), as well as in a number of other cases. In Scotland it was explained that there would be increases in the powers of the sheriff court and the High Court.

The Government resisted suggestions in the Lords that the Offshore Safety Act 1992 should effect a blanket increase in all penalties under the HSWA 1974 and also opposed amendments requiring a court to take into account, when sentencing an employer, the extent to which it had consulted safety representatives of employees. Nor would it accept an amendment designed to add to the penalties the sanction of disqualifying directors of companies (*cf.* s.37 of the HSWA 1974). The reason for the refusal was that s.2 of the Company Directors Act 1986 was considered capable of applying to health and safety matters, as the expression "management", in s.2(1), could include the management of health and safety.

Subsection (1) adds a new para. (d) to s.15(6) of the HSWA 1974 allowing new offshore safety regulations to carry punishments on indictment of up to two years' imprisonment, or an unlimited fine, or both.

Subsection (2) increases the maximum fine that a magistrates' court can impose for breaches of the basic obligations set out in ss.2–6 of the HSWA 1974 to £20,000. The current maximum penalty is £2,000. These basic obligations relate to matters such as the general duties on employers and employees to ensure health and safety at work. Offences under these sections are likely to be more serious than other offences and this was thought to justify higher maxima. Apparently, about 25 per cent. of all health and safety cases are taken under ss.2–6 of the HSWA 1974 (see *Hansard*, H.L. Vol. 532, col. 1426).

Subsection (3) increases the maximum penalty that a magistrates' court can impose for failure to comply with a prohibition or improvement notice, or a court remedy order, under the HSWA 1974 to a £20,000 fine, or six months' imprisonment, or both. The current maximum penalty is £2,000. In a Crown Court there is to be a maximum penalty of up to two years' imprisonment, or an unlimited fine, or both. Again, the higher penalties were thought justified as there may well be a deliberate flouting of a duty, even when specific issues have been brought to a person's attention by an inspector. The subsection also repeals s.33(5) of the HSWA 1974, which allowed for cumulative fines of £50 per day. The Government stated that this repeal was to recognise the general move away from daily fines in sentencing policy, partly because it had the tendency to focus courts' attention on but one aspect of an offence—its longevity.

Subsection (6) makes it clear that the new punishments are not to be retrospective in effect.

Directions for preserving security of petroleum and petroleum products

5.—(1) The Secretary of State may, after consultation with the Health and Safety Executive and with a person to whom this section applies, give to that person such directions of a general character as appear to the Secretary of State to be requisite or expedient for the purpose of preserving the security of any offshore installation, onshore terminal or oil refinery.

(2) If it appears to the Secretary of State to be requisite or expedient to do so for the purpose mentioned in subsection (1) above, he may, after consultation with the Health and Safety Executive and with a person to whom this section applies, give to that person a direction requiring him (according to the circumstances of the case) to do, or not to do, a particular thing specified in the direction.

(3) A person to whom this section applies shall give effect to any direction given to him by the Secretary of State under this section notwithstanding any other duty imposed on him by or under any enactment.

(4) The Secretary of State shall lay before each House of Parliament a copy of every direction given under this section unless he is of the opinion that disclosure of the direction is against the interests of national security or the commercial interests of any person.

(5) A person shall not disclose, or be required by virtue of any enactment or otherwise to disclose, anything done by virtue of this section if the Secretary of State has notified him that the Secretary of State is of the opinion that disclosure of that thing is against the interests of national security or the commercial interests of some other person.

(6) This section applies to any person who is the operator of an offshore installation, onshore terminal or oil refinery.

(7) In this section—

"offshore installation" has the same meaning as in section 1 above;

"oil refinery" includes an installation for processing petroleum products;

"onshore terminal" means an onshore terminal which receives petroleum directly or indirectly from an offshore installation;

"petroleum" has the same meaning as in the Petroleum (Production) Act 1934;

"petroleum products" has the same meaning as in the Energy Act 1976.

DEFINITIONS

"offshore installation": subs. (7).
"oil refinery": subs. (7).
"onshore terminal": subs. (7).
"person": subs. (6) and Interpretation Act 1978.
"petroleum": subs. (7).
"petroleum products": subs. (7).
"Secretary of State": Interpretation Act 1978, Sched. 1.

GENERAL NOTE
   This section is designed to give the Secretary of State powers to deal with security matters, such as terrorist threats, affecting offshore platforms and onshore terminals or refineries.
   The Aviation and Maritime Security Act 1990 was designed to tighten up the regulation of security on ships, offshore platforms and aircraft as well as in ports and at aerodromes (see generally N.J.J. Gaskell, The Aviation and Maritime Security Act 1990, in Current Law Statutes Annotated 1990). In particular, it gave effect to the Rome Convention for the Suppression of Unlawful Acts against the Safety of Maritime Navigation, 1988 and the Protocol for the Suppression of Unlawful Acts against the Safety of Fixed Platforms located on the Continental Shelf 1988. The latter is most relevant here. In general, it can be said that, as enacted in the 1990 Act, it penalised acts of terrorism against platforms such as those covered by the Offshore Safety Act 1992. Part III of the 1990 Act extended to most maritime activities the type of regulatory framework over security issues that had already been applied to aviation under the Aviation Security Act 1982. In outline, the Secretary of State was given wide powers to require information, to create restricted zones in harbours and to require searches to be undertaken. More particularly, s.24 gave the Secretary of State extensive powers to issue "directions" to a wide category of persons involved in shipping. The directions could require these persons to undertake virtually any measures that the Secretary of State considered could guard against terrorism. However, Pt. III of the Aviation and Maritime Security Act 1990 was deliberately *not* extended to platforms. The justifications for this omission always seemed rather thin, given that Pt. II of the 1990 Act had created new offences in relation to offshore platforms. Part of the explanation was said to be that the DEn already had the matter under control.
   Section 5 of the Offshore Safety Act 1992 has remedied the omission by giving the Secretary of State for Employment powers, similar to those under the 1990 Act, to give general directions relating to security. In fact, the powers are more closely modelled on those applying to the telecommunications, electricity and water industries. Section 208 of the Water Industry Act 1991 and s.207 of the Water Resources Act 1991, for instance, deal with directions relating to national security or civil emergencies. The Telecommunications Act 1984, s.94, is directed towards national security or relations with foreign governments. It might be thought that these purposes are somewhat different in character from the general security question referred to in s.5 of the Offshore Safety Act 1992. The latter seems most closely modelled on s.96 of the Electricity Act 1989, which refers to preserving the security of buildings or mitigating the effects of civil emergencies. In debates the Government stated that it had not been necessary to invoke the similar provisions in respect of the telecommunications, water or electricity industries.
   Subsection (1) requires the Secretary of State to consult not only the HSE, but also the very persons to whom the directions will apply. The Government resisted amendments in the Lords and Commons designed to require the directions to be "consistent with the health and safety of workers employed" at the places concerned. It was said that this point was already taken care of by the obligation to consult the HSE.
   The persons to whom the section applies are defined in subs. (6) to be the operators of offshore installations, onshore terminals or oil refineries. Such facilities are defined in subs. (7) to ensure some consistency with the rest of the Act. However, the onshore facilities—the oil refineries and oil terminals—could also be within a port area, so there is a potential overlap with the powers given to a different minister under the Aviation and Maritime Security Act 1990.
   The directions can be either general (under subs. (1)) or specific (under subs. (2)). General directions might reflect a warning that the industry faced a particular threat, or they might address a widespread shortcoming that had been brought to light: specific directions might be given to an individual if the Secretary of State came to the conclusion that there were particular shortcomings at the site which needed to be rectified (*Hansard*, H.L. Vol. 532, col. 633). Examples given by the Government included directions to instal security fences or remove car parks from beside key buildings (*Hansard*, H.L. Vol. 532, col. 1433). Copies of directions must be laid before Parliament, unless this is against the interests of national security or the commercial interests of an operator (see subs. (4)). Clearly, there would not be much point in publicising details of specific measures designed to deter terrorists. Subsection (5) supplements subs. (4) by prohibiting operators from disclosing the confidential national security or commercial information. It would appear from subs. (6) that the prohibition on disclosure in subs. (5) only applies to operators and not to others who might have acquired the information. There were some misgivings in debates about the possible conflict between the issue of safety, the security of the installation and any direction that might be given under s.5, particularly where secrecy is maintained not for national security reasons, but to protect commercial interests.
   The power to give directions arises whenever the Secretary of State considers it to be "requisite or expedient" to preserve the security of the facility in question. "Security" is not defined, but could encompass the most extreme form of threat from external terrorist groups as well as dangers resulting from acts of vandalism from those employed, or visiting, on board.

The directions might also relate to circumstances where security is "threatened" by workers taking industrial action who occupy a platform. They might already be guilty of offences under ss.10 and 11 of the Aviation and Maritime Security Act 1990 if they seize, damage or destroy a platform (see Gaskell, *loc. cit.* p. 31–42).

Operators are required by subs. (3) to comply with directions, even if they are under a duty to do something else imposed by another enactment. It is not immediately apparent what the sanction is for failing to obey a direction. Like s.96 of the Electricity Act 1989, on which it is modelled, s.5 of the 1992 Act contains none of the elaborate enforcement provisions of the aviation or maritime security legislation. In both the 1989 and 1992 provisions there is no reference to penalties, whereas there are in the Water Industry Act 1991, the Water Resources Act 1991 and the Telecommunications Act 1984, mentioned above. Moreover, it is difficult to see how disobedience to a s.5 direction can fall to be an offence under s.33 of the HSWA 1974. That section sets out the general offences for non-compliance with the HSWA 1974, but also lists specific offences, for instance, contravening a prohibition notice. If disobedience of a direction under s.5 of the Offshore Safety Act 1992 was to be an offence under s.33 of the HSWA 1974, one would have expected an amendment of (or addition to) that section.

The UKOOA apparently opposed clause (now section) 5 on the basis that it was unnecessary. It was mindful of the costs involved and preferred that national security should be funded by the Government and not private industry.

Corresponding provisions for Northern Ireland

6. An Order in Council under paragraph 1(1)(b) of Schedule 1 to the Northern Ireland Act 1974 (legislation for Northern Ireland in the interim period) which contains a statement that it is only made for purposes corresponding to the purposes of this Act—

(a) shall not be subject to paragraph 1(4) and (5) of that Schedule; but
(b) shall be subject to annulment in pursuance of a resolution of either House of Parliament.

GENERAL NOTE

Under s.7(4) the Act does not extend to Northern Ireland, which has its own health and safety law. Note also the effect of s.1(5). Section 6 enables the existing legislation for Northern Ireland to be amended by Order in Council, using the negative resolution procedure, so that it may be aligned in due course with the amendments or repeals brought about by the Offshore Safety Act 1992 for the rest of Great Britain.

Short title, repeals, commencement and extent

7.—(1) This Act may be cited as the Offshore Safety Act 1992.

(2) The enactments mentioned in Schedule 2 to this Act are hereby repealed to the extent specified in the third column of that Schedule.

(3) The following provisions of this Act, namely—

(a) section 2(3)(b) and (c);
(b) section 3(1)(a) and (e), (2) and (3)(b); and
(c) subsection (2) above so far as relating to the repeal in the Continental Shelf Act 1964 and the second repeal in the Gas Act 1986,

shall not come into force until such day as the Secretary of State may by order made by statutory instrument appoint, and different days may be appointed for different provisions or for different purposes.

(4) This Act, except section 6 above, does not extend to Northern Ireland.

DEFINITIONS

"Secretary of State": Interpretation Act 1978, Sched. 1.

GENERAL NOTE

Commencement. Most of the provisions of the Act entered into force on the day the Act received the Royal Assent, March 6, 1992. The provisions listed in subs. (3) will enter into force on a date to be appointed. The Government gave an assurance that an order will not be laid until the "Safety Case" regulations are in place (see *Government response to the Cullen Report*, in the Introduction and General Note to the Act, above).

For Northern Ireland, see subs. (4) and the General Note to s.6, above.

SCHEDULES

Section 3(2)

SCHEDULE 1

MODEL CLAUSES REFERRED TO IN SECTION 3(2)

Petroleum (Production) Regulations 1935

The clause entitled "Health and safety of workers and employees" in the model clauses set out in Part I of Schedule 2 to the Petroleum (Production) Regulations 1935.

Petroleum and Submarine Pipe-lines Act 1975

Clause 24 of the model clauses set out in Part II of Schedule 2 to the Petroleum and Submarine Pipe-lines Act 1975 (Schedule 4 to the Petroleum (Production) Regulations 1966 as amended).

Clause 24 of the model clauses set out in Part II of Schedule 3 to that Act (Schedule 3 to those regulations as amended).

Petroleum (Production) Regulations 1976

Clause 24 of the model clauses set out in Schedule 4 to the Petroleum (Production) Regulations 1976.

Clause 24 of the model clauses set out in Schedule 5 to those regulations.

Petroleum (Production) Regulations 1982

Clause 24 of the model clauses set out in Schedule 4 to the Petroleum (Production) Regulations 1982.

Clause 23 of the model clauses set out in Schedule 5 to those regulations.

Clause 11 of the model clauses set out in Schedule 7 to those regulations.

Petroleum (Production) (Landward Areas) Regulations 1984

Clause 15 of the model clauses set out in Schedule 3 to the Petroleum (Production) (Landward Areas) Regulations 1984.

Clause 21 of the model clauses set out in Schedule 4 to those regulations.

Clause 22 of the model clauses set out in Schedule 5 to those regulations.

Petroleum (Production) (Seaward Areas) Regulations 1988

Clause 26 of the model clauses set out in Schedule 4 to the Petroleum (Production) (Seaward Areas) Regulations 1988.

Clause 11 of the model clauses set out in Schedule 5 to those regulations.

Section 7(2)

SCHEDULE 2

REPEALS

Chapter	Short title	Extent of repeal
1964 c. 29.	The Continental Shelf Act 1964.	Section 1(4).
1974 c. 37.	The Health and Safety at Work etc. Act 1974.	In section 33, subsections (4)(d) and (5). Section 84(5).
1975 c. 74.	The Petroleum and Submarine Pipe-lines Act 1975.	Section 28(2)(b). Section 29(2), so far as relating to proceedings for offences created by regulations under section 26 or 27 of that Act.
1982 c. 23.	The Oil and Gas (Enterprise) Act 1982.	Section 27(3), so far as relating to prosecutions for offences under the Mineral Workings (Offshore Installations) Act 1971 or section 23 of the Petroleum Act 1987.

Chapter	Short title	Extent of repeal
1986 c. 44.	The Gas Act 1986.	Section 18(1). Section 47(5), so far as relating to proceedings for offences created by regulations made or having effect under section 16 of that Act so far as relating to standards affecting safety.

INDEX

References are to sections

NURSES, MIDWIVES AND HEALTH VISITORS ACT 1992*

(1992 c. 16)

ARRANGEMENT OF SECTIONS

The Central Council

An Act to amend the Nurses, Midwives and Health Visitors Act 1979; and for connected purposes. [6th March 1992]

PARLIAMENTARY DEBATES
Hansard, H.L. Vol. 532, cols. 484, 495, 1279; Vol. 533, col. 526; H.C. Vol. 201, col. 697; Vol. 205, col. 387.
The Bill was discussed in Standing Committee B between January 28 and 30, 1992.

INTRODUCTION AND GENERAL NOTE

This Act restructures the professional organisations of nursing, midwifery and health visiting. The origin of most of its provisions lies in the *Review of the United Kingdom Central Council and the four National Boards for Nursing, Midwifery and Health Visiting* (1989) carried out by Peat Marwick McLintock on behalf of the Department of Health, the Scottish Home and Health Department, the Welsh Office and the Department of Health and Social Services (Northern Ireland). For the most part, the conclusions of the Review were adopted, but the decision to devolve responsibility for training to the regional health authorities was in direct conflict with the proposals. The Act was drafted in consultation with the UKCC and the National Boards and received all-party support. It is intended to strengthen the principle of professional self-regulation (*Hansard*, H.L. Vol. 532, col. 485).

---

* Annotations by Jonathan Montgomery, B.A., LL.M., Lecturer in Law, University of Southampton.

The Act has five main effects. First, it provides that the United Kingdom Central Council for Nursing, Midwifery and Health Visiting (UKCC) should become a body consisting primarily of members elected directly by members of the professions rather than appointed by the National Boards for England, Wales, Scotland and Northern Ireland (s.1). This ensures that the UKCC will be directly accountable to the members of the professions, who fund it through subscription. Under the old scheme the professions elected two-thirds of the members of the National Boards, but had no say in which of them were nominated to serve on the UKCC. Although it indicates the overall shape of the new Council (s.1, Sched. 1), the Act does not specify the methods of election but obliges the Council to propose an electoral scheme to the Secretary of State for Parliamentary approval within six months of the Act being passed (s.2).

Second, the Act reconstitutes the four National Boards as bodies appointed by the Secretary of State rather than elected by the professions (s.4). Under the new scheme, the National Boards will have a far more limited function, and will become executive rather than policy-making bodies, accountable to the Secretary of State, not the professions. Standards are to be the responsibility of the UKCC; the rôle of the National Boards is to be restricted to implementing and monitoring them.

Third, it alters the nature of the responsibility of the National Boards for professional education (s.5(2)). Whereas previously the Boards provided or arranged for the provision of courses, after the Act is implemented this will fall to the regional health authorities. The function of the Boards will now be to approve institutions which offer such courses. The Government argued that this was more appropriate because planning on human resources could only be done at a local level; thus regional health authorities will be better able to assess how many new professional staff will be needed than the centralised National Boards (Standing Committee B, January 28, 1992, col. 34). This reform may prove to have far-reaching consequences for nurse education, making it vulnerable to neglect in the face of more pressing claims on health authority budgets. Considerable pressure to amend the Act so that the regional health authorities would be under a statutory obligation to fund nurse education was exerted in Parliament. It was resisted, although the Government stated its commitment to ring-fence the education budgets for "as long as necessary".

Fourth, the Act transfers to the UKCC, from the National Boards, the responsibility for preliminary investigations into allegations of professional misconduct or unfitness to practise (ss.5(4), 8). This ensures that all aspects of professional discipline are dealt with by the UKCC and avoids the division of functions that existed under the old law whereby preliminary investigations were carried out by the National Boards and full hearings by the UKCC. This reform is intended to rationalise costs, reduce delays and ensure consistency. The UKCC already bore the cost of the professional conduct investigations carried out by the National Boards, but had no way of monitoring or controlling expenditure. Centralising the procedure will reduce overheads. It is also expected to reduce difficulties arising from poor communication between the UKCC and the National Boards. In addition to these benefits, the other constitutional changes will help reduce delays in professional disciplinary hearings. The old system required most UKCC members to be also on one of the National Boards, making their duties unnecessarily onerous, and was leading to it becoming difficult for them to give the necessary time to hearing allegations of professional misconduct. With more time to commit to disciplinary hearings, it should be possible to reduce the backlog of cases waiting to be heard. It is hoped that this (in conjunction with the other reforms) will lead to the reduction of the time taken to hear cases from two-and-a-half years to six months. This will be assisted by the new power to co-opt persons from outside the Council to make up some of the membership of professional conduct committees (s.8(3)). So far as consistency is concerned, the *Review* noted that it had been suggested that the standards applied to determine whether cases should be forwarded to the UKCC varied between the four National Boards. Although the *Review* found no evidence of such inconsistency, it noted that centralising proceedings would remove any problem that might have existed.

Finally, the Act gives new powers to suspend and caution practitioners (ss.7, 9). The former will enable a practitioner who is unfit to practise for health reasons to be suspended. Previously there was no intermediate option between taking no action and removing the practitioner from the register. The power to issue a formal caution is included to resolve a conflict of legal advice. The Department of Health took the view that it was strictly unnecessary to include an express power because the right to strike a nurse, midwife or health visitor from the register implied the power to administer a caution. However, the UKCC had been told that it could not include a power to suspend in the professional conduct rules because the 1979 Act did not expressly contain one. This new Act clarifies the position.

As the Act does not specify how the electoral scheme for the newly elected UKCC will be constituted, the existing scheme will continue (s.15) until the UKCC has drawn up the new one and it has been approved by Parliament. Sections 2 and 15 came into force on March 6, 1992; the rest of the Act will be brought into force by the Secretary of State by statutory instrument. It is intended that the new bodies will be functioning from April 1993.

The Act extends to Scotland and Northern Ireland.

Changes to constitution

1.—(1) In the Nurses, Midwives and Health Visitors Act 1979 ("the 1979 Act") in section 1 (constitution etc. of United Kingdom Central Council for Nursing, Midwifery and Health Visiting) for subsections (2) to (7) there shall be substituted—

"(2) The Council shall consist of such number of members, not greater than 60, and a multiple of three, as is proposed and approved in accordance with section 2 of the Nurses, Midwives and Health Visitors Act 1992.

(3) Two-thirds of the members of the Council shall be appointed by the Secretary of State on being elected under the electoral scheme ("elected members").

(4) Appointments otherwise than for the purposes of subsection (3) shall be made by the Secretary of State from among persons who—

   (a) are registered nurses, midwives, health visitors or medical practitioners, or

   (b) have such qualifications and experience in education or other fields as, in the opinion of the Secretary of State, will be of value to the Council in the performance of its functions.

(5) In making appointments for the purposes of subsection (4), the Secretary of State shall have especially in mind—

   (a) the need to secure that the members of the Council include registered nurses, midwives and health visitors and persons living or working in each part of the United Kingdom, and

   (b) the need to secure that qualifications and experience in the teaching of nursing, midwifery and health visiting are adequately represented on the Council.

(6) The Council shall have a president and a vice-president appointed by the Council from among its members.

(7) Schedule 1 to this Act shall have effect with respect to the constitution and administration etc. of the Council.

(8) For the purposes of subsection (3), a person appointed as a replacement for an elected member shall be treated as an elected member."

(2) For Schedule 1 to that Act there shall be substituted the Schedule set out in Schedule 1 to this Act.

DEFINITIONS
   "Council": Nurses, Midwives and Health Visitors Act 1979, ss.1, 23.
   "registered": Nurses, Midwives and Health Visitors Act 1979, s.10.

GENERAL NOTE
   This section alters the constitution of UKCC leaving it bigger (raising the maximum size from 45 to 60) and predominantly elected rather than appointed. More members will be needed in order to carry the additional workload arising from the transfer of disciplinary functions to the UKCC from the National Boards.
   Technically speaking, all members of the UKCC are to be appointed by the Secretary of State. However, the effect of the obligation (under s.1(3)) to appoint those elected under the scheme to be approved under s.2 is that two-thirds of the Council will be elected by the profession. Although the UKCC itself is bigger than before, this constitutes a reduction in the total number of elected representatives, because previously there were direct elections to four bodies, the National Boards.
   The remaining one-third of the members of the UKCC will be appointed by the Secretary of State without reference to elections. This is the only point at which lay members may be included. In contrast to the provisions of the Medical Act 1983 (Sched. 1, para. 4) there is no requirement that any of the appointed members come from outside the professions of nursing,

midwifery and health visiting. The only statutory guidance to the Secretary of State on the exercise of these powers is the need to secure representation for the four parts of the U.K. (s.1(5)(a)) and experience in education (s.1(4), (5)(b)). In the Standing Committee, the Health Minister indicated that she expected lay representation on the UKCC to continue as at present (three persons on the present Council) but that at least half of the members appointed under this power would have a professional interest (Standing Committee B, January 28, 1992, col. 15).

Schedule 1 to the 1979 Act is replaced by Sched. 1 to this Act, to reflect the new arrangements.

Section 1: preparatory

2.—(1) Before the end of the period of six months beginning with the day on which this Act is passed, the United Kingdom Central Council for Nursing, Midwifery and Health Visiting ("the Council") shall submit to the Secretary of State for his approval—

    (a) a proposal with respect to the number of members of which the Council is to consist after the coming into force of section 1 above, and

    (b) a scheme for the election of persons to be appointed to the Council.

(2) A scheme under subsection (1)(b) above shall include provision determining the professional, residential or other qualifications which a person must have to be eligible to vote or to be elected in an election held under the scheme.

(3) The provision to be included in pursuance of subsection (2) above with respect to the qualifications which a person must have to be eligible to be elected in an election held under the scheme shall be such as to exclude from eligibility anyone who is not a registered nurse, midwife or health visitor living or working in the United Kingdom.

(4) If the Secretary of State approves a proposal submitted to him under subsection (1)(a) above he shall signify his approval by order.

(5) If the Secretary of State approves a scheme submitted to him under subsection (1)(b) above he shall give effect to it by order.

(6) Orders under this section shall be made by statutory instrument subject to annulment in pursuance of a resolution of either House of Parliament.

DEFINITION
"registered": Nurses, Midwives and Health Visitors Act 1979, s.10.

GENERAL NOTE
This section ensures that the UKCC will bring forward a new electoral scheme before September 6, 1992. The scheme will comprise two parts. The first (subs. (1)(a)) will determine the size of the new Council. The second (subs. (1(b)) will establish the electoral mechanism, which must ensure that only those nurses, midwives and health visitors living or working in the U.K. are eligible (subs. (3)). Both aspects of the scheme will be approved by statutory instrument, subject to the negative resolution procedure in Parliament.

Constitution of standing committees

3. In section 3(3) of the 1979 Act (power of Secretary of State to constitute standing committees)—

    (a) at the beginning there shall be inserted "If the Council (having regard to the duty imposed by section 2(6)) requests him to do so,", and

    (b) the words from "including" to the end shall be omitted.

DEFINITIONS
"Council": Nurses, Midwives and Health Visitors Act 1979, ss.1, 23.
"the 1979 Act": ss.1(1), 17.

GENERAL NOTE
The amendments to the 1979 Act effected by this section ensure that the Secretary of State

has no power to constitute standing committees of the UKCC unless the Council requests him to do so. This increases the independence of the professions from Government control. The duty imposed by s.2(6) of the 1979 Act requires the Council to consider the interests of all groups within the professions. Subsection (b) ends the inclusion of specific categories of matters: training, clinical nursing studies, mental nursing and occupational health nursing. This is in line with the principle that the professions should themselves determine what they need, rather than have it laid down by law.

The National Boards

Changes to constitution

4. In section 5 of the 1979 Act (constitution of National Boards for Nursing, Midwifery and Health Visiting) for subsections (2) to (10) there shall be substituted—

"(2) A National Board shall consist of—
(a) a chairman appointed by the Secretary of State from among persons who are registered nurses, midwives or health visitors,
(b) such number of other members appointed by the Secretary of State as he may specify by order,
(c) the person for the time being appointed in pursuance of subsection (6)(a) to be the chief executive officer of the Board, and
(d) any person for the time being appointed in pursuance of subsection (6)(b) to an office under the Board which is specified for the purposes of this paragraph by the Secretary of State by order.

(3) Appointments to a National Board for the purposes of subsection (2)(b) shall be made from among persons who—
(a) are registered nurses, midwives or health visitors, or
(b) have such qualifications and experience in education or other fields as, in the opinion of the Secretary of State, will be of value to the Board in the performance of its functions.

(4) The Secretary of State shall so exercise his powers under this section as to secure in relation to a National Board that a majority of the members of the Board are registered nurses, midwives or health visitors.

(5) The Secretary of State may, with the consent of the Treasury—
(a) pay such remuneration as he thinks fit to any person who is a member of a National Board by virtue of appointment by the Secretary of State, and
(b) make such provision as he thinks fit for the payment to or in respect of any such person of pensions, allowances or gratuities.

(6) A National Board shall have—
(a) a chief executive officer, and
(b) such other officers as the Secretary of State may by order specify for the purposes of this paragraph,
appointed by the Board.

(7) The Secretary of State may by order make such further provision with respect to the constitution and administration of a National Board as he thinks fit.

(8) Without prejudice to the generality of subsection (7), provision under that subsection may include—
(a) provision with respect to qualification for membership;
(b) provision for the appointment of a deputy chairman and with respect to his powers;
(c) provision with respect to tenure of office of chairman, deputy chairman and other members;
(d) provision with respect to the appointment of officers;
(e) provision requiring payments to employees to be such as the

Secretary of State may, with the consent of the Treasury, approve;
(f) provision requiring powers with respect to the employment of staff to be exercised in accordance with written directions of the Secretary of State;
(g) provision with respect to procedure, including the constitution of committees;
(h) provision authorising the appointment of person who are not Board members to committees of the Board.

(9) Orders under subsection (7) may include provision with respect to proof of documents.

(10) Orders under this section may make different provision in relation to different Boards."

DEFINITIONS
"registered": Nurses, Midwives and Health Visitors Act 1979, s.10.
"the 1979 Act": ss.1(1), 17.

GENERAL NOTE
This section alters the composition of the National Boards. They will become smaller, be appointed by the Secretary of State rather than elected, and be directly accountable to the Secretary of State. Their functions will be executive only (see s.6 of the 1979 Act as amended by s.5 of this Act). Although the Boards must have a professional chairman (subs. (2)(a)) and majority (subs. (4)), they will no longer automatically contain representatives of all three branches. The Government has said that in practice each of the National Boards will need to contain such persons, and it has given a commitment that this will be the case (*Hansard*, H.L. Vol. 532, col. 1287; H.C. Vol. 205, col. 394).

Functions

5.—(1) Section 6 of the 1979 Act (functions of National Boards) shall be amended as follows.

(2) In subsection (1), in paragraph (a), for "provide, or arrange for others to provide, at institutions approved by the Board-" there shall be substituted "approve institutions in relation to the provision of-"

(3) In that subsection, after "and" at the end of paragraph (d) there shall be inserted—

"(da) perform such other functions relating to nurses, midwives or health visitors as the Secretary of State may by order prescribe."

(4) In that subsection, paragraph (e) (investigation of cases of alleged misconduct) shall be omitted.

(5) In subsection (2), for the words from "have" to the end there shall be substituted "take account of any difference in the considerations applying to the different professions".

DEFINITIONS
"National Board": Nurses, Midwives and Health Visitors Act 1979, ss.5(1), 23.
"the 1979 Act": ss.1(1), 17.

GENERAL NOTE
This section amends the functions of the National Boards, as prescribed by s.6 of the 1979 Act, to reflect the new executive rôle of the National Boards.

Subs. (2)
This provides that it will no longer be the task of the National Boards to provide training courses. Instead, it is intended that the regional health authorities will do it, subject to the monitoring of institutions by the National Boards. Budgets for education will be ring-fenced budgets for an undefined period (*Hansard*, H.L. Vol. 532, cols. 1289–95).

Subs. (3)
This discretionary power was included in order to allow the Secretary of State to continue the

responsibility of the Northern Ireland National Board for offering training courses as under the old system.

Subs. (4)

Under s.8, the UKCC is to take over the preliminary investigations into misconduct allegations, previously the responsibility of the National Boards. The Boards' functions in this respect are therefore repealed.

Subs. (5)

The National Boards' original obligation to have regard for the interests of all groups within the three professions is removed as inappropriate for their new executive rôle. That duty concerned functions now confined to UKCC (*Hansard*, H.L. Vol. 532, col. 487). The new phrase emphasises differences in relation to implementation rather than policy-making. The duty to take account of differences between the professions was intended to protect the interests of health visitors and, in particular, midwives. It was said in the House of Lords debates that the types of differences that might be relevant to this provision are "such matters as their respective size, history, tradition, culture, training, knowledge base, style of practice and organisations" (*Hansard*, H.L. Vol. 533, col. 526).

Committees

6. The following provisions of the 1979 Act shall cease to have effect—
(a) section 7 (standing committees of National Boards),
(b) section 8 (joint committees of Central Council and National Boards), and
(c) section 9 (local training committees of National Boards).

DEFINITIONS

"Central Council": Nurses, Midwives and Health Visitors Act 1979, ss.1, 23.
"National Board": Nurses, Midwives and Health Visitors Act 1979, ss.5(1), 23.
"the 1979 Act": ss.1(1), 17.

GENERAL NOTE

The new National Boards will have only executive functions and these committees are no longer appropriate.

Registration

Suspension

7.—(1) Section 12 of the 1979 Act (proceedings about the register) shall be amended as mentioned in subsections (2) to (4) below.

(2) In subsection (1) (duty of Central Council to determine by rules when and how certain steps in relation to a person's registration may be taken) for the word "and" immediately following paragraph (b) there shall be substituted—
        "(ba) a person's registration in the register or a part of it may be directed to be suspended, that is to say, not to have effect during such period as may be specified in the direction;
          (bb) the suspension of a person's registration in the register or a part of it may be terminated; and".

(3) In subsection (2) (proceedings to be heard and determined by committees of the Council) after "register" there shall be inserted ", for the suspension, or termination of the suspension, of a persons's registration in the register".

(4) At the end there shall be inserted—
        "(6) Where a person's registration in the register or a part of it is suspended under subsection (1)(ba), he shall be treated as not being registered in the register or part notwithstanding that his name still appears in it."

(5) In section 13(1) of that Act (decisions which a person may appeal against) after "register" there shall be inserted ", or to direct that his registration in the register be suspended,".

DEFINITIONS
"Council": Nurses, Midwives and Health Visitors Act 1979, ss.1, 23.
"register": Nurses, Midwives and Health Visitors Act 1979, s.10.
"the 1979 Act": ss.1(1), 17.

GENERAL NOTE
This section adds a power of suspension to the existing disciplinary powers of UKCC. The intended purpose of the power of suspension was for cases where medical reasons indicated that the practitioner was unfit to practise (*Hansard*, H.L. Vol. 532, col. 508) but there is nothing in the wording to prevent it being used as a sanction as under s.36(1) of the Medical Act 1983.

Subs. (4)
This amendment specifies the effect of a suspension.

Subs. (5)
This amendment ensures that appeal will lie against decisions to suspend practitioners.

Proceedings about the register: procedure

8.—(1) Section 12 of the 1979 Act shall be amended as follows.

(2) In subsection (2) (committees of the Council to be constituted to hear and determine proceedings about the register) for "hear and determine" there shall be substituted "deal with".

(3) In subsection (3) (constitution of committees dealing with proceedings about the register)—
  (a) for "The committees shall be constituted from members of the Council; and" there shall be substituted "The committees need not be constituted exclusively from members of the Council, but the rules shall provide, in relation to committees constituted by them, that there shall only be a quorum if a majority of those present are members of the Council."; and
  (b) the remainder of the subsection shall become subsection (3A).

DEFINITIONS
"Council": Nurses, Midwives and Health Visitors Act 1979, ss.1, 23.
"register": Nurses, Midwives and Health Visitors Act 1979, s.10.
"the 1979 Act": ss.1(1), 17.

GENERAL NOTE
This section empowers the UKCC to deal with all stages of inquiries into allegations of professional misconduct (subs. (2)) and provides that professional conduct committees may include persons who are not members of the UKCC, provided that they do not constitute a majority (subs. (3)).

Subs. (2)
The alteration of the phrase "hear and determine" to "deal with" reflects the introduction of a preliminary procedure, which does not determine a case, but only decides whether it should be referred to the professional conduct committee. Preliminary investigations were previously the responsibility of the National Boards, but are no longer among their functions (s.5).

Cautions

9. After section 12 of the 1979 Act there shall be inserted—

"Cautions
  12A.—(1) Without prejudice to the generality of section 12, rules under that section may make provision with respect to the giving, in the course of disciplinary proceedings, of cautions as to future conduct.

  (2) Rules under section 12 may also make provision with respect to the keeping by the Council of a record of any caution as to future conduct given in the course of disciplinary proceedings.

  (3) For the purposes of this section, "disciplinary proceedings" means proceedings for removal from the register or a part of it for misconduct."

DEFINITIONS
"Council": Nurses, Midwives and Health Visitors Act 1979, ss.1, 23.
"disciplinary proceedings": subs. (3).
"register": Nurses, Midwives and Health Visitors Act 1979, s.10.

GENERAL NOTE
The power to caution was not originally included as the Government's legal advice was that it was not necessary to do so, but since the UKCC had previously been advised that they had no such power it was accepted that the text of the statute should clarify the matter.

The power to caution will prevent the unnecessary pursuit of less serious cases before the professional conduct committee and will thus help to reduce the backlog of cases before the UKCC. At present, only 45 per cent. of cases result in striking practitioners off. The stark choice between no action and the severity of suspension or erasure compares unfavourably with the more flexible sanctions available to other professions (*Hansard*, H.L. Vol. 532, cols. 1296–99; H.C. Vol. 201, col. 701). It should be noted that there is still no power to make continued registration conditional on compliance with directions from the professional body, as under the Medical Act 1983, s.36(1).

Provisions relating to midwifery

Midwifery practice rules: consultation

10. In section 4(3) of the 1979 Act (which requires the Council to refer proposals regarding midwifery practice rules to its Midwifery Committee) paragraph (b) (which requires the Council to consult the National Boards before acting on the Midwifery Committee's report) shall be omitted.

DEFINITIONS
"Central Council": Nurses, Midwives and Health Visitors Act 1979, ss.1, 23.
"Midwifery Committee": Nurses, Midwives and Health Visitors Act 1979, s.4.
"National Board": Nurses, Midwives and Health Visitors Act 1979, ss.5(1), 23.
"the 1979 Act": ss.1(1), 17.

GENERAL NOTE
This amendment is consequential upon the change to the nature of the National Boards. As they are now executive bodies it would be inappropriate to require consultation on all policy matters.

Notices of intention: notification of receipt

11. In section 15(2) of the 1979 Act (local supervising authority to inform National Board of receipt of notice of intention to practise) for "National Board" there shall be substituted "Council".

DEFINITIONS
"Central Council": Nurses, Midwives and Health Visitors Act 1979, ss.1, 23.
"National Board": Nurses, Midwives and Health Visitors Act 1979, ss.5, 23.
"the 1979 Act": ss.1(1), 17.

GENERAL NOTE
Under s.15 of the 1979 Act and r. 36 of the Nurses, Midwives and Health Visitors Rules 1983 (S.I. 1983 No. 873, as amended) every practising midwife must give notice each year of her intention to practise to the local supervisor of midwives. The supervisor of midwives was previously required to inform the relevant National Board of the notices given. This amendment ensures that the supervisor of midwives will report the notifications to the UKCC.

Advice under section 16(4) of the 1979 Act: standards

12. In section 16 of the 1979 Act (local supervision of midwifery practice) there shall be inserted at the end—
  "(5) The Council may by rules prescribe standards to be observed with respect to advice and guidance provided under subsection (4)."

DEFINITIONS
   "Central Council": Nurses, Midwives and Health Visitors Act 1979, ss.1, 23.
   "the 1979 Act": ss.1(1), 17.

GENERAL NOTE
   Under s.16(4) of the 1979 Act, the National Boards are responsible for giving guidance on the supervision of midwives. Under the new régime the National Boards will be executive bodies only. They are responsible for ensuring that the standards prescribed by the Council are met. The Council is the body that determines what standards are to be expected.
   The drafting of the new s.16(5), which this section inserts, may prove obscure. It appears that the Council is empowered only to prescribe standards for the way in which advice and guidance is given, not standards of supervision or practice. This is unlikely to have been the intention, but the phrase received no discussion in Parliament.

Miscellaneous

Finances of Central Council and National Boards

13.—(1) Section 19 of the 1979 Act (finances of Central Council and National Boards) shall be amended as follows.
   (2) In subsection (3) (power of Secretary of State to make grants to Central Council and National Boards in respect of certain expenditure)—
   (a) paragraph (a) (expenses in connection with initial establishment) shall be omitted, and
   (b) at the end there shall be inserted—
         "(d) the coming into force (whether in whole or part) of any provision of the Nurses, Midwives and Health Visitors Act 1992."
   (3) Subsection (4) (duty of Central Council to reimburse certain expenditure of National Boards not otherwise met) shall cease to have effect.

DEFINITIONS
   "Central Council": Nurses, Midwives and Health Visitors Act 1979, ss.1, 23.
   "National Boards": Nurses, Midwives and Health Visitors Act 1979, ss.5, 23.
   "the 1979 Act": ss.1(1), 17.

GENERAL NOTE
   These amendments permit the Secretary of State to make grants towards the expenses of bringing the new Act into force (subs. (2)) and remove financial responsibility for the National Boards from the UKCC (subs. (3)).

Central Council rules: consultation

14. In section 22 of the 1979 Act (duty of Central Council to consult about rules) after subsection (3) there shall be inserted—
      "(3A) Subsection (3)(b) shall not require the Council to consult a National Board if the proposed rules do not appear to the Council to be relevant to the Board's functions."

DEFINITIONS
   "Central Council": Nurses, Midwives and Health Visitors Act 1979, ss.1, 23. .
   "National Board": Nurses, Midwives and Health Visitors Act 1979, ss.5(1), 23.
   "the 1979 Act": ss.1(1), 17.

GENERAL NOTE
   This amendment is consequential upon the change to the nature of the National Boards. As they are now executive bodies it would be inappropriate to require consultation on all policy matters.

General and supplementary

Transitional provisions

15.—(1) Notwithstanding paragraph 2(2) of Schedule 1 to the 1979 Act (period of office of member of Central Council), where a person is a member of the Council immediately before the day on which this Act is passed, the appointment by virtue of which he is then a member of the Council shall have effect as an appointment for a period ending immediately before the day on which section 1 above is brought into force.

(2) Notwithstanding paragraph 2(1) of Schedule 2 to the 1979 Act (period of office of member of National Board), where a person is a member of a National Board immediately before the day on which this Act is passed, the appointment by virtue of which he is then a member of the Board shall have effect as an appointment for a period ending immediately before the day on which section 4 above is brought into force in relation to the Board.

(3) Where immediately before ceasing to have functions under section 6(1)(e) of the 1979 Act a National Board is investigating in pursuance of that provision a case of alleged misconduct, it shall, as soon as practicable after ceasing to have functions under that provision, notify the Central Council of the case and supply to the Council such information about its investigation of the case as the Council may require.

(4) In this section—
"the Central Council" means the United Kingdom Central Council for Nursing, Midwifery and Health Visiting; and
"National Board" means a body established by section 5(1) of the 1979 Act.

DEFINITIONS
"Central Council": subs. (4) and Nurses, Midwives and Health Visitors Act 1979, ss.1, 23.
"National Boards": subs. (4) and Nurses, Midwives and Health Visitors Act 1979, ss.5, 23.
"the 1979 Act": ss.1(1), 17.

GENERAL NOTE
These transitional provisions ensure that members of the existing Council and National Boards continue in post until, but not after, the provisions of the new Act are brought into force.

Subs. (3)
This obliges the National Boards to notify the Council as soon as is practicable of any investigations into allegations of professional misconduct that are outstanding when the Act takes effect.

Amendments and repeals

16.—(1) Schedule 2 to this Act (minor and consequential amendments) shall have effect.

(2) The enactments specified in Schedule 3 to this Act (which include certain provisions which are already spent) are hereby repealed to the extent specified in the third column of that Schedule.

Short title etc.

17.—(1) This Act may be cited as the Nurses, Midwives and Health Visitors Act 1992.

(2) In this Act "the 1979 Act" has the meaning given by section 1(1) above.

(3) This Act, except sections 2 and 15, shall come into force on such day as the Secretary of State may by order made by statutory instrument appoint; and different days may be appointed in pursuance of this subsection for different provisions or different purposes of the same provision.

(4) This Act extends to Northern Ireland.

GENERAL NOTE

Subs. (3)
This provision ensures that the old scheme will continue until the new one takes over by bringing the transitional provisions (s.15) into immediate effect. It also brings into force the obligation on the existing UKCC to draw up a new electoral scheme (s.2).

SCHEDULES

SCHEDULE 1

SUBSTITUTED SCHEDULE 1 TO THE 1979 ACT

"SCHEDULE 1

CONSTITUTION ETC. OF CENTRAL COUNCIL

Variation of membership

1.—(1) If the Secretary of State approves a proposal submitted to him by the Council with respect to the number of its members, he shall by order amend section 1 as he thinks fit for the purpose of giving effect to the proposal.

(2) The Secretary of State may not approve a proposal under this paragraph if the number proposed—

(a) is greater than 60, or

(b) is not a multiple of 3.

Variation of electoral scheme

2.—(1) The Council may vary the electoral scheme with the approval of the Secretary of State.

(2) The Secretary of State may not approve a variation under this paragraph if it would have the effect of making anyone other than a registered nurse, midwife or health visitor living or working in the United Kingdom eligible to be elected in an election held under the scheme.

(3) The Secretary of State shall signify his approval of a variation under this paragraph by order.

Tenure of office of members and president etc.

3.—(1) Appointment as a member of the Council shall be for a period prescribed by the Secretary of State by order.

(2) The period prescribed by the Secretary of State for the purposes of sub-paragraph (1) above shall not be less than 3 nor more than 5 years.

4.—(1) This paragraph applies where a person ("the former member") ceases to be a member of the Council before the end of the period for which he was appointed.

(2) The vacancy left by the former member shall be filled by a person appointed by the Secretary of State for the remainder of the period for which the former member was appointed.

(3) If the former member was an elected member, the Secretary of State shall appoint under sub-paragraph (2) above a person nominated by the Council who shall have the same qualification for election under the electoral scheme as the former member had at the time of his appointment.

(4) If the former member was not an elected member, the Secretary of State shall, in making an appointment under sub-paragraph (2) above, have regard to the qualification by virtue of which the former member was appointed.

(5) In sub-paragraphs (3) and (4) above, references to an elected member include a replacement for such a member.

5.—(1) Where a member of the Council or any of its committees is absent from meetings for more than 6 months consecutively or is disqualified from practising as a nurse, midwife or health visitor, the Council may by resolution declare that he has ceased to be a member.

(2) An elected member shall cease to be a member if he ceases to hold any qualification by virtue of which he was elected.

(3) A person appointed as a replacement for an elected member shall cease to be a member if he ceases to hold any qualification by virtue of which he was appointed.

6. If the president or vice-president ceases to be a member of the Council he shall also cease to be president or vice-president.

Procedure

7.—(1) The Council may act notwithstanding—

(a) any vacancy among its members, or

(b) that by reason of one or more vacancies, less than two-thirds of the members of the Council are elected members (or their replacements).

(2) At any meeting of the Council the quorum shall be 20 members including, in the case of each part of the United Kingdom, at least one member living or working in that part.

(3) The Council may constitute committees of itself for the purpose of transacting particular business of the Council.

(4) Persons who are not members of the Council may be appointed by it as members of such committees; but not more than one-third of the members of such a committee shall be persons appointed by virtue of this sub-paragraph.

(5) The Council may, by means of standing orders, regulate its own procedure, that of its standing committees and that of any committees constituted under sub-paragraph (3) above, and may, to such extent and in such cases as may be permitted or required by orders of the Secretary of State or by its rules and standing orders, act through those standing and other committees.

(6) No defect in the appointment of any member shall invalidate any proceedings of the Council or of its committees.

Remuneration, allowances and pensions

8.—(1) The Council may pay to its President such remuneration, and make such provision for the payment of pensions, allowances or gratuities to or in respect of him, as it thinks fit.

(2) The Council may pay to its members and to other persons appointed to serve on its committees such travelling and other allowances as it thinks fit.

Documents

9. A document purporting to be duly executed under the seal of the Council or to be signed on its behalf shall be received in evidence and shall be deemed to be so executed or signed unless the contrary is proved."

Section 16　　　　　　　　　SCHEDULE 2

Minor and consequential amendments

1. In Part III of Schedule 1 to the House of Commons Disqualification Act 1975 (disqualifying offices) in the entry relating to the Chairman of any of the National Boards, for the words from "if" to the end there shall be substituted "or member of any of those Boards appointed at a salary".

2. In Part III of Schedule 1 to the Northern Ireland Assembly Disqualification Act 1975, in the entry relating to the chairman of the National Board for Nursing, Midwifery and Health Visiting for Northern Ireland there shall be inserted at the end "or member of that Board appointed at a salary".

3. In section 2(3) of the 1979 Act (duty of Central Council to make rules about training) after "kind" there shall be inserted "content".

4. In section 6(1)(b) of that Act (duty of National Boards to ensure training courses meet Central Council's requirements) after "their" there shall be inserted "kind,".

5. In section 16(2)(b) of that Act (duty of local supervising authority to report prima facie cases of misconduct by midwives) for "to the National Board for the part of the United Kingdom in which the authority acts" there shall be substituted "to the Council".

6. In section 17(3) of that Act, for "Subsections (1) and (2) do" there shall be substituted "Subsection (1) does".

7. In section 20(5) of that Act (duty to make annual report) there shall be inserted at the end "; and a report under this subsection shall, in the case of a report by any of the Boards, be in such form as the Secretary of State may require".

8.—(1) Section 23(1) of that Act (interpretation) shall be amended as follows.

(2) In the definition of "elected members" for "section 5(4)(b)" there shall be substituted "section 1(3)".

(3) After that definition there shall be inserted—

" "electoral scheme" means the scheme submitted and approved as set out in section 2 of the Nurses, Midwives and Health Visitors Act 1992 (with any variations under paragraph 2 of Schedule 1 to this Act);".

9.—(1) Schedule 6 to that Act (adaptations for Northern Ireland and its National Board) shall be amended as follows.

(2) In paragraph 1, for "7, 9, 17," there shall be substituted "6,".

(3) In paragraph 2, the Table shall be amended as follows—

(a) in the first entry, in column 1, for "5(3), (4)(a), (5), (6) and (8)(a)" there shall be substituted "5(8)(e) and (f)";

(b) in the second entry, in column 1, for "7, 9, 17(2)," there shall be substituted "6(1)(da),";

(c) in the fourth entry, in column 1, for "Section" there shall be substituted "Sections 5(8)(e) and"; and

(d) in the sixth entry, in column 1, for "20(5)" there shall be substituted "20(6)".

(4) After paragraph 2 there shall be inserted—

"2A. In section 5, for subsections (2) to (7) substitute—

"(2) The National Board for Nursing, Midwifery and Health Visiting for Northern Ireland shall consist of—

    (a) a chairman appointed by the Head of the Department of Health and Social Services for Northern Ireland from among persons who are registered nurses, midwives or health visitors;

    (b) such number of other members appointed by the Head of the Department of Health and Social Services for Northern Ireland as that Department may specify by order;

    (c) the person for the time being appointed in pursuance of subsection (6)(a) to be the chief executive officer of the Board; and

    (d) any person for the time being appointed in pursuance of subsection (6)(b) to an office under the Board which is specified for the purposes of this paragraph by the Department of Health and Social Services for Northern Ireland by order.

(3) Appointments to the Board for the purposes of subsection (2)(b) shall be made from among persons who—

    (a) are registered nurses, midwives or health visitors, or

    (b) have such qualifications and experience in education or other fields as, in the opinion of the Head of the Department of Health and Social Services for Northern Ireland, will be of value to the Board in the performance of its functions.

(4) The powers conferred by this section shall be so exercised as to secure that a majority of the members of the Board are registered nurses, midwives or health visitors.

(5) The Department of Health and Social Services for Northern Ireland may, with the consent of the Department of Finance and Personnel in Northern Ireland—

    (a) pay such remuneration as the Department of Health and Social Services for Northern Ireland thinks fit to any person who is a member of the Board by virtue of appointment by the Head of that Department, and

    (b) make such provision as the Department of Health and Social Services for Northern Ireland thinks fit for the payment to or in respect of any person who is a member of the Board by virtue of such appointment of pensions, allowances or gratuities.

(6) The Board shall have—

    (a) a chief executive officer, and

    (b) such other officers as the Department of Health and Social Services for Northern Ireland may by order specify for the purposes of this paragraph,

appointed by the Board.

(7) The Department of Health and Social Services for Northern Ireland may by order make such further provision with respect to the constitution and administration of the Board as it thinks fit."

(5) In paragraph 3(a), for "7 or 9" there shall be substituted "5 or 6".

(6) In paragraph 4, in the inserted section 23(2)(c), for "7 or 9" there shall be substituted "5 or 6".

Section 16   SCHEDULE 3

REPEALS

Chapter	Short title	Extent of repeal
1975 c. 24	The House of Commons Disqualification Act 1975.	In Schedule 1, in Part IV, the entry relating to the Chairman of the United Kingdom Central Council for Nursing, Midwifery and Health Visiting.
1979 c. 36.	The Nurses, Midwives and Health Visitors Act 1979.	In section 3(3), the words from "including" to the end. Section 4(3)(b). Section 6(1)(e). Sections 7 to 9. In section 17, subsection (2) and, in subsection (4), the words "or (2)". In section 19, subsections (3)(a) and (4). In section 23(2), the words "Schedule 2, Part I,". In Schedule 2, paragraphs 1 to 4 and 6 to 8.

Chapter	Short title	Extent of repeal
1979 c. 36— *cont.*		In Schedule 6, in paragraph 1, the word "2", in paragraph 2, in the Table, in the first entry, in column 1, the words "and Schedule 2, paragraph 3", in the second entry, in column 1, the words "and Schedule 2, paragraphs 6(5) and 7", the third entry and the eighth entry.

INDEX

References are to sections

COAL INDUSTRY ACT 1992

(1992 c. 17)

An Act to make provision for extending the duration of, and increasing the limit on, grants under section 3 of the Coal Industry Act 1987 and to repeal the Coal Mines Regulation Act 1908.   [6th March 1992]

PARLIAMENTARY DEBATES
    Hansard, H.C. Vol. 198, col. 1247; Vol. 201, col. 985; H.L. Vol. 534, col. 1554; Vol. 353, col. 845; Vol. 536, col. 987.
    The Bill was discussed in Standing Committee B between December 3 to 12, 1991.

INTRODUCTION
    This Act provides for the amendment of the Secretary of State's powers under s.3 of the Coal Industry Act 1987 to make grants to the British Coal Corporation. The Secretary of State is empowered to make grants in connection with the re-deployment and reduction of the Corporation's workforce and the maintenance of social welfare arrangements. The limit on grants under s.3 of the 1987 Act is raised from £1,250 million to £2,500 million and the amount to which the limit may be raised by order from £1,500 million to £3,000 million.
    The period in respect of which grants may be paid is extended to include the Corporation's 1993/4, 1994/5 and 1995/6 financial years. The Coal Mines Regulation Act 1908 which regulates hours of work below ground is repealed.

Further grants for workforce redeployment and reduction etc.

1.—(1) Section 3 of the Coal Industry Act 1987 (grants to British Coal Corporation towards expenditure on workforce redeployment and reduction etc. in respect of costs falling to be charged to accounts in respect of relevant financial years) shall be amended as follows.
    (2) In subsection (4)(a) (which defines "relevant financial year" as a year ending not later than March 1993) for the words "March 1993" there shall be substituted the words "March 1996".
    (3) In subsection (6) (aggregate grants not to exceed £1,250 million or, if an order so provides, £1,500 million) for the words "£1,250 million" there shall be substituted the words "£2,500 million" and for the words "£1,500 million" there shall be substituted the words "£3,000 million".

Repeal of Coal Mines Regulation Act 1908

2. The Coal Mines Regulation Act 1908 (which makes provision for limiting hours of work below ground) shall cease to have effect.

Citation, repeals, commencement and extent

3.—(1) This Act may be cited as the Coal Industry Act 1992.
    (2) This Act and the Coal Industry Acts 1946 to 1990 may be cited together as the Coal Industry Acts 1946 to 1992.
    (3) The enactments mentioned in the Schedule to this Act are repealed to the extent specified in the third column of that Schedule.
    (4) Section 2 above, Part II of the Schedule to this Act and so much of subsection (3) above as relates to that Part shall not come into force until such day as the Secretary of State may appoint by an order made by statutory instrument; and any such order may appoint different days for the coming into force of those provisions in relation to different cases and contain such transitional provisions as the Secretary of State thinks necessary or expedient.
    (5) This Act does not extend to Northern Ireland.

SCHEDULE

REPEALS

PART I

REPEAL CONSEQUENTIAL ON SECTION 1

Chapter	Short title	Extent of repeal
1990 c. 3.	The Coal Industry Act 1990.	Section 2.

PART II

REPEALS CONSEQUENTIAL ON SECTION 2

Chapter	Short title	Extent of repeal
8 Edw.7 c. 57.	The Coal Mines Regulation Act 1908.	The whole Act.
7 & 8 Geo.5 c. 8.	The Coal Mines Regulation (Amendment) Act 1917.	The whole Act.
9 & 10 Geo.5 c. 48.	The Coal Mines Act 1919.	The whole Act.
21 & 22 Geo.5 c. 27.	The Coal Mines Act 1931.	The whole Act.
22 & 23 Geo.5 c. 29.	The Coal Mines Act 1932.	The whole Act.
2 & 3 Eliz.2 c. 70.	The Mines and Quarries Act 1954.	Section 187. In Schedule 4, the entry relating to the Coal Mines Regulation Act 1908.
1975 c. 65.	The Sex Discrimination Act 1975.	Section 21(2).
1986 c. 48.	The Wages Act 1986.	In Schedule 4, paragraphs 1 to 3.

INDEX

References are to sections

LICENSING (AMENDMENT) (SCOTLAND) ACT 1992*

(1992 c. 18)

An Act to amend the provisions of the Licensing (Scotland) Act 1976 relating to the transfer of licences; and for connected purposes.

[6th March 1992]

PARLIAMENTARY DEBATES
Hansard, H.L. Vol. 535, col. 978.
The Bill was discussed in Second Scottish Standing Committee on January 29, 1992.

INTRODUCTION AND GENERAL NOTE
This Act re-amends s.25 of the Licensing (Scotland) Act 1976 as amended by s.51 of the Law Reform (Miscellaneous Provisions) (Scotland) Act 1990. The provisions of s.25 (as amended), which provided first for a temporary transfer of a licence to be followed by a permanent transfer at next appropriate meeting of the board, proved unworkable in practice (see *"Licensing Nightmare"* 1990 S.L.T. (News) 374 and *"Licensing Transfers"* 1991 S.L.T. (News) 58). *Kerr* v. *McAuslin* 1991 G.W.D. 37–2272 confirmed that a temporary transfer was a prerequisite of a permanent transfer and that the licensing board had no discretion to shorten the time limits imposed by the amended section.

To remedy that defect, this Act, by providing that the word "temporarily" shall cease to have effect in s.25(1) reverts the law to the previous situation. A licensing board at a quarterly meeting may now grant an immediate permanent transfer without first having had to grant a temporary transfer. The substituted subss. (1A), (1B) and (1C) provide that a licensing board "may" make a temporary transfer which has effect to the next appropriate meeting of the board. Thus a temporary transfer now becomes an option available in appropriate circumstances.

The Secretary of State is empowered to bring the Act into force to make orders as to incidental and transitional provisions. See note to s.2.

Amendment of section 25 of 1976 Act

1.—(1) Section 25 of the Licensing (Scotland) Act 1976 (transfer of licences) shall be amended as follows—
(a) in subsection (1), the word "temporarily" shall cease to have effect;
(b) for subsections (1A) to (1C) there shall be substituted the following subsections—

"(1A) At any time, a licensing board may make such a transfer on a temporary basis and the licence so transferred shall have effect until the appropriate meeting of the board, which shall be—
(a) the next meeting of the board; or
(b) where the temporary transfer has been made within the period of 6 weeks before the first day of the next meeting, the next following meeting of the board.

(1B) At the appropriate meeting and on an application for a permanent transfer, the licensing board shall make a decision on the permanent transfer of the licence transferred temporarily under subsection (1A) above.

(1C) Where a board refuses to make a permanent transfer of a licence which has been temporarily transferred under subsection (1A) above, the licence so transferred shall have effect until the time within which an appeal may be made has elapsed or, if an appeal has been lodged, until the appeal has been abandoned or determined.";
(c) in subsection (7), after the word "subsection" there shall be inserted the words "(1) or".

---

* Annotations by Sir Crispin Agnew of Lochnaw Bt, Advocate

(2) In section 19(1) of that Act (prohibition of canvassing board members), for the words "or permanent transfer" there shall be substituted the words ", permanent transfer, temporary transfer under section 25(1A) of this Act or confirmation of transfer under subsection (4) of that section".

(3) In section 51 of the Law Reform (Miscellaneous Provisions) (Scotland) Act 1990 (amendment of section 25 of the Licensing (Scotland) Act 1976) paragraph (a) of subsection (2) and subsection (3) shall cease to have effect.

GENERAL NOTE

Subsection (1)(a) provides that the word "temporarily" in s.25(1) shall cease to have effect, thus returning the wording of that subsection to its position prior to amendment by the 1990 Act. A permanent transfer may only be applied for at a quarterly meeting; s.5(6). Subsection (1)(b) substitutes new subss. (1A), (1B) and (1C) for those incorporated into s.25 of the 1976 Act by s.51 of the 1990 Act. These new provisions provide that a licensing board "may make" a temporary transfer which has effect until the next appropriate meeting. For a consideration of "next appropriate meeting" see *Kerr* v. *McAuslin, supra.* From the terms of subs. (1B) a temporary transfer need not be followed by an application for a permanent transfer, but if no application for a permanent transfer is made the license will cease to have effect at the next appropriate meeting, see subs. (1A). The provisions of these amended subsections, apart from alterations made necessary to reflect the fact that the procedure is now optional, mirror the provisions as enacted in s.51 of the 1990 Act; see notes to s.51 of the 1990 Act and notes to s.25 in Allan and Chapman's The Licensing (Scotland) Act 1976, 3rd Ed by Agnew of Lochnaw and Baillie.

Subs. (2)

This is a consequential amendment to s.19(1) to take account of the fact that there can be either a permanent or a temporary transfer. See note to s.2.

Subs. (3)

This subsection provides that the relevant amendments introduced by the 1990 Act shall cease to have effect.

Citation, extent and commencement

2.—(1) This Act, which extends to Scotland only, may be cited as the Licensing (Amendment) (Scotland) Act 1992.

(2) The provisions of section 1 of this Act shall come into force on such day as the Secretary of State may appoint by order made by statutory instrument; and such an order may contain such incidental and transitional provisions and savings as appear to him to be necessary or expedient.

GENERAL NOTE

The Act was brought into force on April 15, 1992 by the Licensing (Amendment) (Scotland) Act 1992 (Commencement and Savings) Order 1992 (S.I. 1992 No. 819). The Secretary of State is empowered to make orders in relation to incidental and transitional provisions. The enabling Statutory Instrument provides, by para. 4, that the provisions of subss. (1A), (1B) and (1C) as originally enacted shall continue to apply to any licence temporarily transferred before April 15, 1992.

INDEX

References are to sections

LOCAL GOVERNMENT ACT 1992*

(1992 c. 19)

ARRANGEMENT OF SECTIONS

PART I

CITIZEN'S CHARTER PROVISIONS

Performance standards of local authorities etc.

PART II

LOCAL GOVERNMENT CHANGES FOR ENGLAND

The Local Government Commission

PART III

GENERAL

* Annotations by Professor Stephen Bailey, Department of Law, University of Nottingham.

29. Consequential amendment, repeals and saving.
30. Short title, commencement and extent.

SCHEDULES:
    Schedule 1—Amendments of Competition Provisions.
    Schedule 2—The Local Government Commission for England.
    Schedule 3—Amendments consequential on Part II.
    Schedule 4—Repeals.
        Part I—Repeals relating to Part I
        Part II—Repeals relating to Part II.

An Act to make new provision, by giving effect to proposals in Cm. 1599 (The Citizen's Charter) relating to publicity and competition, for securing economy, efficiency and effectiveness in the manner in which local authorities carry on certain activities; and to make new provision in relation to local government in England for effecting structural, boundary and electoral changes.   [6th March 1992]

PARLIAMENTARY DEBATES
   Hansard, H.L. Vol. 532, cols. 709–798; Vol. 533, cols. 11–72, 79–90, 102–168, 175–218, 332–343, 345–387, 393–452; Vol. 533, cols. 1194–1262, 1273–1326, 1466–1530, 1540–1553; Vol. 534, cols. 13–78; Vol. 536, cols. 990–1012.
   H.C. Vol. 202, cols. 37–116; Vol. 204, cols. 78–125; Vol. 204, cols. 832–920.
   The Bill was considered by the House of Commons Standing Committee D from January 28 to February 18, 1992.

INTRODUCTION AND GENERAL NOTE
   The Act comprises two main Parts. Part I includes various provisions implementing proposals in *The Citizen's Charter* (Cm. 1599, 1991) and the White Paper *Competing for Quality* (Cm. 1730, 1991) which are intended to make local authorities more accountable. Part I itself has two themes. The first theme is that of strengthening the audit process. Sections 1 to 4 introduce requirements for the publication by local authorities (and other specified bodies) of information concerning performance standards, under the direction of the Audit Commission or the Scottish Accounts Commission. Sections 5 and 6 impose a new duty on authorities to consider certain reports or recommendations by the auditor. Section 7 enables the Audit Commission to publish information concerning contraventions of the duty under s.1 or of accounts regulations, or concerning the making of an auditor's report.
   The second theme of Part I is the extension and clarification of the framework for compulsory competitive tendering. The new provisions are based on proposals in *Competing for Quality. Competition in the Provision of Local Services: A Consultation Paper*, published by the Department of the Environment, the Scottish Office and the Welsh Office in November 1991.
   Compulsory competitive tendering was first introduced by Pt. III of the Local Government, Planning and Land Act 1980. Local authorities which wished to use their own workforce to undertake works of new construction, building maintenance and highways work were required to carry out a competitive tendering process. Local authority workforces which won the contracts were required to meet a rate of return specified by the Secretary of State.
   Part I of the Local Government Act 1988 extended compulsory competitive tendering to other services. The Act specified refuse collection, building cleaning, street cleaning, schools and welfare catering, other catering, ground maintenance, and repair and maintenance of vehicles. The management of sports and leisure facilities was subsequently added by an order made by the Secretary of State. The 1988 Act also included provisions concerning anti-competitive behaviour, gave the Secretary of State sanction powers, and added similar provisions by amendment to the 1980 Act.
   The introduction and extension of compulsory competitive tendering was politically controversial, with opposition not confined to Labour authorities. The Government claims that the introduction of competition under the 1988 Act has led to average savings of some six per cent. overall in the annual cost of work subject to the Act, while standards of service have been maintained or improved (*Competition in the provision of local services: A Consultation Paper*, 1991, para. 1.5). This is apparently based on the research report by K. Walsh, *Competitive Tendering for Local Authority Services: Initial Experiences* (Institute of Local Government Studies, HMSO, 1991), Chap. 13. The fuller picture in the Report shows that the position varies significantly from service to service and authority to authority.

The *Consultation Paper* noted that while "many local authorities have readily adopted the spirit of the competition legislation" others have "sought to bend the rules laid down by the legislation, to cushion their workforce against the full force of competition" (para. 1.6). Accordingly, the framework of compulsory competitive tendering required clarification. The benefits of tendering, according to the Government, included improvements in the management of services as well as value for money: these should be extended to other services. Thus, further manual services not already subject to the procedures should be included, and the procedures should be extended to certain of the professional services. It was, however, recognised that the procedures applicable to manual services might need to be modified when it came to professional services.

Accordingly, Pt. I of the Act provides for the extension of the application of compulsory competitive tendering (s.8); gives the Secretary of State power to define conduct as competitive or anti-competitive (s.9); requires publicity to be given for tender specifications (s.10); and makes a series of amendments to the competition provisions of the Local Government, Planning and Land Act 1980 and the Local Government Act 1988 (s.11, Sched. 1).

Part II concerns the structure of local government in England. It represents the latest in a long series of attempts to establish a generally acceptable pattern for local government in England and Wales. The current arrangements can be traced to the reorganisation of local government in London under the London Government Act 1963 (with effect from 1965) and elsewhere in England and Wales under the Local Government Act 1972 (with effect from 1974). Each Act was preceded by a Royal Commission (the Herbert Royal Commission on Local Government in Greater London 1957–60 (Cmnd. 1164, 1960); the Redcliffe-Maud Royal Commission on Local Government in England 1966–69 (Cmnd. 4040, 1969)). However, particularly in the case of the Redcliffe-Maud report, there were significant differences between the recommendations of the Royal Commission and the ultimate outcome (see the White Papers *London Government: Government Proposals for Reorganisation* (Cmnd. 1562, 1961), *Local Government in England* (Cmnd. 4585, 1971) and *The Reform of Local Government in Wales* (HMSO, 1971)). The standard pattern established for local government was a two-tier structure. In London, powers were divided between the London borough councils and the Common Council of the City of London (which exercised the powers of a London borough council) on the one hand, and the Greater London Council on the other. The G.L.C. was responsible for such matters as metropolitan roads, traffic management, refuse disposal, fire prevention, land drainage and flood protection. It shared responsibility in planning and housing matters with the London boroughs and the Common Council. Education was the responsibility of London borough councils in outer London. In inner London, education was managed by the Inner London Education Authority, a special committee of the Greater London Council.

Outside London, a distinction was drawn between the six metropolitan counties (Greater Manchester, Merseyside, South Yorkshire, Tyne and Wear, West Midlands and West Yorkshire) and the 47 non-metropolitan counties. Each county was divided into districts, but the allocation of functions was different in metropolitan and non-metropolitan areas, with the bulk of the powers being exercised by metropolitan district and non-metropolitan county councils. In particular, it was these councils that were responsible for education, personal social services and libraries.

The major structural change since then has been the abolition of the Greater London Council and the metropolitan county councils by the Local Government Act 1985. This was not strictly a complete move away from a two-tier structure, as a number of the functions of the abolished councils were transferred to joint authorities established by the Act. Part III of the 1985 Act established the Inner London Education Authority as a directly elected authority; Part IV provided for joint authorities to be established to act as (1) police, (2) fire and civil defence and (3) passenger transport authorities in the metropolitan counties and as the fire and civil defence authority for London. Joint authorities are not directly elected; their members (other than for a police authority) are all members of the constituent district or London borough councils appointed by those councils to be members of the authority. The Inner London Education Authority was itself abolished by the Education Reform Act 1988, with the inner London borough councils and the Common Council becoming local education authorities.

Apart from the structural changes to the pattern of local authorities, there have also been perceived changes to the rôle of local authorities in England and Wales.

"The Government's model for local government in the 1990s and into the 21st century is that of the enabling authority. The task of local authorities lies in identifying requirements, setting priorities, determining standards of service and finding the best way to meet those standards and ensuring they are met."

(White Paper, *Competing for Quality* (Cm. 1730, 1991, p. 22)).

This involves

"a move away from the traditional model of local authorities providing virtually all services directly and a greater separation of the functions of service delivery from strategic responsibilities" (*ibid.*).

Particular features of this move that have been secured by Government legislation include the requirements for compulsory competitive tendering (see above); the provisions for the local management of schools and colleges, where responsibility for the management of the budget is delegated to the governing body, and for grant-maintained schools, which are maintained by the Secretary of State and not the local education authority (see *Cross on Local Government Law* (8th ed., 1991), paras. 17–51 to 17–55; 17–62 to 17–67); the transfer of polytechnics and larger colleges out of local authority control (see *Cross*, paras. 17–80 to 17–84); provisions enabling council estates to be privatised (see *Cross*, paras. 15–21 to 15–24); and the "ring-fencing" of housing revenue accounts (see *Cross*, para. 15–29).

Critics have argued that the trend in the relationship of central and local government has been one of increasing centralisation, with a reduction in the significance of the rôle of local authorities. They point to such matters as the removal of responsibility for particular services from local authorities (see above); the replacement of a number of elected authorities by authorities whose members are appointed (see above); the reduction in the proportion of local expenditure raised from locally set taxes, with the reduction in community charge levels (matched by a VAT increase) by virtue of the Community Charge (General Reduction) Act 1991 and the assumption by central government of responsibility for setting the business rate; and the increasingly wide powers of the Secretary of State to "cap" community charge levels (Pt. VII of the Local Government Finance Act 1988, as amended by the Local Government Finance and Valuation Act 1991).

Part II addresses the question of structural reform of local government. The Government decided that it was not appropriate to refer the matter to a Royal Commission or departmental committee for independent consideration. (The questions of finance, the electoral system, structure and functions were excluded from the terms of reference of the Widdicombe *Committee of Inquiry into the Conduct of Local Authority Business* (Cmnd. 9797, 1986).) Instead, Pt. II establishes a Local Government Commission to review such areas in England as are specified by the Secretary of State and to consider what structural, boundary or electoral changes, if any, should be recommended. The Commission is also to take over the responsibilities of the Local Government Boundary Commission for England to conduct periodic reviews of electoral arrangements and make recommendations. The Secretary of State may, if he thinks fit, give effect to all or any of the recommendations, with or without modifications. The Secretary of State may give directions and guidance to the Commission.

The Government believes "that there should be a move towards unitary authorities where these do not already exist" (*Local Government Review: The Structure of Local Government in England: A Consultation Paper*, DOE, April 1991, p. 1). Accordingly, it has "no plans" to change the general structure of local government in London and the metropolitan counties (*ibid.* p. 7). In the non-metropolitan or "shire" counties, it has identified a number of respects in which the current two-tier system is "unsatisfactory". First, some authorities which emerged in 1974 "are still not wholly accepted by all the local communities which they serve. There is still a feeling in some areas that history and tradition were perhaps disregarded in a search for administrative uniformity" (*ibid.* p. 5). Sometimes it is the county which has not been accepted, sometimes one or more of the districts. Secondly, the existence of two tiers can cause confusion over which tier is responsible for which service. Thirdly, the necessary close coordination of functions can be impeded where they are the responsibility of different tiers (*e.g.* housing and social services), and where functions are shared between the two tiers (*e.g.* planning) conflict and tension can arise between the policies of county and district councils (*ibid.*).

Nevertheless, the Government was not prepared simply to impose a system of unitary authorities in non-metropolitan counties, with the wholesale abolition of county or district councils. It accepts that different patterns may be suitable to different areas.

"In some places, it may be best for existing authorities to be merged; in others the best approach may be to create or recreate quite different authorities. In some areas there could be a case for two tiers. The aim will be to achieve the structure which best matches the particular circumstances of each area." (*ibid.* p. 6).

Accordingly, the Government will "set guidelines for the process of moving towards more unitary authorities which reflect community loyalties" (*ibid.* p. 8).

In November 1991, the DOE published for consultation draft Guidance to the Local Government Commission for England.

It will be noted that Pt. II does not make analogous changes to the arrangements for Wales. The Secretary of State for Wales (David Hunt) commenced discussions with the local authority associations in January 1991. In June 1991, he issued a consultation paper in which he said that unitary authorities represented the best way forward for local government in Wales. Following further discussions, on March 3, 1992, he announced proposals whereby the existing eight county councils and 37 district councils would be replaced by 23 unitary authorities (*Hansard*, H.C. Vol. 205, cols. 171–183). Themes in the proposals were the restoration to the largest centres of population (Cardiff, Swansea, Newport and Wrexham) of full control over their affairs; for local government in rural areas to be based on the traditional counties; and for account to be taken of the "intense local loyalties" in the South Wales valleys (although some of the present district councils would have to come together to form new unitary authorities (*ibid.* col. 171).

Part III contains general provisions concerning interpretation, consequential amendment, repeals and saving and short title, commencement and extent.

Scheme of the Act

Part I: Citizen's Charter Provisions
Sections 1 and 2 enable the Audit Commission and the Scottish Accounts Commission to give directions requiring relevant bodies to publish information as to performance standards.
Section 3 extends the functions of auditors to include considering whether a relevant body has complied with any s.1 direction, and extends the range of studies which are to be undertaken by the Commissions.
Section 4 enables the Secretary of State to apply ss.1–3 to parish and community councils and charter trustees.
Section 5 imposes new duties on relevant bodies to consider and respond to an auditor's report or recommendation.
Section 6 imposes publicity requirements for meetings held under s.5.
Section 7 extends the power of the Audit Commission to publish information concerning contraventions of obligations imposed by a s.1 direction or accounts regulations or the making of an auditor's report.
Sections 8–11 concern competition provisions.
Section 8 enables compulsory competitive tendering to be extended to certain professional services.
Section 9 enables the Secretary of State to define conduct as competitive or anti-competitive, and to make regulations making express provision in respect of aspects of the tendering process.
Section 10 extends publicity requirements in respect of tender specifications.
Section 11 introduces Sched. 1, which amends the competition provisions of Pt. III of the Local Government, Planning and Land Act 1980 and Pt. I of the Local Government Act 1988.

Part II: Local Government Changes in England
Section 12 establishes a new Local Government Commission in England.
Section 13 sets out the Commission's functions, which include duties to conduct reviews and make recommendations in accordance with the directions of the Secretary of State (for structural, boundary or electoral changes) or within a timetable established by the Act (for electoral changes).
Section 14 defines structural, boundary and electoral changes.
Section 15 establishes the procedure to be followed on a review.
Section 16 provides for the Commission to consult with the Audit Commission.
Section 17 provides for the implementation of the Commission's recommendations by order of the Secretary of State.
Section 18 makes provision in respect of certain consequences of structural changes.
Section 19 gives the Secretary of State power to make regulations for supplementing orders under s.17.
Section 20 enables public bodies affected by an order under Pt. II to enter agreements as to incidental matters.
Section 21 enables the Secretary of State to establish joint authorities where satisfactory joint arrangements cannot otherwise be made.
Sections 22 and 23 enable the Secretary of State to establish one or more residuary bodies and one or more staff commissions.
Section 24 abolishes the Local Government Boundary Commission for England.
Section 25 enables the Secretary of State to modify the provisions of Pt. II in their application to the Isles of Scilly.
Section 26 contains further provision in respect of orders, regulations and directions under Pt. II.
Section 27 introduces Sched. 3, which contains consequential amendments in connection with Pt. II.

Part III: General
Section 28 sets out the definitions of a number of words and phrases in the Act.

Section 29 makes a further consequential amendment and provides for repeals (Sched. 4) and a
    saving.
Section 30 provides for the short title, commencement and extent of the Act.
Schedule 1 contains amendments of the competition provisions of the 1980 and 1988 Acts.
Schedule 2 provides for the constitution of the Local Government Commission for England.
Schedule 3 makes further consequential amendments.
Schedule 4 provides for a number of repeals.

PART I

CITIZEN'S CHARTER PROVISIONS

Performance standards of local authorities etc.

Publication of information as to standards of performance

1.—(1) The Audit Commission and the Scottish Accounts Commission
shall each give such directions as it thinks fit for requiring relevant bodies to
publish such information relating to their activities in any financial year as
will, in that Commission's opinion, facilitate the making of appropriate
comparisons (by reference to the criteria of cost, economy, efficiency and
effectiveness) between—
    (a) the standards of performance achieved by different relevant bodies in
        that financial year; and
    (b) the standards of performance achieved by such bodies in different
        financial years.
    (2) Where a relevant body are required by a direction under this section to
publish information in relation to any financial year, it shall be the duty of
that body—
    (a) to make such arrangements for collecting and recording the informa-
        tion as secure that the information is available for publication and, so
        far as practicable, that everything published in pursuance of the
        direction is accurate and complete;
    (b) within the period of nine months beginning with the end of that
        financial year, to publish the information, in accordance with the
        direction, in a newspaper circulating in the area of that body; and
    (c) to keep a document containing any information published in pur-
        suance of the direction available for inspection by interested persons.
    (3) The Secretary of State may by order made by statutory instrument
vary the period for the time being specified in paragraph (b) of subsection
(2) above so as to fix the latest time for the publication of information in
accordance with that paragraph at any such time, within the period of nine
months after the end of the financial year in question, as may be specified in
the order; and a statutory instrument containing an order under this subsection shall be subject to annulment in pursuance of a resolution of either
House of Parliament.
    (4) An interested person shall be entitled—
    (a) at all reasonable times and without payment, to inspect and make
        copies of the whole or any part of a document kept available for
        inspection under subsection (2)(c) above; and
    (b) to require copies of the whole or a part of any such document to be
        delivered to him on payment of a reasonable sum for each copy.
    (5) Any person having custody of any document kept available for inspec-
tion under subsection (2)(c) above who—
    (a) obstructs a person in the exercise of his rights under subsection (4)
        above; or
    (b) refuses to comply with a requirement under subsection (4)(b) above,
shall be guilty of an offence and liable, on summary conviction, to a fine not
exceeding level 3 on the standard scale.

(6) References in this section to an interested person, in relation to any document which is required to be kept available by a relevant body in England and Wales, are references to any local government elector (within the meaning of the 1972 Act) for the area of that body.

(7) References in this section and sections 2 and 3 below to a relevant body are references—

   (a) in relation to England and Wales, to any body with which the Audit Commission is concerned, other than one falling within subsection (8) below; and

   (b) in relation to Scotland, to any local authority, joint board or joint committee, within the meaning of the 1973 Act.

(8) Subject to section 4 below, the bodies with which the Audit Commission is concerned which shall not be relevant bodies for the purposes of this section and sections 2 to 3 below are—

   (a) parish and community councils and any parish meeting of a parish not having a separate parish council;

   (b) charter trustees constituted under section 246 of the 1972 Act;

   (c) health service bodies within the meaning of Part III of the 1982 Act;

   (d) port health authorities;

   (e) licensing planning committees;

   (f) internal drainage boards;

   (g) probation committees; and

   (h) Passenger Transport Executives.

DEFINITIONS

   "the 1972 Act": s.28(1).
   "the 1973 Act": s.28(1).
   "the 1982 Act": s.28(1).
   "the Audit Commission": s.28(1).
   "financial year": s.28(1).
   "interested person": subs. (5).
   "relevant body": subss. (7) and (8); s.4.
   "the Scottish Accounts Commission": s.28(1).

GENERAL NOTE

This is the first of a group of four sections which concern the publication of information by local authorities and other specified bodies as to standards of performance. This will enable those such as electors who may be interested in the performance of local authorities to compare the performance of different authorities, and to evaluate the performance of one authority over time. In order that a common approach is adopted by all the authorities among which comparisons might be made, the information to be published is to be specified in directions made by the Audit Commission, or its equivalent in Scotland, the Scottish Accounts Commission. The Audit Commission for Local Authorities and the National Health Service in England and Wales (as it is now called) was established by the Local Government Finance Act 1982, and performs a variety of functions, including the appointment of auditors of local authorities and other bodies, preparing a code of audit practice and undertaking studies for improving economy, efficiency and effectiveness in local authority services and examining the impact of statutory provisions and ministerial guidance on economy, efficiency and effectiveness (the 1982 Act, Pt. III). The Commission for Local Authority Accounts in Scotland was established by the Local Government (Scotland) Act 1973, s.97, and its functions include securing the audit of local authority accounts, considering reports arising out of audits, making recommendations to or advising the Secretary of State in relation to local authority accounting and undertaking studies and making recommendations for improving economy, efficiency and effectiveness in the provision of services (the 1973 Act, ss.97, 97A, 97B, as inserted by the Local Government Act 1988, s.35(3)).

Subs. (1)

The Audit Commission or Scottish Accounts Commission must give such directions as it thinks fit requiring relevant bodies to publish information as to performance standards.

Relevant body. This term is defined by subss. (7) and (8) as being, for England and Wales, any body with which the Audit Commission is concerned, other than one falling within subs. (8), and for Scotland, any local authority, joint board or joint committee within the meaning of the

Local Government (Scotland) Act 1973. Section 4 enables the Secretary of State by order to provide that parish and community councils in England and Wales, or charter trustees under s.246 of the Local Government Act 1972, shall be relevant bodies.

Subs. (2)
Where a direction has been made to a relevant body, the body must arrange for the collection and recording of the information, and ensure that the information is, so far as practicable, accurate and complete; it must publish the information in a local newspaper within nine months of the end of the financial year; and must keep the information available for inspection by interested persons (*i.e.* local government electors: subs. (5)).

Subs. (3)
The Secretary of State may vary the period within which the information must be published.

Subss. (4), (5) and (6)
Local government electors have rights to inspect and copy, or pay for copies of, documents kept under this section, analogous to their rights to inspect statements of account and auditor's reports under s.24 of the Local Government Finance Act 1982.

A local government elector may exercise his right through an agent (*cf. R.* v. *Bedwellty Urban District Council* [1934] 1 K.B. 333 (inspection of accounts by professional accountant acting on behalf of a ratepayers' association)); *R.* v. *Glamorganshire County Council*, ex p. *Collier* [1936] 2 All E.R. 168).

Subs. (5)
Level 3 on the standard scale. See the Criminal Penalties etc. (Increase) Order 1984 (S.I. 1984 No. 447). The maximum fine at level 3 (£400) is to be replaced by the Criminal Justice Act 1991, s.17 (£1,000) from a day to be appointed.

Subs. (6)
Local government elector (within the meaning of the 1972 Act). By s.270(1) of the Local Government Act 1972, " 'local government elector' means a person registered as a local government elector in the register of electors in accordance with the provisions of the Representation of the People Acts". On the franchise in local elections and the registration of electors, see *Cross on Local Government Law* (8th ed., 1991), paras. 13–03 to 13–06; Registration of the People Act 1983, ss.2–7, 9–17, and the Representation of the People Regulations 1986 (S.I. 1986 No. 1081).

Subss. (7) and (8)
Body with which the Audit Commission is concerned. By s.28(2), references to a body with which the Audit Commission is concerned are references to any body any of the accounts of which are required to be audited under Pt. III of the Local Government Finance Act 1982 (including the Common Council of the City of London). These bodies are listed in the 1982 Act, s.12. All accounts of the following bodies are audited under Pt. III: a local authority, a joint authority, a parish meeting, a committee of a local authority, a joint committee of two or more local authorities, the Council of the Isles of Scilly, a body specified in s.98(1) of the National Health Service Act 1977, a port health authority, the Broads Authority, a combined police authority, a fire authority constituted by a combination scheme, a licensing planning committee, an internal drainage board, and a probation committee (except that for Inner London). In addition, the accounts of the collection fund of the Common Council, the accounts of the City fund, the accounts relating to the superannuation fund established by the Common Council and certain other health service accounts are also audited under Pt. III.

So far as England and Wales is concerned, "relevant" bodies are those with which the Audit Commission is concerned other than those bodies listed in subs. (8).

Subs. (7)
Any local authority, joint board or joint committee. By s.235(1) of the Local Government (Scotland) Act 1973, "local authority" means "a regional, islands or district council"; "joint board" means "a body corporate, constituted for the purposes of a combination of local authorities under this Act or by or under any other enactment, consisting exclusively of persons appointed by the local authorities"; and "joint committee" has the same meaning as "joint board" except that the body in question is not a "body corporate".

Subs. (8)
Charter trustees. See note to s.17(5).

Directions under s.1

2.—(1) A direction under section 1 above requiring the publication of information shall—

(a) identify the financial year or years in relation to which the information is to be published;

(b) specify or describe the activities to which the information is to relate; and

(c) make provision as to the matters to be contained in the information and as to the form in which it is to be published.

(2) A direction under section 1 above—

(a) may be given so as to apply either to all the relevant bodies with which the Commission giving the direction is concerned or to all such bodies as are of a description specified in the direction; and

(b) may be varied or revoked by any subsequent direction under that section.

(3) Before giving a direction under section 1 above which imposes a new requirement on any relevant body as to the publication of any information the Audit Commission or Scottish Accounts Commission shall consult such associations of relevant bodies and such other persons as it thinks fit.

(4) A direction under section 1 above imposing a new requirement on any relevant body as to the publication of any information shall not be given any later than the 31st December in the financial year which precedes that in relation to which the information is to be published.

(5) Where the Audit Commission or the Scottish Accounts Commission gives a direction under section 1 above, it shall—

(a) publish the direction in such manner as it considers appropriate for bringing it to the attention of members of the public; and

(b) send a copy of the direction to every relevant body on whom duties are imposed by virtue of the direction.

(6) References in this section to the imposition of a new requirement on a relevant body as to the publication of information are references to—

(a) the imposition of any requirement by the first direction under section 1 above to apply to that body; or

(b) any subsequent extension of, or addition to, either—

(i) the matters to be contained in the information which that body are required to publish in relation to any financial year in pursuance of directions under section 1 above; or

(ii) the activities to which any such information is to relate.

DEFINITIONS

"the Audit Commission": s.28(1).

"financial year": s.28(1).

"imposition of a new requirement": subs. (6).

"relevant body": s.1(7), (8); s.4.

"the Scottish Accounts Commission": s.28(1).

GENERAL NOTE

This section sets out various matters concerning directions by the Audit Commission or Scottish Accounts Commission under s.1.

Subs. (1)

Directions must identify the financial year(s) (*i.e.* 12 months ending with March 31: s.28(1)) in relation to which the information must be published; the activities to which the information must relate; and the matters to be contained in the information and the form of publication.

Subs. (2)

A direction may relate to all or some of the bodies with which the commission is concerned, and may be varied or revoked.

Body with which the Commission . . . is concerned. See note to s.1(7), (8).

Subs. (3)

Before giving a direction which imposes a new requirement (as to which see subs. (6)) the Commission must consult such associations of relevant bodies and such other persons as it thinks fit.

Consult. On the meaning of "consultation" see, *e.g. Rollo* v. *Minister of Town and Country Planning* [1948] 1 All E.R. 13; *R.* v. *Secretary of State for Social Services*, ex p. *Association of Metropolitan Authorities* [1986] 1 W.L.R. 1.

Subs. (4)

A direction imposing a new requirement (see subs. (6)) must be issued no later than December 31 in the year immediately preceding the financial year in respect of which the information is to be published. Accordingly, bodies must be given at least three months to prepare and collect the information required in a new direction.

Subs. (6)

This explains what is meant by the term "new requirement".

Functions of auditor and studies by the Commissions

3.—(1) In section 15(1) of the 1982 Act (duties of auditors), at the end of paragraph (c) there shall be inserted "and

(d) in a case where that body are required to publish information in pursuance of a direction under section 1 of the Local Government Act 1992 (publication of performance information), that that body have made such arrangements for collecting and recording the information, and for publishing it, as are required for the performance of their duties under that section."

(2) In section 99 of the 1973 Act (which makes corresponding provision for Scotland), at the end of paragraph (c) there shall be inserted "and

(d) in a case where that body are required to publish information in pursuance of a direction under section 1 of the Local Government Act 1992 (publication of performance information), that body have made such arrangements for collecting and recording the information, and for publishing it, as are required for the performance of their duties under that section."

(3) The comparative and other studies which the Audit Commission is required to undertake or promote under section 26(1) of the 1982 Act, and those which the Scottish Accounts Commission is required to undertake or promote under section 97A(1) of the 1973 Act, shall include, in particular—

(a) studies designed to enable the Audit Commission or, as the case may be, the Scottish Accounts Commission to determine what directions it should give under section 1 above; and

(b) studies of information published in pursuance of directions under section 1 above which are designed to enable the Commission in question to determine, in relation to each financial year, what comparative information to publish itself about the standards of performance achieved by relevant bodies;

but neither Commission shall be required by section 26(4) of the 1982 Act or section 97A(3) of the 1973 Act to consult any person before undertaking or promoting a study falling within paragraph (a) or (b) above.

DEFINITIONS

"the 1973 Act": s.28(1).
"the 1982 Act": s.28(1).
"the Audit Commission": s.28(1).
"financial year": s.28(1).
"the Scottish Accounts Commission": s.28(1).

GENERAL NOTE

This section amends provisions concerning the duties of auditors and the powers of the Audit

Commission and the Scottish Accounts Commission to take account of the new obligations of local authorities arising from directions under s.1.

Subs. (1)
Under s.15(1) of the Local Government Finance Act 1982, which applies in England and Wales, the auditor is (*inter alia*) required to satisfy himself that the accounts audited are prepared in accordance with the accounts regulations, that proper practices have been observed in compiling the accounts, and that the body the accounts of which are being audited has made proper arrangements for securing economy, efficiency and effectiveness in its use of resources. This subsection adds the further requirement that the auditor satisfy himself that the body has complied with its obligations under any s.1 direction.

Subs. (2)
Section 99 of the Local Government (Scotland) Act 1973, as amended by the Local Government Act 1988, s.35(4), requires the auditor to satisfy himself that the accounts have been prepared in accordance with accounts regulations and other applicable enactments and instruments, that proper accounting practices have been observed in the preparation of the accounts, and that the authority has made proper arrangements for securing economy, efficiency and effectiveness in its use of resources. This subsection adds the further requirement that the auditor satisfy himself that the body has complied with its obligations under any s.1 direction.

Subs. (3)
The Audit Commission and the Scottish Accounts Commission are each required to undertake or promote comparative and other studies designed to enable it to make recommendations for improving economy, efficiency and effectiveness in the provision of local authority services and for improving the financial or other management of local authorities and other bodies. This is to include studies designed to enable the Commission to determine what directions it should give under s.1, and studies of the information published in response to s.1 directions designed to enable the Commission to determine what comparative information to publish itself about performance standards. The consultation requirements that apply to other studies conducted in pursuance of each Commission's duties do not apply to studies under this subsection (although there must be consultation before the Commission gives a direction imposing a new requirement: see s.2(3)).

Application to parish and community councils and charter trustees

4.—(1) The Secretary of State may by order provide for sections 1 to 3 above to have effect as if—
(a) parish and community councils in England and Wales; and
(b) charter trustees constituted under section 246 of the 1972 Act,
were relevant bodies for the purposes of those sections.
(2) The power to make an order under this section shall be exercisable by statutory instrument subject to annulment in pursuance of a resolution of either House of Parliament.
(3) The power to make an order under this section shall include power—
(a) to make such incidental, consequential, transitional or supplementary provision as the Secretary of State thinks necessary or expedient; and
(b) to make different provision for different cases, including different provision for different localities and for different bodies.

DEFINITIONS
"the 1972 Act": s.28(1).

GENERAL NOTE
The Secretary of State may by order apply ss.1–3 to parish and community councils in England and Wales and to charter trustees under s.246 of the Local Government Act 1972. These bodies otherwise fall within the list of exclusions set out in s.1(7). An order is to be made by statutory instrument, subject to the negative resolution of either House of Parliament.

Subs. (1)
Charter trustees. See note to s.17(5).

Auditors' reports and recommendations

Duty to consider auditor's report or recommendation

5.—(1) Where, at any time after the coming into force of this section, a body to which this section applies or, in the case of a parish meeting, their chairman is sent, in connection with the audit of that body's accounts—

(a) a report under section 15(3) of the 1982 Act (an auditor's report) or, in Scotland, a copy of a report from the Controller of Audit under section 102(1) or (2) of the 1973 Act; or

(b) such a written recommendation to that body by an auditor as is stated, in the document containing the recommendation, to be one which, in the auditor's opinion, should be considered under this section or, in Scotland, a recommendation to that body from the Scottish Accounts Commission under section 103(1) of the 1973 Act,

it shall be the duty of the body concerned to consider the report or recommendation in accordance with the following provisions of this section and section 6 below.

(2) The duty under this section of any body to consider a report or recommendation is a duty—

(a) to consider it at a meeting held before the end of the period of four months beginning with the day on which the report or recommendation was sent to that body or, as the case may be, to their chairman; and

(b) to decide at that meeting—

(i) whether the report requires that body to take any action or whether the recommendation is to be accepted; and

(ii) what, if any, action to take in response to the report or recommendation.

(3) If—

(a) an auditor is satisfied, in the case of any body in England and Wales to which, or to whose chairman, any report or recommendation has been sent, that it is reasonable to allow more time for the body to comply with their duties under subsection (2) above in relation to that report or recommendation;

(b) the Controller of Audit is so satisfied in the case of any body to which a copy of a report under section 102(1) or (2) of the 1973 Act has been sent; or

(c) the Scottish Accounts Commission is so satisfied in the case of any body to which a recommendation under section 103(1) of the 1973 Act has been sent,

the auditor, Controller of Audit or, as the case may be, Scottish Accounts Commission may, in relation to that report or recommendation, extend the period of four months mentioned in subsection (2)(a) above or (where it has already been extended under this subsection on one or more previous occasions) further extend it.

(4) Nothing in section 101 of the 1972 Act (delegation of functions) shall apply to any duty imposed by this section on a body to which this section applies; and the duty imposed by this section on any body in Scotland shall be discharged only by that body.

(5) In subsection (3) of section 18 of the 1982 Act (which imposes an obligation to take an auditor's report into consideration as soon as practicable after it is received), for the words from "as soon as" to the end of the subsection there shall be substituted the words "in accordance with sections 5 and 6 of the Local Government Act 1992, or in the case of a body to which that section 5 does not apply, as soon as practicable after they receive the report".

(6) This section applies—
(a) to every body with which the Audit Commission is concerned, other than one falling within any of paragraphs (b) to (h) of section 1(8) above; and
(b) to every local authority, joint board or joint committee, within the meaning of the 1973 Act.

(7) This section shall be without prejudice to any duties (so far as they relate to the subject-matter of a report or recommendation sent to a body to which this section applies) which are imposed by or under Part III of the 1982 Act or Part VII of the 1973 Act (accounts and audit in England and Wales and in Scotland), sections 114 to 116 of the Local Government Finance Act 1988 (functions and reports of finance officers), section 5 of the Local Government and Housing Act 1989 (functions of monitoring officers) or any other enactment.

DEFINITIONS
"the 1972 Act": s.28(1).
"the 1973 Act": s.28(1).
"the 1982 Act": s.28(1).
"auditor": s.28(1).
"the Scottish Accounts Commission": s.28(1).

GENERAL NOTE
Under s.15(3) of the Local Government Finance Act 1982, an auditor must consider whether, in the public interest, he should make a report on any matter coming to his notice in the course of the audit in order that it may be considered by the body concerned or brought to the attention of the public. This may be an "immediate report" rather than a report at the conclusion of the audit. The report must be sent by the auditor to the body concerned or, in the case of a parish meeting, to the chairman; and (at present) the body must take it into account as soon as practicable after it has received it (the 1982 Act, s.18(3)). The report must also be sent to the Audit Commission and included in the agenda supplied to members for the meeting at which it is to be considered (the 1982 Act, s.18(4), (5)), and it may be inspected by members of the public (the 1982 Act, s.18A, inserted by the Local Government Finance (Publicity for Auditors' Reports) Act 1991, s.1(2)).

In Scotland, the Controller of Audit (an officer appointed by the Scottish Accounts Commission) must make to the Commission such reports as it may require, and may make a report to the Commission on any matter arising out of the accounts in order that those matters may be considered by the local authority concerned or brought to the attention of the public. The report must be sent to any local authority named in it, and may be sent to any other person; the local authority must supply a copy to each member and make additional copies available for inspection (the 1973 Act, s.102, as amended by the Local Government and Housing Act 1989, s.185). The Commission must consider any report made to it by the Controller of Audit, and may thereafter make to the Secretary of State or any local authority such recommendation as appears to it appropriate in the light of the report (the 1973 Act, s.103(1)). (The Controller of Audit must also make a special report to the Commission where (*inter alia*) he is of the opinion that any item of account is contrary to law; this may lead to an order by the Secretary of State, acting on the recommendation of the Commission, that the person responsible reimburse the local authority: the 1973 Act, ss.102(3), (4); 103(2)–(7). This procedure is not affected by the present section.)

The present section, implementing proposals in the *Citizen's Charter* (Cm. 1599, 1991) paras. 38–39, strengthens the obligations of certain bodies which are the subject of an auditor's report. In the case of every body with which the Audit Commission is concerned (other than those listed in s.1(8)(*b*) to (*h*)), and every local authority, joint board or joint committee within the meaning of the Local Government (Scotland) Act 1973, the body must consider the auditor's report in accordance with ss.5 and 6 of the present Act. The same obligations apply, in England and Wales, to other written recommendations made by the auditor under subs. (1)(*b*) or, in Scotland, a recommendation made by the Scottish Accounts Commission under s.103(1) of the 1973 Act. Where s.5 does not apply (*i.e.* in respect of the bodies listed in s.1(8)(*b*) to (*h*)), the obligation under the 1982 Act, s.18(3), remains that of considering the report as soon as practicable (see subs. (5)).

Where s.5 does apply, the obligation is for the body to consider the report within four months, and to decide what action should be taken in response (subs. (2)). The time limit may be extended (subs. (3)). The duties under this section cannot be delegated (subs. (4)).

Subs. 1(b)

This provision introduces a new power for the auditor, in England and Wales, to make a written recommendation which is to be considered in accordance with the procedure laid down by ss.5 and 6.

Subs. (4)

Section 101 of the Local Government Act 1972 gives wide powers whereby local authorities may arrange for the discharge of functions by a committee, sub-committee or officer, or by another local authority. These powers are excluded in relation to the exercise of a number of functions of which this is the latest. Others include the power to levy on issue a precept for a rate (the 1972 Act, s.101(6), as amended), and functions in setting amounts for personal community charges and issuing a precept under the Local Government Finance Act 1988 (s.139).

Subs. (6)

Body with which the Audit Commission is concerned. See note to s.1(7), (8).
Local authority, joint board or joint committee. See note to s.1(7).

Subs. (7)

The present section applies without prejudice to the duties imposed in connection with accounts and audit, the functions and reports of finance officers and the functions of monitoring officers, or by any other enactment. Part III of the Local Government Finance Act 1982 and Pt. VII of the Local Government (Scotland) Act 1973 regulate the accounts and audit of local authorities. Sections 114 to 116 of the Local Government Act 1988 impose duties on the chief finance officer (*i.e.* the person having responsibility for the administration of the financial affairs of a local authority under the Local Government Act 1972, s.151 (county, district, London borough, parish or community councils), the Local Government Act 1985, s.73 (joint authorities), or the 1988 Act, s.112 (combined police or fire authorities)). The *chief finance officer* must make a report where it appears to him that the authority, a committee or officer of the authority, or a joint committee on which the authority is represented, has made or is about to make a decision which will lead to unlawful expenditure, or will involve unlawful action likely to cause a loss or deficiency, or is about to enter an item of account the entry of which is unlawful. He must also make a report where it appears to him that the authority's expenditure is likely to exceed its available resources. The *monitoring officer* must make a report where it appears to him that any proposal, decision or omission by the authority, a committee, sub-committee or officer of the authority, or by any joint committee on which the authority is represented may contravene any enactment, rule of law or code of practice, or constitute maladministration. Reports must be considered by the relevant authority.

Publicity requirements for meetings under s.5

6.—(1) A meeting shall not be held for the purposes of section 5 above unless, at least seven clear days before the meeting, there has been published, in a newspaper circulating in the area of the body concerned, a notice which—
> (a) states the time and place of the meeting;
> (b) indicates that the meeting is to be held in order for consideration to be given to a report by an auditor or the Controller of Audit or, as the case may be, to a recommendation of an auditor or of the Scottish Accounts Commission; and
> (c) describes the subject-matter of that report or recommendation.

(2) It shall be the duty of a body who have held a meeting for the purposes of section 5 above to ensure—
> (a) that the relevant authority is notified, as soon as practicable after the end of the meeting, of the decisions made at that meeting in pursuance of subsection (2)(b) of that section; and
> (b) that a notice containing such a summary of those decisions as has been approved by the relevant authority is published, as soon as practicable after the end of the meeting, in a newspaper circulating in that body's area.

(3) A notice published for the purposes of subsection (2)(b) above in relation to any meeting—
> (a) shall not be required to summarise any decision made while the public were excluded from the meeting—

       (i) under section 100A(2) of the 1972 Act or section 50A(2) of the 1973 Act (confidential matters);
       (ii) in pursuance of a resolution under section 100A(4) of the 1972 Act or section 50A(4) of the 1973 Act (exempt information); or
       (iii) in pursuance of a resolution under section 1(2) of the Public Bodies (Admission to Meetings) Act 1960 (protection of public interest);
  but

(b) in a case where sections 100C and 100D of the 1972 Act or sections 50C and 50D of the 1973 Act (availability for inspection after meetings of minutes, background papers and other documents) apply in relation to the meeting, shall indicate the documents in relation to that meeting which are open for inspection in accordance with those sections.

(4) In subsection (2) above "the relevant authority"—

(a) in relation to a meeting of any body with which the Audit Commission is concerned, means the auditor of that body's accounts;

(b) in relation to a meeting for the consideration of a report of the Controller of Audit, means the Controller of Audit; and

(c) in relation to a meeting for the consideration of a recommendation from the Scottish Accounts Commission, means that Commission.

(5) This section, so far as it has effect in relation to a meeting under section 5 above, shall so have effect without prejudice to, and in addition to, any provision made in relation to meetings of the body in question by section 18(5) of the 1982 Act (information in advance of meetings to consider auditor's report) or by or under the 1972 Act, the 1973 Act, the Public Bodies (Admission to Meetings) Act 1960 or any other enactment.

DEFINITIONS
  "the 1972 Act": s.28(1).
  "the 1973 Act": s.28(1).
  "the 1982 Act": s.28(1).
  "the Audit Commission": s.28(1).
  "auditor": s.28(1).
  "the relevant authority": subs. (4).
  "the Scottish Accounts Commission": s.28(1).

GENERAL NOTE
  This section imposes publicity requirements in respect of meetings of local authorities and other bodies held to consider auditor's reports or recommendations in accordance with s.5. Public notice must be given in a local newspaper at least seven clear days before the meeting, and a notice summarising the decisions made at the meeting must also be published as soon as practicable thereafter. The latter notice is not required to summarise any decision made while the public are excluded from the meeting. The auditor (in England and Wales) or the Controller of Audit or the Scottish Accounts Commission (in Scotland) must also be notified.

Subs. (1)
  Seven clear days. The day on which the notice is given and the day of the meeting are excluded: see *R. v. Hereford Justices* (1820) 3 B. & Ald. 581.

Publication of information by the Audit Commission

Publication of information by the Audit Commission

7.—(1) Subject to the following provisions of this section, the Audit Commission shall have power to publish such information as it thinks fit with respect to any of the matters mentioned in subsection (2) below.

(2) The matters referred to in subsection (1) above are—

(a) a contravention by a body with which that Commission is concerned of any obligation imposed on that body by virtue of subsection (2) of section 1 above;

(b) the making by an auditor of a report under section 15(3) of the 1982 Act to any such body, the subject-matter of any such report and the decision made and other action taken by any such body in response to the receipt of any such report or to anything contained in it;

(c) a contravention by any such body of any regulations made under section 23 of the 1982 Act (regulations with respect to accounts).

(3) The information that may be published by virtue of subsection (2)(b) above shall not include—

(a) information with respect to a report made to a health service body, within the meaning of Part III of the 1982 Act, or to any decision or other action by such a body; or

(b) information excluded under subsection (3)(a) of section 6 above from any notice published for the purposes of subsection (2)(b) of that section.

(4) The information that may be published under this section shall include information with respect to a contravention which occurred, to a report which was made and to any decision or action which was made or taken before the coming into force of this section.

(5) Before publishing any information under this section relating to—

(a) the conduct or decisions of any body with which it is concerned; or

(b) a report made to any such body,

the Audit Commission shall notify that body of its proposal to publish the information.

(6) Information published under this section shall be published in such manner as the Audit Commission considers appropriate for bringing the information to the attention of those members of the public who may be interested.

DEFINITIONS
"the 1982 Act": s.28(1).
"the Audit Commission": s.28(1).
"auditor": s.28(1).
"contravention": s.28(1).

GENERAL NOTE
The Audit Commission is given power to publish in any way it considers appropriate for bringing it to the attention of the public, information relating to the contravention of any obligation imposed by s.1(2); the making of an auditor's report and the response of the body concerned to it; and the contravention of any accounts regulations (currently the Accounts and Audit Regulations 1983 (S.I. 1983 No. 1761)). The information is not to include information in respect of a report made to a health service body or information excluded by s.6(3)(a) from any notice published under s.6(2)(b). The Audit Commission must first notify the body concerned of its proposal to publish the information.

Competition

Application of competitive tendering to professional services etc.

8.—(1) The Secretary of State may by order make such provision in relation to proposals for the carrying out of work to which this section applies as he considers appropriate for facilitating or requiring separate procedures to be followed for—

(a) the evaluation for the purposes of Part I of the 1988 Act of the quality of the services which persons willing to carry out the work are able to provide and of their fitness to provide them; and

(b) the evaluation for those purposes of the financial terms on which such persons would carry out the work.

(2) This section applies to any work which—
(a) by virtue of an order under section 2(3) of the 1988 Act, falls within a defined activity for the purposes of Part I of that Act; and
(b) consists in, or involves, the provision of professional advice or of other professional services or the application of any financial or technical expertise.

(3) Before making an order under this section the Secretary of State shall consult such representatives of local government as appear to him to be appropriate.

(4) The power to make an order under this section shall be exercisable by statutory instrument; and no such order shall be made unless a draft of the order has been laid before, and approved by a resolution of, each House of Parliament.

(5) The power to make an order under this section shall include power—
(a) to make such incidental, consequential, transitional or supplementary provision as the Secretary of State thinks necessary or expedient; and
(b) to make different provision for different cases, including different provision for different localities and for different authorities;
and the power conferred by virtue of paragraph (a) above shall include power, for the purposes of, or in connection with, any separate procedures for which an order under this section provides, to modify any of the provisions of Part I of the 1988 Act.

(6) The powers conferred by this section shall be without prejudice to the power conferred by section 15(8)(a) of the 1988 Act (power to make incidental modifications in connection with an order extending the defined activities).

DEFINITIONS
"the 1988 Act": s.28(1).

GENERAL NOTE
This section enables the Secretary of State to extend the scope of compulsory competitive tendering to certain professional and other services. The Government's provisional proposals for the extension of CCT, as explained in *Competing for Quality. Competition in the Provision of Local Services: A Consultation Paper* (November 1991), fell into two groups. The first group were those where extension could be achieved by an order under Pt. I of the Local Government Act 1988. These included, firstly, manual activities which were either not included in or exempted from the original arrangements under the 1988 Act: the cleaning of police buildings, and the maintenance of police vehicles, the maintenance of fire service vehicles and the provision of home-to-school transport; and secondly, the management of theatres and arts facilities, public library support services (*i.e.* the tasks of acquisition, cataloguing and processing of books and other materials), and the provision and management of local authority parking services under the Road Traffic Act 1991. The second group comprised professional services related to construction, and corporate services. The present section deals with the first of these matters: the extension of CCT requirements to a proportion of corporate services (corporate and administrative services, legal services, financial services, personnel services and computing services) in the view of the Government depends on the prior establishment (by further primary legislation) of a system of internal trading accounts (*Consultation Paper*, pp. 25–34). What is intended to be covered at this stage are architectural, engineering and property management services (*Consultation Paper*, pp. 21–25). The Government acknowledged that the tendering framework of Pt. I of the 1988 Act would require modification. In particular, "the assessment of quality in professional services is more complicated because the services are more difficult to specify and performance is harder to measure" (Robert Key, Parliamentary Under-Secretary of State for the Environment, Standing Committee D, February 11, 1992, col. 243). The modified tendering procedures contemplated by the Government were that "tenderers would have to cross an initial quality threshold, and that the choice between tenders that had crossed the threshold would be made solely on the basis of price" (*Consultation Paper*, p. 22). This could be achieved by a "double-envelope" procedure, whereby unpriced tenders are critically evaluated against a pre-set quality threshold, and the lowest-priced tender among those meeting or exceeding the quality threshold is automatically accepted. (This was in essence the

scheme for the allocation of Channel 3 television licences by the Independent Television Commission under the Broadcasting Act 1990.)

Accordingly, the section also enables the Secretary of State to modify the application of Pt. I of the 1988 Act to the services to which the section applies.

Subs. (1)

This subsection enables the Secretary of State to make an order setting out tendering procedures for the categories of work set out in subs. (2) that involve separate procedures for (1) the evaluation of the quality of services which tenderers may provide; and (2) the evaluation of the price of those services.

Subs. (2)

The section applies to the provision of professional services or the application of financial or technical expertise in relation to activities which are "defined activities" for the purposes of Pt. I of the Local Government Act 1988 by virtue of an order made by the Secretary of State under s.2(3) of that Act (power to add to the list of defined activities). Accordingly it does not apply to the defined activities set out in s.2(2) of the 1988 Act (collection of refuse; cleaning of buildings; other cleaning; catering for purposes of schools and welfare; other catering; maintenance of ground; and repair and maintenance of vehicles), where related professional and financial services are already covered by the 1988 Act. The intention is to apply the section to professional services relating to construction work, which is subject to the different régime for competitive tendering under Pt. III of the Local Government, Planning and Land Act 1980. Accordingly, an order under s.2(3) of the 1988 Act will be necessary as well as an order under the present section for implementation of the Government's proposal.

Subs. (3)

Consult. See *Rollo* v. *Minister of Town and Country Planning* [1948] 1 All E.R. 13 and *R.* v. *Secretary of State for the Environment*, ex p. *Association of Metropolitan Authorities* [1986] 1 W.L.R. 1.

Subs. (4)

An order under this section requires an affirmative resolution of each House of Parliament.

Subs. (5)

An order under this section may make incidental, consequential, transitional or supplementary provision, and may modify provisions of Pt. I of the 1988 Act in relation to any separate procedures established by such an order.

Power to define conduct as competitive or anti-competitive

9.—(1) The Secretary of State may by regulations make provision, for the purposes of one or more of the conditions mentioned in subsection (2) below, for conduct described in the regulations to be regarded, in accordance with the regulations and in such circumstances as may be so described—

(a) as conduct which has the effect of restricting, preventing or distorting competition or is likely to have that effect; or

(b) as conduct which does not have that effect and is not likely to have that effect.

(2) The conditions referred to in subsection (1) above are—

(a) the condition specified in section 7(1A) of the 1980 Act (competition condition in the case of certain works contracts);

(b) the condition specified in section 9(aaaa) of the 1980 Act (competition condition applying in the case of prescribed construction or maintenance work);

(c) the condition set out in section 4(5) of the 1988 Act (competition condition in the case of works contracts relating to work falling within a defined activity);

(d) the condition set out in section 7(7) of the 1988 Act (competition condition in the case of functional work falling within such an activity).

(3) Without prejudice to the generality of subsection (1) above or to any power conferred by section 8 of the 1988 Act (regulations with respect to fulfilment of conditions), regulations under this section may—

(a) prescribe the matters which are to be taken into account, or disregarded, in the course of any evaluation made for the purpose of deciding who should undertake or carry out particular work;

(b) prescribe the manner in which, or extent to which, any matter described in the regulations is to be so taken into account or disregarded;

(c) prescribe maximum and minimum periods for the periods which are required, by virtue of paragraphs (b) and (d) of subsection (2) of section 7 of the 1988 Act, to be specified in a notice published for the purposes of subsection (1) of that section (periods for inspection of specification and for notifying an authority of a wish to tender);

(d) prescribe a maximum and a minimum period for the period which is to elapse, in a case where a notice has been so published, between—

(i) the announcement of the decision as to who should carry out the work in question; and

(ii) the beginning of the period during which the work is to be carried out;

(e) make provision for the issue by the Secretary of State for guidance as to how conduct restricting, distorting or preventing competition is to be avoided in the doing of anything under or for the purposes of Part III of the 1980 Act or Part I of the 1988 Act; and

(f) require the extent (if any) to which there has been a contravention of guidance issued by the Secretary of State under the regulations to be taken into account in any determination of whether or not a condition mentioned in subsection (2) above has been fulfilled.

(4) The power to make regulations under this section shall be exercisable by statutory instrument subject to annulment in pursuance of a resolution of either House of Parliament; and that power shall include power—

(a) to make such incidental, consequential, transitional or supplementary provision as the Secretary of State thinks necessary or expedient; and

(b) to make different provision for different cases, including different provision for different localities and for different bodies.

DEFINITIONS
"the 1980 Act": s.28(1).
"the 1988 Act": s.28(1).
"contravention": s.28(1).

GENERAL NOTE
This section gives the Secretary of State a further broad regulation-making power to define conduct as competitive or anti-competitive and to structure the tendering process. A number of provisions in existing legislation (those set out in subs. (2)) impose a "competition condition", *i.e.* a condition that either the local authority or the other party to the contract has not acted "in a manner having the effect or intended or likely to have the effect of restricting, distorting or preventing competition". This form of provision was introduced in the Local Government Act 1988, and that Act inserted similar provisions into the Local Government, Planning and Land Act 1980. The 1988 Act did not give the Secretary of State power to specify matters which might be deemed to be anti-competitive (*cf.* his power under s.19(1) of the 1988 Act to add to the list of "non-commercial" matters for the purposes of s.17 of that Act). Instead, the Secretary of State gave detailed guidance in DOE Circular 1/91, *Local Government Act 1988 Part I. Competition in the Provision of Local Authority Services*, as to matters which might provide prima facie evidence that competition had been restricted, distorted or prevented. The Secretary of State would take these matters into account when considering whether to use his powers to impose sanctions under ss.13 and 14 of the 1988 Act.

In the paper *Competing for Quality. Competition in the Provision of Local Services: A Consultation Paper*, the Government stated (p. 4) that too many authorities had sought to "bend the rules" to cushion their workforces against the full force of competition. In the 18 months following the first deadline for competition under the 1988 Act, directions were given to 10 local authorities for anti-competitive behaviour. The Government's aim was therefore to introduce "greater clarity about what constitutes anti-competitive behaviour" and "more effective action where it appears that such behaviour has occurred" (*ibid.*).

Subs. (1)
This subsection gives the Secretary of State power to make regulations defining conduct as competitive or anti-competitive for the purposes of one or more of the "competition conditions" specified in subs. (2).

Subs. (2)
This subsection specifies the "competition conditions" to which regulations under subs. (1) may apply. In the 1980 Act, such a condition is found in s.7(1A) in relation to works contracts (*i.e.* contracts for construction or maintenance work carried out by a local authority for another public body) and in s.9(4) (*aaaa*) in relation to functional work (*i.e.* construction or maintenance work undertaken by a local authority otherwise than under a works contract). In the 1988 Act, a competition condition is found in s.4(5) in relation to works contracts (*i.e.* contracts for the carrying out of work by "defined authorities", such as local authorities (s.1)) where the work falls within the scope of a "defined activity" (see note to s.8(2)). Such a condition is also found in s.7(7) in relation to functional work (*i.e.* work carried out by a defined authority other than under a works contract) falling within a defined activity.

Subs. (3)
This subsection sets out further matters which may be included in regulations made under subs. (1). These matters relate in various ways to the tendering process.

Subs. (3)(a), (b)
These matters are concerned with the evaluation of tenders for work subject to CCT requirements. The Secretary of State may use his power to make regulations prescribing both *what* matters are to be taken into account or disregarded during the evaluation of tenders, and the *manner* in which this is to be done. It is intended to use this power to specify cost items which local authorities can, or cannot, take into account in tender evaluation (*Consultation Paper*, pp. 8–9). Thus regulations would exclude from consideration a number of items (already identified in guidance contained in DOE Circular 1/91) as not to be taken into account: frozen holiday payments; immediate payment of accrued superannuation benefits or pension increase payments in respect of and costs arising from discretionary awards of compensation to staff made redundant; and costs of accommodation, storage or central administration which may not be immediately saved where a service is taken over by an external contractor. In addition, the Government proposes to use regulations to exclude the cost of losses incurred if an incoming contractor does not wish to make use of depots and vehicles that have been made available to him; and that the cost of a performance bond should be subtracted from the external bid. On the other hand, the regulations would provide that the costs of disabled people, apprentices and trainees, and identified extra supervision costs may still be taken into account. The regulations would also make more detailed provision for the calculation of actual costs and/or savings incurred when comparing an external with an internal bid.

Subs. (3)(c), (d)
These matters are concerned with the timing of different stages of tendering exercises for work under the 1988 Act. The Government's *Consultation Paper* identified five main stages in the tendering exercise required by the 1988 Act:
(i) from publication of notice to notification of interest;
(ii) from notification of interest to invitation of tenders;
(iii) from invitation, to submission, of tenders;
(iv) from submission of tenders to announcement of award;
(v) from announcement of award to start of contract.
The Secretary of State has certain powers under existing legislation to specify minimum and maximum periods for some of these stages. The present section adds to these powers.
By s.7(1) of the 1988 Act, local authorities are required to publish a notice setting out their intention to invite tenders for work described in the notice, and stating certain other matters, including that any person may inspect and be supplied with a copy of a detailed specification of the work during a period specified in the notice, and that any person who may wish to carry out the work should notify the authority within a period specified in the notice (stage (i)). By s.7(3), the periods must be "reasonable". Subsection 3(c) enables the Secretary of State to prescribe

maximum and minimum periods for these purposes. The Government's *Consultation Paper* noted (p. 6) that it may prove anti-competitive if an authority sets too tight a timescale for the tendering process: the in-house workforce knows the work comprised in the contract and has a "head-start" if a tender has to be prepared quickly.

Under s.7(4) of the 1988 Act, local authorities must issue invitations to tender between three and six months after publication of the notice of the intention to go out to tender. Under s.8(2), the Secretary of State already has power to make regulations relating to such invitations, and the Government may use this power to specify minimum periods for the time allowed for tenders to be submitted (stage (iii)).

A further stage where there has not been a power to prescribe minimum and maximum periods is the period between the announcement of the decision to allocate work and the time when the work is to start. The Government's *Consultation Paper* noted (p. 6) that external contractors are less well-placed than in-house workforces to begin work at short notice, given, for example, the possible need to recruit staff or to acquire premises. Subsection (3)(*d*) gives the Secretary of State power to prescribe minimum and maximum periods for what the *Consultation Paper* refers to as the "mobilisation period" (stage (v)).

The Secretary of State has previously issued guidance in respect of stages (iii) and (v): DOE Circular 1/91, para. 35. He suggested a minimum of three months for stage (iii) where a contract represents a sizeable proportion of the authority's work, and one month for small jobs; and at least three months for stage (v) where substantial contracts are involved (see to the same effect Scottish Office Environment Department Circular 6/1991, Annex, para. 31, and Welsh Office Circular 10/91, para. 33). The Government intends to adopt a similar approach when exercising the new regulation-making powers, specifying three months for stages (iii) and (v) (unless the annual value of a contract is £250,000 or less, in which case a shorter period may be specified) (*Consultation Paper*, p. 7). It is also minded to specify a minimum of two months for stage (i) (*ibid.*).

Subs. (3)(e)
Regulations may be made to enable the Secretary of State to give guidance as to how anti-competitive conduct is to be avoided for the purposes of both Pt. III of the 1980 Act and Pt. I of the 1987 Act.

Subs. (3)(f)
Regulations may require that contravention of guidance issued by virtue of subs. (3)(*e*) be taken into account in determining whether a competition condition has been fulfilled.

Subs. (4)
Regulations under this section are subject to annulment by either House of Parliament.

Publicity for tender specifications

10.—(1) This section applies where a relevant authority make a decision in consequence of which any work is required to be carried out (whether by the authority themselves or by some other person) in accordance with a specification which has been either—

(a) prepared for the purposes of an invitation issued for the purposes of section 9(4)(a) of the 1980 Act (competitive tendering for construction and maintenance work); or

(b) made available for inspection in accordance with a notice published for the purposes of section 7(1) of the 1988 Act (competitive tendering for other functional work).

(2) Where this section applies, it shall be the duty of the authority making the decision—

(a) to make arrangements for—
    (i) a copy of the specification; and
    (ii) a document containing a summary of the main requirements of the specification,
    to be kept available, throughout the period during which the work in question is to be carried out, for inspection by members of the public, at all reasonable hours, at the principal office of the authority; and

(b) to give such publicity to those arrangements as they think sufficient for drawing the attention of members of the public who may be interested to the fact that the specification and that document are so available.

(3) In this section "relevant authority" means any body which is a local authority or development body within the meaning of Part III of the 1980 Act or a defined authority within the meaning of Part I of the 1988 Act.

DEFINITIONS
"the 1980 Act": s.28(1).
"the 1988 Act": s.28(1).
"relevant authority": subs. (3).

GENERAL NOTE
This section extends the requirements as to publicity for tender specifications.

Subs. (1)
Section 9(4)(*a*) of the 1980 Act, as amended by Sched. 1 of the present Act, requires the preparation of a detailed specification of functional work which is subject to competitive tendering requirements under the Act. Section 7(1), (2) of the 1988 Act requires publication of a notice stating that a detailed specification of functional work subject to competitive tendering requirements under the Act will be made available for inspection; s.7(3)(*b*) requires the specification to be made available for inspection. Additional requirements in respect of these specifications are imposed by the remainder of this section.

Subs. (2)
Under s.7(1)–(3) of the 1988 Act, the detailed specifications may be inspected by "any person" during the period specified in the notice published under s.7(1). In practice, "the ability to look at tender specifications has been used mainly by potential tenderers in advance of the deadline for the submission of tenders" (*Consultation Paper*, p. 13). This subsection requires the authority to arrange for a copy of the detailed specification, and a summary, to be kept available for inspection by members of the public throughout the period of the contract. The authority must publicise these arrangements. This will enable "the public for whom the services are being provided" to "ascertain whether the standards set for those services are being met" as part of implementation of the Citizen's Charter (*Consultation Paper*, p. 13).

Schedule 1 amends s.9(4) of the 1980 Act by introducing requirements for the preparation of detailed specifications on the pattern of those required under the 1988 Act. The publicity requirements of the present section will also apply to specifications prepared for the purposes of the 1980 Act.

Subs. (3)
Defined authority. "Defined authorities", for the purposes of Pt. I of the 1988 Act, are listed in s.1 of that Act.
Local authority or development body. "Local authorities" and "development bodies", for the purposes of Pt. III of the 1980 Act, are defined in s.20(1) of that Act.

Amendments of competition provisions

11. Part III of the 1980 Act and Part I of the 1988 Act (competition provisions) shall have effect with the amendments specified in Schedule 1 to this Act.

DEFINITIONS
"the 1980 Act": s.28(1).
"the 1988 Act": s.28(1).

GENERAL NOTE
Schedule 1 amends provisions of Pt. III of the 1980 Act and Pt. I of the 1988 Act.

PART II

LOCAL GOVERNMENT CHANGES FOR ENGLAND

The Local Government Commission

The Local Government Commission for England

12.—(1) There shall be a body corporate to be known as the Local

Government Commission for England (in this Part referred to as "the Local Government Commission") for the purpose of carrying out the functions assigned to it by section 13 below.

(2) Schedule 2 to this Act shall have effect with respect to the Local Government Commission.

GENERAL NOTE
    This section establishes the Local Government Commission as a body corporate. It is to consist of between five and 15 members appointed by the Secretary of State, one member being appointed as chairman (Sched. 2, para. 1). The Commission is to appoint a chief executive, subject to the consent of the Secretary of State, and may appoint other staff (Sched. 2, para. 3). There are provisions, analogous to those applicable to local authorities, covering such matters as incidental powers, delegation of powers and members' interests (Sched. 2, paras. 4, 6, 7). The Commission is subject to investigation by the Parliamentary Commissioner for Administration, and its members are disqualified from membership of the House of Commons (Sched. 2, paras. 11, 12).
    The Commission is the fourth of its kind in the post-war period. There was, first, the Local Government Boundary Commission of 1945, brought to an end by the Local Government Commission Dissolution Act 1949; secondly, the Local Government Commission for England and the Local Government Commission for Wales set up in 1958 and dissolved by the Local Government Termination of Reviews Act 1967; and, thirdly, the Local Government Boundary Commission for England, established by Pt. IV of the Local Government Act 1972 and abolished by the present Act (s.24).
    The Commission is to perform the functions set out in s.13.
    In Wales, the Local Government Boundary Commission for Wales, also established by Pt. IV of the 1972 Act, is to continue.

Functions of the Local Government Commission

Duty to conduct reviews and make recommendations

    13.—(1) If the Secretary of State so directs, the Local Government Commission shall, in accordance with this Part and any directions given under it—

   (a) conduct a review of such areas in England as are specified in the direction or are of a description so specified; and

   (b) recommend to the Secretary of State as respects each of those areas either—

      (i) that he should make such structural, boundary or electoral changes as are specified in the recommendations; or

      (ii) that he should make no such changes.

    (2) It shall also be the duty of the Local Government Commission—

   (a) independently of any reviews under subsection (1) above, to conduct periodic reviews of every principal area in England for the purpose of determining whether recommendations should be made for electoral changes in that area; and

   (b) as respects any area reviewed, to recommend to the Secretary of State either—

      (i) that he should make such electoral changes as are specified in the recommendations; or

      (ii) that he should make no such changes.

    (3) So far as reasonably practicable, the first periodic review of any area under subsection (2) above shall be conducted not less than ten or more than fifteen years after the report of the Local Government Boundary Commission for England on a review under Schedule 9 to the 1972 Act (initial review of counties) was submitted to the Secretary of State in relation to the county in which that area, or the greater part of it, was comprised.

    (4) So far as reasonably practicable, subsequent reviews under subsection (2) above shall be conducted within the period of not less than ten or more than fifteen years from the submission to the Secretary of State of the last

report on a review under that subsection of any area comprising the whole or a substantial part of that area.

(5) Any structural, boundary or electoral changes recommended to the Secretary of State under this section shall be such as appear to the Local Government Commission desirable having regard to the need—

(a) to reflect the identities and interests of local communities; and

(b) to secure effective and convenient local government.

(6) The Secretary of State may give directions as to the exercise by the Local Government Commission of any functions under this section; and such directions may require that Commission to have regard to any guidance given by the Secretary of State as respects matters to be taken into account.

DEFINITIONS

"boundary change": s.14(1)(*b*), (3).
"electoral change": s.14(1)(*c*), (4).
"the Local Government Commission": s.28(1).
"principal area": s.28(1).
"structural change": s.14(1)(*a*), (2).

GENERAL NOTE

This section sets out the functions of the Local Government Commission. There are two main aspects of the Commission's work. First, it is to conduct reviews of areas in accordance with the directions of the Secretary of State and make recommendations for structural, boundary or electoral changes, as defined in s.14 (or that no changes should be made) (s.13(1)). This is intended to facilitate a move to unitary authorities in non-metropolitan counties, as explained in the General Note to the Act.

Secondly, the Commission is to take over responsibility for periodic reviews of electoral arrangements from the Local Government Boundary Commission for England (which is abolished by s.24). Section 50 of the Local Government Act 1972 required the Local Government Boundary Commission for England to undertake reviews of the electoral arrangements for counties not less than 10 or more than 15 years from the initial review of electoral arrangements made under Sched. 9 of the 1972 Act. This time-scale is now imposed on the Commission (s.13(3), (4)).

The changes recommended by the Commission must be such as appear to it desirable having regard to the need (a) to reflect the identities and interests of local communities and (b) to secure effective and convenient local government (s.13(5)).

The Secretary of State may give directions to the Commission, and these may require the Commission to have regard to guidance given by him as regards matters to be taken into account (s.13(6)).

In November 1991, the Secretary of State published for consultation draft *Guidance to the Local Government Commission for England*. This "policy guidance" follows the lines foreshadowed in the *Consultation Paper on The Structure of Local Government in England* (April 1991) and develops the points set out in s.13(5). Thus, local authority areas should be "based on communities", the Commission using its own judgment as to the best method of gauging community identities. The Government believes that this assessment "will suggest that unitary authorities could be the most beneficial structure for local government in most areas" (Draft Guidance, para. 5). The Commission should therefore "look for structures consisting of unitary authorities . . . unless there are clear reasons for different arrangements" (*ibid.*).

There need be no maximum or minimum size, but the areas must be such that authorities can carry out their functions effectively, and in ways which reflect community interests (*ibid.* para. 6). The structure should enable individual authorities to be responsible for all local government functions (except law and order), but without the presumption that each authority should deliver all its services in-house (*ibid.* paras. 6, 8). As regards law and order services, arrangements should be made if necessary for local government areas to be combined, in order to preserve as far as possible the existing structures for law and order services (*ibid.* para. 9). If necessary, the Commission should consider joint arrangements, but these "detract from accountability" and the Government intends them to be "very much the exception" (*ibid.* para. 11). Authorities must have an adequate tax and grant base so that they have financial stability (*ibid.* para. 13). Moreover, changes should be worthwhile and cost-effective (*ibid.* para. 14). (The Commission can seek advice from the Audit Commission on the impact of proposed structural changes on "economy, efficiency and effectiveness" (s.16)). The question of boundaries should be considered in "broad terms"; detailed boundary changes will normally be considered in due course after structural change has taken place (Draft Guidance, para. 15).

The Commission should also consider whether traditional counties might usefully be retained or recreated for non-administrative purposes, "including perhaps maps, boundary signs and appropriate heritage, cultural and sporting purposes" (*ibid.* para. 18).

The Draft Guidance also sets out considerations relevant to structural changes specific to the main local government services (Annex A).

Subs. (4)

Subsequent mandatory reviews of electoral arrangements must take place between 10 and 15 years from the last review under subs. (2).

Subs. (5)

The criterion in subs. (5)(*a*) is new; that in subs. (5)(*b*) is based on the terms of reference of the Local Government Boundary Commission.

Subs. (6)

This enables the Secretary of State to give directions to the Commission as to the exercise of its functions. By virtue of s.26(3), the power includes power to make different provision for different cases, including different provision for different localities and for different bodies. A direction may be varied or revoked by a subsequent direction, and there is power to rectify mistakes by order (s.27(6)).

Changes that may be recommended

14.—(1) For the purposes of this Part—

(a) a structural change is the replacement, in any non-metropolitan area, of the two principal tiers of local government with a single tier;

(b) a boundary change is any of the changes specified in subsection (3) below, whether made for the purpose of facilitating a structural change or independently of any such change; and

(c) an electoral change is a change of electoral arrangements for any local government area, whether made in consequence of any structural or boundary change or independently of any such change;

and recommendations by the Local Government Commission for any structural or boundary changes shall include such recommendations as to the matters mentioned in subsection (5) below as the Commission thinks appropriate in connection with the recommended changes.

(2) In subsection (1)(a) above—

(a) the reference to a non-metropolitan area is a reference to any area which is or, as a result of any recommended boundary change would be, a non-metropolitan county or a non-metropolitan district; and

(b) the reference to the replacement, in any such area, of the two principal tiers of local government with a single tier is a reference to either—

(i) the transfer to a council for a county consisting of that area of the functions in relation to that area of district councils; or

(ii) the transfer to a district council for that area of the functions in relation to that area of a county council.

(3) The changes mentioned in subsection (1)(b) above are—

(a) the alteration of a local government area, including the alteration of so much of the boundary of any such area as lies below the high-water mark of medium tides, but excluding the extension of any local government area into Wales;

(b) the constitution of a new local government area of any description outside Greater London by the amalgamation of two or more such areas of the like description or by the aggregation of parts of such areas of the like description or by the separation of part of any local government area;

(c) the abolition of a principal area of any description outside Greater London, or of a metropolitan county, and its distribution among other areas of the like description;

(d) the constitution of a new London borough by the amalgamation of two or more London boroughs or by the aggregation of parts of London boroughs or by the separation of part of a London borough;

(e) the abolition of a London borough and the distribution of its area among other London boroughs;

(f) the constitution of a new parish by—
    (i) the establishment as a parish of any area which is not a parish or part of one; or
    (ii) the aggregation of the whole or any part of any such area with one or more parishes or parts of parishes; and

(g) the abolition of a parish, with or without the distribution of its area among other parishes.

(4) In subsection (1)(c) above "electoral arrangements" means—

(a) in relation to a principal area—
    (i) the number of councillors of the council for that area;
    (ii) the number and boundaries of the electoral areas into which that area is for the time being divided for the purposes of the election of councillors;
    (iii) the number of councillors to be elected for any electoral area in that principal area and the years in which they are to be so elected; and
    (iv) the name of any electoral area;

(b) in relation to a parish council—
    (i) the number of councillors;
    (ii) the question whether or not the parish or (in the case of a common parish council) any of the parishes should be divided into wards for the purposes of the election of councillors;
    (iii) the number and boundaries of any such wards;
    (iv) the number of councillors to be elected for any such ward or, in the case of a common parish, for each parish; and
    (v) the name of any such ward.

(5) The matters mentioned in subsection (1) above are—

(a) the abolition of any local authority whose functions would all vest in another as a result of any recommended structural change or whose area would be abolished or otherwise substantially affected by any recommended boundary change;

(b) the establishment, as a county or district concil, of a new authority for any area which would result from any recommended boundary change involving the amalgamation or aggregation of areas or parts of areas or involving other substantial alterations of areas;

(c) the extent to which a structural or boundary change requires (whether because functions become vested in an authority for a smaller area or for any other reason connected with the change) that joint arrangements should be made in relation to functions affected by the change; and

(d) whether, in connection with any recommended structural change, any authority should, for the purpose of the vesting of functions under Part II of the Town and Country Planning Act 1990 (development plans) in that authority—
    (i) be treated as an authority to whose area Chapter I of that Part (unitary plans) applies, instead of Chapter II (structure and local plans); or
    (ii) be authorised to include any of the policies mentioned in section 37 or 38 of that Act (mineral and waste plans) in their local plan.

(6) For the purposes of this Part the establishment of a new authority as the county or district council for any area shall be taken to include provision, subject to any necessary electoral changes—

(a) for an existing county council to become the district council for any area comprising a part of a county or for any two or more such areas; or

(b) for an existing district council to become the county council for an area comprising any one or more districts.

(7) For the purposes of this section—

(a) a metropolitan district and a non-metropolitan district shall be regarded as local government areas of a like description and so shall a metropolitan county and a non-metropolitan county; and

(b) any county or district resulting from the amalgamation or aggregation of the whole or any part of a metropolitan area with the whole or any part of a non-metropolitan area shall be regarded as a non-metropolitan county or, as the case may be, district.

DEFINITIONS
"boundary change": s.14(1)(*b*), (3).
"electoral change": s.14(1)(*c*), (4).
"local authority": s.28(1).
"local government area": s.28(1).
"the Local Government Commission": s.28(1).
"principal area": s.28(1).
"structural change": s.14(1)(*a*), (2).

GENERAL NOTE
This section sets out the definitions of "structural", "boundary" and "electoral" changes for the purposes of Pt. II of the Act. Structural changes are those that comprise the establishment of a unitary authority in a non-metropolitan area (subss. (1)(*a*) and (2)). Boundary changes include the alteration or creation of a local government area; the abolition of a principal area outside Greater London or a metropolitan county; and the creation or abolition of a London borough or parish (subss. 1(*b*) and (3)). Such changes may be designed to facilitate a structural change, but may also arise independently (hence the inclusion of references to London and metropolitan counties). Electoral changes include changes in the numbers of councillors and the numbers and boundaries of electoral areas (subss. (1)(*c*) and (4)). Such changes may be made in consequence of a structural or boundary change, but may also arise independently.

Subs. (1)
This subsection introduces the concepts of structural, boundary and electoral changes, which are further defined in the remainder of the section. Where the Commission recommends structural or boundary changes, it must also include such consequential recommendations as it thinks appropriate concerning the matters set out in subs. (5).

Subs. (2)
A structural change is one that involves the establishment of a single tier of local government in a non-metropolitan area. Thus the county council may become the sole authority for the area of a non-metropolitan county, and a district council may become the sole authority for a non-metropolitan district. In each case, the area may be an existing area or an area as altered by boundary changes recommended by the Commission. No other structural changes, such as establishing an additional tier of local government or moving to a new two-tier arrangement, are possible under the Act.

Subs. (3)
Local government area. By virtue of s.28(1) this means a non-metropolitan county in England, a district in England, a London borough, a metropolitan county, Greater London, the City of London, the Inner Temple, the Middle Temple or a parish.
Principal area. By virtue of s.28(1) this means a non-metropolitan county in England, a district in England or a London borough.
"Boundary changes" include changes to a local government area; the constitution of a new local government area outside Greater London; the abolition of a principal area outside Greater London or a metropolitan county; the constitution of a new London borough or parish; the abolition of a London borough or parish. As with the forerunner to this section, s.47 of the Local Government Act 1972 (repealed by Sched. 4), there is no provision for the abolition of Greater London as a local government area or the creation of a county in it, and no provision for the abolition of the City of London or the Temples. However, the boundaries of Greater

London, the City and the Temples can be altered by virtue of subs. (3)(*a*) as these are "local government areas".

Possible changes under this subsection that may facilitate the move to unitary authorities include the amalgamation of or the aggregation of parts of two or more local government areas of the like description (such as the areas of two or more district councils), and the abolition of a principal area outside London and its distribution among other areas of the like description. A metropolitan district and a non-metropolitan district, and a metropolitan county and a non-metropolitan county are to be regarded, respectively, as local government areas of a like description (subs. (7)).

Subs. (3)(a)

In the case of some authorities, seaward boundaries are fixed by local Act, but generally speaking they are fixed by reference to the limit of medium tides. Section 71 of the Local Government Act 1972 enabled the Local Government Boundary Commissions for England and Wales to review so much of the boundary of a county that lies below the high-water mark of medium tides and does not form a common boundary with another county. Subsection (3)(*a*) gives a similar power to the Local Government Commission for England. Section 71 is amended by Sched. 3, para. 16, to apply only to the Local Government Boundary Commission for Wales.

In *Blackpool Pier Co.* v. *Fylde Union* (1877) 41 J.P. 344 it was held that the part of a pier lying beyond low-water mark was not part of the parish within the meaning of a provision substantially reproduced by s.71 of the 1972 Act.

A local government area cannot be extended into Wales by virtue of this section. Provision for the alteration of boundaries between English and Welsh counties was formerly made by the Local Government Act 1972, s.62, which is repealed by Sched. 4. This provided for joint reviews by the Local Government Boundary Commissions of England and Wales.

Subs. (5)

Recommendations by the Commission for structural or boundary changes must include such consequential recommendations as to the matters set out in this subsection as it thinks appropriate. These are the abolition of an authority that is no longer required; the establishment of a new county or district council for an area resulting from the amalgamation or substantial alteration of areas; the extent to which joint arrangements should be made in respect of the discharge of particular functions; and whether the arrangements for unitary plans or for structure and local plans under Pt. II of the Town and Country Planning Act 1990 should be applied, and whether an authority should be authorised to include mineral or waste plans in its local plan.

Subs. (5)(c)

The Commission may, if appropriate, recommend that joint arrangements be made in relation to functions affected by a structural or boundary change. If the recommendation is accepted by the Secretary of State, and it appears to him that satisfactory arrangements have not been made by the authorities concerned or will not be in force when the change comes into force, or have ceased or will cease, he may make an order establishing a joint authority (s.21).

Subs. (5)(d)

Part II of the Town and Country Planning Act 1990, as amended by Sched. 4 to the Planning Compensation Act 1991, applies the provisions governing unitary development plans to Greater London and the metropolitan counties and those concerning structure and local plans to the non-metropolitan counties. Sections 37 and 38 of the 1990 Act, as substituted by the 1991 Act, Sched. 4, para. 17, provide for the making of minerals local plans by mineral planning authorities (and by the local planning authority for a National Park), and for the inclusion of policies in respect of the deposit of refuse or waste (other than mineral waste) in waste local plans or minerals local plans. The Commission must decide whether a new unitary authority should prepare a unitary development plan, or whether the provisions as to structure and local plans should apply adjusted as appropriate to unitary authorities. In the latter case, it may be desirable for the local plan to include minerals or waste policies.

Subs. (6)

This subsection provides that the establishment of a new authority as the county or district council for an area may involve provision for the existing county council to become the district council for part of a county, or for an existing district council to become the county council for any one or more districts.

Subs. (7)

Metropolitan and non-metropolitan districts and metropolitan and non-metropolitan counties are to be regarded, respectively, as local government areas of a like description. There is thus no restriction on boundary changes involving both metropolitan and non-metropolitan areas. In such a case, the new area is to be regarded as non-metropolitan.

Procedure on a review

15.—(1) As soon as reasonably practicable after being directed to conduct a review, the Local Government Commission shall take such steps as it considers sufficient to secure that persons who may be interested in the review are informed of—

(a) the direction requiring that review to be conducted;

(b) any other directions under this Part which are relevant to the review; and

(c) the period within which representations with respect to the subject-matter of the review may be made.

(2) As soon as reasonably practicable after deciding to conduct a periodic review of any area under section 13(2) above, the Local Government Commission shall take such steps as it considers sufficient to secure that persons who may be interested in the review are informed of—

(a) the fact that the Commission is to conduct a periodic review of that area;

(b) any directions under this Part which are relevant to the review; and

(c) the period within which representations with respect to the subject-matter of the review may be made.

(3) In conducting a review, the Local Government Commission shall—

(a) take into consideration any representations made to it within the period mentioned in subsection (1)(c) or (2)(c) above;

(b) prepare draft recommendations and take such steps as it considers sufficient to secure that persons who may be interested in the recommendations are informed of them and of the period within which representations with respect to them may be made;

(c) deposit copies of the draft recommendations at the principal office of any principal council appearing to that Commission to be likely to be affected by them; and

(d) take into consideration any representations made to that Commission within that period.

(4) As soon as the Local Government Commission is in a position to submit to the Secretary of State a report on a review, it shall—

(a) submit such a report to him together with its recommendations;

(b) take such steps as it considers sufficient to secure that persons who may be interested in the recommendations are informed of them and of the period within which they may be inspected; and

(c) deposit copies of the recommendations at the principal office of any principal council appearing to that Commission to be likely to be affected by them.

(5) Copies of any draft recommendations deposited at the principal office of a principal council under subsection (3)(c) above, and of any recommendations deposited at any such office under subsection (4)(c) above, shall be kept available for inspection at that office throughout the period within which representations with respect to them may be made or, as the case may be, within which they may be inspected.

(6) Where the report on a review is submitted to the Secretary of State under subsection (4) above, he may, if he thinks fit, direct the Local Government Commission to conduct a further review of any area to which the report relates and to make revised recommendations as respects that area; and this section shall apply in relation to the further review with such modifications as may be specified in the direction.

(7) The Secretary of State may give directions as to the exercise by the Local Government Commission of any functions under this section; and

such directions may require that Commission to have regard to any guidance given by the Secretary of State as respects matters to be taken into account.

(8) This section shall have effect as if the Common Council of the City of London were a principal council and the City of London included the Inner Temple and the Middle Temple.

DEFINITIONS
"the Local Government Commission": s.28(1).
"principal council": s.28(1).

GENERAL NOTE
This section sets out the procedure for the conduct of a directed or a periodic review. Persons who may be interested in a review must be informed that it is to take place, of any relevant directions and of the period within which representations may be made. The Commission must take such representations into account, prepare draft recommendations, inform interested persons of them and deposit copies at the offices of affected councils and take into account further representations which are then made. The Commission then submits a report to the Secretary of State, and there are similar requirements to inform interested persons and deposit copies of the recommendations at the offices of affected councils. Deposited copies of recommendations must be available for inspection throughout the period within which representations may be made or within which they may be inspected. Following the submission of a report, the Secretary of State may direct the Commission to conduct a further review.

Subss. (3) and (4)
Council . . . likely to be affected. By s.28(3), references to a body affected by any recommendations, changes or orders under Pt. II include references to a body whose area or functions are so affected, or to a body which is to cease to exist in pursuance of the recommendations.

Subss. (6) and (7)
These subsections give the Secretary of State power to give directions to the Commission requiring a further review or as to the procedure of a review. (*Cf.* the power to give directions as to the principles governing recommendations for change under s.13(6)). By virtue of s.26(3), a power to give directions includes power to make different provision for different cases, including different provision for different localities and for different bodies. A direction may be varied or revoked by a subsequent direction, and there is power to rectify mistakes by order (s.26(6)).

Subs. (8)
The Common Council of the City of London is treated as a principal council, and the Temples as part of the City, for the purpose of the deposit of copies of recommendations.

Consultation with the Audit Commission

16.—(1) The Audit Commission shall, if so required by the Local Government Commission, provide it with a written opinion as to the likely impact of any proposed structural changes on economy, efficiency and effectiveness in the provision of services provided by such bodies with which the Audit Commission is concerned as are likely to be affected by the changes.

(2) The Audit Commission may require any body with which it is concerned to supply the Audit Commission with all such information as it may reasonably require for the provision of an opinion under this section.

(3) The Audit Commission shall charge the Local Government Commission such fees for opinions provided under this section as will cover the full cost of providing them.

DEFINITIONS
"the Audit Commission": s.28(1).
"the Local Government Commission": s.28(1).
"structural change": s.14(1)(*a*), (2).

GENERAL NOTE
The Audit Commission may be required by the Local Government Commission to give its opinion on the likely impact of proposed structural changes on economy, efficiency and

effectiveness. The Audit Commission's expenses are to be met by the Local Government Commission.

Subss. (1) and (2)
  Body with which the Audit Commission is concerned. See note to s.1(8).

Subs. (1)
  Body . . . likely to be affected. See s.28(3).

Implementation of recommendations

Implementation of recommendations by order

17.—(1) Where the Local Government Commission submit to the Secretary of State a report on a review together with its recommendations, he may, if he thinks fit, by order give effect to all or any of the recommendations, with or without modifications.

(2) No order under this section shall be made before the end of the period of six weeks beginning with the submission of the report; and before making such an order, the Secretary of State may by a direction require the Local Government Commission to supply him with such additional information as may be described in the direction.

(3) An order under this section may, in particular, include provision which, for the purpose of giving effect (with or without modifications) to recommendations of the Local Government Commission, makes provision with respect to—

(a) the area of any authority and the name of any such area;

(b) the name of any authority;

(c) the establishment of any new authority for any county or district or the winding up and dissolution of any existing authority;

(d) the total number of councillors of any authority, the apportionment of councillors among electoral areas, the assignment of existing councillors to new or altered electoral areas, and the first election of councillors for any new or altered electoral area;

(e) without prejudice to paragraph (d) above, the holding of a fresh election of councillors for all electoral areas in a local government area where substantial changes have been made to some of those areas, or the order of retirement of councillors for any electoral areas in the local government area in question;

(f) in the case of an order relating to the system of election of district councillors, the ordinary year of election and the order of retirement of parish councillors for any parish situated in the district;

(g) the constitution and election of public bodies in any area affected by the order;

(h) the abolition or establishment, or the restriction or extension, of the jurisdiction of any public body in or over any part of any area affected by the order.

(4) The power to make an order under this section shall include power to make any such provision in relation to the other provisions of that order, or to the provisions of any previous order under this section, as is equivalent to that which may be contained in regulations under section 19 below or in an agreement under section 20 below.

(5) Without prejudice to the preceding provisions of this section, where charter trustees have been constituted under section 246 of the 1972 Act for an area which is altered by an order under this section and subsection (8) of that section (incorporation of whole or part of trustees' area in parish) does not apply, the order may make such provision with respect to the charter trustees as appears to the Secretary of State to be appropriate.

DEFINITIONS
"the 1972 Act": s.28(1).
"local government area": s.28(1).
"the Local Government Commission": s.28(1).
"public body": s.28(1).

GENERAL NOTE
This section provides for the implementation of the Local Government Commission's recommendations by an order made by the Secretary of State. The Secretary of State has a discretion whether to give effect to the recommendations, and he may give effect to all or any of them, with or without modifications. The section is modelled on s.51 of the Local Government Act 1972, which is repealed by Sched. 4.

Subs. (1)
This enables the Secretary of State to make orders implementing recommendations by the Commission. Orders are to be made by statutory instrument; such a statutory instrument is to be subject to annulment by either House of Parliament unless it effects a structural change, establishes a joint authority or effects only electoral changes or relates only to parishes (s.26(1)). Orders effecting a structural change or establishing a joint authority require the affirmative resolution of each House (s.26(2)). The order may make provision for different cases, including different provision for different localities and different bodies (s.26(3)).

Subs. (2)
A period of six weeks must elapse between the submission of a report and the making of an order, allowing time for objections to be made to the proposals. The Secretary of State may require additional information from the Commission. See further s.26(3), (6), on powers to give directions.

Subs. (3)
This subsection sets out the matters which may be included in an order made by the Secretary of State under subs. (1).

Subs. (4)
An order under subs. (1) may include provision equivalent to that which may be contained in supplementary regulations made by the Secretary of State under s.19 or agreements made by public bodies affected by a Pt. II order under s.20.

Subs. (5)
Charter trustees were established under s.246 of the Local Government Act 1972 where the powers, privileges and rights of an existing city or borough did not pass to a district council (under s.245 of the 1972 Act) or to a parish council constituted by reference to the area of the former city or borough. Charter trustees may elect one of their number to be city or town mayor and another to be deputy city or town mayor, and may exercise any powers to appoint local officers of dignity or other ceremonial rights. Where charter trustees have been constituted under s.246 for an area altered by an order under subs. (1), and all or part of the area becomes part of a parish, the charter trustees cease to act for that area or part (the 1972 Act, s.246(8)). Otherwise, the Secretary of State may include in the order such provision as appears to him appropriate (subs. (5)).

Consequences of structural changes etc.

18.—(1) Where an order under section 17 above gives effect to any structural change by which the functions of district councils in relation to any area are transferred to a council for a county consisting of that area, then the county council—

    (a) shall, for any financial year beginning at the same time as or after the coming into force of the change, be a billing authority for the purposes of Part I of the Local Government Finance Act 1992 in relation to their area; and

    (b) shall not, for any such year, be a major precepting authority for those purposes.

(2) An order under section 17 above which contains provision for a structural change—

(a) shall include provision for any district the council for which are, under the order, to have the functions of a county council in relation to that district to be treated as a county for the purposes of the Police Act 1964; and

(b) may provide, for the purposes of the approval or making of an amalgamation scheme under Part I of that Act, that the area of a district in relation to which the council of any county affected by the order are to have any functions is to be treated as an area that would become a police area by virtue of the order.

(3) An order under section 17 above which contains provision for a structural change—

(a) shall provide that, subject to any combination scheme under the Fire Services Act 1947, any district the council for which are, under the order, to have the functions of a county council in relation to that district is to become the area of a fire authority for the purposes of that Act; and

(b) may provide, for the purposes of the making of any combination scheme under that Act, that the area of any district in relation to which the council of any county affected by the order are to have any functions is to be treated as an area that would become the area of a fire authority by virtue of the order.

(4) It shall be the duty of the Secretary of State to have regard to any recommendations made by the Local Government Commission by virtue of section 14(5)(c) above in determining whether and how to exercise—

(a) his powers under Part I of the Police Act 1964 to approve or make an amalgamation scheme; or

(b) his powers under the Fire Services Act 1947 to approve or make a combination scheme,

in relation to any areas which have been or are to be affected by any order under section 17 above, or in relation to any such area and other areas.

(5) This section shall be without prejudice to the power to make any provision by order under this Part or to any power to make incidental, consequential, transitional or supplementary provision in connection with the provisions of any such order.

DEFINITIONS
"financial year": s.28(1).
"the Local Government Commission": s.28(1).
"structural change": s.14(1)(a), (2).

GENERAL NOTE
This section deals with certain matters consequent on structural changes included in an order under s.17.

Subs. (1)
Where, by virtue of a structural change, the functions of district councils are transferred to a county council, the county council becomes a billing authority responsible for collecting the council tax rather than a major precepting authority for the purposes of the Local Government Finance Act 1992 in relation to its area.

Subs. (2)
Where, by virtue of a structural change, a district council is to have the functions of a county council, the order under s.17 is to provide that the district is to be treated as a county for the purposes of the Police Act 1964 (under which police areas are made up by reference to counties). Moreover, the order may provide for the purposes of the approval or making of an amalgamation scheme under Pt. I of the Police Act 1964, that the area of a district in relation to which a county council affected by the order is to have any functions is to be treated as an area that would become a police area by virtue of the order. This will permit the retention of existing police areas which would otherwise be divided by county boundary changes (see further the note to subs. (3)).

Subs. (3)

Where, by virtue of a structural change, a district council is to have the functions of a county council, the order under s.17 is to provide that the district is to become the area of a fire authority for the purposes of the Fire Services Act 1947. Moreover, the order may provide for the purpose of the making of a combination scheme under the 1947 Act (*i.e.* a scheme made by the Secretary of State where two or more fire authorities wish to combine for fire fighting purposes), that the area of any district in respect of which the county council is to have any functions is to be treated as an area that would become the area of a fire authority by virtue of the order. In the House of Lords, Baroness Blatch explained:

> "The intention is that where any devolution of county functions to smaller unitary authorities is to take place, my right honourable friend the Home Secretary should have the power to amalgamate the new authorities to create viable police and fire authorities. In many cases it is likely that this will involve the re-creation of existing police and fire authorities" (*Hansard*, H.L. Vol. 533, col. 1522) (see further Sched. 3, paras. 1–5).

Subs. (4)

In exercising powers to approve or make an amalgamation scheme under the Police Act 1964 or a combination scheme under the Fire Services Act 1947, the Secretary of State must have regard to any recommendations concerning joint arrangements made by the Local Government Commission under s.14(5)(*c*).

Subs. (5)

Section 18 is without prejudice to the power to make any provision by order under Pt. II, or any power to make incidental, consequential, transitional or supplementary provision in connection with such an order. For lists of these powers see the note to s.26.

Regulations for supplementing orders

19.—(1) The Secretary of State may by regulations of general application make such incidental, consequential, transitional or supplementary provision as he thinks necessary or expedient for the purposes or in consequence of any orders under section 17 above, or for giving full effect to orders under that section.

(2) Regulations under this section may, in particular, include provision of general application with respect to—

    (a) the transfer of functions, property, rights or liabilities from a local authority for any area to another local authority whose area consists of or includes the whole or any part of that area;

    (b) the transfer of property, rights or liabilities, and of related functions, from an authority which ceases to exist to a residuary body established under section 22 below;

    (c) the management or custody of transferred property (whether real or personal);

    (d) the functions or areas of jurisdiction of any public body or of any of the following persons—

        (i) any justice of the peace, stipendiary magistrate, coroner or keeper of the rolls for a commission area (within the meaning of the Justices of the Peace Act 1979);

        (ii) any lord-lieutenant, lieutenant or high sheriff;

        (iii) any other officers (including police officers) within the area of any local authority affected by any such order,

and the costs and expenses of such public bodies and persons.

(3) In their application in relation to any order under section 17 above, regulations under this section shall have effect subject to any provision made under that section.

(4) Any regulations under section 67 of the 1972 Act (regulations in connection with implementation of proposals under Part IV of that Act) which are in force at the commencement of this section shall have effect, without prejudice to their operation in relation to any order made under that Part after the commencement of this section (whether by virtue of section 24(3) below or otherwise) and subject to any regulations under this section, as if orders under section 17 above were orders under that Part.

"the 1972 Act": s.28(1).
"public body": s.28(1).

GENERAL NOTE
The Secretary of State is given a wide power to make regulations to supplement orders under Pt. II.

Subs. (1)
Regulations made by the Secretary of State may make incidental, consequential, transitional or supplementary provision in connection with orders under s.17. By virtue of s.26(4), this includes power to apply (with or without modifications), to extend, exclude or amend, or to repeal or revoke, any enactment, or instrument made under any enactment, or any charter.

Subs. (2)(a), (b)
Transfer of functions, property, rights or liabilities. Powers to provide for the transfer of these matters includes power to provide for the continuation of legal proceedings, the transfer of staff, compensation for loss of office, pensions and other staffing matters, and for the transferee body to be treated for some or all purposes as the same person in law as the body from which the transfer is made (s.26(5)).

Subs. (3)
Regulations under s.19 have effect subject to any order made under s.17.

Subs. (4)
Section 67 of the Local Government Act 1972 enables the Secretary of State to make regulations concerning consequential and transitional arrangements in connection with the implementation of proposals under Pt. IV of the 1972 Act. These regulations are to have effect as if orders under s.17 were orders under Pt. IV of the 1972 Act.

Agreements as to incidental matters

20.—(1) Any public bodies affected by an order under this Part may from time to time make agreements with respect to any property, income, rights, liabilities and expenses (so far as affected by the order) of, and any financial relations between, the parties to the agreement.

(2) Such an agreement may provide—

(a) for the transfer or retention of any property, rights and liabilities, with or without conditions, and for the joint use of any property;

(b) for the making of payments by either party to the agreement in respect of property, rights and liabilities so transferred or retained, or of such joint use, and in respect of the remuneration or compensation payable to any person; and

(c) for the making of any such payment either by way of a capital sum or of a terminable annuity.

(3) In default of agreement as to any disputed matter, the matter shall be referred to the arbitration of a single arbitrator—

(a) agreed on by the parties; or

(b) in default of agreement, appointed by the Secretary of State;

and the award of the arbitrator may make any provision that might be contained in an agreement under this section.

(4) In subsection (3) above "disputed matter" means any matter which—

(a) might be the subject of provision contained in an agreement under this section; and

(b) is the subject of such a dispute between two or more public bodies as is not resolved by or under provision contained in any order or regulations under this Part.

DEFINITIONS
"public body": s.28(1).

GENERAL NOTE
This section is modelled on the Local Government Act 1972, s.68 (Transitional agreements as to property and finance under Pt. IV of the Act). Public bodies affected by an order under

Pt. II may make agreements as to incidental matters. These matters are any property, income, rights, liabilities and expenses (as affected by the order) of and any financial relations between the parties to the agreement. The agreement may provide for the matters set out in subs. (2), and disputes not resolved by an order or regulations under Pt. II are to be settled by arbitration (subss. (3) and (4)).

Joint authorities

21.—(1) This section applies to any functions which are to be or have become functions of any authority as a result of any structural or boundary change if the Secretary of State considers, having regard to any recommendations to that effect made by the Local Government Commission by virtue of section 14(5)(c) above, that they should be carried out in accordance with joint arrangements.

(2) Where it appears to the Secretary of State that joint arrangements, or satisfactory joint arrangements, with respect to any functions to which this section applies—

(a) have not been made by the authorities in whom those functions are to be or have been vested;

(b) will not be in force when the structural or boundary change in question comes into force; or

(c) have ceased or will cease to be in operation,

he may, for the areas of those authorities, by order establish a joint authority, which may be a body corporate, to carry out those functions, from a date specified in the order until such joint arrangements as appear to him to be satisfactory are brought into force.

(3) An order under this section may make provision for enabling the Secretary of State to require the joint authority to submit to him a scheme for the winding up of the joint authority and for the transfer—

(a) to any of the authorities for whose areas the joint authority is established; or

(b) to any body established in pursuance of any joint arrangements made by or in relation to those authorities,

of any of the joint authority's property, rights and liabilities or of any functions which it carries out.

(4) The Secretary of State may by order provide—

(a) for excluding any functions, or any functions in any area, from those falling to be carried out by a joint authority; and

(b) for giving effect (with or without modifications) to any scheme submitted to him under a provision made by virtue of subsection (3) above and for the dissolution of a joint authority.

(5) The power to make an order under any of the preceding provisions of this section shall include power to make such incidental, consequential, transitional or supplementary provision as the Secretary of State thinks necessary or expedient, including provision for the transfer of property, rights and liabilities.

DEFINITIONS

"boundary change": s.14(1)(*b*), (3).
"the Local Government Commission": s.28(1).
"structural change": s.14(1)(*a*), (2).

GENERAL NOTE

This section provides that if the Secretary of State considers that in consequence of a structural or boundary change joint arrangements should be made for the discharge of any functions, and it appears that satisfactory joint arrangements have not been made by the authorities concerned, will not be in force when the change comes into force, or have ceased or will cease, he may establish a joint authority by order. The joint authority may be a body corporate. (*Cf.* the power to make joint arrangements for waste disposal functions under the Local Government Act 1985, s.10). There is also provision for the Secretary of State to require the joint authority to be wound up (subs. (3)).

Subss. (3) and (5)
Transfer... of... property, rights and liabilities or functions. See notes to ss.19(2)(a), (b) and 26(5).

Subs. (5)
Incidental, consequential, transitional or supplementary provision. See notes to ss.19(1) and 26(4).

Residuary bodies

22.—(1) The Secretary of State may by order establish one or more bodies ("residuary bodies"), which shall be bodies corporate, for the purpose of taking over any property, rights or liabilities, and any related functions, of local authorities which cease to exist by virtue of orders under section 17 above.

(2) An order under subsection (1) above may—

(a) make provision with respect to the constitution and membership of a residuary body;

(b) make provision with respect to the powers of a residuary body to make levies and to borrow and lend money and the treatment and distribution of capital and other money by such a body;

(c) make provision with respect to the keeping and auditing of accounts of a residuary body;

(d) make provision with respect to directions which may be given by the Secretary of State in relation to the carrying out by a residuary body of any of its functions;

(e) make provision for enabling the Secretary of State to require a residuary body to submit to him a scheme for the winding up of the body and the disposal of its property, rights and liabilities and related functions; and

(f) without prejudice to the generality of paragraphs (a) to (e) above, make any such provision with respect to a residuary body as was made by Part VII of the Local Government Act 1985 with respect to the residuary bodies established by that Part.

(3) The Secretary of State may by order provide—

(a) for the transfer to any other body or bodies (including any body or bodies corporate established under the order for the purpose) of any property, rights or liabilities, and any related functions, of a residuary body; and

(b) for giving effect (with or without modifications) to any scheme submitted to him under a provision made by virtue of subsection (2)(e) above and for the dissolution of a residuary body.

(4) The power to make an order under any of the preceding provisions of this section shall include power to make such incidental, consequential, transitional or supplementary provision as the Secretary of State thinks necessary or expedient.

GENERAL NOTE
This section enables the Secretary of State to establish residuary bodies to take over any property, rights or liabilities and related functions of local authorities abolished by an order under s.17. The power is modelled on the power under Pt. VII of the Local Government Act 1985 to establish and wind up residuary bodies for the areas of the metropolitan counties and Greater London, following the abolition of the metropolitan county councils and the Greater London Council. The residuary bodies for the metropolitan counties have now been abolished; the London Residuary Body continues to exercise functions consequent on the abolition of the Inner London Education Authority.

Subs. (4)
Incidental, consequential, transitional or supplementary provision. See notes to ss.19(1) and 26(4).

Staff commissions

23.—(1) The Secretary of State may by order establish one or more staff commissions for the purpose of—

    (a) considering and keeping under review the arrangements for the recruitment of staff by relevant authorities affected by orders under this Part and for the transfer, in consequence of the provisions of any such order, of staff employed by such authorities;

    (b) considering such staffing problems arising in consequence of such an order, and such other matters relating to staff employed by any such authority, as may be referred to the staff commission by the Secretary of State; and

    (c) advising the Secretary of State on the steps necessary to safeguard the interests of such staff;

and such a commission may be established either for the whole or for any part of England.

(2) The Secretary of State may give directions to a staff commission as to their procedure and to any relevant authority affected by an order under this Part with respect to—

    (a) the supply of any information requested and the implementation of any advice given by a staff commission; and

    (b) the payment by such an authority of any expenses incurred by a staff commission in doing anything requested by the authority.

(3) Any expenses incurred by a staff commission under this section and not recovered from a relevant authority shall be paid by the Secretary of State out of money provided by Parliament.

(4) The Secretary of State may by order provide for the winding up of any staff commission established under this section.

(5) In this section "relevant authority" means a local authority or a joint authority or residuary body established under section 21 or 22 above.

DEFINITIONS
"relevant authority": subs. (5).
"staff": s.28(1).

GENERAL NOTE
    This section is modelled on s.50 of the Local Government Act 1985. The Secretary of State may establish one or more staff commissions to review the arrangements for the recruitment of staff by authorities affected by orders under Pt. II, and for the transfer of staff employed by such authorities; to consider staffing problems and other matters referred by the Secretary of State; and to advise the Secretary of State on the steps necessary to safeguard the interests of such staff.

Subs. (2)
    A direction may be varied or revoked by a subsequent direction, and there is power to rectify mistakes by order (s.26(6)).

Supplemental provisions of Part II

Abolition of the Local Government Boundary Commission for England

24.—(1) The Local Government Boundary Commission for England ("the predecessor Commission") shall cease to exist with the commencement of this section.

(2) Any property, rights or liabilities to which the predecessor Commission was entitled or subject immediately before the commencement of this section shall become property, rights or liabilities of the Local Government Commission.

(3) Without prejudice to sections 16 and 17 of the Interpretation Act 1978 (effect of repeals)—

    (a) where any report or proposals were submitted by the predecessor Commission to the Secretary of State under Part IV of the 1972 Act before the commencement of this section, the provisions of that Part, and of any regulations made under that Part, that cease to have effect for other purposes by virtue of this Act shall continue to have effect for the purpose of enabling effect to be given (with or without modifications) to those proposals and otherwise in relation to that report and those proposals; and

(b) where the Local Government Commission undertakes a review under this Part of any area which was the subject of a review which was being conducted by the predecessor Commission at the commencement of this section, the Secretary of State may, by a direction to the Local Government Commission, dispense in relation to that review with such of the requirements of section 15 above as appear to him to be inappropriate in the light of any steps taken before the commencement of this section by the predecessor Commission.

(4) If, in the case of any member of the predecessor Commission who ceases to hold office by virtue of subsection (1) above, the Secretary of State determines that there are special circumstances which make it right that that member should receive compensation, he shall pay to that member a sum by way of compensation of such amount as he may determine.

(5) The approval of the Treasury is required for any determination of the Secretary of State under subsection (4) above; and the sums required by the Secretary of State for making any payment under that subsection shall be paid out of money provided by Parliament.

DEFINITIONS
"the Local Government Commission": s.28(1).

GENERAL NOTE
The Local Government Boundary Commission for England established under Pt. IV of the Local Government Act 1972 is replaced by the Local Government Commission for England established by s.12. The Local Government Boundary Commission for Wales, also established by Pt. IV of the 1972 Act, continues in operation. There is provision for the compensation of any member of the predecessor Commission who loses office, if this is justified by special circumstances, and subject to the approval of the Treasury (subss. (4) and (5)).

Subs. (3)
This subsection makes transitional provision in respect of reports or proposals submitted by the Local Government Boundary Commission for England under Pt. IV of the 1972 Act before the commencement of the section. Provisions of Pt. IV that would otherwise cease to have effect, continue in force in relation to such reports or proposals. This enables the Secretary of State to give effect to proposals made before abolition. Where a review is being conducted by the Boundary Commission prior to the commencement of the section, the Secretary of State may direct the new Commission to dispense with requirements of s.15 that appear to him inappropriate in the light of steps taken by its predecessor.

Application of Part II to the Isles of Scilly

25. The Secretary of State may by order provide that, in their application in relation to the Isles of Scilly, the provisions of this Part shall have effect subject to such modifications as he considers appropriate.

GENERAL NOTE
The provisions of Pt. II may be applied to the Isles of Scilly by order of the Secretary of State, subject to such modifications as he considers appropriate. The Council of the Isles of Scilly was established by the Local Government Act 1888, s.49, and continued by the Local Government Act 1972, s.265, and is neither a county nor a district council. An order under s.265 may apply to the Isles of Scilly any other public general Act relating to local government (s.265(3), which does not contain an express power to make modifications).

Orders, regulations and directions under Part II

26.—(1) The powers of the Secretary of State under this Part to make orders or regulations shall be exercisable by statutory instrument; and a statutory instrument containing any order or regulations under this Part shall be subject to annulment in pursuance of a resolution of either House of Parliament unless—

(a) it effects a structural change;

(b) it establishes a joint authority for two or more local government areas; or

(c) it effects only electoral changes or relates only to parishes.

(2) No order under this Part effecting a structural change or establishing a joint authority for two or more local government areas shall be made unless a draft of the order has been laid before, and approved by resolution of, each House of Parliament; but an order effecting such a change or establishing a joint authority shall, if apart from this subsection it would be treated for the purposes of the standing orders of either House of Parliament as a hybrid instrument, proceed in that House as if it were not such an instrument.

(3) Every power of the Secretary of State under this Part to make orders or regulations, or to give directions, shall include power to make different provision for different cases, including different provision for different localities and for different bodies.

(4) Any power of the Secretary of State by order or regulations under this Part to make incidental, consequential, transitional or supplementary provision shall include power for any incidental, consequential, transitional or supplementary purposes—

(a) to apply with or without modifications;

(b) to extend, exclude or amend; or

(c) to repeal or revoke with or without savings,

any enactment, any instrument made under any enactment or any charter, whenever granted.

(5) Any power of the Secretary of State under this Part to make by order or regulations provision for the transfer of any functions, property, rights or liabilities or to make transitional provision in connection with any such transfer or with the establishment of any body shall include, in particular, power to provide—

(a) for legal proceedings commenced by or against any body to be continued by or against a body to whom functions, property, rights or liabilities are transferred;

(b) for the transfer of staff, compensation for loss of office, pensions and other staffing matters; and

(c) for treating any body to whom a transfer is made for some or all purposes as the same person in law as the body from whom the transfer is made.

(6) A direction under any provision of this Part may be varied or revoked by any subsequent direction under that provision; and where the Secretary of State is satisfied that—

(a) a mistake has occurred in the preparation of an order under any provision of this Part; and

(b) the mistake is such that it cannot be rectified by a subsequent order made under that provision by virtue of section 14 of the Interpretation Act 1978 (implied power to amend),

he may by order under this subsection make such provision as he thinks necessary or expedient for rectifying the mistake.

(7) In this section—

"enactment" includes an enactment contained in a provision of this Act (other than a provision of this Part) or in any enactment contained in an Act passed after this Act; and

"mistake", in relation to an order, includes a provision contained in or omitted from the order in reliance on inaccurate or incomplete information supplied by any public body.

DEFINITIONS
"electoral change": s.14(1)(c), (4).

"enactment": subs. (7).
"local government area": s.28(1).
"mistake": subs. (7).
"public body": s.28(1).
"staff": s.28(1).
"structural change": s.14(1)(*a*), (2).

GENERAL NOTE
   This section makes general provision in respect of orders, regulations and directions made under Pt. II. Powers to make orders are found in ss.17; 21(2), (4); 22(1), (3); 23(1), (4); and 25. Powers to make regulations are found in s.19. Powers to make directions are found in ss.13(1), (6); 15(6), (7); 17(2); 23(2); and 24(3)(*b*).

Subs. (1)
   Orders or regulations under Pt. II are made by statutory instrument. They are subject to a negative resolution of either House of Parliament unless (1) it effects a structural change; (2) it establishes a joint authority; or (3) it effects only electoral changes or relates only to parishes. In the case of (1) and (2), the statutory instrument is subject to the affirmative resolution of each House (subs. (2)).

Subs. (2)
   For the avoidance of doubt it is provided that instruments effecting a structural change or establishing a joint authority are not to be treated as hybrid.

Subs. (4)
   Powers to make incidental, consequential, transitional or supplementary provision are found in ss.19(1), 21(5) and 22(4). These powers are to include power to apply (with or without modifications), to extend, exclude or amend or to repeal or revoke any enactment or instrument made under any enactment.

Subs. (5)
   Powers to provide for the transfer of any functions, property, rights or liabilities are found in ss.19(2)(*a*), (*b*); 21(3), (5); and 22(3). These are to include power to provide for the continuation of legal proceedings, the transfer of staff, compensation for loss of office, pensions and other staffing matters, and for treating the transferee body as the same person in law as the body from which the transfer is made.

Amendments relating to local government changes

   27.—(1) Schedule 3 to this Act (which contains consequential amendments in connection with the provisions of this Part) shall have effect.
   (2) In considering the electoral arrangements for any local government area for the purposes of this Part the Secretary of State and the Local Government Commission shall comply, so far as is reasonably practicable, with the rules set out in Schedule 11 to the 1972 Act (rules to be observed in considering electoral arrangements); and accordingly, in that Schedule, references to "either of the Commissions" shall have effect—
   (a) until the commencement of section 24 above, as including a reference to the Local Government Commission; and
   (b) thereafter, as if they were references to the Local Government Commission or the Local Government Boundary Commission for Wales.
   (3) In subsection (2) above "electoral arrangements" has the meaning given by subsection (4) of section 14 above for the purposes of subsection (1)(c) of that section.

DEFINITIONS
   "the 1972 Act": s.28(1).
   "electoral arrangements": subs. (3); s.14(4).
   "local government area": s.28(1).
   "the Local Government Commission": s.28(1).

GENERAL NOTE
   Schedule 3, made by virtue of this section, makes consequential amendments. In considering

electoral arrangements, the Secretary of State and the Commission must comply, so far as is reasonably practicable, with the rules set out in Sched. 11 to the Local Government Act 1972. These rules make separate provision for counties, districts and London boroughs, and parishes and communities. In *Enfield London Borough Council* v. *Local Government Boundary Commission for England* [1979] 3 All E.R. 747, the House of Lords held that in view of the words "so far as reasonably practicable" in s.78(2), the provisions of Sched. 11 were not the overriding consideration; the overriding consideration was "the interests of effective and convenient local government" in s.47(1) of the 1972 Act (*cf.* now the Commission's obligations under s.13(5)).

PART III

GENERAL

Interpretation

28.—(1) In this Act, except where the context otherwise requires—
"the 1972 Act" means the Local Government Act 1972;
"the 1973 Act" means the Local Government (Scotland) Act 1973;
"the 1980 Act" means the Local Government, Planning and Land Act 1980;
"the 1982 Act" means the Local Government Finance Act 1982;
"the 1988 Act" means the Local Government Act 1988;
"the Audit Commission" means the Audit Commission for Local Authorities and the National Health Service in England and Wales;
"auditor" means any person who, within the meaning of Part III of the 1982 Act, is an auditor of the accounts of a body with which the Audit Commission is concerned;
"contravention" includes a failure to comply;
"financial year" means the twelve months ending with 31st March;
"local authority" means a principal council, the Common Council of the City of London, the sub-treasurer of the Inner Temple, the under treasurer of the Middle Temple or a parish council;
"local government area" means a principal area, and any of the following as for the time being constituted, that is to say, any metropolitan county, Greater London, the City of London, the Inner Temple, the Middle Temple or a parish;
"the Local Government Commission" means the Local Government Commission for England;
"modifications" includes additions, alterations and omissions;
"principal area" means any of the following as for the time being constituted, that is to say, a non-metropolitan county in England, a district in England or a London borough;
"principal council" means a council elected for a principal area;
"public body" includes any local authority, any joint authority or residuary body established under Part II of this Act and any other body which is a public body for the purposes of Part IV of the 1972 Act;
"the Scottish Accounts Commission" means the Commission for Local Authority Accounts in Scotland or, in relation to any time after the coming into force of paragraph 3 of Schedule 7 to the National Health Service and Community Care Act 1990, that Commission as re-named by that paragraph;
"staff" includes officers and employees.

(2) References in this Act to a body with which the Audit Commission is concerned are references to any body any of whose accounts are required to be audited under Part III of the 1982 Act (including the Common Council of the City of London).

(3) References in this Act (however framed) to a body affected by any recommendations, changes or order under Part II of this Act include references to a body whose area or functions are so affected or to a body which

is to cease to exist in pursuance of the recommendations, changes or order and, in relation to an order, include a body which is established under or in consequence of the order.

GENERAL NOTE
This section contains definitions for the purposes of the Act.

Consequential amendment, repeals and saving

29.—(1) Part III of the 1982 Act and Part VII of the 1973 Act shall each have effect as if any functions under this Act of an auditor, of the Audit Commission, of the Controller of Audit or of the Scottish Accounts Commission were included in any references in that Part to the functions under that Part of an auditor, of the Controller of Audit or of the Commission in question.

(2) The enactments mentioned in Schedule 4 to this Act are hereby repealed to the extent specified in the third column of that Schedule.

(3) Without prejudice to sections 16 and 17 of the Interpretation Act 1978 (effect of repeals), the repeal by this Act of any provision contained in Part IV of the 1972 Act shall not affect the continuing validity, after the coming into force of that repeal, of any provision contained in any order made under that Part.

DEFINITIONS
"the 1972 Act": s.28(1).
"the 1973 Act": s.28(1).
"the 1982 Act": s.28(1).
"auditor": s.28(1).
"the Audit Commission": s.28(1).
"the Scottish Accounts Commission": s.28(1).

GENERAL NOTE
This section provides that references to the functions of an auditor, the Audit Commission, the Controller of Audit and the Scottish Accounts Commission under Pt. III of the Local Government Finance Act 1982 and Pt. VII of the Local Government (Scotland) Act 1973 are to include functions under this Act. It also introduces Sched. 4 (repeals) and ensures the continuing effect of orders made under the Local Government Act 1972.

Short title, commencement and extent

30.—(1) This Act may be cited as the Local Government Act 1992.

(2) Sections 1 to 7 above and, in Part I of Schedule 4 to this Act, the repeal in the 1982 Act shall come into force at the end of the period of two months beginning with the day on which this Act is passed.

(3) The following provisions of this Act, that is to say—
(a) sections 8 to 11, Schedule 1 and, in Part I of Schedule 4, the repeals in the 1980 Act and the 1988 Act; and
(b) section 24, Schedule 3 and Part II of Schedule 4,
shall come into force on such day as the Secretary of State may by order made by statutory instrument appoint; and different days may be appointed under this subsection for different provisions and for different purposes.

(4) The following provisions of this Act do not extend to Scotland, that is to say—
(a) sections 4 and 7;
(b) Part II, apart from the amendments contained in paragraphs 11 and 12 of Schedule 2 and in paragraphs 21 and 22 of Schedule 3; and
(c) Schedule 4, apart from so much of Part II as makes a repeal in the House of Commons Disqualification Act 1975.

(5) Except for the purposes of—
(a) the amendments contained in paragraphs 11 and 12 of Schedule 2 and in paragraph 21 of Schedule 3; and

    (b) so much of Part II of Schedule 4 makes a repeal in the House of Commons Disqualification Act 1974,

this Act does not extend to Northern Ireland.

DEFINITIONS
  "the 1980 Act": s.28(1).
  "the 1982 Act": s.28(1).
  "the 1988 Act": s.28(1).

SCHEDULES

Section 11   SCHEDULE 1

AMENDMENTS OF COMPETITION PROVISIONS

The Local Government, Planning and Land Act 1980 (c. 65)

1. In section 7(1B) of the 1980 Act (no failure to fulfil competition condition unless local authority are aware of failure when they propose to enter into contract), for the words from "unless" to "aware" there shall be substituted the words "unless the local authority have become aware, before entering into the contract,".

2.—(1) In subsection (2) of section 9 of the 1980 Act (obligation to prepare written statement as to the amounts that will be credited to an authority's DLO revenue account in respect of certain work), after the word "first" there shall be inserted the words ", in accordance with such requirements (if any) as may be contained in regulations made by the Secretary of State,".

(2) In subsection (4)(a) of that section (obligation to invite offers to undertake work in accordance with specified conditions), for the words "conditions specified by them" there shall be substituted the words "a detailed specification prepared for the purposes of the invitation".

(3) In subsection (6) of that section (statement under subsection (2) to be consistent with conditions specified for the purposes of subsection (4)(a)), for the words "conditions corresponding to those specified in" there shall be substituted the words "the requirements of the specification prepared for the purposes of".

3. In section 13(2) of the 1980 Act (documents to be prepared by every local authority or development body who undertake construction or maintenance work), for paragraph (c) (statement of rate of return) there shall be substituted the following paragraph—

    "(c) a statement showing whether the local authority or development body have complied with section 16(1) below."

4.—(1) In subsection (1) of section 16 of the 1980 Act (obligation to secure that revenue from certain work shows such positive rate of return as the Secretary of State may direct), for the words from "their revenue" to the end of the subsection there shall be substituted the words "such financial objective as the Secretary of State may specify for that year is met by their revenue (as adjusted in such manner as he may so specify) for all the work of that description which is carried out in that year."

(2) After that subsection there shall be inserted the following subsection—

    "(1A) Where the Secretary of State specifies a financial objective under this section, he may define that objective by reference to such factors as he thinks fit."

5. In section 18(2B) of the 1980 Act (auditor's obligation to consider statement of rate of return), for the words "statement of rate of return" there shall be substituted the words "statement referred to in section 13(2)(c) above".

6. In section 19A(1) of the 1980 Act (conditions of enforcement)—
    (a) after the word "work", in the first place where it occurs, there shall be inserted the words ", or have decided to do so, in a case in which the carrying out or undertaking of that work has been or (if effect is given to the proposals to which the decision relates) will be"; and
    (b) in paragraph (a), for the words "they have entered into" there shall be substituted the words "into which that authority have entered".

7.—(1) In section 19B of the 1980 Act (power to give directions restricting a power to carry out work or imposing conditions with respect to the carrying out of work), after subsection (5) there shall be inserted the following subsection—

    "(5A) The conditions that may be imposed by a direction given under this section in relation to the carrying out of any work include a condition restricting the carrying out of the work to cases where—
      (a) the Secretary of State has been satisfied as to any matter specified or described in the direction or;
      (b) the work is carried out under and in accordance with an authorisation or consent given for the purposes of the direction by the Secretary of State."

(2) In subsection (6) of that section (power to give direction to be exercised in writing), at the end there shall be inserted the words "and, without prejudice to subsection (4) above, shall include power, at any time, to make such variations of a direction under this section as may be agreed with the authority or body to which the direction relates".

8. In section 20(2) of the 1980 Act (exclusion from references to construction and maintenance work of routine maintenance of specific building etc. by person employed for the purpose), for the words from "employed" in paragraph (b) to the end of the subsection there shall be substituted the words "who—

(i) is employed to perform duties in relation to that building or structure, or those buildings or structures; but

(ii) spends the greater part of the time required for performing the duties of his employment in the carrying out of work which is neither routine maintenance nor work of any other description falling within the meaning, for the purposes of this Part of this Act, of construction or maintenance work".

9. In section 23(1) of the 1980 Act (power to make different provision for different parts of Great Britain), after the word "Act" there shall be inserted the words "and the power under section 16(1) above to specify a financial objective for local authorities and development bodies,".

The Local Government Act 1988 (c. 9)

10. In section 2(3) of the 1988 Act (power to add a paragraph to the list of defined activities), at the end there shall be inserted the words "or by modifying any provision of Schedule 1 to this Act which for the time being excludes anything from the activities falling within any of those paragraphs".

11. In subsection (6) of section 4 of the 1988 Act (no failure to fulfil conditions of entering into works contract unless bidding authority are aware of failure when they propose to enter into contract), for the words from "unless" to the end of the subsection there shall be substituted the words "unless the bidding authority have become aware of the failure before entering into the contract".

12. In section 6(3) of the 1988 Act (application confined to work specified in regulations) at the end there shall be inserted the words "and regulations under this section may describe work by reference to a specified proportion of work of a particular description".

13. In section 13(1) of the 1988 Act (conditions of enforcement), for paragraph (b) there shall be substituted the following paragraphs—

"(b) have carried out work as regards which the conditions set out in section 7 above have to be but, in the circumstances, have not been fulfilled,

(ba) have decided to carry out work as regards which (if the work is carried out in accordance with the decision) those conditions will have to be but, in the circumstances in which it is proposed to carry it out, will not be fulfilled,".

14. In section 14 of the 1988 Act (power to give directions restricting a power to carry out work or imposing conditions with respect to the carrying out of work), after subsection (4) there shall be inserted the following subsections—

"(4A) The conditions that may be imposed by a direction given under this section in relation to the carrying out of any work include a condition restricting the carrying out of the work to cases where—

(a) the Secretary of State has been satisfied as to any matter specified or described in the direction, or

(b) the work is carried out under and in accordance with an authorisation or consent given for the purposes of the direction by the Secretary of State.

(4B) Where a direction under this section imposes any condition in relation to the carrying out of any work, that direction may provide that the requirement that the condition is fulfilled is to have effect, in relation to that work, instead of any requirement which (apart from the direction) would have effect in relation to that work by virtue of this Part.

(4C) Without prejudice to subsection (3) above, the power to give a direction under this section shall include power, at any time, to make such variations of a direction under this section as may be agreed with the authority to which the direction relates."

DEFINITIONS
 "the 1980 Act": s.28(1).
 "the 1988 Act": s.28(1).

Amendments to the Local Government, Planning and Land Act 1980

Para. 1

As originally drafted, s.7(1B) of the 1980 Act provided that a local authority is not prevented from entering a contract unless "at the time it is proposed to be entered into" it is aware of a failure to fulfil the competition condition (*i.e.* the requirement that the other party has not acted in a manner having the effect or intended or likely to have the effect of restricting, distorting or preventing competition). This paragraph changes the time at which the question is to be judged.

Para. 2(1)

Sub-paragraph (1) amends s.9(2) of the 1980 Act and requires a local authority, in preparing written statements of the amounts that will be credited to its DLO revenue account in respect of certain work, or of the method by which it intends to calculate that amount, to comply with any requirements contained in regulations made by the Secretary of State.

Para. 2(2)

This sub-paragraph amends s.9(4)(*a*) of the 1980 Act to require the preparation of detailed specifications for the purposes of invitations to outside contractors to offer to undertake functional work. Section 9(4)(*a*) previously referred to offers to undertake work "in accordance with conditions specified" by the local authority. The requirement for detailed specifications is modelled on such a requirement under s.7 of the 1988 Act. For publicity requirements in respect of tender specifications, see s.10 of the present Act.

Para. 2(3)

Section 9(6) of the 1980 Act requires that the written statement prepared in accordance with s.9(2) (see note to para. 1) must be consistent with the conditions specified in the invitation issued under s.9(4)(*a*). This sub-paragraph substitutes a reference to the detailed specification, now required in accordance with para. 2(2), for the reference to specified conditions.

Para. 3

Section 13(2) of the 1980 Act requires every local authority or development body which undertakes construction or maintenance work to prepare documents comprising a revenue account and a statement of rate of return. This paragraph substitutes for the latter a requirement to prepare a statement showing whether the local authority or development body has complied with s.16(1), as amended by para. 4 of the present Schedule (see below).

Para. 4(1), (2)

Section 16 of the 1980 Act requires authorities to show in respect of specified descriptions of work such a positive rate of return on the capital employed as may be directed by the Secretary of State. This sub-paragraph amends s.16 so as to give the Secretary of State instead power to specify the financial objective to be met by an authority undertaking construction and maintenance work during the year in question. He may define that financial objective by reference to such factors as he thinks fit.

Para. 5

Section 18(2B) of the 1980 Act requires the auditor to consider the statement of rate of return prepared in accordance with s.13(2)(*c*). This paragraph substitutes a reference to the statement showing whether the local authority or development body has complied with s.16(1) now required by s.13(2)(*c*), as amended by para. 3 of the present Schedule.

Para. 6

Section 19A of the 1980 Act enables the Secretary of State to serve a written notice, requiring a written response, if it appears to him that a local authority or development body has carried out or undertaken construction or maintenance work in contravention of specified requirements of Pt. III. The response must either show that the allegation is unjustified, or admit that it is correct and show why the Secretary of State should take no further action. If he receives no written response, or is not satisfied with it, he may give directions under s.19B that the authority or body shall cease to have power to carry out the work identified in the direction, or shall only have such power if specified conditions are fulfilled.

This paragraph amends s.19A to enable the Secretary of State to serve a notice at an earlier stage, as soon as an authority or body decides that it will carry out work subject to competitive tendering requirements in circumstances which appear to the Secretary of State to constitute a breach of those requirements.

Para. 7

This paragraph amends the Secretary of State's power to give directions under s.19B of the

1980 Act by providing expressly that a condition imposed by the Secretary of State may restrict the carrying out of work to cases where he has been satisfied as to any matter set out in the direction or the work is carried out in accordance with an authorisation or consent given by the Secretary of State. There is also to be an express power to vary a direction. Analogous amendments are made by para. 14 to s.14 of the 1988 Act: see further the notes to that paragraph.

Para. 8

Section 29(2)(*b*) of the 1980 Act provides an exemption from the requirements of the legislation where a person is employed to maintain a specific building or block. In the *Consultation Paper* (p. 11), the Government expressed the view that this exemption was appropriate in the case, for example, of a caretaker whose work typically included some routine maintenance; however, the exemption should not extend to whole groups of workers, such as estate-based maintenance teams. Accordingly, para. 8 amends s.29(2)(*b*) to limit exempt maintenance work to cases where it is carried out by an employee as a secondary, rather than a primary task.

Para. 9

This paragraph enables the Secretary of State to make different provision in relation to local authorities in England, Wales and Scotland when specifying the financial objective to be achieved under s.16(1), as amended by para. 4 of the present Act.

Amendments to the Local Government Act 1988

Para. 10

Section 2(3) of the 1988 Act enables the Secretary of State to add to the list of defined activities (see note to s.8(2)). This paragraph extends this power by empowering the Secretary of State to remove or modify any exemptions from defined activities set out in Sched. 1 to the 1988 Act. Such exemptions may include such matters as the cleaning of police buildings, and the maintenance of police and fire service vehicles (see General Note to s.8).

Para. 11

This paragraph makes an amendment to s.4(6) of the 1988 Act analogous to that made by para. 1 to s.7(1B) of the 1980 Act (see note to para. 1).

Para. 12

Section 6(3) of the 1988 Act provides that the CCT requirements applicable to functional work only apply where work which falls within a defined activity is of such description, is proposed to be carried out by a defined authority, and is proposed to be carried out after a date specified in regulations made by the Secretary of State. This paragraph amends s.6(3) by making it clear that the Secretary of State may apply the requirements to a specified proportion of a defined activity.

Para. 13

Sections 13 and 14 of the 1988 Act set out a procedure for the service of a notice followed by the giving of a direction, where it appears to the Secretary of State that a defined authority has contravened the requirements of Pt. I of the Act. Similar provision is made for the purposes of the 1980 Act by s.19A and 19B (see note to para. 6). This paragraph makes similar changes to those effected by para. 6, enabling the Secretary of State to serve a notice as soon as an authority decides that it will carry out work in circumstances which appear to the Secretary of State to constitute a breach of CCT requirements.

Para. 14

This paragraph makes several changes to the Secretary of State's power to give directions under s.14 of the 1988 Act. Section 14(2) gives express power to attach conditions. According to the Government's *Consultation Paper* (p. 12), directions have frequently required that the directed authority carries out a re-tendering exercise for the work in question, and have included the conditions that the authority must seek the Secretary of State's consent to any decision to assign the re-tendered work to the authority's own Direct Services Organisation. In *R.* v. *Secretary of State for the Environment*, ex p. *Knowsley Metropolitan Borough Council, The Times*, September 25, 1991, the Court of Appeal held (reversing Popplewell J.) that s.14(2) did authorise the imposition of a consent condition. The new s.14(4A) gives the Secretary of State express power to attach such a condition.

The new s.14(4B) enables the direction to provide that a condition specified in the direction is to have effect instead of any requirement which would otherwise apply by virtue of Pt. I. The

Consultation Paper (p. 12) explained that this would, for example, allow the Secretary of State, if he had required a re-tendering exercise, to provide that an authority could invite tenders at a date sooner than three months, or alternatively later than six months, after publication of the tendering notice (thus overriding the period specified by s.9(4)(*a*) of the 1988 Act).

The new s.14(4C) enables the Secretary of State to vary a direction by agreement with the authority to which the direction relates. This will, for example, make clear the Secretary of State's power to defer the deadline for completion of a re-tendering exercise if an authority demonstrated that the date originally set would cause clear difficulties (*Consultation Paper*, p. 12).

Section 12   SCHEDULE 2

THE LOCAL GOVERNMENT COMMISSION FOR ENGLAND

Membership

1.—(1) The Local Government Commission ("the Commission") shall consist of not less than five and not more than fifteen members who shall be appointed by the Secretary of State; and the Secretary of State shall appoint one of the members to be chairman.

(2) Subject to the provisions of this paragraph, a member of the Commission shall hold and vacate office in accordance with the terms of his appointment.

(3) A person who ceases to be a member of the Commission shall be eligible for re-appointment.

(4) A member of the Commission may resign his office by notice in writing to the Secretary of State.

(5) The Secretary of State may remove a member of the Commission from office if he is satisfied that he—

(a) is unable or unfit to carry out the functions of a member; or

(b) has not complied with the terms of his appointment.

(6) A person shall cease to be chairman of the Commission—

(a) if he resigns as such by notice in writing to the Secretary of State; or

(b) if he ceases to be a member of the Commission.

Remuneration, pensions etc.

2.—(1) The Commission shall pay to its members such remuneration, and such allowances, as the Secretary of State may determine.

(2) The Commission may—

(a) pay such pensions, allowances or gratuities to or in respect of any persons who have been or are its members as the Secretary of State may determine;

(b) make such payments as the Secretary of State may determine towards provision for the payment of pensions, allowances or gratuities to or in respect of any such persons.

(3) If, when any member of the Commission ceases to hold office, the Secretary of State determines that there are special circumstances which make it right that that member should receive compensation, the Commission shall pay to him a sum by way of compensation of such amount as the Secretary of State may determine.

(4) The approval of the Treasury is required for any determination of the Secretary of State under this paragraph.

Staff

3.—(1) The Commission shall appoint a person to act as chief executive of the Commission and may appoint such other staff as it may determine.

(2) No person shall be appointed by the Commission to act as chief executive unless the Secretary of State has consented to the appointment of that person.

(3) The terms and conditions of appointment of any person appointed under this paragraph shall be determined by the Commission with the consent of the Secretary of State.

(4) The Commission shall pay to members of its staff such remuneration, and such allowances as the Secretary of State may determine.

(5) The Commission may—

(a) pay such pensions, allowances or gratuities to or in respect of any persons who have been or are members of its staff as the Secretary of State may determine;

(b) make such payments as the Secretary of State may determine towards provision for the payment of pensions, allowances or gratuities to or in respect of any such persons.

(6) Any reference in sub-paragraph (5) above to pensions, allowances or gratuities to or in respect of any such persons as are mentioned in that sub-paragraph includes a reference to

payments by way of compensation to or in respect of any members of the Commission's staff who suffer loss of office or employment or loss or diminution of emoluments.

(7) The approval of the Treasury shall be required for the giving of any consent under sub-paragraph (3) above or for the making of any determination under sub-paragraph (4) or (5) above.

Incidental powers

4.—(1) Without prejudice to any powers exercisable apart from this paragraph, the Commission shall have power to do anything (whether or not involving the acquisition or disposal of any property or rights) which is calculated to facilitate, or is conducive or incidental to, the carrying out of any of its functions.

(2) The Commission shall not by virtue of this paragraph have power to borrow money or to cause any local inquiry to be held.

(3) Where the Commission requests a public body to supply the Commission with any information which the Commission reasonably requires in connection with any of its functions, it shall be the duty of that body to supply the Commission with that information.

(4) The Secretary of State may give directions as to the exercise by the Commission of any of its powers under this paragraph.

Proceedings

5.—(1) Subject to the following provisions of this Schedule, the Commission may regulate its own procedure (including quorum).

(2) The validity of any proceedings of the Commission shall not be affected by a vacancy amongst its members or by a defect in the appointment of a member, or by a contravention of paragraph 7 below.

(3) The Secretary of State may give directions as to the exercise by the Commission of its power under this paragraph to regulate its procedure.

Delegation of powers

6. Anything authorised or required by or under this Act to be done by the Commission may be done by any member of the Commission, or of its staff, who has been authorised for the purpose, whether generally or specially, by the Commission or may be done by any committee or sub-committee of the Commission which has been so authorised.

Members' interests

7. A member of the Commission who is directly or indirectly interested in any matter brought up for consideration at a meeting of the Commission shall disclose the nature of his interest to the meeting; and where such a disclosure is made the member shall not take part in any deliberation or decision of the Commission with respect to that matter.

Application of seal and proof of instruments

8.—(1) The application of the seal of the Commission shall be authenticated by the signature of any member of the Commission, or of its staff, who has been authorised by the Commission, whether generally or specially, for the purpose.

(2) Every document purporting to be an instrument issued by the Commission and to be duly sealed with the seal of the Commission or to be signed on behalf of the Commission shall be received in evidence and, unless the contrary is shown, shall be deemed to be an instrument so issued.

Finances of the Commission

9.—(1) The Secretary of State shall, in respect of each accounting year, pay to the Commission such amount as he may, with the approval of the Treasury, determine to be the amount required by the Commission for the carrying out during that year of its functions under this Act.

(2) Any sums required by the Secretary of State for making a payment under sub-paragraph (1) above shall be paid out of money provided by Parliament.

(3) In this paragraph and paragraph 10 below "accounting year" means the period beginning with the day on which the Commission is established and ending with the financial year current on that date, and each successive financial year.

Accounts

10.—(1) The Commission shall—

(a) keep proper accounts and records in relation to the accounts; and

(b) prepare in respect of each accounting year a statement of accounts in such form as the Secretary of State, with the approval of the Treasury, may direct.

(2) The accounts of the Commission shall be audited by persons appointed for the purpose for each accounting year by the Secretary of State.

(3) A copy of any accounts of the Commission audited under sub-paragraph (2) above and the report made on those accounts by the persons appointed to audit them shall be sent to the Secretary of State as soon as reasonably practicable after the report is received by the Commission; and the Secretary of State shall lay before Parliament a copy of any accounts or report sent to him under this sub-paragraph.

The Parliamentary Commissioner

11. In the Parliamentary Commissioner Act 1967, in Schedule 2 (departments and authorities subject to investigation), there shall be inserted, at the appropriate place, the following entry—

"Local Government Commission for England."

House of Commons disqualification

12. In Schedule 1 to the House of Commons Disqualification Act 1975 (bodies of which all members are disqualified for membership of the House of Commons), in Part II there shall be inserted, at the appropriate place, the following entry—

"The Local Government Commission for England";

and the like insertion shall be made in Part II of Schedule 1 to the Northern Ireland Assembly Disqualification Act 1975.

DEFINITIONS

"accounting year": para. 9(3)
"financial year": s.28(1).
"the Local Government Commission": s.28(1).
"public body": s.28(1).
"staff": s.28(1).

GENERAL NOTE

This Schedule makes provision for the constitution, staff, powers and proceedings of the Local Government Commission for England established by s.12.

Section 27   SCHEDULE 3

AMENDMENTS CONSEQUENTIAL ON PART II

The Fire Services Act 1947 (c. 41)

1. In section 6 of the Fire Services Act 1947 (power of the Secretary of State to make combination schemes)—

(a) in subsection (2), after the word "thereto" there shall be inserted the words "or sub-section (2A) of this section applies"; and

(b) after that subsection there shall be inserted the following subsection—

"(2A) If, in a case where the authorities to whom notice of a proposed scheme has been given under subsection (2) of this section do not assent thereto—

(a) it appears to the Secretary of State that the proposed scheme contains only such provision as is appropriate in consequence of an order under Part II of the Local Government Act 1992 containing provision for giving effect to a structural change (within the meaning of that Part); and

(b) the period (if any) that has elapsed between the making of that order and the giving of that notice does not exceed twelve months,

the Secretary of State shall be under a duty to consider any representations made by those authorities with respect to the proposed scheme within such period as may have been specified in the notice, but shall not be required under that subsection to cause a public local inquiry to be held."

2. In section 10 of that Act (schemes for combination of fire areas in advance of alterations of local government areas)—

(a) for the words from "constituting" to "a county" there shall be substituted the words "or Part II of the Local Government Act 1992 affecting any area";

(b) for the words "that date" there shall be substituted the words "the date on which that order gives effect to any transfer of functions or alteration of boundaries in relation to that area"; and

(c) for the words from "as if" onwards there shall be substituted the words "as if—

    (a) references to the area of a fire authority included references to any area which (apart from any combination scheme under this section) would become such an area by virtue of such an order or which, in accordance with such an order, is to be treated, for the purposes of the making of any combination scheme, as an area which would become the area of a fire authority by virtue of that order; and

    (b) references, in relation to such an area, to the fire authority were references to the fire authority for any area the whole or any part of which will be included in that area."

The Police Act 1964 (c. 48)

3.—(1) For paragraphs (a) and (b) of subsection (1) of section 23 of the Police Act 1964 there shall be substituted the words "with respect to any two or more prospective police areas".

(2) For subsection (1B) of that section there shall be substituted the following subsection—

"(1B) In this section—

'prospective police area' means any area which (apart from any amalgamation scheme) would become a police area by virtue of an order under Part II of the Local Government Act 1992 or Part IV of the Local Government Act 1972 or which, in accordance with such an order, is to be treated, for the purposes of the approval or making of any amalgamation scheme, as an area which would become a policy area by virtue of that order; and

'the relevant date', in relation to a prospective police area, means the date on which the order in question gives effect to structural or boundary changes affecting the area comprised in the prospective police area;

and in this subsection the reference to a structural or boundary change is a reference to any structural or boundary change within the meaning of Part II of that Act of 1992 or, in relation to an order under Part IV of that Act of 1972, to the constitution of a new county or the alteration of an existing county."

(3) In subsection (2) of that section (modifications for the purposes of an amalgamation scheme), for paragraphs (a) to (c) there shall be substituted the following paragraphs—

"(a) any reference to a police area shall include a reference to a prospective police area;

(b) any reference, in relation to a prospective police area, to a constituent authority shall be a reference to the police authority for any police area the whole or any part of which will be included in the prospective police area and the council of any county the whole or any part of which will be so included; and

(c) any reference, in relation to a prospective police area, to the police authority (except a reference to which paragraph (b) above applies) shall be a reference to any constituent authority (within the meaning of that paragraph) other than the council for a county for which there is a separate police authority."

(4) For subsection (3) of that section there shall be substituted the following subsection—

"(3) For the purposes of the approval or making of any amalgamation scheme with respect to any area, any steps required by this Act to be taken before an amalgamation scheme is approved or made may be taken at any time—

(a) after any report affecting that area, together with proposals or recommendations, has been submitted to the Secretary of State under Part II of the Local Government Act 1992 or Part IV of the Local Government Act 1972; and

(b) before an order is made to give effect to the proposals or recommendations,

if the Secretary of State has notified the general nature of the order he intends to make to give effect to the proposals or recommendations to every authority which for the purposes of sections 21 and 22 above (as modified by subsection (2) above) would be a constituent authority in relation to that scheme."

4. In paragraph 7 of Schedule 1 to that Act—

(a) in sub-paragraph (a), for the words for "of the new" to the end of the sub-paragraph there shall be substituted the words "for any relevant area, that is to say, any area which under the order in question is (within the meaning of section 23 of this Act) a prospective police area and to which the scheme is to apply; and

(b) in sub-paragraph (b), for the words from "each of the following" to the end of the sub-paragraph there shall be substituted the words "every council which is the council for a county the whole or any part of which is included in a relevant area."

5—(1) In paragraph 3 of Schedule 3 to that Act (obligation to hold public inquiry before making amalgamation scheme if an objection is made), at the beginning there shall be inserted the words "Subject to paragraph 3A below".

(2) After that paragraph there shall be inserted the following paragraph—

"3A. If, in a case where a notice of objection with respect to any proposed scheme is received by the Secretary of State as mentioned in paragraph 3 above—

(a) it appears to the Secretary of State that the proposed scheme contains only such provision as is appropriate in consequence of an order under Part II of the Local Government Act 1992 containing provision for giving effect to a structural change (within the meaning of that Part); and

(b) the period (if any) that has elapsed between the making of that order and the giving of the notice which is required to be given under paragraph 1 above in relation to that scheme does not exceed twelve months,

the Secretary of State shall be under a duty to consider that objection but shall not be required to cause a local inquiry to be held in respect of it."

The Local Government Act 1972 (c. 70)

6. In section 6(2)(c) of the 1972 Act (term of office and retirement of councillors), for the words "Part IV of this Act" there shall be substituted the words "Part II of the Local Government Act 1992".

7.—(1) In subsection (6) of section 7 of the 1972 Act (election of councillors), for the words "section 51 below" there shall be substituted the words "section 17 of the Local Government Act 1992".

(2) In subsection (7) of that section—

(a) for the words "ask the English Commission to make proposals" there shall be substituted the words "direct the Local Government Commission for England to conduct a review and make recommendations"; and

(b) for the words following paragraph (b) there shall be substituted the words—

"and the provisions of Part II of the Local Government Act 1992 shall apply accordingly".

8. In section 9(4) of the 1972 Act (parish meetings and councils), for the words "section 10 or 11 or Part IV below" there shall be substituted the words "section 10 or 11 below or Part II of the Local Government Act 1992".

9. In section 11(5)(a) of the 1972 Act (orders for grouping parishes, dissolving groups and separating parishes from groups), for the words "Part IV below" there shall be substituted the words "Part II of the Local Government Act 1992".

10. In subsection (2) of section 12 of the 1972 Act (provision supplementary to sections 9 to 11 of that Act), for the words from "section 68 below" to the end of the subsection there shall be substituted the words "section 20 of the Local Government Act 1992 shall apply as if the order were made under Part II of that Act".

11. In section 30(1)(b) and (3) of the 1972 Act (restriction on community applications during and after reviews under Part IV of that Act), for the words "the Commission or Commissions", in each place where they occur, there shall be substituted the words "the Welsh Commission".

12. In section 54(1)(e) of the 1972 Act (proposals for change in local government areas in Wales), for the words "a substantive change" there shall be substituted the words "a change (hereafter in this Part referred to as a substantive change) which is independent of any change in local government areas so proposed".

13.—(1) In subsection (1) of section 60 of the 1972 Act (procedure for reviews), for the words "A Commission or" there shall be substituted the words "The Welsh Commission or a".

(2) In subsections (2) to (7) of that section, for the words "a Commission", in each place where they occur, there shall be substituted the words "the Welsh Commission".

14. In section 61(1) of the 1972 Act (local inquiries), for the words "A Commission or" there shall be substituted the words "The Welsh Commission or a".

15.—(1) In subsection (1) of section 65 of the 1972 Act (delegation of functions), for the words "A Commission" there shall be substituted the words "The Welsh Commission".

(2) In subsection (2) of that section, for the words "a Commission" there shall be substituted the words "the Welsh Commission".

16.—(1) In subsection (1) of section 71 of the 1972 Act (modification of seaward boundaries of local government areas), for the words "A Commission" there shall be substituted the words "The Welsh Commission".

(2) In subsection (2) of that section, for the words "a Commission", in each place where they occur, there shall be substituted the words "the Welsh Commission".

17. In section 73(2) of the 1972 Act (alteration of local boundaries consequent on alteration of water course), for the words "the English Commission" there shall be substituted the words "the Local Government Commission for England".

18.—(1) In subsection (1) of section 78 of the 1972 Act (supplementary), in the definition of "substantive change" for the words "section 47(1)(i)" there shall be substituted the words "section 54(1)(e)".

(2) In subsection (2) of that section, for the words "each of the Commissions" there shall be substituted the words "the Welsh Commission".

19.—(1) In paragraph 7(1)(b) of Schedule 2 to the 1972 Act (constitution of London borough councils), for the words "Part IV of this Act" there shall be substituted the words "Part II of the Local Government Act 1992".

(2) In paragraph 7(2) of that Schedule, for the words "Part IV of this Act", in the first place where they occur, there shall be substituted the words "Part II of the Local Government Act 1992".

20. In paragraph 10 of Schedule 3 to the 1972 Act (establishment of local authorities in England), for the words "Part IV of this Act", in each place where they occur, there shall be substituted the words "Part II of the Local Government Act 1992".

The Interpretation Act 1978 (c. 30)

21. In Schedule 1 to the Interpretation Act 1978, in the definition of "London borough" after the words "the Local Government Act 1972" there shall be inserted the words "or Part II of the Local Government Act 1992".

The Banking Act 1987 (c. 22)

22. In section 103(6)(b) of the Banking Act 1987 (effect of change of local government area on connection between local authority and municipal banks), for the words "or Part II" there shall be substituted the words "or Part II of the Local Government Act 1992 or under Part II".

GENERAL NOTE

This Schedule amends Acts including the Fire Services Act 1947, the Police Act 1964 and the Local Government Act 1972, in consequence of Pt. II. The amendments enable schemes for the combination of fire authority areas under the 1947 Act or for amalgamating police areas under the 1964 Act to be made in advance of alterations to local government structure, as well as in advance of alterations to local government boundaries, which is already possible. The 1972 Act is amended by the substitution of references to Pt. II of this Act for references to Pt. IV of the 1972 Act, and to limit the application of Pt. IV of that Act to Wales. The Interpretation Act 1978 is amended to make the definition of a London borough in Sched. 1 to that Act subject to any alterations under Pt. II of this Act as well as any made under Pt. IV of the 1972 Act. The Banking Act 1987 is amended to extend the definition of successor authority following changes to local government areas in s.103(6)(*b*) to include authorities whose areas are altered by Pt. II of this Act.

Section 29   SCHEDULE 4

REPEALS

PART I

REPEALS RELATING TO PART I

Chapter	Short title	Extent of repeal
1980 c. 65.	The Local Government, Planning and Land Act 1980.	Section 13(6). In section 16, subsections (2) and (3). In section 19A(1)(f), the words "(1) to (3)".
1982 c. 32.	The Local Government Finance Act 1982.	In section 15(1), the word "and" immediately preceding paragraph (c).
1988 c. 9.	The Local Government Act 1988.	In section 7(3)(a), the word "periods".

PART II

REPEALS RELATING TO PART II

Chapter	Short title	Extent of repeal
1972 c. 70.	The Local Government Act 1972.	Sections 46 to 52. In section 60(2)(b), the words "50(4) or". Sections 62 and 63. Section 66. Section 196(7) and (8). In section 197(5), the words "and for the words" onwards. In section 270(1), the definitions of "the Commission" and "the English Commission". Schedule 7. Schedule 9.
1975 c. 24.	The House of Commons Disqualification Act 1975.	In Part II of Schedule 1, the entry relating to the Local Government Boundary Commission for England.
1985 c. 51.	The Local Government Act 1985.	In Schedule 16, paragraphs 4 to 6.

INDEX

References are to sections

FINANCE ACT 1992*

(1992 c. 20)

An Act to grant certain duties, to alter other duties, and to amend the law relating to the National Debt and the Public Revenue, and to make further provision in connection with Finance.   [16th March 1992]

PARLIAMENTARY DEBATES
Hansard, H.C. Vol. 205, cols. 1094, 1132; H.L. Vol. 536, col. 1569.

INTRODUCTION
    This Act, rushed through Parliament in two days, implemented those of the proposals in Mr Norman Lamont's second Budget which were either agreed or considered essential by the Government to enact prior to the General Election on April 9.

ABBREVIATIONS
    ICTA 1988: Income and Corporation Taxes Act 1988.

Excise duties

Spirits, beer, wine, made-wine and cider

    1.—(1) In section 5 of the Alcoholic Liquor Duties Act 1979 (spirits) for "£18.96" there shall be substituted "£19.81".

    (2) In section 36 of that Act (beer) as that section has effect apart from section 7(1) of the Finance Act 1991 for "£1.06" there shall be substituted "£1.108".

    (3) For the Table of rates of duty in Schedule 1 to that Act (wine and made-wine) there shall be substituted the Table in the Schedule to this Act.

---

* Annotations by Ian Ferrier, M.A., Barrister.

(4) In section 62(1) of that Act (cider) for "£20.40" there shall be substituted "£21.32".

(5) This section shall be deemed to have come into force at 6 o'clock in the evening of 10th March 1992.

GENERAL NOTE

Together with the Schedule, this implements an increase of 4.5 per cent. in the excise duties on alcoholic drinks, in line with the rate of inflation. The changes, which are equivalent to a penny on a pint of beer or cider, five to 10 pence on a bottle of wine and 28p on a bottle of spirits, will raise £160m in 1992–93.

Tobacco products

2.—(1) For the Table in Schedule 1 to the Tobacco Products Duty Act 1979 there shall be substituted—

"TABLE

1. Cigarettes...............	An amount equal to 21 per cent. of the retail price plus £44.32 per thousand cigarettes.
2. Cigars	£67.89 per kilogram.
3. Hand-rolling tobacco	£71.63 per kilogram.
4. Other smoking tobacco and chewing tobacco	£29.98 per kilogram."

(2) This section shall be deemed to have come into force at 6 o'clock in the evening of 10th March 1992.

GENERAL NOTE

Reflecting official concern regarding the harmful effects of tobacco, the increase in excise duties is generally well above the rate of inflation. Duty on cigarettes is increased by 10.4 per cent. and on cigars and hand-rolling tobacco by 10 per cent. Only on pipe and chewing tobacco is the increase kept to the 4.5 per cent. justified by the rate of inflation. The effect, exemplified by a 13p increase in the cost of a packet of 20 cigarettes, will be to raise £540m in 1992–93.

Hydrocarbon oil

3.—(1) In section 6(1) of the Hydrocarbon Oil Duties Act 1979 for "£0.2585" (duty on light oil) and "£0.2187" (duty on heavy oil) there shall be substituted "£0.2779" and "£0.2285" respectively.

(2) In section 11(1) of that Act (rebate on heavy oil) for "£0.0091" (fuel oil) and "£0.0129" (gas oil) there shall be substituted "£0.0095" and "£0.0135" respectively.

(3) In section 13A(1) of that Act (rebate on unleaded petrol) for "£0.0344" there shall be substituted "£0.0437".

(4) In section 14(1) of that Act (rebate on light oil for use as furnace fuel) for "£0.0091" there shall be substituted "£0.0095".

(5) This section shall be deemed to have come into force at 6 o'clock in the evening of 10th March 1992.

GENERAL NOTE

The rates of duty on most hydrocarbon oils are increased by 4.5 per cent., in line with inflation, but the duty on leaded petrol is increased by 7.5 per cent., raising the tax differential in favour of unleaded petrol from 4.0p per litre to 5.1p per litre. The changes will raise £665m in 1992–93.

Vehicles excise duty

4.—(1) The Vehicles (Excise) Act 1971 shall be amended as follows.

(2) In the Table set out in Part II of Schedule 1 (annual rate of duty on certain vehicles not exceeding 450 kilograms in weight unladen) for paragraph 4 (£50 duty on tricycles) there shall be substituted—

"4. Tricycles of which the
cylinder capacity of the
engine does not exceed
150 cubic centimetres   15.00
5. Tricycles not included
above   50.00".

(3) In Schedule 2 (annual rates of duty on hackney carriages) in the second column of the Table set out in Part II, for "100" (rate of duty on hackney carriages with seating capacity under nine) there shall be substituted "110".

(4) In Schedule 5 (annual rate of duty on vehicles not falling within Schedules 1 to 4) in the second column of the Table set out in Part II, for "100.00" (rate of duty on vehicles not constructed before 1947) there shall be substituted "110.00".

(5) This section shall apply in relation to licences taken out after 10th March 1992.

GENERAL NOTE
The rate of vehicle excise duty on cars, light vans and taxis is raised by £10, the first increase since 1985, raising an additional £240m. A separate tax band for tricycles under 150cc is reintroduced, bringing such tricycles into the same rate band as a comparable moped.

General betting duty

5.—(1) In section 1(2) of the Betting and Gaming Duties Act 1981 (rate of general betting duty) for "8 per cent." there shall be substituted "7.75 per cent."

(2) This section shall apply in relation to bets made on or after 1st April 1992.

GENERAL NOTE
The rate of duty on the total stake on bets in "off course" betting shops is reduced from eight per cent. to 7.75 per cent. at an annual cost of £15m. This facilitated an increase in the yield from the Horserace Betting Levy Scheme determined by the Home Secretary under the Horserace Betting Levy Act 1969, s.1.

Value added tax

Payments on account

6.—(1) In the Value Added Tax Act 1983 the following section shall be inserted after section 38B—

"Payments on account
38C.—(1) The Treasury may make an order under this section if they consider it desirable to do so in the interests of the national economy.

(2) An order under this section may provide that a taxable person of a description specified in the order shall be under a duty—
  (a) to pay, on account of any tax he may become liable to pay in respect of a prescribed accounting period, amounts determined in accordance with the order, and
  (b) to do so at such times as are so determined.

(3) Where an order is made under this section, the Commissioners may make regulations containing such supplementary, incidental or consequential provisions as appear to the Commissioners to be necessary or expedient.

(4) A provision of an order or regulations under this section may be made in such way as the Treasury or, as the case may be, the Commissioners think fit (whether by amending provisions of or made under the enactments relating to tax, or otherwise).

(5) An order or regulations under this section may make different provision for different circumstances."

(2) In section 45(4) of that Act (orders subject to Commons approval) in paragraph (a) after "3(4)" there shall be inserted "or 38C".

GENERAL NOTE

Under the new arrangements coming into force from January 1, 1993, businesses will no longer have to fund the VAT due on imports from EEC countries before they are able to reclaim the tax as an input tax deduction under the normal rules. To offset the resulting shortfall to the Exchequer, large businesses (to be defined as those with an annual VAT liability of more than £2m) will be required to make monthly payments on account.

Serious misdeclaration, default surcharge, etc.

7.—(1) In section 14(1) of the Finance Act 1985 (penalty equal to 20 per cent. of tax lost imposed for serious misdeclaration or neglect resulting in understatements or overclaims), for "20 per cent." there shall be substituted "15 per cent."

(2) In section 19(5) of that Act (specified percentages for default surcharge), for the words from "and" at the end of paragraph (b) to the end of the subsection there shall be substituted—

> "(c) in relation to the third such period, the specified percentage is 15 per cent.; and
>
> (d) in relation to each such period after the third, the specified percentage is 20 per cent."

(3) Subject to subsection (4) below, subsection (1) above shall apply where a penalty is assessed after 10th March 1992 in relation to a prescribed accounting period beginning on or after 1st April 1990.

(4) Subsection (1) above shall not apply in the case of a supplementary assessment if the original assessment was made on or before 10th March 1992.

(5) Subsection (2) above shall apply in relation to any liability to a surcharge arising on or after 1st April 1992.

GENERAL NOTE

The operation of the serious misdeclaration penalty and default surcharge has been severely criticised as imposing a further burden on businesses already in difficulties due to the recession. The serious misdeclaration penalty, reduced from 30 per cent. to 20 per cent. last year, is further reduced to 15 per cent. and will not normally be levied unless the misdeclaration in a prescribed accounting period exceeds £2,000. The maximum rate of default surcharge, payable in respect of returns rendered late, is reduced from 30 per cent. to 20 per cent. The cost of these relaxations is estimated at £33m per annum. The Chancellor has also published a consultation paper on possible further long-term reform of the serious misdeclaration penalty.

Car tax

Reduction of rates

8.—(1) In section 1(2) of the Car Tax Act 1983 (rates of tax) for "10 per cent." in both places where the words occur there shall be substituted "5 per cent."

(2) This section shall apply in relation to vehicles on which car tax becomes due after 10th March 1992.

GENERAL NOTE

Car tax, levied at 10 per cent. on the wholesale value of cars since its introduction in 1973, is reduced to 5 per cent. to assist a hard-pressed motor industry, at an annual cost estimated at £635m for 1992–93.

Income tax

Lower rate

9.—(1) Section 1 of the Taxes Act 1988 (the charge to income tax) shall be amended as mentioned in subsections (2) to (8) below.

(2) In subsection (2) the following paragraph shall be inserted before paragraph (a)—
"(aa) in respect of so much of an individual's total income as does not exceed £2,000, at such rate as Parliament may determine to be the lower rate for that year;".

(3) In paragraph (a) of subsection (2) after "within" there shall be inserted "paragraph (aa) above or".

(4) The following subsection shall be inserted after subsection (2)—
"(2A) The amount up to which an individual's income is by virtue of subsection (2) above chargeable for any year at the lower rate shall be known as the lower rate limit."

(5) In subsection (3) after "at the" there shall be inserted "lower rate or the".

(6) In subsection (4) for "the amount specified" there shall be substituted "each of the amounts specified".

(7) In subsection (6) for "amount" there shall be substituted "amounts".

(8) The following subsection shall be inserted after subsection (6)—
"(6A) Where income tax at the basic rate has been borne on income chargeable at the lower rate any necessary repayment of tax shall be made on the making of a claim."

(9) In section 832(1) of the Taxes Act 1988 the following shall be inserted after the definition of "local authority association"—
" "lower rate", in relation to the charging of income tax for any year of assessment, means the rate of income tax determined in pursuance of section 1(2)(aa), and any reference to the lower rate limit shall be construed in accordance with section 1(2A);".

(10) This section shall apply for the year 1992–93 and subsequent years of assessment.

(11) This section shall not require any change to be made in the amounts deductible or repayable under section 203 of the Taxes Act 1988 (PAYE) before 18th May 1992.

GENERAL NOTE
This, the most controversial item in the Budget, introduces a new 20 per cent. tax rate on the first £2,000 of taxable income at an annual cost of over £2 billion. It was seen by the Government as a first step towards its objective of reducing the standard rate from 25 per cent. to 20 per cent.

Charge etc. for 1992–93

10.—(1) Income tax shall be charged for the year 1992–93, and for that year—
(a) the lower rate shall be 20 per cent.,
(b) the basic rate shall be 25 per cent., and
(c) the higher rate shall be 40 per cent.

(2) For the year 1992–93 the basic rate limit shall be £23,700, and for that year—
(a) section 1(4) of the Taxes Act 1988 (indexation) shall not apply;
(b) section 1(2)(b) of that Act (higher rate) shall apply as if the amount specified in it were £23,700.

(3) Section 257C(1) of the Taxes Act 1988 (indexation), so far as relating to section 257A(1) of that Act (married couple's allowance), shall not apply for the year 1992–93; and section 257A(1) of that Act shall apply for the year 1992–93 as if the amount specified in it were £1,720.

(4) For the year 1992–93 the qualifying maximum defined in section 367(5) of the Taxes Act 1988 (limit on relief for interest on certain loans) shall be £30,000.

(5) This section shall not require any change to be made in the amounts deductible or repayable under section 203 of the Taxes Act 1988 (PAYE) before 18th May 1992.

GENERAL NOTE

The basic rate limit, the married couple's allowance and the limit for mortgage interest relief remain unchanged. Personal allowances under ICTA 1988, s.257, will be indexed by statutory order in line with inflation.

General

Short title and interpretation

11.—(1) This Act may be cited as the Finance Act 1992.

(2) In this Act "the Taxes Act 1988" means the Income and Corporation Taxes Act 1988.

Section 1   SCHEDULE

TABLE OF RATES OF DUTY ON WINE AND MADE-WINE

Description of wine or made-wine	Rates of duty per hectolitre
	£
Wine or made-wine of a strength not exceeding 2 per cent.	12.60
Wine or made-wine of a strength exceeding 2 per cent. but not exceeding 3 per cent.	20.99
Wine or made-wine of a strength exceeding 3 per cent. but not exceeding 4 per cent.	29.39
Wine or made-wine of a strength exceeding 4 per cent. but not exceeding 5 per cent.	37.80
Wine or made-wine of a strength exceeding 5 per cent. but not exceeding 5.5 per cent.	46.19
Wine or made-wine of a strength exceeding 5.5 per cent. but not exceeding 15 per cent. and not being sparkling	125.96
Sparkling wine or sparkling made-wine of a strength exceeding 5.5 per cent. but not exceeding 15 per cent.	208.00
Wine or made-wine of a strength exceeding 15 per cent. but not exceeding 18 per cent.	217.25
Wine or made-wine of a strength exceeding 18 per cent. but not exceeding 22 per cent.	250.59
Wine or made-wine of a strength exceeding 22 per cent.	250.59 plus £19.81 for every 1 per cent. or part of 1 per cent. in excess of 22 per cent.

INDEX

References are to section and Schedule number

CONSOLIDATED FUND (NO. 2) ACT 1992

(1992 c. 21)

An Act to apply certain sums out of the Consolidated Fund to the service of the years ending on 31st March 1991 and 1992.   [16th March 1992]

PARLIAMENTARY DEBATES
  Hansard, H.L. Vol. 536, col. 1496; H.C. Vol. 205, col. 1093.

INTRODUCTION
  This Act provides for the issue of £418,563,447.96 from the Consolidated Fund of the U.K. for the year ending March 31, 1991 and for the issue of £3,059,340,000 for the service of the year ending March 31, 1992.

Issue out of the Consolidated Fund for the year ending 31st March 1991

1. The Treasury may issue out of the Consolidated Fund of the United Kingdom and apply towards making good the supply granted to Her Majesty for the service of the year ending on 31st March 1991 the sum of £418,563,447·96.

Issue out of the Consolidated Fund for the year ending 31st March 1992

2. The Treasury may issue out of the Consolidated Fund of the United Kingdom and apply towards making good the supply granted to Her Majesty for the service of the year ending on 31st March 1992 the sum of £3,059,340,000.

Short title

3. This Act may be cited as the Consolidated Fund (No. 2) Act 1992.

INDEX

References are to section numbers

CITATION, 3

CONSOLIDATED FUND,
    issue out of, for year ending 31 March
      1991, 1
    issue out of, for year ending 31 March
      1992, 2

APPROPRIATION ACT 1992

(1992 c. 22)

An Act to apply certain sums out of the Consolidated Fund to the service of the years ending on 31st March 1992 and 31st March 1993, to appropriate the supplies granted in this Session of Parliament, and to repeal certain Consolidated Fund and Appropriation Acts.   [16th March 1992]

PARLIAMENTARY DEBATES
Hansard, H.C. Vol. 205, col. 1233; H.L. Vol. 536, col. 1605.

INTRODUCTION
This Act provides for the issue of £241,460,000 out of the Consolidated Fund for the service of the year ending March 31, 1992 and for the issue of £109,478,692,000 for the service of the year ending March 31, 1993. The Schedules to this Act detail the allocation of moneys so appropriated.

GRANTS OUT OF THE CONSOLIDATED FUND

Issue out of the Consolidated Fund for the year ending 31st March 1992

1. The Treasury may issue out of the Consolidated Fund of the United Kingdom and apply towards making good the supply granted to Her Majesty for the service of the year ending on 31st March 1992 the sum of £241,460,000·00.

Issue out of the Consolidated Fund for the year ending 31st March 1993

2. The Treasury may issue out of the Consolidated Fund of the United Kingdom and apply towards making good the supply granted to Her Majesty for the service of the year ending on 31st March 1993 the sum of £109,478,692,000·00.

APPROPRIATION OF GRANTS

Appropriation of sums voted for supply services

3. All sums granted by this Act and the other Acts mentioned in Schedule (A) annexed to this Act out of the said Consolidated Fund towards making good the supply granted to Her Majesty amounting, as appears by the said schedule, in the aggregate, to the sum of £192,144,456,447·96 are appropriated, and shall be deemed to have been appropriated as from the date of the passing of the Acts mentioned in the said Schedule (A), for the services and purposes expressed in Schedule (B) annexed hereto.

The abstract of schedules and schedules annexed hereto, with the notes (if any) to such schedules, shall be deemed to be part of this Act in the same manner as if they had been contained in the body thereof.

In addition to the said sums granted out of the Consolidated Fund, there may be applied out of any money directed, under section 2 of the Public Accounts and Charges Act 1891, to be applied as appropriations in aid of the grants for the services and purposes specified in Schedule (B) annexed hereto the sums respectively set forth in the last column of the said schedule.

Repeals

4. The enactments mentioned in Schedule (C) annexed to this Act are hereby repealed.

Short title

5. This Act may be cited as the Appropriation Act 1992.

ABSTRACT
OF
SCHEDULES (A) and (B) to which this
Act refers

Section 2   SCHEDULE (A)

Grants out of the Consolidated Fund.............................£192,144,456,447·96

Section 2   SCHEDULE (B)—Appropriation of Grants

	Supply Grants	Appropriations in Aid
	£	£
1990–91 and 1991–92		
Part 1. Defence and Civil (Excesses), 1990–91	418,563,447·96	48,187,520·24
Part 2. Supplementary, 1991–92	7,178,084,000·00	408,791,000·00
1992–93		
Part 3. Class I	24,239,800,000·00	1,895,892,000·00
Part 4. Class II	3,041,675,000·00	115,227,000·00
Part 5. Class III	784,020,000·00	2,057,489,000.00
Part 6. Class IV	1,617,011,000·00	772,512,000·00
Part 7. Class V	1,209,739,000·00	1,253,457,000·00
Part 8. Class VI	3,200,872,000·00	764,782,000·00
Part 9. Class VII	5,531,377,000·00	225,788,000·00
Part 10. Class VIII	43,186,726,000·00	1,649,980,000·00
Part 11. Class IX	7,143,236,000·00	131,097,000·00
Part 12. Class X	2,036,111,000·00	550,633,000·00
Part 13. Class XI	8,322,109,000·00	2,082,305,000·00
Part 14. Class XII	617,186,000·00	22,000·00
Part 15. Class XIII	24,350,298,000·00	7,018,969,000·00
Part 16. Class XIV	33,971,124,000·00	1,436,899,000·00
Part 17. Class XV	10,028,402,000·00	1,021,227,000·00
Part 18. Class XVI	5,894,399,000·00	310,308,000·00
Part 19. Class XVII	2,604,423,000·00	9,586,000·00
Part 20. Class XVIII	4,945,103,000.00	1,508,719,000·00
Part 21. Class XIX	348,274,000·00	38,839,000·00
Part 22. Class XIXA	87,924,000·00	518,000·00
Part 23. Class XIXB	38,000,000·00	5,100,000·00
Part 24. Class XX	1,350,000,000·00	—
Total	184,547,809,000·00	22,849,349,000·00
Grand Total	192,144,456,447·96	23,306,327,520·24

SCHEDULE (A)

GRANTS OUT OF THE CONSOLIDATED FUND

	£
For the service of the year ended 31st March 1991—	
Under Act 1992 c..	418,563,447·96
For the service of the year ending 31st March 1992—	
Under Act 1991 c. 68	3,427,284,000·00
Under Act 1992 c. 1	450,000,000·00
Under Act 1992 c. 21	3,059,340,000·00
Under this Act..	241,460,000·00
For the service of the year ending on 31st March 1993—	
Under Act 1991 c. 68	75,069,116,000·00
Under Act 1992 c. 1	1,000·00
Under this Act..	109,478,692,000·00
TOTAL..	192,144,456,447·96

SCHEDULE (B)—Part 1

———

Defence and Civil
(Excesses), 1990–91

Defence and Civil (Excesses), 1990–1991

Sums granted, and sums which may be applied as appropriations in aid in addition thereto, to make good excesses on certain grants for defence and civil services for the year ended 31st March 1991, viz.:—

	Supply Grants	Surplus receipts available to be applied as Appropriations in Aid
Vote	£	£
Class I		
1. Defence: personnel costs, support and other services......................	157,869,854·68	—
4. Defence works services etc.	30,152,515·61	—
5. Defence: ship refitting and repair	8,093,358·58	—
Class VI		
5. Sale of Skills Training Agency	4,534,415·54	—
Class VIII		
13. Property Services Agency of the Department of the Environment: PSA Services..	15,148,322·01	44,402,432·99
Class X		
10. Treasury Solicitor's Department: operational costs........................	48,759·35	62,335·23
Class XIII		
3. Department of Health administration, miscellaneous health services and personal social services, England...............	1,000·00	—
Class XIV		
2. Income support etc.	202,715,222·19	3,722,752·02
Total, Defence and Civil (Excesses) 1990–91............................	418,563,447·96	48,187,520·24

SCHEDULE (B).—PART 2

———

SUPPLEMENTARY, 1991–92

SCHEDULE OF SUPPLEMENTARY SUMS granted, and of the sums which may be applied as appropriations in aid in addition thereto, to defray the charges for the Services herein particularly mentioned, for the year ended 31st March 1992, viz.:—

	Sums not exceeding	
	Supply Grants	Appropriations in Aid
	£	£
Vote		
CLASS I		
1. For expenditure by the Ministry of Defence on personnel costs etc., of the Armed Forces and their Reserves and Cadet Forces etc. (including provision for Naval Service to an additional number not exceeding 75), personnel costs etc. of Defence Ministers and of certain civilian staff employed by the Ministry of Defence, movements, certain stores, supplies and services, plant and machinery, charter of ships, certain research, lands and buildings, sundry grants, and payments abroad	145,848,000	* – 125,335,000
2. For expenditure by the Procurement Executive of the Ministry of Defence in operating its Headquarters and Establishments and for its other common services; for research, etc. by contract; for lands and buildings; for development by contract, production, repair etc. and purchases for sale abroad of sea systems, land systems, air systems and associated equipment; for certain contingent liabilities, and for sundry other Procurement Executive services including those on repayment terms to non-exchequer customers	329,257,000	35,704,000
3. For expenditure by the Ministry of Defence on retired pay, pensions and other payments, etc.	1,000	—
4. For expenditure by the Ministry of Defence on new construction and maintenance works and related services at defence establishments and on fees and some works costs for visiting forces	1,000	* – 95,152,000
5. For expenditure by the Ministry of Defence on the refit and repair of ships, associated capital facilities, on contractors' redundancy costs and administration.....	18,371,000	* – 6,326,000
CLASS II		
1. For expenditure by the Foreign and Commonwealth Office on its salaries, building and other accommodation services, and administration, and those of HM Diplomatic Service, official information services, sundry services and loans and payments in connection with catering services............................	8,209,000	* – 11,600,000

	Sums not exceeding	
	Supply Grants	Appropriations in Aid
	£	£

Vote

2. For expenditure by the Foreign and Commonwealth Office on grants and subscriptions, etc., to certain international organisations, special payments and assistance, scholarships, military aid and sundry other grants and services . . . . | 142,296,000 | 1,660,000 |

4. For expenditure by the Foreign and Commonwealth Office on a grant in aid of the British Council . . . . | 463,000 | — |

5. For expenditure by the Foreign and Commonwealth Office: Overseas Development Administration under the Overseas Development and Co-operation Act 1980 on the official United Kingdom aid programme; economic assistance to Eastern Europe and the USSR (now described as the former Soviet Union); and global environmental assistance; including financial and technical assistance to governments, institutions, voluntary agencies and individuals; pensions and allowances in respect of overseas service including contributions to pension funds; capital and other subscriptions and contributions, including payments under guarantee, to multilateral development banks and other international and regional bodies; emergency, refugee and other relief assistance; loans to the Commonwealth Development Corporation; and running costs, related capital expenditure and other administrative costs including for the Natural Resources Institute (an executive agency). . . . . | 87,413,000 | 19,645,000 |

6. For expenditure by the Foreign and Commonwealth Office (Overseas Development Administration) on pension and superannuation payments, etc. in respect of overseas service and sundry other services and expenses . . . . | 1,500,000 | *− 1,679,000* |

CLASS III

1. For expenditure by the Intervention Board—Executive Agency in giving effect in the United Kingdom to the agricultural support provisions of the Common Agricultural Policy of the European Community and for other services . . . . | 1,000 | 155,051,000 |

2. For expenditure by the Intervention Board—Executive Agency on central administration and miscellaneous services | 2,046,000 | 30,000 |

3. For expenditure by the Ministry of Agriculture, Fisheries and Food on market support, grants and loans for capital and other improvements, support for agriculture in special areas and compensation to sheep producers, animal health and certain other services . . . . | 51,042,000 | *− 564,000* |

4. For expenditure by the Ministry of Agriculture, Fisheries and Food on commissioned research and development and advice, education and training services, botanical

	Sums not exceeding	
	Supply Grants	Appropriations in Aid
	£	£

Vote

services, assistance to production, marketing and processing, and certain alternative land uses, support for the fishing industry, arterial drainage, flood and coast protection, emergency and strategic food services, protective, agency, administrative, scientific and policy advice, and other services..............................

| | 1,000 | 3,000,000 |

CLASS IV

1. For expenditure by the Department of Trade and Industry on regional development grants, regional selective assistance, selective assistance to individual industries and firms, UK contributions arising from its commitments under the International Natural Rubber Agreement, a strategic mineral stockpile, support for the film, aerospace, and shipbuilding industries, assistance to redundant steel workers, and other payments......................

| | 1,000 | * – 707,000 |

2. For expenditure by the Department of Trade and Industry on central and miscellaneous services (including running costs, capital expenditure, consultancy advice and legal costs, paid publicity, and grants to the fund for sub-postmasters), business development (including the consultancy initiatives, support for representative organisations and the regional enterprise grant scheme), enterprise and job creation (the inner cities initiative), support for industry, (including industrial research and development, civil aircraft research and demonstration, education, training, design, quality, marketing, management best practice and standards, and support for telecommunications and posts), inward investment, space technology programmes, international trade (including export promotion, trade co-operation, the Single European Market campaign and international exhibitions), the regulation of financial and trading practices, investor information and education, copyright, consumer protection, research establishments major works and other expenditure (including expenditure by the National Engineering Laboratory Executive Agency and the National Weights and Measures Laboratory Executive Agency measurement and technology support, Radiocommunications Executive Agency, Warren Spring Laboratory Executive Agency, the Laboratory of the Government Chemist Executive Agency, the National Physical Laboratory Executive Agency, the Patent Office Executive Agency (net running costs), Companies House Executive Agency (net running

	Sums not exceeding	
	Supply Grants	Appropriations in Aid
	£	£
Vote		
cost), English Industrial Estates Corporations, loans to the Patent Office and Companies House Trading Funds, provision of land and buildings, loan, grants and other payments	1,000	163,000
4. For expenditure by the Export Credits Guarantee Department on administration	2,880,000	233,000
5. For expenditure by the Export Credits Guarantee Department in connection with interest support to banks and other lenders of export finance, cover under the tender to contract/forward exchange supplement scheme, grants towards financing of exports to match foreign competition and residual commitments under discontinued guarantees offered to banks and external trade agencies	3,171,000	* – 6,741,000
6. For expenditure by the Export Credits Guarantee Department in connection with export credits guarantees, other guarantees given in the national interest or to render economic assistance to overseas countries, overseas investment insurance and trading expenses	1,000	77,971,000
7. For expenditure by the Export Credits Guarantee Department in connection with the sale of the short term insurance services operation	1,000	49,999,000
9. For expenditure by the Office of Telecommunications on administrative and operational costs	618,000	1,000
CLASS V		
9. For expenditure by the Department of Energy in connection with the privatisation of the coal industry	4,000,000	—
CLASS VI		
1. For expenditure by the Department of Employment, including expenditure via Training and Enterprise Councils and local enterprise companies, on training, including the provision of training programmes for young people and adults and initiatives within education; on the promotion of enterprise, tourism and the encouragement of self-employment and small firms; on help for unemployed people; the improvement of industrial relations; industrial tribunals; compensation for persons disabled by certain industrial diseases; payments towards expenses of trade union ballots; on residual liabilities and disposal of the remaining assets of the former National Dock Labour Board; on the costs of maintaining and disposing of the former Skills Training Agency; administration, central and miscellaneous services including		

	Sums not exceeding	
	Supply Grants	Appropriations in Aid
	£	£

Vote

assistance on employment issues to eastern Europe in cooperation with the Foreign and Commonwealth Office . . . . | 81,067,000 | 5,057,000

2. For expenditure by the Employment Service of the Department of Employment on help for unemployed people, support for people with disabilities, assistance on employment issues in eastern Europe in cooperation with the Foreign and Commonwealth Office, on research, publicity and on administration . . . . | 35,032,000 | 35,293,000

3. For expenditure by the Department of Employment on grants in aid to the Health and Safety Commission and to the Advisory, Conciliation and Arbitration Service | 339,000 | —

CLASS VII

1. For expenditure by the Department of Transport on the construction, improvement and maintenance of motorways and trunk roads, including the acquisition of land, scheme design and preparation, archaeological survey and rescue work, compensation, the purchase of maintenance vehicles and equipment, expenditure on priority routes in London, the maintenance and operation of the Woolwich Ferry, and highways, safety, and traffic administration . . . . | 1,000 | 31,078,000

2. For expenditure by the Department of Transport on grants for freight facilities and travel concessions; shipping; civil aviation; central administration and miscellaneous services; the Vehicle Certification Agency and loans to the Vehicle Inspectorate Executive Agency (Trading Fund); research and development; road safety, publicity and certain other transport services, including traffic censuses, civil defence, residual expenses associated with the privatisation of transport industries and expenses associated with the sale of the Trust Ports . . . . | 5,170,000 | 1,811,000

3. For expenditure by the Department of Transport on support to nationalised transport industries and to ports; rebate of fuel duty to bus operators; and costs of driver testing and training . . . . | 207,189,000 | 499,000

4. For expenditure by the Department of Transport in connection with driver and vehicle registration and licensing, the collection of revenue and on compensation and payments towards the pension of local authority staff employed in Driver and Vehicle Licensing before the setting up of

	Sums not exceeding	
	Supply Grants	Appropriations in Aid
	£	£

Vote

DVLC; and the development and maintenance of information technology systems for other parts of the Department . . . . — 8,660,000 — * – 8,660,000

5. For expenditure by the Department of Transport on transport supplementary grants to highway authorities in England and certain other grants and payments in support of local roads and transport expenditure; and on grants to the Humber Bridge Board to cover the Board's liabilities . . . . — 7,600,000 — —

CLASS VIII

1. For expenditure by the Department of the Environment on subsidies, improvements and investment, payments to the Housing Corporation and other sundry services . . . — 359,541,000 — 250,000

2. For expenditure by the Department of the Environment on housing administration, including payments to the Housing Corporation and housing action trusts; housing for the single homeless and for special needs accommodation; housing management and mobility; housing, building and construction research; rent officers and Rent Assessment Panels; grants to home improvement agencies; grants and payments for sundry housing services and projects. . . . . — 1,700,000 — —

3. For expenditure by the Department of the Environment on city grants to the private sector for urban regeneration, derelict land reclamation, city action teams, payments in connection with inner cities and urban land research, the urban programme, urban development grant, payments to urban development corporations, transitional grants for voluntary bodies and payments to the Manchester Olympics Bid Committee . . . . — 27,765,000 — 40,000

6. For expenditure by the Department of the Environment on Royal Palaces, Historic Royal Palaces Agency (including administration), Royal Parks, Royal Armouries etc. (including administration), historic buildings, ancient monuments and certain public buildings, the national heritage, on the inspection of historic wreck sites; on payments to the Inland Revenue covering assets accepted in lieu of tax and on the assessment of possible listed buildings. . . . — 3,521,000 — —

7. For expenditure by the Department of the Environment (Property Holdings) on acquisitions, public building work, accommodation services, administration and certain other services for Civil purposes in the United Kingdom, for Ministry of Defence, for civil purposes required in connection

	Sums not exceeding	
	Supply Grants	Appropriations in Aid
	£	£

Vote

with the channel fixed link and for sponsorship of The Buying Agency............	1,000	28,675,000
8. For expenditure by the Department of the Environment on administration, including royal commissions, committees, etc., and by the Building Research Establishment on building and other research and surveys ..	201,000	* – 4,586,000
9. For expenditure by the Department of the Environment on revenue support grant, residual payments of rate support grants, payments of non-domestic rates to charging authorities in England, on a grant providing transitional support for certain charging authorities, on payments to specified bodies and the Commission for Local Administration in England, on payments for Inland Revenue Valuation Office rating and valuation services, and on payments to meet the expenses of valuation and community charge tribunals........	78,232,000	30,000
12. For expenditure by the Ordnance Survey on the survey of Great Britain and other mapping services......................	1,848,000	* – 2,100,000
13. For expenditure by PSA Services on works and similar services for other government departments and certain other clients; administrative costs; transitional and restructuring costs; residual costs of The Crown Suppliers; costs of the PSA Services privatisation programme	135,106,000	44,665,000
14. For expenditure by the Department of the Environment on grants to local authorities in respect of the community charge; on rate rebate grants; on emergency financial assistance to local authorities; and on repayments of excess contributions made by local authorities and other bodies in respect of non-domestic rates in 1990–91	16,901,000	—

CLASS IX

1. For expenditure by the Home Office on court services, compensation for criminal injuries, probation, police and superannuation payments for police and fire services............................	199,675,000	2,807,000
2. For expenditure by the Home Office in England and Wales on prisons (including central administration and other costs arising from the detention of prisoners), the Parole Board, the storage and maintenance of equipment (including certain civilian emergency equipment), and transport management	137,000,000	* – 8,692,000
3. For expenditure by the Home Office on police, the forensic science service, civil defence, fire, the Football Licensing Authority, the Arson Prevention Bureau,		

	Sums not exceeding	
	Supply Grants	Appropriations in Aid
	£	£
Vote		
court services, the Royal Commission on Criminal Justice, other services related to crime, probation and after-care, certain broadcasting services, data protection and other miscellaneous services, prevention of drug abuse, control of immigration and nationality, issue of passports etc., community services; and on administration (excluding prisons)	1,000	142,000
4. For expenditure by the Home Office on payments to the British Broadcasting Corporation for home broadcasting, and balance of payments in respect of the collection and enforcement of licence fees for 1990–91, which fall due in 1991–92	42,000,000	—
6. For expenditure by the Home Office in connection with the sale of the Independent Broadcasting Authority's transmission system.........................	1,000	406,000
CLASS X		
1. For expenditure by the Lord Chancellor's Department on the Court Service, the Law Commission, the Office of the Special Commissioners of Income Tax, the Office of the Social Security Commissioners, the VAT tribunals, the Immigration Appellate Authorities, the Transport Tribunal, the Banking and Building Societies' Appeals Tribunals, the Statutory Publications Office, the Public Trust Office, certain other legal services, the administration of legal aid, site acquisitions, the development and construction of court buildings and the acquisition, disposal, refurbishment and adaptation of office and general accommodation.....................	1,000	9,871,000
2. For grants to the Legal Aid Fund and for expenditure by the Lord Chancellor's Department on legal aid in criminal cases and costs paid from central funds........	218,850,000	* – 40,000
3. For expenditure by the Northern Ireland Court Service on court services and certain other legal services	560,000	725,000
4. For expenditure by the Northern Ireland Court Service on legal aid and court services............................	2,266,000	—
5. For expenditure by the Crown Prosecution Service on administrative costs..........	300,000	—
7. For expenditure by the Serious Fraud Office on administrative costs..........	1,180,000	—
8. For expenditure by the Serious Fraud Office on investigations and prosecutions.	1,687,000	—
9. For expenditure by the Legal Secretariat to the Law Officers and the Department of the Procurator General and Treasury Solicitor on administration costs	743,000	501,000
10. For expenditure by the Department of the Procurator General and Treasury Solicitor on costs and fees for legal services.......	1,395,000	4,874,000

	Sums not exceeding	
	Supply Grants	Appropriations in Aid
	£	£

Vote

12. For expenditure by the Public Record Office on administrative and operational costs .... | 255,000 | 200,000

13. For expenditure by the Lord Advocate's Departments on administrative costs, including fees paid to temporary Procurators Fiscal......................... | 447,000 | —

14. For expenditure by the Crown Office on witnesses' expenses and other costs associated with crown prosecutions......... | 750,000 | —

CLASS XI

1. For expenditure by the Department of Education and Science on the assisted places scheme, voluntary and special schools, City Technology Colleges, grant maintained schools, music and ballet schools, direct grant schools, adult education, youth services, grants for miscellaneous international and other educational services including the provision of a school in Armenia, research, sport and central government grants to local authorities ... | 5,607,000 | 30,500,000

2. For expenditure by the Department of Education and Science on payments to the Universities Funding Council and the Polytechnics and Colleges Funding Council and for certain other higher education institutions, payments for higher and further education, and payment of certain licence fees to the Home Office................... | 12,706,000 | 461,000

3. For expenditure by the Department of Education and Science on student awards and fees, provision of loans to students (including administration costs); access funds; reimbursement of fees for qualifying European Community students; legal expenses; and compensation payments to redundant teachers and staff of certain institutions......................... | 10,118,000 | * – 2,000

4. For expenditure by the Department of Education and Science on administration . | 7,925,000 | 1,000

5. For expenditure by the Department of Education and Science on payments to the Agricultural and Food Research Council, the Medical Research Council, the Natural Environment Research Council, the Science and Engineering Research Council, the Social and Economic Research Council, the Royal Society, the Fellowship of Engineering, the Advisory Board for the Research Councils, and the Centre for Exploitation of Science and Technology including the payment of certain licence fees to the Home Office................ | 11,484,000 | 337,000

	Sums not exceeding	
	Supply Grants	Appropriations in Aid
	£	£

Vote

CLASS XII

1. For expenditure by the Office of Arts and Libraries on payments to the national and other museums and galleries, to the Museums and Galleries Commission; for improvements and for related research, surveys and other services . . . . | 339,000 | — |
2. For expenditure by the Office of Arts and Libraries on payments to the Arts Council and other bodies; on payments to the Inland Revenue for assets accepted in lieu of tax; on the Government Art Collection; and on certain other services for the benefit of the arts . . . . | 14,870,000 | — |
3. For expenditure by the Office of Arts and Libraries on payments to the British Library and the Royal Geographical Society; on the British Library St. Pancras project; the Royal Commission on Historical Manuscripts; on payments in respect of Public Lending Right; and for a development incentive scheme . . . . | 1,000 | 1,447,000 |

CLASS XIII

1. For expenditure by the Department of Health on hospital, community health, family health and family health service administration services, and on related services . . . . | 110,667,000 | * − 176,000 |
2. For expenditure by the Department of Health on family health services, on medical treatment given to people from the United Kingdom in other countries of the European Community and on welfare food | 339,473,000 | * − 167,768,000 |
3. For expenditure by the Department of Health on administration, including certain expenditure on behalf of the Department of Social Security, on the national health service in England, on family health administration and related services, on miscellaneous health, personal social and other services (some of which are administered on a United Kingdom basis), including mental health, medical, scientific and technical services, services for disabled persons, grants to voluntary organisations, etc., and a contribution to the International Peto Institute . . . . | 6,961,000 | * − 226,000 |
4. For expenditure by the Department of Health on National Health Service trusts and on family health services . . . . | 202,151,000 | * − 36,926,000 |
6. For the expenditure of the Office of Population Censuses and Surveys on administrative and operational costs . . . . | 263,000 | 336,000 |

	Sums not exceeding	
	Supply Grants	Appropriations in Aid
	£	£

Vote

CLASS XIV

1. For expenditure by the Department of Social Security on non-contributory retirement pensions, Christmas bonus payments to pensioners, pensions etc., for disablement or death arising out of war, or service in the armed forces after 2 September 1939 and on sundry other services, on attendance allowance, invalid care allowance, severe disablement allowance, mobility allowance; on pensions, gratuities and sundry allowances for disablement and specified deaths arising from industrial causes; on income support, transitional payment, child benefit, one parent benefit, family credit, and on the vaccine damage payment scheme .... **2,484,572,000** | | **28,513,000**

2. For expenditure by the Department of Social Security on rent rebate, rent allowance, community charge benefit, community charge rebate and rate rebate subsidies to housing, charging, levying and local authorities and residual expenditure on subsidies towards the administrative costs incurred by these authorities in operating the former housing benefit scheme, on transitional payments to help certain housing benefit claimants significantly affected by the changes to the housing benefit scheme and certain supplementary benefit claimants not entitled to benefit under the income support scheme; on payments to authorities in respect of completed enquiry forms returned to the Transitional Payments Unit, on sums payable into the National Insurance Fund as compensation in respect of statutory sick pay and statutory maternity pay and on sums payable into the Social Fund for expenditure on maternity expenses, funeral expenses and heating expenses in exceptionally cold weather............................. **282,431,000** | | ***– 16,730,000**

3. For expenditure by the Department of Social Security on sums payable as grants to the Independent Living Fund; on subsidies to housing and local authorities towards the costs of administering the housing benefit scheme and to charging and levying authorities towards the costs of administering the community charge benefit scheme, as grants to Motability towards their administrative costs and to enable them to assist invalid vehicle users and others to have adapted and/or to purchase or lease cars from them, and on sums payable to the Social Fund to finance

	Sums not exceeding	
	Supply Grants	Appropriations in Aid
Vote	£	£
budgeting loans, crisis loans and community care grants	32,918,000	—
4. For expenditure by the Department of Social Security on administration, for agency payments, and for certain other services including grants to local authorities and voluntary organisations	42,505,000	43,973,000
CLASS XV		
1. For expenditure by the Scottish Office Agriculture and Fisheries Department on market support, assistance for structural measures, support in special areas, compensation to sheep producers and certain other services including animal health. . . .	8,000,000	102,000
2. For expenditure by the Scottish Office Agriculture and Fisheries Department on education and advisory services, botanical services, assistance to production, marketing and processing, and certain alternative land uses, assistance to crofting communities, administrative and land management services, assistance to the Scottish fishing industry, fishery protection and certain other services including accruing superannuation liability charges, research and development and special services	963,000	* – 1,845,000
3. For expenditure by the Scottish Office Industry Department on Scottish Enterprise and Highlands and Islands Enterprise; on regional enterprise grants; on technical and vocational education; on the promotion of tourism; on financial assistance to the electricity industry and on local enterprise; on residual expenditure for the Scottish Development Agency and the Highlands and Islands Development Board; on consumer protection; on roads and certain associated services, including the acquisition of land, lighting, road safety and related services; on assistance to local transport; on support for transport services in the Highlands and Islands; on piers and harbours, and on certain other transport services and grants; on advisers' fees relating to the privatisation of passenger transport companies; and on other sundry services in connection with trade and industry, etc.	23,037,000	—
5. For expenditure by the Scottish Office Environment Department on roads and certain associated services, including the acquisition of land, lighting, road safety and related services, on assistance to local transport, on support for transport services in the Highlands and Islands, piers and harbours and on certain other transport		

	Sums not exceeding	
	Supply Grants	Appropriations in Aid
	£	£

Vote

services and grants, on historic buildings and monuments (including administration), expenditure on the countryside and on other central and environmental services.................................... **1,000** **175,000**

7. For expenditure by the Scottish Office Environment Department on housing subsidies, funds for Scottish Homes and a range of other Exchequer contributions and grants relating to housing........... **7,690,000** **—**

9. For expenditure by the Scottish Office Industry Department in connection with the privatisation of the electricity supply industry in Scotland **1,000** **89,598,000**

10. For expenditure by the Scottish Courts Administration on court services, the Scottish Law Commission and certain legal services........................... **1,000** **1,185,000**

11. For expenditure by the Scottish Office Home and Health Department on legal aid, criminal injuries compensation (excluding administration), police, police and fire services superannuation and welfare food............................ **13,279,000** **—**

12. For expenditure by the Scottish Courts Administration on costs and fees in connection with legal proceedings .... **9,650,000** **—**

13. For expenditure by the Scottish Office Home and Health Department on legal aid administration; certain services relating to crime including the Parole Board for Scotland, prison, fire and police services (excluding grants to local authorities and superannuation); civil defence (including grants) and other protective and miscellaneous services; miscellaneous health services; social work services including the provision of residential and secure accommodation for children; services for offenders including probation and supervised attendance orders; grants to voluntary organisations; training and research; unemployed voluntary action fund; other grants to local authorities **6,155,000** **728,000**

14. For expenditure by the Scottish Office Education Department on: schools, including establishment of self-governing schools; higher and further education; compensation payments; special educational needs; community education; curriculum development, educational services, including support for School Boards, training and research; sport; Gaelic broadcasting; arts, libraries, museums and galleries, including purchase grants and payments to Royal Society of Edinburgh, Royal Scottish Geographical Society and Scottish

	Sums not exceeding	
	Supply Grants	Appropriations in Aid
	£	£

Vote

Film Production Fund; publicity; indemnities; administration; central government grants to local authorities, including the Careers Service; and EC agency payments | 2,000,000 | —

15. For expenditure by the Scottish Office Education Department on student loans including administration and related access funds, student awards and fees and reimbursement of fees for qualifying European Community students.................. | 15,000,000 | —

16. For expenditure by the Scottish Office Home and Health Department on provision of services under the National Health Service in Scotland and certain other services and compensation payments to dental practitioners who opt for early retirement .... | 54,596,000 | * – *14,511,000*

17. For the expenditure of the Scottish Record Office on administrative costs and a grant to the Business Archives Council of Scotland...................................... | 50,000 | —

18. For expenditure of the General Register Office for Scotland on administrative and operational costs..................... | 852,000 | —

19. For the expenditure of the Registers of Scotland on administrative costs......... | 1,000 | 1,284,000

20. For expenditure by the Scottish Office on administrative costs .... | 466,000 | —

21. For expenditure by the Scottish Office Environment Department for revenue and rate support grants and for council tax valuation grants in Scotland .... | 170,000 | 2,833,000

22. For expenditure by the Scottish Office Environment Department on grants to local authorities in respect of community charge and certain related administrative expenses; on rate rebate and transitional relief grants; and the special payments scheme to local authorities in Scotland ... | 76,575,000 | —

23. For expenditure by the Scottish Office Home and Health Department on superannuation allowances and gratuities etc, in respect of teachers, and the widows, widowers, and dependants of deceased teachers .... | 3,484,000 | 500,000

24. For expenditure by the Scottish Office Home and Health Department on superannuation allowances and gratuities etc, in respect of National Health Service employees and the widows, widowers and dependants of deceased employees ...... | 19,127,000 | * – *9,911,000*

25. For expenditure by the Scottish Office Environment Department and the Scottish Office Industry Department on advisers' fees and other costs in connection with the sale by the Scottish Transport Group of Scottish Bus operating subsidiaries ...... | 1,000 | —

	Sums not exceeding	
	Supply Grants	Appropriations in Aid
	£	£

Vote

26. For expenditure by the Scottish Office Home and Health Department on hospital, community health, family health services and other health services, including central health services and civil defence.........   23,084,000   3,385,000

CLASS XVI

1. For expenditure by the Welsh Office on market support, grants for capital and other improvements, support for agriculture in special areas and compensation to sheep producers and animal health   10,610,000   —

4. For expenditure by the Welsh Office on a contribution to the Department of Employment in relation to training activities in Wales   5,159,000   —

5. For expenditure by the Welsh Office on tourism, roads and transport and certain associated services, housing, historic buildings and ancient monuments, Cadw Agency (including administration), other environmental services (including civil defence and national parks), education, arts, libraries and museums, health and personal social services, EC agency payments, other grants and certain other services, including research.............   1,000   33,000

6. For expenditure by the Welsh Office on housing, other environmental services, welfare food payments, EC agency payments and certain other services.........   2,000   447,000

7. For expenditure by the Welsh Office on family health services under the National Health Service........................   33,882,000   ** – 11,330,000*

8. For expenditure by the Welsh Office on hospital, community health, family health (part) and family health service administration services and on related services   12,783,000   ** – 438,000*

9. For expenditure by the Welsh Office on central administration and other services .   304,000   —

10. For expenditure by the Welsh Office on revenue support grant, payment of national non-domestic rates income to local authorities in Wales, payments to specified bodies, payments following recalculations of rate support grant for prior years, payments to the Valuation Office for services including council tax banding work and the running costs of valuation and community charge tribunal offices, etc.   10,521,000   4,000

11. For expenditure by the Welsh Office on grants to local authorities in Wales in respect of the community charge and certain related administrative expenses, residual rate rebate grants, on special grants to local authorities following natural emergencies, and on repayments of excess contributions

	Sums not exceeding	
	Supply Grants	Appropriations in Aid
	£	£

Vote

made by local authorities and other bodies in respect of non-domestic rates in 1990–91 — 5,227,000 / —

CLASS XVII

1. For expenditure by the Northern Ireland Office on central and miscellaneous services, services related to crime, civil defence, police training schools, probation and after-care etc, compensation schemes, crown prosecutions and other legal services and certain other grants............... 11,236,000 / 25,000
2. For expenditure by the Northern Ireland Office on a grant in aid of the Northern Ireland Consolidated Fund and other transfers........................... 395,000,000 / —

CLASS XVIII

1. For expenditure by Her Majesty's Treasury on economic, financial and related administration; on computers and general telecommunications; payments to certain parliamentary bodies and the National Economic Development Council; and certain other services including general expenses of certain pay review bodies and expenses in connection with Honours and Dignities; and the cost of the Inquiry into the supervision of the Bank of Credit and Commerce International .... 2,000 / 262,000
3. For expenditure of the Civil Service Catering Organisation (HM Treasury) and Forward Civil Service Catering (HM Treasury) in connection with the provision of catering services .... 1,000 / 6,229,000
4. For expenditure by Her Majesty's Treasury on the superannuation of civil servants, pensions, etc. in respect of former members of the Royal Irish Constabulary and other pensions and non-recurrent payments; and for certain other services..... 7,242,000 / * – 32,800,000
5. For expenditure by the Customs and Excise Department on the administration of taxation, the operation of customs and revenue controls and other customs and excise work .... 8,656,000 / 210,000
6. For expenditure by the Inland Revenue Department on the management and collection of the direct taxes; the provision of rating and valuation services; and services provided for other Departments......... 6,509,000 / 86,980,000
9. For expenditure of the Department for National Savings on administration, publicity costs and certain other expenses 2,082,000 / —

	Sums not exceeding	
	Supply Grants	Appropriations in Aid
	£	£

Vote

11. For expenditure by the National Debt Office and Public Works Loan Commission on administrative costs and relocation expenses..............................   449,000   * – 236,000

12. For expenditure by the Paymaster General's Office on administrative costs..   90,000   210,000

13. For expenditure by the Central Statistical Office on the provision of national accounts and other statistics and on departmental administration, including contributions on behalf of HM Government to international organisations   2,126,000   101,000

14. For expenditure by the Central Office of Information on allied service work and in respect of the anticipated difference between values of assets and liabilities on the establishment of the C.O.I. as a Trading Fund   7,430,000   —

15. For the expenditure of the Department of the Government Actuary on administrative costs............................   50,000   —

19. For expenditure by the Treasury in connection with the sale of shares in British Telecommunications plc...................   1,000   163,598,000

CLASS XIX

1. For the expenditure by the Office of the Minister for the Civil Service on the central management of the civil service, on the Offices of the Prime Minister, the Government Chief Whip and the Parliamentary Counsel and certain other services.......   4,390,000   34,000

2. For the expenditure by the Cabinet Office, including the Office of the Chancellor of the Duchy of Lancaster, on administrative costs and payment to Co-operation on Science and Technology and to the British National Committee for the History of the Second World War....................   850,000   —

7. For the expenditure of the House of Commons on Members' salaries, allowances, pensions etc, financial assistance to Opposition parties and an Exchequer contribution to the Members' Fund   200,000   —

CLASS XX

1. For expenditure by Her Majesty's Treasury on contributions to the Budget of the European Communities not covered by direct charges on the Consolidated Fund under Section 2(3) of the European Communities Act 1972. (New Estimate)......   450,000,000   —

TOTAL SUPPLEMENTARY 1991–92 .. £	7,178,084,000	408,791,000

Deficit

SCHEDULE (B).—PART 3   CLASS I
                                                 1992–93
—————
CLASS I

SCHEDULE OF SUMS granted, and of the sums which may be applied as appropriations in aid in addition thereto, to defray the charges of the several Services herein particularly mentioned, which will come in course of payment during the year ending on 31st March 1993, including provision for numbers of personnel as set out hereunder, viz.:—

	Sums not exceeding	
	Supply Grants	Appropriations in Aid
	£	£
Vote		
1. For expenditure by the Ministry of Defence on personnel costs etc. of the Armed Forces and their Reserves and Cadet Forces etc. (including provision for the Naval Service to a number not exceeding 65,400, provision for Army Service to a number not exceeding 165,645, for the Individual Reserves to a number not exceeding 121,000, for the Territorial Army to number not exceeding 79,600, and for the Ulster Defence Regiment to a number not exceeding 6,970, and provision for Air Force Service to a number not exceeding 88,620, for Royal Air Force Reserve to a number not exceeding 19,350, and for the Royal Auxiliary Air Force to a number not exceeding 2,800); personnel costs etc of Defence Ministers and of certain civilian staff employed by the Ministry of Defence, movements, certain stores, supplies and services, plant and machinery, charter of ships, certain research, lands and buildings, sundry grants and payments abroad .	10,576,703,000	1,237,347,000
2. For expenditure by the Procurement Executive of the Ministry of Defence in operating its Headquarters and Establishments and for its other common services; for research etc by contract; for lands and buildings; for development by contract, production, repair etc and purchases for sale abroad of sea systems, land systems, air systems and associated equipment; for certain contingent liabilities, and for sundry other Procurement Executive services including those on repayment terms to non-exchequer customers	9,593,000,000	485,208,000
3. For expenditure by the Ministry of Defence on retired pay, pensions and other payments etc	1,933,308,000	1,869,000
4. For expenditure by the Ministry of Defence on new construction and maintenance works and related services at defence establishments and on fees and some works costs for visiting forces	1,577,000,000	142,623,000
5. For expenditure by the Ministry of Defence on the refit and repair of ships, associated capital facilities, on contractors' redundancy costs and administration.	559,789,000	28,845,000
TOTAL, CLASS I . . . . £	24,239,800,000	1,895,892,000

SCHEDULE (B).—PART 4

CLASS II

SCHEDULE OF SUMS granted, and of the sums which may be applied as appropriations in aid in addition thereto, to defray the charges of the several Services herein particularly mentioned, which will come in course of payment during the year ending on 31st March 1993, viz.:—

	Sums not exceeding	
	Supply Grants	Appropriations in Aid
	£	£

Vote

1. For expenditure by the Foreign and Commonwealth Office on its salaries, building and other accommodation services, and administration, and those of HM Diplomatic Service, official information services, sundry services and loans and payments in connection with catering services.............................. 721,101,000   19,785,000

2. For expenditure by the Foreign and Commonwealth Office on grants and subscriptions, etc., to certain international organisations, special payments and assistance, scholarships, military aid and sundry other grants and services............... 178,791,000   14,937,000

3. For expenditure by the Foreign and Commonwealth Office on payments to the British Broadcasting Corporation for external broadcasting and monitoring services and for contractual services in connection with FCO relay stations......... 162,711,000   3,650,000

4. For expenditure by the Foreign and Commonwealth Office on the British Council . 88,669,000   —

5. For expenditure by the Foreign and Commonwealth Office: Overseas Development Administration under the Overseas Development and Co-operation Act 1980 on the official United Kingdom aid programme; assistance to eastern Europe and the former Soviet Union; and global environmental assistance; including financial and technical assistance to governments, institutions, voluntary agencies and individuals; pensions and allowances in respect of overseas service including contributions to pension funds; capital and other subscriptions and contributions, including payments under guarantee, to multilateral development banks and other international and regional bodies; emergency, refugee and other relief assistance; loans to the Commonwealth Development Corporation; and running costs, related capital expenditure, and other administrative costs including for the Natural Resources Institute (an executive agency)......... 1,743,015,000   76,701,000

| | Sums not exceeding | |
	Supply Grants	Appropriations in Aid
	£	£
Vote		
6. For expenditure by the Foreign and Commonwealth Office (Overseas Development Administration) on pension and superannuation payments etc., in respect of overseas service and sundry other services and expenses............................	147,388,000	154,000
TOTAL, CLASS II ....£	3,041,675,000	115,227,000

SCHEDULE (B).—PART 5   CLASS III
1992–93

CLASS III

SCHEDULE OF SUMS granted, and of the sums which may be applied as appropriations in aid in addition thereto, to defray the charges of the several Services herein particularly mentioned, which will come in course of payment during the year ending on 31st March 1993, viz.:—

	Sums not exceeding	
	Supply Grants	Appropriations in Aid
	£	£
Vote		
1. For expenditure by the Intervention Board—Executive Agency in giving effect in the United Kingdom to the agricultural support provisions of the Common Agricultural Policy of the European Community and for other services	46,459,000	1,885,570,000
2. For expenditure by the Intervention Board—Executive Agency on central administration and miscellaneous services	47,629,000	1,363,000
3. For expenditure by the Ministry of Agriculture, Fisheries and Food on market support; miscellaneous payments and loan guarantees; support for agriculture in special areas and compensation to sheep producers; and animal health	58,581,000	13,850,000
4. For expenditure by the Ministry of Agriculture, Fisheries and Food on commissioned research and development; advice, education and training services; botanical services; assistance to production, marketing and processing; support for the fishing industry; flood and coast protection and arterial drainage; emergency and strategic food services; protective, agency, administrative, scientific and policy advice services; grants and loans for capital and other improvements and alternative land uses and other services.................	368,256,000	35,296,000
5. For expenditure by the Ministry of Agriculture, Fisheries and Food on departmental research, advisory services and administration and certain other services	263,095,000	121,410,000
TOTAL, CLASS III ....£	784,020,000	2,057,489,000

SCHEDULE (B).—PART 6 CLASS IV
1992–93

CLASS IV

SCHEDULE OF SUMS granted, and of the sums which may be applied as appropriations in aid in addition thereto, to defray the charges of the several Services herein particularly mentioned, which will come in course of payment during the year ending on 31st March 1993, viz.:—

	Sums not exceeding	
	Supply Grants	Appropriations in Aid
	£	£
Vote		
1. For expenditure by the Department of Trade and Industry on regional development grants, regional selective assistance, selective assistance to individual industries and firms, UK contributions arising from its commitments under the International Natural Rubber Agreement, a strategic mineral stockpile, support for the aerospace and shipbuilding industries, assistance to redundant steel workers, and other payments	184,977,000	86,011,000
2. For expenditure by the Department of Trade and Industry on departmental administration, central and miscellaneous services; business development and film projects, the inner cities initiative; industrial research and support; the promotion of inward investment; space technology programmes; the promotion of international trade; consumer protection and the regulation of trade; the operational costs of departmental executive agencies; loans to the Department's trading funds; measurement and technology support and standards; financial support for the English Industrial Estates Corporation; the provision of land and buildings; loans, grants and other payments	778,523,000	181,469,000
3. For Government support for British Shipbuilders for the costs associated with the remedial measures in Sunderland........	1,351,000	350,000
4. For expenditure by the Export Credits Guarantee Department on administration	26,564,000	1,258,000
5. For expenditure by the Export Credits Guarantee Department in connection with interest support to banks and other lenders of export finance, cover under the tender to contract/forward exchange supplement scheme, grants towards financing of exports to match foreign competition, residual commitments under discontinued guarantees offered to banks and external trade agencies, and cost escalation cover .	115,941,000	85,760,000
6. For expenditure by the Export Credits Guarantee Department in connection with export credits guarantees, other guarantees given in the national interest or to render economic assistance to overseas		

	Sums not exceeding	
	Supply Grants	Appropriations in Aid
	£	£
Vote		
countries, overseas investment, insurance and trading expenses	483,696,000	417,380,000
7. For expenditure by the Office of Fair Trading on administrative and operational costs	18,020,000	168,000
8. For the expenditure by the Office of Telecommunications on administrative and operational costs	7,939,000	116,000
TOTAL, CLASS IV .... £	1,617,011,000	772,512,000

SCHEDULE (B).—PART 7   CLASS V
                                                          1992–93
CLASS V

SCHEDULE OF SUMS granted, and of the sums which may be applied as appropriations in aid in addition thereto, to defray the charges of the several Services herein particularly mentioned, which will come in course of payment during the year ending on 31st March 1993, viz.:—

	Sums not exceeding	
	Supply Grants	Appropriations in Aid
	£	£
Vote		
1. For expenditure by the Department of Energy on assistance to the coal industry including grants and loans to the British Coal Corporation and payments to mineworkers made redundant before 29 March 1987..............................	753,000,000	1,136,400,000
2. For expenditure by the Department of Energy in connection with energy related programmes including research and development; energy efficiency; selective assistance to industry; promotion and security of oil and gas supplies; grants and certain other services........................	340,374,000	2,495,000
3. For expenditure by the Department of Energy on salaries and other administrative costs...........................	43,263,000	4,040,000
4. For expenditure by the Department of Energy on the proportionate payment of proceeds from petroleum licensing and royalties; refunds and repayments and other associated expenditure...........	1,000	23,195,000
5. For payment of pensions, etc., to members of the United Kingdom Atomic Energy Authority's superannuation schemes and other related expenditure	49,442,000	65,277,000
6. For expenditure by the Department of Energy in connection with the privatisation of the electricity supply industry in England and Wales....................	1,000	20,999,000
7. For expenditure by the Department of Energy in connection with the privatisation of the coal industry....................	10,000,000	—
8. For expenditure by the Office of Gas Supply on administrative costs	2,941,000	21,000
9. For expenditure by the Office of Electricity Regulation on administrative and operational costs..........................	10,717,000	1,030,000
TOTAL, CLASS V ....£	1,209,739,000	1,253,457,000

Class VI

Schedule of Sums granted, and of the sums which may be applied as appropriations in aid in addition thereto, to defray the charges of the several Services herein particularly mentioned, which will come in course of payment during the year ending on 31st March 1993, viz.:—

	Sums not exceeding	
	Supply Grants	Appropriations in Aid
	£	£
Vote		
1. For expenditure by the Department of Employment, including expenditure via Training and Enterprise Councils and local enterprise companies and amounts retained by them as surpluses, on training, including the provision of training programmes for young people and adults and initiatives and programmes within education; on the promotion of enterprise, tourism and the encouragement of self-employed and small firms; on help for unemployed people; inner city initiatives; the improvement of industrial relations; industrial tribunals; compensation for persons disabled by certain industrial diseases; payment towards expenses of trade union ballots; on residual liabilities and disposal of the remaining assets of the former National Dock Labour Board; on the costs of maintaining and disposing of the former Skills Training Agency; administration, central and miscellaneous services including assistance on employment issues to eastern Europe in cooperation with the Foreign and Commonwealth Office; on research and publicity	2,481,254,000	125,742,000
2. For expenditure by the Employment Service of the Department of Employment on help for unemployed people; assistance to eastern Europe on labour market issues, in cooperation with the Foreign and Commonwealth Office; support for services for people with disabilities; and on research and publicity	522,682,000	638,985,000
3. For expenditure by the Department of Employment on grants in aid to the Health and Safety Commission and to the Advisory, Conciliation and Arbitration Service	196,936,000	55,000
Total, Class VI . . . . £	3,200,872,000	764,782,000

Schedule of Sums granted, and of the sums which may be applied as appropriations in aid in addition thereto, to defray the charges of the several Services herein particularly mentioned, which will come in course of payment during the year ending on 31st March 1993, viz.:—

	Sums not exceeding	
	Supply Grants	Appropriations in Aid
	£	£
Vote		
1. For expenditure by the Department of Transport on the construction, improvement and maintenance of motorways and trunk roads, including the acquisition of land, scheme design and preparation, a grant to English Heritage in respect of archaeological survey and rescue work, compensation, the purchase of maintenance vehicles and equipment, a grant to the Traffic Director for London and other expenditure on priority routes in London, the maintenance of the Woolwich Ferry, highways, safety, and traffic administration, highways research and development and licence refunds....................	2,124,258,000	138,079,000
2. For expenditure by the Department of Transport on central administration and miscellaneous services; shipping; ports; civil aviation; road safety, publicity; the Transport and Road Research Laboratory and Driver Vehicles and Operators Information Technology Executive Agencies: the Vehicle Certification Agency and loans to the Vehicle Inspectorate (Trading Fund); grants for freight facilities and travel concessions and certain other transport services including non highways research and development, traffic censuses, civil defence, residual expenses associated with the privatisation of transport industries and expenses associated with the sale of the Trust Ports and privatisation of British Rail..........................	211,882,000	53,035,000
3. For expenditure by the Department of Transport on support to nationalised transport industries and rebate of fuel duty to bus operators; and costs of driver testing and training	2,584,799,000	249,000
4. For expenditure by the Department of Transport in connection with driver and vehicle registration and licensing, the collection of revenue and compensation and payments towards the pension of Local Authority staff employed on driver and vehicle licensing before the setting up of DVLC..............................	171,657,000	19,500,000
5. For expenditure by the Department of Transport on transport supplementary grants to Highway Authorities in England and certain other grants and payments in		

	Sums not exceeding	
	Supply Grants	Appropriations in Aid
	£	£
Vote		
support of local roads and transport expenditure and on grants to the Humber Bridge Board to cover the Board's liabilities	438,781,000	14,925,000
Total, Class VII..............£	5,531,377,000	225,788,000

CLASS VIII

SCHEDULE OF SUMS granted, and of the sums which may be applied as appropriations in aid in
addition thereto, to defray the charges of the several Services herein particularly mentioned, which will come in course of payment during the year ending on 31st March 1993,
viz.:—

	Sums not exceeding	
	Supply Grants	Appropriations in Aid
	£	£
Vote		
1. For expenditure by the Department of the Environment on subsidies, improvements and investments, payments to the Housing Corporation, payments to commute loan charges on grants to local authorities including the urban programme and urban development grant, and other sundry services	10,186,117,000	1,151,000
2. For expenditure by the Department of the Environment on housing administration, including payments and grants to the Housing Corporation; housing for single homelessness and special needs accommodation; housing management and mobility; housing research; construction research; rent officers and Rent Assessment Panels; grant in aid to housing action trusts; grants to home improvement agencies and for sundry housing services and projects	285,893,000	121,000
3. For expenditure by the Department of the Environment on city grants to the private sector for urban regeneration, derelict land reclamation, city action teams, payments in connection with inner cities and derelict land research, grants for urban and housing projects under the city challenge initiative, urban programme grant, urban development grant and payments to urban development corporations	825,472,000	10,598,000
4. For expenditure by the Department of the Environment on road infrastructure required for the development of new towns, gypsy sites, smoke control, planning redevelopment and other environmental services and on other water supply, conservation and sewerage services	48,525,000	—
5. For expenditure by the Department of the Environment on countryside and environment, including research and support to the environmental protection industry, on grants to the Development Commission, National Rivers Authority and British Waterways Board, on bridge works, on other water supply and sewerage services including civil defence, on national parks, on grants to voluntary bodies and on residual services in connection with the privatisation of the water supply industry	315,931,000	343,000

	Sums not exceeding	
	Supply Grants	Appropriations in Aid
	£	£

Vote

6. For expenditure by the Department of the Environment on Royal Palaces, Historic Royal Palaces Agency (including administration), Royal Parks, Royal Armouries etc. (including administration), historic buildings, ancient monuments and certain public buildings, the national heritage, on the inspection of historic wreck sites; on payments to the Inland Revenue covering assets accepted in lieu of tax and on the assessment of possible listed buildings. . . .

| | 190,595,000 | 25,526,000 |

7. For expenditure by the Department of the Environment (Property Holdings and central support services) on acquisitions, public building work, accommodation services, administration and certain other services for Civil purposes in the United Kingdom, for Ministry of Defence and for civil purposes required in connection with the Channel Fixed Link and for loans to The Buying Agency . . . .

| | 1,000 | 914,926,000 |

8. For expenditure by the Department of the Environment and its agencies on administration including research, royal commissions, committees, etc., and by the Planning Inspectorate Executive Agency on appeals, and by the Building Research Establishment Executive Agency on building and surveys . . . .

| | 211,621,000 | 63,520,000 |

9. For expenditure by the Department of the Environment on revenue support grant, on residual payments of rate support grants, on payment of non-domestic rates to charging authorities in England, on a grant providing transitional support for certain charging authorities, on a grant to compensate 75% of the expenditure incurred by authorities on preparation work for the council tax, on payments to specified bodies and the Commission for Local Administration in England, on payments for Inland Revenue Valuation Office rating and valuation services, on payments to meet the expenses of valuation tribunals, and on payments in respect of expenditure by the Local Government Commission . . .

| | 29,473,833,000 | 1,608,000 |

10. For expenditure by the Office of Water Services on administrative and operational costs . . . .

| | 7,520,000 | 12,000 |

11. For expenditure by the Ordnance Survey on the survey of Great Britain and other mapping services. . . . .

| | 17,570,000 | 61,847,000 |

12. For expenditure by PSA Services on works and similar services for other government departments and certain other clients; administrative costs; transitional, residual,

	Sums not exceeding	
	Supply Grants	Appropriations in Aid
	£	£
Vote		
and restructuring costs; and privatisation expenses..........................	128,884,000	570,328,000
13. For expenditure by the Department of the Environment on the community charge reduction scheme, on final payments of the community charge grant and preparation and administration grants for 1991–92, on final payments of rate rebate grants, on emergency financial assistance to local authorities, and on repayments of excess contributions made by local authorities and other bodies in respect of non-domestic rates in 1991–92......................	1,494,764,000	—
TOTAL, CLASS VIII..............£	43,186,726,000	1,649,980,000

SCHEDULE (B).—PART 11   CLASS IX
1992–93

CLASS IX

SCHEDULE OF SUMS granted, and of the sums which may be applied as appropriations in aid in addition thereto, to defray the charges of the several Services herein particularly mentioned, which will come in course of payment during the year ending on 31st March 1993, viz.:—

	Sums not exceeding	
	Supply Grants	Appropriations in Aid
	£	£
Vote		
1. For expenditure by the Home Office on compensation for criminal injuries, probation, police and superannuation payments for police and fire services..............	2,940,177,000	20,482,000
2. For expenditure by the Home Office in England and Wales on prisons (including central administration and other costs arising from the detention of prisoners), the Parole Board, the storage and maintenance of equipment (including certain civilian emergency equipment), and transport management	1,363,448,000	24,913,000
3. For expenditure by the Home Office on police, the forensic science service, emergency planning, fire, the Fire Service College, the Football Licensing Authority, the Arson Prevention Bureau, court services, other services related to crime, probation and after-care, certain broadcasting services, data protection and other miscellaneous services, prevention of drug abuse, control of immigration and nationality, issue of passports etc., community services; and on administration (excluding prisons)............................	1,243,473,000	85,689,000
4. For expenditure by the Home Office on payments to the British Broadcasting Corporation for home broadcasting and balance of payments in respect of the collection and enforcement of licence fees for 1991–92, which fall due in 1992–93; and payments to the Welsh Fourth Channel Authority..........................	1,575,450,000	—
5. For the expenditure of the Charity Commission for England and Wales on administrative costs.......................	20,688,000	13,000
TOTAL, CLASS IX ....£	7,143,236,000	131,097,000

Appropriation Act 1992

CLASS X

SCHEDULE OF SUMS granted, and of the sums which may be applied as appropriations in aid in addition thereto, to defray the charges of the several Services herein particularly mentioned, which will come in course of payment during the year ending on 31st March 1993, viz.:—

	Sums not exceeding	
	Supply Grants	Appropriations in Aid
	£	£
Vote		
1. For expenditure by the Lord Chancellor's Department on the court service, magistrates' courts, legal aid administration, tribunals, the court building programme and certain other legal services	756,376,000	250,846,000
2. For grants to the Legal Aid Fund and for expenditure by the Lord Chancellor's Department on legal aid in criminal cases and costs paid from central funds........	873,466,000	796,000
3. For expenditure by the Northern Ireland Court Service on court services, legal aid administration, tribunals, the court building programme and certain other legal services.............................	19,086,000	6,940,000
4. For expenditure by the Northern Ireland Court Service on legal aid and court services.............................	14,021,000	—
5. For expenditure by the Crown Prosecution Service on administrative costs including the hire of private prosecuting agents	199,846,000	219,000
6. For expenditure by the Director of Public Prosecutions on Crown prosecutions and in connection with the confiscation of the proceeds of crime	63,344,000	18,000,000
7. For expenditure by the Serious Fraud Office on administrative costs...........	10,272,000	—
8. For expenditure by the Serious Fraud Office on investigations and prosecutions.	10,957,000	330,000
9. For expenditure by the Legal Secretariat to the Law Officers and the Department of the Procurator General and Treasury Solicitor on administration costs	9,627,000	21,230,000
10. For expenditure by the Department of the Procurator General and Treasury Solicitor on costs and fees for legal services.......	1,706,000	5,831,000
11. For expenditure by the Land Registry on administrative costs	1,000	245,780,000
12. For expenditure by the Public Record Office on administrative and operational costs	33,739,000	590,000
13. For expenditure by the Lord Advocate's Departments on administrative costs, including fees paid to temporary Procurators Fiscal.............................	36,912,000	71,000
14. For expenditure by the Crown Office on witnesses' expenses and other costs associated with Crown prosecutions	6,758,000	—
TOTAL, CLASS X ....£	2,036,111,000	550,633,000

SCHEDULE (B).—PART 13   CLASS XI
1992–93

CLASS XI

SCHEDULE OF SUMS granted, and of the sums which may be applied as appropriations in aid in addition thereto, to defray the charges of the several Services herein particularly mentioned, which will come in course of payment during the year ending on 31st March 1993, viz.:—

	Sums not exceeding	
	Supply Grants	Appropriations in Aid
	£	£
Vote		
1. For expenditure by the Department of Education and Science on the assisted places scheme, voluntary and special schools, City Technology Colleges, grant maintained schools, music and ballet schools, direct grant schools, youth services, grants for miscellaneous international and other educational services, administration costs of the Student Loans Company, research, sport and central government grants to local authorities ...	766,485,000	528,557,000
2. For expenditure by the Department of Education and Science on payments to the Universities Funding Council, the Polytechnics and Colleges Funding Council and the planned funding council for higher education in England; and for certain other higher education institutions; payments of bursaries for students attending courses of initial teacher training in certain subjects; other payments for higher and further education, including payments to the planned funding council for further education in England; and payment of certain licence fees to the Home Office...............	3,034,485,000	2,698,000
3. For expenditure by the Department of Education and Science on student awards and fees; provision of loans to students; access funds; reimbursement of fees for qualifying European Community students; legal expenses; and compensation payments to redundant teachers and staff of certain institutions	2,399,483,000	3,000
4. For expenditure by the Department of Education and Science on administration.	108,426,000	2,211,000
5. For expenditure by the Department of Education and Science on payments to the Agricultural and Food Research Council, the Medical Research Council, the Natural Environment Research Council, the Science and Engineering Research Council, the Economic and Social Research Council, the Royal Society, the Fellowship of Engineering, the Advisory Board for the Research Councils, and the Centre for Exploitation of Science and Technology, including the payment of certain licence fees to the Home Office...............	1,050,180,000	1,200,000

	Sums not exceeding	
	Supply Grants	Appropriations in Aid
	£	£
Vote		
6. For expenditure by the Department of Education and Science on superannuation allowances and gratuities, etc, in respect of teachers, and the widows, widowers, children and dependants of deceased teachers	963,050,000	1,547,636,000
TOTAL, CLASS XI .... £	8,322,109,000	2,082,305,000

SCHEDULE (B).—Part 14   Class XII
1992–93

Class XII

Schedule of Sums granted, and of the sums which may be applied as appropriations in aid in addition thereto, to defray the charges of the several Services herein particularly mentioned, which will come in course of payment during the year ending on 31st March 1993, viz.:—

	Sums not exceeding	
	Supply Grants	Appropriations in Aid
Vote	£	£
1. For expenditure by the Office of Arts and Libraries on payments to the national and other museums and galleries, to the Museums and Galleries Commission, to the National Heritage Memorial Fund; to the Inland Revenue for assets accepted in lieu of tax; and for improvements and for related research, surveys and other services..............................	220,682,000	—
2. For expenditure by the Office of Arts and Libraries on payments to the Arts Council and other bodies; on the Government Art Collection; and for research, surveys and other services for the benefit of the arts ..	252,902,000	5,000
3. For expenditure by the Office of Arts and Libraries on payments to the British Library and the Royal Geographical Society; on the British Library St. Pancras project; the Royal Commission on Historical Manuscripts; on payments in respect of Public Lending Right; and for a development incentive scheme.................	141,157,000	—
4. For expenditure by the Office of Arts and Libraries on administration.............	2,445,000	17,000
Total, Class XII...............£	617,186,000	22,000

Appropriation Act 1992

SCHEDULE (B).—PART 15

CLASS XIII
1992–93

CLASS XIII

SCHEDULE OF SUMS granted, and of the sums which may be applied as appropriations in aid in addition thereto, to defray the charges of the several Services herein particularly mentioned, which will come in course of payment during the year ending on 31st March 1993, viz.:—

	Sums not exceeding	
	Supply Grants	Appropriations in Aid
	£	£
Vote		
1. For expenditure by the Department of Health on hospital, community health, family health and family health service administration services, and on related services	18,544,309,000	3,856,704,000
2. For expenditure by the Department of Health on family health services, on medical treatment given to people from the United Kingdom in other countries of the European Community and on welfare food	1,138,378,000	991,590,000
3. For expenditure by the Department of Health on administration, including certain expenditure on behalf of the Department of Social Security, on the national health service in England, on family health administration and related services, on miscellaneous health, personal social and other services (some of which are administered on a United Kingdom basis), including mental health, medical, scientific and technical services, services for disabled persons, grants to voluntary organisations, etc. and a contribution to the International Peto Institute	801,053,000	26,883,000
4. For expenditure by the Department of Health on National Health Service Trusts and on family health services	3,417,578,000	772,780,000
5. For expenditure by the Department of Health on pensions, allowances, gratuities, etc, to or in respect of persons engaged in health services or in other approved employment	411,924,000	1,341,061,000
6. For the expenditure of the Office of Population Censuses and Surveys on administrative and operational costs	37,056,000	29,951,000
TOTAL, CLASS XIII ....£	24,350,298,000	7,018,969,000

SCHEDULE (B).—PART 16

———

CLASS XIV

SCHEDULE OF SUMS granted, and of the sums which may be applied as appropriations in aid in addition thereto, to defray the charges of the several Services herein particularly mentioned, which will come in course of payment during the year ending on 31st March 1993, viz.:—

	Sums not exceeding	
	Supply Grants	Appropriations in Aid
	£	£
Vote		
1. For expenditure by the Department of Social Security on non-contributory retirement pensions, Christmas bonus payments to pensioners, pensions etc., for disablement or death arising out of war or service in the armed forces after 2 September 1939 and on sundry other services, on attendance allowances, invalid care allowance, severe disablement allowance, mobility allowance; disability living allowance; disability working allowance; on pensions, gratuities and sundry allowances for disablement and specified deaths arising from industrial causes; on income support, child benefit, one parent benefit, family credit, and on the vaccine damage payment scheme	25,623,405,000	236,672,000
2. For expenditure by the Department of Social Security on rent rebate, rent allowance, community charge benefit, community charge rebate and rate rebate subsidies to housing, charging, levying and local authorities; on transitional payments to help certain housing benefit claimants significantly affected by the changes to the housing benefit scheme and certain supplementary benefit claimants not entitled to benefit under the income support scheme; on sums payable into the National Insurance Fund as compensation in respect of statutory sick pay and statutory maternity pay and on sums payable into the Social Fund for expenditure on maternity expenses, funeral expenses and heating expenses in exceptionally cold weather . . .	5,725,652,000	18,158,000
3. For expenditure by the Department of Social Security on sums payable as grants to the Independent Living Fund; on subsidies to housing and local authorities towards the costs of administering the housing benefit scheme and to charging and levying authorities towards the costs of administering the community charge benefit scheme, as grants to Motability towards their administrative costs and to enable them to assist invalid vehicle users and others to have adapted and/or to purchase or lease cars from them, and on sums		

	Sums not exceeding	
	Supply Grants	Appropriations in Aid
	£	£
Vote		
payable to the Social Fund to finance budgeting loans, crisis loans and community care grants	351,991,000	7,000
4. For expenditure by the Department of Social Security on administration, for agency payments, and for certain other services including grants to local authorities and voluntary organisations	2,270,076,000	1,182,062,000
TOTAL, CLASS XIV.............£	33,971,124,000	1,436,899,000

SCHEDULE (B).—PART 17   CLASS XV
1992–93

CLASS XV

SCHEDULE OF SUMS granted, and of the sums which may be applied as appropriations in aid in addition thereto, to defray the charges of the several Services herein particularly mentioned, which will come in course of payment during the year ending on 31st March 1993, viz.:—

	Sums not exceeding	
	Supply Grants	Appropriations in Aid
	£	£
Vote		
1. For expenditure by the Scottish Office Agriculture and Fisheries Department on market support, support for agriculture in special areas, compensation to sheep producers and certain other services including animal health........................	45,387,000	10,944,000
2. For expenditure by the Scottish Office Agriculture and Fisheries Department on agricultural education, advisory, research and development services; botanical and scientific services; assistance to production marketing and processing; administration and land management services and other agricultural services; assistance in special areas including crofting communities; assistance for structural measures; assistance to the Scottish fishing industry; fishery protection; and certain other services including fisheries research and development and special services..............	126,684,000	13,330,000
3. For expenditure by the Scottish Office Industry Department on Scottish Enterprise and Highlands and Islands Enterprise; on regional enterprise grants; on technical and vocational education; on the promotion of tourism; on financial assistance to the electricity industry and on local enterprise; on consumer protection; on roads and certain associated services, including the acquisition of land, lighting, road safety and related services; on assistance to local transport; on support for transport services in the highlands and islands; on piers and harbours, and on certain other transport services and grants; on advisers' fees relating to the privatisation of passenger transport companies; and on other sundry services in connection with trade and industry, etc.	712,741,000	11,817,000
4. For expenditure by the Scottish Office Industry Department on regional development grants and regional selective assistance.............................	76,760,000	2,600,000
5. For expenditure by the Scottish Office Environment Department on housing subsidies, financial support for Scottish Homes, other contributions and grants related to housing; on historic buildings		

	Sums not exceeding	
	Supply Grants	Appropriations in Aid
	£	£

Vote

and monuments (including administration); on the countryside and on other central and environmental services **423,453,000**   **7,122,000**

6. For expenditure by the Scottish Office Environment Department on water and sewerage, flood and storm emergencies, and other environmental services, residual payments of grants to housing associations and sites for travelling people ....   **54,974,000**   —

7. For expenditure by the Scottish Office Industry Department on assistance to local transport, piers and harbours, on grants to New Town Development Corporations in connection with housing and other services on the urban programme and economic development, other urban regeneration initiatives, on expenses connected with the New Towns' wind up and grants for ethnic minority groups.....................   **132,538,000**   —

8. For expenditure by the Scottish Office Industry Department in connection with the privatisation of the electricity supply industry in Scotland **1,000**   **13,999,000**

9. For expenditure by the Scottish Courts Administration on court services, the Scottish Law Commission and certain legal services............................   **47,226,000**   **16,120,000**

10. For expenditure by the Scottish Office Home and Health Department on legal aid, criminal injuries compensation (excluding administration), police, police and fire services superannuation and welfare food..........................   **363,412,000**   **233,000**

11. For expenditure by the Scottish Courts Administration on costs and fees in connection with legal proceedings ....   **32,868,000**   —

12. For expenditure by the Scottish Office Home and Health Department on legal aid administration; certain services relating to crime including the Parole Board for Scotland, prison, fire and police services (excluding grants to local authorities and superannuation); civil defence (including grants) and other protective and miscellaneous services; miscellaneous health services; social work services including the provision of residential and secure accommodation for children; services for offenders including probation and supervised attendance orders; grants to voluntary organisations; training and research; unemployed voluntary action fund; other grants to local authorities **247,302,000**   **10,524,000**

13. For expenditure by the Scottish Office Education Department on: schools, including establishment of self-governing schools; higher and advanced further

	Sums not exceeding	
	Supply Grants	Appropriations in Aid
	£	£

Vote

education; the planned Scottish higher education funding council; compensation payments; special educational needs; community education; non-advanced further education, curriculum development, international and other educational services, including support for School Boards, training and research; the transitional costs incurred by further education colleges in preparation for direct central government funding; sport; Gaelic broadcasting; arts, libraries, museums and galleries, including purchase grants; cultural activities and organisations including the Royal Society of Edinburgh, Royal Scottish Geographical Society; Scottish Film Production Fund; publicity; indemnities; administration; central government grants to local authorities, including the Careers Service; and EC agency payments.............. 259,024,000   900,000

14. For expenditure by the Scottish Office Education Department on student loans including administration, access funds, student awards and fees and reimbursement of fees for qualifying European Community Students 332,238,000   3,000

15. For expenditure by the Scottish Office Home and Health Department on provision of services under the National Health Service in Scotland including National Health Service trusts and certain other services and compensation payments to dental practitioners who opt for early retirement 558,665,000   158,905,000

16. For the expenditure of the Scottish Record Office on administrative costs and a grant to the Business Archives Council of Scotland................................ 3,871,000   685,000

17. For expenditure of the General Register Office for Scotland on administrative and operational costs...................... 7,912,000   2,249,000

18. For the expenditure of the Registers of Scotland on administrative costs......... 1,000   32,408,000

19. For expenditure by the Scottish Office on administrative and operational costs 152,875,000   6,544,000

20. For expenditure by the Scottish Office Environment Department for revenue support grants and grants relating to council tax valuation in Scotland............... 3,458,500,000   —

21. For expenditure by the Scottish Office Environment Department on rate rebate grants and payments in connection with the community charge transitional relief scheme, the community charge reduction scheme and the special payments scheme to local authorities in Scotland 162,014,000   —

	Sums not exceeding	
	Supply Grants	Appropriations in Aid
	£	£
Vote		
22. For expenditure by the Scottish Office Home and Health Department on superannuation allowances and gratuities, etc, in respect of teachers, and the widows, widowers and dependants of deceased teachers	74,182,000	176,357,000
23. For expenditure by the Scottish Office Home and Health Department on pensions, allowances, gratuities, etc, to or in respect of persons engaged in health service or in other approved employment ...	67,572,000	166,871,000
24. For expenditure by the Scottish Office Industry Department on advisers' fees and other costs in connection with the sale by the Scottish Transport Group of Scottish Bus operating subsidiaries, and the disposal of other interests..................	13,000	3,000
25. For expenditure by the Scottish Office Home and Health Department on hospital, community health, family health and other health services, including central health services and civil defence..............	2,590,645,000	387,913,000
26. For payments to Forestry Fund	97,544,000	1,700,000
TOTAL, CLASS XV...............£	10,028,402,000	1,021,227,000

CLASS XVI

SCHEDULE OF SUMS granted, and of the sums which may be applied as appropriations in aid in addition thereto, to defray the charges of the several Services herein particularly mentioned, which will come in course of payment during the year ending on 31st March 1993, viz.:—

	Sums not exceeding	
	Supply Grants	Appropriations in Aid
	£	£
Vote		
1. For expenditure by the Welsh Office on market support, support for agriculture in special areas and compensation to sheep producers, and animal health	32,204,000	7,682,000
2. For expenditure by the Welsh Office on assistance to agricultural production, marketing and processing, grants for capital and other improvements, certain alternative land uses, support for the fishing industry, protective, agency and other miscellaneous agricultural services, arterial drainage, flood and coast protection; on industrial development and other activities undertaken by the Welsh Development Agency and the Development Board for Rural Wales; support for medium and small sized firms and certain other services and expenses	116,577,000	3,678,000
3. For expenditure by the Welsh·Office on regional development grants, regional selective assistance, small firms measures and housing subsidy for the Development Board for Rural Wales.................	70,266,000	2,800,000
4. For expenditure by the Welsh Office including expenditure via Training and Enterprise Councils and amounts retained by them as surpluses on training, including the provision of training programmes for young people and adults and initiatives and programmes within education; on the promotion of enterprise, and the encouragement of self-employed and small firms; on help for unemployed people; on Careers Service, publicity and research	156,095,000	—
5. For expenditure by the Welsh Office on tourism, roads and transport and certain associated services, housing, historic buildings and ancient monuments, Cadw Agency, other environmental services (including civil defence, national parks, and Planning Inspectorate Agency), education, arts, libraries and museums, health and personal social services, EC agency payments, other grants and certain other services, including research	496,482,000	12,418,000
6. For expenditure by the Welsh Office on housing, other environmental services,		

	Sums not exceeding	
	Supply Grants	Appropriations in Aid
	£	£
Vote		
welfare food payments, EC agency payments, the commutation of loan charge grants to local authorities and certain other services............................	1,139,608,000	2,018,000
7. For expenditure by the Welsh Office on National Health Service trusts and on the family health services under the National Health Service.......................	310,256,000	80,432,000
8. For expenditure by the Welsh Office on hospital, community health, family health (part), and family health service administration services and on related services ...	1,265,078,000	199,570,000
9. For expenditure by the Welsh Office on central administration and other services .	60,297,000	1,706,000
10. For expenditure by the Welsh Office on revenue support grant and payment of non-domestic rates income to local authorities in Wales, payments of council tax preparation grant, payments to specified bodies, payments following recalculations of rate support grant for prior years, payments for Inland Revenue Valuation Office rating and valuation services including council tax banding work, on running costs of Valuation Tribunals and on publicity costs, etc.	2,172,936,000	4,000
11. For expenditure by the Welsh Office on grants to local authorities in Wales in respect of the community charge and certain related administrative expenses, residual rate rebate grants, on special grants to local authorities following natural emergencies, and on repayments of excess contributions made by local authorities and other bodies in respect of non-domestic rates in previous years.............................	74,600,000	—
TOTAL, CLASS XVI..............£	5,894,399,000	310,308,000

SCHEDULE (B).—PART 19   CLASS XVII
1992–93

CLASS XVII

SCHEDULE OF SUMS granted, and of the sums which may be applied as appropriations in aid in addition thereto, to defray the charges of the several Services herein particularly mentioned, which will come in course of payment during the year ending on 31st March 1993, viz.:—

	Sums not exceeding	
	Supply Grants	Appropriations in Aid
	£	£
Vote		
1. For expenditure by the Northern Ireland Office on central and miscellaneous services, services related to crime, police, prisons, training schools, probation and after-care etc, compensation schemes, crown prosecutions and other legal services and certain other grants...............	844,423,000	9,586,000
2. For expenditure by the Northern Ireland Office on a grant in aid of the Northern Ireland Consolidated Fund and other transfers............................	1,760,000,000	—
TOTAL, CLASS XVII.............£	2,604,423,000	9,586,000

SCHEDULE (B).—PART 20   CLASS XVIII
————   1992–93
CLASS XVIII

SCHEDULE OF SUMS granted, and of the sums which may be applied as appropriations in aid in addition thereto, to defray the charges of the several Services herein particularly mentioned, which will come in course of payment during the year ending on 31st March 1993, viz.:—

	Sums not exceeding	
	Supply Grants	Appropriations in Aid
	£	£
Vote		
1. For expenditure by Her Majesty's Treasury on economic, financial and related administration; on computers and general telecommunications; payments to certain parliamentary bodies and the National Economic Development Council; and certain other services including general expenses of certain pay review bodies and expenses in connection with Honours and Dignities, and expenses in connection with the enquiry into the handling of the closure of the Bank of Credit and Commerce International.	93,689,000	40,307,000
2. For expenditure by Her Majesty's Treasury in connection with the manufacture, storage and distribution of coinage for use in the United Kingdom	40,000,000	6,000,000
3. For expenditure of Forward Civil Service Catering (HM Treasury) in connection with the provision of catering services. . . .	1,000	30,942,000
4. For expenditure by Her Majesty's Treasury on the superannuation of civil servants, pensions, etc, in respect of former members of the Royal Irish Constabulary and other pensions and non-recurrent payments; and for certain other services	1,657,090,000	530,000,000
5. For expenditure by the Customs and Excise Department on the administration of taxation, the operation of customs and revenue controls and other customs and excise work	815,159,000	19,075,000
6. For expenditure by the Inland Revenue Department on the management and collection of the direct taxes.	1,615,071,000	95,554,000
7. For expenditure by the Inland Revenue Department Valuation Office (Executive Agency) on the provision of rating and valuation services for government departments and other public bodies	1,365,000	184,948,000
8. For expenditure of the Inland revenue Department on life assurance premium relief, mortgage interest relief, private medical insurance premium relief and vocational training relief	386,000,000	—
9. For rates and contributions in lieu of rates paid by Inland Revenue in respect of property occupied by the Crown and		

	Sums not exceeding	
	Supply Grants	Appropriations in Aid
	£	£

Vote

premises occupied by representatives of Commonwealth and foreign countries and international organisations	64,500,000	578,750,000
10. For expenditure of the Department for National Savings on administration, publicity costs and certain other expenses	195,066,000	1,117,000
11. For expenditure on administrative costs by the Registry of Friendly Societies on behalf of the Building Societies Commission and the Central Office of the Registry	5,685,000	4,450,000
12. For expenditure by the National Debt Office and Public Works Loan Commission on administrative costs and relocation expenses...........................	1,000	1,512,000
13. For expenditure by the Paymaster General's Office on administrative costs..	25,321,000	1,563,000
14. For expenditure by the Central Statistical Office on the provision of national accounts and other statistics and on departmental administration	40,237,000	2,231,000
15. For expenditure by the Central Office of Information on allied service work	1,181,000	—
16. For the expenditure of the Department of the Government Actuary on administrative costs...........................	726,000	4,872,000
17. For expenditure by the Controller of Her Majesty's Stationery Office to compensate the HMSO Trading Fund for the provision of reports of Parliamentary debates at less than full cost, and for the price concessions to public libraries; to meet the cost of goods and services provided on repayment to public sector bodies within the European Community, and elsewhere; and to meet the cost of government and other publications supplied to United Kingdom members of the European Assembly	2,711,000	199,000
18. For the salaries of the Crown Estate Commissioners and the expenses of their Office	1,299,000	—
19. For expenditure by Her Majesty's Treasury in connection with the sale of shares in British Telecommunications plc	1,000	7,199,000
TOTAL, CLASS XVIII ....£	4,945,103,000	1,508,719,000

SCHEDULE (B).—PART 21   CLASS XIX
1992–93

CLASS XIX

SCHEDULE OF SUMS granted, and of the sums which may be applied as appropriations in aid in addition thereto, to defray the charges of the several Services herein particularly mentioned, which will come in course of payment during the year ending on 31st March 1993, viz.:—

	Sums not exceeding	
	Supply Grants	Appropriations in Aid
	£	£
Vote		
1. For the expenditure by the Office of the Minister for the Civil Service on the central management of the civil service, on the Offices of the Prime Minister, the Government Chief Whip and the Parliamentary Counsel and certain other services.......	38,023,000	32,795,000
2. For the expenditure by the Cabinet office, including the Office of the Chancellor of the Duchy of Lancaster, on administrative costs and payment to Co-operation on Science and Technology and to the British National Committee for the History of the Second World War....................	23,646,000	5,422,000
3. For Her Majesty's foreign and other secret services............................	185,000,000	—
4. For expenditure of the Department of Her Majesty's Privy Council on administrative costs	2,127,000	25,000
5. For expenditure of the Office of the Parliamentary Commissioner for Administration and the Health Service Commissioners for England, Scotland and Wales on administrative costs	3,527,000	—
6. For expenditure of the House of Lords on Peers' expenses and administrative costs, including staff pensions, security, stationery and printing.......................	26,951,000	385,000
7. For the expenditure by the House of Lords on accommodation services; including a payment to the House of Commons Commission in respect of administration......	7,699,000	212,000
8. For the expenditure of the House of Commons on Members' salaries, allowances, pensions, etc. financial assistance to Opposition parties and an Exchequer contribution to the Members' Fund	61,301,000	—
TOTAL, CLASS XIX..............£	348,274,000	38,839,000

SCHEDULE (B).—PART 22   CLASS XIXA,
                                                  1992–93

CLASS XIX,A

SCHEDULE OF SUMS granted, and of the sums which may be applied as appropriations in aid in addition thereto, to defray the charges of the several Services herein particularly mentioned, which will come in course of payment during the year ending on 31st March 1993, viz.:—

	Sums not exceeding	
	Supply Grants	Appropriations in Aid
	£	£
Vote		
1. For expenditure by the House of Commons Commission on administration; including security, broadcasting, publicity, stationery and printing......................	67,319,000	—
2. For expenditure by the House of Commons Commission on accommodation services, including administration	20,605,000	518,000
TOTAL, CLASS XIX,A ....£	87,924,000	518,000

SCHEDULE (B).—PART 23   CLASS XIXB,
                                          1992–93
CLASS XIX,B

SCHEDULE OF SUMS granted, and of the sums which may be applied as appropriations in aid in
addition thereto, to defray the charges of the several Services herein particularly mentioned, which will come in course of payment during the year ending on 31st March 1993,
viz.:—

	Sums not exceeding	
	Supply Grants	Appropriations in Aid
	£	£
Vote		
1. For expenditure of the National Audit Office	38,000,000	5,100,000
TOTAL, CLASS XIX,B ....£	38,000,000	5,100,000

SCHEDULE (B).—PART 24   CLASS XX
                                          1992–93
CLASS XX

SCHEDULE OF SUMS granted, and of the sums which may be applied as appropriations in aid in addition thereto, to defray the charges of the several Services herein particularly mentioned, which will come in course of payment during the year ending on 31st March 1993, viz.:—

	Sums not exceeding	
	Supply Grants	Appropriations in Aid
	£	£
Vote		
1. For expenditure by Her Majesty's Treasury on contributions to the Budget of the European Communities not covered by direct charges on the Consolidated Fund under Section 1(3) of the European Communities Act 1972	1,350,000,000	—
TOTAL, CLASS XX .... £	1,350,000,000	—

SCHEDULE (C)

ENACTMENTS REPEALED

Chapter	Short title
1989 c. 46	Consolidated Fund (No. 2) Act 1989
1990 c. 4	Consolidated Fund Act 1990
1990 c. 28	Appropriation Act 1990

INDEX

ACCESS TO NEIGHBOURING LAND ACT 1992*

(1992 c. 23)

ARRANGEMENT OF SECTIONS

An Act to enable persons who desire to carry out works to any land which are reasonably necessary for the preservation of that land to obtain access to neighbouring land in order to do so; and for purposes connected therewith. [16th March 1992]

PARLIAMENTARY DEBATES
Hansard, H.L. Vol. 533, col. 819; Vol. 535, col. 869; Vol. 536, cols. 346, 755.

INTRODUCTION AND GENERAL NOTE
This measure was introduced first in 1991 and the original Bill lost for want of parliamentary time to improve the deficient drafting when the new session started in October 1991. The present Bill was reintroduced in the House of Lords at the end of November 1991. The purpose of the legislation is for once clear from the title. It aims to provide necessary access to neighbouring land for the carrying out of works required on the applicant's land. It is important to note when considering the usefulness of the Act the following three factors:
 (1) The concepts involved—as to the work that can be carried out—are defined in words that are at times detailed and technical but which also at times contain sufficiency of loose definition to provide ample scope for further dispute.
 (2) The Act gives rights which can be defined and enforced only through the courts. The court has also an important rôle in quantifying any price or compensation which is to be paid in respect of the right of access granted.
 (3) The rights that can be granted are in some ways quite limited. The text of the Act will in most cases require exact and exacting study. It must, in particular, be noted that the Act gives no right to create new permanent structures on neighbouring land. It does not, for example, solve the problem of the "ransom" strip, which prevents access of water pipes over neighbouring land in many cases without permission from the owner of that land.
The Act follows in large parts the recommendations of Law Commission Report No. 151 and persons struggling with its interpretation may on occasion find that helpful—with the *caveat* that its recommendations are not always followed.
The procedures introduced by this Act are very much a remedy of last resort. The measure will do little to reduce the phenomenon known to lawyers as "the neighbour dispute". Indeed, in reality it may even encourage such disputes to lead to costly and lengthy negotiation. The lawyer advising on use of this Act will have to use very great caution before leading an eager client to court. It remains axiomatic that such disputes are best resolved by negotiation.

Access orders

1.—(1) A person—
 (a) who, for the purpose of carrying out works to any land (the "dominant land"), desires to enter upon any adjoining or adjacent land (the "servient land"), and
 (b) who needs, but does not have, the consent of some other person to that entry,

---

* Annotations by Professor Phillip H. Kenny LL.B., Dip. Crim., LL.M., Property Law Consultant, Messrs. Dickinson Dees, Newcastle upon Tyne.

may make an application to the court for an order under this section ("an access order") against that other person.

(2) On an application under this section, the court shall make an access order if, and only if, it is satisfied—

(a) that the works are reasonably necessary for the preservation of the whole or any part of the dominant land; and

(b) that they cannot be carried out, or would be substantially more difficult to carry out, without entry upon the servient land;

but this subsection is subject to subsection (3) below.

(3) The court shall not make an access order in any case where it is satisfied that, were it to make such an order—

(a) the respondent or any other person would suffer interference with, or disturbance of, his use or enjoyment of the servient land, or

(b) the respondent, or any other person (whether of full age or capacity or not) in occupation of the whole or any part of the servient land, would suffer hardship,

to such a degree by reason of the entry (notwithstanding any requirement of this Act or any term or condition that may be imposed under it) that it would be unreasonable to make the order.

(4) Where the court is satisfied on an application under this section that it is reasonably necessary to carry out any basic preservation works to the dominant land, those works shall be taken for the purposes of this Act to be reasonably necessary for the preservation of the land; and in this subsection "basic preservation works" means any of the following, that is to say—

(a) the maintenance, repair or renewal of any part of a building or other structure comprised in, or situate on, the dominant land;

(b) the clearance, repair or renewal of any drain, sewer, pipe or cable so comprised or situate;

(c) the treatment, cutting back, felling, removal or replacement of any hedge, tree, shrub or other growing thing which is so comprised and which is, or is in danger of becoming, damaged, diseased, dangerous, insecurely rooted or dead;

(d) the filling in, or clearance, of any ditch so comprised;

but this subsection is without prejudice to the generality of the works which may, apart from it, be regarded by the court as reasonably necessary for the preservation of any land.

(5) If the court considers it fair and reasonable in all the circumstances of the case, works may be regarded for the purposes of this Act as being reasonably necessary for the preservation of any land (or, for the purposes of subsection (4) above, as being basic preservation works which it is reasonably necessary to carry out to any land) notwithstanding that the works incidentally involve—

(a) the making of some alteration, adjustment or improvement to the land, or

(b) the demolition of the whole or any part of a building or structure comprised in or situate upon the land.

(6) Where any works are reasonably necessary for the preservation of the whole or any part of the dominant land, the doing to the dominant land of anything which is requisite for, incidental to, or consequential on, the carrying out of those works shall be treated for the purposes of this Act as the carrying out of works which are reasonably necessary for the preservation of that land; and references in this Act to works, or to the carrying out of works, shall be construed accordingly.

(7) Without prejudice to the generality of subsection (6) above, if it is reasonably necessary for a person to inspect the dominant land—

(a) for the purpose of ascertaining whether any works may be reasonably necessary for the preservation of the whole or any part of that land,

(b) for the purpose of making any map or plan, or ascertaining the course of any drain, sewer, pipe or cable, in preparation for, or otherwise in connection with, the carrying out of works which are so reasonably necessary, or

(c) otherwise in connection with the carrying out of any such works,

the making of such an inspection shall be taken for the purposes of this Act to be the carrying out to the dominant land of works which are reasonably necessary for the preservation of that land; and references in this Act to works, or to the carrying out of works, shall be construed accordingly.

DEFINITIONS
"the court": s.8(3).
"entry": s.8(1).
"land": s.8(3).

GENERAL NOTE
An "access order" is the order which the court makes permitting the applicant to carry out specified works. The procedure under the Act is, as is usual, not spelled out in the Act itself. Procedural rules will be made. However, it must be clear that an application under this Act will have to specify the order required. This will require skilled drafting. An application will normally identify the dominant and servient land on a plan. Because of the financial implications of the conditions that may be attached to an access order, expert valuation assistance is likely also to be required. The existence of the possibility of an eventual access order and the complexity of it will very much affect the strategy to be used in negotiating such disputed rights.

Subs. (1)
The applicant clearly does not have to be the estate owner of the dominant land. The provision is widely phrased and capable of application to a very wide range of situations where any person, in order to do work he has power to do in some particular land, requires entry to other land. It is perfectly clear literally, for example, that A, who has an easement over some part of Whiteacre, may use the legislation to obtain a right of entry over other parts of Whiteacre which he requires to repair or maintain that easement. In the same way a tenant in a block of flats may be able to use the provision to enter into any other flat to repair a conduit which runs through that flat. The conduit itself (or, more accurately, the easement to use it) is the dominant land and each of the other flats the servient land.

It appears also that a mere licensee may be an applicant under this Act, as may a statutory undertaker who has power to do things on some land but not to enter on other land.

Subs. (1)(b)
Where the servient land is mortgaged, the applicant will not ordinarily require the consent of the mortgagee. However, if subsequently the mortgagee sells, or even goes into possession, the applicant, having obtained an access order, will not necessarily be able to enforce it. Is the mortgagee or persons claiming it a "successor in title" within s.4(1)(a) below? It would be odd if this were so, as the interest is granted before the access order. This point is discussed further in the note on s.4. However, it is at least recommended that if the access order is one requiring prolonged right of entry, the respondent's mortgagee should also be made a respondent.

Any tenant in possession or licensee having the right to exclude the applicant from the land may be made a party to an application.

Subss. (2) and (4)
These form the heart of the Act and describe when an access order may be made. Examples may readily be given of works which fall within s.1(2)(a) and are reasonably necessary to the preservation of the dominant land, but no exhaustive listing would ever be possible. What is clear is that improvements in themselves cannot fall within this provision—thus, work to carry out new installations, such as an extension or computer cables, the laying of which on the dominant land requires access to the servient is excluded. Equally, entry to demolish a building would generally not fall within s.1(2)(a) (but see subs. (5)(b)).

Subs. (2)(b)
This is not very clear in its effect. The applicant has to prove that it is either impossible or *substantially more difficult* to carry out the preservation works without this right of entry. Presumably the fact that it is more expensive without the right does not in itself mean it is substantially more difficult.

Subs. (3)

This subsection provides, as it were, two defences to the application for an access order. In both cases it is clear that the onus must be on the respondent to satisfy the court.

Subs. (3)(a)

Under this paragraph the court has to be satisfied that the degree of interference or disturbance the order would cause is such that it would be unreasonable to make the order. This test is extremely vague. From the respondent's point of view it will always be satisfied, or else there would never be any litigation under this legislation. In effect, it gives the court a very wide discretion as to the balance between the nuisance to the respondent of an order and the nuisance to the applicant if no order is made. The court would be unwise and wrong to fetter this exercise of judgment and this, together with the other loosely worded parts of the Act, will make an application under the Act a time-consuming, costly and uncertain adventure.

Subs. (3)(b)

Under this paragraph the respondent has to satisfy the court that he or another occupier would suffer hardship to such a degree that it would be unreasonable to make the order. The applicant will try to avoid the effect of this paragraph by suggesting conditions (*e.g.* as to noise abatement) which will make the work tolerable.

Subs. (5)

This subsection describes the very limited circumstances in which the works permitted by an access order include works which involve alterations, adjustments or improvements to the dominant land or demolition work on the dominant land. Such activities as these must only be incidental to a scheme which does involve preservation work within subss. (2) or (4). Some ingenuity can be expected by would-be developers who may indirectly be able to obtain entry for a purpose which does not fall directly within the spirit of the Act. In this regard presentation of the application is everything.

Subs. (6)

The purpose of this subsection is to enable an access order to permit the right of entry to be used to do any works incidental to or consequential to the necessary preservation works. It must be remembered that the effect of this is only to permit an access order to allow for the carrying out of such activities. The applicant must ensure that the access order requires from the time of its making all the rights he will require. A second and subsequent order may, of course, be applied for but the applicant who makes a meal of this must surely bear a heavy risk as to the costs involved and a solicitor who advises badly as to the detailed contents of an access order is at great risk of an action in negligence or even a personal costs order under Order 62 if further costs are unnecessarily incurred.

Subs. (7)

This subsection needs to be approached with circumspection. Its effect is to permit an access order to include the right to involve inspection visits and visits to make maps and plans and so on. Such visits will not be permitted unless specified in the necessary order. However, subs. (7)(a) clearly envisages that such inspections may be necessary to discover if work is "reasonably necessary". The following scenario may be common. A has some works on his land which are clearly blocked or defective. Entry on B's land may be necessary to repair them but A cannot be sure without an access order. Subsection (7) envisages that an access order may be made to permit inspection. Will A usefully be able to apply for a "rolled-up order", *i.e.* an order to inspect and if a specified condition is found to remedy it, to avoid a second court application? Thus, "to inspect the ditch marked between points "x" and "y" on the servient land *and if* this ditch is blocked to unblock the same . . ."? The question will arise whether the court has the power to make the second part of this order until the condition is found to be satisfied.

Terms and conditions of access orders

2.—(1) An access order shall specify—
  (a) the works to the dominant land that may be carried out by entering upon the servient land in pursuance of the order;
  (b) the particular area of servient land that may be entered upon by virtue of the order for the purpose of carrying out those works to the dominant land; and
  (c) the date on which, or the period during which, the land may be so entered upon;

and in the following provisions of this Act any reference to the servient land is a reference to the area specified in the order in pursuance of paragraph (b) above.

(2) An access order may impose upon the applicant or the respondent such terms and conditions as appear to the court to be reasonably necessary for the purpose of avoiding or restricting—

(a) any loss, damage, or injury which might otherwise be caused to the respondent or any other person by reason of the entry authorised by the order; or

(b) any inconvenience or loss of privacy that might otherwise be so caused to the respondent or any other person.

(3) Without prejudice to the generality of subsection (2) above, the terms and conditions which may be imposed under that subsection include provisions with respect to—

(a) the manner in which the specified works are to be carried out;

(b) the days on which, and the hours between which, the work involved may be executed;

(c) the persons who may undertake the carrying out of the specified works or enter upon the servient land under or by virtue of the order;

(d) the taking of any such precautions by the applicant as may be specified in the order.

(4) An access order may also impose terms and conditions—

(a) requiring the applicant to pay, or to secure that such person connected with him as may be specified in the order pays, compensation for—

(i) any loss, damage or injury, or

(ii) any substantial loss of privacy or other substantial inconvenience,

which will, or might, be caused to the respondent or any other person by reason of the entry authorised by the order;

(b) requiring the applicant to secure that he, or such person connected with him as may be specified in the order, is insured against any such risks as may be so specified; or

(c) requiring such a record to be made of the condition of the servient land, or of such part of it as may be so specified, as the court may consider expedient with a view to facilitating the determination of any question that may arise concerning damage to that land.

(5) An access order may include provision requiring the applicant to pay the respondent such sum by way of consideration for the privilege of entering the servient land in pursuance of the order as appears to the court to be fair and reasonable having regard to all the circumstances of the case, including, in particular—

(a) the likely financial advantage of the order to the applicant and any persons connected with him; and

(b) the degree of inconvenience likely to be caused to the respondent or any other person by the entry;

but no payment shall be ordered under this subsection if and to the extent that the works which the applicant desires to carry out by means of the entry are works to residential land.

(6) For the purposes of subsection (5)(a) above, the likely financial advantage of an access order to the applicant and any persons connected with him shall in all cases be taken to be a sum of money equal to the greater of the following amounts, that is to say—

(a) the amount (if any) by which so much of any likely increase in the value of any land—

(i) which consists of or includes the dominant land, and

(ii) which is owned or occupied by the same person as the dominant land, as may reasonably be regarded as attributable to the carrying out of the specified works exceeds the likely cost of carrying out those works with the benefit of the access order; and

(b) the difference (if it would have been possible to carry out the specified works without entering upon the servient land) between—

(i) the likely cost of carrying out those works without entering upon the servient land; and

(ii) the likely cost of carrying them out with the benefit of the access order.

(7) For the purposes of subsection (5) above, "residential land" means so much of any land as consists of—

(a) a dwelling or part of a dwelling;

(b) a garden, yard, private garage or outbuilding which is used and enjoyed wholly or mainly with a dwelling; or

(c) in the case of a building which includes one or more dwellings, any part of the building which is used and enjoyed wholly or mainly with those dwellings or any of them.

(8) The persons who are to be regarded for the purposes of this section as "connected with" the applicant are—

(a) the owner of any estate or interest in, or right over, the whole or any part of the dominant land;

(b) the occupier of the whole or any part of the dominant land; and

(c) any person whom the applicant may authorise under section 3(7) below to exercise the power of entry conferred by the access order.

(9) The court may make provision—

(a) for the reimbursement by the applicant of any expenses reasonably incurred by the respondent in connection with the application which are not otherwise recoverable as costs;

(b) for the giving of security by the applicant for any sum that might become payable to the respondent or any other person by virtue of this section or section 3 below.

DEFINITIONS
"access order": s.1(1).
"court": s.8(3).
"dominant land": s.1(1)(a).
"servient land": s.1(1)(a).

GENERAL NOTE
Great care will be needed by the applicant in framing his application for an access order. This, when the procedure is clear will inevitably involve drafting the access order required. The respondent, if contesting the matter, will similarly exercise much creative skill in this area. Because of the infelicitous wording of this part of the Act, it will often be desirable to apply for more than one access order and this may clearly be done in the same application.

Subs. (1)(a)
The applicant has to be careful to specify all the works, including preliminary entry to draw plans and to carry out inspections which may be necessary.

Subs. (1)(b)
This definition is important. Once the area of servient land is specified then where the expression "servient land" is used in the rest of the Act it is only the area so specified which is meant. The singular is used—"the particular area". There will very probably be cases where more than one area is necessary. If it is necessary to enter more than one particular area then more than one access order should be applied for, each specifying its "particular area".

Subs. (1)(c)
The order may specify either "a date" or "the period". This appears to exclude the possibility of it specifying more than one separate date or more than one separate period. It seems to suggest that if the work must be done in separate chunks then separate access orders must be

obtained, although there seems to be no reason why they cannot be applied for in the same action.

A more fundamental question is certain to be asked. Can the period be over the whole length of a lease or in fee simple? A person may wish to have a right of access for such a way, for example to repair a wall. It seems clear that the court does literally have such a power. The order may thus say, "The works are entry on the red land to repair the wall on the blue land and the period during which this right may be exercised is at any future time on reasonable notice".

Subs. (4)

If works are done which are not permitted by an access order then an action for trespass can be maintained. If works are done which are permitted then they might still cause loss to the servient owner. For example, the works may cause the loss or diminution in value of a crop. If no provision is made in the access order for compensation in such respect then it seems that the servient owner will not be able to recover this in the future. It is consequently very important for the respondent to ensure that terms are imposed under this subsection. The terms may include compensation for damage which "might" be caused—presumably the order will make provision for the parties to apply to have such compensation assessed. If it is possible to persuade the court, an order could sensibly allow for this compensation to be determined by an independent expert without recourse to the court.

Subss. (5)–(7)

These provisions all deal with the possibility of the servient owner's recovering a price in respect of the access order. This is not possible if the dominant land is "residential land" as defined in subs. (7).

Subs. (5)

There is no way of guessing what kind of orders will be made under this section. The servient owner is entitled to a "fair and reasonable" consideration, taking into account subs. (5)(a) and (b).

Subs. (6)

The court has to assess the "likely financial advantage of an access order" as one factor in calculating any consideration to be paid for it. This subsection asks the court to consider quite a difficult question of causation. Suppose A purchases land with a factory and requires an access order to repair a flank wall. The court must consider if there is any increase in value of the factory attributable to carrying out those works.

Subs. (6)(a)

The likely financial advantage is then, taking the example above, that sum less the likely cost of carrying out the works. However, if the works can be carried out all without the access order then the court has to deduct the likely cost of carrying out the works with the access order from the cost without the order. The likely financial advantage will be that sum if it is greater than the sum in subs. (6)(a) (see subs. (6)(b)).

It should be noted that subs. (6)(b) asks if it is "possible" to carry out these works without entering upon the servient land and not if it is practicable or sensible.

Subs. (7)

This definition of "residential land" is crucial, as where the dominant owner is doing works on residential land, no consideration will be payable under subs. (5). An estate owner, such as the Grosvenor Estate, may still take advantage of subs. (7)—the commercial purpose of the applicant is irrelevant. Difficult issues will arise—suppose the building consists of shops on the ground floor and then six stories of flats, topped by a defective roof. If the landlord wishes to have access to adjoining land to repair the roof, he will argue that this is "residential land" within subs. (7)(c). Is the roof used "wholly or mainly" with the dwellings? Even a caretaker's flat in a factory may be residential land for this purpose—but this affects the compensation only to the extent that the works are for its benefit (see *Hansard*, H.L. Vol. 535, col. 889).

Subs. (9)

The question of costs of applications under this Act is a sensitive one. Normally in England and Wales costs follow the result. However, is it reasonable for the respondent who has an access order made against him to have to pay the applicant's costs? This subsection does not alter the general discretion that the court has as to costs. However, it extends that discretion further by allowing the respondent to recover other expenses reasonably incurred. Since costs will fall to be dealt with under Supreme Court Rules 1965, Ord. 62 (which applies both to the

High Court and County Court—County Court Rules 1981, Ord. 38, r. 1(3)) then the court in any event has a discretion to allow costs on an indemnity basis (see Ord. 62, r. 12). It is not until any particular rules as to costs are made that it will be possible to see the extent to which subs. 9(a) is otiose. However, it appears to make clear that the purpose is to allow the court to order the applicant to reimburse the respondent's expenses in cases where a cost order is made against the respondent or in cases where the expenses fall outside the scope of a costs order.

Effect of access order

3.—(1) An access order requires the respondent, so far as he has power to do so, to permit the applicant or any of his associates to do anything which the applicant or associate is authorised or required to do under or by virtue of the order or this section.

(2) Except as otherwise provided by or under this Act, an access order authorises the applicant or any of his associates, without the consent of the respondent,—

(a) to enter upon the servient land for the purpose of carrying out the specified works;

(b) to bring on to that land, leave there during the period permitted by the order and, before the end of that period, remove, such materials, plant and equipment as are reasonably necessary for the carrying out of those works; and

(c) to bring on to that land any waste arising from the carrying out of those works, if it is reasonably necessary to do so in the course of removing it from the dominant land;

but nothing in this Act or in any access order shall authorise the applicant or any of his associates to leave anything in, on or over the servient land (otherwise than in discharge of their duty to make good that land) after their entry for the purpose of carrying out works to the dominant land ceases to be authorised under or by virtue of the order.

(3) An access order requires the applicant—

(a) to secure that any waste arising from the carrying out of the specified works is removed from the servient land forthwith;

(b) to secure that, before the entry ceases to be authorised under or by virtue of the order, the servient land is, so far as reasonably practicable, made good; and

(c) to indemnify the respondent against any damage which may be caused to the servient land or any goods by the applicant or any of his associates which would not have been so caused had the order not been made;

but this subsection is subject to subsections (4) and (5) below.

(4) In making an access order, the court may vary or exclude, in whole or in part,—

(a) any authorisation that would otherwise be conferred by subsection 2(b) or (c) above; or

(b) any requirement that would otherwise be imposed by subsection (3) above.

(5) Without prejudice to the generality of subsection (4) above, if the court is satisfied that it is reasonably necessary for any such waste as may arise from the carrying out of the specified works to be left on the servient land for some period before removal, the access order may, in place of subsection (3)(a) above, include provision—

(a) authorising the waste to be left on that land for such period as may be permitted by the order; and

(b) requiring the applicant to secure that the waste is removed before the end of that period.

(6) Where the applicant or any of his associates is authorised or required under or by virtue of an access order or this section to enter, or do any other thing, upon the servient land, he shall not (as respects that access order) be

taken to be a trespasser from the beginning on account of his, or any other person's, subsequent conduct.

(7) For the purposes of this section, the applicant's "associates" are such number of persons (whether or not servants or agents of his) whom he may reasonably authorise under this subsection to exercise the power of entry conferred by the access order as may be reasonably necessary for carrying out the specified works.

DEFINITIONS
  "access order": s.6(1).
  "associates": subs. (7).

GENERAL NOTE
  This section is stated to deal with "the effect of an access order". In most situations each access order will be peculiar in its effect, depending on the precise drafting.

Subs. (1)
  The respondent has to permit the access order to be carried out "so far as he has power to do so". This means, presumably, so far as he has power in law to do so.

Subs. (2)
  This subsection needs careful consideration. The key words are the opening clause "except as otherwise provided by or under this Act". The effect of the provision is to imply certain terms into an access order unless the access order or this Act says otherwise. The general licence given by the subsection is so wide that in every case the respondent will wish to see it cut down. This will be a prime concern in drafting the reply to the applicant's originating application.
  The proviso to subs. (2) is very important. Nothing can be left "in or over the servient land ...". This means there can be no pipes, wires, cables or other conduits left in or over the servient land. Nor can there be any props, supports, foundations or footings left on the servient land. Even a metal tie or boss on a wall which actually forms the boundary will fall foul of this proviso. It is, given the purpose of the Act, an obvious failure to provide such a complete ban on the provision of such structures (but for a qualification of this ban, see subs. (5) below).

Subs. (3)
  All the requirements of this subsection may be varied or excluded under subs. (4). Each paragraph of the subsection contains the imprecise words or concepts that will make this Act very difficult to operate in practice. From both parties' point of view greater clarity than these "fall-back" provisions is desirable. For example, in para. (a), what is "waste", and when is "forthwith"?

Subs. (4)
  This subsection makes it clear which of the terms implied in access orders by subss. (2) and (3) can be varied or excluded. The effect is that they all can except for subs. (2)(a), which gives the right of entry itself.

Subs. (5)
  This at first sight otiose provision appears to be made necessary by the clear wording of the proviso to subs. (2), with which it is literally in conflict. To make clearer sense of the two provisions there could be added to subs. (2), after "land" in the brackets "and except as permitted under subsection (5) below".

Subs. (6)
  This curious subsection is inserted because of the effect of the *Six Carpenters'* case (1610) 8 Co.Rep. 146a (see *per* Lord Murton, *Hansard*, H.L. Vol. 535, col. 893 and also para. 4.111 of the Law Commission Report No. 151). This ancient rule is that if a person enters upon land with lawful authority but then abuses that authority he becomes a trespasser *ab initio* and his original entry is said to be tortious. If that rule had been applied in the case of entry under an access order, which is most unlikely, then this subsection appears apt to negate it.

Subs. (7)
  It is to be hoped that the court will accept that it has jurisdiction to set out in an access order in appropriate cases exactly who is entitled to enter upon the servient land to carry out the order. That this is so is not entirely clear, as the effect of subs. (4) is to imply that subs. (2)(a) cannot be

varied. That it might be argued gives "associates", as defined by subs. (7), their rôle in exercise of the right of entry. However, the opening words of subs. (2) give rise to a more liberal expectation; that is, that associates have a right of entry "except as otherwise provided ...". Clearly, there will be many cases when the respondent to an order reasonably requires that particular persons will not be involved in exercise of the order; so many of these cases come to court only when there is already very bad blood between the parties. Again, the respondent might well seek (to avoid later argument) to persuade the court that the number of persons for particular purposes who can be involved in exercise of the right of entry should be clearly stated.

Persons bound by access order, unidentified persons and bar on contracting out

4.—(1) In addition to the respondent, an access order shall, subject to the provisions of the Land Charges Act 1972 and the Land Registration Act 1925, be binding on—

(a) any of his successors in title to the servient land; and

(b) any person who has an estate or interest in, or right over, the whole or any part of the servient land which was created after the making of the order and who derives his title to that estate, interest or right under the respondent;

and references to the respondent shall be construed accordingly.

(2) If and to the extent that the court considers it just and equitable to allow him to do so, a person on whom an access order becomes binding by virtue of subsection (1)(a) or (b) above shall be entitled, as respects anything falling to be done after the order becomes binding on him, to enforce the order or any of its terms or conditions as if he were the respondent, and references to the respondent shall be construed accordingly.

(3) Rules of court may—

(a) provide a procedure which may be followed where the applicant does not know, and cannot reasonably ascertain, the name of any person whom he desires to make respondent to the application; and

(b) make provision enabling such an applicant to make such a person respondent by description instead of by name;

and in this subsection "applicant" includes a person who proposes to make an application for an access order.

(4) Any agreement, whenever made, shall be void if and to the extent that it would, apart from this subsection, prevent a person from applying for an access order or restrict his right to do so.

DEFINITIONS
"access order": s.6(1).
"land": s.6(1).
"servient land": s.1(1).

GENERAL NOTE
This section contains a number of scarcely related provisions. It deals with making access orders binding on successors in title; it allows certain persons not parties to the proceedings to enforce access orders; it assists in the discovery of possible respondents to an application; and, lastly, it prohibits contracting out of the Act.

Subs. (1)
There are two groups of persons against whom, in addition to any respondents, an access order is binding.

(a) "Successors in title to the servient land". This is not so straightforward as it appears and the following points arise:

(i) the access order should be registered or it will not bind successors in some cases (see s.5 of this Act and the notes thereon);

(ii) a more difficult question arises as to what is meant by the "servient land" in this context. The land owned by the respondent may well be sub-divided. Presumably in such a case the owner of each part remains liable for the performance and financial consequences of non-performance only of the part of the access order which falls to be exercised over his part of the original servient land.

(b) The persons falling within subs. (1)(b) are clearly intended to be a wider and different class of persons than in subs. (1)(a). To what extent is this group wider than successors in title? First, it includes persons claiming under the respondent but who have no title, such as licensees. Secondly, it includes all persons with a derivative title, such as lessees and underlessees. Curiously, it includes all those people who have such a right or interest "over the whole or any part of the servient land". But, surely, as with para. (ii) immediately above, their liability must extend only to the part of the access order which is over *their part* of the quondam undivided servient land. Thus, the servient land is a field bordering the dominant land and the access order permits entry to repair a boundary wall along that boundary. The field is sold as to half to A and half to B. The one access order binds both A and B. But each is clearly bound only in respect of the right to access on *his* part of the boundary.

Subs. (2)
This at first sight opaque provision makes sense when it is borne in mind that the respondent has rights as well as duties. Someone who by virtue of subs. (1) becomes subject to an access order may wish to claim financial compensation under s.1(5) or reimbursement under s.1(9). It seems unlikely that subs. (2) will extend to him the benefit of those provisions. However, the access order will attach conditions to exercise of the right of entry and it is these that are enabled by subs. (2) to be enforced. For example, the right of entry may be subject to the taking out of insurance or the lodging of security. Someone becoming bound by an access order by virtue of subs. (1) may enforce such conditions, but only if to do so is "just and equitable". This last restriction seems quite monstrous, as it puts upon the person seeking to insist upon a condition laid down by the court being honoured a new condition which, however small in practice, is a further unwarranted reduction of his rights as a landowner and in its open-endedness a further incitement to litigation on the part of the owner of the dominant land.

Subs. (3)
Rules of court may permit an applicant to proceed without naming, or presumably serving in the usual way, the respondent. These rules will presumably be very restrictive and the power exercised infrequently. When can the applicant reasonably ascertain the name of an absentee landowner?

Subs. (4)
This subsection forbids agreements contracting out of the Act. It applies to any agreement, whether made before or after the Act. This means that no form of words, however clear, can prevent a person applying to the court for an access order. However, this is not to say that there is no point in including such a provision—in considering whether the interference that entry causes makes it *unreasonable* to make an order (s.1(3)), surely it must be relevant that the applicant has agreed to manage without such a right of entry?

Registration of access orders and of applications for such orders

5.—(1) In section 6(1) of the Land Charges Act 1972 (which specifies the writs and orders affecting land that may be entered in the register) after paragraph (c) there shall be added—
> "(d) any access order under the Access to Neighbouring Land Act 1992."

(2) In section 49 of the Land Registration Act 1925 (rules to provide for certain rights, interests and claims to be protected by notice) in subsection (1) (which specifies those rights, interests and claims) after paragraph (h) there shall be added—
> "(j) Access orders under the Access to Neighbouring Land Act 1992 which, notwithstanding section 59 of this Act, it may be deemed expedient to protect by notice instead of by caution."

(3) In section 64 of that Act (production of certificates for noting on certain dealings etc.) after subsection (6) there shall be added—
> "(7) Subsection (1) above shall also not require the production of the land certificate or of any charge certificate when a person applies for the registration of a notice in respect of an access order under the Access to Neighbouring Land Act 1992."

(4) In any case where—
(a) an access order is discharged under section 6(1)(a) below, and

(b) the order has been protected by an entry registered under the Land
Charges Act 1972 or by a notice or caution under the Land Registration Act 1925,

the court may by order direct that the entry, notice or caution shall be
cancelled.

(5) The rights conferred on a person by or under an access order are not
capable of constituting an overriding interest within the meaning of the Land
Registration Act 1925, notwithstanding that he or any other person is in
actual occupation of the whole or any part of the servient land in question.

(6) An application for an access order shall be regarded as a pending land
action for the purposes of the Land Charges Act 1972 and the Land Registration Act 1925.

DEFINITIONS
"access order": s.6(1).

GENERAL NOTE
This section deals with the steps consequential on the application for and making of access
orders which involve application for registration in either the Land Charges Registry or the
Land Registry. It contains within its separate subsections important procedural points.

Subs. (1)
An access order is registrable in the case of unregistered land as a writ or order under s.6(1) of
the Land Charges Act 1972. The correct form is Form K4. The onus is on the person with the
benefit of an order to apply for registration. This will not be done by the court.

Subs. (2)
This simply provides for access orders to be protected by registration of a notice in registered
land. The applicant may choose instead to register a caution but there is no good reason ever to
do so.

Subs. (3)
This subsection enables the person with the benefit of an access order to register it as a notice
in the Land Registry without production of the Land Certificate. The position is less straightforward if the servient land is subject to a registered charge—this issue is discussed in the note
on s.4(1) and s.1(1)(b).

Subs. (4)
Where a person applies under s.6(1)(a) for discharge of an access order a request for an order
under this subsection will be included in the application—the court will not make the necessary
order if it is not.

Subs. (5)
This important subsection prevents the rights of a person having the benefit of an access order
from becoming an over-riding interest in registered land under s.70(1)(g) of the Land Registration Act 1925. This reinforces the need for registration to be effective under subs. (1) or (2), as
the case may be.

Subs. (6)
An applicant for an access order will be advised to effect registration of the order as a pending
land action in the Land Charges Registry or Land Registry, as the case may be. In unregistered
land a pending land action will not bind a purchaser without express notice unless it is registered
(s.5(7) of the Land Charges Act 1977). In registered land a pending action may be registered
only by a caution under s.59(1) of the Land Registration Act 1925.

Variation of orders and damages for breach

6.—(1) Where an access order or an order under this subsection has been
made, the court may, on the application of any party to the proceedings in
which the order was made or of any other person on whom the order is
binding—

(a) discharge or vary the order or any of its terms or conditions;
(b) suspend any of its terms or conditions; or
(c) revive any term or condition suspended under paragraph (b) above;
and in the application of subsections (1) and (2) of section 4 above in relation to an access order, any order under this subsection which relates to the access order shall be treated for the purposes of those subsections as included in the access order.

(2) If any person contravenes or fails to comply with any requirement, term or condition imposed upon him by or under this Act, the court may, without prejudice to any other remedy available, make an order for the payment of damages by him to any other person affected by the contravention or failure who makes an application for relief under this subsection.

DEFINITIONS
   "access order": s.6(1).
   "court": s.6(1).

GENERAL NOTE
   This innocuous-looking section packs two distinct and powerful punches. Subsection (1) contains an open-ended power to vary and amend access orders and subs. (2) creates a wide-ranging remedy of damages for failure to comply with access orders.

Subs. (1)
   This permits any person bound by an access order to apply for its discharge, variation, suspension or, once suspended, revival. There is no time limit within which such an application may be made. However, and perhaps oddly, the making of such an application in itself has no effect on the continuity in force of an existing access order. An applicant, accordingly, may wish to make an application under this subsection and in the course of it make an interlocutory application to restrain continued access. The court has power to grant such relief under County Court Rules 1981, Ord. 13, r. 6. Ordinarily the application will first be issued and served but the court has power to make such an order *ex parte* and before the issue of the application if the case is one of urgency (Ord. 13, r. 6(4)).

Subs. (2)
   This creates a remedy of damages. The applicant has to show contravention of or failure to comply with a requirement, term or condition imposed by or under this Act. This seems to include breaches both of access orders themselves and of any interlocutory order made under the Act. The subsection is worded very widely indeed and the following should be noted:
   (a) There is not a single clue as to how damages are to be assessed under this provision.
   (b) Any person affected by the "breach" may claim such damages. He does not have to have been a party to the proceedings or to own neighbouring or adjoining land. All he has to do is show that he has been "affected" by the breach.
   (c) There is no fault required on the part of the person accused of such a breach. The applicant must show that a person has contravened or failed to comply with a requirement, etc., but that is all the applicant has to show. Neither is there any "best efforts" or "due diligence" defence. This is very important for the respondent to an application for an access order. The respondent must seek to have the order as drafted qualified so that a claim for damages for breach under subs. (1) is the less likely. For example, compliance with time limits should not be left an absolute requirement.

Jurisdiction over, and allocation of, proceedings

7.—(1) The High Court and the county courts shall both have jurisdiction under this Act.

(2) In article 4 of the High Court and County Courts Jurisdiction Order 1991 (which provides that proceedings in which the county courts and the High Court both have jurisdiction may, subject to articles 5 and 6, be commenced either in a county court or in the High Court) for the words "and 6" there shall be substituted the words ", 6 and 6A"; and after article 6 of that Order there shall be inserted—

   "6A. Applications under section 1 of the Access to Neighbouring Land Act 1992 shall be commenced in a county court."

(3) The amendment by subsection (2) above of provisions contained in an order shall not be taken to have prejudiced any power to make further orders revoking or amending those provisions.

GENERAL NOTE

All applications under this Act will be commenced in the County Court but may thereafter be transferred to the High Court.

Interpretation and application

8.—(1) Any reference in this Act to an "entry" upon any servient land includes a reference to the doing on that land of anything necessary for carrying out the works to the dominant land which are reasonably necessary for its preservation; and "enter" shall be construed accordingly.

(2) This Act applies in relation to any obstruction of, or other interference with, a right over, or interest in, any land as it applies in relation to an entry upon that land; and "enter" and "entry" shall be construed accordingly.

(3) In this Act—

"access order" has the meaning given by section 1(1) above;

"applicant" means a person making an application for an access order and, subject to section 4 above, "the respondent" means the respondent, or any of the respondents, to such an application;

"the court" means the High Court or a county court;

"the dominant land" and "the servient land" respectively have the meanings given by section 1(1) above, but subject, in the case of servient land, to section 2(1) above;

"land" does not include a highway;

"the specified works" means the works specified in the access order in pursuance of section 2(1)(a) above.

GENERAL NOTE

Subs. (1)

This provision needs careful attention. Its effect at first seems to be to cure weaknesses in the drafting of an access order by permitting works which are not specified in the order. This is clearly not so, however, as the access order *must* specify the works that may be carried out (see s.2(1)).

Subs. (2)

This makes it clear that an access order may permit interference with rights such as restrictive covenants, easements, etc.

Short title, commencement and extent

9.—(1) This Act may be cited as the Access to Neighbouring Land Act 1992.

(2) This Act shall come into force on such day as the Lord Chancellor may by order made by statutory instrument appoint.

(3) This Act extends to England and Wales only.

INDEX

References are to sections

OFFSHORE SAFETY (PROTECTION AGAINST VICTIMISATION) ACT 1992*

(1992 c. 24)

An Act to protect employees working on offshore installations against victimisation when acting as safety representatives or members of safety committees.   [16th March 1992]

PARLIAMENTARY DEBATES
Hansard, H.L. Vol. 534, col. 567; Vol. 535, col. 808; Vol. 536, cols. 349, 990; H.C. Vol. 203, col. 679; Vol. 205, col. 619.

INTRODUCTION AND GENERAL NOTE

Relationship to Offshore Safety Act 1992
The Offshore Safety (Protection Against Victimisation) Act 1992 was the result of a private member's bill introduced into the House of Lords by Baroness Turner of Camden on January 20, 1992, fairly shortly before the General Election. The Offshore Safety (Protection Against Victimisation) Act 1992 ought to be read together with the Offshore Safety Act 1992 (c.15), as Baroness Turner introduced her Bill to remedy a deficiency that some critics had perceived in the Offshore Safety Bill 1992 (as it then was). To avoid unnecessary repetition, reference should be made to the annotations of the Offshore Safety Act 1992 (see N.J.J. Gaskell, *Current Law Statutes Annotated 1992*) where the full background to both Acts is explained. For convenience, a brief introduction to the Acts is given below, so that the context of the Offshore Safety (Protection Against Victimisation) Act 1992 may be more easily understood.

Piper Alpha Disaster
The Offshore Safety Act 1992 was enacted mainly to give effect to the recommendations in the report made by Lord Cullen into the Piper Alpha Disaster in 1988, in which there had been great loss of life following fires and explosions aboard an offshore oil and gas platform (see *The Public Inquiry into the Piper Alpha Disaster*, Department of Energy, Cm. 1310, HMSO, 1990, hereafter the Cullen Report). There had been real concerns expressed to Lord Cullen in the course of his inquiry that workers who complained about safety matters offshore might be victimised by their employers.
Lord Cullen responded to trade union concerns about victimisation of workers who complained about health and safety by stating that it was appropriate for the type of protection provided in the case of trade union activities under s.58(1)(b) of the Employment Protection (Consolidation) Act 1978 to be afforded to the activities of an employee as a safety representative (Cullen Report, para. 21.86). Section 58(1)(b) of the Employment Protection (Consolidation) Act 1978 provides that a dismissal shall be regarded as having been unfair if the reason for it was that the employee "had taken, or proposed to take, part at any appropriate time in the activities of an independent trade union . . .".

Government reluctance to legislate
At the Second Reading in the Commons of the Offshore Safety Act 1992, the Secretary of State for Employment explained that the victimisation recommendation of Lord Cullen was not being implemented in the Offshore Safety Act 1992 as the Act was dealing with *safety* and not *employment* issues. It was intended to introduce a provision "as soon as a suitable legislative vehicle becomes available" (*Hansard*, H.C. Vol. 213, col. 682). The Secretary of State clearly indicated that victimisation of workers raising safety matters was unacceptable, but seemed content to rely on the fact that workers could contact the Health and Safety Executive (HSE) anonymously and the HSE could be relied on to investigate matters. Yet an example was given in debates of an employee who had done just that, but who was unable to find work in the North Sea—which is notorious for the short-term nature of its contracts. It was rumoured that the letters NRB ("not required back") were written on to the employment cards of workers who complained (and see generally the evidence given to the Seventh Report of the Energy Committee on "Offshore Safety Management", July 17, 1991, H.C. 343 1990–1991, p. 80 *et seq.*). There are some 36,000 persons employed in the U.K. offshore sector, of whom only 25 per cent. are employees of the oil companies, as opposed to contractors engaged by them. Some 50 to 90 per cent. of the workforce on platforms is made up of contractors' employees. Half of

---

* Annotations by Nicholas Gaskell, Reader in Maritime Law, Institute of Maritime Law, Faculty of Law, University of Southampton.

the offshore installations are owned and operated by contractors. The sanction of being able to sue for unfair dismissal before an industrial tribunal might be some help, if victimisation can actually be proved. There were said to be doubts as to the extent to which refusal to work in unsafe conditions could already found a case for unfair dismissal under the existing law. Thus, in the Lords, Lord McCarthy cited *Power Packing Casemakers* v. *Faust* [1983] Q.B. 471 and *Wilkins* v. *Cantrell and Cochrane (G.B.)* [1978] 1 I.R.L.R. 483, although the cases give minimum support to the proposition, being concerned with dismissals justified as a result of strike action (see *Hansard*, H.L. Vol. 532, col. 1420). Suggestions that it should be a criminal offence on the part of an employer to practise victimisation were raised during debates on the Offshore Safety Act 1992, but not supported by the Government.

The hesitant attitude of the Government was not entirely convincing and it is debatable whether there was any valid reason for not including a suitable amendment in the Offshore Safety Act 1992. Nevertheless, the procedural objection of the Government was outflanked by the actions of Baroness Turner of Camden in introducing her private member's bill into the House of Lords specifically to deal with the issue. In the Commons on February 10, 1992, the Secretary of State for Employment maintained his attitude towards dealing with victimisation in the Offshore Safety Bill 1992, but stated that he was prepared to listen to the debates before deciding the Government's attitude towards Baroness Turner's Bill. Two days later, at Second Reading of the Offshore Safety Bill 1992 in the Lords on February 12, 1992, Viscount Ullswater (the Parliamentary Under-Secretary of State, Department of Employment) agreed that Baroness Turner's Bill might prove a more promising vehicle to give effect to Recommendation 30 of the Cullen Report than the Offshore Safety Act 1992 (see *Hansard*, H.L. Vol. 535, col. 816). By the time of the Committee stage in the Commons of the Offshore Safety Bill 1992 the Parliamentary Under-Secretary of State for Employment, Eric Forth, was able to state that the Government had accepted that Baroness Turner's Bill was the appropriate vehicle to deal with the victimisation issue. He added that it had been agreed with her to introduce amendments in the Lords that would form the basis of a Bill that would not be opposed by the Government, provided that no attempt was made by members to oppose the Bill.

Accordingly, on February 26, 1992 the Government introduced an amendment to Baroness Turner's Bill which, in effect, was a complete redraft of the first clause. Even so, the amended version was quite acceptable to her and the Opposition and passed through Parliament unopposed. Lord Wedderburn of Charlton was able to comment, wryly, that this was the first employment proposal from the Labour side of the House that had seen favour with the Conservative Government since 1980. From First Reading in the Lords on January 20, 1992 to Third Reading in the Commons on March 6, 1992, the Act enjoyed a remarkably quick passage through Parliament, no doubt speeded by the impending dissolution for the General Election of April 9, 1992. Indeed, it received its Second Reading, Committee Stage, Report Stage and Third Reading in the Commons on March 6, 1992 without debate.

Summary of the Act
The Offshore Safety (Protection Against Victimisation) Act 1992 gives effect to the specific recommendation of Lord Cullen that offshore safety representatives should be protected against victimisation by a provision similar to s.58(1)(b) of the Employment Protection (Consolidation) Act 1978. The Act gives more protection than envisaged in the Cullen Report in that (i) it also applies to members of safety committees (see s.1(2)) and (ii) it allows for a remedy where victimisation short of dismissal occurs (see s.1(1)(a)).

Commencement
The Act received the Royal Assent on March 16, 1992.

Protection against victimisation

1.—(1) In relation to an offshore employee, the Employment Protection (Consolidation) Act 1978 and the Trade Union and Labour Relations (Consolidation) Act 1992 shall each have effect as if—
   (a) the purposes specified in section 146(1) of the 1992 Act (action short of dismissal on grounds related to union membership or activities) included preventing or deterring him from carrying out any relevant functions, or penalising him for doing so; and
   (b) the reasons specified in section 152(1) of the 1992 Act (dismissal on grounds related to union membership or activities) included the reason that he had carried out, or proposed to carry out, any such functions.
   (2) In this section—

"offshore employee" means an employee (within the meaning of the 1978 Act) who is or was employed on an offshore installation;
"offshore installation" means any installation which is an offshore installation within the meaning of the Mineral Workings (Offshore Installations) Act 1971, or is to be taken to be an installation for the purposes of sections 21 to 23 of the Petroleum Act 1987;
"relevant functions", in relation to an offshore employee, means any functions conferred on him, as a safety representative or as a member of a safety committee—
  (a) by the Offshore Installations (Safety Representatives and Safety Committees) Regulations 1989; or
  (b) by any corresponding regulations made under Part I of the Health and Safety at Work etc. Act 1974.
(3) In relation to any time before the commencement of the 1992 Act, subsection (1) above shall have effect as if—
  (a) the reference to that Act were omitted; and
  (b) the references to sections 146(1) and 152(1) of that Act were references to sections 23(1) and 58(1) respectively of the 1978 Act.

DEFINITIONS
"offshore employee": subs. (2).
"offshore installation": subs. (2).
"relevant functions": subs. (2).

GENERAL NOTE
Viscount Ullswater explained the intention of the section at Committee Stage in the House of Lords (*Hansard*, H.L. Vol. 536, cols. 350–352, February 26, 1992). The overall effect of subs. (1)(b) is to provide that the dismissal of offshore employees shall be regarded as unfair if the reason, or the principal reason, for it was that they had carried out, or proposed to carry out, any functions conferred on them as safety representatives or as members of a safety committee. No qualifying period of employment or upper age limit applies. The employee could also qualify for higher levels of compensation, including the special award of compensation, where employees are dismissed for belonging to a union.

The overall effect of subs. (1)(a) is to give offshore employees the right not to have action short of dismissal taken against them for the purpose of preventing them or deterring them from carrying out any functions conferred on them as safety representatives or as members of a safety committee or penalising them for so doing. The latter protection, deriving from s.23(1) of the Employment Protection (Consolidation) Act 1978, goes beyond the specific recommendation of the Cullen Report and was welcomed by the Opposition. It follows that where an industrial tribunal upholds a complaint of action short of dismissal, it will make a declaration to that effect. It can award such compensation as is appropriate, having regard to the infringement of the employee's rights and any subsequent loss suffered. There is no upper limit on the amount of compensation that might be awarded.

Relevant functions
Lord Cullen's recommendation in para. 21.86 referred only to safety representatives, but the definition of "relevant functions" in subs. (2) also includes members of safety committees. What has not been covered is the position of an individual worker (not a safety representative or member of a safety committee) who complains, for example, directly to the HSE. Section 1(1)(b) of the original Bill, as introduced by Baroness Turner, deemed a dismissal to be unfair if the employee "invoked or seeks to invoke the aid of an independent trade union ... or of a member of the health and safety inspectorate".

In 1989 the E.C. produced, under Art. 118a of the Treaty of Rome, what has been known as the "Framework Directive" 89/391 on the safety and health of workers (the Council Directive of June 12, 1989 on the introduction of measures to encourage improvements in the safety and health of workers at work, O.J. L/183, March 29, 1989). The E.C. Framework Directive provisions relating to victimisation go further than the Cullen Report. For example, Art. 8 indicates that the individual should have the right to stop work and Art. 11 gives the right to approach the inspectorate. Under Art. 7(2), workers designated to carry out activities relating to the protection and prevention of occupational risks "may not be placed at any disadvantage because of their activities". Similarly, Art. 11(4) states that workers or workers' representatives with specific responsibility for safety and health may not be placed at a disadvantage because of activities such as asking employers to take appropriate safety measures or submitting proposals for improving safety. The Government recognised that when it had to implement the Directive (by the end of 1992) the provisions in the Offshore Safety (Protection Against Victimisation) Act 1992 would be overtaken. Still, it was not prepared to act before then to fully implement the Directive provisions, for example, giving rights to individual workers.

Subsection (2) paras. (a) and (b) refer to the functions of safety representatives and committees under two different pieces of legislation. Under the Safety Representatives and Safety Committees Regulations 1977 (S.I. 1977 No. 500) made under the Health and Safety at Work etc. Act 1974, the safety representatives emerge from the machinery of recognised trade unions. Under the Offshore Installations (Safety Representatives and Safety Committees) Regulations 1989 (S.I. 1989 No. 971) the constituencies for election of safety representatives are organised by the management under a statutory framework. It has already been noted that there is resistance from operators to recognising unions offshore. This explains the Government's reluctance to extend the 1977 Regulations to the offshore sector. Lord Cullen was reluctant to recommend the extension himself as a review of the 1989 Regulations was then under way. It is expected that the review will be completed by the spring of 1993. The amendments to the 1989 Regulations would be made under the Health and Safety at Work Act 1974 by virtue of the new powers given in the Offshore Safety Act 1992.

The Trade Union and Labour Relations (Consolidation) Act 1992 was expected to repeal those parts of the 1978 Act to which the Cullen Report referred. The reference to both the Employment Protection (Consolidation) Act 1978 and the Trade Union and Labour Relations (Consolidation) Act 1992 was because the latter was expected to achieve Royal Assent after that of the present Act and it was necessary for the existing employment legislation to be applied in the interim period. Accordingly, subs. (3) deals with the potential overlap by referring to the equivalent provisions of the 1978 legislation. Unfortunately, the Trade Union and Labour Relations (Consolidation) Bill 1992 failed to achieve Royal Assent before the prorogation of Parliament on March 16. Given the re-election of the Conservative Government, it seems likely that the failed legislation may be reintroduced. In the meantime, the Offshore Safety (Protection Against Victimisation) Act 1992 has the distinction of referring to a non-existent Act. Section 58(1) of the Employment Protection (Consolidation) Act 1978 would be replaced by s.152(1) of the Trade Union and Labour Relations (Consolidation) Act 1992 (if subsequently enacted): s.23(1) of the 1978 Act would similarly be replaced by s.146(1) of that 1992 Act.

Short title and extent

2.—(1) This Act may be cited as the Offshore Safety (Protection Against Victimisation) Act 1992.

(2) This Act does not extend to Northern Ireland.

INDEX

References are to sections

PRISON SECURITY ACT 1992*

(1992 c. 25)

An Act to make provision for an offence of prison mutiny and for a new offence and new penalties in connection with escapes from prison.

[16th March 1992]

PARLIAMENTARY DEBATES

Hansard, H.C. Vol. 200, col. 167; Vol. 202, col. 834; H.L. Vol. 535, col. 963; Vol. 536, cols. 800, 1205.

The Bill was discussed in Standing Committee D on December 17 and 19, 1991.

INTRODUCTION AND GENERAL NOTE

The Prison Security Act 1992 is part of the Government's response to a series of violent disturbances which occurred at various prisons during 1990. Strangeways Prison was virtually destroyed and some 200 prisoners and officers were injured. Other disturbances followed in Glen Parva, Dartmoor, Cardiff, Bristol and Pucklechurch: see *Hansard*, H.C. Vol. 200, col. 167.

Upon his conviction for riot, contrary to s.1(1) of the Public Order Act 1986, Paul Taylor was sentenced to 10 years' imprisonment in respect of his involvement at Strangeways Prison. It was the maximum term that could be imposed under the 1986 Act. Significantly, such a term is the maximum for the offence of "mutiny" under s.1 of the 1992 Act— so what has Parliament sought to achieve by creating yet another offence?

The Government's campaign against prison unrest has been conducted on two fronts. The first is the substantial overhaul of the way prisons are managed and the conditions in which prisoners are kept: see the reports of Lord Justice Woolf, "*Prison Disturbances*" (April, 1990), and H.H. Judge Tumin; and see the Government's White Paper "*Custody, Care and Justice*". The second front is the prosecution and punishment of prisoners who take part in serious disturbances at prisons.

During the debates in both Houses of Parliament, the primary objection taken to s.1 of the Act was that an offence of prison mutiny is unnecessary and, in any event, unduly wide and Draconian (see *Hansard*, H.C. Vol. 200, cols. 173 and 176; H.L. Vol. 535, cols. 968 and 971; Vol. 536, col. 1207). Both Roy Hattersley M.P. and Lord Donaldson of Kingsbridge effectively described s.1 as "window-dressing" (*Hansard*, H.C. Vol. 200, col. 173 and H.L. Vol. 535, col. 971 respectively). There is some support for this view but the hope of the Government seems to be that such a window will act as a "warning signal" and a deterrent to prisoners. Thus, the Home Secretary said: "The new offence will bring home to prisoners the severe consequences of mutinous behaviour . . . a prisoner may be vaguely aware of a range of public order or criminal damage offences . . . However, the warning signals are not in my view clear enough. All prisoners are given an information pack on their reception into prison . . . In future, prisoners will also receive a notice describing the offence of prison mutiny and the penalties available to the courts if a prisoner is convicted of it. This will be drawn specifically to the attention of prisoners". Lord Hesketh made similar observations in the House of Lords (*Hansard*, H.L. Vol. 535, col. 964).

Lord Richard when commenting on the Bill, said "It is difficult to think of an example of mutiny for which the offence is needed" (*Official Report*, November 6, 1991, col. 230). However, it should be carefully noted that in certain respects the s.1 offence of prison mutiny is significantly broader in scope than either "riot" or "violent disorder" under s.1(1) or s.2(1) respectively of the Public Order Act 1986. First, only two persons are required to be proved to have engaged in conduct with the intention set out in s.1(2) of the 1992 Act. Secondly, it would seem that once the fact of mutiny is proved, any other prisoner taking part in that conduct is guilty of the offence of mutiny irrespective of whether he personally intended to further the common purpose set out in s.1(2): see the wording of s.1(1). Furthermore, he shall be deemed to have "taken part" in the mutiny unless he establishes a reasonable excuse for failing to submit to lawful authority once such an opportunity is afforded to him: s.1(4). The rationale for this provision seems to rest in the difficulty encountered by investigators distinguishing between culprit and bystander. "It is not unknown for ring-leaders to try and pass themselves off as bystanders" (*per* Earl Ferrers, *Hansard*, H.L. Vol. 536, col. 807). Thirdly, conduct includes

---

* Annotations by Rudi Fletcher Fortson, LL.B.(Lond.) of the Middle Temple, Barrister.

"omissions", *e.g.* a failure to stop the mutiny: s.1(6). Fourthly, the offence of mutiny can be committed even where no violence or threatened violence has taken place: "taking part" in a mutiny will include both active and passive participation (see *Hansard*, H.L. Vol. 536, col. 804; see also *Hansard*, H.L. Vol. 535, col. 966 and *Field* v. *Receiver of Metropolitan Police* [1907] 2 K.B. 859). As originally drafted, the Bill sought to include conduct where two or more prisoners "collectively resist, impede or disobey any exercise of lawful authority in the prison in such circumstances as to make their conduct subversive of order in the prison" (cl. 1(2)(b)). This part of the Bill was dropped after the Committee stage.

As the Act now stands, where a serious disturbance occurs at a prison, it is likely that prosecutors will seek a conviction for an offence of mutiny under s.1 of the 1992 Act and that charges under the Public Order Act 1986 will be drafted in the alternative. Whether the offence be one of mutiny or riot, the maximum is the same—10 years' imprisonment. However, because an offence of violent disorder requires participation by at least three persons, it is conceivable that conduct which would otherwise be charged as affray (maximum three years) might be tried as mutiny and, upon conviction, expose the accused to the peril of the higher *maxima*.

The History of "Mutiny" as a Proposed Offence
See "mutiny" under the Army Act 1955.

In 1985, the *Prior Committee* recommended the creation of an offence of prison mutiny. However, in 1986 the Public Order Act 1986 was enacted which created the four offences of riot (s.1(1)); violent disorder (s.2(1)); affray (s.3(1)) and threatening, abusive or insulting words or behaviour (s.4). Riot was once punishable at common law. The Riot Act 1714 under which rioters could be called to disperse was repealed by the Statute Law Repeals Act 1973. The provisions of the Public Order Act 1986 were followed by the Government's White Paper "*The Prison Disciplinary System of England and Wales*", published in response to the Prior Committee's report. The White Paper stated that "Given the restructuring of public order offences in the Public Order Bill, the Government's view is that there is no need for a further specific offence of prison mutiny".

In April 1990, Lord Justice Woolf published his report "*Prison Disturbances*" in which he made 204 recommendations. However, the creation of an offence of prison mutiny was not one of them (see also *Hansard*, H.C. Vol. 200, col. 174).

On November 11, 1991 the Prison Security Bill was presented before Parliament and it received Royal Assent on March 16, 1992. It will come into force two months after that date: s.3(2).

Offence of prison mutiny

1.—(1) Any prisoner who takes part in a prison mutiny shall be guilty of an offence and liable, on conviction on indictment, to imprisonment for a term not exceeding ten years or to a fine or to both.

(2) For the purposes of this section there is a prison mutiny where two or more prisoners, while on the premises of any prison, engage in conduct which is intended to further a common purpose of overthrowing lawful authority in that prison.

(3) For the purposes of this section the intentions and common purpose of prisoners may be inferred from the form and circumstances of their conduct and it shall be immaterial that conduct falling within subsection (2) above takes a different form in the case of different prisoners.

(4) Where there is a prison mutiny, a prisoner who has or is given a reasonable opportunity of submitting to lawful authority and fails, without reasonable excuse, to do so shall be regarded for the purposes of this section as taking part in the mutiny.

(5) Proceedings for an offence under this section shall not be brought except by or with the consent of the Director of Public Prosecutions.

(6) In this section—
"conduct" includes acts and omissions;
"prison" means any prison, young offender institution or remand centre which is under the general superintendence of, or is provided by, the Secretary of State under the Prison Act 1952, including a contracted out prison within the meaning of Part IV of the Criminal Justice Act 1991;

"prisoner" means any person for the time being in a prison as a result of any requirement imposed by a court or otherwise that he be detained in legal custody.

DEFINITIONS
"conduct": subs. (6).
"mutiny": subs. (2).
"prison": subs. (6).
"prisoner": subs. (6).

GENERAL NOTE

Subss. (1), (2) and (4)
The offence is triable only on indictment. The offending conduct must take place within a prison as defined by s.1(6). Subsection (1) must be read in conjunction with subs. (2), which defines "mutiny". The involvement of two prisoners was the minimum number recommended by the Prior Committee: it also follows the definition of mutiny in the Army Act 1955 which the Prior Committee took as its model (*Hansard*, H.L. Vol. 535, col. 966).

One construction of the combined effect of those two provisions is that once the fact of mutiny is established, the prosecution need do no more than prove that other prisoners were present and "took part" in that mutiny—irrespective of whether or not they themselves intended to further the common purpose. Such prisoners have a defence under s.1(4) but the burden is on them to establish that they had a reasonable excuse not to submit to lawful authority (see the observations of Earl Ferrers, *Hansard*, H.L. Vol. 536, col. 808). If this construction is correct then the result is startling. However, it is submitted that the better view is that each participating prisoner must share the common purpose of overthrowing lawful authority. Such a construction is consistent with the effect of subs. (3) which caters for the situation where the same prisoners do not act in unison but do different things in different parts of a prison with the common purpose of overthrowing lawful authority (see *Hansard*, H.L. Vol. 536, col. 806).

"Taking part" appears to have a non-literal meaning because the section includes both active and "passive" participation in the sense that "conduct" is defined to include acts and omissions. This would seem to include in certain circumstances a failure to stop the offending conduct, or where by their presence prisoners add "fuel to the mutiny" (*per* Earl Ferrers, *Hansard*, H.L. Vol. 536, col. 808). Furthermore, the effect of subs. (4) means that specific acts of violence, or participation, do not have to be proved against individual prisoners. Where a general order has been given for prisoners to submit to authority (which has been disregarded) the burden will be on the prisoner to give account of his conduct in order to found a defence under subs. (4).

Although a "classic" act of prison mutiny would involve violence or the threat of violence, neither subs. (2) nor subs. (6) is phrased in those restricted terms. The lines between "overthrowing", "usurping" and "subverting" lawful authority are not always easy to draw. Would a mass hunger strike amount to the "overthrow" of lawful authority if repeated requests to submit to lawful authority (*i.e.* to obey instructions) were not only ignored but where other prisoners were encouraged to join in the protest?

Subs. (3)
Subsection (3) caters for the situation where the same prisoners do not act in unison but do different things in different parts of a prison with the common purpose of overthrowing lawful authority (see *Hansard*, H.L. Vol. 536, col. 806).

Subs. (4)
Subsection (4) does not reverse the burden of proof as to whether or not a mutiny existed. It merely provides a defence in circumstances where the prosecution have proved the existence of a mutiny. No guidance has been given in the Act as to what may or may not amount to a "reasonable excuse". Presumably, the fact that a prisoner was in fear of other prisoners at the material time is a "reasonable excuse".

Offences relating to escape

2.—(1) In section 39 of the Prison Act 1952 (offence of assisting prisoner to escape)—
   (a) after the word "prisoner", in the third place where it occurs, there shall be inserted the words "sends any thing (by post or otherwise) into a prison or to a prisoner"; and

(b) for the words "five years" there shall be substituted the words "ten years".

(2) In section 22(2)(b) of the Criminal Justice Act 1961 (penalty on indictment for harbouring or assisting a person unlawfully at large), for the words "two years" there shall be substituted the words "ten years".

(3) In that Act of 1961, section 22(1) and the entry in Schedule 4 relating to section 39 of the Prison Act 1952 (which increased from two years to five years the maximum term of imprisonment for an offence under section 39) are hereby repealed.

(4) This section shall not affect the penalty for any offence committed before the commencement of this Act.

GENERAL NOTE

Subs. (1)

Prior to the amendment, s.39 of the Prison Act 1939 made it an offence to ". . . convey any thing into a prison or to a prisoner". Parliament did not think that those words were necessarily sufficiently wide to include articles smuggled into prison by post or by a courier acting on behalf of the accused. The amendment puts the matter beyond doubt.

Subss. (1)(b), (2) and (3)

The penalty for assisting an offender to escape is increased to 10 years' imprisonment.

The penalty under s.22(2)(b) of the Criminal Justice Act 1961 is increased from two years' to 10 years' imprisonment. The reason for the amendment was not only to mark society's disapproval of such conduct but to bring the sentences into line with the related offence of impeding the apprehension of a person believed to be guilty of an arrestable offence under the Criminal Law Act 1967 (*Hansard*, H.L. Vol. 535, col. 966).

Short title, commencement and extent

3.—(1) This Act may be cited as the Prison Security Act 1992.

(2) This Act shall come into force at the end of the period of two months beginning with the day on which it is passed.

(3) This Act extends to England and Wales only.

INDEX

References are to sections

TOURISM (OVERSEAS PROMOTION) (WALES) ACT 1992

(1992 c. 26)

An Act to enable the Wales Tourist Board to carry on abroad activities to promote tourism to and within Wales.   [16th March 1992]

PARLIAMENTARY DEBATES
  Hansard, H.L. Vol. 535, col. 1434; Vol. 536, col. 990.
  The Bill was discussed in Standing Committee C on January 29, 1992.

INTRODUCTION
  This Act provides for the extension of the powers of the Wales Tourist Board under the Development of Tourism Act 1969 in relation to promoting tourism in Wales, to include activities outside the U.K.
  The power may only be extended with the consent of the Secretary of State, who will consult the British Tourist Board before granting such extension. The money available under the 1969 Act will be increased accordingly.

Power of the Wales Tourist Board to engage outside the UK in the promotion of tourism in Wales

1.—(1) Notwithstanding the provisions of subsection (3) of section 2 of the Development of Tourism Act 1969, the powers of the Wales Tourist Board under the other provisions of section 2 of that Act shall include the power to carry on any activities outside the United Kingdom for the purpose of encouraging people to visit Wales.

(2) The Wales Tourist Board shall exercise the power referred to in subsection (1) above to carry on activities outside the United Kingdom only with the consent (which may be given from time to time with or without conditions) of the Secretary of State who shall, before giving or withholding such consent, consult the British Tourist Authority.

(3) Nothing in this section shall—
  (a) affect the power of the British Tourist Authority to carry on any activities outside the United Kingdom for the purpose of encouraging people to visit Wales; or
  (b) prevent the Wales Tourist Board from acting on behalf of the Authority as mentioned in section 2(3) of the Development of Tourism Act 1969.

Finance

2. There shall be paid out of moneys provided by Parliament any increase attributable to this Act in the sums so payable under the provisions of the Development of Tourism Act 1969.

Short title and commencement

3. This Act may be cited as the Tourism (Overseas Promotion) (Wales) Act 1992 and shall come into force at the end of the period of two months beginning with the day on which it is passed.

INDEX

References are to sections

PARLIAMENTARY CORPORATE BODIES ACT 1992

(1992 c. 27)

ARRANGEMENT OF SECTIONS

An Act to establish corporate bodies to hold land and perform other functions for the benefit of the Houses of Parliament; to make provision for and in connection with the transfer of certain property, rights and liabilities to those corporate bodies; and for purposes connected therewith.   [16th March 1992]

PARLIAMENTARY DEBATES
Hansard, H.C. Vol. 204, col. 778; H.L. Vol. 536, cols. 1109, 1224.

INTRODUCTION

This Act establishes corporate bodies for each House of Parliament and provides for the transfer of property to them from the Secretary of State for the Environment. The person who is for the time being the Clerk of the Parliaments and the person who is the Under Clerk of the Parliaments are to become corporations (The Corporate Officer of the House of Lords/House of Commons) and the Corporate Officers' powers are to include the power to acquire property and to enter into contracts (ss.1, 2).

The Secretary of State is empowered to transfer property, rights and liabilities to the new corporations, which are associated or held in connection with the Parliamentary Works Office of the Department of the Environment. Any person employed by the Parliamentary Works Office who is transferred to employment under the new corporations will not be entitled to redundancy compensation on that transfer.

Establishment of a corporation to be known as "the Corporate Officer of the House of Lords"

1.—(1) By virtue of this Act there shall be a corporation sole, by the name of "The Corporate Officer of the House of Lords", having perpetual succession, an official seal and power to sue and be sued under that name like any other corporation sole; and in the following provisions of this Act that corporation is referred to as "the Corporate Officer of the Lords".

(2) The individual who for the time being is by letters patent appointed to the office of the Clerk of the Parliaments shall be the Corporate Officer of the Lords.

(3) The Corporate Officer of the Lords shall have power—

(a) to acquire, hold, manage and dispose of land and other property of any description for any purpose of the House of Lords;

(b) to enter into contracts for any purpose of that House;

(c) to do any other thing which, in relation to the House of Lords, the Clerk of the Parliaments can do by virtue of his office; and

(d) to do anything reasonably necessary or expedient for, or incidental to, any of the matters referred to in paragraphs (a) to (c) above.

(4) During any vacancy in the office of the Clerk of the Parliaments, the functions of the Corporate Officer of the Lords may be exercised by the Clerk Assistant.

(5) As regards the seal of, and any contract entered into by, the Corporate Officer of the Lords,—

(a) the seal may be authenticated by the signature of, and

(b) the contract may be signed on behalf of the Corporate Officer of the Lords by,

the Clerk of the Parliaments, the Clerk Assistant, the Reading Clerk or any other officer of the House of Lords authorised in that behalf by the Clerk of the Parliaments.

(6) Except in so far as Her Majesty may by Order in Council otherwise provide, the Corporate Officer of the Lords shall not be regarded as the servant or agent of the Crown or as enjoying any status, immunity or privilege of the Crown and property vested in the Corporate Officer of the Lords shall not be regarded as property of, or property held on behalf of, the Crown.

(7) A statutory instrument made in the exercise of the power conferred by subsection (6) above shall be subject to annulment in pursuance of a resolution of either House of Parliament.

Establishment of a corporation to be known as "the Corporate Officer of the House of Commons"

2.—(1) By virtue of this Act there shall be a corporation sole, by the name of "The Corporate Officer of the House of Commons", having perpetual succession, an official seal and power to sue and be sued under that name like any other corporation sole; and in the following provisions of this Act that corporation is referred to as "the Corporate Officer of the Commons".

(2) The individual who for the time being is by letters patent appointed to the office of the Under Clerk of the Parliaments (and who is customarily referred to as the Clerk of the House of Commons) shall be the Corporate Officer of the Commons.

(3) The Corporate Officer of the Commons shall have power—

(a) to acquire, hold, manage and dispose of land and other property of any description for any purpose of the House of Commons;

(b) to enter into contracts for any purpose of that House;

(c) to do any other thing which the Under Clerk of the Parliaments can do by virtue of his office; and

(d) to do anything reasonably necessary or expedient for, or incidental to, any of the matters referred to in paragraphs (a) to (c) above.

(4) During any vacancy in the office of the Under Clerk of the Parliaments, the functions of the Corporate Officer of the Commons may be exercised by the Clerk Assistant.

(5) As regards the seal of, and any contract entered into by, the Corporate Officer of the Commons,—

(a) the seal may be authenticated by the signature of, and

(b) the contract may be signed on behalf of the Corporate Officer of the Commons by,

the Under Clerk of the Parliaments, any Clerk Assistant or any other officer of the House of Commons authorised in that behalf by the Under Clerk.

(6) Except in so far as Her Majesty may by Order in Council otherwise provide, the Corporate Officer of the Commons shall not be regarded as the servant or agent of the Crown or as enjoying any status, immunity or privilege of the Crown and property vested in the Corporate Officer of the Commons shall not be regarded as property of, or property held on behalf of, the Crown.

(7) A statutory instrument made in the exercise of the power conferred by subsection (6) above shall be subject to annulment in pursuance of a resolution of either House of Parliament.

Schemes for transfer of property etc. to the corporations

3.—(1) The Secretary of State may make a scheme or schemes for the transfer to either of the corporations constituted under sections 1 and 2 above, or to both of them jointly, of any property, rights and liabilities—
  (a) to which, immediately before the appointed day, the Secretary of State or, in the case of copyright, Her Majesty is entitled or subject;
  (b) which on that day subsist for the purposes of or in connection with or are otherwise attributable to the Crown service known as the Parliamentary Works Office of the Department of the Environment; and
  (c) which are not rights or liabilities relating to a person's employment.
(2) In the following provisions of this Act—
  (a) a scheme made under this section is referred to as a "transfer scheme"; and
  (b) "the transferee corporation" means, in relation to any property, rights or liabilities transferred by a transfer scheme, the corporation or, as the case may be, the corporations to whom a scheme provides for the property, rights or liabilities to be transferred.
(3) A transfer scheme shall come into force on such day as may be specified for the purpose in the scheme; and in this section "the appointed day", in relation to a transfer scheme, means the day so specified.
(4) On the appointed day such of the property, rights and liabilities falling within subsection (1) above as may be specified in or determined in accordance with the transfer scheme shall be transferred and vest in accordance with the scheme.
(5) A certificate issued by the Secretary of State—
  (a) that any property, rights or liabilities specified in the certificate subsist as mentioned in subsection (1)(b) above, or
  (b) that by virtue of a transfer scheme any property, rights or liabilities specified in the certificate have vested in the transferee corporation specified in the certificate,
shall be conclusive evidence for all purposes of that fact.

Transferred staff

4. Where, by reason of the operation of the Transfer of Undertakings (Protection of Employment) Regulations 1981 in relation to the transfer of any property, rights or liabilities by virtue of a transfer scheme, a person ceases to be employed in the civil service of the State and becomes employed by the transferee corporation—
  (a) he shall not, on so ceasing, be treated for the purposes of any scheme under section 1 of the Superannuation Act 1972 as having retired on redundancy; and
  (b) his ceasing to be employed in that service shall not be regarded as an occasion of redundancy for the purpose of the agreed redundancy procedures applicable to persons employed in that service.

Schemes and transfers: supplementary provisions

5.—(1) A transfer scheme may contain such supplementary, incidental, consequential or transitional provisions as appear to the Secretary of State to be necessary or expedient and may revoke or vary any provision of an earlier transfer scheme.
(2) An agreement, transaction or other thing (not contained in an enactment) which has been made, effected or done by, to or in relation to the Secretary of State (or has effect as if so made, effected or done) and which—

(a) immediately before the appointed day is in force or effective, and

(b) relates to any property, right or liability to be transferred from the Secretary of State in accordance with a transfer scheme,

shall on and after that day have effect as if made, effected or done by, to or in relation to the transferee corporation.

(3) Where any agreement, transaction or other thing has effect in accordance with subsection (2) above, any reference to the Secretary of State in any document incorporating or otherwise connected with the agreement, transaction or other thing (and any reference required to be construed as such a reference) shall on and after the appointed day be construed as a reference to the transferee corporation.

(4) Stamp duty shall not be chargeable on any instrument which is certified to the Commissioners of Inland Revenue by the Secretary of State as being a transfer scheme.

(5) Nothing in subsection (4) above affects the provisions of the Stamp Act 1891 so far as they make an instrument which is not duly stamped inadmissible in evidence unless it is stamped with a particular stamp denoting that it is not chargeable to duty.

(6) In this section "the appointed day" has the meaning given by section 3(3) above.

Gifts to either House to take effect as gifts to corporate officers

6.—(1) Where, by will or otherwise, any property is (by whatever words used) expressed to be given to the House of Lords the gift shall take effect as a gift to the Corporate Officer of the Lords.

(2) Where, by will or otherwise, any property is (by whatever words used) expressed to be given to the House of Commons the gift shall take effect as a gift to the Corporate Officer of the Commons.

Transitional and consequential provisions

7.—(1) Any agreement—

(a) which has been entered into for any purpose of the House of Lords by the Clerk of the Parliaments or any other officer of the House of Lords, and

(b) which, immediately before the day on which this section comes into force, is in force or effective,

shall on and after that day have effect as if made by the Corporate Officer of the Lords.

(2) Where an agreement has effect in accordance with subsection (1) above, any reference to the Clerk of the Parliaments or an officer of the House of Lords in any document incorporating or otherwise connected with the agreement shall on and after that day be construed as a reference to the Corporate Officer of the Lords.

(3) Any agreement—

(a) which has been entered into for any purpose of the House of Commons by the Under Clerk of the Parliaments or any other officer of the House of Commons, and

(b) which immediately before the day on which this section comes into force is in force or effective,

shall on and after that day have effect as if made by the Corporate Officer of the Commons.

(4) Where an agreement has effect in accordance with subsection (3) above, any reference to the Under Clerk of the Parliaments or an officer of the House of Commons in any document incorporating or otherwise connected with the agreement shall on and after that day be construed as a reference to the Corporate Officer of the Commons.

(5) With effect from such day as the Secretary of State may by order made by statutory instrument appoint, section 21 of the Crown Lands Act 1851 (by virtue of which the Secretary of State has certain functions once discharged by the Surveyor General of Her Majesty's Works and Public Buildings) shall cease to have effect in relation to the Palace of Westminster.

Short title and extent

8.—(1) This Act may be cited as the Parliamentary Corporate Bodies Act 1992.

(2) This Act extends to Northern Ireland.

INDEX

References are to section number

MEDICINAL PRODUCTS: PRESCRIPTION BY NURSES ETC. ACT 1992*

(1992 c. 28)

An Act to make provision with respect to medicinal products prescribed or otherwise ordered by registered nurses, midwives and health visitors.

[16th March 1992]

PARLIAMENTARY DEBATES
Hansard, H.C. Vol. 202, col. 1196; H.L. Vol. 536, cols. 533.
The Bill was discussed in Standing Committee A on February 12, 1992.

INTRODUCTION AND GENERAL NOTE
This Act provides for regulations to be made permitting specified categories of nurses, midwives and health visitors to prescribe medicinal products and pharmacists to dispense medicines under such prescriptions (s.1). It obliges Family Health Services Authorities (in England and Wales; s.2) and Health Boards (in Scotland; s.3) to arrange for provision of drugs prescribed by nurses, midwives and health visitors for National Health Service use. Section 1 extends to England, Wales, Scotland and Northern Ireland. Provision is made for the creation of obligations equivalent to those in ss.2 and 3 for Northern Ireland (s.4). The Act is to come into force on days to be appointed by the Secretary of State (s.6). The Government hopes to implement the Act by October 1993.

The therapeutic use of medicines involves four stages (United Kingdom Central Council for Nursing, Midwifery and Health Visiting, *Administration of Medicines* 1986): prescription, dispensation, administration and patient acceptance. The last is governed by the laws of consent to treatment. Administration is regulated through malpractice law, especially the tort of negligence. This Act alters the legal framework dealing with the first two stages. Some medicines, listed in the Medicines (Products Other than Veterinary Drugs) (Prescription Only) Order 1983 (S.I. 1983 No. 1212) are available only on prescription. Under s.58 of the Medicines Act 1968 these may only be administered under the direction of a doctor or dentist. Regulations to be made under this Act will permit nurses to authorise the administration of some of these drugs in specified circumstances. In practice, however, the effect of these reforms on the dispensing of drugs may be the most significant. The nursing formulary is not expected to include many prescription-only medicines (the legislative advisory group's illustrative list included only four such drugs; *Hansard*, H.L. Vol. 536, col. 543). Most of its contents would be available over the counter on payment by the patient. However, these same items would be provided free under NHS prescriptions, subject to the payment of standard prescription charges. This Act will enable nurses to make out those prescriptions. At present, doctors have to sign them, even when the medicines are not particularly dangerous and when nurses assess the need for them. Allowing nurses to prescribe will remove an unnecessary administrative process and is expected to save a considerable amount of professional time.

The principle of nurse prescribing has been accepted for some time. Limited provisions already exist in relation to midwives and occupational health nurses (Medicines Act 1968, s.58(4); Misuse of Drugs Regulations 1985 (S.I. 1985 No. 2066), r. 11; Medicines (Products Other than Veterinary Drugs) (Prescription Only) Order 1983 (S.I. 1983 No. 1212), art. 9 and Sched. 3). These are less significant than the wider powers envisaged by this Act. Midwives are permitted to possess and use prescription-only drugs under a "midwives' supply order" signed either by a doctor or a supervisor of midwives, but they are not permitted to prescribe them for others to use. Occupational health nurses are allowed to use prescription-only drugs without immediate direction, but only in circumstances specified in writing by a medical practitioner. Again, this power does not extend to prescription itself.

The extension of independent powers of prescription to nurses, midwives and health visitors had been proposed by a number of reports and accepted in principle by the Government. The most important of these were the *Report of the Review of Community Nursing* (1986) (the Cumberlege Report) and the *Report of the Advisory Group on Nurse Prescribing* (1990). Following the recommendations of the latter document, it is intended that the Act will initially be extended only to nurses with district nurse or health visitor qualifications who are working in the community. A list of items that they will be able to prescribe is being drawn up by a sub-committee of the Joint Formulary Committee. It is expected to be completed in the summer of 1992 (*Hansard*, H.C. Vol. 202, col. 1229).

* Annotations by Jonathan Montgomery, B.A., LL.M., Lecturer in Law, University of Southampton.

The main benefit that the Act is expected to produce is the saving of time such that health professionals will be released for other tasks and patients will receive the medicines they need more quickly. The Act should also increase the job satisfaction of the nurses who are permitted to prescribe, by enabling them to use their skills more fully.

Prescription only drugs etc.: authorisation of registered nurses, midwives and health visitors

1.—(1) In section 58 of the Medicines Act 1968 (medicinal products on prescription only) in subsection (1) (which specifies who are to be appropriate practitioners in relation to specified descriptions or classes of medicinal products) at the end of paragraph (c) there shall be inserted "and

    (d) registered nurses, midwives and health visitors who are of such a description and comply with such conditions as may be specified in the order".

(2) In subsection (4) of that section (orders providing for exemptions etc.) at the end of paragraph (a) there shall be inserted the words "or, where the appropriate practitioner is a registered nurse, midwife or health visitor, such modifications as may be so specified".

(3) In subsection (5) of that section (exemptions may be subject to conditions or limitations)—

    (a) after the words "exemption conferred" there shall be inserted the words "or modification made", and

    (b) after the word "conferred", in the second place where it occurs, there shall be inserted the words "or made".

DEFINITIONS

"medicinal products": Medicines Act 1968, s.130.

"registered nurses, midwives and health visitors": Nurses, Midwives and Health Visitors Act 1979, s.10.

GENERAL NOTE

This provision does not give a general power of prescription to nurses, midwives and health visitors by reason of their professional status. No nurses will be permitted to prescribe until regulations are made under this section. The regulations will define the category of nurses to which they apply (subs. (1)) and the powers to prescribe may be subject to conditions or modifications (subss. (2), (3)).

Extension of pharmaceutical services in England and Wales

2. In section 41 of the National Health Service Act 1977 (which imposes a duty on Family Health Services Authorities to arrange for the provision of drugs and medicines etc. ordered by medical practitioners and dental practitioners) the word "and" at the end of paragraph (c) shall be omitted and after that paragraph there shall be inserted the following paragraph—

    "(cc) listed drugs and medicines and listed appliances which are ordered for those persons by a prescribed description of registered nurse, midwife or health visitor in pursuance of functions in the health service, the Scottish health service or the Northern Ireland health service or the armed forces of the Crown (excluding forces of a Commonwealth country and forces raised in a colony); and".

DEFINITIONS

"listed": National Health Service Act 1977, s.41.

"registered nurses, midwives and health visitors": Nurses, Midwives and Health Visitors Act 1979, s.10.

GENERAL NOTE

These amendments will oblige Family Health Services Authorities to ensure that medicines prescribed by nurses will be supplied to the patients under the National Health Service.

Extension of pharmaceutical services in Scotland

3. In section 27 of the National Health Service (Scotland) Act 1978 (which imposes a duty on Health Boards to arrange for the provision of drugs and medicines etc. ordered by medical practitioners and dental practitioners) the word "and" at the end of paragraph (c) shall be omitted and after that paragraph there shall be inserted the following paragraph—

"(cc) listed drugs and medicines and listed appliances which are ordered for those persons by a prescribed description of registered nurse, midwife or health visitor in pursuance of functions in the health service, the health service for England and Wales, the Northern Ireland health service or the armed forces of the Crown (excluding forces of a Commonwealth country and forces raised in a colony); and".

DEFINITIONS

"listed": National Health Service (Scotland) Act 1978, s.27.
"registered nurses, midwives and health visitors": Nurses, Midwives and Health Visitors Act 1979, s.10.

GENERAL NOTE

These amendments will oblige Health Boards to ensure that medicines prescribed by nurses will be supplied to the patients under the National Health Service.

Provision as to Northern Ireland

4. An Order in Council under paragraph 1(1)(b) of Schedule 1 to the Northern Ireland Act 1974 (legislation for Northern Ireland in the interim period) which contains a statement that it is made only for purposes corresponding to those of section 2 above—

(a) shall not be subject to sub-paragraphs (4) and (5) of paragraph 1 of that Schedule (affirmative resolution of both Houses of Parliament); but

(b) shall be subject to annulment in pursuance of a resolution of either House of Parliament.

GENERAL NOTE

This section provides for the extension of the duties on health authorities to arrange for the supply of medicines prescribed by nurses, midwives and health visitors (ss.2, 3) to Northern Ireland by Order in Council. Such an order is to be subject to the negative resolution procedure rather than requiring affirmative resolution as is envisaged by the Northern Ireland Act 1974.

Financial provision

5. There shall be paid out of money provided by Parliament any increase attributable to this Act in the sums so payable under any other enactment.

GENERAL NOTE

The report commissioned by the Government from Touche Ross estimated that the provisions of the Act would result in an increase of expenditure of £15 million in England. This was based on the expectation that there would be a significant increase in the number of prescriptions. This figure was based on a survey of 18 district health authorities, with an overall response rate of only 15 per cent. of district nurses and 23 per cent. of health visitors (*Hansard*, H.C. Vol. 202, col. 1203). It may, therefore, not be wholly reliable. It is expected that the considerable savings in time which will result from the implementation of the Act will lead to more work being carried out rather than to cost savings.

Short title, commencement and extent

6.—(1) This Act may be cited as the Medicinal Products: Prescription by Nurses etc. Act 1992.

(2) Sections 1 to 3 above shall come into force on such day as the Secretary of State may by order made by statutory instrument appoint, and different days may be so appointed for different provisions or for different purposes.

(3) Section 2 above extends to England and Wales only and section 3 above extends to Scotland only.

(4) This Act (except sections 2 and 3) extends to Northern Ireland.

GENERAL NOTE

The Government hopes to bring the Act fully into force in October 1993 (*Hansard*, H.C. Vol. 202, col. 1228; H.L. Vol. 536, col. 545).

INDEX

References are to sections

STILL-BIRTH (DEFINITION) ACT 1992*

(1992 c. 29)

An Act to amend the law in respect of the definition of still-birth; to make certain consequential amendments of the law; and for connected purposes.   [16th March 1992]

PARLIAMENTARY DEBATES
Hansard, H.L. Vol. 536, cols. 546.

INTRODUCTION AND GENERAL NOTE

This Act reduces the age at which the loss of a baby during pregnancy is defined by law as a stillbirth rather than a miscarriage from 28 weeks' gestation to 24 weeks (s.1). This reduces the impact of the anomaly whereby a child born breathing at less than 28 weeks, even if it dies immediately afterwards, is classified as a person who has died, but a foetus of the same age that is dead at delivery is not recognised as ever having existed as a legal person. The consequences of this distinction is that in the latter situation the parents are denied the rights to register the child's birth, give it a name, receive a stillbirth certificate and arrange for a formal burial or cremation. These formalities are often greatly valued by the parents and help them come to terms with their loss. In some areas voluntary arrangements had been made for burials and cremations, but generally the remains of miscarriages have merely been incinerated (*Hansard*, H.L. Vol. 536, col. 546). This Act ensures that all parents suffering the tragedy of the stillbirth of a viable child will be able to avail themselves of such procedures.

The Act also extends statutory maternity pay and maternity allowance to those suffering a stillbirth at 24 weeks' gestation or later (s.2). The Act applies to England, Wales and Scotland and will come into force on October 1, 1992. Provision is made for it to be extended to Northern Ireland by Order in Council (s.3).

The original definition of stillbirths in the Births and Deaths Registration Acts 1926 and 1953, covering babies born after 28 weeks' gestation, was fixed in order to be consistent with the presumption that a foetus was "capable of being born alive" at that age, enshrined in the Infant Life (Preservation) Act 1929. The White Paper *Registration: proposals for change* (Cm. 939, 1990, paras. 4.22–4.25) rejected earlier calls for reform, arguing that there should be consistency between the Acts. Although the presumption in the Infant Life (Preservation) Act 1929 remains fixed at 28 weeks, the argument for linking the definition of stillbirth to it has become increasingly problematic. First, the 1929 Act created a presumption which could be rebutted on the facts. Recent cases have indicated that foetuses would now normally be capable of being born alive earlier than 28 weeks (*C.* v. *S.* [1988] Q.B. 135, *Rance* v. *Mid-Downs H.A.* [1991] 1 All E.R. 801). Most commentators now believe that 24 weeks is the stage at which it can be expected that a foetus is capable of sustaining life (*Hansard*, H.L. Vol. 536, col. 546). The new definition of stillbirth is therefore in line with the practical effects of the 1929 Act. Second, the amendments made to the Abortion Act 1967 by the Human Fertilisation and Embryology Act 1990 introduced a 24-week limit to terminations of pregnancy on the so-called "social grounds". In practice, the main function of the presumption of viability before this reform of the ground for abortion was to limit the availability of that justification. The logic of linking the definition of stillbirth with the presumption in the 1929 Act therefore became less compelling, and it is more appropriate to harmonise it with the 24-week limit in the Abortion Act 1967.

The reforms implemented by this Act will not remove all the anomalies in this area. The parents of babies stillborn at 23 weeks will continue to face the problems that those suffering stillbirths at 27 weeks met under the old law. As long as a fixed date is used, advances in medical technology that enable babies to survive at a younger age will lead to pressure to lower the age once again. It has been suggested that future legislation will therefore be needed (*Hansard*, H.L. Vol. 536, col. 546). The use of alternative viability tests based on the weight of the foetus rather than age limits has not received general support (*Registration: proposals for change*, Cm. 939, 1990, para. 4.22) and would not avoid this problem.

Meaning of "still-born child", etc.

1.—(1) In section 12 of the Births and Deaths Registration Act 1926 (definitions) and section 41 of the Births and Deaths Registration Act 1953 (interpretation), in the provisions which relate to the meaning of "still-born

---

* Annotations by Jonathan Montgomery, B.A., LL.M., Lecturer in Law, University of Southampton.

child" for the words "twenty-eighth week", in both places where they occur, there shall be substituted "twenty-fourth week".

(2) In section 56(1) of the Registration of Births, Deaths and Marriages (Scotland) Act 1965 (interpretation) in the definition of "still-born child" for the words "twenty-eighth week" there shall be substituted "twenty-fourth week".

GENERAL NOTE

These amendments ensure that the definitions of stillbirth in the registration statutes are amended so that a stillborn child of 24 or more weeks' gestation is included.

Twenty-fourth week. The statute does not make clear the point from which a pregnancy should be dated. The usual medical practice is to date pregnancies from the first day of the woman's last menstrual period. As this is the normal meaning of the term, it is probably that method of dating that should be used. However, embryologists use the date of conception, usually some 14 days later, as the beginning of a foetus's life and it is possible that this date would be adopted. The same difficulty arises in interpreting the 24-week limit under the Abortion Act 1967 (s.1(1)(a)). Commentators on this provision have argued that the date of conception is the significant point (A. Grubb, *"The new law of abortion: clarification or ambiguity?"* [1991] Crim.L.R. 659, 665–666; J. Murphy, *"Cosmetics, eugenics and ambivalence: the revision of the Abortion Act* 1967" (1991) J. Social Welfare and Family Law 375, 386–391). However, the Abortion Regulations 1991 (S.I. 1991 No. 499) assume that the date of the last menstrual period is the relevant time for dating purposes, adjusted if necessary after ultrasonic scan. This is in accordance with the principle that words which are terms of art should be given their usual technical meanings. Consistency between the two statutes would be in accordance with the policy of linking the dates together.

Meaning of "confinement" for certain social security purposes

2.—(1) In the Social Security Contributions and Benefits Act 1992 (in this section referred to as "the 1992 Act")—
  (a) in subsection (6) of section 35 (definition of "confinement" for the purpose of maternity allowance), and
  (b) in section 171(1) (interpretation of Part XII—statutory maternity pay), in the definition of "confinement",
for the words "28 weeks" there shall be substituted "24 weeks".

(2) If the 1992 Act is not in force at the commencement of this section, then, in relation to any time before the commencement of the 1992 Act—
  (a) subsection (1) above shall not have effect; and
  (b) in section 50(1) of the Social Security Act 1986 (which, until the provisions referred to in paragraphs (a) and (b) of subsection (1) above come into force, has effect corresponding to those provisions), for the words "28 weeks" there shall be substituted "24 weeks".

GENERAL NOTE

This section makes amendments, corresponding to those effected by s.1, to the qualifications for maternity allowance and statutory maternity pay. These ensure that all mothers suffering stillbirths within the new definition are entitled to receive these benefits. The alternative provisions of the two subsections are necessary because the existing provisions of the Social Security Act 1986 are due to be replaced by those in the Social Security Contributions and Benefits Act 1992, but that Act may not have been brought into force by October 1, 1992, when the Still-Birth (Definition) Act 1992 takes effect.

24 weeks. The same problem of dating arises as in relation to s.1: see the note to that section above.

Provision for Northern Ireland

3. An Order in Council under paragraph 1(1)(b) of Schedule 1 to the Northern Ireland Act 1974 (legislation for Northern Ireland in the interim period) which contains a statement that it is made only for purposes corresponding to those of sections 1 and 2 above—
  (a) shall not be subject to paragraph 1(4) and (5) of that Schedule (affirmative resolution of both Houses of Parliament); but

(b) shall be subject to annulment in pursuance of a resolution of either House of Parliament.

GENERAL NOTE
   This section provides for the extension of the provisions of the Act to Northern Ireland by Order in Council. Such an order is to be subject to the negative resolution procedure rather than needing affirmative resolutions as is envisaged by the Northern Ireland Act 1974.

Short title, commencement and extent

4.—(1) This Act may be cited as the Still-Birth (Definition) Act 1992.

(2) This Act (except section 3 above) shall come into force on 1st October 1992.

(3) Subsection (1) of section 1 above extends to England and Wales only and subsection (2) of that section extends to Scotland only.

(4) This Act, other than section 3 and this section, does not extend to Northern Ireland.

INDEX

References are to sections

TRAFFIC CALMING ACT 1992

(1992 c. 30)

An Act to make provision about the carrying out on highways of works affecting the movement of vehicular and other traffic for the purposes of promoting safety and of preserving or improving the environment; and for connected purposes.   [16th March 1992]

PARLIAMENTARY DEBATES
  Hansard, H.C. Vol. 202, col. 610; H.L. Vol. 536, cols. 533, 1172.
  The Bill was discussed in Standing Committee C on February 11, 1992.

INTRODUCTION
  This Act amends the Highways Act 1980, ss.62, 90F and 329 to facilitate the construction and removal of traffic calming works. The Roads (Scotland) Act 1984 is also amended to include further powers to carry out such traffic calming works. The Secretary of State is empowered in both jurisdictions to make regulations prescribing the works to be undertaken.

Amendment of Highways Act 1980

1.—(1) In section 62 of the Highways Act 1980 (general power of improvement) in subsection (3) (description of works for which specific powers are given and to which the general power does not apply) after paragraph (ff) there shall be inserted—
  "(fg) the construction and removal of such traffic calming works as may be specially authorised by the Secretary of State under section 90G below or prescribed by regulations made by him under section 90H below;".
  (2) After section 90F of that Act there shall be inserted the provisions set out in Schedule 1 to this Act.
  (3) In section 329 of that Act (interpretation) after the definition of "traffic" there shall be inserted—
  "traffic calming works", in relation to a highway, means works affecting the movement of vehicular and other traffic for the purpose of promoting safety or preserving or improving the environment through which the highway runs".

Amendment of Roads (Scotland) Act 1984

2.—(1) After section 39 of the Roads (Scotland) Act 1984 (status of road humps) there shall be inserted the provisions set out in Schedule 2 to this Act.
  (2) In section 40 of that Act (interpretation)—
  (a) for the words "39" there shall be inserted the words "39C";
  (b) the word "and", where it occurs immediately after the definition of "road hump", shall cease to have effect; and
  (c) at the end there shall be added the words—
    "; and
  "traffic calming works", in relation to a road, means works affecting the movement of vehicular and other traffic for the purpose of promoting safety or preserving or improving the environment through which the road runs."

Commencement

3. This Act shall come into force at the end of the period of two months beginning with the day on which it is passed.

Extent

4. This Act does not extend to Northern Ireland.

Short title

5. This Act may be cited as the Traffic Calming Act 1992.

SCHEDULES

Section 1   SCHEDULE 1

PROVISIONS TO BE INSERTED IN HIGHWAYS ACT 1980

"Other traffic calming works

Powers to carry out traffic calming works
90G.—(1) A highway authority may, in a highway maintainable at the public expense for which they are the highway authority, construct traffic calming works which—
(a) are of a description prescribed by regulations under section 90H below, or
(b) are specially authorised by the Secretary of State,
and may remove such works (whenever constructed).

(2) A highway authority shall not exercise the powers conferred by subsection (1) above except in accordance with any requirements imposed by the regulations or authorisation concerned.

(3) Requirements imposed by a special authorisation given by the Secretary of State under this section may relate to any matter with respect to which regulations may be made under section 90H below.

(4) Nothing in this section shall prejudice any power of a highway authority to construct or remove traffic calming works which are neither of a description prescribed by regulations under section 90H below nor specially authorised by the Secretary of State.

Prescribing of works
90H.—(1) The Secretary of State may make regulations—
(a) prescribing any description of traffic calming works for the purposes of section 90G above, and
(b) making such provision (if any) as appears to him necessary or expedient in relation to the construction, maintenance and removal of works of a prescribed description.
(2) Regulations under this section may in particular—
(a) provide that works of a prescribed description shall be constructed only in highways of such descriptions and in such circumstances as may be prescribed by the regulations;
(b) impose requirements as to—
(i) the dimensions and location of works;
(ii) the placing of signs;
(iii) the carrying out and maintenance of ancillary or consequential works;
(c) impose requirements as to consultation and publicity in respect of proposed works.
(3) Regulations under this section may make different provision for different cases.

Status of works authorised by section 90G
90I. Works (whenever constructed) of a description prescribed by regulations under section 90H above or specially authorised under section 90G above which conform to any requirements imposed by the regulations or authorisation shall not be treated as constituting an obstruction to the highway but as part of the highway, so that in particular—
(a) the obligation of any person to maintain the highway, and
(b) the obligation of any person having power to break open the highway to make good any damage or otherwise reinstate the highway,
extend to maintaining or, as the case may be, making good any damage to or otherwise reinstating the works."

SCHEDULE 2

PROVISIONS TO BE INSERTED IN ROADS (SCOTLAND) ACT 1984

"Other traffic calming works

Powers to carry out traffic calming works

39A.—(1) A roads authority may, in a road maintainable by them, construct traffic calming works which—

(a) are of a description prescribed by regulations under section 39B of this Act, or

(b) are authorised,

and may remove such works (whenever constructed).

(2) A roads authority shall not exercise the powers conferred by subsection (1) above except in accordance with any requirements imposed by the regulations or authorisation concerned.

(3) Requirements imposed by an authorisation given under this section may relate to any matter with respect to which regulations may be made under section 39B of this Act.

(4) Nothing in this section shall prejudice any power of a roads authority to construct or remove traffic calming works which are neither of a description prescribed by regulations under section 39B of this Act nor authorised.

Prescribing of works

39B.—(1) The Secretary of State may make regulations—

(a) prescribing any description of traffic calming works for the purposes of section 39A of this Act, and

(b) making such provision (if any) as appears to him necessary or expedient in relation to the construction, maintenance and removal of works of a prescribed description.

(2) Regulations under this section may in particular—

(a) provide that works of a prescribed description shall be constructed only in roads of such descriptions and in such circumstances as may be prescribed by the regulations;

(b) impose requirements as to—

(i) the dimensions and location of works;

(ii) the placing of signs;

(iii) the carrying out and maintenance of ancillary or consequential works;

(c) impose requirements as to consultation and publicity in respect of proposed works.

Status of works authorised by section 39A

39C. Works (whenever constructed) of a description prescribed by regulations under section 39B, or authorised under section 39A, of this Act, which conform to any requirements imposed by the regulations or authorisation shall not be treated as constituting an obstruction to the road but as part of the road, so that in particular—

(a) the obligation of any person to maintain the road, and

(b) the obligation of any person having power to break open the road to make good any damage or otherwise reinstate the road,

extend to maintaining or, as the case may be, making good any damage to or otherwise reinstating the works.

Interpretation: Road humps and other traffic calming works."

INDEX

References are to sections

FIREARMS (AMENDMENT) ACT 1992

(1992 c. 31)

An Act to empower the Secretary of State to extend the period for which firearm and shot gun certificates are granted or renewed.

[16th March 1992]

PARLIAMENTARY DEBATES
Hansard, H.L. Vol. 536, cols. 562, 1172.
The Bill was discussed in Standing Committee B on February 13, 1992.

INTRODUCTION

This Act inserts subss. (3A), (3B) and (3C) into s.26 of the Firearms Act 1968, extending the period for which firearm and shotgun certificates can be granted or renewed. The extension of the period will be effected by Order by the Secretary of State and these new provision will only apply to certificates granted or renewed after the date of such Order. The Firearms (Amendment) Act 1988 is also amended to take into account these new provisions.

Duration of firearm and shot gun certificates

1.—(1) In section 26 of the Firearms Act 1968—

(a) in subsection (3) the words ", or such shorter period as may be prescribed," and the words ", or a further prescribed period," shall be omitted; and

(b) after the subsection there shall be inserted—

"(3A) The Secretary of State may by order provide that subsection (3) above shall have effect as if the references to three years were references to such other period as is specified by the order.

(3B) An order made under subsection (3A) above shall apply only to certificates granted or renewed after the date on which the order comes into force.

(3C) The power to make orders under subsection (3A) above shall be exercisable by statutory instrument and any statutory instrument containing such an order shall be subject to annulment in pursuance of a resolution of either House of Parliament."

(2) In section 11(1) of the Firearms (Amendment) Act 1988 for the words "or prescribed under section 26(3)" there shall be substituted the words "subsection (3), or in an order made under subsection (3A), of section 26".

Northern Ireland

2.—(1) Section 1 above does not extend to Northern Ireland.

(2) An Order in Council under paragraph 1(1)(b) of Schedule 1 to the Northern Ireland Act 1974 (legislation for Northern Ireland in the interim period) which states that it is made only for purposes corresponding to those of section 1 above—

(a) shall not be subject to paragraph 1(4) and (5) of that Schedule (affirmative resolution of both Houses of Parliament); but

(b) shall be subject to annulment in pursuance of a resolution of either House.

Citation

3.—(1) This Act may be cited as the Firearms (Amendment) Act 1992.

(2) This Act and the Firearms Acts 1968 to 1988 may be cited together as the Firearms Acts 1968 to 1992.

INDEX

References are to section numbers

CHEQUES ACT 1992

(1992 c. 32)

An Act to amend the law relating to cheques.   [16th March 1992]

PARLIAMENTARY DEBATES
Hansard, H.L. Vol. 536, cols. 344, 1223.
The Bill was discussed in Standing Committee C on February 4, 1992.

INTRODUCTION

This Act amends s.80 and 81 of the Bills of Exchange Act 1882 in relation to non-transferable cheques. Where a cheque is crossed and bears the words "account payee only" or "a/c payee", either with or without the word "only", the cheque will not be transferable. Section 80 of the 1882 Act is amended to take account of the amendment to s.81 in relation to the protection to a banker and drawee where a cheque is crossed.

Amendment of Bills of Exchange Act 1882: non-transferable cheques

1. After section 81 of the Bills of Exchange Act 1882 there shall be inserted the following section—

> **"Non-transferable cheques**
>
> 81A.—(1) Where a cheque is crossed and bears across its face the words "account payee" or "a/c payee", either with or without the word "only", the cheque shall not be transferable, but shall only be valid as between the parties thereto.
>
> (2) A banker is not to be treated for the purposes of section 80 above as having been negligent by reason only of his failure to concern himself with any purported indorsement of a cheque which under subsection (1) above or otherwise is not transferable.".

Amendment of Bills of Exchange Act 1882: protection to banker and drawer where cheque is crossed

2. In section 80 of the Bills of Exchange Act 1882 (protection to banker and drawer where cheque is crossed) after "crossed cheque" there shall be inserted "(including a cheque which under section 81A below or otherwise is not transferable)".

Amendment of Cheques Act 1957

3. In section 4(2)(a) of the Cheques Act 1957 (protection of bankers collecting payment of cheques, etc.) there shall be inserted after the word "cheques" the words "(including cheques which under section 81A(1) of the Bills of Exchange Act 1882 or otherwise are not transferable)".

Citation and commencement

4.—(1) This Act may be cited as the Cheques Act 1992.

(2) This Act shall come into force at the end of the period of three months beginning on the day on which this Act is passed.

INDEX

References are to sections

SOCIAL SECURITY (MORTGAGE INTEREST PAYMENTS) ACT 1992

(1992 c. 33)

An Act to make provision for requiring, in certain cases where interest on a loan secured on land is payable by a person who is entitled, or whose partner, former partner or qualifying associate is entitled, to income support, the applicable amount in respect of which includes a sum in respect of that interest, that a part of the benefits to which any of those persons is entitled under the enactments relating to social security shall be paid directly to the lender and applied towards the discharge of the liability in respect of the interest; and for purposes connected therewith.

[16th March 1992]

PARLIAMENTARY DEBATES
  Hansard, H.C. Vol. 203, col. 423; H.L. Vol. 536, cols. 78, 1042, 1479.

INTRODUCTION
  This Act amends the Social Security Act 1986 to enable regulations to be made providing for sums allowed for mortgage interest relief to be paid directly to the lender by the Secretary of State where a person is entitled to income support. The Social Security Administration Act 1992 is amended accordingly. These arrangements may relate to entitlements of the borrower, his partner, former partner or qualifying associate.

Payment out of benefit of sums in respect of mortgage interest etc.

1.—(1) After section 51B of the Social Security Act 1986 (general provisions about administration of benefits) there shall be inserted—

"Payment out of benefit of sums in respect of mortgage interest etc.
   51C.—(1) This section applies in relation to cases where—
   (a) mortgage interest is payable to a qualifying lender by a person ("the borrower") who is entitled, or whose partner, former partner or qualifying associate is entitled, to income support; and
   (b) a sum in respect of that mortgage interest is or was brought into account in determining the applicable amount for the purposes of income support in the case of the borrower or the partner, former partner or qualifying associate;
   and any reference in this section to "the relevant beneficiary" is a reference to the person whose applicable amount for the purposes of income support is or was determined as mentioned in paragraph (b) above.
   (2) Without prejudice to paragraphs (k) and (r) of section 51(1) above, regulations may, in relation to cases where this section applies, make provision—
   (a) requiring that, in prescribed circumstances, a prescribed part of any relevant benefits to which the relevant beneficiary is entitled shall be paid by the Secretary of State directly to the qualifying lender and applied by that lender towards the discharge of the liability in respect of the mortgage interest;
   (b) for the expenses of the Secretary of State in administering the making of payments under the regulations to be defrayed, in whole or in part, at the expense of qualifying lenders, whether by requiring them to pay prescribed fees or by deducting and retaining a prescribed part of the payments that would otherwise be made to them under the regulations or by such other method as may be prescribed;
   (c) for requiring a qualifying lender, in a case where by virtue of

paragraph (b) above the amount of the payment made to him under the regulations is less than it would otherwise have been, to credit against the liability in respect of the mortgage interest (in addition to the payment actually made) an amount equal to the difference between—

(i) the payment that would have been so made, apart from paragraph (b) above; and

(ii) the payment actually made;

and, in any such case, for treating the amount so credited as properly paid on account of benefit due to the relevant beneficiary;

(d) for enabling a body which, or person who, would otherwise be a qualifying lender to elect not to be regarded as such for the purposes of this section, other than this paragraph;

(e) for the recovery from any body or person—

(i) of any sums paid to that body or person by way of payment under the regulations that ought not to have been so paid; or

(ii) of any fees or other sums due from that body or person by virtue of paragraph (b) above;

(f) for cases where the same person is the borrower in relation to mortgage interest payable in respect of two or more different loans; and

(g) for any person of a prescribed class or description who would otherwise be regarded for the purposes of this section as the borrower in relation to any mortgage interest not to be so regarded, except for the purposes of this paragraph;

but the Secretary of State shall not make any regulations under paragraph (b) above unless he has consulted with such organisations representing qualifying lenders likely to be affected by the regulations as he considers appropriate.

(3) The bodies and persons who are "qualifying lenders" for the purposes of this section are—

(a) any authorised institution, within the meaning of the Banking Act 1987, to which section 67 of that Act applies (companies and partnerships which may describe themselves as banks etc.),

(b) any building society incorporated under the Building Societies Act 1986,

(c) any body or person carrying on insurance business, within the meaning of the Insurance Companies Act 1982,

(d) any county council, district council, islands council or London Borough Council,

(e) the Common Council of the City of London,

(f) the Council of the Isles of Scilly,

(g) any new town corporation,

and such bodies or persons not falling within the above paragraphs as may be prescribed.

(4) In this section—

"mortgage interest" means interest on a loan which is secured by a mortgage of or charge over land, or (in Scotland) by a heritable security, and which has been taken out to defray money applied for any of the following purposes, that is to say—

(a) acquiring any residential land which was intended, at the time of the acquisition, for occupation by the borrower as his home;

(b) carrying out repairs or improvements to any residential land which was intended, at the time of taking out the loan, for occupation by the borrower as his home;

(c) paying off another loan; or

(d) any prescribed purpose not falling within paragraphs (a) to (c) above;

but interest shall be regarded as mortgage interest by virtue of paragraph (c) above only to the extent that interest on that other loan would have been regarded as mortgage interest for the purposes of this section had the loan not been paid off;

"partner" means—

(a) any person to whom the borrower is married and who is a member of the same household as the borrower; or

(b) any person to whom the borrower is not married but who lives together with the borrower as husband and wife, otherwise than in prescribed circumstances;

and "former partner" means a person who has at some time been, but no longer is, the borrower's partner;

"qualifying associate", in relation to the borrower, means a person who, for the purposes of income support, falls to be treated by regulations under Part II above as responsible for so much of the expenditure which relates to housing costs (within the meaning of those regulations) as consists of any of the mortgage interest payable by the borrower, and who falls to be so treated because—

(a) the borrower is not meeting those costs, so that the person has to meet them if he is to continue to live in the dwelling occupied as his home; and

(b) the person is one whom it is reasonable, in the circumstances, to treat as liable to meet those costs;

"relevant benefits" means such of the following benefits as may be prescribed, namely—

(a) benefits under the Social Security Act 1975;

(b) income support;

"residential land" means any land which consists of or includes a dwelling.

(5) For the purposes of this section, regulations may make provision—

(a) as to circumstances in which residential land is or is not to be treated as intended for occupation by the borrower as his home; or

(b) as to circumstances in which persons are to be treated as being or not being members of the same household."

(2) For the purpose of incorporating provisions of this Act into the Social Security Administration Act 1992 (which consolidates certain enactments relating to the administration of social security and which comes into force on 1st July 1992) that Act shall have effect, and be taken always to have had effect, as if it had originally been enacted with the amendments specified in the Schedule to this Act; and subsection (1) above shall accordingly cease to have effect on the coming into force of that Act.

Short title, supplementary provisions and extent

2.—(1) This Act may be cited as the Social Security (Mortgage Interest Payments) Act 1992.

(2) Any administrative expenses incurred by a Minister of the Crown in consequence of this Act shall be defrayed out of money provided by Parliament.

(3) Any sums recovered by a Minister of the Crown by virtue of this Act shall be paid—

(a) into the Consolidated Fund, to the extent that the Secretary of State estimates that those sums relate to payments out of money provided by Parliament; and

(b) into the National Insurance Fund, to the extent that he estimates that they relate to payments out of that Fund;

and any other sums received by a Minister of the Crown by virtue of this Act shall be paid into the Consolidated Fund.

(4) The Secretary of State may by regulations make such transitional or consequential provision, and such savings, as he considers necessary or expedient for, or in connection with, the coming into force of any provision of this Act.

(5) Subsections (1) to (3A) of section 166 of the Social Security Act 1975 (general provisions about regulations and orders) shall apply in relation to the powers to make regulations conferred by subsection (4) above as they apply in relation to any power conferred by that Act to make regulations, but as if for references to that Act there were substituted references to that subsection.

(6) A statutory instrument—

(a) which contains (whether alone or with other provisions) any regulations made under subsection (4) above, and

(b) which is not subject to any requirement that a draft of the instrument be laid before and approved by a resolution of each House of Parliament,

shall be subject to annulment in pursuance of a resolution of either House of Parliament.

(7) An Order in Council under paragraph 1(1)(b) of Schedule 1 to the Northern Ireland Act 1974 (legislation for Northern Ireland in the interim period) which states that it is made only for purposes corresponding to those of this Act—

(a) shall not be subject to paragraph 1(4) and (5) of that Schedule (affirmative resolution of both Houses of Parliament); but

(b) shall be subject to annulment in pursuance of a resolution of either House of Parliament.

(8) Subsections (1) and (7) above and this subsection extend to Northern Ireland; but, except as provided by this subsection, this Act does not extend to Northern Ireland.

Section 1(2)   SCHEDULE

CORRESPONDING AMENDMENT OF THE SOCIAL SECURITY ADMINISTRATION ACT 1992

1. After section 15 of the Social Security Administration Act 1992 there shall be inserted—

"Payments in respect of mortgage interest etc.

Payment out of benefit of sums in respect of mortgage interest etc.
15A.—(1) This section applies in relation to cases where—

(a) mortgage interest is payable to a qualifying lender by a person ("the borrower") who is entitled, or whose partner, former partner or qualifying associate is entitled, to income support; and

(b) a sum in respect of that mortgage interest is or was brought into account in determining the applicable amount for the purposes of income support in the case of the borrower or the partner, former partner or qualifying associate;

and any reference in this section to "the relevant beneficiary" is a reference to the person whose applicable amount for the purposes of income support is or was determined as mentioned in paragraph (b) above.

(2) Without prejudice to paragraphs (i) and (p) of section 5(1) above, regulations may, in relation to cases where this section applies, make provision—

(a) requiring that, in prescribed circumstances, a prescribed part of any relevant benefits to which the relevant beneficiary is entitled shall be paid by the Secretary of State directly to the qualifying lender and applied by that lender towards the discharge of the liability in respect of the mortgage interest;

(b) for the expenses of the Secretary of State in administering the making of payments under the regulations to be defrayed, in whole or in part, at the expense of qualifying lenders, whether by requiring them to pay prescribed fees or by deducting and retaining a prescribed part of the payments that would otherwise be made to them under the regulations or by such other method as may be prescribed;

(c) for requiring a qualifying lender, in a case where by virtue of paragraph (b) above the amount of the payment made to him under the regulations is less than it would otherwise have been, to credit against the liability in respect of the mortgage interest (in addition to the payment actually made) an amount equal to the difference between—

(i) the payment that would have been so made, apart from paragraph (b) above; and

(ii) the payment actually made;

and, in any such case, for treating the amount so credited as properly paid on account of benefit due to the relevant beneficiary;

(d) for enabling a body which, or person who, would otherwise be a qualifying lender to elect not to be regarded as such for the purposes of this section, other than this paragraph;

(e) for the recovery from any body or person—

(i) of any sums paid to that body or person by way of payment under the regulations that ought not to have been so paid: or

(ii) of any fees or other sums due from that body or person by virtue of paragraph (b) above;

(f) for cases where the same person is the borrower in relation to mortgage interest payable in respect of two or more different loans; and

(g) for any person of a prescribed class or description who would otherwise be regarded for the purposes of this section as the borrower in relation to any mortgage interest not to be so regarded, except for the purposes of this paragraph;

but the Secretary of State shall not make any regulations under paragraph (b) above unless he has consulted with such organisations representing qualifying lenders likely to be affected by the regulations as he considers appropriate.

(3) The bodies and persons who are "qualifying lenders" for the purposes of this section are—

(a) any authorised institution, within the meaning of the Banking Act 1987, to which section 67 of that Act applies (companies and partnerships which may describe themselves as banks etc.),

(b) any building society incorporated under the Building Societies Act 1986,

(c) any body or person carrying on insurance business, within the meaning of the Insurance Companies Act 1982,

(d) any county council, district council, islands council or London Borough Council,

(e) the Common Council of the City of London,

(f) the Council of the Isles of Scilly,

(g) any new town corporation,

and such bodies or persons not falling within the above paragraphs as may be prescribed.

(4) In this section—

"mortgage interest" means interest on a loan which is secured by a mortgage of or charge over land, or (in Scotland) by a heritable security, and which has been taken out to defray money applied for any of the following purposes, that is to say—

(a) acquiring any residential land which was intended, at the time of the acquisition, for occupation by the borrower as his home;

(b) carrying out repairs or improvements to any residential land which was intended, at the time of taking out the loan, for occupation by the borrower as his home;

(c) paying off another loan; or

(d) any prescribed purpose not falling within paragraphs (a) to (c) above;

but interest shall be regarded as mortgage interest by virtue of paragraph (c) above only to the extent that interest on that other loan would have been regarded as mortgage interest for the purposes of this section had the loan not been paid off;

"partner" means—

(a) any person to whom the borrower is married and who is a member of the same household as the borrower; or

(b) any person to whom the borrower is not married but who lives together with the borrower as husband and wife, otherwise than in prescribed circumstances;

and "former partner" means a person who has at some time been, but no longer is, the borrower's partner;

"qualifying associate", in relation to the borrower, means a person who, for the purposes of income support, falls to be treated by regulations under Part VII of the Contributions and Benefits Act as responsible for so much of the expenditure which relates to housing costs (within the meaning of those regulations) as consists of any of the mortgage interest payable by the borrower, and who falls to be so treated because—

(a) the borrower is not meeting those costs, so that the person has to meet them if he is to continue to live in the dwelling occupied as his home; and

(b) the person is one whom it is reasonable, in the circumstances, to treat as liable to meet those costs;

"relevant benefits" means such of the following benefits as may be prescribed, namely—

(a) benefits, as defined in section 122 of the Contributions and Benefits Act;

(b) income support;

"residential land" means any land which consists of or includes a dwelling.

(5) For the purposes of this section, regulations may make provision—

(a) as to circumstances in which residential land is or is not to be treated as intended for occupation by the borrower as his home; or

(b) as to circumstances in which persons are to be treated as being or not being members of the same household."

2.—(1) In section 164 of that Act, in subsection (6) (which consolidates certain enactments making provision about the destination of receipts similar to that made by section 2(3) of this Act) for the words "paid to the Secretary of State" there shall be substituted the words "recovered by the Secretary of State under section 15A above or paid to him".

(2) At the end of that section there shall be added—

"(7) Any sums received by the Secretary of State under regulations made by virtue of section 15A(2)(b) above shall be paid into the Consolidated Fund."

INDEX

References in roman type are to sections of this Act; references in italic are to sections of the Social Security Act 1986

SEXUAL OFFENCES (AMENDMENT) ACT 1992

(1992 c. 34)

An Act to make provision with respect to anonymity in connection with allegations of, and criminal proceedings relating to, certain sexual offences.   [16th March 1992]

PARLIAMENTARY DEBATES
Hansard, H.L. Vol. 536, col. 1496.
The Bill was discussed in Standing Committee B on March 3, 1992.

INTRODUCTION
This Act will extend the law which gives statutory anonymity to victims of rape to victims of sexual offences. Section 2 contains a list of all offences to which this new provision will now apply.

Provision is also made for the lifting of restrictions if it is deemed necessary to induce witnesses to come forward. Special consideration is given to a situation where the complaint is incest or buggery as there may be no "victim" in such situation.

Anonymity of victims of certain offences

1.—(1) Where an allegation has been made that an offence to which this Act applies has been committed against a person, neither the name nor address, and no still or moving picture, of that person shall during that person's lifetime—

(a) be published in England and Wales in a written publication available to the public; or

(b) be included in a relevant programme for reception in England and Wales,

if it is likely to lead members of the public to identify that person as the person against whom the offence is alleged to have been committed.

(2) Where a person is accused of an offence to which this Act applies, no matter likely to lead members of the public to identify a person as the person against whom the offence is alleged to have been committed ("the complainant") shall during the complainant's lifetime—

(a) be published in England and Wales in a written publication available to the public; or

(b) be included in a relevant programme for reception in England and Wales.

(3) Subsections (1) and (2) are subject to any direction given under section 3.

(4) Nothing in this section prohibits the publication or inclusion in a relevant programme of matter consisting only of a report of criminal proceedings other than proceedings at, or intended to lead to, or on an appeal arising out of, a trial at which the accused is charged with the offence.

Offences to which this Act applies

2.—(1) This Act applies to the following offences—

(a) any offence under any of the provisions of the Sexual Offences Act 1956 mentioned in subsection (2);

(b) any offence under section 128 of the Mental Health Act 1959 (intercourse with mentally handicapped person by hospital staff etc.);

(c) any offence under section 1 of the Indecency with Children Act 1960 (indecent conduct towards young child);

(d) any offence under section 54 of the Criminal Law Act 1977 (incitement by man of his grand-daughter, daughter or sister under the age of 16 to commit incest with him);

(e) any attempt to commit any of the offences mentioned in paragraphs (a) to (d).

(2) The provisions of the Act of 1956 are—
  (a) section 2 (procurement of a woman by threats);
  (b) section 3 (procurement of a woman by false pretences);
  (c) section 4 (administering drugs to obtain intercourse with a woman);
  (d) section 5 (intercourse with a girl under the age of 13);
  (e) section 6 (intercourse with a girl between the ages of 13 and 16);
  (f) section 7 (intercourse with a mentally handicapped person);
  (g) section 9 (procurement of a mentally handicapped person);
  (h) section 10 (incest by a man);
  (i) section 11 (incest by a woman);
  (j) section 12 (buggery);
  (k) section 14 (indecent assault on a woman);
  (l) section 15 (indecent assault on a man);
  (m) section 16 (assault with intent to commit buggery).

Power to displace section 1

3.—(1) If, before the commencement of a trial at which a person is charged with an offence to which this Act applies, he or another person against whom the complainant may be expected to give evidence at the trial, applies to the judge for a direction under this subsection and satisfies the judge—
  (a) that the direction is required for the purpose of inducing persons who are likely to be needed as witnesses at the trial to come forward; and
  (b) that the conduct of the applicant's defence at the trial is likely to be substantially prejudiced if the direction is not given,
the judge shall direct that section 1 shall not, by virtue of the accusation alleging the offence in question, apply in relation to the complainant.
  (2) If at a trial the judge is satisfied—
  (a) that the effect of section 1 is to impose a substantial and unreasonable restriction upon the reporting of proceedings at the trial, and
  (b) that it is in the public interest to remove or relax the restriction,
he shall direct that that section shall not apply to such matter as is specified in the direction.
  (3) A direction shall not be given under subsection (2) by reason only of the outcome of the trial.
  (4) If a person who has been convicted of an offence and has given notice of appeal against the conviction, or notice of an application for leave so to appeal, applies to the appellate court for a direction under this subsection and satisfies the court—
  (a) that the direction is required for the purpose of obtaining evidence in support of the appeal; and
  (b) that the applicant is likely to suffer substantial injustice if the direction is not given,
the court shall direct that section 1 shall not, by virtue of an accusation which alleges an offence to which this Act applies and is specified in the direction, apply in relation to a complainant so specified.
  (5) A direction given under any provision of this section does not affect the operation of section 1 at any time before the direction is given.
  (6) In subsections (1) and (2), "judge" means—
  (a) in the case of an offence which is to be tried summarily or for which the mode of trial has not been determined, any justice of the peace acting for the petty sessions area concerned; and
  (b) in any other case, any judge of the Crown Court.
  (7) If, after the commencement of a trial at which a person is charged with an offence to which this Act applies, a new trial of the person for that offence is ordered, the commencement of any previous trial shall be disregarded for the purposes of subsection (1).

Special rules for cases of incest or buggery

4.—(1) In this section—

"section 10 offence" means an offence under section 10 of the Sexual Offences Act 1956 (incest by a man) or an attempt to commit that offence;

"section 11 offence" means an offence under section 11 of that Act (incest by a woman) or an attempt to commit that offence;

"section 12 offence" means an offence under section 12 of that Act (buggery) or an attempt to commit that offence.

(2) Section 1 does not apply to a woman against whom a section 10 offence is alleged to have been committed if she is accused of having committed a section 11 offence against the man who is alleged to have committed the section 10 offence against her.

(3) Section 1 does not apply to a man against whom a section 11 offence is alleged to have been committed if he is accused of having committed a section 10 offence against the woman who is alleged to have committed the section 11 offence against him.

(4) Section 1 does not apply to a person against whom a section 12 offence is alleged to have been committed if that person is accused of having committed a section 12 offence against the person who is alleged to have committed the section 12 offence against him.

(5) Subsection (2) does not affect the operation of this Act in relation to anything done at any time before the woman is accused.

(6) Subsection (3) does not affect the operation of this Act in relation to anything done at any time before the man is accused.

(7) Subsection (4) does not affect the operation of this Act in relation to anything done at any time before the person mentioned first in that subsection is accused.

Offences

5.—(1) If any matter is published or included in a relevant programme in contravention of section 1, the following persons shall be guilty of an offence and liable on summary conviction to a fine not exceeding level 5 on the standard scale—

(a) in the case of publication in a newspaper or periodical, any proprietor, any editor and any publisher of the newspaper or periodical;

(b) in the case of publication in any other form, the person publishing the matter; and

(c) in the case of matter included in a relevant programme—

(i) any body corporate engaged in providing the service in which the programme is included; and

(ii) any person having functions in relation to the programme corresponding to those of an editor of a newspaper.

(2) Where a person is charged with an offence under this section in respect of the publication of any matter or the inclusion of any matter in a relevant programme, it shall be a defence, subject to subsection (3), to prove that the publication or programme in which the matter appeared was one in respect of which the person against whom the offence mentioned in section 1 is alleged to have been committed had given written consent to the appearance of matter of that description.

(3) Written consent is not a defence if it is proved that any person interfered unreasonably with the peace or comfort of the person giving the consent, with intent to obtain it.

(4) Proceedings for an offence under this section shall not be instituted except by or with the consent of the Attorney General.

(5) Where a person is charged with an offence under this section it shall be a defence to prove that at the time of the alleged offence he was not aware,

and neither suspected nor had reason to suspect, that the publication or programme in question was of, or (as the case may be) included, the matter in question.

(6) Where an offence under this section committed by a body corporate is proved to have been committed with the consent or connivance of, or to be attributable to any neglect on the part of—

(a) a director, manager, secretary or other similar officer of the body corporate, or

(b) a person purporting to act in any such capacity,

he as well as the body corporate shall be guilty of the offence and liable to be proceeded against and punished accordingly.

(7) In relation to a body corporate whose affairs are managed by its members "director", in subsection (6), means a member of the body corporate.

Interpretation etc.

6.—(1) In this Act—

"complainant" has the meaning given in section 1(2);

"picture" includes a likeness however produced;

"relevant programme" means a programme included in a programme service, within the meaning of the Broadcasting Act 1990; and

"written publication" includes a film, a sound track and any other record in permanent form but does not include an indictment or other document prepared for use in particular legal proceedings.

(2) For the purposes of this Act—

(a) where it is alleged that an offence to which this Act applies has been committed, the fact that any person has consented to an act which, on any prosecution for that offence, would fall to be proved by the prosecution, does not prevent that person from being regarded as a person against whom the alleged offence was committed; and

(b) where a person is accused of an offence of incest or buggery, the other party to the act in question shall be taken to be a person against whom the offence was committed even though he consented to that act.

(3) For the purposes of this Act, a person is accused of an offence if—

(a) an information is laid alleging that he has committed the offence,

(b) he appears before a court charged with the offence,

(c) a court before which he is appearing commits him for trial on a new charge alleging the offence, or

(d) a bill of indictment charging him with the offence is preferred before a court in which he may lawfully be indicted for the offence,

and references in section 3 to an accusation alleging an offence shall be construed accordingly.

(4) Nothing in this Act affects any prohibition or restriction imposed by virtue of any other enactment upon a publication or upon matter included in a relevant programme.

Courts-martial

7.—(1) This Act shall have effect with the modifications set out in subsection (2) in any case where, in pursuance of any provision of the Army Act 1955, the Air Force Act 1955 or the Naval Discipline Act 1957, a person is charged with an offence to which this Act applies.

(2) The modifications are—

(a) any reference to a trial shall be read as a reference to a trial by court-martial;

(b) in section 1 after the word "Wales", in each of the places where it occurs in subsections (1) and (2), there shall be inserted "or Northern Ireland";

(c) subject to subsection (3), in section 3(1) any reference to a judge, in relation to the person charged with the offence, shall be read as a reference to the officer who is authorised to convene, or has convened, a court-martial for the trial of the offence;

(d) in section 3(2), any reference to a judge shall be read as a reference to the court;

(e) in section 5(4), the reference to the Attorney General shall be read, in the case of an offence under section 5 which is alleged to have been committed in Northern Ireland, as a reference to the Attorney General for Northern Ireland; and

(f) for section 6(3)(a) to (d) there shall be substituted "he is charged, in pursuance of any provision of the Army Act 1955, the Air Force Act 1955 or the Naval Discipline Act 1957, with an offence to which this Act applies".

(3) Where, after convening a court-martial, the officer concerned has ceased to hold the appointment by virtue of which he convened that court-martial, any reference to a judge in section 3(1) shall be read as a reference to the officer holding that appointment.

(4) In section 36(1) of the Courts-Martial (Appeals) Act 1968 (which provides that certain powers of the Courts-Martial Appeal Court may be exercised by a single judge) after the words "section 5(1)(d) of that Act" there shall be inserted "or section 3(4) of the Sexual Offences (Amendment) Act 1992".

Short title, commencement and extent, etc.

8.—(1) This Act may be cited as the Sexual Offences (Amendment) Act 1992.

(2) This Act and the Sexual Offences Acts 1956 to 1976 may be cited together as the Sexual Offences Acts 1956 to 1992.

(3) This section comes into force on the passing of this Act but otherwise this Act comes into force on such date as may be appointed by order made by the Secretary of State.

(4) The power to make an order under subsection (3) shall be exercisable by statutory instrument.

(5) Different dates may be appointed for different provisions of this Act and for different purposes.

(6) This Act shall not extend to Scotland, except so far as it relates to courts-martial and the Courts-Martial Appeal Court.

(7) This Act shall not extend to Northern Ireland, except so far as it relates to courts-martial and the Courts-Martial Appeal Court and to such a publication in, or such an inclusion of matter in a relevant programme for reception in, Northern Ireland as is mentioned in section 1(1) or (2) as adapted by section 7(2)(b).

INDEX

References are to sections

TIMESHARE ACT 1992

(1992 c. 35)

ARRANGEMENT OF SECTIONS

An Act to provide for rights to cancel certain agreements about timeshare accommodation.   [16th March 1992]

PARLIAMENTARY DEBATES
Hansard, H.C. Vol. 203, col. 574; Vol. 204, col. 304; H.L. Vol. 536, col. 1542.
The Bill was discussed in Standing Committee C on February 18, 1992.

INTRODUCTION
    This Act makes various provisions to protect persons entering into timeshare agreements. A person proposing to enter into an agreement conferring rights as a timeshare user on another party must give the other party notice of his right to cancel the agreement. Failure to do so is a criminal offence, liable to a maximum fine of £2000 on summary conviction and an unlimited fine on indictment. An offence is also created of obstructing or refusing to cooperate with an enforcement officer or giving false information to an enforcement officer. The penalties are the same as for an offence under s.2.
    The recipient of such notice is given, under ss.5 to 7, fourteen days to cancel the agreement. On cancellation he is entitled to recover any money paid under the agreement. Provision is also made for avoiding the payment of interest on sums borrowed in the case of credit agreements.
    A person charged with an offence under s.2 may present a defence of due diligence.
    The Act is to be enforced by local weights and measures authorities in Great Britain and the Department of Economic Development in Northern Ireland.

Application of Act

    1.—(1) In this Act—
    (a) "timeshare accommodation" means any living accommodation, in the United Kingdom or elsewhere, used or intended to be used, wholly or partly, for leisure purposes by a class of persons (referred to below in this section as "timeshare users") all of whom have rights to use, or participate in arrangements under which they may use, that accommodation, or accommodation within a pool of accommodation to which that accommodation belongs, for intermittent periods of short duration, and
    (b) "timeshare rights" means rights by virtue of which a person becomes or will become a timeshare user, being rights exercisable during a period of not less than three years.
    (2) For the purposes of subsection (1)(a) above—
    (a) "accommodation" means accommodation in a building or in a caravan (as defined in section 29(1) of the Caravan Sites and Control of Development Act 1960), and

(b) a period of not more than one month, or such other period as may be prescribed, is a period of short duration.

(3) Subsection (1)(b) above does not apply to a person's rights—

(a) as the owner of any shares or securities,

(b) under a contract of employment (as defined in section 153 of the Employment Protection (Consolidation) Act 1978) or a policy of insurance, or

(c) by virtue of his taking part in a collective investment scheme (as defined in section 75 of the Financial Services Act 1986),

or to such rights as may be prescribed.

(4) In this Act "timeshare agreement" means, subject to subsection (6) below, an agreement under which timeshare rights are conferred or purport to be conferred on any person and in this Act, in relation to a timeshare agreement—

(a) references to the offeree are to the person on whom timeshare rights are conferred, or purport to be conferred, and

(b) references to the offeror are to the other party to the agreement,

and, in relation to any time before the agreement is entered into, references in this Act to the offeree or the offeror are to the persons who become the offeree and offeror when it is entered into.

(5) In this Act "timeshare credit agreement" means, subject to subsection (6) below, an agreement, not being a timeshare agreement—

(a) under which a person (referred to in this Act as the "creditor") provides or agrees to provide credit for or in respect of a person who is the offeree under a timeshare agreement, and

(b) when the credit agreement is entered into, the creditor knows or has reasonable cause to believe that the whole or part of the credit is to be used for the purpose of financing the offeree's entering into a timeshare agreement.

(6) An agreement is not a timeshare agreement or a timeshare credit agreement if, when entered into, it may be cancelled by virtue of section 67 of the Consumer Credit Act 1974.

(7) This Act applies to any timeshare agreement or timeshare credit agreement if—

(a) the agreement is to any extent governed by the law of the United Kingdom or of a part of the United Kingdom, or

(b) when the agreement is entered into, one or both of the parties are in the United Kingdom.

(8) In the application of this section to Northern Ireland—

(a) for the reference in subsection (2)(a) above to section 29(1) of the Caravan Sites and Control of Development Act 1960 there is substituted a reference to section 25(1) of the Caravans Act (Northern Ireland) 1963, and

(b) for the reference in subsection (3)(b) above to section 153 of the Employment Protection (Consolidation) Act 1978 there is substituted a reference to article 2(2) of the Industrial Relations (Northern Ireland) Order 1976.

Obligation to give notice of right to cancel timeshare agreement

2.—(1) A person must not in the course of a business enter into a timeshare agreement to which this Act applies as offeror unless the offeree has received, together with a document setting out the terms of the agreement or the substance of those terms, notice of his right to cancel the agreement.

(2) A notice under this section must state—

(a) that the offeree is entitled to give notice of cancellation of the agreement to the offeror at any time on or before the date specified in the notice, being a day falling not less than fourteen days after the day on which the agreement is entered into, and

(b) that if the offeree gives such a notice to the offeror on or before that date he will have no further rights or obligations under the agreement, but will have the right to recover any sums paid under or in contemplation of the agreement.

(3) A person who contravenes this section is guilty of an offence and liable—

(a) on summary conviction, to a fine not exceeding the statutory maximum, and

(b) on conviction on indictment, to a fine.

Obligation to give notice of right to cancel timeshare credit agreement

3.—(1) A person must not in the course of a business enter into a timeshare credit agreement to which this Act applies as creditor unless the offeree has received, together with a document setting out the terms of the agreement or the substance of those terms, notice of his right to cancel the agreement.

(2) A notice under this section must state—

(a) that the offeree is entitled to give notice of cancellation of the agreement to the creditor at any time on or before the date specified in the notice, being a day falling not less than fourteen days after the day on which the agreement is entered into, and

(b) that, if the offeree gives such a notice to the creditor on or before that date, then—

(i) so far as the agreement relates to repayment of credit and payment of interest, it shall have effect subject to section 7 of this Act, and

(ii) subject to sub-paragraph (i) above, the offeree will have no further rights or obligations under the agreement.

Provisions supplementary to sections 2 and 3

4.—(1) Sections 2 and 3 of this Act do not apply where, in entering into the agreement, the offeree is acting in the course of a business.

(2) A notice under section 2 or 3 must be accompanied by a blank notice of cancellation and any notice under section 2 or 3 of this Act or blank notice of cancellation must—

(a) be in such form as may be prescribed, and

(b) comply with such requirements (whether as to type, size, colour or disposition of lettering, quality or colour of paper, or otherwise) as may be prescribed for securing that the notice is prominent and easily legible.

(3) An agreement is not invalidated by reason of a contravention of section 2 or 3.

Right to cancel timeshare agreement

5.—(1) Where a person—

(a) has entered, or proposes to enter, into a timeshare agreement to which this Act applies as offeree, and

(b) has received the notice required under section 2 of this Act before entering into the agreement,

the agreement may not be enforced against him on or before the date specified in the notice in pursuance of subsection (2)(a) of that section and he may give notice of cancellation of the agreement to the offeror at any time on or before that date.

(2) Subject to subsection (3) below, where a person who enters into a timeshare agreement to which this Act applies as offeree has not received

the notice required under section 2 of this Act before entering into the agreement, the agreement may not be enforced against him and he may give notice of cancellation of the agreement to the offeror at any time.

(3) If in a case falling within subsection (2) above the offeree affirms the agreement at any time after the expiry of the period of fourteen days beginning with the day on which the agreement is entered into—

(a) subsection (2) above does not prevent the agreement being enforced against him, and

(b) he may not at any subsequent time give notice of cancellation of the agreement to the offeror.

(4) The offeree's giving, within the time allowed under this section, notice of cancellation of the agreement to the offeror at a time when the agreement has been entered into shall have the effect of cancelling the agreement.

(5) The offeree's giving notice of cancellation of the agreement to the offeror before the agreement has been entered into shall have the effect of withdrawing any offer to enter into the agreement.

(6) Where a timeshare agreement is cancelled under this section, then, subject to subsection (9) below—

(a) the agreement shall cease to be enforceable, and

(b) subsection (8) below shall apply.

(7) Subsection (8) below shall also apply where giving a notice of cancellation has the effect of withdrawing an offer to enter into a timeshare agreement.

(8) Where this subsection applies—

(a) any sum which the offeree has paid under or in contemplation of the agreement to the offeror, or to any person who is the offeror's agent for the purpose of receiving that sum, shall be recoverable from the offeror by the offeree and shall be due and payable at the time the notice of cancellation is given, but

(b) no sum may be recovered by or on behalf of the offeror from the offeree in respect of the agreement.

(9) Where a timeshare agreement includes provision for providing credit for or in respect of the offeree, then, notwithstanding the giving of notice of cancellation under this section, so far as the agreement relates to repayment of the credit and payment of interest—

(a) it shall continue to be enforceable, subject to section 7 of this Act, and

(b) the notice required under section 2 of this Act must also state that fact.

Right to cancel timeshare credit agreement

6.—(1) Where a person—

(a) has entered into a timeshare credit agreement to which this Act applies as offeree, and

(b) has received the notice required under section 3 of this Act before entering into the agreement,

he may give notice of cancellation of the agreement to the creditor at any time on or before the date specified in the notice in pursuance of subsection (2)(a) of that section.

(2) Subject to subsection (3) below, where a person who enters into a timeshare credit agreement to which this Act applies as offeree has not received the notice required under section 3 of this Act before entering into the agreement, he may give notice of cancellation of the agreement to the creditor at any time.

(3) If in a case falling within subsection (2) above the offeree affirms the agreement at any time after the expiry of the period of fourteen days beginning with the day on which the agreement is entered into, he may not at

any subsequent time give notice of cancellation of the agreement to the creditor.

(4) The offeree's giving, within the time allowed under this section, notice of cancellation of the agreement to the creditor at a time when the agreement has been entered into shall have the effect of cancelling the agreement.

(5) Where a timeshare credit agreement is cancelled under this section—

(a) the agreement shall continue in force, subject to section 7 of this Act, so far as it relates to repayment of the credit and payment of interest, and

(b) subject to paragraph (a) above, the agreement shall cease to be enforceable.

Repayment of credit and interest

7.—(1) This section applies following—

(a) the giving of notice of cancellation of a timeshare agreement in accordance with section 5 of this Act in a case where subsection (9) of that section applies, or

(b) the giving of notice of cancellation of a timeshare credit agreement in accordance with section 6 of this Act.

(2) If the offeree repays the whole or a portion of the credit—

(a) before the expiry of one month following the giving of the notice, or

(b) in the case of a credit repayable by instalments, before the date on which the first instalment is due,

no interest shall be payable on the amount repaid.

(3) If the whole of a credit repayable by instalments is not repaid on or before the date specified in subsection (2)(b) above, the offeree shall not be liable to repay any of the credit except on receipt of a request in writing in such form as may be prescribed, signed by or on behalf of the offeror or (as the case may be) creditor, stating the amounts of the remaining instalments (recalculated by the offeror or creditor as nearly as may be in accordance with the agreement and without extending the repayment period), but excluding any sum other than principal and interest.

Defence of due diligence

8.—(1) In proceedings against a person for an offence under section 2(3) of this Act it shall be a defence for that person to show that he took all reasonable steps and exercised all due diligence to avoid committing the offence.

(2) Where in proceedings against a person for such an offence the defence provided by subsection (1) above involves an allegation that the commission of the offence was due—

(a) to the act or default of another, or

(b) to reliance on information given by another,

that person shall not, without the leave of the court, be entitled to rely on the defence unless he has served a notice under subsection (3) below on the person bringing the proceedings not less than seven clear days before the hearing of the proceedings or, in Scotland, the diet of trial.

(3) A notice under this subsection shall give such information identifying or assisting in the identification of the person who committed the act or default or gave the information as is in the possession of the person serving the notice at the time when he serves it.

Liability of persons other than principal offender

9.—(1) Where the commission by a person of an offence under section 2(3) of this Act is due to the act or default of some other person, that other person is guilty of the offence and may be proceeded against and punished by virtue of this section whether or not proceedings are taken against the first-mentioned person.

(2) Where a body corporate is guilty of an offence under section 2(3) of this Act (including where it is so guilty by virtue of subsection (1) above) in respect of an act or default which is shown to have been committed with the consent or connivance of, or to be attributable to neglect on the part of, a director, manager, secretary or other similar officer of the body corporate or a person who was purporting to act in such a capacity, he (as well as the body corporate) is guilty of the offence and liable to be proceeded against and punished accordingly.

(3) Where the affairs of a body corporate are managed by its members, subsection (2) above applies in relation to the acts and defaults of a member in connection with his functions of management as if he were a director of the body corporate.

(4) Where an offence under section 2(3) of this Act committed in Scotland by a Scottish partnership is proved to have been committed with the consent or connivance of, or to be attributable to neglect on the part of, a partner, he (as well as the partnership) is guilty of the offence and liable to be proceeded against and punished accordingly.

Enforcement

10. The Schedule to this Act (which makes provision about enforcement) shall have effect.

Prosecution time limit

11.—(1) No proceedings for an offence under section 2(3) of this Act or paragraph 4(3) or 5(1) of the Schedule to this Act shall be commenced after—

(a) the end of the period of three years beginning with the date of the commission of the offence, or

(b) the end of the period of one year beginning with the date of the discovery of the offence by the prosecutor,

whichever is the earlier.

(2) For the purposes of this section a certificate signed by or on behalf of the prosecutor and stating the date on which the offence was discovered by him shall be conclusive evidence of that fact; and a certificate stating that matter and purporting to be so signed shall be treated as so signed unless the contrary is proved.

(3) In relation to proceedings in Scotland, subsection (3) of section 331 of the Criminal Procedure (Scotland) Act 1975 (date of commencement of proceedings) shall apply for the purposes of this section as it applies for the purposes of that.

General provisions

12.—(1) For the purposes of this Act, a notice of cancellation of an agreement is a notice (however expressed) showing that the offeree wishes unconditionally to cancel the agreement, whether or not it is in a prescribed form.

(2) The rights conferred and duties imposed by sections 2 to 7 of this Act are in addition to any rights conferred or duties imposed by or under any other Act.

(3) For the purposes of this Act, if the offeree sends a notice by post in a properly addressed and pre-paid letter the notice is to be treated as given at the time of posting.

(4) This Act shall have effect in relation to any timeshare agreement or timeshare credit agreement notwithstanding any agreement or notice.

(5) For the purposes of the Consumer Credit Act 1974, a transaction done under or for the purposes of a timeshare agreement is not, in relation to any regulated agreement (within the meaning of that Act), a linked transaction.

(6) In this Act—

"credit" includes a cash loan and any other form of financial accommodation,

"notice" means notice in writing,

"order" means an order made by the Secretary of State, and

"prescribed" means prescribed by an order.

(7) An order under this Act may make different provision for different cases or circumstances.

(8) Any power under this Act to make an order shall be exercisable by statutory instrument and a statutory instrument containing an order under this Act (other than an order made for the purposes of section 13(2) of this Act) shall be subject to annulment in pursuance of a resolution of either House of Parliament.

Short title, etc.

13.—(1) This Act may be cited as the Timeshare Act 1992.

(2) This Act shall come into force on such day as may be prescribed.

(3) This Act extends to Northern Ireland.

Section 10   SCHEDULE

ENFORCEMENT

Enforcement authority

1.—(1) Every local weights and measures authority in Great Britain shall be an enforcement authority for the purposes of this Schedule, and it shall be the duty of each such authority to enforce the provisions of this Act within their area.

(2) The Department of Economic Development in Northern Ireland shall be an enforcement authority for the purposes of this Schedule, and it shall be the duty of the Department to enforce the provisions of this Act within Northern Ireland.

Prosecutions

2.—(1) In section 130(1) of the Fair Trading Act 1973 (notice to Director General of Fair Trading of intended prosecution by local weights and measures authority in England and Wales), after "the Property Misdescriptions Act 1991" there is inserted "or for an offence under section 2 of the Timeshare Act 1992".

(2) Nothing in paragraph 1 above shall authorise a local weights and measures authority to bring proceedings in Scotland for an offence.

Powers of officers of enforcement authority

3.—(1) If a duly authorised officer of an enforcement authority has reasonable grounds for suspecting that an offence under section 2 of this Act has been committed, he may—

(a) require a person carrying on or employed in a business to produce any book or document relating to the business, and take copies of it or any entry in it, or

(b) require such a person to produce in a visible and legible documentary form any information so relating which is contained in a computer, and take copies of it,

for the purposes of ascertaining whether such an offence has been committed.

(2) If such an officer has reasonable grounds for believing that any documents may be required as evidence in proceedings for such an offence, he may seize and detain them and shall, if he does so, inform the person from whom they are seized.

(3) The powers of an officer under this paragraph may be exercised by him only at a reasonable hour and on production (if required) of his credentials.

(4) Nothing in this paragraph requires a person to produce, or authorises the taking from a person of, a document which he could not be compelled to produce in civil proceedings before the High Court or (in Scotland) the Court of Session.

4.—(1) A person who—

(a) intentionally obstructs an officer of an enforcement authority acting in pursuance of this Schedule,

(b) without reasonable excuse fails to comply with a requirement made of him by such an officer under paragraph 3(1) above, or

(c) without reasonable excuse fails to give an officer of an enforcement authority acting in pursuance of this Schedule any other assistance or information which the officer has reasonably required of him for the purpose of the performance of the officer's functions under this Schedule,

is guilty of an offence.

(2) A person guilty of an offence under sub-paragraph (1) above is liable on summary conviction to a fine not exceeding level 5 on the standard scale.

(3) If a person, in giving information to an officer of an enforcement authority who is acting in pursuance of this Schedule—

(a) makes a statement which he knows is false in a material particular, or

(b) recklessly makes a statement which is false in a material particular,

he is guilty of an offence.

(4) A person guilty of an offence under sub-paragraph (3) above is liable—

(a) on summary conviction, to a fine not exceeding the statutory maximum, and

(b) on conviction on indictment, to a fine.

Disclosure of information

5.—(1) If a person discloses to another any information obtained in the exercise of functions under this Schedule he is guilty of an offence unless the disclosure was made—

(a) in or for the purpose of the performance by him or any other person of any such function, or

(b) for a purpose specified in section 38(2)(a), (b) or (c) of the Consumer Protection Act 1987 (enforcement of various enactments; compliance with Community obligations; and civil or criminal proceedings).

(2) A person guilty of an offence under sub-paragraph (1) above is liable—

(a) on summary conviction, to a fine not exceeding the statutory maximum, and

(b) on conviction on indictment, to a fine.

Privilege against self-incrimination

6. Nothing in this Schedule requires a person to answer any question or give any information if to do so might incriminate him.

INDEX

References are to sections

ACCOMMODATION,
  definition, 1(2)(a)

BODIES CORPORATE,
  liability of officers, 9(2)–(3)

CANCELLATION,
  duty to give notice of right, 2, 3
    exceptions, 4
    failure to give,
      legal effect on agreement, 4(3)
      offence, 2(3)
    form of notice, 12(1)
  timeshare agreement, 5
    affirmation after 14 days, 5(3)
    before agreement entered into, 5(5)
    credit provision included, 5(9)
    exercise of right, effect of, 5(4)–(8)
    non-receipt of notice, 5(2)
    notice of right of, 2
    time for notice, 5(1)
  timeshare credit agreement, 6
    affirmation after 14 days, 6(3)
    exercise of right, effect of, 6(4)–(5)
    non-receipt of notice, 6(2)
    notice of right of, 3
    time for notice, 6(1)
CARAVANS, 1(2)(a)
COMMENCEMENT, 13(2)
CONSUMER CREDIT ACT 1974,
  application of, 1(6), 12(5)
COURSE OF BUSINESS,
  offeree acting in, 4(1)
CREDIT,
  definition, 12(6)
  repayment of, 7

DEFENCES, 8
DILLIGENCE, DEFENCE OF, 8
  fault of another, 8(2)
  notice required, 8(3)
  reliance on another's information, 8(2)

ENFORCEMENT, 10, SCHED.
  authority, Sched., para. 1
    powers of, Sched., paras., 3–4
  disclosure of information, Sched., para. 5
  privilege against self-incrimination, Sched., para. 6
  prosecutions, Sched., para. 2
EXTENT, 13(3)

FAULT OF ANOTHER,
  defence, 8
  liability of other, 9

INTEREST,
  payment of, 7

LIABILITY OF PERSONS OTHER THAN PRINCIPAL OFFENDER, 9

NORTHERN IRELAND,
  application of Act, 1(8)
NOTICES,
  of cancellation, 4(2)
  form of, 4, 12(1)
  meaning, 12(6)
  right of cancellation,
    content of, 2(2), 3(2)
  service, 12(3)
  See also Cancellation

OFFEREE,
  definition, 1(4)(a)
OFFEROR,
  definition, 1(4)(b)
ORDERS UNDER ACT, 12(7)–(8)

PRIVILEGE AGAINST SELF-INCRIMINATION, Sched. para. 6
PROSECUTION TIME LIMIT, 11

RIGHTS AND DUTIES CONFERRED,
  additional to other rights and duties, 12(2)

SCOTTISH PARTNERSHIPS,
  liability of partners, 9(4)
SHORT DURATION, PERIOD OF,
  definition, 1(2)(b)
SHORT TITLE, 13(1)

TIMESHARE ACCOMMODATION,
  definition, 1(1)(a)
TIMESHARE AGREEMENT,
  application of Act, 1(7)
  definition, 1(4)
  See also Cancellation

35–9

SEA FISHERIES (WILDLIFE CONSERVATION) ACT 1992

(1992 c. 36)

An Act to require appropriate Ministers and relevant bodies to have regard to the conservation of flora and fauna in the discharge of their functions under the Sea Fisheries Acts.   [16th March 1992]

PARLIAMENTARY DEBATES
  Hansard, H.L. Vol. 536, col. 1555.
  The Bill was discussed in Standing Committee C on February 25, 1992.

INTRODUCTION
  This Act is intended to increase consideration of conservation in the exercise of sea fisheries functions. The Minister of Agriculture, Fisheries and Food and the Secretaries of State respectively concerned with the sea fishing industry in Scotland, Wales and Northern Ireland and the Department of Agriculture for Northern Ireland are required, when discharging any functions conferred or imposed upon them by or under the Sea Fisheries Acts, to have regard to the conservation of marine flora and fauna and to try and achieve a balance between those considerations and others.

Conservation in the exercise of sea fisheries functions

1.—(1) In discharging any functions conferred or imposed on him or them by or under the Sea Fisheries Acts, the Minister or Ministers or any relevant body shall, so far as is consistent with the proper and efficient discharge of those functions—
  (a) have regard to the conservation of marine flora and fauna; and
  (b) endeavour to achieve a reasonable balance between that consideration and any other considerations to which he is or they are required to have regard.
  (2) In this section—
    "enactment" does not include an enactment contained in Northern Ireland legislation;
    "the Minister or Ministers" means any one of the following or any two or more of them acting jointly, namely—
        (a) the Minister of Agriculture, Fisheries and Food;
        (b) the Secretaries of State respectively concerned with the sea fishing industry in Scotland, Wales and Northern Ireland; and
        (c) the Department of Agriculture for Northern Ireland;
    "relevant body" means any local fisheries committee constituted under the Sea Fisheries Regulation Act 1966 or any authority exercising the powers of such a committee;
    "the Sea Fisheries Acts" means any enactments for the time being in force relating to sea-fishing, including any enactment relating to fishing in the sea for shellfish, salmon or migratory trout.

Short title, commencement and extent

2.—(1) This Act may be cited as the Sea Fisheries (Wildlife Conservation) Act 1992.
  (2) This Act shall come into force at the end of the period of two months beginning with the day on which it is passed.
  (3) This Act extends to Northern Ireland.

INDEX

References are to sections